Also by Robert M. Parker, Jr.:

BORDEAUX: THE DEFINITIVE GUIDE
FOR THE WINES PRODUCED SINCE
1961
THE WINES OF THE RHÔNE VALLEY
AND PROVENCE
PARKER'S WINE BUYER'S GUIDE
1987–1988

PARKER'S WINE BUYER'S GUIDE

ROBERT M. PARKER, JR.

A Fireside Book
Published by
Simon & Schuster

NEW YORK   LONDON   TORONTO   SYDNEY   TOKYO   SINGAPORE

SIMON AND SCHUSTER/FIRESIDE
Simon & Schuster Building
Rockefeller Center
1230 Avenue of the Americas
New York, New York 10020

Portions of this book were previously published in the author's
bimonthly newsletter, *The Wine Advocate.*

Designed by Levavi & Levavi
Maps by Jeanyee Wong
Drawings by Christopher Wormell
Manufactured in the United States of America

10   9   8   7   6   5   4   3   2   1
10   9   8   7   6   5   PBK

Library of Congress Cataloging-in-Publication Data
Parker, Robert M.
   [Wine buyer's guide]
   Parker's wine buyer's guide/Robert M. Parker, Jr.
       p.   cm.
   "A Fireside book."
   Includes index.
   1. Wine and wine making.   I. Title.   II. Title: Wine
buyer's guide.
TP548.P287   1989
641.2'22—dc 19   88-37688
                                                      CIP

ISBN 0-671-67648-2
      0-671-67649-0 pbk

ACKNOWLEDGMENTS

I WOULD LIKE TO ESPECIALLY THANK THE FOLLOWING PERSONS WITHOUT WHOSE HELP THIS BOOK WOULD NOT HAVE BEEN POSSIBLE.

To KERRI CONAN—for never letting a deadline pass.

To PAUL EVANS—for his remarkable insight into the world of wine as well as his generosity.

To CAROLE LALLI—for her exemplary efforts as my trusted editor and friend.

To BOB LESCHER—for his "sagesse," wit and constant friendship and support.

To JEAN-FRANÇOIS MOUEIX—for his kindness and friendship.

To PATRICIA—for being my light and inspiration.

To my MOTHER and FATHER—for always being there.

To SARAH—for providing the much needed therapy during anxious times.

To JOAN PASSMAN—for always having my best interests at heart.

To DOMINIQUE RENARD—for treating me like the brother I never had.

To the SUBSCRIBERS of *The Wine Advocate*—for always wanting, even requiring, the best wines and the best wine values.

To JEANYEE WONG—for the easily readable and helpful maps.

AND, TO THOSE WINE MAKERS OF THE WORLD WHO HAVE DECIDED TO PLACE QUALITY OVER QUANTITY, TASTE AND CHARACTER OVER THE INSIPIDNESS CAUSED BY HIGH TECHNOLOGY, AND COMMITMENT TO AUTHENTICITY OVER GREED AND COMPLAISANCE.

To Maia

CONTENTS

HOW TO USE
THIS GUIDE

This book is both an educational and buying manual; it is not an encyclopedic listing of wine producers and growers. It is intended to make you a more formidable, more confident wine buyer by providing sufficient insider's information to permit the most intelligent choices possible when buying wine. The finest wine producers and growers in the world's greatest viticultural regions are evaluated, as well as most of the current releases available in the marketplace. If you cannot find a specific vintage of a highly regarded wine, you still have at your fingertips a wealth of information and evaluations concerning the best producers for each viticultural area. You should feel confident in knowing you will rarely make a mistake (unless, of course, the vintage is absolutely dreadful) with a producer rated "outstanding" or "excellent" in this manual. These producers are the finest and most consistent in the world.

However, to make the most of this guide, you must know how to use it.

Organization

The general organization of each specific viticultural region covered in this manual is arranged as follows:

1. The name of the viticultural region
2. A short introduction to the area, including a buying strategy for 1989 and 1990
3. A summary of the quality of the appropriate vintages for the area
4. A quick reference chart to the area's best producers/growers
5. And, where deemed relevant, tasting commentaries, a numerical rating for the wine, and a code letter that represents the general retail price range for a 750 ml bottle of the wine. (See the Wine Price Guide, on page 18, which explains the coding system.)

The Viticultural Areas Covered

This guide covers the world's major viticultural regions. In Western Europe, France receives the most detailed coverage, followed by Italy, Spain, Portugal, and Germany. In North America, California receives much more significant coverage than other viticultural areas, with the exception of America's new emerging wine star, Oregon. The wine regions of the world that dominate the marketplace are given priority and much more detailed coverage than minor areas whose wines are rarely seen or exported to the United States. Consequently, the sections dealing with Bordeaux, Burgundy, Champagne, Alsace, and the Rhône in France, Piedmont and Tuscany in Italy, Rioja, Penedès, and the Duero in Spain, the northern viticultural area of California, and the Mosel in Germany receive an inordinate amount of coverage herein simply because those regions produce the world's greatest wines.

Rating the Producers/Growers

Who's who in the world of wine becomes readily apparent after years of tasting and visiting the vineyards and wine cellars of the world's producers and growers. Great producers are, unfortunately, still quite rare, but certainly more growers/producers today are making better wine, with better technology and more knowledge than ever before. The charts that follow rate the producers on a five-star system; five stars and an "outstanding" rating are awarded to those producers deemed to be the very best, four stars to those producers who are "excellent," three stars to "good" producers, and two stars or one star to "average" and "below average" producers. Since the aim of the book is to provide you with the names of the very best producers, the content is dominated by the top producers rather than the less successful ones. To some extent well-known producers whose reputations exceed the quality of their wines are covered for the obvious reason that extra guidance is needed in such cases.

Those few growers/producers who have received five-star ratings are indeed those who make the world's finest wines. They have been selected for this rating because they make the greatest wine of their particular viticultural region, and because they are remarkably consistent and reliable even in mediocre and poor vintages. Ratings—whether they be specific numerical ratings of individual wines or classifications of growers—are always likely to create controversy not only among the growers but among wine tasters themselves. But if done impartially, with a global viewpoint and with firsthand, on-the-premises *("sur place")* knowledge of the wines, of the producers, and of the type and quality of the winemaking, such ratings can be reliable and powerfully informative. The important thing for readers to remember is that those growers/producers who receive a five- or four-star rating are producers to search out; I suspect few consumers will ever be disappointed with one of their wines. The three-star-rated growers/producers are less consistent, but can be expected to make fine wines in the very good to excellent vintages. Their weaknesses come either from the fact that their vineyards are not as strategically placed, or because for financial or other reasons they are unable to make the severe selections necessary to make only the finest quality wine.

The rating of the growers/producers of the world's major viticultural regions is perhaps the most important point to this book. Years of wine tasting have taught me many things, but the more one tastes and assimilates the knowledge of the world's regions, the more one begins to isolate the handful of truly world-class growers and producers who seem to rise above the crowd in great as well as mediocre vintages. I always admonish consumers against blind faith in one grower or producer, or one specific vintage, but the producers and growers rated "outstanding" and "excellent" are as close to a guarantee of high quality as you are likely to find.

Vintage Summaries

Although wine advertisements proclaiming "a great vintage" abound, I have never known it to occur that more than several viticultural areas in the world have a great vintage in the same year. The chances of a uniformly great vintage are extremely remote simply because of significantly different micro-climates, soils, and so on, in every wine-producing region. It is easy to fall into the trap of thinking that because Bordeaux had a great vintage in 1982, every place else in Europe did too. Nothing, of course, could be further from the truth. Nevertheless, a Bordeaux vintage's reputation unfortunately seems to dictate what the world thinks about many other wine-producing areas. This obviously creates many problems, since in poor Bordeaux vintages the Rhône or Alsace or Champagne could have excellent vintages, and in great Bordeaux vintages those same areas could have bad years because of poor climate conditions. For California, many casual observers seem to think *every* year is a top year and this image is, of course, promoted by that state's publicity-conscious Wine Institute. It may be true that California rarely has a disastrous vintage, but tasting certainly proves that 1981, 1982, and 1983 are different in style and more irregular in quality than either 1984, 1985, 1986, or 1987. In this guide, there are vintage summaries for each viticultural area because the vintages are so very different in both quantity and quality. Never make the mistake of assuming that one particular year is great everywhere or poor everywhere. I know of no year where *that* has been the case.

Tasting Notes and Ratings

For many of the major viticultural areas, the growers/producers are listed alphabetically and their current wines are reviewed, scored, and commented upon. In this instance, great attention has been given to trying to provide an overview of the style and quality level of the producer/grower. Such factors as whether the producer is steadily improving the wine's quality, resting on its allegedly superior reputation, or slipping in quality because of mismanagement, replanting, or simple negligence are issues that I deem extremely important for consumers to be aware of.

Virtually all of my tastings are done in peer group, double-blind conditions—meaning that the same type of wines are tasted against each other and the producers' names are not known. The ratings reflect an independent, critical look at the wines. Neither price nor the reputation of the producer/grower affect the rating in any manner. I spend three months of every year tasting in vineyards both here and abroad. During the other nine months, six- and sometimes seven-day workweeks are devoted solely to tasting and writing. I do not participate in wine judgings or trade tastings for many reasons, but principal among these are the following: (1) I prefer to taste from an entire bottle of wine, (2) I find it essential to have properly sized and cleaned professional tasting glasses, (3) the temperatures of the wine must be correct, and (4) I alone will determine the time allocated to the number of wines to be critiqued.

The numerical rating given is a guide to what I think of the wine vis-à-vis its peer group. Certainly, wines rated above 85 are very good from the ambience, gorgeous setting, excellent food, and fine company that may accompany it.

Quoted Prices

For a number of reasons there is no single suggested retail price for a particular wine that is valid throughout the country. Take Bordeaux as an example. Bordeaux is first sold as "wine futures" two full years before the wine is bottled and shipped to America. This opening or base price can often be the lowest price one will encounter for a Bordeaux wine, particularly if there is a great demand because the vintage is reputed to be excellent or outstanding. Prices will always vary for Bordeaux, as well as for other imported wines, according to the quality of the vintage, the exchange rate of the dollar against foreign currencies, and the time of purchase by the retailer, wholesaler, or importer. Was the Bordeaux wine purchased at a low futures price in the spring following the vintage, or was it purchased when it had peaked in price and was very expensive?

Another consideration in pricing is that in many states, wine retailers can directly import the wines they sell and thereby bypass the middlemen, such as wholesalers, who usually tack on a 25% markup of their own. The bottom line in all this is that in any given vintage for Bordeaux, or any imported wine, there is no standard suggested retail price. Prices can differ by at least 50% for the same wine in the same city. However, in cities where there is tremendous competition among wine shops, the retail markup for wines can be reduced to as low as 10% or even 5% versus the normal 50%–55%. This can result in significantly lower overall prices for wine, whereas in cities where there is little competition, the prices often charged are full retail and can be more expensive. I always recommend that consumers pay close attention to the wine advertisements in major newspapers. For example, every Wednesday, the *New York Times*'s Living Section is filled with advertisements that are a wonderful barometer of the market price of a given wine. Readers should remember, however, that prices differ considerably, not only within the same state but also within the same city. The approximate price range that is reported here reflects the suggested retail price with a 40–60% markup by the retailer in most major metropolitan areas. Therefore, in many states in the Midwest and less populated areas where there is little competition among wine merchants, the price may be significantly higher. In major marketplaces where there is brisk competition, such as Washington, D.C., New York, San Francisco, Boston, Los Angeles, Chicago and

Dallas, prices are often lower because of the discount wars that frequently occur. The key for you as the reader and consumer is to follow the advertisements in major newspapers and to shop around. Most major wine retailers feature sales in the fall and spring; summer is the slow season and generally the most expensive time to buy wine.

Following is the price guide I have used throughout the book.

WINE PRICE GUIDE

CODE
A: Inexpensive/less than $8
B: Moderate/between $8 and $15
C: Expensive/between $15 and $25
D: Very expensive/between $25 and $50
E: Luxury/in excess of $50

ABOUT WINE

How to Buy Wine

On the surface, buying wine seems simple enough: Having made your choices in advance, you go to your favorite wine merchant and purchase a few bottles. However, there are some subtleties that must be kept in mind to ensure that the wine in the bottle you are about to buy is in healthy condition and is unspoiled.

To begin with, take a look at the bottle. Poor storage is generally revealed by a bottle's condition. The first sign indicating that a bottle has been poorly stored is when its cork has popped above the rim and is pushed out on the lead or plastic capsule that covers the top of the bottle. Wines that have been exposed to very high temperatures expand, which puts pressure on the cork and pushes it upward against the capsule. And it is the highest quality wines, those that have not been overly filtered or pasteurized in order to stabilize them, that are the most vulnerable to poor transportation or storage conditions, and the most likely to show these kinds of effects. A wine that has been frozen in transit or storage will likewise push the cork out. The freezing of wine is less damaging than the boiling of it, but both are hazardous to its health. Thus, any cork that is protruding above the rim of the bottle is a bad sign, indicating that you should return that bottle to the shelf and look for another one to buy.

Another sign indicating that a wine has been poorly stored is the presence of seepage, "legs," around the rim of the bottle. This is the sometimes sticky, dried residue of wine that has expanded and seeped around the cork and dripped onto the rim. This condition is almost always due to excessively high temperatures in transit or storage. Few merchants take the trouble to wipe the legs off, and they can often be spotted, particularly in wines that are shipped during the heat of summer or brought into the United States through the Panama Canal in un-airconditioned containers. In any case, avoid buying any wine that shows dried seepage legs originating under the capsule and trickling down the side of the bottle.

Also be on the alert for young wines (those less than four years old) that have more than ½ inch of air space, or ullage, between the cork and the liquid level in the bottle. Modern bottling operations generally fill bottles to within ⅛ inch of the cork, so that more than ½ inch of air space is something to be suspicious of. Although the contents of the bottle may still be very sound, why take the risk if you can buy other bottles with better fills?

Finally, there is a sign indicating poor storage conditions that can generally be determined only after the wine has been decanted, though sometimes it can be spotted in the neck of the bottle. If a wine has been exposed to very high temperatures—particularly if it is a deep, rich, intense red wine—a heavy coat of film of coloring material will often form on the inside of the glass. With a Bordeaux that is less than three years old, a coating such as this generally indicates that the wine has been subjected to very high temperatures and has undoubtedly been damaged. However, one must be careful here because this type of sediment does not always indicate a poor bottle of wine; vintage port regularly throws it as do the huge, rich Rhône wines and the Piedmontese wines.

With these in mind, let's consider two erroneous notions consumers have about wines, leading them to believe a wine is flawed when nothing could be further from the truth. Many consumers return bottles to the store for the very worst reason: a small deposit or sediment in the bottom of the bottle. Paradoxically, this is the healthiest sign one can find in many bottles of wine. (Keep in mind that white wines rarely throw a deposit, and it is rare to see a deposit in young wines that are less than 2–3 years of age.) The tiny particles of sandlike sediment that precipitate to the bottom of a bottle simply indicate that the wine has been naturally made and has not been subjected to filtration, which is traumatic and removes flavor and character from the wine. Naturally made wine is truly alive and usually full of all its natural flavors.

Consumers also return bottles to the store because of the presence of small crystals called tartrate precipitates. Such crystals are found in all types of wines but appear most commonly in white wines from Germany and Alsace. The crystals often shine and resemble little slivers of cut glass, but in fact are only indicative of a bottle of wine that somewhere along its journey was exposed to temperatures below 40° F. They are harmless and tasteless, and are a totally natural occurrence in many bottles of wine. They have no effect on the wine's quality and usually signify that the wine has *not* been subjected to an abusive, sometimes damaging, cold stabilization treatment by the winery solely for cosmetic purposes.

Fortunately, most of the better wine merchants, wholesalers, and importers are more cognizant today of the damage that can be done by shipping wine in unrefrigerated containers, especially in the middle of summer. (Again, heat generally is more damaging to fine wines than cold.) However, far too many wines are still tragically damaged by poor transportation and storage—and it is the consumer who suffers. There are still plenty of wine merchants, wholesalers, and importers around who treat wine no differently than beer or liquor. Thus, the consumer should become as well informed as possible before buying wine.

How to Store Wine

Wine must be stored properly if it is to be served in a healthy condition. All wine enthusiasts know that a subterranean wine cellar that is vibration-free, dark, damp, and kept at a constant 55° F is considered perfect for wine. However, few of us have our own castles and such perfect accommodations for our beloved wines. While such conditions are ideal, most wines will thrive and develop well under other conditions. I have tasted many old Bordeaux wines that have been perfect, even though they have been stored in closets and basements that have reached 65–70° F in summer. When cellaring wine, keep the following rules in mind.

First, to safely cellar wines for ten years or more keep them at 65°

F and *no* higher. If the temperature in the storage area gets up to 70° F or higher, be prepared to drink your red wines within 10 years. Under no circumstances should you store and cellar white wines for more than 1–2 years at temperatures above 70° F. Wines kept at temperatures above 65° F will age faster, but unless the temperature exceeds 70° F, they will not age badly. If you can somehow get the temperature down to 65° F or below, you will never have to worry about the condition of your wines. At 55° F, the ideal temperature according to the textbooks, the wines actually evolve so slowly that your grandchildren are more likely to benefit from the wines than you. Moreover, constancy in temperature is most essential; any changes in temperature should occur slowly. White wines are much more fragile than red wines, and are much more sensitive to temperature changes and higher temperatures. Therefore, if you do not have ideal storage conditions, buy only enough white wine to drink over a 1–2 year period.

Second, be sure that your storage area is odor- and vibration-free, and that it is dark. A humidity level above 50% is essential; 80–90% is ideal. The problem with a humidity level over 80% is that the labels become moldy and deteriorate. A humidity level below 50% will keep the labels in great shape but will cause the corks to become very dry, thus threatening the life of your wines. Low humidity is as great a threat to a wine's health as is high temperature.

Third, keep in mind that wines from vintages that have produced powerful, rich, concentrated, full-bodied wines travel and age significantly better than wines from vintages that produced lighter, more fragile wines. It is often more traumatic for a lighter-styled wine from Europe or California to be transported transatlantically or cross-country.

Fourth, assuming that you have tasted a wine and like it, I always recommend buying it as soon as it appears on the market, since there are still too many American wine merchants, importers, wholesalers, and distributors who are indifferent to the way wine is stored. Thus, after inspecting each bottle, you should stock up on wines as quickly as they come on the market, and you should approach older vintages with a great deal of caution unless you have absolute faith in the wine merchant. Further, you should be confident that your merchant will stand behind the wine in the event it is flawed due to poor storage.

How to Serve Wine

There are really no secrets concerning proper wine service—all one needs is a good corkscrew, clean, odor-free glasses, a sense of order as to how wines should be served, and knowing whether a wine needs to be aired or allowed to breathe. The major mistakes most Americans, as well as most restaurants in the United States, make are that they serve fine white wines much too cold, they serve red wines much too warm, and they give too little attention to the glass into which the wine is poured. These mistakes can do much more to damage the impact of a fine wine and its subtle aromas than you might imagine.

Most people tend to think that a wine must be opened and allowed to "breathe" well in advance of serving. Some even think that a wine must be decanted, a rather elaborate procedure but essential only if sediment is present in the bottle. I am not sure anyone has all the answers regarding the airing of wine. Certainly, no white wine requires any advance opening and pouring. With red wine, all that is necessary is that it be poured into a clean, odor- and soap-free wine decanter within 15–30 minutes of being opened. Of course there are examples that can be cited where the wine improves for 7–8 hours, but these are quite rare and unusual.

Although these topics seem to dominate much of the discussion in wine circles, a much more critical aspect for me is the appropriate temperature of the wine and of the glass in which it is to be served. With red wines temperature is very important; in America's generously heated dining rooms, temperatures are often 75–80° F, higher than is good for fine red wine. A red wine served at such a temperature will taste flat and flabby, with its bouquet diffuse and unfocused. Its alcohol content will also seem higher than it should. The ideal temperature for most red wines is 62–67° F; light red wine such as Beaujolais should be chilled to 55° F. For white wines, 55–60° F is perfect, since most of them will show all their complexity and intensity at this range. If a white wine is chilled to below 45° F, it will be difficult to tell, for instance, whether the wine is a Riesling or a Chardonnay.

Regarding the glass in which the wine is to be served, an all-purpose tulip-shaped glass that holds 8–12 ounces is ideal for just about any type of wine. Be sure to rinse glasses and decanters with unchlorinated well or mineral water just before they are to be used, no matter how clean they look. Decanters or glasses left sitting out or in a closed cabinet are wonderful traps for odors that are detectable only after the wine has been poured. Such odors, as well as soapy residues, have ruined more wines than has any defective cork or, I suspect, any poor storage treatment. I have put considerable strain on one friendship simply because I continue to complain at dinner parties about the soapy glasses that interfere with the enjoyment of the wonderful Bordeaux being served.

Food and Wine Matchups

The art of serving the right bottle of wine with a specific course or type of food has become one of the most overly legislated areas, all to the detriment of the enjoyment of both wine and food. Newspaper and magazine articles, and even books, are filled with precise rules that practically make it a sin not to choose the perfect wine for a particular meal. Thus, instead of enjoying their dinner party, most hosts and hostesses fret, usually needlessly, over choosing the wine.

The basic rules of the wine/food matchup game are not difficult to master. These are the tried-and-true, allegedly cardinal principles, such as young wines before old, dry before sweet, white before red, red with meat, and white with fish. However, these principles are qualified by many exceptions; your choices are a great deal broader than you have been led to believe. One of France's greatest restaurant proprietors once told me that if people would simply pick their favorite wines to go along with their favorite dishes, they would all be a great deal happier. Furthermore, he would be pleased not to have to see so much anxiety and apprehension on their faces. I'm not sure that I can go that far, but given my gut feeling that there are more combinations of wine and food that work reasonably well than there are that do not, let me share some of my basic observations with you. There are several important questions you should consider:

• *Does the food offer simple or complex flavors?* The two favorite grapes of wine drinkers in the United States are Chardonnay and Cabernet Sauvignon, both of which are able to produce majestic wines of exceptional complexity and depth of flavor. However, as food wines they are remarkably one-dimensional. As complex and rewarding as they can be, they work well only with dishes that contain relatively simple flavors. Cabernet Sauvignon marries beautifully with basic meat-and-potato dishes: filet mignon, lamb filets, steaks, and so forth. Furthermore, as Cabernet Sauvignon and Merlot-based wines get older and more complex, they require increasingly simpler dishes to complement their complex flavors. Chardonnay goes beautifully with most straightforward fish courses, but once different aromas and scents are added, either from grilling or from ingredients in an accompanying sauce, Chardonnays often compete with rather than complement the food. Thus, the basic rule is: simple wines with complex dishes, and complex wines with simple dishes.

• *What are the primary flavors in the wine and the food?* An appropriate wine choice can often be made if one knows what to expect from the primary flavors in the food to be served. The reason that creamy and buttery sauces with fish, lobster, and even chicken or veal, work well with Chardonnay or white burgundies is because of the buttery vanillin aromas in the fuller, richer, lustier styles of Chardonnay. On the other hand, a mixed salad with an herb dressing and pieces of grilled fish or shellfish beg for a herbaceous, smoky, Sauvignon Blanc or French Sancerre or Pouilly Fumé from the Loire Valley. For the same reason, a steak au poivre in a creamy brown sauce with its intense, pungent aromas and complex flavors requires a big, rich, peppery Rhône, such as a Châteauneuf-du-Pape or Gigondas.

• *Is the texture and flavor intensity of the wine proportional to that of the food?* Did you ever wonder why fresh, briny, sea-scented oysters that are light and zesty taste so good with a Muscadet from France or a lighter-styled California Sauvignon Blanc or Italian Pinot Grigio? It is because these wines have the same weight and light texture as the oysters. Why is it that the smoky, sweet, oaky, tangy flavors of a grilled steak or loin of lamb work best with a Zinfandel or Rhône Valley red wine? While the full-bodied, supple, chewy flavors of these wines go well with a steak or loin of lamb cooked over a wood fire, the same steak or lamb sautéed in butter or baked in the oven will require a well-aged Cabernet Sauvignon or Merlot-based wine from California, Bordeaux or Australia.

Similarly, regarding fish, the intense flavors and fatty texture of salmon, lobster, shad, and bluefish require a similarly styled, lusty, oaky, buttery Chardonnay. On the other hand, trout, sole, turbot, and shrimp are leaner and more delicately flavored, and therefore require lighter, less-intense wines, such as non-oaked Chardonnays from France's Mâconnais region or Italy's Friuli-Venezia Giulia area. In addition, a lighter-styled champagne or German Riesling (a dry Kabinett works ideally) goes extremely well with trout, sole, or turbot but falls on its face if matched against salmon, shad, or lobster.

One further example of texture and flavor matchups is the classic example of drinking a heavy, unctuous, rich, sweet Sauternes with foie gras. The extravagantly rich and flavorful foie gras cannot be served with any other type of wine, as it would overpower a dry red or white wine. The fact that both the Sauternes and the foie gras have intense, concentrated flavors and similar textures is the very reason why this combination is so decadently delicious.

• *What is the style of wine produced in the vintage that you have chosen?* Several of France's greatest chefs have told me they prefer

off years of Bordeaux and Burgundy to great years, and have in-
structed their sommeliers to buy the wines for the restaurant accordingly. How can this be true? From the chef's perspective, the food,
not the wine, should be the focal point of the meal. Many chefs feel
that a great vintage of Burgundy or Bordeaux, with wines that are
exceptionally rich, powerful, and concentrated, not only takes attention away from their cuisine, but makes matching a wine with the food
much more troublesome. Thus, chefs prefer a 1980 or 1984 Bordeaux
rather than a superconcentrated 1982 Bordeaux. For the same reasons, they prefer a 1982 or 1984 red burgundy over a 1983 or 1985.
Thus, the great vintages (1961, 1982, or 1986 Bordeaux or 1976 and
1985 red burgundy, for example), while being marvelous wines, are
not always the best vintages to choose when considering the matchup
with food. Lighter weight yet tasty wines from unexceptional years
can complement delicate and understated cuisine considerably better
than the great vintages, which should be reserved for very simple
food.

• *Is the food to be served in a sauce?* Ten years ago when eating
at Michel Guerard's restaurant in Eugénie-les-Bains, I ordered a fish
served in a red wine sauce. Guerard recommended a red Graves from
Bordeaux since the sauce was made from a reduction of fish stock and
a red Graves. The combination was immensely successful and opened
my eyes to the possibilities of fish with red wine. Since then I have
had tuna in a green peppercorn sauce with California Cabernet Sauvignon (the matchup was great), and salmon sautéed in a red wine
sauce that did justice to a young vintage of red Bordeaux. A white
wine with any of these courses would not have worked. Similarly, I
have enjoyed veal in a creamy Morilles sauce with a Tokay from
Alsace. As with the choice of red Graves above, you can choose the
same specific wine that the food is prepared with, often with marvelous results. For example, coq au vin, an exquisite peasant dish, can
be cooked in either a white wine or red wine sauce. When I've had
coq au vin au Riesling, a dry Alsace Riesling with it has been simply
extraordinary. In Burgundy I have often had coq au vin in a red wine
sauce consisting of a reduced burgundy wine, and the choice of a red
burgundy makes the dish even more special.

• *When you travel, do you drink locally produced wines with the
local cuisine?* It is no coincidence that the regional cuisines of Bordeaux, Burgundy, Provence, and Alsace in France, and Tuscany and
Piedmont in Italy seem to enhance and complement the local wines.
In fact, most restaurants in these areas rarely offer wines from outside
the local region. One always wonders which came first, the cuisine or

the wine. Certainly, the United States is beginning to develop its own regional cuisines, but except for California and the Pacific Northwest few areas promote local wines as appropriate matchups with the local cuisine. For example, in my Maryland neighborhood a number of small wineries make an excellent white wine called Seyval Blanc, which is the perfect foil for both the oysters and the blue channel crabs from Chesapeake Bay. Yet, few restaurants in the Baltimore–Washington area promote these local wines. Drinking regional wines with regional foods should not only be a top priority when traveling in Europe, but also when traveling in America's viticultural areas.

• *Have you learned the best and worst wine and food matchups?* If the whole subject of wine and food combinations still seems too difficult to grasp, then your best strategy might be simply to learn some of the greatest combinations as well as some of the worst. I can also add a few pointers I have learned through my own experience. Certain wine and food relationships of contrasting flavors can be sublime. Perhaps the best example is a sweet, creamy textured Sauternes with a salty aged Stilton or Roquefort cheese. The opposite flavors and textures complement one another beautifully. Another great combiantion is Alsace Gewürztraminers and Rieslings with ethnic cuisine such as Indian and Chinese. The juxtaposition of sweet-and-sour combinations, as well as the spiciness, of Oriental cuisine seems to work quite well with these Alsatian wines.

One of the great myths about wine and food matchups is that red wines work well with cheese. The truth is that they rarely ever do. Most cheeses, especially such favorites as Brie and double and triple creams, have such a high fat content that most red wines suffer horribly when drunk with them. Although it may shock your guests, with cheese I recommend serving a white wine made from the Sauvignon Blanc grape, such as a Sancerre or Pouilly Fumé from France. The dynamic personalities of these two wines and their tangy, zesty acidity stand up well to virtually all types of cheese, and they especially go well with fresh goat cheese.

Another myth is that dessert wines go best with desserts. Most people seem to like champagne, sweet Riesling, sweet Chenin Blanc, or a Sauternes with dessert. Setting aside the fact that chocolate-based desserts are always in conflict with any type of wine, I find that dessert wines are best served *as* the dessert or after the dessert. I've always enjoyed dessert wines more when they are the centerpiece of attention.

If wine and food matchups still seem too complicated for you, remember that in the final analysis a good wine served with a good dish to good company is always in good taste. *A votre santé.*

What's Been Added to Your Wine?

Over the last decade people have become much more sensitive to what they put in their bodies. The hazards of excessive smoking, fat consumption, and high blood pressure are being taken seriously by increasing numbers of people in the United States and in Europe. While this movement is to be applauded, one extremist group, labeled by observers as "neo-prohibitionists" or "new drys," are exploiting this concern for good health and are promoting the message that the consumption of *any* alcoholic beverage is inherently dangerous and undermines society and family. These groups do not care for moderation; they want to totally remove wine (and any alcoholic beverage) from the marketplace. In this attempt, they have misrepresented wine and have ignored data that demonstrates that moderate wine drinking is more beneficial than harmful. Unfortunately, the law prohibits the wine industry from publicizing this information.

Although wine is one of the most natural of all beverages, additives are often found in it (and the neo-prohibitionists are claiming that these are potentially lethal). Following is a list of the most common additives.

Acids. Most vineyards in cool climates never have the need to add acids to wine. In California and Australia, however, acids are often added to give balance to the wines, as grapes from these hot climates often lack enough natural acidity. Most serious wineries add tartaric acid, which is the same type of acid found naturally in wine. Less quality-oriented wineries dump in pure citric acid, which makes the wine taste like a lemon-lime sorbet.

Clarification Agents. Items that are dumped into wine to cause suspended particles to coagulate include dried ox blood, isinglass, casein (milk powder), kaolin (clay), bentonite (powdered clay), and the traditional egg whites. These fining agents are designed to make the wine brilliant and particle-free, and they are harmless. Nevertheless, top wineries use them sparingly or don't use them at all.

Oak. Many top-quality red and white wines spend most of their lives aging in oak barrels. It is expected that wine stored in wood will take on some of the toasty, smoky, vanillin flavors of wood. These aromas and flavors, if not overdone, add flavor complexity to a wine. Cheap wine can also be marginally enhanced by the addition of oak chips to provide a more aggressive, raw flavor of wood.

Sugar. In most of the viticultural regions of Europe, except for southern France, Portugal, and Spain, the law permits the addition of sugar to the fermenting grape juice in order to raise the alcohol levels. This practice, called chaptalization, is resorted to in cool years when the grapes do not attain sufficient ripeness. It is never needed in the hot climate of California or in most of Australia, where low natural acidity —not low sugar—is the problem. Judicious chaptalization raises the alcohol level by 1–2%.

Sulfates. All bottles must now carry labels indicating that the wine contains sulfates. Sulfate (also referred to as SO_2, or sulphur dioxide) is a preservative used to kill bacteria and micro-organisms, and is sprayed on virtually all fresh vegetables and fruits. A small percentage of the population, especially asthmatics, is allergic to SO_2. The fermentation of wine produces some sulfur dioxide naturally, but it is also added to oak barrels by burning a sulphur stick inside the barrel in order to kill any bacteria; it is added again during bottling to prevent the wine from oxidizing. Quality wines should never smell of sulphur (a burning match smell) because serious winemakers keep the sulphur level very low, and some do not employ sulphates at all. When used properly, sulphates impart no smell or taste to the wine, and are harmless to the general population (excepting, of course, those who are allergic to them). Used excessively, sulphates impart the aforementioned unpleasant smell and a prickly taste. Obviously, people who are allergic to sulphates should not drink wine, just as people who are allergic to fish roe should not eat caviar.

Tannin. Tannin occurs naturally in the skins and stems of grapes, and the content from the crushing of the grape skins and subsequent maceration of the skins and juice is usually more than adequate to provide sufficient natural tannin. Tannin gives a red wine grip and backbone, while also acting as a preservative. However, on rare occasions tannin is added to an otherwise spineless wine.

Yeasts. While many winemakers rely on the indigenous wild yeasts in the vineyard to start the fermentation, it is becoming more common to employ cultured yeasts for this procedure. This is no health hazard here, but the increasing reliance on the same type of yeast in wineries throughout the world is leading to wines with similar bouquets and flavors.

WINE TRENDS IN THE MARKETPLACE

Some General Observations About American Wine

• California will continue to be the most popular wine region due to four stunning vintages in a row (1984, 1985, 1986, and 1987), which range in quality from excellent to superb.

• Chardonnay, the hottest wine for over the last three years, may be in danger of losing its popularity, because it is overpriced and at least half the wines on the market are neutral-tasting, bland, and overly acidified ripoffs.

• Zinfandel, the red claret style but not the white (actually rosé), will continue to surge in popularity as more and more consumers discover the wonderful up-front, raspberry fruit and delicious, supple textures the best of these wines offer. At its best, Zinfandel provides a much more accessible, tastier wine than the more astringent Cabernet Sauvignon.

• Merlot, for very much the same reasons as for the Zinfandel (easy, succulent, supple drinkability), has become a very popular wine.

• Luxury proprietary red wines are in vogue, but all of them are overpriced and are playing on their mystique and on the consumer's perception that higher prices means higher quality. Most proprietary red wines are very good, and some are even superb, but at $35–50 a bottle they are approximately 30–40% too expensive.

• Given the splendid quality of Rhône Valley grapes grown in California by innovative wineries such as Bonny Doon, Edmunds St. John, Sean Thackrey, Kendall-Jackson, Qupé, Sierra Vista, Ojai, and Zaca Mesa, one has to anticipate more vineyards dedicated to grapes such as Syrah, Mourvedre, and Grenache. These varietals have awesome potential in California, and it would appear their time has come.

• Sooner or later consumers will begin to realize that most California sparkling wine has no flavor or character. An overwhelming number of these wines are appallingly mediocre, yet the wine media and industry continue to play them up. I expect a growing resistance to these wines until they offer more flavor and character.

• With the exception of Oregon, America's other viticultural areas will continue to exist in the giant shadow cast by the California wine industry.

• Oregon will continue to generate excitement for its Pinot Noir and Pinot Gris, but its producers must keep their prices reasonable and resist the temptation to increase their yields per acre in the face of increased demand.

• Expect a growing movement toward naturally made, low-tech, unfiltered, minimally processed—even organic—wines to meet with great demand and success. High technology and oenologists with food processor mentalities have already eviscerated a great many wines of their taste and personality. Consumers will demand more flavor and more personality to their wines as they become better educated. Taste and flavor, in both wine and food, are making a strong comeback, and the overly filtered, stabilized, centrifuged, expensive Chardonnays, Pinot Noirs, and Cabernet Sauvignons of the era of high-tech wine processing will be the big losers. Expect to see more wine labels that say "unfiltered" or "handled with minimal clarification to preserve the natural flavors."

• Foreign investment, acquisition, and ownership of American vineyards and wineries will continue at a strong pace. Following is a list of American wineries/vineyards owned or partially owned by foreign companies.

WINERY/VINEYARD	*PRIMARY OWNER*
BELGIUM	
De Moor Winery	DeSchepper-De Moor
CANADA	
Callaway	Hiram Walker
Parsons Creek	Cabrela Wines
Quail Ridge	Quail Ridge
Sterling	Seagram
Monterey Vineyards	Seagram
Winery Lake	Seagram
Domaine Mumm	Seagram
FRANCE	
Domaine Carneros	Taittinger
Domaine Chandon	Moët-Hennessy
Dominus (John Daniel Society)	Joint venture

Domaine Drouhin	Joseph Drouhin
Michel Tribaut	Michel Tribaut
Napa Creek	Joint venture
Opus One	Robert Mondavi/Mouton Rothschild
Piper Sonoma	Piper Heidsieck
RMS (brandy)	Remy Martin
Roederer U.S.	Louis Roederer
Simi Winery	Moët-Hennessy
Skalli Venture (land)	Skalli S.A.

GREAT BRITAIN

Almaden	Grand Metropolitan
Beaulieu	Grand Metropolitan
Inglenook	Grand Metropolitan
San Martin Winery	Guinness
Sonoma Vineyards	Guinness
Sugarloaf Ridge	Peter Michael

JAPAN

Chateau St. Jean	Suntory
Firestone	Firestone (Suntory minority)
Markham	Sanraku
Ridge Vineyards	Otsuka Pharmaceutical
St. Clement	Sapporo

SPAIN

Codorniu (land)	Codorniu S.A.
Gloria Ferrer	Freixenet
Torres (land)	Bodegas Torres

SWITZERLAND

Beringer	Wine World (Nestlé)
Chateau Souverain	Wine World (Nestlé)
Cuvaison	A. G. Inselhold
Domaine Michel	Jean-Jacques Michel
Estrella River Winery	Wine World (Nestlé)
Hess Collection	Donald Hess
Tonio Conti	Chat Botté

THAILAND

Domaine St. George	Four Seas Investment

WEST GERMANY

Buena Vista	A. Racke
Franciscan	Peter Eckes/Augustin Huneeus
Langguth Winery	F. W. Langguth

JOINT VENTURES

France/Switzerland

Maison Deutz	Deutz & Geldermann/Nestlé

Great Britain/Italy/France

Atlas Peak (land)	Whitbread-Antinori-Bollinger

Some General Observations About European Wine

• Buying wine "futures" of Bordeaux has not made sense since 1983, and given the glut of high-quality wine now on the market it still doesn't make sense.

• If buying Bordeaux "futures" and "general" wine investment are out of fashion, so are German wines, due to lack of consumer interest plus less-than-exciting vintages in 1986 and 1987.

• Hedonistic, boldly flavored wines that provide great pleasure are in style. Burgundies (despite their high prices), Rhône wines, Beaujolais, the top Spanish red wines, and Tuscany's new breed of Sangiovese/Cabernet blends are all very popular.

• Regrettably, the era of the designer wine bottle is upon us. There is no doubt that the new super heavy, embossed signature bottles are attractive sights, but the consumer is needlessly under-writing their cost. Italy started this trend and is still the leader in putting mediocre wines in expensive bottles in the hopes of giving them prestige and snob appeal. France and California have been slower to catch on, but I see this as a hot new area. Investors in bottle manufacturing take note!

• Champagne—good old French champagne—continues to have no real competition and remains the top choice for anyone who wants the best in bubbly; but be careful, many of the biggest firms have sacrificed quality as they have expanded internationally.

• Port—vintage port in particular, but 20- and 30-year-old tawny port as well—is in fashion, principally because it is so seductive and rewarding to drink. However, buyers of young vintage port should realize that the best port needs a decade of cellaring before it is ready to drink.

• The most exciting new European viticultural regions for top wine values in the 90s are Tuscany in Italy, the Languedoc-Roussillon corridor in France, the Ribera del Duero and Toro in Spain, and the Douro and Alentejo in Portugal.

• Great wines that consumers are missing out on: Southern Rhônes and Bandols, both of which offer great flavors, exciting aging potential, and realistic prices along with gobs of hedonistic pleasure, lead the lot. They are followed by Alsatian white wines, Italian Barolos and Barbarescos, Italian Dolcettos, and Italy's most refreshing white wine, the Vernaccia di San Gimignano.

• Organic wines, as well as low-processed, unfiltered, unrefined wines, will continue to increase in number. Many wines from Provence are organically made and have met with great commercial success. American importers such as Kermit Lynch and Martine Saunier, both of California, Neal Rosenthal of New York City, and Robert Kacher of Washington, D.C., are now buying wines from their growers by the barrel and insisting that they not be filtered.

• After the boom cycle of 1981–1984, European wines will continue to fall behind California wines in terms of sales and popularity unless the dollar strengthens and makes them more competitively priced.

Some General Observations About Wine of the Southern Hemisphere

• Australia, which has had unprecedented success in the foreign marketplace, particularly in England and the United States, will find it more difficult in 1989–1990. Smaller than normal crops in 1987 and 1988 have led to price hikes that diminish the competitive edge Australian wines have had. Nevertheless, this is still a very good source for reasonably priced Chardonnays, Sauvignons, Cabernet Sauvignons, and Shiraz wines.

• Chile, one of the world's greatest yet untapped viticultural areas, will continue to provide the very best values in Sauvignon Blanc and Cabernet Sauvignon, and it is only a matter of time before a highly capitalized American or French wine producer decides to make a luxury cuvée of Chilean Cabernet Sauvignon.

• Despite progress in quality, Argentina, trying to jump on the South American wine bandwagon, has not yet reached the point where its wines can compete internationally.

• Despite all the hype about New Zealand's cool-climate wines, only a handful have the quality to be competitive internationally. Too much of the praise seems to be the result of all-expense-paid wine writers' junkets.

Some Final Thoughts

THE GROWING INTERNATIONAL NEUTRALIZATION OF WINE STYLES

While technology allows winemakers to produce wines of increasingly better quality, the continuing obsession with technical perfection is stripping wines of their distinctive character. Whether it is due to the excessive filtration of wines or to the excessive emulation of winemaking styles, the tragedy of modern winemaking is that it has become increasingly difficult to tell a Chardonnay made in Italy from one made in France or California or Australia. When all the corporate winemakers throughout the world begin to make their wines the same way, designing them to offend the least number of people, wines will doubtless lose their fascinating appeal and individuality. They will become indistinguishable from one another like most brands of whiskey, gin, scotch, or vodka. One must not forget that wine's great appeal is that it provides a unique experience every time one drinks it. Winemakers and winery owners, particularly in the United States, should be willing to take risks in order to preserve the individual character of their wines, even if some consumers find the wines unusual. It is the distinctive quality of wine that will ensure its future.

THE INFLATED WINE PRICING OF RESTAURANT OWNERS

Given the vast sums that are being spent in restaurants, it would seem that a restaurant would be an ideal place to promote the consumption of wine and to foster awareness about wine. However, most restaurants treat wine as a luxury item, marking it up an exorbitant 200–500%, thereby effectively discouraging the consumption of wine. This practice of offering wines at huge markups also serves to reinforce the mistaken notion that wine is only for the elite and the super rich.

The wine industry does little about this practice, being content to see its wines placed on a restaurant's list. But the consumer would do well to avoid those restaurants that charge exorbitant wine prices, no matter how sublime the cuisine. I stopped going to New York's Le Bernardin because of wine prices that reflect a 400–500% markup, even though the food is spectacular.

Fortunately, things are slightly better today than they were a decade ago, as some restaurant owners are now regarding wine as an integral part of the meal, and not merely as a device used to increase the bill.

THE NEGLECT ON THE PART OF WINE IMPORTERS, WHOLESALERS, RETAILERS, AND RESTAURATEURS TO ENSURE OR PROVIDE FOR PROPER STORAGE CONDITIONS

As previously mentioned, many people in the wine industry carelessly ignore the fundamentals of good wine storage, and it is the consumer who suffers. Wine, especially handcrafted fine wine, is a fragile, living beverage. If it has not been overly processed, pasteurized, or filtered, several days of storage at temperatures above 80° will cause a loss of bouquet and a lack of focus in its flavors. Several weeks at this temperature will give it a baked, hollow, astringent flavor; several months will render it lifeless.

Thousands of bottles and cases of damaged or dead wine are bought each year by you, the unsuspecting wine consumer, and much of it is not drunk for five or ten years. Wine importers who fail to ship their wines in temperature-controlled containers, called "reefers," which adds about 25 cents per bottle to their cost, and continue to ship wines from Europe in the summer or through the Gulf of Mexico and Panama Canal year-round, are guilty of negligence. (I would go so far as to suggest that victims of this type of negligence should consider legal action against these importers.) Wineries who send wines from California, Washington State, or Oregon back East between May and September in unrefrigerated trucks are also at fault, as are wholesalers, retailers, and restaurateurs who poorly store fine wine. The culprits are often liquor and beer distributors who handle wine as a sideline and who care little for how wine is stored.

Wineries and wine brokers who fail to accept responsibility for wine after it has been sold are often as guilty as importers, wholesalers, retailers, and restaurateurs. To compound the problem, when the winery receives complaints about the quality of its wine, it then begins to overly process the wine, often through sterile filtering or perhaps pasteurization, thereby killing the wine's personality and flavors long before it even leaves the winery. Fortunately, poorly treated wine can often be spotted by visual examination (see pages 18–20), but this is a serious problem well worth the serious attention on the part of consumers, government agencies, and, of course, the wine industry itself.

THE 25 GREATEST RED WINES OF RECENT YEARS

L'Arrosée 1986 St.-Émilion	France
Chave 1985 Hermitage	France

Domaine de la Romanée-Conti 1985 Romanée-Conti	France
Domaine de la Romanée-Conti 1985 La Tâche	France
Domaine de la Romanée-Conti 1985 Richebourg	France
Dominus 1985 Proprietary Red Wine	California
Dunn 1985 Cabernet Sauvignon Napa Howell Mountain	California
Angelo Gaja 1985 Barbaresco Sori Tilden	Italy
Bruno Giacosa 1982 Barbaresco Santo Stefano	Italy
Guigal 1985 Côte Rôtie La Mouline	France
Guigal 1985 Côte Rôtie La Landonne	France
Domaine Henri Jayer 1985 Richebourg	France
Leroy 1985 Mazis-Chambertin Hospices de Beaune	France
Château Margaux 1986 Margaux	France
Château Montelena 1985 Cabernet Sauvignon	California
Château Mouton-Rothschild 1986 Pauillac	France
Penfolds 1982 Grange Hermitage	Australia
Pichon Longueville Comtesse de Lalande 1986 Pauillac	France
Château Rayas 1985 Châteauneuf-du-Pape	France
Ridge 1984 Cabernet Sauvignon Monte Bello	California
Joseph Roty 1985 Charmes Chambertin	France
Silver Oak 1985 Cabernet Sauvignon Alexander Valley	California
Silver Oak 1985 Cabernet Sauvignon Napa	California
Spottswoode 1985 Cabernet Sauvignon Napa	California
Stag's Leap 1985 Cask 23 Proprietary Red Wine	California

THE 20 GREATEST WHITE WINES OF RECENT YEARS

Chalone 1985 Chardonnay Reserve	California
Coche-Dury 1986 Corton Charlemagne	France
Coche-Dury 1986 Meursault Perrières	France
Domaine Comte Lafon 1986 Meursault Perrières	France
Domaine Comte Lafon 1986 Meursault Genevrières	France
Domaine Comte Lafon 1986 Meursault Charmes	France
Joseph Drouhin 1985 Montrachet Marquis de la Laguiche	France
Hospices de Beaune 1985 Meursault Cuvée Baudin	France
Hospices de Beaune 1985 Corton Charlemagne F. Salins	France

Louis Jadot 1985 Chevalier Montrachet Les Demoiselles	France
Vincent Leflaive 1986 Chevalier Montrachet	France
Vincent Leflaive 1986 Puligny Montrachet Les Combettes	France
Lequin-Roussot 1985 Bâtard Montrachet	France
Michel Niellon 1985 Bâtard Montrachet	France
Ramonet 1982 Montrachet	France
Ramonet 1983 Montrachet	France
Zind-Humbrecht 1985 Gewürztraminer Gueberschwihr	France
Zind-Humbrecht 1985 Gewürztraminer Hengst	France
Zind-Humbrecht 1986 Tokay d'Alsace Vieilles Vignes	France
Zind-Humbrecht 1985 Tokay Clos Saint-Urbain Rangen	France

THE GREATEST WINE VALUES: 180 WINES FOR UNDER $8 A BOTTLE

Anselmi 1987 Soave (white)	Italy
Apremont 1986 Vin de Savoie (white)	France
Baron Jaquab de Herzog 1987 Sauvignon Blanc Sonoma (white)	California
Baron Jaquab de Herzog 1987 Gamay Sonoma (red)	California
Becassonne 1987 Côtes du Rhone (white)	France
De Belcier 1985 Côtes de Castillon (red)	France
De Belcier 1986 Côtes de Castillon (red)	France
René Berrod 1987 Beaujolais-Villages (red)	France
Bonny Doon 1987 Vin Gris de Mourvedre (rosé)	California
Bonny Doon 1987 Clos de Gilroy (red)	California
Brown Bros. 1985 Cabernet Sauvignon-Family Select (red)	Australia
Brown Bros. 1985 Shiraz (red)	Australia
Brown Bros. 1984 Shiraz/Mondeuse/Cabernet (red)	Australia
Brown Bros. 1987 Sauvignon Blanc (white)	Australia
Brown Bros. N.V. Lexia Muscat (dessert)	Australia
Marqués de Cáceres 1985 Rioja (red)	Spain
Marqués de Cáceres 1982 Rioja Reserva (red)	Spain
Cadiz N.V. Reserva Brut (sparkling white)	Spain
Canepa 1987 Sauvignon Blanc (white)	Chile

Carmenet 1986 French Colombard (white)	California
Castillo di Almansa 1982 (red)	Spain
Caves Coopératives d'Aléria N.V. Réserve du Président Corsica (red)	France
Cazes 1983 Côtes de Roussillon (red)	France
Cazes 1984 Côtes de Roussillon (red)	France
Cazes 1985 Côtes de Roussillon (red)	France
Domaine Challon 1987 Bordeaux Blanc (white)	France
Columbia 1987 Semillon (white)	Washington
Columbia 1987 Pacifica (white)	Washington
Columbia Crest 1984 Merlot (red)	Washington
Columbia Crest 1984 Cabernet Sauvignon (red)	Washington
Conde de Valdemar 1986 Rioja Tinto (red)	Spain
Conde de Valdemar 1982 Rioja Reserva (red)	Spain
Conde de Valdemar 1980 Rioja Reserva (red)	Spain
Corbans 1986 Chardonnay (white)	New Zealand
Domaine le Couroulu 1984 Vacqueyras Cuvée Spéciale (red)	France
Domaine le Couroulu 1985 Vacqueyras (red)	France
Domaine le Couroulu 1986 Vacqueyras (red)	France
Court des Muts 1985 Bergerac (red)	France
Cousino Macul 1987 Chardonnay (white)	Chile
Cousino Macul 1981 Cabernet Sauvignon Antiguas Riserva (red)	Chile
Georges Duboeuf 1988 Beaujolais-Villages (red)	France
Domaine Durieu 1986 or 1985 Côtes du Rhone (red)	France
Etang des Colombes 1985 Cuvée Bicentenaire Corbières (red)	France
Estancia 1985 Cabernet Sauvignon (red)	California
Errazueiz Panquehue 1988 Sauvignon Blanc (white)	Chile
Falchini 1986 or 1987 Vernaccia di San Gimignano (white)	Italy
Charles de Fere N.V. Brut Reserve (white)	France
Charles de Fere N.V. Brut Rosé (rosé)	France
Fetzer 1987 Chardonnay Sundial (white)	California
Fetzer 1985 Zinfandel Lake County (red)	California
Fetzer 1985 Cabernet Sauvignon Lake County (red)	California
Folie à Deux 1987 Chenin Blanc Napa (white)	California
Gamla 1987 French Colombard Galil (white)	Israel
Gamla 1986 Sauvignon Blanc Special Reserve (white)	Israel

Garland Ranch 1985 Cabernet Sauvignon Monterey (red)	California
Domaines Gavoty 1987 Rosé Cuvée Clarendon (rosé)	France
Domaines Gavoty 1987 Blanc Cuvée Clarendon (white)	France
Domaines Gavoty 1986 Rouge Cuvée Clarendon (red)	France
Graville-Lacoste 1986 or 1987 Graves (white)	France
Josmeyer 1987 Pinot d'Alsace Mise du Printemps (white)	France
Kendall-Jackson 1987 Sauvignon Blanc Clear Lake (white)	California
Lancer's N.V. Brut Sparkling Wine (white)	Portugal
Louis Latour 1986 Chardonnay Ardèche (white)	France
Château Launay 1987 Entre Deux Mers (white)	France
Château Lauretan 1986 Blanc (white)	France
Château Lauretan 1985 Rouge (red)	France
Lembey 1984 Spanish Sparkling (white)	Spain
Liberty School N.V. Cabernet Sauvignon Lot 16 (red)	California
Liberty School 1987 Sauvignon Blanc Lot 6 (white)	California
Lindeman 1987 Chardonnay Bin 65 (white)	Australia
Lindeman 1985 Cabernet Sauvignon Bin 45 (red)	Australia
Los Vascos 1984 Cabernet Sauvignon (red)	Chile
Château Louvie 1986 Bordeaux Blanc (white)	France
Maculan 1987 Breganze di Breganze (white)	Italy
Mâitre d'Estournel 1986 or 1987 Blanc Générique Bordeaux (white)	France
Mâitre d'Estournel 1985 Rouge Générique Bordeaux (red)	France
La Margolaine 1986 Chardonnay (white)	California
Mas de Cadenet 1985 Côtes de Provence Rouge (red)	France
Mas de Cadenet 1986 Côtes de Provence Blanc (white)	France
Masa Barril 1986 Priorato Spain (red)	Spain
McDowell Valley Vineyards 1985 Grenache Rosé (rosé)	California
Château de Mille 1985 Côtes du Lubéron (red)	France
Montesierra 1987 (red)	Spain

Mont Marcal N.V. Brut Tradition Sparkling (white)	Spain
Domaine de Montmarin 1987 Marsanne Côtes de Thongue (white)	France
Domaine de Montmarin 1987 Rosé de Cabernet (rosé)	France
Mont-Redon 1985 or 1986 Côtes du Rhône (red)	France
Mountain View N.V. Zinfandel Amador (red)	California
Mountain View 1986 Pinot Noir Carneros (red)	California
Muga 1982 Rioja Tinto (red)	Spain
Muga 1983 Rioja Tinto (red)	Spain
Château de Padère 1986 Côtes de Buzet (red)	France
Château de Paraza 1986 Minervois Cuvée Spéciale (red)	France
Château de Paraza 1986 Minervois Cuvée Chêne Neuf (red)	France
Château de Paraza 1986 Minervois Kosher Cuvée (red)	France
Parducci 1987 Sauvignon Blanc Mendocino (white)	California
Parducci 1986 or 1987 Chardonnay Mendocino (white)	California
Parducci 1984 Cabernet Sauvignon Mendocino (red)	California
Parducci 1986 Zinfandel Mendocino (red)	California
Pedroncelli 1986 Chenin Blanc Sonoma (white)	California
Pedroncelli 1984 Cabernet Sauvignon Sonoma (red)	California
Periquita 1983 (red)	Portugal
Periquita 1985 (red)	Portugal
Picpoul de Pinet 1985 or 1986 Languedoc Cuvée Ludovic Gaujal (red)	France
Pine Ridge 1987 Chenin Blanc Napa (white)	California
Château Pitray 1985 Côtes de Castillon (red)	France
Pitray 1986 Côtes de Castillon (red)	France
Plagnac 1985 Médoc (red)	France
Plagnac 1986 Médoc (red)	France
Château Pontac Monplaisir 1987 Graves (white)	France
Preston Vineyards 1987 Cuvée de Fumé Dry Creek (white)	California
Preston Vineyards 1987 Chenin Blanc Dry Creek (white)	California
Domaine la Rosière 1986 Syrah Coteaux des Baronnies (red)	France
Domaine la Rosière 1986 Syrah (red)	France

Rosemount 1986 Diamond Reserve Red Table Wine (red)	Australia
St. Morillon 1983 Cabernet Sauvignon (red)	Chile
Salice Salentino 1981 Reserve (red)	Italy
Santa Rita 1985 Cabernet Sauvignon Medalla Real (red)	Chile
Santa Rita 1985 Cabernet Sauvignon 120 Estate (red)	Chile
Santa Rita 1985 120 (red)	Chile
Sarda-Mallet 1985 or 1986 Côtes du Roussillon Black Label (red)	France
Sauvion Château du Cléray 1987 Muscadet (white)	France
Seghesio 1987 Chardonnay Sonoma (white)	California
Seghesio 1984 Zinfandel N. California (red)	California
Seghesio N.V. Lot 3 Sonoma Red (red)	California
Seppelt 1986 Chardonnay Reserve Bin (white)	Australia
Seppelt 1987 Chardonnay Reserve Bin (white)	Australia
Seppelt 1985 Cabernet Sauvignon Black Label (red)	Australia
Seppelt 1985 Shiraz Black Label (red)	Australia
Château Souverain 1986 Chardonnay Sonoma (white)	California
Château Tahbilk 1984 or 1985 Cabernet Sauvignon Victoria (red)	Australia
Château Tahbilk 1984 Shiraz Victoria (red)	Australia
Château Talbot 1987 Caillou Blanc (white)	France
Château Talbot 1986 Caillou Blanc (white)	France
Domaine du Talmard 1986 Macon Villages (white)	France
Domaine du Tariquet 1987 Vin de Pays Ugni Blanc (white)	France
Château Tayac 1985 Côtes de Bourg (red)	France
Château Thieuley 1987 Bordeaux Rosé Clairet (rosé)	France
Château Thieuley 1986 Bordeaux Rouge (red)	France
Château Thieuley 1987 Bordeaux Blanc (white)	France
Château Thieuley 1987 Cuvée Francis Courselle (white)	France
Toro 1985 or 1986 Colegiata (red)	Spain
Toro 1985 Gran Colegiata (red)	Spain
Toro 1986 Gran Colegiata (red)	Spain
Torres 1985 Coronas (red)	Spain
Torres 1985 Sangre de Toro (red)	Spain
Torres 1983 Sangre de Toro Reserva (red)	Spain

Trefethen N.V. Eshcol Red (red)	California
Trefethen N.V. Eshcol White (white)	California
Marini 1987 Pinot Grigio di Veneto (white)	Italy
Marini 1987 Chardonnay di Veneto (white)	Italy
Tyrrell 1984 Long Flat Red (red)	Australia
Vallana 1982 Spanna (red)	Italy
M.G. Vallejo 1985 Cabernet Sauvignon (red)	California
Vidal-Fleury 1985 or 1986 Côtes du Rhône (red)	France
La Vieille Ferme 1986 Côtes du Rhône Réserve Gold Label (white)	France
La Vieille Ferme 1986 Côtes du Rhône Réserve Gold Label (red)	France
La Vieille Ferme 1986 Côtes du Lubéron (white)	France
La Vieille Ferme 1986 Côtes du Ventoux (red)	France
Vietti 1987 Moscato d'Asti Cascinetta (white)	Italy
Willow Creek 1986 Chardonnay (white)	California
Willm 1986 or 1985 Pinot Blanc Cordon d'Alsace (white)	France
Wyndham Estate 1985 Pinot Noir Hunter Valley (red)	Australia
Wyndham Estate 1985 Merlot Hunter Valley (red)	Australia
Wyndham Estate 1984 Hermitage Bin 555 Hunter Valley (red)	Australia
Wyndham Estate 1984 Cabernet Sauvignon Bin 444 (red)	Australia
Wyndham Estate 1985 Botrytis Riesling Late Harvest (dessert)	Australia
Yalumba Clocktower Port (Hill-Smith) (port)	Australia

THE WINES OF WESTERN EUROPE

France

Alsace
Bordeaux
Burgundy
Champagne
The Loire Valley
Languedoc and Roussillon
Provence
The Rhône Valley
Bergerac and the Southwest

Italy

Piedmont
Tuscany
Other Significant Red Wines of Italy
Other Significant White Wines of Italy

Germany

Portugal

Spain

1. FRANCE

ALSACE

*France's Least-Known Great
White Wines*

The Basics

TYPES OF WINE

Everytime I have served a wine from Alsace to guests they have loved it. Why, then, do these remarkably good dry wines, ideal with food, continue to fail in gaining popularity with consumers? The best of Alsatian wines are white table wines, ranging from crisp, medium-bodied Pinot Blancs to extravagantly rich, flamboyant Gewürztraminers. Powerful, slightly sweet Vendange Tardives (from grapes harvested especially late) and nectarlike sweet dessert wines, called Sélection de Grains Nobles, come from this region. Inexpensive and very good sparkling white wines, called Crémant d'Alsace, are produced, but the watery, insipid rosé-colored Pinot Noirs that come from Alsace should largely be avoided.

GRAPE VARIETIES

Alsace makes it easy for the consumer. As is done in California, the wines here are named after the variety of grape used to make them. Least expensive—and least interesting—is Edelzwicker (from a blend of grapes) and Sylvaner. Inexpensive and very interesting is

45

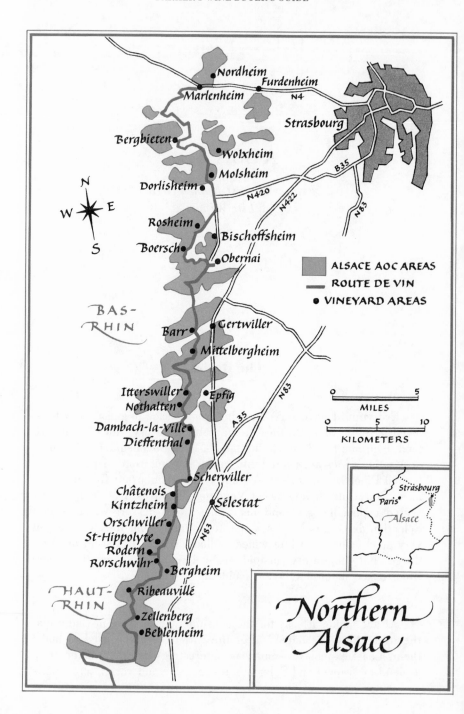

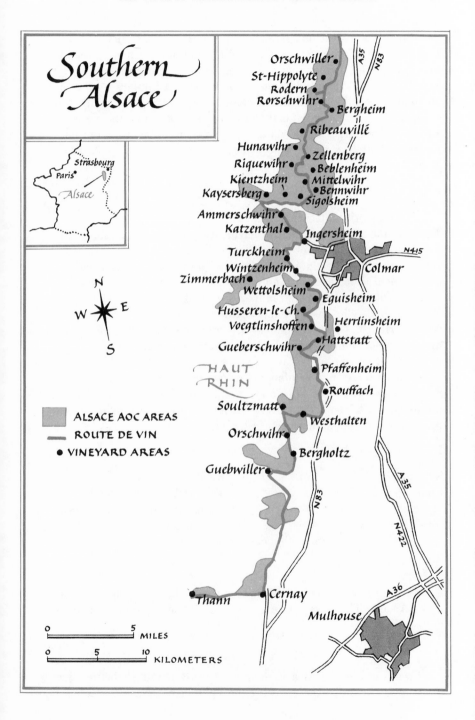

Southern
Alsace

Strasbourg
Paris
Alsace

N
W — E
S

ALSACE AOC AREAS
ROUTE DE VIN
VINEYARD AREAS

Orschwiller
St-Hippolyte
Rodern
Rorschwihr
Bergheim
Ribeauvillé
Hunawihr
Zellenberg
Riquewihr
Beblenheim
Kientzheim
Mittelwihr
Kaysersberg
Bennwihr
Sigolsheim
Ammerschwihr
Katzenthal
Ingersheim
Turckheim
Wintzenheim
Colmar
Zimmerbach
Wettolsheim
Eguisheim
Husseren-le-Ch.
Herrlinsheim
Voegtlinshoffen
Hattstatt
Gueberschwihr
HAUT
RHIN
Pfaffenheim
Rouffach
Soultzmatt
Westhalten
Orschwihr
Bergholtz
Guebwiller

Thann   Cernay
Mulhouse

0   5   MILES
0   5   10   KILOMETERS

the Pinot Blanc. Riesling renders wines that are bone-dry and full, and Pinot Gris (often called Tokay d'Alsace) offers smoky, creamy, rich, and opulent wines that are loaded with fruit, are quite dry, and would embarrass many white burgundies. Gewürztraminer reaches its greatest heights in Alsace and produces intense, pungent, heady, fragrant wines of great individual character. The dry Muscats of Alsace are the finest in the world, yet few people seem to be aware of them. Alsace is largely a white wine lover's paradise, except for its Pinot Noir.

FLAVORS

Alsace's dry table wines generally have a wide range of flavors. There is the green and neutral flavor of Sylvaner; the fresh, stony, floral, and fruity flavor of Pinot Blanc; the applelike, floral, lemony, zesty, and mineral-scented flavor of Riesling; and the spring flowers and tropical fruit flavor of the dry Muscats. The two richest wines of Alsace, Tokay and Gewürztraminer, are totally different. The Tokay is smoky and rich, has a creamy texture, is full-bodied, and has buttery overtones. Gewürztraminers are intensely aromatic, with bouquets suggestive of rose petals, lychee nuts, and grapefruit, and with luscious, often unctuous flavors and a full body. When these same wines are offered in a Vendange Tardive format (meaning a late harvested wine where the grapes are extremely ripe), the alcohol level jumps from 11.5%–12% to 14.5%–16%, and their personality trademarks are then much more concentrated.

AGING POTENTIAL

Sylvaner: 1–5 years   Riesling: 3–10 years
Pinot Blanc: 3–6 years   Tokay (Pinot Gris): 3–12 years
Muscat: 3–6 years   Gewürztraminer: 5–20 years
Note: If the wine is a Vendange Tardive, add 5 years to its longevity span. If the wine is a Sélection de Grains Nobles, add 7–10 years.

OVERALL QUALITY LEVEL

Few of France's viticultural areas have as high a standard of quality as Alsace. The wines are extremely well made, even at the cooperative level.

MOST IMPORTANT INFORMATION TO KNOW

First, the wines of Alsace, though put in German-style bottles, are *dry* wines. The only exceptions are the Vendange Tardives, which are off-dry, and the sweet dessert wines, the Sélection de Grains Nobles. Second, despite the price hikes, Alsatian Pinot Blancs are still reasonably priced and are among the best dry white table wines in the world for less than $10. When made in the dry, full-bodied style preferred by vignerons in Alsace, Pinot Gris, or Tokay, is a remarkably complex, creamy, smoky wine that can rival most white burgundies. The two wine stars of Alsace are the dry, steely Rieslings and the exotic, flamboyant Gewürztraminers. The Rieslings have plenty of flavor and much more body than their German counterparts; they age very well and offer considerable flexibility with food. As for the Gewürztraminers, I have often described them as the "love them or leave them" wines. I adore Gewürztraminer from Alsace and probably go through 3–5 cases per year in my own household; however, there are those who think the wine has too much personality and flavor intensity. I find it to be one that ages well and nicely accompanies Oriental dishes, duck, pheasant, and, of course, smoked meat dishes, particularly the ubiquitous choucroute garnie, which is encountered in virtually every Alsatian restaurant.

Pay strict attention to the labels of Alsatian wines. Most producers make wine of various levels of quality, starting with their regular cuvée, or basic level, followed by their special lots called Cuvée Prestige, Cuvée Réserve, or Réserve Personnelle. Those growers who make wine from any of Alsace's three dozen plus "Grand Cru" vineyards will also list the name of the vineyard. Finally, wines marked "Vendange Tardive" are off-dry, extremely powerful, and often quite amazing. Those wines marked "Sélection de Grains Nobles" are sweet, hedonistic dessert wines.

1989–1990 BUYING STRATEGY

After having an exceptional vintage in 1983, Alsace had another excellent year in 1985 and a decent vintage in 1986. However, the 1983s, bought with a dollar that was 50% stronger than it is today, were outstanding bargains. In fact, many of them still are, since many retailers still have them in stock. The 1985s are virtually as good as the 1983s, less opulent and powerful, but very flavorful and with slightly better acidities. As fine as they are, prices average 30–40% higher per bottle. There is nothing wrong with the 1986s, but they do not compare favorably with the 1985s and 1983s. If one compares the top Alsation white wines with white burgundies of similar quality, the prices look reasonable, but compared with the values that existed for the 1983s, they are expensive. Nevertheless, there is much to recommend, as the 1983 and 1985 vintages produced a bevy of exciting wines. I just wish that more consumers would try these wines and find out just how good they are.

ALSACE
VINTAGE GUIDE

1987—A difficult year in Alsace, but the wines appear better than the growers anticipated. They are light, agreeable, and pleasant, but will have to be drunk young. In many cases the wines may turn out to be as good as the 1986s.

1986—Because of significant rainfall, as well as rot, Alsace's 1986 crop ranges in quality from average to above average. The size of the crop was much smaller than in 1985 or 1983 because of the rot and hailstorms that plagued the area. Most growers felt that the wines would turn out as good as the light, charming 1979s. My tastings appear to confirm their assessment, but there appears to be a great irregularity in quality.

1985—An excellent vintage, nearly as good as the exceptional 1983s. There was a less-intense and less full-bodied Vendange Tardive wine made in 1985; thus the wines are less opulent, rich, and alcoholic than the 1983s, but otherwise this lovely, richly fruity vintage should drink well for 5–7 years, if not longer. Interestingly, the Rieslings of 1985 looked overall to be the weakest group of wines; the Gewürztraminers and Tokays, the strongest.

1984—As in all of France, a difficult but not disastrous year, as press reports had indicated. Most wines are quite light, a trifle too acidic, and less intensely fruity than their 1983 and 1985 counterparts. If priced reasonably, the best of these wines offer decent drinking for the next few years.

1983—A great vintage, the best since 1976 and 1971, the 1983s have everything—intense, pungent, aromatic bouquets, long, rich, ripe flavors, plenty of body, and great balance and length. At the top levels, the wines will last until the mid- to late '90s. It was also a splendid year for the titans of Alsace, the right, alcoholic, heady Vendange Tardives.

1982—A huge crop of rather sound, commercial wines that are soft, fruity, and pleasant. They are aging fast and should, by and large, be drunk up before the end of this decade.

1981—Forgotten in all the (justifiable) hype surrounding 1983 and 1985, this is a good, sometimes very good, vintage of medium-bodied, fruity, well-defined wines. They have good acidity and structure, and though now at their peak, can be drunk with a good deal of pleasure over the next 4–5 years.

1980—A mediocre to below-average-quality vintage. Interestingly, the wines, which were tart and green when first released in 1982–1983, have mellowed substantially with aging. Nothing exciting is to be found here, but as elsewhere in France the wines are better than their initial reputation purported them to be.

1979—A huge crop of sound, fruity, medium-bodied wines were produced in 1979. The wines have aged nicely, surprising most observers who felt they would not last. All of the wines should be drunk up over the next 4–5 years. This vintage can render a number of surprises, particularly the Gewürztraminers, the Tokays, and the Rieslings.

Older Vintages

The 1976s are luscious—intense, full-blown, rather powerful wines of great dimension. The sweet, nectarlike Sélection de Grains Nobles wines are just now coming of age. Two other great vintages for Alsace were 1971 and 1967. But except for the well-cellared examples of Gewürztraminer, Tokay and Riesling, particularly the richer, fuller-bodied Vendange Tardive wines, the glory days have passed.

A GUIDE TO ALSACE'S BEST PRODUCERS

***** *(OUTSTANDING PRODUCERS)*

Marcel Deiss (Bergheim)
Dopff "Au Moulin" (Riquewihr)
Kuentz-Bas (Husseren-les-
    Châteaux)

Josmeyer (Wintzenheim)
Weinbach (Kientzheim)
Zind-Humbrecht (Wintzenheim)

**** *(EXCELLENT PRODUCERS)*

J. Becker (Zellenberg)
Léon Beyer (Eguisheim)
Rolly Gassmann (Rorschwihr)
Hugel (Riquewihr)
Marc Kreydenweiss (Barr)
Kuehn (Ammerschwir)
Landmann-Ostholt (Soultzmatt)
Gustave Lorentz (Bergheim)
Ostertag (Epfig)

René Schaefle (Rouffach)
Martin Schaetzel
    (Ammerschwihr)
Charles Schleret (Turckheim)
Schlumberger (Guebwiller)
Pierre Sparr (Sigolsheim)
Trimbach (Ribeauvillé)
A. Willm (Barr)
A. Zimmerman (Orschwiller)

*** (GOOD PRODUCERS)

Lucien Albrecht (Orschwihr)
Aussay (Eguisheim)
E. Boekel (Mittelbergheim)
Bott Frères (Ribeauvillé)
Joseph Cattin (Voegtlinshoffen)
Dopff & Irion (Riquewihr)
W. Gisselbrecht (Dambach-La-Ville)
Gerard Hartmann (Voegtlinshoffen)
Bruno Hertz (Eguisheim)

Klipfel (Barr)
Klug (Eguisheim)
Laugel (Marlenheim)
Muré-Clos St.-Landelin (Rouffach)
Preiss Henny (Mittelwihr)
Salzmann (Riquewihr)
Edgard Schaller (Mittelwihr)
René Schmidt (Riquewihr)
Sick-Dreyer (Ammerschwihr)
Louis Sipp (Ribeauvillé)

** (AVERAGE PRODUCERS)

Baumann (Mittelwihr)
F. Brucker (Wettolsheim)
La Cigogne (Seva)
Pierre Frick (Pfaffenheim)

Jean Geiler (Ingersheim)
Klack (Riquewihr)
H. Krick (Wintzenheim)

A GUIDE TO THE BEST WINES OF ALSACE

Gewürztraminer

Léon Beyer Comtes d'Eguisheim
Marcel Deiss Bergheim
Marcel Deiss Mittelwihr
Marcel Deiss Saint Hippolyte
Dopff & Irion Les Sorcières
Dopff "Au Moulin" Eichberg
Hugel Réserve Personnelle
Josmeyer Hengst
Marc Kreydenweiss Kritt
Kuentz-Bas Réserve Personnelle
Gustave Lorentz Altenberg
Muré Clos St.-Landelin
Ostertag Moenchberg
Schaetzel Kaefferkopf
Schleret Cuvée Spéciale

Schlumberger Kessler
Schlumberger Christine Schlumberger
Sick-Dreyer Kaefferkopf
Pierre Sparr Mambourg
Trimbach Ribeaupierre
Weinbach Cuvée Théo
Weinbach Réserve Personnelle
Willm Clos Gaensbroennel
Zind-Humbrecht Hengst Wintzenheim
Zind-Humbrecht Gueberschwihr
Zind-Humbrecht Herrenweg Turckheim
Zind-Humbrecht Rangen

Riesling

Léon Beyer Ecaillers
Marcel Deiss Altenberg
Marcel Deiss Saint Hippolyte
Marcel Deiss Schoenenburg
Dopff "Au Moulin"
  Schoenenberg
Hugel Réserve Personnelle
Josmeyer Hengst
Kuentz-Bas "Réserve
  Personnelle
Gustave Lorentz Altenberg
Ostertag Moenchberg
Schaetzel Kaefferkopf
Schlumberger Saering

Schmidt Schoenenberg
L. Sipp Kirchberg
Pierre Sparr Altenbourg
Trimbach Frédéric Emile
Trimbach Clos Ste.-Hune
Weinbach Schlossberg
Weinbach Sainte Catherine
Willm Kirchberg
Zind-Humbrecht Rangen
Zind-Humbrecht Herrenweg
  Turckheim
Zind-Humbrecht Brand
Zind-Humbrecht Clos Hauserer

Tokay d'Alsace (Pinot Gris)

L. Beyer Réserve
Hugel Réserve Personnelle
Kuentz-Bas Réserve Personnelle
Gustave Lorentz Altenberg
Schaetzel

Weinbach
Zind-Humbrecht St. Urbain
  Rangen
Zind-Humbrecht Rangen
Zind-Humbrecht Vieille Vigne

Alsace's Very Best Wine Values—Pinot Blanc and Crémant

Virtually all of Alsace's white wines offer good values in the world-wide wine market, but two stand out as particularly fine values: Pinot Blanc and Crémant d'Alsace, the sparkling wine of Alsace. Pinot Blanc is the poor man's Chardonnay—fresh, lively, crisp, and pleasantly fruity. It is not a wine to buy in lean, tart vintages such as 1984 and 1980 because it is too acidic. However, it flourishes in vintages such as 1983, 1985, 1986, and 1988, rivaling in quality the Chardonnays that sell for two or three times the price. Pinot Blanc, a dry, spicy wine, but not one to age well, is best drunk up within 3–4 years of the vintage. Alsace's other bargain, Crémant d'Alsace, is hardly known outside of the area where it is produced. This inexpensive, sparkling alternative to champagne can be a delicious, fairly priced, dry wine. It rarely sells for more than $10 a bottle.

Alsace's Best Pinot Blancs

Josmeyer Hengst
Josmeyer Les Lutins

Josmeyer Cuvée Vieilles Vignes
Hugel Cuvée les Amours

Marc Kreydenweiss   Weinbach Réserve
M. Schaetzel   Willm Cordon d'Alsace
Schlumbeger Princess Abbes

                    Alsace's Best Crémants
Aussay   Muré Brut Réserve
Dopff "Au Moulin"   Willlm
Landmann Ostholt Vintage

LUCIEN ALBRECHT (ORSCHWIHR)* * *

1985 Gewürztraminer Pfingstberg	B	86
1986 Muscat	B	85
1986 Pinot Blanc	A	75
1985 Riesling	B	85
1986 Riesling	B	79
1985 Riesling Clos Himmelreich	B	85
1986 Riesling Cuvée Henri Albrecht	B	80
1986 Tokay-Pinot Gris	B	74

The 1985 Gewürztraminer Pfingstberg is very elegant—fresh, spicy, and rich, but restrained and balanced. It has developed well with breathing and has exhibited well-focused varietal character; it should age well for 4–5 years. Both Rieslings are quite perfumed and flowery, with some stony mineral scents intermingled. Tightly knit, medium-bodied wines, both have good flavor, depth, and quite a long finish. As for the 1986s, they are not nearly as impressive as Albrecht's 1985s except for the dry yet highly perfumed Muscat. That particular wine is medium-bodied, has a bouquet of spring flowers, and is loaded with fruit. The 1986 Pinot Blanc is dull and boring; of the two Rieslings, the Cuvée Henri Albrecht is the most stylish, but both wines could use more intensity. Lastly, the Tokay also lacks depth and richness for this varietal in Alsace. All in all, the 1985 Albrecht wines are much more impressive than the 1986s.

J. BECKER (ZELLENBERG)* * * *

1985 Gewürztraminer	B	82
1986 Gewürztraminer	B	84
1986 Gewürztraminer Froehn	B	87
1985 Gewürztraminer Vendange Tardive	C	84
1986 Pinot Blanc	A	83
1985 Riesling	B	83

The 1985 regular Gewürztraminer has a flowery, ripe, attractive nose, but tails off on the palate. It should be drunk up over the next two years. The 1985 Gewürztraminer Vendange Tardive has a big, floral, spicy, interesting bouquet, and ripe, round, full-bodied flavors that lack varietal authority. It is good but misses the mark. Drink it over the next 3–4 years. The 1985 Riesling has a good, open, moderately intense, flowery bouquet and is followed by medium-bodied, delicate flavors with good freshness and a polite personality. With respect to Becker's 1986s, surprisingly, I prefer them to his 1985s. The Pinot Blanc has good body and length, and should be consumed over the next several years for its chunky fruitiness. The two 1986 Gewürztraminers are very good, especially the Grand Cru Gewürztraminer from the Froehn vineyard, which shows loads of a lychee nut and grapefruit character in its aromas and flavors. Both wines should be drunk over the next 4–6 years.

LÉON BEYER (EGUISHEIM)* * * *

1986 Gewürztraminer	B	73
1985 Gewürztraminer Cuvée Particulière	B	87
1986 Gewürztraminer Sélection de Grains Nobles	E	92
1985 Pinot Blanc de Blancs	A	84
1985 Riesling	B	80
1986 Riesling	B	84

1985 Riesling Cuvée Particulière	B	86
1986 Riesling Les Écaillers	B	88
1985 Tokay Cuvée Particulière	B	87
1986 Tokay-Pinot Gris Sélection de Grains Nobles	E	?

Fairly powerful, but not overblown, Beyer's 1985 Gewürztraminer Cuvée Particulière is spicy, ripe, and full-bodied, with a smoky, bacon fat bouquet, a long finish, and considerable depth. Drink it over the next 4–6 years. The Pinot Blanc de Blancs is a lighter-styled, yet crisp, refreshing wine with good zesty acidity, and some flavor depth and length. The regular Riesling of 1985 is fresh and well made, but seems to tail off on the palate with a watery finish. On the other hand, the Riesling Cuvée Particulière is very good, with a complex nose of mineral scents and apple blossoms. On the palate, the wine is loaded with ripe fruit, has crisp acidity, and an impressive finish. Drink it over the next 4–5 years. As for the Tokay Cuvée Particulière, I cannot remember a better Tokay from Léon Beyer than this richly buttery, smoky, full-bodied wine. With respect to Beyer's 1986s, most of his wines stood out as being among the most successful made in that vintage. In particular, the 1986 Riesling Les Écaillers is a superb Riesling, with an intense flowery bouquet, crisp, dry, medium-bodied flavors, and excellent length. The 1986 regular cuvée of Gewürztraminer was green and lean, but the decadently sweet Gewürztraminer Seléction de Grains Nobles is pure nectar with huge, massive, honeyed flowers, unbelievable depth and a very sweet, long finish. For whatever reason, the 1986 Tokay Seléction de Grains Nobles tasted heavy, cloying, and sweet without sufficient acidity.

F. BRUCKER (WETTOLSHEIM)* *

1985 Gewürztraminer Cuvée Tradition	A	75
1985 Riesling	A	74

The 1985 Gewürztraminer is a rather bland, simple wine with only a hint of varietal character. Drink it over the next 2–3 years. Brucker's 1985 Riesling has a cheesy nose, which is not very varietal. On the palate, the wine is simple and straightforward. Brucker's 1986 Rieslings and Gewürztraminers were tasted and found to range in quality from mediocre to below average.

JOSEPH CATTIN (VOEGTLINSHOFFEN)* * *

1986 Gewürztraminer	B	83
1985 Gewürztraminer Hatschburg	B	92
1986 Gewürztraminer Hatschburg	B	84
1986 Muscat	B	85
1986 Riesling	B	81
1986 Riesling Hatschburg	B	85
1985 Sylvaner	A	78
1985 Tokay-Pinot Gris	B	84
1985 Tokay-Pinot Gris Hatschburg	B	89
1986 Tokay-Pinot Gris Hatschburg	B	86

I have not been to Cattin's cellars, but his two great 1985s, both from the Grand Cru vineyard Hatschburg, exhibited astonishing richness and balance, as well as great complexity. His 1986s are not as exciting, but are crisp, ready-to-drink, moderately concentrated wines that represent the varietal character of the grape authentically and are quite cleanly made. From a consumer's perspective, I would search for the 1985s that remain in stock before looking at any of the 1986s. Should you be unable to find any of the 1985s, Cattin's 1986 Pinot Gris from the Hatschburg vineyard is excellent.

LA CIGOGNE (SEVA)* *

1985 Gewürztraminer	A	79
1986 Gewürztraminer	A	83
1986 Pinot Blanc	A	76
1985 Riesling	A	80
1986 Riesling	A	73

La Cigogne is one of the better cooperatives in France, and the 1985 Gewürztraminer has a light intensity and a fruity, clean nose; however, some bitterness on the palate lowers the rating. The 1985 Riesling is pleasant and fresh, with a light-intensity perfume of flowers. It is a cleanly and correctly made wine, although short in flavor dimension. La Cigogne made adequate 1986s, with the best being the Gewürztraminer, which while not a blockbuster did exhibit light, spicy, varietal fruit in a medium-bodied format.

MARCEL DEISS (BERGHEIM)* * * * *

1986 Gewürztraminer Bergheim	B	89
1985 Gewürztraminer Mittelwihr	B	86
1986 Gewürztraminer Mittelwihr	B	88
1986 Gewürztraminer Saint Hippolyte	B	90
1986 Pinot Blanc	A	75
1985 Pinot Blanc Bergheim	A	85
1986 Riesling	A	82
1986 Riesling Altenberg	B	87
1985 Riesling Bennwihr	B	85
1985 Riesling Bergheim Engelgarten	B	87
1986 Riesling Bergheim Engelgarten	B	84
1986 Riesling Burg	B	84
1986 Riesling Grasberg	B	78
1986 Riesling Saint Hippolyte	B	85
1986 Riesling Schoenenburg	B	87

The 1985 Gewürztraminer Mittelwihr from Marcel Deiss is a lovely, opulent, luscious Gewürztraminer with considerable depth and fruit.

It is a full-bodied wine, slightly larger scaled than many 1985s, but it offers a chewy mouthful of exuberant Gewürztraminer. The 1985 Pinot Blanc has plenty of fruit, a dry, crisp, elegant, well-balanced palate, good length, and 2–3 years of aging potential. As for the two Rieslings produced in 1985, the Bergheim Engelgarten has a complex bouquet, offering up scents of cinnamon, clove, apple, and flowers. Fresh and flavorful, this medium-bodied wine has a lot of style, plenty of depth, and should offer fine drinking over the next 3–4 years. The Bennwihr Riesling is more tart and less extroverted, but is still a stylish, graceful dry Riesling. Regarding Deiss's 1986s, while the regular cuvée Pinot Blanc and Riesling were compact and austere wines, the other Rieslings and Gewürztraminers were excellent and among the top wines of the 1986 vintage. Virtually all of the single-vineyard Rieslings and Gewürztraminers represented classic wines for their types. Among the 1986 Rieslings, the Grasberg lacked ripeness and was too green, but the stony fruit of the Burg, the floral, rich mineral character of the Schoenenburg, the lemony, apple-like character of the Hippolyte, and the richness of the Altenberg all showed the excellent character of the dry style of Alsace Rieslings. The single-vineyard Gewürztraminers were even better. The Saint Hippolyte, Bergheim, and Mittelwihr wines are very exotic, rich, and opulent, and represent some of the stars of the vintage.

DOPFF & IRION (RIQUEWIHR)* * *

1985 Gewürztraminer	B	82
1985 Gewürztraminer Les Sorcières	B	87
1986 Gewürztraminer Les Sorcières	B	78
1985 Pinot Blanc	A	84
1986 Pinot Blanc	A	82
1985 Riesling	B	84
1986 Riesling Cuvée René Dopff	B	72
1985 Riesling Les Murailles	B	86
1986 Riesling Les Murailles	B	82

1985 Tokay Les Maquisards	B	86

The 1985 regular Gewürztraminer is a light, pleasant, straightforward wine that is dry, well-made, and correct, but lacks a bit of excitement. The top-of-the-line 1985 Les Sorcières is loaded with exotic, spicy, rich fruit, is full-bodied, long, well-balanced, and while quite intense, is not overblown or flabby, as some big, rich, Gewürztraminers can be. I would drink it over the next 5–7 years. Dopff & Irion's 1985 Pinot Blanc is light straw in color, with a flowery, delicate bouquet and medium body, crisp flavors, a dry finish, and good length. Neither powerful nor intense, it offers a lighter-styled Pinot Blanc, which would be ideal as an aperitif wine. As for the 1985 Rieslings, the regular cuvée is crisp, delicate, and tightly knit, but shows good fruit and ripeness. The more expensive Les Murailles Riesling is a more serious wine, with a moderately intense, spicy bouquet of apples and flowers, good crisp acidity, plenty of length, and a dry finish. The Tokay Les Maquisards is firmly structured, with loads of fruit, a buttery hazelnut aroma, and medium to full body; it can be drunk now or aged for 4–6 years. In 1986 the Dopff & Irion wines were of average quality and did not display the richness and breadth of flavor of the 1985s. Certainly, the Pinot Blanc was attractive in 1986, but I was slightly disappointed by the Gewürztraminer Les Sorcières, as it usually tends to be one of the better wines from this house.

DOPFF "AU MOULIN" (RIQUEWIHR)* * * * *

1986 Gewürztraminer	B	74
1986 Gewürztraminer Brand	C	83
1985 Gewürztraminer Brand de Turckheim	C	90
1985 Gewürztraminer Réserve	B	87
1986 Riesling	B	72
1985 Riesling Schoenenberg	B	87

This house is one of the finest in Alsace, and I thought their 1985s were every bit as good as their very successful 1983s. The 1985 Gewürztraminer Réserve balances power and finesse beautifully. It is rich and full-bodied, but remains lively on the palate because of very good acidity. The 1985 Gewürztraminer Brand de Turckheim is a profound wine, with layers of flavor, full body, tremendous extract and palate presence, and a sensational finish. The Schoenenberg is an excellent Riesling that admirably displays what Alsatian Rieslings are all about. Bone-dry, with considerable body and flavor authority, this spicy, fragrant, mineral-scented wine marries power and finesse expertly. It delivers all the fruit and flavor one could want from a dry Riesling. Given the great success of Dopff "Au Moulin" in 1983 and 1985, one would have expected a bit more richness and depth to the 1986s than they currently exhibit. None of the wines showed a great deal of concentration or length except for the Grand Cru Brand Gewürztraminer, but given the standards of this house and the quality of the vineyard, even this wine is unexciting.

PIERRE FRICK (PFAFFENHEIM)* *

1985 Pinot Blanc Klevener	A	55
1985 Riesling	B	74
1985 Tokay	B	74

The 1985 Riesling from Frick is very tart, green, even spritzy, and the unripe character of this wine gives it little appeal. The Tokay is a one-dimensional wine with solid fruit, a spicy, light-intensity bouquet, and a short finish. The Pinot Blanc Klevener is a defective, badly made wine with a flawed bouquet and thin, meager flavors.

ROLLY GASSMANN (RORSCHWIHR)* * * *

1985 Gewürztraminer	B	86
1985 Riesling Réserve	B	84
1985 Riesling Silberberg	B	85

This respected producer tends to produce very elegant, less powerful examples of Alsatian wines that recall the stylish wines of the Trimbach firm. The 1985 Gewürztraminer has a smoky, bacon fat aroma intertwined with a honeyed yet dry fruitiness, medium to full body, and a soft finish. It should be drunk over the next 2–3 years. The Réserve Riesling is fully developed, open knit, flowery, and fresh, in a light to medium bodied, delicate manner. The Silberberg Riesling is more tightly knit and closed, but is a richer, deeper, more promising wine because of its depth and length.

JEAN GEILER (INGERSHEIM)* *

1986 Gewürztraminer Cuvée Prestige	B	87

1986 Pinot Blanc	A	74

1986 Riesling Cuvée Prestige	B	73

The best of the Geiler 1986 wines is the Gewürztraminer, which stood out in my peer group tastings of this varietal for its sheer ripeness, creamy texture, and huge, fragrant bouquet of roses and Oriental spices. It should drink nicely for 2–3 years.

GERARD HARTMANN (VOEGTLINSHOFFEN)* * *

1986 Gewürztraminer Hatschburg	B	87

1986 Tokay-Pinot Gris Hatschburg Vendange Tardive	C	87

I know little about this producer; however, I was very impressed by these two wines. The Gewürztraminer displays classic aromas of grapefruit and lychee nuts, is surprisingly full and rich for a 1986, and has good acidity. The 1986 Tokay is quite full, and intense, with a deeper color than the Gewürztraminer. It has plenty of fruit, full body, and excellent concentration and length. Both wines should drink well for 5–7 years.

HUGEL (RIQUEWIHR)* * *

1985 Gewürztraminer	B	86

1986 Gewürztraminer	B	76

1985 Gewürztraminer Réserve Personnelle	C	87

1985 Gewürztraminer Vendange Tardive	C	84

1985 Pinot Blanc Cuvée les Amours	A	85

1986 Pinot Blanc Cuvée les Amours	A	85

1985 Riesling	B	78

1986 Riesling	B	82

1985 Riesling Réserve Personnelle	C	82

1985 Tokay-Pinot Gris	B	84

One of the most famous firms in Alsace, Hugel produces wines that are quite successful. The firm specializes in big, rich, yet remarkably graceful Gewürztraminers. The 1985 regular Gewürztraminer is quite delicious, offering a flowery, ripe, full-intensity bouquet, nicely concentrated flavors, and good acidity. The 1985 Réserve Personnelle Gewürztraminer, always slower to develop, is a much more closed wine that seems very good, but lighter and less powerful than usual. It opens up somewhat with air, but I think it needs 1–2 years of further aging in the bottle. The 1985 Gewürztraminer Vendange Tardive is thick and heavy, with little complexity, but it has plenty of intense fruit. I have never felt that Hugel tries very hard with its Rieslings. Both the 1985s have a pleasant, light-intensity bouquet of green apples, tart, rather high acidic flavors, and short finishes. The Réserve Personnelle should develop more flavor dimension with 1–3 years of cellaring. The 1985 Tokay-Pinot Gris is a stylish, rather elegant wine, with good freshness and acidity, medium body, and a long, lush finish. It should be drunk over the next 3–4 years. Hugel's 1985 Pinot Blanc Cuvée les Amours is round, fruity, medium to full bodied, with good intensity and balance. Drink it over the next 2–3 years. Overall, I thought Hugel's 1983s greatly superior to the 1985s. As for the 1986s, while I did not taste the top-of-the-line Réserve Personnelle wines in time for this book, the regular cuvées of 1986 revealed a straightforward Riesling and a rather flabby, soft Gewürztraminer. However, a very successful, stylish, elegant, fruity, and medium-bodied Pinot Blanc was made in 1986.

JOSMEYER (WINTZENHEIM)* * * * *

1985 Gewürztraminer Les Archenets	B	85

1986 Gewürztraminer Les Archenets	B	84

1985 Gewürztraminer Hengst	C	88

1986 Gewürztraminer Hengst Vendange Tardive	C	84

1985 Gewürztraminer Herrenweg	C	87

1985 Gewürztraminer Vendange Tardive	C	85

1985 Pinot d'Alsace Les Lutins	A	85
1986 Pinot d'Alsace Les Lutins	A	84
1987 Pinot d'Alsace Mise du Printemps	A	85
1985 Pinot Auxerrois Hengst-Vieilles Vignes	B	88
1986 Pinot Auxerrois Hengst-Vieilles Vignes	B	85
1985 Pinot Gris Vieilles Vignes	C	88
1985 Riesling Hengst	B	87
1986 Riesling Hengst	B	85
1985 Riesling Herrenweg	B	83
1986 Riesling Herrenweg	B	85
1985 Riesling Les Pierrets	B	85
1986 Riesling Les Pierrets	B	77
1986 Tokay-Pinot Gris Hengst	B	85

Josmeyer is one of the trusted names for Alsatian wine, particularly for Pinot Blanc, the finest in Alsace, and Gewürztraminer. Among the Gewürztraminers, the 1985 Vendange Tardive is round, slightly sweet, fat, and quite delicious to drink. The 1985 Les Archenets is a dry wine, but still luscious, fruity, and smoky, with a very forward personality. I would drink it over the next 1–3 years. Both the 1985 Hengst and Herrenweg Gewürztraminers are deep, profound, exuberant, textbook wines with layers of intense, spicy fruit, full body, and luscious, even extravagant textures. I give a slight edge to the Hengst. With the exception of the Herrenweg, which is fresh and flowery, but somewhat short on the palate, the Riesling offerings in 1985 are impressive dry wines. The Les Pierrets is steely and austere, but concentrated and long. The Hengst is even finer, with more flavor, depth, length, and aging potential. Josmeyer made an excellent Pinot Gris in 1985. It exudes an intense aroma of buttery nuts, bacon fat, and very ripe fruit. On the palate, the wine has a good zesty acidity to carry the powerful, rich, full-bodied assertive finish. Unquestionably, Josmeyer is Alsace's finest producer of Pinot Blanc. The wines have a richness that surpasses any other such wine produced in this enchanted viticultural area. The 1985 Les Lutins has a big, flowery bouquet, a good deal of body, plenty of depth, and a dry, crisp fruit. The Vieilles Vignes of 1985 is the finest Pinot Blanc from Alsace I have ever tasted, with a gorgeous bouquet of ripe fruit, flowers, and mineral scents. On the palate, it retains an elegance despite authoritative flavors and plenty of body. Josmeyer's 1986s stood out in all my tastings as among the very best wines of this average to above-average quality vintage. Although there are several mediocre wines, these wines generally show good fruit, are well balanced, and are significantly lighter and less intense than the 1985s or 1983s. They may well turn out much like Josmeyer's 1979s. In particular, the 1986 Pinot Gris and Riesling from the Hengst Vineyard should be sought out, as well as the 1986 Pinot Blanc Vieilles Vignes. All the Josmeyer 1986s should be consumed over the next 3–4 years.

MARC KREYDENWEISS (BARR)* * * *

1985 Gewürztraminer Kritt	B	87
1986 Gewürztraminer Kritt	B	72
1985 Pinot Blanc Kritt Klevener	B	87
1986 Pinot Blanc Kritt Klevener	B	82
1985 Riesling Andlau	B	80
1985 Riesling Weibelsberg	B	86
1986 Riesling Weibelsberg	B	75
1986 Tokay-Pinot Gris Moenchberg	C	85

The Kreydenweiss 1985 Gewürztraminer has a full-intensity bouquet of exotic tropical fruit and spices, followed by a well-balanced, full-bodied wine of distinction. It is wonderfully ripe, yet the delicate flavors show depth and precision. In 1985, Kreydenweiss produced one of the best Pinot Blancs I have ever tasted, with a bouquet of spring flowers and ripe fruit. On the palate, the wine has a creamy, lush texture, plenty of fruit, and a soft finish. Drink it over the next 1–2 years. While the 1985 Andlau Riesling is excessively tart and lacking in personality, the Weibelsberg shows considerable character. From its perfumed flowery bouquet of moderate intensity to its concentrated, crisp, applelike fruitiness and long finish, it is a high-quality, dry Riesling that should age well for 4–5 years. The great success Kreydenweiss enjoyed in 1985 was not repeated in the more difficult, leaner-styled vintage of 1986. Certainly, the Pinot Blanc from the Kritt vineyard was a well-made wine, but it is one-dimensional when compared with the stunning 1985. The 1986 Riesling Weibelsberg was extremely high in acidity, tart, and showed very little length. Even worse was the 1986 Gewürztraminer, which was not only tart and lean, but bordered on being thin. Kreydenweiss's best 1986 would appear to be his Tokay which had much the style, character, and length of a fine white burgundy. Deep in fruit with crisp acidity but a fresh, long, ripe finish, it should age well for 5–7 years.

KUENTZ-BAS (HUSSEREN-LES-CHÂTEAUX)* * * * *

1985 Gewürztraminer Cuvée Tradition	B	86
1986 Gewürztraminer Cuvée Tradition	B	83
1986 Gewürztraminer Eichberg	C	90
1985 Gewürztraminer Réserve Personnelle	B	87
1986 Gewürztraminer Réserve Personnelle	B	85
1985 Muscat Réserve Personnelle	B	85
1986 Muscat Réserve Personnelle	B	85
1985 Pinot Blanc Cuvée Tradition	A	83
1986 Pinot Blanc Cuvée Tradition	A	80
1985 Riesling Réserve Personnelle	B	83
1986 Riesling Réserve Personnelle	B	78
1985 Tokay-Pinot Gris Réserve Personnelle	B	87

1986 Tokay-Pinot Gris Réserve Personnelle	B	85

This moderately sized firm designates its wines in three ways: The Cuvée Tradition wines are those made from purchased grapes; the Réserve Personnelles represent wines that are estate bottled from the firm's own vineyards; and the Vendange Tardives are called Cuvée Caroline. The general quality of Kuentz-Bas wines seems to be extremely high, especially with the Gewürztraminers, Tokays, and Muscats. In my tastings, the Tokay-Pinot Gris not only showed its inimitable Alsatian character, but the smoky, buttery, creamy texture of a fine white burgundy as well. Kuentz-Bas's 1985s are generally more successful than their 1986s, but given the vintage, the 1986, except for the Riesling, have proven to be quite good. I would drink the 1985 Gewürztraminers over the next 4–5 years, and the 1986s over the next 2–3 years.

LANDMANN-OSTHOLT (SOULTZMATT)* * * *

1986 Crémant Brut Sparkling	B	84

1985 Gewürztraminer	B	86

1985 Gewürztraminer Zinnkoepfle	C	87

1986 Gewürztraminer Zinnkoepfle	B	90

1986 Riesling	B	79

1985 Riesling Vallé Noble	C	84

1985 Riesling Zinnkoepfle	B	86

1986 Riesling Zinnkoepfle	B	84

1986 Sylvaner	A	78

1985 Tokay-Pinot Gris	B	83

1986 Tokay-Pinot Gris	B	84

1985 Tokay-Pinot Gris Bollenberg	C	82

1985 Tokay-Pinot Gris Bollenberg-Vendange Tardive   C   88

The regular 1985 Gewürztraminer offers oodles of spicy, charming
fruit and a long, exuberant finish, but has slightly higher acidity than
its sibling, the 1985 Gewürztraminer Zinnkoepfle, which is a big, exotic, very dramatic wine that oozes with opulent fruit. Full-bodied,
ripe, long and powerful, it should be reserved for equally flamboyant
dishes. The Zinnkoepfle vineyard's Riesling has a captivating, intense
bouquet of honeysuckle and flowery fruit. Forward, ripe and already
quite delicious, this medium-bodied wine should continue to drink
well for 2–4 years. The Vallé Noble Riesling is less ripe, a bit more
tart and reserved, but may in 1–2 years turn out to be as fine as the
Zinnkoepfle. Landmann-Ostholt's regular 1985 offering of Pinot Gris
smells like a fine Chassagne-Montrachet, but the impressive bouquet
does not follow through on the palate, as the wine is austere and a bit
lean. The same problem afflicts the Bollenberg, which tasted good but
seems too tart and understated. However, the Bollenberg-Vendange
Tardive offers oodles of rich, luxurious, buttery, opulent fruit, full
body, and a very long, velvety finish. Regarding the 1986 Landmann-
Ostholts, the wines do not offer much excitement, with the exception
of the outstanding, concentrated, rich Gewürztraminer from the
Zinnkoepfle vineyard. The remaining 1986s are correct and pleasant,
but largely undistinguished. However, do try the excellent 1986 Crémant; frothy, light, and tasty, it is a very fine value.

GUSTAVE LORENTZ (BERGHEIM)* * * *

1985 Gewürztraminer	B	82
1985 Gewürztraminer Altenberg	B	80
1985 Gewürztraminer Vendange Tardive	C	?
1985 Pinot Blanc Réserve	A	73
1985 Riesling	B	78
1985 Riesling Altenberg	B	86
1985 Riesling Réserve	B	84
1985 Riesling Vendange Tardive	C	90

Normally some of the best Alsatian wines, Lorentz's offerings did not fare as well in my tastings as I would have expected. The 1985 Gewürztraminer Vendange Tardive was flawed by excessive sulphur in the nose. The normally first-class Gewürztraminer Altenberg tasted a trifle unripe, yet ended with a hefty dosage of alcohol. The best of the Gewürztraminers, at least for now, is the regular cuvée, which is not complex but loaded with spicy, ripe fruit and has a lush, generous texture. The 1985 Pinot Blanc Réserve, dominated by extremely high acidity, is a lean, hard-edged wine of little charm. The progression in quality among the Lorentz Rieslings in 1985 is quite interesting to follow. The basic 1985 Riesling is straightforward and tart, but adequate. The Réserve Riesling has a more intense bouquet of flowers, good zesty acidity, and a longer finish. However, the single vineyard Altenberg Riesling raises the level of flavor extract and offers a complex bouquet, fine balance, and 5–7 years of additional aging potential. At the summit is the 1985 Vendange Tardive, an intensely fragrant wine with layers of well-delineated Riesling fruit and medium to full body, as well as a long, crisp, first-class finish. It is a super Riesling that should keep for upwards of a decade.

MURÉ-CLOS ST.-LANDELIN (ROUFFACH)* * *

1985 Gewürztraminer	B	86
1986 Gewürztraminer Zinnkoepfle	B	83
1986 Pinot Blanc	A	76
1986 Riesling	B	81
1985 Riesling Vorbourg	B	84
1986 Riesling Vorbourg	B	85
1985 Tokay-Pinot Gris	B	86
1986 Tokay-Pinot Gris	B	87

The 1985 is one of the best Clos St.-Landelin Gewürztraminers in years. Representative of the big, spicy, classic style, with power and dramatic flavors, this lush, full-bodied wine is quite concentrated and long; it is superior to the 1983. The 1985 Vorbourg Riesling improves dramatically in the glass as it breathes. At first it appears to be very dull, but with time it reveals good floral scents and crisp fruit. Muré's 1985 Tokay is an extremely elegant, more restrained style of Pinot Gris. Rich in fruit, medium-bodied, crisp and flavorful, this polished wine will drink well for 2–4 years. Muré's success in 1985 has been followed up with good wines in 1986, with the Tokay-Pinot Gris being one of the top wines of that varietal in the vintage. It has smoky, rich, deep, well-balanced flavors that show good acidity. Additionally, the Riesling from the Grand Cru Vorbourg vineyard is also a textbook, stony, mineral-scented Riesling with zesty applelike fruit in a medium-bodied, dry, austere format. The Gewürztraminer from the Zinnkoepfle Grand Cru vineyard is good in 1986, but lacks the great depth the Gewürztraminers obtained in 1985 and 1983. Muré's 1986s should be drunk over the next 2–3 years; the 1985s over the next 4–5 years.

OSTERTAG (EPFIG)* * * *

1985 Gewürztraminer	B	85
1985 Gewürztraminer Fronholzt Vendange Tardive	C	86
1986 Gewürztraminer Nothalten	B	70
1986 Pinot Blanc Barriques	B	69
1985 Riesling	A	82
1986 Riesling D'Epfig	B	84
1985 Riesling Fronholtz	B	82
1986 Riesling Fronholtz	B	85
1986 Riesling Heissenberg	B	85
1985 Riesling Moenchberg	B	87
1986 Riesling Moenchberg	B	85
1985 Tokay Barriques	B	85
1986 Tokay Barriques	B	86

The quality of Ostertag's wines struck me as particularly good when I first tasted the 1983s. The success of 1983 has been followed by some lovely 1985s and a mixed range of 1986s. The two Gewürztraminers in 1985 offer good, ripe, spicy, exotic fruit in a medium- to full-bodied format. The regular bottling is dry, fleshy, and should drink well for 4–5 years. The more powerful and opulent, somewhat off-dry Vendange Tardive is larger scaled and richer. Ostertag's 1985 Tokay Barriques represents an interesting idea—taking Tokay with its buttery, smoky character, and aging it in toasty new oak barrels. I like the thought—and the wine—but the oak is a little too intrusive for the level of fruit in the 1985, and it destroyed the fruit in the 1986 Pinot Blanc, but worked adequately with the Tokay. Both the 1985 and 1986 Tokays are big, spicy, rich, well-made wines that should drink well for 4–5 years. Very fine Riesling was made in 1985 from the Moenchberg vineyard. A complex, moderately intense bouquet of mineral scents, spring flowers, and ripe apples is seductive enough. On the palate, the wine has plenty of ripe fruit, crisp acidity, and a long, dry finish. It is one of the best 1985 Rieslings I tasted. The Fronholtz will age well, but for now tastes too tart, green, and unyielding; if there is sufficient fruit behind the high acids, it will merit a higher rating in 2–3 years. The regular bottling of Riesling is well made, straightforward, pleasant, but a bit simple. As for the other 1986s, again, the Rieslings from the Moenchberg and Fronholtz vineyards exhibit classic mineral-scented, flowery, stony fruit. In addition, the Riesling from the Heissenberg vineyard also showed well, with its apple blossom, lemony, zesty fruit. Not all of Ostertag's 1986s were this well made. The Pinot Blanc tasted like a new oak barrel, while the Gewürztraminer from the Nothalten vineyard tasted thin and poorly nourished.

SALZMANN (RIQUEWIHR)* * *

1985 Gewürztraminer	88

Although I am not that familiar with the wines of this producer, I was remarkably impressed by this stunning Gewürztraminer. It had all the opulence and fragrance that Gewürztraminer should have, and it is well balanced. But it is not for the timid, as it is quite intense.

MARTIN SCHAETZEL (AMMERSCHWIHR)* * *

1985 Gewürztraminer	B	83
1986 Gewürztraminer Cuvée Isabelle	B	87

1986 Gewürztraminer Cuvée Mathieu	B	85
1986 Gewürztraminer Kaefferkopf Cuvée Catherine	B	90
1985 Pinot Blanc	A	86
1986 Pinot Blanc	A	84
1985 Riesling Kaefferkopf	B	78
1986 Riesling Kaefferkopf Cuvée Nicolas	B	90
1985 Tokay d'Alsace	B	73
1986 Tokay d'Alsace Cuvée Réserve	B	85

The 1985 Gewürztraminer from Martin Schaetzel smells spicy and richly fruity, but finishes with a touch of bitterness that lowered its otherwise good rating. Drink it over the next 1–2 years. Schaetzel made very good Pinot Blanc in 1985. It is one of the bigger, ripe, more opulent styles of Pinot Blanc on the market. Full-bodied, deep and rich, with a floral, honeyed fruitiness and velvety texture, but enough acidity for balance, this full-flavored wine should be drunk over the next 1–2 years. With respect to the Riesling in 1985, the positive impression created by the wine's bouquet is not followed up by the wine's flavors. Slightly too tart and diluted, this light-styled Riesling should be drunk over the next several years. The golden color of Schaetzel's Tokay looks premature, suspicious for such a young wine. On the palate, the wine is flabby, low in acidity, and tails off in the finish. As for the 1986s, Schaetzel has turned in one of the best overall efforts in all of Alsace—from the crisp, stony, fleshy, flavorful Pinot Blanc to the Grand Cru Kaefferkopf vineyard's classic, exquisite, slate-and-flint-scented, apple-and-lemon-flavored Riesling. All three Gewürztraminers exhibit surprising opulence and intensity for 1986s, but the Cuvée Catherine from the Kaefferkopf vineyard shows marvelous depth and a very delineated, well-focused character. All of Schaetzel's 1986s should be drunk over the next 3–4 years.

EDGARD SCHALLER (MITTELWIHR)* * *

N.V. Crémant d'Alsace	B	87
1986 Gewürztraminer Cuvée des Refelingen	B	75

1986 Muscat	B	?

1986 Pinot Blanc	A	84

1986 Riesling Cuvée des Amandiers	B	82

I have had little experience with the wines of Edgard Schaller, but I can say with certainty that in 1986 he made a good, frothy, light, tasty Crémant d'Alsace and Pinot Blanc. The Riesling has classic scents of green apples, high acids, and a steely texture. The Gewürztraminer tastes watery and quite thin, and the Muscat suffers from excessive sulphur in the nose.

CHARLES SCHLERET (TURCKHEIM)* * * *

1985 Gewürztraminer	B	86

1986 Gewürztraminer Cuvée Exceptionnel	B	86

1986 Pinot Blanc	A	82

1986 Tokay-Pinot Gris Cuvée Exceptionnel	B	87

Schleret is one of the best, yet least known, growers in Alsace. He made very fine 1983s and surprisingly good 1984s. The 1985 Gewürztraminer has a full-intensity bouquet of honeysuckle and exotic spices on the palate, and good acidity to balance the rich, forward, intense fruit. Schleret's remarkable consistency from one vintage to another is well demonstrated by his 1986s, which are all very successful. His Pinot Blanc is refreshingly dry and austere, but very long, with a great deal of ripeness and rich fruit on the palate. It should drink nicely for 3–4 years. His Tokay in 1986 exhibited a very broad, rich, almost Vendange Tardive style, with an unctuous, medium to full body, and quite concentrated character. Certainly it was one of the top wines made from Pinot Gris that I tasted in 1986. Lastly, his 1986 Gewürztraminer Cuvée Exceptionnel shows exceptional ripeness and intensity for a 1986, has quite a long finish, and has more in common with the 1985 than a 1986. It should drink nicely for 4–5 years.

SCHLUMBERGER (GUEBWILLER)* * * *

1985 Gewürztraminer Cuvée Christine Schlumberger	D	92

1985 Gewürztraminer Kessler	B	90
1985 Gewürztraminer Kitterlé	B	87
1986 Gewürztraminer Kitterlé	B	85
1985 Pinot Blanc	A	79
1986 Pinot Blanc	A	?
1985 Pinot Gris Réserve Spéciale	A	85
1985 Riesling Kitterlé	B	88
1985 Riesling Princess Abbes	B	86
1985 Riesling Saering	B	87
1986 Tokay-Pinot Gris	B	85

Schlumberger, one of the biggest and best-known of Alsatian wine firms, tends to produce robust, full-throttle Gewürztraminers, the richest of which is the nectarlike, sweet, profound Cuvée Christine Schlumberger (the only recent vintages made were 1976 and 1985), the dry yet massive wine from the Kessler vineyard, and the stylish yet opulent Gewürztraminer from the family's vineyard, called Kitterlé. The Gewürztraminer is still a full-flavored, rather big and bold wine, which has a very unique mineral and earthy flavor that some tasters may find unusual. Unctuous and lush for a 1985, it should be drunk over the next 3–4 years. Schlumberger's Pinot Blanc of 1985 suffers from a lack of acidity, which gives it a flat, flabby character; otherwise, it has good fruit and ripeness. The Pinot Gris Réserve Spéciale is fully mature and offers smooth, ripe, buttery flavors in a soft, full-bodied format. It is quite tasty and would make a fine accompaniment to fish and poultry dishes. There is a strong lineup of Rieslings in 1985. The star is the Kitterlé, perhaps because it is more forward than the other two wines. It could serve as a benchmark for the Alsatian style—dry, spicy, full-bodied, loaded with fruit, and capable of aging 5–7 more years. The Saering is more tart and closed, but has a lot of substance behind the acidity. It should develop nicely over the next 2–4 years. The Princess Abbes is a full-bodied, opulent style of Riesling whose texture resembles some of the 1983s. It is the most overtly powerful wine of this trio of Rieslings, and therefore requires equally assertive food. With respect to Schlumberger's 1986 wines,the Pinot Blanc, normally quite reliable, was tasted twice; both times the wine showed traces of oxidation and was not reviewable. Certainly the firm's Tokay-Pinot Gris has the trademarks of a Schlumberger wine—rich, oily, unctuous, creamy texture and an exotic perfume; it should be drunk over the next 3–4 years. Lastly, the 1986 Gewürztraminer from the Kitterlé vineyard is not quite as big and boldly styled as the 1985, but seems to have plenty of finesse and character. It is less overwhelming than previous vintages of this particular wine.

RENÉ SCHMIDT (RIQUEWIHR)* * *

1986 Gewürztraminer Cuvée Particulière	B	81

1986 Riesling Schoenenbourg	C	74

1986 Tokay d'Alsace Réserve	B	82

René Schmidt's wines rarely do well in blind tastings when they are young because they are made in such a bone-dry, austere, lean manner. Although they improve with age, they are not among my favorites. All the 1986s share Schmidt's very restrained, understated, virtually too polite style of winemaking; a little more excitement would have been preferred. They should keep for 3–4 years.

SICK-DREYER (AMMERSCHWIHR)* * *

1985 Gewürztraminer Kaefferkopf	B	86

1986 Gewürztraminer Kaefferkopf	B	77

1985 Pinot Blanc	A	85

1986 Pinot Blanc	A	84

1986 Riesling Kaefferkopf	B	85

The 1985 Gewürztraminer Kaefferkopf is stylish, very refined and floral-scented, with authoritative but generally restrained flavors. If the aromas do not jump out of the glass, they still offer plenty of complex flower and exotic fruit scents. On the palate, the wine is medium to full bodied, polished, and well focused. Dreyer's 1985

Pinot Blanc is a big, fleshy, smoky wine that is reminiscent of a good white burgundy. Somewhat similar to the 1983s in style (because of its chewy, opulent character), this rich, medium to full bodied wine offers considerable style and flavor interest. Regarding the 1986 wines, the Pinot Blanc was one of the better wines in my blind tastings of this varietal from the 1986 vintage. It still had a trace of CO_2, but showed immense amounts of round, flavorful, fresh apple-and-honey-scented fruit. The 1986 Riesling from the Grand Cru vineyard Kaefferkopf also demonstrated a moderately intense, attractive floral, complex aroma with suggestions of apples on the palate. It is quite dry and medium bodied. Lastly, the Gewürztraminer from the same vineyard was very austere and lacked the depth and richness of the 1985.

PIERRE SPARR (SIGOLSHEIM)* * *

1986 Gewürztraminer	B	85
1985 Gewürztraminer Mambourg	B	87
1986 Gewürztraminer Mambourg	B	87
1985 Gewürztraminer Réserve	B	82
1986 Pinot Blanc	A	72
1986 Riesling Altenbourg	B	87

Sparr made wonderful 1983s, and his 1985s are only slightly less impressive. The 1985 Gewürztraminer Réserve is fruity and lush, but lacks depth and complexity. However, the 1985 Mambourg looks impressive, although young and relatively unevolved. A blossoming bouquet of apricots and lychee nuts is followed by a firmly structured Gewürztraminer that has fine length and flavor intensity. Sparr, who does not get the credit he deserves, also made very fine 1986s, except for the thin, rather hollow Pinot Blanc. In particular, the Riesling Altenbourg has a very stony, petrol taste, is loaded with fruit, is quite full, and should drink well for 5–6 years. The 1986 regular cuvée Gewürztraminer is stylish, ripe, fat, and tasty, and of course the 1986 Mambourg Gewürztraminer is more opulent, even unctuous, in a big, ripe, full-bodied style that some may find excessive.

TRIMBACH (RIBEAUVILLÉ)* * * *

1985 Gewürztraminer	B	85
1985 Gewürztraminer Cuvée Ribeaupierre	C	88
1985 Pinot Blanc	A	80
1985 Riesling	B	81
1985 Riesling Cuvée Frédéric Émile	C	87

This firm can always be counted on to produce a reliable group of wines. Its wine style tends to be one of understatement and subtlety, so I was somewhat surprised by the boldness of flavor displayed by both of the 1985 Gewürztraminers. The regular bottling has surprising depth, a big, smoky, spicy, ripe bouquet, complex, crisp, well-balanced flavors, and a long finish. The top-of-the-line Cuvée Ribeaupierre has more of everything—a profound, intense bouquet, broad, rich, long flavors, an opulent yet still lively texture, and tremendous length. The 1985 Pinot Blanc is a light-bodied, very delicate wine with a pleasant floral bouquet and easy, uncomplicated, fruity flavors. Drink it over the next 1–2 years. As for the 1985 Rieslings, the normal bottling is very austere, a bit citric and lean, but well made and delicate; as a straightforward aperitif, it is quite pleasant. On the other hand, the Frédéric Émile has a beautiful bouquet of steely, flowery Riesling fruit, moderately intense flavors suggestive of apples and grapefruit, and a delicate yet authoritative finish. This wine should age nicely over the next 3–4 years.

DOMAINE WEINBACH (KIENTZHEIM)* * * * *

1985 Gewürztraminer Cuvée Théo	D	87
1986 Gewürztraminer Cuvée Théo	D	76
1985 Gewürztraminer Réserve Personnelle	C	88
1986 Gewürztraminer Réserve Personnelle	C	78
1986 Pinot Blanc	B	83

1985 Riesling Cuvée de la Sainte-Catherine	D	90
1986 Riesling Cuvée de la Sainte-Catherine	D	84
1986 Riesling Réserve Personnelle	C	86
1985 Riesling Schlossberg	D	88

One of the great estates not only of Alsace but of France as well, Domaine Weinbach is run with meticulous care by Madame Faller. The wines can be brilliant. For example, the 1983s were among the greatest Alsatian wines I have ever tasted. The 1985 Gewürztraminers are quite expensive, but are wonderfully rich, balanced, and powerfully assertive wines. Normally, the Cuvée Théo is the flagship Gewürztraminer, but in 1985 I thought the Réserve bottling to be every bit as rich, and with slightly better overall balance; hence the marginally higher rating. The bouquets, which seem to suggest rose petals, lychee nuts, and ripe grapefruit, are intense and lingering. As in 1983, the two Rieslings of 1985 are about as well made as Alsatian Rieslings can be. The Schlossberg is a lovingly proportioned dry wine that has an intense fragrance of spring flowers. On the palate, there is zesty acidity, considerable depth and length, and a purity of fruit. It should drink well for 3–4 years. The Sainte-Catherine has a very complex bouquet, clean, concentrated, medium-bodied flavors, and a very long finish. Both Rieslings are quite dry and can be matched with many dishes, especially fish and poultry, but are also ideal as aperitif wines. With respect to the 1986s, despite a good Pinot Blanc, a very well-made Riesling Réserve Personnelle, and an attractive Riesling Sainte-Catherine, I must confess my disappointment over the general quality of the wines, especially given my great admiration and respect for Madame Faller and the success she has had. The Gewürztraminers in particular tasted extremely tart and lean, and lacked character, which I do not think will come out with aging. I tasted the wines blind, twice, to be sure, so you would do well to search out the firm's remarkable 1985s and 1983s.

A. WILLM (BARR)* * * *

1985 Gewürztraminer	B	85
1986 Gewürztraminer	B	82

1985 Gewürztraminer Clos Gaensbroennel	B	87
1986 Gewürztraminer Clos Gaensbroennel	B	87
1985 Pinot Blanc Cordon d'Alsace	A	82
1986 Pinot Blanc Cordon d'Alsace	A	84
1986 Pinot Gris	B	85
1986 Riesling	B	80
1986 Riesling Kirchberg	B	84

Willm's Gewürztraminer, called Clos Gaensbroennel, is one of the longest-lived wines of Alsace. Recent tastings of the superb 1967 and 1971 suggest that the wine can last for up to 20 years. The 1985 tastes more precocious than previous efforts, but still offers dramatic and exotic aromas of ripe fruit and Oriental spices, and a full-bodied, deeply concentrated feel on the palate; it has low acidity. I do not believe it will last as long as the 1983, but for drinking over the next 5–7 years, one can hardly complain. The 1985 regular Gewürztraminer is also a big, succulent, juicy mouthful of wine that shows nearly the same amount of depth and richness as its more famous sibling. Light intensity and floral aromas dominate the 1985 Riesling Kirchberg. On the palate, the wine is fruity, round, very forward, and cleanly made. It is precocious, so I suggest drinking it over the next 1–2 years. Willm continued to turn out successful wines in 1986 despite a more difficult vintage. Furthermore, its prices remain among the more reasonable for Alsatian wine. All of the 1986s showed well in my tastings but for value, certainly the attractively fruity, fleshy, fruit-filled yet well-balanced Pinot Blanc should be searched out by consumers looking for a great value. Willm's Rieslings often excite me less than Rieslings from other producers, but certainly the 1986s were soundly made. With respect to Willm's Pinot Gris, it showed a great deal of tropical fruit and a chewy, fat, intense texture with good length. As with all the better Alsatian Pinot Gris, it is a wonderful and less expensive alternative to French white burgundy. Lastly, Willm always does a top-notch job with Gewürztraminer; the regular cuvée in 1986 shows the exotic lychee nut and grapefruit aroma, and while lighter than the firm's 1985, it has good fruit and crisp acidity. It

should be drunk over the next several years. The top-of-the line Gewürztraminer from the Clos Gaensbroennel should certainly improve
over the next 7–8 years, and while it doesn't quite have the drama and
exotic aromas of the 1985 or 1983, it is still concentrated, fleshy, and
very true to its type.

ZIND-HUMBRECHT (WINTZENHEIM)* * * * *

1986 Gewürztraminer Clos Saint-Urbain Rangen Sélection de Grains Nobles	E	96
1986 Gewürztraminer Goldert	C	86
1985 Gewürztraminer Goldert Vendange Tardive	D	90
1985 Gewürztraminer Gueberschwihr Vendange Tardive	D	90
1986 Gewürztraminer Heimbourg Sélection de Grains Nobles	E	93
1985 Gewürztraminer Hengst	D	92
1986 Gewürztraminer Hengst Vendange Tardive	D	85
1986 Gewürztraminer Herrenweg Sélection de Grains Nobles	E	90
1985 Gewürztraminer Herrenweg Turckheim	D	91
1986 Gewürztraminer Herrenweg Turckheim	D	89
1986 Gewürztraminer Herrenweg Turckheim Vendange Tardive	D	85
1985 Gewürztraminer Rangen Vendange Tardive	D	88
1985 Gewürztraminer Réserve	C	89
1986 Muscat Goldert	C	86
1985 Pinot d'Alsace	B	84

1986 Pinot d'Alsace	B	85
1986 Riesling Brand	C	87
1985 Riesling Brand Vendange Tardive	C	90
1985 Riesling Herrenweg Turckheim	D	89
1986 Riesling Herrenweg Turckheim	C	84
1986 Riesling Rangen	C	87
1985 Riesling Rangen Clos Saint-Urbain	C	90
1985 Tokay d'Alsace Vieilles Vignes	C	90
1985 Tokay Clos Saint-Urbain Rangen	D	92
1986 Tokay-Pinot Gris Clos Saint-Urbain	D	90
1986 Tokay-Pinot Gris Vieilles Vignes	C	92

Without a doubt the most gifted winemaker of Alsace is the prodigious Léonard Humbrecht, who produces a remarkable array of wines. Few winemakers anywhere in the world could claim such a splendid lineup. Humbrecht is a fanatic and insists on his best wines being vineyard-designated. The quantities of each are small and prices are high (there is a great demand for his wines), but the quality is exceptional. As outstanding as Humbrecht's 1983s are, I think his 1985s are even better. For starters, there is the Réserve Gewürztraminer, which has the unmistakable bouquet of smoky bacon fat and rich, unctuous flavors, but adequate acidity for balance. It was one of the finest Gewürztraminers in my tastings, but was overwhelmed by many other wines of Zind-Humbrecht. The two full-bodied, dry Gewürztraminers —the Herrenweg Turckheim and the Hengst—are monumental wines with layers of smoky, complex smelling fruit, staggering concentration, and the length of a great white burgundy. Both wines should age well for 5–10 years. As for the three Vendange Tardives, they are enormously concentrated, full-tilt, intense wines that are stunning to taste, but because of their overwhelming concentration, present problems with regard to food matchups. The slightly lower rating for the Rangen reflects a less complex bouquet than that of either the smoky, exotic, sublime Gueberschwihr or the honeysuckle-and-rose-scented Goldert.

With respect to the 1985 Rieslings, the late-harvest Brand tastes dry, and has remarkable depth for a Riesling. It has fresh, honeyed, applelike flavors, zesty acidity, and 5–8 years of aging potential. The Herrenweg-Turckheim is leaner and more tart, has a complex mineral-scented fragrance, loads of fresh, applelike fruit, and medium body, and seems to need 1–2 years of bottle age to reveal all its character. The Rangen has a spicy, intense, earthy, mineral-scented aroma, great flavor depth, and superb balance and length. It is a very young wine that needs several more years to reach its apogee, but if you adore the dry, fuller-bodied style of Alsatian Riesling, this wine is a must-buy.

Zind-Humbrecht's Tokay from the Rangen vineyard is one of the world's greatest wines. The 1985 comes close to rivaling the sensational 1983. It is a big, powerful, profoundly concentrated wine that in 1985 seems more tightly structured than usual. It will improve in the bottle for 7–10 years, but already offers intense, spicy, buttery fruit, full body, layers of complex flavors, and a long, mouth-filling finish. It must be tasted to be believed. The 1985 Vieilles Vignes is more evolved, offering a full-intensity bouquet of exotic Oriental spices. Opulent and extremely rich on the palate, this deeply flavored wine goes on and on. There are few dry white table wines in the world with this degree of length.

The 1985 Pinot d'Alsace is very crisp with somewhat high acidity, which gives this wine a narrow, compact feel on the palate. Nevertheless, it has good fruit, medium body, and a very well-focused character.

Not surprisingly, Léonard Humbrecht made Alsace's greatest wines in 1986. In fact, having tasted every vintage of the gentleman's wines in the eighties has led me to believe that he is probably one of the two or three greatest winemakers in France, if not the world. His wines are sterling masterpieces, which include those wines low in the hierarchy, such as his Pinot Blanc; as one moves up to the single-vineyard Rieslings, Tokays, or Gewürztraminers, the quality is mind-boggling. In 1986, his top dry table wine is the extraordinary Tokay Vieilles Vignes, which rivals what a great producer of Montrachet, such as Ramonet, can accomplish. It is a staggeringly rich, highly extracted wine, but impeccably balanced; it should last 10–15 years. In fact, there are only a handful of Montrachets that could ever be this complex or concentrated. While I never tasted any of Humbrecht's Trockenbeerenauslese-styled Sélection de Grains Nobles wines of 1985, the three astonishing examples in 1986 are so rich and intense, yet have such high acids and alcohol, that they will no doubt last for 25–30 years. The quantities are quite scarce and the prices are unbelievably high, but, to me, they are as significant as some of the art in the Louvre. If you have the good fortune to try just one of them, make it the Gewürztraminer Clos Saint-Urbain Rangen, an awesomely deep, fabulously scented wine of extraordinary dimension and intensity. The wines of Zind-Humbrecht are the ultimate expression of the art of winemaking. Léonard Humbrecht is a genius and his wines are quite extraordinary.

BORDEAUX

The Basics

TYPES OF WINE

Bordeaux is the world's largest supplier of high-quality age-worthy table wine, which is produced in the region's many châteaux. The production in the eighties has ranged from 25 million to 60 million cases of wine a year, 75% of which is red.

Red Wine—Much of Bordeaux's fame rests on its dry red wine. And much of the best red wine comes from appellations such as Margaux, St.-Julien, Pauillac and St.-Estèphe—all located in the Médoc—and from Graves, Pomerol, and St.-Émilion. These wines are very high in quality and, correspondingly, expensive.

White Wine—Bordeaux produces sweet, rich, honeyed white wines from a famous district called Sauternes, which includes the area of Barsac. A great deal of dry white wine is also produced, most of it insipid and neutral in character, except for the excellent dry white wines made in the Graves area.

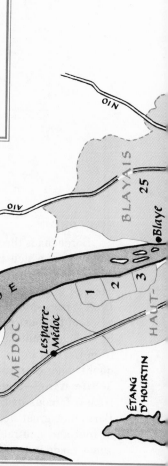

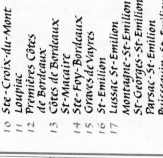

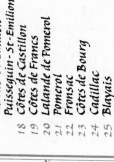

The Bordeaux Appellations

Bordeaux
1 St-Estèphe
2 Pauillac
3 St-Julien
4 Listrac
5 Moulis
6 Margaux
7 Cérons
8 Barsac
9 Sauternes

10 Ste-Croix-du-Mont
11 Loupiac
12 Premières Côtes de Bordeaux
13 Côtes de Bordeaux
14 St-Macaire
Ste-Foy-Bordeaux
15 Graves de Vayres
16 St-Emilion
17 Lussac St-Emilion
Montagne-St-Emilion
St-Georges-St-Emilion
Parsac-St-Emilion
Puisseguin-St-Emilion
18 Côtes de Castillon
19 Côtes de Francs
20 Lalande de Pomerol
21 Pomerol
22 Fronsac
23 Côtes de Bourg
24 Cadillac
25 Blayais

N W E S

GIRONDE

MÉDOC

Soulac

Lesparre-Médoc

HAUT-

BLAYAIS

Blaye

25

N10

A10

ÉTANG D'HOURTIN

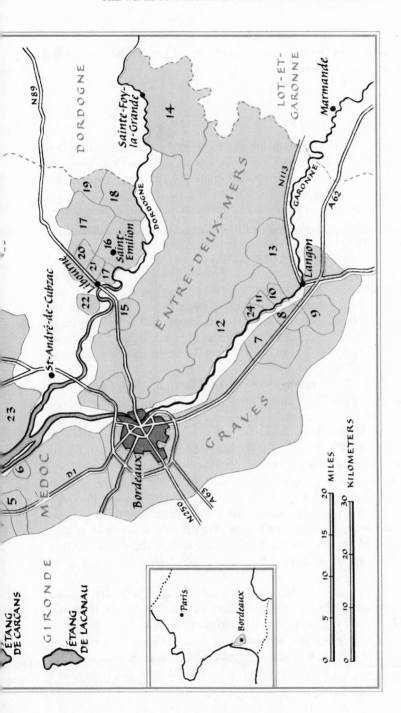

GRAPE VARIETIES

Following are the most important types of grapes used in the red and white wines of Bordeaux.

RED WINE VARIETIES

For red wines, three major grape varieties are planted in Bordeaux, as well as two minor varieties, one of which—Petit-Verdot—will be discussed below. The type of grape used has a profound influence on the style of wine that is ultimately produced.

Cabernet Sauvignon A grape that is highly pigmented, very astringent and tannic, Cabernet Sauvignon provides the framework, strength, dark color, character, and longevity for the wines in most of the vineyards in the Médoc. The grape ripens late, is resistent to rot because of its thick skin, and has a pronounced blackcurrant aroma that is sometimes intermingled with subtle herbaceous scents, and that, with aging, takes on the smell of cedarwood. Virtually all the Bordeaux châteaux blend Cabernet Sauvignon with other red grape varieties. In the Médoc the average percentage of Cabernet Sauvignon in the blend is 40–85%; in Graves 40–60%; in St.-Émilion, 10–50%; and in Pomerol, 0–20%.

Merlot Planted in virtually every wine château in Bordeaux because of its ability to provide a round, generous, lush, supple and alcoholic wine, Merlot usually ripens 1–2 weeks earlier than Cabernet Sauvignon. In the Médoc this grape reaches its zenith, and several châteaux there use high percentages of it (Palmer and Pichon-Lalande), but its fame rests on the wines it renders in Pomerol, where it is used profusely. In the Médoc the average percentage of Merlot in the blend is 5–45%; in Graves, 20–40%; in St.-Émilion, 25–60%; and in Pomerol, 35–98%. Merlot produces wines that are lower in acidity and tannin than Cabernet Sauvignon, and as a general rule wines with a high percentage of Merlot are drinkable much earlier than wines with a high percentage of Cabernet Sauvignon, but frequently age just as well.

Cabernet Franc A relative of Cabernet Sauvignon that ripens slightly earlier, Cabernet Franc (called Bouchet in St.-Émilion and Pomerol) is used in small to modest proportions in order to add complexity to a wine's bouquet and flavor. Cabernet Franc has a pungent, often very spicy, sometimes weedy, olivelike aroma. It does not have the fleshy, supple character of Merlot, or the astringence, power, and color of Cabernet Sauvignon. In the Médoc the average percentage of

Cabernet Franc used in the blend is 0–30%; in Graves, 5–25%; in St.-Émilion, 25–66%; and in Pomerol, 5–50%.

Petit-Verdot A red grape used in Bordeaux winemaking, but generally a difficult one because of its very late ripening characteristics, Petite-Verdot provides intense color and mouth-gripping tannins. It also makes for a wine that is high in sugar—and thus high in alcohol when it ripens fully, as it did in 1982 and 1983 in Bordeaux. When unripe it provides a nasty, sharp, acidic character. In the Médoc few châteaux use more than 5% in the blend, and those that do are, like Palmer and Pichon-Lalande, properties that also use high percentages of Merlot.

WHITE WINE VARIETIES

Bordeaux produces both dry and sweet white wine. Usually only three grape varieties are used: Sauvignon Blanc and Semillon, for dry and sweet wine, and Muscadelle, which is used sparingly for the sweet wines.

Sauvignon Blanc Used for making both the dry white wines of Graves and the sweet white wines of the Sauternes/Barsac district, Sauvignon Blanc renders a very distinctive wine with a pungent, somewhat herbaceous aroma, and crisp, austere flavors. For the dry white Graves, a few châteaux employ 100% Sauvignon Blanc, but most blend it with Semillon. Less Sauvignon Blanc is used in the winemaking blends in Sauternes than in Graves.

Semillon Very susceptible to the famous *pourriture noble* (noble rot) called *Botrytis cinerea*, which is essential to the production of excellent sweet wines, Semillon is used to provide both the dry wines of Graves and the rich sweet wines of Sauternes with a rich, creamy, intense texture. Semillon is quite fruity when young, and wines with a high percentage of Semillon seem to take on weight and viscosity as they age. For these reasons, higher percentages of Semillon are used in making the sweet wines of the Sauternes/Barsac district than in the white wines of Graves.

Muscadelle The rarest of the white wine grapes planted in Bordeaux, Muscadelle is a very fragile grape that is quite susceptible to disease, but when healthy and mature produces a wine with an intense, flowery, perfumed character. It is used only in tiny proportions by châteaux in the Sauternes/Barsac district, and it is not used at all by the producers of white wine in Graves.

FLAVORS

Following are the general flavor characteristics of Bordeaux's most notable types of wines.

MÉDOC

St.-Estèphe While the wines of St.-Estèphe are known for their hardness because of the heavier, thicker soil in the area, the châteaux here have more Merlot planted in their vineyards than do the châteaux elsewhere in the Médoc. Although generalizations can be dangerous, most St.-Estèphe wines do have a tougher character and are more stern and tannic than those found elsewhere in the Médoc. They are usually imbued with a great deal of body.

Pauillac A classic Pauillac seems to define what most people think of as a Bordeaux—a rich blackcurrant, cedary bouquet, followed by medium- to full-bodied flavors with a great deal of richness and tannin.

St.-Julien One can say that St.-Julien wines are virtually indistinguishable from the wines of Pauillac, with perhaps a caveat that they are a bit lighter. However, readers should not take this to mean that they are by any means light wines, as most St.-Juliens are filled with rich curranty fruit and have an aroma of cedar and spices.

Margaux The lightest wines of the Médoc, but in the great vintages perhaps the most seductive. Although the overall quality of the winemaking here is lower than in any other appellation in the Médoc, a great Margaux in a great vintage has an undeniably floral, berry-scented bouquet backed up by the smell of new oak. In body and tannin, despite elevated percentages of Cabernet Sauvignon, Margaux tend to mature more quickly than a St.-Julien, Pauillac, or St.-Estèphe, but are more elegant and lighter.

GRAVES

Textbook red Graves wines are the easiest of all Bordeaux wines to pick out in blind tastings, as they have a distinctive mineral and tobacco aroma, as well as the taste of tobacco and cedar.

The top-notch white Graves are aged in oak and made from the Sauvignon Blanc and Semillon grapes. They often start off excessively oaky, but fill out beautifully with age and develop very creamy, rich flavors that marry beautifully with the oak. Other white wines of Bordeaux are often totally neutral and insipid in character, tasting simply of acidity and water.

ST.-ÉMILION

It is very difficult to generalize about the taste of St.-Émilions given the divergent styles, but most of them tend to be softer and fleshier wines than Médocs, but not as succulent and lush as Pomerols. Because of the elevated percentages of Cabernet Franc planted here, St.-Émilions often have a distinctive herbaceous, cedary bouquet.

POMEROL

Pomerols are often called the burgundies of Bordeaux because of their rich, supple, more monolithic personalities. They age extremely well and are undeniable choices for connoisseurs, as they provide oodles of rich blackcurrant, sometimes blackberry, fruit and very opulent textures in the great vintages.

SAUTERNES/BARSAC

Sauternes and Barsacs can vary a great deal, depending on the vintage. These sweet wines can either taste fat, ripe, and lacking in character in those years of little botrytis, or wonderfully exotic with a bouquet of honeyed tropical fruits and buttered nuts in the great vintages, which had plenty of the noble rot.

AGING POTENTIAL

Médocs	Red Graves: 8–30 years
St. Estèphe: 8–35 years	St.-Émilion: 8–25 years
Pauillac: 8–40 years	Pomerol: 5–30 years
St.-Julien: 8–35 years	White Graves: 5–20 years
Margaux: 8–30 years	Sauternes/Barsac: 10–50+ years

OVERALL QUALITY LEVEL

Of all the great viticultural regions of the world, Bordeaux consistently produces wine of the highest level of quality. Although one-dimensional, innocuous wine can be found, bad wine is rare. For the world's top producers of Cabernet Sauvignon, Merlot, and Cabernet Franc, Bordeaux is the standard-bearer.

THE MOST IMPORTANT INFORMATION TO KNOW

For the wine consumer trying to develop some expertise about the wines of Bordeaux, the most important information to know is, of course, which châteaux are producing the best wines today. A review of my guide to Bordeaux's wine producers (pages 109–115) is a quick way to find out which producers have a high commitment to quality. However, consumers should also familiarize themselves generally with the wine styles from the different appellations. Some people prefer a more austere, sterner style of Bordeaux (such as a St.-Estèphe or a Pauillac), whereas others adore the lushness and opulence of a Pomerol. It has been my experience that the Graves wines, with their distinctive mineral scent and tobacco bouquet, are often the least-favored wines among neophytes, but for those with more experience these characteristics are much admired. And as for the famous official classifications of 1855 that purport to rank wines according to quality, they are now out of date and should only be of academic interest to the consumer. These classifications were once used to promote wines and to establish well-delineated, quality benchmarks, but they have lost their meaning. As a result of negligence, incompetence, or simple greed, some of these châteaux produce mediocre and poor wines that hardly reflect their placement in the classifications. A more valid assessment of the quality of Bordeaux wines can be found in the aforementioned guides, which reflect the overall quality of the wines rather than their historical pedigree.

1989–1990 BUYING STRATEGY

Except for wines of very limited production (certain top Pomerols and St.-Émilions), it is no longer necessary to buy Bordeaux wines two years in advance of their delivery, as "futures." The 1987s are inexpensive and when well chosen will offer delightful, soft, supple drinking immediately. In that sense, they complement the great 1986 Médocs and Graves, which will require 10–15 years of cellaring. Be sure to look for the outstanding Cru Bourgeois wines from vintages such as 1986, and the sweet white wines of 1986 and 1983. In designing a buying strategy, keep these two suggestions in mind: For drinking over the next decade some 1987s and the 1985s make sense; for drinking between 1995 and 2010, the 1986s should be sought out.

BORDEAUX
VINTAGE GUIDE

1987—Notwithstanding all the dreadful reports, this vintage produced another large crop, due to the September heat and sunshine, which saved the day. The better wines of the vintage are more appealing and of higher quality than this decade's two other mediocre years, 1980 and 1984. The results of two weeks of intensive tastings revealed that the early-picked Merlot was ripe, healthy, and rendered good, fruity, soft, and commercial, but pleasant, wines. The harvest rains virtually ruined the Cabernet Franc and early-picked Cabernet Sauvignon, but the very late harvesters did salvage some decent Cabernet Sauvignon from their vineyards. Overall, the 1987 clarets will need to be drunk very young, between 1989 and 1996, but they can be charming wines of medium body. We can be thankful that they have none of the vegetal, austere characteristics of such years as 1984 and 1980. The top successes are in Graves, Pomerol, and in the classified-growths of the Médoc, which were able to make very severe selections. The dry white wines of Bordeaux, harvested under excellent conditions, are very good—better than the 1986s—and while lighter, are not far behind the tasty 1985 whites. It is too early to judge the sweet white wines of Sauternes and Barsac, but it was certainly a very difficult year for them.

All things considered, 1987 is likely to provide some surprisingly pleasant, soft, clean, fruity wines, but the market appears incapable of digesting them at the moment, and anyone, whether consumer or member of the wine trade, would be foolish to buy them until they appear in the bottle in late 1989 and early 1990.

TOP WINES FOR 1987

Ducru-Beaucaillou, Gruaud-Larose, Haut-Brion, Léoville-Las Cases, Margaux, La Mission-Haut-Brion, Mouton-Rothschild, Pétrus, Pichon Lalande, Talbot

1986—In the Médoc, from Margaux to St.-Estèphe, the overall level of quality of the 1986 vintage is very good and sometimes exceptional. The amount of wine produced at many classified châteaux was less than in 1985, the selection process extremely severe, and the resulting wines denser in color than the 1985s, as well as very powerful and rich. The wines are marked by the Cabernet Sauvignon grape, which flourished in this vintage, and have the highest level of tannins ever measured. Three things that stand out about this vintage are the extraordinary potential for 25–35 years of longevity of many of the wines, as a result of their fierce tannins and concentration; far deeper color and much more concentrated flavors than the 1985s; and the sobering thought that only a few of the top wines will be enjoyable to drink before the year 2000. In short, this is a very complementary vintage to the fruity, soft, medium-bodied 1985s. But before you get excited about the top 1986 Médocs, ask yourself whether you have the patience to wait a decade or more for these tannic behemoths. It is a vintage that most closely resembles 1975, but winemaking is significantly better now. While some 1986s will no doubt provide disheartening drinking in 8–10 years because of their sharp, aggressive tannins, there are a dozen or so wines that will in the year 2005 be challenging the greatest 1982s, and will probably outlive the legends of that extraordinary vintage. While the Médoc was clearly the favored area in this vintage, especially in Pauillac and St.-Julien, there are some very fine Graves, good Pomerols, and a number of St.-Émilions that are much deeper and richer than their 1985 counterparts. Lovers of sweet wine will no doubt rejoice over the 1986 Barsacs and Sauternes. While less powerful than the 1983s, they are more aromatic and complex because the essential botrytis was greater than in 1983.

TOP WINES FOR 1986

L'Arrosée, Beychevelle, Canon, Certan de May, Chambert-Marbuzet, Chasse-Spleen, Cheval Blanc, Cos d'Estournel, Ducru-Beaucaillou, L'Eglise-Clinet, Figeac, Gruaud-Larose, Haut-Brion, Lafleur, Léoville-Las Cases, Margaux, Meyney, Montrose, Mouton-Rothschild, Pape-Clément, Pétrus, Pichon Lalande, Sociando-Mallet, Talbot, Vieux Château Certan

1985—Overall 1985 is a lovely vintage of wines that are medium-bodied, very fragrant, soft, and in large part destined to be consumed over the next 15 years while awaiting the hard and powerful 1986s to shed some of their tannins. The record-setting crop in the Médoc in 1985 has effectively prevented most of these wines from reaching greatness. As charming, round, forward—even opulent—as the 1985 Médocs are, any extensive tasting of them will reveal the following weaknesses: (1) they lack grip and are low in acidity and tannin, and (2) the famous first-growths, except for Haut-Brion, Mouton-Rothschild and Margaux, have performed well below the super-seconds. At their best, wines such as the extraordinary Cos d'Estournel, Lynch-Bages, Léoville-Barton, Ducru-Beaucaillou, Léoville-Las Cases, and Margaux may turn out to be modern-day versions of their 1953s, but most of the 1985 Médocs taste like watered-down 1982s or riper, fruitier 1979s. As for the wines of Pomerol and St.-Émilion, there are some undeniable superstars; certainly Pétrus, Lafleur, Certan de

May, Cheval Blanc, and L'Arrosée made their finest wines since 1982. L'Evangile made as great a wine as its 1982, and L'Eglise-Clinet made the finest wine I have ever tasted from this property. Yet, once past most of the famous names, I have to admit to a degree of disappointment with other Pomerols and St.-Émilions, which seem to show, in various degrees, the problems caused by an excessively abundant crop. Both the red and white Graves are excellent, but the Barsacs and Sauternes lack character and complexity.

In general, 1985 will be remembered as a very good vintage that will provide early drinkability. While it is clearly nowhere near the quality of the stupendous 1982s, or many of the powerfully rich 1986 Médocs, 1985 should prove to be as good as 1983, and certainly better than 1978, 1979, and 1981. No one who bought the top wines (for drinking) will regret his or her purchases.

TOP WINES FOR 1985

L'Arrosée, Canon, Certan de May, Cheval Blanc, Cos d'Estournel, Ducru-Beaucaillou, L'Eglise-Clinet, L'Evangile, Haut-Brion, Lafleur, Léoville-Las Cases, Lynch-Bages, Margaux, Mouton-Rothschild, Pétrus, Rausan-Ségla, Le Tertre-Roteboeuf

1984—The late pickers in the Graves and the Médoc harvested surprisingly sound Cabernet Sauvignon and produced wines that have adequate ripeness and color, medium body, and moderate tannins. Because the Merlot crop was largely ruined by the summer's poor weather, Pomerol and St.-Émilion are not the appellations to look for when searching out good 1984s, although several exceptions exist, most notably L'Arrosée. The 1984s are compact, narrowly constructed wines that lack a certain lushness, charm and fruitiness, but for those consumers who like their Bordeaux on the austere side, there are some wines to consider. Pichon-Lalande is the wine of the vintage. Prices, initially absurdly high for such mediocre quality, have now come down, as those in the wine trade attempt to reduce their inventories.

TOP WINES FOR 1984

L'Arrosée, Cos d'Estournel, Gruaud-Larose, Haut-Brion, Latour, Lynch-Bages, Margaux, La Mission-Haut-Brion, Mouton-Rothschild, Pichon-Lalande

1983—If the torrid heat, high precipitation, and tropical humidity that persisted throughout the month of August 1983 had occurred twenty years ago, they would have spelled ruin for a vintage. But thanks to modern sprays, the onslaught of rot was avoided in 1983, and the growers were rewarded with a stunningly perfect, albeit hot month of September and a glorious October; the late harvesters fared the best. This was an excellent year for the Médoc, wherein the Cabernet Sauvignon was excellent. In particular, the appellation of Margaux, a perennial underachiever in the Bordeaux firmament, had its best vintage since 1961, while such notoriously inconsistent châteaux as Brane-Cantenac, Durfort Vivens, Rausan-Ségla, and Kirwan made better wines than they had in years. The early cask tastings of the 1983s not only showed the strength of the vintage in the Médoc, but also revealed wines that, while ripe and full, were much more noticeably tannic than the opulent 1982s. The crop was again enormous; although 8% less than in 1982, in the major Médoc appellations the production per hectare was surprisingly higher than in 1982, and the better châteaux ended up putting much more wine under their second labels than in 1982.

After recently retasting the 1983s, I was surprised to note that the wines have not closed up as much as one might expect. The tannins, once thought much more aggressive than the 1982s, seem to be falling away rather quickly, whereas the higher level of tannins in the 1982s, initially concealed by the extraordinary fleshiness and opulence of fruit of those wines, is becoming more apparent. At present, most 1983s taste much less concentrated and structured for the long haul than the 1982s.

Overall, this vintage will be fully mature before the 1982s. The strengths of the vintage are clearly in the Margaux appellation, followed by St.-Julien and Pauillac. The Pomerols and St.-Émilions are certainly good, but rarely have the succulent excitement that these wines can attain in top years. The Graves can also be fine. I find the overall personality of most of the St.-Estèphes quite boring. For the Barsacs and Sauternes, 1983 is, however, a much-needed, top vintage, although as of today, 1986 is shaping up as an even better year for that much-neglected district.

Five years after the vintage, 1983 looks to be a very good year. Yet save for a handful of wines, it rarely achieves greatness. In the context of the vintages of the eighties, it is clearly superior to 1981, and in appellations such as Margaux and Sauternes, is better than 1982 and 1985, but overall it will have to take a backseat to 1982, 1986, and 1985. One caveat: The top 1983s remain realistically priced, as they were purchased when the dollar was twice its current strength. Consequently, some true bargains are still to be found.

TOP WINES FOR 1983

L'Arrosée, Ausone, Canon, Cantemerle, Cheval Blanc, Ducru-Beaucaillou, L'Evangile, Gruaud-Larose, Haut-Brion, Lafite-Rothschild, Lafleur, Latour à Pomerol, Léoville-Las Cases, Lynch-Bages, Margaux (the wine of the vintage), Mouton-Rothschild, Palmer, Pichon Lalande, Rausan-Ségla

1982—While the 1982s remain the most concentrated, complex, and interesting wines since the 1961 vintage, questions still arise regarding their potential longevity vis-à-vis other great vintages of this century —1929, 1945, and 1961. I have had a chance in the past year to taste most of the 1982s on several occasions, and I believe unequivocally that these are the most exhilarating wines of this the last three decades. Despite a handful of writers who have steadfastly remained critical of this vintage, the majority view is that 1982 is clearly the greatest Bordeaux vintage since 1961. There is, however, no question that many wines can be drunk early with an extraordinary degree of pleasure that, except for the 1929s, cannot be matched by any of the other great Bordeaux vintages of this century. However, I find most of the 1982 Médocs from St.-Julien, Pauillac, and St.-Estèphe to be firming up considerably, but despite their dense black/purple color, fragrant, opulent bouquets, and intense richness on the palate, they remain very undeveloped and little different from the way they tasted from the cask. Most of the Médocs, including all of the first-growths and the super-seconds (except for the soft, somewhat unstructured Palmer) will not be ready until the end of the nineties, which is somewhat longer than I had originally estimated. Saying this, I fear, will not prevent many of them from being drunk much earlier. The Pomerols and St.-Émilions are also beginning to show more structure, but it is hard to resist the opulent, exotic pleasures of wines such as Cheval Blanc, Canon, L'Evangile, Le Pin and Trotanoy, despite the fact that they seem little evolved from their days in the cask. Of course one hears from the likes of Harry Waugh and Jean-Pierre Moueix that most of the 1947 Pétrus and the 1947 Cheval Blanc was also drunk within the first 7–8 years of that historic vintage; but for the life of me I cannot think that those wines, no matter how decadently rich and tasty, could have been more enjoyable in 1954–1955 than today (I recently gave both of them perfect scores in a blind tasting in Bordeaux). Nevertheless, I suspect the debate concerning the longevity of the 1982 clarets will go on for another 20–30 years. But if the ultimate criteria for the greatness of a wine or vintage is the degree of pleasure it can provide, and the span of years over which it can provide this pleasure, then 1982 has, in effect, no modern-day peer. I, for one, plan to start drinking the Cru Bourgeois (except for Sociando-Mallet and Poujeaux) around 1990–1992, the Pomerols and St.-Émilions around 1992–1995, and the Graves, St.-Juliens, Pauillacs, and St.-Estèphes in 1995. The 1982 Margauxs are very forward and can be drunk in 1–2 years. All of the top 1982s, when purchased and stored properly, will drink gorgeously for another 10–25 years, perhaps longer. Despite their precociousness, their great fruit and depth will enable them to outlive all of the recent vintages except the 1986s. Finally, this vintage over the long term will be remembered primarily for the following wines, which are likely to be considered on the same level as the 1929 and 1945 Mouton-Rothschild, the 1928, 1945, and 1961 Latour, the 1945, 1947, and 1961 Pétrus, the 1947 Cheval Blanc, the 1900 Margaux, and the 1953 and 1959 Lafite-Rothschild.

TOP WINES FOR 1982

Ausone, Beychevelle, Bon Pasteur, Canon, Certan de May, Cheval Blanc, Cos d'Estournel, Ducru-Beaucaillou, L'Evangile, Figeac, Grand-Puy-Lacoste, Gruaud-Larose, Haut-Marbuzet, Lafite-Rothschild, La Lagune, Latour, Léoville-Las Cases, Léoville-Poyferré Lynch-Bages, Margaux, Mouton-Rothschild, Pétrus, Pichon Lalande, Sociando-Mallet, Trotanoy

1981—I have found that many of the wines from the 1981 vintage lack generosity and richness, but for admirers of the lighter-styled, less-intense and less-powerful Bordeaux vintages, there are a number of fine choices to be found, particularly in the appellations of St.-Julien, Pauillac, and Pomerol. In St.-Estèphe, Margaux, Graves, and St.-Émilion, the wines are patchy in quality. This vintage, which looked so promising and potentially great, was diluted by the rains that caught everyone off-guard, just as the harvest was ready to commence. This is not a very pleasant vintage for the Crus Bourgeois. Most of the 1981s should be approaching full maturity by 1990–1991, and will keep if well stored, for 5–12 years thereafter.

TOP WINES FOR 1981

Certan de May, Cheval Blanc, La Conseillante, Ducru-Beaucaillou, Gruaud-Larose, Lafite-Rothschild, Latour, Léoville-Las Cases, Margaux, Mouton-Rothschild, Pétrus, St.-Pierre-Sevaistre

1980—Sandwiched between a number of fine vintages, the 1980 Bordeaux crop has largely been a forgotten stepchild. However, the adventurous wine enthusiast can probably tell a few tales about some surprisingly soft, supple wines that were much tastier than any critic led him or her to believe.

The crop of 1980 was a late harvest that suffered from a poor summer, particularly the terrible flowering that diminished the size of the Merlot crop. The weather improved dramatically in September, which allowed the grapes to mature; however, the vintage that commenced on October 14 met with rain once again.

The resulting wines are light; some are rather diluted and disappointing, but a number of sound, fruity, supple wines were produced that, if well chosen, offer immediate drinkability and charm. A very fine wine was made at Margaux, which continued its record of producing one of the finest wines of the vintage since the Mentzelopoulos family took over the estate in 1977. If the vintage was decidedly uninspiring for red wines, the late-harvest sweet wines of Barsac and Sauternes turned out quite well, with most properties picking into late November under ideal weather conditions.

Most 1980s are fully mature now, but only a handful of them will last past 1990.

TOP WINES FOR 1980

Branaire-Ducru, Chasse-Spleen, Cheval Blanc, Domaine de Chevalier. Climens, Cos d'Estournel, La Dominique, Fargues, Giscours, Gruaud-Larose, d'Issan, Lafite-Rothschild, Langoa-Barton, Latour, Léoville-Barton, Margaux, La Mission-Haut-Brion, Pétrus, Pichon Lalande, Siran, Talbot, d'Yquem

1979—Not only was the 1979 crop enormous in size, but the quality was quite good. I thought the wines were a trifle light when I first did my cask tastings in late March of 1980, particularly when tasted against the fuller-bodied, richer 1978s. However, the wines have continued to put on weight and richness during their time in both cask and bottle, and while they are not big, rich, full-bodied wines, they are graceful, nicely concentrated, and well-balanced.

The weather conditions that led up to the 1979 harvest were hardly exceptional. The summer was unusually cold, but fortunately quite dry. The harvest did not start until early October. The weather during the harvest was mixed, with generally good weather interlaced with showery periods. The grapes were considered healthy and mature in all regions of Bordeaux.

The initial reaction was that 1979 was a "Merlot year" and that therefore the top successes were in that region. However, time has proven that the top wines seem to be concentrated in the appellations of Margaux, St.-Julien, and Pauillac.

The 1979 red wines have shown consistently well in tastings. They are not powerful but are, rather, fruity, medium-bodied wines with good concentration and moderate tannins. Most of them will be fully mature and ready to drink between 1990 and 2005. The top wines will, of course, last longer.

For the sweet white wines, the late harvest permitted enough botrytis to form so that some successful wines were made. However, most of the Barsacs and Sauternes were not nearly as good as the 1980s.

TOP WINES FOR 1979

Ausone, Canon, Certan de May, Chasse-Spleen, Cheval Blanc, Domaine de Chevalier, Cos d'Estournel, L'Evangile, Fargues, Giscours, Gloria, Gruaud-Larose, Haut-Bailly, Haut-Brion, Haut-Marbuzet, Lafite-Rothschild, Lafleur, Latour, Latour à Pomerol, Léoville-Las Cases, Margaux, Meyney, La Mission-Haut-Brion, Palmer, Pavie, Pétrus, Pichon Lalande, St.-Pierrre-Sevaistre, du Tertre, Trotanoy, d'Yquem

1978—This vintage turned out to be an excellent one for the red wines of the Médoc and Graves, a good one for the red wines of St. Émilion and Pomerol, and a fair one for the sweet white wines of Barsac and Sauternes. Extremely poor weather throughout the spring and in June, July, and the first part of August had many growers thinking that 1978 would be a repeat of the poor vintage of 1977. However, in mid-August the weather became sunny, hot, and dry. For the next 9 weeks this weather continued virtually uninterrupted except for some light rain. The harvest commenced very late, October 7, and the grapes were brought in under ideal conditions. The astonishing turnaround in the weather and the resulting excellent vintage caused Harry Waugh, the peripatetic English wine authority, to dub the vintage "the miracle vintage," a name that has stuck. The top red wines of 1978 have almost always come from the Médoc and Graves. The wines of Pomerol and St.-Émilion, with a few exceptions, seem noticeably less successful, although they are certainly good. The 1978s at first appeared intensely fruity, very deeply colored, moderately tannic, and medium to full bodied. In style and character they seemed to resemble the lovely wines of the 1970 vintage, only slightly lighter and more herbaceous. Most of the top wines of 1978 should be fully mature by 1990–2005.

The lesser Crus Bourgeois of 1978 are less successful than in such vintages as 1982 and 1983.

As for the sweet wines in Sauternes and Barsac, this was a difficult year, and most of the wines lack the honeyed botrytis character.

TOP WINES FOR 1978

Ausone, Canon, Certan de May, Cheval Blanc, Domaine de Chevalier, Climens, Cos d'Estournel, La Dominique, Ducru-Beaucaillou, L'Evangile, Figeac, Les Forts de Latour, Giscours, Grand-Puy-Lacoste, Gruaud-Larose, Haut-Brion, d'Issan, Lafite-Rothschild, Lafleur, La Lagune, Latour, Léoville-Barton, Léoville-Las Cases, Margaux, La Mission-Haut-Brion, Palmer, Pétrus, Pichon Lalande, Prieuré-Lichine, Raymond-Lafon, St.-Pierre-Sevaistre, Talbot, du Tertre, La Tour-Haut-Brion, Trotanoy

1977—This is the worst vintage for Bordeaux between 1973 and 1987. A wet, cold summer played havoc with the crop. In addition, the Merlot crop was devastated by a spring frost. While warm, dry weather arrived prior to the harvest, there was just not enough of it to save the vintage, although—considering the raw materials—several wines did turn out to be relatively decent. It was also a very poor year for the sweet wine producers.

Any of the 1977 wines listed below should be drunk over the next 2–3 years, as they will not last. Most of the wines are rather high in acidity, with herbaceous, vegetal aromas and flavors. The following are some of the more successful wines produced in the vintage, although I cannot personally recommend any of them.

TOP WINES FOR 1977

Domaine de Chevalier, Cos d'Estournel, Ducru-Beaucaillou, Figeac, Giscours, Gruaud-Larose, La Lagune, Latour, Margaux, La Mission-Haut-Brion, Pichon Lalande, Talbot

1976—The very highly publicized vintage of 1976 has never quite lived up to its reputation, although all the ingredients for a superb vintage were present. September 13 signaled the earliest harvest since 1945. The weather during the summer had been torridly hot, as the average temperatures for the months of June through September were only exceeded by those of the hot grueling summers of 1949 and 1947. However, even with many vignerons predicting a "vintage of the century," very heavy rains fell between September 11 and 15, which bloated the grapes.

The harvested crop was very large, the grapes were very ripe, and while the wines had good tannin levels, the acidity levels were low and the pH was dangerously high. The top wines of 1976 offer wonderfully soft, supple, fruity drinking now and certainly can be said to have more charm than the more publicized 1975s. At present, the top 1976s are among the most enjoyable clarets for drinking in 1989–1993, as they have matured very rapidly.

However, many 1976s, having lacked color from the beginning and being very fragile, have taken on a disturbing brown cast, while others have lapsed into premature senility long before their 10th birthday. For the red wines, the vintage is strongest in St.-Julien, Pauillac, St.-Estèphe, and Margaux. It is weakest in Graves.

This vintage can offer wonderful wine for drinking now, but one must select very carefully.

As for the sweet wines, 1976 is an excellent vintage—providing rich, intense, full-bodied wines with plenty of botrytis and character.

The following are the top 1976s. With few exceptions, these wines are ideal for drinking over the next 4–5 years because few will still be alive thereafter.

TOP WINES FOR 1976

Ausone, Beychevelle, Branaire-Ducru, Cheval Blanc, Climens, Clos des Jacobins, Cos d'Estournel, Ducru-Beaucaillou, Fargues, Figeac, Giscours, Gloria, Guiraud, Haut-Bages-Libéral, Haut-Brion, d'Issan, Lafite-Rothschild, La Lagune, Latour, Latour à Pomerol,

Léoville-Las Cases, Montrose, Nairac, Palmer, Pétrus, de Pez, Pichon Lalande, Rieussec, Suduiraut, Talbot, Trotanoy, d'Yquem

1975—This vintage followed three large vintages of generally poor or mediocre crops (1972, 1973, and 1974). The 1975 crop was small, due to spring frosts and the zealous pruning of vines by many growers who feared another large crop. The months of July, August, and September were hot, but not excessively so. However, the latter two months were punctuated by several huge thunderstorms that delivered enormous amounts of rainfall. In fact, when one looks at the rainfall in the critical months of August and September, it was approximately the same as that of Bordeaux's worst vintages—1969, 1968, and 1965. This caused some observers to question those who claimed that 1975 was the best Bordeaux vintage since 1961.

The harvest began on September 22 and continued until mid-October in good weather except for a hailstorm that ravaged the central Médoc communes of Avensan, Moulis, Arcins, and Lamarque.

While the vintage has been highly touted, my conclusion is that while some very great wines were produced, 1975 is much more irregular in quality than was initially believed.

The wines continue to be tannic, full bodied, and backward, yet show signs of opening up over the next 2–3 years. The top wines have the richness and depth of fruit and dark color to go along with the high level of dry, sometimes astringent tannins. Other wines surprisingly lack color and seem to have an excess of tannin, Certainly, the 1975 vintage will provide some of the longest-lived Bordeaux wines of the last three decades, but also, unfortunately, a number of disappointments.

The wines of Pauillac and Pomerol appear to be the most successful of the vintage. I do not expect most of the great 1975s to be mature before 1990–1995. The top wines have the potential to last another 10–15 years.

With regard to the Sauternes, this was an excellent vintage with just about every estate producing a fine wine.

TOP WINES FOR 1975

Balestard-La-Tonnelle, Branaire-Ducru, Cadet-Piola, Calon-Ségur, Cheval Blanc, Climens, L'Enclos, L'Evangile, Fargues, Figeac, La Fleur Pétrus, Le Gay, Giscours, Gloria, Gruaud-Larose, Haut-Bages-Libéral, Haut-Marbuzet, Lafite-Rothschild, Lafleur, La

Lagune, Langoa-Barton, Latour, Latour Haut-Brion, Léoville-Barton, Léoville-Las Cases, Magdelaine, Meyney, La Mission-Haut-Brion, Mouton-Rothschild, Palmer, Pétrus, Pichon Lalande, Raymond-Lafon, Rieussec, Sociando-Mallet, Soutard, Trotanoy, Vieux Château Certan, d'Yquem

1974—While the crop was large, as the result of a good flowering and a dry, sunny May and June, the weather from late August through October was rainy. Despite the persistently soggy conditions, some surprisingly good wines were made in Graves, clearly the vintage's most successful appellation. Most 1974s are rather hard, tannic, hollow wines that lack flesh and richness. They have kept fairly well because of their good tannin and acidity levels, but overall these wines, except for the top wines listed below, have little to offer.

The vintage was terrible in the Barsac and Sauternes district, and many properties declassified their entire crop.

TOP WINES FOR 1974

Branaire-Ducru, Domaine de Chevalier, Ducru-Beaucaillou, Figeac, Gruaud-Larose, Haut-Brion, Latour, La Mission-Haut-Brion, Trotanoy

1973—At one time in the mid-seventies, the 1973s had some value as agreeably light, soft, simple Bordeaux wines. Today, except for a handful of wines like Latour and Pétrus, these wines have faded into oblivion.

This was another of the Bordeaux vintages in which the summer had been ideal and all of Bordeaux was set for a big crop of good-quality grapes. However, as so often happens there, the heavens opened up; in the course of the three weeks that followed the commencement of the harvest, September 25, a good vintage was turned into a rain-bloated swollen crop of mediocre grapes. The crop was large, but the wines lacked color, extract, acidity, and backbone. The great majority of them were ready to drink when released in 1976, and by 1979 many were beginning to fall apart. Nevertheless, there were some good, round, fruity ones that had some concentration to them. However, buying any 1973 now would be extremely dangerous unless it were Pétrus (clearly the wine of this vintage) or Latour.

As a general rule, the sweet wines of Barsac and Sauternes turned out a little better, but most of them should have been drunk by now.

TOP WINES FOR 1973

Beychevelle, Ducru-Beaucaillou, Giscours, Latour, Latour Haut-Brion, Latour à Pomerol, Montrose, Pétrus, de Pez, Trotanoy, d'Yquem

1972—The unusually cool, cloudy summer months, with an abnormally rainy August, were followed by dry, warm weather in September, but it was too late to salvage the crop. The vintage produced the worst wines of the decade—acidic, green, raw, and vegetal tasting. Their high acidity has indeed kept many of them alive, but their deficiencies are too great for mere age to overcome. As in any poor vintage, some châteaux managed to produce wines far better than those of their neighbors. In 1972, there were only half a dozen or so worthy of consumer interest, and then only at very low prices. Certainly, no appellation in 1972 did better or worse than any other.

TOP WINES FOR 1972

Branaire-Ducru, Cheval Blanc, Climens, Figeac, Giscours, Latour, Léoville-Las Cases, La Mission-Haut-Brion, Rausan-Ségla, Trotanoy

1971—Unlike 1970, 1971 was a rather small vintage because of a poor flowering in June, which caused a significant reduction in the Merlot crop. By the end of the harvest, the crop was a good 40% less than the huge crop of 1970.

Early reports on the vintage have proven to be overly enthusiastic. Some experts, relying on the small production yields as compared to those of 1970, even claimed the vintage was better than 1970. Again, this has proven to be totally false. Certainly the 1971s were forward and delicious, as were the 1970s when first released, but unlike the 1970s, the 1971s lacked the great depth of color, concentration, and tannic backbone. The vintage was rather mixed in the Médoc, but it was certainly a fine year for Pomerol, St.-Émilion, and Graves.

Buying 1971s now is quite dangerous. There are only a few wines that are not fully mature, and even such superb wines as Pétrus, Latour, Trotanoy, La Mission-Haut-Brion, all examples of very well preserved wines from this vintage, are not likely to improve. Yet, when the top 1971s have been well cellared, they can provide the best *current* drinking of any vintage in the 1970s.

The 1971 vintage was originally portrayed as one of those really fine years that gets overlooked because of the publicity and hoopla given to the vintage that preceded it—in this case the marvelous 1970. The 1971 vintage is very irregular, as a handful of really sensational wines were produced along with a horde of mediocre ones. The sweet wines of Barsac and Sauternes were extremely successful. Contrary to their red siblings, the white wines have aged beautifully and will easily outlast the great majority of the red wines produced in 1971.

TOP WINES FOR 1971

Beychevelle, Cheval Blanc, Climens, Coutet, La Dominique, Ducru-Beaucaillou, Fargues, Giscours, Haut-Brion, Lafleur, Lafleur Pétrus, Latour, La Mission-Haut-Brion, Montrose, Mouton-Rothschild, Palmer, Pétrus, Talbot, Trotanoy, d'Yquem

1970—Of all the vintages between the two great ones—1961 and 1982—1970 has proven to be the best. The 1970s are more attractive and charming than the austere 1966s and the hard, tannic, big 1975s. The 1970 vintage was unusual in that it produced high volume and very high quality. It was splendidly uniform and consistent throughout Bordeaux, with every appellation being able to claim its share of superstars. It was also an outstanding year for the lesser growths of Bordeaux.

The weather conditions during the summer and fall of 1970 were perfect.There was no hail, no weeks full of drenching downpours, no frost, and no spirit-crushing deluge at harvesttime. Everything went well and Bordeaux's châteaux harvested one of the biggest and healthiest crops of grapes ever.

From the earliest days, the wines showed great color, an intense richness of fruit, full body, and good tannin. However, because the wines showed so well while young, some writers began to say that they were precocious, a product of the "nouvelle vinification," and would not last until 1980. Some of the greatest Bordeaux vintages—1929, 1947, 1949, 1953 and 1961—all showed extremely well while young, causing many so-called experts to falsely assume they would not last. Like these older vintages, the 1970s have slowed down in development, and in 1989 many of the top wines are just now entering their mature plateau.

The sweet wines, although not as good as the 1971s, were quite successful.

The 1970s will provide great drinking pleasure for years to come. Of the vintages of the last 25 years, only the 1982 and the 1961 can lay claim to being better.

TOP WINES FOR 1970

L'Arrosée, Branaire-Ducru, Chasse-Spleen, Cheval Blanc, Domaine de Chevalier, La Conseillante, Cos d'Estournel, Ducru-Beaucaillou, L'Evangile, Figeac, Fourcas-Hosten, Giscours, Gloria, Gruaud-Larose, Haut-Bailly, Haut-Batailley, Haut-Marbuzet, d'Issan, Lafleur, Lafleur Pétrus, Lafon Rochet, La Lagune, Latour, Latour à Pomerol, Léoville-Barton, Les-Ormes-de-Pez, Lynch-Bages, Magdelaine, Meyney, La Mission-Haut-Brion, Montrose, Mouton-Rothschild, Palmer, Pétrus, de Pez, Pichon Lalande, Poujeaux, Rausan-Ségla, St.-Pierre-Sevaistre, Sociando-Mallet, Trotanoy, d'Yquem

1969—After Bordeaux suffers through a disastrous vintage as it did in 1968, there seems to be a tendency to lavish indiscriminate praise on the next vintage. After a horrible year in 1968, Bordeaux badly needed a fine vintage in 1969. But despite the optimistic proclamations by some of the leading Bordeaux experts at the time, 1969 has turned out to be one of the least attractive Bordeaux vintages of the last two decades.

The crop was small, and while the summer was sufficiently hot and dry to ensure a decent maturity, torrential September rains ruined the chances for a good vintage. Nevertheless, investors irrationally moved in to buy these insipid, nasty, acidic, sharp wines; consequently, these poor wines were quite expensive when they first appeared on the market.

I can honestly say that I have never tasted a red wine from 1969 I have liked. Harsh and hollow, with no flesh, fruit or charm, these wines are anything but palatable. I cannot recommend any of them.

In the Barsac and Sauternes district, a few proprietors managed to produce acceptable wines.

1968—This was another of the very poor vintages Bordeaux had to suffer through in the sixties. As usual, the culprit was heavy rains (it was the wettest year since 1951), which bloated the grapes. However, I have found some 1968s that were much better than anything produced in 1969, a vintage with a "better" reputation. Should anyone run across these wines today, the rule of caveat emptor would most certainly be applicable, as I doubt that any of them have much life left in them.

TOP WINES FOR 1968

Cantemerle, Figeac, Les Forts de Latour, Giscours, Gruaud-La-rose, Haut-Brion, Latour, La Mission-Haut-Brion, Talbot

1967—Even though 1967 cannot be considered a great or even very good vintage, it was a large vintage of soft, quick-maturing wines that provided agreeable drinking between 1970 and 1978. Most 1967s should have been consumed by the start of this present decade, although a handful of wines like Latour, Pétrus, Trotanoy, and Palmer should continue to give pleasure for another 2–3 years.

The strongest wines of 1967 were produced in Pomerol and St.-Émilion, as well as in Graves and Sauternes.

Should one find some of the top wines listed below in the larger-type bottles (magnums, double magnums, and so forth), they could well provide lovely drinking.

TOP WINES FOR 1967

Calon-Ségur, Canon, Cantemerle, Cheval Blanc, Ducru-Beaucail-lou, La Fleur Pétrus, Giscours, Gruaud-Larose, Haut-Bailly, Haut-Brion, La Lagune, Latour, Magdelaine, La Mission-Haut-Brion, Montrose, Palmer, Pavie, Pétrus, Pichon Lalande, Suduiraut, Trotanoy, La Violette, d'Yquem

1966—While there is general agreement that 1966 is the second-best vintage of the sixties (after 1961), its wines have not developed as well as many of its proponents would have liked. Now coming up on their 25th birthday they have never really blossomed out. Many remain rather austere, lean, unyielding, tannic wines that seem to be in danger of losing their fruit before their tannin. This is rather surprising in view of the early reports on the vintage, which called the wines precocious, charming, and early maturing. Yet if the vintage is not as consistent as was initially believed, there are still some wonderfully rich, well-balanced, medium-weight classic wines that were produced in 1966. The Médoc is clearly the strongest district for the top wines of this vintage, but there are many successes in Pomerol as well. It was a mediocre year for the wines of Barsac and Sauternes.

With regard to the climatic conditions that shaped the vintage, the flowering in June went slowly, July and August were intermittently hot and cold, and September was dry and sunny. A large crop was harvested under sound weather conditions.

Most of the 1966s should continue to drink well for another decade, although I worry that the less-balanced wines will dry out. This is a very good vintage, but proper selection is extremely important.

TOP WINES FOR 1966

Beychevelle, Branaire-Ducru, Canon, Cantemerle, Cheval Blanc, Domaine de Chevalier, Ducru-Beaucaillou, Giscours, Gruaud-Larose, La Lagune, Latour, Léoville-Barton, Léoville-Las Cases, La Mission-Haut-Brion, Montrose, Mouton-Rothschild, Palmer, Pape-Clément, Pétrus, Pichon Lalande, La Tour à Pomerol, Trotanoy

1965—This, a vintage produced in rot and rain, is considered by most experts to be one of the worst vintages of the post-World War II era. Its wet summer was bad enough, but its real undoing was the incredibly wet and humid September, which caused the rot to voraciously devour the vineyards. Obviously, these wines should be avoided. I myself have had little experience tasting them.

1964—One of the most intriguing vintages of Bordeaux, 1964 produced a number of splendid, generally underrated and underpriced wines in Pomerol, St.-Émilion and Graves, where many proprietors had the good fortune to have harvested their crops before the rainy deluge began on October 8. However, this downpour caught many other Médoc châteaux by surprise—with unharvested vineyards. Thus, 1964 has never been regarded as a top Bordeaux vintage. While the vintage can be notoriously bad for the properties of the Médoc and the late-harvesting Sauternes/Barsac district, it is excellent to outstanding for the appellations of Pomerol, St.-Émilion, and Graves.

The summer of 1964 had been extremely hot and dry, and when the harvest commenced many proprietors thought that a great vintage was in the making. Since the Merlot grape ripens first, the harvest began in the areas where Merlot is planted in abundance, in St.-Émilion and Pomerol. When the rains came, not all of the Médoc properties were still picking. Consequently, there were some excellent wines made in the Médoc, but because of the famous failures of Lafite-Rothschild, Mouton-Rothschild, Lynch-Bages, Calon-Ségur and Margaux, many wine enthusiasts have apprehensively shied away from the vintage.

The successful wines are quite rich, full-bodied, and concentrated, which are more deeply colored and significantly richer than the leaner, more austere 1966s. While most of the 1964s are now at full maturity, they will certainly hold another 5 years. It may seem incredible that I have enjoyed the best wines of 1964 more than those of 1966, a vintage with a much greater reputation.

TOP WINES FOR 1964

L'Arrosée, Cheval Blanc, La Conseillante, L'Evangile, Figeac, Gruaud Larose, Haut-Bailly, Haut-Brion, Lafleur, Lafleur Pétrus, La Lagune, Latour, Magdelaine, La Mission-Haut-Brion, Montrose, Pétrus, de Pez, Pichon Lalande, Soutard, Trotanoy, Vieux Château Certan

1963—Bordeaux's châteaux have never been able to decide whether 1963 or 1965 was the worse vintage of the sixties. As in 1965, rain and rot ruined this vintage.

1962—It might be expected that 1962, coming after the great vintage of 1961, would be underrated, which it has been; also it is probably the most undervalued Bordeaux vintage of the last three decades. The crop size was large due to a hot and sunny summer with just enough rain. Elegant, supple, and very fruity, the 1962s are neither too tannic nor too big, but have been consistently pleasurable and charming. Because of their balance, they have kept longer than anyone could have ever imagined, and while most of the 1962s now require drinking up, the well-cellared top wines of the vintage can be kept for several more years.

This vintage is especially good for the sweet wines of Barsac and Sauternes, which are now at their decadently rich best.

TOP WINES FOR 1962

Cantemerle, Ducru-Beaucaillou, Figeac, Gruaud-Larose, Haut-Brion, Lafleur, Latour, Lynch-Bages, La Mission-Haut-Brion, Magdelaine, Montrose, Mouton-Rothschild, Palmer, Pape-Clément, Pétrus, Pichon Lalande, Trotanoy, La Violette, d'Yquem

1961—Until the advent of the 1982 vintage, there was little one could offer to refute the argument that 1961 was the finest vintage of the post-World War II era. Even though the 1982s are differently styled, the best of them will be able to hold their own with the finest 1961s. The 1961s have sensational concentration, the magnificent, penetrating bouquets of ripe fruit, rich, deep, long flavors, and outstanding deep colors. Even though they are now 24 years old, the top wines are capable of aging for at least another decade, and the very best wines will still be marvelous by the year 2000.

The weather pattern was nearly perfect in 1961, with spring frosts reducing the crop size, followed by sunny, hot weather throughout the summer and harvest, resulting in splendid maturity levels for the grapes. The small harvest guaranteed very high prices for these wines.

The vintage was excellent throughout all appellations of Bordeaux except for the Barsacs and Sauternes, which have benefited greatly from the vintage's reputation but are in reality quite mediocre. Some of the St.-Émilions are also not what they might have been because the vineyards there had not fully recovered from the killer freeze of 1956.

TOP WINES FOR 1961

Beychevelle, Cantemerle, Cheval Blanc, Ducru-Beaucaillou, Figeac, Gruaud-Larose, Haut-Bailly, Haut-Brion, Latour, Latour à Pomerol, Léoville-Barton, Lynch-Bages, Magdelaine, Malescot St.-Exupéry, Margaux, La Mission-Haut-Brion, Montrose, Mouton-Rothschild, Palmer, Pape-Clément, Pétrus, de Pez, Pichon Lalande, Pontet-Canet, Trotanoy

A GUIDE TO BORDEAUX'S BEST PRODUCERS OF DRY RED WINES

***** *(OUTSTANDING PRODUCERS)*

L'Arrosée (St.-Émilion)
Ausone (St.-Émilion)
Canon (St.-Émilion)
Certan de May (Pomerol)
Cheval Blanc (St.-Émilion)
Domaine de Chevalier (Graves)
Cos d'Estournel (St.-Estèphe)
Ducru-Beaucaillou (St.-Julien)
L'Eglise-Clinet (Pomerol)
L'Evangile (Pomerol)
Figeac (St.-Émilion)
La Fleur de Gay (Pomerol)
Gruaud-Larose (St.-Julien)
Haut-Brion (Graves)

Haut-Marbuzet (St.-Estèphe)
Lafite-Rothschild (Pauillac)
Lafleur (Pomerol)
La Lagune (Ludon)
Latour (Pauillac)
Latour à Pomerol (Pomerol)
Léoville-Barton (St.-Julien)
Léoville-Las Cases (St.-Julien)
Lynch-Bages (Pauillac)
Château Margaux (Margaux)
La Mission-Haut-Brion (Graves)
Mouton-Rothschild (Pauillac)
Palmer (Margaux)
Pétrus (Pomerol)

Pichon-Longueville, Comtesse
de Lalande (Pauillac)
Le Pin (Pomerol)

Sociando-Mallet (Haut-Médoc)
Trotanoy (Pomerol)

* * * * (EXCELLENT PRODUCERS)

Beychevelle (St.-Julien)
Bon Pasteur (Pomerol)
Boyd-Cantenac (Margaux)
Branaire-Ducru (St.-Julien)
Cadet-Piola (St.-Émilion)
Calon-Ségur (St.-Estèphe)
Cantemerle (Macau)
Chambert-Marbuzet (St.-
Estèphe)
Chasse-Spleen (Moulis)
La Conseillante (Pomerol)
La Dominique (St.-Émilion)
La Fleur Pétrus (Pomerol)
Les Forts de Latour (Pauillac)
Le Gay (Pomerol)
Grand-Puy-Lacoste (Pauillac)
Haut-Bailly (Graves)
d'Issan (Margaux)

Lagrange (St.-Julien)
Langoa-Barton (St.-Julien)
Larmande (St.-Émilion)
Lascombes (Margaux)
Leoville-Poyferré (St.-Julien)
Magdelaine (St.-Émilion)
Marquis-de-Terme (Margaux)
Montrose (St.-Estèphe)
Pavillon Rouge de Margaux
(Margaux)
De Pez (St.-Estèphe)
Prieuré-Lichine (Margaux)
St.-Pierre-Sevaistre (St.-Julien)
Tayac Prestige (Côtes de Bourg)
Talbot (St.-Julien)
Tertre-Roteboeuf (St.-Émilion)
La Tour-Haut-Brion (Graves)
Vieux Château Certan (Pomerol)

* * * (GOOD PRODUCERS)

L'Angélus (St.-Émilion)
d'Angludet (Margaux)
Annereaux (Lalande-de-
Pomerol)
Bahans Haut-Brion (Graves)
Balestard-La-Tonnelle (St.-
Émilion)
Batailley (Pauillac)
Beau-Séjour-Bécot (St.-Émilion)
Beaumont (Haut-Médoc)
Beauséjour (Duffau-Lagarrosse)
(St.-Émilion)
Bel Air (Lalande-de-Pomerol)
Belair (St.-Émilion)
de Belcier (Côtes de Castillon)
Belles Graves (Lalande-de-
Pomerol)

Berliquet (St.-Émilion)
Bertineau St.-Vincent (Lalande-
de-Pomerol)
Le Boscq (Médoc)
Branas-Grand Poujeaux (Moulis)
Brane-Cantenac (Margaux)
Brillette (Moulis)
Camensac (Haut-Médoc)
Canon (Canon-Fronsac)
Canon de Brem (Canon-
Fronsac)
Canon-La-Gaffelière (St.-
Émilion)
Canon Moueix (Canon-Fronsac)
Cantenac-Brown (Margaux)
Cap de Merle (Lussac-St.-
Émilion)

Cap de Mourlin (St.-Émilion)
Carbonnieux (Graves)
Cardeneau (Fronsac)
de Carles (Fronsac)
Les Carmes Haut-Brion
  (Graves)
Certan-Giraud (Pomerol)
Chantegrive (Graves)
Châtain (Lalande-de-
  Pomerol)
Cissac (Haut-Médoc)
Clarke (Listrac)
Clerc-Milon (Pauillac)
Clinet (Pomerol)
Clos du Clocher (Pomerol)
Clos Fourtet (St.-Émilion)
Clos des Jacobins (St.-Émilion)
Clos René (Pomerol)
La Clotte (St.-Émilion)
Corbin (St.-Émilion)
Corbin-Michotte (St.-Émilion)
Cormeil Figeac (St.-Émilion)
Coufran (Haut-Médoc)
Couvent-des-Jacobins (St.-
  Émilion)
La Croix (Pomerol)
La Croix de Gay (Pomerol)
La Croix St. André (Lalande-de-
  Pomerol)
Croque-Michotte (St.-Émilion)
Dalem (Fronsac)
Dassault (St.-Émilion)
La Dauphine (Fronsac)
Destieux (St.-Émilion)
Duhart-Milon-Rothschild
  (Pauillac)
Duplessis-Fabre (Moulis)
Durand-Laplagne (Puisseguin-
  St.-Émilion)
Durfort-Vivens (Margaux)
Domaine de L'Eglise (Pomerol)
L'Enclos (Pomerol)

Faurie-de-Souchard (St.-
  Émilion)
Ferrand (St.-Émilion)
Les Fiefs de Lagrange (St.-
  Julien)
de Fieuzal (Graves)
Fonbadet (Pauillac)
Fonplégade (St.-Émilion)
Fonreaud (Listrac)
Fonroque (St.-Émilion)
Fontenil (Fronsac)
Fourcas-Dupré (Listrac)
Fourcas-Hosten (Listrac)
Franc Mayne (St.-Émilion)
La Gaffelière (St.-Émilion)
Gazin (Pomerol)
Giscours (Margaux)
Gloria (St.-Julien)
Grand Mayne (St.-Émilion)
Grand-Ormeau (Lalande-de-
  Pomerol)
Grand-Puy-Ducasse (Pauillac)
La Grave Figeac (St.-Émilion)
La Grave Trigant de Boisset
  (Pomerol)
Gressier Grand-Poujeaux
  (Moulis)
Greysac (Médoc)
La Gurgue (Margaux)
Haut-Bages-Averous (Pauillac)
Haut-Bages-Libéral (Pauillac)
Haut-Batailley (Pauillac)
Haut-Brisson (St.-Émilion)
Haut-Conseillants (Lalande-de-
  Pomerol)
Haut-Sarpe (St.-Émilion)
Hortevie (St.-Julien)
La Jurade (St.-Émilion)
Kirwan (Margaux)
Labégorce-Zédé (Margaux)
Lafon-Rochet (St.-Estèphe)
Lalande Borie (St.-Julien)

Lanessan (Haut-Médoc)
Larose-Trintaudon (Haut-
    Médoc)
Latour du Pin Figeac (St.-
    Émilion)
Liversan (Médoc)
La Louvière (Graves)
Maison Blanche (Montagne-St.-
    Émilion)
Malescasse (Médoc)
Malescot St.-Exupéry (Margaux)
Marbuzet (St.-Estèphe)
Maucaillou (Moulis)
Mazeris (Canon-Fronsac)
Meyney (St.-Estèphe)
Monbrison (Margaux)
Moulin Haut-Laroque (Fronsac)
Moulin Rouge (Médoc)
Moulin à Vent (Moulis)
Mouton-Baronne-Philippe
    (Pauillac)
Nenin (Pomerol)
Les-Ormes-de-Pez (St.-Estèphe)
Les Ormes-Sorbet (Médoc)
Pape-Clément (Graves)
Patache d'Aux (Médoc)
Pavie (St.-Émilion)
Pavie-Decesse (St.-Émilion)
Petit-Village (Pomerol)
Phélan Ségur (St.-Estèphe)
Pichon (Haut-Médoc)
Pichon Longueville, Baron de
    Pichon Longueville (Pauillac)
Picque Caillou (Graves)
de Pitray (Côtes de Castillon)
Plagnac (Médoc)

Pontet-Canet (Pauillac)
Potensac (Médoc)
Pouget (Margaux)
Poujeaux (Moulis)
Rahoul (Graves)
Rausan-Ségla (Margaux)
Rauzan-Gassies (Margaux)
Rocher Bellevue (St.-Émilion)
Roudier (Montagne-St.-Émilion)
Rouet (Fronsac)
Rouget (Pomerol)
de Sales (Pomerol)
Siran (Margaux)
Soudars (Haut-Médoc)
Soutard (St.-Émilion)
Tayac Prestige (Côtes de Bourg)
Terrey-Gros-Cailloux (St.-
    Julien)
du Tertre (Margaux)
Tertre-Daugay (St.-Émilion)
La Tonnelle (Côtes de Blaye)
La Tour de By (Médoc)
La Tour Figeac (St.-Émilion)
La Tour-de-Mons (Margaux)
La Tour St.-Bonnet (Médoc)
Tronquoy-Lalande (St.-Estèphe)
Troplong-Mondot (St.-Émilion)
Trottevieille (St.-Émilion)
Verdignan (Haut-Médoc)
La Vieille Cure (Fronsac)
Vieux-Château Guibeau
    (Puisseguin-St.-Émilion)
Villars (Fronsac)
Villemaurine (St.-Émilion)
La Violette (Pomerol)

* * (AVERAGE PRODUCERS)

d'Agassac (Haut-Médoc)
Andron Blanquet (St.-Estèphe)
Arnauld (Médoc)
L'Arrivet-Haut-Brion (Graves)

Bel-Orme-Tronquoy-de-Lalande
    (Haut-Médoc)
Belgrave (Haut-Médoc)
Bellegrave (Pomerol)

Belloy (Fronsac)
Bonalgue (Pomerol)
Bourgneuf-Vayron (Pomerol)
Bouscaut (Graves)
La Cardonne (Médoc)
Caronnne-Ste.-Gemme (Haut-
  Médoc)
Chauvin (St.-Émilion)
Clos l'Eglise (Pomerol)
Clos des Templiers (Lalande-de-
  Pomerol)
La Commanderie (St.-Émilion)
Cos Labory (St.-Estèphe)
Coustolle (Canon-Fronsac)
Le Crock (St.-Estèphe)
Croizet-Bages (Pauillac)
Curé-Bon-la-Madeleine (St.-
  Émilion)
Dauzac (Margaux)
Desmirail (Margaux)
Ferrière (Margaux)
Feytit Clinet (Pomerol)
La Fleur Gazin (Pomerol)
Fombrauge (St.-Émilion)
Gaby (Fronsac)
du Glana (St.-Julien)
Gombaude-Guillot (Pomerol)
Grand-Corbin-Despagne (St.-
  Émilion)
Grand-Pontet (St.-Émilion)
La Grave (Fronsac)
Hanteillan (Médoc)
Haut-Bergey (Graves)
Haut-Châtain (Lalande-de-
  Pomerol)
Haut-Plantey (St.-Émilion)
Haut-Sarget (Lalande-de-
  Pomerol)

Haut-Sociando (Côtes de Blaye)
Jeandeman (Fronsac)
Labégorce (Margaux)
Lagrange (Pomerol)
Lamarque (Haut-Médoc)
Larcis-Ducasse (St.-Émilion)
Lestage (Listrac)
Loudenne (Médoc)
Malartic-Lagravière (Graves)
Marquis d'Alesme-Becker
  (Margaux)
Mazeris Bellevue (Canon-
  Fronsac)
Monbousquet (St.-Émilion)
Moulin du Cadet (St.-Émilion)
Moulin des Carruades (Pauillac)
Moulin Pez-Labrie (Canon-
  Fronsac)
Pey Labrie (Fronsac)
Peyrabon (Haut-Médoc)
Plince (Pomerol)
La Pointe (Pomerol)
Puy Blanquet (St.-Émilion)
Ramage La Bâtisse (Haut-
  Médoc)
Ripeau (St.-Émilion)
La Rivière (Fronsac)
Roullet (Canon-Fronsac)
Roumagnac La Maréchale
  (Fronsac)
Rousselle (Fronsac)
Ségur (Haut-Médoc)
Smith-Haut-Lafitte (Graves)
Tailhas (Pomerol)
Taillefer (Pomerol)
La Terrasse (Côtes de Castillon)
La Tour-Carnet (Haut-Médoc)
Vraye-Croix-de-Gay (Pomerol)

* *(OTHER PRODUCERS)*

Beauregard (Pomerol)
Bel-Air-Marquis d'Aligre
  (Margaux)
Bourseau (Lalande-de-Pomerol)
La Bridane (St.-Julien)
La Cabanne (Pomerol)
Citran (Haut-Médoc)
Clos des Demoiselles (Listrac)
Colombier Monpelou (Pauillac)
Ferrande (Graves)
La Garde (Graves)
Garraud (Lalande-de-Pomerol)

Lambert (Fronsac)
Lynch-Moussas (Pauillac)
Moulinet (Pomerol)
Olivier (Graves)
St. Bonnet (Médoc)
Le Sablard du Grand Maine
  (Lalande-de-Pomerol)
Tayac (Margaux)
Les Templiers (Lalande-de-
  Pomerol)
La Tour-Martillac (Graves)
Villegeorge (Haut-Médoc)

A GUIDE TO BORDEAUX'S BEST PRODUCERS OF DRY WHITE WINES

* * * * * *(OUTSTANDING PRODUCERS)*

Domaine de Chevalier (Graves)
Fieuzal (Graves)

Haut-Brion Blanc (Graves)
Laville-Haut-Brion (Graves)

* * * * *(EXCELLENT PRODUCERS)*

Couhins-Lurton (Graves)
La Louvière (Graves)
Malartic-Lagravière (Graves)

Pavillon Blanc de Château
  Margaux (Margaux)
La Tour-Martillac (Graves)

* * * *(GOOD PRODUCERS)*

L'Arrivet-Haut-Brion (Graves)
Bouscaut (Graves)
Caillou Blanc de Talbot
  (Bordeaux)
Carbonnieux (Graves)
Domaine Challon (Bordeaux)
Chantegrive (Graves)
Ferrand (Graves)
Loudenne (Bordeaux)
Château de Malle (Graves)

Château Millet (Graves)
Olivier (Graves)
Numéro 1 (Bordeaux)
Pape-Clément (Graves)
Pirou (Graves)
Pontac-Monplaisir (Graves)
Rahoul (Graves)
Respide (Graves)
Smith-Haut-Lafitte (Graves)
Thieuley (Bordeaux)

** *(AVERAGE PRODUCERS)*

Cruzeau (Graves)

Doisy-Daëne (Barsac)

A GUIDE TO BORDEAUX'S BEST PRODUCERS
OF SAUTERNES/BARSACS

* * * * * (OUTSTANDING PRODUCERS)

Fargues (Sauternes)	Rieussec (Sauternes)
Raymond-Lafon (Sauternes)	d'Yquem (Sauternes)

* * * * (EXCELLENT PRODUCERS)

Climens (Barsac)	Lafaurie-Peyraguey (Sauternes)
Coutet (Barsac)	Suduiraut (Sauternes)
Gilette (Sauternes)	

* * * (GOOD PRODUCERS)

Bastor-Lamontagne (Sauternes)	Guiraud (Sauternes)
Doisy-Daëne (Barsac)	Nairac (Barsac)
Doisy-Védrines (Barsac)	Sigalas Rabaud (Sauternes)

* * (AVERAGE PRODUCERS)

d'Arche (Sauternes)	Rabaud-Promis (Sauternes)
Broustet (Barsac)	Rayne-Vigneau (Sauternes)
Caillou (Barsac)	Romer du Hayot (Sauternes)
Filhot (Sauternes)	La Tour Blanche (Sauternes)
de Malle (Sauternes)	

THE BEST WINE VALUES IN BORDEAUX

Côtes de Blaye
Haut-Sociando   La Tonnelle

Côtes de Bourg
La Grolet   Tayac

Côtes de Castillon
de Belcier   Pitray

Côtes de Francs
Puyqueraud   de Francs

Fronsac and Canon-Fronsac

Canon
Canon de Brem
Cardeneau
Dalem
La Dauphine
Fontenil

La Grave
Mazeris
Moulin Haut Laroque
Rouet
La Vieille Cure
Villars

Graves

Bahans Haut Brion
Carmes Haut Brion
Chantegrive
Cheret-Pitres

Haut-Bailly
La Louvière
Picque-Caillou
Rahoul

Lalande-de-Pomerol

Bel Air
Belles Graves
Bertineau St.-Vincent

La Croix St. André
Grand-Ormeau
Clos des Templiers

Lussac St.-Émilion

Bel Air
Cap de Merle
Carteyron

Tour de Grenat
Villadière

Margaux

d'Angludet
La Gurgue
d'Issan

Labegorcé Zédé
Monbrison
du Tertre

Médoc, Haut-Médoc, Moulis, and Listrac

Beaumont
Chasse-Spleen
Cissac
Fourcas Hosten
Lanessan
Liversan
Moulin Rouge
Les Ormes Sorbet

Plagnac
Potensac
Poujeaux
La Rose-Trintaudon
Sociando-Mallet
Soudars
La Tour St.-Bonnet
Verdignan

Montagne St.-Émilion

Roudier
Tour Musset

Pauillac

Fonbadet
Grand-Puy-Ducasse
Haut-Bages-Averous

Haut-Bages-Libéral
Haut-Batailley

Pomerol

Clinet
Clos du Clocher
La Croix
L'Enclos

Clos René
Rouget
de Sales

St.-Émilion

L'Arrosée
Balestard-La-Tonnelle
Cadet-Piola
Cap de Mourlin
Destieux
La Dominique
Ferrand

Grand Mayne
Clos des Jacobins
Larmande
Latour du Pin Figeac
Rocher Bellevue Figeac
Le Tertre-Roteboeuf

St.-Estèphe

Chambert Marbuzet
Haut-Marbuzet

Meyney
Les-Ormes-de-Pez

St.-Julien

Branaire-Ducru
Clos du Marquis
Les Fiefs de Lagrange
Gloria
Gruaud-Larose

Hortevie
Lalande Borie
Léoville-Barton
St.-Pierre
Talbot

Sauternes/Barsac

Bastor-Lamontagne
Doisy-Daëne

Les Justices

Bordeaux—Trends

THE PROLIFERATION OF SECONDARY LABELS

Because of the large crops of the eighties, the number of second-ary labels (wherein 30–45% of the crop can end up) has increased. Concurrently, the quality of these second labels has also increased, and some good bargains are to be found. The best second labels are:

- Haut-Brion: Bahans Haut-Brion
- Margaux: Pavillon Rouge de Margaux
- Léoville-Las Cases: Clos du Marquis
- Pichon Lalande: Réserve de la Comtesse
- Latour: Les Forts de Latour
- Cos d'Estournel: Marbuzet
- Lynch-Bages: Haut-Bages Averous

INCREASINGLY HIGHER QUALITY DRY WHITE WINES FROM GRAVES AND OTHER AREAS

For most of the last several decades, the dry white Bordeaux being produced was either spectacular and expensive, as in the cases of Haut-Brion Blanc, Laville-Haut-Brion and Domaine de Chevalier, or it was over-sulphured, thin, and quite insipid. Then along came Denis Dubourdieu, now 38 years old, who set out to change the style of white Bordeaux by using more Semillon along with Sauvignon Blanc, barrel fermentation, and extended juice contact with the wines' lees. These efforts have resulted in a marked improvement in the quality of much of the white Bordeaux. Not only have prestigious estates such as de Fieuzal, La Tour-Martillac, and Clos Foridene begun to produce fabulous white wines capable of challenging the best, but some of the lower-priced white Bordeaux, such as Château Thieuley and Dourthe's Numero 1, have improved significantly.

AN END TO THE PRICE ESCALATION OF THE EIGHTIES

With the 1986 vintage, Bordeaux's wine châteaux began to realize that they had to reduce prices, since the global marketplace was badly saturated. As a result, prices came down by 15% over the 1985 opening prices. With the mediocre but commercially acceptable soft, fruity, agreeable wines of 1987, prices have generally come down 30–35%. Realistic pricing of Bordeaux wine is finally returning to the marketplace.

Bordeaux's Red Wines

D'AGASSAC (HAUT-MÉDOC)* *

1985	B	79
1986	B	78

This estate never seems to provide the consumer with particularly interesting wines. Both of these wines are correct and adequate, but are essentially one-dimensional. Drink them over the next 2–4 years.

ANDRON BLANQUET (ST.-ESTÈPHE)**

1985	B	67
1986	B	74

The Audoy family, which owns this property, also manages Château Cos Labory, another mediocre wine that hardly merits its status as a fifth-growth. The 1985 is a shallow, somewhat thin and watery wine that is medium bodied, has a light, innocuous fragrance of diluted fruit, and a soft, ready-to-drink texture. The 1986 is also quite light for the vintage, but is a deeper wine, with a bit more stuffing, than the feeble 1985. Improvement should be a top priority at this estate.

L'ANGÉLUS (ST.-ÉMILION)* * *

1985	C	89
1986	C	87

In the seventies this estate made one of St.-Émilion's least distinguished wines, but in this decade the young and serious Mr. de Bouard has taken over from his father and has added a hefty percentage of new oak barrels and instituted a selection policy; as a result, in recent vintages the wine has improved dramatically. Both of the above vintages are impressively rich, full-flavored wines. The 1985 is a seductively smooth, supple, broadly flavored wine with aromas and flavors of berry fruit. Full-bodied, quite concentrated, but forward and delicious, this luscious wine will drink and evolve well over the next 7–8 years. The 1986 is remarkably similar in style, quite long and fleshy with excellent richness, full body, a trifle more tannin and acidity, plus an extremely long finish.

D'ANGLUDET (MARGAUX)* * *

1985	B	83

Of recent vintages, the 1983 d'Angludet remains the pacesetter for measuring other vintages of this wine. The 1985 lacks depth and seems to have a slight hole in its mid-range. Otherwise, it has good color, a plummy, spicy, obvious bouquet, soft, medium-bodied flavors, and light tannins in the finish.

DES ANNEREAUX (LALANDE-DE-POMEROL)* * *

1985	A	85
1986	A	84

The Milhade family, who makes Bordeaux's greatest Bordeaux Superior wine, Château Recougne (I had a super 1955 recently), owns this estate in Lalande-de-Pomerol. The 1985 is round, ripe, soft, supple, and quite tasty. It is medium bodied and should drink well for 3–4 years. The 1986 also has ripe, sweet fruit, a lush texture, and will provide immediate gratification.

ARNAULD (MÉDOC)* *

1985	A	84
1986	A	?

The 1985 has a deep ruby color, plenty of soft, fleshy, supple fruit, full body, low acidity, and immediate appeal. Although the 1986 tasted flat, clumsy, and unstructured, I am sure that the wine is better than this, so I will wait to taste it after bottling. Judgment reserved.

L'ARRIVET-HAUT-BRION (GRAVES)* *

1985	B	84
1986	B	82

This well-placed estate in southern Graves, near Leognan, recently changed hands and rumors abound in Bordeaux about a renaissance in the wine's quality. The 1985 has merit in the sense that the bouquet of tobacco and ripe fruit is textbook Graves. However, I would have liked to see more flesh and substance, but for drinking over the next 3–5 years, this wine fits the bill. The 1986 tastes surprisingly light for the vintage and should also be ready to drink very early on. It is, nevertheless, quite an agreeable, fruity wine.

L'ARROSÉE (ST.-ÉMILION)* * * * *

1985	C	92

1986	C 94

L'Arrosée is a remarkable wine, and while few observers would agree with proprietor François Rodhain's assertion that it is the finest wine of this appellation, there can be no doubt that in blind tastings only Cheval Blanc seems consistently as complex and rich. This is due to a combination of factors: old vines, a knowledgeable, hard-working, and passionate proprietor, 100% new oak, and an unusual blend of grapes for a St-Émilion from the *"Côtes,"* or hillsides of the town— 35% Cabernet Sauvignon, 50% Merlot, and the rest Cabernet Franc. The wine seems to combine the sumptuous richness and depth of Cheval Blanc with a perfume and Cabernet Sauvignon-based character of its own. Recent vintages have all been exhilarating: a great 1982, a wonderful 1983, the top wine of the appellation in 1984, and a staggeringly exotic, fleshy, aromatic, flashy 1985. Each time I taste the 1985 I am even more impressed. The awesome bouquet most recently seemed to suggest the exquisite Richebourg of Henri Jayer. Aside from the intense perfume of raspberries and new oak, the texture of the 1985 is one of extravagant richness of fruit, full body, great depth and length, and remarkable complexity. The wine is already quite delicious, but I suspect this beauty will age well for another decade. The 1986, if you can believe it, is potentially even more dazzling, but despite its stupendous richness and intensity, it also has a great deal more tannin and is less open and flattering than the 1985. However, the 1986 L'Arrosée should turn out to be the finest wine made at this property since the great 1961.

AUSONE (ST.-ÉMILION)* * * * *

1985	E 86?

1986	E 88

Ausone is one of the more difficult wines to evaluate early on. Like Pétrus in Pomerol, it tends to close up and show little of its prebottling character when tasted after the *mise en bouteille* (bottling of the wine). The 1982, spectacular from the cask, is just now beginning to return to form. In blind tastings of the so-called "Big Eight"of Bordeaux, I always (after the bottling) rank Ausone and Pétrus last. That being said, I found the 1985 a little light, supple, pleasant, attractive, but somewhat one-dimensional by the standards of this splendid estate. The 1986 exhibits more of the exotic spice and mineral scents in its bouquet, has medium body, and a good, ripe, moderately long finish. My gut feeling is that in a decade these ratings may look far too conservative. Both wines would appear to be at their plateau of maturity between 1993 and 2005.

BAHANS HAUT-BRION (GRAVES)* * *

1985	C 87
1986	C 87

Bahans is the second wine of Haut-Brion and has become, since the 1982 vintage, the finest of the secondary labels of the first-growths. Its quality is excellent in these two vintages. The 1985 is a sexy wine with its Haut-Brion-like bouquet of smoked meat, tobacco, and ripe fruit. Rich and creamy on the palate, with excellent depth as well as structure, this is a wine to seek out. The 1986 is even better, and I believe superior to some of the vintages made by Haut-Brion during 1966–1975. The intense mineral and tobacco bouquet is very complex and penetrating. On the palate, there is exquisite balance, a wonderful depth of very ripe fruit, and just enough tannin to ensure 5–8 years of further evolution.

BALESTARD-LA-TONNELLE (ST.-ÉMILION)* * *

1985	B 86
1986	B 85

The wines of Balestard are not for the timid. Usually quite robust, brawny, alcoholic, and fleshy, they can deliver a powerful amount of fruit and body. Both of the above vintages are faithful to this style of St.-Émilion. The 1985 is a hefty, fat, rich, but not ponderous wine, with plenty of husky fruit and body. The 1986 shares the same style, but one should expect more tannin and intensity here, characteristics of this vintage.

BATAILLEY (PAUILLAC)* * *

1985	C 86
1986	C 85

It can be argued that Batailley rarely gets the praise it deserves. Batailley is not an easy wine to fully appreciate when young, as it is then always firm and tannic. But it rarely disappoints when it is older and, except for certain vintages, seems capable of aging for 15–20 years. Not surprisingly, the 1985 has the ripeness of the vintage well displayed but also has the Batailley firmness and tannic toughness. It is well made, reserved, and stylish. The 1986 is fuller and more concentrated, but the intrusive tannins preclude drinking this wine for at least a decade.

BEAU-SÉJOUR BÉCOT (ST.-ÉMILION)* * *

1985	C	85
1986	C	87

Pity poor Beau-Séjour, the only St.-Émilion to suffer the ignominious fate of being dropped from the ranks of the Premiers Grands Crus Classés (justifiably so, in my opinion). Happily, however, the response by Bécot has been to make better wine. The 1985 is a rich, ripe, relatively alcoholic wine that possesses a charming, precocious personality, medium to full body, low acidity, but plenty of flesh and fruit. The 1986 is the finest wine from this property I have ever tasted. Smelling more like a Côte Rôtie than a claret, the huge bouquet of raspberries and smoky oak is undeniably enticing. On the palate, the wine is quite rich, full bodied, oaky, and well balanced.

BEAUMONT (HAUT-MÉDOC)* * *

1985	A	82
1986	A	85

A name to watch, Beaumont now enjoys the same ownership and commitment to high quality as Château Beychevelle in St.-Julien. The 1985 is an expansive, sweet, ripe, supple, very tasty wine with immediate crowd appeal. The 1986 is very deep, structured, long, rich, intense, and clearly the finest Beaumont I have ever tasted.

BEAUSÉJOUR (DUFFAU-LAGARROSSE) (ST.-ÉMILION)* * *

1985	C	84
1986	C	77

Neither of these wines exhibited as much depth as I would have expected. The 1985 is lighter weight, medium bodied, with a good, spicy fruitiness, soft texture, and pleasant length. However, for its class, it is uninspiring. The 1986, which tasted a little shallow and short last year, again came up lacking depth and richness this year. Medium ruby, with some woody overtones, it is a one-dimensional wine that will require consumption over the next 4–5 years.

BEL-AIR (LALANDE-DE-POMEROL)* * *

1985	B	84
1986	B	86

The 1985 is a big, thick, rich, intense wine that borders on being over-ripe, but delivers quite a bit of power and a long finish. The 1986 has an old-vine intensity, rich layers of fruit, full body, and soft yet notice-able tannins in the finish. Overall, it is slightly more impressive and age-worthy than the 1985. This is clearly one of the names to search out from Lalande-de-Pomerol.

BEL-ORME-TRONQUOY-DE-LALANDE (HAUT-MÉDOC)* *

1985	B	84
1986	B	?

The two "ancient" vintages (1928 and 1945) of this wine that I have tried have proven they can age extremely well. This is a hard, tannic style of wine that I doubt is much appreciated in the United States, but the wine may have merit for those who have patience. The 1985 is dark ruby, peppery, spicy, full bodied, chunky, and typically dense. It lacks finesse, but has plenty of muscle and tannin. It should mature between 1992 and 2000. The 1986 is simply impenetrable—dark, ex-tremely tannic, even savage on the palate, so I find it impossible to evaluate at present.

BELAIR (ST.-ÉMILION)* * *

1985	C	78
1986	C	82

Last year I reserved judgment on Belair's 1985 because it did not show especially well in my tasting. Now that it is in the bottle, the wine is quite light, soft, rather one-dimensional, and compact. The 1986 is slightly superior, but once again lacks grip and seems surprisingly light for a top St.-Émilion and a winemaker of the quality of Pascal Delbeck. What's going on here?

DE BELCIER (CÔTES DE CASTILLON)* * *

1985	A	83
1986	A	85

The Côtes de Castillon, adjacent to Bordeaux's famous St.-Émilion appellation, is a good source for finding wine values. Anybody who has tried the wonderful Château Pitray knows this already. Belcier offers a rich, uncomplex, meaty style of wine with plenty of guts. Both the round, fat, ripe 1985 and slightly more intense and complex 1986 offer up clean, pure, supple flavors at a great price.

BELGRAVE (HAUT-MÉDOC)* *

1985	B	85
1986	B	86

Of all the classified-growths, Belgrave is the least known. Though neglected for decades, the property is now a model of impeccable management under the large *négociant* firm of Dourthe. The brilliant oenologist from Libourne, Michel Rolland, has recently been brought in to oversee the wines, so quality will, I suspect, continue to improve. The 1985 is well colored, fruity, and medium bodied, with a nice touch of oak. It has an elegance and style that make it very attractive for drinking over the next 4–5 years. The 1986 is a bigger, more aggressive Belgrave with impressive length, excellent richness, full body, and good mid-term aging potential of 5–9 years.

BELLES GRAVES (LALANDE-DE-POMEROL)* * *

1985	B	86
1986	B	86

One of the very best wines of Lalande-de-Pomerol, Belles Graves is frequently better than many of the second-tier Pomerols at one-third the price. The 1985 is a worthy competitor to the very fine 1982 made here. Deep ruby, with a full intensity bouquet of sweet new oak and ripe berry fruit, this concentrated, lush, flavorful wine provides an excellent alternative to the more expensive Pomerols. The 1986 is just as concentrated, slightly more structured and tannic, but long and quite serious.

BELLEGRAVE (POMEROL)* *

1985	B	83
1986	B	79

I have had little experience with this particular Pomerol, but I certainly found the 1985 attractively sweet, plummy, soft, medium bodied, and ideal for drinking over the next 3–4 years. The 1986 is deeper in color, tastes less fat, and has some harder tannins in the finish.

BELLOY (FRONSAC)* *

1985	B	84
1986	B	75

The 1985 could easily be mistaken for a raspberry-scented, perfumed, soft, expansive, fully mature 1982 red burgundy. It is supple and delicious, and I would opt for drinking it over the next 1–3 years. The 1986 is ripe, concentrated, and medium to full bodied, but a little flat.

BERLIQUET (ST.-ÉMILION)* * *

1985	B	81
1986	B	78

I had heard that Berliquet was on the verge of stardom, so I paid a visit to this well-placed property. There are exceptional underground caves wherein the wine is kept in oak casks, 50% of which are new. The 1985 has an open-knit character, a moderately intense, ripe, cherry-scented bouquet, medium body, and soft tannins. The 1986 tasted hard and tannic, and while well made, I am a little concerned about the level of tannins vis-à-vis the depth of fruit.

BERTINEAU ST.-VINCENT (LALANDE-DE-POMEROL)* * *

1985	A	83

Owned by Michel Rolland, Bertineau St.-Vincent is a good, ripe, supple, fruity wine with a precocious personality and pleasant finish. The

1985 will not make anyone forget the gorgeous 1982 made here, but it is, nevertheless, a very agreeable wine.

BEYCHEVELLE (ST.-JULIEN)* * * *

1985	D	87
1986	D	92

This lovely château that guards the southern entrance into St.-Julien came under a new ownership in 1984; consequently, the quality has improved, with the 1986 entering the league of super-seconds that includes wines such as Léoville-Las Cases and Ducru-Beaucaillou. As for the 1985, it admirably reflects the character of this charming vintage. Deep ruby, low in acidity, ripe, round, fruity and precocious, this medium-bodied, supple wine is very tasty and shows the cedary, blackcurrant fruit so common among the wines of St.-Julien. The 1986 is superb, perhaps the finest Beychevelle in 30 years. Still very tannic, black/ruby in color, with a huge bouquet of roasted fruit, this full-bodied, concentrated, stupendous wine should be a joy to drink if one has the patience and good cellar it will require.

BON PASTEUR (POMEROL)* * * *

1985	C	84
1986	C	87

Michel Rolland is now an international superstar due to his remarkable ability to turn around the fortunes of so many estates, but he has hardly changed since I first met him almost a decade ago. His list of clients, while including famous Pomerols such as L'Evangile and La Conseillante, also include Simi in California (the 1985 and 1986 Reserve Cabernets illustrate his talents), and more recently Château Ste. Michelle in Washington. At his own property, Bon Pasteur, he feels his 1986 is vastly superior to his 1985 and I could not agree more. The 1985 is ready to drink; it is soft, fruity, and medium bodied, but lacks the concentration and structure of the top years. The 1986 has a very deep color, a big, toasty, oaky, plummy bouquet, and complex, rich flavors with quite a bit of tannin. It is the best wine made here since the great 1982 Bon Pasteur.

BONALGUE (POMEROL)* *

1985	B 85

1986	B 82

This is not one of the better-known Pomerols, but certainly the quality is quite reliable. Certain vintages, for example the 1985, are very good. The 1985 shows a healthy dosage of toasty new oak barrels and has lush, medium-bodied flavors that are packed with berry fruit, and soft tannins in the finish. The 1986 is a solidly made wine that shows fine ripeness, but lacks the dimension and charm of the 1985.

LE BOSCQ (MÉDOC)* * *

1985	A 84

1986	A 84

This is a reliable, succulent Cru Bourgeois that makes attractive, gusty wines with little elegance, but with much exuberant fruit and body. The 1985 is a concentrated, round, generous, soft, medium-bodied wine that is not very complex but scores high for value and satisfaction. The 1986 is cut from the same cloth, but the vintage is more structured and tannic than usual. It is a deep, richly fruity wine that should win many fans.

BOURGNEUF-VAYRON (POMEROL)* *

1985	B 82

1986	B 82

This is rarely an interesting Pomerol, as it does not have the rich, full-bodied, concentrated feel of a top-notch Pomerol, and is always lacking finesse. The 1985 is somewhat typical. It is thick, plummy, four-square, but essentially simple and grapy. The 1986 borders on being overripe, with a full-throttle bouquet of extremely ripe fruit. This viscous, rich, chewy wine has a great deal of extract, but could use a bit more elegance and charm.

BOURSEAU (LALANDE-DE-POMEROL)*

1985	A 70

1986	A 66

Both wines here offer light, watery, meager fruity flavors in a loosely knit framework.

BOYD-CANTENAC (MARGAUX)* * * *

1985	C 83
1986	C 78

I see no reason why this well-known and respected property could not produce a more serious and complex wine. The 1985 after bottling shows better than it did from the cask, as it exhibits good ruby color and has a sweet, tasty, plummy fruitiness, medium body, low acidity, and a dull finish. It is good, but not exciting. The 1986 is also lacking zip and comes across on the palate as thick, clumsy, and casually made.

BRANAIRE-DUCRU (ST.-JULIEN)* * * *

1985	C 85
1986	C 86

Branaire, the rather stoic-looking château across the road from the impressive gardens of Château Beychevelle, has provided me with plenty of fine drinking over the years, most notably its 1975 and 1976. Recent vintages have taken on a softer, more commercial texture, and I have noticed that the wines do not seem as concentrated or structured. Is the château producing too much wine? Having raised my concerns, I still find the 1985 a spicy, plummy, tasty wine with undeniable appeal because of its precocious fruitiness. Once one gets past all the up-front charm and makeup, there is not much depth or tannin. Nevertheless, for drinking over the next 5–7 years, it is a pleasant enough wine. Restaurants will love it. The 1986 wants to emulate the 1985, but the vintage personality marked by ripe Cabernets with a lot of tannin gives this example of Branaire more grip. For its class, however, it could have been more concentrated.

BRANAS-GRAND POUJEAUX (MOULIS)* * *

1985	B 85
1986	B ?

This can be a very good wine, as its owner is a serious proprietor with high standards. The 1985 exhibits rich, ripe, supple fruit, medium to full body, and a long, stylish finish. It is more forward than many wines of Moulis tend to be. The 1986 is impossible to judge, as its huge size, while clearly apparent, is dominated by excruciatingly high tannin levels, at least for now.

BRANE-CANTENAC (MARGAUX)* * *

1985	C	87
1986	C	89

After years of criticizing the overall lack of quality and inconsistency of this famous second-growth, let me be the first to say that in the eighties, particularly since 1982, things have improved dramatically. The 1985, made in a succulent, forward, sweet, seductive style, is oozing with scents of oak and velvety, super-ripe fruit. One might argue that more grip and tannin might be expected, but the style of the 1985 vintage is well delineated in this attractive wine. The 1986 is probably this château's best wine in over 30 years. Deeper and richer —and with a more expansive palate—than the 1985, the 1986 is an intensely flavored, relatively powerful, ripe, delicious, medium-bodied wine that shows plenty of class.

BRILLETTE (MOULIS)* * *

1985	B	83
1986	B	85

This well-run property produces classic wines that are marked by new oak, but are also richly fruity and tasty. Although the 1985 does not have the grip and concentration of the best vintages of Brillette, it does have some charm and ripe fruit. The 1986 is much more concentrated and powerful, and is altogether a more impressive wine. Full-bodied, with plenty of spicy oak in evidence, it should age well for 5–12 years.

LA CABANNE (POMEROL)*

1985	B	74
1986	B	72

As this estate has made a very mediocre, undistinguished, simple style of wine for some time, one wonders whether the machine harvesters used here have a negative effect on the wine's quality. The 1985 has a light-intensity bouquet of cherry fruit and simple, pleasant, somewhat boring flavors. The 1986 shows some toasty new oak in its aroma but fades away on the palate and is quite bland.

CADET-PIOLA (ST.-ÉMILION)* * * *

1985	C	86

1986	C	87

This is a long-lived, very classic St.-Émilion that deserves a much wider audience, as the wines are consistently well made. Most of the top vintages of Cadet-Piola—1983, 1982, and 1975—remain very young wines. The 1985 is a tannic, well-built wine for the vintage. Deep ruby, with a spicy, plummy, intense bouquet, this is a full-bodied, dense, chewy wine with plenty of character. The 1986 is nearly black in color, very tannic and full bodied, and admirably concentrated with a long, chewy finish. It needs to be cellared for at least 6–8 years.

CALON-SÉGUR (ST.-ESTÈPHE)* * * *

1985	C	86

1986	C	89

Philippe Gasqueton has one of the most promising estates in the Médoc, but the wines have rarely provided excitement since the brilliant ones of the late forties and the fifties. The 1985 was bottled very late (January, 1988), which I feel was a mistake, although the wine is ripe and fruity. With a little more depth, the 1985 Calon-Ségur could have been special. The 1986 appears to be the best wine made at this property since the 1982 (which is still considered by Gasqueton to be the finest of his wines since 1947), but the 1982 is quite hard and closed up at the moment. As for the 1986, it has an unusually high percentage of Cabernet Sauvignon—90%—with the rest being Merlot. It is deeply colored, big framed, and concentrated, but also hard and tannic; it will require serious patience. It should be excellent—perhaps outstanding—when it is ready.

CANON (ST.-ÉMILION)* * * * *

1985	D	90

1986	D	91

Under the expert guidance of Eric Fournier, Canon has earned quite a few supporters who believe that the estate has made the finest wines in St.-Émilion since 1982. The wines generally age quite slowly and are beautifully perfumed, as well as marked by the scent of smoky new oak (65% new wood was used in 1985 and 1986). The 1985 has the deepest color of all the St.-Émilions save for Le Tertre Roteboeuf. The intense fragrance of oak combines with aromas of ripe plums and cherries. On the palate, the wine is rich, full bodied, deep, and alcoholic. If not quite the 1982 in stature, the 1985 is not far behind. The 1986 is one of the superstars of Bordeaux's right bank, explosively rich, quite powerful, oaky, long, dense, and truly exciting.

CANON DE BREM (CANON-FRONSAC)* * *

1985	B	86

1986	B	86

Canon de Brem has an extremely fine reputation within Canon-Fronsac. The wines are indeed quite good and potentially very long-lived. The 1985 has closed up considerably since last year, and despite its impressive display of power and wealth of fruit, it seems a good 5–6 years away from maturity. It is a big, deep, backward wine. The 1986 is even more tannic, quite inaccessible, but on the palate there is quite a bit of size, weight, and length. This wine might turn out to merit a better rating.

CANON-LA-GAFFELIÈRE (ST.-ÉMILION)* * *

1985	C	85

1986	C	87

In the seventies this property offered up a disturbing array of insipid, watery wines that were poorly made. The quality began to improve in the early eighties. In 1984 a German-schooled, very serious young man, Stephan de Peipperg, arrived and has taken on the challenge of turning out wines proportional to the vineyard's potential. The results, made in a fully climatized cellar and aged in 65% new oak, are an excellent, rich, age-worthy 1986, the finest Canon-La-Gaffelière in over three decades, and a good supple, richly fruity, tasty, expansively flavored 1985. This is a property to watch.

CANON MOUEIX (CANON-FRONSAC)* * *

1985	C 87
1986	C 85

This tiny 12-acre vineyard is run with great care by Christian Moueix. With respect to the 1985, the moderately intense bouquet of sweet, ripe raspberry fruit and toasty new oak is exciting. On the palate, the wine is elegant, deep, well balanced, and long. The 1986 shows a healthy dosage of new oak, perfumed, ripe aromas, good depth and flesh, and some firm tannins in the finish. It is less accessible than the 1985.

CANTEMERLE (MACAU)* * * *

1985	C 85
1986	C 84

This lovely château, which sits in a small park just 20 minutes north of Bordeaux, is making medium-weight, extremely stylish and suave wines, though given the soil the wines will never be powerful blockbusters. The 1985 is Cantemerle at its most polite and stylish. Quite supple, medium-ruby in color, with an open-knit bouquet of raspberries and oak, it seemed more like a Volnay than a Médoc when I tasted it. The 1986 is similarly styled, graceful and medium bodied, but the hard tannins of this vintage do not mesh well with the lighter, more delicate style of Cantemerle.

CANTENAC-BROWN (MARGAUX)* * *

1985	C 86
1986	C 88

This property is beginning to reassert itself as one of the potential leaders in the Margaux appellation. After some lackluster wines during a period in the seventies, recent efforts have shown that the new owner's infusion of capital into the property is beginning to pay off. The 1985 has excellent color, a ripe, curranty, big bouquet, medium to full body, and sufficient tannin to warrant 8–10 years of cellaring. The 1986 is richer and more tannic, and appears to be the finest wine made here in over 20 years.

CAP DE MOURLIN (ST.-ÉMILION)* * *

1985	B	86
1986	B	85

Cap de Mourlin—made and owned by Jacques Capdemourlin, who also owns Balestard-La-Tonnelle—is a full-throttle, rich, powerful, ruby/purple-colored wine that lacks elegance, but never flavor. Both vintages above share these characteristics. The dense color, the fat, unctuous texture, the powerful, very ripe, portlike bouquets from *surmaturité* (over-ripeness), and full body are all characteristic of Cap de Mourlin. This rich wine should be consumed with stews, cassoulets, and the like. It is not a complicated wine that requires much introspection.

CARBONNIEUX (GRAVES)* * *

1985	C	85
1986	C	86

For years, the red wine of Carbonnieux tasted as if it were trying to imitate a Beaujolais-Villages. Starting in 1985 there has been a dramatic increase in this wine's character and the results are markedly more interesting. The 1985 has sweet, soft, expansive flavors of cherries and toasty oak that made me think of a Premier Cru Beaune, not a Graves. It is a light but tasty wine. The 1986 is the best red Carbonnieux in years—deep in color, with a smoky, rich, aromatic bouquet, impressively deep flavors, medium body, and ripe tannins in the finish.

CARDENEAU (FRONSAC)* * *

1985	B	85
1986	B	86

I have never visited this Fronsac estate, but I was certainly impressed by the quality of these two vintages of Cardeneau. The 1985 is packed with ripe, rich, sweet curranty fruit, has medium to full body, a deep color, excellent balance, and a long finish. The 1986 is slightly more tannic but very concentrated, deep, multidimensional, and has an old-vine intensity to its flavors. Very impressive!

DE CARLES (FRONSAC)* * *

1985	B	85
1986	B	87

This is another of the leading estates of Fronsac. The 1985 is a soft, expansive, medium-bodied wine with a very dark color, gobs of curranty fruit, and a silky finish. The 1986 is a much larger wine, quite full bodied, loaded with extract, rich, tannic and muscular, but impeccably balanced.

LES CARMES HAUT-BRION (GRAVES)* * *

1985	C	87
1986	C	86

I remember drinking with great pleasure several magnums of the 1959 Carmes Haut-Brion. The wine rarely shows up in tastings, so I was eager to taste the 1985 and 1986. Both are impressively constituted wines, deep in color with the unmistakable mineral, tobacco-scented bouquet so typical of the top wines of this appellation. As one would expect, the 1985 is more supple and smoother and easier to appreciate for its delicious intense fruit and length. The 1986 is similar but much more tannic.

CERTAN-GIRAUD (POMEROL)* * *

1985	C	86
1986	C	78

Certan-Giraud is always a plump, immensely satisfying style of Pomerol that requires drinking within 5–7 years of the vintage. If it seems to lack structure and tastes too soupy and soft, few tasters seem to mind, as the sweet, ripe, hedonistic level of fruit is a joy to behold. The 1985 is loaded with fruit and is very low in acidity, so take advantage of its creamy-textured style over the next 5 years. The 1986 is displaying a bit more tannin, but it also seems a little shallow in its mid-range and is short in the finish.

CERTAN DE MAY (POMEROL)* * * * *

1985	E	94

1986	E	92

Although I have been advocating the fine quality of wine from this splendid little estate on the Pomerol plateau for almost a decade, I find gaining access to it is becoming increasingly troublesome (Madame Badar, the proprietor, can be a very difficult person). *C'est la vie!* Certan de May is clearly one of the top three or four Pomerols. The voluptuous 1985, with its staggering bouquet of cedar, plums, toasty oak and herbs, and a wealth of opulent fruit, is truly remarkable. Very deep, very concentrated, with a finish that just goes on and on, this wine will provide splendid drinking over the next 10–15 years. The 1986 is awesomely proportioned, black/ruby, sensationally concentrated, but also much more tannic and backward than the 1985. I cannot see it being ready to drink before the late nineties.

CHAMBERT-MARBUZET (ST.-ESTÈPHE)* * * *

1985	C	86

1986	C	90

The rating of the 1985 may be a little conservative, as I thought it to be a slightly better wine in the cask prior to bottling. It is a deep, powerful wine packed with jammy fruit, an overt spicy oakiness, medium to full body, and a soft texture. The 1986 is a remarkably impressive wine containing all the elements of the 1985, but possessing more color, depth, richness, length, and tannins. Huge and muscular, with quite a dosage of new oak, Chambert-Marbuzet's 1986 is one of the great bargains of this vintage.

CHANTEGRIVE (GRAVES)* * *

1985	B	85

1986	B	83

I doubt that my scores here will create a surge in sales for the red wine of Chantegrive, but I think it is a very tasty, supple Graves. (I often drink it in the restaurants of Bordeaux.) Always well-made, Chantegrive, while not terribly complex, does indeed still satisfy the palate with authentic tobacco and berry flavors. Do not ignore the estate's white wine, which is also a fine value.

CHASSE-SPLEEN (MOULIS)* * * *

1985	B	90
1986	B	92

These vintages are the finest Chasse-Spleens I have ever tasted (with the possible exception of the 1949), and I have long been an admirer of this property. Often known for their density and slow-to-evolve style, these wines have kept their outstanding concentration, but have become increasingly more complex. The 1985 is fabulously deep in color with a full-intensity, scented bouquet of spicy new oak and rich curranty fruit and plums. On the palate, the wine is very concentrated, long, and big framed, but impeccably balanced, with quite a finish. As splendid as the 1985 is, the 1986 looks to be even deeper, more powerful and long on the palate, but more tannic and backward. Both wines have the classic bouquets and fabulous ripeness and concentration one associates with the super-seconds and first-growths.

CHÂTAIN (LALANDE-DE-POMEROL)* * *

1985	B	84
1986	B	82

Both well-made wines, the 1985 and 1986 are fleshy, fat, quite satisfying, attractively ripe, and flavorful. The 1985 has a silky texture. The 1986 shows more tannin.

CHAUVIN (ST.-ÉMILION)* *

1985	B	76
1986	B	81

The 1985 is quite one-dimensional, with a simple, ripe fruitiness, medium body, and a soft, undistinguished finish. The 1986 is more expansive on the palate, has some tannin, good fruit, and is a much better and more interesting wine than the 1985.

CHEVAL BLANC (ST.-ÉMILION)* * * * *

1985	E	90

1986   E   91

Each time I visit Cheval Blanc and the proprietor, Monsieur Hébrard, I am asked if I would like to meet the dog. Readers may remember that this nasty mongrel took a bite out of my ankle after my initial and incorrect so-so review of the 1981 Cheval Blanc. Cheval Blanc is by far the most flattering wine to taste among Bordeaux's "Big Eight," and early in its life always seems to come out on top in blind tastings. As is the case for its rival Figeac, it is remarkably easy to drink when young. Typically then, the 1985, while not a big or boldly concentrated wine, is quite delicious, ripe, and a total joy to drink. It is very aromatic, soft, and medium bodied, and should turn out to resemble the 1976 or 1979, but be even better. The 1986 is considerably deeper and richer, more powerful, and very age-worthy, and stays splendidly long in the mouth. Hébrard prefers the lighter 1985; I like the richer, more classic 1986, and the dog . . . well, I did not ask him his opinion.

DOMAINE DE CHEVALIER (GRAVES)* * * * *

1985   D   87

1986   D   90

This estate usually produces one of the three or four best red and white Graves every vintage and also has an impeccable record in off-years (i.e., 1984 and 1980). A lot of new oak is preferred here and the wines consistently display plenty of the toasty, vanillin, spicy character that is imparted by the new barrels. I also sense that there has been a deliberate attempt in the eighties to give the wines more tannin and structure. The 1985 has the sweet, ripe, rich fruit that is the hallmark of this vintage, but also has more tannin than most Graves. As a 1985, it will be slow to mature. The 1986 is dominated by the smell of new wood, but on the palate there is explosive richness, depth, great length, and intensity. This may be the finest Domaine de Chevalier in years. A real *vin de garde* (age-worthy wine).

CLERC-MILON (PAUILLAC)* * *

1985   C   87

1986   C   89

The decade of the eighties has witnessed a significant upgrade in the quality of all wines of the Domaines Rothschild in Pauillac, including

Mouton-Rothschild itself. Clerc-Milon has been making considerable strides in quality and the two best examples I have ever tasted are the 1985 and 1986. The 1985 is a gorgeous wine, deep in color with a complex bouquet of blackcurrants, minerals, and smoky oak. On the palate, the wine is rich, full bodied, powerful, and surprisingly structured and long for a 1985. It is one of the top sleepers of the vintage. The 1986 looks to be even better, with a black/ruby color, gigantic bouquet of ripe fruit, plums, coffee, and spices. Forbiddingly tannic, but packed with fruit and body, this deep, impressive, large-proportioned wine will require substantial cellaring.

CLINET (POMEROL)* * *

1985	C 87
1986	C 85

For years, the wines of Clinet were distressingly vapid and thin, but due to successful vinification changes the 1985 is certainly the finest Clinet in years. Quite packed and concentrated with jammy berry fruit encased in a veil of toasty oak, this enticing fleshpot of a wine has broad, creamy flavors and is an absolute joy to drink. The 1986 is, as expected more tannic and less flattering to taste, but it, too, exhibits intelligent winemaking and good, ripe fruit.

CLOS DU CLOCHER (POMEROL)* * *

1985	C 85
1986	C 84

One always hears comparisons to burgundy when certain Pomerols are tasted or drunk. Here is a nice little property that seems to turn out Pomerols that taste as if they are from Volnay or Beaune. The 1985 has vivid cherry fruit, a fragrant, enticing bouquet, medium body, an elegant feel in the mouth, and considerable charm. This wine is more satisfying to drink than my score might indicate. The 1986 is approximately equal in quality, offers more muscle and tannin, but much less charm and up-front fruit.

CLOS DES DEMOISELLES (LISTRAC)*

1985	B 77

| 1986 | B | 75 |

I find this wine to be made in such a hard, tannic way that in the young vintages, the wine lacks charm and grace. Both the 1985 and 1986 show a stern, hard personality, in which fruit is submerged beneath a wall of aggressive tannins.

CLOS L'EGLISE (POMEROL)* *

| 1985 | C | 78 |

| 1986 | C | 79 |

Due to the unusually high percentage of Cabernet Sauvignon in this wine, it tends to stick out in a tasting of Pomerols. Perhaps because of this, I tend to underrate it, but knowing this, I found the 1985 light, medium bodied, and elegant, but a little short on substance and length. The 1986 exhibited a healthy dosage of new oak, but lacked distinction and class.

CLOS FOURTET (ST.-ÉMILION)* * *

| 1985 | C | 82 |

| 1986 | C | 78 |

In spite of being a top-rated St.-Émilion, Clos Fourtet's wines, although improved from two decades ago, remain far below the quality of the best estates of this appellation. The 1985 is certainly the lightest of all the Premier Grand Cru Classé wines. It is medium to dark-ruby, with a supple, obvious taste, and soft tannins; it has an easy, agreeable finish. The 1986 is quite similar in style—overtly fruity, one-dimensional, but pleasurable and ideal for uncritical drinking over the next 5–6 years.

CLOS DES JACOBINS (ST.-ÉMILION)* * *

| 1985 | C | 84 |

| 1986 | C | 86 |

This is certainly an underrated estate, which makes very fine, supple, fleshy wine from a vineyard just outside the town of St.-Émilion. The wines have always been sound, but have taken on more concentration and have gained more class in the eighties. The 1985 is very soft, quite fruity, medium bodied, pleasant, and ideal for drinking over the next 3–4 years. The 1986 has much more muscle, depth, alcohol, and better color. Spicy, cedary, and herbaceous, this medium- to full- —bodied wine has excellent length and presence on the palate.

CLOS RENÉ (POMEROL)* * *

1985	C 87
1986	C 85

This is a consistently good Pomerol that has improved considerably in the eighties. Excellent wines were made in 1985 and 1986. The 1985 has broad, ripe, rich, plummy fruit, long, lush, medium- to full-bodied flavors, a silky, lengthy finish, and impressive concentration. The 1986 has much more tannin to fight through, good fruit, and medium body, but not the fat and charm of the 1985.

COLOMBIER MONPELOU (PAUILLAC)*

1985	C 74
1986	C 83

I have never been impressed with this wine, although, to its credit, it is usually reasonably priced. The 1985 is a decent, soft, undistinguished claret that does not taste like a Pauillac, but, rather, like a minor Cru Bourgeois. The good 1986 may signal a new era of higher-quality winemaking here. It is the best effort so far. Powerful, well-colored, ripe and fruity, this medium- to full-bodied tannic wine should keep well for 8–10 years.

LA CONSEILLANTE (POMEROL)* * * *

1985	D 90
1986	D 87

La Conseillante is strategically located near L'Evangile, Pétrus and Cheval Blanc and produces a lovely, gloriously perfumed wine, but I often wonder if it could become even better. Certainly the 1985 is the type of Pomerol that wins many friends. The big, rich, expansive perfume of sweet raspberry fruit and smoky, new oak will steal just about anyone's heart. On the palate, a purist might quibble over a lack of grip, but for pure hedonistic drinking, this supple, velvety wine fills the bill. The 1986 seems to lack a little depth in its mid-range to be truly thrilling, but it is very good, fruity, and slightly more tannic than the 1985.

CORBIN (ST.-ÉMILION)* * *

1985	C 83
1986	C 75

This can be an especially good St.-Émilion (I remember a fine 1970), but several of the recent vintages have been loosely knit and, frankly, too supple and unfocused. The 1985 exhibits the overripe character that I find common in Corbin, a soft, exuberantly fruity, very agreeable constitution, and a finish that is a trifle short and too alcoholic. The 1986 seems more diluted and lacking the necessary acidity and tannin for balance. These two wines are not up to previous standards.

CORMEIL FIGEAC (ST.ÉMILION)* * *

1985	C 85
1986	C 84

Although this wine lacks consistency from one vintage to another, in the better years it is packed with fruit and character (the 1982 is superb). The 1985 has medium to full body, a deep-ruby color, open-knit texture, and a ripe, plummy bouquet and generous suppleness. It is already quite tasty. The 1986 will probably be just as good. It has quite a bit of tannin and more pure power and muscle than the 1985, but for now, less charm and fruit. It will need 3–5 more years.

COS D'ESTOURNEL (ST.-ESTÈPHE)* * * * *

1985	D 95
1986	D 95

Cos d'Estournel has been making wines as grand as the famous Bordeaux first-growths since 1982. And in both of the above vintages, Cos d'Estournel represented one of the few wines that merited buying as a "future," for the simple reasons that it is priced fairly and is of supreme quality. The 1985, a wine that is 60% Cabernet Sauvignon and 40% Merlot, and was aged in 100% new oak for the first time, is cast from the same mold as the 1982 and 1953 vintages. It is forward, with a fabulously scented bouquet of toasty new oak and concentrated red fruit. On the palate, it is very rich, lush, long, and full bodied, and in spite of its youthful appeal, should age beautifully for 12–18 years. The 1986, which is a blend of 68% Cabernet Sauvignon, 30% Merlot and 2% Cabernet Franc, is also a great wine, but its beauty is built on power, weight, tannin, and great extraction of fruit. Nearly black/ruby in color, it is another superstar from this property.

COS LABORY (ST.-ESTÈPHE)* *

1985	C	78
1986	C	83

For decades this property has produced one of the worst wines in St.-Estèphe, and the results of recent attempts to improve the quality have hardly been reassuring. The 1985 is light, simple, fruity, and ready to drink. Thankfully, the 1986 exhibits some depth and richness, but Cos Labory remains a poignant reminder of how misleading the 1855 Classification of the Wines of the Gironde can be.

COUFRAN (HAUT-MÉDOC)* * *

1985	B	82
1986	B	85

Jean Miailhe, the head of the association of Crus Bourgeois, runs this distinctive property. Its uniqueness is due to the extremely high percentage of Merlot (85%) used in the blend. The wine has been much more consistent in the eighties than in prior decades. The 1985 is a fruity, well-focused wine of medium body, soft tannins, and decent concentration. The 1986 looks to be much more serious, as it has a deeper color, an intense, rich concentration, medium to full body, and plenty of depth. It is certainly the best Coufran since the 1982.

COUSTOLLE (CANON-FRONSAC)* *

1985	B	75
1986	B	82

This Canon-Fronsac seems capable of aging a long time, but to date I have found the wine overly hard and tannic, and occasionally too severe. The 1986 seems to be an improvement over the harder 1985, as the former wine is supple, with an exotic bouquet and a ripe, tasty finish.

COUVENT-DES-JACOBINS (ST.-ÉMILION)* * *

1985	C	86
1986	C	87

No visitor to Bordeaux should miss seeing the ancient, scenic village of St.-Émilion (40 minutes' drive from Bordeaux's center), with a stop at the impeccable underground cellars of the Couvent-des-Jacobins. This is a splendid property that is within (actually a part of) the fortified walls that surround the town. The winemaking is also meticulous. The 1985 is a textbook St.-Émilion—supple, generous, easy to appreciate, with gobs of blackcurrant fruit interlaced with a touch of toasty oak. This medium- to full-bodied wine offers both complexity and a mouth-filling plumpness. The 1986 shows more new oak, an uncommon degree of elegance and class for a St.-Émilion, rich, deep fruit, medium to full body, and excellent length.

LE CROCK (ST.-ESTÈPHE)* *

1985	B	73
1986	B	74

The Cuvelier family, which has done so much to restore the fortunes of Léoville-Poyferré, owns and manages this lovely hillside château, just down the road from Cos d'Estournel. Improvements have been made here, but I certainly have found the 1985 and 1986 to be uninspired. The 1985 has medium body, moderately deep flavors, and some hard astringence in the finish—perhaps too much press wine in the blend? The 1986 is also hard, but seemed slightly less dull, although it, too, lacked generosity and length.

LA CROIX (POMEROL)* * *

1985	B	84
1986	B	84

The Janoueix family runs this estate and produces a somewhat underrated wine of both charm and substance. I have had very good experience with the 1982, 1979, and 1976. The 1985 is an exuberantly plump, fruit-filled wine with full body, a sweet, round, generous texture, not much complexity, but a lot of clean, opulent, mouth-filling berry fruit. The 1986 is dense, with a bouquet of tobacco and cassis. On the palate, it is a bigger wine than the 1985, but also tougher and more tannic.

LA CROIX DE GAY (POMEROL)* * *

1985	C	85
1986	C	86

In the eighties, this estate has begun to make increasingly better wine; both the 1985 and 1986 vintages are resounding successes. The 1985 has a moderately intense, elegant, ripe, spicy bouquet, attractive flavors wrapped gently in new oak, medium body, and a velvety finish. The 1986 seems to have a bit more of everything: more fruit, more new oak, more body, more length, and more tannin. It will be slower to evolve.

LA CROIX ST. ANDRÉ (LALANDE-DE-POMEROL)* * *

1985	B	87
1986	B	86

This is one of the new stars of Lalande-de-Pomerol. The Carayon family is aiming to make a deep, rich, age-worthy wine, which is being aged in oak barrels, some of them new. The 1985 came out on top in my tastings of Lalande-de-Pomerols, and is an impressive, serious wine—deep in color, ripe, rich, long, and very well balanced. The 1986 is also a complex, complete wine. A big bouquet of sweet, toasty oak and lush berry fruit makes the wine enticing. On the palate, the wine is exotic, spicy, rich, and full.

CROIZET-BAGES (PAUILLAC)* *

1985	C	73
1986	C	76

This estate, although classified a fifth-growth, never seems capable of making a very serious wine. Most of the recent vintages have shown a glaring lack of concentration and an insipid, dull personality. The 1985 is soft, one-dimensional, and no better than most generic Bordeaux red wines. The 1986 has a bit more stuffing and length, but for its reputation is a disappointment.

CROQUE-MICHOTTE (ST.-ÉMILION)* * *

1985	C	87
1986	C	85

Both of these vintages offer plenty of hedonistic, rich fruit, succulent textures, long, heady finishes, and intoxicating, intense bouquets. They are immensely enjoyable wines. The 1985, while not a long-lived wine, has oodles of berry fruit, a gorgeous silky texture, and a smooth finish. The 1986 has a vivid black cherry-scented bouquet and tastes like a very fine Pomerol.

DALEM (FRONSAC)* * *

1985	B	88
1986	B	86

This estate, one of the finest in Fronsac, is run with great flair and enthusiasm by Michel Rullier. I have appreciated his wines for some time, and a recent vertical tasting at the château proved quite convincingly that even older vintages like the 1964 and 1970 are still full of fruit. The 1985 is deep in color with a broad, expansive, rich, intense fragrance, sweet, deep, plummy flavors, excellent depth, and quite a finish. The 1986 is potentially even finer, but one will need to wait for it, as it is imbued with a great deal more tannin. It too, however, exhibits oodles of very ripe, intense fruit. This is a property to search out.

DASSAULT (ST.-ÉMILION)* * *

1985	B	83
1986	B	84

This is the sort of St.-Émilion that makes for a pleasant luncheon wine. It is neither disappointing nor terribly exciting. The 1985 is light, ripe, and effusively fruity, but it lacks grip and focus. It should be drunk up over the next 2–3 years. The 1986 is similarly styled, very soft and easygoing (especially for a 1986), but has more depth and length on the palate.

LA DAUPHINE (FRONSAC)* * *

1985	B	85

1986	B	84

The wines of La Dauphine tend to be ripe, rich, fruity and supple—always among the easiest of the Fronsacs to drink when young. The 1985 is soft, supple, tasty, medium bodied, and attractive. The 1986 is a thicker, more tannic wine that has good, ripe, supple fruit beneath a veneer of tannin.

DAUZAC (MARGAUX)* *

1985	C	81

The 1985 Dauzac is a compact, deeply colored wine that seems tightly knit and concentrated, but I was hard-pressed to find much charm or complexity. Perhaps I have been too stern, but time will tell.

DESTIEUX (ST.-ÉMILION)* * *

1985	B	87

1986	B	87

This is another of St.-Émilion's up-and-coming estates. The force behind the recent string of successes here is both the owner, Monsieur Dauriac, and consulting oenologist Michel Rolland. Despite a less favorable *terroir* (soil base for the vineyard), the wines of Destieux share a power and elegance that comes closest to those of the great Canon. The 1985 has shed much of its tannin since I tasted it in 1987. Still broodingly dense and dark, this full-flavored wine has a sumptuous amount of ripe fruit, a voluptuous texture, and moderate aging potential. The 1986 is nearly black in color, more aggressive and powerfully built, and deep and long with an impressive finish.

LA DOMINIQUE (ST.-ÉMILION)* * * *

1985	C	74

1986	C	90

For years, La Dominique (next door to Cheval Blanc) was one of the most seriously underrated and undervalued properties in Bordeaux. The great vintages 1955, 1970, 1971, 1982, 1983, and 1986—have been notable for their sheer opulence of fruit interwoven with plenty of new oak. The 1985 is a disappointment, tasting of green sap from improperly cured barrels and too large a crop. Avoid it. The 1986 will prove to be the finest wine since the great 1982. Ruby/purple, with a giant bouquet of smoky oak and plummy fruit, this well-built, very rich, and powerful wine has 15–20 years of aging potential.

DUCRU-BEAUCAILLOU (ST.-JULIEN)* * * * *

1985	D	91

1986	D	94

Being the most elegant and complex wine of St.-Julien, Ducru-Beaucaillou has rarely been a disappointment. But since 1978 its quality has been raised to an even greater level by Jean-Eugène Borie, its amiable and classy proprietor. The 1985 does not have the sheer power of either of the great Ducrus made in 1982 or 1986, yet it has a wonderfully rich, ripe, generous curranty fruitiness, medium to full body, a creamy texture backed by ripe tannins, and a long, balanced, impressive finish. This is one 1985 that may well turn out to be a clone of this property's 1953—high praise indeed. The 1986 is a very great wine, slightly harder and more tannic than the 1982, but packed with fruit and exceptionally deep and rich, as well as full bodied. You won't need to worry about the tannins outliving the fruit in this 1986.

DUHART-MILON-ROTHSCHILD (PAUILLAC)* * *

1985	C	86

1986	C	87

Duhart is always a fuller bodied, denser wine than its more prestigious sibling, Lafite-Rothschild. The 1985 is a good, medium-bodied wine that is showing slightly less intensity from the bottle than it did out of cask. It is a medium, deep ruby wine with an open-knit, spicy oak, curranty bouquet. Upon tasting, one can sense an elegance and stylish fruitiness. The 1986 may be superior to the 1985, as it is full bodied and deep, but still stylish.

DUPLESSIS-FABRE (MOULIS)* * *

1985	B	84

1986	B	?

Run by the same owners as Fourcas-Dupré, this property is a source of huge, powerful, backstrapping, tannic wines that seem out of place today. The 1985 is typically big, brawny, dense, concentrated, long, and tough. Give it 3–10 years of cellaring. The 1986 may be as good, but I would not want to gamble on its overall balance, as the tannin level is painfully high—and I mean that literally. Judgment reserved.

DURAND-LAPLAGNE (PUISSEGUIN-ST.-ÉMILION)* * *

1985	A	84
1986	A	82

This serious estate is a reliable source for inexpensive Bordeaux. Both the 1985 and 1986 show good fruit, medium body, plump texture, and aging potential of 2–3 years. I thought the 1985 had more charm and depth than the 1986.

DURFORT-VIVENS (MARGAUX)* * *

1985	C	87
1986	C	84

Durfort-Vivens is another perennial underachiever (for over two decades) that is making a serious effort in the eighties to restore its reputation. The 1985 has a deep ruby color, and a fragrant, spicy, rich, intense bouquet of fruit and oak. On the palate, the wine has a creamy richness, medium to full body, and light tannins, but fine length. The 1986 is tannic and has a healthy, deep ruby color, but is quite closed and unevolved. It has medium body, plenty of depth, and mouth-coating tannins.

L'EGLISE-CLINET (POMEROL)* * * * *

1985	C	95
1986	C	91

Denis Durantou, the young new proprietor of L'Eglise-Clinet, has only several vintages under his belt, but based on his extraordinary success in 1985 and 1986, this well-placed vineyard may well be emerging as the next superstar from Pomerol. Made from 80% Merlot and 20%

Cabernet Franc (the vines average 40 years in age) the wine is fabulous in 1985, as it has the exceptional richness and depth of a very great wine. Dark ruby, with a full intensity bouquet of crushed berries and toasty oak, it is explosively rich and has layers of extract; while undeniably impressive now, it will really be in its prime between 1990 and 2005. The 1986 is almost as sublime; black ruby in color, extremely rich, deep and long, it is more powerful and tannic than the 1985. Curiously, it is also lower in acidity. These very great wines are clearly on a par with Pétrus in these vintages.

L'ENCLOS (POMEROL)* * *

1985	B	85
1986	B	84

This is another consistently good to very good, smooth, silky Pomerol that never disappoints. The great vintages here have been 1961, 1975, 1979, and 1982. The 1985 is delectably rich, long, expansive, velvety, and already a complete pleasure to drink. Medium-bodied, with oodles of caramel and berry fruit, this Pomerol gives an impression not unlike biting into candy. The 1986 is virtually identical in style, perhaps less precocious and more structured, but supple, rich, and fruity.

L'EVANGILE (POMEROL)* * * * *

1985	D	95
1986	D	86

For sheer class, complexity and a magnificent perfume, L'Evangile is the top wine of Pomerol in 1985. Although it does not have the power and massive texture of Pétrus or Lafleur, or the exceptional concentration of L'Eglise-Clinet, its dark ruby color and hugely complex, multidimensional bouquet of blackcurrants, raspberries, exotic spices, and oak are unbelievably exciting. Rich, medium to full bodied, quite concentrated, well balanced and moderately tannic, the 1985, along with the splendid 1982, is the finest wine to come out of this estate in over three decades. The 1986 is similar to the seductive, medium-weight 1979 made here—ripe, sweet, forward, low in acidity, but complex and tasty.

FERRAND (ST.-ÉMILION)* * *

1985	C 89

1986	C 86

Baron Bich, owner of the ballpoint pen empire, has put an immense amount of money into this impeccably run estate. The 1985, which I thought to be a sleeper of the vintage several years ago, has indeed turned out to be the finest Ferrand I have ever tasted. Deep ruby, with a forward, classic bouquet of blackcurrants and toasty oak, this medium- to full-bodied, rich yet well balanced, elegant wine has quite a bit of staying power on the palate. The 1986 does not have the fat and charm of the 1985, but is, nevertheless, a deep, rich, long, interesting bottle of wine that will age well.

FEYTIT CLINET (POMEROL)* *

1985	C 84

1986	C 85

Located in the northwestern section of Pomerol on relatively light soil, this property produced good wines in 1985 and 1986. The 1985 has an intense bouquet of bing cherries and toasty oak, good richness, firm tannins, and some elegance. The 1986 is a fuller, larger-proportioned wine, with deep fruit and fine ripeness. It seems slightly deeper and more complete than the 1985. Perhaps this estate, long known for its mediocre wines, is beginning to get serious about its reputation.

LES FIEFS DE LAGRANGE (ST.-JULIEN)* * *

1985	B 84

1986	B 86

This is the second wine of the newly renovated Château Lagrange. The 1985 is elegant, fruity, well made, deep in color, and medium to full bodied. The 1986 is a very serious "second wine"—powerful, deep, long and tannic, with considerable clout and complexity.

DE FIEUZAL (GRAVES)* * *

1985	C 86

1986   C   87

Fieuzal has begun to make increasingly better wine, as the vintages
since 1983 demonstrate. The 1985 is an elegantly wrought, fruity,
deeply colored wine that has a generous, plump texture, and smooth,
concentrated flavors. It is the finest Fieuzal in over a decade. The
1986 is much bolder and dramatic, with considerable power and tannic
clout. Very deep in color and admirably concentrated, this vintage of
Fieuzal should be very long-lived.

FIGEAC (ST.-ÉMILION)* * * * *

1985   D   87

1986   D   90

I believe that Thierry Manoncourt, the aristocratic, articulate owner
of Figeac, has been making some of his finest wines in the eighties.
His wine is always unique because over two-thirds of the blend is
Cabernet Sauvignon and Cabernet Franc. The 1985, while not as deep
or powerful as either the 1982 or 1986, is still an exceptionally elegant,
smoky, cedary-scented wine with a healthy dosage of new oak. On the
palate, the wine is smooth, velvety, very forward and seemingly ready
to drink, but I am sure it will age well for 10–12 years. The 1986 is a
great bottle of Figeac. An extremely complex bouquet is followed by
a wine that has greater depth, richness, length, and structure than the
1985. It is the finest Figeac since the wonderful wines made here in
1970, 1975, and 1982.

LA FLEUR DE GAY (POMEROL)* * * * *

1985   D   89

1986   D   90

Dr. Raynaud, the handsome proprietor who always has a tan,
launched this luxury cuvée of La Croix de Gay in 1983. The wine
comes from a small parcel of very old vines situated between Pétrus
and Vieux Château Certan. Aged in 100% new oak, the wine is characterized by a remarkable opulence and sweetness as well as a purity
of fruit. The 1985 exhibits super-richness, a stunningly intense bouquet, luxurious flavors, full body, and melted tannins, which give it a
silky texture. Given its softness, I hesitate to advise long-term cellaring, but over the next 6–8 years, this treasure should provide for quite

memorable drinking. The 1986 (which Raynaud prefers) is very dense in color, shows quite a bit of new oak, is rich, closed, very tannic, and —for this property—an exceptionally big, powerful, and promising wine.

LA FLEUR PÉTRUS (POMEROL)* * * *

1985	D	85
1986	D	83

Of the bevy of fine Pomerols from the house (or should I now say empire) of the legendary Jean-Pierre Moueix, La Fleur Pétrus is one of the most graceful and elegant. I found the 1985 to be fruity, stylish, suave, and very tasty for drinking today. It exhibits very good ripeness, medium body, an aromatic bouquet, and a soft, velvety finish. The 1986 seems lighter than the 1985 but has more aggressive tannins. It is quite forward and evolved for a 1986.

FONBADET (PAUILLAC)* * *

1985	C	80
1986	C	85

Although Fonbadet usually has been a reliable, though expensive, Cru Bourgeois, the most recent vintages have not been as impressive as those of the past. The 1985 has a good, deep ruby color and an attractive berry perfume, but also chunky flavors that show little complexity. The 1986 is the most successful Fonbadet since the 1982— concentrated, tasty, full bodied and tannic, with a fine balance between the aggressive, hard tannins of the 1986 vintage and the fruit.

FONPLÉGADE (ST.-ÉMILION)* * *

1985	B	85
1986	B	?

This property is located in one of the best vineyard sites of St.-Émilion, and while the wine is good, there is no reason (along with a bit more attention to detail) why Fonplégade cannot be superb. The 1985 is a typical and very good example of the 1985 vintage. Richly fruity, plump, tasty, fat and medium to full bodied, it will provide delicious drinking over the next 5–6 years. The 1986 was closed and impossible to judge.

FONREAUD (LISTRAC)* * *

| 1985 | B | 85 |

An extremely dense, typical Listrac, Fonreaud's 1985 is deep in color, full bodied, tannic, and in need of very long cellaring.

FONROQUE (ST.-ÉMILION)* * *

| 1985 | B | 86 |
| 1986 | B | 85 |

This well-placed St.-Émilion property, owned by the Libourne firm of Jean-Pierre Moueix, has been making increasingly better wine during the eighties. The percentage of new oak barrels has been increased, and the wine is now one of the better St.-Émilions. The 1985 shows the broad, rich, ripe fatness of the vintage, whereas the 1986 is firmer and more tannic. Drink the 1985 over the next 5–7 years, and the 1986 over the next decade.

FONTENIL (FRONSAC)* * *

| 1985 | B | 78 |
| 1986 | B | 87 |

Now owned by the gifted oenologist Michel Rolland, Fontenil made a tough-textured, burly, tannic 1985 that lacks fat and charm. The 1986 is one of the stars of the appellation. Its huge, smoky, rich, deep bouquet filled with currant fruit is top-notch. On the palate, the wine is quite impressive—rich, full bodied, deep, age-worthy, and long.

LES FORTS DE LATOUR (PAUILLAC)* * * *

| 1978 | C | 90 |
| 1979 | C | 84 |

Traditionally this has been one of the finest of the "second" wines of famous Bordeaux châteaux (it is not released by Château Latour until it is deemed somewhat ready to drink). The great vintages of Forts de Latour have been the 1975, 1978, and 1982 (which has not yet been released). The 1978 is showing all of the classic personality characteristics of Latour—the deep walnut and blackcurrant-scented bouquet, full body, super-concentration, and a generous velvety texture. It should drink well for 7–8 years. The 1979 is good, but much lighter and fully mature.

FOURCAS-DUPRÉ (LISTRAC)* * *

1985	A	85
1986	A	86

Fourcas-Dupré is generally reliable. Previously run with great enthusiasm by the late Guy Pages, the estate is now being excellently managed by his son. The 1985 is oozing with ripe fruit, shows just enough tannin, and a long, smooth, creamy texture plus a spicy, interesting bouquet. The 1986 looks to be even deeper and is probably the finest wine to have come out of this estate in several decades. It has a wealth of fruit to balance out the tannins, a deep color, and fine balance.

FOURCAS-HOSTEN (LISTRAC)* * *

1985	B	85

The fine 1985 Fourcas-Hosten recalls the tannic, well-made, concentrated 1970 made here. Deep in color, with a spicy, blackcurrant scented bouquet intermingled with aromas of new oak, this elegant, medium-bodied wine admirably balances power with finesse.

FRANC MAYNE (ST.-ÉMILION)* * *

1986	B	82

Jean Michel Cazes, the affable and extremely competent owner of Lynch-Bages, purchased this small estate of 17 acres next to Clos-des-Jacobins only last year, so he did not make the 1986, which has good color, a ripe, tasty fruitiness, medium body, and good length. Given the past record of the new owner, Franc Mayne should be an estate to watch.

GABY (FRONSAC)* *

1985	B	72?
1986	B	84

I did not care for the 1985 when I first tasted it, and on retasting it more recently I found it very peppery and vegetal with a *goût de terroir* (taste of the soil) that can only be described as rustic and coarse. It will keep well, as it is very tannic. The 1986 is rich, very full bodied, tannic, and potentially much more interesting and complex than the 1985.

LA GAFFELIÈRE (ST.-ÉMILION)* * *

1985	C 85
1986	C 86

The Comte Léo de Malet-Roquefort has made tremendous strides in quality in the eighties after permitting this property to decline in the seventies. Recent vintages have been consistently fine, although this remains one of the lighter, more elegant styles of St.-Émilion. The 1985 has a full intensity, spicy, herbaceous, richly fruity bouquet, medium body, soft tannins, and a supple finish. The 1986 has more tannin, more grip, a deeper concentration, and should keep longer.

LE GAY (POMEROL)* * * *

1985	C 86
1986	C 87?

Among the range of Pomerols, Le Gay always stands out for its rustic, tough, dense, old style of winemaking. With age, the finesse and breed come through, but I have never enjoyed tasting this particular Pomerol when young. The 1985 is mean, moody and murky, as well as terribly tannic. It is full bodied, deep, and exhibits good richness, but how long is one expected to wait? The rating may turn out to be conservative if this wine pulls itself together and smooths out. The 1986 is equally forbidding, as the tannins assault the senses and palate. Big, beefy and bulky, the 1986 Le Gay will strike the hearts of those with nineteenth-century tastes.

GAZIN (POMEROL)* * *

1985	C 76
1986	C 75

The 1985 has adequate ripeness, but is somewhat dull, medium bodied, and, overall, a mediocre, one-dimensional wine. The 1986 seems to promise more complexity in its bouquet of weedy, tobacco and tea scents, but falls away on the palate.

GISCOURS (MARGAUX)* * *

1985	C	84
1986	C	87

Pierre Tari, head of the union of the classified-growths (Union des Grands Crus) is responsible for the fame that Giscours has enjoyed since his family acquired the estate in 1952. The wine has always been one of my favorites, with a record of being surprisingly good in mediocre years, such as 1980 and 1973. However, in the eighties, much of the structure of the wine has been sacrificed in favor of a lighter, fruitier, ready-to-drink wine. This is especially evident with both the 1985 and 1986 vintages. Frankly, I think the quality has suffered because of this change in winemaking. The 1985 is quite light, fruity, agreeable and charming, but shouldn't one expect just a bit more depth and class for a wine of this price? The 1986 tasted awkward and disjointed when tasted from the barrel, but now that it is in the bottle, the wine is displaying excellent ripeness, depth, and a very smooth supple finish.

DU GLANA (ST.-JULIEN)* *

1985	B	82
1986	B	83

For me, the only problem with this estate's wines is that I have detected far too much bottle variation. The style is one that features soft, supple, ripe berry fruit, no evidence of oak, and light tannins. The wines have a tendency to be soupy and lack grip, but good bottles are always pleasant, although they must be drunk over their first 6–7 years of life.

GLORIA (ST.-JULIEN)* * *

1985	B	86
1986	B	86

A staple of many American tables, Gloria began in 1976 to lighten its style and make a softer, less-structured wine that could be drunk when released, but seemed to lack the character and complexity of top years such as 1971, 1970, and 1966. The 1985 after bottling (it was a little clumsy from the cask) is showing more depth and richness than any Gloria since 1975. Deep in color, with a weedy, herbaceous, cedary, blackcurrant bouquet, it offers up a rich mouthful of succulent claret. As for the 1986 Gloria, it shows a surprising amount of structure, deep ruby color, a touch of oak, medium to full body, and will likely be the first Gloria in over a decade that will have to be cellared for several years prior to consumption.

GRAND-MAYNE (ST.-ÉMILION)* * *

1985	B	84
1986	B	86

This is an estate to keep an eye on, as the quality appears to be improving. The 1985 has very good color, a moderately intense bouquet of spicy oak and ripe fruit, medium body, well-focused flavors, and an overall elegant feel. Drink it over the next 4–5 years. The 1986 has greater color, much more stuffing and depth, a deft touch of new oak, and a powerful, long finish. It is quite impressive.

GRAND-ORMEAU (LALANDE-DE-POMEROL)* * *

1985	B	86
1986	B	85

Consistently one of the top two or three Lalande-de-Pomerols, this seriously run property made an excellent, absolutely delicious wine in 1985. Deep ruby, it has a big, rich, plum-scented bouquet that also exhibits some new oak. This perfumed, luscious, fleshy wine will drink well for 5–6 years. The 1986 is equally rich, full, well balanced and deep, but comes across as less forward and slightly more tannic. Looking for excellent values from Bordeaux? Try Grand-Ormeau.

GRAND-PONTET (ST.-ÉMILION)* *

1985	B	77
1986	B	83

The 1985 is a light, simple, fruity wine without a great deal of body, but it has good, straightforward appeal. Drink it over the next 2–4 years. The 1986 has more color, depth and richness, with a round, generous texture and fine length. Like the 1985, it is forward, but there is much more to it.

GRAND-PUY-DUCASSE (PAUILLAC)* * *

1985	B	86
1986	B	85

This property tends to be overlooked, and its wines are actually undervalued in the scheme of Pauillac's high prices. The 1985 is a textbook Pauillac, not a blockbuster in any sense, but, rather, a cedary, spicy, fragrant wine with very fine depth, a supple texture, an exciting fatness to the flavor, and a smooth, graceful finish. The 1986 is more tannic and closed, seems to have less fat and charm, but is a well-made, medium-bodied, ripe, chewy wine that properly expresses the character of the Pauillac appellation.

GRAND-PUY-LACOSTE(PAUILLAC)* * * *

1985	C	88
1986	C	91

When I visited with the proprietor, Monsieur Borie, recently, he said that his 1986 and 1985 were the finest wines he had made at Grand-Puy-Lacoste since his wondrous 1982. The 1985 is a big, juicy, beefy, rich, supple Pauillac oozing with aromas of blackcurrants and new oak. Seductive and full-bodied, with excellent ripeness, this lusty wine will drink well between 1989 and 2005. The 1986 (the finest wine from this estate since 1982) has everything the 1985 has, but is even deeper and richer, more tannic, chewy, and rather old-style in the sense of its huge structure and power. It should be a required purchase for those searching out a great wine for a fair price.

LA GRAVE (FRONSAC)* *

1985	B	82
1986	B	?

La Grave is generally a soundly made wine with lots of color and tannin. The 1985 is full bodied and compact, but very tannic. The

1986 also seems excruciatingly tannic and severe, and I would prefer to taste it again in several years before making a final judgment.

LA GRAVE FIGEAC (ST.-ÉMILION)* * *

1985	B	80
1986	B	72

This property proved quite a discovery a number of years ago, and I have cellared and drunk with great pleasure the outstanding 1982 and 1983. Unfortunately, the proprietor has begun to produce too much wine and the quality has slipped in both 1985 and 1986. The 1985 lacks depth, structure and complexity, but does offer a straightforward appeal. The 1986 is diluted and is only a shadow of the former level of quality attained here. What a shame!

LA GRAVE TRIGANT DE BOISSET (POMEROL)* * *

1985	C	84
1986	C	84

True to form, La Grave Trigant de Boisset's 1985 is an elegant, soft, fruity wine that should be drunk over the next 4–7 years. The 1986 shows more new oak and seems more concentrated and tannic. It, too, is a lighter-styled Pomerol that will drink nicely at a young age.

GRESSIER GRAND-POUJEAUX (MOULIS)* * *

1985	B	87
1986	B	89

The 1985 is showing excellent potential now that it has been bottled. A sleeper of the vintage, this black/ruby-colored wine is loaded with extract, has tremendous tannic clout, a long, rich finish, full body, and 10–15 or more years of further evolution. The 1986 is similarly styled, but much more promising. These are brilliant old-style wines that should be bought only by those who have patience and a fine, cool cellar.

GRESYAC (MÉDOC)* * *

1985	B	81

1986   B   77

Greysac was one of my favorite bargain Bordeaux wines in the mid-
and late-seventies, but its huge popularity led to a considerable expansion of the vineyard area, and the recent vintages have exhibited a
much lighter, somewhat diluted style. Neither the 1985 nor 1986 are
as good as the 1975, 1976, 1978, or 1979, and both should be drunk
over the next 2–3 years.

GRUAUD-LAROSE (ST.-JULIEN)* * * * *

1985   C   90

1986   C   92

Georges Pauli, the brilliant oenologist for Cordier, likens the 1985 St.-
Juliens to the 1979s, but I have to think this is a very conservative
comparison. The 1985 Gruaud-Larose has evolved beautifully, and in
the bottle it exhibits a lovely, sweet, fragrant bouquet of berry fruit,
truffles, and smoky oak. On the palate, the wine is fat, long, quite
forward for Gruaud, medium to full bodied, and quite deep. It will
drink well young. The 1986 is believed by the Cordiers to be similar
to their 1928, 1945, 1961, and 1982. It is a huge, mammoth-structured
wine with a fabulous wealth of fruit, black/ruby color, significant body,
and a finish that goes on and on. This wine, in complete contrast to
the open-knit 1985, is very backward and tannic, and will require
considerable cellaring.

LA GURGUE (MARGAUX)* * *

1985   B   87

1986   B   87

This little estate of just under 30 acres is clearly a property to watch
as Bernadette Villars, the architect behind the resurgent quality of
Chasse-Spleen and Haut-Bages-Libéral, is also responsible for this
luscious, amply endowed wine. The 1985 has gobs of blackcurrant
fruit and is deep, velvety, lush, medium to full bodied, and intensely
concentrated. This lovely wine should drink well over the next 7–8
years. The 1986 is no better, has much the same concentration and
depth, but the tannins are more aggressive and the wine will need
several years to soften.

HANTEILLAN (MÉDOC)* *

1985	A	80

1986	A	79

I always find this wine stubbornly stern, unyielding and lacking charm
—which cannot be said about the proprietor, Madame Blasco. The
1985 has good color, a spicy, light-intensity bouquet, medium body,
and tightly knit, compact flavors. The 1986 is not dissimilar, but tastes
softer than one might expect given the vintage.

HAUT-BAGES-AVEROUS (PAUILLAC)* * *

1985	B	85

1986	B	84

Haut-Bages-Averous, the second label of Lynch-Bages, should be considered seriously by those looking for a smooth, ready-to-drink claret
that is packed with plump, blackcurrant fruit. The 1985 offers delicious, immediate appeal. Deep ruby, with a plump, fruity, tobacco-
and-peppery-scented bouquet, this attractive wine has good body,
light tannins, and a pleasant, soft finish. The 1986 is more powerful,
more concentrated, and more tannic. It is also more age-worthy.

HAUT-BAGES-LIBÉRAL (PAUILLAC)* * *

1985	C	89

1986	C	91

This well-placed property is emerging as one of the top new stars of
the Médoc. Run with considerable attention to detail by Bernadette
Villars, this relatively obscure Pauillac fifth-growth turned in two brilliant efforts in 1985 and 1986. The black/ruby-colored 1985 is a rich,
dense, full-bodied wine with great color, loads of extract, and a powerful, long, ripe finish. The 1986 is the property's finest effort since
1975. Powerfully built for the long haul, this ruby/purple-colored wine
has exceptional depth and power, great concentration and enough
tannin to carry it for three more decades.

HAUT-BAILLY (GRAVES)* * * *

1985	C	86

1986   C   88

For me, Haut-Bailly is always among the lightest of the Graves wines. It is an intensely fruity wine that always suggests early drinkability, but has the cunning ability to age well. The 1985 will no doubt live longer than I thought it would, and I find it hard to ignore its precocious, charming berry fruitiness backed up with sweet toasty oak. It is medium bodied, with very soft tannins and moderate length. The 1986 looks and tastes more serious, as the color is deeper and there is more tannin, fat, and length; yet the wine has retained its charm and elegance. It would appear to be the finest Haut-Bailly since the glorious 1961.

HAUT-BATAILLEY (PAUILLAC)* * *

1985   C   85

1986   C   87

Of all the classified-growth Pauillacs, Haut-Batailley seems the most like St.-Julien. The 1985 is a soft, agreeable, elegantly wrought wine that is quite fruity, medium bodied, and tasty, but is likely to be rather short-lived. On the other hand, the 1986 is about as powerful and tannic as this wine is capable of being. Deep ruby in color, with a concentrated, rich, deep palate impression, the 1986 Haut-Batailley seems to be the finest wine made at this estate in some time.

HAUT-BERGEY (GRAVES)* *

1985   B   78

1986   B   84

I have not tasted this wine in some time, and while the 1985, with its one-dimensional grapy flavors, is hard to get excited about, the 1986 shows a judicious use of new oak, a lovely, soft fruity quality, an elegance, and an attractive suppleness.

HAUT-BRION (GRAVES)* * * * *

1985   E   91

1986   E   94

Jean Delmas, the handsome manager of Haut Brion since 1961, is one of Bordeaux's most forward-thinking men. His experiments with clonal selections and his remarkable new winery for La Mission-Haut-Brion (designed to his specifications) qualify him as a great innovator. More importantly, his efforts at Haut-Brion since 1978 have resulted in an increasingly stronger lineup of wines, culminating in superb efforts in 1985 and 1986. The 1985, along with the flamboyant Mouton-Rothschild, is one of the finest first-growths of the vintage. The epitome of elegance and finesse, the 1985, a deep ruby-colored wine, has a full-intensity bouquet of jammy fruit, spices, and tobacco. On the palate it exhibits a soft, very generous texture, super-concentration, exquisite balance, and a long, impressive finish. While it does not have the power of the 1982 or 1986, it is a gorgeously elegant wine. The 1986 has evolved fabulously over the last year and is a remarkably concentrated and powerful Haut-Brion that now appears to be, along with the 1982, the most promising and long-lived wine from this estate since the 1959 and 1961. Very deep in color, with a staggering wealth of fruit and dimension of flavor, this powerful wine should prove to be a classic.

HAUT-BRISSON (ST-ÉMILION)* * *

1985	B	85
1986	B	84

Haut-Brisson is not a well-known property, but the quality of the wine is quite good and it is a reasonably priced, very faithful example of a St.-Émilion. The 1985 is a succulent, deeply fruity, soft, spicy wine that should be drunk over the next 4–5 years. The 1986 is probably as rich as the 1985—and more firm—but for now, at least, it is less pleasing to taste.

HAUT-CHÂTAIN (LALANDE-DE-POMEROL)* *

1985	A	72
1986	A	78

While the 1985 lacks concentration and grip, the 1986 shows more style, some elegance, and a healthy measure of fruit.

HAUT-CONSEILLANTS (LALANDE-DE-POMEROL)* * *

1985	B	83

1986	B 84

Haut-Conseillants is another reliable wine from the underrated appellation of Lalande-de-Pomerol. The 1985 has fine ripeness, a soft, creamy, supple taste, medium body, and pleasant finish. The 1986 appears a trifle deeper, has good ripeness, medium body, and a touch more tannin.

HAUT-MARBUZET (ST.-ESTÈPHE)* * * * *

1985	B 88
1986	B 88

Haut-Marbuzet has again produced two top vintages of Bordeaux's most decadent and exotic wine. In 1987 I thought the 1986 was showing better than the 1985, but I appear to have underestimated its quality. The 1985 has the fleshpot personality that makes this wine so sexy and appealing. Its big, toasty, plummy-scented bouquet offers generous amounts of fruit. On the palate, the wine is supple, spicy, rich, and immensely tasty. It is a delight to drink now, but should keep 6–9 years. The 1986 is similarly styled, but the tannins seemed more intrusive, suggesting that it will have to be cellared 2–3 years prior to one's devouring its rich, full-bodied, exotic flavors of ripe plums, sweet vanillin, and smoky oak.

HAUT-SARGET (LALANDE-DE-POMEROL)* *

1985	A 83
1986	A 76

The 1985 is an attractive, easy-to-drink, and easy-to-understand wine, with a smooth, pleasant, ripe taste. The 1986 is chunky, but lacks the charm and flavor concentration of the 1985.

HAUT-SOCIANDO (CÔTES DE BLAYE)* *

1985	A 83
1986	A 80

One of the better estates from the Côtes de Blaye, Haut-Sociando offers soft, medium-bodied wines that are spicy and sometimes a trifle herbaceous. Both the fruity 1985 and more narrowly focused 1986 should be drunk over the next 2–3 years.

HORTEVIE (ST.-JULIEN)* * *

1985	B	85
1986	B	86

This wine is, in essence, a selection of wine made by Terrey-Gros-Cailloux and represents a cuvée of old vines. It is not aged in the barrel, which is somewhat of a shame given its richness and density. The 1985 is deep in color, fat, supple, big, chunky, and a full-intensity bouquet of road tar and blackberries. It is a meaty, hefty wine, short on finesse but big on flavor. The 1986 may be even better. It is loaded with sweet blackcurrant fruit, and is full bodied, concentrated, powerful, and more noticeably tannic than the 1985.

D'ISSAN (MARGAUX)* * * *

1985	C	88
1986	C	86

D'Issan, a tranquil-looking château surrounded by a moat, is one of the prettiest properties in the Médoc. The wine is not a powerhouse or tannic behemoth, but, rather, a delicate, fruity, perfumed wine of distinction. The quality of wines here has improved in the eighties. The 1985 is a real charmer and is undeniably appealing to drink in its youth. Deep ruby in color, it has a highly scented floral and berry bouquet, interwoven with scents of toasty oak. Fat, soft, richly fruity flavors show excellent ripeness and mellow tannins. The 1986 exhibits less muscle and depth than the 1985, yet is more tannic and less charming.

JEANDEMAN (FRONSAC)* *

1985	B	74

This is a straightforward, simple, pleasant wine that should be drunk over the next 2–3 years.

LA JURADE (ST.-ÉMILION)* * *

1985	B	81

1986	B 86

This small property of only 17 acres is now administered by the Cordier family. The vineyard is near the Pomerol border and is planted with 60% Merlot and 40% Cabernet Franc. The 1985 is a pleasant, medium-bodied wine—supple, agreeable, but not very distinguished. It should be drunk over the next 2–4 years. The first vintage vinified by the brilliant oenologist for Cordier, Georges Pauli, was the 1986. It has more serious color, evidence of toasty new oak in the bouquet, a ripe, long, lush texture, and an impressive finish.

KIRWAN (MARGAUX)* * *

1985	C 85

1986	C 78

The 1985 is one of the best examples of Kirwan I have ever tasted. It has very fine color and a moderately intense bouquet of blackcurrants and new oak. Firm and elegant, with well-delineated flavors, this medium-bodied wine should age nicely. The 1986 looks light, and without the richness of fruit to balance out the tannins. It may need some time in the bottle to fill out.

LABÉGORCE-ZÉDÉ (MARGAUX)* * *

1985	B 85

1986	B ?

Since 1979 this well-situated Cru Bourgeois in Margaux has been run by the Thienpont family. The 1985 is showing quite well, an elegant perfumed wine of medium body, ripe fruit, excellent balance, and a moderately tannic finish. The 1986 is quite severe and backward, and while impressively colored, it tasted so hard and unyielding that I don't dare try to speculate if it is just too tannic or in an awkward stage of development. Judgment reserved.

LAFITE-ROTHSCHILD (PAUILLAC)* * * *

1985	E 86

1986	E 90

Although there have been some ethereal vintages of Lafite-Rothschild
—1953, 1959, 1975, 1976, 1981, and 1982—one might ask about the
other years between 1945 and today. Even though Lafite is always a
lighter (some would argue more delicate) wine than Mouton or Margaux, are its consistent inconsistency and lack of depth pardonable
when selling at such a high price? I say they are not. The 1985 should
be better, but for followers of fashion, its extravagant price will provide a moderately intense, cedary, woody, herbaceous, leather-
scented bouquet and attractive flavors displayed in a medium-bodied
format. The finish is tannic, and after a pensive sip, one is likely to
wonder whether that is all there is. The 1986 is richer, deeper in color,
with medium body and very fine length. It is quite unevolved but
should last a long time.

LAFLEUR (POMEROL)* * * *

| 1985 | E | 94 |
| 1986 | E | 92 |

I suppose I am indirectly responsible for the depressingly high prices
now asked for Lafleur, since no one ever mentioned the wine until I
launched *The Wine Advocate* a decade ago. The wine is, as Jean-Pierre
Moueix and son, Christian, have always contended, the only other
Pomerol that can match the intensity and richness of Pétrus. It may
be an even bigger wine, as I believe it is in both 1985 and 1986. The
1985 has a very special bouquet, suggesting ripe plums and violets,
and an intensity that comes only from old vines. Deep ruby/purple
with an exceptional richness and depth of fruit, full body and a powerful, long finish, this wine rates with the great vintages of Lafleur—
the 1982, 1979, 1975, and 1964. The 1986 is another gigantic wine with
very great intensity, formidable power, a scent of oak, and plenty of
mouth-searing tannins. It is undoubtedly a superstar of the vintage,
but how long will it take to mature?

LAFON-ROCHET (ST.-ESTÈPHE)* * *

| 1985 | C | 83 |
| 1986 | C | ? |

The Tesseron family is making significant investments into improving
the wines of Lafon-Rochet as well as their well-known Pauillac,
Pontet-Canet. Second labels have been inaugurated, and I anticipate

an augmentation in quality of Lafon-Rochet (Pontet-Canet is already a much finer wine). That being said, the 1985 Lafon-Rochet is fleshy and chewy, has good color, firm tannins and medium body, but seems a little one-dimensional. The 1986 is still too forbiddingly tannic to properly evaluate. There is more to it, as the color and power on the palate demonstrate, but I wonder if it is not too hard and tannic for its own good.

LAGRANGE (POMEROL)* *

1985	C	83
1986	C	78

This is one of the least distinguished Pomerols within the Jean-Pierre Moueix stable. The 1985 and 1986 Lagranges could not be more different. The 1985 is an easygoing, fruity, supple wine that offers immediate gratification. The 1986 displays good ripeness, but tastes a little dull and perhaps too tannic.

LAGRANGE (ST.-JULIEN)* * * *

1985	C	89
1986	C	90

Château Lagrange has been turned into a magnificent property since its acquisition by a Japanese firm in 1983. More importantly, the wines are being looked after by none other than Michel Delon of Léoville-Las Cases, who is attempting to bring Lagrange to the top echelon of St.-Julien producers. Delon does not make soft, fruity, commercial wines, so Lagrange's recent vintages are powerfully constructed wines made to survive several decades of aging with grace and complexity. The 1985 is deep, rich, long, and surprisingly backward and tannic for a 1985. Medium-bodied, elegant and packed with fruit, it is a long-distance runner. The 1986 is even more powerful and tannic, with great color, full body, plenty of depth and length, but—wow!—the tannins are forbidding.

LA LAGUNE (LUDON)* * * * *

1985	C	87
1986	C	90

Initially, I thought the 1986 a bit too sinewy and tough, and in 1985 the epitome of charm and fruit. More recently, these wines seem to have reversed their positions. The 1985, which I thought to be out-standing, is showing very fine rather than great depth, whereas the 1986 has filled out considerably and now appears the better wine, although the 1985 has more near-term appeal. The 1985 is soft, ripe, fleshy, and aromatic, and is better than the 1983, 1981 and 1979, but nowhere near the quality of the opulent, explosively rich 1982. The 1986, dense purple in color, is an atypically powerful wine, the most structured, tannic, and enormous La Lagune I have ever tasted.

LALANDE BORIE (ST.-JULIEN)* * *

1985	B	84
1986	B	87

Although some people continue to think this is a "second" wine of Ducru-Beaucaillou, it is, rather, a small vineyard in St.-Julien that was planted in 1970. The 1985 is very accessible—soft, fruity, pleas-ant, medium bodied, and quite charming; drink it over the next 5–7 years. The 1986 is the finest wine yet made at the property, an asser-tion with which the owner, Mr. Borie, unequivocally agrees. Deep dark ruby in color, the wine is rich, full bodied, quite tannic, and powerful. Very deep and splendidly concentrated, it is undoubtedly one of the sleepers of this vintage.

LAMARQUE (HAUT-MÉDOC)* *

1985	A	77
1986	A	84

Lamarque, the most striking fortress in the Médoc, can make attrac-tively supple wines that age nicely for up to a decade. The 1985 did not impress me, as it tasted a little diluted and undistinguished, but the rich, full-bodied, deep and concentrated 1986 looks promising.

LAMBERT (FRONSAC)*

1985	B	75
1986	B	66

Neither of these two wines offers much in the way of exciting drinking. The 1985 is one-dimensional but does offer soft, fruity, supple flavors and a short finish. The 1986 is extremely tart, very tannic, and in need of an infusion of fruit.

LANGOA-BARTON (ST.-JULIEN)* * * *

1985	C	86
1986	C	?

The 1985 Langoa-Barton is a stylish wine, deep in color and medium bodied, with an elegant bouquet of blackcurrant fruit and spicy oak. It is not a big, rich, blockbuster sort of wine and seems somewhat shy at the moment. Judging from its impressive color, the 1986 may well be a better wine, but it is so closed and tannic that I wonder if the requisite fruit is present to balance out the tannin. I am really a little perplexed by this wine. Judgment reserved.

LARCIS-DUCASSE (ST.-ÉMILION)* *

1985	C	84
1986	C	78

Given the superb location of this vineyard, the wine should be among the top ten wines of St.-Émilion. However, it is overproduced and lacks focus, depth, and definition—very true for the marginally diluted 1985 and 1986 vintages.

LARMANDE (ST.-ÉMILION)* * * *

1985	B	87
1986	B	87

I have been following this estate for almost a decade. It is impeccably run by Philippe Meneret, who has been turning out a bevy of fine wines (55% Merlot, 45% Cabernet Franc). The 1985 competes favorably with the 1982 and 1983 as the best Larmande of the last decade. A deep color, an intense bouquet of bing cherries, and a ripe, fat, concentrated texture give the deceiving impression of early maturity, but there is quite a lot of tannin in the finish. The 1986 is lower in acidity, also fat and rich, with plenty of succulent berry fruit.

LAROSE-TRINTAUDON (HAUT-MÉDOC)* * *

1985	A 78

1986	A 75

There is nothing wrong with Larose-Trintaudon's goal to make soft, light, fruity wines for drinking within the first 5–6 years of their lives, but the 1985 is just too simple and completely lacking in grip and substance. One does not expect a powerhouse wine from this estate, but some length and depth would be welcome. The 1986 is also a one-dimensional, very fruity, but simple, innocuous wine that will require drinking over the next 3–5 years.

LASCOMBES (MARGAUX)* * * *

1985	C 86

1986	C 82

Since 1983 the owners of Lascombes have become more serious about their wine. The percentage of new oak casks have been increased, a secondary label inaugurated, and tighter management of the cellars begun. Today, the wine is considerably better, although it is not one of the leaders. The 1985, while lacking some grip and structure, is very representative of the vintage. Ripe, round, fruity and medium bodied, this lush, aromatic wine will drink well for 6–9 years. The 1986 has good fruit but does not seem to have the richness to balance out the hard tannins in the finish, which give the wine a dry, somewhat harsh finish.

LATOUR (PAUILLAC)* * * * *

1985	E 86

1986	E 87

Latour—like Margaux between 1967 and 1977, and Lafite-Rothschild between 1961 and 1974—has been going through a brief slump, starting with 1983 and running through 1987. Some changes have already been made, and other improvements, especially a much-needed larger winemaking facility, are being planned; with them Latour will no doubt quickly reassert itself as a leader in Pauillac. That being said, the above two wines, while very good as fine wines are concerned, are weak when considered in the context of what Latour is capable of achieving. The 1985 is medium bodied, has a good but not dense ruby color, a moderately intense berry fragrance, and fine depth and length, but is surprisingly light and accessible for the style of this estate. The 1986 is much more backward and tannic, and has more depth and power than the 1985. However, in the context of what the top properties produced in 1986, Latour's wine, while very fine, does not quite measure up to the other first-growths.

LATOUR DU PIN FIGEAC (ST.-ÉMILION)* * *

1985	B 87
1986	B 88

I rarely have this wine in my tastings, although I did visit the château in 1979 (it lies on St.-Émilion's border with Pomerol). The wines tend to be quite full bodied, rich, deep, and age-worthy. Both the 1985 and the 1986 performed extremely well in my tastings. The 1985 is an altogether impressive St.-Émilion, with grip and very fine balance. Quite powerful, concentrated, rich, opaque in color, full bodied and already soft enough to drink, this boldly flavored wine will keep well for another decade. The 1986 has even more fruit, body, and tannins. Much less forward than the 1985, the 1986 will require cellaring.

LATOUR À POMEROL (POMEROL)* * * * *

1985	D 89
1986	D 87

I continue to see a resemblance between the rich, full-bodied, concentrated, ripe, and sexy 1985 and the brilliant wine made here in 1970. Full, long and powerful, this expansively flavored wine has considerable length, plenty of tannin, and will require some cellaring prior to consumption. The 1986 is a more burly and tannic example of the 1985. Dark in color, rich and full bodied, its charm and flesh should be well preserved by the ample amount of tannin.

LÉOVILLE-BARTON (ST.-JULIEN)* * * * *

1985	C 90
1986	C 87

Anthony Barton, the handsome proprietor of Léoville and Langoa-Barton, deserves a great deal of credit for his investment of time and money in the two estates. Furthermore, he is one of only a handful of owners to have wisely kept wine prices well below those of other St.-Julien properties, despite the fact that the quality here is surging upward. Wines such as the 1985 are probably underpriced; in fact, the 1985 may well turn out to be a remake of the 1953. Deep ruby, with a complex, complete bouquet of curranty fruit, minerals, and oak, this medium-bodied wine has exceptional balance, fine length, super fruit, and good firm tannins in the finish. The 1986 is frightfully tannic, deep in color, broodingly rich and full, but will mature slowly and at least for now lacks the charm of the 1985.

LÉOVILLE-LAS CASES (ST.-JULIEN)* * * * *

1985	D	92
1986	D	94

Michel Delon, the lionlike owner of Léoville-Las Cases, is not very popular among Bordeaux *négociants*. They feel he charges too much for his wine and has an arrogant attitude toward the long-term health of the Bordeaux marketplace. Also, they do not like the marble floors in his brand-new million-dollar wine cellar. But no one ever faults the wine Delon turns out, as he is fanatical about quality. His 1985 seems to get better every time I go back to it. It looks to be better than either the 1981 or 1983, which is saying something. Quite deep in color, as well as ripe and forward, which is rare for a Las Cases, this medium-to full-bodied, concentrated wine will mature quickly, but hold nicely. The 1986 is, according to Delon, reminiscent of his 1966 and 1961. It needs a minimum of 10–15 years of cellaring, but one can easily appreciate its super-richness, depth, and lavish fruit backed up by an armada of tannins.

LÉOVILLE-POYFERRÉ (ST.-JULIEN)* * * *

1985	C	85
1986	C	87

The 1985 Léoville-Poyferré has good color, a soft, round, fruity, medium-bodied feel on the palate, a toasty, new oaky bouquet, ripe, melted tannins, and a moderately long finish. The 1986 is tasting much better this year and seems potentially superior to the 1985, although one will have to exercise a bit of restraint, as it will not be ready to drink until the late nineties. It is quite powerful, deep in color, and very backward and tannic, but it does exhibit excellent depth of fruit.

LESTAGE (LISTRAC)* *

1985	A	77
1986	A	75

Both of these wines are light, commercial, fruity, and uncomplex; they are decent, but no better than many shipper's blends.

LIVERSAN (MÉDOC)* * *

1985	B	86
1986	B	85

Prince Guy de Polignac, an affable young man, is serious about the quality of wine in his well-placed vineyard, just behind the Pauillac appellation. The 1985 is an interesting wine, which exhibits a complex bouquet of new oak and plummy fruit. On the palate, the wine is deep, full bodied, admirably concentrated, and has a good lashing of tannin. The 1986 seems less stylish, obviously more tannic, but while rich and deep, it lacks zip and tastes a trifle dull. Given the meticulous attention to detail here, I suspect the 1986 may just be going through an awkward stage.

LA LOUVIÈRE (GRAVES)* * *

1985	B	85
1986	B	85

I find this estate's red and white wine to be terribly underrated, and therefore good values. The 1985 shows more structure than usual (somewhat surprising in view of the loose-knit character of the vintage), but it has generous portions of ripe, plummy, tobacco-scented and flavored fruit in a medium-bodied format. The 1986 should prove to be just as good, maybe even better. It is a soft wine for a 1986, but is rich in flavor, quite well made, deeply colored, and has a long, sweet, deep finish.

LYNCH-BAGES (PAUILLAC)* * * * *

1985		C	90
1986		C	90

Lynch-Bages has been on a hot streak since 1982, and both the 1985 and 1986 are among the finest wines of the vintage. The 1985 tastes as if it were a toned-down 1982. Dense ruby/purple in color, with a big, full-intensity bouquet of blackcurrant fruit and smoky oak, this corpulent, rich, intense, brawny wine has gobs of flavor and full body, and should mature nicely for 12–15 years. The 1986 may well turn out to be even better, but there is no question that it is far too tannic and backward to be enjoyed before the middle of the next decade. Black/ruby in color, this mammoth-sized wine has a dense, powerful structure, excruciatingly high levels of tannin, and super length.

LYNCH-MOUSSAS (PAUILLAC)*

1985		B	78
1986		B	77

This estate is owned and distributed by the *négociant* firm of Borie-Manoux. The wines tend to be rather light and early maturing, true for both vintages above. The 1985 is soft and fruity, but quite one-dimensional. The 1986 is much tougher and more tannic, but it, too, seems shy for the vintage.

MAGDELAINE (ST.-ÉMILION)* * * *

1985		D	86
1986		D	?

This Merlot-dominated wine (80% Merlot, 20% Cabernet Franc) normally requires 4–5 years after bottling to show well, a peculiarity of a number of the wines from the house of Jean-Pierre Moueix. Perhaps the 1985, which I thought to be better last year, is in an awkward stage. Moderately deep ruby with medium body, this ripe, stylish, fruity wine has good rather than great depth. It is stylish but a bit underwhelming. The 1986 has been consistently inconsistent. I have rated it between the low 80s and the low 90s. It is certainly quite tannic and powerful, but I am simply unsure of how much fruit is behind the tannin. Judgment reserved.

MALARTIC-LAGRAVIÈRE (GRAVES)* *

1985		C 84

Although I am very fond of the white wine made here, I think that the red wine, while technically flawless, lacks flesh and depth. The 1985 is very pleasant—ripe, modestly fruity, with a healthy dosage of new oak—but it has little length or grip.

MALESCASSE (MÉDOC)* * *

1985		B 85
1986		B 86

The Tesseron family (who is restoring the fortunes of Pontet-Canet and Lafon-Rochet) runs this Cru Bourgeois. Both the 1985 and 1986 look to be very good. The 1985 displays richness, deep color, medium to full body, and plenty of stuffing and length. The 1986 is extremely powerful and tannic, and if the requisite depth of fruit is present to balance out the tannins it could turn out to be better than the 1985. Both wines are excellent values.

MALESCOT ST.-EXUPÉRY (MARGAUX)* * *

1985		C 74

A dominating smell of leafy vegetation and new oak seems to obscure the depth of ripe fruit that this medium-bodied, rather compact wine may have. Some of my friends in Bordeaux have a good opinion of Malescot, but I have yet to taste a fine example of the 1985.

MARBUZET (ST.-ESTÈPHE)* * *

1985		B 85
1986		B 85

Marbuzet, the home and the entertainment center for foreign guests of the Prats family, is a separate vineyard, but has its wine blended with that of Cos d'Estournel not deemed special enough for the latter's château's primary label. The quality of Marbuzet has been increasing in the eighties. The 1985 is a deeply colored, juicy, intensely fruity wine that offers excellent ripeness, good body, and plenty of charm. The 1986 looks and tastes a bit more serious, as there is more power, tannin, and, I think, a trifle more depth.

CHÂTEAU MARGAUX (MARGAUX)* * * * *

1985	E	90
1986	E	99

No one is making better wine than Château Margaux. One easily senses the excitement among the staff here, as the commitment to excellence is unsurpassed. Although the 1985 is not in the same league as the 1982, 1983, or 1986, it is still a lovely, seductive, medium-bodied wine that has a gorgeous bouquet of toasty new oak, berry fruit, and violets. On the palate, it is not that concentrated when compared to the 1982, 1983 or 1986, but the balance is superb; it is to be hoped that this wine will evolve along the lines of the château's famous 1953. The 1986 is the most powerful, dense, concentrated, and tannic wine yet made under the Mentzelopoulos regime, and offers up an extraordinary level of extract and virtually perfect balance. However, as majestic and sublime as it is, I wonder how many buyers will wait the 15–20 years minimum for it to reach its apogee.

MARQUIS-DE-TERME (MARGAUX)* * * *

1985	C	88
1986	C	90

One of the least known and, until several years ago, most disappointing classified-growths of Margaux, Marquis-de-Terme has received an infusion of much-needed money to improve the cellars and put the wine in 50% new wood; the château has also instituted a stricter selection policy. The result is a 1985 that is showing better and better after bottling and a 1986 that is the finest wine made at this estate in 40–50 years. In 1987, the 1985 tasted unyielding and rustic, but now it is showing a great concentration of fruit, full body, a super finish, and considerable aging potential. It has turned out to be one of the best Margauxs of 1985. The 1986 is nearly black in color and very tannic, but has enormous richness and depth, and should prove to be sensational, provided one can wait for a decade.

MAUCAILLOU (MOULIS)* * *

1985	B	85

Of all the wines of Moulis, this one displays the most elegance and style, although it will never have the power and depth of a Chasse-

Spleen or Poujeaux. The 1985 is a stylish, rich, graceful wine with medium to full body, a perfumed, aromatic character, a long finish, and just enough tannins to ensure 5–8 years of longevity.

MAZERIS (CANON-FRONSAC)* * *

1985	B	89
1986	B	85

This vineyard has quite a few old vines, which produce a powerful, backward, rich wine with considerable aging potential. The 1985 is a sleeper of the vintage—very deep, rich, and full bodied, with sensational extract, a huge finish, and great promise. The 1986 also has that sublime intensity suggesting old vines, deep color, a powerful tannic, tough texture, and a very youthful, hard finish. It will need plenty of time to age.

MAZERIS BELLEVUE (CANON-FRONSAC)* *

1985	B	75
1986	B	84

This well-located property is producing wines that everyone tells me need 5–7 years to fully show their quality, largely because the percentage of Cabernet Sauvignon is quite high (nearly 50%). That being said, perhaps my ratings are a little conservative. The 1985 is too herbaceous—even vegetal—for my taste, but on the palate the wine does show good strength, body, and ripeness. The 1986 shows none of the vegetal character that intrudes on the 1985. It is a soft, medium- to full-bodied wine with good ripeness and a soft, well-balanced finish.

MEYNEY (ST.-ESTÈPHE)* * *

1985	B	88
1986	B	90

The Cordier wines continue to demonstrate brilliance under the direction of Georges Pauli. Furthermore, the Cordiers are among the minority of producers in Bordeaux who have kept a rein on prices, and their wines are still some of the best values in all of France. Both of these vintages of Meyney may well surpass the fine 1982 made here. The 1985 is surprisingly rich, ripe, supple—even voluptuous—for such a young Meyney, normally a slow, stubborn wine to mature. A crushed blackcurrant bouquet, elegantly wrought flavors, and excellent length all combine to make this one of the finest bargains and wines of the vintage. The 1986 is a huge, powerful, black/purple-colored wine with enormous extract and even greater depth and concentration than the 1982, plus additional tannins. It will need plenty of cellaring, but the necessary balance of fruit is present.

LA MISSION-HAUT-BRION (GRAVES)* * * * *

1985	E 88
1986	E 90

These two wines are the last La Missions to have been made in the old winery that possessed the small, squat cuves originally installed by the late winemaking genius Henri Woltner. The 1987, one of the few stars of that vintage, was made in a state-of-the-art wine cellar designed by Jean Delmas. The 1985 La Mission-Haut-Brion is a rich, ripe, smooth, and flavorful wine with oodles of berry fruit, toasty new oak, and a full-bodied, fleshy texture. It will drink well young. The 1986 does not have the complexity of Haut-Brion, but does share the enormous power and density that are characteristic of this vintage. Long, rich, deep ruby/purple, this is a very muscular, rich, full-bodied La Mission. For me, it is the first wine made under the new owners to fully express the personality of La Mission-Haut-Brion.

MONBRISON (MARGAUX)* * *

1985	B 86
1986	B 87

Monbrison, run by the Davis family of the United States, has been consistently singled out by me as one of the up-and-coming Cru Bourgeois estates in the Médoc. There is a commitment to quality here, a second label (Cordat), and the use of new barrels; the result is a rich, supple, well-structured wine that is better than many of the more famous classified-growths. The 1985 is rich and full, but nicely balances its deep fruit with an elegant bouquet of spicy oak and berries. On the palate, it is soft, creamy, and already tasty. The 1986 is clearly a more powerful and richer wine, with a ruby/purple color, deep flavors, full body, and quite a bit of tannin in the finish. It will age very well and is a sleeper of the vintage.

MONTROSE (ST.-ESTÈPHE)* * * *

1985	C	85
1986	C	90

The 1985 Montrose has an elevated amount of Merlot (40%) and therefore tastes surprisingly soft, elegant, and actually ready to drink. It is a far cry from the behemoth wines fashioned at this estate in the fifties and sixties; it continues in the lighter, commercial style that this estate began to develop with the 1978 vintage. It is a good but not a great Montrose. On the other hand, the 1986, whether due to the vintage or to Mr. Charmolue's decision to return to the big brawny wines of years past, is the finest Montrose since the great years of 1961, 1959, and 1953. The 1986 Montrose is vast and intense on the palate, with a deep, full-bodied, chewy texture, super length, and a superb sweetness of fruit.

MOULIN DU CADET (ST.-ÉMILION)* *

1985	B	78
1986	B	82

The famous firm of Jean-Pierre Moueix just purchased this 11-acre estate, so one can certainly expect to see some changes (for the better) with respect to the wines. The 1985 is dull and uninteresting. The 1986 is fruity, well made, elegant and tasty, but will have to be drunk over the next 4–5 years.

MOULIN HAUT-LAROQUE (FRONSAC)* * *

1985	B	87
1986	B	87

In March 1988, proprietor Jean-Noël Hervé served a 1918 and 1929 Moulin Haut-Laroque (not re-corked) to prove the aging potential of the wines of this soon-to-be-famous appellation. The 1918 was quite fragile, with some volatile acidity, but the 1929 was splendidly rich and deep, and in much better condition than many of the more famous Médocs from what was probably the true vintage of the century for Bordeaux. This is a very seriously run property, and the supple, fat, rich, and deeply flavored 1985 has plenty of extract and body, as well as complexity. The 1986 also has deep fruit, firmer tannins, more acidity, but also a rich, long finish and good aging potential.

MOULIN PEZ-LABRIE (CANON-FRONSAC)* *

1985	B	82
1986	B	?

This is a very tough style of Canon-Fronsac with plenty of color and body, but gobs of hard tannins and a severe, stern personality. The wines seem to lack charm and fat, but should age well given their high acid and tannin levels. The 1986 tasted impossibly high in tannins, making a realistic appraisal impossible.

MOULIN ROUGE (MÉDOC)* * *

1985	B	87
1986	B	86

Over the last several years, I have become increasingly enamored of the wines from this estate, which shares the same name as the famous nightclub in the Pigalle section of Paris. The 1985 is a sleeper of the vintage, with very rich, deep, intense flavors, surprisingly good structure for a 1985, full body, and a luxurious texture filled with ripe fruit. It is delicious to drink now, but should age well for another 5–6 years. The 1986 avoids the hard tannins so common with the wines of this vintage and also offers up sumptuous amounts of berry fruit in a full-bodied format. It should be as good as the 1985, but for now the latter wine is showing extremely well.

MOULIN À VENT (MOULIS)* * *

1985	B	85
1986	B	85

This is another up-and-coming estate in Moulis that should merit increasingly more attention from consumers looking for complex, age-worthy wines at realistic prices. Both the 1985 and 1986 are deeply colored, dense, rich, full-bodied wines that offer more brute force than finesse, but are concentrated and age-worthy.

MOULINET (POMEROL)*

1985	B	82

1986	B	79

As Moulinet's vineyard sits on rather light, sandy soil, its wines tend to lack the depth and richness of many Pomerols. The 1985 is an above-average wine with a soft, somewhat obvious, commercial fruitiness, medium body, but agreeable, ripe, easy-to-appreciate and easy-to-understand flavors. The 1986 is a more narrowly built wine, with an austere personality and good tannins, but less charm and appeal.

MOUTON-BARONNE-PHILIPPE (PAUILLAC)* * *

1985	C	86

1986	C	87

This property has benefited from the efforts of administrator Philippe Cottin and winemaker Patrick Léon to raise the quality of all the late Baron Philippe de Rothschild's estates. The 1985 is a creamy textured, fat, lush, lovely wine with a seductive, rich fruitiness, precocious personality and low acidity; it is gorgeous for drinking over the next decade. The 1986 is the best Mouton-Baronne-Philippe that I have ever tasted. More powerful and dense than usual, this dark, ruby-colored wine has excellent color, full body, and plenty of mouth-searing tannins.

MOUTON-ROTHSCHILD (PAUILLAC)* * * * *

1985	E	92

1986	E	99

For now, both Margaux and Mouton-Rothschild seem to be pushing their aspirations for high quality to the maximum. Both have surpassed Lafite-Rothschild and Latour in this decade. Mouton-Rothschild has an impeccable record of brilliance that started with the legendary 1982. The 1985 that they now compare with the 1959 is to me more akin to their 1953. The rich, complex bouquet of Oriental spices, toasty oak, and ripe fruit is wonderful. On the palate, the wine is very rich and forward, but long and sexy, and should be at its best between 1993 and 2010. It is clearly the best first-growth in the Médoc in 1985. The 1986 looks to be another legend in the making. While it may not have quite the overwhelming intensity of the 1982, it is a compelling wine in every sense. The black/ruby color, the extraordinary perfume of Oriental spices, ripe fruit and oak, the layers of concentrated fruit, the length, the balance are—well—nearly perfect. This wine is quite tannic, but the requisite depth of fruit will easily outlive the tannins. This is an exemplary effort that should prove to be one of the great wines of our generation. However, it is sad that the architect behind Mouton-Rothschild, Baron Philippe de Rothschild, died at the age of 86 in January 1988.

NENIN (POMEROL)* * *

1985	C	84
1986	C	83

Between 1976 and 1983, Nenin's approach to winemaking was casual and, as a result, the wines suffered. Now a serious effort is being made to improve the quality. Both the 1985 and the 1986 show good fruit, richness, and fine winemaking. These are not blockbuster Pomerols, but, rather, charming, supple, fruity, medium-bodied wines with attractive, open-knit personalities. The 1985 has slightly more depth than the 1986.

LES-ORMES-DE-PEZ (ST.-ESTÈPHE)* * *

1985	B	83
1986	B	86

The 1985 has turned out to be an agreeable, soft, pleasant, fruity wine without a great deal of depth; it can be drunk up immediately. The 1986 appears altogether more substantial and serious, quite full, deep and, like all of the 1986 Médocs, rather tannic. This is an estate to search out for top Bordeaux values.

LES ORMES-SORBET (MÉDOC)* * *

1985	B	86
1986	B	85

This Cru Bourgeois has dramatically turned things around and is now producing stylish and delicious wines. The 1985 is showing a healthy dosage of spicy new oak, a rich, velvety texture oozing with ripe, berry fruit, medium body, fine balance, and another 7–8 years of cellaring potential. The 1986 is equally as good, perhaps even deeper, but the tannins are also much more aggressive and the wine is fuller bodied.

PALMER (MARGAUX)* * * * *

1985	D	87
1986	D	88

Palmer is the perfect synthesis between the elegant, stylish, perfumed style of Margaux and the plump, succulent, fleshy wines of Pomerol (a result of a very elevated percentage of Merlot, 40%). Of the château's wines in this decade, only the 1983 looks to be extra-special, and one must ask why the 1981, 1982 and 1985, while good, have not been up to previous standards. I have a theory, which I believe is the same reason why Latour has slipped in quality since 1983. A look at the production figures for Palmer during this decade shows a huge increase in the amount of wine made per acre, and the modest cellars at Palmer do not appear large enough to hold these huge crops. Consequently, I suspect the wines are being pulled out of their fermentation tanks too soon so that the next batch of grapes can be put in. The 1985 is a very good wine, but it shows a little dilution in its mid-range (the expression in French is *un peu liquide*). Deep in color, with a moderately attractive bouquet of jammy fruit and oak, this is a stylish wine with a good finish. By Bordeaux standards it is very good, but by the standards of Palmer in the sixties and seventies it is not exciting. The 1986 is, however, showing depth from start to finish and more structure than any Palmer since 1975. Deep ruby, with a perfumed bouquet, this ripe, concentrated, fleshy wine has plenty of length and excellent aging potential. I still prefer the 1983, but this is the second-best Palmer of the decade.

PAPE-CLÉMENT (GRAVES)* * *

1985	C	87
1986	C	90

After a wretched period of poor performances between 1976 and 1983 (I noted that the musty, poor 1981 was recently served at a Reagan White House dinner), Pape-Clément has rebounded with a very good 1985 and a great 1986. The 1985, the best Pape-Clément since the 1975, is a fragrant, supple, tasty wine with a great deal of finesse and charm. Deeply concentrated, medium bodied, long and complex, it should be at its best between 1990 and 2000. The 1986, which I had initially judged to be good, not great, was tasted four times in March 1988 with similar ecstatic results. It is the greatest Pape-Clément since the 1961. A huge, textbook Graves bouquet is followed by a wine that is both powerful and elegant, fabulously concentrated, rich, and extra-special. The 1986 Pape-Clément is a watershed, historic vintage.

PATACHE D'AUX (MÉDOC)* * *

1985	A	79
1986	A	85

Regardless of vintage, this wine seems to offer up a very Californian bouquet of intense, weedy, herbaceous, blackcurrant fruit. The 1985 is a little diluted and just too weedy, but soft and ideal for drinking over the next 2–4 years. The 1986 is the finest Patache d'Aux since the lovely 1982 and 1970. The vegetal, weedy character is nonexistent and the wine is rich, full bodied, powerful, and concentrated. It also has 10–12 years worth of aging potential.

PAVIE (ST.-ÉMILION)* * *

1985	C	86
1986	C	90

Pavie is clearly on the upswing in terms of quality, as proprietor Jean-Claude Valette and his son have continued to make improvements in their wine. The 1985 is firm, tannic, and unyielding, particularly for a wine from this vintage. Deep in color, ripe, medium bodied, but needing time, this wine will provide graceful drinking if cellared. The 1986 is the finest Pavie since the 1982, and should turn out to be even better. It is deep in color, extremely tannic, but packed with fruit and richness. This is a very impressive Pavie, and one of the stars of St.-Émilion in 1986.

PAVIE-DECESSE (ST.-ÉMILION)* * *

1985	B	88
1986	B	86

The 1985 Pavie-Decesse has turned out to be even better than Pavie. Very deep in color, with an intense aroma of blackcurrant fruit, toasty oak and tarlike scents, this rich, long, very big and structured wine has loads of fruits that is tightly bound in a full-bodied format. It should be a very long aged 1985. The 1986 is also impressive, but less so than the 1985. Dark ruby, rich, long, deep, but less structured, the 1986 should be at its best between 1991 and 2000.

PAVILLON ROUGE DE MARGAUX (MARGAUX)* * * *

1985	C	85
1986	C	89

At present, Pavillon Rouge, the second wine of Château Margaux, is the finest among Bordeaux's *deuxièmes marques* (second labels). The 1985 reflects the very severe selection process that was employed by the château that year. It has a lovely perfume of berry fruit and is quite supple, smooth, and ideal for drinking over the next 5–6 years. In contrast, the 1986 is surprisingly powerful, backward, intense, and will no doubt last for 7–12 years.

PETIT-VILLAGE (POMEROL)* * *

1985	C	88
1986	C	86

Bruno Prats, the highly competent and respected owner of Château Cos d'Estournel in the Médoc, makes wines of excellent quality at his estate in Pomerol. The style here stresses gobs of ripe, rich, opulent blackberry, plummy fruit wrapped in smoky, toasty, vanillin oak. The 1985 offers irresistible suppleness and should drink well for another 5–7 years. The 1986 is similarly expensive and round on the palate, but finishes with less fruit and more tannin.

PÉTRUS (POMEROL)* * * *

1985	E	95
1986	E	93

Pétrus, the darling of wine speculators, made a splendid wine in 1985, but I do not believe that it is superior to L'Evangile or L'Eglise Clinet. Of the relatively recent vintages of Pétrus, the 1961, 1964, 1975 and

1982 are superior to the 1985, which is now quite closed and firm, and cannot be fully appreciated yet. Contrary to what most observers think, Pétrus is always the most difficult of all the top first-growths to drink young despite its nearly 100% Merlot content. Many enthusiasts falsely assume that Pétrus is easy to drink young because of all the Merlot. The 1985 is dense in color, very rich and broodingly deep; it has gobs of extract and tannin, and a heady finish. The 1986 has hardly evolved at all since I first tasted it in 1987. It is a huge, dense, very powerful Pétrus with a hefty amount of tannins. Clearly it is the most backward vintage of Pétrus since 1975 and should last for 25–30 years.

PEY LABRIE (FRONSAC)* *

1985	A	?

1986	A	85

The 1985 has performed inconsistently since I first tasted it in March, 1986. In 1987 it showed excellent depth and length, but from the bottle it tasted musty and off. Judgment reserved. The 1986 has huge fruit and color but also mouth-searing tannin, a brooding personality, and a long finish. It will need plenty of time.

PICHON LONGUEVILLE BARON DE PICHON LONGUEVILLE (PAUILLAC)* * *

1985	C	83

1986	C	88

Since 1987, the wine of Pichon Baron has been made by Jean-Michel Cazes and his competent staff at Lynch-Bages. Given the excellence of this vineyard, its wine will soon be one to watch. Previously, Pichon Baron had a very patchy record. The 1985 is fruity, and agreeable but diffuse and a bit unstructured. The 1986 is one of the best wines from this perennial underachiever in years. Deep black/ruby in color, fragrant, rich, long and intense, this beefy, brawny wine has plenty of tannin and should be at its best between 1991 and 2005.

PICHON-LONGUEVILLE, COMTESSE DE LALANDE (PAUILLAC)* * * *

1985	D	90

1986	D	97

I appear to have slightly overrated the 1985 Pichon Lalande based on my earlier cask tastings. It is an outstanding wine, but having tasted it three times from the bottle, I did not think it to be at the same level of quality as the 1986, 1983, 1982, or 1978. In actuality, it has more aging potential than the 1984, but is no more delicious than that lovely wine. The 1985 has a deep ruby color and a ripe, oaky, curranty bouquet with a trace of herbaceousness. On the palate, the wine is rich, elegant, supple, and not dissimilar from the style of either the 1979 or 1981. It is a lovely wine. The 1986 is fabulous and one of the three greatest wines of that vintage. Black/ruby with an astonishing level of richness and a bouquet of remarkable dimensions, the depth and length of this wine just go on and on. It would appear to be even better than the great 1982 made there.

PICQUE CAILLOU (GRAVES)* * *

1985	B	86
1986	B	86

This vineyard, the only one near Bordeaux's airport at Merignac, has been making very stylish wines of late that are very reasonably priced and ready to drink upon release. The 1986 shows the use of some new oak barrels, a generous, supple, tobacco-and-berry-fruit-laden taste, soft tannins (surprisingly so for a 1986), and a smooth finish. The 1985 is similarly seductive as a result of its juicy cherry fruit, medium body, pleasing ripeness and creamy, lush texture.

LE PIN (POMEROL)* * * * *

1985	E	90
1986	E	91

This micro-estate, the jewel of the Thienpont family, has developed quite a cult following. Made from 100% Merlot and aged in 100% new oak, Le Pin is the most exotic wine of Pomerol. If you missed the otherworldly 1982 made here, there may still be a chance to latch onto some 1985 and 1986. The 1985 is more forward, with a deep ruby color and full-throttle bouquet of sweet, ripe berry fruit, toffee, and toasty oak. On the palate, the wine has a lavish texture, unctuous flavors, and a ripe, sweet, fleshy finish. The 1986 is definitely less flattering to taste, but may well outlive the 1985 by 5–10 years. Deep in color, with Le Pin's characteristic exotic, toasty, oaky nose, this wine is deeply concentrated and more powerful and tannic than usual, but intense and quite special.

DE PITRAY (CÔTES DE CASTILLON)* * *

1985	A	86

1986	A	85

This is the leading estate of the Côtes de Castillon, and I am very fond of the 1985–an opulent, richly fruity, supple wine that competes favorably with wines costing four times as much. The 1986 is also very good, but the tannins are more noticeable; ideally, I would cellar it for 1–2 years before drinking. It is just as concentrated as the 1985 and should keep well for 5–7 years.

PLAGNAC (MÉDOC)* * *

1985	A	84

1986	A	84

One of the properties within the Cordier stable, Plagnac is frequently a well-made wine and a very fine value. The 1985 has a moderately intense, herbaceous blackcurrant-scented bouquet, medium body, and soft, plump, fruity flavors. The 1986 is very spicy, a trifle more tannic, but also deeper and richer.

PLINCE (POMEROL)* *

1985	C	84

1986	C	82

Although this is not the most well-situated estate, located near Nenin on light, sandy soil, it seems that Plince does the best it can given its location. The 1985 is a very ripe, succulent, plump wine with a fat, full-bodied texture, low acidity, low tannins, and a tasty finish. The 1986 is equally forward, spicy, ripe, and medium bodied, but while tasty, lacks a certain complexity and finesse.

LA POINTE (POMEROL)* *

1985	C	83

1986	C 84

La Pointe is a minor Pomerol winery that has benefited from the advice of famous oenologist Michel Rolland. Despite a *terroir* that is not one of the most desirable, the wine has improved considerably in recent years. The 1985 is quite light, but well balanced, richly fruity, and medium bodied; it is an agreeable luncheon or picnic wine. The 1986 may be the best La Pointe in years. Spicy, with an attractive, plummy fruitiness, medium body and good finish, it will provide easy and pleasurable drinking early on.

PONTET-CANET (PAUILLAC)* * *

1985	C 86

1986	C 88

The Tesseron family is making tremendous strides at Pontet-Canet, the lovely château that sits among a group of trees opposite the entrance to Mouton-Rothschild. The 1985 is very good and well colored, with a moderately intense blackcurrant, toasty oak bouquet. Slightly less impressive now than from the cask, this elegant, tasty, stylish wine will evolve nicely and is one of the best Pontet-Canets in years. The 1986 is even denser and fuller, with an opaque color and mouth-shattering tannins, and is quite intense and powerful. It will be very slow to develop.

POTENSAC (MÉDOC)* * *

1985	B 85

1986	B 86

Michel Delon, the conscientious owner of Léoville-Las Cases, also makes this wine, which is usually one of the finest of the Cru Bourgeois. The 1985 is a lovely, elegant, supple wine imbued with a good measure of blackcurrant fruit, a deft touch of spicy oak, medium body, fine length, and 7–8 more years of drinkability. The 1986 is more tannic and much firmer, and while less fat and charming to drink now, has plenty of depth and richness. However, it needs some cellaring.

POUJEAUX (MOULIS)* * *

1985	B 87

1986	B 90

This has always been an excellent wine, clearly on a par with a number of the Médoc classified-growths. The 1985 is a lush, rich, full-bodied wine with a good lashing of tannin in the finish. It should age well for 10–15 years. The proprietors, the diminutive Theils, rank it the best Poujeaux made since the 1982 and the 1986. As for the 1986, it was aged in 60% new oak and is a dense, powerful, rich, tannic, full-bodied wine that can be cellared for 10–12 years. It is one of the great bargains and sleepers of the 1986 vintage.

PRIEURÉ-LICHINE (MARGAUX)* * * *

1985	C 84

1986	C 89

Alexis Lichine, who has done so much to promote the benefits of wine-drinking in the United States, has just celebrated his thirty-sixth vintage at his beloved Prieuré-Lichine. His thirty-fifth vintage, the 1986, is, I believe, his finest wine in over two decades. It is certainly much more impressive than the lightish, somewhat shallow 1985, which, while charming and fruity, lacks some grip and depth, particularly for a classified-growth. The 1986 (which has a modified new label to celebrate the thirty-fifth harvest) is rich, deep, very complex, and quite concentrated and long. Surprisingly deep in color for a Lichine, this amply endowed wine should age as graciously as Mr. Lichine has. It appears to be the finest wine made at Prieuré-Lichine since 1978.

PUY BLANQUET (ST.-ÉMILION)* *

1985	C ?

1986	C 74

The 1985 tasted quite awkward and not quite right. Judgment reserved. The 1986 has good color but a very hard, tannic finish that seems to overwhelm the meager amount of fruit.

RAMAGE LA BÂTISSE (HAUT-MÉDOC)* *

1985	A 78

1986	A 77

This Cru Bourgeois has recently been purchased by a French insurance company, and it is to be hoped that the undernourished, emaciated style of wine that has been made here in recent years will take on some weight. The 1985 is showing adequate fruit and some attractive scents of new oak, but it lacks the smooth, ripe charm of most 1985s. The 1986 is quite tannic, but shows some decent ripeness, medium body, and an adequate finish.

RAUSAN-GASSIES (MARGAUX)* * *

1985	C	84
1986	C	86

More like a St.-Estèphe than a Margaux, this wine is always somewhat burly, tough, and tannic, yet concentrated and deep, offering chewy, meaty flavors rather than finesse and elegance. The 1985 should be drunk over the next 5–6 years; the 1986 should be cellared 5–6 years before drinking.

RAUSAN-SÉGLA (MARGAUX)* * *

1985	C	85
1986	C	89

Rausan-Ségla has one of the finest vineyards in Médoc and a lofty reputation based on the 1855 classification in which it was rated just behind all the first-growths and Mouton-Rothschild. The years 1961–1981 were not kind to this estate, which had lacked proper management and direction. However, since 1983 the wine has generally been in top form. The 1985 showed wide variation prior to bottling and now seems richly fruity, supple, and precocious. If it lacks a little structure and aging potential, there can be no doubt that the wine will offer delicious drinking for the next 6–7 years. The 1986 is much more concentrated and powerful, with plenty of tannin, excellent depth and length, medium to full body, and an aromatic bouquet. It appears to be the finest Rausan-Ségla in over three decades.

LA RIVIÈRE (FRONSAC)* *

1985	B	84

This vast estate in Fronsac, with its splendid château and endless miles of deep caves, should be visited by tourists to the region. The quality of the wine varies a bit, but in good Merlot years the wine is plump, ripe, and pleasant, although somewhat rustic. The 1985 will offer delightful drinking for 5–6 more years.

ROCHER BELLEVUE FIGEAC (ST.-ÉMILION)* * *

1985	B 89

Rocher Bellevue Figeac is clearly one of the sleepers of the vintage. Deep ruby/purple in color, this lush, voluptuous, full-bodied wine has an intense bouquet of ripe plums, blackberries, and oak. It is exceptionally concentrated, rich, supple and velvety, and should age gracefully for 6–10 years. It reminds me of the very fine 1982 and 1983 La Grave Figeac.

ROUDIER (MONTAGNE-ST.-ÉMILION)* * *

1985	A 85
1986	A 85

The underrated château of Roudier is an excellent source for rich, beefy, full-bodied, concentrated wines that are bargain-priced. Both the 1985 and 1986 may be a little short on finesse and elegance, but for an extroverted, muscular, chewy mouthful of claret, they are pleasing to both the palate and the purse.

ROUET (FRONSAC)* * *

1985	A 84

Rouet, the estate of the ebullient, baritone-voiced Patrick Danglade, produces soft, delicious, fruity, plump wines that offer immediate gratification. The 1985 is elegant, medium bodied, juicy, and quite tasty.

ROUGET (POMEROL)* * *

1985	C 84
1986	C 82

Rouget tends to be a hard, tannic, slow-to-mature Pomerol made in a rather old style with quite a bit of the coarse press wine added in, as well as aged in old casks. The 1985 showed considerably better from the cask, but after bottling, the wine has gone into a shell. It has a good ruby color, but its charm and depth are concealed behind a wall of rustic tannins. By 1985 standards, it is tough and backward. The 1986 seems more precocious and oriented in the direction of a softer, fruitier, more modern style. The tannins are less obtrusive and the fruit is clean and supple.

ROULLET (CANON-FRONSAC)* *

1985	B	79
1986	B	76

Neither of these vintages of Roullet is a particularly inspired example of the wines of Canon-Fronsac. The 1985 is soft, simple, and fruity, and should be drunk over the next 2–3 years. The 1986 is adequately fruity and medium bodied, but essentially one-dimensional and compact.

ROUMAGNAC LA MARÉCHALE (FRONSAC)* *

1985	B	84
1986	B	79

I prefer the 1985 because of its generous, ripe, plummy fruitiness, good tannins, and overall sense of balance. The 1986 has an attractive perfume of cherry fruit, but comes across on the palate as one-dimensional and simple.

ROUSSELLE (FRONSAC)* *

1986	B	85

I have not tasted the 1985, but the 1986 clearly exhibited rich, sweet, ripe fruit, full body, considerable power and tannin, and excellent aging potential.

LE SABLARD DU GRAND MAINE (LALANDE-DE-POMEROL)*

1985	B	75
1986	B	74

Both vintages of this Lalande-de-Pomerol are four-square, innocuous, rather bland wines that should be consumed over the next 1–2 years.

ST.-BONNET (MÉDOC)*

1985	A	67
1986	A	?

In the sixties, seventies, and early eighties, this property was known by Bordeaux lovers for its good wines at very low prices. Since 1983, the quality appears to have deteriorated badly, and recent vintages have been flawed by the smell of what appears to be old musty barrels in the wine cellar. The 1985 and, even more so, the 1986 suffer inexcusably from this problem. What a shame!

ST.-PIERRE-SEVAISTRE (ST.-JULIEN)* * *

1985	C	87
1986	C	90

I am certainly remiss in not giving this impeccably made, usually fairly priced wine more attention. I suspect it is because there are so many outstanding wines in St.-Julien, and perhaps because I always taste this one at a *négociant*'s office rather than *au château*. My tasting notes for the last year noted that the 1985 is showing better from the bottle than from cask samples. Typically rich, chewy, fat, and deep, with just the right amount of new oak, the 1985 St.-Pierre reminds me of the fine 1981 made here. The 1986 has gobs of rich, dense, sweet fruit, an opaque dark ruby color, powerful, full-bodied palate impression, and a long, rich finish. It is not as hard and tannic as some 1986s. Given the realistic—even modest—pricing policy of this property, both of these wines merit considerable interest.

DE SALES (POMEROL)* * *

1985	B	83
1986	B	81

While rarely a profound Pomerol, de Sales is made in a style that offers immediate drinkability and, in top vintages, 5–8 years of cellaring potential. The 1982 is the best recent example and is now in full bloom. Both of these vintages are very soft, easygoing, supple, fruity wines that are meant to be drunk young. The 1986 has less depth than the 1985, which could use more grip and length, but for uncomplicated drinking at a decent price, it is hard to beat.

SÉGUR (HAUT-MÉDOC)* *

1985	A	80
1985 (cuvée aged in new oak)	A	85
1986	A	76
1986 (cuvée aged in new oak)	A	86

This Cru Bourgeois has begun to produce a special cuvée that is aged in new oak barrels. The differences are remarkable. In both vintages, the special cuvée displays far greater color, ripeness, richness, depth, and aging potential. In fact, the 1986 special cuvée bears a striking resemblance to the decadently rich wines of Mr. DuBoscq's Château Haut-Marbuzet. For the difference in price, I would opt for the oak-aged wine any day.

SIRAN (MARGAUX)* * *

1985	C	86
1986	C	87

Siran, a showpiece property, is run with great attention to detail by a member of Bordeaux's famous Miailhe family, who has interests in various other châteaux, most notably Pichon-Lalande and Palmer. I have consistently liked the 1985 and 1986 vintages, but the price is rather high for a Cru Bourgeois. The 1985 is surprisingly powerful for the vintage—rich in fruit, elegant, long and aromatic; it should age well for 8–10 years. The 1986 is also an impressive wine with a black/ruby color, full body, plenty of mouth-watering tannins, and excellent length. It is less open and fat than the 1985, but may ultimately have more depth and richness.

SOCIANDO-MALLET (HAUT-MÉDOC)* * * *

1985	B	90
1986	B	92

Sociando-Mallet is making wine that is closest in quality to a second-growth Médoc. The problem here is that the proprietor, Jean Gautreau, believes in making wine for drinking in 20–30 years, not tomorrow. His 1973 and 1976 are likely to turn out to be the longest-lived and among the top half dozen wines of these two quick-maturing vintages. His greatest wines to date have been his 1982, followed by the 1986 and 1985. The 1985 is a typically dense ruby/purple, has a rich, blackcurrant classic Médoc bouquet, full body, and sensational concentration and balance. The 1986 is an enormously rich, full wine that is imbued with so much intensity, power, and tannin that I wonder if it will be drinkable before the turn of the century.

SOUDARS (HAUT-MÉDOC)* * *

1985	A	85
1986	A	84

Soudars produces the kind of wine that is very easy to taste and appreciate. The plump, fat, fruity, soft, full-bodied wines that are made here can be drunk young or aged 5–10 years. The 1985 has the vintage's suppleness and ripe fruit, shows good concentration, low acidity, and a very satisfying finish. The 1986 is very similarly styled, but as one would expect, there is more tannin present, and the type of tannin is harder.

SOUTARD (ST.-ÉMILION)* * *

1985	C	90
1986	C	87

It is an axiom in Bordeaux that a château's proprietor gets all of the credit for a successful wine. Yet, a number of talented cellar masters who are behind the scenes are probably just as responsible for a wine's success. At Pichon-Lalande there is Mr. Godin; at Gruaud-Larose, Talbot, and Meyney, Mr. Pauli; at L'Evangile, Mr. Rolland; and at L'Arrosée and Soutard, Mr. Oiseau. Soutard aims for classic, long-lived wines of power and richness. The 1985 is a sensationally rich, tannic, deep, multidimensional wine that balances muscle and grace; it should age well for two decades. The 1986 is even more tannic, but is also very rich, deep, concentrated, powerful, and quite age-worthy.

TAILLEFER (POMEROL)* *

1985	C 76
1986	C 73

Neither of these two vintages of Taillefer inspires much enthusiasm. Compared to other Pomerols, these two wines lack depth to their color, have an undernourished feel to them, and taste quite light and commercial.

TALBOT (ST.-JULIEN)* * * *

1985	C 89
1986	C 91

Talbot, a model of consistency and value, must always stand in the gigantic shadow of its neighbor, Gruaud-Larose (both are owned by the Cordier family). Talbot is not as powerful or tannic as the beefy Gruaud-Larose and usually matures a good 3–5 years earlier. The 1985 is a down-sized version of the 1982 and is quite good to taste and drink. Very deep in color, with a ripe, rich, berrylike fragrance, this supple, fleshy, medium-bodied wine has loads of fruit, a smooth, graceful finish, and excellent balance. The 1986 is quite simply the finest Talbot I have ever tasted (perhaps a magnum I once drank in 1945 was as good). Deeper, than the 1982, and more classically structured, with the depth and length of a great wine from a great year, the 1986 Talbot is indeed superb.

TAYAC PRESTIGE (CÔTES DE BOURG)* * * *

1982	B 88

The leading estate in the Côtes de Bourg, Tayac produces several cuvées of good wine, but the top wine is always the Cuvée Prestige. The 1982 is drinking beautifully, showing a huge, lush berry fruitiness, long, opulent flavors, and excellent length.

LES TEMPLIERS (LALANDE-DE-POMEROL)*

1985	73
1986	74

Of these two very mediocre wines, the 1985 is supple, but dull and diluted; the 1986 is also very simple and one-dimensional.

LA TERRASSE (CÔTES DE CASTILLON)* *

1985	A 83
1986	A 82

La Terrasse is a fine wine to explore when looking for one that is easy to drink, fruity, soft, and inexpensive. The quality here has been consistent in the eighties, and both the 1985 and 1986 have a pleasing, spicy, soft, fruity personality; both should be drunk over the next 1–2 years.

TERREY-GROS-CAILLOUX (ST.-JULIEN)* * *

1985	B 85
1986	B 86

This Cru Bourgeois is consistently well made and is known for its plump, fleshy, chunky style of St.-Julien that is short on finesse but not flavor. Both vintages are close in style. The 1985 is rich, ripe, sweet, low in acidity, meaty, and quite tasty. My notes for the 1986 read nearly the same—a sweet, ripe, deep, four-square wine with gobs of roasted fruit, but more tannin.

DU TERTRE (MARGAUX)* * *

1985	C ?
1986	C 87

I have tasted the 1985 seven times, five from cask and twice from the bottle, and I have never seen a wine behave so differently. My scores range from slightly above average to outstanding. This type of bottle variation is very rare in Bordeaux. Judgment reserved. The 1986 has consistently proven to be rich, powerful, long, and concentrated, with enough tannins to carry it 10–15 years, perhaps longer. Furthermore, the wine has the requisite depth of fruit to stand up to the vintage's strong, aggressive tannins.

TERTRE-DAUGAY (ST.-ÉMILION)* * *

1985	C 85

The owner of La Gaffelière has spared no expense in restoring this property, which is beginning to show signs of turning out excellent St.-Émilions. The 1985 offers up succulent fruit, plenty of toasty oak, a meaty, chewy texture, and a long, velvety finish.

LE TERTRE ROTEBOEUF (ST.-ÉMILION)* * * *

1985	B	90
1986	B	90

The Pétrus of St.-Émilion? Mr. Mitjaville, thin and intense, is as passionate a winemaker as I have ever met, and his splendidly situated 12-acre vineyard, planted with 80% Merlot and 20% Cabernet Franc, is turning out some dazzling wines. He has begun using new oak (50% in 1985 and 100% in 1986), a much-needed component to these full-throttle, exceptionally rich, expressive wines. The 1985 has an astonishing level of richness, a perfume that is reminiscent of a wine costing 3–4 times as much, a full body, an opulent texture that recalls a great 1982, and a taste that is first-class and quite remarkable. The 1986 is equally prodigious and has a fascinating bouquet of roasted cassis and smoky oak. Powerful, rich, and multidimensional, this superb wine should drink well for 10–12 years.

LA TONNELLE (CÔTES DE BLAYE)* * *

1985	A	82
1986	A	80

La Tonnelle is a name to search out when looking for soft, agreeably fruity wines that require being drunk up within 2–4 years of the vintage.

LA TOUR-CARNET (HAUT-MÉDOC)* *

1986	C	85

This fourth-grown is now trying to regain some of its lost prestige. The 1986 looks rich, full, concentrated, and among the more impressive wines to come from this château in some time.

LA TOUR-HAUT-BRION (GRAVES)* * * *

1985	C	84

1986   C   86

Under the château's new owners, the Dillon family, and their manager, Jean Delmas, this wine is no longer the second wine of La
Mission-Haut-Brion, but is made from its own vineyard, which is curiously 100% Cabernet Sauvignon. The 1985 is good but a little short,
a trifle too tannic for the amount of fruit present, and lacks length and
excitement. The 1986 is much richer, very fruity, and softer than
many wines of this aggressive vintage, but long and stylish.

LA TOUR-DE-MONS (MARGAUX)* * *

1985   B   75

1986   B   86

In the forties, fifties, and early sixties, this Cru Bourgeois had an
excellent reputation and was considered by members of the wine trade
to be the equivalent of a classified-growth. Recently the property has
been in decline, and the 1985 shows the effects of a wine that has not
been given the proper care. It is adequate, but rustic and tough in
style. Fortunately, the 1986 is a complete reversal of past form. The
deep, dense color, the intense bouquet of smoky oak and vanillin from
new wood, the rich, concentrated feeling on the palate, and deep,
well-balanced finish suggest that this well-placed vineyard has returned to form.

LA TOUR ST.-BONNET (MÉDOC)* * *

1985   B   85

1986   B   84

For over a decade I have enjoyed the well-made wines from this Cru
Bourgeois in the northern Médoc. The wines always seem to have
excellent color, plenty of ripeness, and a full-flavored as well as full-
bodied appeal. Both the 1985 and 1986 should be drunk over the next
5–6 years.

TROPLONG-MONDOT (ST.-ÉMILION)* * *

1985   C   87

1986   C   87

After plunging in quality in the seventies, this estate has begun to benefit from the considerable talents of Michel Rolland, who is the consulting oenologist. The 1985, with its deep ruby color and complex bouquet of spicy oak and ripe currants, offers extremely well-balanced and well-delineated flavors, medium body, excellent depth, and firm, but soft tannins. The 1986 exhibits a bit more new oak, lavish richness, good structure, and impressive depth.

TROTANOY (POMEROL)* * * * *

1985	E	87
1986	E	85

I appear to have seriously overrated the 1985 Trotanoy. Tasted a number of times in 1986 and 1987, I thought it had the potential to be in the same class as the 1971. However, unless I have misread the wine, it looks to be very good, but more in line with the 1981 or 1979 than any other vintage. It is somewhat light by the standards of this estate, elegant and medium bodied with good color, but I keep wondering where the richness and length have gone. Is the wine going through an awkward stage or have I made an error in judgment? Nor am I terribly excited by the 1986, a wine that also seems a bit light and insubstantial. The hard tannins in the finish seem elevated for the amount of fruit present.

TROTTEVIEILLE (ST.-ÉMILION)* * *

1985	C	86
1986	C	87

I vividly recall many a wretched bottle of Trottevieille that seemed to prove the ludicrousness of the St.-Émilion wine classification. Now, however, Bordeaux *négociant* Borie-Manoux has gotten serious about the quality of his estate, and the results are a very good 1985 and a 1986 that have the potential to be the finest Trottevieille since before the 1956 freeze destroyed this vineyard. The 1985 displays very ripe berry aromas, some evidence of new oak, a sweet, supple, round and generous texture, medium to full body, and soft tannins in the finish. The 1986 has an impressive deep ruby color and a big, rich, exotic bouquet of berry fruit and smoky oak. On the palate, the wine is full bodied, powerful, complex, rich, and quite long. What a pleasure to see this property return to form.

VERDIGNAN (HAUT-MÉDOC)* * *

1985	A 84
1986	A 84

The wines of this Cru Bourgeois, which is run with care by Jean Miailhe, are good though not complex, and are savory, fat, and fruity with fine color and body and a mouth-filling plumpness. The 1985 is round, sweet, generous, and ideal for drinking over the next 3–5 years. The 1986 is a bit more structured, has fine depth, medium to full body, and good length. It should drink nicely for 4–6 years.

LA VIEILLE CURE (FRONSAC)* * *

1985	B 85
1986	B 85

According to the local cognoscenti, this property has enormous potential. Several years ago an American syndicate acquired La Vieille Cure and has seemingly spared no expense; a new winery is just about complete. The 1985 is a juicy, succulent, ripe, elegant, tasty wine with good extract, medium body, and an attractive finish. The 1986 is a more powerful, age-worthy, deeper wine with great color, plenty of tannin, and a long, youthful finish.

VIEUX CHÂTEAU CERTAN (POMEROL)* * * *

1985	D 89
1986	D 91

When the young, studious Alexandre Thienpont took over the management of this famous Pomerol château, several of the appellation's old-timers scoffed at his lack of experience. However, in a brief two years, he instituted crop-thinning to reduce the yield and a program of very meticulous attention to the cellar. The result is the 1986, the finest Vieux Château Certan since the 1964, and, yes, better than the 1982. As for the 1985, it is richly fruity, as are most wines from this vintage, and is long, deep, complex, medium to full bodied, light in tannins, but delicious and seductive. The 1986 impeccably balances power and finesse, has exceptional depth and length, and a very impressive finish.

VILLARS (FRONSAC)* * *

1985	B	85
1986	B	85

This is a very good example of a Fronsac. The wine, aged in oak barrels of which one-third are new, has plenty of fruit, good structure, and never an excess of tannin. The 1985 has a textbook bouquet of new oak and blackcurrants, medium to full body, a soft, supple texture, and good balance. The 1986 is virtually identical except for more noticeable tannins and a stronger scent of new oak. It is a handsomely made wine that will age well for 6–8 years.

LA VIOLETTE (POMEROL)* * *

1985	C	74

This is a perplexing wine. Some vintages have been rich, complex and promising, whereas others have been light, diluted, and insipid. The 1985, unfortunately, falls within the latter category—dull, over-cropped, soft, and loosely knit.

BORDEAUX'S DRY WHITE WINES

BOUSCAUT (GRAVES)* * *

1985	B	82
1986	B	79

Although over 2,000 cases of white Château Bouscaut are produced each year from a blend of 52% Semillon and 48% Sauvignon, the wine has never shown particularly well in my white Graves tastings. Reports continue to circulate that the quality is on the upswing, but this is not apparent in either the 1985 or the 1986, both of which are correct but unexhilarating wines to taste. Both should be drunk over the next 3–4 years.

CARBONNIEUX (GRAVES)* * *

1986	C	82
1987	C	84

Although Château Carbonnieux produces both red and white Graves, it is more widely known for its large yearly production of over 15,000 cases of white wine, made from a blend of 65% Sauvignon Blanc, 30% Semillon, and 5% Muscadelle. The wine is often excellent (I recently drank the 1971 and the 1975 with great pleasure). However, the vintages in the eighties have tended to be more commercial in their orientation and significantly less concentrated. For example, the 1986 seems light and watery and not nearly as good as the 1985. However, the 1987 looks to be better than the 1986, with a pronounced Sauvignon, herbaceous smell interwoven with the scent of new oak. This wine can age, but I have been reluctant to cellar the vintages of the eighties for more than 5–7 years.

DOMAINE CHALLON (BORDEAUX)* * *

1986	A	83
1987	A	86

The production of this little gem, which has only a simple appellation Bordeaux contrôlée, is 3,000 cases a year. The wine is made by the famous winemaker of Château Ausone, Pascal Delbeck, for his boss, Madame Dubois Challon, also the co-owner of Ausone. The wine, made from 70% Semillon, 15% Ugni Blanc, and the rest Muscadelle, is barrel-fermented and is a wonderful example of an *appellation d'origine contrôlée* (AOC) Bordeaux property making wine significantly better than many of the more famous white Graves. The 1987 is creamy and rich, with a lovely fragrant bouquet and medium to full body. The 1986 is slightly less concentrated and lower in acidity, but still refreshing and fruity.

CHANTEGRIVE (GRAVES)* * *

1985	B	84
1986	B	78
1987	B	85

This is a terribly underrated property that yearly produces over 17,000 cases of white Graves from a blend of 50% Semillon, 30% Sauvignon Blanc and 20% Muscadelle. It is a wine I often search for on Bordeaux wine lists, as both the charming, fruity red and the crisp, aromatic white are remarkably good values. Just over 20% new oak is used, and the wine always has good body, an aromatic bouquet, and plenty of plumpness, no doubt from the high percentage of Semillon used in the blend. The 1987 would be the best recent vintage to search out.

DOMAINE DE CHEVALIER (GRAVES)* * * * *

1983	D	94
1984	D	89
1985	D	90
1986	D	88

Many connoisseurs of white Graves prefer Domaine de Chevalier. It is a wine of great style, with a pungent, herbaceous aroma of Sauvignon Blanc and new oak barrels. It spends more time—18 months— in new oak casks than any other white Graves, and has unbelievable aging potential, as a recent vertical tasting back through 1961 proved quite conclusively. In fact, I don't recommend drinking the wine young, although most of its tiny yearly production of 800 cases is probably consumed within 4–5 years of the vintage. When young, Domaine de Chevalier tastes aggressively oaky and almost always lacks the richness and depth that begins to develop around its seventh birthday. The great recent vintages here include a truly spectacular 1983, which will probably not be ready to drink until the early nineties, and the 1985. The off year of 1984 is also an extremely charming, elegant example of Domaine de Chevalier. The blend at Chevalier remains 70% Sauvignon Blanc and 30% Semillon.

COUHINS-LURTON (GRAVES)* * * *

1986	B	84
1987	B	85

Unfortunately, only 450 cases of this wine are made each year. It sells for a reasonable price and is made by André Lurton, who has had quite a positive impact on the Graves appellation. The wine, fermented in new oak casks, has always had an excellent amount of richness and fruit. I have enjoyed the 1983 and 1985 more than the 1986 or 1987, but both latter vintages are good, medium-weight, white Graves for drinking over the next 4–5 years.

CRUZEAU (GRAVES)* *

1985		B	86
1986		B	82

Château de Cruzeau is another property owned by André Lurton, who has built himself quite an empire in the Graves region. Approximately 4,000 cases of white Graves are made each year from a blend of 90% Sauvignon Blanc and 10% Semillon. The wine, while less aromatic and complex than Couhins-Lurton, is nevertheless a tasty, medium-bodied, white Graves that is meant to be consumed very young.

DOISY-DAËNE (BARSAC)* *

This well-known producer in Barsac produces an exceptionally crisp, dry, well-made, fruity wine from Sauvignon Blanc and Semillon. It is a wine that must be drunk within the first 3–4 years of the vintage, but offers outstanding value and has a style not unlike a white Graves.

FERRANDE (GRAVES)* * *

1985		B	83
1986		B	78

This is a fairly well-known white Graves that each year produces 5,000 cases of wine from a blend of 60% Semillon and 40% Sauvignon Blanc. It is one of the white Graves that is extremely dry—even austere—and has a pronounced earthy flavor that sets it apart from many other white Graves. On occasion, I have noticed that some bottles seem overly sulphured. The 1985 is significantly better than the somewhat lightish, dull 1986.

FIEUZAL (GRAVES)* * * *

1985		C	91
1986		C	87
1987		C	90

Fieuzal has made great strides in the eighties to improve the quality not only of its white wine, but of its red wine as well. The production of white wine is very limited, less than 800 cases each year, and the wine is made from a blend of 60% Sauvignon Blanc and 40% Semillon. The quality has improved considerably starting with the 1985 vintage, which was fermented and aged in new oak barrels. The result was a smashingly rich, intense, yet impeccably well-balanced, complex wine, which offered a challenge to the great names of the Graves appellation. This was followed by a very good but lighter 1986, and one of the top stars of the vintage in 1987. Guessing the aging potential of Fieuzal is difficult. Given its richness and balance, 10–15 years of cellaring potential does not seem impossible.

HAUT-BRION (GRAVES)* * * * *

1985	E	96
1986	E	85
1987	E	87

Approximately 1,400 cases are made each year of the most famous white Graves in the world, Haut-Brion Blanc. It is one of the few white Graves that with age can have the richness of a great white burgundy. Aged in 100% new oak, and made from 55% Semillon and 45% Sauvignon Blanc, the great vintages for Haut-Brion Blanc have been the 1985, followed by the 1983, 1979, and 1978. The 1986 is good but a little light, and although the 1987 is a charming, elegant, medium-bodied wine with superb fruit, it does not have the lasting power and richness of a great vintage such as 1985.

LAVILLE-HAUT-BRION (GRAVES)* * * * *

1985	E	93
1986	E	85
1987	E	87

Made at the famous La Mission-Haut-Brion, Laville-Haut-Brion is always a bit different from the famous Haut-Brion Blanc, as it is fatter and richer, but also has remarkable staying power. It is made from 60% Semillon and 40% Sauvignon Blanc. Some of the vintages such as the 1962, 1966, 1975, and 1976 have been legendary. More recently, the 1982, 1983, 1985, and 1987 have all been in top form. Certainly the 1985, with its remarkable power and richness, gets my vote as the top recent Laville-Haut-Brion, but the 1987 is filled with fruit and charm, and for long-term development one has to consider both the 1983 and 1982.

LA LOUVIÈRE (GRAVES)* * * *

1985	B	85
1986	B	75
1987	B	85

La Louvière, known for its reasonably priced, supple, richly fruity red wine, also yearly produces nearly 8,000 cases of an excellent white Graves that is well priced. In fact, of all the top-quality white Graves, this is perhaps the most reasonably priced. Made from a blend of 85% Sauvignon Blanc and 15% Semillon, it is an overt, fat, supple, delicious white Graves that can hold up for 7–10 years despite its precocious charm.

CHÂTEAU DE MALLE (GRAVES)* * *

1985	B	86
1986	B	83

Each year, Château de Malle produces 3,000 cases of a lovely white Graves called M. de Malle, which is aged in new oak casks. Typical of the vintage, the 1986 shows a little dilution, but is still an enjoyable, creamy textured, overtly oaky white wine. The 1985 has greater depth and more fatness and fruit, and the amount of oak seems complementary to the amount of fruit. These are wines that should be drunk over their first 5–7 years of life.

MALARTIC-LAGRAVIÈRE (GRAVES)* * * *

1985	C	87
1986	C	84
1987	C	84

Located in the southern region of Graves near the town of Léognan, this property each year produces fewer than 1,000 cases of an interesting, extremely dry, white Graves fermented in new oak and made from 100% Sauvignon Blanc. It is one of the leanest and most austere of the white Graves, but ages extremely well and seems especially consistent in the off years. Of the three vintages above, the 1985 has the most flavor and fruit, and also the most potential for longevity. It should be drunk within the first decade of its life.

CHÂTEAU MILLET (GRAVES)* * *

1985	B	82
1986	B	75

Made from 50% Sauvignon Blanc and 50% Semillon this white wine is an average white Graves that is rarely exhilarating.

NUMÉRO 1 (BORDEAUX)* * *

1987	A	86

In 1987, the large, very successful *négociant* firm of Dourthe launched this special cuvée of generic Bordeaux white wine that is aged in oak casks and made with cold fermentation and extended lees contact. It is a delicious wine that competes favorably with some of the best white Graves. There appears to be a healthy percentage of Semillon in the wine, and it has surprising length and complexity for a wine of its class. It should be drunk over the first 3–4 years of its life.

OLIVIER (GRAVES)* * *

1985	B	78
1986	B	75

Approximately 10,000 cases of this dry white Graves are produced each year, made from a blend of 65% Semillon, 30% Sauvignon Blanc, and 5% Muscadelle. Despite its rather fine reputation, the wine seems thin and lacking in distinction. New management has taken over and one hopes that the quality will improve.

PONTAC-MONPLAISIR (GRAVES)* * *

1986	A	80
1987	A	83

For sheer value, the crisp, pure, 100% Sauvignon Blanc character of Pontac-Monplaisir seems to beg for a plate of fresh oysters to show off its zesty acidity and crisp, herbaceous Sauvignon flavors. Neither the 1986 nor the 1987 are as rich or flavorful as the 1985. Nevertheless, the wine is a fine bargain for high-quality white Graves.

RAHOUL (GRAVES)* * *

1985	C	87
1986	C	85

This Australian-owned property has made quite a name for itself, given Danish oenologist Peter Vinding-Diers' experimental—and successful—approach to making both white and red Graves. At first, I felt that the white wines were over-oaked and just out of balance, but recent vintages, such as the 1985 and 1986, suggest that while the wines are marked by a tremendous percentage of new oak barrels, the 100% Semillon seems to be asserting itself more and more in the winemaking and in the balance of the wine. This wine gives every indication of being able to age for up to 10 years, and certainly the 1985 looks to be quite a success.

THIEULEY (BORDEAUX)* * *

1986	A	83
1987	A	85
1986 Cuvée Francis Courselle	B	86
1987 Cuvée Francis Courselle	B	87

Thieuley is known for its very good values, and its new special Cuvée Francis Courselle should also be applauded, as the wine is competing with some of the best—and more expensive—white Graves. Aged in new oak, it is a surprisingly rich, flavorful wine that is very marked by Sauvignon Blanc (the special cuvée and the regular white Bordeaux are made from 100% Sauvignon Blanc). The special cuvée should age nicely for 2–4 years. Both the 1987s showed more fruit, balance, and crispness than the 1986s.

LA TOUR-MARTILLAC (GRAVES)* * * *

1986	C	79

1987   C   89

This well-known property produces a white wine from 55% Semillon, 30% Sauvignon Blanc, and the balance from a field blend of other grape varieties. The 1987 represents an attempt by the proprietors to raise the quality of the wine and compete with the top white Graves such as Haut-Brion Blanc, Laville-Haut-Brion, and Fieuzal. It is quite sensational and probably the best La Tour-Martillac that I have ever tasted. Fermented in new oak barrels and aged in new casks, the wine is extremely rich and full, and has immense potential. The 1986 is straightforward and one-dimensional.

BORDEAUX'S SWEET WHITE WINES: SAUTERNES AND BARSACS

D'ARCHE (SAUTERNES)* * *

1983   B   87

1985   B   80

1986   B   86

This under-publicized property tends to produce rather fat, rich, intense wines that, while lacking a bit in finesse, offer a plump mouthful of very rich Sauternes. Each year about 4,500 cases are made from a blend of 80% Semillon, 15% Sauvignon Blanc, and 5% Muscadelle. The 1983 is an extremely powerful and rich wine, and although it is more concentrated than the 1986, the 1986 seems to have more complexity and more evidence of botrytis. Both should drink well for some time.

BASTOR-LAMONTAGNE (SAUTERNES)* * *

1983   B   87

1985   B   79

1986   B   87

Although unclassified, Bastor-Lamontagne deserves to be elevated in any realistic classification of the wines of Barsac and Sauternes. Approximately 8,000 cases are made each year from a blend of 70% Semillon, 20% Sauvignon Blanc, and 10% Muscadelle. While obviously making rich, intense, unctuous wines in the top Sauternes vintages, such as 1983 and 1986, this property has also been successful in years such as 1980 and 1982. The 1985 lacks botrytis and just seems thick and sweet, as opposed to the first class 1986 and 1983.

BROUSTET (BARSAC)* *

1983	C	62
1985	C	78
1986	C	85

It seems odd that the proprietor of Broustet, Eric Fournier, who impeccably runs the famous Château Canon in St.-Émilion, has never quite brought the quality of Broustet's wines up to the level of his red wines. This is a tiny estate, producing fewer than 2,000 cases each year from a blend of 65% Semillon, 25% Sauvignon Blanc, and 10% Muscadelle. The 1983 has tasted consistently disappointing and the 1985 one-dimensional and boring, but the 1986 shows elegance and rich, oaky, long flavors.

CLIMENS (BARSAC)* * * *

1983	D	92
1985	D	85
1986	D	94

This famous Barsac property often produces wine of remarkable elegance and finesse. While wine made from 98% Semillon and only 2% Sauvignon Blanc would suggest a heavy, oily, viscous wine, Climens is just the opposite. It is perhaps the most elegant of all the wines of Sauternes/Barsac, and even in great vintages, such as 1971 and 1975 or 1983, it is never heavy-handed or overly powerful. Of the recent vintages, the 1983 has improved considerably after bottling and looks to be a great Climens. The 1985 lacks the botrytis and complexity of a great vintage. The 1986 is quite superb and given its fascinating richness and balance, it could be the finest Climens made in several decades.

COUTET (BARSAC)* * * *

1983	C	87
1985	C	84
1986	C	89

Coutet, one of the more famous estates in Barsac, makes a wine from the same blend of grapes used at d'Yquem—80% Semillon and 20% Sauvignon Blanc. The wine tends to be lighter than most Sauternes, but is always elegant and rich, with a very floral, honeyed bouquet. In certain vintages the property produces tiny quantities of a special Cuvée Madame, which is nothing short of sensational and, in my opinion, often exceeds d'Yquem itself for pure quality and complexity. Of the recent vintages, the 1986 and 1983 stand out as being the top two years, with the 1986 showing more botrytis.

DOISY-DAËNE (BARSAC)* * *

1983	B	90
1985	B	82
1986	B	88

While rated only as a second-growth, Doisy-Daëne often produces wine of a far higher quality than do the properties rated above it. Interestingly, the wine is made from 100% Semillon, and the result is a splendidly rich yet fresh, complex wine with a great deal of length and richness. My favorite recent vintage has been the extraordinary 1983, which is perhaps the finest Doisy-Daëne I have ever tasted, but the 1986 promises well. Certainly, the 1985 is good even though there was very little botrytis; it is rather fat but not complex.

DOISY-VÉDRINES (BARSAC)* * *

1983	C	86
1985	C	81
1986	C	87

The textbook blend of 80% Semillon and 20% Sauvignon Blanc produces a rich, oily wine that can sometimes be a bit heavy-handed, but in vintages such as 1983 and 1986 comes across as powerful, complex, and mouth-filling. It also ages well.

FARGUES (SAUTERNES)* * * *

1981	D	90
1983	D	92

Unfortunately, the tiny production of under 1,000 cases each year from this historic property, owned by the proprietor of d'Yquem and given similar treatment and elevage, keeps this wine from being better known. It tastes remarkably similar to d'Yquem and can often be more complex, as it matures earlier. The 1981 seems to be even better than the d'Yquem of that year, but as great as the 1983 Fargues is, it is no match for the extraordinary wine produced by d'Yquem in that vintage. Fargues is produced from 80% Semillon and 20% Sauvignon Blanc, and is aged 3 years in new oak casks. Some of the older vintages such as the 1976 and 1975 are remarkably successful wines, very similar to d'Yquem but selling for one-third the price.

FILHOT (SAUTERNES)* *

1983	C	82
1985	C	78
1986	C	82

Although it is one of the most extraordinarily situated and beautiful properties in Sauternes, Filhot is not making wines that fulfill the potential of the vineyard. The 1986 is surprisingly light, although elegant, but cloyingly sweet in the finish and just a bit top-heavy. The same can be said for the dull but less complex 1985, and the fat, very sweet 1983. These are good rather than special wines, and it is unfortunate that the quality is not better. Perhaps the production of 10,000–11,000 cases is excessive for the size of the vineyard.

GILETTE (SAUTERNES)* * * *

1959	E	94
1961	E	87

1962	E 90

Each year fewer than 1,000 cases are produced of this wine, which is held 20–25 years in tanks prior to bottling by its owner, Christian Medeville. It is well worth the wait, as the wine is often quite astonishingly rich and, of course, fully mature when released. The 1959 has the honeyed sweetness and richness of a great Sauternes. The 1961, although a very good wine, is less rich and shows significantly less botrytis in its bouquet. The 1962 is the newest release and offers more complexity and honeyed botrytis in its full-bodied flavors than the 1961. Should you see any of the older vintages, such as the 1955, 1953, or 1950, don't hesitate to try them, as they have the potential to last another 20–25 years after bottling.

GUIRAUD (SAUTERNES)* * *

1983	C 88

1985	C 87

1986	C 92

The owners of this property have made a great effort to bring their wines to the very top of the Sauternes hierarchy. A great deal of new oak has been used, and the wine has begun to receive an exceptional amount of publicity. Each year about 7,000 cases are made from a blend of 55% Semillon and 45% Sauvignon Blanc. Of the recent vintages the 1983 is very good, showing quite a lot of muscle and intensity; the 1985 shows less finesse but a great deal of sweetness, ripeness, and new oak. However, top marks must go to the 1986, which would appear to be the finest Guiraud made under the new regime. It is quite concentrated, very aromatic, and has exceptional staying power on the palate.

LAFAURIE-PEYRAGUEY (SAUTERNES)* * * *

1983	C 92

1985	C 85

1986	C 93

Owned by the Cordiers since 1913, and now under the guidance of the brilliant oenologist Georges Pauli, this spectacular château has begun to make an extraordinary wine in the eighties. The quality improved significantly starting with a very good 1981. This was followed by an extraordinarily rich, honeyed, complex wine in 1983. The 1985 is good, although it lacks complexity due to the lack of botrytis, but it is concentrated, ripe, and rich. The 1986 is exceptionally promising and may in the long run turn out to be better than the 1983, although it doesn't have quite the muscle of the 1983. It does have a sensational bouquet of honey, nuts, and flowers. Prices have yet to catch up with the quality, so this is a Sauternes to seek out. The blend currently employed by the Cordiers is 90% Semillon, 5% Sauvignon Blanc, and 5% Muscadelle, and the wine is aged in 50% new oak. Approximately 4,000 cases are made each year.

DE MALLE (SAUTERNES)* *

1985	B	79
1986	B	84

This is another beautiful château, well worth a visit, but the wines tend to be rather light in style and are sometimes a bit too short on the palate. The 1986 is a medium-bodied, fruity wine that should be drunk young, whereas the 1985 seems slightly one-dimensional and innocuous.

NAIRAC (BARSAC)* * *

1983	C	90
1985	C	85
1986	C	89

While rated only a second-growth, this property is making much higher quality wine than its classification would indicate. Believing in lots of new oak and a great deal of Semillon (90% is used in the blend, along with 6% Sauvignon Blanc and 4% Muscadelle), Nairac has gone from one strength to another in the last 10 years. Certainly the 1985 is good given the lack of botrytis in this particular vintage, but both the powerful, concentrated 1983 and the elegant, very aromatic, complex 1986 are two of the best Nairacs of the last decade.

RABAUD-PROMIS (SAUTERNES)* *

1983	C	85

1986   C   86

After a prolonged period during which this property turned out many disappointing wines, the quality since 1983 has begun to improve markedly. Prices have remained reasonable, so this could well be a Sauternes to seek out. It is not one of the more powerful styles of Sauternes, but the 1983 and 1986 have exhibited an attractive, unctuous, full-bodied character with good complexity and adequate acidity for balance. Each year, approximately 4,000 cases of wine are made from a blend of 80% Semillon, 18% Sauvignon Blanc, and 2% Muscadelle.

RAYMOND-LAFON (SAUTERNES)* * * * *

1983   D   93

1985   D   87

1986   D   90

This little gem of a property produces only 2,000 cases of wine each year from a textbook blend of 80% Semillon and 20% Sauvignon Blanc. The wine is made by Pierre Meslier, who is also responsible for the making of d'Yquem. As the wines have been given meticulous care, one can hardly go wrong with any of the great vintages, such as 1983 and 1986, but the 1985 is also attractively fat, ripe, and tasty. Both the intense, sublime 1983 and extremely aromatic, botrytis-filled 1986 promise splendid drinking in about a decade.

RAYNE-VIGNEAU (SAUTERNES)* *

1983   C   82

1985   C   80

1986   C   87

This is one of the larger estates in Sauternes, which produces just over 12,000 cases of wine each year. For some time, I have found Rayne-Vigneau to be too light and lacking in richness and character. The blend of grapes includes a hefty amount of Sauvignon Blanc—50%—to go along with 50% Semillon. The 1986 is one of the most reassuring examples of Rayne-Vigneau in years; it exhibits a deft touch of toasty new oak, an elegant yet concentrated, flavorful style, and a great deal of finesse. The 1985 and 1983 are rather straightforward, fruity wines that lack the character appropriate to the reputation of this property.

RIEUSSEC (SAUTERNES)* * * * *

1983	D	92
1985	D	86
1986	D	91

For years, this property was considered to have the finest potential in Sauternes after d'Yquem. It is a gorgeous estate, adjacent to d'Yquem, and was acquired by the Rothschild family (of Lafite-Rothschild) in 1984. Since then the quality seems to have been maintained but prices have almost doubled. The 1985 is very good for the vintage but lacks the complexity necessary to be considered great. However, the extraordinary 1983 is perhaps the best Rieussec in over two decades, and the 1986 should be a less muscular but perhaps more complex and elegant successor to the wonderful 1983.

ROMER DU HAYOT (SAUTERNES)* *

1985	B	80
1986	D	86

I have always found that this property makes consistently good Sauternes, which have a great deal of freshness and excellent concentration. Furthermore, they sell at very reasonable prices. The blend is 70% Semillon, 25% Sauvignon Blanc, and 5% Muscadelle. This is not a Sauternes to lay away for two decades, but rather, one to drink over its first 10 years of life.

SIGALAS RABAUD (SAUTERNES)* * *

1983	C	86
1985	C	78
1986	C	85

This is a well-known Sauternes that each year produces about 2,000 cases of wine from a blend of 90% Semillon and 10% Sauvignon Blanc.

Although there have been some excellent vintages, the property is quite inconsistent in its quality. The two most recent vintages include a very complex, elegant 1986, and a fine 1983, the latter having a wonderful aromatic bouquet of honeyed pineapples. The 1985 is rather one-dimensional and boring. This tends to be an elegant, medium-bodied Sauternes that requires drinking within the first 10–12 years of its life.

SUDUIRAUT (SAUTERNES)* * * *

1982	D	92
1983	D	86
1985	D	79
1986	D	87

Each year this famous property produces just over 10,000 cases of usually rich, intense Sauternes from a blend of 80% Semillon and 20% Sauvignon Blanc. It is very inconsistent in terms of quality; the 1983 is, shockingly, not nearly as intense and interesting as the 1982. The reverse is true for virtually every other estate in the Sauternes/Barsac district. The 1985 looks to be quite light and lacking in concentration and depth, whereas the 1986, while very good, should have been a classic. Should you find any of the great 1976 on the shelves, don't hesitate to buy it. It was probably the finest Suduiraut made in the last 20 years.

LA TOUR BLANCHE (SAUTERNES)* *

1985	C	87
1986	C	88

This estate belongs to France's Ministry of Agriculture and is run as a training school. The wine can be very good but has been inconsistent over the last several decades, although both the 1985 and 1986 look to be two of the best examples made here in many years. The wine, of which approximately 600 cases are produced in a good vintage, is made from a blend of 70% Semillon, 28% Sauvignon Blanc, and the rest Muscadelle. It is never the richest, most intense Sauternes, but it does have a great deal of flavor and elegance, as the most recent two top vintages demonstrate. In fact, the 1985 looks to be one of the top vintages in this region.

D'YQUEM (SAUTERNES)* * * * *

1982	E	93
1983	E	99

As everyone knows, this is the world's most difficult and expensive wine to produce. The owner, the Comte Alexandre de Lur-Saluces, seems to have realized this fact as he doubled the price for his exceptionally rich, virtually perfect 1983. Approximately 6,000 cases of d'Yquem are made each year from a blend of 80% Semillon and 20% Sauvignon Blanc. The 1982 is also a marvelous wine, but it seems to me that one has to go back to 1980 to find an exceptional d'Yquem at a less-than-painful price. These wines last 40–50 years, or perhaps even longer, although most seem to be drunk within their first decade by rich collectors who love to buy and taste them.

BURGUNDY AND BEAUJOLAIS

Higher Quality, Higher Price, and Higher Interest

Burgundy is the world's most difficult wine region to understand, as well as the most difficult wine to make. And something has happened there that has not occurred since the excellent four-year streak of 1969–1972—four consecutive fine vintages: 1985, 1986, 1987, and 1988. Of these, the 1985 is undoubtedly great; 1988 may be almost as fine. These fine vintages coincide with a general increase in the quality of Burgundy's wines, but this does not mean that the consumer has it any easier. Despite higher quality overall, far too many burgundies still are insipid wines that lack both taste and character. Given the relatively small quantities of wine produced, and the proportionately large representation of mediocre wine, burgundy remains a wine for masochists—those who do not mind spending a great deal of money and tasting a lot of mediocre burgundies to find the finest ones.

The Basics

TYPES OF WINE

This modestly sized viticultural area in France's heartland, three hours south of Paris by car, yearly produces, on average, 22 million cases of dry red and white wine, as well as tiny quantities of rosé. This represents only 3% of France's total wine production.

Red Wine Burgundy's dry red wines come from the Côte d'Or, which is divided into two areas: the Côte de Nuits, the northern part, and the Côte de Beaune, the southern portion. A bit farther south, red wines are made in the Côte Chalonnaise and even farther south in Mâconnais and Beaujolais.

White Wine Dry white wine is made throughout Burgundy, but most of it is produced in the Côte de Beaune, in the Côte Chalonnaise, in Mâconnais, and in Burgundy's most northern area, Chablis.

GRAPE VARIETIES

Mostly three grapes are used in Burgundy. The red burgundies are made from the Pinot Noir, the most fickle and troublesome of grapes. Although it is an extremely difficult grape to make into wine, when handled with care the Pinot Noir produces the great, sumptuous, velvety, red burgundies of the Côte d'Or. The Gamay, another widely planted grape, offers up the succulent, effusively fruity, easy-to-drink and easy-to-understand wine of Beaujolais. The Chardonnay, the other major grape, makes the great white wines of Chablis and of the Côte de Beaune. Grapes grown in smaller quantities in Burgundy include the Aligoté grape—planted in less hospitable sites—and the Pinot Blanc and Pinot Beurrot, also called Pinot Gris (planted in minute quantities).

FLAVORS

When it is great, the Pinot Noir grape produces the most complex, hedonistic, and remarkably thrilling red wine in the world, but only a tiny percentage of Burgundy's wines attain this level. The bouquet of such wines is filled with red fruits and exotic spices, and the taste is

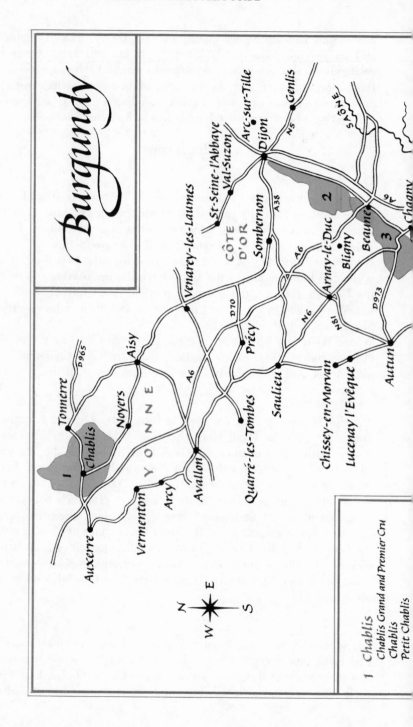

Burgundy

1 *Chablis*
Chablis Grand and Premier Cru
Chablis
Petit Chablis

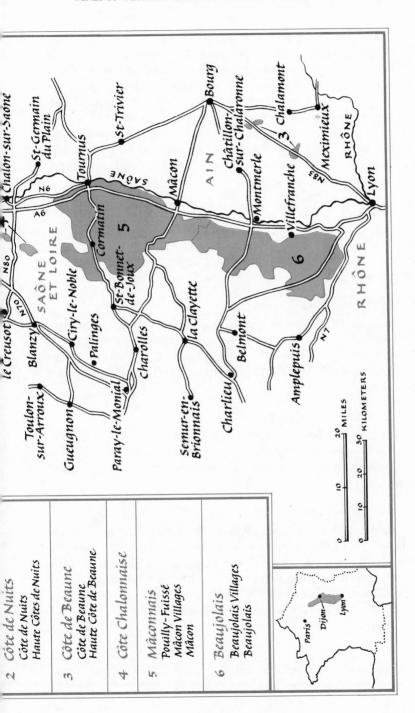

2 Côte de Nuits
Côte de Nuits
Haute Côtes de Nuits

3 Côte de Beaune
Côte de Beaune
Haute Côte de Beaune

4 Côte Chalonnaise

5 Mâconnais
Pouilly-Fuissé
Mâcon Villages
Mâcon

6 Beaujolais
Beaujolais Villages
Beaujolais

broad, expansive, round, lush, and soft. Great burgundy always tastes sweeter than Bordeaux and has a significantly lighter color. Rarely ever does young burgundy have more than a medium cherry color. Gamay is not drunk for its complexity but, rather, for its heady, direct, ripe, soft, fleshy, exuberant fruitiness and easygoing texture. Chardonnay can range from stony and mineral-scented—with high acidity —in wines of Chablis, to buttery, smoky, creamy, decadently rich, and tasting of sautéed almonds and hazelnuts in great Côte de Beaune white burgundies, to refreshingly light, lemony, floral and thirst-quenching in the wines of Mâconnais.

AGING POTENTIAL

Red Wines
Côte de Nuits: 4–30 years
Côte de Beaune: 4–20 years
Beaujolais: 1–5 years

White Wines
Chablis: 1–10 years
Côte de Beaune: 4–15 years
Mâconnais: 1–5 years

OVERALL QUALITY LEVEL

In each appellation in Burgundy, wines range widely in quality, from those that are watery, poorly made, and incompetent to those of great flavor and dimension. While the number of poor and mediocre wines has decreased significantly, these wines still greatly outnumber the fine wines.

THE MOST IMPORTANT INFORMATION TO KNOW

Consult the guides to Burgundy's best producers on pages 234– 238 to avoid buying poor and mediocre wine. There are many pitfalls awaiting uninformed consumers who are seeking out the wines of Burgundy.

1989–1990 BUYING STRATEGY

If you can still find and afford them, the 1985 red burgundies are must-buys. The 1986s and, to a lesser extent, the 1987s must be chosen with great care, but all of my top-rated producers have done very well. The 1988s, when released in late 1990, promise to be almost as rich and succulent as the 1985s. Don't ignore the good values from appellations such as Givry, Rully, and Mercurey for both red and white burgundy.

RED BURGUNDY
VINTAGE GUIDE

1987—One of the biggest surprises in France is how good the 1987 red burgundies have turned out. The marvelous hot, sunny month of September ripened the grapes and allowed many growers to begin their harvest before the rains came. Nevertheless, it did rain, and heavily. Rather than tasting diluted, however, the wines exhibit good ripeness, an aromatic, scented character, low acidities and light tannins, but surprising depth. They have nowhere near the weight or richness of the sexy, glamorous 1985s, but most growers and *négociants* prefer them to the irregular, sometimes good, sometimes mediocre 1986s. They will be medium-bodied wines to drink within their first decade of life. As a general rule, the Côte de Beaune appears to have had slightly greater success than the Côte de Nuits.

1986—Two heavy rainstorms in September seemed to forebode great difficulties for the huge, record-breaking crop of grapes that was to be harvested. In truth, the early pickers did bring in swollen grapes, which were low in flavor concentration, color, acids, and tannin. But those who waited were rewarded with excellent weather throughout the first half of October and were able to bring in drier, riper, more concentrated fruit. The growers of the Côte de Nuits were the principal beneficiaries of the fine early October weather since they harvest later than the growers in the Côte de Beaune. The red wines are very patchy, ranging from mediocre, diluted, low-acidic wines to very good, ripe, tasty ones that have both body and tannin. Some critics and connoisseurs have compared the 1986s to the 1982s, but in fact the finest 1986s resemble the 1979s, and they are even richer and deeper in color. For certain, the 1986s will mature quickly and will likely be at their best between 1990 and 1998. The top wines are from the Domaine de la Romanée-Conti, A. Rousseau, Bruno Clair, Dujac, Georges Mugneret, Groffier, Roumier, Pernin-Rossin, Jean Gros, and Mongeard-Mugneret.

1985—I am hardly the first to tell you how great the 1985 red burgundies are. However, when I first tasted them in 1986, many seemed to be too soft and lacking in the structure needed to be considered exceptional. Needless to say, they have put on weight, length, and structure in the last 24 months, and I have no hesitation in saying that they are the deepest, richest, most seductive and delicious red burgundies I have ever tasted. This is not to say that all growers made great wine, but as the ratings demonstrate, no viticultural area has produced as many great wines since Bordeaux in 1982. The 1985s are so exceptional because the growing season was ideal—quite hot—and, more important, it was free of hail and rot. Most of the wines are the deepest-colored burgundies I have ever seen. The wines explode with pure Pinot Noir fruit, are lush and full bodied, quite concentrated, and moderately tannic. Because of the exceptional ripeness and opulent textures of the wines, the acids are not high, but neither are they too low. The great ripeness and richness of the wines, combined with the low but adequate acids, give them a stunning appeal and accessibility today. However, the best wines will not reach their plateau of maturity until 1990–1995, and will last 5–15 years thereafter, if properly stored in a cool, humid area.

1984—All of us remember 1984, which, like 1980, was declared by several wine writers to be a major catastrophe long before they ever tasted the wines. In 1980, the source of information was the *négociant* Louis Latour, who had all sorts of problems with the vintage, and indeed made poor wine that year. As all burgundy-lovers know, 1980 has turned out some of the most delicious and best-balanced wines of the last 7–8 years, and some of the wines from the Côte de Nuits (e.g., Domaine de la Romanée-Conti and Robert Arnoux) are superb. Be that as it may, 1984 is not likely to be as good as 1980, but many of the good growers have made wines that I predict will be better-balanced and richer than the 1982s. The vintage was late, and everyone had to chaptalize because the natural alcohol contents were only 9–10%. However, the resulting red wines are often quite elegant, very cleanly made, fruity, soft, and agreeable. The yields were low because of a poor flowering. There is the normal irregularity, but the wines of the Côte de Nuits are better colored and richer than those of the Côte de Beaune. The good 1984s will be at their best between now and 1994. They will certainly not be long-lived, but when well chosen, will be very pleasant. The top wines of 1984 are from the Domaine de la Romanée-Conti, Jean Gros, Philippe Leclerc, Georges Mugneret, A. Rousseau, Trapet, Robert Chevillon, Faiveley, and George Roumier.

1983—At harvesttime, before any wine could be tasted, a number of critics were calling this vintage one of the greatest ever, solely on the basis of some astonishing levels of sugars in the very ripe grapes. Other critics based their praise on actual tasting notes. After tasting the wines in May 1985, one well-known English critic said. "This is the sort of Burgundy vintage the world has been anxiously waiting for. [The wines] have a concentration of ripe fruit which is exhilarating. These are wines of depth, character, complexity and length." For about 15% of the red burgundies, this assessment was correct; as for the rest, I have to differ, as I advised readers of *The Wine Advocate* in August, 1984. Over three-fourths of the red burgundies I tasted in 1984, and again in 1985, were quite flawed—either from the rampant rot or the severe hailstorm that wreaked havoc on some of the Côte d'Or's most famous vineyards. Six years after the vintage it is safe to say that 1983 is largely a failure as a red wine vintage. Far too many wines smell and taste of rot and/or are unbelievably tannic and astringent. Nevertheless, the great 1983s, from producers such as Roumier, the Domaine de la Romanée-Conti, Henri Jayer, Maume, Hubert Lignier, Mongeard-Mugneret, Faiveley and Ponsot, should provide some of the longest-lived wines of the last three decades. Yet, this is a vintage to approach with great caution and with the knowledge that even the finest wine will require cellaring until the late nineties.

1982—A huge crop of grapes was harvested in 1982. Had it not been for the extremely wet month of August, this year could have been quite special. However, the enormous yield produced very fragile wines, somewhat watery but generally charming, soft, and fruity. Where the conscientious growers were able to pick before the harvest rains and control the vinification temperature, some good, round, adequately concentrated wines were produced. As for the white wines, they have turned out to be extremely successful—fat, lush, and ripe; they are good for drinking over the next 2–3 years while waiting for the 1981s to open.

In general, the wines of the Côte de Beaune are more consistent than those of the Côte de Nuits. However, the Domaine de la Romanée-Conti and Georges Mugneret, both in Vosne-Romanée; Armand Rousseau, Maume, and both Philippe and René Leclerc, all of Gevrey-Chambertin; Domaine Dujac and Pierre Amiot, in Morey St.-Denis; as well as the *négociant* Faiveley, in Nuits St.-Georges, did quite well in the Côte de Nuits.

1981—A difficult vintage, certainly, the great majority of 1981 red burgundies lack flesh and charm, and are too hard, shallow, and austere. Several optimistic reports have indicated the 1981s will turn out like the 1972s, but the 1972s had significantly more concentration. For white burgundies it is a very good year, but for reds one must choose very carefully. Notable successes among the small growers include the wines of Philippe Leclerc, in Gevrey-Chambertin; Pierre Amiot and Domaine Dujac, in Morey St.-Denis; Robert Chevillon, in Nuits St.-Georges; and Domaine de la Pousse d'Or and Michel Lafarge, in Volnay. Among the *négociants*, the wines of Faiveley are excellent.

1980—A disappointing to mediocre year for the white wines, and an average year for the reds of the Côte de Beaune. As for the Côte de Nuits, this is a vastly underrated vintage in which there are many rich, medium-bodied, very elegant, cleanly made, technically sound red burgundies that can be drunk now or cellared for another 3–5 years. The reds of the Côte de Nuits are probably the best bargains for burgundy today.

1979—A good to very good year for white burgundy. The wines are fully mature now and should be consumed. For the red burgundies, the wines are generally showing their age, and are soft, rather frail, and best drunk up.

1978—The most consistently pleasing and successful vintage for Burgundy over the period 1972–1984. The whites, which are just now reaching full maturity, are classic wines with power, richness, depth, and balance. The reds from the Côte de Beaune are quite good and ready to drink; from the Côte de Nuits, the red wines can be drunk, but the best of them need a few more years.

1977—For red burgundies, a terrible year, in which even the most conscientious growers could not overcome Mother Nature's cruel blows. For the white burgundies, it is a surprisingly good year; the wines that seemed acidic at first have matured well. They are in beautiful condition today and are real sleepers.

1976—Along with the 1983, 1976 must surely be the most controversial burgundy vintage of recent years, in which a hot drought year resulted in tiny berries with thick skins. Its major difference from 1983 is that there was no hail or rot damage. The reds, very deeply colored, very tannic and very concentrated, continue to lack charm and character, but they have all the characteristics necessary to age well. Since they have richer, more concentrated fruit than the 1983s, I suspect that all they need is more time—4–7 more years. As for the whites, they are low in acidity, and are powerful, rich, alcoholic wines that resemble the 1983s in size, but without the taint of rot. They should be drunk immediately, since they are beginning to decline.

1975—An indisputably terrible vintage for virtually everyone. Several surprisingly good wines were made in Chablis; otherwise, this is a vintage to avoid.

1974—When it rains, it pours, and 1974 was another very bad year for the growers and *négociants* of Burgundy. The palatable wines I have tasted have been white burgundies from Meursault and Chassagne-Montrachet.

1973—A very good, sometimes excellent vintage for the white wines. Like the 1982s, they tasted good from the beginning and, while lacking some firmness and acidity, were full of fruit and charm. They should have been consumed by now. The reds were watery, pale, light, and generally in full retreat into oblivion by 1978. There is no life left in them now.

1972—Like 1980, at first a maligned, poorly regarded vintage, 1972 has developed so well that lovely vinous surprises are everywhere and the vintage's reputation is clearly on the rise. The reds, deeply colored but high in acidity when first assessed in 1973–1974, have developed slowly but surely. The top wines have rich, complex bouquets, deep flavors, and a touch of firmness. A vintage to keep, the 1972s should be drunk over the next 5–8 years. The whites were less successful, but certainly good. They must be drunk now.

1971—A splendid vintage of ripe, rich, voluptuous, deeply scented red and white wines. The only disappointment has been how fast they have matured. Virtually all of them have been mature for several years, and the telltale orange/amber colors have become apparent. The whites are somewhat risky unless stored in a cold cellar. The reds are just beginning to lose some fruit, but those that are well preserved are delectably opulent and fragrant.

1970—A good vintage of round, fruity, soft wines was produced throughout Burgundy. Although both the whites and the reds lacked greatness, there were still plenty of satisfying wines produced. They should be drunk without delay, as they matured quickly.

1969—An excellent vintage for the red wines, and a very good one for the whites. The wines were slow to mature because they were powerful, but also backward and quite firm. All the reds are mature and should be drunk up. The white burgundies I have tasted recently seem to be losing their fruit and becoming oxidized. Nevertheless, this is a vintage to look for in the auction market.

110 OF BURGUNDY'S BEST RED WINES

Comte Armand Pommard Clos des Epeneaux
Robert Arnoux Vosne-Romanée Les Suchots
Bichot-Clos Frantin Grands-Echézeaux
Bichot-Clos Frantin Vosne-Romanée Les Malconsorts
Pierre Bourée Charmes-Chambertin
Pierre Bourée Clos de la Roche
Jean Chauvenet Nuits St.-Georges Les Vaucrains
Robert Chevillon Nuits St.-Georges Les Saint-Georges
Robert Chevillon Nuits St.-Georges Les Vaucrains
Bruno Clair Gevrey-Chambertin Les Cazetiers

Edmond Cornu Corton Bressandes
Courcel Pommard Rugiens
Joseph Drouhin Charmes-Chambertin
Joseph Drouhin Griottes-Chambertin
Drouhin-Larose Chambertin Clos de Bèze
Drouhin-Larose Bonnes Mares
Dujac Bonnes Mares
Dujac Charmes-Chambertin
Dujac Clos de la Roche
Dujac Clos St.-Denis
René Engel Grands-Echézeaux
Faiveley Chambertin Clos de Bèze
Faiveley Charmes-Chambertin
Faiveley Corton Clos des Cortons
Faiveley Mazis-Chambertin
Forey Vosne-Romanée Les Gaudichots
Bertrand de Gramont Nuits St.-Georges Les Haut Pruliers
Machard de Gramont Nuits St.-Georges Les Damodes
Machard de Gramont Pommard Le Clos Blanc
Jean Grivot Clos Vougeot
Jean Gros Clos Vougeot
Jean Gros Richebourg
Jean Gros Vosne-Romanée Clos des Réas
Hospices de Beaune Beaune Clos des Avaux*
Hospices de Beaune Beaune Nicolas Rolin
Hospices de Beaune Corton Charlotte Dumay
Hospices de Beaune Corton Docteur Peste
Hospices de Beaune Mazis-Chambertin
Hospices de Beaune Pommard Dames de la Charité
Hospices de Beaune Savigny-les-Beaune Arthur Girard
Hospices de Beaune Volnay Blondeau
Hospices de Beaune Volnay Santenots Jehan de Massol
Hudelot-Noëllat Clos Vougeot
Louis Jadot Beaune Clos des Ursules
Louis Jadot Bonnes Mares
Louis Jadot Chambertin Clos de Bèze
Louis Jadot Chambolle-Musigny Les Amoureuses
Louis Jadot Chapelle-Chambertin

* The Hospices de Beaune wines are sold in cask to different buyers. Since 1978 the quality of the new wine from these cuvées has been superbly made and among the finest wines of each vintage.

Louis Jadot Clos Vougeot
Louis Jadot Gevrey-Chambertin Clos St.-Jacques
Henri Jayer Echézeaux
Henri Jayer Nuits St.-Georges Meurgers
Henri Jayer Richebourg
Henri Jayer Vosne-Romanée Les Brûlées
Henri Jayer Vosne-Romanée Clos Parantoux
Jayer-Gilles Echézeaux
Philippe Leclerc Gevrey-Chambertin Les Cazetiers
Philippe Leclerc Gevrey-Chambertin Combe aux Moines
Leroy Beaune Grèves
Leroy Chambertin
Leroy Clos Vougeot
Leroy Mazis-Chambertin
Leroy Nuits St.-Georges Les Perdrix
Leroy Nuits St.-Georges Richemonde
Leroy Pommard Epenots
Leroy Ruchottes-Chambertin
Leroy Savigny Les Serpentières
Hubert Lignier Clos de la Roche
Maume Mazis-Chambertin
Méo-Camuzet Clos Vougeot
Méo-Camuzet Richebourg
Méo-Camuzet Vosne-Romanée Les Brûlées
Moine-Hudelot Richebourg
Mongeard-Mugneret Clos Vougeot
Mongeard-Mugneret Grands-Echézeaux
Mongeard-Mugneret Richebourg
Hubert de Montille Pommard Rugiens
Georges Mugneret Clos Vougeot
Georges Mugneret Echézeaux
Georges Mugneret Ruchottes-Chambertin
A. Mussy Pommard Epenots
Pernin-Rossin Morey St.-Denis Mont Luisants
Pernin-Rossin Nuits St.-Georges Les Richemondes
Pernin-Rossin Vosne-Romanée Les Beaumonts
Ponsot Chambertin
Ponsot Clos de la Roche Vieilles Vignes
Ponsot Clos St.-Denis Vieilles Vignes
Ponsot Griotte-Chambertin
Ponsot Latricières-Chambertin
Pothier-Rieusset Pommard Rugiens

Pousse d'Or Volnay La Bousse d'Or
Domaine de la Romanée-Conti Grands-Echézeaux
Domaine de la Romanée-Conti Richebourg
Domaine de la Romanée-Conti Romanée-Conti
Domaine de la Romanée-Conti Romanée-St.-Vivant
Domaine de la Romanée-Conti La Tâche
Joseph Roty Charmes-Chambertin
Joseph Roty Mazy-Chambertin
Georges Roumier Bonnes Mares
Georges Roumier Chambolle-Musigny Les Amoureuses
Georges Roumier Ruchottes-Chambertin
Armand Rousseau Chambertin
Armand Rousseau Chambertin Clos de Bèze
Armand Rousseau Clos des Ruchottes
Armand Rousseau Gevrey-Chambertin Clos St. Jacques
Bernard Serveau Chambolle-Musigny Les Amoureuses
Robert Sirugue Grands-Echézeaux
Jean Tardy Clos Vougeot
Tollot-Beaut Corton Bressandes
J. Trapet Chambertin Vieilles Vignes

Rating the Growers, Producers and *Négociants*

It is usually difficult to successfully select a bottle of burgundy unless one has knowledge of Burgundy's finest growers and *négociants*. The most meticulous producers often make better wine in mediocre vintages than many less dedicated growers and producers make in great vintages. Knowing who are the finest producers of burgundy is the most important factor in finding the best wines.

The following is a guide to the best producers of red burgundy. Consistency from one year to another among the producers' total range of wines was the most important consideration. One should be cognizant of the fact that many lower-rated producers may make specific wines that are qualitatively above their placement here.

A GUIDE TO THE BEST PRODUCERS OF RED BURGUNDY

***** (OUTSTANDING PRODUCERS)*

Dujac (Morey St.-Denis)   Hospices de Beaune Cuvées
Faiveley (Nuits St.-Georges)   Henri Jayer (Vosne-Romanée)
Jean Gros (Vosne-Romanée)   Leroy (Meursault)

Domaine de la Romanée-Conti
(Vosne-Romanée)

Joseph Roty (Gevrey-
Chambertin)

* * * * *(EXCELLENT PRODUCERS)*

Comte Armand (Pommard)
Robert Arnoux (Vosne-
Romanée)
Bichot-Clos Frantin (Beaune)
Bitouzet-Prieur (Volnay)
Bourée Père et Fils (Gevrey-
Chambertin)
Cathiard Molinier (Vosne-
Romanée)
Robert Chevillon (Nuits St.-
Georges)
Bruno Clair (Marsannay)
Edmond Cornu (Ladoix)
Courcel (Pommard)
Joseph Drouhin (Beaune)
Drouhin Larose (Gevrey-
Chambertin)
Michel Gaunoux (Pommard)
Pierre Gelin (Fixin)
Gelin-Molin (Fixin)
Bertrand de Gramont (Nuits St.-
Georges)
Machard de Gramont (Nuits St.-
Georges)
Jean Grivot (Vosne-Romanée)
Gros Soeur et Frère (Vosne-
Romanée)
Haegelen-Jayer (Vosne-
Romanée)
Hudelot-Noëllat (Vosne-
Romanée)
Louis Jadot (Beaune)
Domaine Jacqueline Jayer
(Vosne-Romanée)
Lucien Jayer (Vosne-Romanée)
Jayer-Gilles (Hautes Côtes de
Nuits)
Michel Lafarge (Volnay)

Philippe Leclerc (Gevrey-
Chambertin)
René Leclerc (Gevrey-
Chambertin)
Hubert Lignier (Morey St.-
Denis)
Maume (Gevrey-Chambertin)
Jean Méo-Camuzet (Vosne-
Romanée)
Prince Florent de Mérode
(Ladoix-Serrigny)
Moine-Hudelot (Chambolle-
Musigny)
Mongeard Mugneret (Vosne-
Romanée)
Hubert de Montille (Volnay)
Albert Morot (Beaune)
Georges Mugneret (Vosne-
Romanée)
Mussy (Pommard)
P. Naddef (Couchey)
Pernin-Rossin (Vosne-
Romanée)
Ponsot (Morey St.-Denis)
Pothier-Rieusset (Pommard)
Pousse d'Or (Volnay)
Philippe Rossignol (Gevrey-
Chambertin)
Georges Roumier (Chambolle-
Musigny)
Armand Rousseau (Gevrey-
Chambertin)
Bernard Serveau (Morey St.-
Denis)
Jean Tardy (Vosne-Romanée)
Tollot-Beaut (Chorey-les-
Beaune)
Tollot-Voarick (Aloxe-Corton)

Louis Trapet (Gevrey-
Chambertin)

Vadey-Castagnier (Morey St.-
Denis)

*** (GOOD PRODUCERS)

Bernard Amiot (Chambolle-
Musigny)
Pierre Amiot (Morey
St.-Denis)
Pierre André (Aloxe-Corton)
Marquis d'Angerville (Volnay)
Ballot-Millot (Meursault)
Barthod Noëllat (Chambolle-
Musigny)
Adrian Belland (Santenay)
Denis Berthaut (Fixin)
Bertheau (Chambolle-Musigny)
Besancenot-Mathouillet
(Beaune)
Billard-Gonnet (Pommard)
Simon Bize (Savigny-les-
Beaune)
Henri Boillot (Volnay)
Lucien Boillot (Gevrey-
Chambertin)
Bouchard Aîné (Beaune)
Bouchard Père (Beaune)
J. M. Bouley (Volnay)
L. J. Bruck (Nuits St.-Georges)
Georges Bryczek (Morey St.-
Denis)
Alain Burguet (Gevrey-
Chambertin)
Château de Chambolle-Musigny
(Chambolle-Musigny)
Champy Père (Beaune)
Domaine Chandon des Briailles
(Savigny-les-Beaune)
Domaine de la Charrière
(Santenay)
J. Chauvenet (Nuits St.-
Georges)
George Clerget (Vougeot)

Clos des Lambrays (Morey St.-
Denis)
Delarche Père et Fils (Pernand-
Vergelesses)
Deroubaix-Indelli (Clos
Vougeot)
Armand Douhairet (Monthelie)
Dubreuil-Fontaine (Pernand-
Vergelesses)
Duchet (Beaune)
M. Ecard (Savigny-les-Beaune)
René Engel (Vosne-Romanée)
Domaine Forey Père et Fils
(Vosne-Romanée)
Geoffrey Père et Fils (Gevrey-
Chambertin)
Armand Girardin (Pommard)
Robert Groffier (Morey St.-
Denis)
J. Guitton (Beaune)
Antonin Guyon (Savigny-les-
Beaune)
Domaine Jacqueson (Chagny)
Jaffelin (Beaune)
Domaine Joblot (Givry)
Philippe Joliet (Fixin)
Domaine Comte Lafon
(Meursault)
Henri Lamarche (Vosne-
Romanée)
Lamy-Pillot (Chassagne-
Montrachet)
Louis Latour (Beaune)
Yves de Launay (Mercurey)
Lejeune (Pommard)
Lequin-Roussot (Santenay)
Georges Lignier (Morey St.-
Denis)

Château de la Maltroye
(Chassagne-Montrachet)
Manière-Noirot (Vosne-
Romanée)
J. P. Marchand (Gevrey-
Chambertin)
Joseph Matrot (Meursault)
Mestre (Santenay)
Alain Michelot (Nuits St.-
Georges)
Moillard (Nuits St.-Georges)
Charles Moncault (Beaune)
Denis Mortet (Gevrey-
Chambertin)
Gerard Mugneret (Vosne-
Romanée)
André Nudant (Nuits St.-
Georges)
Jacques Parent (Pommard)
Jean Pichenet (Savigny-les-
Beaunes)
Château de Pommard
(Pommard)
Pierre Ponnelle (Beaune)
M. Prunier (Auxey-Duresses)
Rapet (Savigny-les-Beaune)
Gaston et Pierre Ravaut (Aloxe-
Corton)

Henri Rebourseau (Gevrey-
Chambertin)
Remoissenet (Beaune)
Daniel Rion (Nuits St.-Georges)
Rion Père et Fils (Nuits St.-
Georges)
Maurice Rolland (Pernand-
Vergelesses)
Emmanuel Rouget (Nuits St.-
Georges)
Hervé Roumier (Chambolle-
Musigny)
Saier (Mercurey)
Daniel Senard (Aloxe-Corton)
C. Serafin (Gevrey-Chambertin)
Servelle Tachot (Clos Vougeot)
Robert Sirugue (Vosne-
Romanée)
Robert Suremaine (Monthelie)
Gabriel Tortochot (Gevrey-
Chambertin)
Domaine des Varoilles (Gevrey-
Chambertin)
Michael Voarick (Aloxe-Corton)
Comte de Vogüé (Chambolle-
Musigny)
L. Volpato (Chambolle-Musigny)

* * *(AVERAGE PRODUCERS)*

Arlaud (Nuits St.-Georges)
Bernard Bachelet (Chassagne-
Montrachet)
Bertagna (Vougeot)
Chanson (Beaune)
Chanzy Frères (Beaune)
F. Chauvenet (Nuits St.-
Georges)
Chevalier (Aloxe-Corton)'
Coron (Beaune)
Damoy (Gevrey-
Chambertin)

Albert Derey (Marsannay)
Henri Gouges (Nuits St.-
Georges)
Jaboulet-Vercherre (Beaune)
Labouré Roi (Beaune)
Lupé Cholet (Nuits St.-
Georges)
J. P. Magien (Gevrey-
Chambertin)
Mommessin (Macon)
Naigeon-Chauveau (Gevrey-
Chambertin)

Charles Noëllat (Vosne-
  Romanée)[1]
Patriarche (Beaune)
Pernot-Fourrier (Gevrey-
  Chambertin)
Jacques Prieur (Meursault)
Prosper Maufoux (Santenay)
Charles Quillardet (Gevrey-
  Chambertin)

A. Rodet (Beaune)
Vachet Rousseau (Gevrey-
  Chambertin)
Charles Viénot (Nuits St.-
  Georges)
Henri de Villamont (Beaune)

* (OTHER PRODUCERS)

Thomas Bassot (Gevrey-
  Chambertin)
Robert DuBois (Nuits St.-
  Georges)

Geisweiler (Nuits St.-Georges)
Pascal (Meursault)
La Reine Pedanque (Beaune)

The Best Values for Red Burgundy

The glamour appellations of the Côte de Nuits and the Côte de Beaune offer exorbitant prices as well as irregular quality. Consequently, more and more consumers are looking elsewhere for Pinot Noir wines, or are considering some of the less glamorous appellations of Burgundy where good wine values can still be found. The following list includes the best red burgundy appellations and producers.

Fixin (Côte de Nuits): The only reasonable value left among the extravagantly expensive wines of the Côte de Nuits. Located next to Gevrey-Chambertin, the wines of Fixin tend to be big, rustic, rather full red burgundies. The top four producers to look for are Pierre Gelin, Philippe Joliet, Dennis Berthaut, and Bruno Clair.

Ladoix (Côte de Beaune): Although this appellation gets very little attention, the wines are excellent, especially from producers such as Cornu or Ravault.

Savigny-les-Beaune (Côte de Beaune): A terribly underrated appellation, Savigny produces wines that often have a good, ripe, rich, strawberry-and-cherry fruitiness. Simon Bize, Guitton, Ecard, Tollot-Beaut, Bruno Clair, and Tollot-Voarick have very high standards.

Pernand-Vergelesses (Côte de Beaune): Perhaps the varying assessments of this appellation have kept its wines from receiving more notoriety. They are light, fragrant, aromatic wines, which resemble good Beaunes or Aloxe-Cortons, but at a much lower price. Four

[1] Purchased by the Maison Leroy in 1987; quality should ultimately be superb.

producers stand out here—Robert Rapet, Dubreuil-Fontaine, Domaine Chandon des Briailles, and Delarche.

Monthelie (Côte de Beaune): Unlike its neighbor Volnay, whose wines are much sought after as being elegant, suave and lush, Monthelie is terribly underrated, even though it produces robust, fragrant, high-quality Pinot Noir. Robert Suremain and Armand Douhairet are two notable growers.

Auxey-Duresses (Côte de Beaune): An up-and-coming appellation for both red and white burgundy, Auxey-Duresses does not have one of the best known names, but the firms of Leroy and Michel Prunier make very fine wine here.

Chassagne-Montrachet (Côte de Beaune): Although internationally famous for its splendidly perfumed, rich, white wines, Chassagne-Montrachet does not get enough recognition for its fragrant, supple, red wines, produced by such top growers as Château de la Maltroye and Lequin-Roussot.

Santenay (Côte de Beaune): Although Santenay is perhaps the most underrated appellation in the entire Côte d'Or, the quality of wine made there is particularly high. The wines are sturdy and age-worthy, particularly for Côte de Beaunes, with rather deep, rich, long flavors. The best producers are Lequin-Roussot, Adrian Belland, Domaine de la Charrière, Domaine de Pousse d'Or, Phillipe Mestre, and the *négociants* Joseph Drouhin and Remoissenet. All make delicious Santenays in the good vintages.

Values from the Côte Chalonnaise

For decades, smart Europeans who enjoy red burgundy but cannot afford the luxurious prices of the famous wines have been turning to the wine of the Côte Chalonnaise. There is much good—not great—red burgundy made there that normally sells for under $15 a bottle, often for less than $10. The following list includes the best appellations and the best producers. The 1982s, 1985s, and 1987s from these appellations are more consistently successful than the 1983s and 1984s.

St. Aubin: Henri Prudhon's St. Aubin red has plenty of style and character.

Rully: Rully is best known for its being the closest wine village to the drab town of Chagny, where one of France's greatest restaurants, Lameloise, is located. The best producers of Rully are the Domaine de la Folie and Henri Jacqueson, followed by Jean-François Delorme, Chanzy, and the *négociant* Faiveley.

Mercurey: Though hardly world famous, Mercurey is the most well-known appellation of the Côte Cnalonnaise. The best wines are made by the *négociant* Faiveley, as well as by growers Michel Juillot, Yves de Launay, Chanzy Frères, and A. Rodet.

Givry: Some of my favorite wines of the Côte Chalonnaise come from Givry. They have more richness and color than those of the other appellations. The Givry from Baron Thénard is first-class, followed by that of Gardin, who owns a vineyard called Clos Saloman.

Montagny: Of the Côte Chalonnaise's red wines, those of Montagny offer the least appeal, but they are not expensive. I know of no grower here making red wine as good as the aforementioned producers. However Jean Vachet and Maxime Millet are the two best producers.

BERNARD AMIOT (CHAMBOLLE-MUSIGNY)* * *

1985 Chambolle-Musigny	C	85
1985 Chambolle-Musigny Les Charmes	D	85

These are very forward, ripe, richly scented, lush burgundies that have plenty of fat and soft tannins. The "villages" Chambolle-Musigny seemed every bit as good as the Premier Cru Les Charmes. The latter tasted slightly more alcoholic and marginally more tannic.

PIERRE AMIOT (MOREY ST.-DENIS)* * *

1985 Clos de la Roche	E	90
1985 Gevrey-Chambertin aux Combottes	D	87
1985 Morey St.-Denis	D	83
1985 Morey St.-Denis aux Charmes	D	87
1985 Morey St.-Denis Les Baudes	D	85
1985 Morey St.-Denis Millandes	D	85

Pierre Amiot, from a different family and village than the above-mentioned Bernard Amiot, is one of the best-known growers in Burgundy. A man whose girth is almost equal to his height, he produces wonderfully fruity, elegant wines that drink very well when young. They are never particularly tannic or powerful, and age less successfully than others. His 1985s are his best wines since 1978—very fruity, supple, precocious wines that are undeniably charming and will drink well for 5–7 years. Both the Morey St.-Denis and the Morey St.-Denis Millandes are well-colored, richly fruity, soft wines that are drinking well now. The Morey St.-Denis aux Charmes has more depth and gives a broader, more expansive, almost sweet impression. By comparison, the Les Baudes is more tannic and firmer structured, but promising. The Gevrey-Chambertin aux Combottes combines a bit more power and tannin with the opulent, ripe fruit of the vintage to offer a bigger, more robust style of wine. The Clos de la Roche is outstanding—rich, sweet, and quite concentrated, with a penetrating bouquet of berry fruit, Oriental spices, and layers of soft fruit. It should age well for 6–7 more years. Amiot's 1986s, tasted prior to bottling, also looked good.

PIERRE ANDRÉ (ALOXE-CORTON)* * *

1985 Corton Clos du Roi	D	87
1985 Corton Pougets	D	86
1985 Savigny-les-Beaune Clos des Guettes	D	75

Pierre André, from whose vineyards the above wines are made, is also the founder of the *négociant* firm of La Reine Pedauque in Beaune, for whose wines I have little praise. Among the 1985s, the Savigny is lean, light, and decent, but unexhilarating. The Corton Pougets is significantly better, with a bouquet of cherries and toasty new oak. It is medium bodied, ripe, tasty, and ready to drink, with a good measure of alcohol in the finish. The Corton Clos du Roi is much more backward, but has fine power and depth. Don't touch it until 1992–1993.

MARQUIS D'ANGERVILLE (VOLNAY)* * *

1985 Volnay Champans	D	84
1985 Volnay Clos des Ducs	D	86

This is one of the historic estates of Burgundy, as the d'Angerville family was among the first to estate-bottle its wines. For over six decades they have been guardians of authentic, unadulterated burgundies. The 1985s are very stylish, lighter-weight examples of the vintage, with light- to medium-ruby color, a touch of vanillin from their aging in 25% new oak barrels, and elegantly wrought cherry fruit flavors. The Champans should be at its peak in 2–3 years and keep for 5–6 years thereafter. The Clos des Ducs is richer and deeper, with denser color and plenty of ripe cherry fruit.

COMTE ARMAND (POMMARD)* * * *

1985 Pommard Clos des Epeneaux	D	88

As Serena Sutcliffe says in her excellent *Pocket Guide to the Wines of Burgundy*, this wine "is for those who say that the present burgundy is too light." The 1985 has a dense, rich, ruby/purple color, a big, oaky, plummy, intense bouquet, significant flavor interest, and considerable body. It should mature between 1991 and 1998. From the barrel, the 1986 looked to be almost as good as the 1985.

ROBERT ARNOUX (VOSNE-ROMANÉE)* * * *

1985 Clos Vougeot	E	86
1985 Nuits St.-Georges Les Corvées-Paget	D	87
1985 Nuits St.-Georges Les Poisets	D	86
1985 Nuits St-Georges Les Procès	D	87
1985 Romanée St.-Vivant	E	88
1985 Vosne-Romanée Les Chaumes	D	87
1985 Vosne-Romanée Maziers	D	84
1985 Vosne-Romanée Les Suchots	D	90

The tall, robust Robert Arnoux is capable of producing exceptional Pinot Noir. The 1985 is his best vintage since the marvelous 1978. The Maziers is fruity, but straightforward and simple. The Nuits St.-Georges Les Poisets is a bigger, richer, deeper-colored wine, with more length and depth. The Les Procès shows an equally concentrated quality, but has more new wood aromas and more tannin and structure. The Corvées-Paget is rich, creamy, fat, loaded with fruit, and is more supple than the other two wines from Nuits St.-Georges; it is already a joy to drink. Two Arnoux vineyards that always do well are Les Chaumes and Les Suchots, both in Vosne-Romanée. Les Chaumes is always a more open-knit, fruitier, softer version of Les Suchots, and such is the case in 1985. It is already quite round and expansive on the palate, and is well colored, fat yet elegant, ripe, and full-bodied. The Les Suchots is exceptionally concentrated, seductive, very deep in color, and quite aromatic, with 6–10 years of further aging potential. The Clos Vougeot was closed when I tasted it and seemed tough, its personality more akin to 1983 than 1985. It has a dark color and a promising level of concentration, but is extremely tight. Lastly, the Romanée St.-Vivant is the second-best wine from Arnoux in 1985. Rich and alcoholic, supple, expansive, and very complex to smell (raspberries, new oak, and flowers), this wine should age nicely for a decade, yet I can hardly criticize those who want to drink it now. Arnoux's 1986s are not nearly as concentrated or perfumed as his 1985s. Tasted from the cask, they appeared surprisingly light, even in the context of the vintage.

BERNARD BACHELET (CHASSAGNE-MONTRACHET)* *

1985 Chassagne-Montrachet	C	84
1985 Côte de Beaune-Villages	B	85
1985 Santenay	C	85

These are three good examples of richly fruity, pure Pinot Noir that should retail for a reasonable price. The Chassagne-Montrachet has less complexity, more tannin, and may just need more time to show all its attributes. The 1985 Côte de Beaune-Villages and the Santenay are deeply colored, chewy, ripe wines that have silky textures, oodles of clean Pinot fruit, medium to full body, and a seductive sweetness and lushness.

BALLOT-MILLOT (MEURSAULT)* * *

1985 Beaune Epenots	D	85
1985 Pommard Pezerolles	D	90
1985 Pommard Rugiens	D	90
1985 Volnay Santenots	D	85
1985 Volnay Taille Pieds	D	87

Judging by the success of its 1985 red wines, this estate is able to wear two hats quite successfully. All of the 1985s possess broad, sweet, supple, expansive (and in the case of the two Pommards, explosively rich) flavors, medium to full body, gobs of ripe, hedonistic fruit, plenty of toasty new oak, and 5–7 years of cellaring potential.

BARTHOD NOËLLAT (CHAMBOLLE-MUSIGNY)* * *

1985 Bourgogne	B	83
1985 Chambolle-Musigny Les Beaux Bruns	C	86
1985 Chambolle-Musigny Les Charmes	C	87
1985 Chambolle-Musigny Les Cras	C	88

Like many other small growers in Burgundy, the elderly Monsieur Barthod has a one-family operation. He and his wife and daughter plow and prune the vineyards, and look after the wine. Barthod prefers to let his wines speak for him. They are handcrafted, unfiltered wines that are rarely profound, but are richly satisfying. According to Barthod, his 1985s are the best wines he has made since his 1978s and 1959s. The generic Bourgogne is deep in color, plummy, and pleasant for imbibing over the next 3–5 years. The Les Charmes has very good color, a rich, spicy, pure bouquet bursting with Pinot fruit, medium to full body, and plenty of length. It will be at its best between 1990 and 1995. The wine from Les Cras, a Premier Cru vineyard near Bonnes Mares, tasted less seductive, but richer, more tannic, and loaded with ripe fruit. It should reach full maturity between 1990 and 1996. Lastly, the Beaux Bruns seems to fall in style somewhere between the silky, voluptuous finesse and fruitiness of Les Charmes and the fuller bodied, more tannic Les Cras.

ADRIAN BELLAND (SANTENAY)* * *

1985 Chambertin	E	86
1985 Corton Clos de la Vigne Sainte	D	86
1985 Corton Grèves	D	87
1985 Corton Perrières	D	86
1985 Santenay Clos Genêt	D	85

1985 Santenay La Comme	D	86

1985 Santenay Les Gravières	D	85

The shy, gentle, reserved Adrian Belland, who would look like Santa Claus were he to grow a beard, has his serpentine cellars in the village of Santenay, a terribly underrated appellation for both red and white wine. Belland produces chunky, fleshy, well-colored wines that are reasonably priced and quite flavorful. My only criticism is that the wines have much the same taste, texture, and character whether they are from Santenay or Chambertin. Belland's 1985s, if not exceptional, are full-bodied, rich, flavorful, dark ruby-colored wines with much palate presence. Given the ratings, which are approximately the same, the best values above are his Santenays. The Clos Genêt, from a less publicized vineyard, has broad, fat, creamy flavors, wads of fruit, plenty of color, and a full-bodied, lengthy finish. It should last 5–10 years. The La Comme has a similar texture, but tasted slightly more concentrated. The Gravières had a spicy note to its bouquet, and a more dusty, tannic texture. Regarding the three Cortons, the Grèves, made from 25-year-old vines, had loads of rich black cherry fruit, impressive length and depth, and easily 10 years of aging potential. By comparison, the Perrières tastes fat, but less complex. The Clos de la Vigne Sainte, certainly the most famous of the three Cortons, has very high acidity, and an austere, tart personality, but plenty of underlying fruit and depth. It is the only wine here that requires 5–7 years of cellaring before drinking. The Chambertin is quite good, but hardly lives up to its name. The sweet, ripe bouquet offers plenty of appeal, but the wine seems to lack concentration and has a soupy texture. It had been bottled only two months before I tasted it, so perhaps it was not at its best. The 1986s here tasted pleasant but undistinguished.

DOMAINE DENIS BERTHAUT (FIXIN)* * *

1985 Fixin	B	81

1985 Fixin Les Arvelets	C	86

1985 Fixin Les Clos	C	85

1985 Fixin Les Crais	C	83

1985 Gevrey-Chambertin   C   84

The tall, open-faced Denis Berthaut is always worth visiting. Responsive and surprisingly candid, Berthaut is a refreshing young man. His wines, always decent values, are robust, yet interesting and stylish. They spend plenty of time in oak (about 24–26 months) and are never filtered. Although you won't find great wine here, you will find good, forceful burgundy with excellent aging qualities. His 1985s are softer and more openly fruity than usual, with medium to full body, good tannins for 2–6 years of cellaring, and clear, pure Pinot Noir flavors. The Les Crais is distinguished by a minty, very spicy bouquet; the Les Clos is rich, berry-scented and lush; and the Arvelets is the best and most concentrated wine of the Berthaut stable.

DOMAINE BERTHEAU (CHAMBOLLE-MUSIGNY)* * *

1985 Bonnes Mares   E   88

1985 Chambolle-Musigny   D   85

1985 Chambolle-Musigny Les Amoureuses   D   88

Until the 1985s, the wines from this estate did not greatly appeal to me. Very rustic in style, they often tasted as if the barrels used for aging were too old. The 1985s look very good—supple, richly fruity, almost jammy, with loads of sweet, smoky, raspberry fruit. They are unfiltered and already have thrown a small sandy sediment. The "villages" wine, the Chambolle-Musigny, will have to be drunk over the next 4–5 years, but given its round, generous ripe flavors and velvety texture, no one will object. The Les Amoureuses is utterly delicious —rich, sweet, round, fat, and bursting with fruit, as well as fuller and deeper than the Chambolle-Musigny. It is only surpassed by the Bonnes Mares, a dark ruby-colored, opulent, abundantly fruity wine that has excellent ripeness and length, as well as 5–8 years of further cellaring potential.

DOMAINE BESANCENOT-MATHOUILLET (BEAUNE)* * *

1985 Beaune Cent Vignes   C   87

1985 Beaune Clos du Roi   C   86

This small domaine, located just outside the walls of the medieval city of Beaune, is terribly underrated. The wines made here are textbook

Côte de Beaune burgundies. The 1985s are bursting with ripe berry fruit and are quite soft, rich and an absolute joy to drink today, although one suspects that in a cool cellar they will age quite gracefully for another 7–8 years. The Beaune Cent Vignes seemed to be showing a bit more fruit than the fuller-bodied, more massive Clos du Roi. These are excellently made wines from a very good cellar, still priced within reason.

BICHOT-CLOS FRANTIN (BEAUNE)* * * *

1985 Bichot Beaune Montée Rouge	B	55
1985 Bichot Château de Dracy	B	65
1985 Bichot Pommard Rugiens	C	72
1985 Clos Vougeot Clos Frantin	D	90
1985 Echézeaux Clos Frantin	D	87
1985 Gevrey-Chambertin Clos Frantin	D	78
1985 Grands-Echézeaux Clos Frantin	E	90
1985 Nuits St.-Georges Clos Frantin	D	76
1985 Vosne-Romanée Les Malconsorts Clos Frantin	D	92

This gigantic *négociant* produces an ocean of insipid, dull wine under the name "Bichot" and several *sous-noms*, or second labels, which I find overpriced and not always representative of Burgundy. Yet, the wines from the Clos Frantin vineyards in the Côte de Nuits and those from the Chablis estate, Long-Depaquit, rank with the finest made in Burgundy. The ratings above are indicative of the range in quality from Bichot-Clos Frantin. The Bichot offerings taste cooked and dull, and are of no interest. The Clos Frantin wines range from standard quality to absolutely superb in the case of the rich, deep, powerful Clos Vougeot, the silky, seductive Echézeaux, the profound Grands-Echézeaux, and the astonishingly rich, deep, sublime Vosne-Romanée Les Malconsorts. Although I did not taste them, the Clos Frantin Richebourg and the Corton are usually outstanding; however, they are made in tiny quantities.

DOMAINE BILLARD-GONNET (POMMARD)* * *

1985 Beaune La Lune Montrevenots	D	83
1985 Pommard	D	83
1985 Pommard Les Chaponnières	D	?
1985 Pommard Clos de Vergers	D	87
1985 Pommard Les Rugiens	D	87

The wines produced by Billard-Gonnet are tannic, lean, classic, and slow to develop. They are among the least impressive wines when young, most of them requiring a good 4–5 years to shed their cloak of tannin, but they do evolve well. Even the 1985s, though precocious and flattering to taste, are firm and introverted. The only wine that can be drunk today is the Beaune, which has well-developed, moderately intense cherry fruitiness, a nice touch of toasty oak, and a soft texture. The Pommard is firm and well structured, but tannic and closed. There is a noticeable leap in quality starting with the Clos de Vergers, which has a lovely oaky, black cherry-scented bouquet, rich, long flavors, but enough tannin to merit cellaring for 4–5 years before drinking. The Les Chaponnières is very tannic and quite closed, though the color is deep. I found this wine very difficult to judge. The top wine is the Rugiens, a deeply colored, full-bodied, rich, concentrated wine that has plenty of extract and quite a finish. It needs 4–5 years of cellaring.

BITOUZET-PRIEUR (VOLNAY)* * * *

1985 Volnay	C	83
1985 Volnay Aussy	C	85
1985 Volnay Clos des Chênes	C	88
1985 Volnay Pitures	C	86
1985 Volnay Taillepieds	C	90

The village of Volnay has many well-known and reliable winemakers, yet one of the best and surprisingly least known is Vincent Bitouzet. His 1985s are the finest wines I have ever tasted from him. Because

Bitouzet uses hot fermentations (35° C) to extract color, tannin and fruit, his 1985s are rich, deeply colored, quite concentrated wines that exhibit considerable flavor purity. All were filtered according to the Kisselguhr system prior to bottling, except for the splendid Taille-pieds. As for the wines themselves, the Volnay is a lively, well-colored, fruity, solid wine with a chunky, fleshy fruitiness. It will make for pleasant drinking over the next 3–4 years. The Volnay Aussy is also drinking very well at the moment—fat, richly fruity, concentrated, and expansive on the palate, with plenty of raspberry fruit. Unlike the precocious Aussy, the Volnay Pitures is tannic, burly, rich and robust, with a good deal of body. It leans toward Pommard in its style. The Volnay Clos des Chênes should be the best wine of the lot, as the vineyard is one of the best in Volnay. It is indeed a gorgeous wine, with layers of rich cherry and raspberry fruit, full body, and a sublime elegance and finesse; it should be at its best between 1989 and 1999. But the star in 1985 is the Volnay Taillepieds, a majestic, rich, deep, layered wine with superb extract and a wonderfully pure balanced feel on the palate. The wine is a near perfect Volnay and, while quite accessible now, should drink well for 10–12 more years.

LUCIEN BOILLOT (GEVREY-CHAMBERTIN)* * *

1985 Côte de Nuits-Villages	B	84
1985 Gevrey-Chambertin	C	78
1985 Gevrey-Chambertin Les Cherbaudes	D	85
1985 Gevrey-Chambertin Les Corbeaux	D	83
1985 Nuits St.-Georges Les Pruliers	D	85
1985 Pommard Les Croix Noires	D	83
1985 Volnay Cru des Angles	D	84

These are respectable 1985s, but, then, Lucien Boillot is not one of my favorite growers. While a handful of the 1982s turned out to be decent wines, his 1983s are excessively astringent and marked by rot. As for the 1985s, they are cleanly made in an ancient style. Tannic and aged in old barrels, they all lean toward coarseness. Perhaps with 4–5 years of cellaring they will reveal more charm and grace. The Côte de Nuits-Villages is almost as good as the other wines. Robust, spicy, and deeply colored, it has plenty of presence on the palate. The Gevrey-Chambertin is especially hard and austere for a 1985. The Les Cherbaudes shows much more fruit and plenty of tannin, yet has better balance and more concentration than the closed, tough Les Corbeaux. I had similar problems with both the lean, sinewy Volnay and the angular Pommard. Potentially the best wine, the Nuits St.-Georges Les Pruliers offers enough rich black cherry fruit to match the fierce tannins. All of these wines will need 3–5 years of cellaring.

JEAN-MARC BOULEY (VOLNAY)* * *

1985 Pommard Pezerolles	C	86
1985 Pommard Rugiens	C	87
1985 Volnay Clos des Chênes	C	87

On my recent—and first—visit to this up-and-coming domaine, located in the back streets of the village of Volnay I tasted only the 1985s and 1987s. Jean-Marc Bouley has 32.5 acres of well-placed vineyards and believes in 75% new oak for his Premier Crus and 50% new oak for his other wines. While Bouley is not well known, his wines are vastly superior to those from many of the glamorous estates of Pommard and Volnay. His 1987s may be better than his excellent 1985s. Look for his Volnays from the Clos des Chênes and Les Caillerets vineyards and his Pommards from the Pezerolles and Rugiens vineyards.

BOURÉE PÈRE ET FILS (GEVREY-CHAMBERTIN)* * * *

1985 Beaune Premier Cru	C	86
1985 Bonnes Mares	E	86
1985 Chambertin	E	87
1985 Chambolle-Musigny	C	84
1985 Chambolle-Musigny Les Amoureuses	E	89
1985 Chambolle-Musigny Les Charmes	E	87
1985 Charmes-Chambertin	E	91

1985 Clos de la Roche	E	96
1985 Côte de Beaune-Villages	B	80
1985 Côte de Nuits-Villages	B	84
1985 Gevrey-Chambertin Cazetiers	D	89
1985 Gevrey-Chambertin Clos de la Justice	C	90
1985 Gevrey-Chambertin Lavaux St.-Jacques	D	90
1985 Morey St.-Denis	D	84
1985 Nuits St.-Georges	C	80
1985 Nuits St.-Georges Les Vaucrains	D	88
1985 Vosne-Romanée	C	80

The Bourée firm is a small *négociant* located right on the main thoroughfare in Gevrey-Chambertin. For some years, this quality enterprise has been run by Mr. Vallet, the nephew of the late Pierre Bourée. The wines are made in what is clearly the *ancienne méthode*, meaning that there is no destemming here, but there is an extremely long cuvaison of 21–36 days, a high temperature fermentation, the least possible racking, never any filtration, and the bottling of the wine by each barrel, as is done by the Domaine de la Romanée-Conti. One wishes there were more people like Vallet in Burgundy. The 1985s were about to be bottled when I tasted them on July 2, 1987. Vallet thinks they are the best wines he has made since 1949. In general, I found his 1985s to be richly colored and very structured, the best of them being quite special. At the lower level of the burgundy hierarchy, the Beaune Premier Cru showed surprising depth, richness and structure; it has 5–10 years of cellaring potential. The Côte de Nuits-Villages was deeply colored, tannic and quite big; it needs 4–5 years of cellaring. Among the "villages" wines from the Côte de Nuits, while the Vosne-Romanée was boring and one-dimensional, the Morey St.-Denis had plenty of power, depth, structure and character, as did the softer, more seductive and perfumed Chambolle-Musigny. The Nuit St.-Georges was extremely tannic, closed, and not at all easy to evaluate. However, the real stars of the Bourée house in 1985 are the

Premier and Grand Crus. Of course, the five-acre Clos de la Justice in Gevrey-Chambertin is not a Premier Cru, but Vallet owns this property and makes what is certainly the finest red burgundy from the "wrong," or eastern, side of the famous Route Nationale, N 74, which runs through Burgundy's famed Côte d'Or. I thought the 1985 Clos de la Justice the finest example of this wine I have ever tasted. Deep ruby, with a super bouquet of ripe plummy fruit and hickory smoke, this full-bodied wine is quite concentrated and very long. It should be at its peak between 1990 and 2005. I preferred it marginally to the Chambolle-Musigny Les Charmes, which has layers of velvety ripe fruit but seemed less complex and concentrated. The Les Amoureuses has great extract of flavor, a rich, supple texture, quite an expansive feel on the palate, and good tannins. The Bonnes Mares inexplicably tasted much lighter, and while certainly very good, lacked the breadth of the Les Amoureuses. The Nuits St.-Georges Vaucrains tasted enormous, but also broodingly backward and tannic; it is loaded with potential if one has the patience to wait 6–10 years. Vallet's selections from the Gevrey-Chambertin appellation are usually his top wines. The two Premier Cru vineyards, Lavaux St.-Jacques and Les Cazetiers, produce real insiders' wines, not only from here but from other producers as well. Both vineyards often approach Grand Cru quality. The difference between these two wines at Bourée is that the Lavaux is more fleshy, supple and open-knit, but has super fruit and length, whereas the Cazetiers is more tannic, more savage, and even deeper and richer, but it will take more time to reach maturity. I would estimate that the Lavaux will peak between 1989 and 1996, and the Cazetiers between 1992 and 2005. For pure elegance and oodles of plump, succulent berry fruit, the Charmes-Chambertin offers a truly hedonistic drinking experience. It is round, generous, and explosively fruity. The Chambertin is tannic and a trifle too oaky and less impressive. Vallet's greatest wine in 1985, and one of the superstars of the vintage, is his Clos de la Roche, of which 100 cases (4 barrels) were produced. The wine is almost black in color, and has the type of flavor intensity and exceptional length and richness that I have rarely encountered in red burgundy. It is a staggeringly great wine that will drink superbly for the rest of this century.

ALAIN BURGUET (GEVREY-CHAMBERTIN)* * *

1985 Gevrey-Chambertin   C   86

As young Burguet continues to make a very impressive wine, it's a shame he doesn't have access to any of the Premier or Grand Cru vineyards of Gevrey-Chambertin. His 1985 has a good, deep ruby/ purple color, a big, spicy, meaty bouquet, lush flavors, and at least 5– 8 more years of drinking potential ahead of it. From the barrel, the 1986 also looked to be successful, although less seductive and charming than the 1985.

CHÂTEAU DE CHAMBOLLE-MUSIGNY (CHAMBOLLE-MUSIGNY)* * *

1985 Bonnes Mares	E	86
1985 Chambolle-Musigny Les Amoureuses	E	85
1985 Le Musigny	E	87
1985 Le Musigny Vieilles Vignes	E	90

This highly reputable domaine produces elegant, rather delicate wines that get a mighty dosage of aging in new oak barrels, too much so in my view. That being said, the 1985s are very fragrant, aromatic wines with a great deal of toasty vanillin aromas. The colors of these wines are deceptively light, but have plenty of graceful, silky, smooth berry fruit flavors, especially the splendid cuvée of old vines from the Grand Cru vineyard of Musigny. Proprietor Mugneret also made good 1986s that resemble the 1979 Côte de Nuits wines, but are superior to them.

CHAMPY PÈRE (BEAUNE)* * *

1985 Beaune Avaux	C	82
1985 Clos de Vougeot	D	85
1985 Savigny-les-Beaune Les Dominaudes	C	84

This is a source for very old-style red wines that are still fermented in old wooden cuvées, kept 12–24 months in old oak (they eschew new barrels at Champy), and are bottled directly from the barrel by hand. I find the wines hard, overly structured and tannic, but interesting and clearly age-worthy. In fact, prospective purchasers would be advised to cellar virtually any Champy wine for 3–4 years before trying to drink it.

CHANZY FRÈRES (BEAUNE)* *

1986 Bourgogne Clos de la Fortune	B	78

1986 Mercurey Clos de Roy	B	80

1986 Rully	B	73

Chanzy Frères' 1987s and 1985s are superior to their 1986s. This large domaine of 100 acres produces sound wines from Rully and Mercurey, appellations that offer great values. The 1986s listed above are rather lean, hard wines that could have benefited from more fat and charm.

DOMAINE DE LA CHARRIÈRE (SANTENAY)* * *

1985 Santenay La Comme	C	87

1985 Santenay La Maladière	C	85

Jean Girardin's Domaine de la Charrière produces reliably good, beefy wines with plenty of character at modest prices. Both 1985s are quite deep ruby in color, full bodied, rich in flavor, and have 8–12 years of cellaring potential. The Maladière is more accessible. In fact, it is delicious now—round, supple, and elegant, with a berry fruit character of Pinot Noir well displayed. The Comme is a really serious wine —dense, ripe, full bodied, very concentrated, and surprisingly long. The tannin level suggests it will keep for at least a decade.

F. CHAUVENET (NUITS ST.-GEORGES)* *

1985 Beaune Theurons	C	78

1985 Charmes-Chambertin	D	87

1985 Clos St.-Denis	D	87

1985 Corton	D	85

1985 Côte de Beaune-Villages	C	82

1985 Echézeaux	D	85

1985 Pommard Epenots	D	84

1985 Nuits St.-Georges La Perrière	D	80

1985 Santenay	C	78

This *négociant* has recently turned out some very good red wines, and some exceptional white ones. The red 1985s are well made rather than exciting. Although they are correct, well colored, very fruity, soft, and tasty, they miss being special because they lack personality and individuality. The best of them are the fat, rich, velvety, succulent Charmes-Chambertin and the more classic Clos St.-Denis. Both wines are hard to resist because of their voluptuous fruit and soft tannins, but both should age nicely for 5–7 years. The lighter, but still effusively fruity, darkly colored Corton and the elegant, fragrant Echézeaux also looked good. As for the other wines, they have very fine deep ruby color and good ripe fruit, but several are straightforward and one-dimensional.

J. CHAUVENET (NUITS ST.-GEORGES)* * *

1985 Nuits St.-Georges	C	85
1985 Nuits St.-Georges Les Bousselots	C	90
1985 Nuits St.-Georges les Vaucrains	C	90
1985 Vosne-Romanée	C	85

Jean Chauvenet, a small grower, should not be confused with the *négociant* F. Chauvenet, reviewed above. The former's 1985s are the finest wines he has ever made, which were bottled without any fining or filtration. The "villages" Vosne-Romanée has a deep color, a lush rich blackberry fruitiness, and a sweet palate impression from the great ripeness attained in the 1985 vintage. The "villages" Nuits St.-Georges is much more tannic and closed. I suspect it will be fine in 3–4 years, but the Vosne-Romanée will still be more seductive. Chauvenet also made two great wines in 1985. His Les Vaucrains, almost black in color, is a wine of enormous richness, expansive pure Pinot Noir flavors, and awesome length. For the price, it is a steal. Expect it to peak between 1990 and 2000. And the Les Bousselots should turn out to be every bit as good. It is also virtually black in color, extremely rich, full bodied, long and packed with flavor, but also much more tannic. I anticipate its plateau of maturity to be between 1992 and 2005.

ROBERT CHEVILLON (NUITS ST.-GEORGES)* * * *

1985 Nuits St.-Georges	C	85

1985 Nuits St.-Georges Les Cailles	D	90
1985 Nuits St.-Georges La Perrière	D	87
1985 Nuits St.-Georges Les Roncières	D	89
1985 Nuits St.-Georges Les Saint-Georges	D	85
1985 Nuits St.-Georges Les Vaucrains	D	92

It is hard not to like either the handsome, friendly Robert Chevillon or his wines. His track record in the eighties is exemplary, particularly in view of the pleasant wines he turned out in 1981, 1982, and 1984. As for the 1985s, they are much more flattering to taste than his large-scaled, massive 1983s. The Nuits St.-Georges is deliciously ripe, fruity, well colored and well endowed for a "villages" wine. Drink it over the next 4–5 years. The Perrière is similarly precocious, opulently fruity, soft, broadly flavored, and ideal for consuming over the next 5–7 years. Chevillon's Roncières has not only sumptuous levels of Pinot fruit, but also more structure, body and tannin, no doubt from an elevated use of new oak. It should offer ideal drinking between 1988 and 1994. Two splendid wines made by Chevillon in 1985 are his Les Cailles and Les Vaucrains. However, his Les Saint-Georges has turned out to be very good rather than special. As for the Les Cailles, this rich, decadent, explosively fruity wine comes from a vineyard where the vines average 50 years of age. The wine is very deep and profound, and can be drunk now or cellared for 8–10 years. The enormous bouquet of smoky oak and stupendous fruit of the Les Vaucrains left me searching for new adjectives. Absolutely gorgeous and bursting at the seams with fruit, this hedonistic wine will be impossible to resist drinking now, but it has the balance and structure to last 8–10 years. Chevillon's 1986s were among the better wines I tasted from the appellation of Nuit St.-Georges.

BRUNO CLAIR (MARSANNAY)* * * *

1985 Côte de Nuits-Villages	B	83
1985 Fixin La Croix Blanche	C	83
1985 Marsannay	B	82

1987 Marsannay Rosé	B	85

1985 Savigny-les-Beaune Dominode	C	85

The young and talented Bruno Clair has moved back into his family's cellars since the Clair-Daü estate was divided, with many of the family's vineyards being sold to Louis Jadot. Starting with the 1986 vintage, one will see Premier Cru Gevrey-Chambertins from Bruno Clair, such as Fonteny, Cazetiers, and Clos St.-Jacques, as well as the Grand Cru, Chambertin Clos de Bèze, since he has retained the right to make some wine from these vineyards as part of the sale of the Clair-Daü estate. As for Bruno Clair's 1985s, the wines had just been bottled when I was there in March of 1988, and seemed less impressive than when I tasted them in 1987. I must admit, however, that his sublime 1987 rosé from Marsannay, which I tasted half a dozen times or more when I was in Burgundy recently, is one of the three or four finest dry rosés I have ever tasted. It is loaded with flavor. As for the red wines of 1985, the Marsannay is good, but simple and uncomplicated. The Côte de Nuit-Villages is round and well colored, but lacking a bit in body (over-filtered?). The Fixin La Croix Blanche seems to have the same absence of mid-range. His Savigny Les Dominodes, made from 85-year-old vines, had a very deep color and seemed rich, but also dry and very tannic in the finish. Normally this wine is a real show stopper. I've noted that Clair has begun to filter his reds (using the modern but tricky Kisselguhr system), as well as fine them at the insistence of his agent, Tim Marshall. I hope this is not the reason for these wines tasting less impressive than I had hoped. Clair has a very impressive lineup of 1986s, particularly his Gevrey-Chambertin Clos St.-Jacques, Les Cazetiers, and Chambertin Clos de Bèze.

DOMAINE CLOS DES LAMBRAYS (MOREY ST.-DENIS)* * *

1985 Clos des Lambrays	E	87

1985 Morey St.-Denis	C	85

The Morey St.-Denis admirably exhibits the traits that make the 1985 vintage for red burgundy so seductive and appealing. Deep in color, with a bouquet full of red fruit, the palate impression is one of generosity and velvety flavors. It will drink well for 5–6 years. On the other hand, the famous Clos des Lambrays is more tannic and closed, has plenty of ripe fruit and underlying depth, but needs several years to shed its cloak of tannin. I was not impressed with the cask samples of 1986s I tasted.

DOMAINE EDMOND CORNU (LADOIX)* * * *

1985 Aloxe-Corton	C	87
1985 Aloxe-Corton Les Moutottes	C	87
1985 Chorey-les-Beaune Les Bons Ores	C	83
1985 Corton Bressandes	D	93
1985 Ladoix	C	85
1985 Savigny-les-Beaune	C	86

The tall, wiry, deep-voiced Edmond Cornu is a very talented and meticulous winemaker who I am sure would be much better known were he not situated in the drab little village of Ladoix, located on the "wrong," or eastern side of the Côte d'Or's Route Nationale, N 74. For those who say that all of Burgundy's wines are expensive, Cornu's prices are hard to beat, particularly in view of the quality of his 1985s. The Chorey-les-Beaune has a straightforward raspberry fruitiness, an elegant framework, and 4–6 years of aging potential. The Ladoix is a big, rich, creamy textured wine with some scents of new oak, great color, and a long, lush finish. The Savigny-les-Beaune tastes much bigger still; it exhibits plenty of tannin, is full bodied, and has excellent concentration. However, it is a long-distance runner; give it 4–6 years to peak. Cornu really excels with his wines from Aloxe-Corton. The Aloxe-Corton is rich, fat, very plump, and succulent, with layers of fruit, but also plenty of tannin and structure. The Aloxe-Corton Les Moutottes offers more concentration, plenty of rich, plummy, ripe fruit, a nice touch of toasty oak, and a powerful, long finish. It should make an excellent bottle between 1990 and 1998. The Corton Bressandes is an astonishingly rich wine with sensational depth and length, a huge bouquet of raspberry fruit, and toasty new oak and flowery scents. It has outstanding balance and seems to explode on the palate because of its concentration. The wine comes from an old 1.3-acre vineyard, where many of the vines were planted in 1920.

DELARCHE PÈRE ET FILS (PERNAND-VERGELESSES)* * *

1985 Corton Renards	D	90
1986 Corton Renards	D	87
1986 Pernand-Vergelesses Ile des Vergelesses	C	76
1986 Pernand-Vergelesses Les Vergelesses	C	75

This small estate, run by Marius Delarche and his son, Philippe, makes very good wine using traditional techniques and 50% new oak. The 1987s are more successful than the 1986s, but certainly the top red wine made here, the Corton Renards, is quite impressive in 1986 and truly great in 1985. This is also an estate to search out the tiny quantities of outstanding white Corton Charlemagne.

ALBERT DEREY (MARSANNAY)* *

1985 Fixin	B	82
1985 Fixin Les Hervelets	B	85
1985 Marsannay Chante Perdrix	B	81

These wines offer uncomplicated Pinot Noir flavors at what I think are decent prices. The Marsannay is a little rough at the edge and by no means delicate, but is fruity and ripe. The Fixin has an earthy, cherry-scented bouquet, rather light to medium body, and a clean, fresh finish. Drink it over the next 2–3 years. The Fixin Les Hervelets, from one of the three best vineyards of this appellation, is a seductive, ripe, rich, soft, lush wine with 4–6 more years of drinkability.

JOSEPH DROUHIN (BEAUNE)* * * *

1985 Aloxe-Corton	C	85
1985 Beaune Champimonts	C	83
1985 Beaune Clos des Mouches	D	87
1985 Bonnes Mares	E	88

1985 Chambertin	E	87
1985 Chambolle-Musigny	C	82
1985 Chambolle-Musigny Premier Cru	C	85
1985 Charmes-Chambertin	E	92
1985 Chassagne-Montrachet	C	83
1985 Chorey-les-Beaune	B	78
1985 Clos de la Roche	E	86
1985 Clos Vougeot	E	88
1985 Corton Bressandes	E	86
1985 Côte de Beaune-Villages	B	78
1985 Echézeaux	E	90
1985 Gevrey-Chambertin	B	81
1985 Gevrey-Chambertin Lavaux St.-Jacques	E	87
1985 Grands-Echézeaux	E	88
1985 Griottes-Chambertin	E	88
1985 Monthelie	B	82
1985 Morey St.-Denis	C	83
1985 Musigny	E	87
1985 Nuits St.-Georges	C	78
1985 Nuits St.-Georges Les Roncières	D	85
1985 Pommard	C	84

1985 Pommard Epenots	D 87
1985 Santenay	C 84
1985 Savigny-les-Beaune	C 83
1985 Volnay	C 84
1985 Volnay Clos des Chênes	D 87
1985 Vosne-Romanée	C 75
1985 Vosne-Romanée Les Beaumonts	D 86
1985 Vosne-Romanée Les Suchots	D 87

The Drouhin firm is indisputedly one of the most significant producers of quality wine—it now sells to 55 countries—and the company's president, Robert Drouhin, is a capable and articulate spokesman for the growers of Burgundy. Drouhin's wines are a product of the modern school of winemaking; fermentation temperatures are low and the wines are bottled very early and, of course, filtered to ensure stability in the bottle while they are being shipped. The white wines are of very high quality, and the reds are certainly quite good. One suspects that with a slightly higher fermentation temperature, and perhaps less of an obsession with technical stability and perfection, the red wines could be more dramatic, but no one will have any complaints about the 1985s. They are all impeccably clean, correct, and well made. Drouhin has managed to preserve the unique identity of each appellation, as the wines do not taste alike. There is a house style, of course, but that can be said of the wines of a small grower as well. With respect to the Côte de Beaunes, the majority of them tasted like ideal restaurant wines—richly fruity, easy-to-drink and easy-to-understand, and totally correct for their appellations, but without much character. However, there are several notable exceptions. The Beaune Clos des Mouches is a deeply colored, broadly flavored wine bursting with ripe cherry fruit. It will drink well for 4–5 years. The Volnay Clos des Chênes has more of a supple, rich raspberry fruitiness that is married nicely with a touch of new oak. It will keep well for 5–10 years. The most impressive of the Côte de Beaune red is the Pommard Epenots. Surprisingly big, bold and forceful, with plenty of underlying depth and body, this concentrated, alcoholic, tannic wine should age well for 10 years. The Corton Bressandes is even more powerful, but I thought I detected a touch of over-ripeness in the bouquet. It is a fleshy, rich, high alcoholic wine that seems a bit out-of-step with Robert Drouhin's winemaking philosophy.

When one tastes through the Côte de Nuits offerings—but past the bland "villages" wines of Nuits-St.-Georges, Chambolle-Musigny, Morey St.-Denis, Vosne-Romanée, and Gevrey-Chambertin—the quality takes a quantum leap. There is more color, substance, and richness to both the Nuits St.-Georges Les Roncières and Chambolle Musigny-Premier Cru. Both should keep well for upwards of a decade. Among the two Vosne-Romanées, the Les Suchots looks especially good, with an intense, spicy, cinnamon-scented bouquet. It is a full-bodied wine with excellent color and depth. Even more robust, age-worthy and tannic, yet concentrated and balanced, is the Lavaux St.-Jacques, a big, chewy wine to put away for 6–10 years.

At the Grand Cru level, all the wines are excellent, save for the Echézeaux and Charmes-Chambertin—which are superb. The Echézeaux has a haunting and heady bouquet of violets, crushed berry fruit, and new oak. Extremely elegant, supple, rich and concentrated, it is so enticing to drink now that one is tempted to ignore the fact that it should get better over the next 5–7 years. The Charmes-Chambertin is a great wine, filled with layers of ripe, rich fruit, a complex, full-intensity bouquet of toasty new oak, a supple, velvety texture, but enough tannins to ensure a decade of longevity. As for the other Grand Crus, the Clos Vougeot is an effusively fruity wine, yet quite powerful and full bodied. Its low acidity suggests current drinkability, but there is plenty of tannin lurking beneath the surface. The Clos de la Roche is very good but herbaceous. On the palate, it is robust and rich, and should be at its best between 4 and 10 years old. The Grands-Echézeaux has a sweet, ripe, broad, plummy fruitiness, medium to full body, superripeness and length, but less complexity and class than the aforementioned Echézeaux. I suspect that the Bonnes Mares will merit a higher score in 5 years, as it is opulent and quite tannic, but deep, well colored, and very long. The Musigny is more open, more perfumed, and easier to evaluate. It is not a big wine, but is harmonious, well balanced, and richly fruity. Few Chambertins live up to the majesty that the name and price tag certainly suggest. Drouhin's Chambertin is dark ruby, has plenty of extract, is ripe and concentrated as well as tannic, but does not seem profound or special. It needs 4–5 years of cellaring, but will keep 10–15 years. Lastly, the Griottes-Chambertin is oozing with berry fruit, has a super bouquet of toasty oak and jammy fruit, full body, a velvety texture, and excellent length. It will peak between 1989 and 1996.

DOMAINE DUJAC (MOREY ST.-DENIS)* * * * *

1985 Bonnes Mares	E	97
1985 Charmes-Chambertin	E	94
1985 Clos de la Roche	E	96
1985 Clos St.-Denis	E	92
1985 Echézeaux	D	90
1985 Gevrey-Chambertin aux Combottes	D	89
1985 Morey St.-Denis	D	86

This is one of the finest estates in Burgundy. Unfortunately, not everyone in the United States understands these wines, and this includes restaurant owners and certain merchants who are at a loss to explain the positive quality of wines with sandy sediment in the bottle. Because Jacques Seysses does not filter his wines, after 6 months to several years, depending on the vintage, a fine sediment forms in them —a natural occurrence in handmade wines. Such wines are also very vulnerable to heat prostration because they are alive. Perhaps America's fanatical obsession with squeaky clean, crystal-clear wines that have had much of their flavor eviscerated by numerous sterile filtrations is why Seysses now sells only 20% of his crop to the United States. What a tragedy! His 1985s are the finest wines he has made in his illustrious career, even finer than his glorious 1978s. While Dujac made lovely 1986s, including a delicious barrel-fermented Chardonnay from Morey St.-Denis, his 1985s are what we should focus on now. The "villages" Morey St.-Denis is good, fragrant, complex, deep, and lush; it has 6–8 more years of drinkability ahead of it. His Gevrey-Chambertin aux Combottes has a full-intensity, very spicy, rich, and multidimensional bouquet; its deep, rich, flowing flavors just go on and on. It will keep for 10–12 years. Among the Grand Crus (all aged in 100% new oak), there are enough splendid wines to satisfy even the most demanding palate. In ascending the ladder of quality, one starts with the lightest and most elegant, the Echézeaux, which is a great wine, particularly in view of the face that the vines are only 5 years old. Ripe, rich aromas of strawberry and cherry fruit jump from the glass. Medium-bodied, with superfinesse, this will be the earliest maturing wine of the Dujac stable. The Clos St.-Denis has a very deep color and an intense, ripe, spicy, very fragrant, penetrating bouquet. Full bodied and rather tannic, it explodes at the finish. It should peak between 1990 and 2000. For the next 6–8 years, the seductive qualities of the Charmes-Chambertin will be hard to pass by. An open-knit, fabulous bouquet of toasty oak, flowers, berry fruit, and Oriental spices is followed by flavors that are very concentrated, long, lush, and exciting. Lastly, the two superstars offer everything one could really ever want in a burgundy. The Clos de la Roche is the most powerful and concentrated wine the domaine made in 1985. It is a blockbuster wine with 10–15 years of further evolution, great color, and a remarkably opulent, expansive texture on the palate. The Bonnes Mares tasted slightly more concentrated and less tannic, and I was not surprised that my original tasting notes contained the word *great* three times and *extraordinary* twice. One can make no mistake with Dujac's 1985s, provided the importers ship them properly. Jacques Seysses also made some of Burgundy's finest 1986s and 1987s.

DOMAINE RENÉ ENGEL (VOSNE-ROMANÉE)* * *

1985 Clos Vougeot	E	89
1985 Echézeaux	E	85
1985 Grands-Echézeaux	E	90
1985 Vosne-Romanée	C	83
1985 Vosne-Romanée Les Brûlées	D	?

The quality of the wines from this famous old estate declined in the seventies. Slowly, yet surely, they have returned to form, largely because of the efforts of the young, bearded Philippe Engel. The old musty barrels I saw here on my first visit have been totally replaced and the percentage of new oak has been increased to a reasonable 33%. Engel thinks that the 1985s are the finest wines to be made at the estate since the 1964s and the 1959s. The Vosne-Romanée tasted alcoholic, but for drinking over the next 2–3 years, there is good fruit and color. While the Echézeaux tastes surprisingly light, the color is dark and the wine exhibits good ripeness. Although the Vosne-Romanée Les Brûlées has excellent flavors and depth, its barnyard aroma is quite bothersome. Certainly no one will complain about the Grands-Echézeaux, a wine that is rich, deep ruby in color and long, with a savory, lush fruitiness. It should age well for 8–10 years. The same can be said for the Clos Vougeot, from Engel's excellent vineyard on the upper slope at Vougeot. The 1985 is opulent, deep, and expansive on the palate, with the most concentration of all of Engel's wines, plus 13.5% natural alcohol.

FAIVELEY (NUITS ST.-GEORGES)* * * * *

1985 Beaune Les Champs Pimont	C	86
1985 Chambertin Clos de Bèze	E	94
1985 Charmes-Chambertin	E	98
1985 Clos de la Roche	E	92
1985 Corton Clos des Cortons	E	93
1985 Echézeaux	E	89
1985 Fixin	B	78
1985 Latricières-Chambertin	E	92
1985 Mercurey Clos des Myglands	B	86
1985 Mercurey Clos des Roy	B	87
1985 Mercurey Les Mauvarennes	B	84
1985 Morey St.-Denis Clos des Ormes	D	94
1985 Nuits St.-Georges	C	85
1985 Nuits St.-Georges Clos de la Maréchale	C	87

1985 Nuits St.-Georges Les Damodes	D	88

1985 Nuits St.-Georges Les Saint-Georges	D	91

Faiveley has always produced outstanding red burgundies, but their quality has soared to the very top since 1978. Much of the credit must go to the young, bushy-haired François Faivieley. With 235 acres of vineyards, the Faiveley firm is one of the largest landholders in Burgundy, and while the firm is officially called a *négociant*, over 87% of its wine comes from the family's vineyards. The wines, particularly the Premier and Grand Crus, are aged in 50% new oak, and many cuvées are not filtered. The results have been stunning. Faiveley made Burgundy's best wines in 1981, good 1982s, rot-free 1983s, good 1984s, and spectacular 1985s. Why there are not more of these wines in the American marketplace is a complete mystery to me; I cannot recommend them highly enough. The Faiveleys have notable vineyards in Mercurey, and their three wines were the best Mercureys I tasted in 1987 except for those of Yves de Launay. The Les Mauvarennes is not terribly distinguished, but offers a soft, ripe, sweet, round texture and good fruit; it will be delightful to drink over the next 3–5 years. The Clos des Myglands, a wine that I used to drink cases of (the 1971 and 1970) in law school, is excellent in 1985; it is quite a ripe, rich, generous wine with a cascade of berry fruit. Even better is the Clos des Roy, a very rich, creamy textured, smoky wine oozing with sweet layers of fruit. Although the Fixin is a decent wine, I could not get excited by it. The Nuits St.-Georges has a rich perfumed bouquet of red fruit, a concentrated, full-bodied feel on the palate, and a lovely finish. The three Premier Crus from Nuits St.-Georges range from excellent to outstanding. The Clos de la Maréchale is surprisingly deep, rich, long, and ripe, with layers of velvety fruit. The wine drinks extremely well today, but should age well for 5–8 years. The Les Damodes is even deeper and more tannic, with a splendid bouquet of red fruit, full body, and plenty of length. It will keep for 8–14 years. The Les Saint-Georges (there were only 100 cases made) is a fabulously rich, multidimensional wine that is extremely concentrated and has superlength. It should be at its best between 1990 and 2000. The Beaune Les Champs Pimont is a fat, plump, seductive wine that offers immediate gratification. The Morey St.-Denis Clos des Ormes is another very special wine (there are only 95 cases). The explosive bouquet of ripe plums, cherries, toasty oak, and violets is followed by a very rich, long, velvety, full-bodied wine that has enough tannin to ensure 10 years of further cellaring. The Faiveley Grand

Crus are all exceptional. The Echézeaux, full of finesse and elegance, as well as an amazing level of fruit, will offer drinking over the next decade. The Clos de la Roche tastes more robust and has great length, a fabulous presence on the palate, and amazing length. It will peak between 1990 and 2000. Shockingly, the Latricières-Chambertin was even better; my notes said "staggering depth." Like all these wines, it has very deep color, more tannin than others, and unbelievable concentration. While the Chambertin Clos de Bèze and Corton Clos des Cortons are the most backward, and both in need of 5 years of cellaring before they approach maturity, they are enormously concentrated and loaded with fruit extract, tannin, and potential. You can be assured I will be putting a few bottles of these wines away. One of the greatest wines of the vintage is the exquisite Charmes-Chambertin (125 cases were produced). It is virtually perfect—a marvelously concentrated wine that has an unbelievable bouquet, superdepth, layers of fruit, and a finish that goes on and on. It should drink well young, but should also age well for 10–15 years. The 1986s are quite successful, among the very best of the vintage. This is surely a firm to watch.

DOMAINE FOREY PÈRE ET FILS (VOSNE-ROMANÉE)* * *

1985 Echézeaux	E	87
1985 Nuits St.-Georges Perrières	D	84
1985 Vosne-Romanée	C	83
1985 Vosne-Romanée Les Gaudichots	D	87

The Forey cellars are adjacent to those of the Domaine de la Romanée-Conti. The Foreys own the Premier Cru Les Gaudichots, which is next to La Tâche and is said to have much the same root stock and soil. In addition, the Foreys make the wine called La Romanée, of the Liger-Belair family, which the *négociant* Bouchard markets. The 1985s had been bottled (unfiltered for the American importer) immediately prior to my visit, and I suspect will show better in 6–12 months. The Vosne-Romanée is good, quite fruity, and charming; the Nuits St.-Georges Perrières is medium bodied, supple, and somewhat alcoholic but good. The Les Gaudichots did not taste like La Tâche, but is certainly very good with long, velvety flavors and a very fine color. The Echézeaux has a deep color and plenty of substance, but it tasted closed yet promising.

DOMAINE GELIN-MOLIN (FIXIN)* * * *

1985 Chambertin Clos de Bèze	E	86

1985 Fixin Clos du Chapitre	C	84

1985 Gevrey-Chambertin	C	85

This firm has provided me with some notable values over the years, particularly with their Premier Cru, Fixins, which is never especially elegant but is rather robust and hearty. That being said, I had hoped that the 1985s would show better. For value, the chewy, chocolaty, deep, spicy, powerful Gevrey-Chambertin will be hard to beat. I prefer it to the Fixin Clos du Chapitre, which tastes compact, lean, and a little too dry and hard-edged. Perhaps 2–4 years of cellaring will bring forth more charm. Lastly, the Chambertin Clos de Bèze had oodles of very ripe, unctuous Pinot Noir fruit. I am a little concerned that it is too ripe, but it does offer a huge mouthful of wine and will last for 10 years.

GEOFFREY PÈRE ET FILS (GEVREY-CHAMBERTIN)* * *

1985 Gevrey-Chambertin	C	83

1985 Gevrey-Chambertin Clos Prieur	C	86

1985 Gevrey-Chambertin Premier Cru	C	85

1985 Mazis-Chambertin	E	88

I had not tasted the wines from this estate until several friends in France told me the quality was on the upswing, and I made a visit to the cellars. Ongoing improvements are being made in the brand-new cellars, with 100% new wood in evidence, and the 1987s look to be Geoffrey's best wines, although the 1986s are also good. Of the 1985s, there is a very fine Gevrey-Chambertin Clos Prieur and a ruby/purple, intensely oaky, powerful Mazis-Chambertin. These are not what I call classic red burgundies, but they are intensely colored, oaky, very satisfying wines.

ARMAND GIRARDIN (POMMARD)* * *

1985 Pommard Charmes	C	87

1985 Pommard Epenots	C 90

1985 Pommard Rugiens	C 90

Except for a flawed 1982 Epenots, I have not tasted this producer's wines, which are made by the mayor of Pommard in tiny quantities, 5 barrels, or 125 cases, of each wine. However, I will say that Girardin's 1985s are among the blackest-colored Pinot Noirs I have ever seen. The Charmes is fat, succulent, sweet, unctuous, and chocolaty; it will be a real crowd pleaser for the next 5–8 years. The Epenots—with its black/ruby color, astonishing bouquet of toasty, smoky oak and ripe fruit, superconcentrated flavors, full body and sledgehammerlike finish—made quite an impression. It will last 8–10 years. Not surprisingly, the Rugiens is even better and more complex; it is incredibly concentrated, pure, and long.

DOMAINE HENRI GOUGES (NUITS ST.-GEORGES)* *

1985 Nuits St.-Georges	C 81

1985 Nuits St.-Georges Les Chaignots	D 83

1985 Nuits St.-Georges Clos des Porrets	D 84

1985 Nuits St.-Georges Les Pruliers	D 86

1985 Nuits St.-Georges Les Saint-Georges	D 87

1985 Nuits St.-Georges Les Vaucrains	D 86

In the fifties and sixties, few estates in Burgundy made better wine than Gouges. On my first visit there in 1975, I tasted all the 1969s and 1966s, and they were indeed astonishing. In 1970, the quality began to slip badly, and only now are things starting to look better. The young Christian Gouges is assuming tighter and tighter control, and while the 1985s will not remind anyone of the 1969s or 1966s, they are, as a group, the best wines to be made in the last 15 years. The straight Nuits St.-Georges, the "villages" wine, has good color, but not much character or depth; it will offer uncomplicated drinking for 4–5 years. The Les Chaignots has a pronounced earthy, spicy character and 4–5 further years of cellaring potential. The Clos des Porrets is somewhat light, but it has the most exotic and exciting bouquet of all these wines, even though it tails off in the finish. The Les Pruliers is a denser, richer wine with good color, an earthy, intense bouquet, lush, deep flavors, and some muscle in the finish. It will keep 6–8 years. The Les Vaucrains should ultimately prove to be even better. For now it's more tannic, but also richer, deeper, and longer-lived. It should be at its best between 1990 and 2000. The Les Saint-Georges raises the level of tannins still higher, has broad, expansive flavors, full body and may prove in 3–4 years to be the finest Gouges wine made since the legendary 1969s.

BERTRAND DE GRAMONT (NUITS ST.-GEORGES)* * * *

1985 Nuits St.-Georges Les Allots	C	86
1985 Nuits St.-Georges Les Hauts-Pruliers	C	90

As a result of a family dispute, this domaine has emerged. It is tiny, all of 7.6 acres of vineyards, but nearly half of it is the Les Hauts-Pruliers vineyard. The wines are vinified and raised in the cellars, much like those of Machard de Gramont, only less new oak is present here. The Les Allots is a smooth, easy-to-drink wine with the hallmark of the 1985 vintage; an opulence of pure fruit is well displayed. Drink it over the next 4–5 years. The Les Hauts-Pruliers is, as the French say, *extra*. Dense in color and extract, the superripeness, sweet, almost jammy intensity of Pinot Noir fruit is a marvel to behold. Drink it over the next 5–7 years.

MACHARD DE GRAMONT (NUITS ST.-GEORGES)* * * *

1985 Aloxe-Corton Les Morais	C	87
1985 Bourgogne La Vierge Romaine	B	84
1985 Chorey-les-Beaune Les Beaumonts	C	86
1985 Nuits St.-Georges Les Damodes	D	90
1985 Nuits St.-Georges Les Hauts-Poirets	C	88
1985 Nuits St.-Georges La Perrière Noblot	C	87
1985 Pommard Le Clos Blanc	D	92

I first became enamored of the wines of Machard de Gramont with his glorious 1978s and lighter-weight 1979s. Then a family dispute seemed to disrupt shipments to the United States. The 1985s should prove to be real crowd pleasers. The Gramont wines are usually reasonably priced when compared to many other red burgundies. I was enchanted by the quality of the 1985s made here, as they have wonderful, deep colors, are bursting with supple, rich fruit, and have the requisite structure to age for 10 years. Gramont keeps 50% of the stems in the fermentation and uses 30% new oak for aging the wines. Even the generic Bourgogne is surprisingly ripe, fat, and filled with flavor. Another fine value will certainly be the Chorey-les-Beaune Les Beaumonts, a dark ruby-colored wine that, for its appellation, has amazing flavor purity and intensity. Its ripe, precocious, opulent character suggests that it will be difficult to resist drinking over the next 5–6 years. The Aloxe-Corton Les Morais is similarly styled, but is slightly deeper and longer; it has a long, sweet, lush finish that is altogether captivating. All three Premier Crus from Nuits St.-Georges had very dark color, sumptuous flavors of ripe berry fruit, and expansive and multidimensional textures. The Damodes, especially, is a wine of breathtaking richness, power, and balance. All of the Premier Crus will keep for upwards of a decade. At the summit of quality is Gramont's Pommard Le Clos Blanc, a wine from a well-placed Premier Cru vineyard that is located next to the famous Les Grands Epenots. The 1985, produced from vines that are between 50 and 70 years old, is packed with ripe cherry fruit and has a magnificent bouquet of toasty oak and grilled almonds. Sensationally concentrated on the palate, this unctuous, deep wine is a privilege to drink. It should be at its best between now and 1995.

JEAN GRIVOT (VOSNE-ROMANÉE)* * * *

1985 Clos Vougeot	D	88
1985 Nuits St.-Georges Les Boudots	D	86
1985 Vosne-Romanée	C	83

The young Etienne Grivot, who now runs this estate in addition to making the wines of the Domaine Jacqueline Jayer, is one of Burgundy's most promising talents. The emphasis here is on pure, elegant, finely etched Pinot Noir fruit. These wines are never too alcoholic or too tannic, but are, rather, prototypes for the delicate style of Pinot. I was unable to taste any of their Premier Crus of Vosne-Romanée, but the "villages" wine, while light in color, offers moderately intense, strawberry-scented fruit and a soft texture. The Nuits St.-Georges Les

Boudots exhibits the same silky, strawberry, cherry fruitiness, a touch of toasty new oak, and plenty of depth underneath some good tannins. The Clos Vougeot needs cellaring, but has exceptionally pure Pinot fruit, medium to full body, fine depth, and plenty of tannin. It needs until 1990–1992 to fully open. Grivot has also excelled with their elegantly wrought 1986s.

ROBERT GROFFIER (MOREY ST.-DENIS)* * *

1985 Bonnes Mares	E	84
1985 Chambolle-Musigny Les Amoureuses	E	83
1985 Chambolle-Musigny Les Sentiers	D	80

For reasons that Robert Groffier himself cannot explain, his 1985s are less successful than his 1986s. None of the three 1985s I tasted are as concentrated as his 1986s. They seem very soft and soupy, and lack definition. They are pleasing enough, but given the outstanding vineyards that Groffier owns, the investment of 100% new oak, and his own talent, they are more 1982-ish than anything else. Drink them over the next 3–4 years.

DOMAINE JEAN GROS (VOSNE-ROMANÉE)* * * * *

1985 Richebourg	E	93
1985 Vosne-Romanée	C	85
1985 Vosne-Romanée Clos des Réas	D	89

One of the most elegant women in all of Burgundy, Madame Gros takes impeccable care in making her wines. The 1985s look as good as the astonishing 1983s, but are clearly much more flattering to taste. Madame Gros thinks it is the best vintage since 1978. The Vosne-Romanée has a deep color, plenty of ripeness and tannin, and needs 2–3 years of cellaring. Clos des Réas, a Monopole (a single vineyard under sole ownership), is rich and perfumed in 1985, has a dark ruby color; makes a very broad palate impression, and should be ideal for drinking between 1990 and 2000. Of course, the Richebourg is extra-special. The complex aroma of ripe fruit, flowers, and new oak (the wine is aged in 100% new casks) is altogether exciting. On the palate, the wine has outstanding richness and plenty of body and tannin that will ensure greatness over the next 10–15 years. From the cask, the

1986s, especially the Clos des Réas and Richebourg, looked to be outstanding.

DOMAINE GROS SOEUR ET FRÈRE (VOSNE-ROMANÉE)* * * *

1985 Clos Vougeot	E	89
1985 Richebourg	E	90
1985 Vosne-Romanée	D	89

It is unfortunate that the proprietor, Bernard Gros, a brusque man, lacks the elegance of the rest of his family. (He is the son of Jean Gros.) However, his wine is interesting and usually is very sweet and perfumed, smelling almost too much of cherry and cassis. The Vosne-Romanée reeked so intensely of apricot and cherries, it seemed as if someone had dumped several liters of *eau de vie* in the barrel. Rich, fat and precocious, it is, however, a joy to drink. Normally a real superstar, as its vineyard is next to Musigny, the Clos Vougeot has an amazing level of jammy fruit, but also a very elevated level of alcohol. There is plenty of tannin in the finish, so this exotic wine should keep 8–10 years. The Richebourg also tastes highly chaptalized, as it is quite sweet, but the level of fruit extract in the wine is quite amazing. The cherry and cassis flavors are remarkably vivid, as is the concentration of the wine. These are highly seductive wines, but I have an uneasy feeling about their exact composition.

JEAN GUITTON (BEAUNE)* * *

1986 Aloxe-Corton	B	86
1986 Beaune Les Sizies	B	87
1986 Ladoix Côte de Beaune	B	86
1986 Pernand-Vergelesses Les Vergelesses	B	84
1986 Savigny Hauts Garrons	B	85
1986 Savigny Hauts Pruliers	C	85

The young, enthusiastic Jean Guitton has 25 acres of unglamorous appellations, but his conscientious commitment to quality, impeccable cellaring techniques, and 50% new wood all contribute to making this domaine a treasure trove for frugal consumers looking for value rather than prestige. Guitton made delicious 1987s, as well as very successful 1986s. The Ladoix is a perfect example of his winemaking style—rich, loaded with ripe cherry fruit, an elegant whiff of toasty oak, medium to full body, and round tannins in the finish. His top wines in each of the last three vintages have been the Ladoix, the Aloxe-Corton, and the Beaune Les Sizies.

ANTONIN GUYON (SAVIGNY-LES-BEAUNE)* * *

1985 Aloxe-Corton Les Vercots	C	83
1985 Bourgogne Hautes Côtes de Nuits	B	80
1985 Corton Clos des Roy	C	87
1985 Pernand-Vergelesses	B	83

This is a highly respected domaine with nearly 120 acres of fine vineyards. The wines usually need time to show well. The Bourgogne has a good color and a compact, yet fruity taste, but it is one-dimensional. The Pernand-Vergelesses shows some new oak in its bouquet, clean, ripe fruit, and a fleshy finish. The Aloxe-Corton Les Vercots has more depth, but also plenty of tannin (it easily has the most tannin of the Guyon wines) and a rough texture. The best wines from Guyon that I tasted included the Corton Clos des Roy, a wine with huge body, deep, long, chewy flavors, a boatload of tannin, and good acidity. It will need 5–6 years to round out.

HAEGELEN-JAYER (VOSNE-ROMANÉE)* * * *

1985 Chambolle-Musigny	C	87
1985 Clos Vougeot	E	90
1985 Echézeaux	E	88

This excellent producer of red burgundy makes wines that have great complexity, length, and aging potential. All three of these 1985s are deeply concentrated, long, expansive, broadly flavored wines that, while already a joy to drink, ideally need 3–4 more years of cellaring to reach their apogee. For a "villages" wine, the Chambolle-Musigny is especially striking with its fragrant bouquet of violets and raspberry fruit. Both the Echézeaux and Clos Vougeot are top-notch wines with a silky smooth lushness and appeal.

A. HUDELOT-NOËLLAT (VOSNE-ROMANÉE)* * * *

1985 Chambolle-Musigny	D	85
1985 Clos Vougeot	E	?
1985 Vosne-Romanée	C	78
1985 Vosne-Romanée Les Malconsorts	D	89

The wines of Hudelot-Noëllat are usually models of elegance and excellence. Consequently, I was a little perplexed by the so-so showing of the Vosne-Romanée and the odd, vegetal, peppery qualities of the Clos Vougeot. Perhaps they were in an awkward stage. Certainly there is nothing wrong with the Chambolle-Musigny, which is full of berry fruit and has considerable charm and a smooth, silky texture. It should be drunk over the next 5–8 years. The nearly outstanding Vosne-Romanée Les Malconsorts has very deep color, excellent depth of fruit, moderate tannins, full body, and a powerful, long finish.

LOUIS JADOT (BEAUNE)* * * *

1985 Beaune Les Boucherottes	C	85
1985 Beaune Clos des Couchereaux	C	87
1985 Beaune Clos des Ursules	C	88
1985 Beaune Hospices de Beaune Cuvée Hospitalières	D	87
1985 Beaune Hospices de Beaune Cuvée Nicolas Rolin	D	90
1985 Bonnes Mares	E	92
1985 Bourgogne	B	84
1985 Chambertin Clos de Bèze	E	93
1985 Chambolle-Musigny	D	83

1985 Chambolle-Musigny Les Amoureuses	E	90
1985 Chapelle-Chambertin	E	92
1985 Chassagne-Montrachet Morgeot Clos de la Chapelle (Magenta)	D	86
1985 Clos Vougeot	D	91
1985 Corton Pougets	D	88
1985 Gevrey-Chambertin	C	82
1985 Gevrey-Chambertin Clos St.-Jacques	E	91
1985 Gevrey-Chambertin Estournelles St.-Jacques	E	90
1985 Musigny	E	87
1985 Nuits St.-Georges	C	85
1985 Nuits St.-Georges Les Boudots	D	89
1985 Nuits St.-Georges Clos des Corvées	D	90
1985 Pernand-Vergelesses	C	?
1985 Vosne-Romanée	C	74

The firm of Louis Jadot, a *négociant*, is turning out some of the finest wines in Burgundy. The firm's acquisition of the impressive Clair-Daü vineyards (42 acres) in 1985 has ensured them an even stronger lineup than before, particularly in terms of Gevrey-Chambertin. Owning top vineyards does not itself guarantee top wine, but Louis Jadot is run with painstaking care by André Gagey, one of the nicest people in Burgundy. As the above ratings demonstrate, this firm is in full command of its product. Its red wine is silky, rich in color and tannin, and relatively full bodied. The 1985s are loaded with aromas and flavors of red fruits, are judiciously complemented by one-third new oak barrels, and have supercolor, thanks in part to a very high fermentation temperature of 35–36° C. With respect to the red wines from the Côte de

Beaune, even the generic Bourgogne shows character. The Pernand-Vergelesses was totally closed, hard, and impossible to evaluate. The Beaune Clos des Ursules tastes even richer, fuller, and more structured, yet has the wonderful opulence that marks this very special vintage. The Corton Pougets tastes similar, although my notes read "explosive cherry fruit." Among the two Hospices de Beaune wines, the Cuvée Nicolas Rolin had superrichness, a haunting perfume of red fruits and flowers, as well as great length. It will keep for 10–12 years. The Cuvée Hospitalières has less complexity, but is very amply endowed with layers of fruit.

Among the selections from the Côte de Nuits, the "villages" wines are of standard quality except for the surprisingly rich, voluptuous Nuits St.-Georges. The Nuits St.-Georges Les Boudots jumped a big notch in quality. Dark ruby, this wine is very rich, spicy, full bodied, plummy, and quite long. It should be gorgeous between 1989 and 1996. The Nuits St.-Georges Clos des Corvées is a great burgundy, offering exceptional depth and length, the characteristic opulent fruitiness of this vintage, but also structure and harmony. Both of the Premier Crus of Gevrey-Chambertin, the Estournelles St.-Jacques and the Clos St.-Jacques, are new offerings from the old Clair-Daü estate. Both are rich, broadly flavored, amazingly deep, pure wines with power adroitly balanced by elegance. I thought the Clos St.-Jacques had just a bit more length. Jadot always makes fine Clos Vougeot and in 1985 it is top-flight, bursting at the seams with juicy, succulent fruit, but full bodied and deceptively tannic in the finish. The Chambolle-Musigny Les Amoureuses is appropriately named in 1985—you will love it for its fleshy depth of fruit, elegance, and charm; it is slightly lighter than the Clos Vougeot, but no less seductive. I thought the Chapelle-Chambertin, made from 40-year-old vines, was one of the three best wines from Jadot in 1985, but I must admit that its cascade of unctuous berry fruit wrapped in toasty oak, and its remarkable precociousness argue that it should be drunk young (within 5–8 years) while some of the other wines shed their tannins. The Bonnes Mares tasted vastly superior to the elegant but polite, understated Musigny. Perhaps the latter wine was overwhelmed by the sheer power and decadent level of fruit extract in the Bonnes Mares. Incidentally, Jadot is now the largest producer of Bonnes Mares. Lastly, the Chambertin Clos de Bèze, from the Clair-Daü vineyards, is the most enormous and structured of the 1985 Jadot red burgundies. It is also admirably concentrated, long, and impeccable. Most of these wines will drink exceptionally well young, but where well stored, will last and evolve for 8–15 more years. The 1986s are good rather than special, and most clearly take a backseat to the 1985s.

DOMAINE HENRI JAYER (VOSNE-ROMANÉE)* * * * *

1985 Echézeaux	E	93
1985 Nuits St.-Georges Meurgers	E	93
1985 Richebourg	E	96
1985 Vosne-Romanée Clos Parantoux	E	91
1985 Vosne-Romanée Les Brûlées	E	91

There are several certainties regarding the wines of Henri Jayer. They are brilliantly made and, in America, exceedingly difficult to find and expensive. Jayer is a winemaker's winemaker. Everything in his cellar is spotless, and tasting wines there is always a great treat. Jayer, who looks a good 15 years younger than 65, is retiring next year and turning over the winemaking to his nephew, Emanuel Rouget. Jayer will still oversee the operations, as well as make the wines for Domaine Méo, which he has just begun doing. Jayer's wines are consistently great in part because, as he says, "I make the kind of wine I like." Aged in 100% new wood, his wines are never filtered and are bottled directly from the barrel. The excellent color and well-delineated, intense Pinot Noir fruit flavor he achieves could well come from his special "cold maceration," which involves putting the totally destemmed grapes in tanks and leaving them to sit for 2–4 days before starting the fermentation. Modern oenologists would no doubt be horrified at such a process, as the risk of oxidation is high, but never have I tasted a volatile or oxidized bottle of wine from Jayer. As Jayer explains, one must assume certain risks if one wants to make great wine. At Chez Jayer, he ranks his finest vintages in this order—1978, 1985, 1980, and 1986. As for the 1985s, they are all quite profound, deeply colored, packed with fruit, and should last and improve for 10–15 years. They are more tannic than many 1985s. The Nuits St.-Georges Meurgers is rich, tannic, deep and backward, but oh so pure. The two Vosne-Romanées—the Clos Parantoux and the Les Brûlées—are very different: The former has a voluptuous raspberry fruitiness, whereas the Les Brûlées is softer, smoky and exceptionally concentrated, no doubt because it comes from 55-year-old vines. The Echézeaux is what one expects of Grand Cru burgundy but rarely gets—an explosively rich yet elegant wine that titillates the palate with exotic flavors. The Richebourg needs 7–8 years to reach its full potential, but the staggering concentration of fruit, the tight structure, and the smashing length of this wine are the sorts of things that make burgundy wine legendary. As one might expect, Jayer made some of Burgundy's best wines in 1986.

DOMAINE JACQUELINE JAYER (VOSNE-ROMANÉE)* * * *

1985 Echézeaux	E	89
1985 Nuits St.-Georges Les Lavières	D	87
1985 Vosne-Romanée	C	85
1985 Vosne-Romanée Les Rouges	D	87

Etienne Grivot, one of Burgundy's most talented young producers, makes wines that exhibit an opulent purity of cherry and raspberry fruit, supple textures, and impeccable balance. All four of the above-listed wines show a delicious, tasty, rich fruitiness, medium to full body, soft tannins, and just the right amount of spicy oak. The Echézeaux is obviously the class wine of this quartet. All of the wines can be drunk now but promise to be even better if cellared for several more years.

JAYER-GILLES (HAUTES CÔTES DE NUITS)* * * *

1985 Côtes de Nuits-Villages	B	85
1985 Echézeaux	E	93
1985 Hautes Côtes de Beaune	B	85
1985 Hautes Côtes de Nuits	B	85

A cousin of Henri, Lucien, and Jacqueline, Robert Jayer makes wine not in Vosne-Romanée like his relatives, but, rather, high up in the hills of the Hautes Côtes de Nuits. He has an impeccable cellar, where the wine is aged in 100% new allier oak. He does not fine the wine, but filters it, using the Kisselguhr system at bottling. I suspect no one makes better Hautes Côtes de Beaune and Nuits red wines than Robert Jayer. Dark in color, ripe, with good sweetness and flesh, these tasty wines are reasonably priced and are good for drinking over the next 4–5 years. The Côte de Nuits-Villages is a more burly wine, but no better in terms of quality. Robert Jayer's Echézeaux challenges that of his cousin Henri for quality. It will last 10–15 years. Deep ruby/purple with super concentration and length, this medium- to full-bodied wine is impeccably balanced and made.

DOMAINE JOBLOT (GIVRY)* * *

1985 Givry Clos du Cellier aux Moines	B	86

This wine is quite a good value for red burgundy. Vinified and aged totally in new oak, it is savory, fat, and supple; the concentrated berry fruit and spicy new oak marry nicely. Drink it over the next 3–4 years.

DOMAINE MICHEL LAFARGE (VOLNAY)* * * *

1985 Beaune Grèves	C	86
1985 Bourgogne	B	78
1985 Volnay	C	82
1985 Volnay Clos des Chênes	C	86
1985 Volnay Premier Cru	C	85

Lafarge, a handsome, gray-haired, blue-eyed gentleman, is certainly one of Volnay's best producers. However, his 1985s tasted less successful than his 1983s, and I even preferred several of his 1981s to them. His 1985s, while attractively fruity and soft, lacked some definition and tasted a little soupy. The Bourgogne is pleasant but too mild-mannered; the Volnay is light, fruity, and simple. The Volnay Premier Cru exhibits more flavor dimension, a ripe, juicy fruitiness, and 5–6 years of further drinkability. The Volnay Clos des Chênes has the most guts and power of this group, but for whatever reason seemed to lack the great depth this wine is capable of attaining. Perhaps the wine was not showing at its best. The Beaune Grèves seemed in full form; oozing with ripe cherry fruit, it has a rich, creamy texture and a gorgeously lush finish. I would drink it over the next 5–7 years. Lafarge used no filtration for his 1985s.

DOMAINE COMTE LAFON (MEURSAULT)* * *

1985 Volnay Champans	D	87

1985 Volnay Santenots	D	87

Most people justifiably think of the Comte Lafon as one of the greatest producers of white burgundy in the world. However, two excellent red burgundies are also produced in the domaine's deep cold cellars. Both the above 1985s burst with rich berry fruit and are full bodied, quite concentrated, and very supple, rich, and tasty. Although quite drinkable now, both should last for at least another decade.

HENRI LAMARCHE (VOSNE-ROMANÉE)* * *

1985 Clos Vougeot	E	85

1985 Vosne-Romanée La Grande Rue	E	85

1985 Vosne-Romanée Les Malconsorts	E	83

A very famous estate with superbly situated vineyards, Lamarche is beginning to make good (not great) wine again, after a decade of spotty performances. Although the wines should be better, particularly in view of the quality of the vineyards, they are still soft and fruity, round and immediately accessible, though not terribly concentrated. François Lamarche is high on his 1987s, which he compares to the 1978s. As for the 1985s, the Vosne-Romanée La Grande Rue has slightly more depth than the other two listings; all three wines should be drunk over the next 3–4 years.

LOUIS LATOUR (BEAUNE)* * *

1985 Aloxe-Corton Chaillots	C	84

1985 Beaune Vignes Franches	C	85

1985 Corton Grancey	D	90

1985 Corton Domaine Latour	D	87

1985 Echézeaux	D	85

1985 Givry	B	84

1985 Mercurey	B	75

1985 Nuits St.-Georges Argillières	C 84

1985 Santenay	C 83

1985 Savigny-les-Beaune Gravains	C 84

1985 Vosne-Romanée Les Beaumonts	D 85

Louis Latour is one of the most important houses in Burgundy, and Louis Latour himself is a fairly imposing figure, given his size and height. Although everyone agrees that the white wines here are first-class, the red wines have been viewed skeptically ever since Anthony Hanson reported, in his book *Burgundy*, that they were pasteurized. This technique (which I have reservations about as well) has been used for almost a century of Louis Latour and involves heating the wine to 70° C for 7 seconds, then cooling it immediately. There is ample evidence that the Burgundian monks used similar techniques 400–500 years ago. Nevertheless, the 1985 red wines here are above-average in quality. I noticed a great similarity in terms of character and taste among them. Whether this is a result of the flash pasteurization or just a Latour house style I cannot say. Certainly the red wines are big, tannic, alcoholic, and age-worthy. The Echézeaux is good, but hardly exciting for a Grand Cru. Latour does very well with his Cortons. The Corton Domaine Latour has a very deep color and layers of rich, ripe fruit, and shows much more individual character than the other red wines. In the case of Latour's flagship wine, the Corton Grancey (from the gorgeous estate of the same name), the quality is exceptional. It exhibits plenty of new oak in its bouquet, super concentration and length, firm tannins, and an opulent, long finish. It should make a great bottle over the next 8–12 years.

YVES DE LAUNAY (MERCUREY)* * *

1985 Mercurey Clos du Château de Montaignu	B 88

1985 Mercurey Meix Foulot	B 85

1985 Mercurey Les Veleys	B 86

These 1985 wines from Mercurey are exceptional, as are those from Faiveley. The Meix Foulot is dark ruby with tons of ripe, fleshy fruit, full body, and 13.5% natural alcohol. It should drink well for 5–7 years. The Les Veleys is a more powerful, full-bodied wine with considerably more tannin, but, again, significant depth and length for a wine from Mercurey. The Château de Montaignu, aged in 33% new oak, is simply the finest Mercurey I have ever tasted. Oozing with raspberry fruit and toasty oak, this serious wine has astonishing concentration and will no doubt age well for 6–7 years. Consumers will no doubt be happy to hear that Launay made very good 1986s and excellent fruity 1987s.

PHILIPPE LECLERC (GEVREY-CHAMBERTIN)* * * *

1985 Gevrey-Chambertin Les Cazetiers	D	95
1985 Gevrey-Chambertin Combe aux Moines	D	97
1985 Gevrey-Chambertin Les Platière	C	87

Philippe Leclerc walks to the beat of a different drummer (probably from a British rock group). And while he could be taken for a member of the Hell's Angels, there is no doubt that he is a great winemaker. There is a fearful intensity to him that is translated to his wines. Along with his brother René, he was the last to bottle the 1985s in the winter of 1988. Aged in 100% new allier oak, the wines are neither fined nor filtered. Leclerc's off-year wines—the 1981s, 1982s, and 1984s—are amazingly successful, so there seems no denying his ability. The 1985s . . . well, he knows they are the best he has ever made. The La Platière, not a Premier Cru like the others, is explosively fat, fruity, and long, and will be a joy to drink over the next 4–5 years. The Les Cazetiers (one of the great vineyards of this appellation) is extravagantly rich and luxurious, is loaded with layers of sumptuous fruit, and has mind-boggling length. As hard as it is to believe, the Combe aux Moines is close to perfection—a magnificent, broad-flavored wine of seemingly endless depth and breadth. Although both of the latter wines will taste delicious young, they will also age well for 10–12 years. The 1986s are also very concentrated, forceful wines for the vintage; they are some of that year's most successful wines.

RENÉ LECLERC (GEVREY-CHAMBERTIN)* * * *

1985 Gevrey-Chambertin	C	84
1985 Gevrey-Chambertin Clos Prieur	C	84
1985 Gevrey-Chambertin Combe aux Moines	D	91

1985 Gevrey-Chambertin Lavaux St.-Jacques	D	87

René Leclerc's approach to winemaking has been the same as that of his brother Philippe, except that René did not use new oak until 1986; at that time he began making wines with 20–25% new oak. Neither of the Leclerc brothers fines or filters his wines. René's "villages" Gevrey-Chambertin has a spicy, meaty aroma, broad flavors, and soft texture. The Clos Prieur tasted a little diluted and slightly weedy despite some appealing jammy fruit. The Lavaux St.-Jacques leaps up in quality. Deep ruby, with a full-intensity bouquet, velvety yet structured flavors, and plenty of body, it will need 3–4 years of cellaring after bottling. The top wine from René Leclerc is his Combe aux Moines, from 50-year-old vines. Deep ruby, with a fascinating bouquet of plummy fruit, this dense, unctuous, full-bodied wine has considerable appeal. The 1986 Lavaux St.-Jacques and Combe aux Moines are excellent for the vintage.

DOMAINE LEQUIN-ROUSSOT (SANTENAY)* * *

1985 Chassagne-Montrachet Morgeot	C	87

1985 Santenay	B	84

1985 Santenay Le Passe-Temps	C	86

This is an excellent but underpublicized producer of both red and white burgundy. The Lequin brothers made decent 1986s, good 1987s, and very good 1985s. The Santenay is elegant, richly fruity, and quite tasty. The Santenay Le Passe-Temps has deeper color and loads of bing cherry fruit elegantly wrapped in oak. Finally, the Chassagne-Montrachet Morgeot has broad, deep flavors and more body, but also more tannin. These three wines should last for 4–7 more years.

LEROY (MEURSAULT)* * * * *

1985 Auxey-Duresses	D	87

1985 Auxey-Duresses Hospices de Beaune Cuvée Boillot	D	86

1985 Beaune	C	87

1985 Beaune Grèves	D	92

1985 Beaune Mignote	D	90
1985 Beaune Perrières	D	83
1985 Beaune Pertuisots	D	88
1985 Beaune Sizies	D	86
1985 d'Auvenay Bourgogne	B	86
1985 Chambertin	E	96
1985 Chambolle-Musigny	C	74
1985 Charmes-Chambertin	E	87
1985 Chassagne-Montrachet	C	82
1985 Chorey-les-Beaune	B	84
1985 Clos Vougeot	E	92
1985 Côte de Beaune-Villages	B	86
1985 Gevrey-Chambertin	C	86
1985 Gevrey-Chambertin Les Champeaux	D	89
1985 Gevrey-Chambertin Corbeaux	D	84
1985 Gevrey-Chambertin Estournelles St.-Jacques	E	90
1985 Gevrey-Chambertin Lavaux St.-Jacques	E	94
1985 Mazis-Chambertin	E	93
1985 Mazis-Chambertin Hospices de Beaune Cuvée Madeleine Collignon	E	100
1985 Mercurey	C	86

1985 Monthelie	C	75
1985 Musigny	E	87
1985 Nuits St.-Georges	D	82
1985 Nuits St.-Georges Les Argillières	E	90
1985 Nuits St.-Georges Clos des Corvées	E	92
1985 Nuits St.-Georges Les Perdrix	E	92
1985 Nuits St.-Georges Richemonde	E	94
1985 Pommard	D	86
1985 Pommard Les Vignots	D	88
1985 Ruchottes-Chambertin	E	94
1985 Santenay	C	87
1985 Savigny Les Beaune	C	85
1985 Savigny Les Marconnets	D	90
1985 Savigny Les Serpentières	D	92
1985 Volnay	D	87
1985 Volnay Brouillards	D	87
1985 Volnay Clos des Chênes	D	88
1985 Volnay Lassolle	D	87
1985 Volnay Premier Cru	D	87
1985 Volnay Taillepieds	D	90

Much has been written about the dynamic Madame Lalou Bize-Leroy, some of it quite malicious and motivated strictly by jealousy. From time to time I have complained of her pricing structure, and only recently was permitted to taste in her cellar. Be that as it may, there should never be any criticism of Mme. Bize-Leroy's philosophy of what burgundy should be, as her wines are among the noblest and purest expressions of Pinot Noir in Burgundy, and are treated with great care. They are never filtered and are bottled barrel by barrel. I have tasted many great wines, but I shall never forget those I tasted here. Many of them (forgetting the prices, of course) are what dream wines are all about. Given the size of her wines, and their power and structure, they will last 20–25 years in a cool, damp cellar. Mme. Bize-Leroy thinks 1985 is one of the two best burgundy vintages in the last 20 years, the other being 1978. Given the range of wines I tasted, 44 in all, 16 were exceptional, and 21 were very good to excellent; I would be proud to own any of them. Here are my tasting notes on the stars of the Leroy house in 1985.

Côte de Beaune (Leroy)

I doubt there has ever been a vintage like 1985, in which so many generic red burgundies tasted so good. For example, take Leroy's d'Auvenay Bourgogne. The 1985 is even better than the 1978; it is a powerful, rich, intense wine loaded with fruit. The Mercurey is a big, tannic, fleshy wine that will keep 10 years. The Côte de Beaune-Villages possesses plenty of ripe raspberry fruit, has surprising depth for a wine of its class, and is ideal for drinking over the next 4–8 years. Both the Santenay and Auxey-Duresses are also quite powerful, expressive wines, filled with great fruit, body, and concentration. The lineup of Volnays is very impressive, and certainly no small grower, not even Gerard Potel of Pousse d'Or, can claim such a high level of success. The most open-knit and accessible wine is the "villages" Volnay, a fat, ripe, yet elegant wine that shows plenty of raspberry fruit. The Volnay Lassolle is more tannic, yet powerful and deep. The Volnay Premier Cru also tasted muscular, tannic, and capable of undergoing a long period in the cellar. The most elegant of this set of wines is the Volnay Brouillards. The cascade of lush, raspberry fruit and supple, seductive texture gives it more near-term appeal. For those who are more patient, the rewards of cellaring the Volnay Clos des Chênes and the Volnay Taillepieds are obvious. The latter is an especially distinguished wine, with fabulous length and depth; it will age for 10–15 years. The Clos des Chênes is every bit as concentrated, but more tannic and very backward. It should be cellared for 8–10 years. The Pommard is rich and full bodied, but the Pommard Les Vignots has outstanding concentration and is a tightly structured,

tannic wine that could prove to be exceptional if one is willing to wait
6–10 years. Mme. Bize-Leroy made several stunning wines from
Beaune in 1985. The Beaune Pertuisots has an aromatic bouquet of
berry fruit, a velvety texture, and considerable style and class. However, it cannot compete with the exquisite Beaune Grèves, which is
fabulously rich. It will drink well for 10–15 years. The Beaune Mignote
has the same superb depth and concentration, but is more structured
and tannic. I suspect no one pays much attention to Savigny Les
Beaune, a terribly underrated appellation near Aloxe-Corton. Mme.
Bize-Leroy's two superstars are from opposite hillsides, the Marconnets and the Serpentières, closer to the village of Savigny. Although I
remember several great bottles of Savigny Les Beaune Cuvée Arthur
Girard from the Hospices de Beaune, these two aforementioned superstars are the most remarkable bottles of Savigny I have ever tasted.
As special and marvelous as the Marconnets is, the Serpentières, with
its awesome concentration, heady perfume of berry fruit and spices,
and significant concentration and size, should still be going strong at
the turn of the century.

Côte de Nuits (Leroy)

Forgetting the above-average quality but unexciting Nuits St.-
Georges and bland Chambolle-Musigny, which prove to Mme. Bize-
Leroy's critics that she is not infallible, her other wines range from
very good to exceptional, and in the case of one wine, to sheer perfection. I was blown away by her Premier Crus of Nuits St.-Georges. The
most supple and easy to drink is the unctuous Les Argillières, a sexy,
flashy, voluptuous wine that has layers of fruit. The Clos des Corvées
is more structured and age-worthy, but once again, mightily constructed with exciting levels of fruit and complexity. How can one
choose between it and the Les Perdrix, another magical, exotic wine
that is dark ruby in color and quite unforgettable? Believe it or not,
the Richemonde, a Premier Cru near the Vosne-Romanée border, is
even more sublime, a wine for toasting the twenty-first century. While
more closed than the others, this wine explodes on the palate with
enough balanced power and finesse to please anyone. There are several superb Premier Cru Gevrey-Chambertins. Both the fabulous Lavaux St.-Jacques and the fragrant, more forward Estournelles St.-
Jacques made the very good Corbeaux and Champeaux seem undernourished. All of these wines will last 20 years. The selection of Grand
Crus will no doubt cost plenty. I enjoyed both the Musigny and the
Charmes-Chambertin, but in comparison to the other wines, they are
not great. The huge fruit and structure of the Clos Vougeot will fool

no one; it is a majestic wine. The Ruchottes-Chambertin is a real powerhouse of a burgundy, with huge extract, sensational intensity, and enough tannin and depth to carry it 25 or more years. The Mazis-Chambertin is savage and wild, with tremendous sweetness of jammy Pinot Noir fruit but also a boatload of tannins. It was tasted next to the Mazis-Chambertin Hospices de Beaune Cuvée Madeleine Collignon. Perfect wines are exceedingly rare, and until these latter two, I had never tasted what I thought to be the quintessential red burgundy. I have no doubt about the Madeleine Collignon; it has everything. It is rich, long, powerful, and deep in color, and its magical perfume and symphony of flavors just go on and on. I suspect it will peak between 1992 and 2010, and I am sure it will be priced to kill. These are sensational red burgundies, and I wish they were cheaper, but the United States is the smallest market for Leroy's wines. Most of it is sold to top French restaurants and collectors in Switzerland and Belgium. Mme. Bize-Leroy knows full well the quality of her wines, and she also knows there will be no shortage of customers willing to pay for them. Her wines are what great burgundy is all about, and it is a tragedy that there are not more people in Burgundy who share her commitment to quality.

GEORGES LIGNIER (MOREY ST.-DENIS)* * *

1985 Bonnes Mares	E	91
1985 Chambolle-Musigny	C	86
1985 Clos de la Roche	E	95
1985 Clos Saint Denis	E	90
1985 Gevrey-Chambertin	C	84
1985 Gevrey-Chambertin aux Combottes	D	88
1985 Morey St.-Denis	D	84
1985 Morey St.-Denis Clos des Ormes	D	87

On the main road leading into Morey St.-Denis from N 74 (the major artery between Dijon and Beaune) one can find the wine cellars of some outstanding small growers. On the left is Dujac and on the right are Hubert Lignier, Pierre Amiot, Bernard Serveau, and Georges Lignier; each produces a totally different style of wine. Serveau and Amiot produce mostly precocious, elegant, delicate wines. Hubert Lignier and Dujac balance power with finesse, and the young Georges Lignier moves more toward unbridled richness and muscle as he works in one of the dampest, moldiest cellars in Burgundy. Not as consistent a winemaker as some of his peers, Georges Lignier is in full form with his 1985s. However, at the insistence of his agent, Tim Marshall, Lignier has begun to filter his wines, fearing that poor storage or shipment would cause the unfiltered wines to spoil. This is unfortunate; the quantities of the great wine made here are so small that they should be sold only to firms that will properly protect them. While the Morey St.-Denis and the Gevrey-Chambertin are good, fruity wines with plenty of substance, it is the Chambolle-Musigny that first grabbed my attention. Quite forward and developed, it has a gorgeous bouquet of ripe fruit, round, generous flavors, and a soft finish. The Morey St.-Denis Clos des Ormes has excellent color, a spicy, peppery bouquet, quite a bit of power and body, and while drinkable now, will keep 6–7 years. Lignier makes 125 cases of Gevrey-Chambertin aux Combottes, which in 1985 is almost as exquisite as the same wine made at Dujac. Quite rich and broadly flavored, it has an expansive, long finish and supersweetness to the Pinot fruit. It will drink well for 6–8 years. Among the three Grand Crus, there is a very powerful Bonnes Mares (14% natural alcohol) that has great depth and richness, oodles of fruit, but plenty of tannin in the finish. It will keep 10–12 years. The Clos St.-Denis tasted more supple— even jammy—with a wealth of berry fruit and a velvety texture. Only 500 cases of it were produced. The best of Lignier's 1985 offerings is the Clos de la Roche, a densely colored, tremendously powerful wine with 14% natural alcohol; it was aged in 100% new oak barrels. Lignier made 250 cases of this majestic wine, which will be a revelation to those who say modern burgundy is too light.

DOMAINE HUBERT LIGNIER (MOREY ST.-DENIS)* * * *

1985 Clos de la Roche	E	94
1985 Morey St.-Denis Premier Cru	D	86

Hubert Lignier is a serious grower who produces only two wines. His Morey St.-Denis Premier Cru is deeply colored, rich in fruit, has no harsh edges, and is quite concentrated. It will offer ideal drinking between 1988 and 1994. The 1985 Clos de la Roche is impeccable, much fatter, richer, and softer than the firmly structured, tannic 1983 and more concentrated than the 1978. Like the great majority of 1985 red burgundies, it has a savory, forward opulence, supercolor, and a cascade of plummy fruit. Neither wine is fined or filtered. I think this wine will be even greater with 5–6 years of cellaring, but it is certainly a treat to drink now.

CHÂTEAU DE LA MALTROYE (CHASSAGNE-MONTRACHET)* * *

1985 Chassagne-Montrachet Clos de la Maltroye	C 85
1985 Chassagne-Montrachet Clos Saint-Jean	C 85

This estate is much better known for its bevy of white burgundies, but good red wines are also made here. They are typical of the southern Côte de Beaune style—round, soft, medium bodied, and dominated by the scent and taste of bing cherries. Both 1985s are soft, seductive, round, fleshy wines, which are a pleasure to drink now but should keep well for 4–6 years.

J. P. MARCHAND (GEVREY-CHAMBERTIN)* * *

1985 Charmes-Chambertin	D 87
1985 Gevrey-Chambertin aux Combottes	D 86
1985 Griottes-Chambertin	D 89

I predict that the young Jean-Philippe Marchand (who runs this domaine of 25 acres of Grand Crus such as Griottes-Chambertin, Charmes-Chambertin and Clos de la Roche, as well as Premier Crus like Combottes) is on the threshold of stardom. Although his 1985s are excellent, they have the brilliant, polished look that comes from too intense a filtration. If Marchand's American importer, Neal Rosenthal, can persuade him to filter less or not at all, there is no telling what he could attain, since the other aspects of his vinification and elevage are impeccable. The Combottes is very supple, lush, fat and ideal for drinking over the next 5–6 years. The Charmes-Chambertin may not approach the quality of Charmes made by Dujac or Faiveley in 1985, but it is still an excellent wine, with plenty of concentrated berry fruit, medium to full body, and a precocious, lush texture. The Griottes-Chambertin is a decadently intense, rich mouthful of wine. There are good tannins submerged behind the fruit, but this is clearly a wine to consume over the next 7–8 years. Marchand made very good 1986s.

JOSEPH MATROT (MEURSAULT)* * *

1985 Blagny La Pièce Sous le Bois	D	88

1985 Volnay Santenots	D	86

Matrot is better known for his white wines, although his reds are often quite good. The Blagny, from a vineyard just northwest of the Meursault Charmes vineyard, is a very silky, intense, richly fruity wine that offers a resounding blast of cherry fruit, toasty oak, and full body. Drink it over the next 3–6 years. The Volnay Santenots is similar in style, only more restrained. It too should be drunk over the next 5–6 years.

DOMAINE MAUME (GEVREY-CHAMBERTIN)* * * *

1985 Gevrey-Chambertin	C	86

1985 Gevrey-Chambertin Lavaux St.-Jacques	D	88

1985 Mazis-Chambertin	E	92

Among connoisseurs, the wines from this tiny estate at the very northern end of the Côte d'Or are some of the most sought-after burgundies. The very low yield per acre and the ancient vines from which the wines are made produce a wine of astonishing concentration and color. The 1985s are less tannic and more supple than typical Maumes, and can be drunk now or aged 10–15 years. The Gevrey-Chambertin shows a good bouquet of licorice, smoke, and earthy, plummy fruit. The Lavaux St.-Jacques is more concentrated and a bit more burly, but is rich and soft enough to drink now. The big star here, as usual, is the Mazis-Chambertin, which has stunning concentration and an exotic smoky bouquet of Oriental spices, smoked duck, and plummy fruit. On the palate it just goes on and on, and whether one drinks it now or holds it for 15 years it will provide an unforgettable gustatory experience.

DOMAINE JEAN MÉO-CAMUZET (VOSNE-ROMANÉE)* * * *

1985 Clos Vougeot	D	91

1985 Nuits St.-Georges Boudots	D	87

1985 Nuits St.-Georges Meurgers	D	88

1985 Richebourg	E	93

1985 Vosne-Romanée Les Brûlées	D	86

Starting with the 1985 vintage, the legendary winemaker Henri Jayer was brought in as a consultant. Thus, this historic domaine, with some of the best-situated vineyards in Burgundy, can be expected to produce increasingly greater wines. Certainly there is no problem with the 1985s, which are unbelievably seductive, exotic, smoky, rich wines that can be drunk with extraordinary pleasure today. The bacon fat-scented, opulent Clos Vougeot, or the unreal Richebourg, or any other of these vines is well worth having, even in the most conscientiously stocked wine cellar. Jayer believes in no filtration and 100% new oak, and the 1985s reflect this philosophy; one will also see very fine wines in 1986, and some delicious, supple red burgundies in 1987 as well. This is certainly an up-and-coming superstar estate in the Côte d'Or.

PRINCE FLORENT DE MÉRODE (LADOIX-SERRIGNY)* * * *

1985 Aloxe-Corton Premier Cru	C	84

1985 Corton Bressandes	D	88

1985 Corton Clos du Roi	D	90

1985 Corton Maréchaudes	D	86

1985 Corton Renardes	D	87

1985 Ladoix	B	83

1985 Pommard Clos de la Platière	C	85

With its 1985s this important domaine has made its best wines since 1978. Yet, I suspect they could even be better with less filtration. All of the 1985s were bottled early, in January 1987. The Ladoix is light ruby, has a pleasant strawberry, supple fruitiness, and will make a decent bottle over the next 3 years. The Aloxe-Corton delivers more cherry fruit, is very easy to taste and appreciate, and should keep 1–5 years. The quality of Cortons is quite impressive. The Maréchaudes, usually the lightest, has good body, plenty of velvety, supple, cherry fruit, a good lashing of tannin in the finish, and 5–10 years of further drinkability. The Renardes exhibits more stuffing, an elevated percentage of new oak, and a lovely, expansive, long finish. Drinkable now, it will keep for a decade. The Bresssandes, made from 40-year-old vines, actually needs several years to shed its tannins, but has a dark ruby color, is seriously concentrated, shows a complex cherrylike and sweet oaky taste, and is full bodied. My guess is that it should mature between 1990 and 1996. There is no doubt that the Clos du Roi is the fullest, deepest, most powerful and concentrated wine Mérode produced in 1985. It combines intensity with finesse; give it 2–7 years to fully develop. Lastly, the Pommard Clos de la Platière has an earthy, superripe character, exudes gobs of cherry jam and oak, and is very tasty.

DOMAINE MOILLARD (NUITS ST.-GEORGES)* * *

1985 Beaune Grèves	C	87
1985 Bourgogne	B	82
1985 Bourgogne Hautes Côtes de Nuits	B	78
1985 Clos Vougeot	D	90
1985 Corton Clos du Roi	D	92
1985 Côte de Nuits-Villages	B	83
1985 Echézeaux	D	91
1985 Gevrey-Chambertin	C	84
1985 Mercurey	B	80
1985 Nuits St.-Georges Clos de Thorey	B	89
1985 Santenay	C	85
1985 Vosne-Romanée Les Malconsorts	D	88

Founded in 1850, Moillard is not old by Burgundian standards. It is quite a large *négociant*, which exports to 45 countries. Many of the lower-level wines are produced with flash pasteurization, cold stabilization, and centrifuges and filter machines, which can be seen throughout the warehouses. This state-of-the-art technology produces technically perfect, characterless, often flavorless wines. However, for their better wines, Moillard uses more traditional techniques, and some of the greatest leaps in the quality of red burgundy have occurred here. The Thomas family, who own Moillard, believe that consumers prefer supple, round, velvety, dark-colored wines, which is the type of wine Moillard delivers. I should also note that prices for Moillard's wines are not unreasonable; thus, given the high quality of their 1985s, Moillard is a good source for some very fine—even exceptional—red burgundy, provided you like their big, meaty, fleshy, deeply colored style of wine. With respect to the specific wines that merit your attention, the Santenay is a rather powerful, chunky, rich wine with a good dosage of alcohol and fruit. It will keep 5–10 years. The Nuits St.-Georges Clos de Thorey has a very dense color, great extract, a huge, tarry, plummy bouquet, broad flavors, and a solid lashing of tannin. It will last 5–12 years. The Clos Vougeot is exceptional. It oozes with a cascade of ripe bing cherry fruit, exhibits plenty of toasty new oak in its aroma, and has sensational concentration and length. It will last 10–15 years. The Beaune Grèves is typical of many top 1985 red burgundies. Opulent—even explosively fruity—this succulent, sensual wine gives enormous pleasure now, but also should keep 5–10 years. I thought the Corton Clos du Roi was the best of the Moillard 1985 red burgundies. Aged in 100% new oak, it has an extraordinary bouquet of exotic spices, and superconcentrated fruit. Deep, rich, long, full-bodied, tannic and exceptionally long, this wine should provide grand drinking over the next 12–15 years. The Vosne-Romanée Les Malconsorts has less power and substance, but is still very concentrated, supple, and long. The big, penetrating, persistent aroma of the Echézeaux offers nothing but joyous ripeness and complex Pinot Noir aromas. Less full bodied and tannic than either the Corton Clos du Roi or the Nuits St.-Georges Clos de Thorey, the Echézeaux is full of elegance and finesse, and should be drunk over the next 10 years.

Among the 1986s, Moillard's top wines are much less successful than in the 1985 vintage. Yet good wines such as the Nuits St.-Georges-Richemonde, Vosne Romanée-Malconsorts, Clos Vougeot, and Chambertin were produced.

MOMMESSIN (MACON)* *

1985 Beaune Bressandes	C 78
1985 Charmes-Chambertin	D 68
1985 Chassagne-Montrachet	B 78
1985 Clos de Tart	E 92
1985 Corton	D 84
1985 Côte de Beaune-Villages	B 81
1985 Echézeaux	D 72
1985 Fixin	B 72
1985 Gevrey-Chambertin	C 78
1985 Pommard	C 75
1985 Santenay	B 80
1985 Volnay Les Angles	C 84
1985 Vosne-Romanée	C 70

This *négociant* owes much of its fame to its gloriously situated Grand Cru vineyard in Morey St.-Denis, called Clos de Tart. The 1985 is everything that great red burgundy should be: a heavenly bouquet of sweet, juicy, red fruit and toasty new oak and spices; on the palate it is luxuriously rich, elegant, and impossible to resist drinking. That being said, most of the other wines in this range were short on flavor and were cooked in aroma; they rarely reflected their appellation and tasted like everyday, generic red burgundy. The Echézeaux and Charmes-Chambertin are disgraceful wines for Grands Crus. Buy the Côte de Beaune-Villages for value and the Clos de Tart for occasions when you want to splurge.

DOMAINE MONGEARD-MUGNERET (VOSNE-ROMANÉE)* * * *

1985 Clos Vougeot	E	92
1985 Echézeaux	E	90
1985 Fixin	B	85
1985 Grands-Echézeaux	E	96
1985 Richebourg	E	90
1985 Vosne-Romanée	C	87
1985 Vosne-Romanée Les Orveaux	C	86
1985 Vosne-Romanée Les Suchots	D	88

The boyish-looking Mongeard is one of my favorite producers, not only because he consistently makes fine wine, but also because he is a pleasure to deal with and is very enthusiastic. He made some of the finest 1983s, but his 1985s are even better, although they will not be as long-lived. The wines here are fined, never filtered, and are aged in at least 50% new oak. His Fixin has a delicious fruity quality, deep ruby color, soft texture, and good finish. The "villages" Vosne-Romanée is excellent, and inexplicably better tasting than the Les Orveaux, a more expensive wine. The Vosne-Romanée has deep, silky fruit, a sweet, plummy richness, and considerable length. It should drink well for 7–8 years. The Les Orveaux is quite tannic and closed. And the Vosne-Romanée Les Suchots is especially rich, expansively flavored, full bodied, packed with fruit, and has at least 7–10 years of life ahead of it. The Echézeaux is outstanding, with a perfumed, sweet, flowery, fruity nose, an expansive palate, and 8–9 years of further cellaring. I thought the Clos Vougeot tasted even better and had more depth and power, an even greater intensity of fruit, plus more tannin and structure. It should keep 10–15 years. As fine as the elegant, velvety, aromatic Richebourg is, it is not as exceptional as the profound Grands-Echézeaux. The latter wine, usually one of the superstars of Burgundy, has an extraordinary bouquet of cassis fruit, violets, and chocolate. Stunningly rich, full bodied and long, it should be at its best between 1990 and 1998.

DOMAINE ALBERT MOROT (BEAUNE)* * * *

1985 Beaune Bressandes	C	88
1985 Beaune Cent Vignes	C	86
1985 Beaune Grèves	C	86
1985 Beaune Marconnets	C	87
1985 Beaune Theurons	C	87
1985 Beaune Toussaints	C	83
1985 Savigny-Vergelesses	C	85

These offerings, which also appear under the label Chopin, are consistently among the better wines of Beaune and, while not inexpensive, remain moderately priced for red burgundy. The wines are aged in approximately 20% new oak and can age for a considerably long time. Although Albert Morot is a *négociant*, all the above wines are from the firm's own vineyards. The 1985s are dark, expressive wines, which have the characteristics of the vintage—a fat, opulent fruitiness, plenty of soft tannins, and adequate but low acidities. They should keep for 10–12 years. The three top wines of 1985, although the difference is largely negligible, are, first, the Beaune Bressandes, with a supercolor and an intense richness marked by aromas of blackcurrants and licorice. It is a very big wine for a Beaune. The other top wines are the Beaune Marconnets and the Beaune Theurons. The Marconnets is a bit more tannic and structured, but has the same impressive power and richness on the palate. The Theurons is the least open and most tannic, but the underlying depth is impressive. All three wines will age for a decade. Morot also produced good 1986s that are less flattering but more structured than the 1985s.

DENIS MORTET (GEVREY-CHAMBERTIN)* * *

1985 Bourgogne	B	84
1985 Chambertin	E	87
1985 Clos Vougeot	E	88

1985 Gevrey-Chambertin	C	84

1985 Gevrey-Chambertin Champeaux	C	87

1985 Gevrey-Chambertin Clos Prieur	C	85

Denis Mortet is another young burgundy winemaker who has taken charge of the family estate, and is trying to upgrade the quality and image of burgundy wine. Mortet uses 50% new oak. He does not fine his wines, but prior to bottling gives them a light filtration through the Kisselguhr system. He made a good, attractive, easy-to-understand Bourgogne in 1985, which I found just as good as his Gevrey-Chambertin. A specialty here is the Gevrey-Chambertin Champeaux, made from 60-year-old vines. It is a big, rich, dense yet tannic and full-bodied wine that will keep the 10–12 years. The Gevrey-Chambertin Clos Prieur tastes less concentrated, but round, supple, elegant, and fruity. I thought Mortet's Clos Vougeot richer, more concentrated, and altogether a more serious *vin de garde* than his famous Chambertin. The latter wine is fruity, elegant and tasty, but for the money the Clos Vougeot and Champeaux are superior wines. The 1986s from Mortet looked every bit as good as his 1985s.

DOMAINE GEORGES MUGNERET (VOSNE-ROMANÉE)* * * *

1985 Bourgogne	B	88

1985 Clos Vougeot	E	96

1985 Echézeaux	E	91

1985 Nuits St.-Georges Les Chaignots	D	91

1985 Ruchottes-Chambertin	E	95

1985 Vosne-Romanée	C	85

Dr. Mugneret is one of the true professionals in Burgundy. His cellars in Vosne-Romanée, adjacent to those of Jean Gros, are impeccable, as are his wines. There is a sense that Mugneret knows precisely what he is doing, but he modestly says that luck is also necessary to make really great wines, which is exactly what he has done in 1985. Mugneret bottled all his 1985s without a filter. The 1985 Vosne-Romanée reminded me of the lovely, elegant 1984 Saintsbury Pinot Noir from

California. Impeccably clean, fruity and pure, it is a delight to drink. The surprising wine is the generic Bourgogne, aged in 100% new oak; it has immense fruit and a sumptuous texture. I have never tasted an ordinary Bourgogne this special. The lineup of great wines starts with the Nuits St.-Georges Les Chaignots, deep in color, profound in aroma, with a broad, deep, rich intensity. This wine should improve for upwards of a decade. The Echézeaux does indeed smell like violets, but the wine has more than just a pretty floral aroma. It is indeed gorgeous, with the opulence of the 1985 vintage well displayed. If that weren't enough, the Ruchottes-Chambertin is out-and-out great stuff. The superb purity of fruit, the remarkable delineation of flavors, the structure, and the length suggest that it will last for 10–15 years and perhaps even improve. And then there is the Clos Vougeot, which is nearly perfect. A truly magical wine that represents a gustatory tour de force, it will last 15 or more years. Dr. Mugneret made some great wines in 1953, 1966, and 1978, but his 1985s are indeed special. The entire lineup of 1986s from Mugneret is worth pursuing, provided you cannot find the 1985s.

PHILIPPE NADDEF (COUCHEY)* * *

1985 Gevrey-Chambertin	C	82
1985 Gevrey-Chambertin Les Cazetiers	D	87
1985 Mazis Chambertin	E	89

Young Philippe Naddef is short on winemaking experience (he is still in his mid-twenties), but he is quickly making a name for himself. Both recent vintages, 1987 and 1986, are good, but not up to the quality of the 1985s. One hundred percent new oak is used, and the wines have excellent color, ripeness, and plenty of toasty oak. They are bold, age-worthy wines that should last 8–10 years in the 1985 vintage.

DOMAINE PARENT (POMMARD)* * *

1985 Corton Renardes	D	85
1985 Pommard Clos Micault	D	82
1985 Pommard Epenots	D	84

1985 Pommard Rugiens	D 85

Founded in 1650, this famous firm has one of the best reputations in Burgundy; its 1964s and 1966s were superb. Today, the style of the wine is less impressive and more commercial, with the emphasis on soft, alcoholic, somewhat diffuse wines, from over 60 acres of vineyards (mostly in Pommard), that have a similar taste and personality. While the wines are estate-bottled, the current generation at Domaine Parent has a *négociant* mentality. These are wines to drink over the next 4–5 years.

PERNIN-ROSSIN (VOSNE-ROMANÉE)* * * *

1985 Morey St.-Denis Mont Luisants	D 85

1985 Nuits St.-Georges Les Richemondes	D 92

This is a very interesting property, yet few Americans know of it. (I learned of it only through reading some ecstatic reviews of the wines by Michel Bettane, France's leading wine writer.) The vinification here is similar to that of Henri Jayer, with the 2–4–day cold maceration of grapes prior to fermentation. This is no doubt a major contributing factor to the intense, jammy fruit these wines have. Some will approach them with a degree of skepticism, for they have a density of color and level of fruit extract that seem unbelievable; but they do taste of Pinot Noir, so I don't think Pernin-Rossin is pulling any tricks. The 1986s from this property may turn out, along with those from the Domaine de la Romanée-Conti, Faiveley and Roumier, to be the best made in the Côte de Nuits. The two 1985s I tasted included a very alcoholic, very fruity, soft, lush Morey St.-Denis Mont Luisants, which delivers immediate gratification. Simply extraordinary is the Nuits St.-Georges Richemondes. It has a sweetness of fruit and unbelievable aromas and flavors of cassis. It also has a good measure of tannin and body that should allow it to age well for 5–9 years. The 1986s from Pernin-Rossin are quite splendid and well worth seeking out.

DOMAINE PERNOT-FOURRIER (GEVREY-CHAMBERTIN)* *

1985 Chambolle-Musigny	C 80

1985 Gevrey-Chambertin	C 79

1985 Gevrey-Chambertin Clos St.-Jacques	D 84
1985 Gevrey-Chambertin Combe aux Moines	D 84
1985 Gevrey-Chambertin Premier Cru	C 80
1985 Griottes-Chambertin	E 84
1985 Morey St.-Denis	D 82
1985 Vougeot Premier Cru	D 79

This famous estate turned out fabulous wines in 1978, 1976, and 1969. However, the current proprietor, Jean-Claude Fourrier, has not equaled the success of his predecessors. The 1985s, which are average in color and too alcoholic, were not bottled until August 1987. In some cellars, the wines can take—even require—extra cask aging, but here the wines should have been bottled months earlier. All of these wines are tasty, ripe, and supple, but they are dangerously low in acidity, have a soupy texture, and lack definition. They will be enjoyable, but they must be drunk young. Fourrier failed to bleed, or *saigner*, his wines in the excessively abundant year of 1986; consequently, the 1986s are even more disappointing than the 1985s. The quality of wines of this famous domaine is in serious decline.

JEAN PICHENET (SAVIGNY-LES-BEAUNE)* * *

| 1985 Savigny-les-Beaune | B 84 |

This is a pretty wine, redolent with the scent of ripe strawberry fruit. It has a creamy texture and plump fatness that will give it appeal over the next 4–5 years.

CHÂTEAU DE POMMARD (POMMARD)* * *

| 1985 Pommard | D 86 |

This impressive château and enclosed vineyard of nearly 50 acres is one of the major tourist attractions in Burgundy and undoubtedly worth a visit. The estate is run with passion by Dr. Jean-Louis Laplanche, a professor at the Sorbonne. His wines are aged in 100% new oak casks and put in very heavy and expensive bottles. Much has been made of the less-than-ideal location of this vineyard, but Laplanche's meticulous attention results in a chunky, long-lived, deeply colored, firm, and tannic wine that can last 15 or more years. The 1985 is certainly the best wine to be made here since 1978. The 1986 is much lighter, but still a sound wine of good quality.

DOMAINE PONSOT (MOREY ST.-DENIS)* * * *

1985 Chambertin	E	99
1985 Chambolle-Musigny Les Charmes	E	90
1985 Clos de la Roche Vieilles Vignes	E	96
1985 Clos St.-Denis Vieilles Vignes	E	92
1985 Griotte-Chambertin Vieilles Vignes	E	96
1985 Latricières-Chambertin	E	96

I have great admiration for the Ponsot wines, although they are to be avoided in overly difficult years, such as 1982 and 1984. Jean-Marie and his son, Laurent, are the ultimate risk-takers, picking as late as possible to push their Pinot Noir to maximum ripeness; they never filter and they bottle as late as possible. The style of burgundy made here is indeed big, but it is also balanced by and imbued with the intensity of old vines and aided by classical winemaking methods. The 1985s were bottled in September 1987, and I think they are stupendous. Interestingly, both father and son believe that the 1983s will outlive the 1985s by 10–15 years, which is not surprising. They both claim that their 1980 Clos de la Roche Vieilles Vignes is the best wine they have ever made—good news for those lucky enough to have bought it. All the above wines will drink well and last 10–15 years. Some of them appear under the label Domaine des Chézeaux (this is not a second label, as the wines are identical). The Chambolle-Musigny Les Charmes smells of sweet, ripe apples and flowers, has a luscious creamy texture, supercolor, and soft tannins. The Griotte-Chambertin (spelled without an "s" here) is a dazzling wine made from 65-year-old vines. Dark ruby, with an intense raspberry fruitiness, extraordinary concentration and depth on the palate, this mind-boggling wine should drink well for a decade. My tasting notes describe the wine as "awesome, unbelievable, staggering, sensational, and frightening." It is what legends are made of. The Latricières-Chambertin may well be as good. It also had a level of concentration more akin to vintage port or 1982 red Bordeaux than to burgundy. It is wilder and more structured and tannic than the Chambertin. Sadly, the Clos St.-Denis is merely an exceptional wine. In the company of such treasures as the Chambertin and Latricières-Chambertin, all I could muster in my tasting notes was "dark ruby, great wine, explosive richness, heady, and splendid." The vines for the Clos St.-Denis were planted in 1925; it is a true Cuvée Vieilles Vignes. The Clos de la Roche Vieilles Vignes has the misfortune of being a great wine but not Ponsot's greatest wine in 1985. It is much more forward than either the backward 1983 or slowly developing 1980. If you have access to it, and have a fat bank account, don't dare pass it up. The 1986s from Ponsot, while not up to the quality of the 1985s, are nearly as fine as the outstanding 1980s.

DOMAINE POTHIER-RIEUSSET (POMMARD)* * *

1985 Beaune Boucherottes	C	83
1985 Bourgogne	B	75
1985 Pommard Charmots	C	85
1985 Pommard Clos des Vergers	D	86
1985 Pommard Epenots	D	89
1985 Pommard Rugiens	D	89

If I had to pick one grower from Burgundy who looked, talked, and behaved like what most Americans perceive as a French winemaker, he would be Virgile Pothier. Very short, red-faced, bright-eyed, talkative, and, of course, philosophical, Virgile Pothier, an adorable little man, is also a winemaker with considerable talents. His wines, which always taste so seductive from the barrel, are very slow to evolve in the bottle. His 1969s and 1972s are just now opening up. His 1985s are considerably softer than his tannic 1983s, but still they are among the most structured 1985s I have tasted. His generic Bourgogne tastes surprisingly lean and tannic. As for the Beaune Boucherottes, it is deep in color, quite full bodied, and tannic as well as concentrated. It should last 6–12 years. The Pommard Clos des Vergers has very good acidity for a 1985, is quite deep in color, very backward, yet dense and promising. It needs cellaring for at least 6–8 years. The Pommard Charmots is dense, chunky, and softer in style than the Vergers. Normally, the Pommard Rugiens is Pothier's top wine and it is nearly great in 1985—very dark ruby, rich in extract, full bodied and tannic, but his best cuvée is the Pommard Epenots. It is splendid, fabulously concentrated, quite profound in aroma, and has a good 10–15 years of life ahead of it. Pothier compares his 1985s to his 1969s. The 1986s, perhaps tasted at an awkward stage in their development, did not show the richness I have come to expect from this estate.

POUSSE D'OR (VOLNAY)* * * *

1985 Pommard Les Jarollières	C	89
1985 Santenay Clos Tavannes	C	84
1985 Volnay Bousse d'Or	D	90
1985 Volnay Les Caillerets	C	87
1985 Volnay Les Caillerets 60 Ouvrées	D	88

For impeccable, elegant, savory wines, few producers can match the consistent quality of the Domaine Pousse d'Or, which is run with great care by Gerard Potel. His stylish wines are never alcoholic or massive, and they age exceedingly well. Potel prefers his 1978s to his 1985s, explaining that the style of his 1985s falls somewhere between such years as 1966 and 1978. The Santenay Clos Tavannes is already ready to drink, as it is supple, smooth, very fruity, and ripe. This medium-bodied wine should drink well for 4–5 years. The Volnay Caillerets is a wonderfully elegant wine—round, supple, yet firm enough to keep 10–12 years. The Volnay Caillerets 60 Ouvrées is even deeper, darker in color, more intense and more tannic, with a very seductive, gorgeous bouquet of cherry fruit and toasty oak already well developed. It should last 10–12 years as well. The Pommard Les Jarollières has great richness of fruit, a succulent, juicy character, full body, and plenty of ripe tannins. Potel's best wine, however, is the Volnay Bousse d'Or, a gloriously ripe, fruity, unctuous wine with layers of berry fruit wrapped gently in a veil of smoky, toasty oak. It will last for 12–14 years; there were only 750 cases of this nectar made. Potel's 1986s are good, rather tannic, but nowhere near the quality of his 1985s.

MICHEL PRUNIER (AUXEY-DURESSES)* * *

1985 Auxey-Duresses Clos du Val	C	87
1985 Auxey-Duresses Premier Cru	C	85
1985 Beaune Les Sizies	C	86
1985 Volnay Caillerets	C	86

If you are looking for well-made, rich, expressive red burgundy that offers value, then remember the name Michel Prunier. I was first impressed by Prunier's 1981s and 1982s, two vintages where the overall quality was mediocre at best. His 1985s are the best wines I have yet tasted from him. Whether it's the soft, lovely, effusively fruity Auxey Premier Cru, or the intense, velvety, seductive Beaune Les Sizies, or the fat but structured Volnay Caillerets, there is something for everyone. These wines are cleanly made, ripe, rich in fruit, deeply colored, and quite tasty. The star is Auxey-Duresses Clos du Val, the most tannic wine, but also the most concentrated and promising one, with a good 8–10 years of cellaring potential.

DOMAINE CHARLES QUILLARDET (MARSANNAY)* *

1985 Gevrey-Chambertin	C	?
1985 Gevrey-Chambertin Le Bel Air	C	85
1985 Marsannay	B	83

Charles Quillardet, a big, playful man, is a well-known producer located right on the main route through Gevrey-Chambertin. I often find his wines perplexing to evaluate and generally not to my liking. He makes the generic burgundy called Montre Cul, which is obviously controversial because of its label that, in poor taste, shows a woman's derrière in full view. He did not show me the 1985 version of this wine, perhaps because I had written that the 1983 had a fecal aroma. His Gevrey-Chambertin has a defective bouquet (probably mercaptans), but on the palate the wine is certainly fruity. The Marsannay exhibits good, clean berry fruit, medium body, and a soft texture. The best wine is the Gevrey-Chambertin Le Bel Air, a densely colored, big, thick wine with considerable tannin. It needs 6–7 years to fully develop.

GASTON AND PIERRE RAVAUT (ALOXE-CORTON)* * *

1985 Aloxe-Corton	C	85
1985 Ladoix	C	85

Both of these wines are ripe and fleshy, without a great deal of finesse, but with solid, muscular flavors and good balance. They should age well for 5–8 years.

REMOISSENET (BEAUNE)* * *

1985 Aloxe-Corton	C	75
1985 Beaune Grèves	C	86
1985 Beaune Marconnets	C	87
1985 Bonnes Mares	E	82
1985 Bourgogne Rouge	B	78
1985 Chambolle-Musigny Les Charmes	C	86
1985 Charmes-Chambertin	E	83
1985 Clos Vougeot	E	86
1985 Gevrey-Chambertin	C	78
1985 Givry	B	85
1985 Grands-Echézeaux	E	87
1985 Mercurey Clos Fourtoul	B	80
1985 Nuits St.-Georges	B	79
1985 Nuits St.-Georges Les Argillets	C	85
1985 Nuits St.-Georges Les Boudots Hospices de Nuits	E	89
1985 Pommard Epenots	D	86

1985 Richebourg	E	84
1985 Santenay Clos de Tavannes	C	85
1985 Santenay La Comme	C	86
1985 Santenay Gravières	C	84
1985 Savigny Les Beaune	C	80
1985 Savigny Les Beaune Gravains	C	84
1985 Savigny Les Beaune Les Guettes	C	82
1985 Savigny Les Beaune Les Marconnets	C	84
1985 Savigny Les Beaune Serpentières	C	82
1985 Volnay	C	80
1985 Vosne-Romanée	C	77
1985 Vosne-Romanée Les Chaumes	C	87
1985 Vosne-Romanée Les Suchots	C	87

Roland Remoissenet is one of the most dashing figures in Burgundy. Handsome, enthusiastic, extroverted and warm, he always makes my visit with him interesting and pleasant. With respect to the wines, I rate them good to very good for the white, and average to very good for the reds. The 1985 reds are all soundly made, correct wines, but only 13 out of 29 had enough personality and character befitting their appellations to get a recommendation. I noticed that the 1985s have more tart acidity at Remoissenet than elsewhere, as well as more noticeable alcohol levels and tannins. They are, like virtually all 1985s, quite well colored. Many seemed to resemble one another. For value, the spicy, fleshy Givry is quite good. While the selection of Savignys is not inspiring, the Santenays are quite good, full-bodied, fleshy, rich, well-made wines that will drink handsomely after 10–12 years of cellaring. Both the Beaune Grèves and the Beaune Marconnets (the latter wine is always top rank here) are lovely, broadly flavored, deep wines with concentrated, rich cherry fruit-scented personalities. I also thought the Pommard Epenots to be very fine, powerful, deep, rich, lovely, and full bodied. Among the Côte de Nuits wines, the best one is clearly the extremely rich, concentrated, long Nuits St.-Georges Les Boudots, which is oozing with ripe berry fruit and is quite complex. Certainly, the fat, alcoholic, but superconcentrated Grands-Echézeaux and the elegant, stylish Chambolle-Musigny Les Charmes are both lush, rich, full-bodied and concentrated wines that can age well. The Vosne-Romanée Les Suchots and the Vosne-Romanée Les Chaumes also stood out above the pack. The Clos Vougeot and Nuits St.-Georges Les Argillets are also good. None of these wines is exceptional, but all are sturdy, reliable, chunky, fleshy wines that will last.

RION PÈRE ET FILS (NUITS ST.-GEORGES)* * *

1985 Clos Vougeot	D	90
1986 Clos Vougeot	D	76
1985 Chambolle-Musigny Les Echézeaux	D	88
1985 Nuits St.-Georges Les Meurgers	D	87
1985 Vosne-Romanée Les Chaumes	D	87
1986 Vosne-Romanée Les Chaumes	D	78

Bernard Rion, a young, red-faced, chunky man, has 15 acres of vineyards in the Côte de Nuits. He believes in the use of 50% new oak and in keeping the wine in the barrel for 18 months. He made mediocre 1986s and very good 1987s which, he says, are nearly as good as the 1985s. The great ripeness and rich, plump fruitiness of the 1985s have married beautifully with the new oak to render rich, concentrated wines with a decade of cellaring potential. The Clos Vougeot is clearly the winner in 1985 for Rion.

MAURICE ROLLAND (PERNAND-VERGELESSES)* * *

1985 Pernand-Vergelesses Ile de Vergelesses	B	86
1985 Pernand-Vergelesses	B	86
1985 Savigny-les-Beaune	B	86

These are notably good values, and are fruity, deeply colored, quite concentrated wines that will keep 5–8 years. The Savigny is especially voluptuous; the Ile de Vergelesses is more powerful, tannic, and long-lived. They are all unfiltered.

DOMAINE DE LA ROMANÉE-CONTI (VOSNE-ROMANÉE)* * * * *

1985 Echézeaux	E	92
1985 Grands-Echézeaux	E	95
1985 Richebourg	E	96
1985 Romanée-Conti	E	100
1985 Romanée-St.-Vivant	E	94
1985 La Tâche	E	98

This fabled estate has had a brilliant track record since 1978, and its 1985 vintage is its best group of wines in decades, even better than the sensational 1978s. As Lalou Bize-Leroy and Aubert de Villaine seem to have everything tightly under control, it is unlikely that the previous lapses in quality control will occur; yet the estate is frequently singled out for malicious attacks (most recently in *The Wine Spectator*). In any event, no one should have any trouble appreciating the DRC's 1985s; the only problem will be coming up with the cash to buy them. The wines are aged in 100% new oak and never filtered. The Echézeaux, normally the lightest and least distinguished wine of the DRC, is the best I have ever tasted from them. Deep ruby, with a fragrant, rich, complex bouquet of violets and spicy oak, this full-bodied wine is quite long, velvety, and will keep 8–12 years. The Grands-Echézeaux is opulent, deep in color, fatter, and more alcoholic than the lovely 1980, and less tannic than the 1983. Its huge fruit, sweetness, and length are terrific. Drink it between 1989 and 2000. The Romanée-St.-Vivant is much more tannic, has the distinctive ironlike scent, cinnamon, and *goût de terroir* that for me make it the most unique wine of the DRC stable. It is quite tannic and needs 6–8 years of cellaring. The Richebourg is enormous, in an old, heavy-weight style, and is a tannic, relatively closed wine with a broodingly deep color and sensational depth and length. It would be a crime to drink it before 1992–1995, and it will last two decades. The La Tâche offers surreal and celestial aromas of Oriental spices and flowers, masses of ripe fruit, scents of truffles(?), dazzling concentration, tremendous breadth of flavor, exquisite length, and 20 or more years of cellaring potential. Tasting the Romanée-Conti just after I had tasted the La Tâche, I thought the former would not be as good, but it is utterly mind-blowing. The heady, intoxicating bouquet delivered penetrating and sublime aromas that were even more intense than those of the La Tâche. On the palate, there is a veritable smorgasbord of earthy and heavenly delights. Needless to say, it is very rich, very opulent, and very concentrated. Red burgundy—and red wine in general—does not get any better than this. My guess is that it will peak between 1990 and 2005, as it is a bit more forward than either the La Tâche or the Richebourg. The 1986s and 1987s here are fabulous, and after the 1985s, 1987 is the finest overall vintage since the wonderful 1980s made at the DRC.

PHILIPPE ROSSIGNOL (GEVREY-CHAMBERTIN)* * * *

1985 Bourgogne	B	86

1985 Côte de Nuits-Villages	B	84

1985 Gevrey-Chambertin	C	86

There is no doubt that the generic Bourgogne is a lovely, rich, unfiltered, intense wine with gobs of sweet oak in the bouquet as well as surprising depth. Drink it over the next 5–6 years. Surprisingly, I liked it better than the Côte de Nuits-Villages, which is quite tannic. The Gevrey-Chambertin is smoky, ripe, full bodied, and shows fine depth and length. It will age well for 5–6 years.

JOSEPH ROTY (GEVREY-CHAMBERTIN)* * * *

1985 Charmes-Chambertin	D	98

1985 Gevrey-Chambertin Les Champchenys	C	88

1985 Gevrey-Chambertin Les Fontenys	C	90

1985 Mazy-Chambertin	D	94

1985 Pinot Noir Les Pressonières	B	84

The extremely active and loquacious Joseph Roty is a fabulous winemaker. While he has been "discovered" numerous times, I doubt he has ever made better wines than these 1985s. The generic Bourgogne has a dark ruby color, an intense, spicy nose, and at least 5–6 years of life. The specialties here are the wines from Roty's own backyard, Gevrey-Chambertin. The Les Champchenys, not a Premier Cru but still a good vineyard near Charmes-Chambertin, is amazing for a "villages" wine from Gevrey. Ruby/purple in color, with a penetrating bouquet of toasty oak, this full-bodied wine is very rich, long, and concentrated, and will last 10–15 years. The Premier Cru, Les Fontenys, is a broodingly rich, smoky, intense, power-laden wine that has the requisite concentration, length, and tannin to carry it 20 years. While Roty's Mazy-Chambertin is undoubtedly a great wine, with its astonishing black/purple color, a huge oaky, intense bouquet of cassis, as well as dazzling power and depth, the Charmes-Chambertin is simply awesome. From the bouquet of violets, intense cherry fruit and toasty new oak to the staggering level of extract and purity of Pinot Noir fruit, this full-bodied yet sensual and elegant wine is one of the most impressive young burgundies I have ever tasted. The Charmes will keep for 15–20 years. The 1986s from Roty are surprisingly mediocre.

EMMANUEL ROUGET (NUITS ST.-GEORGES)* * *

1985 Echézeaux	D	89

1985 Nuits St.-Georges	B	85

In 1987, the young Rouget, nephew of Henri Jayer, began making the wines of Jayer. He also owns several small parcels of land, where he produces the above wines; they are not filtered and are bottled directly from the barrel. The Nuits St.-Georges has a good color, a charming, elegant, berry fruitiness, medium body, and 4–8 years of further cellaring potential. The Echézeaux has exceptional purity of raspberry fruit, deep color, a long, flowing fruitiness, medium to full body, and 10 years of aging potential.

GEORGES ROUMIER (CHAMBOLLE-MUSIGNY)* * * *

1985 Bonnes Mares	E	90

1985 Chambolle-Musigny	D	85

1985 Chambolle-Musigny Les Amoureuses	D	90

| 1985 Clos Vougeot | D | 87 |

| 1985 Morey St.-Denis Clos de la Bussière | D | 87 |

This is one of the best-known estates of Burgundy. For years Jean-Marie Roumier has made the wines, but now his son, Christophe, is taking charge. The 1985s are very good, more flattering to taste young, but not better than the 1983s. The "villages" Chambolle-Musigny has good length, a supple, charming ripeness and berry fruitiness, and 4–5 years of further evolution. The Clos de la Bussière has a deep color, a broad, sweet, smoky, cherry-scented bouquet, velvety texture, full body, and 7–8 more years of life. The Bonnes Mares may turn out to be a great wine. It is quite dark in color, closed and tannic, but it swells in the glass and appears to have significant depth and richness on the palate. Drink it between 1990 and 2000. The Clos Vougeot is similarly tight and closed, but has an impressive color and great potential, as there is oodles of fruit extract and plenty of body and length. Hold it until at least 1990. On the other hand, the Les Amoureuses gushes from the glass with explosive richness, intense aromas of sweet vanillin oak, ripe cherries, and spring flowers. Full bodied, with extravagant fruit, this wine will drink well for 10–12 years. This is one of the rare estates where the 1986s look superior to the 1985s, especially the Bonnes Mares, Les Amoureuses, and Ruchottes-Chambertin.

HERVÉ ROUMIER (CHAMBOLLE-MUSIGNY)* * *

| 1985 Bonnes Mares | D | 85 |

| 1985 Bourgogne | B | 75 |

| 1985 Chambolle-Musigny | C | 79 |

| 1985 Chambolle-Musigny Les Amoureuses | D | 86 |

Hervé Roumier is a cousin of the above-mentioned Christophe and his estate began to bottle its own wines only in 1978. The 1985s ranged from average to quite good. Both the Bourgogne and Chambolle-Musigny are simple, rather undistinguished wines. The Les Amoureuses has a dark ruby color, soft, supple, concentrated fruitiness, medium to full body, and 4–5 years of further evolution. The Bonnes Mares tastes good, but is not special or particularly concentrated given the vintage. Nevertheless, the wine has plenty of appeal because of its pure, velvety Pinot Noir fruitiness.

DOMAINE ARMAND ROUSSEAU (GEVREY-CHAMBERTIN)* * * *

1985 Chambertin	E	91
1985 Chambertin Clos de Bèze	E	90
1985 Charmes-Chambertin	D	87
1985 Clos de la Roche	E	87
1985 Clos des Ruchottes	D	88
1985 Gevrey-Chambertin	C	83
1985 Gevrey-Chambertin Les Cazetiers	C	85
1985 Gevrey-Chambertin Clos St.-Jacques	D	90
1985 Mazis-Chambertin	D	86

The Rousseau domaine ranks as one of Burgundy's most important estates. It was among the first to bottle its wines, in the thirties, thereby setting an example that many of Burgundy's finest producers would subsequently follow. The friendly, baritone-voiced Charles Rousseau runs the property now, and except for some problems in the late seventies, the quality has been extremely high. Rousseau still calls 1983 one of the finest vintages of this century, and prefers his wines of that vintage to his 1985s. However, I found his 1983s to be erratic—some were great and some showed rot—and his 1985s to be consistently very good to excellent, if not spectacular. The Les Cazetiers and the Mazis-Chambertin tasted too supple and lacked some definition. The Charmes-Chambertin is very seductive and expansive, but can be drunk young. The Clos de la Roche is similarly styled, but surprisingly not rich and tannic enough to be great. The Clos St.-Jacques, made from 61-year-old vines, has oodles of black cherry fruit, a deep color, and layers upon layers of extract. It needs 3–4 years to fully develop, but will keep 10–15 years. The Clos des Ruchottes is similar, but even more structured. Two great wines are the Chambertin Clos de Bèze and the Chambertin. Both wines will age for 10–15 years, have deep color, powerful, rich, intense flavors, plenty of spicy new oak, and gobs of tannin, as well as impeccable length. The 1986s are very good, but with the exception of Chambertin and

Clos de Bèze, I did not rate any of the other wines outstanding from the cask.

SAIER (MERCUREY)* * *

1985 Mercurey Champs Martin	B	86

1985 Mercurey Les Chenelots	B	84

The Saier family, also owners of the famous Clos des Lambrays in Morey St.-Denis, has almost 35 acres in Mercurey. The quality of their two 1985 Mercureys is good to very good. The Les Chenelots is soft, ripe, attractively fruity, and offers plenty of soft berry fruit. The Champs Martin, said by some to be produced in the best vineyard in Mercurey, is a much richer wine; it exhibits toasty, plummy scents and flavors, and has medium to full body and a velvety finish. Both wines should drink well for 5–6 years.

DANIEL SENARD (ALOXE-CORTON)* * *

1985 Corton	D	89

1985 Corton Bressandes	D	87

1985 Corton Clos du Meix	D	85

1985 Corton Clos du Roi	D	87

Daniel Senard, one of Aloxe-Corton's most visible proprietors, made delicious 1985s that show vibrant, well-focused black cherry fruit married handsomely with toasty vanillin oak. On the palate, all the wines show the personality characteristics of the 1985 vintage—soft, lush fruit, medium to full body, and very soft, light tannins. My three favorites included the outstanding Corton, Corton Bressandes, and Corton Clos du Roi. All these wines can be drunk now (the wonderful dilemma regarding most 1985 burgundies) or can be cellared for 5–10 years.

C. SERAFIN (GEVREY-CHAMBERTIN)* * *

1985 Gevrey-Chambertin Les Cazetiers	C	88

Aged in 100% new oak, this impressive wine exhibits exceptional finesse, a long, deep, supple fruitiness, nearly great character and concentration, and 5–7 years of longevity.

BERNARD SERVEAU (MOREY ST.-DENIS)* * * *

1985 Bourgogne	B	86
1985 Chambolle-Musigny Les Amoureuses	D	90
1985 Chambolle-Musigny Les Chabiots	C	86
1985 Morey St.-Denis Les Sorbets	C	87

The wines made here are always graceful examples of red burgundy
—supple enough to be drunk young, and structured and concentrated
enough to age 7–10 years. The surprise here is a ripe, juicy, round,
sweet, aromatic generic Bourgogne that has excellent depth and loads
of fruit. In the high-priced world of burgundy, this wine is a real
bargain. In 1986, Serveau's Morey St.-Denis Les Sorbets is more
successful than his Chambolle-Musigny Les Chabiots; in 1985 it is
just the opposite. The 1985 Les Sorbets is pure elegance—ripe, seductive, loaded with scents and flavors of raspberry fruit and new oak,
well structured, and having 7–8 more years of evolution. The Chabiots
is effusively fruity, but less deep and structured, and should be drunk
over the next 5–6 years. Serveau made a glorious Chambolle-Musigny
Les Amoureuses in 1985 that has a dazzling level of fruit extract, a
wonderful purity, elegance, balance, and sensational length. It should
be at its best between 1990 and 1996.

ROBERT SIRUGUE (VOSNE-ROMANÉE)* * *

1985 Grands-Echézeaux	D	90
1985 Vosne-Romanée	C	86
1985 Vosne-Romanée Les Petits Monts	C	86

The tanned, animated, friendly face of Robert Sirugue breaks into a
broad smile when he is asked to talk about his 1985s. He is a very
commercially oriented grower, and one suspects that no 1985s will be
sold here without a portion of the 1984s tacked on as part of the deal.
With respect to these 1985s, the "villages" Vosne-Romanée is sweet
and round, with lovely fruit, and has 4–5 years of further aging potential. The wine of the well-situated Vosne-Romanée Les Petits Monts
(the vineyard touches Romanée-Conti and Richebourg) tasted less rich
and complex than I had hoped, but in all fairness, it had been bottled
only one month before I tasted it. It has very good color, ripe, fruity,

supple flavors, and seemed nearly ready to drink. Certainly the Grands-Echézeaux showed well in spite of recent bottling. Deep ruby in color, with a ripe, rich, perfumed bouquet of berry fruit, spicy new oak, and flowers, this rich, well-structured and well-delineated wine makes a considerable impression on the palate, yet will not be fully mature until 1991–1992, and will keep 5–7 years thereafter.

JEAN TARDY (VOSNE-ROMANÉE)* * * *

1985 Clos Vougeot	D	91
1986 Clos Vougeot	D	89
1985 Nuits St.-Georges Boudots	D	89
1986 Nuits St.-Georges Boudots	D	87
1985 Vosne-Romanée Les Charmes	C	86
1986 Vosne-Romanée Les Charmes	C	83

Jean Tardy, whose looks and sense of humor could make him Burgundy's answer to Johnny Carson, makes excellent—even outstanding—wine from his 11 + acres of well-placed vineyards. A great believer in a long, 3-week maceration and 100% new oak, Tardy's wines are imbued with a superrichness and purity of Pinot Noir fruitiness. His 1986s are very successful, his 1985s even better. Interestingly, Tardy sells his excess production to the *négociants* Drouhin and Jadot. His Nuits St.-Georges Boudots can rival his Clos Vougeot, as the Boudots is made from very old vines.

TOLLOT-BEAUT (CHOREY-LES-BEAUNE)* * * *

1985 Beaune Clos du Roi	C	89
1985 Corton Bressandes	D	90
1985 Côte de Beaune-Villages	B	84
1985 Savigny Lavières	C	85

This is a very special property, with quite a traditional approach to winemaking—wood fermenters, plenty of punching down, high fermentation temperatures, no fining, and only minimal filtration. The

1985s look very good to exceptional in quality. The Côte de Beaune-Villages has a moderately intense bouquet of clean cherry fruit, some appealing fatness, and fine length. It should be drunk over the next 4–5 years. The Savigny Lavières is a big, rather tannic wine with considerable fruit, but also a firm, very well-structured character. It should not be drunk until 1990–1995. The great bouquet, superrich, ripe fruit, powerful, deep, full-bodied character, and explosive nature of the Beaune Clos du Roi suggest that this big wine should be drunk between 1992 and 2000. The Corton Bressandes is even more stupendous—a huge wine of exceptional concentration, full body, very ripe fruit, spicy oak, and an amazing finish. It will be a real keeper; don't drink it until 1990–2000.

DOMAINE LOUIS TRAPET (GEVREY-CHAMBERTIN)* * * *

1985 Chambertin	E	88
1985 Chambertin Cuvée Vieilles Vignes	E	90
1985 Chapelle-Chambertin	D	87
1985 Gevrey-Chambertin	C	85
1985 Gevrey-Chambertin Premier Cru	C	84
1985 Latricières-Chambertin	D	89

Trapet, in Gevrey-Chambertin, is one of the most important estates in the Côte de Nuits. Jean Trapet, an energetic, polite, reserved individual, realizes that his wines have not really been as good as they should have been (some of his 1978s are now brown and undrinkable). As a result, he has made significant changes in the eighties that have improved his wines, giving them more color and extract; also he has stopped filtering his wines at the time of bottling. His 1984s are quite good, and he considers his 1985s his finest overall vintage of the last three decades, even better than his superb 1969s. The 1985s have an elegance and rich berry fruitiness that give them a precocious appeal and charm now, but they should last for at least a decade. The Gevrey-Chambertin has a rich, earthy, berry-scented bouquet, good color, smoky, plummy fruit, medium body, and a long, lush finish. I preferred it to the Gevrey-Chambertin Premier Cru, which tasted slightly less rich and multidimensional. The Chapelle-Chambertin, while having a good structure, is all silky elegance, with a big, penetrating, toasty, earthy bouquet, concentrated, supple fruitiness, a long finish, and 6–9 years of further drinkability. The Latricières-Chambertin is richer and more full bodied and tannic than the Chapelle. In 3–4 years' time, I would not be surprised if this turns out to be Trapet's best wine of 1985. Quite rich, smoky, and earthy, with superlength and ripeness, this is an atypically big wine for Trapet. The Chambertin is long, ripe, and rich, less full bodied than the Latricières, more elegant and fruity, and aged in 50% new oak barrels. It will drink well young, but also age for 7–9 years. The Chambertin Vieilles Vignes has gobs of sweet, ripe berry fruit, a well-structured palate impression, medium to full body, broad, expansive flavors, and a long finish. It is much better colored and more flattering to drink than the tannic 1983. Trapet's 1986s are fruity, soft, flavorful, quite successful wines, but they are not outstanding and will have to be drunk young.

VADEY-CASTAGNIER (MOREY ST.-DENIS)* * *

1985 Chambolle-Musigny	C	86
1985 Charmes-Chambertin	D	88
1985 Clos de la Roche	D	88
1985 Clos Vougeot	D	87
1985 Gevrey-Chambertin	C	86

As the wines of Guy Castagnier are not terribly well known in the United States, my experience with them has been very limited. While I found none of the 1985s to be exceptional, still they are all very good to excellent red burgundies, bursting with ripe aromas and flavors. The Chambolle-Musigny is full of charm, finesse, and has a super, jammy personality and round fruit. It should be drunk over the next 3–4 years. The Gevrey-Chambertin is more smoky and fat, with layers of succulent Pinot Noir fruit. It is quite an excellent "villages" wine and should be drunk over the next 5–6 years. The Clos Vougeot is also very forward and precocious, but more concentrated, full bodied, and longer. It is loaded with sweet, ripe, pure Pinot fruit. It should drink well for 5–8 years. The two best wines from Castagnier are the Clos de la Roche and Charmes-Chambertin. The Clos de la Roche is bigger, more robust, and potentially the longest-lived wine from Castagnier, but packed with velvety, deep, rich fruit and a penetrating sweet, roasted aroma. Drink it over the next 8–10 years. The

Charmes-Chambertin has the identical texture and level of sweet, ripe fruit, but is less robust and more elegant. All of these wines have plenty of hedonistic appeal.

MICHAEL VOARICK (ALOXE-CORTON)* * *

1985 Aloxe-Corton	C	83
1985 Corton Bressandes	D	87
1985 Corton Clos du Roi	D	90
1985 Corton Languettes	D	85
1985 Pernand-Vergelesses	C	85
1985 Romanée-St.-Vivant	E	86

There is no doubt that the chain-smoking Michel Voarick is a serious winemaker. His cellars are right next to the lovely, tranquil new Hôtel Clarion in Aloxe-Corton and are among the dampest and coolest in Burgundy. The wines are made very traditionally, with no destemming, no new oak barrels (Voarick is totally against new oak), and no filtration except when making wine for the American market. I have found that his wines are among the slowest to mature, as well as being among the most structured burgundies; they usually need 5–7 years to show well in top vintages such as 1985 or 1978. Not surprisingly, his 1985s are very tannic, densely colored wines that Voarick compares to the 1964s and 1959s, and not to the 1978s, which he says are lighter and less powerful. The Pernand-Vergelesses needs 5–8 years of cellaring. Powerful and rich, but too closed and tannic, it is quite a sizable wine for its appellation. The Aloxe-Corton has an unusual tarlike aroma; despite its chewy, dense style, it tasted too tannic. I like the Corton Languettes, and although it needs 5–6 years, I thought it suffered in comparison with the other Voarick wines. The Corton Bressandes is sumptuous, fat, very rich and deep, with 5–12 years of further evolution ahead of it. It is quite full bodied and tannic. The Corton Clos du Roi is even better—a huge, intense, rich, concentrated wine of extremely generous proportions. It oozes with scents and flavors of cherries, and needs 5–9 years of cellaring. The Romanée-St.-Vivant, while quite elegant and tasty, does not live up to its price or reputation. It is stylish, but a slight dilution in its mid-range keeps the score lower than a wine of this pedigree should merit.

COMTE DE VOGÜÉ (CHAMBOLLE-MUSIGNY)* * *

1985 Bonnes Mares	E	87
1985 Chambolle-Musigny	D	84
1985 Chambolle-Musigny Les Amoureuses	E	86
1985 Musigny	E	88

The 1985s are the best wines that have been made at this historic estate since the outstanding ones of 1972. Between 1972 and 1985 there were a succession of wines that did not do justice to the reputation of either Burgundy or this famous domaine. The 1985s are not great wines, but they show a marked improvement over other recent vintages. They are velvety, with rich berry fruit, plenty of toasty new oak, and medium body. As one might expect, the Bonnes Mares and the Musigny are the two best wines, showing an extra level of concentration and character. All these wines are silky styles of red burgundy and perhaps should be drunk over the next 4–6 years.

LENI VOLPATO (CHAMBOLLE-MUSIGNY)* * *

1985 Bourgogne Passe Tout Grains	A	86
1986 Bourgogne Passe Tout Grains	A	84
1985 Chambolle-Musigny	C	87
1986 Chambolle-Musigny	C	82

This little-known producer, whose cellars are tucked away in a back alley of the village of Chambolle-Musigny, produces only two wines, one of which may well be Burgundy's best Bourgogne Passe Tout Grains. This wine, which is traditionally two-thirds Gamay with the balance Pinot Noir, is 95% Pinot Noir from Volpato. The 1986 has a deep color, a big, peppery bouquet, and spicy, supple flavors. The 1985 is quite serious, with a rich, deep fruitiness and amazing length for its class. It may be the best wine of its type that I have ever tasted. The other wine that the soft-spoken, shy Volpato produces is a Chambolle-Musigny, of which the 1986 is a little tough and sinewy but deep. However, the 1985 has all the fruit and finesse one could want in a Chambolle-Musigny, and tastes better than many growers' Premier Crus.

Beaujolais

The summer heat and humidity, which affect most areas of the United States in May, June, July, August and September, are not suitable for drinking rich, full-bodied red wines, particularly fine French Bordeaux, Rhônes, and bigger-style burgundies, or Italian Barolos, Barbarescos and California Cabernet Sauvignons and Zinfandels. Like most wine enthusiasts, I do not totally abstain from drinking these wines, even on the most torrid of days, but they are best served in fall, winter, and spring. There is, however, a perfect summer red wine—Beaujolais—the refreshingly forthright, effusively fruity wine from France. In fact, it can be the right wine for any season.

Produced from the Gamay grape, Beaujolais will never be great or profound, but it has the potential to be one of the most flexible, enjoyable, and seductive wines. At its best, served slightly chilled (50° F is a perfect temperature), it is a heady, perfumed, intensely fruity, soft, lush wine that can be rapaciously gulped down without feeling any guilt for not commenting on its bouquet, complexity, or finesse. Simple, lush and delicious, Beaujolais can be a hedonistic summer pleasure for wine drinkers.

The Beaujolais hierarchy is simple. At the lowest echelon is "straight" Beaujolais, followed by Beaujolais-Villages, which is usually better. At the top level of quality are the nine "crus," each offering the inimitable soft, lush fruitiness that has made Beaujolais so popular, but each slightly different in style.

Today the difference between a Moulin-à-Vent, historically the fullest, most age-worthy and richest Beaujolais cru, and Brouilly, the lightest cru, is not always as apparent as the textbooks suggest. However, the other seven crus include Chiroubles, always one of my favorites for decadently fruity wines; Julienas, fleshy and rich; St.-Amour, very fruity and supple; Morgon, among the most age-worthy; Fleurie, lush, silky, and fruity; Côtes de Brouilly, light and delicate, though rarely seen in this country; and Chénas, full, darkly colored, and potentially excellent, but also rarely seen.

Most Beaujolais will be at their best in 1–3 years after the vintage. Some will last longer. Despite this possibility of longevity, the wines do lose fruit and change in character, as the freshness and zesty, exuberant fruitiness of the wines dissipate. They may taste good after 3 years, but clearly their effusively fruity character begs for them to be drunk up over the first 2–3 years.

Recent Vintages

As for recent vintages, 1985 was the best bet, as the wines were ripe, fragrant, rich, and supple. However, they should have been drunk up by the end of 1988. Avoid the 1984s, which are hollow and lack charm. The rather large-proportioned 1983s were atypical Beaujolais—tannic, full-bodied and rich, but "too big"—and are now drying out. The 1986s have always tasted a little hard and tough for Beaujolais, and the 1987s, while aromatic, light and tasty, are not of the same quality as the outstanding 1985s. The 1987s should be drunk over the next 12–18 months. Although the wines are agreeable and pleasant, one should not believe all the hype concerning their quality. After 1985, 1988 appears to be the finest vintage with the quality closely resembling the great 1985s—good news indeed!

A GUIDE TO THE BEST PRODUCERS OF BEAUJOLAIS

* * * * * (OUTSTANDING PRODUCERS)

L. Bassy	Alain Michaud
René Berrod	Petit Pérou
J.P. Bloud	Jean-Paul Ruet
Michel Chignard	Bernard Santé
B. Diochon	Domaine Savoye
Georges Duboeuf	Georges Trichard
Jacky Janodet	

* * * * (EXCELLENT PRODUCERS)

Serge Aujas	Château des Jacques
Jean Bédin	Mathelin
Château de Bellevue	Domaine Matray
Louis Champagnon	Moulin-à-Vent des Hospices
Domaine Dalicieux	Thevenet
Jacques Depagneux	Château Thivin
Pierre Ferraud	Trenel

* * * (GOOD PRODUCERS)

Paul Beaudet	Henry Fessy
Georges Boulon	Sylvain Fessy
Joseph Drouhin	Chanut Frères

Jaffelin   Piat
André Large   Roger Rocassel
Moillard

* * *(AVERAGE PRODUCERS)*
Château de la Chaize   Robert Pain
Château de Corcelles   Pasquier-Desvignes
Loron   Paul Sapin
Mommessin   Louis Tête

The King of Beaujolais

No other person dominates a wine region of France as completely as Georges DuBoeuf, *le grand roi de Beaujolais*. The reasons for his remarkable success are simple—fair prices, consistently high quality, and a huge production. His famous flower-labeled bottle has inspired a new colorful era of wine labels, and his single domaine-designated Beaujolais wines are frequently the best that money can buy. In recent vintages, Duboeuf's wines have been priced at $6 to $10 a bottle.

RATING DUBOEUF'S BEST SINGLE GROWER

Outstanding

Brouilly (de Nervers)   Morgon Jean Descombes
Chiroubles Desmeures   Moulin-à-Vent Heritiers Tagent
Fleurie Les Déduits

Excellent

Beaujolais Regnie (du Potet)   Julienas (des Mouilles)
Beaujolais-Villages (Grand   Julienas (des Vignes)
  Grange)   Morgon (des Versauds)
Brouilly (du Prieuré)   Morgon (Princesse Lieven)
Chiroubles (de Raousset)   Moulin-à-Vent (La Tour du
Chiroubles (de Javernand)   Brief)
Chénas (La Combe Remont)   Moulin-à-Vent (des Caves)
Chénas (Manoir des Journets)   Saint-Amour (du Paradis)
Fleurie (Quatre Vents)

White Burgundy

The worldwide demand for white burgundy is even more insatiable than it is for red burgundy. It is further exacerbated by the fact that the quantities of wine produced are tiny. For example, one taste of a Leflaive, Jadot, Niellon, or Deleger Chevalier-Montrachet 1986 or 1985 will prove to just what splendid heights the Chardonnay grape can reach. However, the entire Chevalier-Montrachet appellation is less than 19 acres in size, scarcely large enough to produce 3,000 cases of wine for the entire world. Even the major white burgundy appellation of Chassagne-Montrachet has only 425 acres to it, and in a bountiful year, it rarely produces more white wine than the moderate-sized California Chardonnay specialist Sonoma-Cutrer. But Sonoma-Cutrer sells most of its wine in America, whereas Chassagne-Montrachet allocates its wines to most of the civilized countries throughout the world. All of this of course leads one to the dismal conclusion that white burgundy prices are high due to simple supply and demand, and if you want to regularly enjoy the best white burgundy, you must have a fat bank account.

QUICK VINTAGE GUIDE

White burgundy vintages are much more consistent and more frequently successful than those for red burgundy because Chardonnay is an easier grape to grow, suffering less in rain and cold than the fickle Pinot Noir. There has not been a bad or even mediocre white burgundy vintage this decade, a testament to how well the hardy Chardonnay grape thrives. Even 1984, a cold, damp year, produced a bevy of good wines. Here is a brief summary of recent vintages for white burgundy.

1987—A difficult year, but as usual the white wines are better than what might have been expected given the weather. They do not have the fat and depth of the 1985s, nor the charm or complexity of the 1986s, but they are medium-bodied, fruity, pleasant, and agreeable. They will have to be drunk early on because of their low acidities.

1986—The growers and *négociants* are comparing 1986, a huge bountiful crop, with the good abundant year of 1979. The wines are consistently very good, often superb. There is plenty of fresh acidity, and the extract levels, while quite variable, have provided wines ranging from slightly diluted to those that are wonderfully concentrated. One hears comments that the 1986s are more "classic" than the fatter 1985s. Certainly there is some additional complexity in the 1986s as a result of the botrytis or noble rot that attacked some of the Chardonnay. In my tastings, the wines showed extremely well, with the strongest wines appearing to be in the appellations of Chassagne

Montrachet, Meursault, Corton-Charlemagne, the Mâconnais, and Pouilly-Fuissé. The wines, because of their high acidity, should age well for 5–10 years. Prices are lower for the 1986s than the 1985s.

1985—Production was significantly below the bumper crop of 1986. Paradoxically, some wines seem to lack complexity and depth. The grapes were so healthy and free of mold and rot that some growers claim the wines are too clean and perfect. At the top levels, the wines are fat and rich but low in acidity; yet there are numerous splendid wines for drinking over the next 5–7 years. However, the quality is much more variable than the vintage's "great" reputation would suggest. For example, some wines from Mâcon and Pouilly-Fuissé are diffuse and too light. Most wines should age rapidly and be fully mature in another 2–3 years. There were great successes in Chablis, as well as Meursault and Chassagne-Montrachet. In comparison with the higher-acid, lighter-bodied 1986s, the 1985s exhibit more power and are richer, yet not always more complex. Prices are extremely high, owing to the acclaim surrounding this vintage.

1984—If the top wines lack length and finish short on the palate, they do offer complex, interesting aromas and enough ripeness to offer pleasant drinking. The high acidities should keep them alive and fresh for 4–5 more years. In isolated cases, one can even find some great wines; Leflaive's Chevalier-Montrachet is one example.

1983—This controversial year offered the growers the deadly duo of hail and rot, but also fabulous heat and sunshine for attaining a super-ripeness. The resulting wines have been extolled by some, condemned bitterly by others. For the top white burgundies, it is an oldstyle, heavyweight vintage of extremely powerful, rich, intense wines that approach 14–15% alcohol naturally. They are oozing with complex aromas and have a sledgehammerlike power and headiness. For those growers who failed to control the rot or who harvested too late, rather grotesque, out-of-balance wines were produced. There are some fabulous wines from Chablis, Corton-Charlemagne, and Chevalier-Montrachet in the vintage. Many Meursaults are problematic, and the Mâcons, initially intense and full-bodied, have begun to crack up.

1982—Aside from 1978 and 1979, this is the best vintage for current drinkability. A large crop of very healthy, ripe grapes was harvested. Where the yield was not excessive, gorgeously lush, supple, intensely fruity wines were produced. Where the yield was excessive, the wines lack concentration. The Chablis, as a general rule, are soft and watery, but there are super wines in Chassagne-Montrachet, Puligny-Montrachet, and Meursault.

Older Vintages

The 1981s are still tightly locked up and have been slow to evolve. Some of the growers have begun to intimate that these wines don't have the concentration of fruit to outlast the high acids and tart framework. Time will tell. The 1980s are the least successful white burgundies of this decade, but the wines are still alive and offer compact, serviceable drinking. The 1979s are lovely, elegant, stylish wines that are ready to drink and seem vastly underrated. However, I see no reason not to drink them up over the next 2–4 years. The 1978s, a near-perfect vintage, have been slow to mature, but they are concentrated and fine. The 1976s are cracking up badly and these low-acid, powerfully constructed yet overblown wines should be consumed quickly.

A GUIDE TO THE BEST PRODUCERS OF PULIGNY-MONTRACHET, CHASSAGNE-MONTRACHET, MEURSAULT, AND CORTON-CHARLEMAGNE

* * * * * (OUTSTANDING PRODUCERS)

Coche-Dury	Leroy
Albert Grivault	Paul Pernot
Louis Jadot	Ramonet
Comtes Lafon	Étienne Sauzet
Vincent Leflaive	

* * * * (EXCELLENT PRODUCERS)

Pierre Bitouzet	Guffens-Heynen
Bitouzet-Prieur	Jaffelin
Bonneau de Martray	Francois Jobard
Roger Caillot	Louis Latour
Louis Chapuis	Lequin-Roussot
Chartron and Trébuchet	Château de Maltroye
Fernand Coffinet	Château de Meursault
Delagrange-Bachelet	Michelot-Buisson
Georges Deleger	Albert Morey
Joseph Drouhin	Bernard Morey
J. A. Ferret	Jean-Marc Morey
Château Fuissé	Pierre Morey
Gagnard	Niellon
Jean Germain	Prieur-Brunet

Henri Prudhon
Ramonet-Prudhon
Remoissenet

Ropiteau
Guy Roulot

*** *(GOOD PRODUCERS)*

Robert Ampeau
B. Bachelet
Bachelet-Ramonet
A. Belland
Henri Boillot
Bouchard Père et Fils
Bouzereau-Gruère
Louis Carillon
F. Chauvenet
Coche-Bizouard
Georges DuBoeuf
Faiveley

Labouré-Roi
Olivier Leflaive
Duc de Magenta
Joseph Matrot
Moillard
Charles Moncaut
Jean Monnier
Perrin-Ponsot
Rougeot
Thevenot-Machal
Jean Vachet
Michel Voarick

A GUIDE TO THE BEST PRODUCERS OF CHABLIS

***** *(OUTSTANDING PRODUCERS)*

René Dauvissat

Long-Depaquit
Raveneau

**** *(EXCELLENT PRODUCERS)*

Domaine Auffray
Jean Collet
Jean Dauvissat
Paul Droin
William Fèvre

Louis Michel
Louis Pinson
Guy Robin
Robert Vocoret

*** *(GOOD PRODUCERS)*

La Chablisienne
Jean-Claude Dauvissat
Jean Daux
Domaine Defaix
Joseph Drouhin
Marcel Duplessis
Domaine de L'Eglantière

Alain Geoffrey
Lamblin
Domaine Laroche
Moillard
J. Moreau
Albert Pic
A. Regnaud

Where Are Burgundy's White Wine Values?

If one is willing to be a bit adventurous and avoid the glamour appellations of white burgundy, values can be found. The little-known Saint-Romain, Auxey-Duresses, Saint-Aubin, and Santenay provide four appellations from which it is still difficult to find a white burgundy for more than $15 a bottle. Farther south, in the area called the Chalonnais, the white wines of Rully and Montagny are where the values are produced. South of Chalonnais, just to the north of Lyon, is the Mâconnais, the consumer's best chance for enjoying fruity, crisp Chardonnay wines for under $8. The Mâcon-Villages wines and the neighboring wines of St.-Véran are increasingly well-made and represent fine values. Following is a list of the best producers of these wines. Vintages should be regarded as approximately the same as in Puligny, Chassagne, Meursault, and Corton-Charlemagne.

Burgundy's Twenty-Four Best White Wine Values

Chanzy Frères (Mercurey)
Chanzy Frères (Rully)
Chartron and Trébuchet (St.-Aubin)
Jean Daux (Rully)
Delorme (Rully)
DuBoeuf (St.-Véran)
DuBoeuf (Mâcon-Villages)
Faiveley (Mercurey)
Faiveley (Rully)
Domaine de la Folie (Rully)
Jean Germain (St.-Romain)
Alain Gras (Auxey-Duresses)
Guffens-Heynen (Mâcon-Pierreclos)
J. Lamy (St.-Aubin)
Lequin-Roussot (Santenay)
Leroy (Auxey-Duresses)
Leroy (St.-Romain)
Prudhon (St.-Aubin)
Prunier (Auxey-Duresses)
A. Rodet (Mercurey)
Domaine de Rully (Rully)
Château de la Saule (Montagny)
Vachet (Montagny)
A. Villaine (Bourgogne le Clous)

BERNARD BACHELET* * *

1985 Chassagne-Montrachet Morgeot	D	83
1986 Chassagne-Montrachet Morgeot	D	76
1985 Meursault Clos du Cromin	D	79
1986 Meursault Clos du Cromin	D	75
1985 Meursault Les Narvaux	D	83

1986 Meursault Les Narvaux	D	86
1985 Meursault Les Vireuils	D	83
1986 Meursault Les Vireuils	D	85
1985 Puligny-Montrachet	C	83
1986 Puligny-Montrachet	C	80

Here is one of a surprising number of examples where certain cuvées of 1986 look more complex and interesting than their counterparts in 1985. The overall quality in both vintages from Bachelet is adequate rather than exciting. Among the 1986s, the Meursault Clos du Cromin is diluted and simple, but both the Meursault Les Narvaux and Meursault Les Vireuils exhibit elegant, medium-bodied textures, good ripeness and character, and early-maturing personalities. The 1986 Puligny-Montrachet has a very good bouquet but tails off on the palate quite quickly. The 1986 Chassagne-Montrachet Morgeot also has a thin, overcropped taste and simple fruitiness. As for the 1985s, they are sound, medium-bodied, perfectly correct wines with compact structures, not much depth or complexity, and 2–4 years aging potential. For the prices asked, these wines are notoriously poor values.

BACHELET-RAMONET* * *

1985 Bienvenues-Bâtard-Montrachet	E	85
1985 Chassagne-Montrachet Caillerets	D	87
1985 Chassagne-Montrachet Les Grandes Montagnes	D	?
1985 Chassagne-Montrachet Morgeot	D	82
1985 Chassagne-Montrachet La Romanée	D	86
1985 Chassagne-Montrachet Les Ruchottes	D	72

Most white burgundy enthusiasts operate under the assumption that the famous name of Ramonet on a label of white burgundy guarantees ecstasy in the bottle. Caveat emptor—particularly with the wines from Bachelet-Ramonet. I have encountered far too many oxidized bottles of wine from this grower, especially from the 1982 and 1983 vintages, and a look at his dreary, unkempt cellar hardly inspires confidence. That being said, his 1985s, if not great, were at least good to very good save for the thin, diluted, flat Ruchottes and bizarre, problematic Les Grandes Montagnes. The Morgeot is a relatively light wine but has an attractive elegance and charm that gives it some appeal. The Caillerets is also racy and charming with more buttery, applelike fruit showing, medium body, crisp acidity, and 4–6 years of further drinkability. La Romanée is more lemony and tart with plenty of zesty acidity to go along with its medium-bodied, concentrated, fruity character. Though an understated wine, it has good flavor concentration and length. The Bienvenues-Bâtard-Montrachet exhibits more new oak in its bouquet, but given the price and high reputation of the vineyard, the wine does not fulfill expectations. Its medium-bodied character and good apple, lemony fruit suggest it should drink well for 4–5 years.

A. BELLAND* * *

1986 Corton-Charlemagne	E	89
1985 Puligny-Montrachet	C	84
1986 Puligny-Montrachet	C	83

Belland, who makes at least ten different red wines, also produces several well-made white wines. The contrast between his 1985 and 1986 Puligny-Montrachet is quite typical of the differences between the vintages. The 1985 is fuller on the palate and lower in acidity, whereas the 1986 is more aromatic, crisper, yet lighter and more delicate. With respect to the Corton-Charlemagne, there are 110 cases of this impressive, powerfully built wine. Aged in 100% new oak, it is very concentrated, rich, high in acidity, yet very young and backward. It will keep for 10–12 years.

C. BERGERET* *

1985 Chassagne-Montrachet	C	75
1985 Chassagne-Montrachet Morgeot	C	78

Both of these wines are inexcusably bland, simple, one-dimensional wines that offer less flavor dimension than many $6 California Chardonnays. Drink them over the next 1–3 years.

PIERRE BITOUZET* * * *

1985 Corton-Charlemagne	E	90
1986 Corton-Charlemagne	E	92
1986 Savigny-les-Beaune Les Goudelettes	B	85

Pierre Bitouzet, a well-dressed, impeccably groomed man, is well-known for the elegant red wines he makes at the Prince de Mérode estate. He also produces approximately 250 cases of a super Corton-Charlemagne, and even smaller quantities of a white Savigny-les-Beaune. His Savigny is a chubby, soft, yet deliciously fruity, medium-bodied wine that offers immediate gratification. A bit more patience is needed for the two Corton-Charlemagnes, but a wait of 3–5 years will be worth it. The 1986 is potentially a better wine than the 1985. It is richer, with a huge bouquet of tropical fruit, more powerful, full-bodied, and long in the finish; it should be kept for a decade. The 1985 tastes more backward but appears to have all the necessary concentration, length, and balance to be quite special in 4–5 years' time. Both wines should last for at least a decade in a good cool cellar.

BITOUZET-PRIEUR* * * *

1985 Meursault	C	86
1985 Meursault Charmes	D	90
1985 Meursault Clos du Cromin	D	89
1985 Meursault Santenots	D	84

This is an impeccable domaine that excels in making both red and white wine. The Meursault Santenots tasted lean, is high in acidity, and lacks the concentration of the other three wines. The "villages" Meursault is very good, a substantial, full-bodied, elegantly wrought wine with flavor and finesse. The two stars in the Bitouzet-Prieur stable are the hazelnut- and tropical-fruit-scented Meursault Clos du Cromin, and the rich, multi-dimensional Meursault Charmes. The Clos du Cromin is more forward and therefore offers more immediate pleasure. It is loaded with rich, ripe fruit and is balanced admirably by fine acidity and a touch of oak. The Charmes is fuller and richer, but it is also more backward and in need of 1–2 more years of bottle age. It is a classic Meursault. Bitouzet made wonderful 1986s, superior to his 1985s.

BOISSON-MOREY* *

1985 Meursault	C	84
1985 Puligny-Montrachet Folatières	D	83

These two wines exhibit correct, lightly toasty, crisp applelike fruit, medium body, and adequate length. Though somewhat understated, they are cleanly made and should keep for 2–3 years. The Meursault, with a trifle more substance and length as well as lower acidity, should therefore be drunk young. At these prices, they are obviously poor values.

BONNEAU DE MARTRAY* * * *

1985 Corton-Charlemagne	E	88
1986 Corton-Charlemagne	E	91

The Corton-Charlemagne made at this famous estate can frequently be counted on to rival the best white wines of Burgundy. The estate's manager, Maurice Bruchon, is enthusiastic about both the 1985 and 1986 vintages. I am not sure either will equal the quality of the exquisite 1983 (I recently rated it 93), but certainly the 1986 with its combination of power, structure, fruit, and acid appears to be a wine that can last 12–15 years. No one will be disappointed with the 1985, a lighter wine than the 1983 or 1986, with a charming, lush, very forward, apple, floral fruitiness and a nice touch of oak. The 1985 is surprisingly soft and resembles the 1982. The 1986 will certainly outlive the 1985 by 5–8 years.

BOUCHARD PÈRE ET FILS* * *

1985 Beaune Clos Saint-Landry	C	72
1985 Bourgogne Aligoté	B	70
1985 Chevalier-Montrachet	E	80?

This venerable old firm in Beaune (founded in 1731) has some of the most magnificent wine cellars my eyes have seen, as well as significant property holdings in the best vineyards of Burgundy. Yet, the wines are, as a whole, neutral tasting and lack depth. The Bouchards claim their style is one that emphasizes lightness and elegance, and that the wines need time in the cellar, yet bottles of their 1981 Montrachet I cellared perfectly are drying out, not opening up. These three offerings include a typically high-acid Bourgogne Aligoté that begs for some crème de cassis to take away its nasty bite. The Beaune smells green and unripe but tastes adequate and does have some Chardonnay fruit. The Chevalier-Montrachet (the Bouchards are the biggest landholder in this superb vineyard), is quite closed, but no matter how hard I tried, I could not find much depth or substance because of its austere, lean, tart character. The 1986s are significantly richer and better.

HUBERT BOUZEREAU* *

1985 Chassagne-Montrachet	C	70
1985 Chassagne-Montrachet Les Chaumées	C	65
1985 Meursault Charmes	D	85
1985 Meursault Genevrières	D	83
1985 Meursault Limozin	D	80
1985 Meursault Les Tillets	D	78
1985 Puligny-Montrachet	C	76

As a group of wines, these offerings were not terribly interesting or pleasant to taste. Bouzereau aims for a very high acid, tart, lean style of wine that gives his wines aging potential. However, just because they keep in the bottle is no guarantee that they will ever provide pleasure—and as so many people (particularly wine writers) forget, this is what wine is all about. Older vintages tasted are fresh and acidic, but not enjoyable. As for the 1985s, the only two wines of Bouzereau that appear to have the flesh and fruit to possibly balance the acidity are the Meursault Charmes and the Meursault Genevrières. The Charmes is a medium-bodied, elegant wine with both good acidity and fruit. The Genevrières has more of a green oaky character, as well as a hard, rigid framework, but also good fruit. Several wines from Bouzereau, particularly the Les Chaumées and Chassagne-Montrachet, showed a faint, musty, old-barrel smell.

ROGER CAILLOT* * * *

1985 Bâtard-Montrachet	E 96

1986 Bâtard-Montrachet	E 91

I have always thought of Caillot as a hit-or-miss producer, but with his Bâtard-Montrachet in both 1985 and 1986, he has been right on target. The 1986 is a lovely, elegant, rich, graceful wine bursting with scents of pineapples, toasty oak, and flowers. It has very good acidity and should age well for 5–8 years. The 1985 is a blockbuster wine with a dazzling level of concentration, a rich, buttery, deep, full-bodied texture, super length, and 4–5 years aging potential. It is a great Bâtard-Montrachet. Approximately 450 cases of each were produced.

LOUIS CARILLON* * *

1985 Puligny-Montrachet	C 85

1986 Puligny-Montrachet	C 83

1985 Puligny-Montrachet Les Champs Canet	D 87

1986 Puligny-Montrachet Les Champs Canet	D 87

1985 Puligny-Montrachet Les Combettes	D 87

1986 Puligny-Montrachet Les Combettes	D 87

1985 Puligny-Montrachet Les Perrières	D 87

1986 Puligny-Montrachet Les Perrières	D 87

This is an important domaine in Puligny-Montrachet as the Carillon family own 54 acres of vineyards, a sizable amount in the morseled world of Burgundy. The wines, aged one year in oak barrels of which 10% are new, are reliably good. The style of the wines produced by the black-haired, round-faced Louis Carillon is one of elegance and graceful, supple flavors. The 1986s were just bottled when I tasted them. They all exhibited a deft touch of new oak, ripe tropical-fruit-scented bouquets, good, crisp acidity (a trait of the 1986s), medium to full body, and 5–7 years of aging potential. The Perrières and Combettes both showed richer, more extravagant textures and very fine length. In contrast to the 1985s, the 1986s have more intense bouquets and crisper acids, but not the flesh and fat of the 1985s. The 1985 Puligny-Montrachet is richly fruity, even opulent for a "villages" wine, stylish and concentrated, as well as excellent to drink now. There are no differences in quality between the three Premier Cru Pulignys, Perrières, Champs Canet, and Combettes. I thought the Combettes the most hazelnut-scented and lush, while the Perrières filled the nose with exotic tropical fruit, and the Champs Canet was a combination in style of the two previous wines. All are flavorful, medium- to full-bodied Chardonnays that should keep well for 3–5 years.

LOUIS CHAPUIS* * *

1985 Bourgogne Blanc	B	87

1985 Corton-Charlemagne	E	92

Louis Chapuis always seems to produce top-quality Corton-Charlemagne. Even the 1984 (rated 89) turned out to be a top success in that vintage. As for the 1985, it is a full-bodied, rich, and powerful wine with admirable balance and good acidity for a 1985. The scents of tropical fruit are backed up by a steely firmness and tight structure. However, this wine has enough appeal to be drunk today without feeling guilty of infanticide. It will age well for 6–8 years. If the Corton-Charlemagne is too pricey, the Bourgogne Blanc from Chapuis tastes like most other producers' Premier Crus. Surprisingly rich and full, it is an excellent wine and a super value.

CHARTRON AND TRÉBUCHET* * *

1985 Bâtard-Montrachet	E	90
1985 Chassagne-Montrachet	C	80
1985 Chassagne-Montrachet Les Morgeots	C	79
1985 Chevalier-Montrachet (Jean Charton)	E	92
1985 Meursault	C	82
1985 Meursault Charmes	D	83
1985 Puligny-Montrachet	C	82

1985 Puligny-Montrachet Clos de la Pucelle (Jean Chartron)	D	88
1985 Puligny-Montrachet Les Folatières (Jean Chartron)	D	87
1985 Saint-Aubin	B	84

This partnership of two skilled winemakers who have a great deal of experience in Burgundy got started only several years ago. After the difficulties presented by the 1983 and 1984 vintages, 1985 was the first easy year in which to measure the progress of this quality-oriented team. The Saint-Aubin is fruity, clean, charming, and a decent value. The Puligny-Montrachet, along with the two wines from Chassagne-Montrachet and both Meursaults, all tasted compact, very clean, and technically sound, but boring undistinguished. Given the price of white burgundy, one should expect more. The four stars of this house in 1985 lead off with a deep, tightly knit, concentrated, elegant, medium-bodied Puligny-Montrachet Les Folatières. It is a wine with more style and grace than sheer size or power. More obvious and forward is the delicious, richly fruity, fuller-bodied Puligny-Montrachet Clos de la Pucelle. It can be drunk now but promises to keep well for 5–8 years. The two bell ringers from Chartron and Trébuchet are the Bâtard-Montrachet and Chevalier-Montrachet. The Bâtard-Montrachet is more open-knit, has a sensational bouquet of ripe, toasty, apricot- and peach-scented fruit, full body, and an unctuous texture and long finish. The Chevalier-Montrachet has even greater length and concentration, the same intense, layered texture, and impeccable balance, but it is still very young and unevolved. I would recommend cellaring it 4–5 years. In 1986, both Bâtard- and Chevalier-Montrachets are again the two superstars.

F. CHAUVENET* * *

1985 Chassagne-Montrachet	C	84
1985 Corton-Charlemagne Hospices de Beaune François Salins	E	96
1987 Mâcon-Villages Les Jumelles	A	82
1985 Meursault Les Casse-Têtes	C	85
1986 Pouilly-Fuissé Clos de France	B	85

1985 Puligny-Montrachet Reuchaux	C	84

1985 Saint-Véran	B	82

While the wines from this *négociant* are clearly the product of the high-tech, superclean, and intensely filtered modern school of wine-making, the results are attractive, stylish, fruity, rather commercial, yet enjoyable wines. Of course, the preposterously priced Corton-Charlemagne was made by the Hospices de Beaune and is a different animal. It is a splendidly rich, profound wine that is one of the greatest white burgundies I have recently tasted, but for the price of one bottle, one can get a case of good California or Australian Chardonnay. Those who do buy it should resist drinking it all up as it can benefit from 4–5 years of cellaring. The other wines are all clean, fruity, round, low-acid examples of white burgundy. The higher-rated wines have more length and richness, but all of the other white burgundies from Chauvenet should be drunk up over the next 2–3 years.

COCHE-BIZOUARD* * *

1985 Meursault Charmes	D	86

1985 Meursault Les Chevalières	D	89

1985 Meursault Limozin	D	87

Alain Coche, the proprietor of this small domaine of 20 acres, is extremely outspoken when it comes to how most white burgundy is being made. He attacks its low acidity, soft, commercial appeal, and those growers who tear out their vines before the vines hit the ripe old age of 50 or 60 years. I have found his wines a bit spotty, but there is no question that his 1985s are excellent across the board. When I last visited this estate, his 1986s were still going through a malolactic fermentation and were impossible to review. In 1985, his Meursault Les Chevalières, not a Premier Cru but rather a named vineyard or place (a *lieu-dit*), is richer, bolder, and more complex as well as less expensive than his delicious but firmer and leaner Meursault Charmes. Both show plenty of buttery fruit and high acidity. The Meursault Limozin, from a well-known vineyard just below the more famous Premier Cru vineyards of Les Charmes and Genevrières, is also better. Tightly knit, zesty, and fresh with good body and underlying length, it should prove to be an uncommonly long-lived Meursault from the 1985 vintage.

J. F. COCHE-DURY* * * * *

1985 Bourgogne	B	83
1986 Bourgogne	B	86
1985 Bourgogne Aligoté	B	82
1986 Corton-Charlemagne	E	96
1985 Meursault	C	87
1986 Meursault (a blend of Narvaux and La Barre)	C	90
1985 Meursault Les Casse-Têtes	D	88
1986 Meursault Les Casse-Têtes	D	92
1986 Meursault Chevalières	D	91
1985 Meursault Perrières	E	91
1986 Meursault Perrières	E	92
1985 Meursault Rougeots	D	89

The tall, thin, bespectacled, young Jean-François Coche-Dury is a follower of the unfiltered style of winemaking practiced by the Comtes Lafon family. He has built his microsized domaine up to 17.3 acres, which now includes a tiny bit of Corton-Charlemagne (the 1986 is mind-blowing). His secret to making great wine (Coche is universally regarded as one of the 5 or 6 best winemakers in Burgundy) is 33% to 50% new allier oak for his white wines, two rackings of the wines, 18–22 months in oak, and absolutely no filtration, a fact proudly displayed on the label. His 1986s are wonderful, superior to the 1985s, and also a full degree lower in alcohol. They are extremely profound from an aromatic standpoint with rich, full body, and intense but balanced, elegant personalities. The toasty, refined-hazelnut bouquets and stunning length and concentration in the cases of the Meursault Les Casse-Têtes (200 cases), Meursault Perrières (225 cases), and Corton-Charlemagne (fewer than 100 cases) are sublime examples of white burgundy at its purest and best. As for the Corton-Charlemagne, it is a heart-stopping beauty—deep, with layers of ripe Chardonnay fruit bursting from the glass. As for the 1985s, I would rank them behind his 1986s and 1981s, but superior to the 1983s and 1984s. The Perrières is outstanding (only 75 cases were made). It has an elegant, complex, full-intensity bouquet, rich flavors, good acidity, and super balance. Almost as good are the Meursault Les Casse-Têtes and Meursault Rougeots, which are both fat, tasty, full-bodied wines with a lovely harmony among their components.

FERNAND COFFINET* * * *

1986 Bâtard-Montrachet   E   90

1986 Chassagne-Montrachet   C   85

These wines are my first experience with the small grower named Fernand Coffinet. I liked both wines quite a bit. The "villages" Chassagne-Montrachet has a bold, intense, spicy, buttery, and apple-blossom bouquet, plenty of soft, lush Chardonnay fruit, and a gentle finish. The Bâtard-Montrachet has excellent ripeness, wonderful length, a creamy, rich, buttery, toasty texture, and 4–6 years of further drinkability.

JEAN COLLET* * * *

1986 Chablis Vaillons   C   86

1986 Chablis Valmur   C   92

Jean Collet has a lofty reputation among several of my French friends who enjoy fine wine, but despite the obvious richness he gets in his wines, I continue to find too many bottles that have been overly sulphured, giving them a skunky, matchstick character. Such was the problem with the 1985 Valmur, which had a great depth and richness, but an annoyingly high level of sulphur in the nose. The Vaillons was quite clean and exhibited lively mineral- and lemon-scented fruit, medium to full body, plenty of high acid, a rich, ripe level of fruit extract, and 5–6 years of aging potential. In 1986, 1987, and 1988 Collet appears to have made some of the finest wines in all of Chablis. His 1986 Valmur is exquisitely rich and balanced.

JEAN DAUVISSAT* * * *

1985 Chablis Les Preuses   C   87

1985 Chablis Les Vaillons	C	87

1985 Chablis Les Vaillons Vieille Vigne	C	89

Burgundy is confusing enough, but what must astound potential consumers is the number of different growers with the same last name. There are the Moreys and Ramonets in Chassagne-Montrachet, the Mugneret, Gros, and Jayer families in Vosne-Romanée, and a bevy of Dauvissats in Chablis. All of these wines from Jean Dauvissat represent very fine examples of Chablis. They are appropriately austere, with zesty acidity, exhibit very good mineral-scented, applelike Chardonnay fruit, medium body, and plenty of length. While the Preuses is a little fuller and perhaps richer, the aromatic complexity of the Vaillons offers just as much appeal. The Vaillons Vieille Vigne has an extra level of depth and length and will keep well. All three wines will keep for 4–5 years.

JEAN-CLAUDE DAUVISSAT* * *

1985 Chablis	C	82

1986 Chablis	C	82

1985 Chablis Mont de Milieu	C	84

1986 Chablis Mont de Milieu	C	84

1985 Chablis Vaulignot	C	86

1986 Chablis Vaulignot	C	81

1985 Chablis Vaulignot Cuvée Daniel Haas	C	87

1986 Chablis Vaulignot Cuvée Daniel Haas	C	85

As opposed to the barrel-fermented style of René Dauvissat, the style of winemaking of Jean-Claude Dauvissat relies on fermentation in stainless steel tanks and early bottling. The results are predictable—good, clean, correct, easy-to-drink and easy-to-appreciate wines that must be drunk quite young. All of the above wines had plenty of zesty acidity, and perfumed, uncomplex smells of lemony, applelike Chardonnay fruit. The wine in both vintages that has more to it is the Vaulignot Cuvée Daniel Haas. Riper and richer than the other cuvées, it was the deepest wine in both 1985 and 1986. These wines should be drunk within 2–3 years.

RENÉ DAUVISSAT* * * * *

1985 Chablis Les Clos	D	90
1986 Chablis Les Clos	D	90
1985 Chablis La Forêt	D	87
1986 Chablis La Forêt	D	88
1985 Chablis Les Preuses	D	87
1986 Chablis Les Preuses	D	87
1986 Chablis Sechet	D	85
1985 Chablis Vaillons	D	86
1986 Chablis Vaillons	D	87

For barrel-fermented, expansively flavored Chablis, the quality of the wines from René Dauvissat is close to that of the great master of Chablis, Jean-Marie Raveneau. After retasting the 1985s with Dauvissat while tasting the 1986s, I came away with the same qualitative ratings, but I was surprised at how much more acidity and aging potential they showed than when I first tasted them. Dauvissat, a balding, friendly, soft-spoken man, says his 1985s will be perfect to drink in 12–15 years; he is currently drinking his 1973s. As for the 1986s, he made 40% more wine, and while the wines lack the power and flesh of the 1985s, they are elegantly wrought, fully ripe, and have a vibrant acidity and well-focused flavors. Among the 1986s, the Sechet has a spicy, oaky, tropical-fruit-scented bouquet, and the Vaillons more of the minerallike wetstone fragrance and a lemony acidity. With respect to La Forêt, this medium-bodied, well-balanced, toasty, lemony, fruity wine has a bit more length and depth as well as more complexity. Both Les Preuses and Les Clos are classic Chablis, not in the blockbuster style of such vintages as 1983 or 1978, but they are admirably balanced wines with just the right amount of toasty new oak, a great deal of tart, stone-scented Chardonnay fruit, and the balance and depth to age for 5–7 years.

GEORGES DELEGER* * * *

1986 Chassagne-Montrachet	C	86
1986 Chassagne-Montrachet Morgeot	D	?
1985 Chevalier-Montrachet	E	90
1986 Chevalier-Montrachet	E	92

With the exception of the Chassagne-Montrachet Morgeot, which showed an odd bouquet that will probably blow off after Deleger racks the wine, the other wines from this small estate look to be extremely good—even superb in the case of the two Chevalier-Montrachets. The 1985 and 1986 Chevalier Montrachets offer marvelous levels of fruit extract, opulent textures, and sumptuous finishes. The 1986 looks a bit more complex than the fleshy, full-bodied, chewy 1985 because it not only has better acidity, but also a vivid pineapple, tropical-fruit-scented bouquet as a result of some botrytis that attacked the Chardonnay in 1986. In short, it has a spectacular bouquet. Both wines should drink well for 5–7 years. The straight 1986 Chassagne-Montrachet is also quite good, richly fruity, lush, supple, and stylistically more akin to a 1985 than 1986.

JOSEPH DROUHIN* * * *

1985 Bâtard-Montrachet	E	92
1985 Beaune Clos des Mouches	D	90
1986 Bourgogne La Forêt	B	78
1985 Chablis Les Clos	D	87
1985 Chassagne-Montrachet	D	84
1985 Chassagne-Montrachet Morgeot	D	86
1985 Corton-Charlemagne	E	88
1985 Meursault Perrières	E	83
1985 Montrachet Marquis de Laguiche	E	96

1985 Puligny-Montrachet	C	85

1985 Puligny-Montrachet Folatières	D	87

As the ratings attest, Drouhin's 1985 white burgundies are quite successful. The only wines I found to be unexciting included the mass-produced 1986 Bourgogne La Forêt; a boring, surprisingly watery, yet adequate light-styled Meursault Perrières; and a decent Chassagne-Montrachet that exhibited an elegant, fruity bouquet but not much substance or length. The Chassagne-Montrachet Morgeot and Puligny-Montrachet show fine lively aromas of flowers, butter, crisp fruit, and medium body, good concentration, and good length. A step above these two wines are the Chablis Les Clos, an excellent wine offering up a mélange of lemony, tropical-fruit scents, crisp acidity, and plenty of flavor, as well as the Puligny-Montrachet Les Folatières, a lush, fat, honeyed wine that reminded me of this firm's 1982. The Corton-Charlemagne comes close to being exceptional. There is plenty of toasty oak, and the wine is dense and full-bodied with a powerful alcoholic finish. It should provide pleasurable drinking early on. The Beaune Clos des Mouches, a house specialty here, is a rich, honeyed, creamy textured wine that is amazingly seductive, no doubt because of its dazzling level of Chardonnay fruit. The 1985 is a delight to drink and again reminds me of the fine 1982. The Bâtard-Montrachet, bargain-priced to go at one thousand dollars a case, is a full-bodied, unctuous, very concentrated wine bursting with creamy, nut-flavored, rich Chardonnay fruit as well as a superlong finish. It should drink superbly for 4–5 years. The Montrachet, despite a price that has caused some to speculate that only Miami drug dealers can afford it, is an awesome bottle of wine. The perfect balance of power and an incredible level of fruit extract make this wine quite special. Despite its weight and presence on the palate, it ideally needs 5–7 years cellaring. Drouhin's 1986s were lighter, less powerful wines than his 1985s, but very good across the entire range, with the top of the line 1986 Montrachet every bit as sublime as the 1985.

GEORGES DUBOEUF* * *

1986 Beaujolais Blanc	A	84

1986 Mâcon-Villages	A	85

1986 Saint-Véran	B	85

1986 Saint-Véran Domaine de la Bâtie	B	84

1986 Saint-Véran Coupe Louis Dailly	B	85

Georges DuBoeuf, the master Beaujolais producer, rarely gets the recognition he deserves for his fresh, exuberant, tank-fermented, non–oak-aged white wines. His 1986s are widely available and frequently discounted in price. All of his 1986 white wines are more plump and richer than the 1985s. Of the three Saint-Vérans (an appellation to note for value and quality today), they all have plenty of crisp, well-focused, applelike, floral, fresh, clean Chardonnay fruit, and they are a delight to drink. His Mâcon-Villages is also a top bargain, elegant, fruity with good depth, medium body, and a round, gentle finish. An ignored possiblity for zesty, light, yet dry and fruity white wines is Beaujolais. DuBoeuf makes the best Beaujolais Blanc, and the solid, lively 1986 is a fine example.

DuBoeuf's 1987s are lighter, much less concentrated wines than his 1986s, but quite agreeable.

FAIVELEY* * *

1986 Corton-Charlemagne	E	90

1986 Mercurey Clos Rochette	B	86

1986 Rully	B	85

The Faiveley firm does not produce much white wine, but two of their best bargains are the supple, yet intensely fruity, generously flavored Rully and Mercurey. Both wines see minimal amounts of oak aging and are to be enjoyed for their crisp, pure Chardonnay fruit and medium-bodied, elegant textures. Both are quite good values. Tiny quantities of an exquisite Corton-Charlemagne are also made, and the 1986 is a brilliantly rendered example of this wine.

J. A. FERRET* * *

1986 Pouilly-Fuissé Les Menestaières (Cuvée hors classe)	D	90

1986 Pouilly-Fuissé Les Perrières (Tête de Cru)	D	88

There are three growers who consistently make great Pouilly-Fuissé. The crazy Belgian Guffens-Heynen, Château Fuissé, and the Domaine Ferret. These two cuvées of Pouilly-Fuissé tasted more like a Premier or Grand Cru Chassagne-Montrachet. The Les Perrières is a bold, rich, intense, buttery, apple-blossom-scented wine that has just enough oak in evidence, full body, and layers of succulent fruit. The Les Menestaières is just sensational, extremely rich, long, balanced, and amazingly complex and tasty for a Pouilly-Fuissé. If you have been a victim of paying too much for an insipid, industrially made wine from this appellation, try these two gems.

CHÂTEAU FUISSÉ (VINCENT)* * * *

1985 Pouilly-Fuissé	C	86
1986 Pouilly-Fuissé	C	87
1985 Pouilly-Fuissé Vieilles Vignes	D	90
1986 Pouilly-Fuissé Vieilles Vignes	D	91

According to most authorities, this is the leading house of Pouilly-Fuissé. There are two cuvées of wine made, a very good, sometimes excellent regular bottling, and a cuvée of old vines that can be magnificent as it was in 1983, 1985, and again in 1986. These wines show a beautiful harmony of toasty oak, exotic fruit, good acids, plenty of depth, and an overall sense of focus and balance. The Cuvée Vieilles Vignes, not cheap at $30 a bottle, is, however, an exemplary brilliant white burgundy. The hazelnut, vanillin, and orange peel, as well as tropical fruit scents in the bouquet and flavors are top drawer. The 1986 is slightly more elegant, yet also more powerful than the 1985. Drink these wines over the next 1–3 years.

JEAN-NOËL GAGNARD* * * *

1985 Chassagne-Montrachet Caillerets	D	88
1985 Chassagne-Montrachet Morgeot	D	87
1985 Chassagne-Montrachet Premier Cru	D	86

These are delicious, well-endowed wines that offer immediate appeal, but also the promise of more complexity if cellared for 3–4 years. Whether they will improve beyond that is unlikely, as their acidities appear too low for extended aging. The rich tropical fruit of all three wines is beautifully integrated with toasty oak, and consequently the impression is one of silky lushness, medium to full body, and a seductive creamy richness. The Caillerets is the most concentrated and fullest, the Morgeot a trifle lighter but still quite meritorious, and the Premier Cru similar to the others, but a bit less intense and more tart.

JEAN GERMAIN* * * *

1985 Bourgogne Clos de la Fortune	B	84
1985 Meursault	D	86
1985 Meursault Meix Chavaux	D	87
1985 Puligny-Montrachet Les Grands Champs	D	87
1985 Saint-Romain Clos sous le Château	C	87

This small *négociant* business is tucked away on a back street of Meursault adjacent to the Comtes Lafon vineyard of Clos de la Barre. The wines are carefully made by Jean Germain, a small, enthusiastic man who operates this enterprise with Englishman Tim Marshall. Together, they produce a bevy of high-quality wines of which the whites are clearly superior. The 1986 whites, tasted from cask, look to be as good, perhaps even better than the 1985s. With respect to the 1985s, there is the Bourgogne, a surprisingly good, generic example of white burgundy. Ripe, fruity, round, and generous, it is a plump, delicious wine. The Saint-Romain is a real sleeper and top value. Vinified and aged in new oak, the wine is opulent, full-bodied, rich, and complex. I have never encountered a better Saint-Romain. The Meursault is also fat, tasty, plump, and fully ready to drink. The Meursault Meix Chavaux has a full-intensity, toasty, ripe, richly fruity aroma, full body, good concentration of nut-and butter-tasting fruit, and a refreshing finish. The Puligny-Montrachet Les Grands Champs has less fat and flesh, but more elegance and a steely, crisp, yet concentrated personality.

ALBERT GRIVAULT* * * * *

1984 Meursault Clos des Perrières	D	88
1985 Meursault Clos des Perrières	D	92
1986 Meursault Clos des Perrières	D	90

I have included my notes on the 1984 because this wine is so delicious
—light golden in color with a big, intense bouquet of butter, fruit, and
spicy oak. Full-bodied and deep on the palate with 5–6 years aging
potential, it is hard to believe this wine is a 1984. The 1985 is a huge
Meursault with remarkable concentration, and intense aromas and
flavors of honeysuckle, butter, and sautéed apples. For its size, it has
zesty acidity and another 5–7 years of further potential. The 1986 is a
more elegant example of the 1985.

GRIVELET* *

1985 Bourgogne	A	60
1985 Meursault	C	55
1985 Rully	B	72

These three wines had various degrees of musty, cardboard aromas
that alone would have been their undoing. However, the Bourgogne
and Meursault also tasted watery, with little evidence that the Chardonnay grape was used to make the wines.

LOUIS JADOT* * * *

1985 Chassagne-Montrachet	C	86
1986 Chassagne-Montrachet	C	83
1985 Chassagne-Montrachet Morgeot Magenta	D	85
1986 Chevalier-Montrachet	E	91
1985 Chevalier-Montrachet Les Demoiselles	E	94
1985 Corton-Charlemagne	E	92
1986 Corton-Charlemagne	E	90
1986 Mâcon-Villages	A	84
1985 Meursault	C	84
1986 Meursault Blagny	C	86

1985 Meursault Genevrières	D	88
1986 Pouilly-Fuissé	B	85
1985 Puligny-Montrachet	C	85
1985 Puligny-Montrachet Clos de la Garenne Magenta	C	86
1985 Puligny-Montrachet Les Combettes	D	88
1985 Savigny-les-Beaune	C	85

The Jadot firm is turning out one serious wine after another as their commitment to quality is as high as anyone's in Burgundy. The general principle of white winemaking at Jadot is to stop the malolactic if they feel the wines will not have enough acidity. They have done this (with great success) in 1982, 1983, and 1985. They ferment at rather high temperatures and give the wines a healthy stay in oak barrels of which a sizable proportion is new. Bottling for the 1985s took place in December, 1986. The 1985s range from good to outstanding. While the Meursault is clean and correct, the Savigny-les-Beaune is crisp, quite fruity, and altogether a lovely fresh example of Chardonnay from an appellation better known for its red wine. I also liked the Chassagne-Montrachet with its creamy, honeyed richness, lush texture, and nice touch of toasty new oak. The Puligny-Montrachet is less fat, more streamlined and stylish, yet still very flavorful and elegant. The Jadot firm markets exclusively the wines of the Duc de Magenta. The two I tasted included the Morgeot from Chassagne-Montrachet and Clos de la Garenne from Puligny-Montrachet. These wines are not vinified at Jadot. Both are lean, understated, polite wines that offer crisp acidity, medium body, and elegant personalities. Both the Meursault Genevrières and Puligny-Montrachet Les Combettes are similarly styled—fat, full-bodied, weighty white burgundies with excellent levels of hazelnut and buttery fruit. Both the Corton-Charlemagne and Chevalier-Montrachet are *hors classe*. The Corton-Charlemagne, which proprietor André Gagey claims is not as superb as the 1983 or 1982, is a splendidly concentrated, deep, intense wine offering up scents of minerals, pineapple, toasty new oak, and honeysuckle. It has gobs of ripe fruit to fill out its full-bodied frame. The Chevalier-Montrachet is even richer and fuller, with greater length and a sensational bouquet. These last two wines should drink well for 8–12 years. As for the 1986s, the Mâcon-Villages and Pouilly-Fuissé are charming, fruity wines with great freshness and vivacity. Both are better than their 1985 counterparts. As for the other 1986s, while less powerful and alcoholic than the 1985 white burgundies, they are extremely successful.

FRANÇOIS JOBARD* * * *

1985 Bourgogne	B	84
1985 Meursault Blagny	C	84
1985 Meursault Charmes	D	87
1985 Meursault Genevrières	D	89
1985 Meursault Poruzot	D	87

François Jobard quietly and meticulously goes about producing textbook, stylish Meursaults with both flavor and finesse. Perhaps his 1985s, by his own high standards, are not as sublime as one might expect from the success he enjoyed in years such as 1981, 1982, and even 1984. Nevertheless, these are all very good wines, although somewhat deficient in acidity. Both the good Bourgogne and Meursault Blagny came across as spicy, nicely concentrated, but chunky, uncomplex wines that should be drunk over the next 4–5 years. The Poruzot jumps up in quality with its hazelnut- and pineapple-scented bouquet, delicate yet soft, creamy fruitiness, and lush finish. The Charmes is fatter and richer on the palate, but despite the increased power and extract, I thought it no better than the more delicate and delineated Poruzot. The Genevrières, year in and year out the best wine from Jobard, has both power and finesse, a long, full-bodied texture and finish, and an admirable mix of new oak and ripe fruit. All of the wines should be drunk over the next 4–5 years.

LABOURÉ-ROI* * *

1985 Meursault Clos des Bouches Chères (René Manuel)	D	88

For years, the wines from this *négociant* firm ranged from mediocre to disappointing. There now seems to be a perceivable increase in quality, best witnessed by this top-of-the-line Meursault. Toasty, oaky, buttery flavors and aromas offer considerable attraction. This is a fat, tasty, somewhat low-acid wine that has loads of concentrated fruit. It should be drunk young—within 2–3 years.

COMTES LAFON* * * * *

1985 Meursault Charmes	E	94
1985 Meursault Clos de la Barre	D	92
1985 Meursault Les Desirées	D	89
1985 Meursault Genevrières	E	95
1985 Meursault Gouttes d'Or	E	87
1985 Meursault Perrières	E	95
1985 Montrachet	E	90

Some of the finest, most elegant, as well as longest-lived wines to be found are made in the very cold, damp cellars of the Comtes Lafon. Modern oenologists are no doubt horrified by the fact that the Lafons never rack their white wines, nor filter them, preferring to leave the wine sit undisturbed on its lees for almost two years. The 1985s were bottled late in 1987. The only other growers to apply similar winemaking techniques are Coche-Dury and Pierre Morey, and not surprisingly, all of these producers' wines are among the most sought-after in France. Such a winemaking philosophy requires risk and constant surveillance, not to mention getting paid for your wine much later. As the young Dominique Lafon points out, most 1986 white burgundies will have been bottled and sold before his family sells their 1985s.

The 1985s are superb at this estate. The Clos de la Barre is sensational, the best example I have yet seen from this 5-acre vineyard solely owned by the Lafons. It has great intensity of flavor, but a complex aroma of spices, minerals, and hazelnuts. It should keep for 6–10 years. The Les Desirées is always a direct, openly fruity wine and in 1985 resembles a flamboyant Condrieu as much as a Meursault; it will be the most approachable of Lafon's 1985s. The Gouttes d'Or is a very dense, fat, unctuous wine that has surprising muscle and power for a Lafon wine, but less finesse and complexity than the other wines. I adore the Meursault Charmes, a wine produced from 65-year-old vines. Its balance is nearly perfect, as the ripe, flowing, flowery, grilled-nut-scented Chardonnay fruit has just enough acidity to ensure 8–10 years of life. The Perrières is fantastic, although at first glance the wine is closed, tightly knit, and more tricky to judge. With some swirling and aeration, the wine opens up sufficiently to reveal great depth, charm, and a formidable finish. It will need 2–3 years after bottling to open and should last 10–15 years. The Genevrières is more developed than the Perrières, and also more forward on the palate. Similar in style to the great 1982s made at this estate, this long, deep, fragrant wine offers a tremendous level of complex, elegant, and full-bodied Chardonnay fruit. The Montrachet (there are 100 cases in 1985) is the least flattering of all the wines to taste, yet it is still easy to evaluate. It is firm, backward, very concentrated, and long, but quite frankly I cannot see its being ready to drink before 1993–1995, which is rather amazing.

The 1986s from Lafon are less fat but equally compelling wines that may well turn out to resemble the outstanding 1979s made there.

LATOUR* * *

1985 Bâtard-Montrachet	E	90
1986 Bâtard-Montrachet	E	87
1985 Bourgogne Cuvée Latour	A	72
1985 Chassagne-Montrachet	C	82
1986 Chassagne-Montrachet	C	85
1986 Chevalier-Montrachet	E	92
1985 Corton-Charlemagne	E	88
1986 Corton-Charlemagne	E	92
1985 Mâcon-Villages Chameroy	A	82
1985 Meursault	C	72
1986 Meursault	C	83
1986 Meursault Château de Blagny	C	82
1986 Meursault Genevrières	D	86

1985 Montagny	B	83

1986 Montrachet	E	94

1985 Puligny-Montrachet	C	80

1986 Puligny-Montrachet	C	85

1986 Puligny-Montrachet Les Referts	C	86

1985 Saint-Véran	B	80

This famous firm is renowned the world over for its full-bodied, expansively flavored white burgundies. Louis Latour calls the 1985 vintage for white wine "very good," but not great. Tasting the 1986s side by side with the 1985s in the bottle, I preferred the overall quality and complexity of their 1986s to the fleshier, but duller Latour 1985s. With respect to the 1985s, there is the soft, fruity Mâcon-Villages; a very light, diluted Saint-Véran; a crisp, flavorful successful Montagny; an odd-smelling Meursault (an aroma reminiscent of glue!); an extremely high-acid Puligny-Montrachet; and a richer, tastier, fruitier Chassagne-Montrachet. There is a significant and serious leap in quality with the Bâtard-Montrachet, a very rich, opulent, almost sweet-tasting wine with a gorgeous level of fruit extract, full body, a finish that goes on and on, and a knockout bouquet. Expect it to drink well for 5–7 years. The Corton-Charlemagne, usually a bell ringer here (the great but young 1983 and stupendous 1979 I remember well), may ultimately merit a higher score, but for now it is very tightly knit, age-worthy, rich, full-bodied but closed-in and seemingly less intense and profound than the 1986. The 1986s from Latour, which were bottled in April, 1988, exhibited more acidity, but also more richness and length as well as aromatic complexity, thus supporting those who claim 1986 is a better vintage than 1985 for Burgundy's white wine producers. Latour's 1986 Corton-Charlemagne, Chevalier-Montrachet, and Montrachet are stunning wines of great finesse, balance, and richness. I hope you have plenty of discretionary income, as they are not cheap.

OLIVIER LEFLAIVE* * *

1985 Bâtard-Montrachet	E	87

1985 Bourgogne Les Setilles	B	80

1985 Chassagne-Montrachet	C	84
1985 Chassagne-Montrachet Les Baudines	D	83
1985 Corton-Charlemagne	E	84
1985 Meursault	C	85
1985 Meursault Charmes	D	81
1985 Puligny-Montrachet	C	84
1985 Puligny-Montrachet Les Garennes	D	84
1985 Rully Raclot	B	86
1985 Saint-Aubin Premier Cru	B	84

Olivier Leflaive is the nephew of Vincent Leflaive, owner of one of Burgundy's most respected domaines. This *négociant* business was started by the affable Olivier several years ago and has been immensely successful, (the Leflaive name tends to ensure instant respect and attention). I found the 1985s from Olivier Leflaive very shy, understated wines that while all good to very good, lacked the excitement and discreetly balanced power, fruit, and personality of his uncle Vincent's wines. The Bourgogne is light, austere, simple, and pleasant. Both the Saint-Aubin and Rully seemed quite good for their class, and every bit as interesting as the Meursault, Chassagne-Montrachet, and Puligny-Montrachet. In particular, the Rully, with its steely, mineral-scented bouquet, and austere, yet flavor-laden texture, is a notably good value. The straight Meursault is also quite good, fat, with a deft touch of oak and hazelnut; it is a stylish wine with good balance. Both the Chassagne-Montrachet Les Baudines and Puligny-Montrachet Les Garennes are terribly polite, laid-back wines that lack a little depth in their midrange, but they are light, fresh, and cleanly made. The Meursault Charmes, from a vineyard that in 1985 produced fat, powerful wines, is quite light, meagerly endowed, but still pleasant. It tastes very like a good Mâcon-Villages, not a Premier Cru Meursault. The Corton-Charlemagne is a good wine, but for a Grand Cru white burgundy, it comes up short, falling off the palate, and having a succinct finish. Don't get me wrong—it is a good wine, but most Mâcons deliver as much. The Bâtard-Montrachet is the best wine from the Olivier Leflaive stable. It has depth and richness, a good midrange, and toasty, buttery, applelike aromas that are complex. It should be drunk over the next 3–4 years.

VINCENT LEFLAIVE * * * * *

1985 Bâtard-Montrachet	E	92
1986 Bâtard-Montrachet	E	91
1985 Bienvenues-Bâtard-Montrachet	E	90
1986 Bienvenues-Bâtard-Montrachet	E	89
1985 Chevalier-Montrachet	E	96
1986 Chevalier-Montrachet	E	94
1985 Puligny-Montrachet	D	84
1986 Puligny-Montrachet	D	86
1985 Puligny-Montrachet Clavoillon	D	87
1986 Puligny-Montrachet Clavoillon	D	87
1985 Puligny-Montrachet Les Combettes	D	92
1986 Puligny-Montrachet Les Combettes	D	90
1985 Puligny-Montrachet Les Pucelles	D	90
1986 Puligny-Montrachet Les Pucelles	D	90

With 52 acres of superbly located vineyards, as well as a fanatical commitment to quality, the Domaine Leflaive has understandably become the beginning and end of many people's search for the best in white burgundy. Run with precision as well as flair by the aristocratic Vincent Leflaive, the wines from this house are perfect models of high flavor extraction, impeccable balance, enormous finesse, and most importantly, great pleasure. I have closely followed (at great cost) the Leflaive wines in every vintage since 1976, and I have the following observations. Leflaive's Chevalier-Montrachet is absolutely extraordinary; I recently rated the 1982 a 93 and the 1983, 98. Even the 1984 merits 92. Then his Bâtard-Montrachet is next and usually the highest in alcohol. In 1985 it reached 13.8%; in 1983, 14.2%. After these two Grand Crus, I find both the Puligny-Montrachet Les Combettes (his smallest vineyard) and Puligny-Montrachet Les Pucelles, both Premier Crus, of not only Grand Cru quality, but consistently better than his Puligny-Montrachet Clavoillon and Bienvenues-Bâtard-Montrachet. Tasting the Leflaive wines is always one of the highlights of a trip to Burgundy. For the record, he ferments his Chardonnay at a low temperature of 16–18° C, uses only 25–33% new allier oak, and bottles his wines after 16–17 months.

As the ratings attest, the 1986s are excellent to outstanding. Vincent Leflaive compares them to the 1982s, whereas his nephew Olivier says they are more like the 1979s. I found them all to have a great deal of tropical fruit, lush textures, yet enough zesty acidity to ensure cellaring. I believe they will turn out to be every bit as fine as the 1985s, but with less weight and alcohol. With respect to the 1985s, the straight Puligny-Montrachet has a steely, acacia-scented bouquet, medium body, good fruit, and a forward, elegant, accessible fruitiness wrapped gently in toasty oak. It is a refined and pleasant wine to drink now and over the next 7–8 years. The Clavoillon is lighter, and while very good, not up to the level of Leflaive's other top 1985s. The Combettes is always a real star here, and the full-intensity bouquet of hazelnuts, tropical fruit, and *pain grillé* is top-notch. On the palate, it is among the fattest and most powerful, but never heavy. The Bienvenues-Bâtard-Montrachet is lighter but full of elegance and sweet, ripe fruit, beautifully backed up in acidity. No one can mistake the greatness of the Bâtard-Montrachet, a deep, rich, full-bodied, honeyed, creamy textured wine with tremendous presence on the palate. It should last for 10 more years. Lastly, the Chevalier-Montrachet is exquisite in all respects. I know it is priced in the stratosphere, but the quality is fabulous. The wine will keep for at least a decade. Very rich, it has a persistent, compelling bouquet of butter, tropical fruit, lemons, oranges, and hazelnuts. Full-bodied (13.7% alcohol), this greatly concentrated wine is only a shade behind the immortal 1983 made here.

LEQUIN-ROUSSOT* * * *

1985 Bâtard-Montrachet	E	92
1985 Chassagne-Montrachet Caillerets	D	91

1985 Chassagne-Montrachet Vergers	D 88

I have visited the Lequin brothers at their cellars in Santenay three times, and I have always regarded them as terribly underrated growers and producers of both red and white wine. One of the greatest white burgundies I have ever tasted was the 1948 Bâtard-Montrachet made by their father. Their 1985s are truly exceptional in quality and will, I predict, turn out to be among the longest-lived wines of the vintage. For starters, there is the Chassagne-Montrachet Vergers, a crisp, oaky, very rich, yet firm, full-bodied wine that has excellent acidity, a super finish, and 4–10 years of further drinkability. Both the Chassagne-Montrachet Caillerets and the Bâtard-Montrachet are exceptional. The smoky, bacon-fat bouquet, the scents of toasty oak, and the enormously concentrated, balanced feel of the Caillerets makes one think a great Côte Rôtie is on the palate, not a white burgundy. This is a beautifully structured wine that is of Grand Cru stature in 1985. It should keep and improve for a decade. Surprisingly, the Bâtard-Montrachet is (at least the bottle I tasted) more forward, but splendidly concentrated, very long, marked by toasty oak, but admirably balanced and bursting with fruit. The Lequins also made very fine 1986s.

LEROY* * * * *

1985 Auxey-Duresses	C 85

1985 Bourgogne d'Auvenay	B 84

1985 Meursault	C 84

1985 Meursault Genevrières	D 86

1985 Meursault Les Narvaux	D 87

1985 Puligny-Montrachet	D 84

As outspoken as Mme. Bize-Leroy is about the greatness of the 1985 vintage for red wines, she is quick to criticize the vintage for white burgundy. Her white wines, like her red wines, seem to last forever in the bottle. Bottles drunk recently of the 1945, 1949, and 1969 Meursault Perrières were not only superrich, but amazingly fresh and alive. Her 1985s will no doubt improve with age, but I found them very tightly knit, elegant but not easy to judge. The Meursault Genevrières, which she says is her best white wine of the vintage, is so locked in and backward that I suspect one should forget it for a decade and then taste it. Her Bourgogne d'Auvenay is clean and fruity, but less impressive than the 1983. The Auxey-Duresses is crisp, concentrated, medium to full bodied, and a value. The Puligny-Montrachet appears to be very good but tastes tight and totally unevolved. The easiest to judge is the Meursault Les Narvaux, a rich, full-bodied, tropical-fruit-scented wine with plenty of depth and acidity to carry it 15–20 years. Leroy's 1986s are superb with a very great Meursault Perrières.

CHÂTEAU DE MALTROYE* * * *

1986 Chassagne-Montrachet	C	82
1986 Chassagne-Montrachet Fariendes	D	84
1985 Chassagne-Montrachet Morgeot Vigne Blanche	D	89
1986 Chassagne-Montrachet Morgeot Vigne Blanche	D	88
1986 Chassagne-Montrachet Ruchottes	D	86

This estate produces ten different appellations of white burgundy. All of the wine sees 40% new oak and is bottled after 12 months in cask. The 1987s looked promising, especially the Vigne Blanche and Bâtard-Montrachet. As for the 1986s, the star is the Chassagne-Montrachet Morgeot Vigne Blanche, a bold, rich, long, deep, full-bodied wine with oodles of applelike, buttery, hazelnut flavors. The 1985 of this same wine is less elegant but very powerful and rich. These are wines that can last 7–10 years in vintages such as 1985 and 1986.

MATROT* * *

1985 Meursault	C	82
1986 Meursault	C	82
1985 Meursault Blagny	C	83
1986 Meursault Blagny	C	84
1985 Meursault Charmes	D	84

1986 Meursault Charmes	D	85

1985 Meursault Les Chevalières	D	81

1985 Puligny-Montrachet Les Chalumeaux	D	84

1986 Puligny-Montrachet Les Chalumeaux	D	85

The tall, blond Thierry Matrot, who sports an earring in his right ear, claims 1985 is a superior vintage to 1986, the latter vintage resembling 1982 in his opinion. As the above evaluations attest, I marginally preferred his 1986s. Matrot's wines are of the lean, austere style. They are shy, require some introspection, yet are often just too one-dimensional—especially for the price. I thought the 1986s had a trifle more fruit than the 1985s. With respect to the 1985s, the Meursault is simple, chunky, clean, and pleasant. The Meursault Chevalières is not as concentrated and is lighter, but correct. The Meursault Blagny also seems to lack depth and tails off on the palate. I doubt that it will age well beyond 2–3 years. Both the Meursault Charmes and Puligny-Montrachet Les Chalumeaux have elegant personalities and enough depth of fruit to balance out the acids and the structure.

CHÂTEAU DE MEURSAULT* * * *

1985 Meursault	D	90

1986 Meursault	D	88

This showpiece property consistently turns out impeccably made wines, and the 1985 rivals the best of their recent successes. Light golden with a pronounced smoky, hazelnut bouquet, this full-bodied wine is concentrated and has adequate acidity and a lengthy finish. It is quite an impressive and delicious wine. The 1986 is very similar but a touch lighter.

LOUIS MICHEL* * * *

1986 Chablis	C	84

1985 Chablis Montée de Tonnerre	D	86

1986 Chablis Montée de Tonnerre	D	87

1985 Chablis Montmain	D	86
1986 Chablis Montmain	D	86
1985 Chablis Vaillons	D	87
1985 Chablis Vaudésir	D	89
1986 Chablis Vaudésir	D	87

Louis Michel's Chablis never see an oak barrel and represent the best of the modern school of tank-fermented and aged Chablis. His wines have a vibrancy and character delineation as well as heaps of crisp, zesty fruit. His 1986s are not as concentrated as his 1985s, but they have very good acidity and an attractive fruitiness. From the lemon- and lime-scented Montmains, to the mineral-scented, exuberantly fruity Vaillons, to the stony, austere, textbook Vaudésir, all of the 1986s will offer excellent fruit and 5–6 years of drinkability. As for the 1985s, the Vaudésir perfectly balances great flavor concentration with crisp acidity. The wines are extremely long, deep, and should age well for 7–8 years. The other star in 1985 is the Vaillons, a steely, austere yet flavorful lime- and lemon-scented wine. The 1985 Montmain is softer, but floral-scented and fruity, whereas the Montée de Tonnerre again has the aroma of damp stones, good, well-focused, snappy flavors, medium body, and a refreshing finish.

MICHELOT-BUISSON* * *

1986 Bourgogne	B	78
1986 Meursault	C	82
1985 Meursault Charmes	D	90
1986 Meursault Charmes	D	88
1985 Meursault Clos St.-Félix	D	87
1986 Meursault Clos St.-Félix	D	81
1985 Meursault Genevrières	D	90

1986 Meursault Genevrières	D	89
1985 Meursault Limozin	D	87
1986 Meursault Limozin	D	85
1986 Meursault Les Narvaux	D	87
1986 Meursault Perrières	D	78
1986 Meursault Les Tillets	D	86

Bernard Michelot, a diminutive yet dynamic man, is the gregarious and animated proprietor of this 49-acre domaine. The wines are immensely popular for they are easy to understand and offer up sumptuous levels of buttery fruit along with a healthy portion of toasty oak. Sometimes the oak (of which 30% is new each year) can get a little out of hand, as with his tasty but decidedly oaky 1984s. In 1985 and 1986, the mixture seems to work well. This is a rich and successful domaine with outstanding underground cellars for housing the considerable volume of wine made. As for the 1986s, with the exceptions of the bottom of the line Bourgogne, the Meursault, and the Meursault Clos St. Félix, they all showed good depth, richness, length, and balance. They may well turn out like his fine 1982s. The Narvaux, Charmes, and Genevrières look to be the stars. The Perrières is not particularly distinguished as it was made from 4-year-old vines and is quite light. As for the 1985s, they are forward, ripe, opulent wines that should be drunk over the next 4–5 years. The Clos St. Félix is rich, nutty, with aromas of *pain grillé* and vanillin. The Limozin is fat, powerful, alcoholic, and quite a succulent mouthful of wine. The Charmes and Genevrières both have much greater volume in the mouth, and they are intensely concentrated, long, very deep, and opulent, a delight to drink. The Charmes is the more assertive and powerful, the Genevrières more elegant and stylish.

MOILLARD* * *

1985 Bourgogne Hautes Côtes de Nuits	B	75
1985 Chassagne-Montrachet La Romanée	C	90
1986 Chassagne-Montrachet La Romanée	E	82

1985 Corton-Charlemagne	E	92
1986 Corton-Charlemagne	E	84
1985 Meursault Perrières	E	87
1986 Meursault Perrières	E	82
1985 Saint-Véran	C	82

Moillard's style of white burgundy is similar to its style of red burgundy: full-throttle, intense wines that offer a great deal of plump fruit at a young age. The 1985 Bourgogne is simple, fresh, acidic, and fruity —quite typical for its appellation. The 1985 Saint-Véran is fat, very soft, and lacking acidity, but cleanly made and pleasant. The 1985 Meursault Perrières exhibits plenty of toasty new oak, an excellent bouquet of grilled hazelnuts, and intense applelike, buttery flavors, but the 1986 is a bit too oaky. The 1985 Chassagne-Montrachet La Romanée is a great wine, loaded with a fabulous amount of unctuous, buttery Chardonnay fruit, full body, and a finish that goes on and on. It has good acidity for a 1985 and should keep for 4–5 years, yet I cannot see how it could get much better. Again, the 1986 is excessively oaky. Moillard's 1985 Corton-Charlemagne stood out as one of the great white burgundies I tasted. It is a huge, dense, unbelievably concentrated, full-bodied wine that just oozes with fruit and character. There are 150 cases of it, and it should drink splendidly for 4–6 years. The 1986 suffered in comparison with the 1985.

BERNARD MOREAU* *

1985 Chassagne-Montrachet Les Chenevottes	C	68
1985 Chassagne-Montrachet La Maltroye	C	69
1985 Chassagne-Montrachet Morgeot	C	65

All three of these wines are quite mediocre. They all showed a musty, old-barrel smell and rather green, acidic flavors. There is some good fruit to the wines, but the musty or damp-cardboard character detracts considerably from their enjoyment.

BERNARD MOREY* * * *

1986 Chassagne-Montrachet Les Baudines	D	86

1986 Chassagne-Montrachet Les Caillerets	D	90

1986 Chassagne-Montrachet Les Embrazées	D	90

1986 Chassagne-Montrachet Morgeot	D	88

Bernard Morey, a scarlet-faced young man who sports the pompadour haircut that was popular in the late fifties, is one of my favorite growers. He has 22 acres of vineyards in Chassagne-Montrachet, and his wines, aged in 25% new allier oak, are always lush, ripe, rich, hedonistic examples of white burgundy. His 1984s are excellent, especially the Les Embrazées, and curiously, all of his 1985s sold out so quickly that I have never had a chance to taste them. He is proud of his 1986s. They are all bold, dramatic wines with a great deal of ripe tropical fruit and subtle, toasty oak. The Les Baudines is a big, rich, opulent wine, and the Morgeot tastes even bigger and deeper next to it. The exceptional concentration of fruit in Les Embrazées makes it a particularly seductive wine to drink now and over the next 4–5 years. Perhaps the most age-worthy wine in Morey's stable is the Les Caillerets, as it is the most structured and tightly knit wine. One of the hallmarks of Bernard Morey's wines is their fascinating level of fruit extract. If they are to be criticized, it is that they are not long-lived by white burgundy standards, but for drinking over the next 4–5 years, few wines will provide more enjoyment.

JEAN-MARC MOREY* * * *

1986 Chassagne-Montrachet	C	85

1986 Chassagne-Montrachet Les Caillerets	D	89

1986 Chassagne-Montrachet Les Charmes	D	87

Jean-Marc Morey is the brother of Bernard Morey. The style of wine here is identical to that of his brother's, although they maintain two separate wine cellars. All three of these wines are exuberantly fruity, rich, long, and delicious and will have plenty of crowd appeal. I thought the straight Chassagne-Montrachet, despite its cascade of unctuous fruit and velvety texture, had a powerful alcoholic finish. The Les Charmes is extremely fruity, ripe, full-bodied, and very easy to drink. The Les Caillerets has a wonderfully sweet, intense bouquet of apricot, orange, and nut-scented fruit, long, flowing flavors, and a smooth, excellent finish.

PIERRE MOREY* * * *

1985 Bâtard-Montrachet	E	90
1985 Meursault	C	84
1985 Meursault Charmes	D	84
1985 Meursault Genevrières	D	87
1985 Meursault Perrières	D	87
1985 Meursault Tessons	C	87

All of the above ratings are very respectable, and perhaps I am being too picky when I say I expected more. I am an unabashed admirer of Pierre Morey's wines. He ferments at a very high temperature and rarely ever filters his wines, which can be dazzling examples of the best white burgundies (e.g., the 1981s and 1982s). I know it lacks logic, but I thought the Meursault Charmes no better than his Meursault. Both are fat, chubby, fruity wines that are lacking not only a bit of structure, but also a bit of length and zip. The Genevrières, Perrières, and Tessons are very good, ripe, lush, rich, and full-bodied wines that are precocious and creamy textured with plenty of appeal. I suggest drinking them over the next 4–5 years. The Bâtard-Montrachet is outstanding. The bouquet of toasty new oak, honey, oranges, and baked apples is compelling. On the palate, it has a fascinating depth, length, full body, and more structure than the other wines. It should drink well for 5–10 years. The 1986s are Pierre Morey's finest wines this decade—look for the super Meursault Charmes.

MICHEL NIELLON* * * *

1985 Bâtard-Montrachet	E	96
1985 Chevalier-Montrachet	E	93
1985 Chevalier-Montrachet Les Vergers	D	87

Niellon has just under 10 acres of vines, and therefore few wine enthusiasts get a chance to taste his expansively flavored, barrel-fermented, bold style of Chardonnay. His 1985s are knockouts. In time, the closed, firmly structured Chevalier-Montrachet may equal or surpass the otherworldly Bâtard-Montrachet, but for now and over the next 4–5 years, the latter wine is awesome. The huge bouquet of buttered fruit, toast, and grilled nuts is followed by an immense, sweet, rich, fabulous wine that has a nectarlike texture. The wine offers sensational drinking now and in the immediate future. The Chevalier-Montrachet is enormous on the palate, but much more closed. It needs a minimum of 5 years cellaring. I also enjoyed the Chassagne-Montrachet Les Vergers, an opulently fruity, husky wine with plenty of fat and flesh. It should be drunk up over the next 3–4 years. This is a cellar that also produced excellent 1986s that are probably superior to the quality of his 1985s, but I have not tasted them since they were bottled.

J. PASCAL* *

1985 Puligny-Montrachet Chalumeaux	C	84
1985 Puligny-Montrachet Les Champsgains	C	86
1985 Puligny-Montrachet Hameau de Blagny	C	76

With the exception of the dull, one-dimensional Hameau de Blagny, the wines from Pascal are correct, stylish, medium-bodied white burgundies with a moderately intense, floral, vanillin-scented bouquet and ripe, somewhat concentrated flavors. The Les Champsgains has more length and depth.

PAUL PERNOT* * * * *

1986 Bâtard-Montrachet	E	92
1986 Puligny-Montrachet Les Pucelles	E	90
1986 Puligny-Montrachet Les Folatières	D	94

Paul Pernot is a small grower who has for years sold the bulk of his crop to the famous firm of Joseph Drouhin. He has finally begun to estate-bottle his wines. His 1986s are stupendous, breathtaking wines of great flavor, intensity, and harmony. The Les Pucelles is the most floral, elegant, and developed of the wines; the Bâtard-Montrachet, the most powerful and massive. However, I gave my top score to the Les Folatières, which has gobs of both flavor and finesse. All three of these exquisite white burgundies can be drunk now, but they promise to improve for 5–10 years.

PERRIN-PONSOT* * *

1985 Meursault	C	82
1985 Meursault Charmes	D	86
1986 Meursault Charmes	D	87
1985 Meursault Perrières	D	88
1986 Meursault Perrières	D	90

This small domaine specializes in Meursault from two Premier Cru vineyards, Perrières and Charmes. While both of the above 1986s have higher acidities than the 1985s, they have still retained their richness, length, and depth. In fact, the 1986 Meursault Perrières could turn out to be a classic wine and one of the stars of the vintage from Meursault. As for the 1985s, the Perrières is again the star with an opulent texture, ripe, round, sweet, fruity aromas and flavors, and considerable depth to go along with its finish. The Charmes is very good, but less concentrated and complex. Both wines should be drunk over the next 3–5 years. The straight Meursault should be drunk sooner as it offers chunky, clean, but essentially one-dimensional fruit and flavor.

POUHIN-SEURRE* *

1985 Meursault Limozan	D	84
1986 Meursault Limozan	D	85
1985 Meursault Poruzots	D	82
1986 Meursault Poruzots	D	85

Here is another cellar where the 1986s may turn out to be better wines than the 1985s. Both 1986s have more lively fruit and more aromatic complexity than the somewhat dull, even watery 1985s. I have had experience with only three vintages of Pouhin-Seurre's Meursaults and have yet to be impressed.

HENRI PRUDHON* * * *

1985 Saint-Aubin	B	87

1986 Saint-Aubin   B   85

The little village of Saint-Aubin can be a surprisingly fertile place to find well-made, reasonably priced wines. Both offerings from Henri Prudhon are excellent. Aged partially in new oak, these deeply flavored, crisp, well-balanced wines offer flavors and breeding well beyond their modest price and humble appellation.

DOMAINE RAMONET* * * * *

1985 Montrachet	E	94

1986 Montrachet	E	96

1986 Chassagne-Montrachet-Les Ruchottes	D	93

1985 Bâtard-Montrachet	E	90

1985 Chassagne-Montrachet Morgeot	D	87

This famous domaine, according to some authorities, is the home of Burgundy's greatest genius, André Ramonet. The wines can be sublime, but there have been some failures as well. The Morgeot is available in two bottlings, one an estate-bottled wine that is excellent, ripe, and rich, and another bottling done by a *négociant* that tastes like a feeble Sauvignon Blanc, so beware. The Bâtard-Montrachet is splendid, intense, full-bodied, long, and honeyed, and capable of lasting 7–10 years. To my palate, Ramonet makes the greatest of all Montrachets. The 1982 remains for me the single finest bottle of white burgundy I have ever drunk. Both his 1985 and 1986 Montrachets are equally splendid, highly extracted, rich, impeccably balanced wines that will evolve for 10–15 years. They are rare and astronomically priced. Ramonet's best value is his Chassagne-Montrachet-Les Ruchottes, an opulent, exotic, toasty, buttery wine that in 1986 is quite superb. It too will last for 8–12 years.

REMOISSENET* * * *

1985 Bienvenues-Bâtard-Montrachet	E	90

1985 Corton-Charlemagne	E	88

1985 Meursault Charmes	D	87
1985 Meursault Genevrières Hospices de Beaune	E	88
1985 Montrachet	E	93
1985 Puligny-Montrachet Champsgains	D	84
1985 Puligny-Montrachet Les Folatières	D	87

While Remoissenet makes good red wine, I have always given their house's white wines higher overall marks. Their white wines are always rather backward, slow to develop and evolve, but like true thoroughbreds, they do indeed come forth after 4–5 years of bottle age. The 1985s showed as much structure and good acidity as anybody's, and they should last far longer than many of the delicious but precocious wines of this vintage. Both Meursaults have a degree of elegance and balance that one rarely sees from the majority of wines from this famous winemaking village. They both have good acidities and seem to need several years of cellaring to open up. I thought the Puligny-Montrachet Champsgains to be lacking a little flavor concentration and midrange. Nevertheless, it should age well but always be on the light side. The Puligny-Montrachet Les Folatières has a great deal more fruit and substance, with good acidity and very fine length. I envision its lasting for 10–12 years. There are three superstars in the Remoissenet stable in 1985. The Corton-Charlemagne (there were 375 cases produced) is still tight, full-bodied, and unevolved, but quite impressively concentrated, rich, long, and at least 5 years away from maturity. The Bienvenues-Bâtard-Montrachet is much more developed, offering up a full-intensity bouquet of hazelnut, buttery fruit, subtle oak, and superlative flavor depth and length. Drink it over the next 8–10 years. With respect to the Montrachet (from the estate of Baron Thénard), it would be a crime to drink this wine before the early 1990s. It is extremely promising, quite rich and full, but despite its immense power and depth, is totally unevolved. It should prove to be great.

GUY ROBIN * * *

1985 Chablis Butteaux	D	85
1986 Chablis Butteaux	D	82

1985 Chablis Les Clos	D	87
1985 Chablis Mont de Milieu	D	82
1985 Chablis Montée de Tonnerre	D	80
1986 Chablis Montée de Tonnerre	D	83
1985 Chablis Valmur	D	85
1986 Chablis Valmur	D	83

I have had some wonderful Chablis from Guy Robin, but an annoying problem with his wines is excessive levels of sulphur dioxide. I did not detect this problem with any of the 1985s or 1986s, so perhaps he is being a bit more careful with the dosage of this antioxidant. His 1986s, tasted from the barrel, are less successful than other houses I saw. They are extremely high in acidity yet seem to have ripe underlying fruit, and a lemon-limelike, as well as mineral, fragrance. Perhaps they will show better after bottling. His 1985s are led by a big, chunky, barrel-fermented Les Clos that has power, concentration, length, and aging potential. Both the Mont de Milieu and Montée de Tonnerre are lean, well-made wines, but they lack depth and stature. I prefer the Butteaux and Valmur as both have good body, crisp, lemony acidity, and a strong, wet-stone or mineral fragrance to go along with their lively fruit.

DOMAINE ROUGEOT* * *

1985 Bourgogne Les Grandes Gouttes	C	82
1985 Meursault Charmes	C	86
1985 Meursault Monatine	C	86

This reliable domaine consistently turns out good to very good, noticeably oaky Meursaults. The 1985 Bourgogne, with a Chablis-like, austere personality, is fresh and lively with decent fruit. The Monatine is a fat, ripe, toasty, buttery style of Meursault without a great deal of complexity, and as such is a prototype for many of the wines from this appellation. The Charmes is a little more reserved and, I suspect, more age-worthy. While it is reticent, it exhibits good concentration, medium to full body, and a long, crisp finish. Both Meursaults should age well for 4–7 years.

GUY ROULOT* * * *

1985 Bourgogne	B	85
1985 Meursault Les Charmes	D	91
1986 Meursault Les Charmes	D	89
1985 Meursault Les Luchets	C	88
1985 Meursault Meix Chavaux	C	88
1986 Meursault Meix Chavaux	C	87
1985 Meursault Les Perrières	D	91
1986 Meursault Les Perrières	D	91
1985 Meursault Les Tessons	C	90
1985 Meursault Tillets	C	87
1985 Meursault Les Vireuils	C	88

This has always been one of my favorite estates, not only in Meursault but in all of Burgundy. Sadly, Guy Roulot, a much beloved man, died following the harvest of 1982. While the 1982s and 1983s were made by the American Ted Lemon, since 1984 the winemaking has been managed by Frank Greux, a tiny-boned, articulate young man who seems much wiser than his youth would suggest. The wines are fermented in oak at low temperatures of 18–19° C, aged in allier oak of which 25% is new each year, and bottled after 10 months. They are impeccably clean, well-balanced wines that have gobs of buttery and nut-scented fruit. The 1986s are very successful here, and Greux compares them to the 1979s. In particular, the Charmes from 40- and 50-year-old vines and the Perrières (there are only 150 cases) are in·a class by themselves. As for the 1985s, even the generic Bourgogne is a lovely, creamy, richly fruity wine that offers instant appeal. The Tillets, from a young vineyard, is an extremely elegant, medium-bodied wine with a honeysuckle bouquet and applelike, buttery Chardonnay fruit. The Les Vireuils is more extroverted with a pronounced smoky, sweet, tropical-fruit-scented bouquet, full body, and a cascade of fruit in the finish. The Les Luchets is dominated by more flowery scents, has a good measure of ripe-pineapple flavor to it, is not as full-bodied as the Vireuils, but is long and extremely fruity. The Meix Chavaux is an elegant, beautifully structured wine with excellent depth, and 5–7 years of further cellaring potential. Les Tessons was Guy Roulot's favorite vineyard as it has the best exposure. In 1985, it is less evolved and open when compared with the other wines, but it has a gorgeous ripe-pineapple scent, full body, heaps of fruit, and at least 4–6 years of further evolution. Both Les Charmes and Perrières are one notch higher on the quality scale. Each has more power, but also more depth, length, and concentration with a superintense bouquet of hazelnuts, *pain grillé*, and a stunning finish. These are all textbook examples of Meursault at its best.

ÉTIENNE SAUZET* * * * *

1985 Bâtard-Montrachet	E	89
1986 Bâtard-Montrachet	E	90
1986 Bienvenues-Bâtard-Montrachet	E	90
1986 Chassagne-Montrachet	D	84
1986 Puligny-Montrachet	D	84
1985 Puligny-Montrachet Champs Canet	D	86
1986 Puligny-Montrachet Champs Canet	D	87
1985 Puligny-Montrachet Les Combettes	D	89
1986 Puligny-Montrachet Les Combettes	D	90
1985 Puligny-Montrachet Les Perrières	D	88
1986 Puligny-Montrachet Les Perrières	D	87
1986 Puligny-Montrachet Les Referts	D	86

1986 Puligny-Montrachet La Truffière   D   89

This is one of the most serious estates in Burgundy. The wines are usually among the very best made. Unfortunately, most of the Sauzet wines are sold to restaurants, so little is to be found at wine merchants. The wines, now made by Sauzet's son-in-law, Gerard Boudot, are kept on their lees for 10 months, aged in 25–30% new allier oak, and bottled after a coarse Kisselguhr filtration. They are textbook white burgundies, brimming with flavor, yet are elegant and well balanced. The 1986s are very successful here and, as Boudot says, "have the best acidities and overall balance since 1978." There are five stars of the 1986 vintage from Sauzet. The Les Perrières is a very complex, hazelnut-scented wine with high acidity but plenty of flavor and medium body. La Truffière (always a winner at this house) is richer and fuller with excellent balance and outstanding ripeness and length. The Les Combettes is a great young white burgundy filled with fruit and finesse, flavor and character (it has a certain Meursault-like character and in fact the vineyard abuts Meursault's well-known Charmes vineyard next door). The Bienvenues-Bâtard-Montrachet is lighter, extremely fresh and delicate, yet long and flavorful. The Bâtard-Montrachet is rich, full bodied with high extract and high acids, and should age well for 5–8 years.

With respect to the 1985s, they have much lower acids and fatter, more obvious personalities. The 1985 Champs Canets is a light but delicious, toasty, buttery scented, medium-bodied wine that is ready to drink. The 1985 Perrières is richer and deeper with a considerably longer finish. It has a delightful taste of grilled nuts. Les Combettes is marginally less concentrated than the 1986, but it is still a full-bodied, full-flavored, delicious bottle of white burgundy for drinking over the next 4–5 years. The Bâtard-Montrachet, which seems every bit as good, is more tightly knit and closed in, but the depth and richness are apparent. Unlike Sauzet's other 1985s, which make excellent drinking today, the Batard should be cellared several years.

J. THEVENOT-MACHAL* * *

1985 Meursault Poruzots   D   90

1985 Puligny-Montrachet Charmes   D   88

Two extremely impressive white burgundies, both wines combine outstanding concentration, full body, a generous use of toasty new oak, and good crisp acidity (especially for a 1985) to deliver classic aromas of new oak, butter, and grilled nuts. Fleshy, well-focused flavors exhibit gobs of fruit and length. Both wines should evolve for 4–6 years.

JEAN VACHET* * *

1985 Montagny Les Coères	B 86

This is a very good white burgundy from an underrated appellation. Crisp, applelike, spicy fruit flavors jump from the glass. On the palate, the wine is fresh, medium-bodied, flavorful, and quite long. Drink it over the next 1–3 years.

MICHEL VOARICK* * *

1985 Corton-Charlemagne	C 86

The chain-smoking Voarick makes 400 cases of this wine. I suspect it is much better than the "very good" rating, but when I tasted it, the wine was quite closed and impenetrable, although its weight and power could easily be detected on the palate. In any event, this wine needs a good 4–5 years (perhaps longer) to open up.

CHAMPAGNE

A vast amount of champagne, the festive wine par excellence, is purchased and drunk by consumers. A few years ago, champagne buyers never had it so good. The strong dollar, bumper crops of solid-quality wine in Champagne, and intense price competition by importers, wholesalers, and retailers all combined to drive prices down. It was a wonderful buyer's market. Now, however, all this has changed. A small, mediocre crop in 1984, a top-quality but tiny crop in 1985, and a sagging American dollar have caused an upward surge in champagne prices. This was evident in 1986 as prices soared a good 20–40% higher in many cases. Price instability appears to be the rule

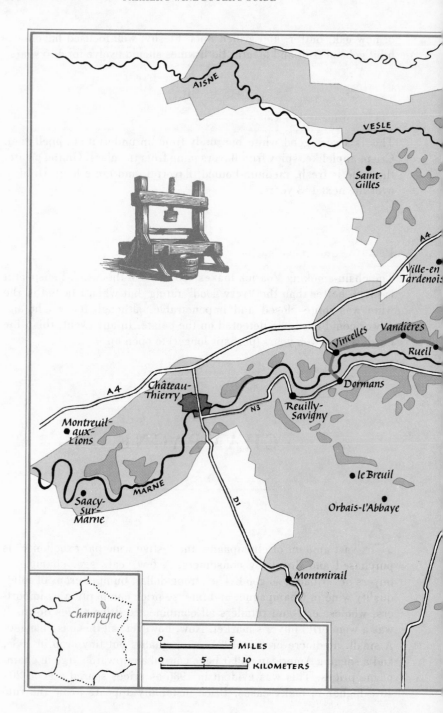

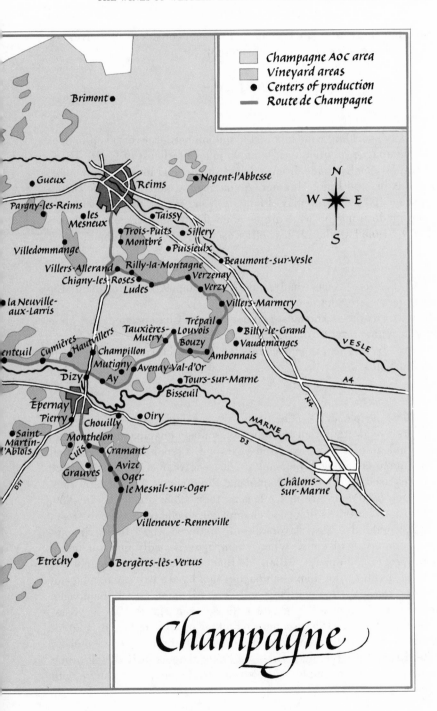

Champagne AOC area
Vineyard areas
• Centers of production
— Route de Champagne

Brimont•

Gueux•

Pargny-les-Reims

•Nogent-l'Abbesse

Reims

•les
Mesneux

•Taissy

Villedommange

•Trois-Puits
•Montbré

•Sillery

•Puisieulx

•Beaumont-sur-Vesle

Villers-Allerand• •Rilly-la-Montagne
Chigny-les-Roses•
Ludes•

•Verzenay
•Verzy

•la Neuville-
aux-Larris

•Villers-Marmery

•Trépail
Tauxières- •Louvois
Mutry Bouzy
•Billy-le-Grand
•Vaudemanges

enteuil Cumières Hautvillers
•Champillon
•Mutigny

•Ambonnais

Dizy• •Ay

Avenay-Val-d'Or

•Tours-sur-Marne

VESLE

A4

N4

Bisseuil

Épernay
Pierry•

•Oiry

Chouilly

MARNE

D3

•Saint-
Martin-
l'Ablois

Monthelon•
Cuis• •Cramant

Grauves• •Avize
•Oger
•le Mesnil-sur-Oger

Châlons-
Sur-Marne

D51

Villeneuve-Renneville

Etrechy• •Bergères-lès-Vertus

Champagne

N
W E
S

now, but those who stocked up in 1985 can consider themselves fortunate, since prices now are considerably higher.

The Basics

TYPES OF WINE

Only sparkling wine (about 180 million bottles a year) is produced in Champagne, a viticultural area 90 miles northeast of Paris. Champagne is usually made from a blend of three grapes—Chardonnay, Pinot Noir, and Pinot Meunier. A champagne called Blanc de Blancs must be 100% Chardonnay. Blanc de Noirs means that the wine has been made from red wine grapes, and the term "Crémant" signifies that the wine has slightly less effervescence than typical champagne.

GRAPE VARIETIES

Chardonnay—Surprisingly, only 25% of the 69,000 acres planted in Champagne are Chardonnay.
Pinot Meunier—The most popular grape in Champagne, Pinot Meunier accounts for 40% of the appellation's vineyards.
Pinot Noir—This grape accounts for 35% of the vineyard acreage in Champagne.

FLAVORS

Most people drink champagne very young. However, some observers would argue that high-quality, vintage champagne should not be drunk until it is at least ten years old. French law requires that nonvintage champagne be aged at least one year in the bottle before it is released, and vintage champagne three years. As a general rule, most top producers are just releasing their 1982s and 1983s in 1989. The reason for this is that good champagne should taste not only fresh, but it should also have flavors akin to buttered wheat toast, ripe apples, and fresh biscuits. When champagne is badly made it tastes sour, green, and musty. A Blanc de Blancs is usually a more delicate, refined, lighter wine than champagnes that have a hefty percentage of the two red grapes, Pinot Noir and Pinot Meunier. Great champagne from houses such as Krug and Bollinger can age for 25–30 years, losing much of its effervescence and taking on a creamy, lush, buttery richness not far different from a top white Burgundy. The exquisite 1964 Krug, 1975 Bollinger R.D., or 1969 Jacquesson R.D. (all drunk in late 1988) are examples of how wonderful champagne can be with some age.

AGING POTENTIAL

Each champagne house has its own style, and the aging potential depends on that style. Below are some aging estimates for a number of the best-known brands. The starting point for measuring the aging potential is 1989, not the vintage mentioned.

N.V. Billecart Salmon Rosé: 3–5 years

1975 Bollinger R.D.: 10–15 years

1979 Charbaut Blanc de Blancs: 5–12 years

1979 Gosset: 5–10 years

1979 Henriot Baccarat: 4–6 years

1981 Krug: 10–15 years

1982 Laurent-Perrier: 5–7 years

1982 Moët Chandon Brut Impérial: 4–5 years

1982 Dom Pérignon: 8–10 years

1982 Pommery: 4–6 years

1982 Louis Roederer Cristal: 7–10 years

1982 Pol Roger: 4–6 years

1982 Dom Ruinart: 5–7 years

1982 Taittinger Brut: 5–8 years

1981 Taittinger Comtes de Champagne: 7–12 years

OVERALL QUALITY LEVEL

French champagne is still the finest sparkling wine in the world, and despite all the hoopla from California, there is really no competition from any other wine-producing region if quality is the primary consideration. Nevertheless, the extraordinary financial success enjoyed by many of the big champagne houses has led, I believe, to some lowering of standards. One can detect this in the increasing number of green-tasting champagnes from many of the big firms that have appeared on the market. In addition, their greed has led to calling every vintage a vintage year. For example, in the fifties there were four vintage years, 1952, 1953, 1955, and 1959, and in the sixties there were five, 1961, 1962, 1964, 1966, and 1969. This increased to eight vintage years in the seventies (only 1972 and 1977 were excluded), and in the decade of the eighties every vintage so far has been a vintage year except 1987. A number of the top champagne houses need to toughen their standards when it comes to vintage champagne.

MOST IMPORTANT INFORMATION TO KNOW

First, you have to do some serious tasting to see which styles appeal to you the most. However, also pay close attention to the following guidelines:

1. The luxury or prestige cuvées of the champagne houses are almost always overpriced (all sell for $55–100 a bottle). The pricing plays

on the consumer's belief that higher price signifies a higher level of quality. In many cases it does not.

2. Purchase your champagne from a merchant who has a quick turn-over in inventory. More than any other wine, champagne is vulnerable to poor storage and bright shop lighting. Buying bottles that have been languishing on the shelves of retailers for 6–12 months can indeed be a risky business.

3. Don't hesitate to try some of the best nonvintage champagnes recommended here. The best of them are not that far behind the quality of the best luxury cuvées, yet they sell for a quarter to a fifth the price.

4. There has been a tremendous influx of high-quality champagnes from small firms in Champagne. Most of these wines may be difficult to find outside of major metropolitan markets, but some of these small houses produce splendid wine worthy of a search of the marketplace. Look for some of the estate-bottled champagne from the following producers: Bonnaire, Lassalle, Legras, Paul Bara, and Michel Gonet.

5. Several technical terms that appear on the label of a producer's champagne can tell you several things about the wine. *Brut* champagnes are dry but legally can have up to 1.5% sugar added (called dosage). *Extra dry* champagnes are those that have between 1.2% and 2% sugar added. Most tasters would call these champagnes dry, but they tend to be rounder and seemingly fruitier than Brut champagnes. The terms *Ultra Brut, Brut Absolu,* or *Dosage Zéro* signify that the champagne has had no sugar added and is bone dry. These champagnes are rarely seen but can be quite impressive as well as austere and lean-tasting.

1989–1990 BUYING STRATEGY

Currently, the consumer has two outstanding vintages on the market. For sheer elegance and harmonious flavors, the medium-bodied 1979s are wonderful. If you want something richer, softer, fuller-bodied, and with gobs of creamy, bubbly fruit, then 1982 is a sensational vintage. Both vintages are as good as champagne gets, and as long as plenty of sublime fizz from these two years is available, why buy 1980s, 1981s, or the feeble 1984s?

QUICK VINTAGE GUIDE

1987—A terrible year, the worst in this decade, 1987 may not be a vintage year—I hope.

1986—This will no doubt be a vintage year, but don't believe all the "vintage of the century" nonsense that the champagne promotion people have been spewing out. This is a good, abundant year of soft, ripe, fruity wines.

1985—After 1982, 1985 appears to be the finest vintage of this decade thanks to excellent ripeness and a good-sized crop.

1984—A lousy year, but I have already seen some vintage champagnes from 1984 in the market. Remember what P. T. Barnum once said?

1983—A gigantic crop of good quality will be descending on the market this year and next. The wines lack the opulence and creamy richness of the 1982s, but they are certainly good to very good.

1982—A great vintage of ripe, rich, creamy, intense wines. If they are to be criticized, it would be for their very forward, lower than normal acids that suggest they will age quickly. No one should miss the top champagnes from 1982—they are marvelously rounded, ripe, generously flavored wines.

1981—The champagnes from 1981 are rather lean and austere, but that has not prevented many a top house from declaring this a vintage year.

Older Vintages

Nineteen eighty is mediocre, 1979 is excellent, 1978 is tiring, 1976, once top-notch, is now fading, 1975 is still superb, as are well-cellared examples of 1971, 1969, and 1964. When buying champagne, whether it is three years old or twenty years old, pay the utmost care to the manner in which it was treated before *you* bought it. Champagne is the most fragile wine in the marketplace, and it cannot tolerate poor storage.

A GUIDE TO CHAMPAGNE'S BEST PRODUCERS

***** *(OUTSTANDING PRODUCERS)*

Bollinger (full-bodied)
Charbaut (light-bodied)
Gosset (full-bodied)
Krug (full-bodied)

Pol Roger (medium-bodied)
Louis Roederer (full-bodied)
Taittinger (light-bodied)

**** *(EXCELLENT PRODUCERS)*

Billecart-Salmon (light-bodied)
Bonnaire (light-bodied)

de Castellane (light-bodied)
Alfred Gratien (full-bodied)

Henriot (full-bodied)
J. Lassalle (light-bodied)
Laurent-Perrier (medium-
bodied)
Lechere (light-bodied)

Moët & Chandon (medium-
bodied)
Bruno Paillard (light-bodied)
Dom Ruinart (light-bodied
Veuve Clicquot (full-bodied)

* * * (GOOD PRODUCERS)

Ayala (medium-bodied)
Paul Bara (full-bodied)
Barancourt (full-bodied)
Bricourt (light-bodied)
Canard Duchêne (medium-
bodied)
Cattier (light-bodied)
Deutz (medium-bodied)
H. Germain (light-bodied)
Michel Gonet (medium-bodied)
Heidsieck Monopole (medium-
bodied)

Charles Heidsieck (medium-
bodied)
Jacquesson (light-bodied)
Lanson (light-bodied)
Launois Père (light-bodied)
R. & L. Legras (light-bodied)
Perrier-Jouët (light-bodied)
Joseph Perrier (medium-bodied)
Philipponnat (medium-bodied)
Piper Heidsieck (light-bodied)
Pommery and Greno (light-
bodied)

* * (AVERAGE PRODUCERS)

Beaumet (light-bodied)
Besserat de Bellefon (light-
bodied)
Boizel (light-bodied)
Nicolas Feuillatte (light-bodied)
Goldschmidt-Rothschild (light-
bodied)
Jacquart (medium-bodied)

Jestin (light-bodied)
Guy Larmandier (medium-
bodied)
Mumm (medium-bodied)
Oudinot (medium-bodied)
Rapeneau (medium-bodied)
Alfred Rothschild (light-bodied)
Marie Stuart (light-bodied)

CHAMPAGNE—FINDING THE BEST WINES

The Best Producers of Nonvintage Brut

Ayala
Bollinger
de Castellane Blanc de Blancs
Charbaut Blanc de Blancs
Michel Gonet
Gosset Brut Réserve
Charles Heidsieck Réserve
Krug Grande Cuvée

Lassalle
Lechere Cuvée Orient Express
Legras
Mumm Crémant
Bruno Paillard Crémant
Joseph Perrier Cuvée Royale
Pol Roger
Louis Roederer Brut Premier

The Best Rosé Champagnes

N.V. Billecart Salmon
1982 Bollinger Grande Année
1982 Charbaut Certificate
1982 Gosset Grand Millésime
N.V. Lassalle
N.V. Laurent-Perrier Rosé
1978 Dom Pérignon
1982 Perrier-Jouët

N.V. Perrier-Jouët Blason de
France
1981 Louis Roederer Cristal
Rosé
1979 Dom Ruinart
1979 Taittinger
1979 Veuve Clicquot La Grande
Dame

The Best Vintage Blanc de Blancs

1982 Billecart Salmon Blanc de
Blancs
1983 Bonnaire Blanc de Blancs
1979 Charbaut
1979 and 1982 Charbaut
Certificate
1982 Jacquesson
1981 Krug Clos de Mesnil
1983 Bruno Paillard Blanc de
Blancs

1982 Pol Roger Blanc de
Chardonnay
1982 & 1979 Dom Ruinart Blanc
de Blancs
1979 Salon
1981 Taittinger Comtes de
Champagne

The Best Vintage Brut Champagnes

1982 Billecart Salmon Cuvée
Billecart
1982 Bollinger Grande Année
1982 Canard Duchêne
1982 Cattier
1982 Gosset Grand Millésime
1982 Heidsieck Dry Monopole
1981 Krug

1982 Laurent-Perrier
1982 Perrier-Jouët
1982 Pol Roger
1982 Pommery
1982 Louis Roederer
1982 Taittinger
1982 de Venoge

The Best Luxury Cuvées or Tête de Cuvées

1975 Bollinger R.D.
1981 Bollinger Vieilles Vignes
1979 and 1982 Charbaut
Certificate
1982 Deutz Cuvée Wm. Deutz
1982 Henriot Cuvée Baccarat
1979 Henriot Réserve de
Philippe de Rothschild

1982 Moët & Chandon Dom
Pérignon
1982 Mumm René Lalou
1982 Pol Roger Winston
Churchill
1982 Pommery Louise
Pommery
1982 Louis Roederer Cristal

1981   Taittinger   Comtes   de   1979 Veuve Clicquot La Grande
     Champagne   Dame

Producers for the Best Champagne Bargains

Ayala   Lanson
Bricourt   Bruno Paillard
Canard Duchêne   Joseph Perrier
Michel Gonet   de Venoge
Charles Heidsieck

THE LOIRE VALLEY

The Basics

TYPES OF WINES

Most wine drinkers can name more historic Loire Valley châteaux than Loire Valley wines. It's a pity, really, because the Loire Valley regions offer France's most remarkable array of wines. The wine-producing region stretches along one-third of the meandering 635-mile Loire River, and the astonishing diversity of grapes planted in the valley is far greater than that in the better-known wine-growing regions of Burgundy or Bordeaux.

With 60 wine appellations and *vin délimité de qualité supérieure* (VDQS) areas, the vastness and complexity of the Loire Valley as a winemaking area should be obvious. Dry white table wines dominate production, as do the three major white wine grapes found in the Loire. The Sauvignon Blanc is at its best in Sancerre and Pouilly-Fumé. The Chenin Blanc, which produces dry, sweet, and sparkling white wines, reaches its zenith in Vouvray, Savennières, Bonnezeaux,

Coteaux du Layon, and Quarts de Chaume. Lastly, there is the Muscadet grape, from which Muscadet wines are made.

There is plenty of light, frank, fruity, herbaceous red wine made from both the Cabernet Franc and Cabernet Sauvignon grapes in appellations with names such as Bourgueil, Chinon, St.-Nicolas-de-Bourgueil, Touraine, and Anjou. Rosés, which can be delicious outside the Loire, are not successful from the appellations of Anjou, Sancerre, Chinon, and Reuilly (the latter made from Pinot Gris).

GRAPE VARIETIES

Chenin Blanc, Sauvignon Blanc, Muscadet, and Gros Plant are the four dominant white wine grapes, but Chardonnay, especially in the VDQS region called Haut-Poitou, is frequently seen. For red wines, Gamay and Pinot Noir are seen in the VDQS vineyards, but in the top red wine Loire appellations it is virtually all Cabernet Sauvignon and Cabernet Franc.

FLAVORS

There is an unbelievable variety of flavors and textures in the wines of the Loire Valley. Below is a quick summary of tastes of the major wines.

DRY WHITE WINES

Muscadet-sur-Lie—A classic Muscadet, sur-Lie has light body, tart, dry, fresh, stony, and delicate flavors with refreshing acidity.

Savennières—A good Savennières is marked by a stony, lemon-and-limelike bouquet with dry, austere yet floral, deep flavors and medium body.

Vouvray—Dry, very flowery and fruity with crisp acidity for balance, a Vouvray is delightful as an aperitif wine.

Sancerre—Assertive aromas of fresh herbs, recently cut grass, wet stones, and gooseberries dominate this crisp, intense, and flavorful wine.

Pouilly-Fumé—Pouilly-Fumé is very similar in aromatic character to Sancerre, but on the palate it is a fuller, more opulent and alcoholic wine.

DRY RED WINES

Bourgueil—Bourgueils are prized for their herb-tinged strawberry and cherry fruit in a light, soft, compact format.

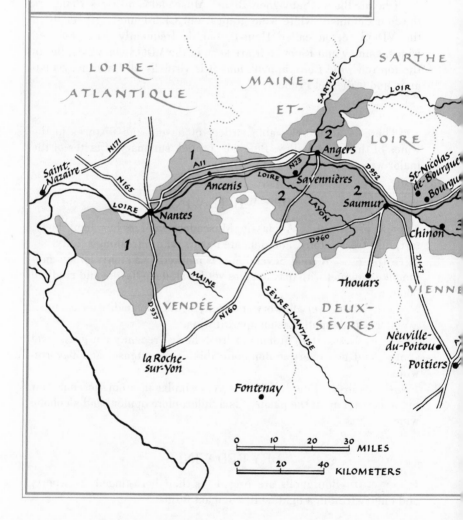

The Loire Valley and Central France

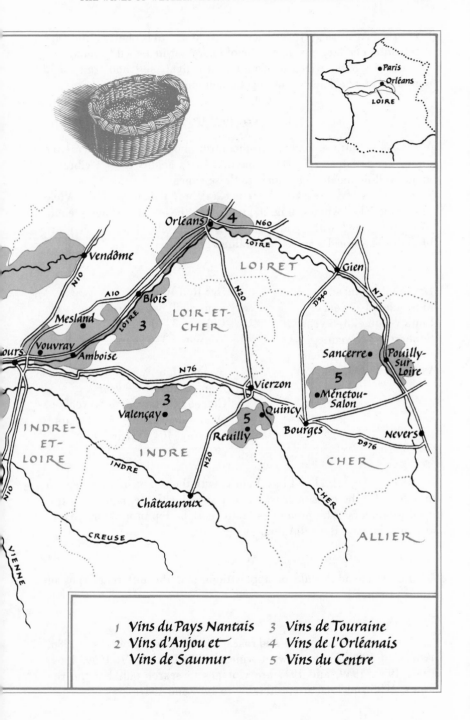

1 **Vins du Pays Nantais**
2 **Vins d'Anjou et**
  Vins de Saumur
3 **Vins de Touraine**
4 **Vins de l'Orléanais**
5 **Vins du Centre**

Chinon—Aggressively herbaceous aromas and cherry fruit age nicely into a cedary/curranty wine of character in a good Chinon.
Touraine—Most wines of Touraine are light, soft and 'fruity, and dominated by herbaceous or vegetal bouquets.

SWEET WHITE WINES

Vouvray—Buttery, overripe tropical fruit, honey, and flowers are the aromas and tastes in a sweet Vouvray. Crisp acidity gives a vibrance and a well-delineated character to these wines.
Coteaux du Layon, Quarts de Chaume, Bonnezeaux—While undistinguished when young, in great years these sweet wines age into honeypots filled with rich, ripe, decadent levels of fruit. They are probably the world's most undervalued great sweet wines.

AGING POTENTIAL

Dry White Wines:
Muscadet: 1–3 years
Pouilly-Fumé: 3–5 years
Sancerre: 3–5 years
Savennières: 3–12 years
Vouvray: 2–6 years

Dry Red Wines:
Bourgueil: 3–7 years
Chinon: 3–10 years
Touraine: 3–6 years

Sweet White Wines:
Bonnezeaux: 5–20 years
Coteaux du Layon: 5–20 years
Quarts de Chaume: 5–20 years
Vouvray: 10–30 years

OVERALL QUALITY LEVEL

Poor to superb. The Loire Valley, with thousands of growers, is a minefield for the consumer who is not armed with the names of a few good producers. The producers chart lists the top proprietors. Avoid anything labeled Rosé d'Anjou.

MOST IMPORTANT INFORMATION TO KNOW

Learn the multitude of appellations and the different types of wines produced.

1989–1990 BUYING STRATEGY

For the dry white wines and rosés, restrict your purchases to 1986, 1987, and 1988. For the sweet wines, 1978, 1976, 1971, 1969, 1964, 1962, 1959, 1949, and 1947 are vintages to search out. For the red wines, 1985 and 1986 are preferable to 1984 and 1987.

Muscadet

Muscadet is made from the grape of the same name in an area just southeast of the city of Nantes in the western Loire Valley. The best Muscadet is called Muscadet de Sèvre-et-Maine, after the two local rivers. Although much maligned by wine snobs, Muscadet is really the perfect white wine for shellfish, particularly briny clams and oysters. Muscadet must be drunk young, always within two to three years of the vintage, when its best attributes can be fully appreciated. Textbook Muscadet is exuberantly fruity, extremely fresh, totally crisp, dry, and light- to medium-bodied. In fact, there is no other wine in the world quite like it.

Consumers in search of top Muscadet should bypass anything older than 1985 (with the exception of the long-lived Château de Chasseloir). Look instead for the successful 1988s and 1987s, which, because of their excellent freshness and crisp fruitiness, are more of a textbook example of Muscadet than the 1986s. Don't buy more Muscadet than you will drink within the next 12 months; these wines don't improve in the bottle.

Finally, there are three basic types of wine from this area. Regular Muscadet is fine, but the best is always called Muscadet-sur-Lie. It is called "sur lie" because the wine is left on its sediment, or lees, over the winter following the harvest. This gives it more flavor and personality than mere Muscadet. The third type is called Gros Plant (after the grape), and it is a very light, acidic wine that I find useful only with some cassis added to make a decent Kir. When buying Muscadet, try to stick to either top firms such as Sauvion or estate-bottled wines from small growers, the best of whom usually have cellars in the two best villages for Muscadet de Sèvre-et-Maine, Vallet and St.-Fiacre.

MUSCADET
QUICK VINTAGE GUIDE

1987—Better than the 1986s, the 1987s are everything Muscadet should be: tart, light, and exuberant.

1986—A good vintage of fresh, tart, well-balanced, typical wines.

1985—A very good vintage, very similar in style to the 1982s, but perhaps superior. Soft, fruity, and delicious, the wines should have been drunk by now.

A GUIDE TO MUSCADET'S BEST PRODUCERS

* * * * (EXCELLENT PRODUCERS)

André-Michel Bregeon	Domaine de la Mortaine
Château de Chasseloir	Domaine des Mortiers-Gobin
Joseph Drouard	Château La Noë
Marquis de Goulaine	Domaine La Quila
Château de la Mercredière	Sauvion Cardinal Richard
Louis Metaireau	Sauvion Château de Cléray

* * * (GOOD PRODUCERS)

Domaine de la Botinière	Domaine de la Grange
Château de la Bretesche	Domaine de l'Hyvernière
Domaine des Dorices	Château de la Jannière
Domaine de la Fevrie	Château l'Oiselinière
Domaine de la Fruitière	Château de la Ragotière
Domaine de la Gautronnière	Sauvion (other cuvées)

Anjou-Saumur

At last count, over 11 million cases of wine were produced annually in the 25 Anjou-Saumur appellations of the Loire Valley. Most of the wines made here are rosés, which can be quite good, but they never quite match the great rosés made in the Tavel in the southern Rhône Valley and in Bandol in Provence. However, there is one Loire rosé that does stand out, and that is the Rosé d'Anjou from Château de Tigné. In any case, this area's reputation is based not so much on its rosés as on its sweet white wines.

Curiously, the dry white wines of the Savennières appellation are hardly known in France, even less so in America. Just southwest of the intriguing city of Angers, Savennières has a winemaking history that dates back to the twelfth century, when monks planted the first vines in the steep, slate-covered hillsides. The grape variety is Chenin Blanc, which here reaches an aristocratic level of excellence unmatched elsewhere in the world. No one makes Savennières any better than Madame Joly, who produces a rare, extremely dry, powerful and rich, age-worthy wine from 17 acres that are entitled to their very own appellation. The Joly Savennières-Coulée-de-Serrant, from her estate called Clos de la Coulée de Serrant, is a wine that does not reveal all of its charms until it is at least 7–8 years old. One suspects that the mouth-puckering acidity of the wine when young and its steep price will keep many a wine adventurer from ever experiencing what a great treasure this wine can be when it is fully mature.

Less expensive, but still quite interesting, are Savennières from the Château d'Epiré and La Bizolière. Both of these wines are dry, clean, yet remarkably fresh and fruity, with mouth-bracing acidity.

There are three special estates worth knowing in this region of the Loire Valley, all noteworthy because they produce very high quality, sweet wines. From the Coteaux du Layon appellation there is the Touchais family, from the Quarts de Chaume appellation the Domaine des Baumard, and from the Bonnezeaux appellation the Château de Fesle. All three estates make surprisingly rich, luscious wines that can often rival the better-known wines from the Sauternes/Barsac region of Bordeaux.

The most remarkable thing about these sweet wines, in addition to their quality, is that few people realize that they even exist, and still fewer realize that they will last for 30 or more years without losing their freshness, delicacy, sweetness, and vigor. Hardly anyone realizes that they are made from the Chenin Blanc grape, a grape that in America is mostly associated with bland, cheap jug wines. Of course, they are wonderful to sip at the end of a meal, but they are also splendid with foie gras, poached chicken, mildly sweet desserts, or as an aperitif.

Like the famous Sauternes/Barsac of Bordeaux, the sweet wines from these Loire appellations can be produced only in years when the climatic conditions are right for the Chenin Blanc grape to be attacked by the famed fungus, *Botrytis cinerea*. Consumers can still find older vintages of the Touchais Coteaux du Layon wines back to 1959, which are all in marvelous condition. Other excellent vintages for the Coteaux du Layon, the Quarts de Chaume and the Bonnezeaux are 1978, 1975, 1971, 1969, and 1964. These limited-production wines are not cheap, but most of the recent vintages, sell for $8–12 a bottle, which is far less than their equals from Bordeaux.

Before leaving the Anjou-Saumur area, it is necessary to mention the booming, sparkling wine industry of Saumur. A number of firms specialize in producing surprisingly good, low-priced, sparkling wines from the Chenin Blanc grape, but no one does it better than Bouvet-Ladubay in St.-Hilaire-St.-Florent. Their sparkling Saumur, highly promoted in this country under the name Bouvet Brut and selling for under $10, is a high-quality alternative to champagne—dry, lively, medium-bodied, and fruity. Other sparkling wines of merit are from Ackerman-Laurence and Gratien and Meyer.

ANJOU-SAUMUR
QUICK VINTAGE GUIDE

1987—The dry rosés and dry white table wines are light but fruity and agreeable. At the time of writing it was too soon to judge the sweet wines.

1986—Another very good vintage, which is close in quality to 1985.

1985—The best vintage since 1978—rich, long-lived, sweet wines from the Coteaux du Layon, Quarts de Chaume, and Bonnezeaux, and remarkably long-lived dry white wine from Savennières.

1984—The balance between fruit and acidity is missing in 1984; the wines lack fruit and are too high in acidity.

1983—Wonderfully mature, ripe grapes produced fat, rich, big wines that lack a little finesse but have plenty of flavor and intensity. For the sweet wines, this could turn out to be a great vintage.

Older Vintages

The sweet wines of the Coteaux du Layon, Bonnezeaux, and Quarts de Chaume do indeed survive and even flourish and improve in the bottle for 15, 20, 25, or more years. Given their modest prices, these wines are undoubtedly the greatest bargains in sweet white wines on the market. The dry Savennières can be drunk young, but it is at its best when 5–10 years old. Older vintages to look for are 1978, 1976, 1971, 1969, 1962, and 1959. The rosés and light, fruity red wines should be drunk up within three years of the vintage.

A GUIDE TO ANJOU-SAUMUR'S BEST PRODUCERS

* * * * * (OUTSTANDING PRODUCERS)
Coulée de Serrant (Savennières)

* * * * (EXCELLENT PRODUCERS)

Domaine des Baumard (Quarts de Chaume)

Château de Chamboureau (Savennières)

Philippe Delesvau (Coteaux du Layon)

Château de Fesles (Bonnezeaux)

Château de Plaisance (Coteaux du Layon)

Château de la Roulerie (Coteaux du Layon)

Touchais (Anjou)

* * * (GOOD PRODUCERS)

Jacques Beaujeau (Coteaux du Layon)

Château de Bellerive (Quarts de Chaume)

Château de la Bizolière (Savennières)

Château Bonin (Coteaux du Layon)

Domaine du Closel (Savennières)

Domaine de la Croix de Mission (Bonnezeaux)

Diot-Autier (Coteaux du Layon)

Château d'Epiré (Savennières)

Vincent Goizel (Coteaux du Layon)

Château de la Guimonière (Coteaux du Layon)

Logis du Prieuré (Coteaux du Layon)

Château des Rochettes (Coteaux du Layon)

Château de Tigné (d'Anjou)

Touraine

Chinon is the first appellation that one encounters in this part of the Loire Valley after leaving Anjou-Saumur to head upriver. Chinon's historic château is reason enough to visit this beautiful area, but Chinon makes the Loire Valley's best red wine, as well as some distinctly fresh, fruity rosés. The region also makes white wines, but they do not compare favorably with the white wines from other parts of the valley.

The best-known producer of Chinon is the firm Couly-Dutheil. Although I have found some of Jacques and Pierre Couly's white wines not impressive enough to warrant their high reputation, their red wines from Chinon and Bourgueil, produced from the Cabernet Franc grape, can be surprisingly complex and interesting. Look for the following trio of fruity, spicy, slightly herbaceous, complex wines, with scents of wild strawberries and vanillin oak: the Chinon Domaine de Versailles and Clos de l'Echo and the Bourgueil Réserve des Closiers—all quite well-made wines that represent excellent value.

My favorite Chinon producer is Charles Joguet. He makes a marvelous rosé; try his stunningly refreshing, lively, fruity Chinon Rosé and you will see what I mean. His loyal following, however, is based on his red wines—all rich, full, complex, and savory—that require 5–6 years of aging to show their real character. This is especially true of his best wine, the Chinon Cuvée Clos de la Dioterie Vieilles Vignes. The 1978 version of this wine could have been confused for an excellent St.-Emilion. Other selections from Joguet to look for are his Chinon Cuvée Clos du Chêne Vert, Chinon Cuvée des Varennes du Grand Clos, and Chinon Cuvée du Clos du Curé.

The other major Loire Valley appellation in Touraine is Vouvray, which is famous for its white wines. They are produced from the Chenin Blanc grape, and range in style from dry to sweet, as well as bubbly. I have enjoyed immensely the Vouvrays from the largest producer of this appellation, Château Moncontour; their Vouvray Sec is a brilliantly made wine, with its vivid, ripe fruitiness counterbalanced against crisp, taut acidity. The small growers of Vouvray, such as Gaston Huet at the Domaine de Haut-Lieu, produce excellent Vouvrays, as does A. Foreau at his property called Clos Naudin. Interestingly, Foreau's Brut Réserve is one of the best sparkling Vouvrays I have tasted, resembling, believe it or not, rich, old vintages of champagne. Foreau also does a nice job with his dry (or *sec*) style of wine. The regular Vouvray is clean, stylish, fruity, with good acidity and at least 5–6 years of positive evolution.

TOURAINE
QUICK VINTAGE GUIDE

1987—Considered by the growers to be better than 1986, but not as good as 1985.

1986—A good to very good year of soft, fruity, spicy wines.

1985—A potentially great year for the sweet wines of Vouvray, and at the very least a very good year for the dry white wines and an excellent year for the red wines.

1984—A poor vintage, with the wines lean, acidic, and thin.

1983—An excellent vintage for Vouvray, both dry and sweet wines, and a very good vintage for the red wine producers since everything ripened well.

1982—The dry white wines are fading quickly. The red wines are perfect for drinking now; the sweet whites are above average but overshadowed by the two recent vintages of 1983 and 1985.

Older Vintages

Gaston Huet's sweet Vouvrays from 1959 and 1962 were tasted last year and are in superb condition. Why don't more people realize just how fine these wines are? Charles Joguet's best cuvées of red wine from his Chinon vineyards, unfiltered and rich, can easily last 10 years. His 1978s are excellent now. The same can be said for Jacques Druet's and Olga Raffault's Chinons. Otherwise, the wines from Touraine should generally be drunk within their first 5–6 years of life for their freshness.

A GUIDE TO TOURAINE'S BEST PRODUCERS

* * * * * (OUTSTANDING PRODUCERS)

Pierre Jacques Druet (Chinon)   Charles Joguet (Chinon)
Gaston Huet (Vouvray)

* * * * (EXCELLENT PRODUCERS)

Couly-Dutheil (Chinon)   Château Moncontour (Vouvray)
A. Foreau Clos Naudin   Domaine du Roncée (Chinon)
(Vouvray)

* * * (GOOD PRODUCERS)

Audebert (Bourgueil)   Jean-Pierre Freslier (Vouvray)
La Berthelonnière (Chinon)   Sylvain Gaudron (Vouvray)
Marc Brédif (Vouvray)   Domaine du Grand-Clos
Caves Coopératives de Haut-   (Bourgueil)
Poitou (Touraine)   Lamé-Delille-Boucard
Domaine de la Charmoise   (Bourgueil)
(Touraine)   Jean Louet (Touraine)
Le Clos Neuf des Archambaults   J. M. Monmousseau (Vouvray)
(Cobeaux)   D. Moyer (Vouvray)
Clos du Parc de Saint-Louans   Prince Poniatowski–Le Clos
(Chinon)   Baudin (Vouvray)
La Croix de Mosny (Touraine)   Olga Raffault (Chinon)

Upper Loire

The upper Loire Valley is synonymous with Sauvignon Blanc. There are other grape varieties planted here, the bland Chasselas and some Pinot Noir, but the real glories are the Sauvignon Blanc-based wines from such appellations as Sancerre and Pouilly-Fumé and from the three little-known appellations of Quincy, Ménétou-Salon, and Reuilly. Sauvignon Blanc, when grown in these appellations, produces dry white wines that are very aromatic, sometimes too aggressively pungent for some tastes, but always smoky, herbal, earthy, and distinctive. They are usually medium- to full-bodied wines, with crisp, high acidity, plenty of fruit, and a dry finish. They are marvelous with fish, poultry, and not surprisingly, the freshly made earthy goat cheeses of the area.

Both 1986 and 1985 were especially kind vintages to these appellations, which often produce wines too high in acidity and too abrasively sharp and angular in texture. In 1985, the hot summer and fall rendered wines slightly lower in acidity than normal, but rich, lush, and oozing with the fruit of the Sauvignon Blanc. From Sancerre and Pouilly-Fumé, the following producers' 1986s and 1985s are excellent choices. First, J. C. Chatelain's Pouilly-Fumé Cuvée Prestige is loaded with intense, ripe Sauvignon fruit, very aromatic, and quite long in the finish. Another excellent Pouilly-Fumé is Ladoucette's Château du Nozet, but this wine tends to be overpriced compared to other Pouilly-Fumés.

From Sancerre, the pickings are even better. Five producers have consistently made excellent, estate-bottled Sancerres that stand far above their peers. All were extremely successful in 1985, 1986, and 1987. Jean Reverdy's Domaine de Villots, Vincent Delaporte's Sancerre from Chavignol, Lucien Crochet's two Sancerres, Clos du Chêne Marchand and Clos du Roy Blanc, Jean-Max Roger's Clos Derveau, and Lucien Thomas's Clos de la Crele—all have the pungent, herbaceous bouquet and dry, lively, fruity flavors that one expects from a fine Sancerre.

Last, the three tiny wine hamlets of Quincy, Ménétou-Salon, and Reuilly also make Sauvignon Blanc-based wines, which can be almost impossible to distinguish from a fine Sancerre. (They also are likely to have the advantage of being unknown to your wine-smart guests.) The only wine from Quincy imported into the United States that I know of is from the highly acclaimed producer Raymond Pipet. From Ménétou-Salon, I know of one producer whose wines are imported into the United States—Henri Pellé, whose wines are excellent. His 1985 and 1986 Ménétou-Salons are quite spicy, pungently herbaceous, dry, medium-bodied, fruity wines, with crisp acidity. The Sauvignon Blancs of Reuilly produced by either Beurdin, Claude Lafond, or Gerard Cordier are excellent. They would do justice to any fish or fowl dish. One thing is certain in this area—the overall quality of winemaking is by far the best of any in the Loire Valley area.

UPPER LOIRE
QUICK VINTAGE GUIDE

1987—Light but crisp, zesty, pungent textbook wines were made that have more varietal character than the 1986s. They will have to be drunk before the end of 1990.

1986—Lighter wines than 1985 were produced in 1986. However, they are well balanced but must be drunk before the end of 1989.

1985—This is a very fine vintage in the same style as the 1982s—

fat, ripe, juicy wines that are a little low in acidity, but concentrated and loaded with fruit. They have more finesse and freshness than the heavy-handed 1983s, more charm and fruit than the 1984s. Drink them over the next 12–36 months.

1984—High-acid wines were made that have kept well. However, the best wines of this vintage should now be drunk up as they will not get better.

1983—Ripe, alcoholic, rather ponderous wines were produced in 1983. When first released, they tasted quite good, although certainly more powerful than normal. However, they are now comatose.

A GUIDE TO THE UPPER LOIRE'S BEST PRODUCERS

* * * * * (OUTSTANDING PRODUCERS)

J.C. Chatelain (Pouilly-Fumé)
Paul Cotat (Sancerre)
Serge Dagueneau (Pouilly-Fumé)

Château du Nozet-Ladoucette (Pouilly-Fumé)

* * * * (EXCELLENT PRODUCERS)

Lucien Crochet (Sancerre)
Vincent Delaporte (Sancerre)
Gitton (Sancerre)
Masson-Blondelet (Pouilly-Fumé)
André Neveu (Sancerre)

H. Reverdy (Sancerre)
Jean Reverdy (Sancerre)
Jean-Max Roger (Sancerre)
Lucien Thomas (Sancerre)
Domaine Vacheron (Sancerre)

* * * (GOOD PRODUCERS)

Henri Beurdin (Reuilly)
Henri Bourgeois (Sancerre)
Clos de la Poussie (Sancerre)
Gerard Cordier (Reuilly)
Paul Figeat (Pouilly-Fumé)
Château de Maimbray (Sancerre)

Roger Neveu (Sancerre)
Henri Pellé (Ménétou)
Raymond Pipet (Quincy)
Michel Redde (Pouilly-Fumé)
Jean Teiller (Ménéton-Salon)
Château de Tracy (Sancerre)

LANGUEDOC AND ROUSSILLON

Great Wine Values for the Adventurous

Introduction

For years, this vast, sun-drenched area running parallel to the Mediterranean between Perpignan near the Spanish border and Arles in Provence was considered the major supplier of inexpensive, high-alcohol red wines for the French supermarket trade. Much of the wine from this area still finds its way into these grapy, thick blends, but a few producers are trying to rise above the tide of mediocrity and produce something with more class and distinction. There are many viticultural regions and appellations in this enormous area, but five seem to have the most potential—Costières du Gard, Faugères, Minervois, Corbières, and Fitou. None produce particularly refined, graceful, long-lived wines, but the best producers make immensely satisfying, round, generous, fruity wines that are very inexpensive and meant to be drunk within their first 4–5 years of life. Don't hesitate to slightly chill any of these red wines, since many seem to taste better when served at a cool temperature. Lastly, there is one red wine producer that is not even in an approved French appellation but is widely recognized for not only making the greatest wines of the Languedoc region but one of the great wines of all France. The red wine of Mas de Daumas Gassac in L'Hérault (which is legally only a *vin de pays*) is an extraordinary wine with great potential for a longevity of 15–20 years. It is primarily a Cabernet Sauvignon-based wine made in a distinctly Bordeaux style. The first vintage was 1978, the most recent 1987, and all have been stunningly rich, powerful, potentially very long-lived wines. To date they have sold for under $15 a bottle. In 1987, Mas de Daumas Gassac added a remarkable white wine to its lineup made from 60% Viognier, 30% Chardonnay, and 10% Muscat. Fermented in new oak, it was one of the finest wines I drank in 1988. Production in 1987 was very limited (fewer than 400 cases), but this wine rivaled the great Condrieus of the Rhône Valley.

The Basics

TYPES OF WINE

The appellations, the wines, the estates, and the areas here are not well-known to wine consumers. Consequently, there are some great wine values. The range in wines is enormous. There is sound sparkling wine such as Blanquette de Limoux; gorgeously fragrant, sweet muscats such as Muscat de Frontignan; oceans of soft, fruity red wines, the best of which are from Minervois, Faugères, Côtes du Roussillon, Costières du Gard, and Corbières; and even France's version of vintage port, Banyuls. These areas have not yet proven an ability to make interesting white wines, except for sweet muscats.

GRAPE VARIETIES

Grenache, Carignan, Cinsault, and Syrah are the major red wine grapes. Small experimental vineyards of Cabernet Sauvignon and Merlot are becoming more common.

FLAVORS

This is a hot, frequently torrid part of France, and the problem is never one of adequate ripeness, but rather of overripeness. The wines vary incredibly in style, but the best examples of dry red wine are made by using the carbonic maceration method, giving them a quick look at some new oak barrels, and then bottling them early. They are filled with the aromas of superripe cherries, oranges, apricots, and herbs.

AGING POTENTIAL

Except for a handful of wines—the Mas de Daumas Gassac, St.-Jean de Bebian, and the portlike wines of Banyuls—the wines of Languedoc and Roussillon should be drunk within their first 5 years of life.

OVERALL QUALITY LEVEL

Long known for monotonous mediocrity in wine, quality levels have increased significantly as the market has realized the potential for well-made, inexpensive wines from these areas.

MOST IMPORTANT INFORMATION TO KNOW

Memorize several of the names of the leading estates and go out and find their wines. Because they are inexpensive, the educational cost is minimal, and finding a wine you like at a low cost is undoubtedly a pleasure.

1989–1990 BUYING STRATEGY

Except for those few wines that can age well for up to a decade— Mas de Daumas Gassac, St.-Jean de Bebian, and the wines of Banyul —look for the 1985, 1986, and 1987 vintages. Don't buy anything older than 5 years.

Super Sparkling Wine Values

It is probably the least-known well-made sparkling wine of France, at least to the Anglo-Saxon world. From an appellation called Blanquette de Limoux, hidden in the Languedoc-Roussillon area just north of Spain's border, comes France's oldest sparkling wine, made a century before a monk named Dom Pérignon was credited with discovering the process for producing champagne. Made primarily from the Chardonnay, Chenin Blanc, and Mauzac grapes, the wines are similar to a high-quality, nonvintage champagne at one-third the price—most dry brut vintage sparkling wines from this appellation retail for $8 a bottle. The best are the Saint-Hilaire Blanc de Blancs, the Maison Guinot, and the two top wines from the Coopérative Aiméry: the Cuvée Aldéric and Cuvée Sieur d'Arques.

The World's Greatest Wine With Chocolate

Some of the unique wines of the world are the late-harvested wines from Banyuls made by Dr. Parcé at his Domaine du Mas Blanc. One Banyuls, labeled "dry," is an explosively rich, full-bodied, Grenache-based wine that should be drunk with hearty fare on cool fall and winter evenings. Another, a dry red wine called Collioure, is a complex table wine, impeccably made from a blend of 40% Syrah, 40% Mourvedre, and 20% Grenache. And then there is Dr. Parcé's famous portlike sweet Banyuls made from very ripe Grenache. Complex, decadent, and the only wine I have found to go well with chocolate desserts, this is a spectacular wine that can age well for 20–25 years. The alcohol content averages 16–18%. Parcé also makes a special cuvée of Vieilles Vignes (old vines) that is even more stunning. Dr. Parcé's sweet Banyuls usually sell for under $15 a bottle, making them an inexpensive alternative to vintage port. His dry Banyuls and Collioure sell for under $10.

A Marvelous Muscat

Looking for a sweet, ripe, honeyed, aromatic, reasonably priced wine to serve with fresh fruit or fruit tarts? Then be sure to try the Muscat de Frontignan from the Château de la Peyrade, which sells for about $10 a bottle. It is a heady drink, but the muscat's seductive charm and power is very evident in this excellent wine.

Recent Vintages

Heat and sun are constants in this region. Vintages are incredibly consistent, and the quality of most wines has more to do with the availability of modern technology to keep the grapes and grape juice from overheating in the intensely hot temperatures. Nevertheless, recent vintages that stand out are 1987, 1986, 1985, 1983, and 1982, with 1984 the closest thing this area has had to a mediocre year.

A GUIDE TO LANGUEDOC AND ROUSSILLON'S BEST PRODUCERS

* * * * * (OUTSTANDING PRODUCERS)

Mas de Daumas Gassac (L'Hérault)

Dr. Parcé Mas Blanc (Banyuls)

* * * * (EXCELLENT PRODUCERS)

Cazes Frères (Roussillon)
Château Etang des Colombes (Corbières)

Château de Paraza (Minervois)
St.-Jean de Bebian (L'Hérault)

* * * (GOOD PRODUCERS)

Gilbert Alquier (Faugères)
Domaine des Bories (Corbières)
Domaine du Bosccaute (L'Hérault)
Domaine de Fontsainte (Corbières)
Château de Gourgazaud (Minervois)
Château de Grezan (Faugères)
Haut Fabrèges (Faugères)
Château de Jau (Roussillon)
Domain des Jougla (St.-Chinian)

Domaine de la Lecugne (Minervois)
Domaine de Mayranne (Minervois)
Caves de Mont Tauch (Fitou)
Château de Nouvelles (Fitou)
Cuvée Claude Parmentier (Fitou)
Château de la Peyrade (Muscat-Frontignan)
Château de Queribus (Corbières)

Sarda-Malet (Roussillon)　　　Château de Villerambert-Julien
St. André (L'Hérault)　　　　(Minervois)

PROVENCE

More Than Just Rosé

It is easy to regard Provence as just the dramatic play-ground for the world's rich and famous, for few wine lovers seem to realize that this vast viticultural region in southern France is at least 2,600 years old. For centuries, tourists traveling through Provence have been seduced by the aromatic and flavorful thirst-quenching rosés that seem to complement the distinctive cuisine of the region so well. Yet today, Provence is an exciting and diverse viticultural region that is turning out not only extremely satisfying rosés but immensely promising red wines and a few encouraging whites.

Provence is a mammoth-size region that has seven specific viticultural areas. The best way to get a grasp on the region is to learn what each of these viticultural areas has to offer, and which properties constitute the leading wine-producing estates. While Provence is blessed with ideal weather for grape growing, not all the vintages are of equal merit. Certainly for the white and rosé wines of Provence, which must be consumed in their youth, only 1988, 1987, and 1986 vintages ought to be drunk today. A super vintage for all of Provence was 1985, but the once-exuberant and tasty rosés and white wines are now beginning to fade in the bottle. However, the top red wines of Provence from 1985 are stunning, as this is the best recent vintage for red wine, followed by 1988, 1982, and 1983. As a general rule, the top red wines of Provence can handle aging for up to a decade in the aforementioned vintages.

Following is a brief synopsis of the seven major wine-producing areas in Provence, along with a list of the top wines from each area that merit trying. While the wines of Provence are not overpriced, the recent collapse of the American dollar against the French franc has made these wines less attractively priced than they were several years ago. Yet, when the top wines are compared with wines of similar quality from France's more famous areas such as Burgundy and Bordeaux, their relative value as French wines is obvious.

Bandol

In France, Bandol is often called the most privileged appellation of France. Certainly, the scenic beauty of this storybook area offers unsurpassed views of the azure Mediterranean Sea with the vineyards spread out over the hillsides overlooking the water. Bandol produces red, rosé, and white wines. It is most famous for its rosé wine, which some people consider the best made in France, and its long-lived, intense, tannic red wine, which is unique in France in that it is made from at least 50% of the little-known Mourvèdre grape. Prices for Bandol have never been cheap, largely because of the never-ending flow of tourists to the area who buy up most of the wine made by the local producers.

There seems to be no doubt among connoisseurs that the best red wines come from such producers as Domaine Tempier, Domaine de L'Hermitage, Domaine de Pibarnon, Domaine Pradeaux, Château Romassan, Château Vannières and two properties called Moulin des Coste and Mas des Rouvière. While most of these producers also make a white wine, it is not one I recommend with great enthusiasm, as it seems to always taste dull and heavy. However, the red wines as well as the fresh, personality-filled rosés from these estates are well worth seeking out and are available in most of the major markets in America. Prices for the rosés now average $10–12 a bottle with the red wines costing $10–15 a bottle. While I have had the good fortune to taste red wines of Bandol as old as 15–20 years, most of the wines seem to hit their peak after 6–7 years in the bottle. Bandol, one of the most strictly regulated appellations in France, is certainly the leading candidate among Provence appellations for producer of the longest-lived and best-known red wines.

Bellet

Like all of the Provence appellations, the tiny appellation of Bellet, tucked in the hillside behind the international seaside resort of Nice, produces red, white and rosé wines. The history of Bellet is rich, as its vineyards were originally cultivated by the Phoenician Greeks in 500 B.C., but unless one spends time on the Riviera, one is unlikely to ever know how a fine Bellet tastes. Most of the wine pro-

Provence

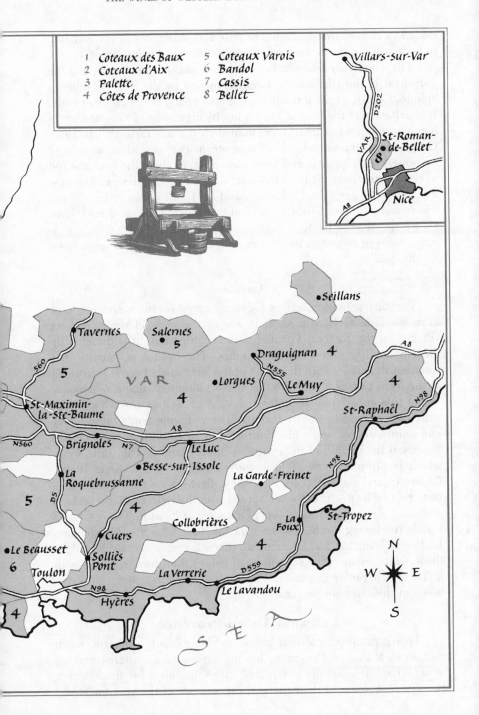

1 Coteaux des Baux
2 Coteaux d'Aix
3 Palette
4 Côtes de Provence
5 Coteaux Varois
6 Bandol
7 Cassis
8 Bellet

Villars-sur-Var
St-Roman-
de-Bellet
8
Nice

Seillans

Tavernes   Salernes
5

VAR   Draguignan 4

Lorgues   Le Muy
4

St-Maximin-
la-Ste-Baume   5

St-Raphaël

N560   Brignoles N7   Le Luc
A8

Besse-sur-Issole

La
Roquebrussanne   La Garde-Freinet

5   4   La
Foux   St-Tropez
Collobrières

Cuers   4

Le Beausset   Solliès
Pont   La Verrerie   Le Lavandou
6   Toulon   N98
4   Hyères

SEA

4

duced in this microappellation of only 100-plus acres never makes it outside of France, as the local restaurant demand is insatiable.

There are only a handful of producers making wine here, and the very best is the Château de Crémat, owned by the Bagnis family, a splendid estate of 50 acres that produces nearly 6,000 cases of wine. It is exported to the United States, but its high price of $15–20 a bottle has insured that few consumers know how it really tastes. Château de Crémat is a unique estate in Provence in that the white wine is of extremely high quality, and local connoisseurs claim the rosé and red wines are the best made in this part of the French Riviera. The best vintages have been the 1985, 1983, and 1981, but I have tasted the red wines from Château de Crémat back through 1978, and they have shown no signs of decline. However, the wines of Bellet remain esoteric, enjoyed by only a handful of people with prices that seem steep for the quality.

Cassis

The tiny fishing village of Cassis, located on the western end of France's famous Côte d'Azur, is one of the most charming fishing villages on the Riviera. Located on a secluded bay, it is dwarfed by the surrounding steep limestone cliffs. The hordes of tourists that frequent the area insure that most of the wine made here is consumed at the local bistros along with the area's ubiquitous *soupe de poisson*. While this appellation includes red wine as well as rosé, it is white wine that has made Cassis famous. The red wine tends to be heavy and uninteresting, and while the rosé can be good, it never seems to approach the quality of its nearby neighbor Bandol. The white wine, which is often a blend of little-known grapes such as Ugni Blanc, Clairette, and Bourboulenc, is a spicy, fleshy wine that often seems unattractive by itself, but when served with the rich, aromatic seafood dishes of the region, it takes on a character of its own. The estates of Cassis producing the best white wines include Clos Ste.-Magdelaine, La Ferme Blanche, and Domaine du Bagnol. Prices average $8–10 for these white wines, which are not bad values, but they are wines with a distinct character that require fairly rich, spicy fish courses to complement their unique personality.

Coteau d'Aix-en-Provence

This gigantic viticultural region, which extends primarily north and west of Aix-en-Provence, has numerous small estates making acceptable but generally overpriced wines that must be drunk within the first 7–8 years of their lives. However, two of the very finest red wine producers in Provence are located here: Domaine Trevallon and the better-known Château Vignelaure. Both producers specialize in red wine, capable of aging 15–20 years, produced from a blend of two great red wine grapes, the Cabernet Sauvignon and Syrah. While other estates have tried to imitate the wines made by Trevallon and Vignelaure, no one has yet succeeded.

The Domaine Trevallon is owned by the ruggedly handsome Eloi Durrbach, who carved his vineyard out of the forbidding and lunarlike landscape near the medieval ghost town of Les Baux. Its first vintage was only in 1978, but that vintage has been followed by other successful vintages that have produced wines that are compellingly rich and intense with enormously complex bouquets and significant concentration, as well as tremendous aging potential. The most recent vintage to be released is the 1986, a fabulously rich wine with a cascade of silky, concentrated cassis and blackberry fruit intermingled with scents of wild thyme.

Not surprisingly, proprietor Durrbach apprenticed at Château Vignelaure, the other great estate of the Coteaux d'Aix-en-Provence. Vignelaure's wines, while not as bold and striking as Trevallon's, are still elegant expressions of Provençal winemaking at its best. They are widely available in America, and the two best recent vintages are the 1985 and 1983.

The wines of Vignelaure and Trevallon both retail in the $10–15 range, making them surprisingly good values for their quality and aging potential.

Côtes de Provence

The Côtes de Provence is the best known and largest viticultural region of Provence, with just under 50,000 acres planted in vines. This appellation is famous for the oceans of dry, flavorful rosé wine that tourists gulp down with great thirst-quenching pleasure. There are many fine producers of Côtes de Provence wines, but the best include the very famous Domaines Ott, which is available on virtually every restaurant wine list in southern France, the Domaines Gavoty, the Domaine Richeaume, and the Domaine Saint-André de Figuière. All these estates, with the exception of the Domaine Richeaume, produce outstanding rosé wine. The Domaine Richeaume specializes in intense, rich, complex red wines that are only surpassed by the aforementioned wines from the Domaine Trevallon and Château Vignelaure. In addition, the very best white wine produced in Provence is made by the Domaine Saint-André de Figuière. All these wines are currently available in most of the major metropolitan markets in the United States, but they are not inexpensive. The Ott wines, no doubt due to their fame in France, sell for fairly hefty prices in the $10–15 range, but I have never heard anyone complain regarding the quality of their superb rosés and underrated red wines. Certainly, the white wine made by Saint-André de Figuière is not overpriced at under $10 a bottle, and the 1987, which has just been released, is an especially fine representative example of just how good a white wine from Provence can be. Saint-André de Figuière also makes a delicious, supple red wine that is well worth trying. The 1985s look to be the best wines made at this estate in the last decade. Should you find a bottle of the Domaine Richeaume's red wine, made by a fanatical German by the name of Henning Hoesch, it is well worth the $10-a-bottle price to taste one of Provence's finest examples of red wine. His serious, densely colored red wines, loaded with heaps of fruit, power, and tannin, give every indication of being capable of aging for over a decade, as they are usually made from a blend of Cabernet Sauvignon and Syrah with some Grenache added at times.

Côtes du Lubéron

Virtually all the wine made in the Côtes du Lubéron is produced by one of the many cooperatives that dominate this region's production. However, this area, which is located in the north of Provence near the villages of Apt and Pertuis, has immense potential. The best estate in the Côtes du Lubéron is the Château de Mille, run with great meticulousness by Conrad Pinatel. However, there is also a new and extremely promising estate called Château Val-Joanis, launched in 1978 with an initial investment of six million dollars to construct a 494-acre vineyard and château near the town of Pertuis. The Chancel family, great believers in the idea that top-quality wines will ultimately be produced from the Côtes du Lubéron, is behind this extraordinary investment. At present, they make a good, fresh white wine, a delicious, fragrant rosé, and an increasingly serious red wine. All sell for under $8 a bottle, making them outstanding values. Consumers should look for their 1985s, which have just been released and are in good distribution in America.

Palette

Palette is a tiny appellation just to the east of Aix-en-Provence that in actuality consists of only one serious winemaking estate, Château Simone. Run by René Rougier, this tiny estate of 37 acres produces a surprisingly long-lived and complex red wine, a fairly oaky, old-style rosé wine, and a muscular, full-bodied white wine that behaves as if it were from the northern Rhône Valley. Simone's wines are not inexpensive, usually averaging $10–12 a bottle, but they do age extremely well and have always had a loyal following in France. Provence is one of France's oldest yet least-known viticultural regions. It remains largely uncharted territory for wine consumers. However, a taste of the best rosés, white wines, and red wines from its bold and innovative new vineyards is certain to cause many consumers to consider Provence more than just an expensive playground for the rich.

The Basics

TYPES OF WINE

A huge quantity of bone-dry, fragrant, crisp rosés are made in Provence, as well as rather neutral but fleshy white wines, and higher and higher quality red wines.

GRAPE VARIETIES

For red wines, the traditional grape varieties have always been Grenache, Carignan, Syrah, Mourvèdre, and Cinsault. Recently, however, a great deal of Cabernet Sauvignon has been planted in the Côtes de Provence and Coteaux d'Aix-en-Provence. The most interesting red wines are generally those with elevated levels of either Syrah, Mourvèdre, or Cabernet Sauvignon. For white wines, Ugni Blanc, Clairette, Marsanne, Bourboulenc, and to a lesser extent Semillon, Sauvignon Blanc, and Chardonnay are used.

FLAVORS

There is immense variation due to the number of microclimates and different grapes used. Most red wines have vivid red fruit bouquets that are more intense in the Coteaux des Baux than elsewhere. In Bandol, the smells of tree bark, leather, and currants dominate. The white wines seem neutral and clumsy when served without food, but when drunk with the spicy Provençal cuisine, they take on life.

AGING POTENTIAL

Rosés: 1–3 years
White wines: 1–3 years, except
  for that of Château Simone

Red wines: 5–12 years, often
  longer for the red wines of
  Bandol and specific wines
  such as Domaine de Trevallon
  and Château Vignelaure

OVERALL QUALITY LEVEL

Quality has increased and in general is well above average, but consumers must remember to buy and drink the rosé and white wines only when they are less than 3 years old.

MOST IMPORTANT INFORMATION TO KNOW

Master the types of wines of each appellation of Provence, as well as the names of the top producers.

1989–1990 BUYING STRATEGY

Concentrate on the red wines of 1985 and 1986, and the whites and rosés of 1987 and 1988.

A GUIDE TO PROVENCE'S BEST PRODUCERS

***** (OUTSTANDING PRODUCERS)

Château de Mille (Côtes du Lubéron)
Château Pradeaux (Bandol)
Domaine Richeaume (Côtes de Provence)

Domaine Tempier (Bandol)
Domaine de Trevallon (Coteaux des Baux)
Château Vignelaure (Coteaux d'Aix-en-Provence)

**** (EXCELLENT PRODUCERS)

Domaine de Beaupré (Coteaux d'Aix-en-Provence)
Château de Crémat (Bellet)
Commanderie de Peyrassol (Côtes de Provence)
Domaine de Feraud (Côtes de Provence)
Domaine Le Gallantin (Bandol)
Domaines Gavoty (Côtes de Provence)
Domaine de L'Hermitage (Bandol)
Mas de la Dame (Coteaux d'Aix-en-Provence)
Mas de Gourgonnier (Coteaux d'Aix-en-Provence)

Mas de la Rouvière (Bandol)
Moulin des Costes (Bandol)
Domaines Ott (Bandol and Côtes de Provence)
Domaine de Pibarnon (Bandol)
Domaine Ray-Jane (Bandol)
Domaine de Rimauresq (Côtes de Provence)
Saint-André de Figuière (Côtes de Provence)
Château Simone (Palette)
Château Val-Joanis (Lubéron)
Château Vannières (Bandol)
La Vieille Ferme (Lubéron)

*** (GOOD PRODUCERS)*

Domaine du Bagnol (Cassis)
Château Barbeyrolles (Côtes de Provence)
Château Bas (Coteaux d'Aix)
La Bastide Blanche (Bandol)
Domaine Caguelouf (Bandol)
Clos Ste.-Magdelaine (Cassis)
Domaine de Curebreasse (Côtes de Provence)
Château de Fonscolombe (Coteaux d'Aix-en-Provence)

Domaine Frégate (Bandol)
Domaine de Lafran-Veyrolles (Bandol)
Domaine La Laidière (Bandol)
Domaine de la Noblesse (Bandol)
Château Sainte-Anne (Bandol)
Domaine des Salettes (Bandol)
Domaine de Terrebrune (Bandol)

DOMAINE DU BAGNOL (CASSIS)* * *

1985 Red	B	75
1986 White	B	82
1986 Rosé	A	84

This is quite a good domaine for white and rosé wines, which are highly appropriate for spicy Provençal dishes. The rosé is extremely fruity but dry, assertive, and full bodied. The white seems to be fairly neutral in character when drunk by itself, but it takes on quite a bit of personality when matched up with dishes that are highly spiced.

CHÂTEAU BEAUPRÉ (COTEAUX D'AIX-EN-PROVENCE)* * * *

1986 Rosé	A	85
1985 Red	B	82

This impeccably run property produces red, white, and rosé wines. I find the rosé the most interesting, followed by the red wine. The rosé tends to have a great deal of flavor, is light, dry, and extremely fragrant. The red wine in 1985 has a scent of Provençal herbs and cherries. Medium bodied and elegant, it should provide another 4–5 years of good drinking.

CLOS STE.-MAGDELAINE (CASSIS)* * *

1986 White	B	84

One of the best white wines made in Cassis comes from this property. The wine, quite full bodied and flavorful, can stand up against the hottest and spiciest dishes from Provence.

COMMANDERIE DE PEYRASSOL (CÔTES DE PROVENCE)* * * *

1986 Rosé	A	84
1985 Rouge Cuvée Eperon d'Or	B	85
1985 Rouge Cuvée Marie-Estelle	B	86

The Commanderie de Peyrassol is one of the finest estates in Côtes de Provence. This large, impeccably kept property produces nearly 20,000 cases of red, rosé, and white wines. The best wines are the refreshing, zesty, dry rosé, and two special cuvées of red wine made primarily from Cabernet Sauvignon, Mourvèdre, Grenache, and Syrah. The 1985 Cuvée Eperon d'Or has a richly fruity bouquet suggestive of bing cherries and spicy oak. The 1985 Cuvée Marie-Estelle is even deeper and richer, with more tannin, body, and a classic Cabernet Sauvignon bouquet of herbaceous black currants. Both wines give every indication of lasting in the bottle for 5–8 years.

CHÂTEAU DE CRÉMAT (BELLET)* * * *

1985 Bandol (red)	C	87
1986 Bandol (white)	B	85
1986 Bandol Rosé	A	85

The finest wines of the microappellation of Bellet (tucked behind the French Riviera's major city of Nice) are made by the Château de Crémat. These wines have surprising complexity and charm. While I've never enjoyed drinking the white wine alone as an aperitif, it is quite delicious with some of the spicy Provençal cuisine, particularly a *soupe de poisson*. The rosé made by Château de Crémat is one of the better rosés of Provence. Their red wine is quite delicious, and in vintages such as 1985, it shockingly resembles an outstanding Volnay from Burgundy. Not inexpensive, given its limited quantities, it retails at prices not unlike a French red burgundy, but the quality is impeccable.

LA FERME BLANCHE (CASSIS)* *

1985 Red	B	72

1986 White	A	83

While the red wine is heavy-handed and lacking in distinction, the white wine is lighter than the other wines from Cassis but still very fragrant and attractive with a great deal of character and fragrance. It should be drunk within 2–3 years of the vintage.

CHÂTEAU DE FONSCOLOMBE (COTEAUX D'AIX-EN-PROVENCE)* * *

1986 Blanc	A	78

1986 Rosé	A	84

1985 Rouge Cuvée Spéciale	B	84

This property produces attractively fruity, clean wines for rather low prices. The white wine has given me more pleasure in vintages other than 1986. The 1986 rosé is exuberant, refreshing, and easy to drink. The red wine, especially the top of the line Cuvée Spéciale, is aged in cask and shows a great deal of generosity and rich, long flavors. It should be drunk over the next 4–5 years.

DOMAINE LE GALLANTIN (BANDOL)* * * *

1985 Bandol (red)	A	87

1987 Bandol Rosé	A	76

This modest-sized estate in Bandol produces adequate rosé and white wines, but a very powerful and flavorful red wine meant to last 10–15 years. The 1985 is the most successful Bandol for the Domaine Le Gallantin since the 1978. This rich, full-bodied wine has a great deal of extract and tannin. The rosé in 1987 is one-dimensional and innocuous.

DOMAINES GAVOTY (CÔTES DE PROVENCE)* * * *

1986 Red Cuvée Clarendon	A	86

1987 Rosé Cuvée Clarendon	A	85

1987 White Cuvée Clarendon	A 85

This outstanding property produces a good rosé, one of the best white wines made in Provence, as well as one of the finest red wines. The 1987 white wine, made from little-known grapes such as Rolle, Clairette, and Ugni Blanc, has excellent flavor depth and is fresh, lively, and altogether a joy to drink. The Cuvée Clarendon, the top cuvée of red wine, made from a blend of Syrah, Cabernet Sauvignon, Grenache, and Mourvèdre, is an excellent red wine with flavors of framboise, spices, and toasty new oak. The 1986 is a slightly lighter but very elegant example of this property's red wine, whereas the 1985 is rich, more intense and has 6–8 years of aging potential.

DOMAINE DE L'HERMITAGE (BANDOL)* * * *

1985 Bandol (red)	B 84

1986 Bandol Rosé	A 79

This reliable source for Bandol wine makes both a red and a rosé. The rosé is extremely dry, even austere, but has flavor and character. The 1985 Bandol red is a full-bodied, compact wine with a lot of flavor but not much complexity.

MAS DE LA DAME (COTEAUX D'AIX-EN-PROVENCE)* * * *

1985 Rouge Cuvée Réserve	B 86

This property, located in the forbidding, eerie, jagged rock outcroppings of southern Provence, produces interesting and well-priced wines made from a blend of the Grenache, Cinsault, Syrah, Cabernet Sauvignon, and Carignan grapes. The 1985 Cuvée Réserve is a round, generously flavored, spicy wine that should be drunk over the next several years.

MAS DE GOURGONNIER (COTEAUX D'AIX-EN-PROVENCE)* * * *

1985 Rouge	A 82

1985 Rouge La Réserve de Mas	B 84

1986 Rouge La Réserve de Mas	B 85

This, one of the better Provence estates, makes a special cuvée, called the La Réserve de Mas, that is mostly Cabernet Sauvignon and Syrah.

Both the 1985 and 1986 showed smoky, deep, impressively rich black-currant bouquets, medium to full body, and good length. While both wines are clearly drinkable now, they should hold and perhaps improve for another 2–3 years. The regular cuvée of red wine, which has a much higher percentage of Grenache, is less intense, but for a soft, commercial, easy-to-drink wine, it is quite enjoyable.

CHÂTEAU DE MILLE (CÔTES DE LUBÉRON)* * * * *

1985 Red	A	87

1986 Red	A	87

Château de Mille, by virtually unanimous agreement, is making one of the finest wines in Provence. In both 1985 and 1986, the proprietor, Conrad Pinatel, made excellent wines exhibiting a great deal of richness, complexity, and a style not unlike a fine Rhône Valley wine. Both wines display an aging potential of 7–10 years. For the quality, the price is amazing.

MOULIN DES COSTES (BANDOL)* * * *
and MAS DE LA ROUVIÈRE

1986 Bandol Blanc de Blancs	B	83

1985 Bandol Cuvée Spéciale Red	B	87

1985 Bandol (red)	B	84

1986 Bandol Rosé	B	85

The wines from the Moulin des Costes and Mas de la Rouvière appear under both labels, but they are the same wines. The estates are run by the outgoing Bunan family, who make their wines in a very modern style. The white is one of the better whites of Bandol and can be appreciated for its floral, lively, dry, fruity style. The rosé has less depth and length than some of the top Bandol rosés, but nevertheless it is an attractively made wine. As for the red wines, the regular cuvée has medium ruby color, a raspberry-scented bouquet, and is of moderate intensity. The 1985 Cuvée Spéciale is a deeper, more concentrated wine with considerably more aging potential and length. It will keep for 8–10 years.

CHÂTEAU DE LA NOBLESSE (BANDOL)* * *

1986 Bandol Blanc	A	79
1985 Bandol (red)	B	85
1986 Bandol Rosé	A	79

While white, rosé, and red wines are made at this estate, the red wine stands out for its powerful, full-bodied, concentrated, firm character that suggests it is capable of lasting for 7–10 years. The vintages since 1983 have been particularly successful, whereas prior to that, the red wine was rather spotty in quality.

DOMAINES OTT (CÔTES DE PROVENCE)* * * *

1986 Bandol Rosé Cuvée Marine	C	86
1987 Bandol Rosé Cuvée Marine	C	86
1986 Bandol Rosé Château Romasson	C	85
1986 Bandol Rosé Château de Selle	C	84
1986 Blanc de Blancs Clos Mireille	C	82
1985 Rouge Cuvée Spéciale Château de Selle	C	86

The Ott family, known to most people as the brothers Marcel and Olivier Ott, have successfully built an empire in Provence, and one sees their wines on virtually every wine list of every top restaurant not only in southern France, but in the entire country. The reason is high quality, and of course, the distinctive bottles that the Otts use for their wines. Their rosés are reference points for the style of dry, medium- to full-bodied rosé wines with flavor. One can hardly go wrong with any rosé here as long as the vintage is a recent one. They have fragrant bouquets of fresh fruit followed by long, flowing, intense flavors and dry, zesty finishes. The white wine from the Clos Mireille, in its heavy, champagne-style bottle, always seems rather undistinctive when tasted alone, but when matched with some of the local specialities of Provence, the wine takes on new life and is quite delicious. While the Ott family gets little recognition for their red wine, there is no question that the regular cuvée of red wine from the Château de Selle is a ripe, deeply colored, fruity wine, but the Cuvée Spéciale with its high percentage of Cabernet Sauvignon is a wine that can last for 20 or more years in the bottle. It is distinguished not only by the words Cuvée Spéciale but also by a distinctive gray label. It is made only in great vintages.

DOMAINE DE PIBARNON (BANDOL)* * * *

1985 Bandol (red)	B	89
1986 Bandol (white)	B	74
1986 Bandol Rosé	B	85

The Domaine de Pibarnon, one of the best known of the Bandol estates is run with great care by the Comte Henri de Saint-Victor. The rosé, usually loaded with a great deal of strawberry fruit, is quite dry and refreshing. The white tends to be made in a severe, high-acid style, which offers little charm or excitement. The 1985 red wine, aged primarily in new oak casks, is quite exceptional with tremendous extract and concentration, and a depth in the finish that suggests it will keep and improve in the bottle until the late 1990s.

CHÂTEAU PRADEAUX (BANDOL)* * * * *

1982 Bandol (red)	C	92
1983 Bandol (red)	C	90

This estate, run by the eccentric Portalis family, does many unusual things, but there is no question that in vintages such as 1983, 1982, and 1979 the quality of their Bandol is among the two or three best in Provence. It is made from an unusually high percentage of Mourvèdre, 95%, with 5% Grenache, and the estate has the oldest vines in Bandol. The wine spends 6–8 years in cask and does not seem to suffer where there is great richness and fruit, but in lighter years the long aging in oak tends to obliterate the fruit. I recently drank the 1969 with Michel Bettane, the noted French wine authority, and it was in remarkable condition. Both the stupendously rich, complex, intense 1982 and the outstanding 1983 suggest they will not be ready to drink before the mid-1990s and should keep well for about 10 years thereafter. These are special, unique wines made uncompromisingly and inflexibly by one of the most eccentrically run estates in France.

DOMAINE RAY-JANE (BANDOL)* * * *

1985 Bandol (red)	B 90

This tiny estate uses 80% Mourvèdre in making a massive, backward, tannic wine that is exemplified by the 1985, which will not be ready to drink before the late nineties. For those with patience and a good, cool cellar, this is a wine to search out.

DOMAINE RICHEAUME (CÔTES DE PROVENCE)* * * * *

1986 Rouge Cuvée Cabernet Sauvignon	B 88

1986 Rouge Cuvée Syrah	B 87

1986 Rouge Cuvée Tradition	A 87

This domaine, run with unbelievable passion and commitment by its proprietor, Henning Hoesch, believes in making intense, rich, age-worthy red wines from varied blends of Syrah, Grenache, and Cabernet Sauvignon. The wines spend up to 18 months in small oak barrels, of which a high percentage is new. Some serious age-worthy wines have been made here in vintages such as 1978, 1982, 1983, 1985, and 1986. As for the 1986s, none is really ready to drink, although a taste of them now will display their intense black/ruby color, aggressive aromas of toasty new oak, spicy Cabernet Sauvignon fruit, and rich blackberry flavors. They are imbued with a great deal of tannin, and aging is recommended for all three of the above cuvées.

CHÂTEAU ROMASSAN (BANDOL)* * * *

1985 Bandol (red)	C 85

1986 Bandol Rosé	B 85

1987 Bandol Rosé	B 87

Run by the ubiquitous Ott family, who have done so much through their estates in Provence to promote the wines of that area, the Château Romassan makes an unsurpassed rosé. The 1987 is an exceptionally flavorful rosé that is quite dry but has an amazing level of berry fruit and a significant length, which sets it apart from virtually every other rosé made in the world, with the exception of the other great Bandol rosé from the Domaine Tempier. As for the red wine, the 1985 is deeply colored with a roasted, black-cherry bouquet and plump, chewy flavors. It will age nicely for 5–10 years.

SAINT-ANDRÉ DE FIGUIÈRE (CÔTES DE PROVENCE)* * * *

1985 Rouge Cuvée Spéciale	B	85
1987 White	A	84

Many observers feel the finest white wine made in the Côtes de Provence appellation is that from Saint-André de Figuière. Extremely fresh and medium-bodied, it has good lively flavors if drunk within 2–3 years of the vintage. As for the red wine, there are several cuvées made, but in general the Cuvée Spéciale, with at least 65% Mourvèdre, is the best wine. The 1985 is a wine capable of lasting 8–10 years. With its rich, herb-scented, blackberry fruit, concentration, and length, it can be drunk now or cellared.

CHÂTEAU SAINTE-ANNE (BANDOL)* * *

1984 Bandol Red	B	85
1986 Bandol Rosé	A	82
1986 Bandol (white)	A	72

This 50-acre estate produces a good red wine, rather dull white wine, and an adequate rosé wine. The 1985 red wine has the Provençal bouquet of fresh herbs and berry fruit. While it can be drunk now, it promises to be even better in 2–3 years.

DOMAINE TEMPIER (BANDOL)* * * *

1986 Bandol (red)	C	84
1985 Bandol Cuvée Spéciale	C	88
1985 Bandol La Migoua	C	90
1987 Bandol Rosé	B	87
1985 Bandol La Tourtine	C	87

The Domaine Tempier, run with remarkable exuberance and enthusiasm by Lucien and Lulu Peyraud, is no doubt Bandol's most famous estate, and one of the area's great champions of the Mourvèdre grape. Their Bandol Rosé, along with the top rosés from the Domaines Ott, are the best made in France, with a distinctive, fragrant bouquet, and an amazing length and character. They produce four separate red wines in top vintages such as 1985, ranging from a regular cuvée of Bandol, which is richly fruity and can be aged up to 10 years, to their Bandol Cuvée Spéciale, which is meant to last 10 to as long as 20 years in certain vintages. This, made with a high percentage of Mourvèdre, has great depth and richness, and the 1985 is a good example. In addition, two single vineyard Bandols are made from the La Tourtine and La Migoua vineyards. These are unique, exotic wines that show great individual style, but since they are produced in such tiny quantities, they are difficult to find. They are well worth the search, however, and should you be lucky enough to buy a bottle, it should be cellared for 8–10 years. Both 1985s are very successful, particularly the La Migoua with its outstanding bouquet of herbs, flowers, licorice, spicy oak, and roasted bing cherries.

DOMAINE DE TREVALLON (COTEAUX D'AIX-EN-PROVENCE)* * * * *

1985 Red	B	90
1986 Red	B	90

This property still rates as one of the greatest discoveries I have made in all my trips to France. The only wine made here is an exciting red from a blend of 60% Cabernet Sauvignon and 40% Syrah. Organically produced, with no fining or filtration, the wine is aged 18 months in small wood casks and displays an incredible richness and intensity that must be tasted to be believed. The vineyard is still relatively young but has shown remarkable potential to produce world-class wines that rival the best in France. The 1985 is a more succulent and lush rendition of the more tannic and structured 1986. For drinking over the next 7–8 years, I would opt for the 1985, and wait 4–5 years before I begin drinking the 1986. Both are outstanding wines that seem to suggest both a great Bordeaux and a great Rhône wine with their intense, black-currant bouquets interwoven with the smell of Provençal herbs. This is a wine to search out.

CHÂTEAU VAL-JOANIS (CÔTES DU LUBÉRON)* * * *

1985 Red	B	84

1986 Red	B 84

1987 Rosé	A 82

1987 White	A 80

This promising new estate has been carved out of the hillsides of the Lubéron Mountains by former business tycoon Jean-Louis Chancel. The vineyards of his huge estate are still young, but he intends to make wines of high quality. The rosé is made in a light, fruity, dry style and is enjoyable quaffing. The 1987 white wine shows good fruit, medium body, and impeccable freshness. The red wines have been deep in color, round, fruity, and generous to date, and they should get better as the vineyard ages. Certainly both the 1985 and 1986 are good, medium-weight wines made primarily from the Syrah grape, and they have 5–8 years aging potential.

CHÂTEAU VANNIÈRES (BANDOL)* * * *

1983 Bandol (red)	B 86

1985 Bandol (red)	B 87

This estate, one of the most beautiful properties in Bandol, produces a stylish, graceful, age-worthy red wine, which in certain vintages is capable of lasting 10–20 years. Both the 1983 and 1985 show fleshy, medium- to full-bodied flavors, a concentrated, silky texture, and a full-intensity bouquet of cedary, herbaceous, smoked-meats aromas.

CHÂTEAU VIGNELAURE (COTEAUX D'AIX-EN-PROVENCE)* * * * *

1983 Red	B 89

1985 Red	B 87

1986 Red	B 86

For years, Château Vignelaure was the benchmark property for measuring the progress of the red wines of Provence. Produced from a blend of 60% Cabernet Sauvignon, 30% Syrah, and 10% Grenache, the wine is rich in cassis fruit with the scent of wild Provençal herbs. It has proven that it can age for 10–15 years in top vintages. The superstar of recent vintages has been the intense, concentrated, profound 1983, but the soft, ripe, jammy 1985 and more tannic, structured 1986 are both textbook examples of this outstanding Provençal red wine that offers both quality and value.

THE RHÔNE VALLEY

The Basics

TYPES OF WINE

In actuality, the Rhône Valley has two halves. The wines of the northern Rhône Valley, from famous appellations such as Côte Rôtie, Hermitage, and Cornas are mostly all age-worthy, rich, full-bodied red wines from the noble Syrah grape. Minuscule quantities of fragrant and delicious white wine is made at Condrieu. White wine is also made at Hermitage, and both good, but not great, red and white wine is made in the appellations of Crozes Hermitage and St.-Joseph.

The southern Rhône, with its Mediterranean climate, primarily produces lusty, full-bodied, heady red wines, but some very fragrant underrated rosés are made here, as well as better and better white wines. In the appellation of Muscat des Beaumes de Venise, a honeyed, perfumed, sweet white wine is made, and in Tavel, France's most famous rosé wine is produced.

GRAPE VARIETIES

RED WINE VARIETALS

Cinsault (grown only in the southern Rhône)—All the growers seem to use a small amount of Cinsault. It ripens early, yields well, and produces wines that offer a great deal of fruit. It seems to offset the high alcohol of the Grenache and the tannins of the Syrah and Mourvèdre. Though a valuable asset to the blend of a southern Rhône wine, it seems to have lost some appeal in favor of Syrah or Mourvèdre.

Counoise (grown only in the southern Rhône)—Very little of this grape exists in the south because of its capricious growing habits. However, I have tasted it at Château Beaucastel in Châteauneuf-du-Pape where the Perrin family is augmenting its use. It had great finesse and seemed to provide deep, richly fruity flavors and a complex perfume of smoked meat, flowers, and berry fruit. The Perrins feel Counoise has at least as much potential as a high-quality ingredient in their blend as Mourvèdre.

Grenache (grown only in the southern Rhône)—A classic hot-climate grape varietal, Grenache is for better or worse the dominant grape of the southern Rhône. The quality of the wines it produces ranges from hot, alcoholic, unbalanced, coarse wines to rich, majestic, long-lived, sumptuous wines. The differences are largely caused by the yield of juice per acre. Where Grenache is pruned back and not overly fertilized, it can do wondrous things. The sensational Châteauneuf-du-Pape Château Rayas is a poignant example of that. At its best, it offers aromas of kirsch, black currants, pepper, licorice, and roasted peanuts.

Mourvèdre (grown only in the southern Rhône, and especially in Bandol)—Everyone seems to agree on the virtues of the Mourvèdre, but few people want to take the risk and grow it. It flourishes in the Mediterranean appellation of Bandol, but in Châteauneuf-du-Pape only Château Beaucastel has made it an important part (one-third) of their blend. It gives great color, a complex aroma, superb structure, and is very resistant to oxidation. However, it ripens late and unlike other grape varietals has no value until it is perfectly mature. When it lacks maturity, the growers say it gives them nothing, being colorless and acidic. Given the eccentricities of this grape, it is unlikely that anyone other than the adventurous or passionately obsessed growers will make use of it. Its telltale aromas are those of leather, truffles, fresh mushrooms, and tree bark.

Muscardin (grown only in the southern Rhône)—More common than Terret Noir, Muscardin provides a great deal of perfume while imparting a solidarity and a good measure of alcohol and strength to a wine. Beaucastel uses Muscardin, but by far the most important plantings of Muscardin at a serious winemaking estate is at Chante Perdrix in Châteauneuf-du-Pape. And the Nicolet family uses 20% in their excellent Châteauneuf-du-Pape.

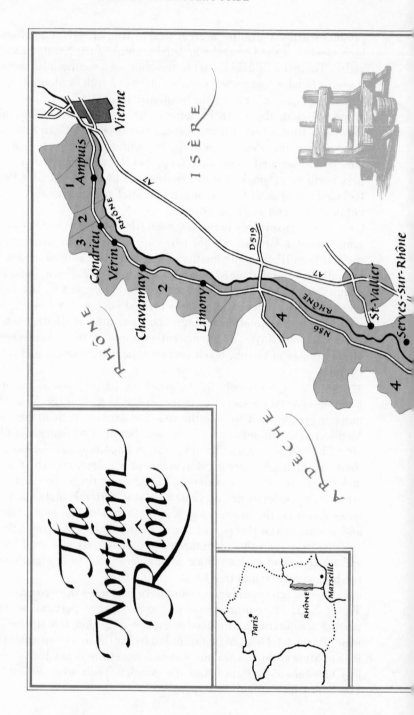

The Northern Rhône

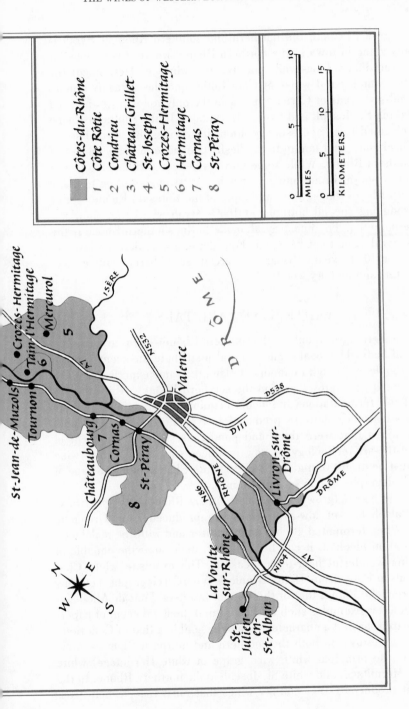

Côtes-du-Rhône
1 Côte Rôtie
2 Condrieu
3 Château-Grillet
4 St-Joseph
5 Crozes–Hermitage
6 Hermitage
7 Cornas
8 St-Péray

MILES
KILOMETERS

Syrah (grown in both the northern and southern Rhône)—Syrah is the only game in town in the northern Rhône, where it is famous for the extraordinary long-lived, massive red wines of Hermitage; the velvety, complex red wines of Côte Rôtie; and the savagely tannic, rich, old-style reds of Cornas. It is also the only red wine grape used for making St.-Joseph and Crozes-Hermitage. In the southern Rhône it is relegated to an accessory position. It provides the needed structure, backbone, and tannin to the fleshy Grenache in many cuvées of the southern Rhône. While some growers believe it ripens too fast in the hotter south, in my opinion, it is a very strong addition to many southern Rhône wines. More and more of the Côtes du Rhône estates are producing special bottlings of 100% Syrah wines that show immense potential. The finest Syrah made in the southern Rhône is the Cuvée Syrah from the Château de Fonsalette, a wine that can last and evolve for 10–15 years. Its aromas are those of berry fruit, coffee, smoky tar, and hickory wood.

WHITE WINE VARIETALS

Bourboulenc (grown only in the southern Rhône)—This grape offers plenty of body. The local cognoscenti also attribute the scent of roses to Bourboulenc, though I cannot yet claim the same experience.

Clairette Blanc (grown only in the southern Rhône)—Until the advent of cold fermentations and modern equipment to minimize the risk of oxidation, the Clairette produced heavy, alcoholic, often deep-yellow wines that were thick and ponderous. Given the benefit of state-of-the-art technology, it now produces soft, floral, fruity wine that must be drunk young. The superb white Châteauneuf-du-Pape of Vieux Télégraphe has 35% Clairette in it.

Grenache Blanc (grown only in the southern Rhône)—Deeply fruity, highly alcoholic yet low-acid wines are produced from Grenache Blanc. When fermented at cool temperatures and with the malolactic fermentation blocked, it can be a vibrant, delicious wine capable of providing wonderful near-term pleasure. The exquisite white Châteauneuf-du-Pape from Henri Brunier's Vieux Télégraphe contains 25% Grenache Blanc; that of the Gonnet brothers' Font de Michelle, 50%. In a few examples such as these, I find the floral scent of paperwhite narcissus and a character vaguely resembling that of Condrieu.

Marsanne (grown in both the southern and northern Rhône)—Marsanne is the principal white wine grape in white Hermitage, white Crozes-Hermitage, and white St.-Joseph in the northern Rhône. In the south it produces rather chunky wines that must receive help from other varietals because it cannot stand alone as well there as in the north. The wine writer Jancis Robinson often claims it smells "not unpleasantly reminiscent of glue."

Roussanne (grown in both the southern and northern Rhône)—For centuries, this grape was the essence of white Hermitage in the northern Rhône, but its small yields and proclivity to disease led to its being largely replaced by Marsanne. It is making something of a comeback in the southern Rhône. With the most character of any of the white wine varietals—aromas of honey, coffee, flowers, and nuts—it produces a wine that can be very long-lived, an anomaly for a white wine in the southern Rhône. The famous Châteauneuf-du-Pape estate Beaucastel uses 80% Roussanne in their wine, which not surprisingly is the longest-lived white wine of the appellation.

Viognier (grown primarily in the northern Rhône and in small quantities in the southern Rhône as well)—This grape is synonymous with Condrieu and Château Grillet in the northern Rhône, where it produces wines that are exotic, with an overwhelming tropical-fruit fragrance intertwined with floral aspects mostly reminiscent of honeysuckle flowers. In the south, there is little of it, but experimental plantings have exhibited immense potential. The finest example in the southern Rhône is the Domaine Ste.-Anne in the Côtes du Rhône village of Gervais. Saint-Estève is another domaine in the Côtes du Rhône that produces a good Viognier.

FLAVORS

NORTHERN RHÔNE

Condrieu—This exotic, often overwhelmingly fragrant wine is low in acidity and must be drunk young, but it offers hedonistic aromas and flavors of peaches, apricots, honey, and an unbelievably decadent, opulent finish.

Cornas—The impenetrable black/ruby color, the brutal, even savage tannins in its youth, the massive structure, and muddy sediment in the bottle are all characteristics of a wine that tastes as if it were made in the nineteenth century. But Cornas wines are among the most virile, robust wines in the world, with a powerful aroma of cassis and raspberries that develops into chestnuts, truffles, licorice, and black currants as it ages. These wines are among the most underrated great red wines of the world, but one must have patience with them.

Côte Rôtie—This is an immense, fleshy, rich, fragrant, smoky, full-bodied, stunning wine with gobs of cassis fruit frequently intertwined with the smell of frying bacon. It is one of France's greatest wines and can last for up to 25 years where well stored.

Crozes-Hermitage—Despite this appellation's proximity to the more famous appellation of Hermitage, the red wines tend to be soft, spicy, fruity, chunky, and rather one-dimensional rather than distinguished. The white wines vary enormously in quality and can be pleasant, but they are often mediocre and too acidic.

Hermitage—At its best, Hermitage is a rich, almost portlike, viscous, very full-bodied, tannic red wine that can seemingly last forever. It is characterized by a great peppery, cassis smell often with a touch of Provencal herbs thrown in for complexity. The white Hermitage can be neutral, but the great examples display a bouquet of herbs, minerals, nuts, peaches, honey, and a stony, wet-slate type of smell.

St.-Péray—Tiny quantities of still and sparkling white wines are made from this forgotten appellation of the Rhône Valley. Neither merit consumer interest as the wines often are dull, heavy, and diffuse.

SOUTHERN RHÔNE

Châteauneuf-du-Pape—An enormous diversity of styles of Châteauneuf-du-Pape are made. It can resemble a Beaujolais, in which case it offers jammy, soft, fruity flavors and must be drunk quite young. If the wine is vinified in a classic manner, it can be very dense in color, quite rich, full-bodied, and can last 15–20 years. It is often characterized by the smell of saddle leather, fennel, licorice, black truffles, pepper, nutmeg, and smoked meats. Wines made by both these methods and then blended together, and dominated by the Grenache grape, often smell of roasted peanuts and overripe bing cherries. The white Châteauneuf-du-Papes can be neutral and uninteresting, but the best examples have a floral and tropical-fruit-scented bouquet. However, they must be drunk extremely young.

Côte du Rhône—The best Côtes du Rhone offer uncomplicated but deliciously succulent, crunchy, peppery, blackberry and raspberry fruit in a supple, full-bodied style that is meant to be consumed within 5–6 years of the vintage.

Gigondas—Gigondas offers up a robust, chewy, full-bodied, rich, generous red wine that has a heady bouquet and supple, rich, spicy flavors. A tiny quantity of a very underrated rosé wine is often made and should be tried by consumers looking for something special.

Muscat de Beaumes de Venise—This sweet, alcoholic, but extraordinarily perfumed, exotic wine offers up smells of peaches, apricots, coconut, and lychee nuts and must be drunk in its youth to be fully appreciated.

AGING POTENTIAL

Northern Rhône

Condrieu: 2–5 years
Cornas: 5–15 years
Côte Rôtie: 5–25 years
Crozes-Hermitage: 3–8 years
Hermitage (red): 5–30 years
Hermitage (white): 3–15 years
St.-Joseph: 3–8 years

Southern Rhône

Châteauneuf-du-Pape (red): 5–20 years
Châteauneuf-du-Pape (white): 1–2 years
Côte du Rhône: 4–8 years
Gigondas: 5–12 years
Muscat de Beaumes de Venise: 1–3 years
Tavel: 1–2 years

OVERALL QUALITY LEVEL

In the northern Rhône appellations of Côte Rôtie, Hermitage, Condrieu, and Cornas, the general level of winemaking is excellent. In the other appellations, it is quite irregular. For the southern Rhône, Châteauneuf-du-Pape has the broadest range in quality, from superb to irresponsible and inept producers. Gigondas has the highest level of quality winemakers.

MOST IMPORTANT THINGS TO KNOW

Develop a sense of taste for the different grapes that are employed in the Rhône Valley. This will take some effort and research, but it will help you immensely when picking a particular producer's wine. Of course it is also important to memorize the names of the finest producers of each type of wine (see the producer's chart on the following pages).

1989–1990 BUYING STRATEGY

For current consumption, the 1985 red Rhônes are wonderfully succulent, juicy wines with immediate appeal. However, they also have another 5 or more years of cellaring potential. The 1986s can be drunk now but are firmer, slightly tougher textured wines than the 1985s. The 1986 southern Rhônes may have the best cellaring potential of any vintage in that area since 1978. Search out the top Côtes du Rhône producers such as Guigal, Coudoulet, and Fonsalette for stunning wines at fair prices. In summary, the consumer is fortunate in

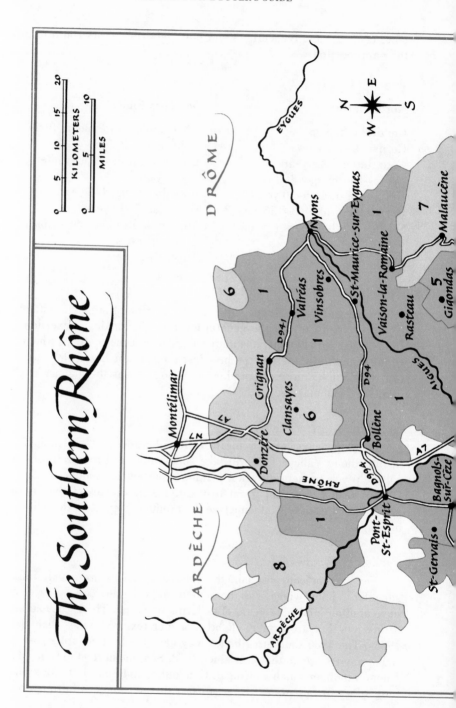

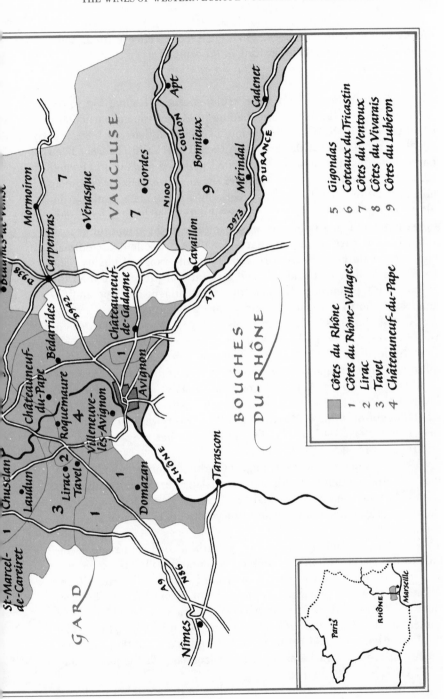

St-Marcel-
de-Careiret

Chusclan

Laudun

Châteauneuf-
du-Pape

Bédarrides

Roquemaure

Villeneuve-
lès-Avignon

Lirac
Tavel

Domazan

GARD

Nîmes

Tarascon

RHÔNE

Avignon

Châteauneuf-
de-Gadagne

Carpentras

Mormoiron

Vénasque

VAUCLUSE

Gordes

Cavaillon

Apt

COULON

N100

Bonnieux

Mérindal

DURANCE

Cadenet

BOUCHES-
DU-RHÔNE

Côtes du Rhône
1 Côtes du Rhône-Villages
2 Lirac
3 Tavel
4 Châteauneuf-du-Pape

5 Gigondas
6 Coteaux du Tricastin
7 Côtes du Ventoux
8 Côtes du Vivarais
9 Côtes du Lubéron

Paris

RHÔNE

Marseille

having two very fine vintages, 1985 and 1986, to choose from, and a potentially great one, 1988, waiting in the wings.

Recent Vintages

1987—A poor to mediocre year in the southern Rhône, but in the northern Rhône, the wines are shaping up. They appear particularly excellent in Côte Rôtie and much more successful than the 1986s.

1986—About 20% of the grapes in the Rhône Valley had not been harvested when the area was inundated with heavy rains on October 12, and the weather that followed over the next two weeks was equally miserable. However, the early pickers did exceptionally well, particularly in the southern Rhône, where quality is at least good, sometimes outstanding. Production was less than in the bountiful year of 1985, but because of the late-harvest deluge, selection was critical, and one sees a great deal of irregularity in the range of quality. The wines are firmer, more tannic, and less fat and precocious than the 1985s. The top southern Rhônes from Châteauneuf-du-Pape and Gigondas appear to have outstanding cellaring potential.

1985—My tastings indicate that this vintage has produced excellent wines in the northern Rhône, and very good wines in the south. For Côte Rôtie, it is a great vintage. The wines are very deep in color, quite rich, but not particularly tannic. The overall impression is one of wines fully ripe, rich in fruit, opulent in style, and quite forward. Overall the vintage is close in quality to 1978. In Côte Rôtie and Châteauneuf-du-Pape it is better than 1983. Everywhere it is certainly better than 1982, 1981, and 1980. The white wines are very powerful and rich but must be drunk young.

1984—A rather mediocre vintage of light- to medium-body wines that will offer straightforward, one-dimensional drinking over the near term. There are many surprisingly good wines from Châteauneuf-du-Pape and Gigondas, and the white wines of the entire region are quite good.

1983—An outstanding vintage in the north, a good yet irregular vintage in the south. A hot, dry summer resulted in fully mature grapes loaded with sugar, flavor extract, and hard tannins. For Hermitage, Crozes-Hermitage, and St.-Joseph, the wines are clearly the best since 1978 and 1961, neither so massive and rich as the 1978s nor as opulent as the 1985s, but more elegant and potentially long-lived. The southern Rhônes should be moderately long-lived since they are ripe, yet full of tannin. In Châteauneuf and Gigondas, 1983 is just behind 1978, 1981, and 1985 in quality.

1982—Initially believed to be outstanding in the north but mediocre in the south, only the latter early prognosis has held true. The great heat during the harvest created significant problems, and those growers not equipped to keep the fermenting grapes cool had problems with volatile acidity. The northern Rhônes are very flavorful but quite forward and will mature quickly. Most will keep until the early nineties, not much longer. At present, they are showing better than the more tannic, more sought-after 1983s. The southern Rhône had many more problems with both the heat and the huge crop. The wines are rather frail and somewhat unstable. However, there are some pleasant surprises, yet one must tread carefully here.

1981—A much better vintage in the southern than northern Rhône, where many vineyards lacked fully mature grapes. Most of the big red wines from Hermitage, Côte Rôtie, and Cornas are lean and lack charm; however, exceptions do exist. In the south it is a good, even excellent vintage for both Gigondas and Châteauneuf-du-Pape, the best between 1978 and 1985. The wines here are quite powerful, deep in color, and offer excellent value.

1980—A large crop of easy-to-drink, medium-weight wines was produced in 1980. They are all relatively mature today and if stored well, will continue to provide delicious drinking for the rest of this decade. Both the north and the south were equally successful in this attractive, commercial vintage of fruity, soft, medium-bodied wines. Clearly, in 1980, the Rhône was France's most successful viticultural district.

1979—A very underrated yet excellent year in both the northern and southern Rhône. Nineteen seventy-nine had the misfortune to follow 1978, the Rhône's greatest vintage since 1961. The wines are just now entering their mature period (where the best of them should remain for another 7–10 years). The wines are rich, full bodied, deep in color, and quite flavorful and scented. The 1979s can still be found at low prices.

1978—An undeniably great vintage in both sectors of the Rhône Valley. Most of the top wines, even though they are just short of their tenth birthday, are still not mature, yet they can be drunk with pleasure because of their explosive fruit and remarkable depth. The 1978s are collectors' items, and the well-cellared examples of Côte Rôtie, Hermitage, Cornas, and Châteauneuf-du-Pape will easily make it into the next century.

1977—Between 1976 and 1986, this is the Rhône's worst vintage. The wines are light, a little green, and lack character and charm. Some of the white wines from the northern Rhône, particularly those of Hermitage, which were very acidic when young, have opened up, but this is by and large a vintage to ignore.

1976—Some reports called this a great vintage, but time has taken its toll on these wines that in reality lacked depth from the beginning. Côte Rôtie was by far the most successful appellation, but many other northern Rhônes were problematic, and the southern Rhônes in most cases lacked balance and were excessively tannic. Whereas 1979 is the Rhône's most recent underrated vintage, 1976 is its most overrated.

A GUIDE TO THE NORTHERN RHÔNE'S BEST PRODUCERS

* * * * * (OUTSTANDING PRODUCERS)

J. L. Chave (Hermitage)
A. Clape (Cornas)
A. Dervieux-Thaize (Côte Rôtie)
Gentaz-Dervieux (Côte Rôtie)
E. Guigal (Côte Rôtie)

Paul Jaboulet Ainé (Hermitage)
R. Jasmin (Côte Rôtie)
R. Rostaing (Côte Rôtie)
N. Verset (Cornas)

* * * * (EXCELLENT PRODUCERS)

G. Barge (Côte Rôtie)
R. Burgaud (Côte Rôtie)
B. Chave (Hermitage)
Delas (Hermitage)
P. Dumazet (Condrieu)
B. Guy (Côte Rôtie)

P. Multier (Condrieu)
J. Pinchon (Condrieu)
M. Sorrel (Hermitage)
Georges Vernay (Condrieu)
Vidal-Fleury (Côte Rôtie)

* * * (GOOD PRODUCERS)

G. de Barjac (Cornas)
Caves des Clairmonts (Crozes-
   Hermitage)
E. Champet (Côte Rôtie)
M. Chapoutier (Hermitage)
R. Clusel (Côte Rôtie)
Courbis (St.-Joseph)
Coursodon (St.-Joseph)
Yves Cuilleron (St.-Joseph)
Desmeures (Hermitage)
A. Drevon (Côte Rôtie)
E. Duclaux (Côte Rôtie)
B. Faurie (Hermitage)
Fayolle (Hermitage)
Ferraton (Hermitage)

Florentin (Crozes-Hermitage)
Gaec de la Syrah (Crozes-
   Hermitage)
A. Gerin (Côte Rôtie)
Gray (Hermitage)
Château Grillet (Condrieu)
B. Gripa (Crozes-Hermitage)
J. L. Grippat (Hermitage)
J. Jamet (Côte Rôtie)
M. Juge (Cornas)
B. Levet (Côte Rôtie)
J. Lionnet (Cornas)
J. Marsanne (St.-Joseph)
R. Michel (Cornas)

La Négociale (Crozes-
Hermitage)
Domaine Pradelle (Crozes-
Hermitage)
R. Roure (Crozes-Hermitage)

C. Tardy (Crozes-Hermitage)
R. Trollat (St.-Joseph)
de Vallouit (Côte Rôtie)
A. Voge (Cornas)

* * (AVERAGE PRODUCERS)

A. Fumat (Cornas)
J. Teysseire (Cornas)

Union des Propriétaires
(Hermitage)

A GUIDE TO THE SOUTHERN RHÔNE'S BEST PRODUCERS

* * * * * (OUTSTANDING PRODUCERS)

Beaucastel (Châteauneuf)
Henri Bonneau (Châteauneuf)
Le Bosquet des Papes
(Châteauneuf)
Clos des Papes (Châteauneuf)
Fortia (Châteauneuf)

Les Gouberts (Gigondas)
Les Pallières (Gigondas)
Raspail (Gigondas)
Rayas (Châteauneuf)
Vieux Télégraphe (Châteauneuf)

* * * * (EXCELLENT PRODUCERS)

Beaumet Bonfils (Gigondas)
Beaurenard (Châteauneuf)
Les Cailloux (Châteauneuf)
Chante Perdrix (Châteauneuf)
Les Clefs d'Or (Châteauneuf)
Clos du Mont-Olivet
(Châteauneuf)
Coudoulet (Côtes du Rhône)
Cuvée du Belvedere
(Châteauneuf)
Durieu (Châteauneuf)
Georges Faraud-Cayron
(Gigondas)
Fonsalette (Côtes du Rhone)

Font de Michelle (Châteauneuf)
Lou Fréjau (Châteauneuf)
Grand Tinel (Châteauneuf)
Longue-Toque (Gigondas)
Mont-Redon (Châteauneuf)
La Nerthe (Châteauneuf)
Roger Sabon (Châteauneuf)
St.-Gayan (Gigondas)
Sénéchaux (Châteauneuf)
Cuvée du Tastevin
(Châteauneuf)
Cuvée du Vatican (Châteauneuf)
Vieux Donjon (Châteauneuf)

* * * (GOOD PRODUCERS)

d'Aqueria (Tavel)
P. Archimbaud (Gigondas)
P. Bérard (Châteauneuf)
Brusset (Côtes du Rhône)

Cabasse (Côtes du Rhône)
Cabrières (Châteauneuf)
Chante Cigale (Châteauneuf)
Chapoutier (Châteauneuf)

Le Clos de Cazaux (Côtes du Rhône)
Clos de l'Oratoire (Châteauneuf)
Clos St.-Jean (Châteauneuf)
Combe l'Ousteau Fauquet (Gigondas)
Le Couroulu (Côtes du Rhône)
Devoy (Lirac)
Fines Roches (Châteauneuf)
Font du Loup (Châteauneuf)
Forcadière (Tavel)
La Fourmone (Côtes du Rhône)
La Gardine (Châteauneuf)
Genestière (Tavel)
du Grand Moulas (Côtes du Rhône)
Guigal (Châteauneuf)
Haut des Terres Blanches (Châteauneuf)
Paul Jaboulet Ainé (Châteauneuf)
Marcoux (Châteauneuf)

Maupertuis (Châteauneuf)
Montmirail (Gigondas)
Mousset (Châteauneuf)
Nalys (Châteauneuf)
Père Caboche (Châteauneuf)
J. Quiot (Châteauneuf)
Relagnes (Châteauneuf)
St.-Roch (Lirac)
Ste.-Anne (Côtes du Rhône)
de Ségriès (Lirac)
La Solitude ((Châteauneuf)
Terre Ferme (Châteauneuf)
Trignon (Côtes du Rhône)
Trinquevedel (Tavel)
Trintignant (Châteauneuf)
Vaudieu (Châteauneuf)
La Vieille Ferme (Côtes du Rhône)
Vieux Chêne (Côtes du Rhône)
Vieux Julienne (Châteauneuf)
Vieux Lazaret (Châteauneuf)

The Rhône Valley

Red Wines

GILLES AND PIERRE BARGE* * * *

1985 Côte Rôtie	C	90
1986 Côte Rôtie	C	86

Deeply colored, the 1985 has concentrated fruit, a fragrant bouquet of blackberries, a touch of vanillin from partial aging in new casks, full body, and a long, ripe tannic finish. The 1986 is more tannic and has less fatness, but it will make a very fine bottle in 2–3 years.

GUY DE BARJAC* * *

1985 Cornas	B	85
1986 Cornas	B	87

As young Cornas wines go, the 1985 is quite flattering due to the lower than normal acidity and ripe tannins. It has very broad, velvety flavors, a big, forward bouquet of peppery, blackberry, earthy fruit, and a sweet, long finish. It is quite seductive. The 1986 is just as concentrated, better structured, and should shed enough of its tannins to be fully mature in 2–4 years.

CHÂTEAU BEAUCASTEL* * * * *

1985 Châteauneuf-du-Pape	C	91
1986 Châteauneuf-du-Pape	C	88

Proprietors François and Jean-Pierre Perrin believe the 1985 is too soft to be a classic Beaucastel. It is more open and accessible, but very opaque ruby/black in color. It has an exciting mélange of flavors, from blackberry to chestnuts. Extremely full-bodied, chewy, dense, opulent, and rich, this wine will drink well young but will also keep for the rest of this century. The 1986 is the most tannic and backward Beaucastel since the 1978. It needs 4–8 years to round out, yet should be excellent by 1995.

DOMAINE DE BEAURENARD* * * *

1985 Châteauneuf-du-Pape	B	87
1986 Châteauneuf-du-Pape	B	86

Proprietor Paul Coulon believes the 1985 is his finest wine since the 1967, and I tend to agree. Deep in color with an intense bouquet of ripe berry fruit, this voluptuous, lush wine is bursting with fruit. Full-bodied and soft, it should drink well for the next 6–7 years. The 1986, almost as tasty but slightly less charming, is still a big, chewy, supple mouthful of Châteauneuf-du-Pape.

DOMAINE DE LA BERNADINE

1985 Châteauneuf-du-Pape	B	84

Relatively one-dimensional, the 1985 from La Bernardine exhibits plenty of ripe, chunky fruit, a soft, lush texture, low acidity, and good near-term drinking potential.

HENRI BONNEAU* * * * *

1985 Châteauneuf-du-Pape	C	94

1986 Châteauneuf-du-Pape   C   93

I believe I was the first wine writer to gain access to Henry Bonneau's
tiny cellar. Several serious growers had told me he made one of the
three or four finest wines in the southern Rhône, but he had no toler-
ance for writers, had a long waiting list of European clients who desired his wine, and was a recluse. However, in the fall of 1986, I saw
him and was permitted to taste three vintages. All of them (the 1978,
1979, and 1981) were spectacular, but Bonneau said he would never
sell his wines to America as he did not make enough wine to satisfy
his European clients. Fortunately, another Frenchman, Alain Junge-
net, persuaded him to sell some of his monumental Châteauneuf-
du-Pape to America, and his 1985 is the wine of the vintage for this
sun-drenched, windy appellation. Astonishingly concentrated (it is
deeper and richer than the 1985 Rayas and Beaucastel), this explosive,
full-bodied, nectarlike wine is quite extraordinary. Drinkable now, it
should last for 10–15 years. Although quite marvelous, it is very limited in quantity. The 1986, just as concentrated and explosively rich
on the palate, is more tannic and backward and will need 5–7 years to
shed its youthful toughness.

LE BOSQUET DES PAPES* * * * *

1985 Châteauneuf-du-Pape   B   89

1986 Châteauneuf-du-Pape   B   88

Both these wines appear to be one of the top dozen or so red wines of
the appellation in 1985 and 1986. They are deep in color with big,
black-cherry-scented bouquets, robust, rich, deep flavors, plenty of
length and depth, as well as 8–10 years of aging potential. The 1986
shows more plums and tobacco in its bouquet, yet for a 1986 it is
remarkably smooth and velvety.

DOMAINE DE BRUSSET* * *

1985 Côtes du Rhône-Villages   A   84

1986 Côtes du Rhône-Villages   A   85

This family-run estate has always been a good source for Côtes du
Rhône. Both the 1986 and 1985 have medium ruby color with forceful,
peppery, spicy bouquets, soft, nicely concentrated flavors, full body,

and provide immediate gratification. The 1986 will keep an additional 2–3 years because of its tannin.

ROGER BURGAUD* * * *

1985 Côte Rôtie	C	91

By comparison with the elegantly wrought wines Burgaud produced in previous vintages, the 1985, a black/purple-colored wine, is rather corpulent, dense, and powerful. Yet the wonderfully clean, ripe blackcurrant fruitiness is abundantly displayed with good acidity as well as marvelous depth and length.

DOMAINE DE CABRIÈRES* * *

1985 Châteauneuf-du-Pape	C	84

The Arnaud family, which runs the Domaine de Cabrières, believes this is among the best vintages of the last three decades. It is a medium-bodied, fruity wine, extremely clean, not that deep, but round and charming.

LES CAILLOUX* * * *

1985 Châteauneuf-du-Pape	B	88

1986 Châteauneuf-du-Pape	B	90

The 1985 is a deeply colored wine that is quite rich and chewy with heaps of fruit and length. It is full bodied, slightly low in acidity, but appealing and forward with a great deal of fragrance and character. The 1986 is superb with stunning richness, an impressive structure and length, and 10–15 years of cellaring potential.

CAVES DES CLAIRMONTS* * *

1985 Crozes-Hermitage	A	80

1986 Crozes-Hermitage	A	82

These quite grapy wines, with good levels of peppery, cherry fruit, and medium body, are overall soft and pleasant.

DOMAINE DE CAYRON* * * *

1985 Gigondas	B	89

Georges and Michel Faraud think this is one of the finest wines they have ever made. With a whopping 14.4% natural alcohol, there is no doubting its ability to grab your attention. Black/ruby with an intense chocolaty, spicy bouquet, heaps of flavor, great depth and length, this should prove to be a propitious effort.

LE CELLIER DES PRINCES

| 1985 Châteauneuf-du-Pape | A | 84 |

Quite a solid wine for the price, this Châteauneuf-du-Pape from a large *négociant* has a moderately intense bouquet of salty seaweed, ripe plums, and pepper. Low in acidity, fully ready to drink, this is a smooth, full-bodied, lush wine for drinking over the next 1–3 years.

EMILE CHAMPET* * *

| 1985 Côte Rôtie | C | 86 |

| 1986 Côte Rôtie | C | 87 |

Champet did not have the great success that many of his peers enjoyed with the 1985 vintage. Nevertheless, this is still an appealing wine with a rustic, full-bodied, intensely spicy, pepper-scented aroma, good concentration and hard tannins, as well as good acidity. It is quite different in style from other 1985s. His 1986 appears marginally more concentrated, better balanced, and more structured. I would drink it between 1990–1996.

DOMAINE CHANTE CIGALE* * *

| 1985 Châteauneuf-du-Pape | B | 83 |

Herbaceous, earthy aromas dominate this chunky, robust wine that seems a bit unstructured and diffuse. Proprietor Christian Favier says he is in the minority, but he believes 1985 is a mediocre year.

DOMAINE DE CHANTE PERDRIX* * * *

| 1985 Châteauneuf-du-Pape | B | ? |

Bottle variation seems to plague this wine. Some is black/ruby in color, intense, opulent, and bursting with blackberry fruit and aromas of sweet fruit and flowers. Quite concentrated as well as alcoholic, the top bottles show a velvety texture that provides delicious drinking and could merit a rating of 88–90. Other bottles are light ruby in color, watery, and appear to be a totally different wine. Is Monsieur Nicolet playing games?

CHAPOUTIER* * *

1985 Côte Rôtie	B	84
1985 Crozes-Hermitage Les Meysonniers	B	75
1985 Hermitage La Sizeranne	C	87
1985 St.-Joseph Deschants	B	83

Potentially, this may be Chapoutier's best Côte Rôtie in years. It will not be long-lived, but for drinking over the next 5–7 years, few could deny its supple, smooth, black-cherry fruitiness and easygoing charm. It also has a great deal of alcoholic punch to it. The 1985 Crozes-Hermitage is soft and simple with jammy fruit flavors. They are the only interesting aspects of this otherwise one-dimensional wine. Like many of the red Hermitage wines from this vintage, Chapoutier's 1985 Hermitage is rather low in acidity but quite richly flavored, full-bodied, deep, velvety, and loaded with peppery, cassis fruit. It will mature quickly. The 1985 St.-Joseph from Chapoutier is an elegant, fruity, soft, cherry- and raspberry-scented wine. It will provide delightful drinking over the next 2–3 years.

BERNARD CHAVE* * * *

1986 Hermitage	D	88

This relatively new, young grower who is not a relative of the internationally famous Gérard Chave, has made an exceptional wine in 1986, a vintage that was good, but rarely great in the Northern Rhône. Very deep ruby with a huge, smoked-meat, Oriental-spice bouquet, this full-bodied, rich, excellent Hermitage should be at its best between 1991 and 2003. Perhaps we have a new star emerging from Hermitage.

J. L. CHAVE* * * * *

1985 Hermitage	D	92
1986 Hermitage	D	88
1985 St.-Joseph	B	86

There is no question that Chave produced the best red Hermitage of this vintage. Yet, for Chave, 1985 was not a year he would like to remember. Holding back tears, he sadly told me that his beloved mother, as well as his faithful sidekick, his dog, both passed away that year. A sentimentalist, Chave is likely to put little of this vintage into the huge reservoir of old vintages the Chave family has faithfully cellared throughout this century. His 1985 avoids the oversupple style of some of the other reds of this vintage. Perhaps similar to the 1982, the 1985 is a voluptuous wine with deep cassis fruit, plenty of body, excellent concentration, and good tannin. The 1986 is more tannic, quite full and promising, but it does not yet show the sheer class of his superb 1985. The 1985 St.-Joseph from Chave is decadently fruity and ripe. The luscious scents of peppery, raspberry fruit are extremely intense. Quite supple, this lovely wine should be drunk over the next 3–4 years. Unfortunately, it is virtually unavailable except at the Chez Panisse restaurant in Berkeley, California.

AUGUSTE CLAPE* * * * *

1985 Cornas	C	90

1986 Cornas	C	87

Clape seems to prefer his 1983 to the 1985, but for me they are equal in quality if different in style. The 1985, with all the great depth and length of the 1983, is fatter, softer, and more lush with an explosive richness. There are plenty of tannins, but they are ripe and round. This is an unctuous, gorgeous Cornas that will provide tantalizing drinking while young but will keep well, too. The 1986 is reminiscent of Clape's excellent 1981, black/ruby in color, quite tannic, full-bodied, but much less seductive than the 1985—at least at the present.

DOMAINE LES CLEFS D'OR* * * *

1985 Châteauneuf-du-Pape	B	88

Very dense in color, the 1985 has a rich, peppery, raspberry and black-cherry bouquet, lush, intensely concentrated flavors, and a sweetness and length on the palate that is most attractive. While not quite as profound as the 1978, this is still a fine bottle of wine.

DOMAINE LE CLOS DES CAZAUX* * *

1985 Vacqueyras Saint Roch Côtes du Rhône-Villages	A	83

1985 Vacqueyras Templiers Côtes du Rhône-Villages   A   87

Vacqueyras is one of the very fine Côtes du Rhône-Villages, and the Archimbaud-Vache family that runs this domaine is as serious as any. The Saint-Roch, which contains 20–30% Syrah, is an exuberantly fruity, peppery wine that is soft and pleasant. On the other hand, the Templiers is black in color and not unlike a good Hermitage as it is nearly 100% Syrah. Quite impressive, rich, intense, and capable of aging 4–6 years, it is a top-rank southern Rhône.

CLOS DU MONT-OLIVET* * * *

1985 Châteauneuf-du-Pape   C   90

1986 Châteauneuf-du-Pape   C   90

The 1985 is a fabulous wine, black/ruby in color with an intense fragrance of berry fruit, floral scents, and exotic spices. Extremely dense and rich, very full-bodied, this sensational wine combines power with finesse and will age well for two decades. The 1986 is just as impressive, but more backward and tannic.

CLOS DE L'ORATOIRE* * *

1985 Châteauneuf-du-Pape   B   83

Deep ruby in color with a jammy, straightforward bouquet of berry fruit, flabby, fat, and low in acidity, this chunky wine will offer good, uncomplicated drinking for 5–7 years.

CLOS DES PAPES* * * * *

1985 Châteauneuf-du-Pape   B   88

1986 Châteauneuf-du-Pape   B   90

The 1985 from Clos des Papes is a rich wine with a huge berry-scented bouquet, very unctuous, fat flavors, heaps of fruit, full body, and excellent length. Winemaker/proprietor Paul Avril believes it is too low in acidity to age more than 10–15 years. Avril thinks his 1986 is even better, and I concur, as it is deep, full-bodied, rich, powerful, and tannic. It would appear to be the finest Clos des Papes since the 1978.

RENÉ AND GILBERT CLUSEL* * *

1985 Côte Rôtie   C   84

For a 1985 Côte Rôtie, Clusel's wine is notably less successful than others. Medium ruby, rather loosely knit, low in acidity but soft and accessible, this wine will have to be drunk over the next 5–6 years.

COLLOGNE-DOMAINE LA NÉGOCIALE* * *

1985 Crozes-Hermitage   A   82

This is a round, generously fruity, plump, medium-bodied wine with a good deal of gutsy fruit.

CRU DE COUDOULET* * * *

1985 Côtes du Rhône   B   87

1986 Côtes du Rhône   B   88

Both of these wines are among the finest Côtes du Rhône I tasted. The vineyard, owned by the Perrins, who make Château Beaucastel in Châteauneuf-du-Pape, is adjacent to their more prestigious estate. The 1985 continues the success this property established by recent years such as 1984, 1983, 1981, and 1978. Quite forward, dense in color, this wine is packed with rich, velvety fruit, is quite full-bodied, extremely long, and should only get better over the next 4–6 years. As hard as it is to believe, I thought the 1986 Coudoulet was as promising and as rich and complex as the 1986 Beaucastel. I know that makes no sense, but that is how well the 1986 Coudoulet is showing.

MAURICE COURBIS* * *

1985 St.-Joseph   B   82

This wine will not age well (no St.-Joseph does), but for drinking over the next 2–3 years, it offers spicy, moderately intense, peppery, chewy fruit, medium body, and low acidity.

DOMAINE LE COUROULU* * *

1985 Vacqueyras   A   86

1986 Vacqueyras   A   86

1984 Vacqueyras Cuvée Spéciale · A 84

All of these wines are from the Côtes du Rhône-Villages of Vacqueyras and are loaded with deep, rich, peppery, raspberry fruit, and have full body as well as surprising length and complexity. The 1984 is well colored, lush, totally mature, and a textbook Côtes du Rhône. The 1985 is fatter, richer, also very soft, and quite a hedonistic mouthful of chewy fruit. In contrast, the 1986, while just as concentrated as the 1985, is firmer, more tannic and age-worthy, although one is hard pressed not to enjoy the intense, peppery, raspberry fruit now. These are all impressive Côtes du Rhône.

PIERRE COURSODON* * *

1985 St.-Joseph · B 85

Despite the low acidity, the 1985 has a deep ruby color, a very perfumed bouquet of rich berry fruit, full body, and a succulent, lush finish. It will be delicious for 2–4 years.

YVES CUILLERON* * *

1985 St.-Joseph · B 87

A super St.-Joseph, the 1985 from Cuilleron has a black/ruby color, an explosive bouquet of smoky, raspberry fruit, full body, soft, concentrated, lush flavors, and a surprisingly long finish.

CUVÉE DU BELVEDERE* * * *

1985 Châteauneuf-du-Pape · B 90

1986 Châteauneuf-du-Pape · B 87

The 1985 is more like a Côte Rôtie than a Châteauneuf-du-Pape. The dense, dark ruby color, the bouquet of roasted raspberry fruit, and the opulent texture bursting with sweet, ripe berry flavors of this seductive wine offer great drinking at an early age. The 1986 is atypical for Châteauneuf-du-Pape, but typical for this estate. Always strutting its charm in an open, up-front, richly fruity, succulent style, this 1986 seems to ignore the firmer, more structured style of the vintage completely, and delivering tremendous levels of hedonistic blackberry/cherry fruit. Drink this hedonistic wine over the next 4–8 years.

DELAS FRÈRES* * * *

1985 Châteauneuf-du-Pape	B	84
1985 Cornas Chante Perdrix	B	87
1985 Côte Rôtie	C	84
1985 Crozes-Hermitage	B	85
1985 Hermitage Cuvée Marquise de la Tourette	C	88

The 1985 Châteauneuf-du-Pape is a solid, rather robust wine with good color, plenty of fruit and body, as well as a firm, tannic balance. Yet, it lacks complexity and character. For a gutsy mouthful of wine, though, it will do quite nicely for 4–5 years. As for the Cornas from Delas, it is one of the most tannic and backward Cornas wines of 1985. A dark ruby color with an earthy, almost truffle-scented bouquet, this full-bodied, chewy wine has heaps of both tannin and fruit but will require patience. It may ultimately merit a higher score. The Côte Rôtie in 1985, less concentrated than other top Côte Rôties in this vintage, is lighter and more supple, surprisingly so for a wine from the hillside of Côte Rôtie called the Côte Brune. Deliciously fruity, quite low in acidity, it is also uncomplicated. Drink it over the next 5–7 years. The Crozes-Hermitage is a deeply colored, sturdy, fleshy wine with plenty of fruit, muscle, and length. It is drinking well now but should hold in the bottle and improve for 2–3 more years. Lastly, the 1985 Marquise de la Tourette is deeply colored, quite forward, fat, ripe, richly fruity, full bodied, low in acidity, but quite concentrated. It will mature quickly, between 1989 and 1996.

ALBERT DERVIEUX-THAIZE* * * * *

1985 Côte Rôtie Fongent	D	87
1985 Côte Rôtie La Garde	D	92
1985 Côte Rôtie La Viaillière	D	92

Dervieux's 1985 La Viaillière is a fabulously promising wine with a deep, dark ruby color, a huge, exotic, earthy, fruity, undeveloped bouquet, superripeness and richness, and great length. It should mature between 1991 and 2004. In contrast to the more sturdy, tannic La

Viaillière from the Côte Brune, Dervieux's La Garde from the Côte Blonde is more supple and velvety, yet still fully capable of a decade or more of evolution in the bottle. It has layers and layers of fruit, sensational intensity and color, and ripe, round tannins. The only problem with the Fongent is that I tasted it in the company of Dervieux's other two wines that are unquestionably superstars in 1985. The Fongent is lush but finishes harder, and while admirably concentrated, it does not have the great depth of La Garde and La Viaillière. From barrel samples, Dervieux's 1986s look to range from good to very good, but not near the quality of his 1985s.

DESMEURE–DOMAINE DES REMEZIÈRES* * *

1985 Hermitage	C	85

This appears to be the best wine I have tasted from Desmeure. Deep in color, clean with oodles of jammy, berry fruit, this medium- to full-bodied wine will mature quickly.

EDMOND DUCLAUX* * *

1985 Côte Rôtie	C	89

Duclaux believes his 1985 is the finest wine he has yet produced. A textbook Côte Blonde (from the Côte Rôtie hillside that produces less tannic wine than the Côte Brune), it has a captivating crushed-berry fragrance, rich, lush, almost sweet, jammy flavors, a long finish, and enough backbone to ensure further evolution.

DOMAINE DURIEU* * * *

1985 Châteauneuf-du-Pape	B	82
1986 Châteauneuf-du-Pape	B	90

Durieu's 1985 is less successful than many other wines from this vintage. Quite low in acidity, on the palate it is intensely fruity and cleanly made, but heavy and alcoholic. The great 1986 is characterized by a huge, chocolaty, exotic, cedary, smoky aroma that creates a sensational bouquet. On the palate this large-scaled wine is exhibiting great richness and depth, a deceptively fruity, lush texture that hides a sizable level of tannins, and 14% alcohol. This is one of the best but least-known estates in Châteauneuf-du-Pape, and Durieu's 1986 is his best wine since his 1978 and 1983.

BERNARD FAURIE* * *

1985 Hermitage	C	88

Very deep in color, this full-bodied, powerful wine admirably balances muscle and finesse. As with many 1985s, there is a precocious succulent appeal, but the tannins are there for longevity.

JULES FAYOLLE ET FILS* * *

1985 Crozes-Hermitage Les Pontaix	B	84
1986 Crozes-Hermitage Les Pontaix	B	84

The 1985 is a big, beefy, concentrated, rather ink-colored Crozes with the smoky, tar-scented bouquet one gets from Hermitage. Its low acidity makes it delicious now. Surprisingly, given the vintage, the 1986 is fat, fruity, and tasing well already.

MICHEL FERRATON* * *

1985 Crozes-Hermitage La Matière	B	87
1986 Crozes-Hermitage La Matière	B	84
1985 Hermitage Cuvée Les Miaux	C	90

Aside from the Crozes produced by Jaboulet's Thalabert vineyard, the 1985 from Ferraton is the best red Crozes I have tasted. Dark ruby in color with an aggressive and intense bouquet of cassis fruit and smoky scents, this lush, supple, unctuous, full-bodied wine is quite impressive. His 1986 is less concentrated, but quite supple and charming. Ferraton's 1985 Hermitage, every bit as concentrated as his 1983, is, however, much softer, very rich and unctuous with a huge bouquet of wild berry fruit and smoky tar. Intense and full-bodied, this wine should keep well despite its precocious appeal.

EMILE FLORENTIN* * *

1985 St.-Joseph Clos de l'Arbalestrier	B	82

The 1985 seems to signal that Florentin is putting more fruit into his wine. Medium-ruby with soft, berry aromas and flavors, this wine is quite attractive.

FONSALETTE* * * *

1985 Côtes du Rhône   B 90

1985 Côtes du Rhône Cuvée Syrah   C 92

The regular cuvée 1985 Fonsalette should prove to be the most tasty
wine from this splendid Côtes du Rhône vineyard since the 1979. A
huge bouquet of ripe plummy fruit, fresh pepper, and cedarwood is
top rank. On the palate, the wine exhibits the 1985 style—power,
lushness, huge fruit, full body, low acids, but an exciting level of taste.
The 1985 Cuvée Syrah is an astonishing example of how great a wine
can be made from the Syrah grape in the southern Rhône. In 1985 it
is as great as any of the Hermitage wines produced farther north. It
should be at its best between 1992 and 2000.

FONT DU LOUP* * *

1985 Châteauneuf-du-Pape   B 88

The 1985 red Châteauneuf-du-Pape from Font du Loup has exceptional depth, great color, a long, persistent palate impression, loads of
black-cherry fruit, and quite a future ahead of it.

FONT DE MICHELLE* * * *

1985 Châteauneuf-du-Pape   B 87

1986 Châteauneuf-du-Pape   B 87

The 1985 is plummy, fat, somewhat low in acidity, but deeply colored,
round, and generous. This peppery and raspberry-flavored, full-bodied wine will make a fine bottle for drinking early on. The 1986 shares
these same characteristics but is exhibiting more tannin and slightly
greater depth.

CHÂTEAU FORTIA* * * * *

1985 Châteauneuf-du-Pape   C 85?

Richly fruity, deep in color, but dangerously low in acidity, this wine,
if it develops more structure to go along with the excellent concentration, will merit a better review. Normally Fortia produces one of the
top 7 or 8 wines of the appellation, so this rating seems low—time will
tell.

LOU FRÉJAU* * *

1985 Châteauneuf-du-Pape	B	90

1986 Châteauneuf-du-Pape	B	88

This tiny estate, run by Serge Chastan, made an unbelievable 1985 that some observers thought was the best wine of the vintage in Châteauneuf-du-Pape. The 1986, with its huge bouquet of crushed raspberries, and deep, sweet, round, full-bodied flavors, reminds me of the style of the famous La Nerthe. Smoky, rich, and multidimensional with plenty of appeal today, this wine will drink exceptionally well for 6–9 years.

GAEC DE LA SYRAH* * *

1985 Crozes-Hermitage Pierrelles	A	85

The 1985 is a delicious, plump, deeply colored wine loaded with smoky, cassis-scented Syrah fruit. Full-bodied, rich, and long, this is what fine Crozes is all about.

CHÂTEAU DE LA GARDINE* * *

1985 Châteauneuf-du-Pape	B	86

The late Gaston Brunel, the proprietor of La Gardine who died tragically in the summer of 1986 in a fishing accident, was quite high on this vintage. Interestingly, the 1985 is more restrained and less obviously opulent than other wines. It still has a good measure of ripe black-cherry fruit, full body, and 5–10 years of further evolution.

MARIUS GENTAZ-DERVIEUX* * * * *

1985 Côte Rôtie	E	94

1986 Côte Rôtie	D	86

The 1985 is an exceptional wine in all respects. Gentaz feels this is his best vintage in the last decade. Very dark ruby with a huge, intensely perfumed bouquet of ripe fruit, a luscious, deep, velvety texture with enough tannin for 10 years of evolution, this wine is already quite accessible. The 1986, less voluptuous and more tannic, is still very good for the vintage.

DOMAINE LES GOUBERTS* * * * *

1985 Côtes du Rhône	A	85
1985 Côtes du Rhône-Villages Beaumes de Venise	A	87
1985 Gigondas	C	90
1985 Gigondas Cuvée Florence	C	93
1986 Gigondas Cuvée Florence	C	92

Jean-Pierre Cartier is well-known both for his superb Gigondas and the baseball cap he constantly sports. He also makes two delicious, fairly priced Côtes du Rhône. The Côtes du Rhône has a healthy, deep-ruby color; big, fragrant, rich, spicy bouquet; soft, concentrated, fruity flavors; and a fine length. The dense, powerful, red Beaumes de Venise made from 65-year-old vines explodes on the palate with peppery, blackberry fruit. Full-bodied and amazingly similar to his Gigondas (made from a vineyard only a few miles away), this exciting wine should provide great pleasure over the next 2–5 years. Oozing with wonderfully ripe raspberry fruit, spicy pepper, and some floral aromas, the regular 1985 Gigondas has great concentration, exceptional length and depth, and good aging potential notwithstanding its precocious appeal. It should mature over the next 2–3 years. Both the 1985 and 1986 Cuvée Florence are the single greatest Gigondas I have tasted. The blend of primarily Grenache, Syrah, and Mourvèdre seems to have benefited immensely from a sojourn in new oak barrels. The 1985 is fragrant and complex, rich and full-bodied, and not lacking acidity and structure as many 1985s are; it is a profound effort. The 1986 is equally prodigious with an intense bouquet of toasty new oak and jammy plum fruit. More powerful and tannic than the 1985, it should keep for 10–15 years.

DOMAINE DU GOUR DE CHAULE* * * *

1985 Gigondas	B	88

This is a luscious wine, black/ruby in color, full-bodied, loaded with peppery blackberry fruit. Lush and fat, it has good ripe tannins in the finish.

CHÂTEAU DU GRAND MOULAS* * *

1985 Côtes du Rhône	A	81

1985 Côtes du Rhône-Villages	A	85

This reliable estate makes consistently good wines with a good measure of Syrah in them. The Côtes du Rhône is 75% Grenache, 25% Syrah, and is a richly fruity, spicy, peppery wine with good body and length. It should be drunk over the next 1–3 years. The Côtes du Rhône-Villages has 50% Syrah and is a much deeper, richer wine that tastes full-bodied and not unlike a mini-Hermitage. It should last 3–4 years.

DOMAINE DU GRAND TINEL* * * *

1985 Châteauneuf-du-Pape	C	90

This is a monster Châteauneuf-du-Pape with the alcohol tipping the scales at 14.7%. An intense bouquet of roasted nuts and peppery raspberry fruit is followed by a huge, concentrated wine of immense size, weight, and clout. It is not for the shy.

BERNARD GRIPA* * *

1985 St.-Joseph	B	84

This is a vibrant, juicy, fruity wine with good body, decent acidity, and a lush texture.

J. L. GRIPPAT

1985 Hermitage	C	83

1985 St.-Joseph	B	82

1985 St.-Joseph Cuvée des Hospices	C	87

The 1985 Hermitage is very soft, medium ruby in color, with a light-intensity bouquet of cherry and strawberry fruit. This wine lacks the depth and richness one normally associates with red Hermitage, but it does have finesse. The St.-Joseph is extremely soft, medium ruby colored, and has an engaging berry fruitiness, silky finish, and no astringency whatsoever. Drink it over the next 2–3 years. The 1985 Cuvée des Hospices is a marvelously fruity, fat, sumptuous St.-Joseph bursting with black-cherry and raspberry fruit. Plump and unctuous, it will provide a delicious mouthful of wine over the next 3–4 years. Unfortunately, the Cuvée des Hospices is not exported.

ÉTIENNE AND MARCEL GUIGAL* * * * *

1985 Châteauneuf-du-Pape	B	86
1984 Côte Rôtie Côte Blonde et Brune	E	85
1985 Côte Rôtie Côte Blonde et Brune	E	90
1985 Côte Rôtie La Landonne	E	100
1985 Côte Rôtie La Mouline	E	100
1985 Côte Rôtie La Turque	E	100
1983 Côtes du Rhône	B	86
1984 Côtes du Rhône	B	84
1985 Côtes du Rhône	B	86
1985 Gigondas	B	87
1985 Hermitage	C	87

Like many northern Rhônes from this vintage, the 1985 Côte Blonde et Brune is a deliciously ripe, round, precocious wine, but quite deep, concentrated, and long, with a creamy texture and smoky bouquet. The 1985 La Mouline is similar in style to the 1982. Decadently ripe, perfumed and rich with layers of sweet, smoky fruit, this hedonistic wine offers as complex and sensuous a taste of wine as money can buy. It should mature between 1989 and 2000. An extraordinary wine, even richer and longer on the palate than the La Mouline, the 1985 La Landonne has a full-intensity bouquet of smoky, plummy fruit and grilled almonds. This is an enormously concentrated wine of remarkable dimension and depth.

The 1985 La Turque is Guigal's first effort from this vineyard and has already received deity status in Western European wine circles. Only 333 cases were produced, and if one were to kill for a wine, this might be the one to do it for. It meets then exceeds all parameters for judging wine—calling it great seems somehow woefully inadequate.

It has the power and enormous concentration of La Landonne, as well as the sheer, decadent, self-indulgent pleasures of the voluptuous La Mouline. It is the quintessential Côte Rôtie. One frightening development concerning Guigal's single-vineyard wines requires comment. These wines, which should normally sell for $50–60 a bottle, are being priced at the ridiculously high level of $125–150 a bottle. This is reprehensible. Unfortunately, Guigal has no control over individual speculators who buy up all existing supplies and sell it at huge profits. Regrettably, the only way to stop this profiteering is to refuse to buy the wines, which is all rather sad given their sublime quality and the great efforts the Guigal family make to turn out such monumental Côte Rôties.

The Côtes du Rhône made by Guigal are some of the best available on the market. In the eighties he has been increasing the amount of Syrah and Mourvèdre in the blend to give the wine more personality. The 1985 and the 1983 are the type of wine that I would drink daily if I were not always tasting. Both are supple, filled with personality and fleshy fruit, aromatic, and a total joy to drink. The 1984, equally deep in color, is, however, more compact and stern, but still a success for the vintage as its peppery, fruity nose and full-bodied taste attest. Guigal, a master winemaker, gives his Côtes du Rhône as much care as his famous Côte Rôties, and the results show.

As for his 1985 Hermitage, Guigal believes it will turn out like his 1982. Quite rich, very dark in color, with an intense bouquet of peppery cassis fruit, this full-bodied wine has a good deal of tannin, but the low acidity gives it a precocious appeal. Lastly, Guigal made two other excellent southern Rhônes that should be sought out by those looking for supple, even sumptuous wines. The 1985 Châteauneuf-du-Pape is quite rich, and a worthy successor to his very fine 1983. His 1985 Gigondas is bursting with rich, peppery, raspberry fruit, is quite full-bodied, long, and chewy. Both wines are ideal for drinking over the next 5–6 years.

BERNARD GUY* * * *

1986 Côte Rôtie   D   89

A new name to follow in Côte Rôtie, Guy's 1986 is certainly one of the leading wines of the Northern Rhône in this vintage. Surprisingly rich and intense for a 1986, this broadly flavored, deeply colored wine exhibits a bouquet of new oak, shows a fat, expansive, sweet fruitiness, and finishes with a long, velvety aftertaste. It should drink well for 7–8 years.

PAUL JABOULET AINÉ* * * * *

1985 Châteauneuf-du-Pape	B	84
1985 Cornas	C	86
1985 Côte Rôtie	D	86
1985 Côtes du Rhône-Villages	A	84
1985 Crozes-Hermitage	A	84
1985 Crozes-Hermitage Thalabert	B	87
1985 Gigondas	B	83
1985 Hermitage La Chapelle	D	90?

A charming and flattering wine for young Cornas, the 1985 is marked by the low acidity of this vintage as well as by a lush, rich, black-cherry fruitiness. Full-bodied yet supple, this wine will develop quickly. The Jaboulets believe their 1985 Côte Rôtie to be the best they have made since their fine 1976. Rather low in acidity and precocious, it has heaps of lush blackberry fruit, medium to full body, and a velvety, long finish. As for the Côtes du Rhône, it is made entirely from vineyards in the Seguret area. A warm, generous, friendly wine, it is not terribly complex, but round, supple, quite fruity and tasty. Most of Jaboulet's southern Rhônes have declined in quality over recent years, but his 1985 Côtes du Rhône-Villages is attractive and interesting. For Jaboulet's straight Crozes, the 1985 is surprisingly good. Quite dark in color, exuberantly fruity, lush, medium-bodied, and extremely satisfying to both palate and purse, this wine shows what intelligent winemaking can produce. Much more voluptuous and opulent than Jaboulet's regular bottling of Crozes, the 1985 Thalabert has very dark color, full body, outstanding concentration, oodles of cassis, peppery fruit, and a velvety finish. Nearly 100% Grenache, the 1985 Gigondas from Jaboulet is a generously fruity, straightforward wine with plenty of body and alcohol. Recent tastings of Jaboulet's famous Hermitage La Chapelle suggest there is a shocking and inexcusable degree of bottle variation. The best examples are quite deep ruby/purple in color with an intense bouquet of cassis fruit and pepper, a concentrated, full-bodied, soft texture that has some charm and appeal already. Low acidity makes aging beyond 15 years a gamble, but this wine could well turn out to resemble the gorgeous 1971. Other examples have been much less deep and full-bodied and taste like a Crozes-Hermitage. Lastly, the 1985 Châteauneuf-du-Pape is better than some of the one-dimensional wines recently produced at Les Cèdres, but it is still a far cry from the great wines made here in the decade of the sixties (i.e., 1961, 1962, 1966, 1967, 1969). Medium deep ruby with a grapy, straightforward bouquet, this wine is fat, soft, quite pleasant, and full-bodied.

JOSEPH JAMET* * *

1985 Côte Rôtie	C 90

Extremely concentrated, this full-bodied wine, which is nearly black in color, shows immense potential. Unlike other 1985s, it is quite closed, but it should age extremely well.

ROBERT JASMIN* * * * *

1985 Côte Rôtie	D 92

Jasmin believes this is his best wine since his father's 1947. Already delicious to drink, broadly flavored with an intense bouquet of ripe berry fruit and floral scents, it will be hard to resist drinking up, but it should hold and develop well for 6–10 years.

MARCEL JUGE* * *

1985 Cornas Cuvée Spéciale	C 92
1985 Cornas Demi-Coteaux	C 84

The 1985 Cuvée Spéciale from Juge is certainly one of the most spectacular young wines of Cornas I have ever tasted. Only 150 cases of this black/ruby-colored, stunningly concentrated, and perfumed wine were made. It is enormous on the palate with staggering length. A totally different wine, the 1985 Demi-Coteaux is a blend of younger vines from both Juge's hillside and valley-floor vineyards. It is a pretty, medium-bodied, elegantly wrought wine with good, soft fruit.

DOMAINE DE LONGUE-TOQUE* * * *

1985 Gigondas   B   85

A heady, quite enjoyable wine, the 1985 Gigondas has good dark-ruby color, a soft, fruity, lush texture, low acidity, but good length and an obvious alcoholic kick. Drink it over the next 4–5 years.

DOMAINE DE MARCOUX* * *

1985 Châteauneuf-du-Pape   B   86

Very deeply colored, the 1985 Marcoux has a powerful, rich, jammy bouquet of cassis, fat, low acid flavors, full body and a soft, generous finish.

JEAN MARSANNE* * *

1985 St.-Joseph   C   84

This is a different and unique style of St.-Joseph. Wild-game–like, smoky, untamed-Syrah aromas predominate. On the palate, the wine is quite full-bodied, spicy, and has at least 5–8 years cellaring potential.

CHÂTEAU MAUCOIL* *

1985 Châteauneuf-du-Pape   B   84

1986 Châteauneuf-du-Pape   B   83

The 1985 Maucoil, a medium deep ruby color, has intense cherry-fruit aromas and is soft, quite alcoholic, ripe, and chewy, but not complex. The 1986 is better structured but not as flattering to taste.

DOMAINE DE MAUPERTUIS* * *

1985 Châteauneuf-du-Pape   B   86

This is a very good, rather big wine with a deep ruby color, a complex, plummy, leather-scented bouquet, tannic, full-bodied flavors, and a muscular, alcoholic finish.

ROBERT MICHEL* * *

1985 Cornas	C 82

1985 Cornas Le Geynale	C 87

The 1985 Cornas from Michel, though quite hard and closed, shows ripe, decent fruit underneath. This tough, aggressive wine seems to be so hard that I sometimes wonder about its balance. At least a decade away from maturity, the Le Geynale is deep ruby/purple in color, very dense and peppery, full-bodied, with considerable tannin.

MOILLARD* *

1985 Crozes-Hermitage	A 85

This Burgundy *négociant* has turned in a very good effort. Deep in color with a pronounced Syrah aroma, lush and rich on the palate with full body and soft tannins, it makes a very satisfying wine with full-flavored dishes.

DOMAINE DE MONT-REDON* * *

1985 Châteauneuf-du-Pape	C 87

Regarded as the best vintage for Mont-Redon since 1978, the 1985 is dense in color, very ripe, quite full-bodied, soft, and lush with a fine finish. This will provide great appeal at a young age.

CHÂTEAU MONTMIRAIL* * *

1985 Gigondas Cuvée Beauchamp	B 83

Very jammy and scented with blackberries, the 1985 is quite low in acidity and fat, with its exuberant fruitiness disguising a good level of tannin. I believe this precocious wine should be drunk over the next 5 years; the staff at Montmirail claims it will last 10–15 years.

DOMAINES MOUSSET* * *

1985 Clos du Roi Châteauneuf-du-Pape	B 82

1985 Clos St.-Michel Châteauneuf-du-Pape	B 87

1985 Fines Roches Châteauneuf-du-Pape	B 87

1985 Font du Roi Châteauneuf-du-Pape   B 85

The 1985 Clos du Roi, though chunky and fruity, is extremely low in acidity and structure. This loosely knit wine will offer enjoyable yet uncomplicated drinking for the next 3–5 years. Because of a high percentage of Syrah, the opaque color and fragrant blackberry, smoky character comes out immediately in the 1985 Clos St.-Michel. Full-bodied, opulent and unctuous, this wine lacks acidity but offers a tremendous mouthful of corpulent Châteauneuf-du-Pape. It should mature over the next 2–4 years. The 1985 Fines Roches is a densely colored, rich wine with loads of peppery, cassis-scented fruit. Quite supple, full-bodied, and low in acidity, it will drink splendidly at a young age. Deep in color, very ripe with a jammy, berrylike nose, the 1985 Font du Roi has heaps of fruit, full body, and a velvety finish.

DOMAINE DE NALYS* * *

1985 Châteauneuf-du-Pape   B 85

The red Châteauneuf-du-Pape of Nalys hit 14.5% natural alcohol in 1985. Richly fruity, ripe, and deep in color, this lush wine will offer delicious drinking for the next 4–5 years.

CHÂTEAU DE LA NERTHE* * * *

1985 Châteauneuf-du-Pape   C 86

The 1985 La Nerthe has a natural alcohol content of 14%, deep, rich, raspberry fruit, an unctuous texture, low acidity, but gobs of body. It will drink well young.

DOMAINE L'OUSTEAU FAUQUET (COMBE)* * *

1985 Gigondas   A 84

Quite fat and fruity with a very deep color, this succulent, plump wine lacks acidity but makes a delicious mouthful of wine.

DOMAINE LES PALLIÈRES* * * *

1983 Gigondas   B 90

1985 Gigondas   B 91

There is no doubt that the 1985 Les Pallières is a super wine, one of the great successes of the southern Rhône in this vintage. Black/ruby in color with an exceptionally intense fragrance of black pepper, raspberry fruit and violets, this full-bodied, powerful yet harmonious wine should provide superb drinking. One should also try the superb 1983 with its huge bouquet of plumlike fruit and Provençal herbs. Both of these wines should drink well for 7–8 years.

PÈRE CABOCHE* * *

1985 Châteauneuf-du-Pape	B	84

1985 Châteauneuf-du-Pape Elisabeth Chambellan	B	86

The 1985 regular cuvée is a typical wine of the vintage in many respects—fat, fruity, rather alcoholic, and deeply colored. It will drink well young. The 1985 Elisabeth Chambellan, more noticeably tannic than the regular cuvée, has more length, stuffing, and character.

PIGNAN* * * *

1985 Châteauneuf-du-Pape	C	87

Pignan is the "other" Châteauneuf-du-Pape of Jacques Reynaud, the eccentric but brilliant, reclusive proprietor of Château Rayas. The 1985 is a fat, full-throttle wine bursting with layers of powerfully scented and flavored black-cherry fruit. Quite rich, succulent and alcoholic, this big wine should drink beautifully over the next 7–8 years.

LA PONTIFICALE* *

1985 Châteauneuf-du-Pape	B	84

A big, intense aroma of kirsch and roasted peanuts as well as bing cherries is quite exciting. On the palate, the wine is too jammy and low in acidity to merit higher marks, but for a hefty Châteauneuf-du-Pape with a good lashing of alcohol, this wine will provide a heady experience over the next 2–3 years.

DOMAINE PRADELLE* * *

1985 Crozes-Hermitage	A	82

A plump, deeply colored, chunky specimen, the 1985 is tannic, has good concentration, quite a bit of body, and seems to need cellaring.

DOMAINE RASPAIL* * * * *

1985 Gigondas	B	90

1986 Gigondas	B	87

The 1985 looks to be the finest vintage for Raspail since the glorious 1978. Ruby/purple in color with a fabulous crushed-raspberry, peppery, even violet bouquet, this full-bodied, concentrated, rich wine has layers of flavors and a sensational finish. The natural alcohol is 14%. The 1986 is less powerful, has more tannin, but is bursting with fruit. It should drink well for 10–12 years.

CHÂTEAU RAYAS* * * * *

1985 Châteauneuf-du-Pape	D	94

1986 Châteauneuf-du-Pape	D	92

It took the 1985 almost a year to finish its malolactic fermentation. Extremely dense and rich with a black/purple color, the wine is slightly low in acidity but very powerful, extremely concentrated with heaps of seductive fruit and the old-vine intensity that gives Rayas so much character and depth of flavor. It will not be as long-lived as the 1978, 1979, or 1986, but it is a very special, hedonistic wine that makes for splendid drinking. The 1986 is the most backward and tannic Rayas since the 1978. Exceptionally concentrated, it should be cellared until 1991–1995. Châteauneuf-du-Pape does not get any better than this!

DOMAINE DES RELAGNES* * *

1985 Châteauneuf-du-Pape	B	84

The 1985 here is not unlike the 1982, very low in acidity with a fat, jammy, effusively fruity character. Quite tasty, it must be drunk young, within 5–6 years of the vintage.

RÉSERVE DES HUGUENOTS* *

1985 Châteauneuf-du-Pape	B	78

This is a beefy, alcoholic, but essentially one-dimensional wine that is mouth-filling and correct, but after one glass I found it boring.

R. ROSTAING* * * * *

1985 Côte Rôtie Côte Blonde	E	92

1985 Côte Rôtie La Landonne	E	93

Black/purple in color with a concentrated, powerful, ripe feel on the palate, the 1985 La Landonne has sensational extract, a fabulous bouquet, and a finish that goes on and on. A great wine! Rostaing's 1985 Côte Blonde is a more velvety, softer wine than the more obviously tannic La Landonne. Voluptuous on the palate with a staggering bouquet of roasted nuts and ripe, jammy fruit, this super wine offers a smorgasbord of exotic aromas and flavors. Quantities are minuscule, so Rostaing's wines are virtually unavailable.

DOMAINE ROGER SABON* * * *

1985 Châteauneuf-du-Pape	B	85

Dark in color, richly fruity with expansive berry-fruit flavors, this soft-textured wine has quite an alcoholic clout to it.

DOMAINE ST.-GAYAN* * * *

1985 Côtes du Rhône-Villages	A	85

1985 Gigondas	B	87

Roger Meffre, the likable producer of top-flight Gigondas, makes good quantities of an exuberant, full-bodied, remarkably tasty Côtes du Rhône. His 1985 has a heady fragrance of berry fruit, pepper, and herbs. On the palate, it is rich, concentrated, long, and a joy to drink now. It should last 2–3 years. The 1985 Gigondas should show very well young. Deep ruby/purple with a full-intensity, portlike bouquet of jammy, berry fruit, the 1985 is quite full-bodied, lush, and long with oodles of fruit.

DOMAINE SÉNÉCHAUX* * * *

1985 Châteauneuf-du-Pape	B	90

This looks to be one of the stars of this vintage. Very deep in color and stunningly concentrated, this blockbuster wine has 14.5% natural alcohol, makes an immense impression on the palate, yet finishes with good acidity and tannins.

DOMAINE DE LA SOLITUDE* * *

1985 Châteauneuf-du-Pape   B 83

Very soft, richly fruity, and well-colored, this wine will provide uncomplicated drinking over the next 3–5 years.

MARC SORREL* * * *

1985 Hermitage   C 85

1985 Hermitage Le Gréal   D 90

The 1985 Hermitage from Sorrel is surprisingly elegant and soft with plenty of black-cherry fruit. A medium-bodied, stylish wine, it has good color, adequate acidity, and low tannins. Significantly deeper and more aromatic than the regular cuvée, the Le Gréal has a smoky, toasty, plummy bouquet of excellent ripeness and complexity, and long, rich, intense flavors of black cherries. This full-bodied wine is loaded with fruit.

DOMAINE TERRE FERME* * *

1985 Châteauneuf-du-Pape   B 86

Well-structured for a 1985, this richly fruity, full-bodied wine has a floral, berry-scented bouquet, gobs of ripe fruit, good acidity, and a decade of evolution ahead of it.

CHÂTEAU DU TRIGNON* * *

1985 Gigondas   B 85

The enthusiastic, genteel, and kind André Roux runs the Château du Trignon, and this is his best wine to date. Sound and bursting with fruit, this rich, supple wine will be delicious to drink over the next 2–3 years.

DOMAINE JEAN TRINTIGNANT* * *

1985 Châteauneuf-du-Pape   B 84

Dense in color with a rich, intense, berry-scented bouquet, this wine borders on being too flabby and low in acidity. It is impressively deep and chewy, not particularly classic, but fun to drink.

RAYMOND TROLLAT* * *

1985 St.-Joseph   B   87

As St.-Josephs go, this is an opulent, ripe, broadly flavored, intensely fruity wine. Deep ruby in color with fruit oozing from within, this wine will provide great hedonistic enjoyment over the next 5–6 years.

UNION DES PROPRIÉTAIRES* *

1985 Crozes-Hermitage   A   84

In the last several years there has been a considerable increase in the quality of the wines from this grower's cooperative in Tain-L'Hermitage. The 1985 red Crozes-Hermitage, while not quite as excellent as the co-op's 1985 white Crozes-Hermitage, is still an attractive, fleshy, concentrated, supple mouthful of pure Syrah. It should age nicely for 3–5 years.

DE VALLOUIT* * *

1985 Côte Rôtie   C   86

1983 Hermitage Greffières   D   90

This luxury cuvée, Hermitage Greffières, from the vineyard spelled Greffieux, is the finest example of its type I have tasted from de Vallouit. Dense in color, aged in new oak barrels, this intense, powerful, concentrated wine from the 1983 vintage has just been released. Remarkably deep and long, this wine should be purchased only by those willing to wait 6–8 years for it to mature. The 1985 Côte Rôtie also shows great style, a huge, forward, well-developed, peppery bouquet, and soft, lush flavors.

CHÂTEAU VAUDIEU* * *

1985 Châteauneuf-du-Pape   B   85

This wine is deep in color, fruity, rich, soft, and full-bodied with heaps of extract, but I wonder if there is enough spine and backbone.

NOËL VERSET* * * *

1985 Cornas   C   93

1986 Cornas   C   86

A blockbuster wine, Verset's 1985 has aromas of violets, jammy blackberry fruit, licorice, and exotic spices. On the palate, it is unbelievably concentrated with layers of flavor that persist and persist. The extraordinary level of ripe fruit actually conceals a very high level of ripe tannins. The 1986 suffers in comparison, yet it is a rich, full-bodied, highly extracted wine that will offer good drinking between 1990 and 2000.

VIDAL-FLEURY* * * *

1985 Châteauneuf-du-Pape	B	85
1985 Côte Rôtie La Chatillonne	D	90
1985 Côte Rôtie Côte Blonde et Brune	D	89
1985 Côtes du Rhône	A	85
1985 Crozes-Hermitage	A	86
1985 Gigondas	B	85

The 1985 Châteauneuf is deep ruby in color; this ripe, round, concentrated, chewy, full-bodied wine has plenty of extract, a powerful finish, and heady fragrance. Not complicated, it is certainly satisfying. Drink it over the next 2–3 years. Ripe and fat with heaps of blackberry fruit, the 1985 La Chatillonne has excellent depth and richness, rather low acidity, but undeniable charm. It will develop quickly. I found the Blonde et Brune Côte Rôtie to be virtually identical in style, perhaps even more supple. The quality and price of the 1985 Côtes du Rhône and Crozes-Hermitage should have consumers buzzing. The 1985 Côtes du Rhône is deep in color, has a lovely bouquet of pepper and intensely ripe fruit, is lush and full-bodied on the palate, loaded with fruit, and finishes quite well. This is an impressive Côtes du Rhône. The excellent Crozes-Hermitage is dense in color with a big, beefy, smoky bouquet and rich, intense, full-bodied flavors. Drinkable now, it should age well for 3–4 years. Lastly, the 1985 Gigondas is deep ruby in color with a smoky, ripe, peppery, even chocolaty bouquet. This full-bodied wine has plenty of extract, a long finish, and a supple texture. Drink it over the next 2–3 years.

ALAIN VOGE* * *

1985 Cornas	C	88

A splendid 1985 Cornas, this deeply colored, full-bodied wine is loaded with exotic spices and jammy, lush fruit. However, the finish has plenty of tannin. It should mature quickly but offer sumptuous drinking for at least another 7–8 years.

LA VIEILLE FERME* * *

1986 Côtes du Rhône Réserve Gold Label	A	85

1986 Côtes du Ventoux	A	85

Jean-Pierre Perrin, the handsome co-owner of the famous Château-neuf-du-Pape estate called Beaucastel, operates this highly successful *négociant* business a few miles away. By carefully vinifying the wines himself, bottling early, and keeping the prices at bargain-basement levels, he has built La Vieille Ferme into one of the most successful brands in France. The quality is in the bottle, and the prices speak for themselves. As a general rule, the red wines are plump, aromatic, rich, and generously flavored. They tend to be better than the whites. The 1986 Côtes du Ventoux should be treated as you would a top Beaujolais Cru. Decadently fruity and vibrant, juicy and succulent, it is quite a charmer. Drink it over the next year. The 1986 Côtes du Rhône Gold Label is more muscular, fuller bodied, rich, and peppery, and extremely well made; it should last for 3–4 years. These wines are both tremendous values.

VIEUX CHÊNE* * *

1986 Côtes du Rhône des Capucines	A	85

1986 Côtes du Rhône La Haie aux Grives	A	86

This is always one of the better Côtes du Rhône wines. The two separate cuvées offer two different styles of wine. For immediate gratification, there is the Capucines, a lovely, supple, expansive wine that is round, concentrated, and totally ready to drink. For drinking now, as well as cellaring 4–5 years, the Haie aux Grives is black/ruby in color, has more Syrah in the blend, and is a bigger, much richer wine. Impressively concentrated and built, this excellent, full-bodied wine is oozing with fruit and personality.

VIEUX DONJON* * * *

1985 Châteauneuf-du-Pape	B	88

1986 Châteauneuf-du-Pape	B	88

Great color, opaque and dense, the 1985 Vieux Donjon is oozing with significant amounts of black-cherry, plummy, peppery fruit. It has an unctuous, full-bodied texture and a powerful finish. The young Michel family that runs this estate thinks it is too low in acidity to last, but for 6–8 years it should be splendid. The 1986 is rich, deep, and as complex as this property's 1985. In comparison to the 1985, this vintage exhibits more tannin and body, slightly better acidity, and greater potential for long-term cellaring.

VIEUX LAZARET* * *

1985 Châteauneuf-du-Pape	B	84

One of the better wines from this estate I have tasted, the 1985 has a vibrant ruby color, moderately intense berry-fruit aromas, a velvety texture, and some muscle in the finish.

DOMAINE DU VIEUX TÉLÉGRAPHE* * * * *

1985 Châteauneuf-du-Pape	C	89

1986 Châteauneuf-du-Pape	C	87

An explosively rich, fruity, deep wine, Vieux Télégraphe's 1985 is quite full-bodied, very alcoholic (14.5%) with a sweet, jammy, almost portlike richness and texture. It will provide hedonistic pleasure for the next 6–7 years. Note that the Cuvée imported by Kermit Lynch has more depth and color than the Cuvée imported by representatives of Cannan and Wasserman. The latter wine would score 2–3 points lower as there is an obvious difference to the wines. The 1986 is the most structured Vieux Télégraphe that has been made in the decade of the eighties. It does not have the size of the 1983, is firmer than the delicious 1985, more concentrated than the 1981 and the 1982, and perhaps is closest in style to the 1979. As usual, it is loaded with salty, peppery, mineral-scented berry fruit, is full-bodied, rich, and deep.

The Rhône Valley

White Wines

1985 Château Beaucastel Châteauneuf-du-Pape	C	90

1986 Château Beaucastel Châteauneuf-du-Pape	C	87

Fewer than 1,000 cases a year are made of the only white wine in Châteauneuf-du-Pape that can last and evolve in the bottle for 10–15 years. The aromas and flavors are reticent at first, but after 7–8 years, smoky, buttery, hazelnut aromas and tremendous tastes of fruit come out on the palate. Both the 1985 and 1986 spent a tiny amount of time in new oak barrels and went to a full malolactic fermentation to give them extra character and finesse. The 1985 is slightly fuller and deeper than the more elegant 1986, but both should prove quite long-lived.

1985 Chapoutier Hermitage Chante-Alouette	C	89

N.V. Chapoutier Hermitage Cuvée de l'Orvée	E	92

N.V. Chapoutier Hermitage Grande Cuvée	C	86

This internationally well-known Rhône wine producer seems to excel when it comes to white wines. Their white Hermitage is always a powerful, alcoholic, intense wine that can age quite well. There are three separate wines made by the Chapoutiers. The nonvintage Grande Cuvée will obviously vary depending on the blend, but at the time I tasted it, it showed wonderful ripeness and richness, smelled of honey and pineapples, and was quite tasty. Even better is the 1985 Chante-Alouette, although its depth and structure suggest it will last for another 10–12 years. The top of the line is the very rare (fewer than 400 cases were produced) Cuvée de l'Orvée, a nonvintage blend from a number of old vintages. The wine is remarkably fresh and represents what Chapoutier feels is the finest white Hermitage he can produce. Extremely rich and long, and not unlike a great white burgundy, it is simply an astonishingly rich wine with a bouquet suggestive of smoky almonds and ripe fruit. On the palate, it is enormously rich but yet impeccably balanced.

1985 J. L. Chave Hermitage	D	92

1986 J. L. Chave Hermitage	D	83

The finest grower and wine producer of red Hermitage also makes an outstanding white Hermitage. Working with a rather traditional blend of 90% Marsanne and 10% Roussanne, and fermenting and aging his white wine in wooden barrels for 14–18 months, Chave's white Hermitage, along with that of Chapoutier, has a tendency to last longer than any other wine in the appellation. The 1986 is leaner and less opulent and fat than the 1985, and it should age quite quickly. The 1985 is a blockbuster with its huge aroma of pineapples, wet stone, spring flowers, and honey. On the palate, it is extremely intense, broadly flavored, and very rich.

1986 Delas Frères Condrieu	D	90

1985 Delas Frères Hermitage Cuvée Marquise de la Tourette	C	87

The modern winery of the *négociant* and vineyard owner Delas Frères has one of the choicest vineyard sites in all of Condrieu, called Le Clos Bouché. From this 5-acre vineyard comes one of the most sensational Condrieus of the appellation. The 1986 is a match for the extraordinary 1985 made here, with an intense, overwhelming fragrance of flowers, pears, and honeysuckle. It should be drunk over the next several years. As for the white Hermitage called Cuvée Marquise de la Tourette, the 1985 is a fairly fleshy, big full-bodied wine with a bouquet of hazelnuts intertwined with the scent of apricots. It should be drunk young rather than aged.

1986 Dumazet Condrieu	D	90

With only one acre of vineyard, why go to all the trouble of reviewing a wine that is available in such microquantities? One taste of Dumazet's Condrieu is enough to make anyone fanatical for his style of wine, which oozes with scents of lychee nuts, apricots, and an intense aroma of overripe melons. The 1986 is a hedonistic wine that must be tasted to be believed.

1986 Font de Michelle Châteauneuf-du-Pape	B	84

This property tends to make floral, fresh, eminently drinkable white Châteauneuf-du-Pape that must be consumed within several years of the vintage. The 1985 was excellent but is now fading. The 1986 should be drunk over the next six months.

1986 Les Gouberts Côtes du Rhône	A	86

Jean-Pierre Cartier, who makes one of the finest Gigondas wines, also excels with his white Côtes du Rhône, a Rhône white wine that is

generally boring and innocuous. Not so here. Obviously made to be
drunk young, the wine is bursting with a floral-scented fruitiness and
is crisp and flavorful on the palate with some surprising character.
Drink it over the next near.

1985 Grippat Hermitage	C	90
1986 Grippat Hermitage	C	88
1985 Grippat St.-Joseph	B	86
1986 Grippat St.-Joseph	B	84

While this producer's white wines are hard to find, thanks to the
voracious appetite of the French for them, they are worth a special
search. His white Hermitage is not meant to age but to be drunk in
the exuberance of youth, being generally fat, sumptuous, and loaded
with flavor. His white St.-Joseph is made from the same mold, being
a flowery, peach-scented wine with quite a bit of flavor. While somewhat lacking in acidity, it drinks gorgeously when young. Both 1986s
have a bit more acidity but less concentration than the full-blown,
intense 1985s.

1987 E. Guigal Condrieu	D	92
1986 E. Guigal Côtes du Rhône	A	82
1985 E. Guigal Hermitage	C	82
1986 E. Guigal Hermitage	C	86

Guigal, the master winemaker and blender of the Rhône Valley, has
been turning out sensational Condrieu that rivals the very finest made
by the small growers. His 1987 is a decadently rich, perfumed wine of
remarkable complexity and flavor. As for his white Hermitages, I have
generally found them rather lean, high in acidity, quite backward, and
difficult to taste when young. Therefore, I have tended to underrate
them, since older examples when tasted show a great deal more richness and intensity and can certainly last for 10–12 years in the bottle.
For example, the 1979, drunk in 1988 with French wine expert Michel
Bettane, was simply superb even though I remember its being quite
closed and dull when tasted after bottling. That being said, both the
1986 and 1985 white Hermitage seem more angular and restrained,
but I suspect they will develop into better wines than the ratings

suggest. Lastly Guigal's white Côtes du Rhône is a chunky, fleshy wine that would go well with grilled or smoked fish.

1985 Domaine de Nalys Châteauneuf-du-Pape   B   87

1986 Domaine de Nalys Châteauneuf-du-Pape   B   88

The white Châteauneuf-du-Pape of the Domaine de Nalys is certainly one of the finest made. While made in the modern style, it is intensely fruity and perfumed and while extremely drinkable young, seems to last 3–4 years in the bottle, which is significantly longer than virtually all of the modern-style white Châteauneuf-du-Papes. The 1986 is a powerful, rich, full-bodied wine, yet it retains its freshness and life. The 1985 is still not showing signs of fatigue, but I would rush to drink this splendidly fruity and fragrant wine with its intense aromas of tropical fruit and wet stones.

1986 Paul Perret Condrieu   D   88

Until the 1986, I was never moved by the quality of Perret's Condrieu. However, his 1986 is an excellent example of this rare wine made from the fickle Viognier grape. Its creamy texture and concentrated, flowery flavors and aroma give it undeniable crowd appeal.

1986 Jean Pinchon Condrieu   D   85

Pinchon is one of the last to bottle his Condrieu, and not surprisingly, it tends to be one of the slowest to develop and longest-lived of the wines from this appellation. The 1986 has a good, firm, acidic backbone, medium to full body, and relatively intense, flowery, and peach-like scents and aromas.

1986 Château du Rozay Condrieu   D   86

These wines from one of the most famous of the Condrieu producers, tend to be opulent and unctuous in texture. The 1986 is slightly less intense than some prior vintages, but it shows the telltale flowery, lychee-nut–scented fruit of very ripe Viognier grapes.

1986 St.-Estève Viognier   B   80

1987 St.-Estève Viognier   B   83

St.-Estève is another of the better Côtes du Rhône estates experimenting with the Viognier grape, and while the vineyard is very young, the wines are beginning to show an authentic honeysuckle, tropical fruit, exotic bouquet that Viognier provide. On the palate, both the

1987 and the 1986 lack the richness that will no doubt come as the vineyard gets older. Drink both over the next 18 months.

1986 Domaine Ste.-Anne Viognier	B	86

This splendid Côtes du Rhône estate has been experimenting with the Viognier grape for some time, and the wines, at one-third the price of most Condrieus, are not far from the Condrieus' quality level. The 1986 is a wonderfully aromatic, complex wine with a great deal of fruit and the luscious texture that makes a wine produced from the Viognier grape so rare and special. It should be drunk over the next 2–3 years.

1986 Georges Vernay Condrieu	C	84

1986 Georges Vernay Condrieu Coteaux de Vernon	D	88

Vernay is the dominant producer of Condrieu, making more of it than anybody else, but the quality is usually impeccably high. He produces two Condrieus for export. The regular bottling in 1986 is leaner and higher in acid than usual, and while lacking the great richness and fabulous fruit of the 1985, it is still an enjoyable wine. His special bottling, from a tiny vineyard across from Condrieu's most famous restaurant and hotel, Beau Rivage, is called the Coteaux de Vernon and can be the very best wine made in Condrieu in vintages such as 1983, 1984, and 1985. The 1986 is slightly less opulent and extraordinary, but all in all it offers a sumptuous mouthful of Viognier fruit in a medium- to full-bodied format. It should be drunk over the next 2–3 years.

1986 Vieux Télégraphe Châteauneuf-du-Pape	B	82

1987 Vieux Télégraphe Châteauneuf-du-Pape	B	82

The white wine made by Vieux Télégraphe is only available in limited quantities of under 1,000 cases, but it is one of the two or three best white wines of the appellation. Therefore, I am a bit disappointed in the rather lightish, diluted 1987, but that has more to do with the difficulties of the vintage in the southern Rhône. The 1986, while just beginning to fade, still offers quite a mouthful of very perfumed and tasty fruit. This is a wine to be drunk in the first 2–3 years of its life.

BERGERAC AND THE SOUTHWEST

The Basics

TYPES OF WINE

This remote corner of France, while close to Bordeaux, remains unexplored territory when it comes to wine. Some appellations have recognizable names, such as Madiran, Bergerac, Cahors, and Monbazillac, but how many consumers can name one good producer from the Côtes du Frontonnais, Gaillac, Pacherenc du Vic Bilh, Côtes de Duras, or Pécharmant. The best wines are serious, broodingly deep red wines from Madiran, Pécharmant, and Cahors; lighter, effusively fruity reds from Bergerac and the Côtes du Frontonnais; and some fine sweet white wines from Monbazillac and Jurançon.

GRAPE VARIETIES

In addition to the well-known varieties such as Cabernet Sauvignon, Merlot, and Syrah, this vast area is the home to a number of grape varieties that are little known and mysterious to the average consumer. In Madiran, there is the Tannat; in the Côtes du Frontonnais, the Mauzac and Negrette. For the white wines of Pacherenc du Vic Bilh and Jurançon, rare varieties such as the Gros Manseng, Petit Manseng, Courbu, and Arrufiac are planted.

FLAVORS

The red wines of Bergerac are light and fruity; those of Madiran and Cahors, dense, dark, rich, and often quite tannic. The red wines from the Côtes de Buzet, Côtes de Duras, and Côtes du Frontonnais, often vinified by the carbonic maceration method, are light, soft, and fruity. The best dry white wines are crisp, light, and zesty. Some surprisingly rich, sweet wines that resemble a fine Sauternes can emerge from Monbazillac and Jurançon.

AGING POTENTIAL

Except for the top red wines of Madiran, Pécharmant, and Cahors, all of the wines from France's southwest corner must be drunk within 5 years.

Bergerac: 2–5 years   Jurançon: 3–8 years
Cahors: 4–12 years   Madiran: 4–12 years
Côtes de Buzet: 1–5 years Monbazillac: 3–8 years
Côtes de Duras: 1–4 years Pécharmant: 3–10 years

OVERALL QUALITY

The overall quality is extremely irregular. Improvements have been made, but most wines are sold for very low prices, so many producers have little incentive to increase their quality. For the top estates listed below, the quality is good to excellent.

MOST IMPORTANT INFORMATION TO KNOW

Learn the top two or three estates for each of the better-known appellations and their styles of wine.

1989–1990 BUYING STRATEGY

These wines are for the shrewd and adventurous consumer who wants to experience different aromas and flavors at a very low price. Stick to only recent vintages, such as 1985 and 1986, although in the case of Madiran and Cahors, one should look for the 1982s and 1983s that may be languishing on retailers' shelves at very low prices.

A GUIDE TO THE SOUTHWEST'S BEST PRODUCERS

Dry Red Wine

* * * * (EXCELLENT PRODUCERS)

Château d'Aydie-Laplace (Madiran)
Domaine Bouscassé (Madiran)
Château Champerel (Pécharmant)

Clos de Gamot (Cahors)
Clos de Triguedina Prince Phobus (Cahors)
Château Montus (Madiran)
Domaine Pichard (Madiran)

* * * *(GOOD PRODUCERS)*

Domaine de Barrejat (Madiran)
Château de Belingrad (Bergerac)
Château de Cayrou (Cahors)
Château de Chambert (Cahors)
Clos de Triguedina (Cahors)
Château Court-les-Mûts
(Bergerac)
Domaine Jean Cros (Gaillac)
Domaine de Durand (Côtes de
Duras)
Domaine du Haut Pécharmant
(Pécharmant)
Domaine de Haute Serre
(Cahors)

Château de la Jaubertie
(Bergerac)
Château Michel de Montague
(Bergerac)
Château de Padére (Buzet)
Château de Panisseau
(Bergerac)
Château du Perron (Madiran)
Château de Peyros (Cahors)
Château St.-Didier Parnac
(Cahors)
Château de Tiregand
(Pécharmant)

Sweet White Wines

* * * *(GOOD PRODUCERS)*

Clos Uroulat (Jurançon)
Cru Lamouroux (Jurançon)
Château Le Fage (Monbazillac)

Château de Treuil-de-Nailhac
(Monbazillac)

2. ITALY

PIEDMONT

The Basics

TYPES OF WINE

The glories of Piedmont (aside from the scenery and white truffles) are the robust, rich, multidimensional red wines made from the Nebbiolo grape. The top wines made from the Nebbiolo—Barbaresco, Barolo, Gattinara, and Spanna—are at their best between 6 and 15 years of age, but they can last up to 25 years. At the opposite extreme are the wines called Dolcetto d'Alba, which are wonderfully supple, rich, and fruity but are meant to be drunk within their first 4–5 years of life. There are also Barbera, often too acidic for New World palates, but some can be splendid and cheap, a rare combination. Lastly, there is Cabernet Sauvignon, and a host of insipid, usually inferior red wines that are less likely to be seen in the international marketplace, namely Freisa, Grignolino, and Brachett. Piedmont's white wine production is growing, and while most of the wines are overpriced and bland, good potential is being shown by the indigenous Arneis grape and Cortese di Gavi. Chardonnay is making its ubiquitous presence felt; Erbaluce di Caluso is underrated; and Moscato, the low alcohol, fizzy, slightly sweet wine, is perhaps Piedmont's best value in white wine. Lastly, there is the ocean of sweet, industrially produced Asti Spumante.

GRAPE VARIETIES

Nebbiolo, Barbera, and Dolcetto are the top red wine grapes in Piedmont, producing the finest wines. For white wines, the Muscat, Arneis, Cortese di Gavi, and Erbaluce di Caluso are the most successful. Of course there are many other grapes, but the wines made from these varietals are generally of little interest.

FLAVORS

RED WINES

Barolo—Barolo is one of the world's most stern, tannic, austere yet full-flavored wines. The aromas of road tar, leather, bing cherries, tobacco, and dried herbs dominate. It is a massive wine to drink.

Barbaresco—Often better balanced than Barolo (less tannin, more fruit), with the same aromas and flavors, Barbaresco often has more intense jammy fruit, and sometimes more cedar and chocolate; it can be sublime.

Dolcetto—Purple in color and not sweet as the name implies, this dry, exuberant, effusively fruity and grapy wine tastes of blackberries, almonds, chocolate, and spices, being very soft and supple.

Barbera—Frequently too acidic, woody, and oxidized, the new-style Barberas, often aged in 100% new French oak, are showing greater fruit and richness to balance out the naturally high acidity.

Gattinara/Spanna—These wines come from Nebbiolo grown in the hills north of Barolo and Barbaresco. Intense tar and earthy aromas dominate, and the bouquet has a pronounced Oriental spice-box character. The wines tend to be softer and fruitier than Barolo, but no less age-worthy.

Carema—The lightest of the Nebbiolo-based wines, Carema, made in a marginally mountainous climate near Valle d'Aosta, can be quite smooth, fruity, and elegant, but adequate ripeness is often a problem.

WHITE WINES

Arneis—The ancient wine of Piedmont, Arneis is a rich, gloriously fruity, mouth-filling wine that is soft, even unctuous. This may seem to imply a certain heaviness, but the best examples are light and a joy to drink.

Gavi or Cortese di Gavi—Often outrageously overpriced and frightfully bland, this supposedly prestigious wine is acidic and has a lemony, flinty, stony character, and in the best examples, full body.

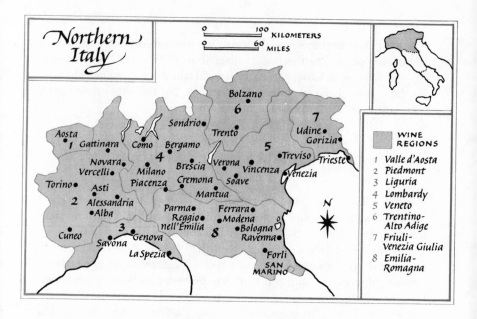

Northern Italy

0 — 100 KILOMETERS
0 — 60 MILES

Bolzano
6
Sondrio
Trento
Aosta
1 Gattinara
Como Bergamo
Udine
Gorizia
7
5
Treviso
Trieste
Novara
Vercelli
Brescia
Verona
Vincenza
Torino
Milano
Cremona
Soave
Venezia
Asti
Piacenza
Mantua
Alessandria
Alba
Parma
Ferrara
Reggio
nell'Emilia
Modena
8
Bologna
Cuneo
3
Genova
Ravenna
Savona
La Spezia
Forlì
SAN
MARINO

N

WINE REGIONS

1 Valle d'Aosta
2 Piedmont
3 Liguria
4 Lombardy
5 Veneto
6 Trentino-Alto Adige
7 Friuli-Venezia Giulia
8 Emilia-Romagna

Southern Italy

San Severo
Manfredonia
Benevento
Foggia
Bari
Napoli
2
Salerno
Rionero
Matera
Ostuni
Brindisi
1
Potenza
Metaponto
Taranto
3
Gallipoli
Cetraro
Paola
Cosenza
Ciro
4
Catanzaro
Caraffa

TYRRHENIAN SEA

WINE REGIONS

1 Campania
2 Puglia
3 Basilicata
4 Calabria
5 Sicily

Palermo
Messina
Reggio di Calabria
Trapani
Marsala
Taormina
5
Catania
Agrigento
Siracusa
Ragusa

N
W E
S

0 — 60 MILES
0 — 100 KILOMETERS

Central Italy

MILES
0   60

0   50   100
KILOMETERS

ADRIATIC SEA

LIGURIAN SEA

•Lucca
•Pisa   •Firenze
•Livorno   Arrezo•
Siena•
8   •Pesaro
•Ancona
•Macerata

1
3   2
Perugia
•Spoleto
Terni•   Ascoli Piceno
•Grosseto

CORSICA

Viterbo•
L'Aquila   •Pescara
•Chieti

5   4
Roma•
Isernia
6
•Latina

TYRRHENIAN SEA

Olbia•
•Sassari
•Alghero
Nuoro   •
•Bosa   7
Tortoli•
•Oristano

Cagliari•

N
W   E
S

WINE REGIONS

1 Tuscany   5 Lazio
2 Marche   6 Molise
3 Umbria   7 Sardinia
4 Abruzzo   8 San Marino

Moscato d'Alba—One of the world's most seductive wines to smell and drink, Moscato d'Alba, when well made and drunk within 18 months of the vintage, is a gorgeously fragrant, apricot- and floral-scented, slightly sweet, crisp, vibrant wine that is ideal as an aperitif. It should not be confused with the cloyingly sweet Asti Spumanti.

AGING POTENTIAL

Barbera: 3–10 years   Arneis: 2–3 years
Barbaresco: 8–25 years   Gavi: 2–4 years
Barolo: 8–25 years   Moscato: 12–18 months
Carema: 6–12 years
Dolcetto: 3–5 years
Gattinara/Spanna: 8–20 years

OVERALL QUALITY LEVEL

The best Piedmont wines are impeccably made, brilliant wines. Producers such as Bruno Giacosa, Angelo Gaja, the Ceretto brothers, and the late Renato Ratti, to name just a few, are winemakers as great as you will find anywhere. But despite the number of great Barolos, Barbarescos, etc., a lot of wine made in Piedmont is technically defective and has a terrible taste. Much of this results from the number of inferior grapes still being made into wine, as well as the primitive winemaking methods of some growers. In short, Piedmont offers the best and the worst in wine quality; you must know the producer in order to shop with confidence.

MOST IMPORTANT INFORMATION TO KNOW

Learning the top producers for each type of Piedmont wine is extremely important. However, in the last decade more and more of the best producers have begun to make single-vineyard wines, so a knowledge of the finest vineyards is also very helpful. Below is a list of forty-two of the major vineyards that consistently stand out in my tastings, and the producer(s) making the best wine from these locations.

Vineyard	Wine	Best Producer
Arborina	Barolo	Elio Altare
Arionda or Vigna Rionda	Barolo	Bruno Giacosa
Asili	Barbaresco	Bruno Ceretto, Produttori di Barbaresco
Basarin	Barbaresco	Castello di Neive

Bernadotti	Barbaresco	Giuseppe Mascarello
Briacca	Barolo	Vietti
Bricco Colonello	Barolo	Aldo Conterno
Bricco Rocche	Barolo	Bruno Ceretto
Brunate	Barolo	Giuseppe Rinaldi, Cogno-Marcarini
Bussia	Barolo	Bruno Giacosa, Clerico, Fenocchio
Camp Gros	Barbaresco	Marchese di Gresy
Cannubi	Barolo	L. Sandrone
Conca	Barolo	Renato Ratti
Costa Russi	Barbaresco	Gaja
Enrico VI	Barolo	Cordero di Montezemolo
Gaiun	Barbaresco	Marchese di Gresy
Gallina	Barbaresco	Bruno Giacosa
Ginestra	Barolo	Clerico, Prunotto
La Serra	Barolo	Cogno-Marcarini
Lazzarito	Barolo	Fontanafredda
Marcenasco	Barolo	Renato Ratti
Martinenga	Barbaresco	Marchese di Gresy
Moccagatta	Barbaresco	Produttori di Barbaresco
Monfalletto	Barolo	Cordero di Montezemolo
Monprivato	Barolo	Giuseppe Mascarello
Montefico	Barbaresco	Produttori di Barbaresco
Montestefano	Barbaresco	Produttori di Barbaresco
Ovello	Barbaresco	Produttori di Barbaresco
Pian della Polvere	Barolo	R. Fenocchio
Pora	Barbaresco	Produttori di Barbaresco
Prapo	Barolo	Bruno Ceretto
Rabaja	Barbaresco	Produttori di Barbaresco
Rio Sordo	Barbaresco	Brovia, Produttori di Barbaresco
Rionda (same as Arionda)	Barolo	Bruno Giacosa

Rocche di Castiglione Falletto	Barolo	Bruno Giacosa, Vietti
Santo Stefano	Barbaresco	Bruno Giacosa, Castello di Neive
Serra Boella	Barbaresco	Cigliuti
Sori d'Paytin	Barbaresco	Pasquero-Secondo
Sori San Lorenzo	Barbaresco	Gaja
Sori Tilden	Barbaresco	Gaja
Villero	Barolo	Giuseppe Mascarello, Bruno Giacosa
Zonchetta	Barolo	Bruno Ceretto

1989–1990 BUYING STRATEGY

There have been three great vintages for the red wines of Piedmont in the eighties, 1982, 1985, and most recently, 1988. Other recent vintages pale in comparison, and these three years should be the subject of any buying frenzy. Avoid 1981, 1983 (grossly overrated by the wine press), and 1984. Buy Dolcetto only from 1985, 1986, and 1988, and Piedmont's white wines only from 1987 and 1988; they do not keep well. Older vintages of Barolo, Barbaresco, Gattinara, and Spanna to look for include 1980 (underrated), 1979 (delicious now), and 1978 and 1971 (both long-term, great vintages).

PIEDMONT
VINTAGE GUIDE

1987—Pessimism was the word of the day during the growing season of 1987, but the wines have turned out surprisingly well, and comparisons with the underrated vintage of 1980 are not invalid. The wines are lighter than usual but do show excellent fruit, ripeness, and a forward, charming personality. The whites have turned out fruity and pleasant. This will be a good commercial vintage to drink early on.

1986—A good year—no better and no worse, despite some perennial Italian wine cheerleaders who are calling 1986 another great year. The red wines, well colored and well balanced, have good depth and tannin to shed. They lack drama and boldness, but this is a good, useful vintage as the quantity of wine produced was quite high.

1985—Gaja, Ceretto, and their peers call this one of the greatest vintages of the century. I believe they said the same thing about 1982, 1978, and 1971. Nevertheless, broker Neil Empson claims it is better than either 1982 or 1978, which is difficult to imagine given the superlative quality of those years. However, one taste of these wines reveals a flamboyant, rich, intense, velvety fruitiness not unlike the opulence of 1982. These rich, lush, sensational wines will drink well over the next 10 years.

1984—Maligned by the press corps (as was the case with this vintage throughout Europe), this is an average to below-average vintage, light and forward, but deficient in fruit.

1983—A vintage of rather tannic, stern wines, the 1983s may turn out to be similar to the unyielding 1974s. Most of the wines have a hollow, eviserated taste and lack fruit.

1982—A great vintage. The wines are loaded with ripe, rich fruit, have plenty of tannins, full body, and a real alcoholic punch. They are tasting surprisingly forward, but given the fact that most great vintages of Barolo and Barbaresco need 10–15 years of bottle age to mature, this might be a rare opportunity to enjoy a rich, dense, ripe, full, and fruity Barolo or Barbaresco before the age of 10. Despite the accessible nature of this vintage, the top wines should keep 25 or more years. A year to buy.

1981—Rain during September ruined what could have been a good year. Many of the best growers declassified their entire crop. My initial tastings have turned up fruity, rather compact, short, rather plain wines.

1980—Somewhat of a sleeper vintage, the 1980s are medium-bodied, rather light wines, but the good growers have produced wines with plenty of fruit, soft tannins, and charm. Drink this vintage over the next 4–5 years. If priced right, 1980 is worth considering.

1979—One of the best vintages for current drinking. Elegant, ripe, fruity wines were produced. They may lack the muscle, power, and great concentration of a vintage such as 1978 or 1982, but they offer plenty of finesse and complexity. Not to be overlooked.

1978—This is a great vintage of long-lived wines, huge in structure, tannic and concentrated. The best of them are still a good 10 years from maturity. The crop was small, the style of the wines aggressive, rich, and tough. Developing slowly, they have caused impatient critics to downgrade them. The 1982s show more ripe, intense fruit than the 1978s did at a similar stage, but this is a great vintage that just needs more time.

1977—A horrendous year of rain and cold weather. Most good growers declassified their entire crops.

1976—Another bad year. The wines lacked ripeness, had excessive tannins, and are now drying out.

1975—The first of a trio of consecutive poor vintages, the 1975s I have tasted have had aromas of tea, light-intensity flavors, and shallow personalities.

1974—This highly praised vintage I find overrated; the wines are too hard and tannic, lacking ripeness and richness. Perhaps time will prove me wrong, but most of the Piedmont wines from 1974 lack length, grace, and charm.

1973—Relatively easy-to-drink, soft, pleasant, light wines were produced in 1973. All should have been drunk by now.

1972—As in most of Europe's viticultural regions, rain was the ruination of this vintage.

1971—Until the advent of the remarkably promising 1982s, the 1971s had been what I consider a classic Piedmont vintage. Rich, perfumed, and deeply concentrated, these wines are now entering their plateau of maturity, which should easily last for another 10–15 years. A great vintage.

Older Vintages

The 1970s are very good, eclipsed in stature by the admittedly greater 1971s; the 1969s are average and best drunk up. The 1968s are disastrous; the 1967s very good, but now beginning to slip; the 1966s and 1965s below average to poor; and the 1964s another great vintage. Well-stored bottles of 1964 Piedmontese wines are gloriously rich and scented.

A GUIDE TO PIEDMONT'S BEST PRODUCERS

* * * * * (OUTSTANDING PRODUCERS)

Elio Altare (Barolo/Barbaresco)
Bruno Ceretto (Barolo/
    Barbaresco)
Clerico (Barolo)

Aldo Conterno (Barolo/Dolcetto)
Angelo Gaja (Barbaresco)
Bruno Giacosa (Barolo/
    Barbaresco/Arneis)
Renato Ratti (Barolo/Dolcetto)

* * * * (EXCELLENT PRODUCERS)

Castello di Neive (Barbaresco)
Cigliuti (Barbaresco)
Cogno-Marcarini (Barolo)
Damonte (Barbera)
Giacomo Conterno (Barolo)

R. Fenocchio (Barbaresco)
Fontanafredda (Barolo)
Marchesi di Gresy (Barbaresco)
G. Mascarello (Barolo)
Pio Cesare (Barolo/Barbaresco)

Produttori di Barbaresco
  (Barbaresco)
Francesco Rinaldi (Barolo)
L. Sandrone (Barolo)

Valentino (Barolo/Dolcetto)
Vallana (Spanna/Gattinara)
Vietti (Barolo/Dolcetto)

* * * (GOOD PRODUCERS)

Mario Antoniolo (Gattinara)
Associati di Rodello (Dolcetto)
Azelia (Barolo)
Brovia (Barolo/Barbaresco)
Carretta (Barolo)
Cerequio (Barolo)
Dessilani (Gattinara, Spanna,
  Ghemme)
Dosio (Barolo)
Luigi Einaudi (Barolo)

Giovannini Moresco
  (Barbaresco)
Pasquero-Secondo (Barbaresco)
Pelissero (Barbaresco)
Prunotto (Barolo)
Ravizza (Gattinara)
Giuseppi Rinaldi (Barolo)
Roagna (Barbaresco)
Scarpa (Barolo)
G. D. Vajra (Barola/Barbara)

* * (AVERAGE PRODUCERS)

Borgogno (Barolo)
Agostino Brugo (Gattinara)
Damilano (Barolo)
Deforville (Barbaresco)
Franco-Fiorina (Barolo)

Elli Giacosa (Barolo)
Granduca (Barolo)
Spinona (Barbaresco)
Travaglini (Gattinara)
G. Voerzio (Barolo)

* (OTHER PRODUCERS)

G. Accomasso (Barolo)
Guido Barra (Gattinara)
Bersano (Barolo)
L. Caldi (Barolo)

B. Colle (Barbaresco)
Kiola (Barolo)
Marchesi di Barolo (Barolo)
Oddero (Barolo)
A. Scavino (Barolo)

Piedmont's Best Red Wines

ELIO ALTARE (BAROLO/BARBARESCO)* * * * *

1982 Barolo Vigna Arborina	C	88
1984 Barolo Vigna Arborina	C	70

1985 Barolo Vigna Arborina		C	92

1985 Vigna Arborina	100% Nebbiolo	C	94

1985 Vigna Larigi	100% Barbera	C	90

Altare's magnificent 1985 Vigna Arborina, available only in tiny quantities, is one of the finest examples of a small-oak–aged, 100% Nebbiolo wine that I have tried. Fabulously concentrated with intense flavors of ripe cherries, this full-bodied, impeccable wine has 10–12 years of aging potential, yet an explosive fruitiness and suppleness give it appeal today. The Vigna Larigi, a small-cask–aged, 100% Barbera, is simply sensational and the finest Barbera (a wine I usually find terribly acidic) I have ever drunk. From the ruby/purple color to the staggering levels of plummy fruit, it is a great wine that should be drunk over the next 3–5 years.

The 1982 Barolo has a big, intense bouquet of dried flowers, roses, leather, and cherries. Full-bodied, rich in fruit, but not astringent, this big, deep, impressive wine can be drunk now or over the next 10 years. As for the 1985 Barolo Vigna Arborina, it is a sensational wine with a velvety quality that is one of the hallmarks of this great vintage for the Nebbiolo grape in Piedmont. Though surprisingly approachable now, it promises to live for 10–15 years—absolutely sensational. The 1984 Barolo Vigna Arborina, however, I cannot recommend, because the vintage has resulted in a skinny, meagerly endowed wine dominated by hard tannins.

ASSOCIATI DI RODELLO (DOLCETTO)* * *

1985 Dolcetto d'Alba		B	83

1986 Dolcetto d'Alba		B	80

These are two pleasant Dolcettos. The 1985 shows much more soft, plump, pleasant fruit, whereas the 1986 is quite agreeable but much leaner and less sexy.

AZELIA (BAROLO)* * *

1980 Barolo Bricco Punta		C	83

1982 Barolo Bricco Punta		C	89

1983 Barolo Bricco Punta   C   62

Deep ruby garnet in color, the 1982 Barolo Bricco Punta is a huge
wine with a full-intensity bouquet of spicy, chocolaty, smoky fruit, a
rich, beefy, large-scaled framework, outstanding concentration, and
enough tannins to warrant cellaring for another decade, although it is
not without accessible fruit today. While the 1982 is an exciting wine,
the 1983 is musty, thin, and hard with unbelievably high acidity, making it unpleasant. Lastly, the 1980, a fully mature Barolo, is lighter
than a Barolo from a top vintage, but it is plummy, easy to drink,
round and soft.

BROVIA (BAROLO/BARBARESCO)* * *

1982 Barbaresco Rio Sordo   B   89

1983 Barbaresco Rio Sordo   B   84

1982 Barolo Rocche   B   88

1983 Barolo Rocche   B   78

The 1982 wines were the most impressive I have tasted from Brovia.
Both the 1982s, with at least 10–15 years of life left, are clearly products of the old school of winemaking in Piedmont. The 1982 Barbaresco from the Rio Sordo vineyard is an extremely rich, full-bodied
wine with a great deal of cherry and saddle-leather aromas and flavors.
Quite full-bodied and drinkable now, it will no doubt be better in 5–6
years when the tannins have softened. The Barolo Rocche is fairly
impenetrable, but the huge fruit comes through on the palate to balance out the hard tannins. An immense wine, it should not be fully
mature until 1992–1995. The 1982s from Brovia are extremely well
made wines, but be sure your bloodline is long. As for the 1983s, they
show the meager concentration of fruit that plagues so many wines of
this vintage. Neither wine merits interest from consumers.

LUIGI CALDI (BAROLO)*

1985 Barbera d'Alba   A   50

1982 Gattinara   B   55

Both of these are appallingly bad wines. The Barbera is caustic, abrasive, and simply horrible, and the Gattinara is flawed by excessive volatile acidity.

CARRETTA (BAROLO)* * *

1982 Barolo Podere Cannubi	C	87
1983 Barolo Podere Cannubi	C	69
1982 Nebbiolo d'Alba Bric Paradiso	B	87
1982 Nebbiolo d'Alba Bric Tavoleto	B	85

This producer's wines are usually consistently good, though made in such a dense, tannic, slow-to-age style that prospective buyers should be prepared to cellar Carretta's wines for 10–12 years. His two 1982 Nebbiolo d'Albas are among the best I have tasted. Both wines should age well for 10–15 more years, rather amazing for Nebbiolo. The rich, backward Bric Paradiso is filled with fruit, extremely powerful and tannic; I liked it as much as the huge, massive, cherry-flavored and leather-scented 1982 Barolo Podere Cannubi, which needs another decade of cellaring. The Bric Tavoleto single-vineyard Nebbiolo d'Alba is the most accessible of these old-style, impressive wines. All these wines do indeed require some patience. Carretta's 1983 Barolo from the Podere Cannubi is another example of wines produced from this vintage—a thin, harsh, hard style of wine that fades quickly on the palate.

CASTELLO DI NEIVE (BARBARESCO)* * * *

1982 Barbaresco Santo Stefano	C	88
1985 Barbaresco Santo Stefano	C	88
1986 Dolcetto d'Alba Basarin	B	85
1985 Dolcetto d'Alba Messoirano	B	85

Castello di Neive is a consistently fine producer of Piedmont wines, particularly Barbaresco and Dolcetto. The 1986 Dolcetto Basarin is a big, beefy, rich wine with a soft underbelly and deep color. The 1985 Dolcetto Messoirano is ripe, has more fat and flesh, and is quite lush and tasty. The flagship wine of this winery is their Barbaresco from the famous Santo Stefano vineyard. The 1982, quite evolved and very fragrant, is a big, rich, velvety wine loaded with spicy, cedary, ripe, plummy fruit. Quite full-bodied and voluptuous for a 7-year-old Barbaresco, it finishes very long. As for the 1985, it is just as rich as the 1982, very velvety and forward, and will keep for at least a decade. Both wines are wonderfully supple, forward, delicious Barbarescos.

CEREQUIO (BAROLO)* * *

1978 Barolo	C	89
1979 Barolo	C	87
1980 Barolo	B	70
1982 Barolo	B	73

The two top Barolos from Cerequio on the market are the 1979 and 1978. Both have an aged, rich maturity with considerable flavor depth and complexity. The 1979 smells of coffee and leather, is full bodied, fleshy, supple, and quite delicious. The 1978 is even richer, with the fruit tasting ripe and sweeter, and the overall impression on the palate is one of a creamy, melted ripeness that lingers and lingers. These are two impressive wines. The 1982, however, was a disappointing wine given the excellence of the vintage. The 1980 is also meagerly endowed, light and disappointing on the palate.

BRUNO CERETTO (BAROLO/BARBARESCO)* * * * *

1985 Barbaresco Asij	D	90
1985 Barbaresco Bricco Asili	D	91
1985 Barolo Bricco Rocche Prapo	D	90
1985 Barolo Zonchetta	D	88
1986 Dolcetto Rossana	B	84

Since 1979, Ceretto's wines have gone from one strength to another. The current Ceretto releases include the superb 1985s, which rival his outstanding 1982s. Ceretto achieves a fragrance and perfume in his wines, plus a wonderful drinkability at an early age, that has caused his critics to say his wines won't last. Only time will tell, but there is no doubt that of all the Piedmontese wines only Ceretto and Ratti offer so much up-front, seductive, luscious berry fruit.

For example, the 1986 Dolcetto Rossana is a wonderfully elegant, scented wine with plenty of tasty fruit and a soft texture. Though not as good as the 1985, it is delicious. The 1985 Barbaresco Asij compares with the monumental 1982. Extremely rich, with tons of berry fruit, spicy oak, and scents of fresh leather, it should be drunk over the next 8–10 years. The 1985 Barbaresco Bricco Asili is an astonishingly rich, very aromatic wine with immense expansion on the palate, great length, and awesome concentration. It should drink well for another 7–8 years.

As for Ceretto's Barolos, the 1985 Barolo Bricco Rocche Prapo is large-framed, spicy, backward wine that has outstanding potential, significant depth, and should last at least a decade. Lastly, the 1985 Barolo Zonchetta, though more closed, has impressive structure, great length, and the huge, tarry, bing-cherry–scented, leathery aromatic complexity that Barolo can provide. Ceretto's wines, among the most elegant and seductive made in Piedmont, are, in spite of their rather high prices, well worth seeking out.

CIGLIUTI (BARBARESCO)* * * *

1983 Barbaresco Seraboella	C	85
1985 Barbaresco Seraboella	C	90

The 1983 Barolos and Barbarescos are in large measure thin and terribly disappointing, but this 1983 is supple and quite tasty. It should be drunk over the next 1–2 years. The 1985 is a gorgeously seductive, deep, velvety Barbaresco that is already showing a creamy texture of ripe, concentrated fruit.

CLERICO (BAROLO)* * * * *

1985 Arté	C	89
1986 Arté	C	90
1985 Barbera d'Alba	B	85
1983 Barolo Bussia	C	75
1985 Barolo Bussia	C	91

1983 Barolo Ginestra	C	80

1984 Barolo Ginestra	C	81

1985 Barolo Ginestra	C	92

Clerico is an emerging star of Piedmont who first came to my attention with his good 1980 Barolo. He followed that wine with two superb Barolos in 1982, and his 1985 Bussia and Ginestra Barolos look to be absolutely stunningly great Barolos, even more explosively rich than his 1982s. He is also making a 100% Nebbiolo that is fermented in new French oak called Arté. The 1985 was excellent, and the 1986 looks to be even better, with a complex, toasty, rich bouquet, great color, outstanding depth, length, and balance. This stunning wine should keep for up to a decade. In addition, the 1985 Barbera d'Alba smells of peanuts and ripe fruit, with good acids and a robust, fleshy flavor. It would go well with tomato-based pasta dishes. As for Clerico's 1984s and 1983s, they reflect the weaknesses of these two vintages, lacking fruit and being overly tannic and less fleshy and rich than his wines in top vintages.

COGNO-MARCARINI (BAROLO)* * *

1982 Barolo Brunate	C	86

1982 Barolo La Serra	C	85

1986 Dolcetto d'Alba	B	50

This producer is quite highly regarded, but I find his wines inconsistent. I wonder if my samples have been poorly transported or stored or if they are typical. His highly rated 1971s were over the hill by the end of that decade, and his 1978s were a disappointment as well, making me wonder what all the acclaim is about. Of the current releases, the Dolcetto, with a spritzy, green, unstable character, is totally repugnant on the palate. As for the 1982 single-vineyard Barolos, they are velvety, soft, and fruity, but lack the depth of wines from other top producers in this vintage.

ALDO CONTERNO (BAROLO/DOLCETTO)* * * * *

1982 Barolo Bricco Bussia Colonnello	C	94
1982 Barolo Bussia Soprano	C	92
1987 Dolcetto d'Alba	A	85
1983 Il Favot	B	73
1985 Il Favot	B	86

Aldo Conterno is highly respected, and while I have always enjoyed his wines, I have never been more impressed with his Barolos than with the 1982s. The Bussia Soprano is splendidly open and rich, displaying a great bouquet of tarlike, spicy, smoky Nebbiolo fruit. On the palate, it is rich, relatively velvety for a Barolo, with a tremendous finish. It will drink well for 10–15 years. The Bricco Bussia Colonnello is even finer. More than any other Barolo it seems to offer as much finesse as muscle and power. Extremely concentrated and rich, its spice-box, cherry-fruit flavors seem to linger and linger on the palate. The 1986 Dolcetto is a ripe and tasty wine from one of the acknowledged masters of this grape. As for Conterno's blend of Barbera and Nebbiolo called Il Favot, the 1985 is quite rich and deep, but the 1983 has thin, hard flavors exhibiting a lack of fruit, a continual problem with the Piedmontese wines from this vintage.

GIACOMO CONTERNO (BAROLO)* * * *

1978 Barolo Monfortino	D	92
1979 Barolo Monfortino	D	90
1982 Barolo Riserva Serralunga	C	91

Conterno—his first name is Giovanni, not Giacomo—is one of the few remaining traditionalists in Piedmont. He will bottle his Barolo only after 6–8 years of cask aging, caring little if it has a bit of volatile acidity. I know his wines well, and they are not for the shy; they are persuasive, intense, full-throttle Barolos that grab you by the throat and say, "This is what nineteenth-century wine tasted like." His new releases consist of the 1982 Barolo Riserva, an unusually huge and powerful wine that has enough depth, tannin, and extract to last 25–30 years. Very deep in color, it is probably his best Riserva since the

1971. The 1979 Monfortino is equally deep, and ferociously tannic with layers of intense fruit, yet the volatile acidity seems slightly elevated for so young a Monfortino. Certainly, the splendid 1978 does not have this level of volatile acidity, and it seems to have even greater richness and depth as well as muscle and power than even the 1979. These are old-style, rather riveting wines that represent a long-gone era of wine-making.

DAMONTE (BARBERA)* * * *

1985 Barbera San Guglielmo, Malvira	B	87

One of the finest Barberas I have ever tasted, the 1985 from Damonte exhibits delicious sweetness, toasty oak, and plummy fruit. A deep, lush, full-flavored Barbera, it offers gobs of flavor and personality.

DEFORVILLE (BARBARESCO)* *

1981 Barbaresco	C	68
1982 Barbaresco	C	86
1985 Barbera d'Alba	B	73
1986 Dolcetto d'Alba	B	78
1983 Nebbiolo d'Alba	B	78

I am rarely moved by the Deforville wines, but certainly the 1982 Barbaresco, with its intense bouquet of cherries and spices, well-balanced nose, and full-bodied taste, would satisfy anyone. Drink it over the next 4–5 years. Other wines include a drying-out, astringent, tea-scented 1981 Barbaresco, and a lean, austere, highly acidic 1985 Barbera d'Alba.

DESSILANI (GATTINARA, SPANNA, GHEMME)* * *

1982 Gattinara	B	86
1982 Ghemme	B	87

Dessilani's wines, usually fine values, are made in a direct, robust, and deeply fruity style lacking finesse, but more than making up for this with their richness, unabashed fruitiness, and intensity. They are not cerebral wines, but rather fleshy wines that in the case of the

Gattinara offer robust, full-bodied flavors with the scents of tar and black cherries. The Ghemme is even more rustic, a large-scaled wine oozing with plummy, intense fruit, a tarry, full-bodied richness, and soft tannins. Both wines will drink well for 7–8 years.

DOSIO (BAROLO)* * *

1985 Barbera d'Alba	A	75
1982 Barolo Vigna Fossati	C	85
1985 Dolcetto d'Alba	A	81
1986 Dolcetto d'Alba	A	78

I have had plenty of experience tasting Dosio's wines, and I find them good, often irregular, but never overpriced. The best Dosio wines tend to be his Barolos, made in a rich, deep but forward style, which can be drunk or cellared for up to 10–15 years. The 1982 single-vineyard Barolo Vigna Fossati shows the lush, plummy, rich fruit of that vintage, full body, and another 7–8 years of aging potential ahead of it.

RICARDO FENOCCHIO (BARBARESCO)* * * *

1985 Barbera d'Alba Pianpolvere	B	75
1982 Barolo Pianpolvere Soprano	C	87
1983 Barolo Pianpolvere Soprano	C	65

Avoid Fenocchio's vegetal 1985 Barbera and excessively hard and tannic 1983 Barolo. Search out his massive, enormously complex 1982 Barolo with a rich bouquet and layers of ripe, intense fruit that caress the palate. Quite intense and full-bodied, this wine has some appeal now, but my bet is that it will be even better in 3–4 years.

FRANCO-FIORINA (BAROLO)* *

1982 Barbaresco	B	82
1983 Barbaresco	B	74
1982 Barolo	B	85

1983 Barolo	B	72

My favorite wine among current vintages from this spotty producer is the 1982 Barolo, a relatively understated wine, but one that can be admired for its soft, spicy, elegantly wrought cherry fruit, and sense of balance. It is a forward, tasty wine for drinking over the next 4–5 years.

FONTANAFREDDA (BAROLO)* * * *

1982 Barolo Bianca	D	87

1982 Barolo Delizia	D	89

1982 Barolo Lazzarito	D	91

1982 Barolo La Rosa	D	90

This modern-style winery perched in the hills of Barolo makes very good, even superb Barolo that used to be applauded for its reasonable prices, as well as high quality. Although the prices have become staggeringly high, the style of Fontanafredda's Barolos remains classic, and the wines need 8–10 years of cellaring in good vintages. Somewhat confusing for the consumer is that Fontanafredda produces at least six different single-vineyard Barolos in top years such as 1982 and 1978. The differences in taste are marginal, at least in their early stages of life. All the 1982s are very dark in color with full body and a velvety, supple, rich opulence that is a hallmark of the 1982 vintage. They have softer tannins than the 1978s, but long, rich finishes. The higher-scoring wines have more developed and complex aromas, but all are excellent to exceptional wines displaying great ripeness and depth, as well as a sense of balance and finesse. They can be drunk now or aged for 12–15 years. I wonder, however, why have prices nearly tripled for the Fontanafredda wines?

ANGELO GAJA (BARBARESCO)* * * * *

1983 Barbaresco	D	82

1985 Barbaresco	D	87

1983 Barbaresco Costa Russi	E	84

| 1985 Barbaresco Costa Russi | E | 92 |

| 1983 Barbaresco Sori San Lorenzo | E | 84 |

| 1985 Barbaresco Sori San Lorenzo | E | 94 |

| 1983 Barbaresco Sori Tilden | E | 85 |

| 1985 Barbaresco Sori Tilden | E | 92 |

| 1982 Cabernet Sauvignon Darmagi | D | 85 |

More than any other Italian winemaker, Angelo Gaja, the unofficial spokesman for the wines of Piedmont, has a knack for always being in the spotlight. His wines are among the finest made, not only in Italy but in the world, and he prices them accordingly. They are boldly flavored, individualistic expressions of winemaking art, and no expense is spared in making them, which is evident by the bottles they come in, the cork (which is the longest I have ever seen in a dry table wine), and the designer label. In top vintages such as 1971, 1978, 1982, and 1985, the quality is extraordinary, and anyone who loves fine wine and has the requisite wealth to afford them should be stashing away a few bottles of Gaja's Barbaresco.

Gaja is not without his critics. There are those who feel his pricing policy is outrageous, and although I once thought that, too, given the limited production of his top wines and the effort that goes into them, I now feel the prices are not out of line when compared to other wines of this quality. There are also those who criticize him for leading an ill-considered charge by producers into aging their wine in small French casks (as practiced in Bordeaux), and more recently, for his lack of allegiance to Nebbiolo, the grape that made him famous, in order to plant Chardonnay and Cabernet Sauvignon on some precious vineyard properties in Piedmont. Nevertheless, these are the wines of an artist, and the difficulty is in trying to determine which vintage is better, the 1985s or 1982s.

Though the 1985s seem slightly less tannic and more dominated by spicy oak, there is no question that the 1985s share the intense, velvety, rich, astonishing level of ripe fruit and opulence of the 1982s, which have closed up considerably since they were released several years ago. Gaja offers four Barbarescos of which his regular bottling is still a good value. The 1985 is showing a deep ruby color, a toasty, vanillin oaky bouquet, and plenty of tarry, rich berry fruit and full body; it should last at least a decade or more.

Of the three single-vineyard Barbarescos, the Sori San Lorenzo is denser than the regular Barbaresco but not as ripe, full-bodied, or powerful as either the Costa Russi or the mammoth-sized Sori Tilden. The Costa Russi tends to be the most unctuous and intensely perfumed initially and often the easiest to taste young. The Sori Tilden is always the darkest, most concentrated, most backward, yet is, in its own way, the most spectacular wine Gaja produces. The 1985 is no exception. There are approximately 1,000 cases produced of each of these single-vineyard Barbarescos, and all of them belong in any conscientiously stocked wine cellar.

Lastly, Gaja's Cabernet Sauvignon is quite good, although the 1982 tasted overoaked and seemed California-like with its medium dark ruby color and herbaceous, black-cherry, curranty fruit, medium-body, crisp acidity, and overly clean, sterile style. Given the fact that it is made from very young vines, it is an encouraging wine. However, the price asked for it is hard to swallow.

BRUNO GIACOSA (BARBARESCO/BAROLO/ARNEIS)* * * * *

1984 Barbaresco	C	60
1982 Barbaresco Gallina	D	89
1985 Barbaresco Gallina	D	92
1982 Barbaresco Santo Stefano Riserva	E	96
1985 Barbera d'Alba Altaville d'Alba	B	84
1979 Barolo Bussia	E	94
1978 Barolo Rionda	E	96
1983 Barolo Serralunga	E	90
1986 Dolcetto d'Alba Plinet di Trezzo	B	74
1985 Nebbiolo d'Alba Valmaggiore	B	80

The wines of Bruno Giacosa have provided this writer with some of the most memorable wine-drinking experiences. His 1964s, 1967s, surreal 1971s (to me the finest Italian red wines I have ever tasted), exceptional 1978s, and extraordinary 1982s are the type of wines from which legends arise. His best wines are usually his Barbaresco Santo Stefano, Barolo Rionda, Barolo Serralunga, Barolo Bussia, Barbaresco Gallina, and his Barolo Villero.

The 1982 Barbaresco Santo Stefano is more forward and less tannic than the great 1978, but don't think for a minute that this explosively rich, impeccably crafted wine with its layers of chewy, spicy, leathery-scented fruit won't last for two decades. It has a stupendous bouquet and as much flavor length and complexity as any recent wine I have tasted. The 1982 Barbaresco Gallina suffers only in comparison with Giacosa's Santo Stefano, as its hallmark is a rich, velvety, intense Nebbiolo fruitiness, full body, and creamy finish. It is a decadently rich Barbaresco for drinking over the next 5–7 years. In comparison, the 1985 seems even richer, more structured, and should also be another astonishing wine from this great producer.

The 1982 Barolo Serralunga is not as celestial as Giacosa's 1978 Barolo from Serralunga that he also vineyard-labeled as Rionda. However, it is a large-framed, dry, intense, formidable wine that needs 5–7 years to shed its considerable tannic clout. No such wait is necessary for the 1979 Barolo Bussia, a complex, multidimensional wine with an immense bouquet of roses, cedar, tar, saddle leather, and plummy fruit. At nine years of age it has just begun to reach its apogee, and the layers of fruit and a finish that lasts several minutes are the sort of things one rarely tastes in wines produced in today's commercial world.

Perhaps Giacosa's greatest achievement with Barolo is the 1978 Barolo from the Rionda vineyard in Serralunga. In Italy it is considered one of the greatest Barolos made in this century. It is easy to see why from its staggeringly rich, sensational bouquet of smoky fruit, cedar, nuts, leather, and exotic spices. Though quite accessible, it should continue to improve throughout the rest of this century, and age well into the next. This monumental wine, if you can find any, belongs in your cellar.

As for the other Giacosa wines, I must admit I was disappointed that he made a Barbaresco in 1984, as it should have been declassified given its thin, harsh, hard character. The 1983 Barbaresco Santo Stefano also shocked me with its excessive sulphur in the nose, but perhaps I tasted a flawed bottle. Other wines include his 1985 Nebbiolo d'Alba Valmaggiore, which is light-bodied with cherry fruit, and his 1986 Dolcetto, rather lean and highly acidic for a wine from Giacosa.

Despite stubbing his toe with a couple of his current offerings, for sheer majesty of flavors, purity of fruit, and overall complexity, Giacosa still makes the finest wines in Piedmont, and they deserve to be recognized as some of the world's greatest wines.

GRANDUCA (BAROLO)* *

1982 Barbaresco	C	75
1983 Barbaresco	C	68
1983 Barilot	C	78
1978 Barolo	C	82
1982 Barolo	C	80
1983 Barolo	C	72

If you enjoy kissing your sister, eating frozen food prepared in your microwave, or listening to Muzak while strolling in suburban shopping centers, then these bland, tame, eviscerated, characterless wines are for you. Don't misunderstand me—there is nothing wrong with the wines. They are remarkably clean, straightforward, and inoffensive, but don't you deserve more, especially when there are so many wines to choose from?

MARCHESI DI GRESY (BARBARESCO)* * * *

1985 Barbaresco Camp Gros	D	90
1985 Barbaresco Gaiun	D	90
1985 Barbaresco Martinenga	D	86
1986 Dolcetto Monte Aribaldo	B	85
1985 Martinenga (100% Nebbiolo)	B	87

I admire this producer's wines, which are among the most elegant and graceful wines of Piedmont. While they are never in the blockbuster style of wines of a Gaja, or the magnificently rich, complex style of a Giacosa, they offer hedonistic levels of ripe, rich fruit in a supple, early-to-mature style with no rough edges. Readers will no doubt like the 1986 Dolcetto with its open-knit, fruity, appealing style, as well as the 1985 Martinenga, which is made from 100% Nebbiolo and fermented in small casks. As for the Barbarescos, they come from some of the best vineyard sites in Piedmont. Single-vineyards such as the Camp Gros, Gaiun, and Martinenga show super bouquets of ripe cherry fruit, spicy oak, tobacco scents, and wonderful balance. While they are delicious to drink today, they give every indication of lasting for 7–10 years. However, I would drink the Barbaresco Martinenga first and cellar the Camp Gros and Gaiun for another several years. For those who find Piedmontese wines almost too overwhelming in their massive style, the wines of Marchesi di Gresy may be the best place to begin to learn how great the Nebbiolo grape really is.

GIUSEPPE MASCARELLO (BAROLO)* * * *

1985 Barbera d'Alba Fasana	B	85
1982 Barolo Dardi	C	86
1982 Barolo Monprivato	C	94
1985 Dolcetto Gagliassi	A	85

The massively proportioned wines of Giuseppe Mascarello are among the great old-style heavyweights of Piedmont. Even his Dolcetto is made in a Rocky Balboa style with its deep purple, opaque color, muscular, rich, chewy flavors, and amazing length. As for his Barolos, the first bottle of Dardi I tasted was coarse, but the second showed huge richness, gobs of tannin, and a ruby/purple color; it was about as backward a wine as I have tasted recently. The greatest wine made by Mascarello is his Barolo from Monprivato vineyard, which shows the ability to last 30–40 years in vintages such as 1978, and 25–30 years in vintages such as 1982 or 1985. The 1982 has everything that fans of these heavyweight, old-style, Piedmont wines desire. The dense ruby/purple color, the huge, smoke, hot-road-tar-scented bouquet, the chewy, beefy flavors that last and last, and the two to three decades' worth of tannins are all seemingly in harmony in this behemoth of a wine. I don't expect it to be ready to drink until the mid to late 1990s. These are wines for the adventurous that offer exciting potential.

ODDERO (BAROLO)*

1982 Barbaresco	B	80
1985 Barbera d'Alba	B	73
1982 Barolo	B	75
1986 Dolcetto d'Alba	A	63

The wines of the Fratelli Oddero have not impressed me over recent vintages as they have tended to be made in a very correct, commercial, but simple, one-dimensional style. They are inexpensive, but there is more flavor for the money from other producers.

PIO CESARE (BAROLO/BARBARESCO)* * * *

1982 Barbaresco Riserva	C	88
1985 Barbera d'Alba	B	85
1982 Barolo Riserva	C	87
1983 Ornato	C	82

This producer has been consistently reliable over the years, and the old, woody, somewhat oxidized style of winemaking has been replaced by a quasi-modern approach that emphasizes a bit more fruit. One can see this in the 1985 Barbera d'Alba, which is a surprisingly supple, tasty wine with none of the annoyingly high acidity that frequently plagues this Piedmontese wine. As for the Barolo and Barbaresco, both the 1982s are excellent. I liked the Barbaresco a bit more because it has more fruit and depth, and the tannins so prominent in the big, beefy, intense, and aggressive Barolo are less obtrusive. Both wines should keep for at least a decade. The 1983 Ornato seems to have less complexity and flavor depth than Pio Cesare's other wines. Although I have not tasted the recent vintages, I would not recommend the Grignolino made by Pio Cesare, or the inconsistent Nebbiolo d'Alba.

PRODUTTORI DI BARBARESCO (BARBARESCO)* * * *

1982 Barbaresco Asili	B	91
1982 Barbaresco Moccagatta	B	90

1982 Barbaresco Monte Stefano	B	90

1982 Barbaresco Pora	B	85

1982 Barbaresco Rabaja	B	87

This cooperative in Piedmont must certainly have the highest standards of winemaking of any co-op in the world. The wines are superbly made, reasonably priced for what they represent, and usually can age well for 10–15 years. The 1982s range from very good to outstanding. As a group of wines, they are more forward and evolved than the very fine 1978s. The Pora and Rabaja are the most ready to drink. I prefer the Rabaja because of its gingery, spicy, intense aromas, rich, full-bodied, chewy flavors, and potential to last for another 8–10 years. The Pora is good but clearly less complex and concentrated than the others. Its suppleness suggests that it should drink well for 3–5 years. The Moccagatta is one of the most backward wines, but extremely promising. The harnessed power is kept in check, and the impression given by this wine is one of immense fruit, body, richness, and length. Expect it to hit its plateau of maturity between 1990 and 2000. The Monte Stefano is similarly proportioned, but slightly smoother in texture and less tannic. It exhibits great richness, an expansive, explosive taste, and the classic leather and cherry spice of the Nebbiolo grape. Perhaps the finest wine of this impressive batch is the Asili, a wine of stupendous depth, richness, length, and harmony, yet still a baby in its development. The most concentrated of these admirably made Barbarescos, I would not expect it to be ready to drink until the late nineties.

ALFREDO PRUNOTTO (BAROLO)* * *

1982 Barbaresco Monte Stefano	C	88

1982 Barolo Podere Cannubi	C	87

I have always felt that if Prunotto could tame down the savage tannins in his wines (have you ever tasted his 1971s, 1978s, or 1979s?), they would have greater appeal as there is always the requisite ripeness and fruit. In essence, he has achieved that with the 1982 Barbaresco and Barolo. The Barbaresco is a rich, alcoholic, broadly flavored wine with gobs of extract and the telltale cherry, saddle-leather, meaty, tar combination of aromas. Drinkable now, this wine should improve for

6–10 years. The Barolo is more tannic, but extremely spicy, large-framed, and in need of 4–5 more years of cellaring.

RENATO RATTI (BAROLO/DOLCETTO)* * * * *

1983 Barbaresco	C	79
1982 Barolo	C	85
1982 Barolo Marcenasco	C	90?
1982 Barolo Marcenasco Rocche	C	92
1985 Dolcetto d'Alba Colombe	B	87
1986 Dolcetto d'Alba Colombe	B	85
1985 Nebbiolo d'Alba Ochetti	B	85

The recently deceased Ratti was one of the most intelligent of Piedmont's winemakers. He seemed to realize that only moderate tannins are necessary for a wine to last and age, provided the depth of fruit and harmony of acid, alcohol, fruit, and concentration are present. Consequently, his wines are infused with a splendid, rich, ripe fruitiness that makes them remarkably seductive when young, yet they age extremely well. His gloriously fruity, rich, decadent Dolcetto is one of Piedmont's two or three finest examples of this grape, and while the 1986 is very good for the vintage, the 1985 is a textbook, classic Dolcetto that flows over the palate far too easily for its 13% alcohol. Ratti's 1982 Barolo, made from purchased grapes, is a good commercial example of a fruity, supple, restaurant-styled wine, but his two Marcenasco Barolos have layers and layers of deep, voluptuous fruit, velvety textures, and dazzling finishes. They both have 10–15 years of further aging potential. The Marcenasco Rocche is even richer and deeper than the Marcenasco, and the question mark next to the score of the latter wine is because one of three bottles tasted had an excessive level of volatile acidity. I hope the bad bottle is an isolated example. As for the 1983 Barbaresco, it is light, simple, and fairly one-dimensional. One hopes his successors will make no changes.

GIUSEPPI RINALDI (BAROLO)* * *

1985 Barbera d'Alba	B	50

1978 Barolo Brunate	C	87

1982 Barolo Brunate	C	89

1983 Barolo Riserva	C	57

Giuseppi Rinaldi is one of the most traditional winemakers in Barolo, and perhaps that explains why his wines are often a hit-or-miss proposition. For example, the 1982 and 1978 Barolo Brunates are huge, intense, aromatic, chewy, tannic, and large-scaled wines that may well intimidate neophyte tasters. These large-framed wines, which have some volatile acidity present, are classic examples of the textbook, big, old-style Barolos that were made earlier in this century. In contrast to these wines is the 1983 Barolo Riserva, with its vinegary aromas and thin, harsh, unpleasant flavors, as well as the 1985 Barbera with its excessive volatile acidity. Nevertheless, well-chosen wines in certain top vintages from Rinaldi are good examples of what wines from the nineteenth century probably tested like.

ROAGNA (BARBARESCO)* * *

1982 Barbaresco	C	78

1985 Barbaresco	C	82

1982 Crichet Pajè	B	80

Despite this producer's excellent reputation, I find his wines, while elegant and pleasant at their best, often too short and insubstantial on the palate to be pleasurable. For example, his 1982s tasted rather lean and, for the vintage, disappointing. The 1985 Barbaresco shows more fruit, but again considering the quality of the vintage, it is not one of the stars. I have not tasted a recent cuvée of his nonvintage Opera Prima, but the first three examples I tried of this Nebbiolo wine, which is vinified and aged in small oak casks, left me wondering where the fruit was, as it had been obliterated by the taste of new oak. Certainly, Roagna has a better reputation than my comments here would indicate.

LUCIANO SANDRONE (BAROLO)* * * *

1982 Barolo	C	90

1983 Barolo	C	73

1984 Barolo	C	82

1985 Barolo Boschis	C	95

This small producer can make astonishingly rich, majestic Barolos in top vintages such as 1982 and 1985. In fact, his 1985 is a candidate for the wine of the vintage with its fabulous extract, great color, and absolutely stunning range of flavors and dimension. The 1984 turned out to be a success, although it is light, fruity, and ready to drink. The 1983 is compact with little length or flavor, which is so typical of this vastly overrated vintage. Sandrone's production is small, but his wines are well worth searching out for their remarkable quality.

SCARPA (BAROLO)* * *

1982 Barbaresco	D	86

1982 Barolo I Tetti di Neive	D	86

I always find the wines of Scarpa among the most backward, tannic, and forbiddingly unapproachable wines of all Piedmont. For that reason, these scores may ultimately turn out to be conservative given the richness and concentration of these wines, but the tannin levels seem quite elevated despite the impressive richness and length. Both these wines need at least another 7–10 years to shed sufficient tannin to be drinkable. Perhaps they are better than I have indicated, but this is a nineteenth-century style of winemaking that seems unsuitable for the demands of the modern world. I wouldn't want to think Scarpa would change, so perhaps the solution is to release his wines at a much later date.

G. D. VAJRA (BAROLO/BARBERA)* * *

1985 Barbera d'Alba	C	79

1982 Barolo	C	87

1985 Dolcetto d'Alba	B	82

In general, Vajra's 1985s, particularly the Dolcetto and the Barbera, were adequate, cleanly made, decent wines, but given the vintage, I had expected more. Certainly, the 1982 Barolo delivers intense fruit,

full body, and plenty of the leathery, hot-tar-scented fruit that the
Nebbiolo grape can render.

VALENTINO (BAROLO/DOLCETTO)* * * *

1983 Barolo	C	80
1982 Barolo Vigna Roul	C	91
1985 Bricco Manzoni	C	90
1985 Dolcetto d'Alba	B	85

Valentino's wines seem to represent a fine synthesis between the traditional and modern styles of winemaking in Piedmont. His blend of
Nebbiolo and Barbera, the Bricco Manzoni, has been absolutely sensational in top vintages such as 1985 and 1982. It's characterized by
its rich, berrylike aromas that are intertwined with scents of saddle
leather and tobacco. On the palate, this is a full-bodied, velvety, expansive wine that is altogether delicious, but it should be drunk within
5–7 years of the vintage. Valentino's Dolcetto is also a vibrant, tasty
wine with a great deal of attractive, up-front fruit, which should be
drunk within 4 years of the vintage. Of his recent Barolos, the 1983 is
adequate, but the best wine he produced is the 1982 Vigna Roul that
has great flavor dimension, and a complex bouquet of licorice, cedar,
tobacco, and roses. The flavors are huge and intense, but relatively
soft, and the wine has a powerful, long finish. It is certainly Valentino's finest Barolo since his outstanding 1978. It can be drunk over the
next 15 years.

VALLANA (SPANNA/GATTINARA)* * * *

1983 Barbera	A	76
1986 Barbera	A	75
1979 Gattinara	B	87
1980 Gattinara	B	85
1982 Gattinara	B	86
1978 Spanna Piemonte	B	87

1982 Spanna Piemonte	B	86

Here are densely colored, rather intense, traditionally made wines that ooze with character, and they are at the opposite end of the spectrum from the great majority of industrially made, vapid wines one sees today. Vallana's wines can age for 20–25 years as evidenced by his 1958s and 1964s, which I recently tasted and found to be still in superb condition. His new releases are all deep-ruby/purple in color with exotic, smoked-meat, tobacco, and intense earthy, trufflelike bouquets. The 1980 Gattinara has high acids, but plenty of extract to go along with its smoky, aggressive personality. The 1982 Gattinara is similar, just more concentrated and backward; it needs 5–8 years of cellaring. For drinking today, the 1982 Spanna has broad, supple flavors, plenty of earthy, mineral, smoky fruit, and a deep-ruby/purple color. Lastly, the 1979 Gattinara and the 1978 Spanna offer concentrated, intense, ripe flavors, full body, and plenty of power and presence on the palate. The 1979 Gattinara seems a little more refined than the robust, spicy Spanna. Both of these wines should continue to improve for 5–10 years. The only wines of Vallana I can't get excited about are his 1986 and 1983 Barberas; they tasted innocuous and clumsy.

VIETTI (BAROLO/DOLCETTO)* * * *

1982 Barbaresco	C	82
1982 Barbaresco Masseria	C	87
1985 Barbera d'Alba Bussia	B	86
1985 Barbera d'Alba Pianromualdo	B	88
1985 Barbera d'Alba Scarrone	B	82
1982 Barolo Rocche	C	90
1983 Barolo Rocche	C	74
1985 Dolcetto d'Alba Disa	A	82
1986 Dolcetto d'Alba Sant Anna	A	73

1985 Nebbiolo d'Alba San Michelle   A   83

I have to admit to a slight degree of disappointment with a number of
the current releases from one of my favorite producers in Piedmont,
Vietti. This winery, run with great passion by the gentlemanly Alfredo
Currado, has consistently turned out some of the benchmark exam-
ples of wine in northern Italy. Therefore, I'm surprised by wines such
as the 1986 Dolcetto d'Alba Sant Anna and the 1983 Barolo Rocche.
However, despite these letdowns, Vietti has produced in 1985 two
sensational Barberas from the Pianromualdo and Bussia vineyards.
The Bussia has a ruby/purple color, rich, deep, spicy fruit, full body,
good but unexcessive acidity, and a long, powerful, rich finish. The
Pianromualdo is even more impressive and may be one of the finest
Barberas I have ever tasted. A huge, richly fruity, smoky, and licorice-
scented bouquet is first class. On the palate, this full-bodied wine has
gobs of fruit, a long finish, and an overall hedonistic appeal to it. As
for Vietti's other wines, his Dolcettos tend to be excellent, but the
1985s are starting to fade a bit and the 1986s do not look to be nearly
as good. His 1983 Barolo from the Rocche vineyard, with old, tealike
aromas, is a short, thin, rather feeble wine. No such problem exists
with the 1982 Barolo Rocche or the 1982 Barbaresco Masseria. Both
are rich, full-bodied, intense wines that should last 15 or more years.

G. VOERZIO (BAROLO)* *

1982 Barolo La Serra di La Morra	C	85
1984 Nebbiolo della Langhe	B	56
1984 Nebbiolo Roscaleto	B	52
1982 Rosso della Serra	C	85

Voerzio is a relatively new firm, and these are the first wines from
them I have tasted. Both Nebbiolos had technical defects as they were
light, spritzy, unstable, and in one case, foaming in the glass. Though
the Nebbiolos were bad, the 1982 Rosso della Serra had a very dark
color, scents of ripe cherry fruit and leather, good body and depth,
and was quite well made. The 1982 Barolo La Serra has lots of acidity
and tannin to shed, but very good flavor extraction, fine ripeness, deep
color, and 5–10 years of evolution ahead of it. While the verdict is
mixed, certainly the Barolo and Rosso della Serra are good wines that
showed fine winemaking.

Piedmont's Best White Wines

In general, the top white wines of Piedmont are vastly overpriced (Gavi is a rip-off) for what one gets in the bottle. The exception is the lovely flower blossom and apricot scented Moscato, and the dry version of Erbaluce. The former wine has low alcohol (usually 5–9%), is slightly sweet and effervescent, and overall is a gorgeous wine to drink as an aperitif or with fresh fruit for dessert. My favorite Piedmont white wines are listed below. As for vintages, concentrate on the last two years only, 1988 and 1987.

Wine	*Producer*
Arneis	Bruno Giacosa
Arneis	Castello di Neive
Arneis	Bruno Ceretto
Arneis	Rabino Vittoria
Chardonnay	Angelo Gaja
Cortesi di Gavi	Pio Cesare
Cortesi di Gavi	Broglia Fasciola
Gavi	La Scolca
Gavi	La Chiara
Erbaluce di Caluso	Carretta
Erbaluce di Caluso	Boratto
Erbaluce di Caluso	Ferrando
Moscato d'Asti	Rivetti
Moscato d'Asti	Ceretto
Moscato d'Asti	Bruno Giacosa

TUSCANY

The Basics

TYPES OF WINES

Beautiful Tuscany is the home of Italy's most famous wine region, Chianti, and Italy's most celebrated wine, Brunello di Montalcino. Both wines can be either horrendous or splendid as quality is shockingly irregular—more so than in other viticultural regions. Yet, it is in Tuscany that Italy's wine revolution is being fought, with adventurous and innovative producers cavalierly turning their backs on the archaic regulations that govern wine production. They are making wines, based on Cabernet Sauvignon and Sangiovese, aged in small oak casks, filled with flavor and personality, and put in designer bottles. I disagree completely with those critics who have called them French look-alikes, and though entitled to be called only Vino da Tavola, these wines are some of the most exciting red wines made in Italy. The same cannot be said for Tuscany's white wines. Except for the light, tasty whites called Vernaccia from the medieval hill town of San Gimignano, Tuscan whites are ultraneutral, boring wines, and the new-breed whites are often excessively priced and overly oaked.

GRAPE VARIETIES

The principal and greatest red wine grape of Tuscany is the Sangiovese, which comes in different clones. The highest yielding, most insipid wine from Sangiovese comes from the most widely planted clone called Sangiovese Romano. The better producers are using clones of Sangiovese with names such as Sangioveto, Prugnolo, and Brunello. These all produce a richer, deeper, more complex wine. Of course, Cabernet Sauvignon and Cabernet Franc from the international school are also making their presence known in Tuscany. As for the white wines, there is the sharp, uninteresting Trebbiano that is used in industrial-strength quantities. It is an inferior grape and the results are distressingly innocuous wines. The Vernaccia has potential, and of course, there are Chardonnay and Sauvignon Blanc. Tuscany, in my mind, means red not white wine, but if you are inclined to try a white wine, then I suggest a Vernaccia di San Gimignano.

FLAVORS

Chianti Classico—It is virtually impossible to provide specific information given the extraordinary range in quality—from musty, poorly vinified, washed-out wines to one with soft, supple, raspberry, chestnut, and tobacco flavors, medium body, and a fine finish. Stick to only the recommended producers that are listed below. Remember, most Chianti, despite tighter regulations governing quality, is appallingly insipid.

Brunello di Montalcino—It should be rich, powerful, tannic, and heady with a huge bouquet of smoky tobacco, meat, dried red fruits, and spices, and have superb concentration. Only a few do. One is more likely to encounter an alarming degree of tannin and old musty oak to the detriment of fruit. Again, selection is critical. Rosso di Montalcino is red wine made from the Brunello clone of Sangiovese that is not aged long enough to qualify as Brunello di Montalcino. It is often much less expensive and considerably fresher.

Carmignano—This is an underrated viticultural area wherein the wines show good fruit, balance, and character. They taste like good Chiantis with more structure. Not surprisingly, Carmignano is made from Sangiovese with 10–15% Cabernet added.

Vernaccia di San Gimignano—Tuscany's best dry white table wine, this nutty, zesty, dry, fruity white is meant to be drunk within 2–3 years of the vintage. It is a satisfying rather than thrilling wine.

Vino Nobile di Montepulciano—A Chianti neighbor with identical characteristics (the grape is the same), Vino Nobile di Montepulciano costs more but rarely gives more in flavor or aging potential.

Other Tuscan whites—The names Bianco di Pitigliano, Bianco Vergine della Valdichiana, Galestro, Montecarlo, Pomino, and any Tuscan producer's name plus the word "bianco" translates into wines that taste ultraclean, wretchedly neutral and bland, and provide no more flavor than a glass of water.

Vino da Tavolas—The most exciting red wines of Tuscany, perhaps in the world, are the designer show wines that are being made by Tuscany's most innovative growers. They can be 100% Cabernet Sauvignon, 100% Sangiovese, or a blend of these two grapes plus Cabernet Franc. They are aged in oak casks (usually new French ones), and in great Tuscan vintages such as 1982, 1983, and 1985, have had remarkable flavor breadth. Following are the best Vino da Tavolas, their top vintages, and the grapes used.

GUIDE TO THE TOP VINO DA TAVOLAS

Name	Producer	Top Vintages	Primary Grape
Ania	Gabbiano	1985	Cab. Sauvignon
Barco Reale	Capezzana	1985	Cab. Sauvignon
Boro Cepparello	Isole e Olena	1982, 1983, 1985	Sangiovese
Brusco di Barbi	Barbi	1982, 1983	Sangiovese
Ca del Pazzo	Caparzo	1983, 1985	50-50 blend
Capannelle Rosso	Capannelle	1982, 1983	Sangiovese
Cetinaia	San Polo in Rosso	1985	Sangiovese
Coltassala	Castello di Volpaia	1983, 1985	Sangiovese
Concerto	Fonterutoli	1985	Sangiovese
Elegia	Poliziano	1985	Sangiovese
Flaccianello della Pieve	Fontodi	1983, 1985	Sangiovese
Fontalloro	Felsina	1983, 1985	Sangiovese
Ghiaie della Furba	Cappezzana	1983, 1985	Cab. Sauvignon
Grifi	Avignonesi	1982, 1983, 1985	Cab. Sauvignon
Grosso Senese	Il Palazzino	1983, 1985	Sangiovese
Il Sodaccio	Monte Vertine	1982, 1983, 1985	Sangiovese
Monte Antico	Monte Antico	1982, 1983, 1985	Sangiovese
Mormoreto	Frescobaldi	1983, 1985	Cab. Sauvignon
Palazzo Altesi	Altesino	1982, 1983, 1985	Sangiovese
Percarlo	San Giusto	1985	Sangiovese
Le Pergole Torte	Monte Vertine	1982, 1983, 1985	Sangiovese
Sammarco	Castello di Rampolla	1982, 1983, 1985	Cab. Sauvignon
Sangioveto Grosso	Monsanto	1977, 1982, 1983	Sangiovese
Sassicaia	Marchese Incisa della Rocchetta	1981, 1982, 1983, 1985	Cab. Sauvignon
I Sodi di San Niccolo	Castellina	1983, 1985	Sangiovese
Solaia	Antinori	1982, 1983, 1985	Cab. Sauvignon
Solatia Basilica	Villa Cafaggio	1983, 1985	Sangiovese
Tavernelle	Villa Banfi	1985	Cab. Sauvignon
Tignanello	Antinori	1981, 1982, 1985, 1986	Sangiovese
Vigorello	San Felice	1983, 1985	Sangiovese
Vinattieri	M. Castelli	1981	Sangiovese

AGING POTENTIAL

Brunello di Montalcino: 8–25
  years
Carmignano: 5–8 years
Chianti Classico: 3–15 years*
Rosso di Montalcino: 5–8 years

Tuscan whites: 1–2 years
Vino Nobile di Montepulciano:
  5–10 years
Vino da Tavolas (red wine
  blends): 5–15 years

OVERALL QUALITY LEVEL

For one of the world's most famous wine regions, the quality, while on the upswing, is depressingly variable. Some famous estates in Brunello continue to live off their historic reputations while making poor wine, and there is an ocean of mediocre Chianti producers. Yet, the exciting new-breed Sangiovese/Cabernet wines can be superb, and the top growers are doing some special things. As for the white wines, the situation is intolerable, and the Italians need to wake up to the fact that high-tech, computerized, stainless-steel tanks, centrifuges, and sterile bottling through micropore filter machines do not make pleasure-giving wine.

MOST IMPORTANT INFORMATION TO KNOW

Forget the Italian wine regulations that are supposed to promote a better product. There are many disgustingly poor wines that carry the government's highest guarantee of quality, the DOCG, or Denominazione di Origine Controllata e Garantita. Many of the Vino da Tavolas are vastly superior wines, and this title is supposedly left for Italy's lowest-level, generic wines. What you need to know is who the top producers of Chianti, Brunello, etc., are. Then and only then will you be able to make your way through the perilous selection process for Italian wines.

1989–1990 BUYING STRATEGY

For Tuscany, 1985 was a better year than any since 1971. Some observers have even said the wines are "too perfect." One European critic went so far as to call the 1985s "overbearingly rich." These are the wines to search out, as even the lowly Chiantis have a wealth of fruit. Avoid 1984, seriously consider 1983 and 1982, especially the latter. For Brunello di Montalcino, 1983 and 1985 offer good wines, but I see no reason to search them out until the stock of 1982s is exhausted.

* Only a handful of Chianti producers make wines that age and last this long.

TUSCANY
VINTAGE GUIDE

1987—Light, agreeable, pleasantly fruity wines for drinking over the next 3–5 years should be the rule of the day.

1986—A good vintage that at present is lost in the hype surrounding 1985, but the wines are well balanced, round, and will probably turn out like the 1981s, only better.

1985—A smashing, no-holds-barred, incredible year with the wines bursting at the seams with a superripe, velvety, opulent, plummy fruitiness, full body, and a lushness and precociousness not seen since 1971. The wines are seductive, glamorous, voluptuous, and fabulously tasty. The light Chiantis will keep for 5–6 years, the serious Chiantis and Vino da Tavolas, 8–15 years, and the Brunellos for 20 years. The wines from the top producers are not to be missed.

1984—A dreadful year, much worse in Tuscany than in Piedmont to the north. Rain and a paucity of sunshine were the culprits. No doubt the trade will say the wines are light and commercial, but at this point, this looks to be a vintage to pass up.

1983—Quite highly regarded. Tuscany had weather similar to that experienced in Bordeaux hundreds of miles to the west. A drought year of intense heat caused sugars and the consequent alcohol level to skyrocket in the grapes. Reports are that the wines are ripe, alcoholic, fat, low in acidity, and jammy, with deep layers of fruit.

1982—Considered more "classic" than 1983, which I suppose means less powerful and less opulently fruity and rich wines. Certainly a very good vintage with firm tannins, good depth, and ripeness. My tasting notes indicate that the vintage is the best since 1975, maybe 1971. A year to be taken seriously, and for Brunello di Montalcino, the best vintage since 1970.

1981—An average vintage of light, pleasant, rather frail wines. Most are fully mature. Only a handful will get better.

1980—An average vintage of light, soft, easy-to-drink wines. They should be drunk up.

1979—A good vintage of wine with more flesh and stuffing than either 1980 or 1981. As in most of Europe, a gigantic crop was harvested.

1978—Rather highly regarded, but I have never found the wines to be terribly exciting, either in Brunello or Chianti.

1977—Rather successful, particularly in view of the negative publicity surrounding this vintage in Europe. Most Brunellos and Chiantis have more fruit and character than the more highly rated wines of 1978.

1976—For Tuscany, a disastrous vintage because of heavy rains that diluted the grapes.

1975—A very good vintage, though not a great one as initially claimed by the producers of Chianti and Brunello. All of the wines are fully mature and should be drunk up over the next several years.

1974—An average year of pleasant but rather charmless wines that have lacked flesh and fruit. Most are now too old to drink.

1973—It has been a good five years since I last tasted a 1973 Chianti or Brunello. The wines, never very attractive, were excessively light and feeble, and I would suspect they are now totally decrepit.

1972—As in most of Europe, a wet, cold summer precluded the grapes from reaching maturity. Most of the better producers did not declare a vintage, preferring to declassify their entire crop. A disaster.

1971—Arguments among Chianti lovers have long raged as to which was a greater vintage, 1971 or 1970. The 1971s, rich, alcoholic, sumptuous wines, drank well young but are now tiring. They can, where well stored, be delicious, voluptuous, rich wines that are full of fruit, but even the best-preserved examples of this vintage should be drunk immediately.

1970—Unquestionably a greater vintage for Brunello di Montalcino than 1971, but in Chianti, most observers have given 1971 the edge. However, the 1970 Chiantis, less flashy and flamboyant in their youth, have opened and blossomed in aging. The Chiantis from this vintage, overshadowed by the 1971s, can offer many surprises. The best Brunellos are sensational and will last at least another decade.

A GUIDE TO TUSCANY'S BEST PRODUCERS OF CHIANTI, BRUNELLO, VINO NOBILE DI MONTEPULCIANO

***** *(OUTSTANDING PRODUCERS)*

Altesino (Brunello)	Pacenti (Brunello)
Caparzo (Brunello)	Pertimali (Brunello)
Costanti (Brunello)	Castello di Rampolla (Chianti)
Il Poggione (Brunello)	San Felice (Brunello)
Monsanto (Chianti)	

* * * * (EXCELLENT PRODUCERS)

Antinori (Chianti)	Monte Antico (Tuscany)
Avignonesi (Vino Nobile)	Monte Vertine (Chianti)
Badia a Coltibuono (Chianti)	Pagliarese (Chianti)
Berardenga (Chianti)	Peppoli (Chianti)
Boscarelli (Vino Nobile)	Ruffino (Chianti)
Capannelle (Chianti)	San Giusto a Rentennano
Caprili (Brunello)	(Chianti)
Castellare di Castellina (Chianti)	San Guido (Tuscany)
Fontodi (Chianti)	Talenti (Brunello)
Il Palazzino (Chianti)	Val di Suga (Brunello)
Isole e Olena (Chianti)	Castello di Volpaia (Chianti)
Lisini (Brunello)	

* * * (GOOD PRODUCERS)

Ambra (Carmignano)	La Fortuna (Brunello)
Barbi (Brunello)	Fossi (Chianti)
Biondi Santi (Brunello)	Montesodi (Chianti)
Boscarelli (Vino Nobile)	Castello di Nipozzano (Chianti)
Castiglion del Bosco (Brunello)	Nozzole (Chianti)
Camigliano (Brunello)	La Poderina (Brunello)
Capezzano (Vino Nobile)	Riecine (Chianti)
Carletti della Giovampaola (Vino	San Filippo (Brunello)
Nobile)	Savignola Paolina (Chianti)
Fanetti (Vino Nobile)	Villa Cafaggio (Chianti)
Fassati (Vino Nobile)	Villa Selvapiana (Chianti)
La Fonterutoli (Chianti)	

Tuscany's Red Wines

The following are all recommended wines from recent tastings and represent the crème de la crème of Tuscany's current wines.

ALTESINO (BRUNELLO)* * * * *

1982 Brunello di Montalcino	D	90
1983 Brunello di Montalcino	D	87
1985 Rosso di Montalcino	B	85
1986 Rosso di Montalcino	B	85

Altesino makes sensational Brunello di Montalcino and its younger, less woody sibling, Rosso di Montalcino. I have followed Altesino's wines since the early seventies, and he is clearly one of the very best. The current releases all share the house style—rich, full-bodied wines with layers of deep, tarry, smoky fruit, and 10–15 years of aging potential still ahead of them. The Rosso di Montalcino do not have the complexity of the Brunello but show nice fatness. The 1982 and 1983 Brunello di Montalcino are top-notch, superb wines, quite full bodied, powerful, and rich. The 1982 shows the vintage's precocious appeal, but don't let that be deceiving—the wine will age well for another 10–15 years. The 1983 shows a little bit less depth, but its other qualities are similar to the 1982.

AMBRA (CARMIGNANO)

1985 Carmignano Riserva	C	88

This small producer has turned out a wonderful Carmignano, deep ruby in color with an intense, ripe, rich, concentrated, tarry, cherry fruitiness, full body, a supple texture, and a further 6–8 years of aging potential.

ANIA (VINO DA TAVOLA)

1983 Vino da Tavola (Castello di Gabbiano)	C	88

When I smelled this wine, I thought of the marvelous Spanish wine called Pesquera from the Duero. The intense bouquet of ripe berry fruit and toasty oak is persistent. On the palate, the wine continues to show a lot of new oak, rich, fat, plummy fruit, and a long velvety finish. Drink it over the next 3–5 years.

AVIGNONESI (VINO NOBILE)* * * *

1983 Vino Nobile di Montepulciano	C	87

1985 Vino Nobile di Montepulciano	C	90

The 1983 has a mellow, sweet, ripe bouquet of fruit that is followed by a wine with deep cherry flavors, lush texture, soft tannins, and a full, intense finish. It is a delicious wine that should be drunk over the next 3–5 years. The newly released 1985 is sensational with its fabulous depth and expansive bing-cherry richness married attractively with spicy, toasty oak. It should drink beautifully for another decade. In my opinion, this is the best producer of Vino Nobile in Tuscany.

BADIA A COLTIBUONO (CHIANTI)* * * *

1985 Chianti Classico	B	85
1982 Chianti Classico Riserva	B	87
1983 Chianti Classico Riserva	B	86
1981 Sangioveto	B	81
1982 Sangioveto	B	88

Badia a Colitbuono is one of the most historic and important of the Chianti estates, having been founded in the eleventh century by monks. Today the property has modernized its very traditional style of Chianti, yet it has not gone totally berserk in producing simply a high-tech wine with no personality. The Badia Chiantis remain among the most expansive and richest of all the Chiantis. From recent vintages one can see that some wonderfully rich, ripe wines are being made here with cellaring potential of 5–10 years. My two favorite wines from recent vintages include the 1982 Chianti Classico, which is a young, broodingly deep, tannic, big wine with rich, intense flavors, burgeoning complexity, and full body. The winery makes a special cuvée called Sangioveto, of which the 1982 smells and tastes like an impressive young Brunello di Montalcino. This big, chewy wine with a tarry, spicy, intense bouquet should last for at least another decade. The 1985 Chianti Classico shows the wonderful ripeness and seductive appeal of that astonishing vintage, and the 1983 Riserva offers close competition in both taste and style to the opulent 1982 Chianti Classico.

BARBI (BRUNELLO)* * *

1982 Brunello di Montalcino	C	86
1985 Chianti	B	85

I remember some stunning Brunellos from Barbi in vintages such as 1964 and 1970, but since the mid-1970s, the style has lightened up considerably, and while this used to be one of the best producers of Brunello di Montalcino, it's now clearly below the top tier of Brunello producers. The newly released 1982 is one of the better Brunellos from Barbi since the early seventies, but given the vintage, one would like to have seen more intensity and concentration. I get the impression that the wine production here might be excessive for the acreage, and that there is no selection process used to insure that only the finest juice from the oldest vines goes into the top wine. The 1985 Chianti produced by Barbi shows the strength of that lovely vintage with its deep color and rich, soft, supple fruitiness; it is an ideal wine to drink over the next 5–6 years.

BERARDENGA (CHIANTI)* * * *

1985 Chianti Classico	A	85
1983 Chianti Classico Riserva	B	87

The finest Chianti I have ever tasted was the 1970 Berardenga Chianti Classico Riserva. This winery lacks some consistency, but the quality of the wines from here, when they are done right, is among the best in Chianti. The 1985 is a charming, rather light Chianti, but it offers plenty of straightforward, ripe, fruity flavors and has a good, supple finish. The 1983 Riserva is a more serious wine altogether with its complex, spicy, cherry-scented bouquet, and relatively deep, intense flavors. It should keep well for 2–3 years.

BIONDI SANTI (BRUNELLO)* * *

1982 Brunello di Montalcino	E	90
1977 Brunello di Montalcino Riserva	E	80
1982 Brunello di Montalcino Riserva	E	92

While this estate has been maligned for its rather hard, overly tannic, austere, inconsistent wines, it would appear that they have made two great wines in the decade of the eighties with their 1982 regular and Riserva bottlings. However, this hardly excuses some of the mediocre wines from 1978 and 1979, as well as the 1977 Brunello di Montalcino Riserva, which is deficient in fruit and simply not concentrated enough to warrant the outrageous price tag it carries. Of course, the winery will tell you that these wines need a good 24–48-hour breathing period, but it seems to me they decline rather than improve after breathing. Certainly, those consumers who want to invest in a famous label should make their reservations now for the 1982s, the best Biondi Santi Brunellos in decades. Their great intensity and wonderful length and richness on the palate suggest both will last a good 20–30 years.

CAMIGLIANO (BRUNELLO)* * *

1982 Brunello di Montalcino	B	86
1985 Rosso di Montalcino	B	87
1986 Rosso di Montalcino	B	85

This producer always seems to keep its prices much more reasonable than other growers and producers of Brunello di Montalcino. The wines can be very good, and certainly in top vintages such as 1985 and 1982 this is an estate to search out for a reasonably priced Rosso or Brunello di Montalcino. The wines listed above are probably the best wines made by this estate since their stunning 1975. The 1986 Rosso does not have quite the incredible richness and ripeness of fruit of the 1985, but it is a good wine for the vintage. Certainly, the 1982 Brunello di Montalcino shows very good richness, fruit, and smoky, spicy flavors.

CAMPOGIOVANNI (BRUNELLO)* * * * *

1979 Brunello di Montalcino	C	90
1982 Brunello di Montalcino	C	92

An up-and-coming star of Brunello, the recent vintages of Campogiovanni from San Felice have been stunningly rich, intense, full-bodied, powerful, and delicious to drink. Both the 1982 and 1979 will last another 10–15 years, but the great pleasure they give now is hard to resist. The 1979, with its bouquet of smoky nuts, tobacco, and rich fruit, is not unlike a fine Graves from France. Of course, the 1982 is less precocious, but it still shows the great richness and super ripeness of fruit that this vintage offers. I would want to cellar it until the early nineties and then drink it over the following 10–12 years. This is one of the great producers of Brunello di Montalcino.

CAPARZO (BRUNELLO)* * * * *

1981 Brunello di Montalcino La Casa	D	88
1982 Brunello di Montalcino La Casa	D	92
1985 Ca del Pazzo	C	87

1985 Rosso di Montalcino	B	85

This is one of the best producers of Brunello di Montalcino, and their wine from the La Casa vineyard can be among the two or three best Brunellos produced in a given year, as it was in 1982 and 1981. (I also remember the 1979 with great satisfaction.) This is concentrated, rich wine with a complex bouquet of chestnuts, ripe fruit, cedar, and smoke. On the palate, these have tremendous length, yet an undeniable appeal even today. For those who do not want to pay the price for the single-vineyard La Casa, Caparzo offers a wonderfully rich, supple Rosso di Montalcino of which the 1985 is a very good example.

CAPRILI (BRUNELLO)* * * *

1982 Brunello di Montalcino	C	92

1983 Brunello di Montalcino	C	88

This small producer has impressed me with every Brunello I have tasted from the late seventies through the early eighties. Certainly the 1982 Caprili is one of the great wines from what was a great vintage in this prestigious appellation of Italy. Its complex bouquet of chestnuts, ripe fruit, cedar, and smoke is dazzling. On the palate, the wine is quite concentrated and rich, with tremendous length, yet is, like the vintage, precociously drinkable. It should last another 12–15 years. The 1983, not quite as richly endowed, still has a powerful, full-bodied, rich, intense bouquet with a chocolaty, smoky, earthy character.

CARLETTI DELLA GIOVAMPAOLA (VINO NOBILE)* * *

1983 Vino Nobile di Montepulciano	C	86

1985 Vino Nobile di Montepulciano	C	89

I don't know much about this producer, but certainly the high quality of these two wines says everything one needs to know—there is a high commitment to quality here. Both wines are big and chewy, with a great deal of depth, full body, and oodles of ripe, plummy fruit to go along with the earthy, tarry scents. The 1983 is fully mature and should drink well for another 5–6 years, whereas the 1985 is just beginning to open up and should last at least a decade.

CASTELLO DI RAMPOLLA (CHIANTI)* * * * *

1983 Chianti Classico Riserva	B 86

1985 Chianti Classico Riserva	B 90

Castello di Rampolla is one of the finest producers in Tuscany, and their Chiantis are among the richest, most complex, and age-worthy wines made in the area. The 1985 Riserva is an astonishingly rich, full-bodied, intense Chianti that should last for another decade. It shares the bouquet of coffee, ripe cherries, and tobacco with its 1983 counterpart, but it is even more concentrated and longer on the palate than the delicious, supple, expansive 1983.

CASTIGLION DEL BOSCO (BRUNELLO)* * *

1982 Brunello di Montalcino	C 85

In 4–5 years this wine will probably merit a higher rating, but for now the hard and high level of tannins precludes a good look at just how much fruit it has. It is certainly a very good, deep Brunello, but it needs several years of cellaring.

COLTASSALA (VINO DA TAVOLA)* * * *

1983 Vino da Tavola (Castello di Volpaia)	C 86

1985 Vino da Tavola (Castello di Volpaia)	C 90

These two wines, made primarily from the Sangiovese grape, show toasty new oak, a rich, deep, plummy fruit, full body, and in the case of the 1985, great length and lushness, making it appealing when young. The 1983 is showing more complexity in its bouquet, but not the richness and depth of the 1985. Both wines are from the excellent Chianti producer Castello di Volpaia.

COSTANTI (BRUNELLO)* * * * *

1982 Brunello di Montalcino	D 90

1983 Brunello di Montalcino	D 88

Costanti, one of the most traditional and finest of the Brunello producers, has made a great wine in 1982 and a very good wine in 1983. The 1982 is deep in color, with a closed yet promising bouquet of oak, spices, and ripe fruit, and is showing admirable depth, but a tremendous lashing of tannin precludes drinking this young, potentially out-standing Brunello for at least 5–6 years. The 1983 shows the same degree of tannin, but not quite the great depth and richness of the 1982; it should be ready to drink a bit sooner.

FLACCIANELLO (VINO DA TAVOLA)* * * *

1983 Flaccianello della Pieve (Fontodi)	C	88

1985 Flaccianello della Pieve (Fontodi)	C	90

Of the new breed of Tuscan red wines, Flaccianello, from the excel-lent Chianti producer Fontodi, has proven in the vintages of the eighties to be among the very best. The wine, made from 100% San-giovese grapes, is fermented and aged in new oak barrels. The 1983 has a big, sweet, oaky, ripe, rich bouquet, and supple, velvety, tasty fruit that is present in generous amounts. This soft, seductive, ripe, and extremely attractive wine should be drunk over the next 4–5 years. The 1985 shows even greater richness and depth, and a huge bouquet of superripe, plummy fruit married adroitly with toasty new oak barrels. It should age well for up to a decade.

FONTALLORO (VINO DA TAVOLO)* * * *

1983 Vino da Tavola (Felsina)	C	86

1985 Vino da Tavola (Felsina)	C	90

Felsina, a very good Chianti producer, enters the luxury cuvée new-breed Italian red wine market with Fontalloro. A Sangiovese-based wine aged in oak casks, it shows wonderful ripe-cherry character married with toasty, smoky, oak barrels. The 1983 is very good, the 1985 quite stunning with a concentration and richness that is rarely seen in wines from Tuscany. It should age gracefully for at least a decade.

FONTODI (CHIANTI)* * * *

1985 Chianti Classico	A	87

This excellent producer has turned out a sumptuous 1985 Chianti that will keep 4–5 years. Medium dark ruby with a fragrant, intense bou-quet of berry fruit, this velvety, nicely concentrated wine offers a plump mouthful of lush fruit, and just the right touch of oak.

FOSSI (CHIANTI)* * *

1982 Chianti Classico Riserva	A	85
1983 Chianti Classico Riserva	A	82

Fossi is a notably reliable producer of Chianti that, while never great, is consistently good. The 1983 Riserva is a straightforward, well-made wine, but the 1982 Riserva has more richness and is quite well endowed, immensely satisfying, and shows a medium- to full-bodied texture. Fossi has recently released a lot of its older vintages into the marketplace, and if you should see either the 1959 or 1961, they are excellent examples of well-aged, rich, complex Chiantis that are selling for less than $25 a bottle.

FRESCOBALDI (CHIANTI)* * *

1982 Montesodi	B	87
1982 Castello di Nipozzano Riserva	B	85

The Frescobaldi family is one of the largest landowners in Tuscany, and two of their finest red wines are their Montesodi and Castello di Nipozzano. The 1982 renditions of these wines are quite well made, tasty wines, with a good measure of ripe-cherry fruit, a spicy, cigar-box aroma, and medium to full body. The Montesodi has a bit more depth and 5–10 years aging potential.

GHIAIE DELLA FURBA (VINO DA TAVOLO)* * *

1985 Vino da Tavola (Capezzana)	C	85

This Cabernet Sauvignon–based wine from Capezzana is very good, showing a lot of new oak, a weedy, curranty fruitiness, and medium to full body. It should be drunk over the next 4–5 years.

GRIFI (VINO DA TAVOLO)* * *

1985 Vino da Tavola (Avignonesi)	C	88
1986 Vino da Tavola (Avignonesi)	C	86

Grifi is one of the more elegantly wrought new-breed Italian red wines. Both the 1986 and 1985 display a good healthy deep ruby color, moderately intense chocolaty berry fruit, somewhat oaky bouquets, and an attractive fleshy suppleness on the palate. The 1985 seems a bit more concentrated and richer than the 1986. Both wines should be drunk on the young side, preferably over the next 4–5 years.

GROSSO SENESE (VINO DA TAVOLO)* * * *

| 1985 Vino da Tavola (Il Palazzino) | C | 91 |

This wine, 100% Sangiovese, has been one of the most spectacular of all of the experimental Tuscan Vino da Tavolas produced. Quite a blockbuster wine in 1985, it was also stunningly rich and intense in 1983 and 1982. The 1985 has a black/ruby color, a magnificent perfume of black-cherry fruit and spicy new oak. Superconcentrated, full-bodied, forward yet tannic enough to last for 10 years, this is a great wine that typifies the best Tuscany can produce. Bravo!

IL PALAZZINO (CHIANTI)* * * *

1985 Chianti Classico	A	87
1982 Chianti Classico Riserva	B	87
1983 Chianti Classico Riserva	B	87
1985 Chianti Classico Riserva	B	90

It is difficult to find better Chianti than that made by Il Palazzino. The 1985 regular Chianti is surprisingly deep in color, rich, fat, full flavored, and ideal for drinking over the next 5–6 years. The 1985 Riserva is a compelling wine and raises the concentration and complexity levels several notches. It is an astonishing, rich, seductive Chianti that should drink beautifully for another decade. As for the 1983 Riserva, it has a full-intensity black-cherry and sweet toasty oak bouquet, expansive, broad, velvety flavors, full body, and enough tannin to ensure another 4–5 years of aging potential. The 1982 Riserva is similarly styled yet more velvety and developed. These are four very impressive Chiantis from one of the best-run small estates of Tuscany.

IL POGGIONE (BRUNELLO)* * * * *

| 1982 Brunello di Montalcino | C | 88 |
| 1985 Rosso di Montalcino | B | 88 |

I know it does not make any sense that the 1985 Rosso could be as good as the 1982 Brunello from Il Poggione, one of the finest producers of Brunello. However, I tasted them side by side, and while the Brunello is excellent, very rich, backward, tannic, and full-bodied as well as needing an additional 4–5 years to reach its apogee, the Rosso is exquisite for its type—deeply fruity, powerful yet lush, dramatic, and just loaded with gobs of leathery, berry-scented fruit. I would not hesitate to drink it over the next 5–7 years. Perhaps in time the Brunello will turn out to be better, but certainly this is one of the finest Rossos I have ever tasted.

IL SODACCIO (VINO DA TAVOLA)* * * *

| 1983 Vino da Tavola (Monte Vertine) | C | 87 |

| 1985 Vino da Tavola (Monte Vertine) | C | 90 |

There are extremely elegantly crafted wines from one of the most impeccable wineries in all of Tuscany, Monte Vertine. The style of this particular wine does not aim for pure power and richness, but rather it offers sensual, graceful cherry flavors wrapped intelligently in toasty oak. The taste of this wine reminds me of a fine Volnay from France.

ISOLE E OLENA (CHIANTI)* * * *

| 1985 Chianti Classico | A | 86 |

| 1983 Chianti Classico Riserva | B | 85 |

While the 1983 is a fully mature, open-knit, soft, raspberry and vanillin-scented wine with a velvety, gentle fruitiness and medium body, the 1985 regular Chianti shows a bit more depth, richness, and fat fruitiness. It should be drunk over the next 4–5 years.

LISINI (BRUNELLO)* * * *

| 1981 Brunello di Montalcino | C | 87 |

| 1982 Brunello di Montalcino | C | 85 |

| 1983 Brunello di Montalcino | C | 84 |

I have fond memories of the 1975 Lisini Brunello, but more recent vintages have been somewhat less impressive. Curiously, of the three vintages listed above, the weakest vintage produced the best wine for

Lisini, and while the 1982 and 1983 Brunellos are good, they do not show the complexity, balance, and richness of the 1981. These are good medium-weight Brunellos that seem less powerful and rich than this producer's wines from the early and mid seventies. Of the three vintages, the 1982 should last 10–12 years, and the 1981 and the 1983, 7–9 years.

MONSANTO (CHIANTI)* * * * *

1982 Chianti Classico	B	87
1981 Chianti Classico Il Poggio	C	88
1982 Chianti Classico Il Poggio	C	90
1983 Chianti Classico Il Poggio	C	90

No estate in Chianti has provided me with more great memories of that region's wines than Monsanto. I have bought, cellared, and drunk with immense pleasure the 1964, 1969, 1970, 1971, and 1975 single-vineyard Chiantis from Monsanto called Il Poggio. These are wonderfully rich, full, big wines with huge, smoky, tobacco-scented bouquets intertwined with plummy, mineral-scented, red fruits. They are wines that in vintages such as 1970 or 1971 easily last close to two decades when stored in a cool cellar. (Curiously, the 1971 in the decade of the seventies seemed head and shoulders above the 1970, but in the eighties, the 1971 has started to decline rapidly while the 1970 has blossomed into a very great wine.)

As for the recent vintages, one can hardly go wrong whether it be the 1981 or 1982. The 1981 shows surprising richness and fullness for the vintage; the 1982 Il Poggio and regular cuvée are both large-scaled, rich, highly extracted wines with quite a bit of body, outstanding concentration, and a sizable, muscular feel on the palate. While drinkable now, they give every indication of being even better in another 2–3 years, and lasting through the end of the century. As for the 1983, though not quite as full and as highly concentrated as the 1982, in many ways it is as good because of its unbelievable perfume of ripe berry fruit, smoky tobacco, and spicy mineral scents. It should last for 7–8 years. These wines are what great Chianti is all about, and it's a shame more producers don't have the same aspirations and commitment to quality as this winery.

MONTE ANTICO (TUSCANY)* * * *

1983 Monte Antico Riserva	A 87

1985 Monte Antico Riserva	B 89

This is one of my favorite producers in Tuscany, as the wines show excellent complexity and broad, expansive, smoky, meaty, fleshy flavors in a full-bodied format. The 1985 is showing more structure than the fully mature 1983, but both wines have very open, rich bouquets, and intense, ripe, deep, lingering flavors. Prices for the Monte Antico wines have never quite caught up with their quality, so this is an estate to search out for extremely well made, distinctive red wines.

PACENTI (CANALICCHIO DI SOPRA) (BRUNELLO)* * * * *

1982 Brunello di Montalcino	C 92

1983 Brunello di Montalcino	C 89

Based on the only two vintages I have tasted from this tiny producer, the 1982 and 1983, Pacenti is making splendid wine in Brunello di Montalcino. Curiously, little information is to be found on Pacenti in any of the major Italian wine books. The 1982 has a huge, chocolaty, cedary, truffle-scented bouquet that is first class. Extremely rich, deep, and full-bodied, this wine is quite serious and should age well for 5–12 more years. The 1983 is not as opulently rich or as lavishly deep as the exceptional 1982, but it does show elegant cedary, spicy aromas, a deep, fruity nose, full body, and a long finish with harder tannins than the 1982.

PALAZZO ALTESI (VINO DA TAVOLA)* * * * *

1983 Vino da Tavola (Altesino)	C 86

1985 Vino da Tavola (Altesino)	C 89

It is not surprising to see that this producer has done so well with its Sangiovese wine. Aged in oak casks, this wine shows a deep, rich ruby color, an exotic, smoky, spicy bouquet of sweet, plummy fruit, and quite a full-bodied, rich texture. Again, the greatness of the 1985 vintage has resulted in a wine with more layers of fruit and depth, and potentially more complexity than the good 1983.

PERCARLO (VINO DA TAVOLA)* * * *

1985 Vino da Tavola (San Giusto a Rentennano)	C 93

An absolute blockbuster wine, this 100% Sangiovese wine from Per-carlo is fermented and aged in small oak casks, and it is as rich and as promising as any Italian wine I have tasted. Deep-ruby/purple in color with a complex, tarry, berry, oak-scented bouquet, this beauti-fully concentrated, long, deep wine rivals virtually anything ever pro-duced in Italy. Made in very limited quantities, it should be at its best between 1990–1996. I can't recommend it highly enough; it's simply fantastic.

LE PERGOLE TORTE (VINO DA TAVOLA)* * * *

1983 Vino da Tavola (Monte Vertine)	C 87

1985 Vino da Tavola (Monte Vertine)	C 90

These Sangiovese wines, aged in oak casks, are quite classy, elegant examples of the new style of Tuscan wine at its best. There is an ample display of rich berry fruitiness combined with spicy new oak that seems to want to resemble a top Ridge Zinfandel from California, or a fine Pomerol from France. The 1983 has layers of cherry, plummy fruit in a soft, luscious, well-balanced texture, and while deliciously pleasurable now, it should last for another 5–6 years. The 1985 is the best Le Pergole Torte I have tasted, displaying sensational ripeness, full body, and superb depth; it should last for at least another 7–8 years.

PERTIMALI (BRUNELLO)* * * * *

1982 Brunello di Montalcino	C 92

1983 Brunello di Montalcino	C 90

Pertimali, perhaps my favorite Brunello producer, has made a great 1982 that is oozing with ripe, smoky, tobacco-scented fruit, has an uncommon, precocious appeal to it, exceptional concentration and length, and enough tannin to guarantee 6–12 years of further evolu-tion. It is a classic wine from a generally overrated viticultural area. As for the 1983, it is a candidate for the top Brunello of the vintage, showing superb ripeness, full body, great length, and again the open-knit, well-evolved, exotic bouquet of fresh tobacco and spicy, plummy, smoky fruit.

LA PODERINA (BRUNELLO)* * *

1982 Brunello di Montalcino	C	87

1983 Brunello di Montalcino	C	84

Though I know little about this producer, both of these wines are quite velvety for a Brunello and are enjoyable for their less aggressive, smooth, rich, ripe, savory characters, which make them drinkable now. But given their depth, they should certainly hold for 5–6 more years. The 1982 has more ripe fruit in evidence than the 1983.

RUFFINO (CHIANTI)* * * *

1982 Chianti Classico Riserva Ducale	C	88

1983 Chianti Classico Riserva Ducale	C	87

Ruffino makes a number of levels of Chianti, but their very best (and most expensive) is the gold label Riserva Ducale. In top vintages, it is a candidate for one of the best wines made in Chianti. Consequently, I was not surprised to see how well the 1982 performed. Nearly exceptional, this expressive, rich wine is filled with ripe, cedary fruit, has considerable depth, and enough concentration to last for at least another decade. The 1983 is close in quality, seemingly a bit less evolved and complex in its bouquet, but still quite full-bodied, concentrated, and powerful on the palate with certainly as much aging potential as the 1982.

SAMMARCO (VINO DA TAVOLA)* * * * *

1983 Vino da Tavola (Castello di Rampolla)	D	93

1985 Vino da Tavola (Castello di Rampolla)	D	94

Of all the experimental Cabernet Sauvignon wines, the Sammarco is undoubtedly the most complex and promising. I even prefer it to the famous Sassicaia. While a small percentage of Sangiovese is blended in for complexity, the Sammarco seems to have a style all its own—I have often called it the Mouton Rothschild of Tuscany. Unbelievably, the 1983 seems even better than the great 1982 and 1981. A stunning bouquet of oak, minerals, and plumlike tobacco-scented fruit is super.

On the palate, this is a rich, deep, long, concentrated, and impeccably well balanced wine, which I would expect to be at its full maturity between 1990–1998. If that's not enough, the 1985 is an even richer, more compelling, profound wine showing astonishing richness and complexity; it should last a good 10 years longer than the 1983.

SAN GIUSTO A RENTENNANO (CHIANTI)* * * *

1985 Chianti Classico	A	88

This is an extremely impressive Chianti from one of the best small producers in Tuscany. It has a deep ruby color, a full-intensity bouquet of toasty, ripe berry fruit, surprising depth and richness, and a long, intense finish. Drink it over the next 5–6 years.

SASSICAIA (VINO DA TAVOLA)* * * * *

1983 Vino da Tavola (Marchesi Incisa della Rocchetta)	E	90
1985 Vino da Tavola (Marchesi Incisa della Rocchetta)	E	92

This famous wine has become such a luxury-priced item that I wonder who really drinks it anymore. Nevertheless, if you are a spendthrift and want what some people think is Italy's best and most historic Cabernet Sauvignon, then take a look at the 1983 and 1985 Sassicaia. Both follow in the great tradition of these wines in vintages such as 1982, 1981, and 1978. Cedary aromas intermixed with scents of blackcurrants are enticing. On the palate, both the 1983 and 1985 show a firm structure, deep, tannic flavors, and quite long futures. Clearly both wines are built for the long term, although the 1985 seems to have slightly softer tannins and a more plump texture than the 1983. I would not want to drink these wines until the mid-nineties or beyond.

SELVAPIANA (CHIANTI)* * *

1981 Chianti Ruffina	A	85
1985 Chianti Ruffina	A	87

The 1985 Chianti Ruffina shows a ripe, rich, raspberry-scented character, plenty of attractive suppleness, and a full-bodied, velvety finish. The 1981 shows more evolution than one might expect, more of a strawberry- and raspberry-scented character, and again, a soft, lush finish. It should be drunk over the next 1–2 years. Both are excellent bargains.

SOLAIA (VINO DA TAVOLA)* * * * *

1982 Vino da Tavola (Antinori)	E	93

1985 Vino da Tavola (Antinori)	E	95

I have yet to see a bottle of this wine on a retailer's shelf, but I have been the beneficiary of some generous friends who have offered it to me in tastings. It is one of the titans of Italy, and I know it has received so much publicity and hype that it has its skeptics. However, Solaia is a fabulous wine, particularly in the two extraordinary vintages of 1982 and 1985; I found both better than I expected. They share a deep-ruby/purple color with a bouquet that is crammed with spicy oak, blackcurrants, Oriental spices, and ripe, even overripe, plums. Both wines have the concentration of the greatest 1982 Bordeaux, a velvety texture, sensational length, and behind a tremendous amount of melted tannins, there is an avalanche of unbelievably opulent, unctuous fruit. What a shame there is so little of this wine available. If you can find some, both the 1982 and 1985 share a similar style because of the velvety, superripeness of the fruit in those vintages. Both should keep for at least a decade.

SOLATIA BASILICA (VINO DA TAVOLA)* * *

1983 Vino da Tavola (Villa Cafaggio)	C	86

1985 Vino da Tavola (Villa Cafaggio)	C	90

This Sangiovese-based wine from one of the better Chianti producers, Villa Cafaggio, is absolutely stunning in 1985 with its full-blown, plummy, oaky bouquet, lush, velvety flavors, and soft tannins. This hedonistic wine offers lovers of decadence a delicious Tuscan red table wine for imbibing over the next 7–8 years. The 1983, also very good, is a downsized version of the powerful, unctuous, lavishly rich 1985.

TALENTI (BRUNELLO)* * *

1981 Brunello di Montalcino	D	90

1982 Brunello di Montalcino	D	92

Piero Talenti is the architect behind the wines of the famous Brunello estate of the Franceschi family called Il Poggione. He also has his own tiny operation, and if the 1981 and 1982 are any indication, Talenti could be a source for some super Brunello di Montalcinos. The 1981 has remarkable strength and size for a vintage that has been called mediocre and light. The wine is dense in color with an unevolved but promising bouquet, intense, full-bodied flavors, outstanding richness, and considerable tannic clout. I don't expect it to be in its prime until 1993–2005. If that sounds good, the 1982 is even more powerful and rich, yet softer because of the style of that vintage. It's crammed with rich, cedary, plummy fruit, and has enormous body and great length. It will probably be drinking better several years before the 1981, but it will last every bit as long given its exceptional richness.

TAVERNELLE (VINO DA TAVOLA)* *

1983 Vino da Tavola (Villa Banfi)	C	82

1985 Vino da Tavola (Villa Banfi)	C	84

Much has been written about the efforts made by Villa Banfi to produce high-quality wines. Given what surely must be an extraordinary commitment of money, I'm optimistic that fine wines will eventually be made here. However, at present, the wines have that high-tech, ultraclean, ultramodern style that I feel eviscerates a wine of its true personality and character. For example, both of these Cabernet Sauvignons from Villa Banfi are technically correct, superclean, and no doubt have the right levels of acidity, pH, tannin, alcohol, etc. However, they lack soul and a feeling that the person who made them truly loves wine as opposed to being a technocrat hired by a gigantic corporation with plenty of money. As the winery becomes more established, I hope some individuality and character will be put into the wines. For now, they taste like anybody's above-average Cabernet Sauvignon made in a squeaky clean, sterile style.

TIGNANELLO (VINO DA TAVOLA)* * * *

1983 Vino da Tavola (Antinori)	C	90

1985 Vino da Tavola (Antinori)	C	90

I lament that the price for Tignanello, like that of a number of Italian wines, has soared into the stratosphere over the last several years, but Tignanello is still one of the finest Sangiovese-based wines. Both the 1985 and 1983 show wonderfully rich, fat, intense flavors that offer a nice blend of cedary fruit and oak. On the palate, they are quite full-bodied, display excellent richness, a spicy, weedy, blackcurrant fruitiness, and long finishes. Drinkable today, they should improve over the next 5–7 years.

VILLA ANTINORI (CHIANTI)* * *

1982 Chianti Classico Riserva	B	85

1983 Chianti Classico Riserva	B	86

1985 Chianti Classico Riserva	B	87

The name "Antinori" is synonymous with the hopes and aspirations of Tuscany, as well as with some of the very best wines that that bucolic and historic viticultural region can produce. While Antinori is famous for his Tignanellos and Solaias, it is his Chiantis, produced in much larger quantities and therefore more accessible to the drinking public, that are better known. One can do a great deal worse than an Antinori Chianti Classico Riserva from the 1985, 1983, or 1982 vintages. All show intelligent winemaking, a supple, rich, ripe fruitiness interwoven with aromas of oak and leather. I'm not sure each reflects its vintage as much as it does the Antinori style, but these are delicious, ready-to-drink wines that will keep another 4–5 years.

Tuscany's White Wines

Over recent years, much has been made of the new Tuscan white wines. There is the Pomino from Frescobaldi, the Galestro of Antinori, the inexpensive Bianco di Pitigliano, and of course, numerous white wines usually made from Trebbiano by the Chianti producers. Italy does indeed make a few lovely white wines today, but none of the aforementioned Tuscan whites are any more exciting than the domestic jug wines that Americans can obtain at lower prices. The only Tuscan white I can stand behind and recommend enthusiastically is the Vernaccia di San Gimignano. Thankfully, it is not made from the bland, tart Trebbiano grape, but rather from the Vernaccia grape, and it comes from the remarkable medieval fortified hill town of San Gimignano. All the Vernaccias today are made in stainless steel, temperature-controlled tanks, and the results are refreshingly crisp, light yet flavorful, dry wines that seem to perfectly match, and are easy to drink with, fish and chicken. For Vernaccia, 1985 was an excellent vintage, but most should have been drunk up by now. The 1986s are better than the 1985s, and the 1987s look to be much better than expected. Reports from Italy indicate that 1988 was excellent for Vernaccia. The best Vernaccias, year in and year out, are the wines from

Falchini, Teruzzi, Strozzi, di Pancole, and Pietraserena. Of these five excellent producers, I find Strozzi's the fruitiest, Falchini's and di Pancole's the lightest, and Teruzzi and Pietraserena the fullest. A double pleasure about Vernaccia di San Gimignano is the price; despite the frail American dollar, they cost no more than $7 a bottle. Following are the best wines of Vernaccia di San Gimignano.

THE BEST WINES OF VERNACCIA DI SAN GIMIGNANO

Producer	Vintage
Falchini	1986, 1987
di Pancole	1986, 1987
Pietraserena	1985, 1986
Strozzi	1986
Teruzzi & Puthod	1986, 1987
Vigna a Solatio	1986

OTHER SIGNIFICANT RED WINES OF ITALY

GIUSEPPE TASCA D'ALMERITA (SICILY)* * *

1982 Regaleali   B   78

This producer is renowned for making Sicily's best red wine. Having attended a vertical tasting recently, I found most of the wines big, often thick, heavy, too alcoholic, and often excessively tannic. The 1982 is robust but lacks finesse and comes across as a rather hefty, somewhat overbearing, coarsely made wine.

D'ANGELO (CAMPANIA)* * * *

1982 Aglianco del Vulture	C	88

1983 Aglianco del Vulture	C	86

While many wine lovers consider the Italian winery of Mastroberardino the best winery in southern Italy, it seems to me that D'Angelo's wines are superior, as evidenced by his chocolate-, coffee-, and leather-scented, rich, full-bodied, powerful but lush and supple 1982, and the somewhat lighter 1983. These are wines for wintertime drinking with a hearty soup or stew.

BONCOMPAGNI LUDOVISI PRINCIPE DI VENOSA* * * * *

1982 Fiorano	C	90

1983 Fiorano	C	88

1985 Fiorano	C	89

Perhaps the best-kept secret of Italy is the tiny quantities of Fiorano, based on Merlot and Cabernet Sauvignon, made south of Rome along the ancient Appian Way. International winebroker Neil Empson represents this estate, which ages its wines two years in oak before releasing them. The result is a wine with the decadent richness and succulence of not just a good but a great Pomerol of France. This serious wine is probably one of Italy's top ten red wines, and certainly the best wine made from Cabernet Sauvignon and Merlot, yet it has received little publicity. The tiny quantities produced are no doubt the reason it lacks celebrity status. A 1970 tasted in 1987 showed just how extraordinary this wine can be when it reaches maturity, but the softness of the Merlot in the blend gives the wine an accessibility while young. This rare, fabulous wine is well worth searching out.

CA' DEL BOSCO (LOMBARDY)* * * *

1985 Rosso	C	84

Maurizio Zanella, the gregarious genius behind Italy's best sparkling wines, also has an interest in producing small-cask–aged red wine. His two red wines of 1984, a Rosso and Franciaforte, were unforgivably vegetal, green, and ghastly, but his 1985 Rosso shows none of this vegetal character. A ripe, round, fruity wine with good intensity and a supple, soft finish, the 1985 is not quite at the level of his white wines, but progress can be seen.

LUNGAROTTI (UMBRIA)* * * *

1982 Rubesco	B	72
1978 Rubesco Riserva Monticchio	C	73

Lungarotti has always been one of my favorite sources for Italian red wines, but I have to admit my disappointment with his 1982 Rubesco, an uncommonly narrow, tart, unpleasant wine with short flavors and excessive acidity. Even more shocking was the showing of several bottles of the 1978 Rubesco Riserva from the vineyard called Monticchio. The 1975 version of this wine was and still is a great classic. The 1978 is rather dull and nowhere near the quality of the 1975. I hope these poor showings are just examples of isolated bad lots of wine, because Lungarotti has been one of the great pioneers of the wines of Umbria and has generally produced high-quality wine.

MASTROBERARDINO (CAMPANIA)* * * *

1985 Lacryma Christi	B	81
1982 Taurasi	D	82
1983 Taurasi	D	85
1977 Taurasi Riserva	E	87

More than a few knowledgeable observers have long believed that Taurasi Riserva is one of Italy's half dozen best red wines. Certainly the winery, which dates from 1580 and is working from probably the most ancient vineyards in all of Italy, is of great historical significance. Furthermore, the wines can be good and sometimes even outstanding, as was the case with the famous 1968 Taurasi Riserva. Over recent years, the quality has been a bit spotty, the wines lacking fruit in vintages such as 1982, 1981, and 1978. In addition, the smell and taste of Taurasi is quite different, having an earthy, almost cheesy nose that seems unusual and at first off-putting. But the wines age extremely well, seeming to fill out and show much more intensity after 7–8 years than they do when tasted young. This seems to be the case with the 1977, which the Mastroberardino family touted highly when it was released, but which I never found to be all that interesting. Now it is starting to blossom and show much more richness and ripeness, and it is certainly a very good wine. Readers wanting to indulge in these peculiar and unique wines may want to first try the 1983 Taurasi regular bottling. The 1983 is considered by the Mastroberardinos as the best vintage since 1977. The Riserva will only increase the intensity factor over the regular cuvée. A lighter red wine called Lacryma Christi is also made, and the 1985 is a medium weight, nice, charming, soft, fruity wine for drinking over the next 3–4 years. These are interesting wines, but they are not inexpensive and seem to require a cultivated taste to be fully appreciated.

EMILIO PEPE (ABRUZZI)* * * *

| 1982 Montepulciano d'Abruzzi | C | ? |

This producer's wines are hard to fathom. I remember an interesting 1974 with a spicy, cigar-box bouquet, and a deep, full-bodied, rustic feel on the palate. However, the 1978 was flawed by excessive volatile acidity, and while some bottles of the 1982 appear quite rich, intense, and not volatile, others are volatile to the point of being undrinkable. This is a good producer making interesting, unmanipulated wines, but consistency is certainly a problem.

QUINTARELLI (VENETO)* * * *

1982 Valpolicella	B	85
1983 Valpolicella	B	86
1985 Valpolicella	B	87

Quintarelli is a great master of Valpolicella, and for those who have been weaned on the ocean of industrial Valpolicella that has been eviscerated of flavor, and often tastes cooked or pasteurized, one taste of a Valpolicella from Quintarelli is enough to inspire confidence in this maligned wine. Whether it be the 1982, 1983, or 1985, this Valpolicella is bursting with deliriously enjoyable succulent red fruit, is supple, fat, even crunchy on the palate, and makes for a totally hedonistic but enjoyable drink.

DR. COSIMO TAURINO (APULIA)* * * *

| 1981 Salice Salentino Riserva | A | 85 |

Looking for a fine value from Italy at under $6 a bottle? There is no better source than the full-bodied, robust, black-cherry-scented-and-flavored, spicy 1981 Salice Salentino Riserva, one of the great red wine values in the world. Not exactly a summer-weight wine, but for drinking fall through spring, it's a red wine with gusto, offering plenty of satisfying flavors.

EDOARDO VALENTINI (ABRUZZI)* * * *

1982 Montepulciano d'Abruzzi	C	88

Valentini is considered by many to be the finest producer of Montepulciano d'Abruzzi, and his 1982 is a wonderfully rich, unfiltered, intense red wine with quite a fascinating array of spicy, cedar-box, vaguely Oriental aromas. There is even a hickory-wood-fired-barbecue scent in the background. This viscous, alcoholic, rich wine is a bit overbearing for light drinking, but when matched with the right robust foods and drunk in cool weather, it is quite pleasurable.

OTHER SIGNIFICANT WHITE WINES OF ITALY

A Guide to the Best of Italy's Other Dry White Table Wines

Producer	Best Wines	Vintages to Buy	Price Code
Abbazia di Rosazzo	Ronco Acacie	1986, 1987	A
	Pinot Bianco	1987	A
	Sauvignon	1987	A
	Tocai	1987	A
Anselmi	Soave	1986, 1987	A

Producer	Best Wines	Vintages to Buy	Price Code
Anselmi	Soave Capitel Foscarino	1987	A
Bellavista	N.V. Brut Sparkling	Nonvintage	B
	Franciacorta Brut	1984, 1985	B
	Gran Cuvée Pas Opere	1983, 1985	D
Berlucchi	Cuvée Imperiale Brut	Nonvintage	B
	Cuvée Rose Imperiale Brut	Nonvintage	B
Bigi	Orvieto Classico	1986, 1987	A
Borgo Conventi	Chardonnay	1986, 1987	B
	Pinot Bianco	1986, 1987	B
	Pinot Grigio	1986, 1987	B
	Tocai	1986, 1987	B
Bortoluzzi	Chardonnay	1986, 1987	B
	Foian Blanc	1986, 1987	B
	Pinot Grigio	1986, 1987	B
Boscaini	Soave	1987	A
Bucci	Verdicchio	1985, 1986	B
Ca' del Bosco	Brut Méthode Champenoise	Nonvintage	C
	Chardonnay	1985, 1986	C
	Dosage Zéro	Nonvintage	C
	Rosé Brut Sparkling	Nonvintage	C
Enofriulia	Müller-Thurgau	1987	A
	Pinot Grigio	1987	A
	Tocai	1987	A
F. Furlan	Pinot Grigio	1986, 1987	A
	Ribolla Gialla	1986, 1987	A
	Tocai	1986, 1987	A
Maculan	Breganze di Breganze	1987	B
	Chardonnay	1987	B
	Prato di Canzio	1987	B
Marini (Trevi)	Chardonnay	1987	A
	Pinot Grigio	1987	A
Mastroberardino	Fiano di Avellino-Vignadora	1986, 1987	C
	Greco di Tufo-Vigna d'Angelo	1986, 1987	C
	Lacryma Christie	1986, 1987	C
	Plinius	1987	C
Maso Poli	Chardonnay	1987	A
	Pinot Grigio	1987	A
Mirafiore	Soave	1987	A
Guerrieri Rizzardi	Dogoli	1986, 1987	A
	Soave Costeggiola	1986, 1987	A
Ronchi di Fornaz	Pinot Bianco	1986, 1987	A
	Tocai	1986, 1987	A
Roncho del Gnemiz	Chardonnay	1986, 1987	A
	Müller-Thurgau	1986, 1987	A
	Pinot Grigio	1986, 1987	A
	Tocai Fiulano	1986, 1987	A
Ruffino	Monte Rossa Rosé Sparkling	Nonvintage	C
Castel Schwanburg	Chardonnay	1986, 1987	A

	Pinot Grigio	1986, 1987	A
Tedeschi	Bianco di Custoza	1986, 1987	A
J. Tiefenbrunner	Chardonnay	1986, 1987	A
	Pinot Grigio	1986, 1987	A
Valentini	Trebbiano d'Abruzzi	1985, 1986	C
Zardetto	Brut Prosecco di Conegliano	Nonvintage	B

3. GERMANY: SEARCHING FOR A NEW FORMULA FOR SUCCESS

The Basics

TYPES OF WINE

With 250,000 acres in vine and a production that hit 115 million cases in the bountiful year of 1982, Germany is a major producer of wine. The wines of consequence are the whites, which usually contain a degree of sweetness, although drier styles aimed at the American and British export markets are appearing with greater frequency. Despite the newer-styled, drier wines such as Novum, created by the famous New York City winebroker Peter M. F. Sichel, and the wine from the five-year-old Association of Charta Estates (a group of Rheingau producers who are making drier, fuller wines), Germany's winedom is still controlled by the 1971 law that divided German wines into seven grades, all based on ascending levels of ripeness and sweetness, as well as price. These seven levels are:

1) Tafelwein
2) Qualitätswein (QbA)
3) Kabinett
4) Spätlese
5) Auslese
6) Beerenauslese
7) Trockenbeerenauslese

In addition to these, there are other generic categories of German wines. The Trocken and Halbtrocken wines are the two generic types of dry German wine. The Trockens tend to be drier, but also boring, thin wines with little body or flavor. Halbtrockens also taste dry but are permitted to have slightly more residual sugar and are marginally more interesting. I rarely recommend either because they are not very good and they are commercial creations made to take advantage of the public's demand for "dry" wine. A third type of wine is called Eiswein, Germany's rarest and most expensive wine. It is made from frozen grapes, generally picked in December or January, or even February. It is quite rare, and a very, very sweet wine, but has remarkably high acidity and can last and improve in the bottle for decades. It does have great character, but one must usually pay an unbelievably steep price to experience it.

There are also the sparkling wines of Germany, called Deutscher Sekt, which should be drunk only by certified masochists as they are a ghastly lot of overly sulphured wines. Lastly, there is the German wine that everyone knows about, the ubiquitous Liebfraumilch. This sugary, grapy drink is to quality German wine what California wine coolers are to that state's serious wine producers.

GRAPE VARIETIES

Müller-Thurgau—Representing 25% of Germany's vineyards, Müller-Thurgau has become the most widely planted grape because it gives prolific yields of juice (90–100 hectoliters a hectare is not uncommon). Ignore all of the self-serving promotion from German wine importers about Müller-Thurgau. It is not a great wine grape, and the Germans have planted it for quantity, not quality.

Riesling—While Riesling accounts for only 20% of the vineyards in Germany, it produces about 95% of that country's finest wines. If the bottle does not say Riesling on it, then chances are you are not getting Germany's best wine. Riesling achieves its greatest pinnacles of success in Germany, whether it be a dry, crisp, tangy Kabinett or decadently sweet, nectarlike Trockenbeerenauslese.

Sylvaner—This unimpressive grape accounts for 10% of Germany's vineyards and rarely results in anything interesting. Most Sylvaners have either a nasty vegetal streak to them or are simply dull and flat.

Other grape varieties—Much of Germany's problem today is that such a large proportion of its vineyards are planted with mediocre grape varieties. The remaining 45% of the vineyards generally consists of grapes that have little personality and names such as Kerner, Gutedel, Morio-Muskat, Bacchus, Faberrebe, Huxelrebe, Optima, and

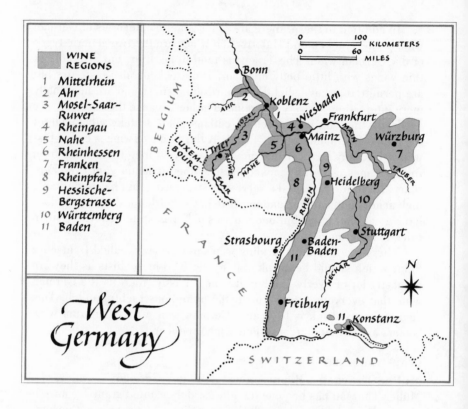

WINE
REGIONS
1 Mittelrhein
2 Ahr
3 Mosel-Saar-
   Ruwer
4 Rheingau
5 Nahe
6 Rheinhessen
7 Franken
8 Rheinpfalz
9 Hessische-
   Bergstrasse
10 Württemberg
11 Baden

West Germany

Rheingau

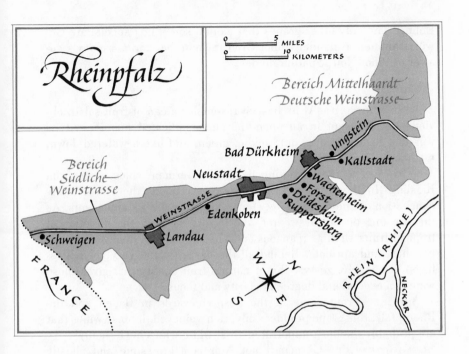

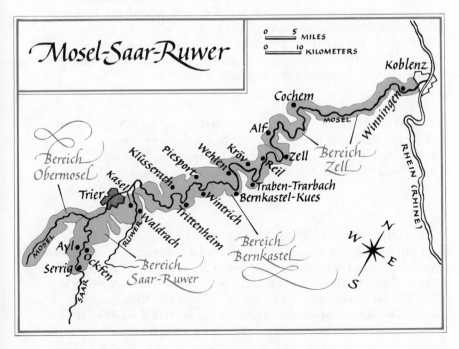

Ebling. The only other grapes that can do something special are Gewürztraminer, Rulander (Pinot Gris), Scheurebe, and Germany's answer to Pinot Noir, Spatburgunder.

FLAVORS

Müller-Thurgau—At its best, it resembles a can of fruit salad, obvious but pleasant in an open-knit, uncomplicated manner. At its worst, it tastes washed out, acidic, green, and like a watered-down, mediocre Riesling.

Riesling—The most exciting flavors in German wines come from Riesling. In the drier and slightly sweet versions there is a lovely concoction of apple, lime, wet stone, and citric flavors and scents. As the Riesling becomes sweeter, the flavors move in the direction of tropical fruits such as mangoes and pineapples, and honeyed apples, peaches, and apricots. Behind all the flavor (in the very good Rieslings) is a steely, zesty, vibrant natural-fruit acidity that gives those wines an exceptional degree of clarity and focus.

Rulander—From some of the best vineyards in Baden and the Rheinpfalz, this grape produces oily, rich, honeyed, intense wines that are probably the most underrated great white wines in Germany.

Spatburgunder—German Pinot Noir is a grotesque and ghastly wine that tastes like dirty, sweet, faded, and diluted red Burgundy from an incompetent producer. Need I say more?

Sylvaner—On occasion, Sylvaner from selected vineyards in Franken and the Rheinhessen can be a rich, muscular, deep wine, but more often it is vegetal, thin, and dull.

AGING POTENTIAL

Auslese: 3–15 years

Beerenauslese: 10–40+ years

Kabinett: 3–6 years

Liebfraumilch: 8–16 months

Qualitätswein (QbA): 2–4 years

Spätlese: 3–10 years

Tafelwein: 8–16 months

Trockenbeerenauslese: 10–40+ years

OVERALL QUALITY LEVEL

At the top level, the quality is impeccably high, but at this level we are talking about small estates that make virtually all their wines from Riesling. High-quality estates that are members of the VDP Estates (Verband Deutscher Prädikats und Qualitätsweingüter), which has 180 members, and the Charta Estates of the Rheingau, with 34 members, are scrupulously trying to put as much quality into the bottle as anyone. However, the German government has been inexcusably remiss over recent decades in allowing too many high-yielding, low-quality grapes to be planted (the 1987 average yield per hectare was an incredible 97 hectoliters), thus causing consumers to become increasingly skeptical about the seriousness of German wine quality. For example, in the mediocre year of 1987, 77% of the wine produced was allowed to be called QbA (Qualitätswein bestimmer Anbaugebiete) and only 2% was declassified as simple table wine (Tafelwein). This is ridiculous. A campaign to promote the top-quality German estates that are making the finest German wines is long overdue. Until the consumer begins to believe that Germany is serious about quality, these wines will be difficult to sell, which is a shame for the growers and producers I have listed in my overall guide to quality.

THE MOST IMPORTANT INFORMATION TO KNOW

As indicated above, the Charta Estate growers from the Rheingau (the labels have two Roman arches and the words Vereinigung der Charta-Weingüter on them) and the VDP Estates (whose labels are distinguished by a bunch of thirteen grapes superimposed on a black eagle with the letters *VDP* surrounding it) represent a current total of 214 growers who are dedicated to producing only the highest-quality Rieslings. Look for their wines, and attempt to memorize the names of the top growers listed in the charts that follow. This is the first and most important step in finding the finest German wines. Secondly, here are some guidelines that attempt to simplify the impossibly complex, overly detailed German wine laws of 1971:

1. There are eleven major wine-producing zones in Germany. Within these zones there are three subdistricts, the most general of which is called a Bereich. This is used to describe a wine from anywhere within the boundaries of that particular Bereich. An analogy that may help clarify this distinction would be the closest French equivalent, a wine entitled to Appellation Bordeaux Contrôlée or Appellation Bourgogne Contrôlée. Within the Bereich there are more specific boundaries called Grosslagen, to which the closest French equivalent would be the generic Appellation St.-Julien Contrôlée or Appellation Morey–St.-Denis Contrôlée. These would be wines not from a specific château or specific vineyard, but from a specific region or collection of sites for vineyards. There are 152 different Grosslagen in Germany. The most specific zone in Germany is called an Einzellage, which is a specific site or vineyard. There are 2,600 of them in Germany, and again, by analogy, the closest French equivalent would be a specific

St.-Julien château such as Ducru-Beaucaillou, or a specific Premiér Cru or Grand Cru Burgundy vineyard in Morey–St.-Denis such as Clos des Lambrays. Perhaps this will help one to understand the breakdown of the German wine zones. However, few people have the patience to memorize the best Einzellagen or Grosslagen, so it is much more important to try to remember the names of some of the best producers.

2. The majority of the best producers in Germany are located in four of the eleven German wine zones. They are the Mosel-Saar-Ruwer, the Rheingau, the Rheinhessen, and the Rheinpfalz. While there are certainly good wines, even some outstanding wines, made in the other seven German wine zones, far and away the great majority of the finest German wines are produced in these four regions, with the Mosel-Saar-Ruwer being the very best region in all of Germany.

3. The best German wines are those produced at the Kabinett, Spät-lese, Auslese, Beerenauslese, and Trockenbeerenauslese levels of ripeness and sweetness. Most consumers tasting a Kabinett wine would not find it particularly sweet, although there is residual sugar in the wine. Because of the high natural acidity found in German wines, a Kabinett generally tastes fresh, fruity, but not sweet to most palates. However, most tasters will detect a small amount of sweet-ness in a Spätlese, and even more with an Auslese. All three of these types of wines are ideal as an aperitif or with food, whereas the wines of the Beerenauslese and Trockenbeerenauslese designations are clearly dessert wines, very rich and quite sweet. One should keep in mind that the alcohol level in most German wines averages 7–9%, so one can drink much more of it without feeling its effects. One of the naïve criticisms of German wines is that they do not go well with food. However, anyone who has tried a fine Kabinett, Spätlese, or Auslese with Oriental food, with roast pork, or even with certain types of fowl such as pheasant or turkey can tell you that these wines work partic-ularly well, especially Spätlese and Auslese.

4. The best German wines age like a fine Bordeaux. In great vintages, such as 1985 or 1983, one can expect a Kabinett, Spätlese, or Auslese from a top producer to evolve and improve in the bottle for 5–10 years. In a great vintage, a Beerenauslese or a Trockenbeerenauslese can improve for two or three decades. This is a fact, not a myth, to which those who have recently tasted some of the great Ausleses from 1959 can easily attest. German wines at the top levels, from the top produc-ers, do indeed improve remarkably in the bottle, though the trend among consumers is to drink them when they are young, fresh, and crisp.

VINTAGE GUIDE

1987—A mediocre vintage followed an unusual growing season that was characterized by a wet, cold summer but glorious September and mixed bag of weather in October. The quality is expected to be better than either 1980 or 1984, and many growers reported harvests close in size to those in 1986. The average production was a whopping 96 hectoliters per hectare, which is excessive. Interestingly, this appears to be a good year for the rare nectarlike Eisweins.

1986—A copious crop of grapes has resulted in pleasant, agreeable, soft, fruity wines that will have broad commercial appeal. Because of the size of this crop, prices dropped, for in 1985 the crop had been smaller than normal. All in all, this vintage will be regarded by the trade as a useful, practical year of good rather than great wines.

1985—The German wine trade has touted this year rather highly, but except for a handful of areas, it is not comparable to the outstanding 1983 vintage. Nevertheless, it is a very good, sometimes great year with a moderate production of wines with good acidity and more typical textures and characteristics than the opulent, richly fruity 1983s. Like 1983, the dryness during the summer and the fall prevented the formation of *Botrytis cinerea*. The Rieslings in many cases are very good but will be firmer and slower to evolve and less open than the more precocious, overt, fruity 1983s. Overall, the 1985s should be at their best between 1988 and 1995. The top successes are in the Middle Mosel, with potentially great wines from villages such as Urzig and Erden.

1984—Fresh, light, very pleasant, straightforward wines that are neither green nor too acidic were produced in this vintage of average quality and below-average quantity. They will not keep, so drink the 1984s over the next 3–4 years. The Mosel estate of Dr. F. Weins-Prüm Erben made excellent wines in 1984, as did Monchof.

1983—Most growers seem to feel that this vintage, which has received the most publicity since the 1976, is the best since then. Though very large throughout all viticultural areas of Germany, this crop was especially large and exceptional in quality in the Mosel-Saar-Ruwer region. The wines have excellent concentration, very fine levels of tartaric rather than green malic acidity, and a degree of precocious ripeness and harmonious roundness that gives the wines wonderful appeal now. However, because of their depth and overall balance, they should age well for at least 10 or more years. The vintage seemed strongest at the Spätlese level, with little Auslese, Beerenauslese, and Trockenbeerenauslese wines produced. For Eiswein, 1983 was also a great year, because as a result of an early freeze, above-normal quantities of this nectarlike, opulent wine were made. However, despite larger quantities than normal, the prices are outrageously high for the Eisweins, but very realistic and reasonable for the rest of the wines.

1982—In 1982 the Germans harvested a record crop of wine. The wines are ready to drink, fruity, somewhat soft, and on occasion, somewhat diluted because of the huge crop, but very cleanly made and fresh. Few wines at the Auslese level and above were produced. Overall, 1982 is a big, commercial vintage with plenty of appeal, and it is priced quite reasonably. The wines should now be drunk up.

1981—The Mosel was particularly blessed in 1981 with a number of excellent Kabinett and Spätlese level wines produced. A little bit of Eiswein of outstanding quality was produced in the Rheingau.

1980—A somewhat maligned vintage, but as in the rest of Europe, there are many successful wines, although few great ones. Certainly the Mosel and the Rheingau seemed to have produced better wines than elsewhere in Germany. These wines are now fully mature and should be drunk before the end of the decade.

1979—Between 1976 and 1983, this is certainly the most successful overall vintage for all of Germany. The quality in the Mosel was very good, even excellent, and the wines extremely well balanced with very good acidity and wonderful fresh, nicely concentrated fruit flavors that are rounding into the full bloom of maturity at the moment. The top Rieslings are fully mature and should be drunk before the end of this decade.

Older Vintages

The great vintage that can still be found in the marketplace is 1976, a vintage that, by German standards, produced incredibly ripe, intense, opulent wines, with a significant amount of wine produced at the Auslese and Beerenauslese levels. These tend to be very sweet and are drinking sensationally well at the moment. The top wines should continue to last for another 5–8 years. Some critics have disputed the greatness of this vintage, saying that the 1976s are low in acidity, but that seems to be a minority point of view. The wines remain reasonably priced at the Auslese level, but the Beerenausleses and the Trockenbeerenausleses from this vintage are soaring into the stratosphere in price. The 1977 vintage should be avoided, and 1978, unlike in France, was not a particularly successful year in Germany. Well-kept 1975s can provide great enjoyment, as can the wines from another great vintage, 1971. I would avoid the wines from 1972, and of course, the 1973s, which were good in the mid-seventies but are now tiring quite a bit.

A GUIDE TO GERMANY'S BEST PRODUCERS

* * * * * (OUTSTANDING PRODUCERS)

F. W. Gymnasium (Mosel-Saar-Ruwer)
F. Haag (Mosel-Saar-Ruwer)
Monchof (Mosel-Saar-Ruwer)
Egon Müller-Scharzhof (Mosel-Saar-Ruwer)

J. J. Prüm (Mosel-Saar-Ruwer)
von Schubert Maximin Grunhaus (Mosel-Saar-Ruwer)
Geltz-Zilliken (Mosel-Saar-Ruwer)

* * * * (EXCELLENT PRODUCERS)

Adelmann (Württemberg)
Aschrottsche Erben (Rheingau)
A. Babach Erben (Rheinhessen)
Bassermann-Jordan (Rheinpfalz)
Bergweiler-Prüm-Erben (Mosel-Saar-Ruwer)
Bischofliches (Mosel-Saar-Ruwer)
H. Braun (Rheinhessen)
Baron von Brentano (Rheingau)
Dr. Burklin-Wolf (Rheinpfalz)
Christoffel-Berres (Mosel-Saar-Ruwer)
Hans Crusius (Nahe)
Deinhard (Mosel-Saar-Ruwer and Rheinpfalz)
O. Dunweg (Mosel-Saar-Ruwer)
G. Siben Erben (Rheinpfalz)
Dr. Fischer (Mosel-Saar-Ruwer)
Forstmeister-Geltz-Erben (Mosel-Saar-Ruwer)
Freiherr von Heddesdorff (Mosel-Saar-Ruwer)
Graf zu Hoensbroech (Mosel-Saar-Ruwer)

Grans-Fassian (Mosel-Saar-Ruwer)
F. Heyl (Rheinhessen)
Hohe Domkirche (Mosel-Saar-Ruwer)
Karthäuserhof (Mosel-Saar-Ruwer)
H. Kerpen (Mosel-Saar-Ruwer)
Koehler-Ruprecht (Rheinpfalz)
Landgraf von Hessen (Rheingau)
Lauerburg (Mosel-Saar-Ruwer)
Licht-Bergweiler-Erben (Mosel-Saar-Ruwer)
Licht-Kilburg (Rheingau)
Dr. Loosen (Mosel-Saar-Ruwer)
Milz-Laurentiushof (Mosel-Saar-Ruwer)
Dr. R. Muth (Rheinhessen)
Dr. Nagler (Rheingau)
Peter Nicolay (Mosel-Saar-Ruwer)
Pleffingen (Rheinpfalz)
S. A. Prüm-Erben (Mosel-Saar-Ruwer)
E. Reverchon (Mosel-Saar-Ruwer)

Ruetter Kunz (Mosel-Saar-
Ruwer)
Willi Schaefer (Mosel-Saar-
Ruwer)
Schloss Johannisberg
(Rheingau)
Schloss Plettenberg (Nahe)
Dr. A. Senfter (Rheinhessen)
Staatlichen Weinbaudomanen
(Mosel-Saar-Ruwer)
Staatsweingüter Eltville
(Rheingau)
J. H. Strub (Rheinhessen)
Dr. H. Thanisch (Mosel-Saar-
Ruwer)

Van Volxem (Mosel-Saar-
Ruwer)
Vereinigte Hospitien (Mosel-
Saar-Ruwer)
von Hövel (Mosel-Saar-Ruwer)
von Kanitz (Rheingau)
von Kesselstatt (Mosel-Saar-
Ruwer)
von Mummisches (Rheingau)
von Simmern (Rheingau)
Dr. Heinz Wagner (Mosel-Saar-
Ruwer)
H. Wirsching (Franken)
Dr. Zenzen (Mosel-Saar-Ruwer)

* * * *(GOOD PRODUCERS)*

S. Adler (Baden)
F. Altenkirch (Rheingau)
P. Anheuser (Nahe)
F. Baumann (Rheinhessen)
Graf von Neippergsches
(Württemberg)
L. Guntrum (Rheinhessen)
Johann Hart (Mosel-Saar-
Ruwer)
D. Hermann (Mosel-Saar-
Ruwer)
Irsch-Ockfen (Mosel-Saar-
Ruwer)
Josefinegrund (Mosel-Saar-
Ruwer)
Josephshof (Mosel-Saar-Ruwer)
Jostock-Thul (Mosel-Saar-
Ruwer)
J. Kock (Mosel-Saar-Ruwer)
Kurfurstenhof (Rheinhessen)
Lehneit-Veit-Erben (Mosel-
Saar-Ruwer)
Max Markgraf (Baden)

Okonomierat Piedmont (Mosel-
Saar-Ruwer)
Okonomierat Rebholz
(Rheinpfalz)
F. Reh (Mosel-Saar-Ruwer)
P. Scherf (Mosel-Saar-Ruwer)
Schloss Groenesteyn (Rheingau)
Schloss Reinhartshausen
(Rheingau)
Schloss Vollrads (Rheingau)
F. Schmitt (Rheinhessen)
R. Schmitt (Franken)
Schumann-Nagler (Rheingau)
Selbach-Oster (Mosel-Saar-
Ruwer)
B. Simon (Mosel-Saar-Ruwer)
Studert-Prüm (Mosel-Saar-
Ruwer)
H. Taprich (Mosel-Saar-Ruwer)
Erbhol Tesch (Nahe)
Usinger-Gunderlach
(Rheinhessen)
von Buhl (Rheinpfalz)

von Hessisches (Rheingau)
von Prittwitz (Mosel-Saar-
Ruwer)
R. Weil (Rheingau)

S. Weiland (Mosel-Saar-Ruwer)
Würzburg Staalichen Hofkeller
(Franken)
W. Zahn (Mosel-Saar-Ruwer)

4. PORTUGAL

Port

Americans have finally begun to realize the great pleasures of a bottle of mature vintage port after a meal. For years, this sumptuous and mellow fortified red wine was seriously undervalued as most of it was drunk in the private homes and clubs of the United Kingdom. Prices have recently soared, reflecting the fact that there is not much vintage port produced, and that there are rarely more than four declared vintages in a decade. Only eight years ago, I could have bought all the marvelous 1963s I wanted for $10–15 a bottle. I was foolish enough to pass up this opportunity, and I am lamenting the fact that these wines now fetch $80–100 a bottle. Demand for vintage port can only increase, and prices will be driven up further unless the producers decide to lower their standards of quality and begin to declare vintages more frequently—which of course would be their undoing over the long term.

The accepted guideline for cellaring a great year of vintage port is 15 to 20 years, but I find most ports easily drinkable around age 10, save for the massive 1977s. The vintage now being touted by the wine trade is the 1985, and while those ports are not cheap, neither are they too expensive. However, before investing a considerable sum of money in the 1985s, keep in mind the following observations:

1. The 1983s, a vintage that shows more aromatic complexity but slightly less weight than the 1985s, are available for the same or a lower price than the 1985s.

2. Wine investors have dumped a good deal of vintage port in recent sales at London's Sotheby's and Christie's, though investors have made money on the great 1977s, which have appreciated by 200% since their release in 1979. Many of the dumped wines may well turn up in America over the next 6–9 months at prices not far above the 1985s. If this happens, why not buy the 1977s, the greatest port vintage since 1963, rather than the very good 1985s? But remember, the 1977s will not be ready until the year 2000.

3. If you are going to buy vintage port, be prepared to wait a minimum of 6–10 years for the wines to develop the lush mellow complexity that makes them so seductive. If you are not prepared to invest this time in them, consider the alternatives—the well-aged tawny ports from Portugal as well as their excellent counterparts from Australia.

VINTAGE GUIDE

The great recent vintages for port are 1963, 1970, 1977, 1983, and 1985. Other years have been declared and are quite good, such as 1982, 1980, 1975, and 1966, but these do not have the same level of sheer intensity and richness, nor do they have the same aging potential. However, the latter vintages are much less expensive.

VINTAGE YEARS FOR MAJOR FIRMS

Cockburn	1947, 1950, 1955, 1960, 1963, 1967, 1970, 1975, 1983, 1985
Croft	1945, 1950, 1955, 1960, 1963, 1966, 1970, 1975, 1977, 1982, 1985
Dow	1945, 1947, 1950, 1955, 1960, 1963, 1966, 1970, 1972, 1975, 1977, 1980, 1983, 1985
Fonseca	1945, 1948, 1955, 1960, 1963, 1966, 1970, 1975, 1977, 1980, 1983, 1985
Graham	1945, 1948, 1955, 1960, 1963, 1966, 1970, 1975, 1977, 1980, 1983, 1985
Quinta do Noval	1945, 1947, 1950, 1955, 1958, 1960, 1963, 1966, 1967, 1970, 1975, 1978, 1982, 1985
Sandeman	1945, 1947, 1950, 1955, 1957, 1958, 1960, 1962, 1963, 1966, 1967, 1970, 1975, 1977, 1980, 1982, 1985

Taylor Fladgate   1945, 1948, 1955, 1960, 1963, 1966, 1970, 1975,
                  1977, 1980, 1983, 1985
Warre   1945, 1947, 1950, 1955, 1958, 1960, 1963, 1966,
                  1970, 1975, 1977, 1980, 1983, 1985

A GUIDE TO PORTUGAL'S BEST PRODUCERS OF PORT

* * * * * (OUTSTANDING PRODUCERS)

Dow   Graham
Fonseca   Taylor Fladgate & Yeatman

* * * * (EXCELLENT PRODUCERS)

Churchill   Quinta do Noval
Cockburn   Sandeman
Croft   Warre
Ferreira

* * * (GOOD PRODUCERS)

Calem   Martinez
Delaforce   Offley Forrester
Gould Campbell   Poças Junior
Quarles Harris   Ramos-Pinto
Hooper   Smith-Woodhouse

CALEM * * *

1985   C 84

Deep-ruby/purple in color, the 1985 Calem is a soft, medium-bodied, relatively lightweight style of wine with a good deal of juicy fruit, soft tannins, and alcoholic finish.

CHURCHILL * * * *

1985   C 88

A new house. Churchill's 1985 showed extremely well in my tastings. Dark-ruby/purple with a projected full-intensity bouquet of ripe plums, licorice, and fruitcake, full-bodied, seductively soft, rich, and concentrated, this overtly fruity wine seems precocious and only 5–7 years away from maturity. It is deep, delectable, and delicious.

COCKBURN* * * *

1963	E	86
1970	E	87
1975	D	82
1983	D	95
1985	D	87

This house tends to produce quite full-bodied, rich, alcoholic, spirited vintage ports that never have a great deal of complexity or finesse but offer meaty, chocolaty, spicy, full-bodied, alcoholic flavors at the expense of elegance. The 1985 was placed in a tasting where I also inserted the 1983 Cockburn as a ringer. I was surprised to find out upon revealing the wines that the massive blockbuster of the tasting was the 1983, and the soft, intensely fruity, forward wine was the 1985. While the 1983 Cockburn is superior to the 1985, the latter wine should offer rich, opulent, multidimensional flavors in 6–8 years. Like the other 1985s, it is low in acidity and a trifle loosely knit, but relatively powerful and heady, with an amazing level of black-cherry fruit. The 1975 is light, a little alcoholic, and not terribly distinguished. The 1970 is big and powerful and just now reaching maturity. The 1963 is fully mature, spicy, with a chocolaty, meaty texture and somewhat hot, short finish.

CROFT* * * *

1963	E	86
1966	E	87
1970	E	85
1975	D	87
1977	D	88
1982	D	90
1985	D	87

Croft never seems to get much publicity since the wines, while always very good, sometimes even excellent, never quite reach the superb level of the top houses in Oporto. However, Croft seems to do surprisingly well, often rivaling the top ports in the less glamorous vintages such as 1975 and 1966. The 1975 is almost as good as Croft's 1977. Both are rich, creamy, intense ports that should be fully mature within 10–12 years, relatively soon for a vintage port. The 1970 is quite good, but in the context of the vintage, marginally disappointing. The 1966 is a sleeper: complex, rich, very aromatic, with long, deep flavors. The 1963, one of the great vintages for port, is good but unexciting. However, the 1982 is superb, a powerful, broadly flavored wine with exhilarating depth and richness on the palate and at least 25 years of life ahead of it. I prefer it to the 1985, which will be an early-developing port. The 1985 shows aromas that border on overripeness and offers scents of plums and black cherries. Full-bodied, rich yet lush and soft, this husky wine has loads of concentration, a very sweet, long finish, and light tannins.

DELAFORCE* * *

Eminence's Choice 16-Year-Old Tawny Port	B	85
1966	E	86
1970	E	84
1975	D	82
1978 Quinta da Corte	D	85
1982	D	85
1985	D	82

This house tends to make good port and sell it at rather reasonable prices. The 16-year-old tawny is soft and pleasant but lacks a bit of character. The 1978 single-vineyard port, Quinta da Corte, is straightforward and chunky, with good length but not much complexity; the same can be said for the 1975 and the 1970, both of which are fully mature. It has been several years since I have tasted a 1966, but my recollection is that it is the best Delaforce port I have had. The 1985 has a heady perfume of sugary fruit, sweet, soft, medium-bodied flavors, good concentration, and an adequate finish. It suffers in comparison with the major ports of 1985 but is not at all bad.

DOW* * * * *

Boardroom 15-Year-Old Tawny Port	B	87
Gold Label 30-Year-Old Tawny	D	90
1963	E	92
1966	D	88
1970	E	86
1975	D	85
1977	E	93
1980	D	88
1983	D	90
1985	D	87

This is an extraordinary house that seems to have been particularly successful with its vintage ports since 1977. Of course, the 1963 is a classic, a monumental, rich, still tannic wine that will last at least another 30 years. The 1966 is also a top success for that vintage; in fact, it would be hard to find a better port from that year. The 1970 is good, but for some reason has never blossomed and developed any complexity, and the same can be said for the fully mature, fruity, soft 1975. However, starting with the 1977, Dow has hit its stride. The 1977, still a baby, is fabulously scented, very rich and concentrated, and has a potential longevity of at least another 30–50 years. The 1980 is very, very good and certainly better than what this house produced in 1975 and 1970. It should mature relatively fast and be ready to drink by 1992. The 1983 is rich, concentrated, very fruity, and magnificently perfumed, suggesting that it is going to mature early, long before the 1977. The 1985 is dark-ruby/purple with a rather closed one-dimensional aroma. On the palate, this Dow is restrained, but rich, tannic, and full-bodied, yet not nearly as concentrated as one would expect. Have I missed something? As for the tawny ports from

Dow, they can also be superb. The 30-year-old tawny has a scent of sweet saddle leather, hazelnuts, and rich fruit. The 15-year-old tawny, for one-third the price, is a somewhat lighter but no less interesting version.

FERREIRA* * * *

Duque de Bragança 20-Year-Old Tawny	B	88
1970	D	85
1975	D	86
1977	D	87
1980	D	85
1983	D	88
1985	D	86

This house is terribly underrated when top ports are mentioned. Their vintage ports tend to lack a bit in complexity and sheer majesty of aromas, but they do offer rich, robust, concentrated flavors of chocolate, spices, and deep, plummy fruit. However, their 20-year-old tawny, Duque de Bragança, must certainly be one of the top tawny ports made in Portugal and is well worth seeking out for those who want something to drink immediately. Their most recent vintage port, the 1985, is deep-ruby/purple and among the more tannic and backward ports of the vintage. Quite robust and brawny, this concentrated, relatively intense wine needs 5–7 years of cellaring to shed its cloak of tannin.

FONSECA* * * * *

Bin 27	B	84
Fonseca 10-Year-Old Tawny	B	86
1963	E	96
1966	E	88

1970	E 93
1975	D 89
1977	D 93
1980	D 87
1983	D 92
1985	D 90

Fonseca is one of the great port lodges, producing the most exotic and most complex port. If Fonseca lacks the sheer weight and power of a Taylor, Dow, or Warre, or the opulent sweetness and intensity of a Graham, it excels in its magnificently complex, intense bouquet of plummy, cedary, spicy fruit and long, broad, expansive flavors. With its lush, seductive character, one might call it the Pomerol of vintage ports. When it is young, it often loses out in blind tastings to the heavier, weightier, more tannic wines, but I always find myself upgrading my opinion of Fonseca after it has had 7–10 years of age. If there is a disappointment for me, it is Bin 27, which, though a huge commercial success, is rather straightforward and simple. However, for vintage ports, the newly released 1985 looks to be one of the top successes of the vintage, yet I believe both the superb 1983 and the otherworldly 1977 are far superior. Dense ruby/purple with the Oriental spice-box aroma, the 1985 is an expansive, sweet, broadly flavored wine with outstanding depth, concentration, and balance. It finishes with a solid lashing of alcohol and tannin. The 1983 is magnificently scented, full-bodied, creamy, rather forward, but showing great length and character. The 1980 is very good, possibly excellent, but tasted lighter than some of the best ports from that vintage. The 1977 has developed magnificently in the bottle, and while it clearly needs another decade to reach its summit, it is the best Fonseca since the 1970 and 1963. Fonseca's 1975, which is fully mature, shows just how good this house can be; it is a port to seek out since the vintage does not have the reputation or the price tag that 1977 and 1970 do. It should drink magnificently for another decade or more. The 1970, of course, is a powerful Fonseca with an exotic bouquet and lush, creamy, multidimensional flavors. The 1966, a top success as well, is fully mature, but will hold for 15 or more years. The 1963, one of the great modern-day classics of vintage port, is an incredibly aromatic, sublime, majestic port that simplyd defines Fonseca's style perfectly.

GOULD CAMPBELL* * *

1977	C	84
1980	C	85
1983	C	82
1985	C	89

My experience with this house is limited, but I have found the 1980 and 1983 rich, full-bodied, well-colored, and complex. The 1985 from Gould Campbell is one of the surprises of this vintage. It has an intense nose of chocolate, berry fruit, and tar. On the palate, the wine is concentrated, powerful, and full-bodied with layers of fruit. It finishes sweeter than some of the other ports with a great deal of tannin. One rarely sees this brand stateside.

GRAHAM* * * * *

Emperor Tawny 20-Year-Old	C	85
Prince Regent's 10-Year-Old Tawny	B	88
1963	E	92
1966	E	88
1970	E	93
1975	D	82
1977	D	96
1980	D	88
1983	D	95
1985	D	96

Graham is another great port house, producing one of the deepest-colored and sweetest styles in vintage port. Along with Taylor and Fonseca, Graham has probably been the most consistent producer of great port in the post–World War II era. Their tawnys are quite good rather than exceptional, but their vintage ports are truly sublime and sumptuous. Graham is the undisputed star and kingpin of the 1985 vintage ports. Yes, it is made in a sweeter style than the other ports, but it is a fabulous wine because of a dazzling level of black-cherry fruit, an enormous structure, and staggering depth, dimension, and length. It is forward, as are all the 1985s, and I would speculate that this port will be approaching maturity by 1992–1993 and will keep 15–20 years thereafter. The 1983, like most vintage ports, seems more forward than normal but has a great depth of very ripe, viscous, unctuous, plummy, tarry fruit and significant tannin in its long finish. It is black-purple in color. I doubt that it will be either as profound or as long-lived as the great 1977, but it is certainly one of the top two or three ports of this vintage, and better than the excellent 1980 that Graham produced. The 1970 is a monumental vintage port and one of the greats of that vintage. It begs to be drunk now, although it will last for at least another two decades. The 1966, which I initially thought rather mediocre, has developed beautifully in the bottle and is a much finer vintage port than I suspected. It should be drunk now as it is not likely to get any better. The 1975 is the only recent vintage of Graham that I find disappointing. It is rather light in color, finishes very short on the palate, and obviously lacks depth and ripeness.

QUARLES HARRIS* * *

1985	B 84

This robust, densely colored port has plenty of muscle, power, and alcohol yet is short on finesse. Slightly disjointed with the alcohol quite noticeable, this port needs 4–5 years to find its balance, but all the component parts are there. It may prove to merit a higher rating in the future.

HOOPER* * *

1985	B 83

Surprisingly opaque and purple, this port has a tightly knit but compact structure, fine depth of fruit, full body, yet seems to tail off in the finish. One of the more tannic and closed ports of this otherwise charming, precocious vintage.

MARTINEZ* * *

1963	D	78
1967	D	85
1975	C	86
1982	B	84
1985	B	86

This house is rarely seen in the United States, and I was unimpressed with the sample of the 1963 that I had in a comparative tasting. However, the recent notes I have for the 1967 and 1975 show that both were good, medium-weight, tarry, plummy ports without a lot of character, but with good ripeness and clean winemaking. The 1982 is light and mature. As for the 1985, it has a deep, juicy fruitiness, excellent color, full body, and firm tannins in the finish. It is not as complex as some ports but offers robust, fruity drinking.

OFFLEY FORRESTER* * *

1970	C	86
1972	C	83
1977	C	86
1980	B	83
1983	B	85

Offley Forrester produces medium-weight ports that, given their reasonable price, offer value rather than great complexity and richness. Curiously, the 1972, a vintage not declared by most port shippers, produced a very good wine, and I have good notes on the 1970, 1977, and 1983.

QUINTA DO NOVAL* * * *

1963	E	82
1970	E	84

1975	D	85
1978	D	84
1982	D	87
1985	D	87

The beautiful Quinta do Noval is undoubtedly the most famous port producer, largely because their 1931 and 1927 were to vintage port what the 1947 Cheval Blanc and 1945 Mouton-Rothschild were to the Bordeaux trade—divine, monumental wines of extraordinary depth of flavor. Also, the Quinta do Noval produces a rare vintage port from a small vineyard of ungrafted, pre-phylloxera vines called Nacional. It is so rare that I have never seen, much less tasted, a bottle of what is supposedly a great port. However, the truth of the matter is that recent vintages of Quinta do Noval have not been nearly as impressive as they should be. Commentators have described the wines as light, elegant, and charming when in fact they lack richness and depth of flavor. The 1963 and 1970, two great vintages for port, are disappointing. The 1975 has turned out charming, fruity, and actually better than the 1970 or 1963, which is inexplicable. The most recent vintages, 1978, 1982, and 1985, have shown more richness of flavor and character in bouquet and aroma. The 1985 is quite concentrated, seductive, and amazingly delicious now, and it should mature quite quickly. The finish is long and flavorful, but I wonder about the lack of tannic structure to this wine.

RAMOS-PINTO* * *

Quinta da Bom Retiro Tawny 20-Year-Old	B	86
Quinta de Ervamoira Tawny 10-Year-Old	C	85
1970	C	86
1980	C	84
1983	C	85
1985	C	79

I know little about this firm other than that both their tawnys are excellent and offer considerable value, and that the two vintage ports currently on the market show a style not unlike that of Fonseca, a lush mellowness and complex, plummy, chocolaty bouquet. Their 20-year-old tawny, the Quinta da Bom Retiro, is really quite sumptuous.

SANDEMAN* * * *

Founder's Reserve	B	80
N.V. Royal Tawny	B	83
1970	D	84
1975	D	84
1977	D	87
1980	C	82
1982	C	87
1985	C	86

Sandeman is one of the biggest and most conspicuous of the port houses, with extensive interests in the sherry business as well. They advertise significantly and their products are well-represented in virtually every American marketplace. The quality is quite good given the quantity of wine produced, but rarely does a Sandeman tawny or vintage port hit the true heights that a Dow, Fonseca, Taylor, or Graham will. Their Royal Tawny has an attractive, nutty, ripe black-cherry character. Their Founder's Reserve, which is highly publicized, is good, inexpensive, straightforward port without much complexity but plenty of mellow, savory, sweet flavors. Their vintage ports have been a bit light, but the 1977 and 1982 show considerable strength and richness. The newest release, the 1985, has less of a deep-ruby/purple color, but it does offer a spice-box, fruitcake sort of aroma, mildly sweet, medium- to full-bodied flavors, and a ripe, tasty finish. Not a heavyweight, this wine represents a lighter style of vintage port. The 1980, 1975, and 1970 are good rather than exciting in quality.

SMITH-WOODHOUSE* * *

1980	C	85
1985	C	90

My experience with Smith-Woodhouse is limited, but I was impressed with the 1980, which showed a lovely, supple, ripe, rich, fruity character in an early-maturing style. Is the 1985 the sleeper of the vintage? An astonishing amount of creamy, black-cherry and chocolate-scented fruit fills the nose. On the palate, this full-bodied wine is loaded with extract, great length, and has super finish with plenty of fruit and tannin in proper balance.

TAYLOR FLADGATE & YEATMAN* * * * *

N.V. Tawny	B	85
10-Year-Old Tawny	C	87
20-Year-Old Tawny	D	90
30-Year-Old Tawny	D	87
1963	E	95
1966	E	88
1970	E	96
1975	D	87
1977	D	96
1980	D	89
1983	D	94
1985	D	?

This house must certainly be the Latour of Portugal. Their ports are remarkably backward yet still impressive when young. Of all the vintage ports, those of Taylor need the longest time to mature and even when fully mature seem to have an inner strength and firmness that keep them going for decades. Their tawnys are also among the very best, though somewhat expensive. For current drinking, the 20-year-old tawny is a wonderfully fragrant, nutty-scented wine with great character and complexity. Among their vintage ports, there has not been an unsuccessful year since 1963. The 1963 is quite fabulous yet still seemingly capable of developing for another decade or more. The 1966 is drinking well now and is a very good rather than an exceptional Taylor. The 1970 is fabulous, a broodingly dense-colored, backward port that has all the signs of future greatness, provided one is willing to cellar it until the early 1990s. The 1975 has turned out richly fruity, supple, and offers delicious drinking for the near future. The 1977 has consistently been at the top of my list of vintage ports in this great vintage, although the Dow, Graham, and Fonseca are equally splendid. It is a mammoth, opaque, statuesque vintage port of remarkable depth and power, but it should not be touched before 2000. The 1980 is probably the best port of the vintage, and the 1983 is wonderfully aromatic and so perfumed (a characteristic of this charming vintage), yet powerful, long, and deep on the palate. It gives every indication of being an early-maturing Taylor, but I wouldn't want to drink it before 1995. As for the 1985, two bottles were tasted and each was different. One was compact and dull, the other beefy, rich, full-bodied, and loaded. While the better bottle clearly was outstanding, it was not as sublime or as sensational as one expects Taylor to be, and not as rich or as profound as the 1983, 1977, or 1970. Perhaps this particular port, usually one of my favorites, is going through an awkward stage. Judgment reserved.

WARRE* * * *

Nimrod Tawny	B	85
1963	E	87
1966	E	86
1970	E	87
1975	D	86
1977	D	92

1980	D	88
1983	D	90
1985	D	90

This house makes rather restrained yet rich, flavorful vintage port and a very good tawny called Nimrod. Their vintage ports seem slow to develop, and while they never quite have the voluptuous richness of a Dow, Graham, or Fonseca, they have a unique mineral-scented character that gives them their own complexity and style. Warre has been making exceptionally fine ports of late, and their 1985 is the sweetest and richest of their recent vintages. Extremely concentrated, rich, even luscious, this full-bodied, intense, opulent wine has layers of fruit, a full-blown bouquet, and impeccable balance. The soft tannins and precocious appeal of the 1985 suggest rapid maturation. The 1983 is richly perfumed and fragrant, which is so typical of the ports from this vintage, and is seemingly more forward than normal. The 1980 is backward, firm, and has yet to reveal its true personality; the 1977 is quite powerful, very deep and intense, particularly for Warre; and the 1975 is soft, supple, and clearly mature. Of the older vintages, the 1970 remains rather unyielding but still impressive; the 1966 fully mature and good but not exciting; and the 1963 very, very good and now fully mature.

Table Wines

Except for the unctuous, rich, almost decadent joys of vintage port, Madeira, and one of the greatest nectars of all, Muscatel de Setubal, the potential for fine wine from Portugal has yet to be discovered by most wine enthusiasts. Of course, the ubiquitous, spritzy, rather sweet Portugese rosés are known the world over and are what many consumers first move on to when they deem themselves too old or too sophisticated for soda pop. But Portugal produces some good red wines that could even be superb if their winemaking was not still adhering to nineteenth-century practices, as well as a few lively, crisp, tart white wines, the best of which are the *"vinho verdes."* For dry red wine, the best are from such regions as Dão, Bairrada, and the Douro.

VINTAGE GUIDE

Vintages in Portugal seem to have relevance only for the port trade. For the dry red table wines, none of the wineries seem to think vintages matter a whole lot, but certainly 1986, 1985, 1983, 1982, 1980, and 1977 would be recent years in which grapes were reputed to ripen evenly and reach perfect maturity.

A GUIDE TO PORTUGAL'S BEST PRODUCERS OF TABLE WINES

* * * * (EXCELLENT PRODUCERS)

Carvalho, Ribeiro, Ferreira (Dão, Serradayres, Garrafeira)

Ferreira (Barca Velha)

J. M. da Fonseca (Periquita and Dão)

João Pires (Cabernet, Muscat, and Tinta da Anfora)

* * * * (GOOD PRODUCERS)

Caves Alianca (Vinho Verde)

Caves Borlido (Garrafeira)

Caves St. Jão (Garrafeira)

Caves Velhas (Dão, Romeira)

M. Champalimaud (Quinta do Cotto)

Grao Vasco (Dão)

Quinta da Aveleda (Vinho Verde)

Reguengos (Garrafeira)

Santa Marta Penaguiao (Douro)

J. Serra (Serra Vidiqueira)

5. SPAIN:
A HOTBED FOR RED WINE
VALUES-BUT BE CAREFUL!

The Basics

TYPES OF WINE

Aside from the glories of sherry, which is synonymous with Spain, this beautiful sun-drenched country is best known as a treasure trove for top red wine values. Forget the white wines, which once tasted musty and oxidized. Now thanks to high technology, they taste like lemon water. And while the booming Spanish sparkling wine business stays in the headlines, as my producers' chart indicates, few makers of sparkling wine actually merit serious interest from those who enjoy good wine. Red wine is king in Spain, but regrettably this country is still one of unrealized potential rather than existing achievement. The best red wines all come from northern Spain. The areas that stand out for quality are the famous Rioja region, the generally well-known Penedès viticultural area in Catalonia near the Mediterranean coast, the Ribera del Duero region, and several emerging areas such as Navarra and Toro. To understand Spanish red wines, one must first realize that the Spanish want their red wines supple, with an aged taste of maturity, as well as a healthy dosage of oak. Once you realize this, you will understand why many Spanish wineries, called *bodegas*, age their wines in huge oak or concrete vats for seven or eight years before they release them. The Spanish are not fond of grapy, tannic,

569

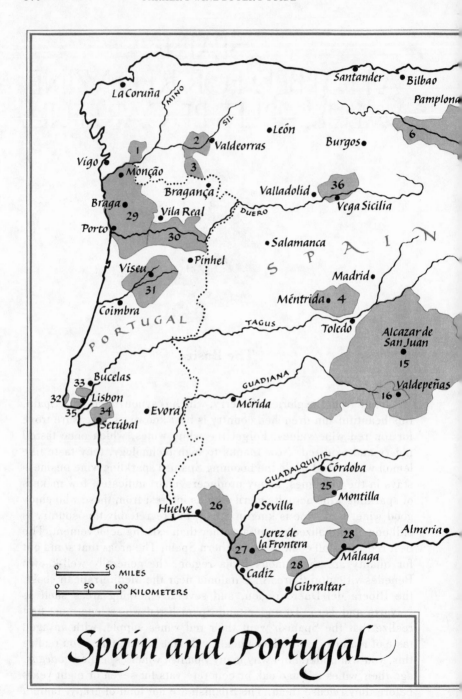

Spain and Portugal

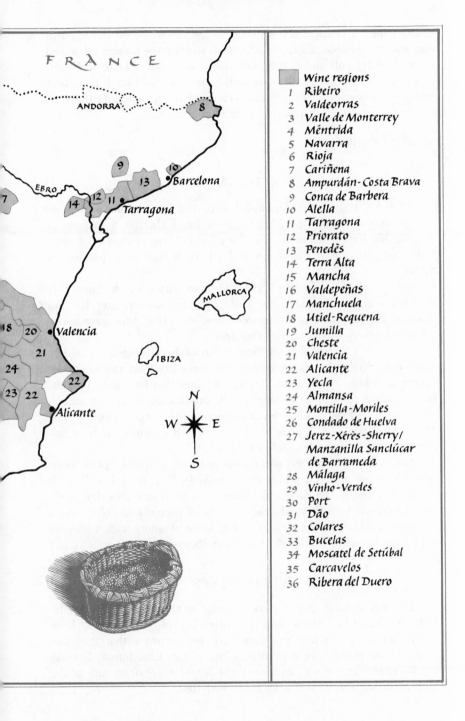

FRANCE

ANDORRA

8

EBRO

9

10

13 Barcelona

14 12 11

Tarragona

7

MALLORCA

18 20 Valencia

21

IBIZA

24

22

23 22

Alicante

N
W E
S

Wine regions
1 Ribeiro
2 Valdeorras
3 Valle de Monterrey
4 Méntrida
5 Navarra
6 Rioja
7 Cariñena
8 Ampurdán- Costa Brava
9 Conca de Barbera
10 Alella
11 Tarragona
12 Priorato
13 Penedès
14 Terra Alta
15 Mancha
16 Valdepeñas
17 Manchuela
18 Utiel-Requena
19 Jumilla
20 Cheste
21 Valencia
22 Alicante
23 Yecla
24 Almansa
25 Montilla-Moriles
26 Condado de Huelva
27 Jerez-Xérès-Sherry/
   Manzanilla Sanclúcar
   de Barrameda
28 Málaga
29 Vinho-Verdes
30 Port
31 Dão
32 Colares
33 Bucelas
34 Moscatel de Setúbal
35 Carcavelos
36 Ribera del Duero

young wines, so expect the wineries to age the wines for the Spanish consumer. Consequently, most Spanish wines have a more advanced color, and are soft and supple with the sweet vanillin taste of American oak well-displayed. Many wineries actually hold back their best lots for a decade or more before releasing them, enabling the consumer to purchase a mature, fully drinkable wine.

GRAPE VARIETIES

RED WINES

Cabernet Sauvignon—An important part of Spain's most expensive and prestigious red wine, the Vega Sicilia, Cabernet Sauvignon is responsible for the great Torres Black Label Gran Coronas. To date, Cabernet Sauvignon has flourished where it has been planted in Spain.

Carinena—In English this is the Carignan grape, and in Spain this workhorse grape offers the muscle of Arnold Schwarzenegger. Big and brawny, the tannic, densely colored wine made from this grape varietal is frequently used as a blending agent.

Garnacha—The Spanish spelling of Grenache, Garnacha is widely planted in Spain. In that country's relentless dry heat and sunshine, it produces huge, rich, alcoholic, dense wines that have gobs of fruit, but not much tannin. Its weakness is its tendency to oxidize quickly.

Monastrell—Frequently seen in Catalonia, this grape, believed to be Mourvedre, provides a great deal of body and tannin as well as fragrance to the wine with which it is blended.

Tempranillo—The finest indigenous red wine grape of Spain, Tempranillo travels under a number of names. In Penedès it is called Ull de Llebre, and in the Ribera del Duero, Tinto. It provides rich, well-structured wines with good acids, plenty of tannin and color, and a raspberry, cedary bouquet. It makes an ideal blending mate with Garnacha but is complex enough to stand on its own.

WHITE WINES

The white wine grapes parade under names such as Parellada, Verdejo, Xarel-Lo, Airen, and the better-known Malvasia and Moscatel, but Spain's white varietals have yet to prove that they can compete internationally with other white wines. Chardonnay is making its presence known, and no doubt it will outperform any of the aforementioned neutral-tasting grape varieties.

FLAVORS

Penedès—The dominant winery here is Torres, which produces a bevy of excellent red wines from the typical Spanish varietals. Yet, the top wine is the 100% Cabernet Sauvignon Black Label Gran Coronas that has a rich, open-knit bouquet of plums, sweet oak, and often licorice and violets. Its chief rival is the Cabernet Sauvignon from Jean León, another concentrated, blackberry-scented and -flavored, full-throttle wine with a whopping influence from sweet, toasty oak.

Ribera del Duero—Two of Spain's greatest red wines are produced in this broad river valley: Pesquera, which comes primarily from the Tempranillo grape, and Vega Sicilia, primarily a Cabernet Sauvignon/Merlot/Malbec wine. What is noticeable about these wines is the remarkable purity of berry fruit that can be found in the top vintages. Take superripe fruit and combine it with a minimum of three years (in the case of Vega Sicilia, 8–12 years) in oak casks, and you have powerfully heady, supple, explosively rich wines that offer a great deal of spicy, sweet, toasty, vanillin-scented oak.

Rioja—When made by one of the best producers, such as the 1973 La Rioja Alta Reserva called 904, Rioja will be a mature wine having a medium-ruby color often with a touch of orange or brown (normal for an older wine), and a huge, fragrant bouquet of tobacco, cedar, smoky oak, and sweet, ripe fruit. On the palate, there will be no coarseness or astringency because of the long aging of the wine in cask and/or tank prior to bottling. Despite its suppleness, the wine will still keep for 5–10 years after its release by the winery. Even a young Rioja, released after just 3–4 years, such as a 1985 Marqués de Cáceres, will show a ripe, fat, rich, supple fruitiness, and soft, sweet, oaky character.

Toro—Once known for overwhelmingly alcoholic, heavy wines, Toro has adopted modern technology, and the results have been some rich, full-bodied, deeply flavored, southern Rhône–like wines from wineries such as Farina and Mateos. They taste like big, lush, peppery Châteauneuf-du-Papes and represent astonishing values.

AGING POTENTIAL

Navarra: 5–7 years   Rioja: 6–25 years*
Penedès: 6–15 years   Sparkling white wines: 3–6
Ribera del Duero: 6–30 years**   years

*Only a handful of Rioja wines, principally the Gran Reservas from La Rioja Alta, Marqués de Murrieta, and CVNE, can age this long.
**Only the wines of Pesquera and Vega Sicilia will keep 25–30 years.

OVERALL QUALITY LEVEL

While it may be fashionable to tout the quality and value of all Spanish wines, the only ones with merit are the red wines, and sadly, only a small percentage can hold up to the best international competition. The whites are atrociously boring, and while the sparkling wines are very cheap, only a few offer value. Despite the fabulous climate and high percentage of old vines, most of Spain's wines have not yet realized their potential, which is formidable.

MOST IMPORTANT INFORMATION TO KNOW

Learning the names of the best producers, and a few top recent vintages (1982, 1985, and 1986), will get you a long way if you avoid the white wines from this country.

1989–1990 BUYING STRATEGY

For Rioja, look for the 1982s, the finest vintage since 1970. Also keep an eye out for the up-and-coming wines from Toro, especially those wines from the Bodegas Farina and Bodegas Mateos. Few red wines in the world offer as much flavor and character for your money as do the Gran Colegiata of Farina and Tío Babu of Mateos.

VINTAGE GUIDE

1986—Considered to be spectacular in the Duero, the crop size was down from 1985. In Rioja it is called a "good" year.

1985—Virtually every wine-producing region of Spain reported 1985 to be a very successful, high-quality vintage. In Rioja, the crop was a record-setting size.

1984—This vintage has a terrible reputation because of a poor, cool European summer, but the better red wines of Spain have turned out to be among the best made in Europe.

1983—A hot, dry year caused some problems, but the wines range from good to very good.

1982—For Rioja and Ribera del Duero, the finest vintage since 1970, and largely regarded as a great year, superior to 1985, and equal to 1986 in the Duero.

1981—A very good vintage.

1980—An average-quality year.

1979—A good year in the Penedès area, but only average in Rioja.

1978—For Rioja, Penedès, and the Ribera del Duero, the best overall vintage between 1970 and 1982.

Older Vintages

For most of northern Spain, 1970 was a great vintage. Prior to that, 1964 was another superb vintage. Well-kept bottles of 1970 and 1964 red wines from Rioja and the Ribera del Duero can be excellent examples of Spanish red wines.

A GUIDE TO SPAIN'S BEST PRODUCERS OF DRY RED TABLE WINES

* * * * * (OUTSTANDING PRODUCERS)

Pesquera (Ribera del Duero)
La Rioja Alta (Rioja)

Torres Black Label Coronas (Penedès)
Vega Sicilia (Ribera del Duero)

* * * * (EXCELLENT PRODUCERS)

Bilbainas (Rioja)
Campo Viejo (Rioja)
Can Rafols del Cans (Penedès)
Cartoixa (Priorato)
CVNE (Rioja)
Farina (Toro)

Jean León (Penedès)
Marqués de Griñon (Rueda)
Muga (Rioja)
Remelluri (Rioja)
Torres Gran Coronas (Penedès)

* * * (GOOD PRODUCERS)

Berberana (Rioja)
Corral (Rioja)
Castillo de Tiebas (Navarra)
Faustino Martinez (Rioja)
Lar de Barros (Tierra de Barros)
Lopez de Heredia Viña
  Tondonia (Rioja)
Marqués de Arienzo (Rioja)
Marqués de Cáceres (Rioja)
Marqués de Murrieta (Rioja)

Marqués de Riscal (Rioja)
L. Mateos (Toro)
Montecillo (Rioja)
Olarra (Rioja)
Perez Pasqua (Ribera del
  Duero)
Rioja Vega-Muerza (Rioja)
Señorío de Sarria (Navarra)
Torres Gran Sangre de Toro
  (Penedès)

* * (AVERAGE PRODUCERS)

Age-Unidas (Rioja)
Masia Bach (Penedès)
R. Barbier (Penedès)
Beronia (Rioja)
Franco Españolas (Rioja)

Gran Condal-Bodegas Santiago
  (Rioja)
Lan (Rioja)
Federico Paternina (Rioja)

A GUIDE TO SPAIN'S BEST PRODUCERS OF SPARKLING WINE

***** (OUTSTANDING PRODUCERS)
None

**** (EXCELLENT PRODUCERS)
None

*** (GOOD PRODUCERS)

Cadiz	Mont Marcal
Ferret	Segura Viudas
Juvé y Champs	

** (AVERAGE PRODUCERS)

Castel Blanch	Freixenet
Paul Cheneau	Lembey
Codorníu	Marqués de Monistrol

AGE-UNIDAS, S.A. (RIOJA)* *

1981 Siglo	A	65

1982 Siglo	A	82

I remember some very fine wines from this firm in the early sixties. In fact, there used to be a rich, fairly intense, ripe wine called the Marqués de Romeral that could compete with the best of the Riojas, but I have not seen it offered by this *bodega* in some time. The current selections in the export market include their wine in a burlap sack called Siglo. The 1981 has consistently tasted feeble and a little oxidized, but the 1982 is showing more ripe fruit, medium to full body, and a nice lush, pleasant texture. The 1982 should be drunk over the next 3–4 years.

RENÉ BARBIER (PENEDÈS)* *

1984	A	72

1983 Reserva	A	75

The firm of René Barbier is not one of the leaders in the viticultural area of Penedès. The wines are made in a commercial, straightforward, fruity, simple style and are meant to be drunk young. While the prices are reasonable, the wines lack excitement and a focal point of interest.

BODEGAS BERBERANA (RIOJA)* * *

1982 Carta de Oro	A 84
1975 Gran Reserva	B 82
1978 Gran Reserva	B 83
1982 Reserva	87

This large producer has undergone a number of changes in the eighties, when it was sold and then taken over by the Spanish government. The wines can be big, supple, and deliciously fruity, but my notes reveal excessive bottle variation, and therefore I have less confidence in recommending these wines than some from other Rioja producers. The Carta de Oro from the excellent 1982 vintage is a rich, fruity wine that is quite pleasant and ready to drink. Even better is the deep, plummy, velvety 1982 Reserva that should drink well for 5–8 years. Both the 1978 and 1975 Gran Reservas have been quite variable from bottle to bottle, sometimes better than the above scores, but other times showing a rather oxidized, dull character. At their best, though, they tend to be richly spicy, fruity, soft wines that should be drunk over the near term.

BODEGAS BILBAINAS (RIOJA)* * * *

1978 Viña Pomal	A 85
1973 Viña Pomal Reserva	A 86
1978 Viña Zaco	A 84

This is one of the better wineries in Rioja for finding rather full-bodied, rich, old-style Spanish reds that still have a great deal of personality, richness, and character. In fact, it is one of the few Rioja wineries where I have had little difficulty in finding consistent bottles in the marketplace. The Viña Pomal is a fuller, richer wine than the Viña Zaco, and the Reserva is aged longer in cask, giving it a rich, mellow, aged maturity. Both 1978s are quite fresh and lively, yet they have the suppleness and complexity that comes from aging. I can hardly wait for the release of the 1982s from this very good *bodega*.

BODEGAS CAMPO VIEJO (RIOJA)* * * *

1970 Gran Reserva Villamagna	B 88
1975 Gran Reserva Villamagna	B 85
1978 Gran Reserva Villamagna	B 86

The Bodegas Campo Viejo is a relatively new enterprise founded only in 1959, but the quality of its wines is consistently excellent. My tasting notes show the 1978, 1975, and 1973 Gran Reservas have rather full, intense bouquets of coffee, leather, spicy fruit, and plenty of the wonderful, sweet oaky smells that make Spanish Riojas so distinctive. The 1970 is still available and has an excellent deep color, a rich, cedary, spice-box bouquet, and full-bodied, fleshy, plump flavors that linger and linger on the palate. Both the 1978 and 1975 are a bit younger but show excellent richness and ripeness and should age nicely for another 6–8 years. This is an excellent, somewhat underrated source for some of the best Rioja from Spain, although I do not recommend Campo Veijo's new-style, innocuous white wine called San Asensio, which is neutral and bland.

CARTOIXA (PRIORATO)* * *

1975 Scala dei Priorato Gran Reserva	A 86
1978 Scala dei Priorato Gran Reserva	A 82
1982 Scala dei Priorato Gran Reserva	A 86

One does not see that many wines from the small viticultural area called Priorato, which is located in Catalonia not far from Penedès. This particular producer's wines, made from 100% Grenache, show a style not unlike that of a rich, intense, peppery, well-made southern Rhône from France. The 1975 is an extremely rich, deep, thick, chewy, full-bodied wine that should be drunk in the winter with a hearty stew or robust game; it is quite a rich, intense wine. The 1982 shows a bit more elegance without losing any of the broad, rich, sweet, fat, berry fruitiness that wines from this area seem to possess. The 1978 is leaner, and while good, does not have the depth or richness of either the 1975 or 1982. One taste of this wine left me with the impression that lovers of southern Rhônes or California Zinfandels would appreciate these excellent values from Priorato.

BODEGAS CORRAL (RIOJA)* * *

1978 Don Jacobo Gran Reserva	B	84
1981 Don Jacobo Reserva	B	85

This firm, which operates out of a new winery at Navarrete six miles southwest of Logroño, produces its best wines under the Don Jacobo label. The style seems to be one that offers plenty of supple, ripe, sweet fruit, with quite a bit of toasty oak preferred by the winery. I favor the 1981 because of its extras measure of fruit to the rather oaky, but still tasty and delicious, 1978. Both wines should be drunk over the next 3–4 years.

CVNE (RIOJA)* * * *

1981 Contino	B	87
1982 Contino	B	90
1975 Imperial Gran Reserva	B	87
1976 Imperial Gran Reserva	B	88
1978 Imperial Gran Reserva	B	89
1985 Rioja Clarete	A	82
1985 Viña Real	A	85
1976 Viña Real Gran Reserva	B	85
1978 Viña Real Gran Reserva	B	87

Established in the late nineteenth century, CVNE, or Compañía Vinícola del Norte de España, is one of the most respected of the Spanish Rioja wineries. Over four million bottles are now produced, of which nearly 70% comes from the firm's over 1,000 acres of vineyards. The wines are still made very traditionally, and there is a wide range of styles and vintages available. The lightest wines are those called the

Rioja Clarete, which is an inexpensive, soft, elegant, fruity wine made to be drunk within several years of its release. The 1985 is a good example of this lighter, picnic-style Rioja. A step up the scale of flavor intensity and fullness is the Viña Real, which in 1985 offers more intensity and robustness but is released early by the winery for those who like a more grapy, fruity, less oaky taste to their wines. At the next level are the Viña Real Gran Reservas, of which the 1978 and 1976 show plenty of toasty oak, a smoky, cigar-box, cedary, plummy fruitiness, full body, and quite a bit of softness. The 1978 seems slightly richer than the more alcoholic and oaky 1976. At the very top level are the Imperial Gran Reservas, which have been among the four or five best Riojas in every vintage I have tasted. I have fond memories of the 1966 and the 1970 vintages of this particular wine. The current releases are the excellent 1978, very fine 1976, and the fully mature 1975. Consumers will note that the Imperial Gran Reservas come in a Bordeaux-styled bottle, whereas the Viña Reals are in burgundy-shaped bottles.

The firm launched a new single-vineyard wine called Contino in the seventies, and this wine, made from 70% Tempranillo, 7% Garnacha, 5% Mazuelo, 5% Graciano, and 13% Viura, has been a tremendous success in each vintage it has been made. The 1975 was excellent and was followed by a very good 1978, a delicious 1980, an excellent 1981, and a superb 1982. The wine shows enormous potential, has a deep ruby color, a very fragrant, oaky bouquet, voluptuous, intense, berry fruitiness, and quite a long, sweet rich finish. In fact, the 1982 should probably not be drunk for another several years, and it should last and improve in the bottle for the rest of this century.

The wines of CVNE are excellent, but I must point out that a number of bottles I have tasted from suppliers in America showed evidence of being poorly shipped, with corks pushed out of the bottle and a sticky residue of dried wine on the outside, which is caused by the bottle's being exposed to extremes of heat. The importer should be much more careful in handling this wine between Spain and retail shops in America. I suspect many consumers have tasted what they thought were bad bottles of CVNE wines when in fact they were tasting badly stored bottles of excellent Rioja.

BODEGAS FARINA (TORO)* * *

1985 Colegiata	A	85
1986 Colegiata	A	85

1985 Gran Colegiata	A 87
1986 Gran Colegiata	A 88

This *bodega* in the up-and-coming viticultural area of Toro was previously known as the Bodegas Porto. The name had to be changed because of complaints from Portuguese authorities claiming the name Porto confused consumers. In any event, this is one of the great discoveries I made recently, as the wines are astonishing values and have the flavors of a top-notch southern Rhône. The grape used is the Tempranillo, called Tinta de Toro in this area. While the region was traditionally known for producing high-alcohol, old-style reds, modern vinification techniques allowing the vinification temperature to be controlled have resulted in wines that are explosively rich, full-bodied, yet well-balanced and loaded to the brim with fruit. The difference between the Colegiata and the Gran Colegiata is that the latter wine sees aging in new oak casks. Both 1985s have deep color, the richness of a top Châteauneuf-du-Pape, robust, plummy, leathery, smoky aromas and flavors, as well as shocking length. The 1986s are even better as they are slightly more structured, but they have every bit as much richness, length, and depth as the 1985s. These wines should keep and possibly improve for another 4–6 years, but it's hard to ignore their sumptuous pleasures now.

LAN (RIOJA)* *

1973 Lanciano Gran Reserva	B 62

My experience with the Bodegas Lan, which was founded in the early seventies and quickly became one of the most modern of the Spanish *bodegas*, has been disappointing. The current release in the marketplace is the 1973, and it is not only astringent but has dried out and lost its fruit; it probably should have been drunk a decade ago. At present, this *bodega*, which was purchased by the Spanish government in 1982 because of its commercial failure, seems to be a major gamble for consumers.

LAR DE BARROS (TIERRA DE BARROS)* * *

1982 Tinto Reserva	A 83
1983 Tinto Reserva	A 77

This very inexpensive red wine remains one of the best Spanish reds I have tasted outside any of the famous viticultural areas. The 1982 continues to drink well, suggesting chocolate/cherry candy, and has the texture of a lush Pomerol with its smooth, velvety fruit. However, the 1983 has consistently tasted clumsy and has nowhere near the finesse or balance of the 1982.

JEAN LEÓN (PENEDÈS)* * * *

1981 Cabernet Sauvignon	B	86
1982 Cabernet Sauvignon	B	88

This American-owned winery continues to make one of the greatest red wine values in all of Spain. I have just begun to break open my case of 1974 Jean León Cabernet Sauvignon, and after 15 years, it is still a youthful but opulent, richly concentrated, powerful wine with a great deal of complexity; it has another decade of evolution ahead of it. The new releases, while not quite as powerful and as concentrated as the vintages of the mid-seventies, are still superbly concentrated, powerfully rich wines. The 1982 shows deep blackcurrant fruit married intelligently with plenty of toasty new oak, which results in a cedary, exotic wine packed with flavor and at least 10–15 years of aging potential ahead of it. The 1981 is a bit lighter and less muscular, but still a deep, full-bodied, complex wine. Shrewd consumers should beat a path to their merchant to stock up on one of Spain's finest red wine values.

LOPEZ DE HEREDIA VIÑA TONDONIA (RIOJA)* * *

I was unable to find any current releases from Lopez de Heredia in any of the major markets of the East Coast. This is a shame because during my college days I stocked up on old vintages from the sixties, and today these wines are still drinking deliciously. The two best red wines made by this very traditionally run *bodega*, founded in 1887, are the Viña Tondonia and Viña Bosconia. These wines are always released as *reservas* with considerable age, and the Bosconia is always a fuller, richer, more velvety, fatter wine than the Tondonia. A small amount of white wine is made, and since no concessions have been made to modern-day tastes, the white tends to be heavy and often oxidized. This producer, with some great vintages from the fifties and the sixties (e.g., 1964, 1953), should be considered an ideal source for top Rioja, but apparently few importers have wanted to represent the wines, which is rather unfortunate.

MARQUÉS DE ARIENZO (RIOJA)* * *

1982	A	83
1983	A	80
1976 Gran Reserva	B	84
1980 Reserva	B	78

The gigantic sherry firm of Pedro Domecq set up this *bodega* in Rioja in the early 1970s, and it has consistently produced a light, relatively commercial but very clean, soft, fruity wine that is easy to drink and very fairly priced. I prefer the 1982 regular bottling to the 1983 as it has a bit more richness and depth. Among the older bottlings, the 1976 Gran Reserva shows a nice sweet, bing-cherry fruitiness, a caramel-candy-type flavor, and plenty of the sweet oak the Spanish adore. These are all inexpensive and excellent values.

MARQUÉS DE CÁCERES (RIOJA)* * *

1984 Rioja	A	84
1985 Rioja	A	85
1981 Rioja Reserva	A	84

The Riojas from the Marqués de Cáceres have always represented the modern school of winemaking in Rioja. They are round, ripe, overtly fruity with the sweet scent of oak noticeable, but under control. The wines generally have mass appeal. Certainly the 1985 is imbued with loads of soft berry fruit, has a good lashing of toasty vanillin oak, medium body, and generous flavors. The 1984 is less fat and concentrated than the deliciously fruity, heady 1985, but the 1981 Reserva shows a lovely aged mellowness, medium body, and a soft, sweet finish. It should be noted, however, that the Bodegas Marqués de Cáceres has not been without its critics, particularly the traditional school of Rioja winemakers, who were quick to charge that proprietor Enrique Forner, a man with interests in Bordeaux also, was changing the way Rioja was made. However, with the help of the famous Bordeaux professor Emile Peynaud, Forner has led the way for a number of innovative producers to turn out Rioja with more fruit than oak, and whether one appreciates its modern style or not, it can be a delicious wine in vintages such as 1985 and 1982.

MARQUÉS DE GRIÑON (RUEDA)* * *

1984 Tinto de Crianza	B	87
1985 Tinto de Crianza	B	89

Owner/proprietor Carlos Falco, an agricultural engineer and graduate of the University of California at Davis, has fashioned one of Spain's most interesting new styles of red wine from a blend of Cabernet Sauvignon and Merlot. Aging it several years in American oak, he has, since the early eighties, produced a wine with a great deal of flavor, and a complex bouquet of cedar and ripe plums that shows the potential to age well in the bottle for 5–10 years. As his vineyard has gotten older, the wines have gotten better, with the 1984 better than the 1983 and the 1985 perhaps the most impressive wine he has yet made. Prices have remained extremely reasonable for one of Spain's finest and most elegant Cabernet Sauvignon–based wines. Falco also makes a white wine from the Verdejo grape, and while it is made in a very fresh, fruity style and is among the better Spanish whites, I still cannot enthusiastically recommend it.

MARQUÉS DE MURRIETA (RIOJA)* * *

1982 Rioja	A	87
1983 Rioja	A	84
1968 Rioja Gran Reserva Castillo de Ygay	D	88

One of the oldest and most respected of the traditional producers of Rioja, the Marqués de Murrieta still produces wine from the original *bodega* built in 1872. While the white wine made here is rather heavy and dull, the red wines show considerable style. The 1983 regular Rioja shows a lively, vibrant, cherry fruitiness, a good dosage of sweet, toasty oak, and a soft, medium-bodied finish. The 1982 is deeper and richer and should last at least another decade. The winery also produces a rare and often superb Gran Reserva called Castillo de Ygay. Selling at prices of $40–50 a bottle, it has been made in only a handful of vintages, including 1917, 1925, 1934, 1942, and most recently, 1968. The 1968 has just been released after having spent 20 years aging in Murrieta's cellars. This very rich, intense wine shows its 20 years of age in a graceful, supple, voluptuous texture, and a bouquet filled with the smells of toasty almonds, rich berry fruit, and sweet American oak; it should drink well for another 5–10 years.

BODEGAS MARQUÉS DE RISCAL (RIOJA)* * *

1982 Rioja	A 84

1970 Rioja Reserva Speciale	D 87

One of Spain's oldest *bodegas*, this winery is known for its outstanding Gran Reservas, which often contain as much as 90% Cabernet Sauvignon, unusual for a Gran Reserva from Rioja. After a recent patch of rather mediocre wines from the late seventies through the early eighties, the newly released 1982 Rioja shows an elegant, richly fruity, stylish nose and well-balanced flavors, though it is somewhat more restrained and less opulent than other Riojas from this outstanding vintage. However, the 1970 Reserva Speciale is close to outstanding with its very ripe, intense bouquet, full body, succulent, mellow, velvety flavors, and long length. This *bodega* also produces an innocuous, bland white wine that I cannot recommend, as well as a decent rosé, which I have not seen in recent vintages.

BODEGAS LOUIS MATEOS (TORO)* * *

1976 Tinto Tío Babu	A 86

1980 Tinto Tío Babu	A 84

1981 Tinto Vega de Toro	A 59

1982 Tinto Vega de Toro	A 82

This is another *bodega* producing excellent wines from Toro, an unknown but promising appellation in northern Spain. While these wines are not quite as good as the Bodegas Farina's, they are still excellent wines of amazing value. The Bodegas Mateos produces two styles of Toro, one a lighter, less-intense style called Vega de Toro, of which the 1981 has tasted very poorly and should be avoided. However, the 1982 shows good fruit, not much complexity, but a rich, full-bodied, heady fruitiness and plenty of muscle. The most powerful style from this *bodega* is called Tío Babu, and the 1976 could easily be confused with a top-notch Rhône wine given its huge richness, full body, massive fruit, and 10–15 years of aging potential. The 1980 is similarly styled with big, deep, chunky fruitiness, but it does not have quite the complexity of the 1976. These wines remain remarkable values, and prices can only go up once the world discovers just how good they are.

BODEGAS MONTECILLO (RIOJA)* * *

1985 Rioja Cumbrero	A	82

1975 Rioja Gran Reserva	B	82

1982 Rioja Reserva Viña Monty	B	85

This winery on the outskirts of Navarrete specializes in making two styles of red wine; a three-year aged Cumbrero, of which the 1985 shows a full, lush, black-cherry flavor and soft, velvet texture, and a more mature Reserva called Viña Monty, of which the 1982 shows excellent richness, a sweet, ripe, American-oak taste, and a medium to full body. Both wines are ideal for drinking now, but certainly the Viña Monty can last another 7–8 years. In certain vintages a Gran Reserva is produced. The 1975 is starting to lose its fruit but still shows a fragrant cherry and oaky bouquet, medium body, and decent flavor concentration. I do not recommend the innocuous, one-dimensional white wine called Cumbrero. It is made from the Viura grape, but it shows little bouquet and watery flavors.

BODEGAS MUERZA (RIOJA)* * *

1978 Rioja Vega Reserva	A	84

1982 Rioja Vega Tinto	A	85

1983 Rioja Vega Tinto	A	84

While this winery is located in one of the less glamorous areas of Rioja known as La Rioja Baja, the wines have consistently offered great value and are made in a rich, full-bodied, effusively fruity, supple style. The wines appear under the Rioja Vega label, and the Tinto often contains as much as 80% Garnacha, whereas the Reserva contains 80% Tempranillo. The wines are never terribly deep in color, but they have seductive, rich, ripe-raspberry-scented bouquets with soft, fat, delicious fruit and flavors. They are not wines for those who love structure and body, but rather for those who prefer charm, suppleness, and seductiveness in their wines. All should be drunk within 3–4 years of their release.

BODEGAS MUGA (RIOJA)* * *

1982 Rioja	A	85

1983 Rioja	A 84

1981 Rioja Prado Enea	B 86

1982 Rioja Prado Enea	B 89

The Muga brothers produce some of my favorite Riojas, which have far greater richness and flavor than one might suspect from their rather light ruby color. Their standard Rioja, simply labeled Muga, is a delicious, almost burgundy-styled wine with a light ruby color, but amazing expansion and flavor breadth on the palate, showing deep cherry and plumlike fruit, plenty of toasty American oak, and a soft, rich finish. The 1982 seems to have a bit more to it than the delicious but lighter 1983. The Reservas, called Prado Enea, are excellent wines with a bit more color but plenty of deep, rich, complex, cedary, tobacco- and berry-scented fruit. The 1981 is quite a spicy, ripe, expansive wine in the mouth with full body and excellent length; it should drink well for another 5–6 years. The 1982 shows even more depth and richness and has more tannin, but with a very voluptuous, velvety texture and gobs of fruit. These wines are quite hedonistic, seductive Riojas that are among my favorites.

BODEGAS OLARRA (RIOJA)* * *

1983 Rioja Anares	A 77

1981 Rioja Anares Reserva	A 81

1981 Rioja Cerro Añon Reserva	A 83

1983 Rioja Tinto	A 75

Founded by a group of entrepreneurs in 1972, this winery quickly established an outstanding reputation for its reasonably priced, rich, velvety Riojas, largely based on the quality of its wines in the seventies, particularly the 1970, 1973, and 1975. However, the quality seemed to dip a bit for a while, but it now looks to be coming back. Though tasty, the wines are made in a rather commercial style that features light tannins, soft, velvety fruit, plenty of American oak in the bouquet and flavor, and 5–7 years of aging potential once the wines are released. Of the current releases, the 1983s and 1981s are good, and although I have not yet seen any 1982s in the marketplace, one would think they should be better than the 1983s or 1981s. Normally, the Cerro Anon has more richness and flavor than the other wines from Olarra; it is the one I would normally recommend. Be sure to avoid Olarra's white wine called Blanco Ruciente, made from 100% Viura, which tastes like lemon water.

BODEGAS FEDERICO PATERNINA (RIOJA)* *

1978 Rioja Gran Reserva	C	75

The Paternina Bodegas is certainly one of the most famous in Spain, having gained a reputation as being the favorite wine of Ernest Hemingway. Much has been made of this over past years, but recent vintages have simply not been as reliable and as complex as they should be. The 1978 Gran Reserva is simply an average-quality wine with adequate fruit and a great deal of oak in its taste, some of which seems to be old, musty wood. Perhaps a better bet would be to try the winery's three-year-old red wine called Banda Azul or its fruity Viña Vial than to spend so much more money for one of its *reservas*. All this is rather sad as I remember some pretty extraordinary wines from Paternina from vintages in the early sixties and late fifties.

BODEGAS HERMANOS PEREZ PASQUA (RIBERA DEL DUERO)* * *

1985 Pedrosa	B	83
1982 Pedrosa Reserva	B	85

These wines from the Ribera del Duero area are made in a very supple, supposedly fruity style that suggests to me it is Spain's answer to Italy's Dolcetto or France's Beaujolais. However, many observers feel that this *bodega* is almost into superstardom in Spain, so it may be a property well worth watching.

BODEGAS PESQUERA (RIBERA DEL DUERO)* * * *

1983 Pesquera	B	87
1984 Pesquera	B	86
1985 Pesquera	C	90
1986 Pesquera	C	92
1982 Pesquera Janus Reserva Speciale	E	85

Owner/proprietor Alejandro Fernandez has become one of the new superstars in Spain and has regrettably wasted no time in doubling the price for his exquisite red wine called Pesquera. Made from the Tempranillo grape and aged 2–2½ years in casks, the wine has remarkable depth and richness, and a texture not unlike a top-notch Pomerol. The rich fruit combined with the sweet oaky smells of Spanish oak (although Fernandez has also begun to use some new French oak casks) has resulted in some opulent and voluptuous wines that are real head turners. The 1986 Pesquera is probably the finest wine Fernandez has yet made, and comparisons to a top Bordeaux are not unjustified. Very deep in fruit, quite tannic and well structured, this wine should last 20 or more years in a good cool cellar. It looks to be even superior to some of his great wines produced in 1982 and 1975. The 1985 is a more supple, lighter, easier and more ready-to-drink wine than the tannic, massive 1986. It shows a great deal of elegance and rich berry fruit, and it should last for another 10–15 years. The 1983 is also drinking deliciously now but should continue to improve for another 5–6 years. In 1982, three different cuvées were made, a regular, a Reserva, and the newly launched Janus, which is a Reserva Speciale made half by the very traditional method of foot-stomping the grapes and half by machine-crushing the grapes. Given its price, one wonders if this is not a bit of a marketing gimmick used to take advantage of all the publicity this winery has received—let's hope it's not. It's an awfully good wine, but I wonder why it's not simply called a Reserva Speciale and why all the hype that Pesquera's importer is trying to generate isn't forgotten. Pesquera is clearly one of Spain's three best red wines, and in certain vintages probably its best, and while success is unlikely to go to the level head of Alejandro Fernandez, one suspects it has gone to the head of his importer.

BODEGAS LA GRANJA REMELLURI (RIOJA)* * * *

1983 La Bastida de Alava	B	87
1984 La Bastida de Alava	B	85
1985 La Bastida de Alava	B	88

Founded in 1970 by Jaime Rodriquez Salis, this tiny *bodega* is dedicated to producing only one red wine from its own 90 acres of vines planted with 80% Tempranillo, 10% Mazuel, and 10% Viura. This is consistently one of my favorite Riojas as it is among the most complex and fragrant wines produced in that area of Spain. There are those who have argued that the Tempranillo has a style more like a Pinot Noir than any other French grape, and one taste of a Remelluri Rioja will support such a belief. The wines have a burgundy-styled lushness and richness, with that wonderful expansion on the palate of sweet, ripe berry flavors intertwined with gobs of toasty oak. Every vintage I have tried from this winery has been good enough to recommend, and that's saying something. The newly released 1985 shows layers of rich berry fruit, plenty of spicy oak, and a smooth, harmonious, velvety texture. It is hard to believe it can get better, but my experience is that it should evolve even further with 4–5 more years in the bottle. The 1984, from a rather disappointing year, is a very attractive wine with plenty of sweet oak, supple berry flavors, and medium body. The 1983 again has a burgundian, full-intensity bouquet of ripe fruit, sweet oak, and marvelously rich, graceful, silky flavors on the palate. These are delicious, seductive Riojas that I find among the finest made in this viticultural area of Spain.

LA RIOJA ALTA (RIOJA)* * * * *

1970 Rioja Gran Reserva 890	C	90
1973 Rioja Gran Reserva 904	C	90
1980 Rioja Reserva Viña Ardanza	A	86
1983 Rioja Viña Alberdi	A	79

Rioja Alta produces the two most classic examples of Rioja made, the Reserva 904 and Reserva 890. Both wines are aged at least a decade before they are released by the winery. The bottom-of-the-line red wines from Rioja Alta are from Viña Alberdi. As in 1983, it is a soft, fruity, rather light wine that is easily drunk but should not be cellared for more than two or three years after it has been released. For enthusiasts of fuller-styled Riojas, the winery makes an excellent, velvety, rich, spicy, full-bodied Viña Ardanza, and the last three vintages released, the 1980, 1978, and 1976, have all been very successful wines with a great deal of fruit, body, fullness, and complexity. However, for tasting what Rioja Alta is capable of achieving, one must spend a few dollars more and try either the Reserva 904 or Reserva 890, the finest two Riojas made. If one were only to smell their bouquets, they could easily be mistaken for a top-notch Graves from Bordeaux such as Haut-Brion or La Mission Haut-Brion. Both have a deeply rich, mineral- and tobacco-scented bouquet bursting with ripe berry fruit.

The oak is there, but it is never the primary player in this wonderful symphony of scents. On the palate, both wines show a rich, velvety, lush texture, excellent length and richness, and while fully mature, should hold in the bottle for at least another decade. Certainly the 1970 Reserva 890 and 1973 Reserva 904 are as fine as Rioja as one is likely to drink, but they are not inexpensive. On the other hand, the winery's white wine is mediocre and cannot be recommended.

BODEGAS SANTIAGO (RIOJA)* *

1983 Gran Condal Rioja	A	75
1984 Gran Condal Rioja	A	76
1985 Gran Condal Rioja	A	80
1978 Gran Condal Rioja Reserva	A	72

I have had very little good fortune with the wines from the Bodegas Santiago, which appear under the name of Gran Condal. Like all of the above, they tend to be very commercial, rather insubstantial wines that are somewhat diluted and lacking flavor depth and complexity.

BODEGAS SEÑORÍO DE SARRIA (NAVARRA)* * *

1973 Gran Reserva	A	83
1981 Gran Reserva	A	78
1982 Reserva	A	83

While the above ratings hardly reflect the enjoyment and value the wines of Señorío de Sarria have provided me, this has generally been a consistent and reliable source for inexpensive Spanish wines from Navarra, another up-and-coming but as yet unknown Spanish viticultural area. The major red wine grape is the Garnacha, and it represents at least 70% of these wines. These are ripe, fruity, soft wines, although the above vintages did not show as well as I would have suspected. Drink these supple wines fairly young, although the older vintages that have been released by the winery have held up well with age.

TORRES (PENEDÈS)* * * * - * * * * *

1985 Coronas	A	82

1982 Gran Coronas Black Label	C	?
1983 Gran Coronas Black Label	C	88
1982 Gran Coronas Reserva	A	89
1983 Gran Coronas Reserva	A	79
1983 Sangre de Toro Reserva	A	87
1985 Sangre de Toro Reserva	A	88

This venerable winery continues to turn out some stunning values in red wines, especially its regular bottling of Coronas, which still has to be one of the great red wine values in the world, and its full-bodied, rich, intense Sangre de Toro, of which the 1985 and 1983 Reservas are bursting with blackberry fruit, have gobs of toasty vanillin oak, and offer quite a mouthful of delicious red wine. Both should easily last another 5–7 years, whereas the regular bottling of Coronas should be drunk within 2–3 years of its release. As for Gran Coronas White Label, the 1983 has proven to be rather mediocre on the three occasions I have tasted it, showing a lack of the rich, fleshy fruit that this wine usually has. However, the 1982 is fairly stunning with a cedary, rich blackcurrant bouquet, plenty of toasty oak, and gobs of rich berry fruit. Of course the flagship wine of Torres is the Gran Coronas Black Label, which over time has evolved into a 100% Cabernet Sauvignon wine from the family's own vineyards. It was exceptional in 1978 and extremely good in 1975, 1976, 1977, and again in 1981. However, despite an amazing amount of hype about how great the 1982 was going to be, after having tasted it a half dozen times, I find it a rather vegetal, overly oaked wine that lacks the great depth of fruit contained in prior vintages of this Spanish classic. In some bottles I have even detected a nasty green-sap character from improperly cured barrels. I'm not sure what the problem is, but this is a very chancy wine to buy, and a disappointing performance from this quality-conscious winery. However, the winery is back in top form with the 1983, a delicious, ripe, rich, cedary, plum-scented, lush wine that, while not as good as the 1978 or 1981, is still a top-notch Cabernet Sauvignon, and one of the two best Cabernets made in Spain. All things considered, Torres is still one of the leaders in providing the world's wine consumers with some tasty wine values.

VEGA SICILIA (RIBERA DEL DUERO)* * * * *

1976 Unico Reserva	E 94

N.V. Unico Reserva Speciale	E 93

1983 Valbuena	D 86

Vega Sicilia has the reputation of producing Spain's greatest red wines. However, the estate has been the target of a great deal of criticism principally because of the high prices charged for its wines, although the quality is such that one suspects if these wines were made in France or Italy, few people would ever question their price. The policy of the winery is to release a wine called Valbuena at either 3 or 5 years of age, and to release the famous vintage Vega Sicilia Unico after 10 years of cellaring at the winery, much of this time spent in oak casks. The 1976 is the current offering of the Unico Reserva. The winery has still not released the 1968 and the 1970, which are reputed to be the two greatest years for Vega Sicilia since World War II; a call to the winery revealed that they will be released within two years. The winery produces a third bottling of red wine that is not vintage-dated but is simply entitled Unico Reserva Speciale. The current nonvintage offering is a blend of the best lots of wine made between 1949 and 1955. It sells for well over $100 a bottle and is available on allocation only. It may be easy to criticize the long cask aging and pricing policy of Vega Sicilia, but if one considers the length of time these wines spend in oak, and the fact that they are generally quite drinkable when released, they are actually a decent value given the extraordinary wines that were produced in vintages such as 1966, 1972, and 1976. One suspects the 1968 and the 1970 will be even better.

As for the 1976 Unico Reserva, it has an absolutely sensational bouquet of sweet oak and ripe, cedary, berrylike fruit that explodes from the glass. On the palate, it has extraordinary depth, richness, and complexity, and it tastes like no other wine made in the world. It is quite full-bodied, powerful, and rich, but the suppleness resulting from its being 12 years old allows it to be drunk with great pleasure now, and it should hold and perhaps improve in the bottle for at least another decade. The 1983 Valbuena is a downsized version of the Unico Reserva with quite a bit of oak and good fruit, but not nearly the flavor dimension and complexity of the Unico Reserva. The nonvintage Reserva Speciale blend is amazingly youthful given its alleged age, but at twice the price of the Unico Reserva, it is a notoriously bad value. It is quite rich, and very sweet with ripe plummy fruit and plenty of the toasty oak the Spanish adore. It is a tremendously seductive wine to drink. How it will age is debatable, but it is certainly drinking sensationally well at present.

THE WINES OF NORTH AMERICA

California
Oregon
Other American
Viticultural Regions

6. CALIFORNIA

The Basics

TYPES OF WINE

Virtually every type of wine seen elsewhere in the wine world is made in California. Fortified port-styled wines, decadently sweet, late-harvest Rieslings, sparkling wines, and major red and white dry table wines from such super grapes as Chardonnay and Cabernet Sauvignon—all are to be found in California.

GRAPE VARIETIES

The fine wines of California are dominated by Cabernet Sauvignon and Chardonnay as much of the attention of that state's winemakers is directed at these two grapes. However, California makes wonderful Zinfandel and increasing amounts of world-class Merlot and Syrah, plus some Petite Sirah. Despite improved quality, Pinot Noir is still a questionable wine in the hands of all but a few California wine producers. As for the white wines, Sauvignon Blanc and Semillon, and blends thereof, can be wonderfully complex and fragrant, but the great majority are nondescript wines. It is a shame that Chenin Blanc has so little sex appeal among consumers, because it can make a very inexpensive, delicious wine. Colombard and Muscat suffer from the same image problems as Chenin Blanc, but shrewd consumers know

597

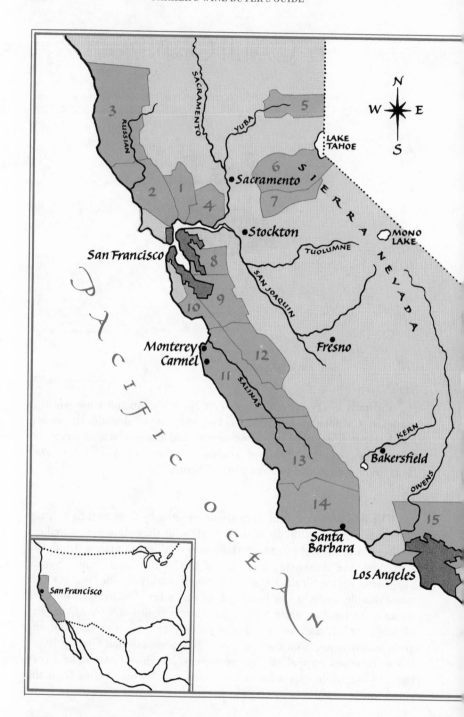

California

Wine regions

1 Napa Valley
2 Sonoma
3 Mendocino
4 Solano
5 Sierra Foothills
6 El Dorado
7 Amador
8 Alameda
9 Santa Clara
10 Santa Cruz
11 Monterey
12 San Benito
13 San Luis Obispo
14 Santa Barbara
15 Los Angeles
16 Riverside
17 San Diego
18 Imperial Valley

NEVADA

MOJAVE DESERT

San
• Bernadino

COLORADO

16

SALTON
SEA

San
Diego 17 18

MEXICO

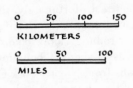

```
0      50    100    150
KILOMETERS

0      50    100
MILES
```

the good ones and seek them out. Gewürztraminer and dry Rieslings have been dismal wines. For years California has made it simple for the consumer, naming its wines after the varietal from which it is made. By law, a Chardonnay or Cabernet Sauvignon must contain 75% of that grape in the wine. The recent trend, accompanied by very high prices, has been to produce luxury-priced proprietary wines with awe-inspiring, often silly names such as Dominus, Opus, Rubicon, Trilogy, and Insignia. These wines are supposed to be the winery's very best lots of wine blended together for harmony. Some of them are quite marvelous, but keep in mind that all of them are overpriced.

FLAVORS

RED WINE VARIETALS

Cabernet Franc—Now being used by more and more wineries to give complexity to their wines' bouquets, Cabernet Franc is a cedary, herbaceous-scented wine that is much lighter in color and body than either Cabernet Sauvignon or Merlot. It can rarely stand by itself, but used judiciously in a blend, it can provide an extra dimension. Two great California wines with significant proportions of Cabernet Franc that have stood the test of time are the 1971 Robert Mondavi Reserve Cabernet and the 1977 Joseph Phelps Insignia red wine. The Santa Cruz winery of Congress Springs and Napa's Chateau Chevre and Cosentino (Crystal Valley Cellars) have recently demonstrated success with this varietal.

Cabernet Sauvignon—Rich, jammy black currants, chocolate, leather, ground meat, minerals, and herbs are all part of a top Cabernet's aromatic complexity. If the wine smells of asparagus or cooked green beans (as many do from Monterey County and the Santa Barbara area), it is a major flaw.

Merlot—More plums, sometimes scents of toffee and tea as well as herbs, particularly garden tomatoes, enter into the picture, but the main difference from Cabernet Sauvignon is the softer, more opulent texture, lower acids, higher alcohol, and less aggressive tannins.

Petite Sirah—Unfortunately, this varietal has fallen from grace. Petite Sirah, in actuality the Duriff grape, is unrelated to the true Syrah, yet it can produce richly colored, very tannic, intense wines with peppery, cassis-scented bouquets. The Ridge and Freemark Abbey Petite Sirahs from Napa's York Creek Vineyard prove the outstanding potential of this grape when planted in the proper soils and grown and vinified with care. Parducci and Guenoc produce a very good, soft, fruity style of this wine that is quite agreeable.

Pinot Noir—Since it is rarely good, the Pinot Noir characteristics most often encountered are washed-out vegetal, tomato-scented fruit, cooked prune and raisin flavors, and an imbalanced feel on the palate. The good Pinot Noirs, the best of which are from wineries such as Calera, Saintsbury, Chalone, and Robert Mondavi, display exotic bouquets filled with Oriental spices, vibrant, well-focused, subtly herbaceous cherry and plum fruit, and velvety, lush textures complemented by the sweet scent of vanillin oak. Progress has been made by California vintners, but a great majority of their Pinot Noirs are unacceptably mediocre and overpriced.

Syrah—Syrah is the great red grape of the Rhône Valley. Few California wineries have toyed with this varietal, which may be more suitable for the climate and soils of more California viticultural districts than any other varietal. Joseph Phelps produces a Syrah in a light, fruity, Beaujolais style, while Bonny Doon in the Santa Cruz Mountains has made exquisite wines from Syrah in 1983, 1984, and 1985. Ojai is another pioneer with this varietal. Brilliant wines have also been made from true Syrah by Sean Thackrey, Edmunds St. John (where it is used in a blend), Kendall-Jackson, Duxoup, Qupé, McDowell, Preston, Sierra Vista, and Zaca Mesa. At its best, Syrah produces a black/ruby-colored wine with a smoky, cassis-scented bouquet, rich, sometimes massive flavors, and 10–15 years of aging potential.

Zinfandel—Despite the great spectrum of styles ranging from soft, light, effusively fruity wines to late-harvest, thick, portlike wines, most of the Zinfandels made in this decade represent a more balanced "claret" style with gobs of direct, ripe, straightforward, spicy, berry fruit that is presented (or should be) in a supple, full-bodied, soft style.

FLAVORS

WHITE WINE VARIETALS

Chardonnay—The great superstar of the white wines, Chardonnay at its best can produce majestically rich, buttery wines with, seemingly, layers of flavors suggesting tropical fruits, apples, peaches, and buttered popcorn. It flourishes in all of California's viticultural districts. The trend in the eighties in California has been to pick the grapes earlier to achieve better natural acidities. Even though Chardonnay definitely produces California's finest white wines, far too many, while technically flawless, tend to lack character and taste like imitations of each other. Also, far too many Chardonnays have had excessive amounts of acidity added to them, giving them a very tart character. Chardonnay is generally aged in oak barrels for several months to a year. The wines can be long-lived in the hands of a producer such as Trefethen, Stony Hill, Mayacamas, Chalone, or Kalin, but the great majority of these wines should be drunk up before they turn 4 years old. Anyone who tells you anything different clearly does not have your best interests in mind.

Chenin Blanc—This maligned, generally misunderstood grape can produce lovely aperitif wines that are both dry and slightly sweet, but in either style, fruity, delicate, perfumed, and light-bodied. However, Chenin Blanc is not in fashion, and sagging sales have caused many premium wineries to abandon it. Dry Creek, Chappellet, Preston, Pine Ridge, Alexander Valley, and Hacienda make some of the best. It deserves more attention from consumers, but given its low sex appeal, it is not likely to get it until wine drinkers put pleasure before prestige.

French Colombard—Like the Chenin Blanc, Colombard is a varietal that is rarely accorded respect by consumers. Its charm is its aromatic character and crisp, light-bodied style. Parducci and Chalone consistently prove its credentials.

Gewürztraminer—Highly promoted and encouraged by the California wine press, this varietal, made in the dry, slightly sweet, and late-harvest (very sweet) style, has to my palate a watery, vague resemblance to the spicy, exotic, flamboyant Gewürztraminers made in Alsace, France. While it is hard to understand the appeal of this grape in California, a few wineries such as St. Francis and Navarro have captured some of its magic.

Muscat—This is a terribly underrated and underappreciated varietal that produces at the top levels slightly sweet, remarkably fragrant, perfumed wines that are usually loaded with tropical-fruit aromas and flavors. Robert Pecota, Louis Martini, and Bonny Doon consistently achieve special results with this grape.

Pinot Blanc—Often indistinguishable from Chardonnay in a blind tasting, Pinot Blanc is usually a more steely, crisper, firmer wine than Chardonnay. Chalone makes the best Pinot Blanc in California followed by Congress Springs, Mirassou, Buehler, and Bonny Doon.

Sauvignon Blanc—In the last several years, the trendy California wine scene made this grape their "great white hope," and now that wineries have taken up its cause, it seems to be falling out of fashion.

It is often called Fumé Blanc. It is a crisp wine with a subtle earthy, herbaceous quality that in many examples becomes grotesquely vegetal, although examples of blatantly vegetal wines are much less extensive today than several years ago. This is a remarkably flexible wine that goes with various foods, and the quality across the board is quite high. Yet, rather unfortunately, far too many wineries aim for the middle-of-the-road, safe style of wine, and as with Chardonnay, one finds an excessive number of fairly neutral, bland, innocuous examples of this wine. Sauvignon Blanc is often blended with Semillon to give it more body and more of a creamy character. Some of California's best Sauvignon or Fumé Blancs are produced by Robert Mondavi, Dry Creek, Kalin, Matanzas Creek, Chateau St. Jean, Spottswoode, and Glen Ellen.

Semillon—This is clearly one of the up-and-coming white varietals of California. It is the perfect partner when added to the crisp, lean, acidic Sauvignon Blanc because it always seems to have plenty of body and a creamy richness. It is difficult to handle entirely by itself, but Kalin Cellars of Marin County has produced a ravishing string of Semillons from old vines planted in Livermore, and Beringer has produced a decadently sweet dessert wine from this varietal.

White Riesling or Johannisberg Riesling—With over 8,000 acres planted with this varietal in California, the wine industry is not likely to tear out the vines; nevertheless, except for the world-class, late-harvest sweet Rieslings made by Joseph Phelps, Chateau St. Jean, Raymond, and a handful of other wineries, the attempts at making dry Kabinett- or Spätlese-styled Rieslings have generally produced dull, heavy wines with little character. The simple truth of the matter is that most of the Riesling is planted in areas where the soil is too rich or the climate too hot. With only a handful of exceptions—Jekel, Trefethen, Kendall-Jackson, and Chateau St. Jean are four that come to mind—California is only suitable for great, sweet, dessert-style Rieslings. No one wants to hear it, but its drier versions have largely been failures.

AGING POTENTIAL

Cabernet Franc: 5–10 years	Muscat: 1–3 years
Cabernet Sauvignon: 5–25 years	Petite Sirah: 5–15 years
Chardonnay: 1–4 years	Pinot Blanc: 1–4 years
Chenin Blanc: 1–3 years	Pinot Noir: 5–8 years
Colombard: 1–2 years	Riesling (dry): 1–3 years
Gamay: 2–4 years	Riesling (sweet): 2–10 years
Merlot: 5–10 years	Sauvignon Blanc: 1–3 years

Semillon: 1–3 years   Syrah: 5–20 years
Sparkling wines: 3–8 years   Zinfandel: 3–10 years

OVERALL QUALITY LEVEL

The top two dozen producers of Cabernet Sauvignon, Merlot, or proprietary red wines, as well as those two dozen or so who produce Chardonnay, make wines that are as fine and as multidimensional as anywhere in the world. However, there are many wines made from poorly placed vineyards, and there are far too many vegetal and over-acidified wines to take lightly. The bold truth is that despite the enormous potential, California makes as much innocuous, charmless, and characterless wines as anywhere in the world. Sadly, it does not have to be that way if more people would just show a little contempt after being ripped off by an excessively acidic and/or innocuous Cabernet or Chardonnay that costs $18.

MOST IMPORTANT INFORMATION TO KNOW

First learn which wineries produce the type and style of wine that you enjoy the most. The fact that a winery makes a delicious Cabernet Sauvignon does not guarantee that its Chardonnay or Sauvignon Blanc is equally as good. Try to memorize the top producers for the different types of wines and then be sure to taste their wines.

1989–1990 BUYING STRATEGY

The California wine industry is in the midst of another boom period (the last one was 1977–1981). The finest run of vintages (1984, 1985, 1986, 1987) in over a decade, plus the exorbitant cost of top imported wines from France, Italy, and Spain, has focused much of the wine consumer's attention on California. In particular, lovers of red wines, especially Merlot, Cabernet Sauvignon, and Zinfandel, have the opulent, explosively rich, forward 1984s; classically structured, marvelously concentrated, long-term agers of 1985; or powerful, intense, full-bodied 1986s to choose from. Amazingly, all three vintages surpass in quality every other Cabernet vintage since 1974. For white wines, 1987 Chardonnays, Sauvignons, Semillons, and Chenin Blancs look to be the best made this decade—combining richness with finesse and structure. California is, for now, loaded with wine riches. If the top producers do not become too greedy and alienate clients with significantly higher prices (which some are already doing), California's boom cycle will go into the next decade with no slowdown in sight.

VINTAGE GUIDE

1987—An early vintage with plenty of accompanying heat to cause grape sugars to soar in August 1987 has turned out to be the fourth very-good-to-excellent vintage in succession. The Cabernets and Merlots may turn out to be as good, perhaps even better than the 1984s, a vintage of similar climatic conditions. The white wines are superb, exhibiting rich, aromatic personalities, and a great deal of depth. This appears to be another vintage with exciting potential.

1986—Overshadowed by the resounding acclaim for 1985, 1986 has produced rich, buttery, opulent Chardonnays that have lower acidities than the 1985s, but frequently more fruit and plumpness. The best examples should drink well through 1990, but as a general rule, the 1986 Chardonnays will not be as long-lived as the 1985s, although they probably will be more enjoyable. The red wines follow a similar pattern, exhibiting a rich, ripe, full-bodied character with generally lower acids than the nearly perfect 1985s, but also more tannins and body. It appears to be an excellent year for red wines that should age quite well.

1985—On overall balance, the finest vintage for California Cabernet Sauvignon since 1974. A perfect growing season preceded near-perfect conditions for harvesting. Napa and Sonoma look to be the best, Santa Cruz and Mendocino just behind in quality. The rich Cabernets are less extroverted and opulent in their youth than the 1984s, but certainly longer-lived. This could prove to be the best overall vintage since 1970 as the top wines will last for 10–20 years.

1984—An excellent year, somewhat overshadowed by 1985, 1984 was one of the hottest years on record with temperatures soaring over 100° F frequently during the summer. An early flowering and early harvest did create problems because many grape varietals ripened at the same time. The style of the Chardonnnays and Cabernets is one of very-good-to-excellent concentration, an engaging, opulent, forward fruitiness that gives the wines appeal in their infancy and good overall balance. Mendocino is less successful than elsewhere, but the ripe, rich, forward character of the wines of this vintage gives them undeniable charm and character. The majority of winemakers call 1985 a more classic year, 1984 a more hedonistic year. The Chardonnays should be consumed by now; the red wines are already drinking extremely well.

1983—An average year for most of California's viticultural regions, and although the Chardonnays from Napa were very good, most are now far too old. The Cabernets are medium-bodied, rather austere, and lack the flesh and richness found in top years. Nevertheless, some stars are to be found (e.g., Hess Collection Reserve, Opus One, Chateau Montelena, and Dunn). The red wines will keep for at least another 4–6 years.

1982—The growing season was plagued by heavy rains, then high temperatures. The press seemed to take a cautionary approach to the vintage, and as it turns out, justifiably so. Sonoma is more consistent than Napa, and Santa Cruz is surprisingly weak in 1982. The Sonoma red wines are ripe, rich, very forward, and much more interesting than those of Napa, which range in quality from outstanding to out of balance. Chardonnays are mediocre, diluted, and lack depth and acidity. They should have been drunk up by now.

1981—Like 1984, a torridly hot growing season that had all varietals ripening at once and the harvest commencing very early. Many fine, ripe, rich, dramatic Chardonnays were produced, but they should have been drunk up by 1987. The Cabernets are good rather than exciting, with the best of them having a decade of life. Most 1981 Cabernets, because of their forward character, should be drunk before 1991–1992.

1980—A relatively long, cool growing season had wineries predicting a classic, great vintage for both Chardonnay and Cabernet. As the wines have matured, the Chardonnays were indeed excellent, but not as good as in 1984 and 1985. The Cabernets are very good, but hardly great. The Cabernets do, however, have good acidity levels and seem by California standards to be evolving rather slowly. A vintage that has a top-notch reputation but in reality appears to be a very fine rather than a monumental year.

Older Vintages

Since I fervently believe California's Chardonnays and Sauvignon Blancs rarely hold their fruit or improve after 4 years, older vintages are of interest only with respect to California red wines, principally Cabernet Sauvignon.

1979—This year produced a good vintage of tannic, well-endowed wines that are now fully mature.

1978—An excellent vintage from a hot year that produced very concentrated, rich, plummy, dense wines that have aged quite quickly. In all but a few cases, they should be drunk up before the end of this decade.

1977—An above-average vintage that rendered elegant, fruity, supple wines that are now just beginning to tire a bit.

1976—A hot, drought year in which production yields per acre were small. The wines are very concentrated and tannic, sometimes out of balance. Nevertheless, the great examples from this vintage (where the level of fruit extract matches the ferocity of the tannins) should prove to be among the longest-lived Cabernets of this generaton. Despite irregularity here, there are some truly splendid Cabernets.

1975—After the great vintage of 1974, few people wanted to believe California could have another good vintage. The wines, noticeably lighter and less alcoholic and opulent than the 1974s, are all fully mature now. They are refined, fruity, very well balanced Cabernets, but they should be drunk up.

1974—A great vintage of rich, big, deep, dramatic, intense wines that have shown well from their first release. Some of the lesser stars have started to fade, and even the greatest wines from this vintage are not likely to get much better. And yet, 1974 offers wine enthusiasts flamboyant, rich, intense wines that should continue to drink seductively and well for at least another 5–6 years.

1973—A very fine vintage of classically structured Cabernet with plenty of fruit, some finesse, and 10- to 12-year life spans. These wines should be drunk up.

1972—A rain-plagued, terrible year except in the Santa Cruz area, which produced a bevy of fine wines.

1971—A mediocre year, although Mondavi's Reserve and the Ridge Montebello are two of the greatest Cabernets I have ever tasted.

1970—Along with 1968, 1974, 1984, and 1985, one of California's most successful vintages. The top 1970s are still in great form, with a decade of life left in them at the top levels.

1969—A good vintage, but the wines did not have the stamina or extract to last more than 10 years. I know of nothing from this vintage that should not have been drunk up by now.

1968—A great vintage: powerful, rich, deep, dense wines that when stored well are close to perfection today. The Heitz Martha's Vineyard is one of the greatest Cabernets I have ever tasted from California.

A GUIDE TO CALIFORNIA'S BEST PRODUCERS OF CABERNET SAUVIGNON, MERLOT, OR BLENDS THEREOF

* * * * * (OUTSTANDING PRODUCERS)

Beaulieu Private Reserve
  Georges de Latour (Napa)
Carmenet (Sonoma)
Caymus Special Selection
  (Napa)

Diamond Creek (Napa)—all 3
  bottlings
Dominus (Napa)
Duckhorn Three Palms
  Vineyard Merlot (Napa)

Dunn (Napa)—both bottlings
Forman (Napa)
Groth (Napa)
Heitz Martha's Vineyard (Napa)
Hess Collection Reserve (Napa)
William Hill Reserve (Napa)
Kistler (Sonoma)
Robert Mondavi Reserve (Napa)
Chateau Montelena (Napa)
Opus One (Napa)

Joseph Phelps Eisele & Insignia
  Vineyards (Napa)
Ridge Monte Bello (Santa Cruz)
Rubicon (Napa)
St. Francis Merlot (Sonoma)
Silver Oak (Napa)—all 3
  bottlings
Simi Reserve (Sonoma)
Spottswoode (Napa)
Stag's Leap Cask 23 (Napa)

* * * * (EXCELLENT PRODUCERS)

Bellerose (Sonoma)
Beringer Private Reserve (Napa)
Buehler (Napa)
Burgess (Napa)
Caymus Estate (Napa)
Chappellet (Napa)
Château Chevre Merlot (Napa)
B. R. Cohn (Sonoma)
De Moor (Napa)
Durney (Monterey)
Field Stone (Sonoma)
Girard (Napa)
Grace Family (Napa)
Gundlach-Bundschu Rhine
  Farm Merlot and Cabernet
  Sauvignon (Sonoma)
Havens (Napa)

Hess Collection (Napa)
Inglenook Reserve and Reunion
  (Napa)
Johnson-Turnbull (Napa)
Laurel Glen (Sonoma)
Long (Napa)
Matanzas Creek Merlot
  (Sonoma)
Mayacamas (Napa)
Monticello (Napa)
Mount Eden (Santa Cruz)
Joseph Phelps Backus Vineyard
  (Napa)
Ravenswood (Sonoma)
Ritchie Creek (Napa)
Sattui (Napa)
Philip Togni (Napa)

* * * (GOOD PRODUCERS)

Alexander Valley (Sonoma)
Baldinelli (Amador)
Beringer (Knight's Valley)
Boeger (El Dorado)
David Bruce (Santa Cruz)
Cakebread (Napa)
Carneros Creek (Napa)
Cassayre-Forni (Napa)
Christian Brothers (Napa)
Clos du Bois (Sonoma)
Clos du Val (Napa)

Clos du Val Reserve (Napa)
Congress Springs (Santa Clara)
Conn Creek (Napa)
Cuvaison (Napa)
Dehlinger (Sonoma)
Dry Creek (Sonoma)
Eberle (Paso Robles)
Far Niente (Napa)
Fetzer Reserve (Mendocino)
Fisher (Sonoma)
Flora Springs (Napa)

Franciscan (Napa)
Glen Ellen (Sonoma)
Grgich Hills (Napa)
Harbor (Yolo)
Jaeger (Napa)
Jordan (Sonoma)
La Jota (Napa)
Robert Keenan (Napa)
Kenwood (Sonoma)
Charles Krug (Napa)
Charles Lefranc (San Benito)
Louis Martini (Napa)
Montevina (Amador)
Mount Veeder (Napa)
Newton (Napa)
Parducci (Mendocino)
Robert Pepi (Napa)
Pine Ridge (Napa)
Quail Ridge (Napa)
Raymond (Napa)
Roudon-Smith (Santa Cruz)
Round Hill (Napa)

Rutherford Hill (Napa)
St. Clement (Napa)
Santa Cruz Mountain (Santa Cruz)
Sebastiani (Sonoma)
Sequoia Grove (Napa)
Shafer (Napa)
Silverado (Napa)
Simi (Sonoma)
Steltzner (Napa)
Sterling (Napa)
Stonegate (Napa)
Sullivan (Napa)
Trefethen (Napa)
Tudal (Napa)
Tulocay (Napa)
Viansa (Sonoma)
Vichon (Napa)
Villa Mt. Eden (Napa)
Whitehall Lane (Napa)
Stephen Zellerbach (Sonoma)

* * *(AVERAGE)*

Cain (Napa)
Chimney Rock (Napa)
Cronin (San Mateo)
Delicato
Freemark Abbey (Napa) (since 1974)
Gallo (Stanislaus)

Guenoc (Lake)
Joanna
Lakespring (Napa)
Paul Masson (Monterey)
McDowell (Mendocino)
Rombauer (Napa)
Spring Moutain (Napa)

A LIST OF CALIFORNIA'S PROPRIETARY RED WINES

Alexandre (Geyser Park)
Cain Five (Cain Cellars)
Carmenet (Chalone)
Cask 23 (Stag's Leap Wine Cellars)
Le Cigare Volant (Bonny Doon)
Cuvée Bellerose (Bellerose)
Dominus (John Daniel Society)

Insignia (Joseph Phelps)
Lyeth (Lyeth Vineyards)
Marlstone (Clos du Bois)
Old Telegram (Bonny Doon)
Opus One (Mondavi-Rothschild)
Pahlmeyer (Pahlmeyer Vineyards)
Pickberry (Ravenswood)

Poet (Cosentino)
Reunion (Inglenook)
Rubicon (Niebaum-Coppola)

Trilogy (Flora Springs)
Victorian (Guenoc)

A GUIDE TO CALIFORNIA'S BEST PRODUCERS OF CHARDONNAY

***** (OUTSTANDING PRODUCERS)

Chalone (Monterey)
Cronin (San Mateo)
De Loach (Sonoma)
Flora Springs (Napa)
Forman (Napa)
Girard (Napa)
Kalin (Marin)
Kistler (Sonoma)
Long (Napa)
Matanzas Creek (Sonoma)

Robert Mondavi Reserve (Napa)
Chateau Montelena (Napa)
Mount Eden (Santa Clara)
St. Francis (Sonoma)
Simi (Sonoma)
Sonoma-Cutrer (Sonoma)
Stony Hill (Napa)
Talbott (Monterey)
Trefethen (Napa)
ZD (Napa)

**** (EXCELLENT PRODUCERS)

Acacia (Napa)
S. Anderson (Napa)
Au Bon Climat (Santa Barbara)
Clos du Bois (Sonoma)
Congress Springs (Santa Clara)
Edna Valley (San Luis Obispo)
Ferrari-Carano (Alexander
  Valley)
Grgich (Napa)
Kendall-Jackson (Mendocino)

Monticello (Napa)
Morgan (Monterey)
Navarro (Mendocino)
Newton (Napa)
Raymond (Napa)
Ritchie Creek (Napa)
Chateau St. Jean (Sonoma)
Saintsbury (Napa)
Sinskey (Napa)
Tiffany Hill (Edna Valley)

*** (GOOD PRODUCERS)

Alderbrook (Sonoma)
Arrowood (Sonoma)
William Baccala (Mendocino)
Balverne (Sonoma)
Beringer (Napa)
Château Bouchaine (Napa)
David Bruce (Santa Cruz)
Buena Vista (Sonoma)
Burgess (Napa)

Chamisal (Edna Valley)
Chappellet (Napa)
B. R. Cohn (Sonoma)
Concannon (Santa Clara)
La Crema Vinera (Sonoma)
Cuvaison (Napa)
Dolan (Mendocino)
Dry Creek (Sonoma)
Eberle (Paso Robles)

Far Niente (Napa)
Fetzer (Mendocino)
Fisher (Sonoma)
Thomas Fogarty (Monterey)
Folie à Deux (Napa)
Freemark Abbey (Napa)
Fritz (Sonoma)
Gainey (Santa Barbara)
Glen Ellen (Sonoma)
Groth (Napa)
Guenoc (Lake)
Gundlach Bundschu (Sonoma)
Hacienda (Sonoma)
Hanna (Sonoma)
Haywood (Sonoma)
Hess Collection (Napa)
William Hill (Napa)
Inglenook (Napa)
Jekel (Monterey)
Robert Keenan (Napa)
Lambert Bridge (Sonoma)
Landmark (Sonoma)
Domaine Laurier (Sonoma)
Leeward (Central Coast)
Charles Lefranc (San Benito)
Manzanita (Napa)

Mayacamas (Napa)
Mazzocco (Sonoma)
Merry Vintners (Sonoma)
Milano (Mendocino)
Mount Veeder (Napa)
Neyers (Napa)
Robert Pepi (Napa)
Perret (Napa)
Joseph Phelps (Napa)
Pine Ridge (Napa)
Quail Ridge (Napa)
Martin Ray (Santa Clara)
Rutherford Hill (Napa)
St. Andrews (Napa)
St. Clement (Sonoma)
Sanford (Santa Barbara)
Sausal (Sonoma)
Shafer (Napa)
Smith-Madrone (Sonoma)
Stag's Leap (Napa)
Sterling (Napa)
Stratford (Napa)
Vichon (Napa)
Château Woltner
Zaca Mesa (Santa Barbara)

* * *(OTHER PRODUCERS)*

Bargetto (Santa Cruz)
Clos du Val (Napa)
Conn Creek (Napa)
Firestone (Santa Barbara)
Gallo (Central Coast)
Jordan (Sonoma)
Château Julien (Monterey)
J. Lohr (Monterey)

Lords and Elwood (Napa)
Michton (Sonoma)
Pellegrini (Sonoma)
R. H. Phillips (Yolo)
Schug (Napa)
Sebastiani (Sonoma)
Rodney Strong (Sonoma)
Mark West (Sonoma)

A GUIDE TO CALIFORNIA'S BEST PRODUCERS OF SAUVIGNON BLANC AND SEMILLON

***** (OUTSTANDING PRODUCERS)

Kalin (Marin)
Long (Napa)
Matanzas Creek (Sonoma)

Robert Mondavi Reserve (Napa)
Spottswoode (Napa)

**** (EXCELLENT PRODUCERS)

Acacia (Napa)
Beaulieu (Napa)
Carmenet (Sonoma & Edna
  Valley)
Dry Creek (Sonoma)
Duckhorn (Napa)
Glen Ellen (Sonoma)
Hanna (Sonoma)
Hidden Springs (Sonoma)

Louis Honig (Napa)
Karly (Amador)
Kendall-Jackson (Lake)
Kenwood (Sonoma)
Lyeth (Sonoma)
St. Clement (Napa)
Chateau St. Jean (Sonoma)
Simi (Sonoma)
Sterling (Napa)

*** (GOOD PRODUCERS)

Alderbrook (Sonoma)
Amizetta (Napa)
Beringer (Napa)
Château Bouchaine (Napa)
Congress Springs (Santa Cruz)
Fetzer (Mendocino)
Flora Springs (Napa)
Fritz (Sonoma)
Frog's Leap (Napa)

Gallo (California)
Parducci (Mondocino)
Robert Pecota (Napa)
Robert Pepi (Napa)
Joseph Phelps (Napa)
R. H. Phillips (Yolo)
Preston (Sonoma)
Stag's Leap (Napa)
Stratford (Napa)

A GUIDE TO CALIFORNIA'S BEST PRODUCERS OF PINOT NOIR

***** (OUTSTANDING PRODUCERS)

Calera (San Benito)

**** (EXCELLENT PRODUCERS)

Bonny Doon (Santa Cruz)
Chalone (Monterey)
Edna Valley (San Luis Obispo)
Hanzell (Sonoma)

Kalin (Marin)
Kistler (Sonoma)
Robert Mondavi Reserve (Napa)
Saintsbury (Napa)

* * * *(GOOD PRODUCERS)*

Acacia (Napa)
Bay Cellars (Alameda County)
Beaulieu (Napa)
Belvedere (Sonoma)
Monticello (Napa)
Mount Eden (Santa Cruz)
Qupé (Santa Barbara)
Richardson (Sonoma)
Sanford (Santa Barbara)

Santa Cruz Mountain (Santa Cruz)
Sea Ridge (Sonoma)
Soleterra (Napa)
Robert Stemmler (Sonoma)
Joseph Swan (Sonoma)
Trefethen (Napa)
Tulocay (Napa)

A GUIDE TO CALIFORNIA'S BEST PRODUCERS OF CHENIN BLANC

Alexander Valley (Sonoma)
Chappellet (Napa)
Dry Creek (Sonoma)
Guenoc (Lake)
Hacienda (Sonoma)
Louis Martini (Napa)

Robert Mondavi (Napa)
Pedroncelli (Sonoma)
Pine Ridge (Napa)
Preston (Sonoma)
Villa Mt. Eden (Napa)

A GUIDE TO CALIFORNIA'S BEST PRODUCERS OF RED ZINFANDEL

* * * * * *(OUTSTANDING PRODUCERS)*

Lytton Springs Reserve (Sonoma)
Ravenswood (Sonoma)

Ridge (Santa Cruz)
Sausal (Sonoma)
Terraces (Napa)

* * * * *(EXCELLENT PRODUCERS)*

H. Coturri (Sonoma)
Edmeades (Mendocino)
Grgich (Napa)
Kendall-Jackson (Mendocino)
Chateau Montelena (Napa)
Monterey Peninsula (Monterey)
Nalle (Sonoma)

Joseph Phelps Alexander Valley (Sonoma)
Rafanelli (Sonoma)
Richardson (Sonoma)
Shenandoah (Amador)
Storybook Mountain (Napa)
Joseph Swan (Sonoma)

* * * *(GOOD PRODUCERS)*

Baldinelli (Amador)
Burgess (Napa)

Calera (San Benito)
Caymus (Napa)

DeMoor (Napa)
Dry Creek (Sonoma)
Fetzer (Mendocino)
Guenoc (Lake)
Hidden Cellars (Mendocino)
Montevina (Amador)

Preston (Sonoma)
Santino (Amador)
Story (Amador)
Sullivan (Napa)
Sutter Home (Napa)

A GUIDE TO CALIFORNIA'S BEST ROSÉ OR "BLUSH" WINES

Beringer White Zinfandel
Bonny Doon Vin Gris
Buehler White Zinfandel
De Loach White Zinfandel
Fetzer White Zinfandel
Grand Cru White Zinfandel
Green and Red White Zinfandel
Karly White Zinfandel

Markham Gamay Blanc
Robert Mondavi Zinfandel Rosé
Sanford Vin Gris Pinot Noir
Sausal White Zinfandel
Sterling Cabernet Blanc
William Wheeler White
  Zinfandel

ACACIA (NAPA)

1986 Chardonnay Carneros	Napa	D	86
1987 Chardonnay Carneros	Napa	D	87
1986 Chardonnay Marina Vineyard	Napa	D	88
1987 Chardonnay Marina Vineyard	Napa	D	89
1985 Merlot	Napa	D	85
1986 Pinot Noir Carneros	Napa	C	84
1985 Pinot Noir Madonna Vineyard	Napa	C	84
1986 Pinot Noir Madonna Vineyard	Napa	C	84
1985 Pinot Noir St. Clair	Napa	C	82
1986 Pinot Noir St. Clair	Napa	C	86

The Acacia winery, founded in 1979 to encouraging reviews from wine critics, was recently sold to the high-quality-oriented Chalone winery.

The first releases showed a style that was clearly inspired by the wines of France. Both the 1987 and 1986 Chardonnays show more austere textures with stony, mineral fragrances, and good crisp acidity; they emulate a top-quality French Chablis. The 1987s look to be richer and slightly longer on the palate than both 1986s. In comparing the two offerings from Acacia, the single-vineyard Marina seems to have a bit more length and richness of fruit in each vintage. Acacia has also garnered praise for its Pinot Noirs, and they certainly are among the better ones in California; however, this does not mean the top French red burgundy producers have much to worry about. They tend to be weedy with smooth, chocolate, cherry, and herbaceous flavors. They are good, but not thrilling, although winemaker Mike Richmond claims the 1986s are the best he has ever made. I thought the 1986s good, more forward and fragrant than the 1985s, but I would not consider them top-flight Pinot Noirs. The winery also produced small quantities of a tart, lean, highly structured Merlot and Cabernet Sauvignon, but under the guidance of the Chalone staff one would expect to see fleshier and richer wines emerge. All in all, this is a good to very good winery that charges relatively high prices for its wines. The Chardonnays should be drunk within the first several years of their lives, and the other wines within six years of the vintage.

ADLER FELS (SONOMA)

1986 Fumé Blanc	Sonoma	B	75
1985 Mélange à Deux	Sonoma	B	55

To date, the releases from this small winery, founded only in 1980, have been mediocre at best. This includes some very vegetal, out-of-balance Cabernet Sauvignons, watery, acidic Chardonnays, and barely adequate Fumé Blancs. The bizarre sparkling wine called Mélange à Deux is an unattractive attempt at combining Gewürztraminer and Riesling in a bubbling format. Unless higher quality is forthcoming, this is not a winery to seek out.

ALDERBROOK (SONOMA)

1986 Chardonnay	Sonoma	B	87
1987 Chardonnay	Sonoma	B	88
1986 Sauvignon Blanc	Sonoma	A	84

1986 Semillon	Sonoma	A	84

This winery has quickly established a reputation for producing richly fruity, fleshy, full-bodied wines with a great deal of flavor that sell for a reasonable price. Founded in 1982, the wines have been consistently enjoyable, and their early success has apparently not inflated the egos of the owners. The 1986 Chardonnay offers muscular, full-bodied, tropical fruit and a touch of oak; the 1987 looks even better. The 1986 Sauvignon has crisp, subtly herbaceous fruit, and medium body; the Semillon has a creamier texture and fleshier flavors. When I'm in restaurants looking for a good, relatively unknown high-quality wine from California at a reasonable price, I always check to see if there is a white Alderbrook on the wine list.

ALEXANDER VALLEY VINEYARD (SONOMA)

1984 Cabernet Sauvignon	Alex. Vly.	B	88
1985 Cabernet Sauvignon	Alex. Vly.	B	78
1986 Chardonnay	Alex. Vly.	B	75
1987 Chenin Blanc	Alex. Vly.	A	80
1984 Merlot	Alex. Vly.	B	87
1985 Merlot	Alex. Vly.	B	78

By California standards, this moderate-sized winery producing 20,000+ cases has been around for a long time (since 1975). It has been run with a good deal of success by the Wetzel family, who have emphasized bold and dramatic flavors in their wines, keeping them priced at a manageable level. They have held to their principles in continuing to make a light, pleasant, off-dry Chenin Blanc that has no snob appeal but remains a delightful aperitif wine to drink. The Chardonnay has never excited me, but certainly some of their Cabernets and Merlots can be rich, intensely flavored wines that can age well for up to a decade. The top recent successes include the 1984 Merlot and 1984 Cabernet Sauvignon. These wines have considerably more depth, richness, and complexity than the 1985s, which tasted lean and rather unimpressive for this winery. A barrel-sample tasting of these two wines in 1986 showed them to be better than the 1985s but not nearly as good as the 1984s.

ALMADEN (SAN JOSE)

1983 Cabernet Sauvignon	Monterey	B	72
1984 Cabernet Sauvignon	Napa	B	75
1986 Chardonnay	Monterey	B	68
1985 Fumé Blanc	Monterey	A	66
1984 Merlot	Monterey	B	75

This gigantic winery in San Jose seemed to be producing more serious wines in the early eighties as evidenced by a couple of excellent wines, particularly the 1981 Cabernet Sauvignon and 1983 Cabernet Sauvignon from San Benito. They also began to release some top wines with Napa Valley appellations. However, the new releases have declined somewhat in quality, and one has to wonder what the intentions of this winery are today regarding its serious wine program.

ALTAMURA (NAPA)

1985 Chardonnay	Napa	C	84
1986 Chardonnay	Napa	C	89

A tiny, specialist producer of Chardonnay, this winery, run by Frank Altamura, gets its grapes from a vineyard south of the Stag's Leap area. The debut wine, a 1985 Chardonnay, had a trifle too much oak, but it showed good depth, ripeness, and a style that was not afraid to offer some personality. The 1986 is an even stronger effort with the rich, pineapple-and-buttery-apple fruit married beautifully with smoky oak. Full-bodied and lush, it should drink well for several years.

AMADOR FOOTHILL WINERY (AMADOR)

1987 Fumé Blanc	Amador	A	77
1987 White Zinfandel	Amador	A	78
1984 Zinfandel	Amador	B	83
1984 Zinfandel Eschen Vineyard	Amador	B	86

Amador Foothill, a modest-sized winery, was founded in 1980 and is dedicated to producing mostly Zinfandel from vineyards in Amador County. A small amount of Fumé Blanc is also produced. To date the wines have been adequate in quality, with the very best being the Zinfandels from the Eschen Vineyard in Fiddletown. They have not been meek wines, but rather full-bodied, alcoholic wines with considerable clout. My favorite to date has been the 1984, which, with its 14.3% alcohol, is not for the shy. All of these wines should be drunk within 3–4 years of their release by the winery.

AMIZETTA (NAPA)

1985 Cabernet Sauvignon	Napa	B	84
1986 Sauvignon Blanc	Napa	B	84

A new winery, Amizetta has released a good rather than exhilarating, spicy, herbaceous Sauvignon Blanc, and a compact but flavorful, well-made Cabernet Sauvignon from the great 1985 vintage. The Cabernet Sauvignon should last for 7–8 years, whereas the Sauvignon Blanc should be drunk within several years of the vintage.

S. ANDERSON (NAPA)

1985 Blanc de Noirs Sparkling Wine	Napa	C	84
1985 Chardonnay	Napa	B	87
1986 Chardonnay	Napa	B	85

This moderately small winery specializes in relatively rich, oaky, well-balanced Chardonnays, and a good, tart, somewhat severe sparkling wine. Of the recent Chardonnays, neither the 1985 nor the 1986 seemed to be as rich as the 1984, but the winery has high hopes for its 1987. The sparkling wine is good, better than many in California, but still relatively one-dimensional though pleasant and agreeable. One would like to see a bit more richness and body to it.

ARROWOOD (SONOMA)

1985 Cabernet Sauvignon	Sonoma	C	85
1986 Chardonnay	Sonoma	C	86

Dick Arrowood, the outstanding winemaker behind all the vintages of

Chateau St. Jean's wines, does double duty at his small winery. His debut release, the 1986 Chardonnay, is a full-bodied wine that has an applelike, buttery, subtle, herb-scented bouquet, good acids, and a crisp finish. The 1985 Cabernet Sauvignon is a graceful, rich, stylish wine with a precocious, supple texture, good acids, and flavors suggestive of bing cherries, spicy oak, and weedy blackcurrants. It should be at its best between 1990 and 1994.

DAVID ARTHUR VINEYARDS (NAPA)

1986 Chardonnay	Napa	B	82

I have had little experience with this producer, but the 1986 Chardonnay is a fairly oaky yet agreeable, chunky wine with a good deal of body and some length, although lacking complexity and finesse. It should be drunk by the end of this decade.

ARTISAN WINES (NAPA)

This company, founded in 1984 to specialize in inexpensive wines that are blended together, has come out with a group of wines under such names as Ultravino and La Cruvinet. The wines, which sell for less than $8 a bottle, have been correct but uninteresting blends that are no better than many of the generic wines on the market that sell for less money. All the wines are meant to be drunk quite young.

ASHLY (SANTA CLARA)

1985 Chardonnay	Monterey	C	?

While I remember tasting a good, boldly flavored, toasty, oaky 1984 from Ashly at a rather elevated price, two bottles of the 1985 showed an oxidized color, an excessive oaky character, and were unpalatable. There is no question that the winery likes oak to dominate the flavor of its wines, but they appear to have gone overboard in 1985.

AU BON CLIMAT (SANTA BARBARA)

1986 Chardonnay	Santa Barbara	B	89
1987 Chardonnay	Santa Barbara	B	90
1985 Pinot Noir	Santa Barbara	B	82

| 1986 Pinot Noir | Santa Barbara | B | 85 |

The wines of this small winery in Los Olivos, California, are hard to find outside of that state. While both the Chardonnay and Pinot Noir get rave reviews from the California wine press, the Chardonnay excites me most. Filled with aromas of tropical fruits such as mangoes and pineapples, and given a judicious sojourn in toasty oak barrels, this exotic, complex Chardonnay is an absolute delight to drink within three years of the vintage. As for the Pinot Noir, I admire its supple, velvety texture, and the obvious talent of the winemaker, but the predilection for this grape to render rather vegetal wines when planted in many regions of California keeps my rating low for the 1985. The 1985 shows delicious smoky, cherry fruit, but the intrusive scents and flavors of vegetables are not what I desire in Pinot Noir. The 1986 is similarly styled, but the winery has thankfully managed to tone down the vegetal components.

BABCOCK VINEYARDS (SANTA BARBARA)

| 1985 Chardonnay Estate | Santa Barbara | B | 80 |

| 1986 Chardonnay Reserve | Santa Barbara | B | 72 |

| 1986 Riesling | Santa Barbara | B | 80 |

The small Babcock Vineyards, founded in 1983, has turned out several standard-quality wines of no great distinction. Their Riesling may be their best, made in a Spätlese, slightly sweet style with a small degree of residual sugar. The Chardonnays have lacked vibrancy and just taste dull and one-dimensional to date.

BARGETTO (SANTA CRUZ)

| 1983 Cabernet Sauvignon | Napa Valley | B | 60 |

| 1985 Cabernet Sauvignon Bates Ranch | Santa Cruz | B | 76 |

| 1987 Chardonnay Cyprus Vyd. | Santa Maria | B | 84 |

| 1987 Gewürztraminer | | A | 73 |

| 1985 Pinot Noir Madonna Vyd. | Carneros | B | 84 |

N.V. Raspberry Wine A 85

Few people realize that the Bargetto Winery just turned 50 years of age and produces 40,000 cases of table wine and sweeter fruit wines that all share a realistic pricing structure and sound quality. Of the new releases, the 1987 Gewürztraminer is symptomatic of most California Gewürztraminers in that it lacks true varietal character. However, the fresh, exuberant, medium-bodied, deliciously fruity Cyprus Chardonnay from the top-notch 1987 vintage is quite tasty. The Cabernets have been plagued by tart acids, lean textures, and in the case of the 1983, a damning vegetal unpleasantness. The winery makes an unfashionable but admirably delicious group of fruit wines, the best of which is their raspberry wine (which always seems to me to make a good Mother's Day present). It's sweet but redolent with aromas and flavors of juicy raspberry fruit. Lastly, this winery also makes a little bit of adequate white Zinfandel, a generally pleasant Riesling, and a sparkling wine that I have not tasted.

BAY CELLARS (ALAMEDA COUNTY)

1985 Chardonnay	Napa	B 79
1985 Pinot Noir	Oregon	B 86

This small winery founded only in 1982 is producing just over 1,000 cases of wine from purchased grapes. The most interesting wine to date has been their Pinot Noir, especially the 1985, which was made from grapes purchased from the Bethel Heights Vineyard in Oregon. Smoky with ripe cherry flavors and spicy new oak, this wine shows a great deal of finesse and elegance, and 5–7 years of further evolution. The Chardonnays to date have been adequate but generally tart and acidic.

BEAULIEU (NAPA)

1986 Cabernet Sauvignon Beau Tour	Napa	A 82
1982 Cabernet Sauvignon Private Reserve	Napa	C 90
1983 Cabernet Sauvignon Private Reserve	Napa	C 85
1984 Cabernet Sauvignon Private Reserve	Napa	C 90

1983 Cabernet Sauvignon Rutherford	Napa	B	65
1984 Cabernet Sauvignon Rutherford	Napa	B	84
1986 Chardonnay Beaufort	Napa	B	78
1986 Chardonnay Los Carneros	Napa	B	85
1986 Sauvignon Blanc	Napa	A	85

Founded in 1900, Beaulieu has throughout this century been one of the historic as well as benchmark producers of Napa Valley wine. The great success this winery has enjoyed is in large part due to the extraordinary Private Reserve Cabernet Sauvignons called Georges de Latour. Certain vintages have virtually defined what the quintessential Napa Valley Cabernet Sauvignon is all about. For example, the 1968, 1970, and 1976, and more recently the 1980, 1982, and 1984, have all been among the top dozen of California Cabernet Sauvignons. Followers of the occult might wonder why this winery seems to excel in even-numbered years while some of the odd-year Cabernets have been good but less concentrated and inspired. The mark of a great Beaulieu Reserve Cabernet Sauvignon is its superripe blackcurrant fruit and depth, married with a healthy dosage of cedary, spicy, vanillin and toasty American oak. They are wines that can be drunk within 5–6 years of the vintage, but the great vintages generally show no signs of decline until they are 15–20 years old. The 1970 at 19 years of age is still in full bloom. Among the other offerings from Beaulieu, the Chardonnays have tended to be light, but the winery certainly seems to be putting a bit more character and flavor into its Los Carneros Chardonnay since 1983. A wine that I happen to find very interesting is Beaulieu's crisp, mineral, and subtly herbaceous Sauvignon Blanc, of which the 1986 is a very good example and priced affordably. Lastly, this winery also turns out a number of other wines, including a good, chewy, rich Pinot Noir from the Carneros region of Napa Valley. It won't remind you of French red burgundy, but it is a hardy, robust wine with a great deal of flavor.

BELLEROSE VINEYARD (SONOMA)

1984 Cuvée Bellerose	Sonoma	B	87
1985 Cuvée Bellerose	Sonoma	B	88

| 1984 Merlot | Sonoma | B | 87 |

| 1985 Merlot | Sonoma | B | 87 |

| 1987 Sauvignon Blanc | Sonoma | B | 86 |

I have been very impressed with the wines from this small (5,000 cases) winery specializing in three wines: a Bordeaux-styled Sauvignon Blanc that generally has a healthy dosage of Semillon added to give it lushness and complexity; a full-bodied, rich, intense, fleshy Merlot; and a stylish proprietary wine called Cuvée Bellerose. They offer complex, rich, intense wines at prices that are not unreasonable. In both the 1984 and 1985 vintages the Cuvée Bellerose has been surprisingly Bordeaux-like with its interesting blend of generally close to three-fourths Cabernet Sauvignon and the rest a mixture of Cabernet Franc, Merlot, and Petit Verdot. Barrel samples of the 1986s were extremely impressive as well. Of the Bellerose wines, the Merlot would appear to have 5–7 years of aging potential, whereas the Cuvée Bellerose should last at least a decade.

BELVEDERE WINE CO. (SONOMA)

| 1983 Cabernet Sauvignon Robert Young Vyd. | B | 79 |

| 1984 Cabernet Sauvignon Robert Young Vyd. | B | 85 |

| 1985 Chardonnay Bacigalupi | B | 65 |

| 1986 Chardonnay Bacigalupi | B | 85 |

| 1986 Chardonnay Carneros | B | 75 |

| 1984 Merlot Robert Young Vyd. | B | 73 |

| 1983 Pinot Noir Bacigalupi | B | 55 |

The Belvedere Wine Company specializes in purchasing grapes from independent owners of vineyards and then designating their top wines according to vineyard. There is also an inexpensive line of wines under the "Discovery" label. I find this winery's products inconsistent, ranging from several top-notch wines such as the now tiring but at one time superb 1981 Winery Lake Pinot Noir, to wretchedly weak, feeble wines such as the 1983 Bacigalupi Pinot Noir. Of the current releases, the 1986 Bacigalupi Chardonnay shows impressive tropical-fruit flavors, a touch of spicy oak, and good, clean winemaking. On the other hand, three bottles of the 1985 were flawed by a damp, cardboard moldiness that is either the result of improperly maintained barrels or filtration pads. The 1984 Merlot from the Robert Young Vineyard is too acidified, which is a shame, but certainly the 1984 Cabernet Sauvignon Robert Young Vineyard is a big, rich, chewy, cedary wine filled with weedy, blackcurrant fruit. The 1983 Cabernet Sauvignon from Robert Young shows more depth than most wines from this disappointing vintage, but it is still on the austere, lean, compact side. This is certainly a winery to approach with a great deal of care; be sure to taste before investing in more than one bottle.

BERINGER (NAPA)

1984 Cabernet Sauvignon	Knight's Valley	B	85
1985 Cabernet Sauvignon	Knight's Valley	B	86
1982 Cabernet Sauvignon Private Reserve	Lemmon-Chabot	C	89
1983 Cabernet Sauvignon Private Reserve	Lemmon-Chabot	C	85
1985 Chardonnay Private Reserve	Napa	C	84
1986 Chardonnay Private Reserve	Napa	C	80
1987 Chenin Blanc	Napa	A	82
1987 Fumé Blanc Estate	Napa	A	84
1987 Sauvignon Blanc	Knight's Valley	A	85
1987 White Zinfandel	Napa	A	82

With its production quickly edging toward 1,000,000 cases of wine per year, the historic Beringer Winery, located in one of the most popular tourist areas of Napa Valley, has something for every wine lover. Their mass-appeal wine, the 1987 White Zinfandel, actually shows stylish winemaking and gobs of round, off-dry, strawberry fruit; it's the perfect picnic rosé. Even the unglamorous Chenin Blanc made at Beringer shows the floral, honeysuckle aromas of this unfairly maligned varietal and crisp, fresh fruit. Obviously both of these wines should be consumed within a year of their release. On a more serious side, this winery's Chardonnays, especially those called Gamble Ranch or Private Reserve, have been dominated, sometimes unsuccessfully so, by the smell of oak barrels. For example, the 1985 Private Reserve Chardonnay had the balance between fruit and oak just right, but the 1986 leaned too much toward the oak side. For a dramatic contrast, Beringer offers two totally different styles of Sauvignon Blanc. The 1987 Fumé Blanc is oriented toward a Loire Valley, subtly herbaceous Pouilly Fumé taste, whereas the 1987 Sauvignon Blanc Knight's Valley has oak as a prominent characteristic and begs comparison with a top white Bordeaux such as the Pavillon Blanc de Château Margaux. On the other hand, the Cabernet Sauvignons, while always good, have never been better than in the decade of the eighties, with the really great wines from the 1984, 1985, and 1986 vintages yet to be released. For starters, one can find a great deal of juicy, crunchy, supple, black-currant fruit in both the 1984 and 1985 Knight's Valley Cabernets. This is the type of Cabernet that offers plenty of authentic varietal character, but without the tannins that make you grab for a glass of water. The two top-of-the-line Cabernets, the Private Reserve and Chabot Ranch Cabernets, have been on a hot streak since the gregarious winemaker, Ed Spragia, took over from the legendary Myron Nightingale. Readers should make a mental note to look for either the Beringer Chabot or Private Reserve Cabernet Sauvignons from the 1984, 1985, or 1986 vintages, as they are all blockbuster wines. For now, one will hardly regret a taste of the 1982 Private Reserve, which is bursting with tarry, spicy, oaky, rich blackcurrant fruit. Intelligently, Beringer recently launched its second line of wines called Napa Ridge, and they have offered strikingly good values in Chardonnay for about $6 a bottle, whereas the Cabernet Sauvignon has been slightly less impressive and perhaps a bit too herbaceous. All in all, this is a winery that is doing a number of things right, although I'd personally like to see more consistency in the balance between fruit and oak in their top-of-the-line Private Reserve Chardonnays.

BOEGER WINERY (EL DORADO)

1984 Cabernet Sauvignon	El Dorado	B	83
1985 Merlot	El Dorado	B	82
1987 Sauvignon Blanc	El Dorado	A	85

1984 Zinfandel	El Dorado	A	72

While I have never been overwhelmed by the wines from this producer, shrewd buyers would certainly argue that the Sauvignon Blanc has a good deal of flavor and is fairly priced, and that the Merlot can be a fleshy, supple wine with attractive chocolaty, weedy, berry-fruit flavors. The Cabernet has the same degree of softness, and the Chardonnays are adequate, but the Zinfandels are rather light, herbaceous, and too simple to merit much interest.

BONNY DOON VINEYARD (SANTA CRUZ)

1986 Chardonnay	B	85
1985 Le Cigare Volant	B	90
1986 Le Cigare Volant	B	88
1987 Clos de Gilroy	A	88
1987 Gewürztraminer Vin de Glacière	C	93
1987 Grenache Vin de Glacière	C	88
1987 Muscat Vin de Glacière	C	96
1986 Old Telegram	B	90
1987 Roussanne	not available	95
1987 Le Sophiste (80% Marsanne, 20% Roussanne)	not available	89
1987 Vin Gris de Mourvedre	A	87

The irrepressible winemaker, Randall Grahm, continues to turn out some of the most stunning and interesting wines not only in America but in all the world. Every time I taste one of his wines, I wonder if there is any more daring and talented winemaker in existence. The above wines all show his remarkable talents and also his love of the grapes that have made the Rhône Valley in France so famous. Virtually any wine is interesting here, including what is one of California's greatest dry, full-flavored rosé wines, Bonny Doon's Vin Gris de

Mourvèdre. One taste of this wine will make anyone a believer in how delicious and seductive a dry, crisp, flavorful rosé wine can be. The wine that probably brought Randall Grahm more attention than any other is his Cigare Volant. This blend of Syrah, Mourvèdre, and Grenache is Grahm's interpretation of what a California Châteauneuf-du-Pape would taste like. The historic 1984 was followed by an even richer, fuller, fleshier, and more seductive 1985, and the 1986 returns to a slightly more structured style without quite the opulence of fruit that characterized the 1985. In the fall of 1988, he released his first Mourvèdre wine from the 1986 vintage, called the Old Telegram. This is also another profound wine with gobs of truffle-scented, earthy, and tree-bark-flavored wood. It's Grahm's homage to one of his favorite estates in Châteauneuf-du-Pape, Vieux Télégraphe. Grahm also makes tiny quantities of Syrah when he can get grapes from the Paso Robles Vineyard of Estrella River Winery. In addition, he has pioneered a process called cyroextraction, or freezing grapes, to make his extraordinary, decadently rich, sweet, unbelievably perfumed Vin de Glacière from the Muscat, Grenache, and Gewürztraminer grapes. They are rather amazingly pure, fresh wines with Beerenauslese-level quantities of sweetness, but I don't know of a more decadent, complex, rich Muscat than Bonny Doon's. The 1987s are available only in half bottles and should be drunk before the end of 1990. Grahm is also increasing his quantities of very rare grape varieties such as Viognier, Marsanne, and Roussanne in his vineyard based on the profound wines he has made in tiny quantities from small plantings of these grapes. For all his experimentation and stunning success, Grahm still makes a Chardonnay to please less adventurous tasters. Randall Grahm's success is one of the great winemaking stories in California in the last twenty years, and based on the quality of his wines to date, he is quickly becoming one of America's national treasures.

BOUCHAINE VINEYARDS (NAPA)

1985 Chardonnay	Napa Valley	B	78
1985 Pinot Noir	Los Carneros	B	75

This winery began producing wine in 1980 with a great deal of fanfare and special bottles designed for its Chardonnays and Pinot Noirs. The wines never seemed to reflect the abilities and talents of former winemaker Jerry Luper, who left to take another position. While the Chardonnays were certainly good, one always wondered why they weren't even better given the talent of the winemaker and the winery's public

assertions that it was trying to do something special. The Pinot Noirs
have been light and weedy, with simple cherry flavors, and are also
quite overpriced. At present, this winery seems to lack direction, and
while certain vintages of the Chardonnays still merit attention, it is far
from being one of the leaders in the competitive wine business of
California.

RICHARD BOYER (MONTEREY)

1986 Chardonnay Ventana	Monterey	B	86
1987 Chardonnay Ventana	Monterey	B	86

Rick Boyer, the winemaker for Ventana Vineyards, has ventured out
on his own, and the results have been these two graceful, elegant,
tasty Chardonnays that have medium to full body and show a restrained use of toasty oak, nice tropical-fruit flavors, and good, crisp
acids. Both wines should last for 2–3 years.

BRANDER VINEYARDS (SANTA BARBARA)

1984 Cabernet Sauvignon	Santa Ynez	B	70
1985 Chardonnay	Santa Ynez	B	72
1986 Sauvignon Blanc	Santa Ynez	A	75

I have always felt this winery did an excellent job working with Sauvignon Blanc from the Santa Ynez Valley. However, the recent releases all tasted dull, and in the case of the Cabernet and Chardonnay,
too vegetal and unpleasant. One wonders what has happened with a
winery that heretofore turned out some surprisingly good wines.

DAVID BRUCE WINERY (SANTA CRUZ)

1984 Cabernet Sauvignon Vintner's Select	California	B	78
1984 Chardonnay	California	B	78
1984 Chardonnay Estate	Santa Cruz	B	84
1985 Pinot Noir Estate	Santa Cruz	B	72

The David Bruce Winery, founded in 1964, was one of California's
first boutique wineries and developed quite a following for its intense,

personality-filled, full-bodied wines that were right on target in certain vintages and grotesquely flawed in others. In the eighties, the winery has claimed to have "awakened," and the new style of wines, while more consistent and even-handed, lack the personality of the old releases. Certainly the overpriced 1985 Pinot Noir shows little of the richness and character one expects in a bottle of wine at its price. The 1984 Cabernet Sauvignon, while pleasant and quite drinkable, is essentially a one-dimensional wine. The Chardonnays remain the best wines from the David Bruce Winery, exhibiting plenty of toasty oak but a more balanced approach to winemaking with tropical fruit and medium to full body. After going too far with many of their wines in the seventies, I wonder if they are not playing it too conservatively today.

BUEHLER VINEYARDS (NAPA)

1984 Cabernet Sauvignon	Napa	B	90
1985 Cabernet Sauvignon	Napa	B	87
1986 Pinot Blanc	Napa	A	78
1987 White Zinfandel	Napa	A	83

This winery has never strayed off its course since the first brawny, rich, intense wines were released from the 1978 vintage. In fact, the 1978 Cabernet Sauvignon from my cool cellar is still not fully mature. The recent releases have all been well made, including one of California's best white Zinfandels and an interesting but subdued Pinot Blanc. No doubt, most lovers of Buehler's wines seek out the Cabernet Sauvignon and the Zinfandel. The Cabernet Sauvignon is for those who do not like shy, wimpish wines. Always dense in color, bursting with tarry, blackcurrant, rich fruit, it can be an overwhelming, even exaggerated wine, but it is a bold expression of California winemaking. The 1984 is lush and rich and should provide delicious drinking for at least a decade. The 1985 is less flattering than the 1984 at present, but despite the lower rating, it may ultimately turn out to be longer-lived and more balanced than the 1984. I would cellar it rather than drink it at the present. A barrel-tasting note on the 1986 indicates it shows the same full-intensity, blackcurrant, earthy bouquet, and deep, full-throttle flavors that define Buehler's style of Cabernet Sauvignon. Not surprisingly, the 1985 Zinfandel behaves in much the same manner, offering plenty of Rambo-styled, robust fruit and body.

BUENA VISTA (SONOMA)

1984 L'Année	Carneros	C	85
1984 Cabernet Sauvignon Estate	Carneros	B	78
1983 Cabernet Sauvignon Reserve	Carneros	B	79
1986 Chardonnay Joanette's Vyd.	Carneros	A	74
1985 Chardonnay Private Reserve	Carneros	B	82?
1984 Merlot Private Reserve	Carneros	B	77
1984 Pinot Noir Private Reserve	Carneros	B	75
1986 Spiceling	Carneros	A	84

This large winery with a production in excess of 120,000 cases has had German owners since 1979. Buena Vista is California's oldest winery. While the newly released proprietary red wine (available only in 1.5-liter bottles) called L'Année showed a bit more personality and character, the high-tech, highly sculptured, frequently too acidic (or overly acidified), totally correct wines made at Buena Vista always strike me as unexciting, commercial examples of wine. If you like your wines lean and high in acidity, you will appreciate this winery's style more than I.

BURGESS CELLARS (NAPA)

1984 Cabernet Sauvignon Vintage Reserve	Napa	B	90
1985 Cabernet Sauvignon Vintage Reserve	Napa	B	88
1986 Chardonnay Triere Vineyard	Napa	B	87
1985 Chardonnay Vintage Reserve	Napa	B	90
1985 Zinfandel	Napa	B	85
1986 Zinfandel	Napa	B	86

Tom Burgess, former airline pilot, burst on the scene in the early seventies with a boldly flavored, dramatically oaky, alcoholic Chardonnay, and heady, intense, rich, and complex Cabernet Sauvignons. The style of his earlier wines has been fine-tuned to a less oaky but still boldly flavored, Meursault-inspired white burgundy type of Chardonnay that still demonstrates a lot of oak but has the fruit to match, particularly in a top vintage such as 1985 or 1986. Burgess has also produced a long string of rich, tannic, and firm Cabernet Sauvignons that have had no trouble lasting for a decade or more. The 1974 Vintage Reserve, for example, is just now blossoming. The best recent Cabernets have certainly been the 1982, 1984, and 1985, all of which demonstrate gobs of blackcurrant fruit, a healthy dose of toasty new oak, and plenty of tannin and body. While the winery rarely gets credit for its fine Zinfandel, it is a wine made in much the same mold as the Cabernet—rich, full-bodied, and packed with berry fruit. The 1986 shows a little more fat and flesh than the 1985.

DAVIS BYNUM WINERY (SONOMA)

1983 Cabernet Sauvignon Reserve	Sonoma	C	77
1985 Chardonnay	Sonoma	B	74
1985 Chardonnay Reserve	Sonoma	B	73
1986 Gewürztraminer Reserve	Sonoma	B	67
1984 Pinot Noir	Sonoma	B	72

Over the last decade, this modest-sized winery with a production in excess of 25,000 cases has experimented with most of the major wine varietals with limited success. While none of the wines are flawed or defective in any manner, neither are they exciting to drink nor ones I would grab when seeking a pleasurable experience. The Chardonnays have tasted like a misguided oenologist's idea of high acid, tart, technically correct wines that have the personality of a rock. The Cabernets have been rather lean, hard, and lacking fruit, and the Gewürztraminer insipid. The labels would win no awards for artistic good taste either. On the bright side, prices for these mediocre wines are not excessive.

BYRON (SANTA BARBARA)

1984 Cabernet Sauvignon	Santa Barbara	B	62
1985 Chardonnay	Santa Barbara	B	82
1985 Pinot Noir	Santa Barbara	B	60
1986 Pinot Noir	Santa Barbara	B	72

There is a feeling among southern California wineries that they do not get a fair shake from the wine press in that state because so much of the media is located in San Francisco. Yet, when one tastes wines such as these, it's hard to find fault with any member of the wine media who would criticize them. First, the wines show a distinctively unpleasant, vegetal character that is at its worst in the red wines such as the Cabernet Sauvignon and the Pinot Noir. The Chardonnay is palatable and would appear to be the wine this producer should concentrate on making, as I don't believe there is a market for Cabernet Sauvignon and Pinot Noir of the quality of the above.

CAIN CELLARS (NAPA)

1982 Cabernet Sauvignon	Napa	B	70
1983 Cabernet Sauvignon	Napa	B	55
1984 Cabernet Sauvignon	Napa	B	67
1985 Chardonnay	Carneros	B	75
1986 Chardonnay	Carneros	B	83
1982 Merlot	Napa	B	55

This winery, with a projected production of 30,000 cases from its sizable (200 acres) parcel on Spring Mountain, started operations in 1981. To date it has specialized in four wines—Sauvignon Blanc, Cabernet Sauvignon, Merlot, and Chardonnay. While one does not like to be overly critical, particularly of a family-owned winery just getting its feet wet, the quality of the early releases of Cain Cellars has been unacceptable with the exception of an adequate Sauvignon Blanc and a Chardonnay. The red wines have tasted as if someone felt that Cabernet Sauvignon's and Merlot's most dominant varietal characteristic is the taste and smell of boiled asparagus. They are clearly the products of young vines, and financial pressures aside, wines of this nature should be sold in bulk rather than released by a winery serious about its quality image. I hope that as the vineyard and wine-making team mature, the reds will show less and less of the annoying and unpleasant vegetal character. As for the white wines, the floral, apple-scented 1986 Chardonnay showed good fruit, an elegant texture, and medium body. I hope this wine's good quality is an encouraging sign.

CAKEBREAD CELLARS (NAPA)

1984 Cabernet Sauvignon	Napa	C	76
1985 Chardonnay	Napa	C	82
1986 Chardonnay	Napa	C	75
1986 Sauvignon Blanc	Napa	B	86

Cakebread Cellars, with a production now approaching 40,000 cases, was founded in 1973 and was originally appreciated for its fairly brawny, tannic, big wines that sold for big prices. In the eighties, proprietor Jack Cakebread and his winemaking team have unfortunately moved in the direction of more compact, narrowly focused wines that offer lean, hard, charmless flavors. At present, the wines are more disappointing than pleasurable, and one wonders why a Napa Valley producer making Chardonnay would try (without success) to out-Chablis a real French Chablis. The only wine in the portfolio that seems to beg for anyone's attention is the austere but subtle, herbaceous-scented, interesting, medium-bodied Sauvignon Blanc. The 1984 Cabernet Sauvignon, from a vintage that produced many profound, richly textured, lush wines, is unbelievably tart and overly acidified—again another example of oenology prevailing over common sense. The wines are currently distributed nationally, and prices are hardly bargains for what one gets.

CALERA WINE CO. (SAN BENITO)

1986 Chardonnay	San Benito	B	82
1986 Pinot Noir	Santa Barbara	B	86

1984 Pinot Noir Jensen	San Benito	C	90
1985 Pinot Noir Jensen	San Benito	C	90
1984 Pinot Noir Reed	San Benito	C	90
1985 Pinot Noir Reed	San Benito	C	90
1984 Pinot Noir Selleck	San Benito	C	90
1985 Pinot Noir Selleck	San Benito	C	90
1984 Zinfandel	Chienga Valley	B	73

While an average-quality Zinfandel and above-average-quality Chardonnay are made at Calera, the glories of this small winery are its three estate-bottled Pinot Noirs from vineyard sites called Selleck, Reed, and Jensen. The 1984s and 1985s are simply the finest Pinot Noirs made in America, even better than the best Pinot Noirs coming out of the Willamette Valley in Oregon. And while the 1986s slip a bit in quality, the unreleased 1987s are spectacular. Owner Josh Jensen, an Oxford-educated man, found in the Gavilan Mountains the limestone soil and microclimate he deemed critical to produce top-quality Pinot Noir. He founded his 10,000-case winery in 1975, and in spite of some enormous failures in the early years, he has never veered from the course of searching for the mystical complexity and sublime quality of Pinot Noir. The differences among the three vineyard Pinot Noirs are marginal, but in general the Selleck tastes more forward, open-knit, and less tannic than either the Reed or Jensen. All these wines are truly outstanding with stunning bouquets of exotic spices and ripe Pinot Noir grapes, full body, and layers of velvety fruit. While all are drinkable now, they should certainly last in the bottle 2–3 more years. Until 1986, the winery had made a vegetal, mediocre Pinot Noir from purchased Santa Barbara grapes, but with the 1986 Pinot Noir from Santa Barbara grapes, they seem finally to have struck gold, as it shows some of the same complexity, richness, and profoundness of the single-vineyard Pinot Noirs. Calera is one of California's most exciting wineries, and its wines merit interest from anyone who loves a fine Pinot Noir. Remember to keep an eye out for the winery's 1987s, which include a fourth vineyard designated Pinot Noir called Mills.

CALLAWAY VINEYARDS (RIVERSIDE COUNTY)

1987 Chardonnay Calla-lees	Temecula	B	81
1986 Chenin Blanc	Temecula	A	73
1984 Chenin Blanc Sweet Nancy	Temecula	B	84
1987 Fumé Blanc	Temecula	A	73

Callaway Vineyards, located in the unfashionable (for wineries) Riverside County in southern California, produces in excess of 150,000 cases of wine and is owned by the giant liquor-and-spirits company Hiram Walker & Sons. The winery's owners have intelligently realized that it would be foolish to try to produce red wine from an area that has failed to make interesting reds, but they have succeeded in introducing to the market a tank-fermented, non–oak-aged, soft, voluptuous Chardonnay called Calla-lees. The 1987 is a very easy-to-drink, soft wine with a good varietal character. The winery's off-dry Chenin Blanc and Fumé Blanc have been less successful and marked by rather simple, one-dimensional flavors. However, for lovers of sweet wines, Callaway's Sweet Nancy is a ripe, rich, dessert-styled Chenin Blanc that tastes and smells of overripe melons. It is meant to be drunk within 5 years of the vintage.

CARMENET VINEYARD (SONOMA)

1986 Colombard Old Vines Cyril Saviez	Napa	A	87
1984 Red Table Wine	Sonoma	A	90
1985 Red Table Wine	Sonoma	C	90
1986 Red Table Wine	Sonoma	C	92
1986 Sauvignon Blanc	Edna. Vly.	A	85
1986 Sauvignon Blanc	Sonoma	A	87

This new mountaintop winery, with caves cut into the hillside for proper aging of the wine, was founded in 1980 by several principals from the hugely successful Chalone winery in Monterey County. Their objectives were to produce a proprietary red wine from a blend of

Cabernet Sauvignon, Cabernet Franc, and Merlot, as well as a
Graves-style white wine from Sauvignon Blanc and Semillon. To date,
the red wine has emerged as one of California's finest despite the fact
that the first release was only in 1982. The wines have exhibited great
richness, length, and character, and the debut 1982 was followed by a
harder and leaner but nevertheless successful 1983; a superb, voluptuous, full-bodied, opulent, exceptionally promising 1984; a more classically structured, brilliant 1985; and an exotically scented, extremely
impressive 1986, which may turn out to be the best of this trio. All of
these wines appear to have 10–15 years of aging potential. Among the
white wines, I have had some severe bottle variations in the Sauvignon
Blanc from Edna Valley, but the recent bottles have shown tremendous depth of fruit and richness. Yet, I still favor the more delicate
but no less rich Sonoma bottling. Lastly, the winery produces a barrel-
fermented Colombard that must be tasted to be believed. The 1986
from old vines is an especially fine example, and for its modest price,
one of the great values in serious white wines from California. This
30,000-case winery has quickly emerged as a star, as one might expect
given the commitment to high quality of the principals of the Chalone
operation. Their wines are not to be missed.

CARNEROS CREEK WINERY (NAPA)

1982 Cabernet Sauvignon Fay Vyd.	Napa	B	70
1987 Chardonnay	Napa	B	82
1984 Merlot	Napa	B	87
1985 Merlot	Napa	B	77
1983 Merlot Truchard Vyd.	Napa	B	65

Carneros Creek Winery has led a roller coaster life. Some of the
earlier vintages of Cabernet Sauvignon were stunning wines, particularly those made during the period between 1974 and 1978. The winery
also stunned tasters with an exceptionally successful Pinot Noir in
1977. All the success seemed to go down the drain with the winery's
releases in the late seventies and early eighties, as the wines lightened
up in style considerably, and lost much of their character. The winery's divorce from its national distributor several years ago has perhaps renewed its commitment to return to the quality of the wines it
produced in the mid-seventies. The Chardonnay remains an unexcit-

ing wine; but certainly the 1984 Merlot showed great style, richness, and gobs of the fleshy, velvety fruit that makes Merlot so sexy. The 1982 Cabernet Sauvignon from the outstanding Fay Vineyard, and the 1983 Merlot from the Truchard Vineyard, were disappointing wines, deficient in flavor and marred by a vegetal character. I hope the 1984 Merlot signals a new era for Carneros Creek, which has seen the best and the worst for its wines.

CARTLIDGE AND BROWN (NAPA)

1987 Chardonnay	Napa	B	75
1987 Chardonnay Canterbury	California	A	77
1986 Sauvignon Blanc	Napa	A	79

This team of winebrokers makes wines under two labels, a modestly priced Stratford label and a less expensive Canterbury label. The early releases showed that they knew how to purchase good grapes and turn them into soft, tasty wines representing good values. Fortunately, they launched their enterprise when there was an excess of good-quality Chardonnay grapes in the marketplace. Now, apparently, the supply of good-quality grapes has dried up, and the recent releases have suffered. After a stunning value with their 1985 Canterbury Chardonnay, both the 1986 and the 1987 tasted light and innocuous. In the cyclical wine business, this will be a constant problem when buying wines from brokers, or, as the French say, *négociants*.

CAYMUS VINEYARD (NAPA)

1984 Cabernet Sauvignon Estate	Napa	B	87
1985 Cabernet Sauvignon Estate	Napa	B	89
1985 Cabernet Sauvignon Napa Cuvée	Napa	B	88
1982 Cabernet Sauvignon Special Selection	Napa	C	90
1983 Cabernet Sauvignon Special Selection	Napa	C	85
1984 Cabernet Sauvignon Special Selection	Napa	C	94
1984 Pinot Noir Special Selection	Napa	B	78

1987 Sauvignon Blanc	Napa	A	84

1985 Zinfandel	Napa	A	86

1986 Zinfandel	Napa	A	85

I somehow think of serious winemaker/owner Charlie Wagner as having always been associated with the Napa Valley, yet this 60,000-case winery has not yet celebrated its twentieth anniversary. Founded in 1971, Caymus achieved its reputation with its rich, amply endowed, intense Cabernet Sauvignons and did as much as anybody in the early seventies to focus attention on viticulture in the Napa Valley. The Cabernets from their early years have also stood the test of time. Today, three Cabernet Sauvignons are made. The Wagners have shown themselves to be quite adept at purchasing grapes from selected Napa Valley locations and blending a wine made therefrom into a wine called Napa Cuvée. The 1984 was delicious, and the 1985 even better, just bursting with blackcurrants and showing a nice touch of toasty oak. The second Cabernet is the estate-bottled, and it comes in two versions, a normal bottling that is released the third year after the vintage, and a special selection that is aged 3½ years in oak casks and released 5 years after the vintage. The latter wine is extremely limited in availability, but it is a remarkable wine that amazingly has not had its cascade of spicy blackcurrant fruit overwhelmed by toasty oak. The 1975, 1976, and 1978 Special Selections are still not fully mature. The 1981 and 1982 are seemingly more forward and less intense, but still delicious, complex wines. The 1984 Special Selection appears to be a very special wine, and perhaps the finest Cabernet that Caymus has produced since their legendary 1976 Special Selection. It should age well for 15 to 20 years. As for the Estate Cabernet Sauvignons, the 1984 is a velvety, lush, rich wine that should age well for another decade, and the 1985 looks to be even better with slightly higher acidity and more obvious tannins, but excellent depth. The winery should also be applauded for its fresh, delicately herbaceous Sauvignon Blanc, and its tasty, full-bodied, brawny, sometimes heady Zinfandel. The only wine that I consistently find uninteresting is the Special Selection Pinot Noir, an overly oaked, rather robust, one-dimensional wine that shows a great deal of fruit but none of the finesse or magical perfume that Pinot Noir can render. The Wagners are admirable also in the sense that except for their Special Selection wines, they have consistently kept a lid on prices. Their second line of wines, under the Liberty School label, represents some of the best wine values in the marketplace. Recently, Caymus has introduced a line of wines from Chile under the Liberty School label. Caymus is certainly one of the top California wineries and deserves all the accolades it consistently receives.

CHALONE VINEYARDS (MONTEREY)

1985 Chardonnay	California	C	92
1986 Chardonnay	California	C	96
1987 Chardonnay	California	D	90
1985 Chardonnay Reserve .	California	C	96
1985 Pinot Blanc	California	C	87
1986 Pinot Blanc	California	C	86
1983 Pinot Noir	California	C	85
1984 Pinot Noir	California	C	87
1985 Pinot Noir	California	C	88

If life were so simple as to require me to drink only one Chardonnay, then mine would be a Chalone. There are other Chardonnays in California that are every bit as good, but this is the most nearly unique, and if one could say there is a Montrachet of California, it has to be the Chardonnays produced at this tiny, isolated property located in the remote Gavilan Mountains about 40 minutes from Soledad, California. I have followed this winery's Chardonnays from the mid-seventies, and while I have had reservations about aging them more than 5–6 years, in early 1988 some friends of mine pulled out bottles of the 1978 and 1980 and served them to me blind. Both wines were absolutely stunning, and I was shocked by how well they had held up. The style of Chardonnay made at Chalone is one of remarkable richness and intensity, barrel-fermented, and with gobs of oaky, buttery, intense fruit. Of recent vintages, both the 1986 and 1985 Chardonnays, which were bursting with fruit after bottling, have gone into a dumb stage and may require several years of cellaring to open up. This would be contrary to what California Chardonnay usually does. The newly released 1987 Chardonnay is less massive than either the

1986 or 1985 but does seem more elegant. It may ultimately turn out to resemble the 1982. The Pinot Blanc is more austere with a more stony, mineral quality to its character. I do not believe the Pinot Noirs are as complex or as compelling as those made by Calera or by Kalin in Marin County, but they are still among the top half dozen Pinot Noirs made in California. Both the 1985 and 1984 show more velvety, rich fruit than the more perfumed but less intense 1983. For those who want to invest in a winery, Chalone might well be a good investment if only to get access to the tiny quantities of Reserve wines made from the oldest vines of the Chalone vineyards. Only stockholders of this publicly traded company are eligible to get any of the Reserve wines, and having tasted them, I can say they are truly spectacular wines, even more concentrated and compelling than the regular cuvées made for the rest of us. This exemplary winery is setting standards for Pinot Blanc and Chardonnay in California, and in believing in unique, individual, personality-filled wines. One wishes more wineries would emulate Chalone.

CHAMISAL VINEYARD (SAN LUIS OBISPO)

1986 Chardonnay Estate	Edna Vly.	B	87

This small, 3,000-case winery in Edna Valley is devoted to Chardonnay and to date has offered up a rich, toasty, buttery, tropical-fruit-scented Chardonnay that should make lovers of the lusty style of this wine salivate. The 1986 is one of the more successful wines to date from this small winery.

DOMAINE CHANDON (NAPA)

N.V. Blanc de Noir	Napa	B	85
N.V. Brut	Napa	B	84
N.V. Brut Reserve	Napa	C	86

The gigantic French conglomerate Moët-Hennessy aggressively set up shop in Napa Valley in 1973 and immediately announced its intentions to produce a sparkling wine in the image of champagne. To do this, the famous chef de caves of Moët-Chandon's operation in Champagne, Edmond Maudier, was brought in to sculptor the first cuvées. Today, Domaine Chandon is as hot a brand name as any 15-year-old winery in California, producing over 400,000 cases of wine a year. If their sparkling wines have not yet reached the heights of finesse and flavor that the Moët champagnes can attain in France, they have been among the two or three best made in California. They are always offered in nonvintage blends from the Napa fruit. Dominated by Chardonnay, but also containing Pinot Blanc and Pinot Noir, both a Blanc de Noir with a pale salmon color and a fuller, toastier, and more complex Brut Reserve are produced. With the exception of the Reserve, Domaine Chandon has kept the prices for its wines within the reach of most wine consumers, which undoubtedly helps account for the immense success this winery continues to have. An extra incentive to try Domaine Chandon is the lovely restaurant the winery owns in Napa Valley.

CHAPPELLET VINEYARD (NAPA)

1984 Cabernet Sauvignon	Napa	B	84
1985 Cabernet Sauvignon	Napa	B	88
1985 Chardonnay	Napa	B	73
1987 Chenin Blanc	Napa	A	85

This gorgeous winery on Pritchard Hill with a spectacular vista of Napa Valley was founded in 1967, and since then it has been dedicated to producing three wines: a dry, underrated, always flavorful, crisp Chenin Blanc; a chunky, rather uninteresting Chardonnay; and an age-worthy, occasionally superb Cabernet Sauvignon. To date, the 1969 Cabernet Sauvignon made at this winery is one of the greatest Cabernets from Napa Valley that I have ever had the pleasure of tasting. Cetainly some fine winemakers—principally, Philip Togni, who now has his own winery, Joe Cafaro, and Tony Soter, the winemaking genius behind the great success of Spottswoode—have passed through Chappellet on their way to establishing their names as prominent winemakers. Of recent vintages, the 1980 and 1985 Cabernet Sauvignons look to be the best, and neither is anywhere near close to maturity. In between the 1980 and 1985, the wines have not been as grand as this winery's reputation and potential would suggest they should be. For example, the 1984 seems surprisingly compact, lean, and tight for a wine from this particular vintage. This winery can hit the heights with its Cabernet Sauvignon, and it's a shame Chenin Blanc is not more in fashion because Chappellet's is one of the best, but all in all there is a lack of consistency in the quality of Chappellet's Chardonnays and Cabernet Sauvignons.

CHATEAU CHEVRE WINERY (NAPA)

1985 Cabernet Franc	Napa	B	86
1984 Merlot	Napa	B	87
1985 Merlot	Napa	B	87
1984 Merlot Reserve	Napa	B	90
1986 Sauvignon Blanc	Napa	A	55

This winery's style has settled down in the mid-eighties with some impressive Merlots. In fact, the 4,000-case production of Chateau Chevre is virtually all Merlot except for a tiny quantity of Sauvignon Blanc and Cabernet Franc. Prices have remained quite reasonable for the quality. Of recent vintages both 1984 Merlots exhibited sensational richness and complexity in a full-bodied, opulent style. The 1985 showed slightly crisper acidity but still retained the rich, voluptuous, sexy, berry fruitiness, married intelligently with spicy new oak. The introduction in 1985 of a Cabernet Franc showed that owner and winemaker Gerald Hazen is willing to take a bit of a risk and make another interesting wine with both finesse and character. Barrel samples of the 1986s look promising as well, so this property's wines should be on the list of anyone who is searching for a sumptuous, rich Merlot. As for the Sauvignon Blanc, the only vintage I tasted was so intensely vegetal that I found it undrinkable.

CHIMNEY ROCK (NAPA)

1985 Cabernet Sauvignon	Napa	B	84
1985 Chardonnay	Napa	B	72
1986 Chardonnay	Napa	B	75

Another showcase winery where the publicity surrounding the wines far exceeds their current quality, Chimney Rock has a talented winemaker, but he seems to be making wine with his hands tied behind his back. In spite of a very polite, understated, graceful 1985 Cabernet Sauvignon, the Chardonnays and debut Cabernet Sauvignons all suffered from being one-dimensional and innocuous, acting as if no one desired to provide any identifiable personality to these wines. A little dynamic winemaking could go a long way given what must be a huge financial commitment to quality on the part of Chimney Rock. At present, these wines offer about as much excitement as kissing your sister.

CHRISTIAN BROTHERS WINERY (NAPA)

1984 Cabernet Sauvignon	Napa	A	86
1985 Cabernet Sauvignon	Napa	A	81
1985 Chardonnay	Napa	A	84
1986 Chardonnay	Napa	A	84
1985 Merlot	Napa	A	77
N.V. Montage Bordeaux–Napa Valley Blend Premier Cuvée		B	76

The Christian Brothers Winery, which dates from 1882 and has over 1,200 acres of premier vineyard land in California's North Coast, has for the last several decades been synonymous with standard-quality, bulk-produced wines of no great consequence. However, the winery seems to be intent on making something a bit more special, and the 1984 Cabernet Sauvignon and 1985 and 1986 Chardonnays are examples of well-made, flavorful, balanced wines, which I hope signal a new era for Christian Brothers. Why the 1985 Merlot and Cabernet Sauvignon did not perform as well as the other wines is anyone's guess. One curious wine I have tasted is Christian Brothers' Montage, a blend of its own Napa Cabernet (40%) with wine produced in Bordeaux (60%). This would appear to be a gimmick of the utmost stupidity, designed to get press attention for the winery. The wine is rather one-dimensional and restrained, and worth about $5–6 a bottle. There is also an insipid Montage white wine made from a blend of Chardonnay and French White Burgundy that should also be avoided. Except for the overhyped Montage, prices remain fair. This winery requires a closer and closer look, as certainly the vineyards this property can draw from are in ideal locations.

CHRISTOPHE VINEYARDS (SAN FRANCISCO COUNTY)

1984 Cabernet Sauvignon	California	A	75
1987 Chardonnay	California	A	78
1987 Joliesse	California	A	80
1987 Sauvignon Blanc	California	A	82

This winery is dedicated to producing inexpensive wines, and the results to date have been agreeable, pleasant, one-dimensional wines that represent decent bargains. I would opt for the fresh, exuberant whites over the often excessively herbaceous and vegetal red wines.

CLINE CELLARS (CONTRA COSTA)

1987 Mourvèdre	B	89
N.V. Oakley Cuvée (70% Mourvèdre/30% Zinfandel)	B	85

This tiny winery producing less than 3,000 cases has made a sensational 1987 Mourvèdre that is a blockbuster wine. Opaque purple in color, and exceptionally rich, intense, and full-bodied, it should evolve well for 10–15 years. The nonvintage Oakley Cuvée shows an imaginative blend of Mourvèdre and Zinfandel. It's a very good wine but does not compare to the 1987 Mourvèdre. The winery also makes a regular and incredibly rich, portlike, late-harvest Zinfandel.

CLOS DU BOIS WINERY (SONOMA)

1984 Cabernet Sauvignon Briarcrest	Alex.Vly.	B	87
1986 Chardonnay Barrel-Fermented	Alex. Vly.	B	78
1986 Chardonnay Calcaire	Alex. Vly.	B	87
1986 Chardonnay Flintwood	Dry Creek	B	87
1986 Chardonnay Proprietor's Reserve	Alex. Vly.	B	84
1984 Marlstone Proprietary Red Wine	Alex. Vly.	B	88

1985 Merlot	Alex. Vly.	B	72
1986 Merlot	Alex. Vly.	B	83
1987 Sauvignon Blanc Barrel-Fermented	Alex. Vly.	A	84

For the last twenty-five years Clos du Bois has intelligently accumulated over 1,000 acres of vineyards in the Dry Creek and the Alexander Valley areas, gradually enlarging its production to well in excess of 200,000 cases of consistently good, sometimes outstanding wine. Much of the success is deservedly credited to Frank Woods, the articulate, handsome, and aggressive founder and owner of Clos du Bois. In addition to the quality, the secret here has been in presenting wines that are delicious to drink when released, yet have the potential in the case of the Cabernets to improve for up to a decade. A recent vertical tasting back through 1974 showed that despite the obvious charm of these wines when young, they stand the test of time as well. The Merlot tends to be less consistent than some of the other red wines and can, in certain vintages, show an annoyingly high level of weedy herbaceousness, which West Coast critics seem to overlook, but it is not a classic wine. The other red wines, which include names such as Briarcrest, are full-bodied, supple, richly fruity, and quite delicious. The Briarcrest is especially successful in 1984 and 1985. In 1981, the winery launched a luxury prioprietary blend of Cabernet Sauvignon, Merlot, and some Cabernet Franc called Marlstone. In most vintages since, it has been the best red wine made at Clos du Bois. The 1984 shows especially rich, seductive, blackcurrant fruit in a forward, voluptuous style. While the Cabernet Sauvignons have been quite consistent, the small quantity of Pinot Noir produced here has been a disappointment. The Chardonnays have been one of the highlights of this grape in California, led by the two single-vineyard Chardonnays called Flintwood and Calcaire. Flintwood, from the Dry Creek area, tends to have a more austere, stony-scented fruit with good aging potential, and quite a bit of complexity. It seems more French in style when compared to the more tropical-fruit-scented, more opulent Calcaire. The winery also produces a barrel-fermented Chardonnay and a Chardonnay called Proprietor's Reserve that tends to be a rather oaky, lush, richly fruity wine. A wine not to be missed here is the Barrel-Fermented Sauvignon Blanc, which has quite a bit of character as well. Prices for Clos du Bois wines are inching upward for their single-vineyard designated Chardonnays and proprietary red wine, but otherwise the prices for wines in the Clos du Bois stable are very reasonable. For introducing potential wine drinkers to the beverage, Clos du Bois wines would be an excellent choice. Clos du Bois also has the distinction of being the only California wine to be served on British Airways (only in first class, however). In 1988, Clos du Bois was sold to the liquor giant Hiram Walker for $40 million, but reports indicate that Frank Woods will stay at the winery—a good sign.

CLOS PEGASE (NAPA)

1986 Cabernet Sauvignon	Napa	B	78
1986 Chardonnay	Napa	B	68
1986 Fumé Blanc	Napa	B	72
1986 Merlot	Napa	B	80

With remarkable publicity and fanfare, a huge temple to viticulture was erected in the Napa Valley and named Clos Pegase. It has become one of Napa Valley's top tourist attractions, and now if only this highly promoted and hyped winery were to turn out good wine, wouldn't we all be happier for it. As so often happens in California, the sculptures and millions of dollars' worth of architecture are put in place first, with the quality of the wines a secondary matter. The initial releases from Clos Pegase have been, for lack of a better word, disappointing. A watery, thin Fumé Blanc and insipid Chardonnay are greatly surpassed in quality by many bulk wine producers selling their wines at one-third the price. The 1986 Merlot seemed to show some promise that adequate wines could be made, but his winery's greatest claim to fame is the amount of money spent building it.

CLOS DU VAL WINE CO. (NAPA)

1984 Cabernet Sauvignon	Napa	B	85
1985 Cabernet Sauvignon	Napa	B	87
1985 Chardonnay	Napa	B	75
1986 Chardonnay	Napa	B	84
1985 Merlot	Napa	B	86

| 1986 Semillon | Napa | B | 78 |

| 1985 Zinfandel | Napa | B | 87 |

Since this winery's first releases in the early 1970s, the French-trained winemaker Bernard Portet was assured of being a star of the California wine industry. The early successes were led by some stunning Cabernet Sauvignons in 1974 and 1975, and some full-blooded, rich, beefy Zinfandels in that period as well. However, in the late seventies, the style of virtually all the wines of Clos du Val took on a one-dimensional, commercial blandness and dullness from perhaps too blind a reliance on high technology. The Chardonnays tasted overly acidified and watery; the Cabernets and Merlots were sad reminders of what they were in the mid-seventies. This unfortunate decline in quality went largely unnoticed by much of the California wine press, which continued to praise what were essentially bland, commercial wines of no great interest or pleasure. In 1984 and 1985 it would appear that Clos du Val has bounced back and is offering wines with a great deal more flavor, personality, and perhaps a less overzealous use of high-tech gimmicks such as the centrifuge and numerous micropore filtrations that eviscerate a wine and strip it of any identifying character and flavor. This is all very encouraging since this winery has over 300 acres of vineyards and has been an important cornerstone in the resurgence of interest in California wines. Of the new releases, the 1985 Zinfandel is a beautifully made, richly fruity, full-bodied wine packed with soft, rich, berry fruit. The new releases of the soft, luscious Merlot and Cabernet Sauvignon show as much flavor as any wine made by Clos du Val since 1978. They should both age nicely for 7–10 years. Only the Chardonnay seems to be lagging behind the renaissance in quality at Clos du Val, but even the 1986 showed more lemony, tart fruit than previous vintages have. The winery still offers a decent Semillon and a Pinot Noir that I find mediocre, but that the West Coast wine writers seem to love. Prices have largely remained fair for the quality of the wine, and consumers should also keep an eye out for the decent second label of wines called Gran Val.

B. R. COHN (SONOMA)

| 1984 Cabernet Sauvignon Olive Hill | Sonoma | B | 91 |

| 1985 Cabernet Sauvignon Olive Hill | Sonoma | B | 90 |

| 1985 Chardonnay Olive Hill | Sonoma | B | 85 |
| 1986 Chardonnay Olive Hill | Sonoma | B | 90 |

This tiny winery in Sonoma has seemingly struck gold with its first releases, an oaky but richly fruity, full-bodied, deeply flavored Chardonnay, of which the 1986 is deeper and more complex, and two compelling multidimensional Cabernet Sauvignons. The 1984 Cabernet Sauvignon has a huge bouquet of toasty new oak and black currants, and on the palate, it is a wine of enormous richness with an expansive, rich, extremely long finish and ripe, round tannins. The winemaker's serious intentions are no better evidenced than by the sidebar on the label, which says the wine is "unfiltered." The 1985 Cabernet has slightly higher acidity and is less opulent at present, but it appears every bit as concentrated as the 1984. Both wines should last 10–15 years. The winery also plans to release a small amount of sparkling wine that it has begun to make. This appears to be an extremely impressive newcomer that connoisseurs of California wines should take notice of immediately.

CONCANNON VINEYARD (ALAMEDA)

1985 Cabernet Sauvignon	Livermore	B	78
1986 Chardonnay	Tepusquet	B	82
1986 Sauvignon Blanc	Livermore	B	84

The Concannon Vineyard can trace its history back to the late nineteenth century. While the wines are far from the top level of quality in California, they are certainly well made, easy to drink, and modestly priced overall. The Chardonnays tend to emphasize crisp, zesty, lemony, and applelike fruit in a medium-bodied, unoaky style. The 1986 Sauvignon Blanc, as in 1985, shows surprising richness and length. The Cabernet Sauvignon has evolved from a mediocre, overly vegetal wine to one that is supple, moderately fruity, cleanly made, and attractive for drinking within its first 5–6 years of life.

CONGRESS SPRINGS WINERY (SANTA CLARA)

| 1986 Brut Sparkling Wine | Santa Cruz | B | 63 |
| 1984 Cabernet Sauvignon | Santa Cruz | B | 85 |

1985 Cabernet Sauvignon	Santa Cruz	B	78
1987 Chardonnay	Santa Clara	B	86
1987 Chardonnay Reserve	San Ysidro	B	90
1987 La Mer Blanc	Santa Clara	A	85
1987 Pinot Blanc	San Ysidro	A	82

The Congress Springs Winery, in existence only since 1976, has an outstanding winemaker of white wines in Dan Gehrs, and the results of the range of wines produced at this property are quite predictable —the whites range from good to superb and the red wines are spotty and inconsistent. The house specialty is its toasty, lavishly rich, luscious Chardonnays, of which there are usually three styles. The regular cuvée of Santa Clara Chardonnay tends to offer gobs of apple- and floral-scented fruit in a medium- to full-bodied, soft style. The Santa Cruz Chardonnay from the estate's own vineyard tends to be a boldly flavored, dramatically oaky, rich wine with a great deal of character in vintages such as 1987, 1986, and 1985. The third type is the Reserve Chardonnay from San Ysidro in Santa Clara County, which is probably the best-balanced and most seductive Chardonnay of all. It has great flavor extract and is certainly among the top dozen or so Chardonnays made in California. The winery also makes a very competent Pinot Blanc, and in 1987 it introduced a fascinating blend of primarily Sauvignon Blanc and Semillon with a tiny percentage of Malvasia added in called La Mer Blanc. It is a deliciously fruity, medium-bodied wine that finishes dry. It would be ideal as an aperitif or seafood wine. The red wines have been less consistently successful. They include an adequate but overly oaked Pinot Noir, and a Cabernet Sauvignon and Cabernet Franc that are sometimes richly fruity, blackcurrant-scented, full-bodied, and oaky, and other times oddly vegetal and thin. The winery has also begun to make sparkling wines, which I have found to be odd and empty of flavor. Overall, production has skyrocketed; the winery is now producing in excess of 25,000 cases, up from a mere 6,000 cases several years ago.

CONN CREEK WINERY (NAPA)

1982 Cabernet Sauvignon	Napa	B	75
1984 Cabernet Sauvignon Private Reserve	Napa	C	88
1986 Chardonnay Barrel Select	Napa	B	75
1986 Chardonnay Château Maja	Napa	A	77
1985 Merlot	Napa	B	72

Conn Creek Winery, which was founded in 1973, has the dubious distinction of not having made its greatest wine itself. This occurred due to an unusual distress sale of a lot of wine from Milton Eisele's vineyard near Calistoga that had been made by another winery. Conn Creek was the successful buyer and proceeded to bottle the wine and put it on the market. It turned out to be one of the greatest California Cabernets made in the decade of the seventies, and it focused attention on the extraordinary Eisele Vineyard, one of the top places for quintessential Napa Valley Cabernet Sauvignon. The 1974 Conn Creek Cabernet Sauvignon was followed by wines indeed made at the winery, and they were great successes in 1976, 1978, and 1980. The decade of the eighties, during which time Conn Creek was sold, has seen less consistent success. While the 1981 Cabernet Sauvignon was good, the 1982 tasted problematic and out of balance. I have not seen a 1983 from the winery, but the 1984 Private Reserve, of which quantities are unfortunately very small, showed great richness, length, and intensity. The winery also makes two Chardonnays, one under its second label called Château Maja and a Barrel Select Chardonnay. The Chardonnays have at best been adequate, displaying somewhat heavy, chunky fruit, some oak, but a lack of finesse and character. The Zinfandel from extremely old vines can be stunning, but the last one I tasted from Conn Creek, the 1980, had more tannin than fruit. This is a winery that appears to be going through numerous changes in direction, and the quality and style of wine that will emerge are impossible to predict.

COSENTINO WINE COMPANY (NAPA)

1986 Cabernet Franc	North Coast	B	87
1985 Cabernet Sauvignon	North Coast	B	82

1986 Chardonnay	North Coast	B	78

1986 Chardonnay—The Sculptor	North Coast	B	84

1986 Merlot	North Coast	B	84

1985 Proprietary Red Wine—The Poet	North Coast	B	87

This is an interesting operation in many respects. The proprietor and winemaker, Mitch Cosentino, markets the wines under the name Crystal Valley Cellars and is producing fairly large quantities of wine and many different lots of it from purchased grapes bought from a broad range of viticultural areas in California. His talents as a blender would appear obvious, as well as his adoration of plenty of toasty oak in his wines. All of the wines I have tasted to date, which are impressively rich and generously flavored, soft and supple, are quite lasciviously oaked. While some tasters may prefer a lighter, less oaky style, there is no doubting that wines such as the 1986 Cabernet Franc, with its complex, sweet, round, generous richness, and the 1985 Proprietary Red Wine called The Poet, with its rich, smoky, robust, oaky, opulent flavors, are rather decadent, hedonistic wines that provide persuasive evidence that Mr. Cosentino believes in having his wines make a statement. His Chardonnays are also very interesting and come in a lighter, more run-of-the-mill North Coast version and one called The Sculptor, which offers oodles of tropical fruit along with plenty of sweet, toasty oak. The wine prices to date have ranged from just under $10 to the mid-teens for the top wines, but I have liked what I have tasted, and I especially admire a winemaker who is willing to make bold, innovative wines such as these. The winery moved from Modesto to Napa Valley in November 1988.

COSTELLO VINEYARDS (NAPA)

1985 Chardonnay	Napa	A	75

1986 Chardonnay	Napa	B	80

1986 Sauvignon Blanc	Napa	A	82

1987 Sauvignon Blanc	Napa	A	84

Founded in 1982, this 40-acre winery owned by John Costello has announced its intention to specialize only in white wines such as Chardonnay and Sauvignon Blanc. The early releases have shown a well-oaked character in the wines with the fruit lacking the crisp, zesty freshness seen at better wineries. It would appear to me the winery needs to make a few improvements in order to compete nationally.

H. COTURRI AND SONS (SONOMA)

1984 Cabernet Sauvignon	Sonoma	B	85
1986 Zinfandel Chauvet Vineyard	Sonoma	B	86
1986 Zinfandel Cooke Vineyards	Sonoma	B	87
1985 Zinfandel Estate	Sonoma	B	87
1986 Zinfandel Les Vignerons	Sonoma	B	87

This tiny winery believes in totally natural, organically made wines and eschews fertilizers, herbicides, pesticides, centrifuges, micropore filters, and fining ingredients that are so much a part of other wine-making operations. What results from these primitive but century-proven ideas are remarkably rich, distinctive, complex wines that require a good 1 to 2 hours of breathing in a decanter before drinking. An argument can be made that the Cabernet Sauvignon actually tastes better the day after than when opened initially. The best wines to date have been the Zinfandels, which display quite complex aromas of smoked meat, damp earth, rich berry fruit, and Oriental spices. These are full-bodied, rich, and intense and they show every indication of being able to age well for up to a decade. However, be forewarned, they need to be decanted because they are neither fined nor filtered and they will throw a heavy, pasty sediment after six months to a year in the bottle. The inky Cabernet Sauvignon has been more puzzling to evaluate. Often weird and impenetrable when opened and decanted, it seems to show much greater character the second day. I admire a winery that is seeking to make authentically handcrafted organic wines, and I hope they succeed. A production of less than 3,000 cases seems to have no difficulty finding its way into the hands of consumers who are looking for individualistic, unique wines that are rare in to-day's world of commercial compromise and the almighty fast buck.

CRESTON MANOR VINEYARDS AND WINERY (SAN LUIS OBISPO)

1985 Cabernet Sauvignon	Central Coast	B	64
1986 Chardonnay	Central Coast	B	61
1985 Pinot Noir Petite D'Noir	Central Coast	A	50
1986 Pinot Noir Petite D'Noir	Central Coast	A	52

If there is ever a case where the quality of the wine in the bottle matches the label, it would be with Creston Manor Vineyards. The garish, almost offensive purple label with high-profile printing is enough to cause one to cringe, but the quality of the wines in the bottle is even worse. The attempt at making a carbonic maceration Pinot Noir called Petite D'Noir has been a disaster as the wines have had a bubbly texture and cooked-asparagus flavors. The Cabernet Sauvignon has been only slightly better with the asparagus character toned down to mere green beans. As for the Chardonnay, I defy any connoisseur to identify it as having the varietal character of this grape. I have heard good things about the winery's Sauvignon Blanc, but I have not as yet had the opportunity to taste it.

CRICHTON HALL VINEYARD (NAPA)

1985 Chardonnay	Napa	B	87
1986 Chardonnay	Napa	B	84

This brand-new winery has only released two wines to date, but both have shown impeccable winemaking and an intelligent use of oak. The 1985 Chardonnay showed richer and deeper-delineated varietal character than the soft, round, attractive 1986. The taste of the Crichton Hall Chardonnays suggests that this winery knows what to do with its grapes, and I look forward to seeing how future vintages turn out. This Napa winery makes only a Chardonnay.

CRONIN VINEYARDS (SAN MATEO)

1983 Cabernet Sauvignon	Napa	B	74
1986 Chardonnay	Alex. Vly.	B	90
1986 Chardonnay	Napa	B	90

1985 Chardonnay Dryer Vineyard	Santa Cruz	B	70
1985 Chardonnay Vanumanutagi Ranch	Santa Cruz	B	65
1986 Chardonnay Ventana Vineyards	Monterey	B	92
1984 Pinot Noir	Monterey	B	62

This tiny winery in Woodside, California, is making sumptuous, rich, and intense Chardonnays from the Ventana Vineyard in Monterey and the Napa and Alexander valleys. When they venture beyond these three areas, such as into the Dryer Vineyard and the Vanumanutagi Ranch, the wines have been unusual, even bizarre, and certainly not pleasant. In addition, the winery has fallen on its face with its attempt at making Cabernet Sauvignon, which has turned out vegetal, tart, and of no interest to serious drinkers. The Pinot Noir also had major shortcomings with its vegetal, thin, hollow character. However, the three top Chardonnays from Cronin are among the top Chardonnays produced in California. They have superconcentrated flavors, a judicious touch of oak, fabulous length, and an unctuous, rich texture, and they are not dissimilar from a great Michel Niellon Batard Montrachet from France, which sells for about four times as much. The three top Chardonnays are indeed compelling, but I would avoid anything else from this small producer.

CUVAISON (NAPA)

1984 Cabernet Sauvignon	Napa	B	85
1985 Chardonnay	Napa	B	86
1986 Chardonnay	Napa	B	85
1985 Merlot	Napa	B	86
1984 Merlot Reserve	Napa	B	88

The Cuvaison Winery has been in business since 1970 but has undergone a number of changes that have probably kept its name somewhat insulated from the public. This is regrettable given the fact that there have been some good wines from here over the last two decades, especially the Chardonnay and Cabernet Sauvignon. In addition, prices have been fair in relation to the quality. The current releases, which are sporting a new, dressier label, include a fleshy, toasty, oaky Chardonnay that is more successful in 1985 than in 1986, although both are quite good. As for the Cabernet Sauvignon, it has tended to represent quite poignantly the hotter end of Napa Valley near Calistoga. Ironically, the winery's 270-acre vineyard is located in the cool Carneros area. Cuvaison's Cabernet Sauvignons are rich in extract, full-bodied, and powerful. The 1984 showed less flavor than I might have expected knowing the personality of the vintage, but it is a good, peppery wine of blackcurrant scents and flavors with a great deal of body that should certainly last for another decade. More impressive, however, is the 1984 Merlot Reserve, which shows gobs of fleshy, seductive fruit in a full-bodied, lush texture. The 1985 Merlot is slightly leaner, but lovely, ripe, and a very attractive wine for drinking over the next 4–5 years. I think wine enthusiasts will also be excited about the 1985 and 1986 Cabernet Sauvignons, which I tasted from the barrel. Both look to be among the best two Cabernet Sauvignons made at Cuvaison in more than a decade.

THE JOHN DANIEL SOCIETY (NAPA)

1983 Dominus	D 93
1984 Dominus	D 92
1985 Dominus	D 96
1986 Dominus	D 94

The long-awaited release of Dominus occurred in February 1988. The partnership of the well-known Christian Moueix—who oversees the winemaking of such Bordeaux superstars as Pétrus, Trotanoy, Latour à Pomerol, and Magdelaine—and Americans Robin Lail and Marcia Smith has from the beginning sought to make wine using traditional Bordeaux techniques and Napa Valley grapes. This has meant minimal clarification, labor-intensive racking, and little or no additions of acidity to the wine. In short, the Moueix philosophy of letting the wine make itself has been employed rather than man's manipulating and dictating the style. Unfortunately, a handful of writers and winery people in California have resented the publicity surrounding this historic venture and have spread a number of vicious rumors. However, it is the quality that matters most, and with Dominus, Moueix has produced a wine of exceptional complexity without sacrificing any of the richness that the favorable Napa Valley climate provides. The tannic, powerful 1983 was followed by an opulent, flattering, very fleshy, and richly fruity 1984; a monumental, nearly perfect 1985; and consumers have every right to get excited about the very rich, heady, full-bodied, and powerful 1986; plus another promising wine in 1987. All of these wines have achieved a rare, elusive level of richness and complexity, and in the case of the 1983, 1985, and 1986 should improve and age gracefully for 10–15 years. The 1984 should be fully mature by 1990 and last at least a decade thereafter. One hopes the retail price of $35 a bottle does not go any higher, but Dominus is certainly the finest and most complex wine yet made by a French/American partnership working in California. Bravo!

DE LOACH VINEYARDS (SONOMA)

1984 Cabernet Sauvignon Dry Creek	Sonoma	B	82
1986 Chardonnay O.F.S.	Sonoma	C	90
1987 Chardonnay O.F.S.	Sonoma	C	92
1986 Chardonnay Russian River	Sonoma	B	88
1987 Chardonnay Russian River	Sonoma	B	87
1985 Pinot Noir Russian River	Sonoma	B	75
1987 White Zinfandel	Sonoma	A	83
1985 Zinfandel Russian River	Sonoma	B	85

No winery's Chardonnay is in any greater demand than that of De Loach. Why? Its unbeatable combination of intense mango, orange, pineapple, and other tropical-fruit scents married deftly with sweet, toasty oak results in a rich, lush, lavishly fruity wine that seduces the taster. The regular Chardonnay is delicious enough, but the special bottling called O.F.S. (meaning, our finest selection) is an unbelievably opulent, exotic Chardonnay that one can seemingly not get enough of. While the Chardonnays are this winery's greatest contribution to the domestic wine scene, they also make a pleasant white Zinfandel; a rich, briary, but essentially one-dimensional Zinfandel; mediocre Pinot Noir; and sometimes good but compact Cabernet Sauvignon. In essence, I'll go a long way to get a bottle of De Loach's Chardonnay, but I'll seek my Pinot Noir, Cabernet Sauvignon, and Zinfandel from other producers, although the 1986 Zinfandel is the most promising red wine De Loach has yet made.

DE MOOR WINERY (NAPA)

1984 Cabernet Sauvignon	Napa	B	88
1982 Cabernet Sauvignon Special Selection	Napa	B	88
1985 Chardonnay	Napa	B	84
1986 Chardonnay	Napa	B	84
1984 Zinfandel	Napa	A	82

The style of wines produced by the De Moor Winery in Napa Valley emphasizes fairly full-throttle flavors, big body, and a great deal of extract. This doesn't seem to work as well with the Chardonnay as it does with the Cabernet Sauvignon, which was quite excellent in both 1984 and 1982. The 1984 Zinfandel lacks flavor dimension but has good varietal character with its vibrant berry flavors and medium to full body. If I had to pick one wine to search out from De Moor, it would be the Cabernet Sauvignon in big, rich years such as 1982, 1984, 1985, and 1986. That seems to be a can't-miss proposition with this particular winery. The Cabernets give every indication of aging well for 8–12 years.

DEHLINGER WINERY (SONOMA)

1986 Chardonnay	Russian River	B	88
1987 Chardonnay	Russian River	B	89
1985 Pinot Noir	Russian River	B	86
1985 Zinfandel	Russian River	B	82

This winery has been making good, sometimes very good, wines since 1976. However, recent releases have shown even higher quality. In recent vintages such as 1985 and 1986, the wonderfully rich Chardonnays show evidence of challenging the finest from California. Beautifully balanced with gobs of buttery, hazelnut-scented fruit, these bold yet balanced wines are quite hedonistic mouthfuls of wine. The 1985 Zinfandel is pleasant but not as exciting as the winery's delicious, velvety, berry-flavored 1985 Pinot Noir, one of the best examples of that varietal I have yet tasted from the Russian River area. It should be drunk over the next 2–4 years.

MAISON DEUTZ (SANTA BARBARA)

N.V. Brut Cuvée	Santa Barbara	B	82

The famous French champagne house Deutz has launched its California sparkling wines, and the result is a mild-mannered, lean wine with decent fruit but of no great excitement or stature. As the French winemaking team from Deutz learns to identify the best vineyards for their grapes and becomes more confident in California, perhaps the quality will increase. However, at present, this is a fairly standard-quality sparkling wine that is living off the reputation of the excellent champagnes made by its sibling house in France.

DIAMOND CREEK VINEYARDS (NAPA)

1985 Cabernet Sauvignon Gravelly Meadow	Napa	C	88
1986 Cabernet Sauvignon Gravelly Meadow	Napa	C	90
1985 Cabernet Sauvignon Red Rock Terrace	Napa	C	89
1986 Cabernet Sauvignon Red Rock Terrace	Napa	C	91
1985 Cabernet Sauvignon Volcanic Hill	Napa	C	87
1986 Cabernet Sauvignon Volcanic Hill	Napa	C	91

Little has changed here with either the winemaking or the wine since the early seventies when owner Al Brounstein and his wife planted 20 acres of vines in the northern end of Napa Valley near Calistoga. From this vineyard come the forceful, rich, intense, aromatic, and dramatic Cabernet Sauvignons that have made this winery so popular with collectors. The wines are made naturally with no filtration and bottled à la Bordeaux after 18–20 months in small casks. In vintages in the eighties, the Diamond Creek Cabernets have excelled in 1980, 1982, 1984, and 1986, all even-numbered vintages. Curiously, as good as the 1985s are, they do not seem to be as profound as either the 1984s or 1986s. In all three Cabernets, the bold, rich, broad, ripe sweet Cabernet Sauvignon flavors dominate, but in most vintages the Gravelly Meadow is the slowest wine to show its character, and it is frequently less concentrated and flamboyant when compared to the Volcanic Hill and Red Rock Terrace. In each vintage the three wines seem to show differently. In 1982, I marginally preferred the Volcanic Hill, in 1983 the Gravelly Meadow, in 1984 the Volcanic Hill, in 1985 the Gravelly Meadow, and in 1986 the Red Rock Terrace. These are clearly limited-production wines (fewer than 3,000 cases are generally produced in a good year), but they are worth a special search of the marketplace to find. In years such as 1984 and 1986, one can expect these wines to evolve and improve in the bottle for at least 10–12 years.

J. PATRICK DORÉ

I have not tasted the most recent examples from J. Patrick Doré, a large company specializing in purchasing wine and selling it under its own name, but my experience with the wines produced in the vintages 1982, 1983, 1984, and 1985 was quite disappointing in spite of attractively low prices. The red wines have ranged from raisiny to vegetal and herbaceous; the whites have been flat and lacking varietal character.

DRY CREEK VINEYARD (SONOMA)

1985 Cabernet Sauvignon	Sonoma	B	84
1986 Chardonnay	Dry Creek	B	84
1987 Chenin Blanc	Dry Creek	A	84
1984 David Stare Reserve Red Wine	Dry Creek	B	87
1987 Fumé Blanc	Dry Creek	A	86
N.V. Zinfandel Old Vines	Dry Creek	B	87

The gregarious David Stare launched Dry Creek Winery in 1972 and has gradually increased his production to close to 60,000 cases, of which two-thirds is one of California's best and commercially most successful, as well as serious, Fumé Blancs. At Dry Creek the style of Fumé Blanc is subtly herbaceous, medium-bodied, and one that can actually age beyond the normal 2–4 years. His other wines are rarely stunning with the exception of his proprietary red wine, called David Stare Reserve, and his newly launched nonvintage Zinfandel from a selection of his oldest vines. The Chardonnays tend to be enjoyable but chunky, fruity, and fairly straightforward. The regular Cabernet Sauvignon from Dry Creek is made in much the same style, slightly herbaceous, richly fruity, but of no great complexity or grandeur. However, Stare has made especially good proprietary red wines in 1982 and 1984, and I applaud the N.V. Old Vine Zinfandel, which is bursting with peppery berry fruit and has a full-bodied, lush texture.

DUCKHORN VINEYARDS (NAPA)

1985 Cabernet Sauvignon	Napa	C	87
1985 Merlot Three Palms Vineyard	Napa	C	90
1985 Merlot Vine Hill Vineyard	Napa	C	90
1987 Sauvignon Blanc	Napa	B	76
1986 Semillon Decoy	Napa	B	78

The Duckhorn Winery attained instant celebrity when its 1978 Cabernet Sauvignon and Merlot were released. From these stunningly rich, graceful wines with exceptional depth, consumers immediately felt that another superstar was in the making. As much as I have been an admirer of Dan Duckhorn's efforts to make top wines since the debut wine in 1978, I have felt a number of Duckhorn's wines released in the 1980s were not as special as the wine released in the 1978–80 era. If the winery was in a minor slump, it clearly came out of it in 1985 with three big, rich, boldly flavored, powerful wines that are among the top successes of even that outstanding vintage. Duckhorn is one of the principals responsible for the Merlot craze over the last several years, and he has exhibited a consistent touch with this grape. The 1985 Merlot from the Three Palms Vineyard is backward and tannic for a Merlot, but for those with enough patience to wait several years, this explosively rich, full-bodied, intense, complex wine should drink beautifully for 10–12 years. It is the most impressive Duckhorn Merlot since the ethereal 1978. Restraint and willpower are not required for the 1985 Merlot from the Vine Hill Vineyard. Quite forward, supple, seductive, and generously flavored, this French-styled, elegant yet richly fruity wine should remain a joy to drink for 5–7 years. As for the 1985 Cabernet Sauvignon, it is quite powerful, backward, and needs a good 4–5 years to show its potential. The 1985s are clearly the best Duckhorn wines since the 1978s, and barrel samples of the 1986s showed similarly fine, ripe, rich, well-balanced wines.

DUNN VINEYARDS (NAPA)

1984 Cabernet Sauvignon	Napa	C	90
1985 Cabernet Sauvignon	Napa	C	92
1986 Cabernet Sauvignon	Napa	C	92
1984 Cabernet Sauvignon Howell Mtn.	Napa	D	95
1985 Cabernet Sauvignon Howell Mtn.	Napa	D	95
1986 Cabernet Sauvignon Howell Mtn.	Napa	D	94

Located on a bucolic, secluded hillside of Howell Mountain is the tiny, 3,000-case winery of Randy and Lori Dunn. No winemaker or wine is in any greater demand today than the red-haired, laid-back Randy Dunn and his two Cabernet Sauvignons. There are no tastings or tours at Dunn Vineyards as he has his hands full just making the wines and trying to satisfy angry wine merchants, suppliers, and consumers who want more of his wines than he can provide. What makes these Dunn Cabernets so special? Certainly the Howell Mountain Cabernet with its explosive blackcurrant fruit, remarkable depth and length is a result of not just top winemaking but of the great fruit that Howell Mountain seems to yield. On the other hand, the Napa Cabernet is often more appealing in its youth than the dense, powerful Howell Mountain. Dunn uses only 30–40% new oak casks and ferments at a high temperature of 90° F. His first vintage was 1979, and in a vertical tasting in 1988, it was the only wine that was fully mature. He followed the 1979 with a tannic 1980; a sweet, ripe 1981 that is approaching full maturity; a fabulous 1982 (the wine of the vintage?); a very good 1983 considering the difficulties of that year; and absolutely extraordinary wines in 1984, 1985, and 1986. The production of 3,000 cases is split between Howell Mountain and his Napa Cabernet. The Napa Cabernet shares very much the rich, powerful, expansive personality of the Howell Mountain, but it is significantly less tannic and more flattering to drink at an earlier age. Prices have jumped, and while I lament this, given the quality of the wines from this producer, few complaints are likely to be heard. These two wines are among the great classics

of Napa Valley and should be sought out by any true lover of Cabernet
Sauvignon.

DUXOUP WINEWORKS (SONOMA)

1987 Gamay	Dry Creek	A	85
1986 Charbono	Napa	B	84
1986 Syrah	Dry Creek	B	86
1985 Zinfandel	Dry Creek	B	83

Fans of the Marx Brothers will no doubt like the name of this small
winery producing less than 2,000 cases of Syrah and Zinfandel, plus a
small amount of Charbono and a deliciously rich Gamay. The wines
made at Duxoup, while not blockbusters, do show excellent harmony
among their component parts with special attention paid by the winemaker to the varietal character of the wines. The 1986 Syrah shows a
lovely peppery, raspberry, spicy bouquet, and long, rich, concentrated flavors. The 1986 Charbono is more earthy, but quite a tasty
wine; the 1985 Zinfandel seems to lack the roundness and richness of
the Syrah and Charbono. Prices are quite reasonable for the quality
of the wine.

EBERLE WINERY (PASO ROBLES)

1984 Cabernet Sauvignon	Paso Robles	B	87
1984 Chardonnay	Paso Robles	B	84

With a production of close to 10,000 cases, this winery rarely gets
much publicity, but there is no doubting that the rich, lush, unctuous,
and opulent Cabernet Sauvignon provides great pleasure within 7–8
years of the vintage. The 1984, bursting with blackcurrant fruit and a
generous, lush texture, is altogether quite a seductive wine. The 1984
Chardonnay shows moderately intense tropical-fruit aromas, a touch
of oak, and finishes with adequate acidity. Winemaker Gary Eberle
seems to know how to make quite a pleasurable wine and has kept
prices at a reasonable level.

EDNA VALLEY VINEYARDS (SAN LUIS OBISPO)

1986 Chardonnay Estate	Edna Vly.	C	89
1987 Chardonnay Estate	Edna Vly.	C	90
1984 Pinot Noir Estate	Edna Vly.	C	78
1985 Pinot Noir Estate	Edna Vly.	C	86

The Edna Valley Vineyard was established in 1980 as a partnership between Chalone Vineyards, who are responsible for the winemaking, and the Paragon group, who are the growers. The first vintage was the 1977, which was made at Chalone. From the beginning, the style of all the wines made here has been of typical Chalonian proportions, meaning bold, barrel-fermented, toasty, buttery Chardonnays, and full-throttle, herbaceous and spicy, sometimes overly exaggerated Pinot Noirs. In the late eighties the Chardonnay has moved to a more balanced but nevertheless rich, intense, unctuous style. Both the 1986 and 1987 are the two best Edna Valley Chardonnays to date, combining the lavishly oaked, full-bodied style of Edna Valley with gobs of tropical fruit and a buttered-nut taste that can only come from barrel fermentation and long aging in oak. The Pinot Noir has missed the mark as often as it has been on target. Certainly the 1984 veered in the direction of excessive herbaceous and earthy, woody notes, but the 1985 shows good balance, and the exotic, rich, herbaceous, Oriental-spice character that makes Pinot Noir so alluring, plus a velvety, lovely texture.

ESTRELLA RIVER WINERY (SAN LUIS OBISPO)

1982 Cabernet Sauvignon	Paso Robles	B	85
1983 Cabernet Sauvignon	Paso Robles	B	82
1986 Muscat	Paso Robles	A	85
1984 Syrah	Paso Robles	B	?
1985 Syrah	Paso Robles	B	73
1984 Zinfandel	Paso Robles	A	72

Estrella River Winery is the largest producer in the Paso Robles area and has extensive vineyard holdings from which it not only draws its own grapes, but also sells grapes to other producers. The wines tend to be made in a relatively straightforward, moderately intense style as if the highest priority is not to offend any taster, nor give them a great deal of pleasure. The 1982 Cabernet Sauvignon surprised me for its ripeness and tastiness. The winery does an outstanding job with a slightly sweet, wonderfully fragrant Muscat, but the Syrahs, from some of the best vineyards for this grape varietal in all of California, have been disappointing. This is especially true when one compares the Syrahs made from Estrella River's grapes by other wineries. It seems unquestionable that the winery's obsession with wine clarification and several filtrations is indeed eviscerating much of the wine's flavor and personality. With close to 600 acres of vineyards, this winery seems to have immense potential to turn out some very good wines at reasonable prices. Unfortunately, at present they seem to be content to follow a path of mediocrity. Perhaps the winery's recent acquisition by the huge Nestle's corporation (owners of Beringer), who are renaming the operation Meridian, will result in higher-quality wines.

FAR NIENTE (NAPA)

1984 Cabernet Sauvignon	Napa	C	85
1985 Cabernet Sauvignon	Napa	C	87
1986 Chardonnay	Napa	C	80

In many respects this winery has typified the excesses of the California wine industry. Despite the fact that the winery was founded only in 1979, the unproven wines of Far Niente were released at the bold prices of $20–25 a bottle. Of course, one look at the expensive packaging and promotional efforts reveals where much of the cost was. This publicity-conscious winery produced a bevy of overpriced Chardonnays that seemed to find favor with those who had more money than good taste. The Cabernets proved to be adequate but hardly inspiring until the 1984 and the 1985, which at last revealed the sort of depth and complexity one might expect when paying $25 for a bottle of wine. Both the 1984 and the 1985 Cabernets displayed rich, weedy, blackcurrant fruit, full body, plenty of depth and intensity, and should last for up to a decade. Despite my reservations about this winery—which seems to live by the motto "Why pay less?"—it is good to see the increased quality of their Cabernet Sauvignon, but it is hard to explain the inconsistent performance of such an expensive Chardonnay.

GLORIA FERRER (SONOMA)

1984 Brut—Royal Cuvée	Sonoma	B	83
N.V. Brut	Sonoma	B	81

This is another example of a famous European sparkling wine producer, in this case Freixenet, setting up shop in California on the theory that America is quickly becoming a sparkling-wine-consuming nation. Their debut nonvintage Brut showed a great deal of character and seemed to me like a very positive step in the right direction for making good sparkling wine in California. The 1984 vintage added more fruit and complexity, an encouraging sign. My only question is where all these wineries are going to sell the large quantities of sparkling wine they plan to make.

FETZER VINEYARD (MENDOCINO)

1986 Cabernet Sauvignon	Lake	A	84
1985 Cabernet Sauvignon Barrel Select	Mendocino	B	84
1984 Cabernet Sauvignon Special Reserve	Mendocino	B	84
1985 Cabernet Sauvignon Special Reserve	Mendocino	B	86
1987 Chardonnay Barrel Select	California	B	86
1987 Chardonnay Reserve	California	B	86
1987 Chardonnay Sundial	Mendocino	A	85
1987 Fumé Blanc Valley Oaks	Lake	A	84
1987 Gewürztraminer	California	A	73
1987 Johannisberg Riesling	California	A	75
1985 Petite Sirah Special Reserve	Mendocino	B	85

1985 Pinot Noir Special Reserve	Mendocino	B	75
1986 Zinfandel	Lake	A	84
1985 Zinfandel Ricetti Vyd. Special Reserve	Mendocino	B	85
1985 Zinfandel Special Reserve	Mendocino	B	79

It is hard to believe that the family-owned Fetzer winery was established only twenty years ago in 1968. The production has expanded to the point where the day is not far off when this one-time small winery will be producing close to 1,000,000 cases of wine a year. The formula for success at Fetzer has been to deliver wines with a very strong quality/price rapport. In doing this, they have been one of the first wineries to realize that Americans desire their white wines fresh, fruity, and light. The white wines, with the exception of their Barrel Select Chardonnay, are bottled as quickly as possible in order to preserve the exuberant varietal character of the grapes, then rushed to market. Consumers have loved this style of wine, ranging from the lemony, citrusy, non–oak-aged Sundial Chardonnay, to the effusively fruity, subtly herbaceous Valley Oaks Fumé Blanc. Their Chardonnays have consistently offered excellent values, as has the Sauvignon Blanc. I am less impressed with the dull, unvarietal-tasting Gewürztraminer, and adequate but unexciting Chenin Blanc and Riesling. The philosophy of making white wines in fresh, lively styles was carried over by the Fetzers to their Lake Country red wines, especially the juicy, berry-scented and berry-flavored Lake Country Zinfandel, and the riper, more intense Cabernet Sauvignon. For those who want something with a bit more body, tannin, alcohol, and wood, the winery offers its Barrel-Select Chardonnay and Mendocino and Reserve Cabernet Sauvignons that still carry the hallmark of this winery: unadulterated, rich, supple, tasty fruit unencumbered by heavy tannins or excessive alcohol. In truth, the Reserve Cabernets can be excellent as in 1985, which is a rich, blackcurrant- and oak-scented wine that should keep for 5–7 more years. The huge, strapping Zinfandels made by the winery in the late seventies have been toned down considerably, but this is still a very reliable source for intense, full-bodied, well-made Zinfandel. Their 1985 Special Reserve Zinfandel displayed quite a bit of oak for the amount of fruit it had, and although the 1985 Ricetti Zinfandel had a huge dose of toasty oak, it also had the requisite fruit needed to carry the wood. I have only seen their 1985 bottling of Pinot Noir Special Reserve, which is correct but quite boring and too oaky. The 1985 Special Reserve Petite Sirah is a good, peppery, ripe, meaty, powerful, interesting wine, and generally a fine value. The winery also produces sound wines under its second label, called Bel Arbres. Someone should tell them, however, that if this is meant to be French, they have spelled the word "Bel" incorrectly. All in all, Fetzer is one of the names that stands out in California for offering solid values in wine, and I encourage frugal shoppers to search out these wines.

FIELD STONE (SONOMA)

1985 Cabernet Sauvignon Home Ranch Vyd.	Alex. Vly.	B	87
1984 Cabernet Sauvignon Hoot Owl Creek Vyd.	Alex. Vly.	B	89
1984 Cabernet Sauvignon Turkey Hill Vyd.	Alex. Vly.	B	88
1985 Petite Sirah	Alex. Vly.	B	86
1987 Rosé of Petite Sirah	Alex. Vly.	A	68

This family-owned winery in Alexander Valley keeps a low profile, but this is an excellent source for Cabernet Sauvignon. In top vintages such as 1984 and 1985, Field Stone offers three vineyard-designated wines—Turkey Hill, Home Ranch, and Hoot Owl. In other vintages, these wines are blended together into an estate blend. The 1987 Rosé did not impress me because of its cloying sweetness and dull, earthy character. The 1984 Hoot Owl Cabernet (850 cases were produced) has a rich curranty, chocolaty, intense bouquet, layers of rich fruit, full body, and quite a long finish. It should drink well for 10–15 years. The 1984 Turkey Hill is more tannic and less opulent, but still a very impressive, blackcurrant-scented, full-bodied wine with at least a decade's worth of aging potential. Interestingly, this vineyard was the source of fruit for Simi's great 1985 and 1986 Reserve Cabernets. The 1985 Home Ranch has rich curranty fruit married beautifully with spicy oak. Quite full-bodied, rich, and impressive, this stylish, intense wine should also age well for 12–15 years. Lastly, the huge, chewy, deep, 1985 Petite Sirah comes from vines planted in 1894. It is a monolithic wine, not complex, but very rich, deep, and intense. These are all impressive wines from a low-profile producer.

FIRESTONE VINEYARDS (SANTA BARBARA)

1983 Cabernet Sauvignon	Santa Ynez	B	81
1984 Cabernet Sauvignon	Santa Ynez	B	80
1985 Cabernet Sauvignon	Santa Ynez	B	83
1987 Cabernet Sauvignon Rosé	Santa Ynez	A	78
1986 Chardonnay	Santa Ynez	B	73
1987 Johannisberg Riesling	Santa Ynez	A	82
1984 Merlot	Santa Ynez	B	75
1986 Merlot	Santa Ynez	B	80
1986 Sauvignon Blanc	Santa Ynez	A	80

This winery, jointly owned by the Suntory firm from Japan and the
Firestone family from America, has been making generally mediocre
wines since its inception in 1973. While other producers have overcome the highly vegetal character found in many of the wines of Santa
Barbara, Firestone has consistently turned out a bevy of vegetal and
herbaceous Cabernets that are unpleasant to drink. Recent encouraging signs are the 1983, 1984, and 1985 Cabernet Sauvignons, and
the 1986 Merlot. Although all these wines still had a distinctive herbaceous streak to them, the cooked-asparagus character of many of
the previous vintages of these varietals was missing. Furthermore, the
wines exhibited very good berry fruitiness. The Santa Barbara viticultural area has produced fine Chardonnays, but Firestone's Chardonnay is a rather empty, insipid wine with little varietal character. As
for the other wines, the 1987 Riesling (and prior vintages as well) was
quite good; the Sauvignon Blanc seems to be improving; and the Rosé
of Cabernet Sauvignon is not unappealing, but again very herbaceous
to smell and taste. Prices are not unreasonable.

FISHER VINEYARDS (SONOMA)

1984 Cabernet Sauvignon Coach Insignia	Sonoma	C	84
1985 Cabernet Sauvignon Coach Insignia	Sonoma	C	85

1986 Chardonnay Coach Insignia	Sonoma	C	84

Fred Fisher must have one of the most striking wineries and vineyard locations in California's North Coast area. Situated in the mountains, right on the Napa County/Sonoma County line, this gorgeous hillside property is dedicated to producing both Chardonnay and Cabernet Sauvignon in the well-drained soil and cooler mountain climate that its peers who operate on the valley floor do not enjoy. The style to date has been one of streamlined, restrained wines of understated varietal character. The Chardonnay has shown a nice touch of oak, medium body, and floral, applelike aromas and flavors. It is quite delicate, but I often ask myself, is the wine just elegant or undernourished? As for the Cabernet Sauvignon, it shares the same rather compact, austere character that Fred Fisher likes for his chardonnay, but it does have a deep color, very crisp, high acids, and medium body. I felt the 1984 and 1985 showed more depth of fruit and slightly greater flavor dimension than prior vintages. If I had one wish, it would be that these wines were a bit bolder and more dramatic, for at their prices I believe the consumer is entitled to just a bit more flamboyant flavors. The winery also produces a less expensive Chardonnay and Cabernet Sauvignon called Everyday Chardonnay and Everyday Cabernet Sauvignon.

FLORA SPRINGS WINE CO. (NAPA)

1984 Cabernet Sauvignon	Napa	B	87
1986 Chardonnay Barrel Fermented	Napa	C	90
1987 Chardonnay Barrel Fermented	Napa	C	90
1985 Merlot	Napa	B	85
1987 Sauvignon Blanc	Napa	B	87
1984 Trilogy	Napa	D	83
1985 Trilogy	Napa	D	86

This winery has just turned 10 years old and is able to draw its best grapes from over 300 acres of prime vineyards located in some of the best parts of Napa Valley. From the beginning the quality of the wines has been demonstrated by Flora Springs' stunning Chardonnays and one of the best Sauvignon Blancs made in California. In particular, the Barrel-Fermented Chardonnay aims at the French white-burgundy style, particularly a Puligny-Montrachet, and succeeds. Its oakiness is kept in check, and the wine offers up gobs of classy, complex, hazelnut-scented fruit. The 1987 appears slightly fatter and richer than the elegant, gracious 1986. The Sauvignon Blanc also shows a great deal more flavor and character than most wines made from this grape in California. The winery's red wine program has been more mixed. After an excellent 1980 Cabernet Sauvignon, the red wines seemed to take on a more compact, austere character lacking richness and charm. In 1984, Flora Springs launched its own luxury-priced, proprietary red wine called Trilogy, an appropriately named blend of one-third each of Cabernet Sauvignon, Merlot, and Cabernet Franc. The 1984 seemed surprisingly light and overpriced for the degree of pleasure it provided. However, starting in 1984, the Cabernet Sauvignon began to show more richness and more of the tobacco, herbaceous, weedy, blackcurrant fruit that certain parts of Napa Valley can provide. In addition, the 1985 Merlot showed attractive lushness and plump, berry flavors. The 1984 Trilogy was succeeded by the 1985, which finally delivered an appealing combination of velvety rich fruit, good structure, and complex tobacco, spice, oak, and fruit notes. The good news is that the 1986 Trilogy looks to be every bit as impressive as the 1985, as do the other wines from Flora Springs. This is a winery that is quickly approaching the very top echelon of quality in California, with, I lament, prices to match.

THOMAS FOGARTY WINERY (SAN MATEO)

It has been several years since I have tasted a Thomas Fogarty wine, but assuming not much has changed, this winery, drawing grapes from the Santa Cruz Mountains, is capable of making very fine Chardonnay and Pinot Noir, although its source for both of its best wines, the Winery Lake Vineyard in Carneros, was sold to Sterling several years ago. One wonders if these vineyard-designated Chardonnays and Pinot Noirs will still be available. Certainly, the style of the Fogarty wines has emphasized fragrant, rich bouquets, broad, dynamic flavors, and a great deal of oak. In most cases, the fruit was more than sufficient to carry the amount of toasty oak.

FOLIE À DEUX WINERY (NAPA)

1984 Cabernet Sauvignon	Napa	B	82
1986 Chardonnay	Napa	B	84
1987 Chenin Blanc	Napa	A	85

This small winery, producing less than 3,000 cases from its production facility in St. Helena, emphasizes three wines. Surprisingly, the star of their portfolio is the wine with the least snob appeal, their Chenin Blanc. For example, the 1987 Chenin Blanc delivers wonderfully fresh, floral, spring-flower aromas and melonlike fruit in a dry, medium-bodied format. It is a delicious aperitif wine. The 1986 Chardonnay is a well-made wine with cunningly measured doses of apple and lemony fruit, spicy oak, and citrusy acidity. The 1984 Cabernet Sauvignon is cut from the same cloth, being medium-bodied, agreeable, and fruity, but lacking enough depth and overall complexity to be considered exciting. There is absolutely nothing wrong with the Cabernet and Chardonnay from Folie à Deux, but the wine simply tastes like too many other California Cabernets and Chardonnays.

LOUIS FOPPIANO WINE CO. (SONOMA)

1983 Cabernet Sauvignon	Sonoma	B	77
1984 Cabernet Sauvignon/Fox Mountain	Sonoma	B	86
1984 Chardonnay	Sonoma	B	68
1985 Chardonnay	Sonoma	B	72
1986 Sauvignon Blanc	Sonoma	A	80

One of California's oldest wineries, the Louis Foppiano winery for decades was a grower providing its 200 acres of grapes to other wineries. Starting in 1970, the winery began marketing varietal wines under its own name. The quality of the wines is sound and correct, but generally uninspiring. The best wines tend to be the red wines: particularly the winery's estate-bottled Petite Sirah, which is full-bodied, robust, and tannic; and the Cabernet Sauvignon made from the Fox Mountain Vineyard in the Russian River Valley. The 1984 version of this wine is quite rich, supple, as well as a notable value. The white wines, especially the Chardonnay and Sauvignon Blanc, lack varietal

character, often tasting too simple and dull. The secondary label of
Foppiano is Riverside Farm. Varietal wines offered under that label
generally retail for less than $5 a bottle.

FORMAN WINERY (NAPA)

1984 Cabernet Sauvignon	Napa	C	90
1985 Cabernet Sauvignon	Napa	C	90
1986 Cabernet Sauvignon	Napa	C	90
1986 Chardonnay	Napa	C	92
1987 Chardonnay	Napa	C	90

Ric Forman was one of the California whiz kid winemakers in the
seventies who became more famous than the wineries for which he
worked. He was the architect behind the impressive Sterling wines in
the mid-seventies, particularly the resounding Reserve Cabernets of
1973, 1974, 1975, and 1976, all of which have stood the test of time
quite impeccably. In fact, the 1974 may turn out to be the top Cabernet from that heralded vintage. Forman, after stops at several other
wineries, now has his own 3,000-case operation specializing primarily
in two wines: a Bordeaux-style Cabernet Sauvignon and some Chardonnay. I say primarily because he made minuscule quantities of a
barrel-fermented, oak-aged Sauvignon Blanc that tastes like a clone
of the rare and famous white Graves, Domaine de Chevalier. I hope
he expands production of this gem. Forman, who has a scholarly look
about him, is indeed a master winemaker who seems quite capable of
handling whatever Mother Nature deals him. His 1986 Chardonnay is
the finest he has ever made—anywhere—combining rich, intense flavors with barrel-fermented, crisp acids, and 5–7 years of potential
longevity. The 1987 is similarly styled and almost as good. The Cabernets to date have ranged from one of the better 1983s made in that
difficult vintage for Napa Valley, to an elegant, lush, gracious 1984; a
stunning 1985; and a powerful, rich, and intense wine in 1986. This is
one of the top wineries in California, and despite its small size, it is
worth a special search of the marketplace to find.

FRANCISCAN VINEYARDS (NAPA)

1984 Cabernet Sauvignon	Oakville Estate	B	86
1987 Cabernet Sauvignon	Oakville Estate	B	86
1985 Cabernet Sauvignon Estancia	Alex. Valley	A	82
1985 Chardonnay	Oakville Estate	B	84
1986 Chardonnay	Oakville Estate	B	85
1986 Chardonnay Estancia	Alex. Valley	A	83
1984 Merlot	Oakville Estate	A	86
1985 Merlot	Oakville Estate	B	78
1987 Merlot	Oakville Estate	B	86

Franciscan is an underrated winery making good to very good wines and selling them at sometimes surprisingly low prices. With a production in excess of 100,000 cases, and with nearly 500 acres of vineyards owned by the winery in both Oakville and Alexander Valley, the potential for outstanding-quality wines is clearly apparent. One might wonder why Franciscan's Napa Valley Cabernet Sauvignon sells for about one-sixth the price of Opus One when their vineyards are only separated by a road. There have been numerous changes of ownership here, but since the beginning of this decade, the winery has been under the fairly steady helm of its German owners and seems to have concluded the best way to win the hearts of wine consumers is to offer good wines at bargain prices. The Estancia line of wines has strikingly good values in both Chardonnay and Cabernet. While the wines may never have quite the complexity and depth of flavor of the best wines of Alexander Valley, at prices of around $6 a bottle their bargain value is indisputable. The winery has always made good Merlot, and certainly the 1984 and 1987 from their Oakville Estate are lush, fleshy, intense wines that can be drunk early. The Cabernet Sauvignon, particularly the lovely 1984 and 1987 Oakville Estate, are also good wines, showing blackcurrant, ripe flavors, full body, and the lushness that is a hallmark of these two vintages. Franciscan also has a modestly priced proprietary red wine in the works. Overall, Franciscan is a

reliable source for good-quality wines at fair prices. Consumers would
be foolish not to take advantage of this winery's pricing philosophy.

FREEMARK ABBEY (NAPA)

1984 Cabernet Sauvignon/Sycamore Vineyards	Napa	C	86
1984 Cabernet Sauvignon Bosché	Napa	C	86
1985 Chardonnay	Napa	C	87
1986 Chardonnay	Napa	C	88
1986 Edelwein Gold	Napa	C	88

Freemark Abbey, founded in 1967, has maintained a relatively modest
production of 30,000 cases a year and has been content to specialize
in only four wines: a boldly flavored, oaky, rich, sometimes excessively heavy Chardonnay; a late-harvest, decadently sweet Johannisberg Riesling called Edelwein Gold; a regular cuvée of Cabernet
Sauvignon; and a single-vineyard Cabernet Sauvignon from the famous, highly respected Bosché Vineyard near Rutherford. On occasion, a very fine Petite Sirah is made from the York Creek Vineyards
in Napa Valley. While I was extremely impressed with the old vintages
of Cabernet Sauvignon from Freemark Abbey in the late sixties and
early to mid seventies, I have found many of the wines in the late
seventies and early eighties to be one-dimensional, somewhat vegetal,
and lacking the richness and depth I had come to expect after experiencing the winery's early releases. Between 1980 and 1983 the Cabernet Sauvignon Boschés were fairly mediocre, but the 1984 would
appear to be the finest wine made from the vineyard in a decade. Deep
ruby with a broad, complex bouquet of weedy blackcurrant fruit and
toasty oak, this full-bodied, intense wine, which is already drinkable,
should age beautifully for 12–15 years. The winery also launched a
new Cabernet Sauvignon from the Sycamore Vineyard in 1984. It is a
brawny, beefy, very tannic, and full-bodied wine that should not be
touched until 1993 or later. The recent Chardonnays have been quite
oaky, but in both 1986 and 1985 the buttery, pineapple-scented flavor
and fruit were more than adequate to carry the healthy dosage of
toasty new oak. Lastly, the 1986 Edelwein Gold, a Trockenbeerenauslese-styled, decadent, sweet wine made from Johannisberg Riesling,
is again quite extraordinary and should age beautifully for another 7–
8 years, although it is hard to resist now. Perhaps this important

winery, after slipping a bit in the late seventies and early eighties, has returned completely to top form. Let's hope so.

FRICK WINERY (SANTA CRUZ)

I have not tasted any Frick wines recently, save for a very one-dimensional 1985 Chardonnay. The winery has tried to specialize in making Pinot Noir from grapes grown in Monterey County, and the results have sometimes been interesting, as in the case of the 1980, which had a penetrating, smoky, earthy, ripe, expansive bouquet that was very burgundian. However, all the promises delivered by the nose were left unfulfilled on the palate as the wine tasted tart and thin. The 1981 Pinot Noir was also quite simple.

FRITZ CELLARS (SONOMA)

This winery was founded in 1979 and has experimented with Cabernet Sauvignon, Pinot Noir, Zinfandel, Chardonnay, and Fumé Blanc. I have no recent tasting experience following the release of the 1985 Chardonnay and Fumé Blanc, but my impression of the wines released early in the eighties was that the quality of the white wines was quite good, that of the red wines spotty and inconsistent. Prices were quite reasonable, especially for the quality Chardonnay and Fumé Blanc that Fritz offered up in the 1984 and 1985 vintages.

FROG'S LEAP WINERY (NAPA)

1985 Cabernet Sauvignon	Napa	B	84

1986 Chardonnay Carneros	Napa	B	86

1987 Sauvignon Blanc	Napa	B	84

If the wines from this eight-year-old winery have never been exhilarating, they have been consistently good, led by a stylish, subtly herbaceous, complex Sauvignon Blanc, tasty, refined, medium- to full-bodied Chardonnay, and an increasingly better weedy, blackcurrant-scented, full-bodied Cabernet Sauvignon. Production, now in excess of 7,000 cases, is expected to peak at around 10,000 cases. This is a good winery.

FULTON VALLEY WINERY (SONOMA)

1984 Cabernet Sauvignon Steiner Vyd.	Sonoma	B	52
1985 Chardonnay	Alex. Vly.	B	74

Initial releases from this small winery have been unimpressive. The Chardonnay tastes one-dimensional and simple, but the Cabernet Sauvignon from the Steiner Vineyard on the Sonoma Mountains reeked of cooked asparagus and excessive new oak, making it unpalatable. In today's competitive wine world, the quality will have to improve for these wines to compete.

GAINEY VINEYARDS (SANTA BARBARA)

1984 Cabernet Sauvignon	Santa Ynez	B	70
1986 Chardonnay	Santa Barbara	B	75
1985 Chardonnay Limited Selection	Santa Barbara	B	85
1986 Sauvignon Blanc	Santa Barbara	A	68

I was impressed when this young winery, started in 1984, released its first wines, but recent releases, save for the Limited Selection Chardonnay, have been disappointing. The problem has been the dominant vegetal smells that plague so many wines from southern California. However, the Limited Selection Chardonnay remains a rich, full-bodied wine loaded with tropical fruit, toasty oak, and plenty of body, and it should be drunk within 3 years of the vintage. The winery also made a very sweet, rich, interesting Select Late-Harvest Johannisberg Riesling in 1985, but I have not seen a more recent vintage.

E. & J. GALLO WINERY (MODESTO)

1981 Cabernet Sauvignon Limited Release	California	A	65
N.V. Chablis Blanc	California	A	78
1986 Chardonnay Reserve	California	A	58
N.V. Hearty Burgundy	California	A	78
N.V. Rhine Wine	California	A	72

1986 Sauvignon Blanc	California	A	70

Gallo Winery advertises aggressively that they produce 60,000,000 cases of wine a year, making them one of the largest producers of wine in the world. While the winery has entered the premium wine market with its varietal wines, the current batch did not show as well in my tastings as the debut releases did several years ago. For example, the 1981 Cabernet Sauvignon had musty, almost dirty flavors and excessive herbaceousness. The 1986 Sauvignon Blanc smelled sour and overtly unripe and green, and the 1986 Chardonnay Reserve was watery and thin. On the other hand, the bulk wine called Hearty Burgundy is slightly sweet, but quite a tasty, full-bodied, grapy wine with much more character than many wines costing 10–20 times as much. If you haven't tasted it in a while, spend the $2–$3 and try it again; it's really quite palatable. The Chablis Blanc is also a pleasant, agreeable wine with a slight amount of residual sugar left in to give it roundness and fullness. It's hard to beat at its price. I find the nonvintage Rhine Wine to be just too sweet and cloying to get excited about. Of course Gallo makes an immense range of wines under other labels, such as Carlo Rossi, Boone's Farm, and its highly successful line of wine coolers called Bartles and James.

GIRARD WINERY (NAPA)

1984 Cabernet Sauvignon	Napa	B	87
1985 Cabernet Sauvignon	Napa	B	87
1984 Cabernet Sauvignon Reserve	Napa	C	92
1985 Cabernet Sauvignon Reserve	Napa	C	93
1986 Chardonnay	Napa	B	90
1985 Chardonnay Reserve	Napa	C	90
1986 Chardonnay Reserve	Napa	C	92
1987 Semillon	Napa	A	88

This modest-sized winery with a total production of 15,000 cases was founded in 1980, but the family vineyards have been the source of grapes for a number of Napa's best wineries. The proprietor is the handsome and boyish-looking Stephen Girard, who along with talented winemaker Fred Payne seems intent on keeping the Girard Winery in the spotlight. This should hardly be a problem given what the winery has done in 1984, 1985, and 1986. When Girard released their 1981 Chardonnay, it seemed as if another star performer had been born. The wine was one of the great Chardonnays of the vintage, but tasted last month, it seemed to be declining. The newest stars are the 1985 and 1986 Reserve Chardonnays and the 1985 and 1986 regular Chardonnays. They are all barrel-fermented, rich, full-bodied, well-focused Chardonnays with a significant amount of buttery, popcorn fruit intertwined with scents of apple blossoms. However, this is not a one-dimensional Chardonnay winery. The 1984 Cabernets offer the consumer two styles of wine. The 1984 regular bottling is loaded with fleshy, soft, blackcurrant fruit, has a lush, full-bodied texture, and plenty of appeal for drinking over the next 4–7 years. The 1984 Reserve Cabernet Sauvignon is simply much deeper, richer, and more profound in every sense. It would appear to be one of the great wines of the vintage. As impressive as this wine was, the 1985 Reserve Cabernet Sauvignon is even richer and deeper. For those readers who live in California and can make a quick trip to the winery, Girard produces about 100 cases of a rich, deep, flavorful Semillon that is a perfect foil for grilled fish and fowl. In addition, there is a tiny quantity of Oregon Pinot Noir made by Girard that is available only at the winery. This is one of California's top wineries, and I highly recommend their wines.

GIUMARRA VINEYARDS (BAKERSFIELD)

This gigantic winery with over 6,000 acres of vineyards produces in excess of 4,000,000 cases of wine, which is sold under numerous labels. Interestingly, much of it makes its way by tanker to European countries where it is sold simply as California Chardonnay, Cabernet Sauvignon, Sauvignon Blanc, etc. The wines sell at unbelievably low prices, and samples I have tasted in Europe show a clean, correct, but essentially neutral, bland style of winemaking that is designed to offend the least number of people. In essence, you get what you pay for.

GLEN ELLEN (SONOMA)

1985 Cabernet Sauvignon Estate	Sonoma	B	81
1985 Cabernet Sauvignon Proprietor's Reserve	Sonoma	A	75

1986 Chardonnay Proprietor's Reserve	California	A	74

1987 Sauvignon Blanc Benziger	Sonoma	A	87

Since the Benziger family launched this winery in 1981, it has had splendid commercial if not critical success. The backbone of the winery's appeal has been the Proprietor's Reserve Chardonnay and Cabernet Sauvignon that were made available to the consumer for $6 a bottle. Even if they were a bit diluted in varietal character and lacked a focal point, consumers nevertheless flocked to buy these wines from the two California supergrapes, and the winery was off and running. While these two wines no doubt make the winery most of its money, the best wine is probably the Estate vineyard's Sauvignon Blanc, which tends to be herbaceous but rich and fruity with significant flavor depth as well as complexity. The Estate Cabernet Sauvignon has more aggressive varietal character, but also a bit too much herbaceousness. The Proprietor's Reserve wines should be drunk within 3 years of the vintage, and the other wines within 3–4 years of the vintage. In the fall of 1988, all of the estate-bottled wines began to appear under a new label called Benziger.

GOOSECROSS CELLARS (NAPA)

1985 Chardonnay	Napa	B	74

1986 Chardonnay	Napa	B	80

Somewhat typical of the California wine scene is this new winery that has just released its first two Chardonnays, both dull, chunky wines selling for a bold mid-teen price. The wines are worth about half the price asked for them. I hope improvement is forthcoming.

GRACE FAMILY VINEYARDS (NAPA)

1982 Cabernet Sauvignon	Napa	D	90

1983 Cabernet Sauvignon	Napa	D	85

1984 Cabernet Sauvignon	Napa	D	90

1985 Cabernet Sauvignon	Napa	E	88

This small Cabernet Sauvignon specialist burst on the scene in the early eighties with some full-bodied, intense, rich, deep Cabernets that were flamboyant and dramatic. The style has never wavered from giving the consumer gobs of cedary, blackcurrant fruit, a mouthful of toasty, smoky oak, and plenty of extract and concentration. It would be hard not to believe that these wines will age well for 10–15 years. The 1985 and 1984 are the two most recent stars in the Grace Family Vineyard crown. The 1984 is more open and opulent than the altogether classic 1985, which tasted closed and very oaky but deep and promising if cellared for 5–7 years. However, the price of $50 plus a bottle is ridiculous.

GRAND CRU VINEYARDS (SONOMA)

1984 Cabernet Sauvignon	Sonoma	B	65
1987 Chenin Blanc	Sonoma	A	82
1987 Sauvignon Blanc	Sonoma	A	77

While this winery has made some interesting late-harvest wines from Gewürztraminer, the overall quality of the wines has been average. The Cabernet Sauvignon has had impressively deep color, but the astringency is excessive for the amount of fruit. This has been a consistent problem with all the vintages I have tasted. The 1987 Sauvignon Blanc is adequate, but again fairly one-dimensional and unexciting. Perhaps the best wine is the Chenin Blanc, which is made in a fairly dry but fresh, crisp style that emphasizes good melony, floral fruit.

GREEN AND RED VINEYARD (NAPA)

Except for their lovely white Zinfandel, I have not seen a wine from Green and Red Vineyards for several years, but this small winery, which launched its first wine in 1977, has a good reputation for producing Zinfandel from the Chiles Valley in Napa. Perhaps I have been unlucky, but the wines I have tasted have not made me want to return to this winery for my Zinfandel.

GRGICH HILLS CELLARS (NAPA)

1983 Cabernet Sauvignon	Napa	C	85
1984 Cabernet Sauvignon	Napa	C	90

1985 Chardonnay	Napa	C	89
1986 Chardonnay	Napa	C	90
1987 Fumé Blanc	Napa	B	86
1984 Zinfandel	Alex. Vly.	B	90

Despite the rather bold pricing for the wines from Grgich Hills, the quality is in the bottle. Run by Miljenko Grgich, who obtained fame but not fortune while making the wines at Château Montelena in the early seventies, this winery does a splendid job with its barrel-fermented, fresh, rich Chardonnays, of which the 1985 and 1986 are as good as they get. Although it is with the Chardonnay that most people associate the Grgich name, the winery also makes a rich yet graceful and refined Sauvignon Blanc that always seems to have the taste of pineapples and figs. Grgich also produces one of the better Zinfandels from old vines in Alexander Valley, a very intense, rich, full-bodied wine that is never heavy to taste but bursts with berry fruit. As for the Cabernet Sauvignon, the best vintages have been the 1980, 1982, and the newly released 1984, which looks to be the best yet made at Grgich. It is an extremely rich, blackcurrant-scented, full-bodied wine intertwined with the scent of oak and understated herbaceous notes. Opulent and quite full, it is a wine that can be drunk now or cellared for 7–10 years.

GROTH VINEYARDS AND WINERY (NAPA)

1984 Cabernet Sauvignon	Napa	B	92
1985 Cabernet Sauvignon	Napa	B	91
1985 Chardonnay	Napa	B	85
1986 Chardonnay	Napa	B	82
1986 Sauvignon Blanc	Napa	A	84

This is another winery in California that has reached the top before it is even a decade old. Groth has leaped into the top ranks of Cabernet Sauvignon producers for no other reason than the owners, Dennis and Judy Groth, had the shrewd sense to hire away from Villa Mount Eden the inspired winemaker Nils Venge. He is also one of Napa Valley's nice guys. While at Villa Mount Eden, Venge had fashioned some legendary Napa Cabernets, particularly the 1974, 1978, and 1980. His arrival at Groth in 1982 subsequently resulted in the release of a very fine 1982, a good 1983, and spectacular wines in 1984 and 1985. There are also reserve wines from both vineyards, which have been aged a longer time in French oak. To the winery's credit, the prices have remained reasonable, given wines of such compelling flavors and aromas. A barrel sample I tasted of the 1986 Cabernet Sauvignon shows there has been no drop in quality despite the increased fame and good fortune that have been directed at the Groth Winery. If the Groth portfolio of wines has a slight weakness, it is perhaps the Chardonnay. Oaky and sometimes lacking fruit in its midrange, it is a pleasant rather than sublime example of Napa Chardonnay. On the other hand, the Sauvignon Blanc shows a touch of oak and lush, well-delineated Sauvignon fruit in vintages such as 1986.

GUENOC WINERY (LAKE COUNTY)

1984 Cabernet Sauvignon	Lake	A	82
1985 Cabernet Sauvignon Premier Cuvée	Guenoc Valley	A	85
1986 Chardonnay Premier Cuvée	Guenoc Valley	A	84
1985 Merlot	Guenoc Valley	A	84
1984 Petite Sirah	Lake	A	84
1985 Petite Sirah	Guenoc Valley	A	84
1983 Victorian Proprietary Red Wine	Guenoc Valley	A	85
1985 Zinfandel	Guenoc Valley	A	85
1985 Zinfandel	Lake	A	84

This is a reliable source for finding good-quality wines at reasonable prices. In particular, the Zinfandel, Petite Sirah, Merlot, and Chardonnay tend to do well consistently in my tastings against wines that are twice the price. The Cabernet Sauvignon sometimes has a tendency to be too vegetal to merit a high rating, but certainly the 1984 and 1985 showed more ripeness and plump, berrylike fruit than some of the prior vintages. The style for all the red wines is similar—the wines are soft, fat, and delicious to drink while young. Production is creeping toward 100,000 cases as the winery draws more and more grapes from its 270-acre vineyard on a ranch that once belonged to Lillie Langtry. The winery launched a proprietary red wine in 1983 called Victorian (a 73% Merlot, 23% Cabernet Sauvignon, 2% Petite Sirah, and 2% Cabernet Franc blend). Also, the better lots are now being designated by the words "Premier Cuvée" on the label.

GUNDLACH-BUNDSCHU WINERY (SONOMA)

1982 Cabernet Sauvignon Rhine Farm Reserve	Sonoma	B	88
1984 Cabernet Sauvignon Rhine Farm Vyd.	Sonoma	B	87
1985 Cabernet Sauvignon Rhine Farm Vyd.	Sonoma	B	90
1986 Chardonnay Sangiacomo	Sonoma	B	79
1986 Chardonnay Sonoma	Sonoma	B	72
1986 Gewürztraminer	Sonoma	A	72
1984 Merlot Rhine Farm Vyd.	Sonoma	B	87
1985 Merlot Rhine Farm Vyd.	Sonoma	B	86
1985 Zinfandel Rhine Farm Vyd.	Sonoma	A	85

This is one of Sonoma's oldest wineries, originally founded in 1858 and resurrected by the Bundschu family in 1973. Production has crept up toward 50,000 cases with nearly all of the top wine made from the winery's 110-acre home property called Rhine Farm. The quality in the late seventies and early eighties was spotty, although I remember drinking a stunning 1980 Merlot that was still aging extremely well when I last tasted it in 1988. However, the vintages in the eighties, particularly for the red wines, have shown a style that is impressively rich, full-bodied, intense, and loaded with rich fruit. Much of the vegetal character that plagued some of the Merlots and Cabernets in the late seventies has been eliminated completely. The top new releases include the 1985s and 1984s from the Rhine Farm Vineyard, which show fat, rich flavors, full body, and robust, powerful finishes. The Merlot, and even more so the Cabernet Sauvignon, tend to have the very intense coffee, chocolaty character that seems to come from the Rhine Farm Vineyard. Barrel samples of the 1986s indicated that the quality has continued to be maintained at a very high level. The winery has also turned out a seductively supple, raspberry-scented 1985 Zinfandel that will drink nicely over the next 3–4 years. As wonderfully rich, fleshy, and muscular as the red wines tend to be, the white wines are still rather compact, lean wines lacking personality. For shrewd shoppers, Gundlach-Bundschu often makes small lots of nonvintage Sonoma white and red table wine, which, at less than $4 a bottle, tend to be well made and an excellent value.

HACIENDA WINE CELLARS (SONOMA)

1983 Cabernet Sauvignon	Sonoma	B	84
1984 Cabernet Sauvignon	Sonoma	B	86
1986 Chardonnay Clair de Lune	Sonoma	B	85
1987 Chenin Blanc	Sonoma	A	85

This modest-sized winery with a production of under 30,000 cases makes one of California's best Chenin Blancs, but unfortunately the market for such tasty, delicate, and flowery wines seems limited. The Chardonnay called Clair de Lune can be the winery's best wine, showing floral- and apple-scented fruit in a medium- to full-bodied, restrained character. The Cabernet Sauvignon has been spotty for the last decade, but I noticed that the 1983 is surprisingly rich and fruity without the hollowness that plagues so many wines from this vintage. Its smooth, tasty flavors suggested to me that it should be drunk over the next 3–4 years. Even better is the 1984 Cabernet, which shows a fuller-bodied, more opulent texture, and some bold, blackcurranty, cedary flavors. This is a good Sonoma winery that for one reason or another does not quite seem to get the publicity it deserves.

HANDLEY (MENDOCINO)

N.V. Brut Sparkling Wine	Mendocino	B	85
1986 Chardonnay	Dry Creek	B	87

While much publicity has been lavished on the Louis Roederer (of French champagne fame) Sparkling Wine venture in Mendocino's Anderson Valley, this small winery is making a very tasty, complex, elegant, wheat-thin–flavored sparkling wine that is clearly better than the great majority of California bubbly. If that is not enough news, the 1986 Chardonnay exhibits rich, stylish apple and citrus fruit, medium to full body, excellent balance, and a generous touch of toasty oak. This looks to be a new winery with a serious commitment to quality wine.

HANNA WINERY (SONOMA)

1985 Cabernet Sauvignon	Sonoma	B	84
1986 Chardonnay	Sonoma	B	87
1987 Chardonnay	Sonoma	B	88
1987 Sauvignon Blanc	Sonoma	B	85

This new winery, with its artistic and colorful high-tech label, entered the market with three relatively impressive wines. Certainly the 1987 and 1986 Chardonnays will get anyone's attention. Judiciously oaked with an abundance of pineapple, hazelnut, and other tropical-fruit flavors, these lush but crisp, medium- to full-bodied Chardonnays indicate that Hanna is quite serious about its winemaking. The 1987 Sauvignon Blanc shows more flavor and body than most, and while the 1985 Cabernet Sauvignon is not one of the leaders, its well-focused, pure, blackcurrant fruitiness, medium to full body, and overall harmony show good winemaking, and its potential to age for another 7–8 years.

HANZELL WINERY (SONOMA)

1983 Cabernet Sauvignon	Sonoma	C	?
1984 Chardonnay	Sonoma	C	?
1985 Chardonnay	Sonoma	C	?
1982 Pinot Noir	Sonoma	C	84
1983 Pinot Noir	Sonoma	C	72
1984 Pinot Noir	Sonoma	C	55

Hanzell Winery has somewhat of a cult following for its wines, but I have found the prices to be high and the quality to be inconsistent. I loved the 1983 Chardonnay produced here, but one bottle of the 1984 tasted too vegetal and cumbersome in style, and the other showed huge amounts of oak and buttery fruit with little of the vegetal quality. Will the real 1984 Chardonnay please come forth? The 1985, tasted only once, also seemed off. As for the Pinot Noirs, they have their admirers, but I am not one of them. They again seem to be dominated by rather raw vegetal characteristics, with an excess of tannin in the finish. Perhaps they will age into something more sublime, but I wouldn't gamble on them. The 1984 is particularly poor. The same charge can be leveled at the 1983 Cabernet Sauvignon, an impressively complex wine to smell and look at, but the tannin level is so elevated I found it impossible to evaluate.

HAVENS (NAPA)

1985 Merlot	Napa	B	85
1985 Merlot Reserve	Napa	C	89
1986 Merlot	Napa	C	87
1986 Merlot Reserve Truchard Vyd.	Napa	C	89

I know little about this producer, but certainly the quality of these Merlots would make a believer out of anyone. All four wines showed a talented winemaker's hand in extracting the ripe, velvety, coffee, herb, and chocolate scented and flavored character out of the Merlot grape and in giving the wine the right amount of spicy oak. The 1986s tend to be a bit bolder, more muscular, and bigger-boned wines than the stylish, graceful 1985s. All of them can be drunk with great pleasure now, but for extended cellaring of 7–10 years, the smoky, fleshy, ripe 1986 Reserve gets the nod over the wonderfully lush, plummy, cedary 1985 Reserve. The regular bottlings from each vintage are also very good with the 1986 showing slightly more depth and power than the 1985. All four wines should prove big sellers given their quality.

HAYWOOD WINERY (SONOMA)

1984 Cabernet Sauvignon	Sonoma	B	85
1985 Cabernet Sauvignon	Sonoma	B	86
1985 Chardonnay	Sonoma	B	82

1986 Chardonnay	Sonoma	B	84
1985 Chardonnay Reserve	Sonoma	B	78
1984 Zinfandel	Sonoma	B	86
1985 Zinfandel	Sonoma	B	85
1986 Zinfandel	Sonoma	B	85

Haywood Winery makes adequate Chardonnays, good to very good Zinfandels, and very good, highly extracted, tannic Cabernet Sauvignons from its 90-acre hillside vineyard above the town of Sonoma. While some of the wines in the early eighties were compact and seemed to be deficient in fruit, but not tannin, the recent vintages of 1984 and 1985 have shown a richer, deeper, berry fruit married nicely with toasty oak. They have not forsaken any of their tannins, a hallmark of this producer's red wines, although the soft, effusively fruity 1986 Zinfandel may indicate a change in style. While this is not one of the leaders in California, the wines are realistically priced, and the potential of the Zinfandels looks to be very good.

HEITZ CELLARS (NAPA)

1983 Cabernet Sauvignon	Napa	B	75
1982 Cabernet Sauvignon Bella Oaks Vineyard	Napa	C	86
1983 Cabernet Sauvignon Bella Oaks Vineyard	Napa	C	84
1982 Cabernet Sauvignon Martha's Vineyard	Napa	C	88
1983 Cabernet Sauvignon Martha's Vineyard	Napa	C	88
1984 Cabernet Sauvignon Martha's Vineyard	Napa	C	90
1985 Chardonnay	Napa	B	65
1986 Chardonnay	Napa	B	85

Based on the uniqueness and greatness of one wine, the mint- and eucalyptus-scented Heitz Cabernet Sauvignon from Martha's Vineyard, this winery has become one of the legendary names of Napa

Valley. There have been some exceptional Martha's Vineyard Cabernet Sauvignons, the 1968, 1970, and 1974 for example, but some vintages have missed the mark completely, including a disappointing 1978, and good but hardly thrilling wines for the price in 1980 and 1981. However, from the 1982 vintage on, the wines look very impressive with the depth and 10–15 years of aging potential one expects of a great Napa Valley Cabernet Sauvignon. Even so, it remains hard to justify some rather mediocre wines that have come from Heitz, including an odd Grignolino, inconsistent Chardonnays such as the moldy, dirty 1985 and 1983, and some inexcusably feeble Zinfandels and Pinot Noirs. However, the high price, the allure of the Martha's Vineyard name, and the mystique of Joe Heitz, as well as the outstanding, even profound quality in the top vintages, keep people coming back for the taste of a Heitz wine. While Heitz may be an institution in Napa Valley, I still wonder how such a great Cabernet Sauvignon winemaker can show so much inconsistency and little ability with white varietals that seem to be made rather easily elsewhere.

HESS COLLECTION WINERY (NAPA)

1983 Cabernet Sauvignon Mt. Veeder	B	87
1985 Cabernet Sauvignon Mt. Veeder	B	89
1983 Cabernet Sauvignon Reserve Mt. Veeder	C	90
1984 Cabernet Sauvignon Reserve Mt. Veeder	C	95
1986 Chardonnay Mt. Veeder	B	86

This new winery's debut releases from its vineyard on Mt. Veeder suggest that its Cabernets may turn out to be among the very best made in California. Certainly a vertical look at the three vintages released in the last year reveals a rich, intense, powerful mountain style of Cabernet that has the extract of the wines of the now-famous Randy Dunn, an elevated percentage of new French oak, rich, ripe, but not astringent tannins, and exceptional aging potential. Excellent Cabernets from California's 1983 vintage are few and far between, as most wines are deficient in fruit while being excessively tannic. Hess produced two excellent 1983s that have great midrange fruit to carry the tannins. The regular cuvée of 1983 is opaque, loaded with fruit, full-bodied, and can be drunk now or cellared for a decade. It is a classic Napa Cabernet. The 1983 Reserve may turn out to be the wine of the vintage. My notes contain comments such as "great stuff, unbelievable richness and fruit, the Dunn of Mt. Veeder." It is a super 1983 that should be at its best between 1992 and 2005. The 1984 Reserve has mind-blowing richness. It held up in the bottle for over six days and showed impeccable balance, fleshy, rich new oak with gobs of pure blackcurrant fruit, sensational length, and 15 or more years of aging potential. It is a monumental effort and astonishingly rich, well-balanced Napa Mountain Cabernet Sauvignon. The regular cuvée of 1985 is rich, broodingly opaque, backward, and has outstanding depth and length. Like the Reserve, it just needs time. All the 1985s and 1984s should be at their best between 1993 and 2005. As for the 1986 Chardonnay, it has quite a bit of oak showing through, but it does have just enough buttery fruit to carry the oak. What a way to open a new winery—with wines such as these! Hess Collection would appear to be one of California's bright new stars.

HIDDEN CELLARS (MENDOCINO)

1985 Chevrignon d'Or—Bailey J. Lovin	Mendocino	B	87
1985 Johannisberg Riesling Late Harvest—Bailey J. Lovin	Mendocino	B	87
1986 Johannisberg Riesling Late Harvest—Bailey J. Lovin	Mendocino	B	90
1986 Sauvignon Blanc	Sonoma	A	85
1984 Zinfandel Pacini Vyd.	Mendocino	B	85
1985 Zinfandel Pacini Vyd.	Mendocino	B	85
1986 Zinfandel Pacini Vyd.	Mendocino	B	86

This winery, with production of just over 10,000 cases, started in 1981 and has quickly gained a following for its very well made dry Sauvignon Blancs, its elegant, graceful, richly fruity, balanced, supple Zinfandels, and sweet late-harvest Rieslings, as well as its homage to the French district of Sauternes called Chevrignon d'Or. There has been some Chardonnay and Cabernet Sauvignon made here, but it has been one-dimensional and lacking the interest of the other wines produced by Hidden Cellars. The winery believes in utilizing Mendocino grapes and has done quite a good job with them. For lovers of nectar, both the apple- and peach-scented 1986 and 1985 Johannisberg Rieslings Late Harvest from the Bailey J. Lovin Vineyard exhibit very rich, sweet flavors, and quite a bit of botrytis (the fungus that makes Riesling so special) in this decadent, rich, intense style. The Chevrignon d'Or is a Sauvignon Blanc and Semillon late-harvest wine with a very unctuous texture and heavy, woody, rich, slightly vegetal flavors. It seemed to work in 1985, but I suspect some tasters might find it too overblown for its own good. Don't ignore either this winery's dry Sauvignon Blanc, which shows a good deal of flavor and character, or its stylish Zinfandel, particularly the 1986 and 1985 from the Pacini Vineyard.

THE WILLIAM HILL WINERY (NAPA)

1984 Cabernet Sauvignon Reserve	Napa	C	86
1985 Cabernet Sauvignon Reserve	Napa	C	90
1986 Cabernet Sauvignon Reserve	Napa	C	88
1985 Cabernet Sauvignon Silver Label	Napa	B	85
1986 Chardonnay Reserve	Napa	C	89
1987 Chardonnay Silver Label	Napa	B	85

Bill Hill, a slim, blond-haired man from Oklahoma with a slight resemblance to country singer John Denver, has been a fervent believer in vineyards in the Mayacamas Mountains for making the winery's two wines, a Cabernet Sauvignon and a Chardonnay, both of which come in two versions. For consumers desirous of a more obviously fruity, supple wine ready for immediate drinking, Hill offers a Silver Label Chardonnay and a Silver Label Cabernet Sauvignon. In particular, the 1985 Silver Label Cabernet Sauvignon may have been the best he has made to date, with delicious, well-focused, blackcurrant fruit that lingers on the palate. Despite its accessibility, I wouldn't hesitate to cellar this wine for another 7–8 years. The wines for which Hill has put forth his greatest efforts include Reserve Gold Label Cabernet Sauvignons, which were launched with an outstanding wine in the 1978 vintage. There has not been a disappointing wine since, with some great wines produced not only in 1978 but in 1980, and of course more recently in 1985 and 1986. Certainly the 1979, 1981, 1982, 1983, and 1984 are all very good Cabernets with at least a decade of aging potential. However, there is no doubting that the 1985 is the best Reserve Cabernet Sauvignon he has made to date, with exceptional richness, great balance, and a style not unlike a textbook St.-Julien from Bordeaux. These are Cabernet Sauvignons that clearly improve in the bottle as the 1978 and 1980 have proven, and I have no doubt the Reserve Cabernets have a life span of 15–20 years in the top vintages.

As for the Chardonnays, the style of Bill Hill has fluctuated considerably. His early Chardonnays in the late seventies and early eighties were so overwhelmingly oaky that they tasted out of balance when released and only got more grotesque as they aged. Despite Bill Hill's great belief in barrel-fermented, toasty, oaky Chardonnays, one taste of the 1980 today will prove what a failure these wines were. He must have realized it because he turned around 180°, making wines with much crisper acidities and the oak kept well in check. Some of these wines turned out to be too one-dimensional and innocuous, but in 1986 he seems to have gotten the blend just right with his Reserve Chardonnay. It has the toasty vanillin oak that one looks for in a great white burgundy, but it has gobs of well-focused and delineated fruit, and a sort of hazelnut, buttery taste that gives it excellent complexity. It is certainly the best William Hill Chardonnay made to date. The William Hill Winery, in spite of its tendency to publicly overstate, via advertising, the case for its wines, is one of California's leading wineries when it comes to age-worthy, classic Napa Valley Cabernet Sauvignon; and if Bill Hill can build on the success of his 1986 Reserve Chardonnay, it will quickly gain ground on the top echelon of Chardonnay producers.

LOUIS HONIG (NAPA)

1986 Sauvignon Blanc	Napa	A	85
1987 Sauvignon Blanc	Napa	A	86

There is something admirable about a winery that decides to make 10,000 cases of only one wine—and it is Sauvignon Blanc. From their own 70-acre vineyard near Rutherford, the Honigs make one of the richer, fuller styles of Sauvignon that offers subtle herbaceous-scented fruit, full body, a good touch of toasty oak, and a lush texture. It is one of the few California Sauvignons that can age past 1–2 years. The 1987 has an extra element of freshness because it is a year younger, consequently the marginally higher score.

HOP KILN WINERY (SONOMA)

1983 Zinfandel	Russian River	B	73
1984 Zinfandel	Russian River	B	84

I have not seen a recent vintage of the wine that this producer is famous for, Petite Sirah, but among the two most recent Zinfandels, the 1983 was quite mediocre and lacking the rich, berry, supple fruit for which Zinfandel is famous. Perhaps the vintage was the culprit in 1983. The 1984 vintage produced a riper and fruitier Zinfandel from the Russian River Valley that should be drunk over the next 2–3 years.

THE ROBERT HUNTER VINEYARD (SONOMA)

1984 Brut de Noir	Sonoma	B	84

I have not seen a vintage of the Robert Hunter sparkling wine since the rather good, cleanly made, technically correct 1984 Brut de Noir. The wines to date from this 8,000-case winery have been attractively packaged but rather unexciting. Perhaps the 1984 signals higher aspirations for quality.

HUSCH VINEYARDS (MENDOCINO)

1983 Pinot Noir	Anderson Valley	B	68
1987 La Ribera Blanc	Mendocino	A	79
1985 La Ribera Cabernet Sauvignon	Mendocino	A	80

The idea of an inexpensive, blended white wine is good, but at nearly $8 a bottle, La Ribera Blanc, usually made from a blend of Chardonnay and Sauvignon Blanc, is priced too high. At $5 it would be a good value. On the other hand, the soft, Beaujolais-styled La Ribera Cabernet Sauvignon is light, fruity, attractive, and meant to be drunk within 2–3 years of the vintage. I do not recommend the vegetal, thin, unattractive Pinot Noir. The winery also makes an uninteresting Gewürztraminer, the 1986, for example, being dull and lacking varietal character.

INGLENOOK VINEYARDS (NAPA)

1983 Cabernet Sauvignon Reserve Cask	Napa	C	86
1984 Cabernet Sauvignon Reserve Cask	Napa	C	87
1983 Charbono Estate	Napa	B	84
1984 Charbono Estate	Napa	B	86
1986 Chardonnay Estate	Napa	B	85
1986 Chardonnay Reserve Cask	Napa	B	87
1984 Merlot Reserve Cask	Napa	C	84
1984 Reunion Red Table Wine	Napa	D	87
1986 Sauvignon Blanc Estate	Napa	B	84
1987 Sauvignon Blanc Estate	Napa	B	85

Founded in 1879, Inglenook is one of the historic, as well as legendary, producers of California wine. In fact, the old vintages of Cabernet Sauvignon made in the fifties and early sixties by the late John Daniel proved to the world that exceptional Cabernet Sauvignon could be made in California's Napa Valley. When Inglenook was purchased by the gigantic Heublein conglomerate in the mid-sixties, production expanded and it was apparent to everyone that the quality suffered immensely. In the eighties there has been renewed effort to strengthen the quality of the winery's top wines, such as the Reserve Cask Chardonnays and Cabernet Sauvignons, and introduce some new high-quality proprietary wines such as the Reunion Red Table Wine and Gravion Proprietary White Wine. The result has been a succession of very good to excellent but not yet outstanding Reserve Cask Cabernet Sauvignons starting with the 1980 and most recently exemplified by the rich, slightly minty, well-structured but dense and concentrated 1984 Reserve Cask Cabernet Sauvignon. In addition, the Chardonnays have taken on a bit more flavor intensity, but the winery still seems to be victimized by the philosophy of playing it too safe and wanting to produce very good but not great wine. Perhaps the unreleased Reserve Cabernet Sauvignons and Reunion from the exceptional 1985 vintage and the powerful vintages of 1986 and 1987 will show even greater flavor dimension and a bolder style. The winery's Reunion, introduced in 1983, is an understated, polite, elegant wine, and the Gravion, the winery's attempt to imitate a white Graves, is good rather than thrilling. One of the best values from Inglenook is its Charbono, although this particular wine has little glamour in the eyes of consumers. Nevertheless, it is a robust, earthy, full-bodied wine with a good deal of character and richness. Both the 1983 and 1984 show a rich, hearty, satisfying character. The Reserve Merlot introduced in the 1983 vintage is good and certainly shows the emphasis on a higher-quality style of wine than what was released in the seventies, but one wishes it were a bit fleshier and riper. In conclusion, Inglenook, such an important viticultural institution in not only Napa Valley but all of California, is making a comeback, and the wines once again deserve attention from consumers.

IRON HORSE RANCH AND VINEYARDS (SONOMA)

1984 Blanc de Noirs	Sonoma	C	88
1984 Blanc de Blancs	Sonoma	C	89
1985 Brut	Sonoma	C	86
1985 Blanc de Noirs Wedding Cuvée	Sonoma	C	87
1985 Brut Rosé	Sonoma	C	90
1985 Cabernet Sauvignon	Sonoma	B	84
1986 Chardonnay	Sonoma	B	73
1986 Fumé Blanc	Alexander Vly.	B	85
1987 Fumé Blanc	Alexander Vly.	B	85

Despite all of the hoopla over the investment in California made by famous champagne firms from France, the best sparkling wine being made in all of California at present comes from Iron Horse, not from one of the French-American hybrid operations. Whether it is the light-salmon-colored Blanc de Noirs with its delicate, berry-scented bouquet, and crisp, dry, medium- to full-bodied flavors; or the fresh Wedding Cuvée; or the winery's delicious, dry, flavorful Brut; the quality of sparkling wines being made at this winery is very high, and the packaging gorgeous, if that matters to you. In fact, Iron Horse has crossed a threshold of quality with the 1985 Brut Rosé. Obviously modeled after the deep salmon-colored rosé of Dom Pérignon, this wine astounded me with its flavor and richness. Rather full, deep, and complex, it has to be the best sparkling wine yet made in California. The other knockout sparkling wine is the 1984 Blanc de Blancs. It exhibits flavor and finesse, has a lovely, creamy apple-butter richness, tiny, persistent bubbles, and a long dry finish. The winery has also enjoyed much success with its Fumé Blanc, which shows a touch of oak and complex, medium-bodied, subtly herbaceous flavors. While these are the most successful wines made by Iron Horse, I have been disappointed with the tart, lean Chardonnay. For example, the 1986 Chardonnay tastes more like a French Colombard than a California Chardonnay. In addition, the Cabernet Sauvignons here have tended to be extremely light and innocuous, although the 1985 showed more midrange depth and fruit than any vintage to date. However, it is far outdistanced by the other top California Cabernets. To me, this is a winery whose sparkling wine should not be missed, and if you like Fumé Blanc, certainly Iron Horse offers one of the better ones. Production has inched up toward 30,000 cases.

JAEGER-INGLEWOOD VINEYARD (NAPA)

1982 Merlot Inglewood	Napa	B	83
1983 Merlot Inglewood	Napa	B	75

This small Merlot specialist is the inspiration of Bill Jaeger, whose family is among the major growers of Napa Valley and who also have large shares in both Freemark Abbey and Rutherford Hills wineries. Production is limited to 4,000 cases of Merlot, which to date have shown deep color but have lacked the rich, chewy, succulent texture that a top-class Merlot should exhibit. The 1983 tastes surprisingly compact with narrowly focused flavors, a great deal of acidity, and a certain hollowness. The 1982 has a bit fatter texture, but again it lacks overall flavor dimension and length.

JEKEL VINEYARD (MONTEREY)

1983 Cabernet Sauvignon	Monterey	B	?
1982 Cabernet Sauvignon Private Reserve	Monterey	B	?

1985 Chardonnay	Monterey	B	85

1984 Chardonnay Private Reserve	Monterey	B	86

1987 Johannisberg Riesling	Monterey	A	86

This 50,000-case winery was founded in 1978 and has quickly become one of the staunchest advocates of the wines from the cooler climate of Monterey County south of San Francisco. To date, there seems to be no doubt that Monterey has turned out some of the best of the dryer styles of California Riesling, and at Jekel in vintages such as 1987, the wine shows crisp, floral, applelike fruit, steely texture, and crisp, zesty acidity; it could easily compete with some of the better Spätlese German wines in the market. The Chardonnay is made in a fairly bold, oaky, dramatic style with a great deal of flavor. The 1985 is quite tightly knit but exhibits good balance and length. The 1984 Reserve is an extroverted, spicy, rich, full wine that is not for the shy. While the winery is very proud of its intense, rich, and one might say, voluptuously fruity and dramatic Cabernet Sauvignons, the fact cannot be ignored that the wines have an intense vegetal or cooked-asparagus character that I find to be a major drawback. Some critics have expressed praise for this style of wine, but for me it is an annoying, unpleasant characteristic of virtually all the Cabernet Sauvignon made from grapes grown in Monterey County. A vertical tasting of all the Jekel Cabernets back through 1978 certainly indicates that it does not go away as the wine ages in the bottle. I just don't believe that Monterey can turn out high-quality Cabernet Sauvignon that is not marked and/or dominated by the smell of excessive vegetation. Therein lies the problem with the 1982 Reserve Cabernet Sauvignon and 1983 regular bottling.

JEPSON VINEYARD (MENDOCINO)

1985 Champagne	Mendocino	C	79

1987 Chardonnay	Mendocino	B	83

1987 Sauvignon Blanc	Mendocino	B	82

This winery, dedicated to producing only white wine (and a brandy from Colombard grapes that has not yet been released), makes fresh, light, crisp, and clean fruity white wines that should be drunk within a year of their release. The idea is to deliver plenty of uncomplicated, unadorned varietal fruit up front, and this winery manages to do just that. The French may have problems with the name of Jepson's 1985 Champagne, but as California sparklers go, it is light, tart, fruity, and clean with good length and a lingering effervescence.

JOHNSON-TURNBULL VINEYARDS (NAPA)

1985 Cabernet Sauvignon	Napa	B	83
1986 Cabernet Sauvignon	Napa	B	86

This small winery with a production of only 2,000 cases draws its only wine, a Cabernet Sauvignon, from a 20-acre vineyard located between Oakville and Rutherford in Napa. From the first vintage, the 1979, the wine has had a striking resemblance to the minty, eucalyptus style made famous by another Napa winery, Heitz, renowned for its Martha's Vineyard Cabernet Sauvignon. While the Johnson-Turnbull wine does not have quite the depth of the Heitz Martha's Vineyard, it does have the telltale characteristics of that wine, and the best vintages to date have been the 1982 and 1986. For whatever reason, the 1985 did not show as well in my tastings as I had expected, exhibiting a restrained, compact, ungenerous character, and very closed-in, hard, tannic flavors. Certainly the 1986 looks to be better balanced, and with more fruit and character. If anyone is lucky enough to see any of the old vintages, such as the 1982 or 1984, they are certainly worth trying, but be warned, the intense, minty, eucalyptus style of this wine does not please everyone.

JORDAN VINEYARD AND WINERY (SONOMA)

1984 Cabernet Sauvignon Estate	Alex. Vly.	C	85
1985 Chardonnay	Alex. Vly.	C	68
1986 Chardonnay	Alex. Vly.	C	78

A huge success story, the Jordan Vineyard, which was founded in 1972 and now boasts a production of over 80,000 cases of wine, leaped to the attention of wine consumers with its herbaceous, supple, seductive 1976 Cabernet Sauvignon. More recently a Chardonnay was added to the winery's portfolio. Backed by an intense publicity program, and the spectacular château built by multimillionaire Thomas Jordan, this winery has never been out of the public eye, but I have often wondered if the wines are as good as they should be. Although the early Cabernet Sauvignons have aged very quickly, they were charming wines filled with berry-scented, herbal fruit, made in a full-bodied, lush style that provided plenty of appeal. The 1976 is now fading, but certainly other vintages such as the 1979, 1980, and 1982 are still drinking well. As for the 1984 Cabernet Sauvignon Estate, it is a good rather than great wine, with plenty of toasty oak, ripe berry fruit, and a telltale weedy character that has to date been an integral part of all of Jordan's Cabernet Sauvignons. If the Cabernets have ranged from good to very good in quality, the Chardonnays have been a huge disappointment and painfully overpriced. One-dimensional, thin, overly acidified, and lacking depth and character, they are wines that I find appallingly deficient in character and interest. One is likely to see the Jordan wines on restaurant wine lists as the winery has been remarkably effective in penetrating many of the top restaurants in the United States. The Cabernet is ideal for such lists, but be forewarned, most vintages should generally be consumed within 6–7 years as they do have questionable longevity.

CHÂTEAU JULIEN (MONTEREY)

1985 Chardonnay	Monterey	B	77
1986 Chardonnay	Monterey	B	86
1984 Chardonnay Reserve Cobblestone Vyd.	Monterey	B	78
1986 Emerald Bay Montonnay Seafood Wine	Monterey	A	73
1984 Merlot	Santa Barbara	B	64
1987 Sauvignon Blanc	Monterey	A	86
1987 Semillon	Monterey	B	85

Château Julien, a new winery that launched its first wines in 1983, has felt the difficulties and birth pangs of trying to get established. The inconsistencies noted in the first several vintages seem to have been corrected, and the newest batch of wines I tasted showed as much character and potential as any released to date. These include a deli-cious, richly fruity, melon- and fig-scented as well as flavored 1987 Sauvignon Blanc, a creamy, lush 1987 Semillon, and a very good, vibrant, effusively fruity, medium- to full-bodied 1986 Chardonnay. Some of the older releases, especially the red wines, should be avoided, but fortunately, the latest crop of white wine may signal a new era of higher-quality wines from Château Julien. I'm sure comedians have had fun with the Château's inexpensive, generic white wine blend called Montonnay—the seafood wine.

KALIN CELLARS (MARIN)

1983 Cabernet Sauvignon	Potter Valley	C	85
1984 Cabernet Sauvignon	Potter Valley	C	84
1985 Cabernet Sauvignon	Potter Valley	C	86
1986 Chardonnay Cuvée L	Sonoma	C	90
1986 Chardonnay Cuvée MV	Potter Valley	C	89
1985 Cuvée d'Or	California	C	90
1986 Cuvée Rosé Brut Sparkling Wine	California	C	88
1983 Pinot Noir Cuvée WD	Sonoma	C	?
1984 Pinot Noir Cuvée WD	Sonoma	C	88
1985 Sauvignon Blanc	Potter Valley	B	88
1986 Sauvignon Blanc	Potter Valley	B	89
1985 Sauvignon Blanc Reserve	Potter Valley	B	90
1986 Sauvignon Blanc Reserve	Potter Valley	B	?
1986 Semillon	Livermore	B	88

If I were to pick California's two most talented as well as adventurous winemakers, Randall Grahm of Bonny Doon and Terry Leighton of Kalin would unquestionably be my choices. Leighton, a silver-haired, middle-aged professional microbiologist, is himself a paradox. Able to converse knowledgeably about the great wine classics of France, he seems equally talented when discussing the merits of modern-day

Oriental cuisine or rock music. His style of winemaking involves buying fruit that comes from cool microclimates and needs little or no acid adjustment. A great believer in the importance of vineyard and specific types of yeast used to start the fermentation, and who also has a proven distrust for the centrifuge and filtration equipment, Leighton produces a bevy of profound wines that improve dramatically in the bottle. Where does the praise begin? Initially, I thought Leighton to be only a white wine genius, but after five years of studying his wines I have come to understand that his red wines simply are slow to develop.

As for the white wines, the glories of this 5,000-case winery are his separate Cuvées of Chardonnay often designated BL from Potter Valley, and Cuvée L and Cuvée LV from Sonoma. Sometimes there is also a Cuvée D from the well-known Dutton Ranch in Sonoma. Kalin has consistently adhered to the principle of no filtration for fear of removing any of the exquisite flavor from its wines, so all of the Kalin wines have sediment in them. If the Chardonnays from Kalin are among the top half dozen of their type for both quality and aging potential, the Sauvignon Blanc and Semillon are the best made in all of California. Recent vintages such as the 1986, 1985, and 1984 have easily shown the potential to last 7–8 years in the bottle. His Sauvignon Blanc Reserve can be spectacular, as it was in 1984 and 1985, however, I found the 1986 to be totally closed and impossible to evaluate. While most Sauvignon Blancs are bottled early and have a shelf life of 1–3 years after the vintage, Kalin's Sauvignon Blancs seem to come to life after 3–4 years of bottle age, giving every indication of lasting up to a decade—something that is simply incredible for California Sauvignon Blanc. And of course, they are unfiltered.

While I have been impressed by Kalin's Pinot Noirs, I rarely gave them my highest marks. Unfortunately, the wines are released 4–5 years after the vintage and taste promising but tightly knit. For example, the 1983 Pinot Noir Cuvée WD from Sonoma seems to be quite unsettled and closed in, and virtually impossible to evaluate at the present. However, the 1984 Pinot Noir Cuvée WD is showing a breathtaking complexity and exoticism rare in California Pinot Noir. Leighton ferments his Pinot Noir in short, squat wood fermenters (a rarity in California), and in addition to a hot, furious fermentation, punches down 2–4 times a day, uses 30–50% new oak, and neither fines nor filters these wines. A 1980 Pinot Noir Cuvée WD tasted in 1988 next to the 1976 Romanée Conti from France was amazingly close in character to the French wine. As for his Cabernet Sauvignons, they have often been vegetal, but he has changed grape sources and in 1983,

1984, and 1985 made very good Bordeaux-styled, elegant wines from Potter Valley. In 1986 he made 800 cases of a smashing Cabernet Sauvignon with grapes from Sonoma.

Perhaps the most intriguing wines from Leighton to date are his sparkling wine called 1986 Cuvée Rosé and his blend of Semillon and Sauvignon called Cuvée d'Or. A barrel-fermented rosé left on its lees for 9 months, made from 40% Chardonnay and 60% Pinot Noir, and harvested at the end of October from a cool vineyard in Marin County, the 1986 Cuvée Rosé is one of the two most complex and flavorful sparkling wines I have yet to taste from California. When you compare it with most of the sparkling wines from there, its quality and flavor dimension become all the more striking for their breadth and complexity. His barrel-fermented, rich blend of Semillon and Sauvignon called Cuvée d'Or is a knockout wine with exotic aromas of smoky, buttery caramel, coconut, and toasty oak. It is a dead ringer for a top Sauternes such as Suduiraut. Finally, the unmistakable European style of Kalin's wines seems to keep him from getting much publicity in his own state, but these are the wines of a genius, and worth every effort to find in the marketplace.

KARLY WINERY (AMADOR)

1986 Sauvignon Blanc	Amador	A	86
1987 White Zinfandel	Amador	A	84
1985 Zinfandel	Amador	A	87
1986 Zinfandel	Amador	A	86

With a small production of under 5,000 cases, one doesn't see enough of the Karly wines. The two recent Zinfandels from the 1985 and 1986 vintages are absolutely delicious, fruit-filled wines bursting with scents of blackberries and spicy oak as well as showing super depth and ripeness. Overall, the 1985 had crisper acids and merited a slightly higher score. The winery has also shown a good touch with Sauvignon Blanc, making a wine with more body and flavor than the great majority of the innocuous, one-dimensional Sauvignons coming out of California. Perhaps the sleeper wine in the entire portfolio of Karly is its White Zinfandel, which tends to be more lively, flavorful, and vibrant than many of the overly sugared rosés parading under the name of White Zinfandel from California.

ROBERT KEENAN WINERY (NAPA)

1984 Cabernet Sauvignon	Napa	B	84
1985 Cabernet Sauvignon	Napa	B	83
1986 Chardonnay Ann's Vineyard	Napa	B	83
1986 Chardonnay Estate	Napa	B	84
1985 Merlot	Napa	B	82

This winery, established in 1977, developed a loyal following for its highly extracted, aggressively tannic, backward style of wines, which to me tasted too astringent and hard to ever develop into harmonious, pleasure-giving beverages. The excruciatingly painful levels of tannin found in some of the red wines have mellowed significantly with recent vintages as the winery seems to be developing a more consistent and more charming style of red winemaking. Both the 1985 Merlot and Cabernet Sauvignon exhibited deep ruby colors, and the depth of fruit needed to match the tannins, which are considerably tamer and less astringent than in years past. They also exhibit much better balance than in prior vintages. As for the Chardonnay, it still seems a bit compact and chunky without the overall depth of ripe fruit it should have, and with perhaps too much acidity for its own good. Certainly the 1986 and 1985 look to be better than the succession of Chardonnays made in 1982, 1983, and 1984. In 1986, a single-vineyard bottling was offered that tastes lean, tight, and in need of some bottle age in order to round out. Production at the Robert Keenan Winery is now approximately 10,000 cases of wine, virtually all of it made from the family-owned 46-acre vineyard on Spring Mountain.

KENDALL-JACKSON VINEYARD (LAKE)

1984 Cabernet Sauvignon	Lake	B	72
1985 Cabernet Sauvignon	Lake	B	80
1984 Cabernet Sauvignon Cardinale	California	B	73
1986 Chardonnay Barrel-Fermented Proprietor's	California	C	90

1987 Chardonnay Barrel-Fermented Proprietor's	California	C	90
1987 Chardonnay Vintner's Reserve	California	B	88
1987 Muscat Canelli	Lake	A	86
1987 Sauvignon Blanc	Lake	A	85
1986 Syrah Durrel Vyd.	Sonoma	B	88
1986 Zinfandel	Mendocino	A	85
1985 Zinfandel Ciapusci	Mendocino	B	87
1986 Zinfandel Ciapusci	Mendocino	B	87
1985 Zinfandel Mariah	Mendocino	B	87

There is no doubting the ability of this Lake County winery to turn out gorgeously proportioned, lush, fresh, exuberantly fruity white wines. Virtually anything made from a white wine grape such as Muscat, Riesling, Sauvignon Blanc, and Chardonnay is guaranteed to be delicious and popular with consumers. In particular, the Vintner's Reserve Chardonnay for under $10 shows abundant amounts of tropical fruit, a touch of oak, and is made in a very soft, fresh, delicious style. Those who like a bit more buttery popcorn and toasty oak in their wine will adore the Barrel-Fermented Proprietor's Chardonnay in vintages such as 1986 and 1987. In fact, one might argue that Kendall-Jackson's best Chardonnays are among the top dozen made in California. The Sauvignon Blanc, with its mineral and herbaceous fruit, has a freshness and lightness on the palate that makes it very appealing. One also cannot forget the well-crafted Rieslings and the Muscat Canelli made here, the latter of which shows a bit of sweetness, but a wonderful spring-flower-garden fragrance; it should be drunk within a year of the vintage.

On the other hand, the winery seems to overacidify some of its red wines, as they taste tart, often too herbaceous, and vegetal. The brilliant winemaker Jed Steele likens several of his Cabernets to some of the red wines of the Loire Valley, but I have found them rather short and excessively vegetal. Fortunately, one cannot accuse the excellent line of Zinfandels made here of the same propensity. The

Zinfandels range from a gorgeously fruity, lighter style simply called Mendocino, to the single-vineyard Zinfandels that offer more forceful fruitiness, power, and body. Both Zinfandels in the 1985 and 1986 vintages from the Ciapusci and Mariah vineyards are richly textured wines loaded with intense berry fruit, and extremely well balanced. I envision both of them drinking extremely well for another 4–5 years. Lastly, the winery makes small quantities of a superb Syrah from the Durrel Vineyard in Sonoma. Winemaker Steele is a great enthusiast of the Rhône Valley wines, having made several interesting wines when he was at Edmeades from blends of Syrah and Grenache. Only 350 cases of the 1986 Syrah were produced, but it has a wonderful smoky, bacon-fat, peppery, cassislike scent and flavors, is superbly balanced, and is a rich, deep wine with a decade or more of aging potential. The wines of Kendall-Jackson, except for the surprisingly mediocre Cabernets, should stir the interest of most wine consumers. I recommend them highly.

KATHERINE KENNEDY WINERY (SANTA CLARA)

1984 Cabernet Sauvignon	Santa Cruz	B	85

This small winery turns out one wine, Cabernet Sauvignon, and it tends to be sold only in California. It is a good wine with an opaque, deep ruby color, rich, lush, full-bodied flavors, and 5–7 years of aging potential.

KENWOOD VINEYARDS (SONOMA)

1984 Cabernet Sauvignon	Sonoma	B	86
1984 Cabernet Sauvignon Artist Series	Sonoma	C	89
1983 Cabernet Sauvignon Jack London	Sonoma	C	86
1984 Cabernet Sauvignon Jack London	Sonoma	C	88
1986 Chardonnay Beltane Ranch	Sonoma	B	72
1987 Chardonnay Beltane Ranch	Sonoma	B	82
1987 Sauvignon Blanc	Sonoma	A	87

1984 Zinfandel	Sonoma	B	85

1985 Zinfandel	Sonoma	B	84

This winery with a production in excess of 100,000 cases was founded in 1970, and I remember criticizing the early releases as the Chardonnays lacked varietal character, the Sauvignon Blancs tasted of vegetal, thick, unctuous fruit, and the Cabernet Sauvignons were grotesquely heavy, thick, and vegetal. The winery began showing consistent improvement in its wines in the late seventies, and in the eighties the overt vegetal character that plagued so many of its wines in the seventies has virtually completely disappeared. The current lineup of releases represents the highest level of quality I have ever tasted from the Kenwood Winery. The Sauvignon Blanc has moved from its thick, vegetal style to a full-bodied, yet vibrant, well-balanced, delicious wine with crisp, subtly herbaceous fruit, a touch of oak, and wonderful flavor length and richness on the palate. The Chardonnays still taste too chunky and lack true varietal character, but they are correct if erring too much on the simple side. The biggest improvement has been with the winery's Cabernet Sauvignons, which have lost none of their intense, full-bodied richness and unctuous as well as voluptuous qualities, but now the vegetal character has been replaced by deep chocolaty, plummy fruit, and a toasty vanillin, spicy character from the judicious use of oak barrels. Furthermore, the winery's top-of-the-line Artist Series Cabernet Sauvignon and Jack London Cabernet Sauvignon have at least 8–10 years of aging potential. Kenwood made good Cabernets in the troublesome 1983 vintage, and excellent wines with opulent flavors in 1984. This is a winery that after almost two decades of practice is making its best wines to date; I can hardly wait for the release of the 1985 and 1986 Cabernets. Lastly, the winery also produces a good rather than outstanding Zinfandel from Sonoma Valley; both the 1984 and 1985 show moderately intense berry fruit and subtle herbs in the nose, with good depth, full body, and plenty of ripeness with no rough edges. They should last at least 3–4 years.

KISTLER VINEYARDS (SONOMA)

1985 Cabernet Sauvignon Kistler Vyd.	Sonoma	C	92

1986 Cabernet Sauvignon Kistler Vyd.	Sonoma	C	90

| 1986 Chardonnay Durrel Vyd. | Sonoma | B | 86 |

| 1987 Chardonnay Durrel Vyd. | Sonoma | B | 87 |

| 1986 Chardonnay Dutton | Sonoma | C | 90 |

| 1987 Chardonnay Dutton | Sonoma | C | 93 |

| 1986 Chardonnay Kistler Vyd. | Sonoma | C | 90 |

| 1987 Chardonnay Kistler Vyd. | Sonoma | C | 95 |

| 1987 Pinot Noir Dutton | Sonoma | B | 86 |

This 8,000-case winery located on a steep mountainside high above the Sonoma Valley floor recently celebrated its tenth anniversary. The early years were a mixed bag for the reserved but handsome Stephen Kistler and his partner, the ebullient Mark Bixler. Their debut Chardonnays, the 1979s, were hailed by critics, but the 1980s were defective, and the winery suffered immensely because of bad publicity surrounding these wines. Yet, Kistler and Bixler have bounced back, and subsequent vintages have gone from one strength to another. In addition, their own steep mountain vineyard has come into maturity. While their 1986 Chardonnays, especially the Dutton Ranch and Kistler Vineyard, were outstanding wines and prized by connoisseurs for their super depth, complexity, and marriage of French winemaking techniques with ripe Sonoma fruit, the 1987s are even richer and deeper with fabulous bouquets of Chardonnay fruit. The 1987 Dutton Ranch and Kistler Vineyard Chardonnays are two of the finest young California Chardonnays I have ever had the pleasure to taste. The third Chardonnay from the Durrel Vineyard is quite good but simply does not have the exceptional depth and richness of Kistler's other two Chardonnays. Chardonnay lovers will also be happy to know that starting in 1988 Kistler will be making Chardonnay from one of Sonoma's finest vineyard sites, the McCrea Vineyard. Although Chardonnays are what most people associate with the Kistler name, the winery's own vineyard is also producing small quantities (fewer than 300 cases) of quite stunning Cabernet Sauvignon, which seems to combine a mineral, gravelly, tobacco-scented character with rich, plummy, exotic fruit. Both the 1985 and 1986 show every indication that they will age well for at least 10–12 years. The winery also makes a very supple, cherry-scented, lush Pinot Noir from grapes from the

Dutton Ranch. Like many wine producers, Stephen Kistler and Mark Bixler have seen both the good and the bad times, but the current level of wine quality coming from the 30-acre Kistler Vineyard, plus the purchased grapes from the Dutton Ranch and soon the McCrea Vineyard, has everyone excited. This is clearly one of California's brightest stars at the moment.

KONOCTI WINERY (LAKE)

1987 Chardonnay	Lake	A	82
1987 Fumé Blanc	Lake	A	82
1987 White Riesling	Lake	A	80

This moderate-sized winery, owned by a number of growers in Lake County, has been making very fresh, lively, vibrant wines, especially from Sauvignon Blanc, Riesling, and Chardonnay, that have been sold at extremely reasonable prices. These are not complicated wines but lovely aperitif ones that emphasize gobs of fresh fruit and crispness. I urge consumers looking for fine wine values to search them out.

F. KORBEL AND BROTHERS (SONOMA)

N.V. Blanc de Blancs Sparkling Wine	B	74
N.V. Blanc de Noirs Sparkling Wine	B	72
N.V. Extra Dry Champagne	B	64

Korbel's sparkling wine products can be found in virtually every wine-shop in America. Founded in the late nineteenth century and currently with a production in excess of three-quarters of a million cases, Korbel is one of the most successful California sparkling wine producers. Nevertheless, the quality is quite mediocre, and the wines dull and bland.

HANS KORNELL CHAMPAGNE CELLAR (NAPA)

1984 Blanc de Noirs	B	52
N.V. Brut Sparkling Wine	B	70
N.V. Rosé	B	55

N.V. Sehr Trocken Sparkling Wine   B   72

With a production close to one-quarter million cases, Hans Kornell
wines are widely known, but unfortunately they taste musty, odd, and
seem to have a chemical bouquet that does not smell like wine. I hate
to think I am being too tough on them, but they are simply not serious
sparkling wines when compared with the alternatives available in the
global marketplace. Furthermore, the prices are in the mid-teens for
most of the wines, which makes them vastly overpriced for their quality.

CHARLES KRUG (NAPA)

1982 Cabernet Sauvignon	Napa	B	73
1979 Cabernet Sauvignon Vintage Reserve	Napa	C	87
1980 Cabernet Sauvignon Vintage Reserve	Napa	C	86
1986 Chardonnay	Los Carneros	B	75
1984 Pinot Noir	Napa	B	63
1987 Sauvignon Blanc	Napa	A	60

With a production of well over one million cases of wine (much of
it under its jug wine label, C. K. Mondavi), and a lineage that goes
back to 1861, one would think the Charles Krug Winery would have a
better reputation in California for high quality than it does today. The
problem seems to be that except for an occasional excellent Reserve
Cabernet Sauvignon such as the 1979 and 1980, the wines are one-
dimensional, sometimes even insipid, and hardly show what this winery can do from its 1,200 acres of vineyards in Napa Valley. I'm not
sure what the problem is, other than perhaps too much wine is being
made from the vineyard, but whether it is the one-dimensional, overly
acidified, bland Pinot Noir; the soft, almost Beaujolais-like regular
bottling of Cabernet Sauvignon; an unvarietal-tasting Chardonnay; or
a grotesquely vegetal Sauvignon Blanc; the quality is not what it
should be. However, with wines such as the 1979 and 1980 Cabernet
Sauvignon Vintage Reserves, the potential for rich, even exceptional
wines can be seen, and it makes one wonder why the winery doesn't
have higher aspirations.

LA CREMA (SONOMA)

1987 Chardonnay	California	B	88
1987 Chardonnay Reserve	Monterey	C	90

After seven years of inconsistent performances, this winery was sold and has been on a steadier path, or so I thought, making richly oaky, barrel-fermented Chardonnay that while lacking finesse offered gobs of butterscotch and toasty oak, and dramatic flavors. The winery is now concentrating primarily on two Chardonnays. A rather oaky, controversial 1987 Reserve Chardonnay suffers from bottle variation, but the better bottles seem to have an explosively fruity, toasty aroma filled with butterscotch and baked buttered-apple flavors, with a whopping amount of dizzying alcohol in the finish. This is a rather old-California-styled Chardonnay that merits attention from the adventurous. For the more timid, there is the 1987 regular bottling, which has balance, freshness, rich tropical-fruit flavors, and less oak than the 1987 Reserve Chardonnay.

LA JOTA VINEYARD (NAPA)

1984 Cabernet Sauvignon Howell Mountain	Napa	C	87
1985 Cabernet Sauvignon Howell Mountain	Napa	C	90
1986 Cabernet Sauvignon Howell Moutain	Napa	C	90
1987 Viognier	Napa	D	87
1985 Zinfandel Howell Mountain	Napa	B	86
1986 Zinfandel Howell Mountain	Napa	B	87

Hidden on the top of Howell Mountain is the small stone winery of Bill and Joan Smith, who have quickly propelled their La Jota wines to the forefront by virtue of a series of rich, dense, full-bodied, age-worthy Cabernet Sauvignons and Zinfandels. One look at the crammed old stone winery would instill confidence in just about any home winemaker. There are no glittering, computer-controlled stainless steel tanks, fancy centrifuges, rows of expensive new oak barrels, nor an army of whiz-kid oenologists to make the fine wine found here. If one didn't know that La Jota was in California, this winery could easily be thought to be somewhere in Burgundy's Côtes d'Or. Each vintage to date of the Howell Mountain Zinfandel has been impressive. My favorite has been the recently released 1984, followed by the rich, peppery, fruity, briary 1986, and the lighter, less muscular 1985. With respect to the Cabernet Sauvignons, the 1985 and 1986 are La Jota's finest two wines to date. Both showed the potential to improve in the bottle for 8–10 years. La Jota has also begun to make tiny quantities of Viognier, the rare Rhône Valley grape responsible for the fragrant, seductive white wines of Condrieu from the northern Rhône Valley. The 1987 Viognier has the gorgeously perfumed bouquet (aroma of pears, peaches, and honeysuckle) so characteristic of Viognier, as well as plenty of fruit. This is one of California's up-and-coming new wineries, but the quantity of wine is still a meager 5,000 cases from the 30-acre vineyard atop Howell Mountain.

LAKESPRING WINERY (NAPA)

| 1985 Cabernet Sauvignon | Napa | B | 81 |

| 1986 Chardonnay | Napa | B | 80 |

| 1985 Merlot | Napa | B | 81 |

Founded in 1980, this winery relies mostly on purchased grapes to produce its nearly 16,000 cases of Cabernet Sauvignon, Merlot, and Chardonnay. The winery prizes its Merlot; I remember receiving a sample of the 1984 with a press release telling me how great it was, only to find upon tasting the wine that it was vegetal, overacidified, and rather bizarre. The 1985 Merlot is a much better wine—rich, quite concentrated, and intense, but has no complexity or finesse. For people who want a big, robust, grapy mouthful it will no doubt prove satisfying. The 1985 Cabernet Sauvignon has herbaceous blackcurrant flavors, is a solidly built, firm, rather toughly structured wine, but it shows good depth and ripeness. I would not want to drink it for two to three more years. The 1986 Chardonnay has a personality similar to the red wines—chunky, full, and robust, but again lacking an interesting bouquet, and just too straightforward and one-dimensional. I must confess that California wine writers seem to find these wines much better than I do, so perhaps I'm missing something.

LAMBERT BRIDGE (SONOMA)

| 1984 Cabernet Sauvignon | Sonoma | B | 83 |

1985 Cabernet Sauvignon	Sonoma	B	85

1986 Chardonnay	Sonoma	B	85

1987 Chardonnay	Sonoma	B	86

Lambert Bridge, a lovely winery tucked in the hills of the Dry Creek area of Sonoma, had never enthused me with the quality of their wines until recently. The Cabernets had been disasters and were known mostly for their incredible weedy and vegetal taste that often resembled a puree of asparagus while showing none of the rich blackcurrant, cassis fruit that one found in other California Cabernets. This has all changed starting with the 1984, and following through with the even better, richer, blackcurranty 1985. In addition, the Chardonnays have taken on more richness and show a judicious use of oak barrels and an intelligent winemaking style. This winery has clearly made quite an improvement over its wines from the late seventies and early eighties. Prices are moderate and production is up to 25,000 cases.

LAMBORN FAMILY VINEYARD (NAPA)

1985 Zinfandel	Howell Mtn.	B	86

1986 Zinfandel	Howell Mtn.	B	87

This tiny Zinfandel specialist is making less than 800 cases a year of powerful, rich, deep, muscular Zinfandel, and for enthusiasts of this underrated grape, I urge serious consideration of this winery's efforts. The 1985 has a firmer structure and more natural acidity; the 1986 is fuller and more opulent, but both are well balanced, age-worthy, very rich, deep wines that should evolve nicely for 5–7 more years.

LANDMARK VINEYARDS (SONOMA)

1986 Chardonnay	Sonoma	B	84

1985 Chardonnay Reserve		B	78

This winery has had an inconsistent performance record since its inception in 1974. Production from its own 80 acres of vineyards has reached 25,000 cases. Although I have not tasted their most recent vintage, one of the best values for inexpensive white wines from California is Landmark's Petite Blanc, a blend of Chardonnay, Sauvignon Blanc, and Chenin Blanc. If you happen to see the 1987, it should be

quite good and usually sells for less than $5 a bottle. The two Char-
donnays are chunky and show a good amount of oak, but lack complexity. I actually preferred the regular cuvée since it has more fruit
than the excessively oaky Reserve bottling.

LAUREL GLEN (SONOMA)

1984 Cabernet Sauvignon	Sonoma Mt.	B	87
1985 Cabernet Sauvignon	Sonoma Mt.	C	91
1986 Cabernet Sauvignon	Sonoma Mt.	C	90
N.V. Counterpoint Cuvée 85/86	Sonoma Mt.	A	85

High in the mountains above the Sonoma Valley, accessible only by a
swirling, dangerous road, is Patrick Campbell's 5,000-case Laurel
Glen Winery and 35-acre vineyard. While Campbell has owned this
property only since 1980, the vineyard is old, with the vines averaging
20 years in age. There is no question that this mature vineyard, which
sits at an elevation of 1,000 feet, renders exceptional fruit. The excellent 1981 Cabernet Sauvignon was followed by less successful wines
in the problematic years of 1982 and 1983, but the 1984 is a clear-cut
success; the last three vintages should have Cabernet fans jumping
with excitement. The 1985 is a sensational wine with terrific richness
and length as well as a good decade's worth of aging potential. The
1986 looks to be equally as fine and every bit as rich and deep, but
perhaps more elegant and less opulent than the 1985. Owner/wine-
maker Patrick Campbell actually prefers his 1986 to his 1985. The
barrel samples I tasted of the 1987 also show super ripeness and
richness, plus a fatter texture than the 1986s, so it would appear that
Laurel Glen has produced four consecutive vintages of superior Cabernet Sauvignon. Campbell also produces small quantities of a second
wine called Counterpoint. For less than $8 a bottle, the current ren-
dition called Cuvée 85/86 is a rich, soft, tasty wine showing a weedy,
blackcurrant fruitiness and medium to full body. Laurel Glen is one
of California's best wineries and has a commitment to quality as high
as any winery in that state.

DOMAINE LAURIER (SONOMA)

1984 Cabernet Sauvignon	Green Valley	B	79

1986 Chardonnay	Sonoma	B	84

1982 Pinot Noir Estate	Sonoma	B	55

1987 Sauvignon Blanc	Sonoma	B	78

While the Domaine Laurier has garnered significant praise for its wine from much of the California-based wine media, I have found the wines too much the product of an overzealous oenologist where form takes precedence over substance. The wines simply taste too acidified, as if the only criteria for making wine is to be sure the acidity levels are high enough. The flavors have been stark, austere, and buried beneath tart acids. Therein lies the problem with the Cabernets and Chardonnays that have been released to date. They are correct wines and technically well done, but they have the personality of a piece of cellulose. The Pinot Noir is even worse, exhibiting grossly vegetal aromas and hard tannins. I fail to see where all the excitement is with the wines from this producer.

LEEWARD WINERY (VENTURA)

1986 Chardonnay	Central Coast	B	84

1986 Chardonnay MacGregor Vineyard	Edna Vly.	B	86

The style of these Chardonnays from Leeward requires that they be drunk within 1–2 years of the vintage. Why? They emphasize tremendous amounts of toasty, buttery oak along with rather low-acid, opulent tropical-fruit flavors. I have found that within 18 months of their release, the fruit seems to fade and the oak becomes more and more dominant. However, for lovers of the lusty, oaky, lush style of Chardonnay, these wines do offer a somewhat decadent style of wine drinking for the first 18 months of their lives. Both 1986s are good, but I actually preferred the MacGregor, which tends to be too buttery and oaky. While I did not have a chance to taste the 1985s, Leeward also produces Cabernet Sauvignon from Alexander Valley and Merlot from Napa Valley. The 1984 Cabernet Sauvignon I tasted showed a ripe, velvety, open-knit character, and precocious fruitiness. The 1984 Merlot, while clean and technically correct, tasted one-dimensional and simple.

LIVINGSTON VINEYARDS (NAPA)

1984 Cabernet Sauvignon Moffett Vyd.	Napa	C	87

1985 Cabernet Sauvignon Moffett Vyd.   Napa   C   90

This new winery specializing in Cabernet Sauvignon has released two impressive vintages of deeply colored, dense, dark, full-bodied, well-structured, rich, and tannic wines that should age nicely for 10–12 years. The 1985 has slightly higher acids and more noticeable tannins than the more opulent and seemingly more powerful 1984. Both are impressive wines from what looks to be an up-and-coming producer of top-notch Napa Valley Cabernet Sauvignons.

J. LOHR WINERY (SANTA CLARA)

1985 Cabernet Sauvignon	California	B	80
1986 Chardonnay Greenfield Vineyards	Monterey	B	86
1987 Chardonnay Greenfield Vineyards	Monterey	B	83
1987 Gamay Greenfield Vineyards	Monterey	A	78

J. Lohr Winery has significant vineyard holdings (in excess of 500 acres), mostly in Monterey's Arroyo Seco district, with some acreage in Napa Valley and Clarksburg in Sonoma. Production is in excess of 300,000 cases, and the wines, especially the Chardonnay, can be quite tasty. The style of Chardonnay is one with round, plump, succulent flavors that offer immediate accessibility and appeal. The Gamay is peppery, fruity, but slightly too herbaceous for my taste, and the Cabernet Sauvignon is fruity, soft, and attractive, but essentially one-dimensional. Prices for J. Lohr's wines have always been reasonable for the quality found in the bottle.

LONG VINEYARDS (NAPA)

1985 Cabernet Sauvignon	Napa	C	91
1986 Cabernet Sauvignon	Napa	C	89
1986 Chardonnay	Napa	C	90
1987 Chardonnay	Napa	C	92
1987 Sauvignon Blanc	Napa	B	87

In an isolated location high on Pritchard Hill in Napa Valley with a spectacular view, Bob Long turns out minuscule quantities of superb wines. Consumers are willing to go to great trouble to find Long's Chardonnays and then pay upwards of $30 a bottle because there are few Chardonnays in California that combine the stylish, rich, barrel-fermented, buttery, applelike fruit in such a powerful yet harmonious style that can age for 4–6 years. The 1981 and 1979 Chardonnays, tasted in 1988, were still in excellent condition and showing no signs of oxidation. Of the recent releases, the 1987 may well turn out to be the best Chardonnay yet made by Long, with a hazelnut-scented bouquet not unlike a fine premier cru Meursault. The 1986 is hardly a weak sister, with its rich, stylish, complex, full-bodied, highly concentrated flavors that show impeccable balance. His Chardonnay has gotten Bob Long a cult following among wine connoisseurs, but he also produces a superb Sauvignon Blanc to which he often adds 15–20% Chardonnay to give it more richness and length. The 1987 is about as complex, long, and delicious a Sauvignon Blanc as one is likely to find in Napa Valley. The Cabernet Sauvignon is made in a very deep, backward, tannic, rather hard style that needs a good 5–6 years after the vintage to begin to open up and drink well. I was extremely impressed by the very concentrated, tannic, well-balanced 1985, and similarly styled but slightly less acidic though just as tannic 1986. Neither wine should be drunk before the mid 1990s. Lastly, this 1,500-case winery also produces a Late-Harvest Johannisberg Riesling that can be stunning, although I have not seen a vintage in the marketplace since the spectacular 1984.

LYETH VINEYARD AND WINERY (SONOMA)

1984 Red Table Wine	Alex. Vly.	B	88
1985 Red Table Wine	Alex. Vly.	B	88
1986 Red Table Wine	Alex. Vly.	B	85
1985 White Table Wine	Alex. Vly.	B	84
1986 White Table Wine	Alex. Vly.	B	87

This 30,000-case winery made headlines with its proprietary Red and White Table Wines that were released in 1985. The White wine, a Bordeaux-like blend of primarily Sauvignon Blanc but with usually at least 20% Semillon and a little bit of Muscat, had more than a close resemblance to a fine white Graves from France. Its creamy, complex character combined with its elegance made it distinctive among California's proprietary white wines. The 1986 is a very good example of this style, although I would recommend that it be drunk before the end of 1990. As for the Red Table Wine, it has generally been a blend of two-thirds Cabernet Sauvignon and the rest a mixture of Cabernet Franc and Merlot. It has been especially successful in years such as 1982, 1984, and 1985, where it combined gracefulness with some fatness, opulence, and a texture and character not unlike a good Pomerol. The production of these two wines has leveled off at 30,000 cases, and in 1988 the winery had to endure the tragedy of the untimely accidental death of its founder, Munro Lyeth. Prices have been reasonable for the quality of wines produced here.

LYTTON SPRINGS (SONOMA)

1985 Zinfandel	Sonoma	B	90
1986 Zinfandel	Sonoma	B	87
1984 Zinfandel Private Reserve	Sonoma	B	90
1985 Zinfandel Private Reserve	Sonoma	B	90

Since the first vintage of Lytton Springs Zinfandel in 1976, these Rambo-inspired Zinfandels have never won any awards for finesse or elegance, but for a resounding blast of massive, peppery, spicy berry fruit with the body of Arnold Schwarzenegger, these huge, intense, powerful, yet balanced wines offer a mouthful of savory delights. There is little difference among the recent three vintages, no doubt because 1984, 1985, and 1986 are all top vintages in California, but certainly these intense, highly interesting wines should last a decade, and they are the type of heady, intense Zinfandel that has made California famous. Let's hope these wines never change in style.

PAUL MASSON VINEYARDS (MONTEREY)

1984 Cabernet Sauvignon	Sonoma	A	72
1986 Chardonnay	Monterey	A	73
1987 Chenin Blanc	California	A	70

1987 Emerald Dry Riesling	California	A	75

1987 Sauvignon Blanc Pinnacles	Monterey	A	78

The Paul Masson Winery located in Monterey produces a staggering amount of wine (8,000,000 cases) from its nearly 4,600 acres of vineyards in Monterey County. While it is fashionable to criticize the winery, which is largely known for its line of jug wines, the quality is quite acceptable across the board, and with certain wines such as the inexpensive Sauvignon Blanc from the Pinnacles Vineyard and the off-dry Riesling called Emerald Dry, there is a freshness and fruity character to the wines that gives them broad appeal. The Cabernet is compact, and the Chardonnay, French Colombard, and Chenin Blanc are adequate. One line of wines that I think needs great improvement is the sparkling wines, which are sweet, flabby, and generally unpleasant to drink. While the quality is hardly inspirational, the low prices and consistency of wines such as the Emerald Dry, Sauvignon Blanc, Chenin Blanc, and French Colombard may well surprise those who turn up their noses at the mention of a Paul Masson wine.

MCDOWELL VALLEY VINEYARDS (MENDOCINO)

1983 Cabernet Sauvignon	Mendocino	B	75

1982 Cabernet Sauvignon Reserve	Mendocino	B	83

1986 Chardonnay	Mendocino	B	72

1986 Fumé Blanc	Mendocino	A	80

1985 Grenache Rosé	Mendocino	A	84

1982 Syrah	Mendocino	B	85

1983 Syrah	Mendocino	B	86

McDowell Valley Winery, a great believer in the potential for Syrah, has some of the oldest vineyards of Syrah (planted in 1950 and 1930) in all of California. The Syrah stands out as their best wine, as a recent vertical tasting back through 1980 indicated. Their other red wine, Cabernet Sauvignon, is adequate, but it always seems essentially one-dimensional, a little too tart, and perhaps a bit weedy. This is definitely not the case with the peppery, rich, intense, full-bodied, age-worthy Syrah made here. As for the white wines, I have never been impressed with the winery's Chardonnay, and the Fumé Blanc is slightly above average quality but hardly exciting. Lastly, McDowell Valley makes a Grenache Rosé that is very dry and is meant to imitate a Tavel from France.

MANZANITA (NAPA)

1982 Cabernet Sauvignon	Napa	B	86
1984 Chardonnay	Napa	B	82

This tiny winery, which specializes in less than 2,000 cases of Chardonnay and Cabernet Sauvignon from Napa Valley, made a very good Cabernet Sauvignon in 1982 that has aged well and is now tasting better than it did several years ago. On the other hand, the 1984 Chardonnay, which started off life rich and buttery with attractive toasty, lemony flavors and good balance, is now starting to lose its fruit. Although it is still a pleasant wine, it should be drunk up immediately.

MARIETTA CELLARS (SONOMA)

1984 Zinfandel	Sonoma	A	84
1985 Zinfandel	Sonoma	A	83

Marietta Cellars is primarily producing Zinfandel, plus a nonvintage "Old Vine Red" that is available in different lot numbers. The Zinfandels have been full-bodied, inky in color, chunky in texture, and pleasant, but lacking a bit in complexity and character. The Old Vine Red offers full-bodied, robust, soft, fruity flavors for a low price. The winery also produces a little bit of white Zinfandel, of which the only vintage I have tasted has been a disappointing 1986.

MARKHAM WINERY (NAPA)

1984 Cabernet Sauvignon	Napa	B	83
1985 Cabernet Sauvignon	Napa	B	84
1986 Chardonnay	Napa	B	78
1987 Chardonnay	Napa	B	79

1987 Gamay Blanc	Napa	A	84
1984 Merlot	Napa	B	75
1985 Merlot	Napa	A	82
1987 Muscat de Frontignan	Napa	A	87
1987 Sauvignon Blanc	Napa	A	82

This winery, founded in 1978, has kept a distinctly low profile despite the fact that proprietor Bruce Markham has 300 acres of vineyards that produce close to 20,000 cases of wine each year. The Muscat and rosé called Gamay Blanc would appear to be the winery's top wines. The Muscat is made in a sweet, rich, unctuous style, has a marvelous perfume of peaches and apricots, and would be ideal as dessert or served with fruit tarts. The other wines all share a rather compact, fruity, rather oaky character and taste as if the winemaker has been told to keep them tightly knit and not show any great expansive flavor or character. If this sounds as though they all tend to be fairly straightforward and uncomplicated in style, then you have the picture of the Markham's Merlots, Cabernets, and Chardonnays. They are correctly made, but one would like to see a bit more personality and charm in the wines.

MARTIN BROTHERS WINERY (SAN LUIS OBISPO)

1982 Nebbiolo	A	58
1984 Nebbiolo	A	62
1985 Nebbiolo	A	68

Winemaker Dominic Martin should be applauded for taking the initiative and trying to make the famous grape of Piedmont in Italy, Nebbiolo, into wine from grapes grown in the Paso Robles area. The wines are a distinct failure, even when judged liberally, as they show none of the Nebbiolo character I have found in the Piedmontese wines. In addition, they have a diluted, virtually sour, tart character that makes them quite unpleasant. Perhaps more recent vintages will show improvement. Despite the low prices for the wines, they are no value.

LOUIS M. MARTINI (NAPA)

1984 Barbera	California	A	83
1983 Cabernet Sauvignon	North Coast	A	65
1984 Cabernet Sauvignon	North Coast	A	70
1982 Cabernet Sauvignon Monte Rosso	Sonoma	B	87
1986 Chardonnay	North Coast	A	70
1987 Chenin Blanc	North Coast	A	84
1985 Johannisberg Riesling	North Coast	A	60
1984 Pinot Noir	Napa	A	65
1984 Merlot	North Coast	A	58
1984 Merlot Los Vinedos del Rio	Russian River	B	78
1984 Zinfandel	Napa	A	80
1984 Zinfandel	North Coast	A	77

This is one of California's better-known wineries, and while I still see writers coming to the defense of the Martini wines, it seems to me that the prices have gone up over the last several years yet the quality has deteriorated. Too often the wines are very short on flavor, pale in color, have rather musty, old-wood flavors, and an oxidized character. I remember some lovely vintages of Cabernet Sauvignon and Barbera from Martini in the fifties, sixties, and seventies, but it is simply not possible that the wines of today are being made at the same level of quality. Two wines that should still be good are the single-vineyard Cabernet Sauvignon La Loma from Napa Valley and the Cabernet Sauvignon Monte Rosso from Sonoma. The current release of the Monte Rosso is the 1982, and it is an impressive, rich, broad, expansively flavored wine that should keep for a decade or more. These are supposedly Martini's top Cabernets, and they are released very late into the marketplace. Among the other vintages of La Loma and Monte Rosso tasted were the 1981 and 1980, both of which were quite good. The winery also produces a gorgeously perfumed, sweet, nonvintage Moscato sparkling wine that is available only at the winery. At present, aside from the single-vineyard Cabernets and certain vintages of the Barbera, which tends to be a good inexpensive red wine for quaffing down, and the aforementioned Moscato, the other wines range from the frail, feeble Chardonnays to rather insipid Merlots and regular cuvées of Cabernet Sauvignon. With a history dating back to 1922, with over 1,500 acres of vineyards producing close to 400,000 cases of wine, and with one of the best-known winemaking families of California, the quality here should be significantly better. The family's motto of an honest wine at an honest price may soon be in jeopardy.

MATANZAS CREEK WINERY (SONOMA)

1986 Chardonnay	Sonoma	C	89
1987 Chardonnay	Sonoma	C	91
1985 Merlot	Napa	C	88
1986 Merlot	Sonoma	C	90
1986 Sauvignon Blanc	Sonoma	B	87
1987 Sauvignon Blanc	Sonoma	B	89
1986 Semillon Botrytis	Sonoma	C	90

In 1989 Matanzas Creek Winery has its eleventh anniversary. The early years were marked by the extraordinary praise this winery received for its flavorful Chardonnays. On the other hand, the red wines were frequently vegetal and clumsy. Starting in 1984 when Pomerol-trained David Ramey replaced Merry Edwards as winemaker, the red wine, now only a Merlot, has taken on far greater character, and the Chardonnays and Sauvignons have continued to perform extremely well. This is not a small winery as it turns out 20,000 cases of wine from its own 45 acres of vineyards, as well as purchased fruit. The owners, Bill and Sandra McIver, seem clearly intent on pushing quality to higher and higher levels as they realize that in the competitive marketplace quality counts more than ever. Under Ramey, the Chardonnays have moved in the direction of a more age-worthy, burgundian style with complete malolactic fermentation, extensive lees contact, and a higher percentage of French-oak barrels. The 1986 is a rich, stylish, graceful wine, but the 1987 is even more complex, deeper and fuller, and shows 5–7 years of aging potential, which is unbelievably long for a California Chardonnay. The Sauvignon Blanc, which usually has a small percentage of Semillon added in, is a fragrant, flavorful, crisp, authoritative, delicate wine with a great deal of palate presence and character. Both the 1986 and 1987 are top successes. Yet, the most dramatic change in this winery has been the conversion of the clumsy, earthy, vegetal Merlot to a Pomerol-inspired, rich, supple, fleshy wine with a large measure of fruit and character. While winemaker Ramey's first vintage was 1984, when a very good wine was produced, the recent vintages, including the deep, outstanding 1985, and dense, creamy, ripe 1986, are full-bodied, lush, complex wines that are everything a stylish Merlot should be. Readers should make a mental note to remember April 1990, when the 1987 Merlot will be released. It has the potential to be the finest red wine ever made at Matanzas Creek as its exceptionally concentrated personality, stunning flavors, and harmony from the barrel attest. Visitors to the winery should also ask to purchase a bottle of the 1986 Semillon Botrytis, which is a barrel-fermented, decadently rich, full-bodied, intense dessert wine that reminded me of a great vintage of Château Rieussec. Unfortunately, only tiny quantities of it are made.

MAYACAMAS VINEYARDS (NAPA)

1983 Cabernet Sauvignon	Napa	C	82
1984 Cabernet Sauvignon	Napa	C	90
1984 Chardonnay	Napa	C	87
1985 Chardonnay	Napa	C	78
1986 Chardonnay	Napa	C	88
1986 Sauvignon Blanc	Napa	B	86

Mayacamas is one of Napa's oldest wineries, having originally been founded in 1889, then resurrected by the Travers family in 1941. The reputation of this house has been built on California's longest-lived Cabernet Sauvignon, a wine that ages as slowly as the great Latour in Pauillac. A vertical tasting attended recently showed such wines as 1968, 1970, and 1974 still evolving, the last vintage not yet close to being ready to drink. Recent vintages have performed less spectacularly than such greats as the 1974, 1973, and 1968, but one always wonders (when tasting this wine) if its true personality and flavor intensity are really showing through since it is such a notoriously slow starter. Of the recent vintages, certainly the 1982 looks like a big winner, but it should not be drunk until the mid-1990s. It has more accessibility than most Mayacamas Cabernets, while the 1981 seems particularly hard, backward, and without the inner core of strength and muscle this wine normally exhibits. The 1984 is a stunning wine, with all the muscle and tannin as well as the opulence a great Napa Cabernet should have.

The Chardonnays are also remarkably slow developers. The 1975 remains in healthy condition, proof that not every California Chardonnay begins to fall apart after 3 or 4 years. It remains one of the best California Chardonnays I have ever tasted. Recent vintages such as the 1986, 1985, and 1984 have been less consistent, although certainly the 1986 looks to be a great success for Mayacamas, whereas the 1985 seems to be tightly knit with good high acidity, and a leaner personality. The powerful 1984 Chardonny, full-bodied, rich, and intense, should last for 6–7 years. The 1986 Sauvignon Blanc is married nicely with toasty, spicy oak, shows good fruit, and seems to be the only Mayacamas wine that one must drink in its first 4 or 5 years. The winery also makes small quantities of a mediocre Pinot Noir that I have been told does improve significantly in the bottle, so perhaps I have been drinking it too young to pass effective judgment on it. Lastly, one should also keep an eye out for the Late-Harvest Zinfandel this winery occasionally makes. It can be one of the best examples of the portlike, intense, overripe style of Zinfandel once famous in California but now facing extinction as wineries have sought a more popular style.

MAZZOCCO VINEYARDS (SONOMA)

1986 Chardonnay Winemakers Cuvée	Sonoma	B	85
1987 Chardonnay Winemakers Cuvée	Sonoma	B	85
1986 Chardonnay River Lane Vineyard	Alex. Vly.	C	84
1987 Chardonnay River Lane Vineyard	Alex. Vly.	C	87

I have consistently been impressed with the Chardonnays released by this winery in Sonoma since I first tasted the 1985s. Two styles of Chardonnay are offered by Mazzocco Vineyards. The less expensive Chardonnay designated Winemakers Cuvée from Sonoma tends to have less oak and more of a supple fruitiness and less structure than the River Lane Vineyard Chardonnay from Alexander Valley. In the three vintages I have tasted, 1985, 1986, and 1987, the River Lane has been a wine with a great deal more oak in its flavors, more structure, and crisper acidities as well as more complex flavors. I felt the 1986 perhaps tasted a bit too oaky, but certainly the 1987 showed beautiful balance and structure. This is a very good source for California Chardonnay that deserves more publicity.

MEEKER VINEYARD (SONOMA)

1984 Cabernet Sauvignon	Dry Creek	B	60
1986 Chardonnay	Sonoma	B	77

The current releases from this relatively new winery in Sonoma County include a round, oaky, medium-bodied, fresh, and quite agreeable but essentially one-dimensional Chardonnay, and an overwhelmingly oaky Cabernet Sauvignon wherein the wood obliterates any taste of fruit in the wine.

MERLION WINERY (NAPA)

1985 Blanc Doux	Napa	B	90
1985 Cabernet Sauvignon	Napa	B	84
1986 Chardonnay	Carneros	B	82
1986 Chevrier	Carneros	B	85

The attractively packaged wines of the relatively new Merlion winery owned by the former winemaker at Napa's Vichon Winery, George Vierra, are led by the 100% Semillon called Chevrier that tastes as elegant and as classy as this grape is capable of tasting. A pretty bouquet of subtle oak, pears, and spring flowers is quite enticing. On the palate the wine is very flavorful but always fresh and crisp. The Chardonnay tasted closed, perhaps too oaky for its depth of fruit, but it is slightly above average in quality. The 1985 Cabernet Sauvignon shows proprietor Vierra's love of lean, high acid, austere red wines. It is a good wine with a very complex and rich bouquet, but I would like to have seen more flesh and depth. Lastly, the gorgeous sweet wine, Blanc Doux, is a dead ringer for a classy French Sauternes. It should be drunk over the next 1–2 years.

MERRY VINTNERS (SONOMA)

1986 Chardonnay	Sonoma	C	?

1986 Chardonnay Vintage Preview	Sonoma	C	70

This new winery specializing in Chardonnay has received much better reviews from other critics than from me, and I wonder why the wines have not shown well in my tastings given the obvious talents of the winemaker here, Merry Edwards, who did such an outstanding job when she was at Matanzas Creek. The wines to date, in my opinion, have tasted overly acidified with excessively narrow, tart, citric flavors and entirely too much oak in both the bouquet and flavors. I found this to be a problem with the 1985s and again with the 1986s. I hope my opinion is the minority's point of view, because at present I am not at all impressed with these wines.

DOMAINE MICHEL (SONOMA)

1984 Cabernet Sauvignon	Sonoma	C	85

1985 Cabernet Sauvignon	Sonoma	C	85

1986 Chardonnay	Sonoma	B	84

1986 Chardonnay La Marjolaine	Sonoma	A	83

This new winery, which claimed its first vintage only in 1982, has received quite a bit of publicity and seems to have high aspirations for producing some of California's better wines. It seems a bit early to ascertain just how good the Domaine Michel wines can be, but the winery has been turning out very inexpensive Chardonnay under the La Marjolaine label that shows good tart flavors, fresh fruit, and medium body. The 1986 Chardonnay had good fruit, crisp acidity, and some body and flavor. The two Cabernet Sauvignons I have tasted to date from Domaine Michel have been deeply extracted, rich, slightly herbaceous, full-bodied wines with a great deal of tannin to shed. Neither the 1984 or 1985 should be drunk before the beginning of the next decade. If this is the style they intend to produce, the quality looks to be good to very good, but consumers will have to have a degree of patience while they wait for these wines to come around.

MILANO WINERY (MENDOCINO)

1982 Cabernet Sauvignon California Reserve	California	A	55
1985 Chardonnay	Sonoma	A	64
1984 Merlot California Reserve	California	A	65

The recent releases from this winery have been quite disappointing, as the red wines have displayed overly vegetal flavors, excessive acidities, and a lack of varietal character. The Chardonnay has hardly fared better, exhibiting a lack of depth and pleasure-giving qualities. The last outstanding wine I tasted from Milano was their 1982 Beerenauslese-styled Late-Harvest Riesling, which was quite superb.

MIRASSOU VINEYARDS (SANTA CLARA)

1982 Cabernet Sauvignon	Napa	B	84
1983 Cabernet Sauvignon	California	A	74
1983 Cabernet Sauvignon Harvest Reserve	Napa	B	74
1986 Chardonnay	Monterey	B	77
1986 Fumé Blanc	California	A	55
1987 White Burgundy	Monterey	A	83

The Mirassou Winery is one of the great old historic wineries in California, having been founded in 1854. It remains family-owned in a time when wineries this size (300,000+ cases) are being gobbled up by large corporations. The quality of the wines here ranges from good to occasionally below average. One of the great buys offered by Mirassou has consistently been their white burgundy, a wine made from Pinot Blanc grown in Monterey County. It has been a success in every vintage I have tried, with the 1986 and 1987 fresh, loaded with fruit and broad flavors, and, at under $6 a bottle, unquestionably a "best buy." The top wines are called Harvest Reserve, and the Chardonnays have tended to be rather oaky and buttery, with a certain earthy character. In some vintages they have turned out slightly thin and vegetal. The Fumé Blanc tends to be very vegetal and smoky, but is certainly interesting. Among the red wines, the Cabernets have been persistent disappointments, extremely herbaceous and green, and rather unpleasant to drink. After decades of drawing their grapes from Monterey for Cabernet, the Mirassous in 1982 began to put their Harvest Reserves under a Napa appellation, and the 1982 Cabernet Sauvignon is their best Cabernet in memory. The winery also dabbles a bit with Zinfandel, which tends to be very high in alcohol, rich, lush, and intense (as the 1981 is). The winery has also made some Pinot Noir, a rather big wine but again painfully green and herbaceous. Sparkling wines are also part of the huge stable of offerings at Mirassou—I have had remarkably thin and again vegetal-tasting wines as well as rather odd, unidentifiable-smelling sparkling wines. Many wine consumers tend to dismiss this winery as not making serious wine, but they can do very well with certain varietals; their decision to go to Napa for their Cabernet Sauvignon can only be looked upon as a positive step in the right direction.

ROBERT MONDAVI WINERY (NAPA)

1982 Cabernet Sauvignon Reserve	Napa	D	83
1983 Cabernet Sauvignon Reserve	Napa	D	79
1984 Cabernet Sauvignon Reserve	Napa	D	88
1985 Cabernet Sauvignon Reserve	Napa	D	89
1986 Cabernet Sauvignon Reserve	Napa	D	90
1987 Chardonnay	Napa	B	85
1985 Chardonnay Reserve	Napa	C	87
1986 Chardonnay Reserve	Napa	C	91
1987 Chenin Blanc	Napa	A	86
1987 Fumé Blanc	Napa	B	85
1985 Fumé Blanc Reserve	Napa	B	87
1982 Pinot Noir Reserve	Napa	C	86

| 1983 Pinot Noir Reserve | Napa | C | 84 |

| 1984 Pinot Noir Reserve | Napa | C | 85 |

| 1985 Pinot Noir Reserve | Napa | C | 88 |

The name Robert Mondavi is entrenched in the minds of most wine consumers as synonymous with high-quality wines from California, particularly Napa Valley. There are few people who have championed the joys of wine as much as Robert Mondavi, and who have been open and candid about what needed to be done to compete on a global basis with the greatest wines made. His significance and contributions to the modern-day success of California wines cannot be overstated. Unlike many of his peers who have shunned publicity or decided to remain outside the limelight, Mondavi has stepped forward and to his credit, taken on sensitive issues such as the anti-alcohol lobby and the growing neoprohibitionist movement. With respect to his wines, perhaps his greatest achievement is how he has projected the image of a small boutique winery when in fact this is one of the giants of California. At the handsome winery in Oakville in Napa Valley, there is generally nothing but exciting wines to be found. Even unfashionable varieties such as Chenin Blanc take on a vibrant, rich fruitiness when handled by Robert Mondavi. My other favorites from Mondavi include his Chardonnays, especially the Reserve bottling, which is a boldly flavored, creamy, oaky, toasty wine that has never aged particularly well, but for drinking within the first 4 years of its vintage, it offers gobs of rich, buttery, popcorn-flavored fruit, and a full-bodied, lush texture. The regular Chardonnay can be rather one-dimensional and boring, but I certainly thought the 1987 showed well, and I can hardly wait for the release of the 1987 Reserve Chardonnay.

As for his red wines, no winery has made more progress with Pinot Noir than Mondavi, and he is constantly experimenting to refine his style. In the top recent vintages, such as the 1985, 1984, and 1982 Reserves, it has reminded me of a delicious, supple, cherry-scented and cherry-flavored Volnay from France. Consumers should definitely look for the new 1985 Reserve Pinot Noir, which is probably Mondavi's most successful Pinot yet. Of course, most connoisseurs judge much of what Mondavi does by his Reserve Cabernet Sauvignon. Despite all the hype that comes from the winery, it seems somewhat uncharacteristic of Mondavi that his best two Cabernet Sauvignons were made in the decade of the seventies, the 1974 and 1978. There has been nothing since then that approaches those two wonderful wines in either aging potential or quality. After some less than exhilarating Reserve Cabernet Sauvignons in 1981, 1982, and 1983, the 1984 shows more richness and opulence than any Mondavi Reserve Cabernet since 1980. The 1985 improves upon that in its greater depth and aging potential, and the 1986 is probably Mondavi's finest Reserve since the 1978. Curiously, in his never ending search for refining his style, I find his Reserve Cabernet has become less intense and perhaps overly sculptured and refined to the point where he may find himself being accused of producing something boring rather than exciting. Time will tell. As for the regular Cabernet Sauvignons, after an absolutely stunning regular cuvée in 1974 (which is still drinking deliciously today), this wine turned into a fairly one-dimensional, commercial wine meant for use by nonadventurous diners at restaurants. The 1985 and 1986 look to be the best regular Cabernets produced by Robert Mondavi. Finally, the winery's rich, delicious, well-balanced Moscato d'Oro should not be missed by those with a sweet tooth. It is extremely well made.

In summary, some of Napa Valley's best Chardonnays, Pinot Noirs, Chenin Blancs, and Reserve Cabernet Sauvignons are being made at the Robert Mondavi Winery. If they are rarely the single greatest wines made in California, they are consistently among the top two dozen wines of their type produced.

CHÂTEAU MONTELENA (NAPA)

1982 Cabernet Sauvignon	Napa	C	90
1983 Cabernet Sauvignon	Napa	C	87
1984 Cabernet Sauvignon	Napa	C	92
1985 Cabernet Sauvignon	Napa	C	94
1986 Chardonnay	Alexander Vly.	C	90
1986 Chardonnay	Napa	C	91
1984 Zinfandel	Napa	B	87
1985 Zinfandel	Napa	B	81

This is an admirable winery in every sense. The owners, the Barrett family, settled on a style of wine in the early seventies, and despite the presence of different winemakers such as Mike Grigich, Jerry Luper, and Bo Barrett, the style of their Chardonnay and Cabernet Sauvignon has remained amazingly consistent. What one gets from Château Montelena is textbook, quintessential Napa Cabernet Sauvignon, Chardonnay, and Zinfandel that says to the taster in bold, dramatic terms, "I'm from California and I'm proud of it." I recently tasted through most of the winery's Cabernets, and the surprising thing is how well they hold up. Even the 1974 Sonoma bottling, which was beautiful to drink in 1978, remains a gorgeous Cabernet in 1988. Of the great recent vintages, the 1978, 1980, 1982, and 1983 may all have more depth and ultimate potential, but I would advise further cellaring rather than consumption. The newly released 1984 Cabernet Sauvignon is a heady, powerful, unctuous wine with excellent depth and richness, but I suspect it will mature more quickly than either the 1983 or 1982. The 1985, which has not yet been released, is probably the finest example of Château Montelena's Cabernet I have ever tasted—a breathtaking wine of stunning depth and richness that is destined to be one of the great classics of Napa Valley. It will not be released until late 1989. As for the Chardonnays, there is the open-knit, fruity, apple-blossom-scented Alexander Valley Chardonnay, and a more tightly knit, more age-worthy Napa bottling. As delicious as the 1985s are, the 1986s are even better. While an alarming number of California Chardonnays seem to fall apart after 3–4 years, certain vintages of Montelena Chardonnays have been among a handful from that state to withstand the test of time. Recently, a 1975 was still quite drinkable at 12 years of age. If you like Zinfandel, then chances are Château Montelena's heady style of Zinfandel will please you. The 1985, for whatever reason, was not up to recent vintages, but certainly the 1984 and barrel samples of the 1986 show excellent potential for this grape variety that is indigenous to California.

MONTEREY PENINSULA WINERY (MONTEREY)

1984 Barbera Vineyard View	California	A	88
1982 Cabernet Sauvignon	Monterey	B	52
1982 Cabernet Sauvignon Dr.'s Reserve Lot 11	Monterey	B	62
1985 Chardonnay Sleepy Hollow	Monterey	B	65
1986 Pinot Blanc Arroyo Seco	Monterey	B	85

1982 Zinfandel Ferrero Ranch Dr.'s Reserve   Amador   B 86

Thank goodness there are innovative wineries such as Monterey Peninsula, which produces well over a dozen and a half separate and often vineyard-designated wines each year. All of the wines are unique and some are delicious, whereas others are bizarre and quite strange. A look at the current releases demonstrates what a schizophrenic winery Monterey Peninsula is. First, there is the best Barbera I have ever tasted from California. Unfortunately, less than 300 cases were made, but it is a stunningly rich, round, delicious, voluptuous wine packed with flavor, and while drinkable now, it should certainly last for another 3–5 years. The Amador County Zinfandel from the Ferrero Ranch also showed extremely well, with deep blackcurrant and berry flavors, plenty of spicy oak, full body, and a lush texture. Then of course there are the Cabernet Sauvignons that the winery has tried to make from Monterey County grapes. I don't know which one is the least appealing. The Dr.'s Reserve Lot 11 is a thick, vegetal wine that smells of cooked asparagus, has the kind of texture and flavor concentration that shows the winery knows how to extract flavor, but has a classic, regrettably incurable, case of the Monterey County "veggies." If it's bad, then the 1982 Cabernet Sauvignon from Monterey is even more appallingly vegetal, and one smell should cause virtually anybody to hold his nose in shock. The winery's white wines can also be inconsistent. The 1986 Pinot Blanc shows a wonderful stony, toasty, complex, earthy, fruity character; however, the 1985 Chardonnay is oxidized and losing its fruit very quickly. All in all, I would not hesitate to try any of the wines from this winery for the simple reason that when they are good, they are extremely good as well as unique and great individual expressions of winemaking art. When they are not, that's another matter. But in my opinion, it is preferable to taste wines such as these and support wineries such as this than to just blindly follow the large commercial wineries that are turning out a bland, standardized product each year that is not bad, but neither is there any personality, character, charm, or appeal in the wine.

MONTEREY VINEYARDS (MONTEREY)

1987 Chardonnay Classic   Monterey   A 85

1986 Chardonnay Reserve   Monterey   B 78

1986 Classic Red   California   A 70

1987 Classic White	Monterey	A	81

Over 100,000 cases a year of the Classic White and the Classic Red table wines are made at Monterey. They have generally been a reliable source for good, inexpensive, sound wine. However, recent vintages of the Classic Red have shown a very annoying vegetal character, and the quality has not been up to some of the earlier vintages. The Classic White still remains a good value for a tasty white wine, and for value-conscious buyers, the 1987 Classic Chardonnay is a delicious, citrusy, pleasant white wine that competes with Chardonnays at twice the price. Monterey Vineyards has also begun to offer a line of vintage-dated varietal wines, but the first several I have tasted were quite mediocre. Increasing amounts of sparkling wine are due to be released, and if the 1984 Brut sparkling wine is any indication of the quality, then it will be another wine to add to the ocean of mediocrity that exists in California.

MONTEVINA (AMADOR)

1984 Zinfandel Winemaker's Choice	Shenandoah	B	85

1985 Zinfandel Winemaker's Choice	Shenandoah	B	86

This winery has gone through a number of changes, but I remember some of its Zinfandels, and surprisingly some of its Cabernets, from the late seventies as being among the top sleepers of those vintages, and aging much better than most people suspected they would. The top-of-the-line Zinfandel made at Montevina is the Winemaker's Choice, and it is richly fruity, full-bodied, and in many ways a typical Amador County Zinfandel with a great deal of character and richness. The 1985 has a bit more balance than the more muscular 1984, but both are quite good examples of Amador County Zinfandel.

MONTICELLO CELLARS (NAPA)

1984 Cabernet Sauvignon Corley Reserve	Napa	C	91

1985 Cabernet Sauvignon Corley Reserve	Napa	C	88

1986 Cabernet Sauvignon Corley Reserve	Napa	C	94

1985 Cabernet Sauvignon Jefferson Cuvée	Napa	B	87

1986 Cabernet Sauvignon Jefferson Cuvée	Napa	B	90
1986 Chardonnay Corley Reserve	Napa	B	84
1986 Chardonnay Jefferson Cuvée	Napa	B	89
1986 Chevrier Blanc	Napa	B	85
1987 Chevrier Blanc	Napa	B	85
1986 Pinot Noir	Napa	B	72
1985 Pinot Noir	Napa	B	82
1984 Pinot Noir Estate	Napa	B	86

While proprietor Jay Corley acquired this large estate (in excess of 200 acres) in 1971, it was not until 1980 that Corley, a Jeffersonian scholar turned grape grower turned winery owner, launched his first wines. The debut releases were sometimes good, sometimes spotty, but in 1983 both the Chardonnays and Cabernets were successful, and this has been followed by an outstanding Corley Reserve Cabernet Sauvignon in 1984, two excellent Cabernets in 1985, and again two superb Cabernet Sauvignons in 1986, especially the multidimensional Corley Reserve. In addition, the Chardonnays from Monticello have been well-balanced, buttery, toasty, apple-blossom-scented wines bursting with ripe, delicious fruit. Both the Corley Reserve and Jefferson Cuvée 1986 Chardonnays had this character, and the 1987s look to be every bit as successful as well. Somewhat surprisingly, the winery also made a delicious, burgundian, seductive, and rich 1984 Pinot Noir, which was followed up by a good but less complex 1985 Pinot. The Semillon-based Chevrier Blanc is one of the better wines of its type, slightly herbaceous but crisp, medium- to full-bodied with attractively balanced flavors. Production has crept up to over 25,000 cases, and except for a watery, bland Gewürztraminer the quality of the wines from Monticello has never been higher. This moderately small winery, which has jumped into the top ranks of California's Cabernet Sauvignon and Chardonnay producers, is also planning to add a sparkling wine to its portfolio to be released under the name Jefferson Cellars.

MORGAN WINERY (MONTEREY)

1986 Chardonnay	Monterey	B	86
1987 Chardonnay	Monterey	B	89
1986 Pinot Noir	California	B	77
1987 Sauvignon Blanc	Alex. Vly.	B	83

This small, high-quality wine producer in Monterey County burst on the scene with its stylish Sauvignon Blanc and elegant yet flavorful, deep Chardonnay. Winemaker/proprietor Dan Lee knows how to put flavor and finesse into his wines, and while neither the Sauvignon Blanc nor Chardonnay would appear to be age-worthy after several years in the bottle, they are sumptuous, well-balanced, complex wines that provide immensely satisfying drinking over the near term. As for Morgan's only red wine, a Pinot Noir, the 1986 showed an attractive, even outstanding bouquet of smoky cherry fruit and toasty oak, but on the palate the wine fell off and ended with a short, tart finish.

J. W. MORRIS WINERY (SONOMA)

1987 Chardonnay Black Mountain Douglas Hill	Alex. Vly.	B	86
1985 Chardonnay Black Mountain Gravel Bar	Alex. Vly.	B	85
1985 Petite Sirah Bosun Crest	Alex. Vly.	B	86
1985 Red Table Wine	California	A	80
1985 Zinfandel Black Mountain Kramer Ridge	Alex. Vly.	B	85

The J. W. Morris Winery started in 1975 as a specialist in port-styled wines and has evolved since into making not only ports but also Sauvignon Blanc, Chardonnay, Zinfandel, Petite Sirah, and some Cabernet Sauvignon. The new Black Mountain label should be successful as the initial wines have shown well, especially the 1985 Chardonnay from the Gravel Bar Vineyard, which is a medium- to full-bodied wine with ripe, chunky flavors, good but not an excessive amount of oak, and crisp acids in the solid, fleshy finish. The Black Mountain Chardonnay from the Douglas Hill Vineyard is a more creamy textured wine with more ripeness than its sibling. As for the Zinfandel from the Kramer Ridge Vineyard, it shows very intense fruit, quite a bit of tannin, and full body, and it seems to need several years in the bottle to reach its apogee. While the Black Mountain wines are apparently J. W. Morris's attempt at establishing a premium wine label, don't ignore the generic Red Table Wine made by this winery. The 1985 is a soft, fruity, attractive wine that tastes good chilled.

MOUNT EDEN VINEYARDS (SANTA CLARA)

1984 Cabernet Sauvignon	Santa Cruz Mts.	C	82
1985 Chardonnay	Santa Cruz Mts.	C	92
1986 Chardonnay	Santa Cruz Mts.	C	96
1986 Chardonnay MEV MacGregor Vyd.		B	88
1987 Chardonnay MEV MacGregor Vyd.		B	89
1984 Pinot Noir	Santa Cruz Mts.	B	83
1985 Pinot Noir	Santa Cruz Mts.	C	88

Located in the Santa Cruz Mountains, this 22-acre vineyard produces one of California's most compelling Chardonnays, as well as a brilliant Chardonnay under its second label, MEV. The Pinot Noir and Cabernet Sauvignon are not nearly of the same quality as the Chardonnays as they tend to be rather herbaceous, sometimes bordering on vegetal. It is the Chardonnay here that has everyone so excited, and certainly in the 1987 and 1986 vintages the wine has demonstrated an explosive buttery, pineapple, and applelike richness, a good lashing of toasty vanillin oak, full body, good, crisp acids, and probably 5–7 years of aging potential, although I see no reason to defer your gratification given the richness and wonderful intensity of these wines. In 1985, the winery also produced a lavishly fruity, seductive Pinot Noir that is one of the finest that I have ever tasted from California. Production is small, and the wine highly sought, so don't expect to see a Mount Eden Chardonnay at your corner liquor store; however, the search for a wine of this character is well worth it.

MOUNT ST. JOHN'S CELLARS (NAPA)

1985 Chardonnay Carneros	Napa	B	84

| 1983 Zinfandel Proprietor's Reserve | Napa | A | ? |

I have had little experience with this winery, but its owner, Louis Bartolucci, has been a well-known grower in Napa Valley for the last forty years. The Chardonnay comes from Carneros, and it is a crisp, technically correct, well-made, medium-bodied wine, but while I enjoyed it, I had no inclination to buy another bottle. On the other hand, the 1983 Zinfandel Proprietor's Reserve seemed clumsy and a bit odd.

MOUNT VEEDER WINERY (NAPA)

| 1984 Cabernet Sauvignon | Napa | B | ? |

| 1986 Chardonnay | Napa | B | 84 |

This 5,000-case winery owned by Henry and Lisille Matheson has the potential to make outstanding wines from its location on Mount Veeder. The wines to date have come very close to the top echelon of California's producers, but they always seem to lack the extra depth of fruit and breadth that one sees in the very finest Chardonnays and Cabernet Sauvignons. The 1986 Chardonnay finishes a little tart, but it shows good, well-focused toasty oak, and pineapple- and buttery-scented fruit. I'm sure the 1984 Cabernet Sauvignon is better than what I tasted, nevertheless, it seemed rather hard, astringent, and lacking charm and concentration. Barrel samples of the 1986 Cabernet Sauvignon looked very promising, as did a proposed proprietary red wine.

MOUNTAIN VIEW WINERY (SANTA CLARA)

| 1985 Cabernet Sauvignon | Mendocino | A | 78 |

| 1986 Cabernet Sauvignon | Mendocino | A | 78 |

| 1986 Chardonnay | California | A | 78 |

| 1987 Chardonnay | California | A | 82 |

| 1986 Pinot Noir | Carneros | A | 85 |

| 1987 Sauvignon Blanc | Mendocino | A | 80 |

| N.V. Sparkling Brut | California | A | 74 |

N.V. Zinfandel   Amador   A   84

This winery knows how to make wines that offer appealing flavors in a forward, fruity, lush style, and it prices them reasonably. Some of the best values in the marketplace in the last year have come from the Mountain View Winery, such as the unbelievably gorgeous, supple, cherry-scented, seductive 1986 Pinot Noir, which is better than 80% of California Pinot Noirs and costs about one-third the price of most. The nonvintage Zinfandel from Amador County is another heady, smooth, silky wine with gobs of fruit, and undeniable charm and appeal. The Chardonnays have been correct, a bit boring, but pleasant wines. The two Cabernet Sauvignons from Mendocino are slightly herbaceous but richly fruity, medium-bodied wines that are supple and easy to drink. The attempt at making a sparkling wine has resulted in a wine that is tart and neutral tasting. All things considered, this is a winery to search out for some outstanding wine bargains, particularly in Pinot Noir, Zinfandel, Chardonnay, and Sauvignon Blanc. It's hard to beat the prices.

DOMAINE MUMM (NAPA)

N.V. Brut   Napa   B   78

Domaine Mumm is another joint venture between the gigantic French champagne producer G. H. Mumm and Company and the Canadian-based Seagram wine company. Significant investments have been made in establishing a winery that will produce large quantities of sparkling wine from Napa Valley grapes. The first releases have been pleasant, agreeable wines that are not extravagantly priced, but neither are they exciting in quality. Given the investment made, I envision the emergence of higher and higher quality wines in the future.

MURPHY-GOODE (SONOMA)

1986 Chardonnay	Alex. Vly.	B	81
1987 Chardonnay	Alex. Vly.	B	84
1986 Fumé Blanc	Alex. Vly.	A	84
1987 Fumé Blanc	Alex. Vly.	A	85

This new wine producer has entered the market with two attractively priced wines, a spicy, pungent, richly fruity yet overtly herbaceous

Fumé Blanc, and a middle-of-the-road, medium-bodied Chardonnay. It's hard to believe that wines with no greater aspirations than these will cause the winery to have great success, but they are reasonably priced and offer adequate drinking.

NALLE (SONOMA)

1985 Zinfandel	Dry Creek	B	85
1986 Zinfandel	Dry Creek	B	87

This Zinfandel specialist has burst onto the wine scene with two intensely fruity, full-bodied, velvety wines that are quite delicious to drink and have the textbook aromas and flavors of the vibrant, berry fruitiness that the Zinfandel grape can offer. I have drunk these wines with great enthusiasm and highly urge readers to try these excellent Zinfandels.

NAPA CREEK WINERY (NAPA)

1982 Cabernet Sauvignon	Napa	B	74
1984 Chardonnay	Napa	B	77
1986 Chardonnay	Napa	B	86
1984 Merlot	Napa	B	83

Founded in 1980, the Napa Creek Winery makes all its wines from purchased grapes. The above wines are middle-of-the-road, standard-quality California wines that are adequately made but have no great charm or personality. The exception is the 1986 Chardonnay, which is loaded with buttery fruit, a lot of toasty oak, and has quite an individual and tasty character. I have also had some good Merlots from this winery. Prices are moderate.

NAVARRO VINEYARDS (MENDOCINO)

1982 Cabernet Sauvignon	Mendocino	B	65
1986 Chardonnay	Mendocino	B	85
1986 Chardonnay Reserve	Mendocino	C	87

1987 Gewürztraminer	Mendocino	A	83

1987 Muscat	Mendocino	A	85

1984 Pinot Noir	Mendocino	B	84

Based on the wines I have had to date from the Navarro Winery in Anderson Valley, the white wines appear to get more attention and are more a specialty of the winery than its red wines. I'm not a great believer in California's ability to translate the elusive character of the Gewürztraminer into interesting, dry wines, but Navarro certainly does as good a job (in a dry style) as anybody with this particular grape variety. In addition, their Muscat should be tasted by anyone who loves the wonderful aromas of spring flowers and honeyed oranges, peaches, and apricots. It is quite a delicious aperitif wine. The 1986 Chardonnay Reserve is a rich wine with an appealing degree of toasty oak and crisp, nicely concentrated, well-focused flavors. The regular 1986 Chardonnay has less oak and more vibrant fruit. As for the red wines, the 1984 Pinot Noir was quite promising with more complexity and character than any I have ever tasted from Mendocino. The 1982 Cabernet Sauvignon, however, is chunky and lacking in varietal character. The winery also produces late-harvest Rieslings and a sparkling wine from grapes grown in the Anderson Valley in Mendocino County.

NEVADA CITY WINERY (NEVADA COUNTY)

1982 Cabernet Sauvignon	Mount Lassen	B	86

1986 Chardonnay	Napa	B	73

1987 Gewürztraminer	Sonoma	A	72

1984 Pinot Noir	Nevada County	B	70

1984 Zinfandel	Nevada County	A	84

1986 Zinfandel	Nevada County	A	78

This innovative winery operating in one of the lesser-known viticultural areas of California believes it is breaking new ground with its Pinot Noir. Based on the 1984, the only vintage I have tasted, I would disagree, as that particular wine had a bizarre, unvarietal character. However, one vintage does not make the reputation of the winery. The other wines here include another uninteresting and insipid Gewürztraminer from California, and a correct but straightforward Chardonnay. The winery does do an excellent job with its rich, velvety Zinfandel, and with its Cabernet Sauvignon, which tends to be a rather full-throttled, rich, interesting wine. Prices of the Nevada City wines are among the most modest for wines of such interesting quality, and while distribution seems to be a problem outside of California, 5,000 cases of these wines are produced and should be sought out. I have old tasting notes on an interesting Petite Sirah and Charbono from the 1980 and 1981 vintages, but I have not seen any recent releases of these two wines.

NEWLAN VINEYARDS (NAPA)

1982 Cabernet Sauvignon	Napa	B	84
1981 Cabernet Sauvignon Reserve	Napa	B	83
1982 Cabernet Sauvignon Reserve	Napa	B	86
1985 Chardonnay	Napa	B	85
1984 Pinot Noir	Napa	B	74

Newlan Vineyards, a small, 3,000-case winery, produces Chardonnay, Sauvignon Blanc, Cabernet Sauvignon, Pinot Noir, and a Johannisberg Riesling that I have never tasted. If the 1981 and 1982 Cabernets are typical of the style owner/winemaker Bruce Newlan is aiming for, they seem to be above-average-quality wines made in a fairly aggressive, full-bodied, tannic, weighty style with good richness, but needing 4–5 years after the vintage before drinking. The 1985 Chardonnay tasted like many other California Chardonnays with a good touch of toasty oak, ripe fruity flavors, and good balance. Though not one of the best, it is certainly among the better Chardonnays made. On the other hand, the Pinot Noir, at least the two vintages I have tasted, has been very herbaceous and extremely tart with compact, uninteresting flavors.

NEWTON VINEYARDS (NAPA)

1984 Cabernet Sauvignon	Napa	B	87
1985 Cabernet Sauvignon	Napa	B	88

1985 Chardonnay	Napa	B	84
1986 Chardonnay	Napa	B	86
1984 Merlot	Napa	B	85
1985 Merlot	Napa	B	90

This is a reliable winery for Cabernet Sauvignon, Chardonnay, and Merlot, as well as Sauvignon Blanc, although I have not seen a recent vintage of that wine to taste. The Newtons first employed the well-known and highly respected Ric Forman to make their wines, but he left in 1983 to start his own winery. The style has been consistent, though, from their first vintage in 1979. This has meant that all the wines, including the Sauvignon Blanc and Chardonnay, have been well-marked by toasty oak and made in a fairly rich, full-bodied, age-worthy style. The Chardonnays seem more closed initially and may take a year or two to open fully, but there is no doubting that both the Merlot and Cabernet Sauvignon admirably marry rich, blackcurrant, plummy fruit with a great deal of new oak, offering early accessibility combined with an aging potential of 8–12 years in the case of the Cabernet Sauvignon and 5–10 years in the case of the Merlot. Certainly both the 1984 and 1985 vintages were great successes for Newton.

NEYERS WINERY (NAPA)

1985 Cabernet Sauvignon	Napa	B	78
1985 Chardonnay	Napa	B	85
1986 Chardonnay	Napa	B	78

Bruce Neyers, the gracious and amiable public relations wizard for the Joseph Phelps winery, produces approximately 4,000 cases of Cabernet Sauvignon and Chardonnay from purchased grapes. To date the Chardonnay has been his best wine, showing a stylish, elegant personality with just enough oak to marry nicely with the medium- to full-bodied texture and fruit. Surprisingly, the 1985 tasted better than the somewhat disappointing, lean, and compact 1986. As for the Cabernet Sauvignons, they have been average-quality wines that, for my taste, are dominated by too much herbaceous fruit and weedy flavors. The good news is that the 1986 Cabernet Sauvignon should prove to be the best red wine yet made by Bruce Neyers. Prices are reasonable.

NIEBAUM-COPPOLA ESTATES (NAPA)

1978 Rubicon	Napa	D	87
1979 Rubicon	Napa	D	90
1980 Rubicon	Napa	D	88
1981 Rubicon	Napa	D	90
1982 Rubicon	Napa	D	92

Of all the luxury-priced proprietary red wines, it seems odd that Rubicon, the product of one of this century's most gifted movie producers/directors, has maintained the lowest profile. Francis Coppola owns this historic estate in Napa, and to date he has refused to release any wine unless it has aged for 7 years after the vintage. Of the wines released so far, the 1981 and 1982 appear to be the finest of the vintages made by Coppola. The initial vintages, particularly the 1978 and 1980, are powerful, dense, tannic, even tarry wines that taste as if Coppola were trying to mold his Napa Cabernet Sauvignon into a Barolo. The 1981 and 1982 have moved in the direction of more finesse without sacrificing any flavor or character. Both are exciting wines, but this is not to denigrate the first three wines, of which the 1978 is now fully mature and still a delicious wine, and the 1979 is turning out to be one of the very top wines of that vintage, displaying quite a bit of richness and intensity for a 1979. The last three vintages, 1980, 1981, and 1982, show exuberant, spicy, ripe bing-cherry fruit, plenty of oak, and a full-bodied, concentrated, deep feeling on the palate. These are impressive wines that should age for at least 10–15 years after the vintage. Production of 3,500 cases is expected to remain stable, as has the price of this wine. The winery also produces a little bit of Cabernet Franc, but based on the two vintages I have tasted, it has been much less impressive than the excellent, often outstanding proprietary red wine, Rubicon.

NOBLE HILL VINEYARDS (SONOMA)

1986 Chardonnay	Sonoma	B	75

1986 Sauvignon Blanc	Sonoma	A	60

I have only tasted two wines from this new operation in Sonoma, and it appears the winery will have to do a bit better to compete in the global marketplace. The 1986 Sauvignon Blanc lacked fruit and tasted entirely too herbaceous; the 1986 Chardonnay was compact and lacking a bit in personality and character, though agreeably fruity and fleshy.

OJAI VINEYARD (VENTURA COUNTY)

1984 Syrah	California	B	84

1985 Syrah	California	B	88

1986 Syrah	California	B	86

One of the most exciting things happening in California is to see how well the major grape varietals of France's Rhône Valley that have been planted in California are turning out. The quality of a number of wines is so exceptionally promising that one has to anticipate that more adventurous individuals will be planting Syrah, Mourvedre, Grenache, and the great white wine grape of the Rhône, Viognier, in selected areas of California. Ojai is an up-and-coming Syrah specialist, and while the wines exhibit less pure power and depth than those of some of the other Syrah producers, such as Sean Thackrey and Bonny Doon, they do share a lovely elegance and finesse. The 1984 is fully mature, supple, medium- to full-bodied, long and well-balanced, but I marked it down slightly for its weedy, herbaceous bouquet, which did not show up in either the 1985 or 1986. The 1985 is the most concentrated and richest, with a huge bouquet of smoky, raspberry fruit, great depth and length, and a personality not unlike a top Hermitage from the Rhône. The 1986 shows a rich, complex, seductive, smoky, raspberry-scented bouquet, with rich, supple, ripe, well-focused flavors; it is softer and less profound than the 1985. All these wines should last another 5–7 years.

OLSON VINEYARDS (MENDOCINO)

1985 Cabernet Sauvignon	Mendocino	A	85

1986 Chardonnay	Mendocino	A	77

1987 Fumé Blanc	Mendocino	A	81
1984 Petite Sirah	Mendocino	A	82
1985 Petite Sirah	Mendocino	A	84
1984 Zinfandel	Mendocino	A	75

The Olson family have been longtime growers in Mendocino's Red-wood Valley, and in 1982 they decided to produce their own wines from their vineyards. Their portfolio of wines includes a light, tart, refreshing but one-dimensional Chardonnay; a dark, dense, powerful, chunky Petite Sirah; an adequate Zinfandel; a lovely, richly fruity, nongrassy Sauvignon Blanc; and a plump, succulent, blackcurrant-flavored, chewy Cabernet Sauvignon. Prices have remained well under $10, so while the wines are hardly among the finest in California, they are good bargains. Aficionados of organically made wines (no chemicals are used in the vineyard) will applaud this winery's strict adherence to organic principles.

OPUS ONE (NAPA)

1979 Opus One	Napa	D	78
1980 Opus One	Napa	D	85
1981 Opus One	Napa	D	80
1982 Opus One	Napa	D	87
1983 Opus One	Napa	D	87
1984 Opus One	Napa	D	90
1985 Opus One	Napa	D	91

No wine or winery received more publicity in the history of California winemaking than the joint venture between Napa Valley's most artic-ulate supporter and spokesman, Robert Mondavi, and the late Baron Philippe de Rothschild of Bordeaux. Their joint venture gave birth to a wine called Opus One, which was to be a synthesis of the finest that Napa Valley grapes and French *savior-faire* could produce. The first vintages were released at expensive press tastings at some of the most outstanding eateries in America. The wine press was greatly receptive to this new style of wine, produced by a cooperative effort of Mondavi's and Rothschild's respective cellars. The wines have gained in finesse and character, clearly showing a personality that is something midway between a French Bordeaux and a Napa Cabernet. However, at a vertical tasting of all the Opus One wines in 1988 (with the wines being provided from Mr. Mondavi's own cellar), it was troubling to see the 1979 beginning to lose its fruit after only 8 years, and the 1980, which was the richest of the first two vintages, taking on a rather dull, one-dimensional character. The 1981 was the lightest of all the early Opus wines, and it is now tasting like a mediocre $8-a-bottle wine rather than the synthesis of two of the most talented winery owners in the world. Perhaps the more recent vintages offer more convincing proof that Opus may be something special, but I continue to have nagging doubts that the wine is more a creation of Robert Mondavi and his philosophy of highly stylized, sculptured, overly filtered wines than that of the Mouton-Rothschild staff. Certainly the 1982 shows good power, richness, and balance and is still drinking well; it should be at its prime between 1990 and 1996. And the 1983 is clearly the most French-inspired of all the Opus wines to date. It gives the taster a whiff of the famous Mouton-Rothschild lead-pencil nose, is lighter than any other previous Opus, and has a certain richness, finesse, and appeal that suggests it should last for at least another 6–7 years. The 1984, in retrospect, looks to be less aromatic than the 1983, but richer, more age-worthy, and potentially one of the best yet released by this winery. I believe the most recent release, the 1985, is the finest Opus yet produced. The suggested retail price of $60 a bottle is paid by few people as this wine has become a favorite of the discounters, and unless the quality jumps significantly, Opus is in danger of being regarded as one of the most overrated and overhyped Franco-American wines of our generation. After seven vintages it is not close in class to the other famous Franco-American wine, Dominus. Certainly the wine has achieved one goal of Mr. Mondavi's, and that was to generate a tremendous amount of attention for his winery and his efforts to produce world-class wine, and to promote the California wine business. There is no doubt that that has been a great success.

PAHLMEYER (NAPA)

1986 Pahlmeyer   Napa   C   90

This newcomer's first vintage of red wine is quite a winner. Dense ruby with a bouquet of violets, minerals, black currants, and toasty oak, this rich, full-bodied, tannic wine needs 2–3 years of cellaring but should last for 10–15 years. It is a very impressive debut!

PARDUCCI WINE CELLARS (MENDOCINO)

1984 Cabernet Sauvignon	Mendocino	B	84
1985 Cabernet Sauvignon	Mendocino	B	84
1986 Chardonnay	Mendocino	A	81
1987 Chardonnay	Mendocino	A	84
1987 French Colombard	Mendocino	A	80
1987 Gewürztraminer	Mendocino	A	72
1986 Sauvignon Blanc	Mendocino	A	84
1987 Sauvignon Blanc	Mendocino	A	86
1985 Zinfandel	Mendocino	A	82
1986 Zinfandel	Mendocino	A	84

Has anyone ever noticed that the great majority of California wineries with Italian names seem to sell their wines at very reasonable prices? Perhaps the Italian heritage of many of the founding families of these wineries has emphasized reasonably priced, drinkable wines. Certainly the Parducci family is a leader when it comes to quality wines of value. In addition, this family has long fought for the recognition of Mendocino as one of the better viticultural areas of California. The winery, founded in 1932, is now producing well over 350,000 cases of wine, most of it from the Parducci's 400 acres of vineyards in Mendocino. The wines all emphasize wonderfully exuberant, fresh fruit in an easily drinkable, medium-bodied format. The Gewürztraminer tends to be a disappointment, as most of them are in California, but the French Colombard is one of the best of its type with an intensely aromatic nose, and very crisp, vibrant, off-dry flavors. The Chenin Blanc is adequate but borders on being dull, and the Chardonnays have shown gradual improvement, culminating with a very fine apple-scented, charming 1987 Chardonnay that is also one heck of a value. Parducci has always done well with Sauvignon Blanc, and this wine, with a little bit of CO_2 intentionally left in, offers gobs of fresh, subtly herbaceous, mineral-scented fruit in a soft, delicious style. The winery's Cabernet Sauvignons have consistently been underrated by everybody, including this writer. I recently tasted the 1970, and it was still drinking beautifully; what a buy it was in the mid-seventies at $2 a bottle. With inflation factored in, current vintages are probably even less expensive. These wines are easily drunk young, perhaps too deceptively so, but they are balanced and have pure, curranty flavors, soft tannins, and enough body and alcohol so that they can easily last 8–10 years, perhaps longer. The winery also produces a very light but charming picnic-styled Zinfandel that provides delicious drinking if consumed within 2–3 years of the vintage. I have not seen a Petite Sirah from Parducci for several years, but it usually is a reliable, chunky, deeply colored wine without much complexity, but with solid, satisfying flavors. The Pinot Noir made here should be avoided. All in all, Parducci is a winery that has a lot to offer, receives little publicity, but deserves all the success it has had as the wines have immense crowd appeal and are sold at unbelievably realistic prices.

PAT PAULSEN VINEYARDS (SONOMA)

1985 Cabernet Sauvignon	Sonoma	B	72
1986 Cabernet Sauvignon	Sonoma	B	76
1985 Chardonnay	Sonoma	B	78
1986 Gewürztraminer	Alex Vly.	A	55
1986 Muscat Canelli	Alex. Vly.	A	86
1987 Muscat Canelli	Alex. Vly.	A	88

It's no laughing matter that the well-known television comedian and frequent candidate for president Pat Paulsen has a vineyard and winery at the upper end of Alexander Valley. And it's no joke either that his best wine is a wonderfully aromatic, off-dry, delicious, and fragrant Muscat Canelli, of which the 1986 and 1987 are about as good as this underrated wine can be. As an aperitif wine, or simply as a glass of wine to finish off a meal, it has few peers. On the other hand, the rest of the wines from Pat Paulsen, while not the laughingstock of the wine industry, are merely innocuous, one-dimensional, correct wines lacking either great depth or personality. The winery was sold in 1988, but Paulsen is expected to remain for purposes of publicity.

ROBERT PECOTA WINERY (NAPA)

1983 Cabernet Sauvignon	Napa	B	78
1984 Cabernet Sauvignon	Napa	B	80
1986 Chardonnay Canepa	Alex. Vly.	C	78
1987 Chardonnay Canepa	Alex. Vly.	C	85
1987 Muscat Blanc	California	A	88
1987 Sauvignon Blanc	Napa	B	85

This winery at the very northern end of Napa Valley near the quaint town of Calistoga excels with its Muscat Blanc, which is arguably one of the two or three best made in California. It offers slightly sweet, deliciously fruity, fragrant aromas and flavors in a very crisp, light, harmonious format. The other white wines have been somewhat spotty, but Pecota generally turns out a subtly oaky, richly fruity, medium-bodied Sauvignon Blanc that at least has personality and character, and an inconsistent Chardonnay, which ranges from lush, rich, oaky, and deeply fruity to one with a pervasive vegetal element that only seems to get worse with age. The 1986 suffered from the latter characteristic. As for the Cabernet Sauvignon, one would expect a wine from the northern end of Napa to be very rich, full-bodied, tannic, and intense, but the Pecota Cabernet has tended to be compact, overly sculptured, and lacking flavor dimension and breadth.

J. PEDRONCELLI WINERY (SONOMA)

1984 Cabernet Sauvignon	Sonoma	A	84
1982 Cabernet Sauvignon Reserve	Sonoma	B	86
1986 Chardonnay	Sonoma	A	84
1987 Chardonnay	Sonoma	A	84

1987 Chenin Blanc	Sonoma	A	84

1986 Sauvignon Blanc	Sonoma	A	72

1987 Sauvignon Blanc	Sonoma	A	80

1987 White Zinfandel	Sonoma	A	83

1984 Zinfandel	Sonoma	A	78

1985 Zinfandel	Sonoma	A	84

Pedroncelli Winery is consistently underrated for its portfolio of well-made, satisfying red, white, and rosé wines. Wines that have usually pleased me have been the winery's reds, ranging from a smooth, graceful regular cuvée of Cabernet Sauvignon, of which the 1982 successfully follows in the same mold as the excellent wine made here in 1980. The Zinfandels are richly fruity, ripe, and round, although I did not think the 1984 was nearly as concentrated as the very tasty, supple 1985. As for the rosés, the winery makes one of the better white Zinfandels in an off-dry style that is brimming with fresh strawberry fruit. The white wines are slightly less successful than the reds (isn't this true of all California wineries with an Italian heritage?), but no one will complain about the easily drinkable and agreeable off-dry, vibrant Chenin Blanc. The Chardonnays tend to be one-dimensional rather than special, as do the winery's Sauvignon Blancs. I have not seen a Pinot Noir in the last several vintages; it was one red wine that the winery slipped with a bit. Overall, Pedroncelli offers immensely satisfying wines at very reasonable prices.

ROBERT PEPI (NAPA)

1983 Cabernet Sauvignon Vine Hill Ranch	Napa	B	84

1984 Cabernet Sauvignon Vine Hill Ranch	Napa	B	87

1985 Cabernet Sauvignon Vine Hill Ranch	Napa	B	90

1985 Chardonnay	Napa	B	75

1986 Chardonnay	Napa	B	84

1987 Sauvignon Blanc	Napa	A	82

1987 Semillon	Napa	A	84

This modest-sized winery with a 15,000-case production was founded in 1981 by the Pepi family, and while they have made a good Sauvignon Blanc and Chardonnay, the winery seems to have quickly gotten on the right track for Cabernet Sauvignon. Ironically, the winery thinks of itself as a white wine rather than red wine specialist. Starting with the initial release of Cabernet Sauvignon from their neighbor's Vine Hill Ranch, one could see that there were outstanding-quality grapes as well as talented winemaking behind the wine. Interestingly, the winemaking genius behind the great Spottswoode Cabernets, Tony Soter, is also the winemaking consultant for the Pepi family. The superb 1981 Vine Hill Ranch Cabernet Sauvignon was followed by a very good 1982, a surprisingly big, rich, tannic, but closed wine in 1983, and rich, opulent, complex wines in both 1985 and 1984. While the Sauvignon Blanc, Semillon, and Chardonnay are certainly good and reasonably priced, it would appear that it is just a matter of time before Robert Pepi produces great Cabernet Sauvignon.

PERRET VINEYARDS (NAPA)

1985 Chardonnay Estate	Napa	B	87

This tiny winery in Carneros specializes in one oaky, well-made Chardonnay. The 1985 is the best wine yet made by owner and winemaker Paul Perret since his debut vintage in 1982. It's a full-bodied wine with plenty of toasty, vanillin oak backed up by buttery, tropical-fruit flavors. It should age nicely for 2–3 years.

JOSEPH PHELPS VINEYARDS (NAPA)

1984 Cabernet Sauvignon	Napa	B	87

1984 Cabernet Sauvignon Backus Vyd.	Napa	C	87

1985 Cabernet Sauvignon Backus Vyd.	Napa	C	90

1986 Cabernet Sauvignon Backus Vyd.	Napa	C	90

1984 Cabernet Sauvignon Eisele Vyd.	Napa	D	90

1985 Cabernet Sauvignon Eisele Vyd.	Napa	D	92
1986 Cabernet Sauvignon Eisele Vyd.	Napa	D	90
1984 Cabernet Sauvignon Insignia	Napa	D	90
1985 Cabernet Sauvignon Insignia	Napa	D	92
1986 Chardonnay	Napa	B	73
1986 Chardonnay Sangiacomo	Sonoma	B	?
1986 Delice du Semillon	Napa	B	78
1986 Johannisberg Riesling Late-Harvest	Napa	B	90
1986 Merlot	Napa	B	?
1983 Syrah	Napa	B	83
1987 Zinfandel	Napa	A	84

This winery, which started off in the mid-seventies to great accolades for its stunning nectarlike late-harvest Johannisberg Rieslings, turned heads with some sensational Cabernet Sauvignons in 1975, and except for a petite slump in 1981 and 1982, fame and fortune have followed the Joseph Phelps Winery since its inception. The current lineup of wines continues to offer stunningly rich, quintessential, full-blooded Napa Valley Cabernets, and some of California's finest late-harvest nectars. The Zinfandel also remains good, but the winery continues to struggle with its Chardonnays, although it will be the first to tell you that no one is working harder to improve the quality of this particular varietal.

One of the great glories of this top-of-the-line winery is its Cabernet Sauvignons, of which there are currently four. The regular Cabernet Sauvignon was sensational in 1975 and then went through a period in which it was adequate but rarely inspirational. I thought the 1984 was the best regular Cabernet Sauvignon I had tasted since the 1975, but due to severe bottle variation I was worried about its consistency. However, the last three bottles tasted have shown great fruit and richness; perhaps the earlier variation was due to recent bottling and shipping to the East Coast. In any event, it is certainly the best

Phelps regular Cabernet since the 1975. It has a touch of mint, wonderfully rich, long, deep flavors, and at least a decade of aging potential. Of the other 1984s, the Backus Vineyard Cabernet has the minty, chocolaty, spicy bouquet that characterizes wines from this vineyard. Deep in color, powerful, and concentrated, it is a full-bodied wine that should be at its best between 1990 and 1997. The 1984 Eisele Vineyard Cabernet Sauvignon lacks the great extract of the super vintages for this particular wine, 1975, 1976, 1978, and 1985, but is still a very powerful, massive, backward wine that should last 12–20 years when well stored. The 1984 Insignia is the best of all the Phelps 1984 Cabernets with its characteristically exotic, minty bouquet, sensational depth and ripeness, and an opulent texture that hides some serious tannins in the finish. As good as the 1984s from Phelps are, each of these wines would appear to be even better in 1985, as that great vintage offers up as much opulence and richness as is found in the 1984s, yet the wines have even better balance and harmony. Barrel samples of the 1986s showed that this winery has three superb vintages in a row for its Cabernet Sauvignons.

In 1986 the winery also released its first Merlot, but it tasted odd and rather clumsy, particularly for a Joseph Phelps red wine. Among the other red wines is a youthful, effusively fruity, Beaujolais-styled 1987 Napa Zinfandel, which should be drunk over the next several years. I have not seen a recent vintage of the Joseph Phelps Alexander Valley Zinfandel, but some of the finest Zinfandels I have ever tasted from California came from this particular vineyard, and readers who had the chance to try the 1975, 1976, or 1980 know full well what I am saying.

The Phelps winery has been a great innovator in experimenting with pure Syrah. The irony is that other wineries have surpassed the quality of the Syrah made at Phelps, as their wine tends to be very light. While I remember a good 1979, the vintages in the eighties have not been as good. This may be due to their practice of filtering the wines after malolactic fermentation, then fining the wine and filtering again prior to bottling, which can remove much of the wines' depth and flavor. Certainly the 1983 Syrah is good, but I wonder if it shouldn't be much better as it just seems too soft and fruity for a wine from this grape varietal. Interestingly, Phelps has begun to plant some of the rare white wine grape of the Rhône Valley, the Viognier, and a sample of their 1987, which was never sold commercially, was stunning. With respect to the 1986 Chardonnays, the winery seems to have finally gotten richness and power into the wines, but I felt both the Napa bottling and the Sangiacomo Vineyard bottling were not quite right. For example, the Sangiacomo had quite a concentrated feel on the palate, but the raw-oak character in the nose made it unappealing to me. As for the Napa bottling, it tasted one-dimensional and fruity with little personality.

Lastly, for almost 15 years the winery has done a spectacular job with its late-harvest sweet wines. Initially, they were simply the Late-Harvest or Select Late-Harvest Johannisberg Riesling, which along with those of Château St. Jean have remained the best made in California. The great success enjoyed by the Phelps winery with these wines later resulted in the addition of a Late-Harvest Scheurebe to their roster; it was also wonderfully fragrant. These Rieslings and Scheurebes have been virtually perfect, with recent vintages such as the 1986 and 1985 being the equivalent of the finest German Beerenauslese and Trockenbeerenauslese wines. They are decadently rich, intense, and fragrant, and very exciting to drink. Recently the winery also launched an imitation of a French Sauternes with its Sauvignon Blanc–Semillon sweet wine called Delice du Semillon. The first vintage in 1983 was quite stunning, being followed by another outstanding wine in 1985. However, the 1986 seems dull and lacking fruit for the amount of oak it has.

All things considered, when it excels, the Joseph Phelps Winery has few true competitors, but there is still room for improvement with the winery's Chardonnays, and the once-impressive Sauvignon Blanc has also taken on a duller character of late. However, this is a winery committed to the finest quality and should be sought out by those seeking fine wines.

R. H. PHILLIPS VINEYARD (YOLO)

1987 Chardonnay	Yolo	A	78
1987 Chenin Blanc Dry	Yolo	A	82
1987 Sauvignon Blanc Night Harvest	Yolo	A	82
1985 Semillon Reserve	Yolo	A	75

Founded only in 1983, the R. H. Phillips Vineyard in Yolo has consistently priced its wines at very affordable levels, and it is quickly obtaining a reputation for producing fresh varietal wines that should be drunk quite young. While tasting through the wines over the last year, I have been disturbed by the surprising amount of bottle variation with Phillips wines. It is virtually impossible to ascertain why, but certain cuvées seem fresh while others seem dull with almost cardboardlike filter-pads smells. The 1985 Semillon Reserve is showing a certain dullness to the fruit, but some bottles are vibrant and well focused. The same can be said for the 1987 Chardonnay, as well as the 1987 Sauvignon Blanc. Only the winery's 1987 Chenin Blanc has been consistently good. The values exist here, but the irregularity in bottle quality is definitely a problem.

PINE RIDGE WINERY (NAPA)

1985 Cabernet Franc Rutherford Cuvée	Napa	B	88
1985 Cabernet Sauvignon Andrus Reserve	Napa	D	90
1986 Cabernet Sauvignon Andrus Reserve	Napa	D	90
1986 Cabernet Sauvignon Diamond Mt. Cuvée	Napa	C	90
1986 Cabernet Sauvignon Rutherford Cuvée	Napa	C	85
1985 Cabernet Sauvignon Stag's Leap Cuvée	Napa	B	83
1986 Cabernet Sauvignon Stag's Leap Cuvée	Napa	B	82
1987 Chardonnay Oak Knoll Cuvée	Napa	B	88
1986 Chardonnay Stag's Leap Vyd.	Napa	B	86
1987 Chenin Blanc	Napa	A	87
1986 Merlot	Napa	B	88

This winery on the Silverado Trail in Napa Valley specializes in several cuvées of Chardonnay and multiple cuvées of Cabernet Sauvignon, as well as one of the two best Chenin Blancs made in California. Production has reached 40,000 cases of wine. Proprietor Gary Andrus had significant training in Bordeaux, and there is no doubt of the French style of his wines. In the early eighties I felt many of his Cabernets and Chardonnays seemed to be playing it too safe and came across as technically well-made wines that did not reflect the character of the vintage nor the credentials of a winemaker with the ability of Andrus. However, since 1985, the wines have gone from one strength to another, and after having been at Pine Ridge and tasting all the wines through the 1987 vintage, I find them to have a super array of 1985 Cabernets, 1986 Chardonnays and Cabernets, and some wonderful wines in 1987. It would appear they are ready to compete with some of the finest wines in California. There is no doubt that the Chenin Blanc is a gorgeously elegant and perfumed wine. With 1.5% residual sugar, it is one of the two best Chenin Blancs made in California. The top-of-the-line red wine is the Andrus Reserve, which is primarily Cabernet Sauvignon, but in most vintages a small amount of Merlot, Cabernet Franc, and Malbec is added to round out the wine. It has been absolutely superb in vintages such as 1980, 1985, and 1986. Among the other cuvées of Cabernet Sauvignon, the Stag's Leap Cuvée tends to be the lightest and often the most polite, even malnourished at times. The Rutherford Cuvée is richer and riper. Andrus has added small quantities of both Merlot, which looks to be outstanding in 1986 and 1987, and an excellently made Cabernet Franc. As for the Chardonnays, the understated style has given way to wines with both flavor and finesse, and while the 1987s look to be the best Chardonnays Pine Ridge has yet made, don't ignore the 1986 Stag's Leap Vineyard, which is an elegantly wrought, medium-bodied wine with a spicy bouquet of spring flowers and apples. It complements favorably the 1987 Oak Knoll Cuvée of Chardonnay, which shows a bit more toasty oak in its bouquet and has very smooth, well-balanced flavors that hint of mangos, pineapples, and baked apples. After a shaky period in the early eighties, this winery has settled into making some of the most interesting and best wines of Napa Valley, and their excellent 1986s and 1987s offer consumers the chance to give Pine Ridge another look.

PIPER SONOMA (SONOMA)

1984 Blanc de Noir	Sonoma	B	72
1985 Brut	Sonoma	B	70
1984 Brut Reserve	Sonoma	B	78

Piper Sonoma, the joint venture of the French champagne house of Piper Heidsieck and Sonoma Vineyards, started off with several auspicious sparkling wines that seemed to show that California was ready to make a serious run at the quality of French champagnes. However, the initial excitement over the first releases was followed by wines that have tasted neutral and devoid of much flavor complexity or interest. In fact, the recent releases have been very tart and citric, and it's hard to see what pleasure anyone could get from drinking them. If these are what we are to expect from what should be one of the leaders of the California sparkling wine industry, then I predict troubled times ahead for both the sparkling wines of California and Piper Sonoma.

PLAM VINEYARDS AND WINERY (NAPA)

1985 Cabernet Sauvignon	Napa	B	87
1986 Chardonnay	Napa	B	84

The early releases from this new winery in Napa Valley have shown that they are aiming for high quality. The Chardonnay has shown well-balanced, buttery, applelike fruit, and a good but not excessive dosage of oak. The Cabernet Sauvignon, particularly the 1985, showed excellent ripeness and depth, some complexity, full body, and plenty of weedy, blackcurrant, luxuriously rich, soft fruit. It should be drunk over the next 3–4 years.

CHÂTEAU POTELLE (NAPA)

1984 Cabernet Sauvignon	Napa	B	76
1986 Chardonnay	Napa	B	81

A French couple has taken up residence in Napa Valley and is trying to produce elegant, French-inspired wines from Napa Valley's two most glamorous grapes. The 1986 Chardonnay has an attractive bouquet of vanillin and tropical fruit, but it finishes rather tart and could use some more depth. The 1984 Cabernet Sauvignon tastes rather polite and emaciated for a wine from this vintage. If it was meant to be elegant, it has turned out to be innocuous instead.

BERNARD PRADEL CELLARS (NAPA)

1984 Cabernet Sauvignon	Napa	B	80
1986 Chardonnay	Napa	B	75
1987 Chardonnay	Napa	B	86

Another newcomer to the wine scene in California, the early releases here have shown an average to above-average Chardonnay, and a compact, elegant, but understated Cabernet Sauvignon. The wines are certainly well made, but they could use a bit more personality and drama. The fine showing of the 1987 Chardonnay may portend a new level of higher quality, more interesting wine.

PRESTON VINEYARDS (SONOMA)

1984 Cabernet Sauvignon	Dry Creek	B	75
1985 Cabernet Sauvignon	Dry Creek	B	?
1987 Chenin Blanc	Sonoma	A	87
1987 Sauvignon Blanc Cuvée de Fumé	Dry Creek	A	85
1987 Sauvignon Blanc Estate	Dry Creek	B	85
1986 Sauvignon Blanc Reserve	Dry Creek	B	82
1985 Sirah-Syrah	Dry Creek	B	76
1986 Sirah-Syrah	Dry Creek	B	85
1985 Zinfandel	Dry Creek	B	82
1986 Zinfandel	Dry Creek	B	86

Preston Vineyards seems to be making better and better quality wine in the last several years, and it should be praised for not only improving its wines but for keeping its prices reasonable. For example, one of my favorite wines from this winery is its least expensive Cuvée de Fumé, which is a blend primarily of Sauvignon Blanc but with Chenin Blanc and Semillon added in for roundness, body, and bouquet. Both the 1987 and the 1986 vintages of this lovely Loire Valley–inspired wine are quite tasty and delicious, perfect for drinking with poultry and fish. This is also a winery that has begun to produce outstanding dry Chenin Blanc that has the body of Chardonnay but the wonderful spring-flower-blossom and melon scents of the delightful Chenin Blanc grape. The 1987 is one of the best Chenin Blancs I have ever tasted from California. The winery has also improved its blend of Petite Sirah and Syrah. Whereas the 1985 tasted compact and one-dimensional, the 1986, with a blend of 71% Syrah and 29% Petite Sirah, showed significantly more richness, muscle, and the peppery, earthy quality of a good Rhône. The Cabernet Sauvignons have tended

to be standard-quality wines, but the 1985, which showed more richness and complexity than any prior vintage, was flawed by too much
sulphur in the nose. The Zinfandels, while always good, have never
been better than in 1986 and 1985. The only wine that does not seem
to be up to the quality one might expect is the rather expensive Reserve Sauvignon Blanc, which seems to lack freshness and tastes too
much of oak. This is a winery that deserves consumer attention for its
well-made, reasonably priced, attractive wines.

QUIVERA (SONOMA)

1986 Sauvignon Blanc	Dry Creek	A	73
1985 Zinfandel	Dry Creek	A	86

The Sauvignon Blancs from Quivera, a new winery, have tasted undernourished, austere, and just simply lacking fruit and pleasure. On
the other hand, the rather dull Zinfandels of 1983 and 1984 have given
way to a very rich, berry-scented, full-bodied, powerful yet well-
balanced Zinfandel in 1985 that sells for a very modest price. It's too
early to say for sure what direction this young winery is heading, but
certainly the 1985 Zinfandel is a very positive sign.

QUPÉ WINERY (SANTA BARBARA)

1986 Chardonnay Reserve	Santa Barbara	B	83
1986 Syrah	Paso Robles	B	85

While this winery also makes a fairly oaky, intense Chardonnay that
will never be accused of shyness, its best wine is a lighter, supple-
styled, pure Syrah that winemaker Bob Lindquist compares to a
St.-Joseph rather than a Hermitage or Côte Rôtie from France. The
1986 has a vivid, rich, briary, peppery, slightly herbaceous nose, medium to full body, soft, supple flavors, and a velvety, attractive finish.
It should be drunk over the next 4 years. As for the Chardonnay, this
winery has a tendency to overemphasize the oak to the detriment of
the wine's fruit and freshness. The 1986 is good but could have been
even better.

A. RAFANELLI WINERY (SONOMA)

1985 Zinfandel Unfiltered	Sonoma	A	86

| 1986 Zinfandel Unfiltered | Sonoma | A | 88 |

This is a terribly underrated producer of sometimes outstanding but always interesting, rich, full-bodied, classic Zinfandel that does justice to the reputation of this grape in California. Rafanelli, a longtime grower in the Dry Creek Valley, makes just under 3,000 cases of Zinfandel and some Gamay (which I have never tasted), bottling it unfiltered so as not to remove any of its flavors. Both the 1986 and 1985 show attractive, rich, berry, spicy bouquets, a very deep, opaque color, and have a full-bodied, supple, expansively flavored palate with a roasted quality. Both wines are gutsy, robust, full-throttle Zinfandels (with balance) that should be drunk over the next 5–6 years.

RAVENSWOOD WINERY (SONOMA)

1985 Cabernet Sauvignon	Sonoma	B	85
1986 Cabernet Sauvignon Pickberry Vyd.	Sonoma Mt.	C	92
1987 Chardonnay Sangiacomo	Sonoma	C	89
1985 Merlot	Sonoma	B	90
1986 Merlot	Sonoma	B	90
1985 Zinfandel	Sonoma	B	91
1986 Zinfandel	Sonoma	B	90
1985 Zinfandel Dickerson Vineyard	Napa	B	92
1986 Zinfandel Dickerson Vineyard	Napa	B	92
1985 Zinfandel Old Hill Vineyard	Sonoma	B	90
1986 Zinfandel Old Hill Vineyard	Sonoma	B	94
1986 Zinfandel Vintner's Blend	Sonoma	A	87

Ravenswood is one of the greatest of the small California wineries. The production of 5,000+ cases is snapped up so fast that winemaker Joel Peterson is under constant pressure to expand his operation. The winery, located in a garage, has actually been in existence since 1976, but its stardom has been established in the eighties, largely on the basis of California's most exciting, exotic, and flavorful Zinfandels. No vineyards are owned here, but Peterson, an articulate, confident man who still works at the Sonoma Valley Hospital, has had considerable experience tasting the great classics of Europe and seems to know precisely what he wants to achieve. Peterson has long believed that Zinfandel from old established vineyards in Sonoma and Napa could easily achieve the greatness of Cabernet Sauvignon. He scoffs at those who claim Zinfandel is an inferior wine, and why shouldn't he? His least-expensive Zinfandel, the Vintner's Blend, was superb in 1984, very good in 1985, excellent in 1986, and looks to again be superb in 1987, yet sells for well under $10 a bottle. His winemaking philosophy is not terribly different from many of the great masters of the craft, such as Henri Jayer and Jacques Seysses of Burgundy, Gerard Chave and François Perrin of the Rhône Valley, and oenologists Michel Rolland and Jean Claude Berrouet of Bordeaux. That philosophy is, get great fruit from the vineyard, and handle and manipulate the wine as little as possible. And by no means overprocess it or strip it of its flavors in the name of commercial stability and deposit-free wine.

The three great Zinfandels made here are totally different in style. While they all see about 30% new oak, the Sonoma balanced oodles of berry fruit with considerable power and harmony. It is a Zinfandel that oozes with character and is never heavy or tiring to drink. The Dickerson Vineyard, with its minty, cedary fragrance and remarkable concentration, is equally awesome, yet totally different. The Old Hill Vineyard, made from 80-year-old Zinfandel vines, is a blockbuster wine with a staggering wealth of fruit and a finish that seems to last several minutes. The 1985s and 1986s are true classics and among the greatest Zinfandels made by any winery except for Paul Draper at Ridge Vineyards. The unreleased 1987s look to be equally as stunning and will no doubt merit outstanding scores when released in 1990. While Peterson, along with Paul Draper at Ridge, is Zinfandel's greatest proponent, he also produces a rich, multidimensional Merlot that has been especially brilliant in 1985 and 1986.

Curiously, I have never been enamored of his green, pickle-scented Cabernet Sauvignon, which was extremely vegetal in 1984, but he finally toned down the veggies in 1985, and in 1986 he made his first proprietary wine called Pickberry Vineyards (a blend of 50% Cabernet Sauvignon, 40% Cabernet Franc, and 10% Merlot) from a vineyard on Sonoma Mountain near that of the well-known winery Laurel Glen. It looks to be exceptional in both 1986 and 1987. Lastly,

Ravenswood also makes a full-bodied, very individualistic Chardonnay that is fermented with wild yeasts from the vineyard, kept 10 months on its lees in the barrel, and then bottled unfiltered, much like Coche-Dury and the Comte Lafon do in Burgundy. The 1985 and 1986 seem to have a bit too much oak, but the 1987 has exquisite fruit to go along with the toasty oak. Prices for Ravenswood's wines are among the most realistic in the business. Given the splendid as well as unique quality and personality of the wines here, they look to be bargains. This winery is making some of the greatest and most unique wines in California, and while availability is tight, they are worth a special effort to find.

RAYMOND VINEYARD AND CELLAR (NAPA)

1984 Cabernet Sauvignon	Napa	B	84
1983 Cabernet Sauvignon Private Reserve	Napa	C	87
1984 Cabernet Sauvignon Private Reserve	Napa	C	89
1986 Chardonnay	Napa	B	85
1986 Chardonnay California Selection	Napa	A	83
1985 Chardonnay Reserve	Napa	B	87
1986 Chardonnay Reserve	Napa	B	87

The Raymond family, grape growers in Napa Valley for the last sixty years, launched their first wine in the early seventies and imediately established a signature style of full-bodied, intense, oaky, buttery, opulently styled Chardonnays, and spicy, intensely oaky, rich, lush Cabernet Sauvignons. On occasion, a splendidly rich late-harvest Johannisberg Riesling is also made, such as the excellent 1982. In addition, Zinfandel is produced by the Raymonds. Production is inching up toward 70,000 cases. The current releases all admirably reflect the Raymond style of winemaking. There are three Chardonnays produced; the modestly priced 1986 California selection shows nice tropical fruit buttressed by abundant quantities of oak. The level of concentration goes up a notch with the 1986 Napa Valley Chardonnay, reaching its peak with the 1985 and 1986 Reserve Chardonnays, which show very rich, full-bodied, concentrated flavors, and plenty of toasty, intense oak. As for the Cabernet Sauvignons, they are made to be drunk within their first decade of life, and I have had no experience with them past that age. Certainly, the 1983 Reserve is an outstanding success for this difficult vintage, showing an exotic, full-throttle intensity; gobs of ripe fruit for a 1983; supple, rich, smoky, oaky flavors; and a soft, pleasing texture. It should be drunk over the next 4–5 years. The 1984 regular bottling of Cabernet Sauvignon is similarly styled and quite approachable now; the 1984 Reserve is perhaps the best Raymond Cabernet Sauvignon I have tasted to date.

REVERE WINERY (NAPA)

1985 Chardonnay	Napa	C	72
1986 Chardonnay	Napa	C	82

This small, new winery is producing a very oaky, highly acidic, expensive Chardonnay that lacks charm and flesh, leading some optimists to conclude (erroneously in my opinion) that it's going to develop into something quite special. Both the 1985 and 1986 simply lack fruit and flavor, being overwhelmed by their oak and high acids.

RICHARDSON VINEYARDS (SONOMA)

1985 Cabernet Sauvignon	Sonoma	B	82
1985 Chardonnay	Sonoma	B	78
1986 Merlot	Los Carneros	B	83
1986 Pinot Noir	Los Carneros	B	82
1985 Zinfandel	Sonoma	B	84

Richardson Vineyards is a tiny winery, producing fewer than 2,000 cases of Chardonnay, Pinot Noir, Zinfandel, and Cabernet Sauvignon. The releases to date have consistently offered good Zinfandel, Merlot, and Pinot Noir, all of which show a touch of new oak, plenty of plummy, rich, berry fruit, and full-bodied textures. Clearly the house style goes for gobs of fruit in a relatively uncomplicated style. The Chardonnay has been compact and lacked depth and fruit.

RIDGE VINEYARDS (SANTA CLARA)

1985 Cabernet Sauvignon Howell Mountain	Napa	B	86

1984 Cabernet Sauvignon Monte Bello	Santa Cruz	D	96
1985 Cabernet Sauvignon Monte Bello	Santa Cruz	D	92
1986 Cabernet Sauvignon Monte Bello	Santa Cruz	D	87
1985 Cabernet Sauvignon York Creek	Napa	B	87
1986 Chardonnay	Santa Cruz	B	82
1984 Petite Sirah York Creek	Napa	B	88
1985 Petite Sirah York Creek	Napa	B	87
1985 Zinfandel Geyserville	Sonoma	B	90
1986 Zinfandel Geyserville	Sonoma	B	87
1985 Zinfandel Lytton Springs	Sonoma	B	92
1986 Zinfandel Lytton Springs	Sonoma	B	85
1985 Zinfandel Park-Muscatine	Napa	B	93

For just over twenty-five years, Ridge Vineyards has been serving up a steady diet of complex, rich, naturally made red wines led by the incomparable Cabernet Sauvignon from Ridge's own Monte Bello Vineyard, and a bevy of classic, relatively long-lived, but always tasty and delicious Zinfandels. California's best Petite Sirah is also made here. This winery should be visited, as the steep, long, winding road (Montebello Ridge Road) affords magnificent views of Silicon Valley and San Jose. While it would be hard to pick California's finest Cabernet Sauvignon, the Ridge Monte Bello has to be one of the two or three best, as well as the most consistent. It also has the aging potential of a fine Bordeaux. Old vintages such as the 1964 are just now in their prime, whereas 18-year-old wines such as the 1970 are not nearly ready to drink. There have been some fabulous Monte Bello Cabernets —the 1964, 1968, 1970, 1971, 1974, 1984, and 1985. Interestingly, all of these vintages still have at least a decade of cellaring potential, with the two superstars in the eighties having at least 20–25 years of aging potential.

While most vintages of Monte Bello require patience, the Zinfandels from Ridge can be drunk young or aged. The three best Zinfandels come from fruit purchased in both Sonoma and Napa. The 1984 and 1985 Zinfandels called Geyserville, Lytton Springs, and York Creek have only those Zinfandels from the small Ravenswood Winery in Sonoma for competition as California's best Zinfandels. Ridge also makes limited lots of Zinfandels such as the 1985 Zinfandel from the Park-Muscatine Vineyard. This particular vineyard produced a lavish, luxuriously rich, intense wine that is one of the greatest Zinfandels from California I have ever drunk. Unfortunately, only 30 barrels of it were made. All the Zinfandels are elegantly wrought with both flavor and finesse, but no lack of power. The Lytton Springs usually has the most muscle, but all are packed with rich, ripe berry fruit, show an intelligent use of oak barrels, and have 6–10 years of aging potential. Both the 1986 Geyserville and Lytton Springs Zinfandels, though less intense and less powerful than in 1984 and 1985, are still wonderfully elegant and stylish.

While the French Syrah grape has shown immense potential from the likes of tiny wineries such as Bonny Doon and Sean Thackrey, Ridge has consistently made California's finest Petite Sirah, a grape that usually produces chunky, peppery, uncomplex wines. In the hands of winemaker Paul Draper, the Petite Sirah from the York Creek Vineyard has proved an extravagantly rich, age-worthy wine with loads of peppery raspberry and blackberry fruit. The 1971 drunk recently was in magnificent shape and only reinforced my thinking that few people age Ridge's Petite Sirah long enough. The philosophy of winemaking at Ridge is that of "hands on" only when it is essential to intervene for the sake of the wine's health. The wines are given minimal clarification for fear of stripping them of flavor and aging potential. Filtration is used as sparingly as is possible. The winery makes several other wines, the most interesting of which are the Howell Mountain and York Creek Cabernets, and a small quantity of toasty, oaky, barrel-fermented Chardonnay that tends to be rather spotty in quality. This is one of the greatest wineries in California, and while some may lament that it is no longer under American ownership, the wines are as brilliant as ever, and Paul Draper is certainly one of the most talented winemakers in the world.

RITCHIE CREEK WINERY (NAPA)

1984 Cabernet Sauvignon	Napa	B	86
1985 Chardonnay	Napa	B	86

1986 Chardonnay	Napa	B	77

1986 Viognier	Napa	B	86

From high atop Spring Mountain emanates less than 1,000 cases of intense, mountain-styled Cabernet Sauvignon, fleshy, full-bodied Chardonnay, and a unique, exotic, and rare Viognier. This tiny winery has quite a cult following for its large-proportioned Cabernet, of which the 1984 seemed closed but very intense, highly extracted, powerful, and packed. The Chardonnnay is prized for its oaky, lush, intense personality, but it can be a bit overblown and clumsy as it was in 1986. The new addition to Ritchie Creek's roster of wines is the rare Viognier, and based on the only vintage I have tasted, 1986, it is an intensely aromatic, dry, luscious, very fragrant wine that will please everyone.

J. ROCHIOLI VINEYARDS (SONOMA)

1986 Chardonnay	Russian River	B	84

1984 Pinot Noir	Russian River	B	65

1985 Pinot Noir	Russian River	B	73

I have had little experience with this winery, but certainly their efforts with Pinot Noir leave a lot to be desired. However, the 1986 Chardonnay showed surprisingly attractive fruit in a medium- to full-bodied, chunky style. I see nothing to get too excited about here, and certainly the weedy, tart Pinot Noir needs improvement.

ROMBAUER VINEYARDS (NAPA)

1984 Cabernet Sauvignon	Napa	B	76

1985 Chardonnay	Napa	B	75

1986 Chardonnay	Napa	B	73

Kerner Rombauer's winery, situated on a high hill overlooking the Silverado Trail, released its first wines with the 1982 vintage and has plans to build up production to 10,000 cases. The wines are technically correct but seem to lack concentration and express no character or personality, which is just the opposite of the proprietor, a likable, serious man who seems committed to making interesting wines. I hope the vintages from 1987 and 1986 will show more richness and personality, as there has been a change in winemakers here.

ROSENBLUM CELLARS (ALAMEDA)

1985 Cabernet Sauvignon	Sonoma	B	85
1984 Zinfandel	Napa	B	87
1986 Zinfandel Cullinan Vyd.	Sonoma	B	86
1985 Zinfandel Reserve	Napa	B	87

This small winery makes interesting purple-colored, intense, full-bodied, berry-filled and berry-flavored Zinfandel. Both the 1985 Reserve and 1986 Cullinan Vineyard emphasized the rich, berry, intense fruit of the Zinfandel grape. In addition, the winery makes a good Cabernet Sauvignon, and an excellent Petite Sirah, although I have not seen a recent vintage of that wine. Apparently there is a sparkling Gewürztraminer and Chardonnay made as well, but I have never seen them in the marketplace. The prices are reasonable and the quality is high for the Rosenblum wines I have tasted. This is a winery to remember, especially if you are a lover of Zinfandel.

ROUDON-SMITH VINEYARDS (SANTA CRUZ)

1984 Cabernet Sauvignon	Santa Cruz	B	76
1986 Chardonnay Nelson Ranch	Mendocino	B	59

Roudon-Smith Winery was started in 1972 and production has remained fairly constant over recent years at about 10,000 cases. The owners purchase grapes from different locations in California and have traditionally made rich, powerful, intense Zinfandels that often carry an excessive amount of tannin along with their powerful personalities. The winery has also made a good Pinot Blanc. The two above-mentioned vintages showed very poorly, the Chardonnay being unbelievably tart and thin, and the Cabernet Sauvignon deep in color but extremely astringent and hard on the palate.

ROUND HILL (NAPA)

1984 Cabernet Sauvignon	Napa	B	79

1985 Cabernet Sauvignon	Napa	B	82
1984 Cabernet Sauvignon Reserve	Napa	B	82
1986 Chardonnay	North Coast	B	75
1986 Chardonnay House	California	A	80
1986 Chardonnay Reserve	Napa	B	78
1986 Chardonnay Van Asperen	Napa	B	68
1987 Fumé Blanc House	Napa	A	82

Round Hill burst on the scene in the late seventies and immediately took consumers by surprise by offering a pleasing number of good quality wines at very modest prices. Whether the production has caused the quality to slip a bit, I do not know, but certainly the current vintages, which are stronger vintages for California than those Round Hill made its reputation on, have rendered wines that are one-dimensional, with simple flavors and adequate depth. The wines are not overpriced, but they no longer represent the good values they once did. The Chardonnays do taste like Chardonnays, the Cabernets like Cabernets, and the Zinfandels like Zinfandels, but the lovely juicy fruit that this winery captured in its wines in the early eighties seems to be missing in the current batch of releases.

RUTHERFORD HILL WINERY (NAPA)

1984 Cabernet Sauvignon	Napa	B	84
1986 Chardonnay Cellar Reserve	Napa	B	83
1986 Chardonnay Jaeger Vineyard	Napa	B	80
1986 Chardonnay Rutherford Knoll	Napa	B	80
1987 Gewürztraminer	Napa	A	72
1985 Merlot	Napa	B	86
1984 Merlot	Napa	B	84

1987 Sauvignon Blanc	Napa	A	82

Rutherford Hill Winery continues to turn out good quality wines with a style that does not sacrifice any flavor, but one that could offer a bit more complexity and finesse. I have tended to prefer the Merlot and Cabernet Sauvignon more than the white wines. In addition, although drinkable when released, the red wines have shown the ability to age gracefully for up to a decade. Older vintages of the Cabernet Sauvignon and Merlot are well worth trying, as they can still be quite good. The Chardonnay has always been a rather chunky, oaky wine and seems to be moving more in the direction of a lighter-styled, more elegant wine. The winery's Sauvignon Blanc is well made, but pass up the very bland Gewürztraminer. Prices on the whole are quite reasonable for the quality of the wines.

ST. ANDREWS WINERY (NAPA)

1984 Cabernet Sauvignon	Napa	B	85

1986 Chardonnay	Napa	B	85

1987 Chardonnay	Napa	B	87

1987 Chardonnay St. Andrews Vineyard	Napa	B	88

While much of the 5,000-case production of this small winery is lovely, rich, deeply concentrated Chardonnays that show an engaging concoction of honey, hazelnut, oaky, and buttered-apple flavors, it has also quietly but successfully been making a lush, plummy, richly fruity Cabernet Sauvignon. Prices seem quite fair given the quality of recent wines from St. Andrews.

ST. CLEMENT VINEYARDS (NAPA)

1984 Cabernet Sauvignon	Napa	B	77

1985 Chardonnay	Napa	B	76

1986 Sauvignon Blanc	Napa	B	85

Aside from a very crisp, lean but tasty Sauvignon Blanc with its melonlike, figlike character, the other wines from St. Clement in the eighties have been mildly disappointing. The lean, overly acidified character of the Chardonnay, and compact, rather hard, charmless character of the Cabernet Sauvignon leave much to be desired from a winery that in the late seventies produced some wonderful Cabernets and Chardonnays. One wonders what the problem is here.

ST. FRANCIS VINEYARD (SONOMA)

1986 Chardonnay	Sonoma	B	86
1987 Chardonnay	California	B	85
1987 Chardonnay	Sonoma	B	87
1986 Chardonnay Reserve	Sonoma	C	90
1987 Chardonnay Reserve	Sonoma	C	90
1987 Gewürztraminer	Sonoma	A	84
1987 Johannisberg Riesling	Sonoma	A	81
1985 Merlot	Sonoma	B	87
1986 Merlot	Sonoma	B	90
1985 Merlot Reserve	Sonoma	C	90
1986 Merlot Reserve	Sonoma	C	91
1987 Muscat Canelli Late Harvest	Sonoma	A	90

St. Francis represents a rather typical story of what frequently happens in the California wine business. In 1973, Joe Martin bought a large 100-acre vineyard near Kenwood in Sonoma County. Martin built up such a reputation for his grapes, especially his Merlot and Chardonnay, that he decided to build his own winery. The first wines came out in the early eighties, but it was in the 1983 vintage that I first noticed a significant leap in quality. That success has been followed by excellent, sometimes brilliant wines in 1984, 1985, and 1986. The strengths of this house are the Merlots and Chardonnays. The Gewürztraminers and occasional Pinot Noirs have been adequate, sometimes even disappointing, rather than exciting like the Merlots and Chardonnays. Robust winemaker Tom Mackey deserves much of the credit for putting the Merlots and Chardonnays of St. Francis in the upper ranks among California producers. The first striking Merlot was the 1983, which was made in a difficult vintage. That wine was followed by spectacularly rich, velvety, chewy Merlots in 1984, 1985, and 1986. They all exhibit gorgeous smoky, opulently full bouquets, creamy, concentrated, lush textures, and stunning finishes. In my opinion, St. Francis is making California's most decadently rich, intense, and thrilling Merlots.

St. Francis also continues to turn out excellent Chardonnays. In the 1986 and 1987 vintages, both the regular bottlings and the Reserve bottlings will be favored by those who love crisp apple blossom and tropical fruit in their wines. The regular bottling emphasizes more of the fruit aspect of Chardonnay, whereas the Reserve bottlings will no doubt appeal to lovers of lusty white burgundy, especially the toasty, buttery Meursaults, as both the 1986 and 1987 Reserves have huge butterscotch, oaky characters imbued with layers of rich, creamy fruit. It's worth pointing out that the style of St. Francis wines seems oriented to giving the consumer a rich, delicious wine for drinking over the near term. The winery made a good Gewürztraminer in 1987 (a rarity in California), and the 1987 Muscat Canelli is a decadently rich, yet fresh and crisp, heavenly perfumed dessert wine with 7.5% residual sugar. While the 1986 Merlots would appear to have more aging potential than the 1985s or 1984s, these are clearly wines to drink young, within 5–7 years of the vintage. St. Francis, which has just celebrated its tenth anniversary, is doing some splendid things with Chardonnay and Merlot—don't miss them.

DOMAINE ST. GEORGE (SONOMA)

1985 Cabernet Sauvignon	Sonoma	A	77

1987 Chardonnay	Sonoma	A	75

This is probably the fastest-growing winery in California, having sold just over 10,000 cases in 1985 and nearly 200,000 cases two years later. How did they do it? By offering sound, bargain-priced varietals that taste like Chardonnay and Cabernet Sauvignon, the Domaine St. George found there is no shortage of customers for a $6 bottle of decent Chardonnay. Their wines are fresh, well made, and should be drunk within 1–2 years of their release.

CHATEAU ST. JEAN (SONOMA)

1987 Chardonnay	Sonoma	B	84

1987 Chardonnay Robert Young Vyd.	Alex. Vly.	C	90
1987 Fumé Blanc La Petite Etoile	Sonoma	B	85
1985 Johannisberg Riesling Select Late-Harvest	Sonoma	C	90
1985 Johannisberg Riesling Special Select Late-Harvest	Sonoma	C	94
1984 Pinot Blanc Robert Young Vyd.	Alex. Vly.	A	86
1985 Semillon d'Or	Sonoma	C	84
1987 Vin Blanc	Sonoma	A	82

Chateau St. Jean is in many ways representative of the high-fashion California wine industry. Founded in 1973, the wines quickly became cult items, and a Chardonnay, Fumé Blanc, and sweet late-harvest Riesling with the name Chateau St. Jean on it was a symbol of connoisseurship and good taste. However, what's in one year is soon out, and followers of California wine fashion were quick to forget Chateau St. Jean in the late seventies and early eighties as a bevy of new stars arrived on the scene. It's the end of the eighties now, and Chateau St. Jean is still one of the forerunners and most important producers of top-quality Chardonnay, Fumé Blanc, and late-harvest wines, particularly Riesling, which this winery does better than anyone else in America. The winery's strength has always been its white wines, largely because winemaker Dick Arrowood seems to have a special talent for translating flavorful and well-balanced white wine grapes into wines with character. While the winery was sold to Suntory of Japan in 1984, the quality of new releases has certainly been as good as before. The Chardonnays have never lacked for flavor, and the Robert Young Vineyard has become famous because of the demand for the Chateau St. Jean Chardonnay from that vineyard. This Chardonnay is quite full, with a buttery, herbaceous quality that sets it apart from other North Coast Chardonnays. The Fumé Blancs have at times erred in the direction of being too vegetal, but more recently, wines such as La Petite Etoile have balanced their aggressive, herbaceous fruit character with good solid body and some finesse. The Gewürztraminers, while winning raves from the California media, have rarely impressed me, but then my teeth were cut on the real stuff from Alsace. As for the late-harvest Rieslings from this winery, it can be argued that these Beerenauslese and Trockenbeerenauslese, decadent, lusciously rich, sweet dessert wines are the finest made in the New World. No one has done it better, and some of the great classics, such as the 1978 Special Select Late-Harvest from the Belle Terre Vineyard, were still drinking spectacularly well at the end of 1988. In 1984 the winery added an impressive Sauternes-like, sweet, late-harvest Semillon/Sauvignon Blanc, and if the 1985 is not as good as the 1984, it is still a tasty, well-balanced wine. While critics may argue that St. Jean's practice of vineyard-designating as many as six different Chardonnays in each vintage is excessive, the quality of this winery has remained high despite its wines having fallen out of fashion in the late seventies and early eighties. Though it is not one of the hottest wineries in California at the moment, the quality justifies continued serious interest in Chateau St. Jean.

SAINTSBURY WINERY (NAPA)

1987 Chardonnay	Carneros	B	86
1986 Chardonnay Reserve	Carneros	C	79
1986 Pinot Noir Carneros	Carneros	B	87
1987 Pinot Noir Garnet	Carneros	B	85

David Graves and Richard Ward, the two owners of the Saintsbury Winery, have done a rather amazing job in the eight years since they released their first Chardonnay and Pinot Noir. Convinced that high-quality Pinot Noir could be made in the Carneros area, they sought a style that was both elegant and flavorful, never deviating from their view of what California Pinot Noir should taste like. Saintsbury's Pinot Noir comes in two versions: a lighter style called Garnet, and their full-fledged, rich, supple Pinot Noir called Carneros. There has been little variety to choose from in recent vintages as the wines have shown a lovely, silky, cherry fruit, complemented beautifully by toasty oak. I have not held any bottles to see how they have aged, but certainly the Garnet Pinot Noir in vintages such as 1986 or 1987 should be drunk within 3–4 years of the vintage, and the Carneros Pinot Noir gives every indication of having the potential to last 5–7 years in the bottle. While I still believe the Calera Winery makes California's finest Pinot Noir, Saintsbury makes one of the most seductive, elegant styles, and certainly it must be considered among the top 2 or 3 producers of Pinot Noir in California. With respect to their Chardonnay, I have liked its exuberant freshness, medium to full body, and layers of apple blossom and floral, buttery fruit. The 1987 is one of their most attractive Chardonnays to date, but I found their 1986 Chardonnay Reserve to be closed and excessively oaky for the amount of fruit that was showing through. Perhaps it just needs more time, but it did not strike me as being in complete balance. Prices for these wines remain quite reasonable for their quality and pleasure-giving aspects.

SANFORD WINERY (SANTA BARBARA)

1987 Chardonnay	Central Coast	B	87
1986 Chardonnay Barrel Select	Santa Barbara	C	90
1987 Chardonnay Barrel Select	Santa Barbara	C	90
1984 Merlot	Santa Barbara	B	65
1985 Merlot	Santa Barbara	B	80
1986 Pinot Noir	Central Coast	B	79
1987 Vin Gris du Pinot Noir	Central Coast	A	83

Historically, I have had a great many problems with the overt, aggressive vegetal character that permeates so many of the wines from the Santa Barbara area. I know that many of the wineries feel as if there is a conspiracy among writers to praise only wines from California's North Coast, but it seems that Santa Barbara is a much better area for Chardonnays than for many of the red varietals, although luminaries such as Julia Child are very high on the wines from this area. Sanford has made tremendous progress with the quality of their wines, and their Chardonnays are now among the most flamboyant and exotic made in California. Both the 1987 and 1986 Barrel Select offer an exceptional amount of rich, tropical fruit, toasty oak, and slight herbaceous scents in a full-bodied, lush, rather explosive format. The open-knit, juicy fruit flavors are hard to ignore. I also like the winery's pale-colored rosé Vin Gris du Pinot Noir; but I still find the regular Pinot Noir to be too stemmy and weedy for my taste. However, significant improvements to its quality are noticeable with each new vintage. The 1984 Merlot has an underlying weedy, herbaceous character, but the 1985 has a fat, rich, ripe, supple fruitiness with less of a weedy character. All in all, this is a winery where I would not hesitate to try the Chardonnay or Vin Gris, but I still feel the reds are an acquired taste.

SANTA CRUZ MOUNTAIN VINEYARD (SANTA CRUZ)

1985 Cabernet Sauvignon Bates Ranch	Santa Cruz	B	88
1986 Cabernet Sauvignon Bates Ranch	Santa Cruz	B	87
1985 Merlot	Central Coast	B	79
1986 Merlot	Central Coast	B	86
1984 Pinot Noir	Santa Cruz	B	85?

I have often suspected that the large-framed, extroverted Ken Burnap makes wines that mirror his own physical characteristics and outgoing personality. His wines can be a combination of fascinating aromas of blackberry fruit, tar, and smoky oak, offering up nearly overripe, rich, unctuous flavors with the body of Sylvester Stallone. They are not wines for the wimpish, so be forewarned. His Cabernet Sauvignons have also stood the test of time, particularly his top Cabernet from the Bates Ranch in the Santa Cruz Mountains. The 1985 and 1986 are similarly styled, being very robust, huge, full-throttle, inky, intensely concentrated wines that are quite gregarious, and have 8–10 years of aging ahead of them. The Merlot from purchased grapes from the Central Coast has been less consistent than the excellent Cabernet Sauvignon. The 1985 seems especially uncomplicated and simple, although it is made in the big, generously flavored style that wine-maker/owner Burnap finds amiable. I prefer the 1986 Merlot to the 1985. Burnap has also made some interesting (some would say grotesque, and others, fascinating) Pinot Noirs that have reached nearly 15% alcohol. They will never quite resemble a burgundy, in fact they seem to have a spiritual similarity to something in northern Italy more than in Burgundy, but they can be immensely powerful, rich, tasty wines that would go well with wintertime cooking and robust cuisine. The most recent vintage, the 1984, is styled in just this manner and should drink nicely for another 7–8 years. The Santa Cruz Mountain Vineyard has consistently kept a low profile on its prices, making them among the better values in California.

SANTINO WINES (AMADOR)

1987 Muscat Canelli	Amador	A	85

1985 Zinfandel Dry Berry Select Late Harvest	Amador	C	90

1984 Zinfandel Fiddletown	Amador	A	79

This winery has specialized largely in Zinfandel and even made an incredibly sweet, syrupy dessert wine from Zinfandel in 1985. Their dry Zinfandel tends to be compact but pleasant. However, it is their Muscat Canelli that strikes me as their best and most consistent wine, offering up springtime flower-garden aromas, the scent of melons, and a lovely balance between crisp acidity and sweetness.

SARAH'S VINEYARD (SANTA CLARA)

1986 Chardonnay	Santa Clara	E	85

Crisp, clean, well-focused, and well-delineated flavors characterize the medium-bodied toasty Chardonnay made by this tiny winery, which specializes in Zinfandel, Chardonnay, and Cabernet Sauvignon from vineyards in Monterey County. The price is mind-boggling.

SAUSAL (SONOMA)

1985 Cabernet Sauvignon	Alexander Valley	B	88

1987 White Zinfandel	Alexander Valley	A	84

1984 Zinfandel	Alexander Valley	B	87

1985 Zinfandel	Alexander Valley	B	89

1984 Zinfandel Private Reserve	Alexander Valley	B	87

1985 Zinfandel Private Reserve	Alexander Valley	B	90

I am not too familiar with this winery's Chardonnays, and I have only recently had experience with their Zinfandels, even though Sausal has been producing wines under its own label for over 15 years. However, the quality of the 1984 and 1985 Zinfandels from Sausal is top-notch, as evidenced by the above ratings. These are all exquisite Zinfandels that display the velvety, rich, berry fruit of this varietal intertwined with complex, toasty oak notes. All four wines are quite full-bodied.

The Reserve wines seem to be a bit more tannic and oaky as a result of slightly longer aging in new wood barrels. Other than that from Ridge and Ravenswood, Zinfandel rarely gets any better than this. These wines should all drink well for at least another 7–8 years. although the 1985s may last longer because of their slightly higher acidities. Lastly, this winery also produces one of California's best white Zinfandels, and in 1985 made a stunningly rich, ripe, deeply flavored Cabernet Sauvignon. Sausal would appear to be on a hot streak.

SCHARFFENBERGER CELLARS (MENDOCINO)

1985 Blanc de Blanc	Mendocino	B	74
N.V. Brut	Mendocino	B	70
N.V. Brut Rose	Mendocino	B	78
N.V. Crémant	Mendocino	B	65

I have a hard time getting excited over most California sparkling wines, and the four wines above are good examples of why this is so. They are quite cleanly made, correct wines, but they lack flavor depth and come across on the palate as simple, tart, innocuous wines. The consumer should expect more for his or her money.

SCHUG CELLARS (NAPA)

1985 Chardonnay A. Hollinger Vineyards	Napa	B	73
1985 Chardonnay Beckstoffer Vineyards	Napa	B	84
1984 Pinot Noir Beckstoffer Vineyards	Napa	B	82

The German-born and -trained winemaker Walter Schug was the superstar winemaker behind the great success the Joseph Phelps Winery had in the decade of the seventies. He began his own winery in 1980, and his first releases, which included Cabernet Sauvignon, Chardonnay, and Pinot Noir from the Beckstoffer Vineyards in Napa, were not bad wines but were disappointing given his abilities and prior track record. The new releases from the much better 1984 vintage are beginning to show more character and personality, but they are still not nearly as impressive as one might expect given the talent involved. The Beckstoffer Chardonnay is a riper, fruitier wine than the A. Hollinger, which is extremely lean and compact. The 1984 Pinot Noir shows a weedy, smoky Pinot character and finishes somewhat short on the palate, but its flavors and aromatic complexity are getting close to what top-notch Pinot Noir is all about. With production expected to reach 8,000 cases, one hopes this winery will show more promise with the release of its remaining 1985s and 1986s.

SEBASTIANI WINERY (SONOMA)

1985 Cabernet Sauvignon	Sonoma	B	79
1985 Cabernet Sauvignon Bell Ranch	Sonoma	C	82
1985 Cabernet Sauvignon Cherry Block	Sonoma	C	84
1985 Cabernet Sauvignon Wildwood Vyd.	Sonoma	C	82
1986 Chardonnay Clark Ranch	Sonoma	C	86
1986 Chardonnay Kinneybrook	Sonoma	C	79
1986 Chardonnay Niles	Sonoma	C	85
1986 Chardonnay Reserve	Sonoma	B	85
1986 Chardonnay Wilson Ranch	Sonoma	C	75
1985 Merlot	Sonoma	B	82
1983 Richard Cuneo Sparkling Wine	Sonoma	C	75
1985 Zinfandel	Sonoma	B	84

Sebastiani Winery, one of California's most famous wineries with a production in excess of two million cases, is trying to find a new identity despite having prospered since its founding of 1904. The family-run operation, built into one of the great giants in California winedom by August Sebastiani, is now run by Don Sebastiani after the highly publicized ousting of his brother Sam in 1985. The new releases, the most publicized of which are all single-vineyard wines, fall under a group called the Estate Wines and are priced in the mid-teens. They are all attractively packaged with new labels, and as a group they are stylish and elegant, but I kept asking myself why they didn't have a bit more flavor depth and boldness. With respect to the Chardonnays, the Clark Ranch has good, rich, stylish, tropical-fruit aromas, an elegant, understated personality, medium body, and a crisp finish. The Niles is leaner, more compact and austere, with a stony, mineral character that reminded me of a French Chablis. Both of these wines should age well for 1–3 years. Of the other Chardonnays, the Kinneybrook tasted entirely too lean and austere and lacked flavor and depth, whereas the Wilson Ranch was simply dull, very simple, and one-dimensional. As for the non–single-vineyard wines, Sebastiani has made a delicious tropical-fruit-scented, fairly full-bodied 1986 Reserve Chardonnay that shows a lot of class and character. I actually preferred it to several of the single-vineyard Chardonnays that are more expensive.

With respect to the Cabernet Sauvignons, the 1985 Sonoma bottling falls off completely on the palate and reveals very narrow, somewhat weedy, compact flavors. The intense cherry flavors of the Cherry Block Cabernet Sauvignon make it easy to see how this vineyard got its name. This is a stylish, elegant wine with a much more subdued character than the Eagle Cabernet that brother Sam Sebastiani launched in the early eighties from the same vineyard. The Bell Ranch Cabernet is a softer, more supple wine without the complexity and character of the Cherry Block, but it is agreeable and pleasant. The 1985 Zinfandel has quite a powerful, full-bodied, muscular appeal on the palate, shows gobs of rich berry fruit, and should drink nicely for another 7–8 years; it's quite well made. As for the 1985 Merlot, it is good, perhaps a little too acidic, but very attractive in the nose though a little tart and short on the palate. Lastly, the sparkling wine called Richard Cuneo is an adequate, serviceable sparkling wine for uncritical drinking, but after one taste I was not in a hurry to go back for more.

SEGHESIO WINERY (SONOMA)

1984 Cabernet Sauvignon	Sonoma	A	75
1986 Chardonnay	Sonoma	A	72
1987 Chardonnay	Sonoma	A	84
1984 Pinot Noir	Sonoma	A	70
N.V. Red Table Wine Lot 3	Sonoma	A	82

| N.V. White Table Wine | Sonoma | A | 77 |

| 1984 Zinfandel | Sonoma | A | 82 |

For much of this century the Seghesio family produced and bottled wine in bulk for other wineries, but starting in 1983 they began to release wine under their own name. While the winery has gotten very little publicity (probably largely because prices are so low), there are some excellent values to be had in Seghesio's roster of wines. For example, the 1987 Chardonnay has good size, plenty of fruit, medium to full body, and surprising character for a wine of its price. The 1984 Zinfandel is made in a lighter, effusively fruity style, but there is no denying the appeal of its soft raspberry flavors, as well as its texture. Also, the N.V. Sonoma Red Table Wine offers hearty, straightforward flavors that are clean, well-balanced, and satisfying. At under $4 a bottle it's quite a bargain. The other wines are all standard quality and sell for very low prices. This is a winery to seek out for finding wines of value that are at least average quality and on occasion better than average, at prices well below the industry average.

WILLIAM SELYEM (SONOMA)

| 1985 Pinot Noir | Sonoma | B | 80 |

| 1986 Pinot Noir | Sonoma | B | 83 |

| 1984 Zinfandel | Sonoma | B | 87 |

The William Selyem winery, operating out of a garage, specializes in a Pinot Noir that has quite a following in California, but while it is fragrant and soft, it seems pleasant and agreeable rather than exciting. Certainly the 1986 appears to have better stuffing than the 1985. Perhaps I am missing something. Of far greater interest, but no longer in style, is Selyem's massive Zinfandel made from the 100-year-old vines of the Martinelli Vineyard. It offers the taster something closer to port than dry table wine, but the 1984 (with 17.5% alcohol, 1.5% residual sugar) is an explosively rich, intense wine that should last 20–25 years.

SEQUOIA GROVE WINERY (NAPA)

| 1984 Cabernet Sauvignon | Napa | B | 78 |

1985 Cabernet Sauvignon	Napa	B	85

1985 Cabernet Sauvignon Estate	Napa	B	87

1983 Cabernet Sauvignon (75% Napa, 25% Alex. Vly.)		B	63

1985 Chardonnay Estate	Napa	B	78

1986 Chardonnay Estate	Napa	B	85

Run by the charming Allen family, the Sequoia Grove Winery has built a good reputation for its Cabernet Sauvignons and Chardonnays, all produced at the family-owned winery near Oakville. The style of the Chardonnays emphasizes generous, buttery, apple-blossom fruit touched gently by subtle, toasty oak. It has never been one of the great North Coast Chardonnays, but in vintages such as 1986 and 1984 it is certainly among the better Chardonnays of the vintage. As for the Cabernet Sauvignon, in top years such as 1985 it is a richly fruity, supple, concentrated, and flavorful wine that has plenty of appeal for early drinking, but can be cellared for 5–7 years. The Estate Cabernet Sauvignon is more generously flavored with bigger, richer, blackcurrant flavors and a bit more tannin, oak, alcohol, and body. It can seemingly last for up to 10 years. The winery's 1986 and 1985 Cabernets look much stronger than any of their other Cabernets in the vintages of the eighties.

SHADOW CREEK CHAMPAGNE CELLARS (SAN LUIS OBISPO)

1984 Blanc de Noir	California	B	82

N.V. Brut Sparkling Wine	California	B	78

The quality of the sparkling wines from this producer tends to be quite ordinary, although the 1984 Blanc de Noir offers a light raspberry-scented bouquet that gives some appeal and a clean, zesty finish. The winery was purchased by Domaine Chandon in late 1988.

SHAFER VINEYARDS (NAPA)

1985 Cabernet Sauvignon	Napa	B	84

1985 Cabernet Sauvignon Reserve	Napa	C	86

| 1986 Cabernet Sauvignon Reserve | Napa | C | 88 |

| 1986 Chardonnay | Napa | B | 84 |

| 1985 Merlot | Napa | B | 78 |

The Shafer Winery quickly established its reputation for a rich, full-bodied Cabernet Sauvignon in 1978, the debut vintage. Production has grown to over 15,000 cases, and the winery continues to specialize in Cabernet Sauvignon, Chardonnay, and at times Merlot. While the winery did make a good Zinfandel, unfortunately they dropped it from their portfolio. Following the great success of the 1978 Cabernet Sauvignon, I found the Shafer wines to show a great deal of bottle variation and an excessive amount of sulphur in the bouquet of some wines. I was especially puzzled by the huge bottle variation of the 1982 Cabernets, and I was not impressed by the vegetal character of the 1983s. It seems that these inconsistencies have been ironed out, as the 1986 Chardonnay is an attractive, medium-bodied wine with scents of pears, toasty oak, and green apples. As for the red wines, the finest Shafer Cabernet Sauvignon made since the 1978 will no doubt be the 1986 Reserve Cabernet. It has an impressive bouquet of rich, weedy, blackcurrant fruit, is quite full-bodied, and is admirably concentrated. It should age for up to a decade. The 1985 Cabernet Sauvignon and Merlot are also good wines, but less intense and complex than the 1986 Reserve. This is a winery that has maintained a fairly moderate pricing structure, and if the wines show greater consistency in the bottle, they will be well worth seeking out.

SIERRA VISTA (EL DORADO)

| 1984 Cabernet Sauvignon El Dorado | A | 82 |

| 1983 Syrah El Dorado | A | 87 |

This winery gets little recognition, but there is little denying the reasonable prices and very good quality of its wines. They offer plenty of richness, show excellent winemaking, and are faithful to the grape variety they are produced from. The 1983 Syrah is an especially promising, age-worthy wine.

SILVER OAK CELLARS (NAPA)

| 1984 Cabernet Sauvignon | Alex. Vly. | C | 92 |

1985 Cabernet Sauvignon	Alex. Vly.	C	92
1986 Cabernet Sauvignon	Alex. Vly.	C	90
1984 Cabernet Sauvignon	Napa	C	95
1985 Cabernet Sauvignon	Napa	C	96
1986 Cabernet Sauvignon	Napa	C	91
1984 Cabernet Sauvignon Bonny's Vineyard	Napa	D	97
1985 Cabernet Sauvignon Bonny's Vineyard	Napa	D	96
1986 Cabernet Sauvignon Bonny's Vineyard	Napa	D	93

These three vintages of Cabernet Sauvignon from Silver Oak Cellars are among the most majestic and complex Cabernets made by any California winery at any time. The experience of sitting down and tasting through all of them was mind blowing. Much if not all the credit for these wines must go to the low-profile, but highly competent owner/winemaker, Justin Meyer. The winery, using 100% American oak, specializes in only one wine, a luscious Cabernet Sauvignon that comes from three locations. About 16,000 cases come from Alexander Valley, about 2,000 cases from Napa Valley, and about 500 cases from the tiny parcel of vines named after Meyer's wife, Bonny. The Cabernets spend nearly 2½ years in American oak barrels, of which 50% is new oak for the Alexander Valley and 100% new oak for the Bonny's Vineyard. The winery has somehow managed to keep a low profile despite the fact that the quality of their Cabernets is outstanding. However, the quiet, reserved Justin Meyer does reluctantly admit that the 1984s, 1985s, and 1986s are the finest wines he has ever made. The 1984 Alexander Valley is a fleshpot of a wine with an exotic, intense, spicy, blackberry, oaky bouquet that explodes from the glass. On the palate there is a marvelous, velvety, rich, multidimensional flavor sensation, and an enormously long, delicious finish. Unbelievably appealing now, it should age well for 7–8 years. The 1984 Napa is even more sensational with greater depth and extract but more tannin and body. It shares the same exotic, extroverted, flashy style of the Alexander Valley, just packing more depth and tannin. The Bonny's Vineyard, several notches more profound, is truly one of the most exciting Cabernets I have ever had the pleasure to taste. It has explosive fruit and power, as well as great extract and the ability to age for 10–15 years. As great as these wines are, the 1985s may in certain cases be marginally superior, although it's hard to see how. Though every bit as splendidly rich, complex, and exotic as the 1984s, they are slightly less opulent, have better acidities, and will probably outlive the 1984s by 3–5 years. Lastly, the 1986s also look to be among the finest wines from that excellent vintage. These accomplishments should not cause one to ignore the very good 1983s and outstanding 1982s made at Silver Oak. Justin Meyer seems totally content to stay out of the limelight and let his wines do the talking for him, and one would be a fool not to stockpile the current and upcoming vintages of the Silver Oak Cabernets.

SILVERADO VINEYARDS (NAPA)

1984 Cabernet Sauvignon	Napa	B	87
1985 Cabernet Sauvignon	Napa	B	88
1986 Chardonnay	Napa	B	88
1987 Chardonnay	Napa	B	87
1984 Merlot	Napa	B	86
1985 Merlot	Napa	B	87
1986 Sauvignon Blanc	Napa	A	85

This Walt Disney-owned winery, which sits on top of a hill with a commanding view of the lower Napa Valley and the Silverado Trail, started off with good wines when the 1981s were released, and it has steadily moved up in quality, culminating with excellent wines in the three vintages of 1986, 1985, and 1984. Furthermore, the winery has not let its high quality and both critical and commercial success go to its head when it comes to prices; they have remained reasonable. Production is expected to peak at 50,000 cases, all from Silverado's own vineyards. Of the current releases, the Chardonnay is showing wonderfully ripe scents of tropical fruit and toasty oak, a lush texture, good acidity, and a winemaker who is not afraid to put some flavor into the bottle. As far as the red wines go, the 1984 Merlot has vivid black-cherry flavors, full body, a soft, plump texture, and a well-delineated varietal character. The 1985 is very similar but has a slightly less opulent texture, higher acids, and five additional years of aging potential. Both the 1985 and 1984 Cabernet Sauvignons are excellent. They both share a blackcurrant, subtle, herbaceous bouquet that shows a judicious use of toasty oak. Dense in color and quite concentrated, these stylish yet authoritatively flavored wines should age gracefully for 7–10 more years, and both establish a new high for this excellent winery.

SIMI WINERY (SONOMA)

1984 Cabernet Sauvignon	Sonoma	B	82
1985 Cabernet Sauvignon	Sonoma	B	84
1985 Cabernet Sauvignon Reserve	Sonoma	D	92
1986 Cabernet Sauvignon Reserve	Sonoma	D	94
1985 Chardonnay	Sonoma	B	86
1986 Chardonnay	Sonoma	B	87
1984 Chardonnay Reserve	Sonoma	C	90
1985 Chardonnay Reserve	Sonoma	C	90
1987 Rosé of Cabernet Sauvignon	Sonoma	A	84

It's no secret that when the outstanding winemaker Zelma Long came to Simi in 1979, this historic winery, founded in 1876, was about to enter a new era of higher quality. Long brought her touch for white wines along with her, and the Simi Chardonnays evolved into a good, commerical, richly fruity, medium-bodied regular cuvée, and an extravagantly rich, intentionally big, lavishly oaky, unctuous, intense, complex, and buttery Reserve Chardonnay, of which both the 1985 and 1984 are textbook examples of this extroverted, large-scaled, creamy, oaky, flavorful style. As for the red wines, there is no doubting the credentials of Zelma Long, and when those are combined with the consultation of the brilliant French oenologist Michel Rolland, the formula for successful Cabernets was discovered. Could the teaming up of Long and Rolland be the reason why both the sublime 1985 and 1986 Reserve Cabernet Sauvignons are close in complexity and style to what Christian Mouiex has accomplished with Dominus? Here is one winery where picking between the 1985 and 1986 Reserves will be difficult, although the 1986 may turn out to be slightly less intense. Complex oak as well as a plethora of Cabernet Sauvignon aromas is remarkably enticing in both vintages of these special wines. On the palate, there is impeccable balance, plenty of finesse and flavor, and enough tannin and length to suggest that both vintages will keep at least 10–15 years. Bravo to Simi, for these two Cabernets are the finest they have made since their historic days early in the century. As for the regular cuvées of Cabernet, they are made for the masses —supple, fruity, easy-to-drink, and quite agreeable. Lastly, don't forget one of the best rosé wines made in California. The 1987 Rosé of Cabernet Sauvignon offers vibrant, poignant, herbaceous, curranty aromas, crisp, well-delineated fruit, and a lovely off-dry taste that makes it an ideal picnic or summertime rosé wine.

SINSKEY (NAPA)

1986 Chardonnay	Carneros	C	88
1986 Pinot Noir	Carneros	C	85

The debut releases from this new enterprise show high aspirations. The winemaker, Joe Cafaro, has top credentials, and the lovely, rich, tropical-fruit-scented Chardonnay with an attractive toasty vanillin perfume is full-bodied, well-structured, and loaded with fruit. The Pinot Noir also looks well done with its vibrant black-cherry fruit married intelligently with toasty oak. My only complaint about these debut wines are the bold prices.

SMITH AND HOOK VINEYARD (MONTEREY)

1985 Cabernet Sauvignon	Monterey	B	?
1986 Cabernet Sauvignon	Monterey	B	?

I don't mean to always be so tough on Cabernet producers in Monterey; however, it saddens me to say that despite the impressive power of these two wines, the vegetal character of both is so overwhelming it makes them quite unappealing. I know there are those who would argue that this is a characteristic of Monterey County, and I am sure it is, but it does not belong in Cabernet Sauvignon. Until the viticulturists learn how to eliminate it, I think these wines are defective as well as bizarre.

SMITH-MADRONE (NAPA)

I have not seen any of this winery's vintages in the marketplace for several years. However, wines I tasted from vintages such as 1982, 1983, and 1984 included a disappointing Pinot Noir, an adequate Cabernet Sauvignon, and a Chardonnay of no great merit.

SODA ROCK WINERY (SONOMA)

1985 Chardonnay	Sonoma	B	78
1986 Chardonnay	Sonoma	B	80

This is a new winery and the only wine I have tasted from it has been a compact, rather neutral-tasting, chunky Chardonnay that will hardly win great praise.

SONOMA-CUTRER WINERY (SONOMA)

1986 Chardonnay Cutrer Vineyard	Sonoma	C	90
1986 Chardonnay Les Pierres	Sonoma	C	92
1986 Chardonnay Russian River Ranches	Sonoma	B	87
1987 Chardonnay Russian River Ranches	Sonoma	B	89

There is no doubt that the Chardonnays that have been released by the youthful Sonoma-Cutrer Winery and its brilliant winemaker Bill Bonetti have had quite a sensational welcome from both the wine press and wine consumers. There are three Chardonnays made, two from single vineyards and one from what the winery calls its Russian River Ranches. They are made in a winery that has more technology than I have ever seen, but the basic philosophy of making the wine is to manipulate it as little as possible. The Russian River Ranches Chardonnay tends to be the more open-knit, opulent, and tropical-fruit-scented, and the easiest to drink initially, whereas the Cutrer Vineyard tends to be very Californian in style with a good lashing of toasty oak, but opulent, rich in fruit, and extremely elegant in a full-bodied style. Perhaps the most interesting of all the Sonoma-Cutrer Chardonnays is Les Pierres Chardonnay, which, as its name may imply, has a pronounced taste of wet stones or minerals, and which is made in a more classic, austere, yet powerful, richly fruity, full-bodied style. These are extraspecial Chardonnays, but I have to admit that at a blind tasting in 1988, the initial wines from the vintages of 1981, 1982, and 1983 were fading much more quickly than what one might have thought given the manner in which they were made. Certainly the recent vintages should age better than the earlier ones. As for the 1987s, Bill Bonetti says they are the finest Chardonnays he has made to date, and that is high praise indeed. Sonoma-Cutrer is one of California's hottest wineries, and one hopes the sparkling wine they are planning on releasing is every bit as good as their outstanding trio of Chardonnays.

CHÂTEAU SOUVERAIN (SONOMA)

1984 Cabernet Sauvignon	Sonoma	B	75
1985 Cabernet Sauvignon	Sonoma	B	78
1986 Chardonnay	Sonoma	B	79
1986 Chardonnay Reserve	Sonoma	B	77

The Souverain winery has been through a great deal of change over the years and is now marketing its wines under the more pretentious-sounding name of Château Souverain. The wines have generally been fairly priced, and on occasion they could be stunning sleepers when tasted against the competition. I especially remember a 1974 Cabernet Sauvignon at $6 a bottle that was one of the top dozen wines of that great vintage. The new wines show clean, correct, technically competent winemaking, though lacking a little personality and individuality. They are pleasant and fairly priced, but a bit bolder, more dramatic style would seem to be in order.

SPOTTSWOODE VINEYARD AND WINERY (NAPA)

1984 Cabernet Sauvignon	Napa	D	90
1985 Cabernet Sauvignon	Napa	D	93
1986 Cabernet Sauvignon	Napa	D	92
1987 Sauvignon Blanc	Napa	B	87

This relative newcomer burst on the California scene with a terrific 1982 Cabernet Sauvignon that won plaudits for its bold blackcurrant fruit, deep, spicy, toasty oakiness, and generous mouth-filling texture.

The quality could not have come as much of a surprise since the winemaker was and continues to be the highly capable Tony Soter, and the vineyard he got his grapes from had already been an important component of the early Cabernet Sauvignon successes turned out by the nearby Duckhorn Winery. The debut Cabernet was followed by a good 1983, an excellent 1984, an otherworldly 1985 that should prove to be the finest wine yet from Spottswoode, and the outstanding 1986, which may ultimately turn out to be every bit as exceptional as the 1985. The Spottswoode Cabernets all show the same personality traits —sensational color, full-intensity bouquets of blackcurrant fruit, tarry, smoky, toasty oak, great flavor extraction from the grapes, full body, and enough tannin to warrant cellaring for 7–15 years. The winery's other wine is a stylish, flavorful, far from bland and boring Sauvignon Blanc that is among the best of its class. Prices for Spottswoode's wines are on the high side, particularly in view of how short the history of the winery is, but the quality is impeccable, and the 1985 and 1986 Cabernets appear to be the finest yet made by this up-and-coming Cabernet superstar in Napa Valley.

SPRING MOUNTAIN VINEYARDS (NAPA)

1982 Cabernet Sauvignon	Napa	B	77
1983 Cabernet Sauvignon	Napa	B	68
1983 Chardonnay	Napa	B	74
1984 Chardonnay	Napa	B	72
1985 Chardonnay	Napa	B	85
1986 Sauvignon Blanc	Napa	B	79

As a result of the Falcon Crest soap opera, which was filmed at this winery, Spring Mountain is better known than ever. Its history goes back to 1968, but in spite of the fact that the wines have been mostly quite mediocre and inconsistent, they seem to have sold well largely because of the winery's notoriety. I hope that when the winery begins to produce wines from its own vineyard (which just recently came into production), the quality will be more consistent and on a higher level. Currently, prices are excessive for what one gets in the bottle.

STAG'S LEAP WINE CELLARS (NAPA)

1985 Cabernet Sauvignon	Napa	B	86
1984 Cabernet Sauvignon Cask 23	Napa	D	94
1985 Cabernet Sauvignon Cask 23	Napa	D	96
1986 Cabernet Sauvignon Cask 23	Napa	D	94
1984 Cabernet Sauvignon Stag's Leap Vineyard	Napa	C	87
1985 Cabernet Sauvignon Stag's Leap Vineyard	Napa	C	89
1986 Cabernet Sauvignon Stag's Leap Vineyard	Napa	C	89
1986 Chardonnay Reserve	Napa	C	87
1987 Chardonnay Reserve	Napa	C	89
1984 Merlot Stag's Leap Vineyard	Napa	B	87
1985 Petite Sirah	Napa	B	85
1987 Sauvignon Blanc	Napa	A	85

The 16-year-old Stag's Leap Wine Cellars is one of California's best-known wineries. Its fame, based largely on the success of its erudite owner Warren Winiarski and his splendid wines, is also the result of the historic wine taste-off in 1976 that was staged by Englishman and wine merchant Steven Spurrier in Paris. Stag's Leap was a big winner against the more prestigious and expensive top châteaux of Bordeaux. Winiarski followed this wine with a succession of strong Cabernets, all displaying velvety fruit and finesse, with particularly outstanding wines in 1976, 1977, and 1978. His wines slumped in quality between 1979 and 1982, bouncing back in the troublesome vintage of 1983 and being clearly outstanding in 1984, 1985, and 1986. Cask 23 is his top wine, and in the last three vintages this proprietary red wine (it's largely a Cabernet Sauvignon–based wine) has been as great and as distinctive a California wine as any red wine I have ever tasted. The 1984 is an opulent, multidimensional, extremely rich wine that displays expansive, complex aromas of coffee, cedar, chocolate, toasty oak, and berry fruit. Supple, seductive, and intense, this full-bodied wine is deceptively easy to drink now, but it will develop for at least a decade. It reminds me somewhat of his famous 1974 Cask 23. The other 1984s from Stag's Leap are slightly less compelling but all rich, velvety wines that will provide wonderful drinking over the next 5–7 years. The 1985 Cask 23 was one of the three or four most impressive young California wines I have ever tasted. Now that it is in the bottle, it seems to have closed up a bit, but it is a profound wine of great flavor dimension, staggering richness and intensity, and should prove to be one of the most monumental bottles of Cabernet Sauvignon ever to be produced in Napa Valley. It should last for a good 10–15 years. The 1986, while a notch below the extraordinary 1985, is still worthy of any conscientiously stocked wine cellar. The huge bouquet jumps from the glass with scents of smoked meats, spicy new oak, and ripe fruit. On the palate it shows great depth, a forward, opulent texture, and an extremely long finish. In style, one might say it falls in between the 1984 and 1985. As for the other Cabernet Sauvignons, they share a similarity with the Cask 23 but do not have its multidimensional character or richness.

While the greatness of Stag's Leap Wine Cellars has been based on its Cabernet Sauvignons, the winery for years was unable to demonstrate the same magical talent with its Sauvignon Blanc or Chardonnay, which were correct rather than thrilling wines. The most encouraging signs are the 1986 and 1987 Reserve Chardonnays made by Stag's Leap, which are certainly the finest Chardonnays made here, both exhibiting considerable style and flavor. In addition, the Sauvignon Blanc has taken on a bit more flavor dimension and complexity. The winery also makes a good, rich, peppery, supple Petite Sirah. For shrewd consumers looking for value, the wines under the Hawk Crest label have gotten increasingly better in the decade of the eighties, with wines such as the 1987 Hawk Crest Chardonnay, and 1985 and 1986 Hawk Crest Cabernet Sauvignons, showing tremendous fruit and up-front richness for wines that can generally be found in the marketplace for under $6 a bottle. While Stag's Leap wines can be expensive, the quality here has been remarkably consistent since 1983, and some of the wines are among the most thrilling and exciting wines being produced in the New World.

STAG'S LEAP WINERY (NAPA)

1984 Cabernet Sauvignon	Napa	B	80

1984 Petite Sirah	Napa	B	86

Carl Doumani produces Cabernet Sauvignon, Petite Sirah, Merlot, and Chardonnay from a vineyard in the Stag's Leap area. He is best known for his rich, age-worthy Petite Sirah that usually takes a half dozen years to reach its peak. I have not been as impressed with his Cabernet Sauvignon, but his Merlot tends to be good. I have not seen a recent vintage of his Chardonnay. The secondary wines made here are called Pedregal.

STELTZNER VINEYARDS (NAPA)

1984 Cabernet Sauvignon	Napa	B	86

1985 Cabernet Sauvignon	Napa	B	87

This famous vineyard, which until 1983 sold its grapes to other California wineries, has been making very elegant, graceful Cabernet Sauvignons since 1982. While the 1984 shows more opulent, forward fruit than either the 1983 or 1982, the best wine yet made at Steltzner appears to be the 1985, which has a deep color, a rich, curranty, restrained bouquet of subtle oak, and weedy, berry fruit, medium to full body, and at least a decade's worth of aging potential. These are rather understated, polite wines that come from one of the better-placed Cabernet vineyards in all of Napa Valley. Production is around 5,000 cases.

ROBERT STEMMLER WINERY (SONOMA)

1985 Pinot Noir	Sonoma	C	84

1986 Pinot Noir	Sonoma	C	84

While Chardonnay is also made at the 10,000-case Stemmler Winery located in the Dry Creek Valley, the pride and joy of the gregarious Robert Stemmler is his Pinot Noir. It has an attractive berry ripeness framed by a moderate sojourn in toasty oak. While it is not the best Pinot Noir in California, it is amazingly consistent from vintage to vintage and always seems to be at its best 3–4 years following the vintage. In addition, its price has remained fair.

STERLING VINEYARDS (NAPA)

1985 Cabernet Sauvignon	Napa	B	82
1984 Cabernet Sauvignon Diamond Mountain	Napa	B	85
1985 Cabernet Sauvignon Diamond Mountain	Napa	B	89
1986 Cabernet Sauvignon Reserve	Napa	C	89
1986 Chardonnay	Napa	B	85
1987 Chardonnay	Napa	B	87
1986 Chardonnay Winery Lake	Napa	C	89
1985 Merlot	Napa	B	85
1986 Pinot Noir	Carneros	B	82
1987 Sauvignon Blanc	Napa	B	85
1985 Three Palms Vineyard (55% Merlot/45% Cabernet Sauvignon)	Napa	C	84

Sterling Vineyards, which has some of the most impressive vineyard holdings in all of Napa Valley, has had a checkered lifestyle since its founding in 1969. The early vintages with winemaker Ric Forman at the helm produced a stunning succession of Chardonnays and Cabernet Sauvignons from 1973 to 1977. In 1978 the winery was sold to Coca-Cola and in 1983 to Seagram, who at first seemed to apply accounting principles to the making of wine. Consequently, the quality of Sterling's wines slipped as production was given precedence over personality. All those early wines have stood the test of time quite well, and it's encouraging that Seagram has now switched gears again, and with winemaker Bill Dyer being given more flexibility, the quality has begun to bounce back in the mid-eighties. I could see some good signs with the 1982 Cabernet Sauvignon from Diamond Mountain, which showed so much potential and richness. However, the most encouraging signs of all are the red wines from the 1984 and 1985 vintages, which show excellent depth, a sense of harmony, and a winemaker who seems committed to putting flavor, finesse, and individuality into the wines. The several Chardonnays produced here have taken on new flavor dimensions and are showing a good dosage of oak and rich, well-focused flavors of apples, oranges, and buttery fruit. Additionally, we can now look forward to a Winery Lake Chardonnay from that superb vineyard acquired by Sterling several years ago. The debut release, the 1986, is an outstanding bottle of Chardonnay. The winery is also producing a regular Cabernet Sauvignon and a Reserve Cabernet Sauvignon, as well as a Merlot. Even a good 1986 Pinot Noir emerged from this winery. I hope the straightforward, compact, rather one-dimensional wines of the late seventies and early eighties from potentially one of the most significant producers of California wine are now history.

STEVENOT VINEYARDS (CALAVERAS)

1984 Cabernet Sauvignon	Calaveras	B	75
1984 Cabernet Sauvignon Grand Reserve	Calaveras	B	68
1986 Chardonnay	California	B	74
1987 Muscat Canelli	San Luis Obispo	B	85

Stevenot Winery produces over 50,000 cases of very reasonably priced (generally under $10 a bottle) wine from Sierra foothill vineyards. The only wine I have truly liked to date has been the moderately sweet Muscat Canelli with its exotic mélange of tropical-fruit flavors and crisp acidity. The other wines from the Stevenot cellar include a compact, rather dull Chardonnay, and two Cabernets that had good color and full body but have been dominated by the smell of spearmint, and in the case of the 1984 Grand Reserve, a medicinal taste and odd personality. Given the prices, I wish I liked the wines more.

STONEGATE WINERY (NAPA)

1984 Chardonnay Spaulding Vineyard	Napa	B	75
1983 Merlot Spaulding Vineyard	Napa	B	82
1984 Merlot Spaulding Vineyard	Napa	B	87
1986 Sauvignon Blanc	Napa	B	78

Stonegate Winery, located near Calistoga in the northern end of Napa Valley, has shown the ability to turn out very plump, tasty Cabernet

Sauvignon and Merlot from its own vineyard, but the white wines have been a mixed bag. Certainly the 1984 Chardonnay from Spaulding Vineyard seems to be losing its fruit at a rather accelerated pace, although it is still palatable. I would definitely look for the Merlot from this winery, and if you can find it, the Cabernet Sauvignon, but choose the Sauvignon Blanc and Chardonnay from someone else.

STONY HILL VINEYARDS (NAPA)

1985 Chardonnay	Napa	C	92
1986 Chardonnay	Napa	C	90

Stony Hill is one of the legendary names in California viticulture. Its reputation was built on one of the few Chardonnays from California that can actually improve in the bottle beyond 3–4 years. There is also white Riesling and Gewürztraminer made at this winery, but I lament the fact that I have never tasted it. The Chardonnay starts off light, closed, compact, and while weighty and rich, just not in full bloom. However, with several years in the bottle, the apple-blossom smells and buttery, ripe richness emerge, and within 5 to 6 years one has an opulent, well-balanced, well-delineated, full-bodied Napa Valley Chardonnay that competes with the very best made in the entire state. Much of the credit for this must go to the remarkable enthusiasm demonstrated by Stony Hill's proprietor, the redoubtable Eleanor McCrea.

STORY BOOK MOUNTAIN VINEYARDS (NAPA)

1981 Zinfandel	Napa	B	85
1983 Zinfandel	Napa	B	84
1985 Zinfandel	Napa	B	86
1986 Zinfandel	Napa	B	87
1984 Zinfandel Reserve	Napa	B	86
1985 Zinfandel Reserve	Napa	B	85
1986 Zinfandel Reserve	Napa	B	90

How many proprietors in California can you name who make only Zinfandel? How many proprietors can you name who make 5,000 cases of Zinfandel and sell 60% of it outside California with 10% going to Switzerland and Germany? Well, the name is Storybook Mountain Vineyards, and owner, Bernard Seps, is as serious about his Zinfandel as California's top producers of Cabernet Sauvignon, Merlot, and Chardonnay are about their wines. He also scoffs at those who claim Zinfandel doesn't age well, and he has the wines to prove it. The style of Zinfandel here is different from other top Zinfandel wineries such as Ravenswood or Ridge. Seps aims for an elegant, very age-worthy style with a great measure of tannin and rather restrained, well-balanced flavors, but intense concentration and full body. There are two Zinfandels made, a regular bottling that appears under a blue label, and a Reserve bottling that has a cream-colored label. Of the Reserves, the 1986 is the best Zinfandel Seps has made to date, showing fabulous richness and length, full body, oodles of the crushed berry fruit that makes Zinfandel so enticing, and enough balance to last the rest of this century. The 1985 Reserve is a tighter, harder, leaner style of wine, but nevertheless impressive. The 1984 Reserve is totally ready to drink, has less color than the 1986 and 1985, but is extremely fruity, soft, and fragrant. Should you see any of his older Reserves on the shelves, don't dare miss the 1980 Reserve that when last tasted, 8 years after the vintage, was showing great complexity and could have been mistaken for a fine burgundy. As far as the regular bottlings go, it again looks as if the 1985 and 1986 are the best two wines under the blue label, with both showing a crushed-raspberry fruitiness in their bouquets, full body, and long, concentrated finishes with plenty of tannin to shed. Both wines should easily last a decade or more. Storybook Mountain Vineyards is one of the best Zinfandel specialists in the state of California, and the wines age as gracefully as anybody's. Prices are modest for the quality in the bottle.

STREBLOW VINEYARDS (NAPA)

1985 Cabernet Sauvignon	Napa	B	79
1986 Sauvignon Blanc	Napa	B	72

A new winery whose first wines revealed a compact but well-made, berry-scented, well-focused, medium-bodied Cabernet Sauvignon and lean, insubstantial, and rather tasteless Sauvignon Blanc, it is too early to judge what Streblow has in mind, but it is well located and has the vineyards to produce good wine.

SULLIVAN VINEYARDS WINERY (NAPA)

1982 Cabernet Sauvignon	Napa	C	88
1983 Cabernet Sauvignon	Napa	C	?
1984 Cabernet Sauvignon	Napa	C	90
1985 Cabernet Sauvignon	Napa	C	?
1985 Chenin Blanc	Napa	A	55
1985 Merlot	Napa	B	?

With a production of 8,000 cases, I wouldn't describe this winery as small, but the Sullivan family has changed from home winemakers to ones turning out seriously rich, big-styled wines from their own vineyards located south of St. Helena and Rutherford. The first vintage was in 1981, and the winery made headlines with its phenomenonly rich, intense 1982 Cabernet Sauvignon, then fell on its face with a defective 1983 Cabernet Sauvignon. It returned to form with a stunning wine in 1984 that showed astonishing concentration and richness in a very big, oaky, full-bodied style. However, neither the 1985 Cabernet Sauvignon nor the Merlot smelled totally clean; they still have a rather unpleasant, off character to their bouquets despite a mouth-filling and attention-getting richness that one rarely sees except in California's very finest Cabernet Sauvignons. This problem needs to be corrected. Clearly the vineyards here are capable of producing mammoth-sized, massive wines that are bold, dramatic, and loaded with character. Sullivan also produces a little bit of Chenin Blanc that is apparently barrel-fermented. At least it tastes that way, and for that reason I find it unacceptable in every sense as the delicate, flowery aromas of Chenin Blanc are obliterated under a tidal wave of coarse oakiness.

SUTTER HOME WINERY (NAPA)

1987 White Zinfandel	California	A	83

Sutter Home has been one of the great overnight success stories in California on the basis of one wine, its white Zinfandel. There have been a horde of imitators of this wine, but no one's white Zinfandel is any more popular than Sutter Home's, notwithstanding the fact that at least a dozen wineries produce a better white Zinfandel. While wine connoisseurs turn their noses up at such products, the fact is that this wine, with its slight percentage of residual sugar, and crisp, fresh, strawberry and cherry flavors, is a decent drink. No, it's not serious, but it is satisfying, and therein lies the reason why Sutter Home is making a fortune with a wine that is remarkably easy to produce. In 1985 a sparkling white Zinfandel was added, but it has not sold as well as the regular bottling. This winery also produces other wines, such as Zinfandel, but I have not seen them in the market.

JOSEPH SWAN VINEYARDS (SONOMA)

1983 Pinot Noir	Sonoma	C	79
1984 Pinot Noir	Sonoma	C	84
1984 Zinfandel	Sonoma	C	87
1985 Zinfandel	Sonoma	C	88

From the first day he opened his winery in 1969, Joseph Swan has been one of the cult figures of California's wine industry. Never one to seek publicity, Swan has continued to make wine, but one rarely hears much about him today. While he also makes Chardonnay and Cabernet Sauvignon, the recent releases I tasted included two rich, deliciously fruity, full-bodied Zinfandels that are ready to burst from the amount of berry fruit he has packed into them. Both should drink well for 5–7 years. The two Pinot Noirs are not as impressive, but I certainly liked the burgundian aromas and flavors that Swan was able to put in these wines—there was just not enough of them. The velvety, richer 1984 gets the nod over the leaner, harder 1983. Swan's wines are available only from the winery, located at 2916 Laguna Road, Forestville, CA 95436.

TAFT STREET WINERY (SONOMA)

1983 Cabernet Sauvignon	Napa	A	73
1984 Cabernet Sauvignon	Napa/Sonoma	A	78
1985 Cabernet Sauvignon	Napa/Sonoma	A	77
1985 Chardonnay	Sonoma	B	72

| 1986 Chardonnay | Sonoma | B | 75 |

| 1983 Pinot Noir | Monterey | A | 52 |

While Taft Street Winery is to be applauded for trying to make wines under $10 a bottle available to the consumer, the quality of their releases to date has generally been mediocre. The Chardonnays have been overly acidified, too tart and compact, and the Cabernet Sauvignons undistinguished with rather rough, harsh finishes, although the 1984 Cabernet showed a soft, alcoholic, fruity character, but no definition or focus. The Pinot Noir was ghastly in its cooked, vegetal, earthy character, all of which makes me question whether these wines are worth the price of admission.

ROBERT TALBOTT VINEYARDS (MONTEREY)

| 1985 Chardonnay | Monterey | C | 87 |

| 1986 Chardonnay | Monterey | C | 92 |

Robert Talbott of necktie fame has specialized in one classically rendered, barrel-fermented, rich, oaky, but well-balanced Chardonnay. From the debut release in 1984 the wine has been a big hit with serious wine drinkers. The 1984 was followed by a more tightly knit but no less impressive 1985. The best wine yet made by this small winery dedicated to Chardonnay is the 1986, which is bursting with rich, lemony, applelike and orange-flavored fruit, with good, crisp acidity, a solid lashing of toasty new oak, full body, and quite a long finish. Given its balance, it may actually age in the bottle much longer than most California Chardonnays, and one may wish to gamble and hold a bottle or two for four or five years. These are immensely impressive wines in what is the most expensive bottle, and one of the most attractive labels, in all of California.

EVAN TAMAS (SANTA CLARA)

| 1985 Cabernet Sauvignon | Mendocino | A | 75 |

| 1986 Cabernet Sauvignon | Mendocino | A | 80 |

| 1987 Chardonnay | Central Coast | A | 78 |

| 1987 Sauvignon Blanc | Napa | A | 80 |

1987 White Zinfandel	Mendocino	A	75

This winery is attempting to find its place in the California wine world by offering its wines at reasonable prices, and making them in a very forward, fruity, easy-to-appreciate-and-drink style. To date the wines have been pleasant, cleanly made, and while hardly thrilling, quite acceptable and reasonably priced. All of the wines, including the Cabernet Sauvignon, should be drunk within 3–4 years of the vintage.

THE TERRACES (NAPA)

1985 Zinfandel Hogue Vyd.	Napa	B	90

The debut wine from a new producer (the wine was made at Caymus) specializing in a hillside-vineyard Zinfandel, the 1985 is an impressive wine. Deep ruby/purple with a moderately intense, oaky, crushed-raspberry-scented bouquet, this rich, full-bodied, beautifully structured wine will age well for 5–10 years. A beauty!

TIFFANY HILL (EDNA VALLEY)

1986 Chardonnay	Edna Valley	C	88

Based on the first release from this new winery in Edna Valley, consumers should have another top-notch Chardonnay producer to look for in the marketplace. This boldly flavored, rich wine filled with aromas of oranges, honey, and toasty oak is quite a delicious, rich, ripe mouthful of wine.

PHILIP TOGNI VINEYARD (NAPA)

1984 Cabernet Sauvignon	Napa	C	86
1985 Cabernet Sauvignon Estate	Napa	C	85
1985 Cabernet Sauvignon Tanbark Hill	Napa	C	89
1986 Ca Togni	Napa	B	?
1987 Sauvignon Blanc	Napa	B	84

Philip Togni, a consultant and winemaker for a number of wineries as well as a grower, developed a reputation for being talented but also difficult. He now has his own line of wines, offering very highly extracted, rich, age-worthy Cabernet Sauvignons with excellent depth and length. The 1984 is loaded with blackcurrant fruit, is full-bodied and intense, and shows a judicious use of oak and 5–7 years of aging potential. The 1985 Tanbark single-vineyard Cabernet is even deeper with a huge, chocolaty, curranty nose, very deep, full, intense flavors, outstanding depth, and 10–15 years of further evolution possible. The 1985 Estate bottling is a leaner, less impressive wine, but still well-made and rich. As for the Sauvignon Blanc, it should prove to be controversial with tasters as it has quite an assertive, herbaceous, varietal nose, and crisp, medium-bodied flavors. The Ca Togni, a very sweet, syrupy, one-dimensional wine made from the black Muscat grape, is rich and full but has no complexity and tastes heavy and cloyingly sweet.

TREFETHEN VINEYARDS WINERY (NAPA)

1984 Cabernet Sauvignon	Napa	B	75
1985 Chardonnay	Napa	B	87
1986 Chardonnay	Napa	B	88
N.V. Eschol Red	Napa	A	84
N.V. Eschol White	Napa	A	84
1984 Pinot Noir	Napa	B	77
1987 White Riesling	Napa	A	87

The Trefethens are significant growers in the Napa Valley with over 600 acres of vineyard, but they only use a tiny portion of their own grapes for wines that appear under their label. Since its first vintage in 1974, the winery has made one of California's most stylish and graceful Chardonnays, which has also proved to be an exception to the rule and has generally aged well for 5–7 years. However, a recent release of the 1981 Library Selection Chardonnay showed it to have a rather dull, oxidized bouquet and fading flavors, raising the question of why the winery would release it for a price of $30 a bottle when it seemed to be falling apart. In addition, two of the best nonvintage blended wines, Eschol Red and Eschol White, are made by Trefethen. These well-made wines sell at low prices, and the white contains a healthy percentage of Chardonnay. They are exactly what inexpensive wines should be—supple, medium-bodied, fresh, fruity, and a joy to drink. As for the other wines, the Cabernet Sauvignon has been a distinctly herbaceous, even vegetal wine at times, although it is made in a very fruity, supple style. I just find the vegetal component excessive for it to merit high marks. I have the same objection to the winery's Pinot Noir, but I must be in the minority as most of the wine press give it rave reviews. However, I find it peppery, herbaceous, and while smooth and silky on the palate, I would never consider it to be classic Pinot Noir. This is a good winery, but frankly I would stick to their two inexpensive Eschol wines, their excellent Chardonnays, and perhaps the finest dry Riesling made in California; the 1987 is lovely.

TRENTADUE WINERY (SONOMA)

1985 Carignan	Sonoma	A	83
1986 Carignan	Sonoma	A	82
1987 Chenin Blanc	Sonoma	A	78
1986 Petite Sirah	Sonoma	A	84
1986 Sangiovese	Sonoma	A	84

This winery, which started off in the mid-seventies, has virtually disappeared from retailers' shelves for no apparent reason. Certainly proprietor Leo Trentadue has significant vineyard holdings in the Alexander Valley, but his admiration for grape varietals that are out of fashion has probably been his undoing commercially. Nevertheless, from the very beginning the Trentadue Winery has offered up wines that are rich, chewy, and robust. They represent an old but interesting style. The current roster includes unpopular wines such as Carignan, Sangiovese, Petite Sirah, and Chenin Blanc, so one can quickly understand why unadventurous wine wholesalers and retailers balk at carrying Trentadue's wines. However, all are well-made, big, intense, rich wines, with the exception of the innocuous Chenin Blanc. I urge consumers to try a Trentadue Sangiovese (perhaps the best expression of this noble Italian grape made in California), and the winery's massive Petite Sirah and Carignan, but be sure to offer them with food that is equally robust and flavorful as these wines are not for the shy.

MICHEL TRIBAUT (MONTEREY)

N.V. Brut	B	84
1984 Brut	B	85
1985 Brut	B	86
N.V. Rosé	B	86
1985 Rosé	B	85

Two Frenchmen, Michel Tribaut and Bertrand Devavry, are making some of the best sparkling wine in California and selling it at modest prices. From their debut releases there have been a sense of style and impressive flavors in their three cuvées of sparkling wine. Unlike many of the California sparklers, the Tribaut wines have some body, flavor depth, and finesse, as opposed to the ocean of mediocre wines that are overly tart, acidified, and simply taste like lemon water with bubbles in it. I highly recommend these wines for those consumers who desire top-quality domestic sparkling wine.

TUDAL WINERY (NAPA)

1982 Cabernet Sauvignon	Napa	B	69
1983 Cabernet Sauvignon Estate	Napa	B	82
1984 Cabernet Sauvignon Estate	Napa	B	88
1985 Cabernet Sauvignon Estate	Napa	B	89

This small winery produces less than 3,000 cases of Cabernet Sauvignon (and occasionally some Chardonnay) from a vineyard north of St. Helena. One has to like the dedication of owner and winemaker Arnold Tudal and the style of his wines, which offer up pure, almost textbook, herbaceous, blackcurrant aromas, judiciously influenced by the smell of toasty oak barrels, and his conviction that Cabernets should be full-bodied, rich in extract, well-balanced, tannic, and deep. Of all his vintages in the eighties, the 1982, for some reason, turned out almost overwhelmingly vegetal, but it is seemingly shedding this as it ages. However, it is my least favorite wine from Tudal. The other vintages have been especially successful, particularly the excellent 1984 and 1985 Cabernet Sauvignons, which should age easily and gracefully for the rest of this century. The 1983, while no great success, is still a good wine for the vintage. I certainly recommend lovers of Cabernet who have patience and a cool cellar to seek out Tudal's very fine 1984 and 1985 Cabernets. An extra incentive is the fact that their prices are not swollen as so many other Napa Cabernets. Tudal is clearly an underrated producer of fine wine.

TULOCAY VINEYARDS (NAPA)

1984 Cabernet Sauvignon Egan Vyd.	Napa	B	87
1985 Cabernet Sauvignon Egan Vyd.	Napa	B	86
1986 Chardonnay de Celles Vyd.	Napa	B	84
1984 Pinot Noir	Napa	B	?

Tulocay, a tiny winery east of the city of Napa, produces four major wines—Cabernet Sauvignon, Zinfandel, small quantities of Chardonnay, and some Pinot Noir, all from purchased grapes. The local cognoscenti claim that owner Bill Cadman has quite the touch with Pinot Noir, but after having tasted four vintages of his Pinot, I would have to disagree, having found it peppery, too vegetal, and just not a good example of classic Pinot Noir in any sense. However, the Cabernet Sauvignon from Tulocay in 1984 and 1985 is an impressive wine with dark ruby color, an intense, cedary, spicy, oaky bouquet, big, well-balanced, full-bodied flavors, and an expansive texture on the palate. The 1984 is more opulent and forward than the more closed 1985. As for the Chardonnay, it generally relies on a generous portion of oak for its flavors, but I thought the medium-bodied 1986 had the pineapple and buttery fruit to stand up to the oak.

VAN DER KAMP CHAMPAGNE CELLARS (SONOMA)

1985 Blanc de Noir	Sonoma	B	72
1984 Brut	Sonoma	B	73

Here is another example of a sparkling wine operation in California in which the wines are terribly undistinguished, overly tart, acidic, and lacking any flavor depth or dimension. It's hard for me to understand how sparkling wines of this quality can effectively make it in the marketplace.

VIANSA (SONOMA)

1984 Cabernet Sauvignon (58% Napa/42% Sonoma)		B	79
1986 Chardonnay	Sonoma	B	76
1986 Sauvignon Blanc	Sonoma	B	73

Viansa is the new label marketed by Sam Sebastiani, and the three wines above all tasted rather one-dimensional and simple. This is surprising in view of Sam Sebastiani's abilities. Could an overzealous oenologist be advising that too much acidity be added to the wines to get the right technical numbers? In any event, Sam Sebastiani is investing $3 million in his new winery, which he hopes will be completed in time for the 1989 crush.

VICHON WINERY (NAPA)

1985 Cabernet Sauvignon	Napa	B	83
1985 Chardonnay	Napa	B	85
1986 Chardonnay	Napa	B	84
1985 Merlot	Napa	B	82

The Vichon winery, founded in 1980, was recently sold to Robert Mondavi. From the beginning, I have been unmoved by these high-tech, overly sculptured, streamlined wines that show no soul or personality, but straightforward, correct, highly acidified, compact flavors, as if an oenologist who had no love of wine was asked to make Chardonnays, Cabernet Sauvignons, and Merlots. All of the wines have been technically perfect and flawless, but they have no pleasure-giving qualities. Under the helm of Mondavi there has been more character and fruit in the wines, but they still seem as if they have all been put in straightjackets with much of their personality and character intentionally suppressed. Nevertheless, the Chardonnay is crisp, fresh, well-balanced, shows a little bit of oak and fruit, and is, I am sure, perfect on the technical charts. The same can be said for the stylized, not too big, not too small Merlot, and the fresh, herbaceous, blackcurrant-scented Cabernet Sauvignon. Doesn't anyone want to take a little bit of risk anymore in order to produce wines with great flavor dimension and individuality?

VILLA MT. EDEN WINERY (NAPA)

1982 Cabernet Sauvignon Reserve	Napa	B	87
1985 Chardonnay	Napa	B	85
1987 Chenin Blanc	Napa	A	83

In the seventies, this winery made some of the most exceptional Cabernet Sauvignons in all of California. Anyone seeing a bottle of the 1974 or 1978 Reserve should not pass up the opportunity to try what are two of the finest Cabernets made in that decade. The winery is now under new ownership and is releasing its wines into the marketplace much later than other wineries. The Chenin Blanc is dry, well-made, and fresh, and the Chardonnay full-bodied and oaky, not great, but a good example of a Napa Chardonnay. The 1982 Cabernet Sauvignon looks to be very good, totally mature, but bursting with rich gobs of blackcurrant fruit, with plenty of spicy oak to go with its full-bodied, concentrated, long taste. The winery has certainly fallen a bit out of favor with consumers, but there seems to be no problem with quality.

WEINSTOCK CELLARS (SONOMA)

1986 Chardonnay	Alexander Vly.	A	84
1987 White Zinfandel	Dry Creek	A	82

All the wines made by Weinstock Cellars are kosher wines, offering good drinking for those who must have a kosher wine with a religious observance. The emphasis is on fresh, clean, lush fruit in a medium-bodied format; both the Chardonnay and white Zinfandel fit this bill. These are well-made wines that should not be dismissed by serious drinkers just because they are kosher.

WENTE BROTHERS WINERY (ALAMEDA)

1983 Brut Sparkling Wine	Monterey	B	75
1986 Chardonnay Reserve	Livermore	B	85
1986 Sauvignon Blanc Special Selection	Sonoma	A	?
1986 Semillon	Livermore	A	83

With some of the most important vineyard holdings in the Livermore Valley, and with a history that dates back to the late nineteenth century, Wente Brothers has always been an important winery in California. Recently, there has been an effort to upgrade the image and quality of the wines, and while far too many wines from this producer still turn out dull, there is no question that the new-look Chardonnay, Semillon, and Sauvignon Blanc are filled with much richer flavors and more personality. Certainly the winery has some of the best and oldest vineyards in all of Livermore Valley, and several people, including Terry Leighton, the genius winemaker of Kalin Cellars, have said the quality of fruit, particularly the Semillon and Sauvignon Blanc, is among the finest in all of California. The 1986 Chardonnay shows a soft, plump, succulent texture, and good, rich, honeyed-pear and apple flavors. The 1986 Sauvignon Blanc comes across as too aggressively herbaceous, but it has gobs of ripe, supple flavors. The Semillon is less herbaceous, fat, and ripe. I am not too impressed with Wente Brothers' sparkling wines, which are typical of California's efforts in this area. The 1983 Brut is simple, one-dimensional, and almost neutral-tasting except for its high acids. Lastly, the winery does make some uninteresting, jammy Petite Sirahs, and dark, dull Cabernet Sauvignons.

WILLIAM WHEELER WINERY (SONOMA)

1984 Cabernet Sauvignon	Sonoma	B	82?
1986 Chardonnay	Sonoma	B	73
1987 White Zinfandel	Sonoma	A	84

Despite the fact that I have tasted nearly all the wines from the first seven vintages of this winery in Sonoma, I don't really feel I know in what direction the winery wants to go. For starters, William Wheeler makes one of the best white Zinfandels in California, and on occasion it has made a very tasty, delicious Chardonnay, but certainly the style has varied significantly with each vintage. Whereas the 1985 was buttery and toasty, the 1986 has dull flavors that are not enhanced by the excessively high, tart acids. As for the Cabernet Sauvignon, it has never lacked personality, but certainly it has often been too herbaceous and bordered on being too vegetal as well. The newest release, the 1984, is simply big, burly, massive, and too tannic. Whether it will come together with age is doubtful. This winery seems to have the potential to do a lot better; I am just uncertain whether they have the will.

WHITEHALL LANE WINERY (NAPA)

1984 Cabernet Sauvignon	Napa	B	86
1985 Cabernet Sauvignon	Napa	B	87
1984 Chardonnay	Napa	B	70
1984 Merlot Knight's Valley Vineyard	Napa	B	87
1985 Merlot Knight's Valley Vineyard	Napa	B	88
1984 Pinot Noir	Napa	B	64

This winery has shown quite a bit of talent when it comes to producing complex, rich, attractive red wines from the Cabernet Sauvignon and Merlot grapes, but it has fallen short with its ghastly Pinot Noir. In addition, its Chardonnays have been dull, insipid wines with little personality. However, one taste of either the 1984 or 1985 Merlot will show you why this is one of the hot wines from California. The deep ruby color, the complex, open-knit bouquet of mint, chocolate, and ripe fruit is very enticing. The 1984 shows more suppleness, but both vintages are full-bodied, rich wines that will continue to drink well for the next 5–6 years. As for the 1984 and 1985 Cabernets, they are both textbook Napa wines with full body, weedy, blackcurrant aromas, and deep, tannic, concentrated flavors that despite being accessible today should be even better with another several years in the bottle, and which will last for up to a decade. The 1985 has a touch more mint in its bouquet than the 1984. Readers should make note of the fact that Whitehall Lane also makes a nonvintage Cabernet Sauvignon for under $6 a bottle that is effusively fruity, soft, supple, cleanly made, and for its type, a good bargain.

J. WILDMAN AND SONS (NAPA)

This *négociant* line of wines, launched by the famous importer from New York City, included a 1986 Chardonnay, 1985 Cabernet Sauvignon, and 1986 Sauvignon Blanc that were all insipid, clean, and correct, but unbelievably boring, compact wines. The prices are low so there is a tendency to wish them well, but the quality was not in the bottle.

CHÂTEAU WOLTNER (NAPA)

1985 Chardonnay Estate	Napa	C	86
1986 Chardonnay Estate	Napa	C	86
1985 Chardonnay St. Thomas Vyd.	Napa	D	64
1986 Chardonnay St. Thomas Vyd.	Napa	D	89
1985 Chardonnay Titus Vyd.	Napa	E	69
1986 Chardonnay Titus Vyd.	Napa	E	89

When the famous Bordeaux château in the Graves region, La Mission-Haut-Brion, was sold, the ex-owners, the Dewavrins, packed their bags and moved to Napa Valley's Howell Mountain, whereupon they established a vineyard dedicated not to making a Bordeaux-styled red wine, but rather a Chardonnay inspired by the great white burgundies of France. Immodestly, the first wines were released at prices that ranged from $18 a bottle for the estate-bottled Chardonnay to nearly $60 for the single-vineyard Chardonnays. They were overoaked, excessively alcoholic, and showed only that the Dewavrins had bought far too many new oak barrels in which to age the delicate Chardonnay fruit. The failures of the first vintage were followed by the 1986s, which showed a more balanced approach to the marriage of fruit and new toasty oak, and I hope that under the guidance of a very talented winemaker by the name of Ted Lemon, this will be one of the up-and-coming great producers of Chardonnay. The prices are entirely disproportionate to the present-day quality, but I hope the quality will soon justify the price. The style of wine for the 1986s is still a very big, alcoholic, buttery, toasty, barrel-fermented, full age-worthy style of Chardonnay, which the owners believe is suitable for the grapes grown on the cool Howell Mountain overlooking Napa Valley.

ZACA MESA WINERY (SANTA BARBARA)

1983 Cabernet Sauvignon Reserve	Santa Barbara	B	82
1985 Chardonnay	Santa Barbara	B	84

1986 Chardonnay	Santa Barbara	B	82
1983 Pinot Noir Reserve	Santa Barbara	B	52
1984 Pinot Noir Reserve	Santa Barbara	B	70
1986 Syrah	Santa Barbara	B	75
1987 Syrah	Santa Barbara	B	86

A lot of people are rooting for this winery in the Santa Ynez Valley to succeed as the owners were among the early believers in the quality of fruit that could be grown in the Santa Barbara area. The winery has gone through a number of changes but seems to have improved the overall quality of its wines in the last several years. In particular, the 1987 Syrah, although not likely to be a huge commercial success, is a lovely wine showing a great deal of personality and character, and the rich, cassis, peppery personality of the Syrah grape. It is a shame so many wine drinkers suffer from Cabernet Sauvignon myopia. The Pinot Noir from Zaca Mesa has consistently been overly vegetal, astringent, and often repugnant. However, the Chardonnays have shown lush tropical-fruit flavors, a nice touch of oak, and an up-front, appealing style. Both the 1985 and 1986 are easy-to-drink-and-appreciate, stylish wines. The Cabernet Sauvignon has been more mixed, but the winery has been making an all-out attempt to tame its vegetal character and produce a wine with more complex, rich, blackcurrant fruit.

ZD WINERY (NAPA)

1986 Cabernet Sauvignon Estate	Napa	B	90
1986 Chardonnay	California	B	90
1987 Chardonnay	California	B	88
1986 Pinot Noir	Napa	B	84

This venerable winery, which has been producing some of California's most luscious, richest, exotic Chardonnays since 1969, continues to score high with consumers for its two new vintages of Chardonnay, the 1986 and 1987. The 1986 should be drunk now, but the 1987 shows a fresher acidity and a more restrained style, but it still has plenty of the wonderful buttery, tropical-fruit scents that ZD seems to produce with regularity in its Chardonnay along with its full-bodied, opulent texture. The red wines have been considered much more controversial than the excellent Chardonnays. The 1986 Pinot Noir from the Carneros region of Napa will never remind you of a burgundy, but its aging in American oak and the tendency of ZD to go for a huge, chewy, fat, ripe, tasty style makes it an undeniably seductive, fleshy wine. While it doesn't even remind me of Pinot Noir, I found myself wanting a second glass of it. The winery has also made some good Cabernet Sauvignons and some bizarre Cabernet Sauvignons, drawing grapes from all over California, such as from Santa Maria in the south and Napa in the north. (I remember a 1981 Santa Maria Cabernet Sauvignon's being repugnant and unattractive, and a 1982 Napa's being delicious and fat in a low-acid style.) In 1986, ZD made its first Estate Cabernet Sauvignon, and it is a blockbuster wine with massive body, huge extract, and fabulous length and richness. It should age gracefully for the rest of this century, if not longer. It will certainly make believers out of those who have said ZD can't make great red wine.

7. OREGON: MARCHING INTO STARDOM?

The Basics

TYPES OF WINE

Oregon makes wine from most of the same grapes as California, although the cooler, more marginal climate in Oregon's best viticultural area, the Willamette Valley, has meant more success with cool-climate varietals, such as Pinot Noir, than with hotter-climate varietals, such as Cabernet Sauvignon, Merlot, Syrah, and Grenache. In fact, Oregon has proven to be the only place outside of Burgundy where high-quality Pinot Noir grapes can be grown with consistent success. Chardonnay, Riesling, and Sauvignon Blanc have done well in Oregon, but the great white hope here is the Pinot Gris, which has shown not only stunning potential but a knack for being the perfect partner for the salmon of the Pacific Northwest. There is also believed to be good potential for high-quality sparkling wine in Oregon, but the efforts to date have generally been insipid. Oregon's wines are distinctive, with a much greater kinship to European wines than to those of California. The higher natural acidities, lower alcohol content, and more subtle nature of Oregon's wines bode well for this area's future.

Oregon

1 Henry
2 Hillcrest
3 Garden Valley
4 Bjelland
5 Giradet

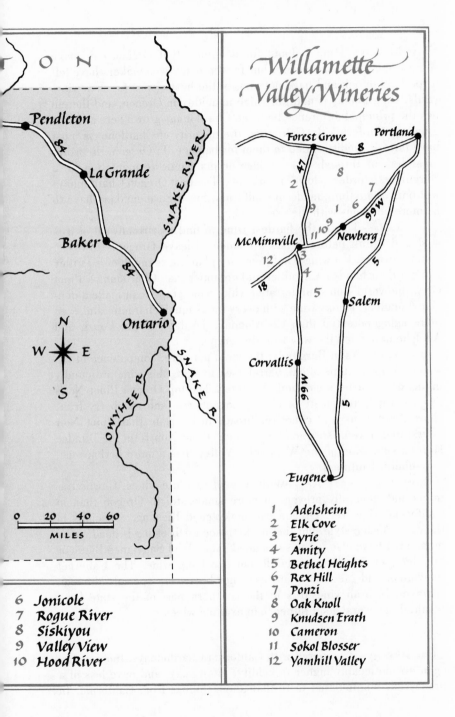

Willamette Valley Wineries

1   Adelsheim
2   Elk Cove
3   Eyrie
4   Amity
5   Bethel Heights
6   Rex Hill
7   Ponzi
8   Oak Knoll
9   Knudsen Erath
10 Cameron
11 Sokol Blosser
12 Yamhill Valley

6   Jonicole
7   Rogue River
8   Siskiyou
9   Valley View
10 Hood River

GRAPE VARIETIES

Chardonnay—I don't doubt for a minute that Oregon can make some wonderful Chardonnay, but far too many winemakers have left it too long in oak and have not chosen the best clones for their vineyards. Chardonnay is naturally high in acidity in Oregon, and therein lies the principal difference between Chardonnay grown here and that grown in California. In California, the majority of Chardonnays must have tartaric acidity added to them for balance. In Oregon, the wines must be put through a secondary or malolactic fermentation, à la Burgundy, in order to lower their acids. The best Oregon Chardonnays will outlive anything made in California, but the winemakers have to be more judicious with the use of oak.

Pinot Gris—This is the hardest wine to find as virtually all of it is sold and drunk before it has a chance to leave Oregon. However, winery owners, knowing a hot item, are planting as much of it as they can get their hands on. Fruitier and creamier than Chardonnay, Pinot Gris, the world's most underrated white wine grape, can make a delicious, opulent, smoky wine with every bit as much character and even more aging potential than Chardonnay. To date, Eyrie, Ponzi, and Adelsheim had led the way with this grape.

Pinot Noir—As in Burgundy, the yield per acre, competence of the winemaker, and type of oak barrel used in aging this wine profoundly influence its taste, style, and character. The top Oregon Pinot Noirs have a wonderful purity of cherry, loganberry, and raspberry fruit, show the expansive, seductive, broad, lush palate that Pinot Noir offers, and have crisp acids for balance. Pinot Noir from the Dundee Hills, a subregion of the Willamette Valley, has a more herbaceous, bing-cherry fruitiness.

Other Grape Varieties—With respect to white wines, Gewürztraminer has generally proven no more successful in Oregon than in California. However, Oregon can make good Riesling, especially in the drier Alsace style, but the marketplace for Riesling is dead at the moment. I have also yet to see a good example of Sauvignon Blanc or Semillon, or for that matter decent sparkling wine. The Cabernet Sauvignon and Merlot to date have not been very special, although some made from vineyards in the southern part of the state have resulted in several good rather than exciting wines.

FLAVORS

Chardonnay—Compared with California Chardonnays, those of Oregon are noticeably higher in acidity, more oaky, and have less of a processed, manipulated taste than their siblings from California. In many cases the oak is excessive, but for the top examples from wineries such as Eyrie, Ponzi, Girardet, and Tualatin, the results are very promising.

Pinot Gris—A whiff of smoke, the creamy taste of baked apples and nuts, and gobs of fruit characterize this white wine that has shown outstanding potential in Oregon.

Pinot Noir—Red-berry fruits dominate the taste of Oregon Pinot Noirs. Aromas and flavors of cherries, loganberries, blackberries, and sometimes plums with a streak of spicy, herbaceous scents characterize these medium-ruby-colored wines. Pinot Noir should never be astringent, harsh, or broodingly deep in color, and it rarely ever is in Oregon.

AGING POTENTIAL

Chardonnay: 4–7 years   Sparkling wines: 2–4 years
Pinot Gris: 2–6 years   Dry/off-dry Rieslings: 2–4 years
Pinot Noir: 5–10 years

OVERALL QUALITY LEVEL

Bearing in mind that most Oregon wineries started as underfinanced, backyard operations where the owners/winemakers learned as they went along, it is surprising that so many wonderful wines have emerged from winemakers who had no textbook training, but plenty of hands-on experience. In fact, many of Oregon's best winemakers, David Lett, Myron Redford, David Ramey, Dick Ponzi, Dick Erath, and Carole Adams, seem to have contempt for many of California's high-tech, university-trained winemakers who have learned to make wine only by the "numbers." Although this pioneering approach to winemaking has resulted in some stunning, individualistic wines, it has also resulted in poor choices of grape clones, poorly placed vineyards, as well as some questionable winemaking decisions. In short, Oregon as a viticultural region is where California was in the late sixties. They are just realizing the great potential for Pinot Noir and Pinot Gris, but also wondering why they planted Riesling, Sauvignon Blanc, and Chardonnay in some of the places they did. This, plus the amazing number of new, meagerly capitalized winery operations, has resulted in a range of quality from poor to spectacular.

MOST IMPORTANT INFORMATION TO KNOW

To purchase good wine, know the best wineries and their best wines. However, some additional information worth knowing is that the finest Pinot Noirs generally come from a stretch of vineyards in the Willamette Valley southwest of Portland. For Cabernet Sauvignon and Merlot, the warmer Umpqua Valley to the south and the Grant Pass area farther south are better regions.

1989–1990 BUYING STRATEGY

The two most recent, sexiest Oregon vintages, 1983 and 1985, disappeared from the marketplace long ago. The winemaking is better today, but both 1986 and 1987 are good rather than thrilling vintages, so keep your selection restricted to the top wines from the top wineries.

VINTAGE GUIDE

1987—A very hot year resulted in good wines, low in acidity, but quite flavorful, ripe, supple, and forward. They are tasty wines but buy them to drink over the next 4–5 years. As a vintage, 1987 is more consistent in quality than 1986.

1986—Rain complicated the harvest, but there are a number of good wines, although they are not as fat and rich as either the 1985s or 1987s. Quality is irregular in this vintage.

1985—After the rainy, disappointing year of 1984, everyone in Oregon was immensely pleased with the 1985 vintage. It is generally a very good to excellent year for all varietals, but particularly Pinot Noir, Chardonnay, and Pinot Gris. It was a vintage to buy, but many of the wines have now disappeared from the marketplace.

1984—A poor year plagued by rain and cool weather. The wines are tart, lean, and lack charm.

1983—The vintage that finally brought Oregon wines their long-deserved publicity. Textbook climatic conditions and sunny, hot weather resulted in fully mature grapes, excellent sugar contents, and an array of very impressive Pinot Noirs and Chardonnays that will age gracefully for 4–8 years. The small quantities produced by the best producers disappeared from the marketplace long ago.

1982—A good, above-average vintage of soft, medium-weight wines with decent ripeness and charm. The wines should be drunk up since they will not be long-lived.

1981—A good, even very good, vintage that produced very fine Pinot Noir and Chardonnay. The wines from the top producers are now in their prime and should be drunk up.

A GUIDE TO OREGON'S BEST PRODUCERS OF PINOT NOIR

* * * * * (OUTSTANDING PRODUCERS)

Amity	Ponzi Vineyards
Eyrie	Rex Hill Vineyards

* * * * (EXCELLENT PRODUCERS)

Adams	Knudsen Erath Vintage Select
Adelsheim	Oak Knoll Vintage Select
Elk Cove Vineyards (since 1986)	Panther Creek
Evesham Wood	

* * * (GOOD PRODUCERS)

Alpine Vintage Select	Knudsen Erath (regular cuvée)
Arterberry	Oak Knoll (regular cuvée)
Bethel Heights	Shafer
Broadly Vineyard	Sokol Blosser
Cameron	Yamhill Valley
Forgeron	

* * (AVERAGE PRODUCERS)

Château Benoit	Hood River Vineyard
Girardet	Pellier
Hidden Springs	Siskiyou Vineyards
Hillcrest Vineyard	Tyee Wine Cellars

A GUIDE TO OREGON'S BEST PRODUCERS OF PINOT GRIS

* * * * * (OUTSTANDING)
None

* * * * (EXCELLENT)
Eyrie   Ponzi

* * * (GOOD)
Adelsheim

A GUIDE TO OREGON'S BEST PRODUCERS OF CHARDONNAY

* * * * * (OUTSTANDING)
None

* * * * (EXCELLENT)

Adams	Ponzi
Eyrie	Shafer
Girardet	Tualatin

* * * (GOOD)

Adelsheim	Rex Hill
Amity	Veritas
Cameron	Yamhill Valley Vineyards

ADAMS VINEYARD AND WINERY

1985 Chardonnay	B	87
1986 Chardonnay	B	72
1985 Chardonnay Reserve	C	95
1986 Chardonnay Reserve	C	?
1985 Pinot Noir	B	87
1986 Pinot Noir Reserve	C	87

This tiny winery burst on the scene with excellent wines in 1981 and 1983 when the wines were being made by one of Oregon's most talented young winemakers, David Ramey. The Adams primarily produces Chardonnay and Pinot Noir that is boldly flavored, age-worthy, and dramatic. Their production is less than 3,000 cases, and their 1985s appear to be the best wines they have produced to date. As for the 1986s, the 1986 Pinot Noir Reserve showed extremely well with a lot of spicy oak, plenty of ripe, sweet fruit, good body and ripeness, and at least 5–6 years of aging potential. It did not seem to develop in the glass as much as the 1985 Pinot Noir, which has a fullintensity, plummy, ripe-berry-fruit-scented bouquet, obvious toasty oak, but a rich, broad, expansive palate. With respect to the Chardonnays, the

1986s did not fare well in my tastings, with the regular bottling showing decent fruit but not much concentration, and a rather closed character. The 1986 Chardonnay Reserve showed traces of acetate in the
nose and seemed odd and off. This wine requires retasting as it is
unlikely this high-quality winery would make an error of this magni-
tude with its wine. However, if you are able to find any of the 1985
Chardonnays from Adams, they are quite excellent, with the regular
bottling being rich, full-bodied, oaky, long, and powerful with an undeniable French taste to it. The 1985 Reserve Chardonnay is exquisite
with significant power and concentration, impeccable balance, and
not unlike an outstanding Corton Charlemagne.

ADELSHEIM VINEYARD

1985 Chardonnay	B	84
1986 Chardonnay	B	86
1985 Merlot Layne Vineyards	B	86
1986 Pinot Noir Polk County	B	86
1986 Pinot Noir Yamhill County	B	87

The small Adelsheim Winery is gorgeously perched on a hilltop overlooking its vineyard, which is run with great care by the husband-and-
wife team of David and Ginny Adelsheim. David Adelsheim is probably the leading spokesperson for the Oregon wine industry, as well as
one of its leading authorities on grape clones, trellising methods, and
overall winemaking methodology. His Pinot Noir, whether by coincidence or not, shows an amazing burgundylike style that closely resembles the Beaune Clos des Mouches of his good friend and famous
burgundy broker Robert Drouhin. Both the 1986 and 1985 from Yamhill County show the classic aromas of ripe bing cherries, toasty, new
oak, and leathery scents. This is one winery where the 1986 is clearly
a bit richer, riper, and maybe longer lasting and more complex than
the 1985. In 1986 Adelsheim also produced a Pinot Noir from Polk
County, which showed extremely well with its deep, more tannic
structure, fuller body, but authentic and pure aromas and flavors of
Pinot Noir. As for the Chardonnays, there has been consistent progress, although they are among the slowest to develop from those made
in Oregon. The 1985 is just beginning to show the ripeness that has
been hidden behind a firm structure of oak and acidity. The 1986 is

showing better at a similar stage in development and may have more fruit and length to it. As for the 1985 Merlot from the Layne Vineyards (located in the hotter Grants Pass area of southern Oregon), it shows how good a wine from this grape can be made from one of the warmer viticultural areas of Oregon. Dense in color, ripe, long, deep, tannic, and full of flavor, it is accessible now but will age well for 5–7 years.

ALPINE VINEYARDS

1986 Chardonnay	B	77
1986 Pinot Noir	B	75
1985 Pinot Noir Vintage Select	B	88

This winery's production of nearly 4,000 cases includes an assortment of wines other than those listed above. Most of the wines are made from Alpine's own 20-acre vineyard. The top wine I have tasted from Alpine is the 1985 Pinot Noir Vintage Select, which would certainly rate as one of the finest Pinot Noirs this winery has ever produced. As it ages, it is turning out to be one of the best from this excellent vintage. It is deep in color with a very intense, ripe-cherry bouquet backed by a judicious touch of oak. Its lush plummy flavors are sweet and expansive, as well as being reminiscent of a top-quality French red burgundy. By comparison, the 1986 Pinot Noir showed a much leaner, less opulent texture and seemed to lack the concentration and richness of the 1985. As for the Chardonnay, it is a correct but rather one-dimensional, Chablis-like, simple wine that is probably best quaffed with oysters.

AMITY VINEYARDS

1985 Chardonnay	B	83
1986 Pinot Noir	B	85
1985 Pinot Noir Estate	C	90
1983 Pinot Noir Winemaker's Reserve	C	90
1985 Pinot Noir Winemaker's Reserve	C	90
1986 Pinot Noir Estate	C	88

Tucked high on a ridge with an outstanding view of the Willamette Valley is the crowded, small winery of Amity. The bearded Myron Redford produces a bevy of wines there. His commercial "cash flow" wines include an interesting fruity and grapy Nouveau wine made from Pinot Noir, of which the 1987 is fresh and exuberant but relatively simple, as well as a generic white wine called Solstice Blanc, which I find rather one-dimensional and simple. In addition, Gewürztraminer, Chardonnay, and Pinot Noir are made here. Amity excels with the latter wine, and there are usually three different bottlings of Pinot Noir produced—one from purchased grapes, an Estate bottling, and his special cuvée called Winemaker's Reserve. These are Pinot Noirs that show more of a robust, spicy, full-bodied character than other Oregon Pinot Noirs, and although slow to develop, they give every indication of aging for up to a decade. If many of Oregon's Pinot Noirs have a sort of cherry-fruit Côte de Beaune style, those of Amity have more of a northern Côte de Nuits style with their cinnamon, smoked-meat, spicy, rich character. Of the two 1986s I tasted from Amity, the nonstate bottling shows very soft, rich, supple flavors, an elegant bouquet of spicy, cinnamon-scented cherry fruit, and medium body; it will certainly not age as well as the 1985. As for the Estate bottling, it shows more sweetness, a touch more oak, and has greater ripeness and richness on the palate. The real gems of Amity appear to be the 1985s, which were released late into the marketplace. For example, the 1985 Estate Pinot Noir is a stunning wine and shows just what amazing potential this area has for producing the finest Pinot Noir outside of Burgundy. It is quite long and rich, with a complete as well as complex bouquet of pure, sensual Pinot Noir fruit, a good backing of spicy oak, and a fabulous length and richness on the palate. It should drink well for another 6–7 years. Amity's 1985 Winemaker's Reserve (which will not be released until the fall of 1990) is every bit as rich and intense, but more tannic and closed, and one can understand the decision to hold it back for another year. The 1983 Winemaker's Reserve, which was made in very small quantities, again shows the fabulous quality that many Oregon Pinot Noirs can reach. It vaguely reminded me of a fine Premier Cru Chambertin from Burgundy with its earthy, animal, meaty, berrylike smells, rich texture, and excellent balance. Myron Redford's Pinot Noirs consistently represent some of the best made in Oregon, but one has to have a bit of patience not only with his policy of releasing the wines late into the marketplace, but also with allowing them to breathe in the glass and develop with a few years in the bottle. As for his Chardonnay, it always shows good structure and crisp acidity, but sometimes it seems to lack a bit of fatness and flesh. The 1985 is a good rather than exciting wine.

ANKENY VINEYARD

1986 Cabernet Sauvignon	B	55
1986 Chardonnay	B	64
1986 Pinot Noir	B	69

I hope this is just a one-vintage failure for this winery, but based on the three wines I tasted, the quality is clearly not of a level to compete in the marketplace with other Oregon wines. Improvements need to be made as the Pinot Noir was watery, light, thin, and stemmy; the Chardonnay harsh and acidic; and the Cabernet Sauvignon very undistinguished and unpleasant. I hope the 1987 vintage will bring higher-quality wines from Ankeny Vineyard.

ARTERBERRY

1986 Chardonnay	B	77
1987 Pinot Noir Maresh/Red Hills Vineyard	B	87
1986 Pinot Noir Winemaker's Reserve	B	87

Unfortunately I did not have a chance to taste the sparkling wine from Arterberry, which is one of their specialties, but I did taste their Pinot Noir and Chardonnay. Arterberry is a very underrated producer of high-quality Pinot Noir. The style they emphasize delivers plenty of up-front, lush, sweet, expansive berry fruit, supple texture, and immediate accessibility. Both the 1987 Maresh/Red Hills Vineyard and the 1986 Winemaker's Reserve show wonderfully lush, ripe, velvety fruit and should be drunk over the next 4–5 years while waiting for some of the more reticent Oregon Pinot Noirs to develop. The 1986 Chardonnay is a pleasant, agreeable, picnic-style Chardonnay that is light and fruity, but not complex or particularly deep.

CHÂTEAU BENOIT

N.V. Brut Sparkling Wine	B	75
1986 Pinot Noir	B	62

| 1987 Sauvignon Blanc | A | 82 |

This winery often seems to march to the beat of a different drummer, producing a different array of wines such as Müller-Thurgau, sometimes a sweet dessert-style Chardonnay, as well as Sauvignon Blanc, sparkling wine, and of course, Pinot Noir. Ironically, the Pinot Noir is their least-attractive wine. For example, the 1986 showed an odd, lactic bouquet, and tart, one-dimensional, somewhat bizarre flavors. The 1987 Sauvignon Blanc is one of the better examples of this varietal from Oregon, with an aggressive, herbaceous bouquet, and fleshy yet crisp, medium-bodied flavors. The sparkling wine is a very austere, crisp, rather one-dimensional wine that is serviceable but provides little excitement.

BETHEL HEIGHTS VINEYARD

| 1986 Chardonnay | B | 67 |

| 1985 Pinot Noir | B | 85 |

| 1986 Pinot Noir | B | 87 |

Growers until 1984, the Bethel Heights Vineyard in Willamette Valley started producing wine under its own label with the 1984 vintage. While grapes are still sold to various producers, even to the eccentric Bonny Doon Winery in California, the emphasis in the future will be estate-bottled wines. When I first tasted the 1985s, I was not that impressed because they were at an awkward stage, but the 1985 Pinot Noir is now showing a very attractive, ripe-berry-fruit character, has dropped some it its excessive tannins, but is still a relatively young, tough, closed-in wine that seems to have a good 6–8 years of aging potential. I prefer the overall balance and style of the 1986 Pinot Noir from Bethel Heights, which was a very Volnay-like, lush, velvety, berry fruitiness, fat, deep flavors, and 4–5 more years of drinkability. The 1986 Chardonnay reeked of raw oak and seemed to have too much wood and acidity for its flavors.

BRIDGEVIEW VINEYARD

| 1986 Pinot Noir Estate | B | 84 |

This is the only wine I have tasted from this winery, and although one might quibble over the fact that it was made in a carbonic maceration style, there is no doubting its seductive nose of jammy, soft fruit and hedonistic, velvety, ripe, effusively fruity flavors. It should be drunk over the next 1–2 years as it does not have the underlying body or structure for aging.

BROADLEY VINEYARD

1986 Chardonnay	B	60

1986 Pinot Noir Reserve	B	85

A new winery, Broadley Vineyard produced a very spicy, meaty, earthy, cinnamon- and berry-flavored 1986 Pinot Noir that had a striking resemblance to a good Gevrey-Chambertin. On the palate it has gobs of fruit and considerable length; it should drink nicely over the next 5–6 years. As successful as their Pinot Noir was in 1986, the Chardonnay had a dirty-dishwater smell and thin, musty, washed-out flavors. If anything, my score seems generous when I read my tasting notes.

CAMERON WINERY

1986 Chardonnay Reserve	B	79

1986 Pinot Noir	B	87

1985 Pinot Noir Reserve	B	84

The tiny Cameron Winery is one of the bright newcomers to the Oregon scene. Its start has been auspicious mainly because of the talent and enthusiasm of its winemaker/owner, John Paul. The 1986 regular cuvée of Pinot Noir (I have not tasted their Reserve) shows a rich, beef-blood nose, spicy, long, deep, velvety flavors, and plenty of body and depth to ensure 4–6 years of further aging. The 1985 Pinot Noir Reserve seems to have a great deal of fruit, but also very high acidity and perhaps excessive wood; it is tightly knit and not as flattering or as opulent to taste as the 1986. The 1986 Chardonnay Reserve also exhibits excessive amounts of oak, which is rather unfortunate given the attractive fruit that seems to lurk behind its veneer of toasty, vanillin, smoky oak. If it had been pulled out of the barrel a little bit sooner, it could have been special rather than average in quality.

ELK COVE VINEYARDS

1986 Chardonnay Estate	B	82
1986 Pinot Noir Dundee Hills Vineyard	B	76
1986 Pinot Noir Estate	B	88
1986 Pinot Noir Wind Hill Vineyard	B	86
1987 Riesling	B	81

For the pure beauty of its setting, no winery in Oregon can match the breathtaking views from Elk Cove's splendid wine-tasting room. The winery specializes in Pinot Noir, Chardonnay, and Oregon's best sweet Rieslings. The production of 12,000 cases is fairly large by Oregon standards. While the Pinot Noirs from Elk Cove have always been good, the 1986s are the best they have yet made, and in the case of the Estate and Wind Hill Vineyard Pinots, they show wonderful opulent fruit and a great deal of complexity. The 1986 Estate Pinot Noir has a rich, deep, ripe, sweet, broadly flavored palate that seems to be bursting with fruit, a voluptuous texture, and a very open-knit, well-developed, intriguing bouquet. It should drink well for the next 3–5 years. The 1986 Wind Hill Vineyard Pinot Noir shows more cinnamon and herbaceous, smoky character in the nose, but again it is quite ripe and fleshy with a bit of tannic toughness in the finish. It may actually outlive the Estate Pinot Noir, but it is less rich and interesting to taste now. I found the 1986 Dundee Hills Pinot to be a little too vegetal and washed-out in flavor, as if it had been caught by the rains of the 1986 vintage. The 1986 Chardonnay is a pleasant, agreeable wine, but with no great pedigree or personality. Its crisp, high-acid flavors suggest it should be drunk as an aperitif with fresh seafood. Lastly, the 1987 Riesling is made in a true German Kabinett style and comes across on the palate as crisp, dry, and well made, but lacking a bit of definition and depth.

ELLENDALE

1986 Chardonnay Willamette Valley	B	83
1986 Pinot Noir Estate	B	81

These are the first wines I have tasted from this relatively new winery. The 1986 Pinot Noir Estate showed a very pretty, cherry fruitiness, a nice touch of new oak, a certain leanness that kept its overall rating down, but a well-defined personality and good Pinot Noir character. The 1986 Chardonnay from Ellendale developed nicely in the glass, although it is hardly a blockbuster wine. Its appeal is its attractive floral bouquet and crisp, well-balanced, understated but pleasant flavors.

EOLA HILLS

| 1986 Pinot Noir | B | 75 |

The only wine I have tasted from Eola Hills, the 1986 Pinot Noir, shows deep color, but rather hard, closed-in, tough flavors that made an evaluation difficult. If the fruit emerges from behind the wall of hard tannins, this wine will merit a higher rating.

EVESHAM WOOD

| 1986 Pinot Noir | B | 90 |

Wow! This tiny winery's debut release of Pinot Noir from the 1986 vintage shows a sensational richness and compelling fragrance of blackberries, plums, and ripe cherries. All of this is backed up by gobs of concentration, medium to full body, good acids, and stunning length. This unfiltered Pinot Noir should be handled with care since it will probably throw a heavy sediment given its sensational extract. Buy it, put it in your cellar for 2–3 years, and then experience the magic. This looks to be a new superstar producer of Oregon Pinot Noir.

THE EYRIE VINEYARDS

| 1985 Chardonnay | B | 88 |

| 1986 Chardonnay | B | 89 |

| 1986 Muscat Ottonel | A | 84 |

| N.V. Pinot Gris | A | 82 |

| 1985 Pinot Noir | B | 87 |

| 1986 Pinot Noir | B | 86 |

1985 Pinot Noir Reserve   C   89

Oregon's most famous estate, the small Eyrie Winery (less than 6,000 cases) sits across the railroad tracks in the two-horse Oregon town of McMinnville. Proprietor David Lett has been making handcrafted special wines for over 20 years. Lett, who has not let his reputation go to his head, routinely turns out a long-lived, elegant Pinot Noir, a slow-evolving Chardonnay that is probably one of the two best made in Oregon, delicious Pinot Gris, and a crisp, perfumed dry Muscat Ottonel that makes an ideal aperitif wine. Be aware that Lett's Pinot Noirs rarely show their full character young and are among the lightest in color of the Oregon Pinots, but after 3–5 years in the bottle they usually blossom magnificently. That being said, the 1986 Pinot Noir showed extremely well, and while quite light ruby in color, it offered up sweet, expansive, ripe, generous, fruity aromas and had a seductive, lush, velvety palate with quite a bit of berry fruit in the finish. It's deceptively easy to drink young, but one suspects it will certainly last 5–6 years. The 1986 Chardonnay is the Chardonnay of the vintage with its rich, buttery, pineapple- and apple-scented bouquet, and opulent, almost unctuous flavors that are balanced beautifully by good acids. It is a worthy successor to the lovely 1985 Chardonnay that was dominated by a buttery, appley fruitiness, had full body, and a rich, lingering finish. Lett's nonvintage Pinot Gris (there is also a 1987 vintage that I have not tasted) is a rather fat, oily wine that shows lower acidity than his vintage Pinot Gris, but it has a nice creamy, smoky ripeness and should be drunk over the next year. The Muscat Ottonel would make an ideal mate to most types of Oriental cuisine with its dry, forceful personality and heady perfume, but as Lett says, most consumers ignore it, which is a shame. In certain vintages, Lett offers his followers a Reserve Pinot Noir, which is meant to age for up to a decade. His 1985 Reserve Pinot Noir has a very striking Volnay-like, oaky, berry-scented perfume with a hint of flowers, a soft, concentrated, ripe-fruit taste, and quite a long finish. While these wines always last longer than most people give them credit for, this one looks as if it should be at its best between 1990 and 1996.

FORGERON VINEYARD

1986 Chardonnay   B   75

1985 Pinot Noir   B   84

The 1985 Pinot Noir from Forgeron shows good ripe fruit, medium body, and an earthy, cinnamon smell with a good bit of acidity and length; it should drink nicely for 5–6 years. The Chardonnay shows some oak, plenty of acidity, and has a correct, rather straightforward bouquet and flavor.

GIRARDET CELLARS

1986 Chardonnay Umpqua Valley	B	85
1986 Chardonnay Reserve Umpqua Valley	B	87
1986 Pinot Noir Umpqua Valley	B	67

While the Swiss-born Philippe Girardet wins plaudits in Oregon for his Riesling, I have yet to see a bottle, but I have consistently found his Chardonnay to be one of the better made in this state. It avoids the overoaked, often too woody style of many Oregon Chardonnays, offering the taster plenty of exotic, lush, tropical fruit in an open-knit, up-front style. The 1986 regular bottling is just such a wine and should be drunk over the next several years, whereas the 1986 Reserve Chardonnay seems just a bit richer and fuller. The 1986 Pinot Noir is overoaked and has rather tired, tealike, spicy flavors that lack varietal purity.

HIDDEN SPRINGS

1983 Chardonnay	B	68
1983 Pinot Noir	B	73
1985 Pinot Noir	B	81

I have found the wines from Hidden Springs, which is run by two very friendly families, the Byards and Alexandersons, to be inconsistent and often below standard quality. The 1985 Pinot Noir is a little tart but has a good perfume of cherry fruit, medium body, and a short finish. The 1983 Pinot Noir is totally mature, quite vegetal, and short. As for the 1983 Chardonnay, it is straightforward, a little thin, and insubstantial.

HILLCREST VINEYARD

1983 Cabernet Sauvignon	B	74
1984 Gewürztraminer	A	78
1982 Pinot Noir	B	68

This winery is located in the Umpqua Valley and is run by Richard Sommer, one of the pioneers in the Oregon wine business who began his 35-acre vineyard in 1963. The lineup of wines includes a Riesling, Gewürztraminer, blush wine, and Cabernet Sauvignon, all of which are sound rather than inspiring.

HOOD RIVER VINEYARDS

1986 Cabernet Sauvignon	B	55
1986 Chardonnay	B	83
1985 Pinot Noir	B	80

This winery, which is also known for its fruit wines, has a growing reputation for its Gewürztraminer and Riesling, which, unfortunately, I was unable to taste, and also produces a very fine Zinfandel. Its vineyards are located in the warm Hood River area. As for the current releases, the 1986 Chardonnay showed a good barrel-fermented, spicy, buttery nose, was rather closed in the mouth, but showed adequate underlying fruit and depth. The 1986 Cabernet Sauvignon was spritzy and tasted of overripe prunes, making it rather unpalatable. The 1985 Pinot Noir, although not one of the stars, does offer soft, pretty, easy-to-appreciate berry flavors.

KNUDSEN ERATH

1986 Chardonnay	B	72
1986 Chardonnay Vintage Select	B	72
1986 Pinot Noir	B	79
1985 Pinot Noir Vintage Select	B	86
1986 Pinot Noir Vintage Select	B	87

It is no secret that Knudsen Erath is usually among Oregon's finest producers of Pinot Noir and Chardonnay. The towering Dick Erath cuts an imposing figure, but he is one of the nicest people in Oregon's wine country. His Pinot Noirs, which seem to start off life delicate and understated, gain richness and length in the bottle. Magical bottles of the 1975 and 1976 tasted in 1987 could easily have been mistaken for $50 bottles of mature red burgundy. As for the 1986s, I was disappointed in both Chardonnays, which exhibited lean, undernourished, austere characters; it was hard to tell the difference between the regular bottling and the more expensive Vintage Select bottling. There seemed to be a great difference between the Vintage Select and the regular 1986 Pinot Noir bottling. The latter was spicy, medium-bodied, fruity, but fairly one-dimensional, whereas the 1986 Vintage Select Pinot Noir had a full-intensity bouquet of rich, raspberry fruit, a touch of oak, and showed a lovely, lush, elegant texture and medium body on the palate. It should drink nicely for the next 4–5 years. It appears to be even better than the fine 1985 Pinot Noir Vintage Select, which had more of a cherry-fruit character, and a personality similar to a stylish Premier Cru from Beaune.

LANGE

1987 Chardonnay Reserve	B	60

The 1987 Chardonnay Reserve is the only wine I have tasted from this new operation. It was made in a very severe, excessively high-acid style with little underlying fruit or charm.

MONTIMORE

1987 Pinot Gris	A	55

If this wine is typical of others from this winery, they are going to have a tough time in the marketplace. The wine was cloyingly sweet, heavy, and frankly, just awful.

OAK KNOLL

1985 Pinot Noir	B	88
1986 Pinot Noir	B	76
1985 Pinot Noir Vintage Select	C	90

1986 Pinot Noir Vintage Select   C   87

One of the greatest non-French Pinot Noirs I have ever tasted was the
1980 Oak Knoll Vintage Select, a profound wine that reminded me of
a great Grands Echézeaux from Mongeard Mugneret. Tasted twice in
1987, the purity and complexity of Pinot Noir fruit found in this wine
was hard to believe. Oak Knoll, run by the Vuylsteke family, is equally
famous for its sweet raspberry wine, which is exceptional in its own
eccentric way. Their Chardonnays have been inconsistent, and I have
not seen the 1986, so I don't know whether it was an improvement
over their rather mediocre 1985. However, the glories of this winery
are its Pinot Noirs. The regular bottling in 1986 showed a lean, attractive cranberry, plummy-fruit-scented character, but very high, tart
acids and a toughness in the finish. On the other hand, the 1986
Vintage Select shows the hallmark of this winery's Pinot Noirs in its
rich, exotic bouquet of blackberry and plumlike fruit. On the palate it
has not yet come together completely and may ultimately deserve a
higher rating, but it shows marvelous richness, full body, and quite a
bit of length in a very deep burgundian style. As for the 1985s, they
are probably the best Pinot Noirs I have yet tasted from Oak Knoll,
which I hope will rival the great 1980 made at this winery. The 1985
regular bottling has deep ruby color, a huge aroma of ripe black-cherry
fruit, and spicy new oak. There are gobs of extract, super length and
balance, and the wine seems to have 6–7 more years of aging potential. The 1985 Vintage Select simply delivers more of a good thing. A
cascade of berry fruit is wrapped deftly in a glove of spicy oak. Rich,
deep, even profound, the wine should offer glorious drinking by 1990–
1991.

PANTHER CREEK

1986 Pinot Noir   B   87

This new winery has made an auspicious debut with its lovely 1986
Pinot Noir, made from the Oak Grove Vineyard (85%) and the Abbey
Ridge Vineyard (15%). Only 600 cases were produced, and the wine
shows a deep ruby color, an interesting black-cherry and spicy-oak-
scented bouquet, velvety, lush, opulent flavors, medium to full body,
and quite a long, well-balanced finish. It should drink nicely for another 4–5 years.

PELLIER

1986 Chardonnay	B	60
1985 Pinot Noir	B	86

Pellier is a relatively new winery in Oregon run by a member of the famous Mirassou family of California. The 45 acres of vineyards, while still young, are in a promising hillside location near the more renowned Bethel Heights Vineyard in the Salem area of Oregon. The 1986 Chardonnay showed excessive oak and very little fruit, making a rather unpleasant impression on the palate. However, the 1985 Pinot Noir is evolving beautifully, and while it has quite a bit of oak in its bouquet, it still has a very attractive, spicy, black-cherry bouquet, supple flavors, and medium body; it should be drunk over the next 3–4 years.

PONZI VINEYARDS

1986 Chardonnay	B	85
1986 Chardonnay Reserve	B	87
1987 Pinot Gris	A	87
1985 Pinot Noir	B	90
1986 Pinot Noir Reserve	C	88
1987 Riesling	A	85

Ponzi Vineyards is emerging as Oregon's top winery. Owner and winemaker Dick Ponzi knows exactly what he wants to do, and his vintages from 1983 on have been among the very best wines made in Oregon, with his Pinot Noir, Pinot Gris, Chardonnay, and white Riesling impeccably made and often quite exciting. Production has now passed 6,000 cases so availability is generally good in most of the major metropolitan markets. The wines, like many produced in Oregon, are given minimal handling in the wine cellar and are only filtered if they do not fall brilliant through the course of aging in cask or tank. These are wines that are often worth a special effort to find. The 1987 dry white Riesling is the best made in Oregon. It leans toward the Alsace style rather than the German style of Riesling, is quite dry and full-flavored, exudes personality and freshness, and should be drunk over the next year. Ponzi's 1987 Pinot Gris continues his tremendous success with this varietal as it is the best example of Pinot Gris made in Oregon, even superior to that made by David Lett at Eyrie Vineyards. The 1987 is a creamy, smoky, richly fruity wine that has just enough acidity for freshness and balance. As for his Chardonnay, the 1986 Reserve is not quite as richly fruity and exotic as his 1985, but again it shows tropical-fruit aromas of oranges and lemons and has a very well-balanced, long feel on the palate with just the right amount of oak. The regular Chardonnay is very similar yet has less oak in evidence. However, although Ponzi does an excellent job with everything he touches, it is his Pinot Noirs that are quite exciting and display a degree of complexity rarely seen outside of Burgundy. His 1986 Reserve Pinot Noir (I did not taste his regular bottling of Pinot Noir in 1986) shows a medium deep ruby color, a rich, complex, smoky, Oriental-spice bouquet, long, velvety, well-balanced flavors, and medium to full body. It is not quite as profound or as compelling as the 1985 and should be drunk over the next 4–5 years. As for the 1985 Pinot Noir, it is a classic example of the immense potential that exists in Oregon for this temperamental grape. The big, forward bouquet offers ripe cherry fruit, flowers, spicy oak, and the indescribable complexity that one associates with the wines of Domaine de la Romanée-Conti. Deep in color, rich and expansive on the palate with a good lashing of tannin, this wine should be at its best between 1990 and 1996.

REX HILL VINEYARDS

1985 Pinot Noir Archibald Vineyard	C	87
1985 Pinot Noir Dundee Hills Vineyard	C	88
1985 Pinot Noir Maresh Vineyard	C	90
1985 Pinot Noir Medici Vineyard	C	90
1985 Pinot Noir Willamette Valley	C	89

The Rex Hill winery, one of the showcase properties of Oregon's Willamette Valley, raised eyebrows with its debut releases of its 1983 Pinot Noirs priced at $20 a bottle. Owner Paul Hart, a studious-looking man, seems surprisingly flexible about pricing his Pinot Noirs. He intends to charge a premium for outstanding vintages, such as 1983 and 1985, and then drop his prices in mediocre years, such as 1984.

One wishes winemakers around the world would adopt such a realistic policy. While I thought the 1983 Pinot Noirs from Rex Hill were very good, I wondered about the winery's obsession with vineyard-designating every Pinot Noir it produces. After tasting the 1985s, it would appear that this winery has leaped into the very top echelons of quality in Oregon, and given how wonderfully these wines are drinking today, I'll be the last to criticize this top-notch Pinot Noir producer for vineyard-designating its wines.

Where does one start with the praise? For openers, there is the 1985 Archibald Vineyard Pinot Noir, which displays quite a bit of oak and almost seems to resemble what a top-notch Spanish Pinot Noir might taste like given the emphasis on exotic, toasty new oak in its bouquet. Nevertheless, this is an opulent, rich, well-structured wine that has tremendous fruit extraction and is a total joy to drink; it should age well for another 4–5 years. Even better is the 1985 Maresh Vineyard Pinot Noir, which, while showing plenty of toasty, smoky oak, has an awesome level of hedonistic black-cherry fruit, a big, exotic, bold, and dramatic bouquet, and sensational concentration and length. I couldn't resist going back to it time after time and watching it develop in the glass. It is one of the best Pinot Noirs to come out of Oregon in the last several years, and it should drink well for another 4–6 years. Rex Hill's regular Pinot Noir from the Willamette Valley shows plenty of oak (which seems to be a personality trademark of this winery's Pinot Noirs), excellent concentration, full body, and again the spicy, exotic, rich, berry fruit that marks all of the 1985s from Rex Hill. As for the 1985 Dundee Hills Pinot Noir, it has a whopping 14% alcohol and displays a vastly different character from the other Rex Hill Pinot Noirs. It is dominated by a rather earthy, smoky, ground-beef bouquet, has rich, ripe flavors, but seems more tightly knit and shows a bit more tannin than the other wines. Though perhaps less opulent and seductive, it shows good aging potential. Lastly, another superstar produced by Rex Hill is the 1985 Medici Vineyard Pinot Noir, which has a sensational bouquet of dense, superripe fruit married judiciously with toasty, smoky oak. On the palate it is a bit closed compared to some of the other 1985s, but it has fabulous potential, which can easily be seen from its rich, deep layers of fruit and extract. This is a Pinot Noir that should not be drunk before 1990 and should last another 5–7 years thereafter. While the prices may look high, Pinot Noir of this quality is rare anywhere in the world, and I enthusiastically applaud Rex Hill's outstanding lineup of 1985 Pinot Noirs.

SCHWARZENBERG

1986 Chardonnay	B	55

This is the second vintage of very disappointing Chardonnay I have tasted from this new winery. The problem is a very simple one— where is the fruit? This wine is simply so high in acidity and so underripe that it's hard to believe anyone could derive pleasure from drinking it.

SERENDIPITY

1986 Chardonnay McCorqudae Vineyard	B	70

From another new producer in Oregon, this wine exhibited fairly ripe fruit on the palate. However, it again reflects a mistake that far too many Oregon wineries are making: excessive oak flavors for the amount of fruit in the wine.

SHAFER VINEYARD CELLARS

1985 Chardonnay	B	86
1986 Chardonnay Estate	B	86
1985 Pinot Noir	B	82
1987 Pinot Noir Blanc	A	85
1986 Pinot Noir Estate	B	84

The shy Harvey Shafer produces Oregon's best blush wine (a rosé made from Pinot Noir that has surprising flavor), one of that state's longest-lived and most stylish Chardonnays, and a variable Pinot Noir, although the 1986 would appear to be the best wine he has yet made from this grape. This has a certain leanness and hardness to its flavors, but underlying the tannin is a very attractive, elegant, spicy, cherry and cinnamon fruitiness. I would not drink this wine before 1990. The 1986 Chardonnay is again one of the best made in Oregon, yet it needs another 6–12 months in the bottle to round out. At present it is austere but shows excellent underlying richness and length, and a character not unlike a good Premier Cru Chablis from France. The 1985 is just now showing its floral, buttery, apple-scented fruit that in 1987 seemed tightly closed and hidden behind the good acidity. Lastly, this winery's blush wine, the 1987 Pinot Noir Blanc, is one of the best rosés made in America. Loaded with berry fruit, crisp and fresh with a charming bouquet, this medium-bodied, slightly sweet wine has considerable appeal but should be drunk over the next year.

SISKIYOU VINEYARDS

1985 Chardonnay	B	78
1985 Pinot Noir	B	76

Oregon's southernmost winery (in Cave Junction), Siskiyou is owned and managed by Suzi David and Donny Devine. The 1985 Pinot Noir has an interesting bouquet of fresh herbs and crushed tomatoes. Medium ruby in color, it is made in a lighter style and tends to lack varietal definition. The 1985 Chardonnay is quite austere and lean with a very tightly knit structure and an ungenerous personality. Perhaps more fruit and charm will emerge with 1–2 years of cellaring.

SOKOL BLOSSER

1986 Chardonnay	B	82
1986 Chardonnay Reserve	C	75
1985 Pinot Noir Hyland Vineyard	B	85
1986 Pinot Noir Hyland Vineyard	B	82
1985 Pinot Noir Red Hills Vineyard	B	87
1986 Pinot Noir Red Hills Vineyard	B	80

Oregon's best-known commercial winery is also one of its largest, producing in excess of 30,000 cases of wine. The quality of the Pinot Noirs is consistently good, but the Chardonnays have tended to vary. Neither of the 1986 Pinot Noirs is as good as the 1985. The 1986 Red Hills Vineyard Pinot Noir has a ripe cherry fruitiness and medium ruby color, but it is lean and rather austere on the palate with tart acids in its finish. It should be drunk over the next 2–3 years. As for the 1986 Hyland Vineyard Pinot Noir, though showing a bit more fruit and fat than its Red Hills sibling, it again suffers from a bit of leanness and hard tannins in the finish. The 1985 Pinot Noirs have different styles, but both are much more interesting wines than the 1986s. The 1985 Hyland Vineyard offers delectable, soft, cherry-fruit flavors, a supple, expansive texture, and good body. It should evolve well for another 3–4 years. Far more age-worthy and serious is the 1985 Red Hills Pinot Noir, which has a deeper color, more noticeable tannin, a longer finish, and a more concentrated feel on the palate. As for the 1986 Chardonnays, the regular bottling shows more fruit and while not a knock-out Chardonnay, is quite palatable and fresh with some oak and a pleasant apple fruitiness. On the other hand, the 1986 Chardonnay Reserve is excessively oaky, and the fruit is buried behind the oak and high levels of acidity.

TUALATIN VINEYARDS

1985 Chardonnay	B	86
1986 Chardonnay Estate	B	76
1985 Pinot Noir Private Reserve	B	85

The square-jawed Bill Fuller, Tualatin's owner, has 83 acres of vineyards and has excelled with his white wine varietals, especially Chardonnay, although the 1986 is surprisingly stern and lacking in fruit. Perhaps it was in an awkward stage when I tasted it. However, the 1985 Chardonnay is a winner with a big, rich, toasty, ripe, apple-butter-scented bouquet and long, rich, creamy flavors, but it should be drunk up soon as it is developing at a fairly rapid pace. While I have not tasted the 1986 Pinot Noir, this winery has rarely excelled with the quality of its Pinot Noirs, although the 1985 Reserve shows good jammy, raspberry, cherry fruit, a touch of toasty oak, and clean, well-defined flavors; it should be drunk over the next 3–4 years.

VERITAS VINEYARD

1986 Chardonnay	B	70
1985 Pinot Noir	B	83
1986 Pinot Noir	B	78

The Veritas winery, located just across the road from Rex Hill, was established in 1984. The owners, the Howiesons, have developed a 20-acre vineyard planted primarily with Chardonnay, Pinot Noir, and Riesling. After making a very fine 1985 Chardonnay, the 1986 proved to be disappointing because the winery fell into the trap of overoaking the wine. Its excessive woody flavors destroyed any scents of Chardonnay fruit, and drinking it is like biting on a wood plank. As for the Pinot Noirs, they have yet to impress me, although the vineyard is certainly located in a good area. Perhaps the vines are still too young to expect the highest level of quality. The 1986 Pinot Noir is perfumed and shows a good deep color, but again it has a leanness and tart, somewhat minty quality I find unusual for Oregon Pinot Noir. On the other hand, the 1985 Pinot Noir has developed a good, straightforward raspberry fruitiness and has a soft, delicate texture, light tannins, but not much complexity. It should be drunk over the next year. This is a winery that is committed to high quality, and it just seems to be a matter of time as the vineyard matures before some exciting wines emerge from Veritas.

YAMHILL VALLEY VINEYARDS

1985 Chardonnay	B	85
1986 Chardonnay	B	84
1985 Pinot Noir	B	87
1986 Pinot Noir	B	86

The debut wine from this winery near McMinnville was a striking 1983 Pinot Noir. Since then the quality has been maintained, and Yamhill Valley Vineyards looks to be one of the up-and-coming stars of Oregon. The 1986 Pinot Noir is one of the bigger, bolder, more muscular Pinot Noirs of the vintage, displaying deep, plummy, raspberry, cherry fruit, a full-bodied, muscular texture, and at least 4–8 years of further aging potential. It is really not that flattering to drink now, but everything is in balance and the future looks promising. As for the 1985 Pinot Noir, it is deep in color, very ripe, rich in extract, tannic, and quite impressive, and although young and undeveloped, it should also age gracefully for the next 5–7 years, but I would not want to drink it before 1990. The 1986 Chardonnay shows an interesting bouquet of pears and ripe fruit, being one of the few Oregon Chardonnays to get the correct balance between the wood and the fruit. It is not a great Chardonnay but is certainly pleasant and agreeable. The 1985 Chardonnay, showing plenty of ripe fruit as well as oak, seems to be a dead ringer for a Meursault from France. Its ripe, buttery, apple- and lemon-tinged fruit seems to jump from the glass, and this big wine should be drunk over the next 3–4 years.

8. OTHER AMERICAN VITICULTURAL REGIONS

One can find vineyards in almost every state in America, most of them tiny and with purely local supporters. While the great majority of the wines I have tasted from other areas outside Oregon and California have left me unimpressed, there are isolated cases in at least thirteen other states of high-quality winemaking as well as potential. Wine consumers should give the following wineries a serious look. Except for the several large wineries in Washington state, most of these wineries' products will rarely be found outside their state of origin.

Connecticut

The standout winery in this state is **Crosswoods** in North Stonington. The Chardonnay ($12) is a delicious, ripe, lemony, buttery wine that shows toasty oak and plenty of body. In power and depth, it is more akin to something from California's Central Coast than New England. This winery also does a surprisingly good job with Merlot made from purchased grapes from Long Island's North Fork; the 1985 was quite delicious. The production here is 4,000 cases.

Idaho

One winery again dominates this state's wine production. The Ste. Chapelle winery in Caldwell produces in excess of 100,000 cases of wine using grapes from growers throughout the state as well as from Washington. Their red wines have been mediocre at best, but the white wines, particularly their moderately sweet Johannisberg Riesling and slightly sweet Chenin Blanc, each priced at $4–7, are quite well made. The winery promotes its Chardonnays, but they have generally been uninspiring, although the 1987s looked improved.

Maryland

There are a number of good wineries in Maryland, yet few are known outside the state because of tiny productions. The most famous winery is Dr. Hamilton Mowbray's **Montbray Vineyard** in Westminster. The crusty and feisty Mowbray produces the finest Seyval-Villard in America, a wine that is easy to confuse with a white burgundy from the Côte Chalonnaise. His Cabernet Sauvignon is also good (the 1982, 1983, and 1985 are excellent), and the barrel-fermented Chardonnay can make many a French Chablis look thin. Mowbray is a very serious winemaker, and his 3,000-case production is quickly sold out to local enthusiasts.

The East Coast's best Cabernet Sauvignon is made by **Byrd Vineyard** in Myersville, Maryland. With hillside vineyards planted in the foothills of the Appalachian Mountains, Byrd's rich, black-ruby-colored, tannic Cabernets are closest in spirit to those of Mayacamas in Napa Valley. They have been immensely impressive young, particularly the 1980, 1982, and blockbuster 1983 and 1984 (all sell for $12–14). Each needs a decade to show its true potential. Unfortunately, most of Byrd's other wines tend to be dull, overoaked, and uninteresting, although he does make tiny quantities of America's very best Gewürztraminer.

The brightest new star in Maryland is **Basignani Vineyards** in Sparks, Maryland. Owner/winemaker Bertero Basignani learned the ropes of winemaking as an amateur, and his newly bonded winery is now turning out lovely, ripe, lush, barrel-fermented, unfiltered Chardonnay for under $10 a bottle, plus one of the two best Seyval Blancs made in Maryland, and a gorgeous, Spätlese-styled, crisp, mineral- and apple-fruit-scented Riesling. His reds, a Merlot, Cabernet Sauvignon, and hybrid blend, have been on the lighter side, but the purity of fruit and focus are there. Basignani is a name to watch.

Other Maryland vineyards to take note of are **Catoctin Vineyards** in Brookeville, which produces above-average Chardonnay and Cabernet, and **Boordy Vineyards**, which has adequate Chardonnay, Seyval-Villard, and some pleasant nouveau-styled wines.

Massachusetts

One taste of the **Commonwealth Winery's** Chardonnay or Riesling is convincing proof that fine wines can be made in this northern state. A cranberry sparkling wine is also produced by this Plymouth winery.

Missouri

The **Mount Pleasant Vineyard** in Augusta, Missouri, with production in excess of 10,000 cases, makes a very good, rich, full-bodied red wine from hybrid grapes, plus an interesting port. The quality is surprisingly high, the prices moderate.

New Jersey

The **Tewksbury Winery** in Lebanon, New Jersey, is the uncontested leader. Again, the red wines are run-of-the-mill, but the white wines are a different story altogether. Seyval-Villard, white Riesling, Gewürztraminer, and Chardonnay all merit interest and sell at reasonable prices of $6.50–8.50 a bottle.

New York

New York has the greatest number of wineries of any state after Oregon and California. The two major viticultural areas are the beautiful Finger Lakes region and Long Island. Like most viticultural regions in the Northeast, the red wines are generally insipid and in many cases frankly repugnant. Many of the best wineries do not even make a red wine, but one winery has miraculously excelled with Cabernet Sauvignon and Merlot. The **Hargrave Vineyard** in Cutchogue, Long Island, makes very good, sometimes excellent Cabernet Sauvignon that is one of the two best red wines produced in the East (the other is Byrd's Cabernet Sauvignon). The winery also does an excellent job with Sauvignon Blanc and Chardonnay.

Elsewhere in New York, Chardonnay, Riesling, and Seyval-Villard are the principal grape varietals that have proved successful. For Chardonnay, the finest producer in the East, and one of the best in the country, is **Wagner Vineyards** in Lodi. Their 1980, 1981, 1984, and 1986 Chardonnays had remarkable depth of flavor as well as complexity. Wagner may be at the summit in terms of Chardonnay, but there are a bevy of fine producers of this wine. **Bridgehampton** on Long Island, **Plane's**, **Casa Larga**, **Finger Lakes Wine Cellars**,

Glenora, and Knapp, all near the Finger Lakes, Pindar on Long Island, Millbrook, Schloss Doepken, West Park, Wickham Vineyards, and Hermann J. Wiemer are all reliable producers of Chardonnay. Other than Wagner's explosively rich Chardonnay, the style of New York Chardonnays is more austere, leaner, and less opulently fruity than those found in California.

Several other wineries of note are Clinton, a producer of very good Seyval, Benmarl, a good producer of Seyval, and the idiosyncratic Bully Hill, a good producer of white wine hybrids.

A GUIDE TO NEW YORK'S BEST PRODUCERS OF CHARDONNAY

* * * * * (OUTSTANDING PRODUCERS)
Wagner

* * * * (EXCELLENT PRODUCERS)
Millbrook   Hermann J. Wiemer

* * * (GOOD PRODUCERS)
Bridgehampton   Hargrave
Casa Larga   Knapp
Finger Lakes   Pindar
Glenora

Ohio

There is a small but flourishing wine industry in Ohio. I have had little experience with many of this state's wineries, but I do recommend one winery that has pleased me time and time again. The Markko Vineyard in Conneaut does a good job with a Chardonnay that has a lemony, fresh-apple fruitiness, good, clean varietal character, and plenty of body. The price is a reasonable $9 per bottle.

Pennsylvania

This state's wineries have never, in my judgment, demonstrated the potential for making fine wine. However, there is one notable exception, the small Allegro Vineyards in Brogue. There is no one more serious about his winemaking than owner John Crouch. If he can overcome the enormous economic strains of financing a new winery, I predict big things for him and his wines. To date, the successes have been a beautiful Cabernet Sauvignon; the 1980, 1982, and 1983 all revealed rich blackcurrant fruitiness married intelligently with toasty new oak. Crouch's Seyval-Villard is also good, and his Chardonnay seems to get better with each passing vintage, the 1984 being the best yet. Prices here range from $6 for the Seyval to $12–15 for the reserve Cabernets. Another good winery to keep an eye out for is Naylor's.

Rhode Island

I have often wondered how the 10,000-case Sakonnet Vineyard in Little Compton can make good wine so far north. Yet this winery makes very interesting, well-made wine ranging from good Riesling and Chardonnay to a particularly interesting Pinot Noir. The winery's very good blush wine in 1985 was called Eye of the Storm after the savage hurricane, Gloria, that wreaked havoc on the northeastern coastline that year. Prices are extremely reasonable, ranging from $4 for the hybrids to $8 for the vinifera-based wine.

Texas

Texans are unusually chauvinistic about anything grown, produced, or located in that state, but everyone should pay more attention to the handful of wineries in this state that are making very fine wine. For Cabernet Sauvignon, the Pheasant Ridge Winery in Lubbock is turning out delicious, lush, intense wines with plenty of character. The bold $15–20 price is Texas-proportioned. For Chardonnay, the Llano Winery in Lubbock made an exquisite 1984 for $12 a bottle. For fruity, fresh, slightly sweet Chenin Blanc, both the aforementioned Llano Winery and Fall Creek in Tow merit attention. There are at least another half-dozen wineries sprouting up in Texas, but for the moment, these three wineries can compete in quality with anybody.

Virginia

The state of Virginia and its producers actively promote the state's wines, but I cannot see any reason for their enthusiasm. A great deal of money has been invested in winery operations, but as it is a state that is quite hot and extremely humid, though lovely, one has to be cautious about the future for quality wine here. To date, the Meredyth Winery in the historic town of Middleburg has done a credible job with the hybrids, but the Chardonnay and Cabernet have left me consistently unimpressed. I have not yet tasted an excellent Cabernet or Merlot from Virginia, but the winery of Mont Domaine in Charlottesville is getting close to producing very good red wines. With respect to Chardonnay, the outlook is better. Virginia has one winery that produces world-class Chardonnay: **The Piedmont Vineyards.** Their 1986 and 1987 Chardonnays compete with the best in America. Other good Chardonnays have come from three wineries: **Ingleside Plantation** in Oak Grove, **Naked Mountain** in Markham, and **Oakencroft Vineyards** in Charlottesville. These Chardonnays tend to be well marked by oak but are correct and pleasant. For Riesling, **Rapidan River Vineyards** in Culpepper has, since 1978, produced a series of very flavorful, interesting wines. Lastly, **Piedmont Vineyards** also produces a very good, interesting Semillon.

I hope these Virginia wineries succeed, but in all truthfulness, the quality of their wines does not stand up well when compared to what else is available from around the world.

Washington

While I still have doubts about the overall quality and potential for Washington state wines, there are some encouraging signs since the last edition of this guide. Most importantly, the huge **Château Ste. Michelle** appears to be consistently upgrading its quality. While St. Michelle's white wines have always been good the Cabernet Sauvignons and Merlots have been irregular in quality. However, since 1983 the quality of the red wines has been very good to excellent, including super Reserve Merlots and Cabernets in 1983 and 1985. In addition, with the introduction of their second line of well-made, inexpensive wines under the Columbia Crest label, this winery appears headed in the right direction. Don't miss Ste. Michelle's recent 1983 and 1984 Reserve Merlots and Reserve Cabernet Sauvignons that are so good that a few of California's top producers may be getting just a little nervous.

Two other sizable wineries also continue to make very good to excellent wines. **Columbia Winery,** with David Lake at the helm, continues to turn out lovely, rich Cabernets, especially from the Red Willow Vineyard, decent Chardonnays, and very fine Sauvignon Blancs and Semillons. The other winery, **Hogue Cellars,** also continues to excel with its Chardonnay, Chenin Blanc, Fumé Blanc, Semillon, and Riesling. To this roster of tasty whites has been added a rich, tasty, medium-weight, effusively fruity Merlot. If that is not enough, this winery also produces some of the best pickled asparagus and green beans that you could ever want to eat.

Other, smaller wineries of note include **Arbor Crest,** which produces one of this country's best Fumé Blancs. For Cabernet Sauvignon, an often too vegetal and troublesome varietal for Washington state wineries, there is the excellent wine of **Woodward Canyon,** followed by **Redford Cellars** and **Quilceda Creek.** I have also been impressed by the excellent Merlot (the 1983 and the 1986) from **Latah Creek Winery.**

There are numerous other wineries in Washington state, but overall the quality of their wines does not compare favorably with the best wines from California or Oregon or of those imported.

A PRODUCER'S GUIDE TO THE BEST WASHINGTON CHARDONNAYS

* * * * * (OUTSTANDING PRODUCERS)
None

* * * * (EXCELLENT PRODUCERS)
Hogue

* * * (GOOD PRODUCERS)

Arbor Crest	Château Ste. Michelle
Columbia	Zillah Oakes

A PRODUCER'S GUIDE TO THE BEST WASHINGTON MERLOTS AND CABERNET SAUVIGNONS

* * * * * (OUTSTANDING PRODUCERS)
Château Ste. Michelle Reserve Bottlings (since 1983)

* * * * (EXCELLENT PRODUCERS)

Château Ste. Michelle	Latah Creek
Columbia "Red Willow"	Leonetti
	Woodward Canyon

* * * (GOOD PRODUCERS)

Arbor Crest	Quilceda Creek
Columbia	Redford Cellars
Hogue	

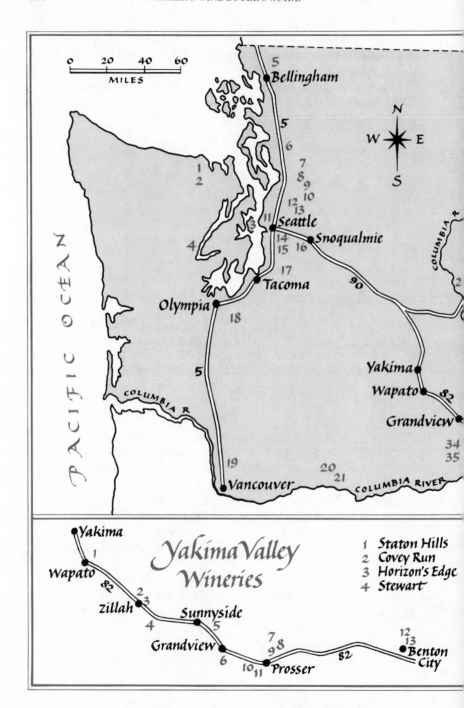

Washington

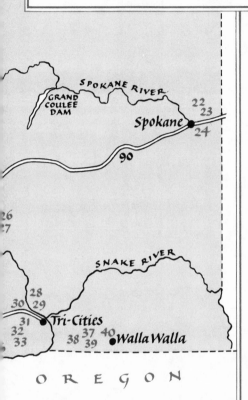

1 Neuharth
2 Lost Mountain
3 Bainbridge Island
4 Hoodsport
5 Mount Baker
6 Pacific Crest
7 Quilceda Creek
8 Haviland
9 Chateau Ste. Michelle
10 French Creek
11 Staton Hills
12 Columbia
13 Paul Thomas
14 E.B. Foote
15 Salmon Bay
16 Snoqualmie
17 Manfred Vierthaler
18 Johnson Creek
19 Salishan
20 Hooper
21 Mont Elise
22 Arbor Crest
23 Latah Creek
24 Worden's
25 Champs de Brionne
26 Hunter Hill
27 F.W. Langguth
28 Preston
29 Gordon Brothers
30 Quarry Lake
31 Bookwalter
32 Barnard Griffin
33 Caroway
34 Mercer Ranch
35 Redford
36 Chateau Ste. Michelle
37 L'Ecole No 41
38 Waterbrook
39 Woodward Canyon
40 Leonetti

5 Tucker
6 Chateau Ste. Michelle
7 Pontin del Roza
8 Hogue
9 Chinook
10 Yakima River
11 Hinzerling
12 Blackwood Canyon
13 Kiona

THE BEST
OF THE
REST

Australia
Argentina
Bulgaria
Chile
Greece
Hungary
Lebanon
New Zealand
Switzerland
United Kingdom
Yugoslavia

9. AUSTRALIA

A Special Report

TYPES OF WINE

You name it and the Australians no doubt grow it, make it into wine, blend it with something else, and give it an odd bin number. Australian wines have been hot for three years, and not just in America. The combination of quality and value that many of them offer is the hottest thing in town from London to New York. Australia, like California in America, and Alsace in France, labels its wine after the grape (or grapes) that it is made from. All the major grape varietals are used here, and amazingly, good wines are turned out from all of them. The major viticultural districts (listed alphabetically) are:

Adelaide Hills—Located in southern Australia, this is a high-altitude, cooler-climate region. Petaluma is its most famous winery, Mountadam makes Australia's finest Chardonnay from Vineyards in the Adelaide Hills.

Barossa Valley—In southern Australia, this huge, well-known viticultural area north of Adelaide is the home of some of the titans of Australia's wine industry (i.e., Penfolds, Henschke, Tollana, Seppelt, Orlando, and Hill Smith).

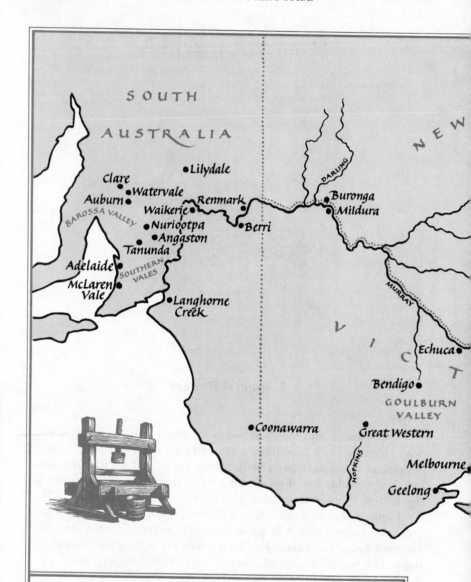

Australia

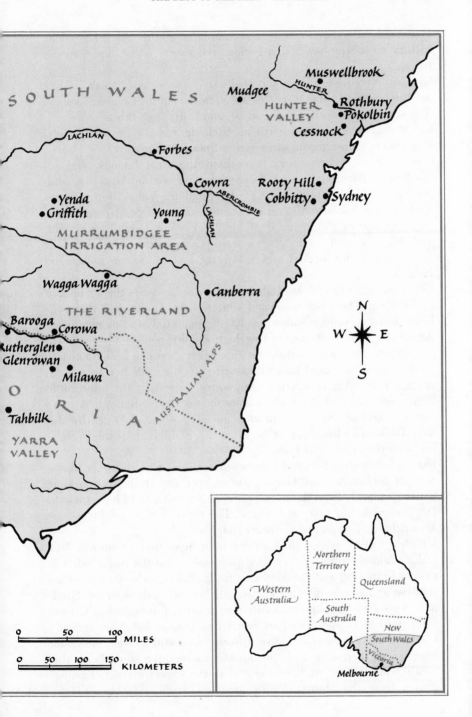

Bendigo—Bendigo is an up-and-coming area, although it has a long history as a wine-producing region. Balgownie is the finest winery there.

Central Victoria—The traditionally styled wines of Château Tahbilk are the best that come from Central Victoria and the Goulburn Valley. The wines are powerful, full-bodied, and fruity from this area.

Clare Valley—Located north of Adelaide and the Barossa Valley, this area is known for its white rather than red wines.

Coonawarra—Coonawarra is perhaps the most famous, and according to some, the best red wine growing area of Australia. Situated in South Australia, west of the Goulburn Valley, top wineries such as Lindeman's (their Limestone Ridge and St. George Vineyards are there), Petaluma, Penfolds, Rosemount, Orlando, Reynella, and Mildara pull their grapes from Coonawarra. The two best wineries actually located in Coonawarra are the Bowen Estate and Hollick.

Geelong—Southwest of Melbourne near the coast is the small area of Geelong. The most renowned wineries are Anakie and Bannockburn, but everyone is talking about the potential of Hickinbotham's Anakie, a winery of impeccable high quality now in the throes of overcoming the tragic death of its winemaker, Stephen Hickinbotham.

Glenrowan—Located in northeastern Victoria, this hot area is famous for its inky, rich, chewy red wines, especially the full-throttle Shiraz from one of Australia's historic producers, Baileys. A more commercial Cabernet and Shiraz is made by Wynn's. At nearby Milawa, Brown Brothers, one of the most successful high-quality Australian wineries, makes its home.

Great Western—Situated between Ararat and Stawell, to the northwest of Melbourne and Geelong, is an area known for its sparkling wines (primarily from the huge producer Seppelt), and for its smooth, fat, low-acid, but tasty red wines. The top red wine producers are Mount Langi Ghiran and Cathcart Ridge.

Hunter Valley—Less than a three-hour drive from Sydney is Australia's famed Hunter Valley. It is to Sydney what the Napa Valley is to San Francisco and the Médoc is to Bordeaux—a major tourist attraction and source of some of Australia's most desired wines. Originally this area was known for its rich, exotic, full-bodied red wines from the Shiraz and Cabernet Sauvignon grapes, but more recently Chardonnay and Semillon have proven successful as well. No doubt because of their size and the intense competitive spirit here, this area's wineries are well represented in the export market. Familiar names from the Hunter Valley include Tyrrell, Rothbury Estate,

Lindeman's, Rosemount, Saxonvale, Lake's Folly, Arrowfield, Hungerford Hill, Brokenwood, Evans, and Wyndham Estate.

Lower Great Southern—In the remote southwestern tip of Australia approximately 150 miles south of Perth is a vast, burgeoning viticultural area called Lower Great Southern. Apple orchards thrive more than vineyards, but wineries such as Mount Barker, Redmond, and Alkoomi have good reputations.

Margaret River—In the very southwestern tip of this country is the Margaret River viticultural zone. Australian wine experts claim that Australia's most French-like Cabernet Sauvignons and Chardonnays come from this area that produces wines with higher natural acidities. There are some superb producers located here, including the likes of Vasse Felix, Moss Wood, Leeuwin Estate, and Cullens.

McLaren Vale—The traditional fare of this hot area south of Adelaide was high-alcohol Grenache wines that were thick and rich. This has all changed in the last ten years with the advent of cold fermentations and the perception that the public yearns for lighter, fruitier wines. Some of the greats of the Australian wine business are in McLaren Vale, including Hardy's and its higher-quality sibling, Reynella. Smaller wineries of note are Wirra Wirra, Woodstock, and Kay Brothers.

Mudgee—Located in New South Wales west of the famed Hunter Valley, Mudgee (an aboriginal name meaning "nest in the hills") with its cool nights and hot days has proven not only to be a top-notch red wine area, but also an excellent source for tropical-fruit-scented, luxuriously rich Chardonnays. For whatever reason, the wines of Mudgee also tend to be less expensive than those from other top areas. One winery, Montrose, dominates the quality scene; two other fine producers are Miramar and Huntington Estate.

Murrumbidgee Irrigation Area—This area, which has to be irrigated, is in New South Wales about 250 miles due west of Sydney. The region has a mediocre reputation for quality wines that appears justified given what I have tasted, although several producers, such as McWilliams and De Bortoli, have managed to turn out interesting wines. When the wines are good they are a bargain, as prices from this area called the MIA are low.

Padthaway—This southern Australian viticultural area has developed a strong following for its white wines, especially the Chardonnay and Sauvignon Blanc. Padthaway is one of Australia's newest "hot" areas, and two of Australia's largest producers, Lindeman's and Seppelt, have shown just how tasty the white wines from this region can be.

Pyrenees—The attractive, rolling-hill countryside of the Pyrenees northwest of Melbourne forms a triangle between Redbank, Moonambel, and Avoca. The top wines are the reds from the Cabernet Sauvignon and Shiraz grapes. The best white wines are from the Sauvignon grape. Wineries of note include Redbank, Taltarni, Mount Avoca, and Château Remy.

Riverland—Located in South Australia, Riverland is to Australia what the San Joaquin Valley is to California. This vast source of grapes of mediocre quality is dominated by huge cooperatives and producers who turn out Australia's jug wines and bag-in-the-box generic wines. Some big enterprises have their jug wine business centered here, including Penfolds, Kaiserstuhl, Angove, Berri, and Renmano. While most of the wines from this area are decidedly insipid, some good-value, fresh whites at bargain-basement prices can be found.

Rutherglen—Rutherglen is synonymous with Australia's fortified sweet wines, many of which are quite extraordinary. The famous sweet, nectarlike, ageless ports and fortified Muscats and Tokays of William Chambers, Campbells, and Seppelt are made from Rutherglen grapes.

Swan Valley—This hot, arid area in Western Australia just northeast of the coastal city of Perth produces large-framed, muscular red wines and increasingly better white wines. Houghton is the area's most famous winery, but good wines are made by Evans and Tate, as well as Moondah Brook.

Yarra Valley—This is the viticultural area most in fashion in Australia, and its proponents argue that the climate and resulting wines come closest in spirit to those of Bordeaux and Burgundy in France. I am not convinced. Located in Victoria, this is a cool-climate area outside Melbourne, and every major red and white glamour varietal is planted, from Cabernet Sauvignon, Merlot, and Pinot Noir, to Chardonnay, Riesling, and Gewürztraminer. The best wineries are Lillydale, Yarra Yering, Coldstream Hills, and St. Huberts.

GRAPE VARIETIES

RED WINES

Cabernet Sauvignon—This varietal excels in Australia and generally produces a very fruity, often jammy, intensely curranty, fat wine, sometimes low in acidity, but round, generous, and surprisingly age-worthy for up to 7–8 years in spite of an acid deficiency.

Pinot Noir—As in California, there are those who claim to have made successful wines from this infinitely fickle varietal, but the great majority of Australian Pinot Noirs to date have been raisiny, unusual, often repugnant wines. Anyone who tells you something different clearly does not have your best interests at heart.

Shiraz—Despite the Aussies' present-day infatuation with Cabernet Sauvignon, Merlot, and Pinot Noir, this is the grape that makes their greatest red wines. The problem is that there is an enormous amount of it in Australia, and only a handful of producers treat Shiraz (Syrah) with the respect and care that is accorded Cabernet. It can produce Australia's greatest red wine when left to stand on its own, as Penfolds Grange Hermitage convincingly proves, or it can offer more dimension and character to a red wine when blended with Cabernet Sauvignon, as Penfolds and Petaluma have proven time and time again.

WHITE WINES

Chardonnay—The shrewd Aussies, taking full advantage of the wine consumer's thirst for Chardonnay wines, have consistently offered plump, fat wines filled with flavors of apples, pears, oranges, and very ripe melons. The tendency to over-oak-age the wines has virtually disappeared, as more and more Australian Chardonnays are fresh and exuberant and bottled early to preserve their youthful grapy qualities. The one major disappointment is the aging potential of these naturally low-acid wines, but most consumers are drinking them within several months of purchase, so this is probably a moot issue.

Gewürztraminer—Contrary to the local salespeople who hype the quality of Gewürztraminer, this grape produces insipid, pale, watery wines that are a far cry from what Gewürztraminer does in France.

Marsanne—Château Tahbilk is the greatest proponent of this wine, which I find to have a one-dimensional, bland taste.

Muscat—This hot-climate grape excels in Australia and is at its best in the decadently rich, sweet, fortified Muscats that seemingly age and improve for ages. It is also made into a medium sweet table wine with which Brown Brothers does a particularly admirable job.

Riesling—Australia has proven to be the New World's best alternative to German-made Rieslings. This grape has done extremely well with Kabinett- and Spätlese-styled drier Rieslings in the Barossa Valley and Adelaide Hills. Wineries such as Petaluma, Pewsey Vale, Rosemount, and Hill Smith have turned out some spectacular Beerenauslese- and Trockenbeerenauslese-styled sweet wines. Overall, this grape gets high marks from me in Australia.

Sauvignon Blanc—The results have been mixed as the very hot climate causes this grape to overripen and take on a grotesque, vegetal, oily, thick fruitiness. However, there are some fresh, tasty, dry Sauvignons coming from Australia; but for now, New Zealand is consistently beating Australia when it comes to quality Sauvignon-based wines.

Semillon—This can be delicious, whether it is blended with Chardonnay or Sauvignon, or whether it stands by itself. It produces big, creamy, rich wines loaded with flavor. Wineries such as Rothbury, Rosemount, Montrose, Peter Lehmann, Henschke, and Evans and Tate have done better with Semillon than anyone. Some great sweet wines have been made from Semillon affected by the botrytis fungus. Look for those from Rothbury, Rosemount, and Peter Lehmann, which are world class.

FLAVORS

RED WINES

Cabernet Sauvignon—Very ripe, often overripe, sweet, intense blackcurrant flavors, supple, fat textures, and oodles of fruit. When poorly made or overly acidified, the wines are musty, dirty, and tart.

Pinot Noir—Raisiny, pruny fruit flavors with no finesse or complexity represent appallingly bad examples of Pinot Noir.

Shiraz—Intense aromas of cassis, leather, licorice, cedar, tar, and pepper are found in wines that have a healthy dose of Shiraz. Quite full-bodied and rich with softer tannins than Cabernet Sauvignon, these wines are drinkable young, but frequently they age better than the more glamorous Cabernet Sauvignons.

WHITE WINES

Chardonnay—Tropical-fruit flavors predominate in this creamy textured, voluptuous wine. Oak is sometimes too noticeable, but better-balanced wines with the fruit in the forefront have been the rule in recent vintages.

Gewürztraminer—Where's the spice and exotic lychee-nut character found in the great Gewürztraminers of Alsace? Watery, thin wines are usually disappointing.

Marsanne—Usually neutral, or as Jancis Robinson says, "reminiscent of glue," aptly describes Marsanne. It usually tastes much better old than young, but because it tastes so uninteresting young, no one ages it.

Muscat—Huge aromas of brown sugar, fruitcake, crème brûlée, buttered and baked apricots, and oranges with honey and nuts give this varietal its appeal.

Riesling—The classic Riesling aromas of spring flowers, green apples, and wet stones are present in the drier versions of this wine. As the wines get sweeter, aromas and flavors of oranges, peaches, apricots, butter, baked apples, and honeyed nuts arise.

Sauvignon Blanc—Unfortunately, these wines seem to be either feeble, bland, and tasteless, or oily, vegetal, and grotesque.

Semillon—In the drier versions, lemon-lime aromas intertwined with honey and toasty oak are often the most interesting. With the sweet versions, buttery nuts and honey-coated-raisin flavors take over.

AGING POTENTIAL

Cabernet Sauvignon: 5–10 years
Pinot Noir: 4–6 years
Shiraz: 5–20 years

Chardonnay: 2–3 years
Gewürztraminer: 1–3 years
Marsanne: 4–12 years
Muscat (Dry): 1–3 years
   (Fortified): 5–50+ years
Riesling (Dry): 3–6 years
   (Sweet): 4–10 years
Sauvignon Blanc: 1–3 years
Semillon (Dry): 2–8 years
   (Sweet): 4–12 years

OVERALL QUALITY LEVEL

At the top level, wines such as the Penfolds Grange Hermitage or Bin 707 Cabernet Sauvignon are as fine as any red wine made in the world. Unfortunately, there are too few of them in Australia. Far and away, Australia's overall wine quality is average to above average with many mediocre and poorly made wines but very few great wines. There are, however, plenty of good, agreeable wines at great prices, and therein lies the secret to the recent success of Australia's wines in the marketplace. Australia today leads the wine world in offering tasty, delicious wines at modest prices. In that area, Australian wines have very little competition.

MOST IMPORTANT INFORMATION TO KNOW

Given the remarkable diversity, the best thing for consumers to do is to memorize the names of some of the better producers and restrict their initial purchases to the surefire successes from that particular winery—usually Chardonnay, Cabernet, and Shiraz. The producers chart for each varietal should be used as a guideline until you have decided which wines and producers you prefer.

1989–1990 BUYING STRATEGY

For 99% of Australia's wines, buy only what you intend to drink over the next year. Except for a few red wines, the open-knit, plump, overtly fruity, low-acid style of Australian wines is ideal for consuming immediately, but their cellaring potential is limited. For white wines, restrict your buying to 1986, 1987, and 1988. For red wines, you can safely buy any vintage in the decade of the eighties without worrying about its senility. Furthermore, keep in mind that Australia does indeed produce sensational, world-class, late-harvest, and fortified wines at a fraction of the price one has to pay for a German Beerenauslese or Trockenbeerenauslese, a French Sauternes, or vintage or tawny port. These wines, as well as the reasonably priced, tasty, dry table wines, are well worth seeking out.

VINTAGE GUIDE

As in California, constant sunny weather virtually guarantees at least good-quality wines in Australia, but each year is different as a result of drought, heat or cold waves, and hail. However, the extremes in quality that one often sees in Europe do not exist in Australia.

1988—Early reports indicate a terrific year for red wines, but a mixed bag for the whites. In some areas the quantity was down considerably, leading to speculation that prices are going to escalate given the smaller than normal crop.

1987—An exceptionally cool and late year all over Australia, the crop size was down, but the quality is considered to be very good to exceptional with some splendid white wines and good, sometimes excellent red wines in Victoria and South Australia.

1986—The crop size varied from average to well above average, but the quality is very good to excellent in all major districts. Many producers rate 1986 and 1987 the two best back-to-back years for both red and white wines in this decade.

1985—The second of four straight cool years, the 1985 vintage is highly regarded for its Cabernet Sauvignons. Overall, a good red wine vintage, particularly in New South Wales, but it is far from a great vintage as most producers prefer 1987, 1986, and 1983 to 1985, although in the Great Southern region growers felt it was a top-notch vintage. It was a cool, very dry year.

1984—A huge crop everywhere translated into lighter, less concentrated wines. In particular, the Hunter Valley suffered because of excessive rainfall.

1983—An exceptionally hot, dry year resulted in some full-blown, now tired, white wines, and some rich, intense, outstanding red wines, especially in the Hunter Valley. Overall, this vintage looks to be the worst of this decade for quality.

1982—A large crop of good wines was produced. No one has called it great, and the successes would appear to be mostly in South Australia.

A GUIDE TO AUSTRALIA'S BEST PRODUCERS OF CABERNET SAUVIGNON AND SHIRAZ

***** (OUTSTANDING PRODUCERS)

Henschke (Barossa)
Penfolds (South Australia)

Petaluma (South Australia)
Château Tahbilk (Goulburn)

**** (EXCELLENT PRODUCERS)

Alkoomi (Western Australia)
Baileys (Glenrowan)
Balgownie (Bendigo)
Brand's Laira (Coonawarra)
Château François (Pokolbin)
Hickinbotham (Geelong)
Hungerford Hill (Hunter Valley)
Huntington Estate (Mudgee)

Lake's Folly (New South Wales)
Leeuwin Estate (Margaret River)
Lindeman's (Coonawarra)
Redbank (Victoria)
Seville Estate (Victoria)
Virgin Hills (Victoria)
Wolf Blass (Victoria)

*** (GOOD PRODUCERS)

Brokenwood (New South Wales)
Bowen Estate (South Australia)
Brown Bros. (Victoria)
Capel Vale (Western Australia)
Cold Stream Hills (Yarra Valley)
Cullens (Margaret River)
Fern Hill (McLaren)
Tim Knappstein (Clare Valley)
Peter Lehmann (Barossa)
Lindeman's (New South Wales)

Geoff Merrill (South Australia)
Mildara (Coonawarra)
Montrose (Mudgee)
Moss Wood (Margaret River)
Mount Langi Ghiran (Victoria)
Redman (Coonawarra)
Rosemount Estate (Coonawarra)
Saxonvale (Hunter Valley)
Seppelt (Barossa)
Taltarni (Victoria)

Vasse Felix (Western Australia)
Wrights (Western Australia)

Wyndham Estates (South
Australia)

A GUIDE TO AUSTRALIA'S BEST PRODUCERS OF CHARDONNAY

***** (OUTSTANDING PRODUCERS)

Clyde Park (Geelong)
Montrose (Mudgee)
Mountadam (Adelaide Hills)

Rosemount Estate (Coonawarra)
Rothbury Estate (Hunter Valley)

**** (EXCELLENT PRODUCERS)

Cassegrain (New South Wales)
Cold Stream Hills (Yarra Valley)
Cullens (Margaret River)
Hungerford Hill (Hunter Valley)
Katnook Estate (Coonawarra)
Krondorf (Barossa)
Lake's Folly (New South Wales)
Leeuwin (Margaret River)
Lindemans (New South Wales)
Mitchelton (Goulburn)

Miramar (Mudgee)
Moss Wood (Western Australia)
Petaluma (South Australia)
Reynella (Southern Vales)
Seppelt (Barossa)
Mark Swann (South Australia)
Tyrrells Vat 47 (New South
Wales)
Yarra Yering (Yarra Valley)
Yeringsberg (Yarra Valley)

*** (GOOD PRODUCERS)

Balgownie (Victoria)
Brown Bros. (Victoria)
Capel Vale (Western Australia)

Mildara (Coonawarra)
Orlando (South Australia)

A GUIDE TO AUSTRALIA'S BEST PRODUCERS OF DRY SAUVIGNON BLANC AND SEMILLON

***** (OUTSTANDING PRODUCERS)
None

**** (EXCELLENT PRODUCERS)

Henschke (Barossa)

Rothbury Estate (Hunter Valley)

*** (GOOD PRODUCERS)

Berri Estates (South Australia)	Peter Lehmann (Barossa)
Evans and Tate (Margaret River)	Lindeman's (Padthaway)
	Mildara (Coonawarra)
Tim Knappstein (Clare Valley)	Rosemount (Hunter Valley)
Krondorf (Barossa)	

A GUIDE TO AUSTRALIA'S BEST PRODUCERS OF SWEET SAUVIGNON BLANC AND SEMILLON

***** (OUTSTANDING PRODUCERS)

Peter Lehmann (Barossa)	Rothbury Estate (Hunter Valley)
Rosemount (Hunter Valley)	

A GUIDE TO AUSTRALIA'S BEST PRODUCERS OF FORTIFIED WINES

***** (OUTSTANDING PRODUCERS)

Wm. Chambers Rosewood Tokay and Muscat	Seppelt Show Wines
Morris Muscat and Tokay Liquor	Yalumba Port

ALKOOMI (WESTERN AUSTRALIA)

1985 Cabernet Sauvignon	B	85
1986 Rhine Riesling	B	75
1986 Semillon/Sauvignon Blanc	B	82

Located in the Lower Great Southern area of Western Australia, Alkoomi produces just in excess of 13,000 cases of wine with the best-quality wines tending to be the Cabernet Sauvignon and Cabernet/Shiraz blend. Of the current releases, the 1986 Rhine Riesling has a dull, somewhat musty nose and rather one-dimensional flavors, whereas the 1986 Semillon/Sauvignon Blanc is rather robust and fleshy, but lacking finesse. The best wine of this trio is the 1985 Cabernet Sauvignon, which shows excellent color, a classic weedy, blackcurranty bouquet backed up with some mineral scents, full body, good tannins, and the ability to age well through the decade of the nineties.

AMBERTON (MUDGEE)

1986 Cabernet Sauvignon	B	85

1986 Chardonnay	B	85

1987 Gewürztraminer	B	75

This relatively small, quality-oriented winery is located in Mudgee, and based on the only three wines I have tasted, the Gewürztraminer seems typical of most New World wines from this particular grape. It lacks the spice and exotic character found in Gewürztraminers from Alsace, France. However, the Chardonnay shows a lovely bouquet with scents of melon, pear, and apple, medium to full body, and soft, lush fruit. It should drink nicely over the next several years. The Cabernet Sauvignon also impressed me with its well-focused, bing-cherry fruit, smoky, toasty oak, and ripe, rich, round, lush flavors.

ANGOVES (SOUTH AUSTRALIA)

1985 Cabernet Sauvignon	A	83

1986 Chardonnay	A	60

1987 Chardonnay	A	70

1987 Rhine Riesling	A	72

1987 Sauvignon Blanc	A	59

This gigantic winery is known for its brandy as well as its inexpensive line of table wines. I found the wines to range from below average to mediocre in quality, with the exception of a good, supple Cabernet Sauvignon. It had well-focused black-cherry fruit, medium body, light tannins, and a soft, agreeable finish. The Chardonnays tasted unbelievably tart and thin; the Sauvignon Blanc, dirty and unpleasant. Prices are low, but selection is extremely critical here.

ARROWFIELD (UPPER HUNTER VALLEY)

1985 Cabernet Sauvignon	A	78

1987 Chardonnay	A	72

1987 Semillon	A	80

Arrowfield, in the Upper Hunter Valley, has a reported production of 10,000 cases, and based on the several vintages I have tasted, the quality appears to be only average. Most of the production is dedicated to white wine varietals such as Semillon, Chardonnay, Sauvignon, and Gewürztraminer. None of the above wines was terribly exciting to drink, but they are certainly fair values. These are clearly wines that must be drunk within 3–4 years of the vintage, with the possible exception of the Cabernet Sauvignon, which may last 6–7 years after the vintage.

BAILEYS (GLENROWAN)

1984 Cabernet Sauvignon	B	75

N.V. Founder's Muscat Liqueur	C	90

N.V. HJT Muscat Liqueur	C	94

1986 Rhine Riesling	A	78

Baileys Winery of Glenrowan produces a bevy of dry table wines that are of average quality. The glories of this moderate-sized winery of 12,000 cases are its spectacular Muscats and Tokays, which rival those of William Chambers as the greatest made in Australia. Of the above wines, the Rhine Riesling is a rather innocuous, simple wine, and the Cabernet Sauvignon a chunky, muscular, intense wine, lacking finesse but exhibiting plenty of power and richness. However, the two Muscats provide fabulous drinking. The Founder's Muscat has a honeyed, caramel sweetness, quite a bit of age to it, a perfume and fragrance that can fill a room, and a long, luxuriously rich finish. As exceptional as it is, the HJT Muscat simply must be tasted to be believed. It has explosive richness, a bouquet of honeyed nuts, caramel, brown sugar, and candied tropical fruits; it is exquisite and will probably live forever.

BALGOWNIE (BENDIGO)

1986 Cabernet Sauvignon	A	86
1987 Chardonnay	A	85
1986 Hermitage	A	86

This 5,000-case winery in Bendigo has an outstanding reputation in Australia, and it is easy to see why. The 1987 Chardonnay displays a restrained yet classic lemony, applelike, complex bouquet of fruit and subtle oak, medium to full body, and plenty of underlying depth and richness of fruit. It is one of the few Australian Chardonnays that I would bet could age for 6 years. Furthermore, the price is unbelievable. The 1986 Cabernet Sauvignon is also an impressive, deeply colored wine, quite tannic, but full-bodied and showing the subtly herbaceous blackcurrant fruit one expects from Cabernet married deftly with subtle oak. The Hermitage is a bigger, denser, even richer wine with a bit more suppleness and even more concentration of fruit hiding the tannins.

BANNOCKBURN (GEELONG)

1983 Cabernet Sauvignon	B	83
1984 Cabernet Sauvignon	B	80
1985 Chardonnay	B	83
1986 Chardonnay	B	84
1986 Pinot Noir	C	78

Bannockburn is a small, 4,000-case winery that is dedicated to making very fine wine. My tastings have shown wines that are richly fruity, soft, and quite agreeable, but the prices seem a little high for what one gets in the bottle, a rarity with Australian wines. Both the 1986 and 1985 Chardonnays show a good lashing of oak and plump, solid, full-bodied fruit flavors. The 1986 shows a bit more length than the 1985. As for the Cabernet Sauvignons, they too show attractive, moderately intense, blackcurranty, sweet, new oaky noses, soft, richly fruity flavors, and 3–4 more years of drinkability. The Pinot Noir, which is reputed to be one of the specialties of this house, shows entirely too much oak for the amount of fruit, and one would be hard pressed to find any varietal character in it. Oddly enough, it is grossly overpriced.

BERRI ESTATES (SOUTH AUSTRALIA)

1986 Cabernet Sauvignon/Shiraz	A	85
1986 Chardonnay	A	75
1987 Chardonnay	A	82
1987 Fumé Blanc	A	86
1987 Semillon	A	86
1985 Shiraz	A	85
1986 Shiraz	A	84

This gigantic cooperative in South Australia makes a tremendous range of wines. The best lots of their varietal wines are surprisingly well done with rich, soft, voluptuous fruit flavors. They are clearly made in a style that emphasizes up-front charm and appeal over aging ability and cellaring potential. Prices are remarkable for the quality. My favorite wines from Berri Estates include their delicious, exuberantly fruity, medium-bodied Fumé Blanc, which has gobs of fruit and a lively acidity; the fat, tasty, concentrated Semillons; the 1985 Shiraz, which lacks finesse but does offer meaty, forward, tasty fruit in a lush, full-bodied framework; and the 1986 Cabernet Sauvignon/ Shiraz, which smells of jammy raspberries, is medium to full bodied, and offers a supple, very smooth glass of wine. All of these wines, including the red wines, should be drunk over the next 2–3 years.

BOWEN ESTATE (SOUTH AUSTRALIA)

1985 Cabernet Sauvignon	B	84
1986 Rhine Riesling	B	76
1985 Shiraz	B	84

This tiny winery with a 4,000-case production has made some excellent wines over recent vintages. I found both the red wines, the 1985 Shiraz and Cabernet Sauvignon, to show good, rich, stylish fruit in a medium- to full-bodied format with 3–5 more years of aging potential. These wines are not made in a blockbuster, powerful, muscular, Australian style, but rather in an elegant, understated but flavorful manner. The only wine that I have not been impressed by is the estate's Riesling, which always tastes a bit clumsy and lacks balance.

BROKENWOOD (NEW SOUTH WALES)

1985 Cabernet Sauvignon	B	85
1985 Hermitage/Cabernet	B	86

This winery has a good reputation for its elegantly rendered wines from the Lower Hunter Valley. The Cabernet Sauvignon has a medium to full body, a pure, well-delineated, oaky, blackcurrant fruitiness, and soft flavors, and it should drink nicely for another 5–6 years. The Hermitage/Cabernet has a more peppery, spicy bouquet, an excellent balance between toasty oak and ripe fruit, and is a lush, full-bodied wine for drinking over the next 5–6 years.

BROWN BROS. (VICTORIA)

1985 Cabernet Sauvignon Family Select	A	85
1987 Chardonnay	B	86
N.V. Lexia Muscat	A	85
1987 Sauvignon Blanc	A	84
1985 Shiraz	A	85
1984 Shiraz/Mondeuse/Cabernet	A	84

This venerable family-owned winery with substantial vineyard holdings in Victoria has consistently priced its wines intelligently for the export markets; therefore, the wines represent some of the best bargains to be found. While the wines from Brown Bros. are rarely complex, they do offer silky, smooth, generous, ripe, rich, fruity flavors that provide plenty of satisfaction. The 1987 Chardonnay shows attractive buttery, apple aromas and flavors, soft acidity, and a ripe, gentle finish. The Sauvignon Blanc is quite dry with a fragrant, lemony, melony, subtle, herbaceous bouquet, medium body, and a crisp, zesty finish. As for the red wines, the 1985 Cabernet Sauvignon is filled with supple blackcurrant and blackberry fruit flavors. The Shiraz adds a peppery, spicy component to the same range of flavors, and the 1984 Shiraz/Mondeuse/Cabernet blend (a specialty of this house) projects a more herbaceous aroma and has a less opulent, more austere texture. Lastly, the Lexia Muscat has the intense, heady, intoxicating perfume of peaches and apricots, a sweet, unctuous texture, and loads of fruit; it should only be drunk with dessert.

CAMPBELLS (VICTORIA)

1985 Cabernet	B	87
N.V. Muscat Liqueur	C	87
N.V. Muscat Rutherglen	C	86

While this winery is known primarily for its fortified wines, its blend of Ruby Cabernet and Cabernet Sauvignon is quite an excellent wine with gobs of curranty, cedary fruit, full body, and a judicious use of toasty new oak. Though the Muscats are not quite up to the quality level of Baileys or William Chambers, they do exhibit the wonderfully unctuous, sweet, fragrant, almost decadent fruit of the Muscat grape in a very sweet, rich, full-bodied, alcoholic style. They are not vintage dated but appear to be capable of lasting 20–40 years.

CAPEL VALE (WESTERN AUSTRALIA)

1985 Chardonnay	B	86
1985 Shiraz	B	87

Reputedly one of the shining stars of Western Australia, Capel Vale produces 7,000 cases of wine, of which the majority is white. The 1985 Chardonnay is still drinking well, showing an intense bouquet of apple, pear, and buttery fruit admirably complemented by oak, as well as a fresh, vibrant, full-bodied feel on the palate. The Shiraz is close to being one of the blockbuster wines from this varietal in Australia with very rich, intense flavors, full body, and a nearly exceptional perfume of plummy, cassis, peppery fruit. It should drink nicely for 4–5 more years.

CASSEGRAIN VINEYARDS (NEW SOUTH WALES)

1987 Chardonnay Hastings Valley	C	90

1986 Pinot Noir Hastings Valley	B	85

I wish I had been able to taste several more vintages of wine from this moderate-sized producer in Hastings Valley in New South Wales. The quality of the Chardonnay is quite impressive with a wonderful marriage of opulent pineapple and buttery fruit integrated nicely with toasty new oak. It is a full-bodied, rich Chardonnay with 4–5 years of aging potential. As for the Pinot Noir, it is one of the two or three best I have tasted from Australia, and it perhaps proves that the supporters of this grape in Australia may have something to be excited about in the Hastings Valley viticultural area.

CLYDE PARK (GEELONG)

1984 Cabernet Sauvignon	B	74

1985 Cabernet Sauvignon	B	82

1986 Chardonnay	B	87

1987 Chardonnay	B	88

The production of this tiny winery in Geelong is less than 1,000 cases, but it has already developed a cult following for its rich, intense, very well made Chardonnay. Both the 1987 and 1986 are quite full-bodied Chardonnays incorporating hefty doses of oak into rich, intense, unctuous flavors, but they are well balanced and should drink well for at least 18 months; they are among Australia's more interesting Chardonnays. As for the Cabernet Sauvignons, the 1985 shows good weedy, blackcurrant fruit, medium body, and a nice, long finish. The 1984, while admirably concentrated, is minty to an extreme, and this mint/eucalyptus character obscures much of its currant fruit.

COLD STREAM HILLS (YARRA VALLEY)

1986 Cabernet Sauvignon	Lilydale	B	85

1986 Chardonnay Three Vineyards Blend	Lilydale	B	83

1986 Chardonnay Yarra Ridge Vineyard	Lilydale	B	86

1986 Pinot Noir Three Vineyards Blend	Lilydale	C	84

1987 Semillon	Lilydale	B	85

This new winery in one of the hottest new viticultural areas of Australia, the Yarra Valley, is the property of one of Australia's two most renowned wine writers, James Halliday. While I have had a chance to try only one vintage of his Pinot Noir and Cabernet Sauvignon, I was impressed with both. The Pinot shows good varietal character, plenty of berry fruit, and 4–5 years of further drinking potential. The 1986 Cabernet Sauvignon has plenty of ripe blackcurrant fruit, full body, and good crisp acidity. It should drink well for 5–6 years. Both the Chardonnay and the Semillon showed rich, ripe, varietal fruit, plenty of depth and length, and should drink nicely over the next 3–4 years. At present, the winery has just over 10 acres of vines, of which the largest portion is dedicated to Pinot Noir, so it will be interesting to see if Halliday is able to turn out high-quality, complex Pinot Noir in Australia.

CULLENS (MARGARET RIVER)

1983 Cabernet/Merlot	B	86

1984 Cabernet/Merlot	B	82

1985 Cabernet/Merlot	B	85

1986 Chardonnay	B	87

1987 Chardonnay	B	87

1987 Sauvignon Blanc	B	84

Based on the wines I have tasted to date, this low-profile winery in Western Australia, which draws its grapes from the Margaret River area, is making very fine, balanced yet distinctive, and personality-filled wines that show vibrant, rich, full-bodied flavors, and a healthy dose of oak as a result of barrel fermentation. The Sauvignon Blanc has some oak to vie with its crisp, aggressive, herbaceous fruit, is medium-bodied, and quite flavorful; it is not for the shy. The two Chardonnays show rich, buttery, toasty, barrel-fermented characters, excellent smoky, ripe bouquets, full body, and plenty of power somewhat at the expense of finesse. Both should be drunk over the next several years. Lastly, the 1983 and 1985 Cabernet/Merlot show wonderful suppleness, and fat, leathery, rich currant flavors, plenty of alcoholic punch, leathery, ground-meat-scented, penetrating bouquets, and soft tannins in the finish. The 1985 looks to be a bit better structured for the long haul than the fully mature 1983. As for the 1984, it seems slightly lighter, but still very delicious and supple in the same style as the 1983 and 1985. This is a winery of which to take note.

DE BORTOLI (MIA)

1984 Botrytis Semillon	B	87

This winery, situated in the less-respected viticultural district called the Murrumbidgee Irrigation Area, turns out one of Australia's best sweet table wines from Semillon grapes that have been infected with the botrytis fungus. The 1984, with its explosive richness and rather heavy, powerful style, is the best wine made by De Bortoli since the 1982. This large-scale producer also makes a huge range of dry table wines of mediocre quality that are sold for relatively low prices. The best I have tasted has been the Merlot, made by the carbonic maceration method.

DENMAN ESTATE (NEW SOUTH WALES)

1983 Cabernet Sauvignon	A	52
1985 Private Bin Chardonnay	A	50
1985 Semillon Bin 3	A	55

Based on what I have tasted, this large winery in New South Wales has a number of very defective wines in the marketplace that are to be avoided. The 1985 Private Bin Chardonnay had a chemical aroma and was a horrendously bad wine. The 1983 Cabernet Sauvignon, with a mercaptan nose of garlic and onions, was a flawed, virtually undrinkable wine; and lastly, the 1985 Semillon Bin 3 was watery and thin, with an extremely sharp taste in the finish. In essence, if these are representative of the wines made by Denman Estate, it is appalling.

ELDERTON (BAROSSA)

1984 Cabernet Sauvignon/Merlot	B	85

1985 Hermitage	B	87

I have only tried two wines from this 20,000-case winery in the Barossa Valley, but I was impressed by the soft, generous, rich fruit of the Cabernet Sauvignon/Merlot; it is a wine for those who require instant gratification. The 1985 Hermitage with its deep ruby/purple color and huge, peppery, cedary bouquet shows a luscious softness to the gobs of fruit it contains in its full-bodied format. The wine style here seems to aim for up-front charm and appeal, so these wines should be drunk over the next 3–4 years.

EVANS AND TATE (MARGARET RIVER)

This winery has quite an excellent reputation in Australia for its Shiraz and Cabernet Sauvignon from Redbrook. My tastings to date have been limited to less than a half dozen wines from several different vintages, and I found the 1984 Shiraz to be very musty with off aromas that spoiled an otherwise concentrated, decent wine. The 1982 (which is no longer available commercially) was a much better wine with soft, rich, plumlike, berry flavors. The 1986 and 1987 Semillon from Redbrook in the Margaret River area have shown zesty, tart acidity, and a floral bouquet with flavors of ripe melons. Certainly there were no bottle variations or flaws in this well-made but lighter-styled Semillon.

HARDY'S (PADTHAWAY)

1985 Hardy Collection Cabernet Sauvignon	A	85

1986 Hardy Collection Cabernet Sauvignon	A	84

1986 Hardy Collection Chardonnay	A	84

1987 Hardy Collection Chardonnay	A	85

1985 Hardy Knottage Hill Claret	A	73

One of the largest wineries in Australia, the quality here is very irregular, as one might expect given the quantities of wine produced. However, no one complains about the prices, which are extremely fair, and one is almost always assured of getting at least an adequate wine from Hardy's. The Collection series represents the best wines made here, with the Chardonnay, especially excellent in recent vintages, showing a very intense, smoky character, rich, sweet, fat fruit, and quite a wallop of alcohol. The Cabernet is similarly big in style with fairly rich, tasty fruit. As for the other wines, such as the Knottage Hill Claret and less expensive non–Collection series wines, they tend to be quite one-dimensional.

HEGGIES VINEYARD (BAROSSA)

1986 Rhine Riesling Late-Harvest Botrytis	B	90

The Heggies Vineyard, well-located at a high elevation in the Barossa Mountain range, is owned by S. Smith and Sons, who also produce wines under the labels Yalumba and Pewsey Vale. The top wine is a Beerenauslese-styled, decadently sweet Riesling that has an enormous bouquet of honeyed tropical fruit and orange peel, excellent acidity for balance, and well-delineated flavors to go along with its rich, long finish. One of the great sweet wines made in Australia, it should be drunk over the next 2–3 years.

HENSCHKE (BAROSSA)

1984 Cabernet Sauvignon Barossa Valley	B	90
1987 Semillon	B	86
1984 Shiraz Hill of Grace Barossa Range	B	89
1984 Shiraz Mt. Edelstone Barossa Range	B	88

I have been impressed with this 40,000-case winery's recent efforts, particularly the red wines made since the 1982 vintage. The personality of the Henschke red wines takes ripeness and extract to the maximum limits, yet the wines stop just short of tasting raisiny or excessively alcoholic. The 1984 Cabernet Sauvignon has a broodingly deep purple color, an intense bouquet of rich cassis fruit, only a faint suggestion of oak, and quite a full, powerful palate impression. The fruit virtually obscures plenty of ripe tannins, which suggest to me that this wine could safely be cellared for another 5–7 years. Between the two Shiraz wines, the Hill of Grace is softer and seems more mature, but both wines, which are deep ruby with big, projected, smoky, toasty, peppery, huge bouquets, are unbelievably concentrated and long on the palate. These hefty, intense wines are not for the shy, but with several more years of cellaring, they could become even more impressive. The winery also produces an excellent Semillon, of which the 1987 and 1986 stood out in tastings for their rich, creamy, waxy fruit, and toasty new oak, which gives them a dimension other tart, more floral Semillons lack. Lastly, Henschke also produces two styles of Riesling, but I have not had the opportunity to taste them.

HICKINBOTHAM (GEELONG)

1985 Cab Mac	B	87

This small winery produces several white wines, principally Chardonnay and Riesling, but is best known for its wine called Cab Mac, which is a rather full-styled Cabernet Sauvignon vinified by the carbonic maceration method. Although most people would think a carbonic macerated wine would be light, the 1985 is a very rich, almost Rhône-like wine with a big, spicy, ground-beef aroma, and long, intense flavors. Lovers of Châteauneuf-du-Pape will appreciate its style immensely.

HILL SMITH ESTATE (BAROSSA)

1984 Cabernet Sauvignon	B	80
1987 Chardonnay Barossa	B	85
1987 Semillon Barossa	B	80
1985 Shiraz Barossa	B	82

The Hill Smith Estate wines offer considerable value, particularly the Chardonnay, which is a delicious, fruity, elegant wine with zesty lemonlike acidity, a deft touch of spicy oak, and plenty of body. The Semillon is light and subdued in character, but very pleasant and agreeable. As for the red wines, they are light and relatively straightforward, but the Shiraz has a seductive and intense bouquet dominated by the scent of crushed raspberries, spicy oak, and pepper. All of these wines are again typically Australian in their very up-front, supple charm and should be drunk within 4–6 years of the vintage.

HOUGHTON (WESTERN AUSTRALIA)

1986 Chardonnay	A	58
1987 Chardonnay	A	65
1984 Shiraz	A	69
1985 Shiraz	A	70
1987 Verdelho	A	60
1987 White Burgundy	A	70

Houghton is one of the first commercial vineyards of Western Australia and is now part of the massive Hardy's conglomerate. The wines showed very poorly in my tastings, lacking varietal character, being thin and often watery. If these are representative of this winery, then despite what are modest prices, the wines are certainly no value.

HUNGERFORD HILL (HUNTER VALLEY)

1982 Cabernet Sauvignon Coonawarra	B	84
1986 Chardonnay	B	68
1987 Chardonnay	B	72

While this winery has an excellent reputation for Chardonnay, I found both the 1987 and 1986 excessively oaky, to the detriment of the fruit in the wine. As for the Cabernet Sauvignon, it showed very supple, lush, berry flavors with a subtle herbaceousness, finishing on the palate with a medium- to full-bodied texture. It should be drunk over the next several years.

HUNTINGTON ESTATE (MUDGEE)

1984 Cabernet/Merlot Bin FB 13	B	85
1985 Cabernet Sauvignon Estate Bin FB 16	B	86

This 10,000-case winery produces an entire range of wines from Semillon to Chardonnay to rosé to even a light carbonic-macerated red wine. However, the stars here are the Bin Cabernet Sauvignon, Cabernet/Merlot blends, and Shiraz. The wines listed above from the

1984 vintage both displayed outstanding richness and ripeness with a velvety texture that makes them appealing now, but they certainly appear capable of aging for another 5–6 years. The Cabernet Sauvignon shows more weedy, curranty aromas, whereas the Cabernet/ Merlot has more plumpness and a more opulent texture.

KATNOOK ESTATE (COONAWARRA)

1984 Cabernet Sauvignon Coonawarra	B	84
1985 Cabernet Sauvignon Coonawarra	B	82
1986 Chardonnay Coonawarra	B	83

Katnook, a large estate in Coonawarra, produces a great deal of wine with the quality consistently slightly above average. Correct, pleasant wines that are tasty but uninspiring are produced here, as evidenced by the above-mentioned wines, with the best marks going to the elegant, blackcurrant- and mineral-scented 1984 Cabernet Sauvignon.

TIM KNAPPSTEIN (CLARE VALLEY)

1984 Cabernet Sauvignon	B	85
1985 Cabernet Sauvignon	B	84
1985 Cabernet/Merlot	B	82
1986 Fumé Blanc	A	82
1986 Gewürztraminer	A	72
1986 Rhine Riesling	A	86

This winery, formerly known as Enterprise Wines, is specializing in reliable-quality wines from the Clare Valley. If the wines rarely provide exhilarating drinking, they are generally quite soundly made with the strength of the wines being the reds, especially the Cabernet Sauvignon, which has a restrained but weedy blackcurrant fruitiness, medium body, and moderately intense flavors. The 1984 shows a bit more stuffing than the 1985. The Gewürztraminer is innocuous and bland, but the Fumé Blanc shows subtle, herbaceous fruit, crisp acidity, and medium body. The Rhine Riesling is one of the better off-dry

Spätlese-style Rieslings made in Australia. Prices are reasonable for the quality.

KRONDORF (BAROSSA)

1985 Cabernet Sauvignon (80%)/Cabernet Franc (20%)	A	85
1986 Chardonnay Barossa Valley	A	85
1986 Chardonnay Burge and Wilson	B	87
1987 Chardonnay Burge and Wilson	B	88
1987 Chardonnay South Australia	A	85
1987 Fumé Blanc South Australia	A	85
1984 Shiraz (65%)/Cabernet Sauvignon (35%)	A	84

Krondorf is a large winery in the Barossa Valley run by two enterprising men, Grant Burge and Ian Wilson, who produce a significant amount of wine, of which 75% is white. I have followed Krondorf's wines for most of the vintages of the eighties, and the quality has been consistently good, the prices remarkably fair. The top wines are their delicious Chardonnays, of which the winery produces three varieties. The least expensive is the Chardonnay South Australia, which shows a trace of new toasty oak, but its appeal is its wonderfully fresh, snappy fruit, crisp finish, and good, fleshy, lemon and apple Chardonnay fruitiness. The 1986 Barossa Valley Chardonnay is quite an elegant, medium- to full-bodied wine with loads of lemony, applelike Chardonnay fruit in a round, long finish. It has a graceful, gentle feeling on the palate and impeccable balance. The best Chardonnay made by Krondorf is always designated Burge and Wilson, and it is a deeper wine with fuller body and greater flavor dimension as well as length. All these Chardonnays should be drunk within three years of the vintage. As for the Sauvignon Blanc, it too is one of the most successful made in Australia, and the 1987 has a fresh, exuberant, fruity, smoky, herbaceous bouquet and medium-bodied, well-balanced, dry flavors. The red wines are made in a very soft, supple style and offer immediate drinking. The 1985 Cabernet Sauvignon/Cabernet Franc blend is a deliciously supple, tasty wine with gobs of blackcurrant fruit in evidence. The 1984 Shiraz/Cabernet Sauvignon blend has a more fragrant, cedary richness, and a smoky, long finish. I have also had a good dry Riesling from Krondorf, so this winery should be sought out by shrewd consumers looking for wines that please both the palate and the purse.

LAKE'S FOLLY (NEW SOUTH WALES)

1985 Cabernet Sauvignon	C	89

1986 Chardonnay	C	87

The wines of Lake's Folly are among the most highly sought-after wines of Australia, and the 5,000-case production of Chardonnay, Cabernet Sauvignon, and a Caberet Sauvignon/Shiraz blend called Folly Red disappears quickly when the wines are released. The quality, based on what I have seen, appears to be excellent, bordering on outstanding. The Chardonnay is made with gobs of rich fruit, plenty of toasty oak, and a full-bodied feel to it. This wine should be drunk within 4 years of the vintage. As for the Cabernet Sauvignon, the 1985 shows a very stylish toasty oak, blackcurrant aroma, medium to full body, good crisp acidity, and a finish that lingers and lingers. It should be at its best between 1990 and 1994.

LEEUWIN ESTATE (MARGARET RIVER)

1984 Cabernet Sauvignon	D	84

1984 Chardonnay	D	87

1984 Pinot Noir	C	75

This 20,000-case winery in the Margaret River region of Western Australia has some of Australia's highest wine prices, and while the quality is good to very good for the Chardonnay and Cabernet Sauvignon, prices seem a little out of line when compared to those of other Australian producers. In any event, there is no doubting the 1984 Chardonnay is a dramatic, boldly styled wine that is full-bodied with plenty of ripe pineapple and tropical fruit, a whopping degree of alcohol, and plenty of aggressive oak. It should drink well for the next 2–3 years. The Cabernet Sauvignon has herbaceous and cedary, blackcurrant aromas, medium to full body, and a touch of acidity in the finish that keeps the overall rating somewhat low, but the wine is quite concentrated. Lastly, the Pinot Noir, which some reckon to be among the very best made in Australia, is a rather one-dimensional, light, some-

what diluted wine that is hardly impressive. It should be drunk quite
soon before it deteriorates any further.

PETER LEHMANN (BAROSSA)

1985 Cabernet Sauvignon Barossa	B	86
1986 Cabernet Sauvignon Barossa	B	85
1986 Semillon	A	85
1987 Semillon	A	83
1985 Semillon Sauternes	B	90
1984 Shiraz	B	85
1985 Shiraz	B	80
1986 Shiraz	B	86
1984 Shiraz/Cabernet Sauvignon	B	84
1985 Shiraz/Cabernet Sauvignon	B	82

Much of the production from the highly respected Barossa winemaker
Peter Lehmann is sold in bulk under private labels to other wineries,
but increasing quantities of the finest lots are bottled under Lehmann's own name and represent outstanding values in good-quality
Australian wine. While I have never tasted Lehmann's Chardonnay,
or even seen a bottle, the dry Semillon is one of the better examples
of this type of wine coming out of Australia, displaying delicate, fresh,
flowery, and limelike scents in its bouquet, and medium body. The
1986 shows a bit more fruit and richness than the 1987. Lehmann also
produces one of the most spectacular sweet Semillons made in Australia, and recent vintages have been quite consistent for this staggeringly sweet, Sauternes-like wine. With prices for French wines such
as Yquem, Rieussec, Raymond Lafon, and Climens soaring from $35
to as much as $150 a bottle, exceptionally made sweet wines such as
Lehmann's should get a very receptive audience. The 1985 shows a
great deal of toasty new oak, which combines beautifully with aromas
of coconut, melon, and honeyed fruit to give the wine a rich, lush,
creamy texture, and stupendous length. This well-balanced wine

should last for 4–10 more years and is an exceptional bargain. As for the red wines from Lehmann, while they are never great, they are consistently very good, and very fairly priced. They combine soft, supple, cedary, blackcurrant fruit, medium to full body, and light tannins seemingly regardless of whether the vintage is 1986, 1985, or 1984. The Shiraz and the Shiraz/Cabernet Sauvignon blend tend to be a bit more burly and chunky wines than the straight but graceful and elegant Cabernet Sauvignon. This is a very reliable name to search out for good, reasonably priced Australian wine.

LINDEMANS (NEW SOUTH WALES)

1985 Cabernet Sauvignon Bin 45	A	82
1986 Cabernet Sauvignon Bin 45	A	83
1985 Cabernet Sauvignon St. George Vineyard Coonawarra	B	88
1986 Chardonnay Bin 65	A	86
1986 Chardonnay Padthaway	B	87
1987 Chardonnay Padthaway	B	88
1986 Pyrus Coonawarra	C	87
1987 Sauvignon Blanc Padthaway	B	85
1986 Semillon	A	75
1985 Shiraz Limestone Ridge Coonawarra	B	87
1987 Griffith Botrytis Semillon	C	92

This gigantic winery is one of the three largest in Australia with vineyards in most of that country's viticultural areas. There are also a number of special single-vineyard, estate-bottled wines that offer some outstanding choices to the consumer. At the very top level are the single-vineyard Cabernet Sauvignon from the St. George Vineyard in Coonawarra and the single-vineyard Shiraz from the Limestone Ridge Vineyard in Coonawarra. The 1985 Limestone Ridge Shiraz is quite a tannic, full-bodied mouthful of wine, but it does show plenty of potential charm with its sweet, cedary, rather Pauillac-like, cigar-box bouquet. Deep in color and rich in extract, this full-bodied, beefy wine has quite a future but should be cellared for several years. The 1985 St. George Vineyard Cabernet Sauvignon shows quite a bit of new oak in its bouquet, has a big, fruitcake, curranty smell, dense, rich, full-bodied flavors, and 8–10 years of further aging potential. In addition to these two wines, Lindemans has introduced its own proprietary wine called Pyrus, a Cabernet Sauvignon/Merlot/Cabernet Franc blend. The 1986 is a very big, jammy, almost overripe wine, but it does not go overboard, and its huge, deep, concentrated flavors are framed admirably with a great deal of new oak; it should certainly last for another 4–7 years. Among the white wines, the best Chardonnays and Sauvignon Blancs from Lindemans are those that are made from the company's vineyards in Padthaway. Both the 1987 and 1986 Padthaway Chardonnays are crisp and flavorful with full body, and more depth and power than the excellent-value Chardonnay made by Lindemans called Bin 65, which seems to gush with exuberant tropical fruit, has a touch of oak, good acids, and medium body, but not the depth of the Padthaway Chardonnays. The same can be said for the 1987 Padthaway Sauvignon Blanc. With aromas of lemons and herbs, it is a medium-bodied, crisp wine with a subtle, herbaceous fruitiness. Several other wines made by Lindemans include a competent Riesling, a rather dull Semillon, and a sometimes very good Semillon/Chardonnay blend. One wine not to miss is the hedonistic, decadently sweet, rich, opulent Griffith Botrytis Semillon. The winery's Pinot Noir, like most from Australia, is boring stuff.

GEOFF MERRILL (SOUTH AUSTRALIA)

1984 Cabernet Sauvignon	B	86
1985 Cabernet Sauvignon	B	85

The Geoff Merrill Winery specializes in two basic wines, a Semillon and a Cabernet Sauvignon. Both the 1984 and 1985 Cabernets show that this winery knows how to make a very good Cabernet Sauvignon, with medium to full body, a spicy, black-cherry-scented bouquet, and a harmonious, elegant feel on the palate. The 1985 is slightly lighter than the more opulent 1984, but both should be drunk over the next 3–4 years.

MILDARA (COONAWARRA)

1984 Cabernet Sauvignon Coonawarra	A	84
1987 Chardonnay Coonawarra	A	85
1987 Rhine Riesling Coonawarra	A	78
1985 Shiraz and Cabernet Coonawarra	A	82

Mildara, a large company making a range of wines that are all rather average in quality, has embarked on an aggressive marketing campaign in the foreign markets with an infusion of capital from the large United Kingdom whiskey company William Grant and Sons. The result has been higher and higher quality wines that are still very reasonably priced. Mildara's wines are not in the top echelon of quality for Australia, but they represent very good values and do justice to the varietal named on the label. While the Riesling is rather one-dimensional, the best wine over the last several vintages has been the Coonawarra Chardonnay with its lemony, citrusy, floral, fruity flavors, medium body, and crisp, vibrant personality. The Cabernet Sauvignon, particularly in 1984, has also been a soft, berry-scented, flavorful wine with a great deal of finesse. These are not wines to stock away in your cellar; the Cabernet and Shiraz should be drunk within 5–6 years of the vintage and the other wines within 2–3 years.

MITCHELTON (GOULBURN)

1984 Cabernet Sauvignon	B	78
1986 Chardonnay Wood-Matured	A	85
1987 Chardonnay Wood-Matured	A	86
1987 Marsanne Wood-Matured	A	84
1986 Rhine Riesling Winemaker's Selection	A	85

This large winery in the Goulburn Valley has three quality levels of wine. The top cuvées of wine made by Mitchelton are designated Winemaker's Selection, and the regular cuvées are designated by the straight Mitchelton label. The secondary label is called Thomas Mitchell, and a number of good values can be found under it. The wines from Mitchelton are generally average to above average in quality. For example, a consistent winner from this winery is its Rhine Riesling, which is a sweet, dessert, Beerenauslese-styled wine with a full-intensity bouquet of peachlike and apricotlike flavors, good crisp acidity, and a long, honeyed finish. The Marsanne is not as neutral-tasting as many that are made in Australia, but rather full-bodied and surprisingly good with food, although rather nondescript when served by itself. The Cabernet Sauvignon tends to be a bit herbaceous, but it is an elegant, lighter-styled wine for drinking within 5–6 years of the vintage. Probably the second-best wine from Mitchelton is the excellent wood-matured Chardonnay, which in both 1987 and 1986 showed lovely scents of oranges, limes, and apricots, with a deft touch of oak that added class to the full-bodied character of these wines.

MONTROSE (MUDGEE)

1984 Cabernet Sauvignon/Shiraz Mudgee	A	85
1985 Cabernet Sauvignon/Shiraz Mudgee	A	86
1984 Cabernet Sauvignon Special Reserve Mudgee	B	87
1985 Cabernet Sauvignon Special Reserve Mudgee	B	88
1987 Chardonnay Mudgee	A	85
1986 Chardonnay Reserve Mudgee	B	90
1987 Chardonnay Reserve Mudgee	B	90
1988 Chardonnay	A	88
1987 Semillon Mudgee	A	85
1983 Shiraz	A	86
1984 Shiraz	A	85

Winemaker Carlo Corino started off making good wines for Montrose, and based on the 1985 through 1987 releases, some of the best Chardonnays being made in Australia come from this moderately sized winery with a production of less than 65,000 cases. Whether its recent sale to Wyndham Estates will affect the quality remains to be seen, but it is unlikely given the fact there has been no change in winemakers. Of the above wines, the Chardonnays from Montrose get the highest marks and consistently showed well in all my tastings. The newly released 1988 Chardonnay may well be the finest regular cuvée of Chardonnay that Montrose has yet made. It is a well balanced, big, rich, deep wine with gobs of flavor and body. The regular 1987 Chardonnay has hefty portions of lemony, buttery fruit, full body, and a judicious use of oak. Its crisp acids give it definition and freshness. The Reserve is just simply much richer, shows more oak, is a deeper, fuller wine, and requires more serious food than the tasty, lighter regular bottling. The 1986 Reserve is drinking gorgeously now and should probably be consumed over the next 2 years as it is fully mature with a style very similar to the 1987. Montrose also does a good job with Semillon, and the 1987 has a very expressive, exuberant, lemon-limelike bouquet that vaguely suggests a gin and tonic. In the mouth there is more ripeness than one might suspect from the bouquet, and it is actually a quite tasty, unique style of Semillon. As for the red wines, they are made in a delightfully fruity, aromatic style offering up-front charm, although there is no question that in the case of the Special Reserve Cabernet Sauvignon the wine can last 4–5 years after it is released by the winery. I especially liked both the 1984 and 1983 Shiraz, which revealed textbook peppery, cassis fruit, good extract, full body, and soft tannins. The 1983 is a bit more concentrated than the 1984. Lastly, the 1985 and 1984 Cabernet/Shiraz are both deeply fruity, husky, supple wines that seduce the taster with their gush of peppery, currany fruit. Montrose is a very consistent winery from top to bottom, and prices for what are often very high quality, very satisfying wines are quite fair.

MOSS WOOD (MARGARET RIVER)

1985 Cabernet Sauvignon	C	87
1986 Semillon Wood-Matured	C	86

This tiny boutique winery with its production of 3,000 cases is located in the Margaret River section of Western Australia. Despite the small quantities available, the wines are in great demand in Australia because of their high quality. The 1985 Cabernet Sauvignon has a big, deep color, an intense, blackcurrany bouquet, full body, and soft tannins. It should last through the mid-nineties. The 1986 Wood-Matured Semillon shows just how well this particular grape variety, with its waxy, spicy fruit, takes to a little bit of aging in oak barrels. Quite a ripe, full-bodied wine with the oak under control, it is an ideal wine with fish or chicken; it should last for another 2–3 years.

MOUNTADAM (ADELAIDE HILLS)

1987 Chardonnay Estate	C	92
1986 Chardonnay Estate	C	90

Mountadam, behind the gifted winemaker/owner David Wynn, was one of the first to pioneer Chardonnay in the cool-climate hillsides near Adelaide. The wines, all barrel-fermented in Trench oak, are from the estate's own vineyards. Aged in one-third new oak barrels, they are quite spectacular, and possibly the finest Chardonnays made in Australia. The 1986 is a generously rich, full-flavored wine with an intense perfume of hazelnut, apples, spicy vanilla scents, and butter. Full bodied and dry, yet so harmonious, it should drink well for 1–2 more years. The 1987 is even richer, with an astounding bouquet of apple blossoms, buttery fruit, and a subtle touch of oak. Very deep, well-balanced and rich, this wine could easily be mistaken for a great Batard-Montrachet from France's Etienne Sanzet.

ORLANDO (SOUTH AUSTRALIA)

I have not seen any recent releases of Orlando wines, and the wines for which I do have tasting notes are no longer commercially available. However, Orlando, which is one of the most significant wineries in Australia, makes an entire range of wines with its Show Reserve and Single Bin wines being the top cuvées and often among the best wines made in Australia. Their second-level wines are designated St. Helga Riesling or St. Hugo Cabernet Sauvignon; these are followed by their third tier of wines, which are designated by the letters RF on the label. My experience with some of Orlando's older vintages has demonstrated that the Show Reserve or Single-Bin Chardonnays can be quite stunning, but they are virtually impossible to obtain in the export marketplace. The winery's St. Hugo Cabernet Sauvignon from Coonawarra is also an excellent wine, and Orlando does one of the best jobs in all of Australia with its Riesling, making it in a multitude of styles, all of which are fresh, exuberant, and lively. This is a winery that I feel deserves far more attention than it has been receiving.

PENFOLDS (SOUTH AUSTRALIA)

1982 Cabernet Sauvignon Bin 707	C	90
1984 Cabernet Sauvignon Bin 707	C	85
1985 Cabernet Sauvignon Bin 707	C	88
1984 Cabernet Sauvignon/Shiraz	B	87
1985 Cabernet Sauvignon/Shiraz	B	88
1987 Chardonnay	B	67
1980 Grange Hermitage	E	94
1981 Grange Hermitage	E	93
1982 Grange Hermitage	E	98
1982 St. Henry Claret	B	83
1983 St. Henry Claret	B	78

The largest winery complex in all of Australia, Penfolds, is largely known in the export market for its sensational Grange Hermitage, undoubtedly the finest wine made south of the equator, and one of the fifty greatest red wines in the world. It is this wine, which has 20–30 years of aging potential, that has built the reputation for outstanding quality of the Penfolds firm. (They don't promote the fact, but they own the huge winery Kaiserstuhl, which makes some rather bland wines.) The Grange Hermitage is a remarkable wine to taste, and despite its price, which has escalated to $50+ a bottle, it is still one of the most amazingly concentrated, highly extracted yet complex wines in the world. The newly released 1982 could turn out to be one of the greats from Penfolds, but then so was the 1981, 1980, 1979, 1978, and 1977. The winery does not seem to miss a beat when it comes to this particular unfiltered wine with its distinctive gray-and-crimson label. A blockbuster wine, the Grange offers up from its dense, opaque, ruby/purple color a smoky, ripe-berry, tarry, cedary nose, great flavor depth and dimension, full body, and a super finish. It usually begins drinking well at about 9 years of age, then gets better and better for the next 10–15 years. Despite its Syrah content, it smells like a Pauillac but tastes like a great Pomerol or Rhône wine.

While the price for the Grange Hermitage is pretty forbidding, it drops considerably for the Cabernet Sauvignon/Shiraz blend, of which the 1985 and 1984 show a generous constitution with supple texture, gobs of spicy black-cherry fruit, and a peppery, spicy finish. The Bin 707 Cabernet Sauvignon can be absolutely sensational in years such as 1982, where it was explosively rich and fruity, but it is hardly ever less than excellent, as it was in 1984 and 1985. The winery also produces a St. Henry Claret, which, for me, because of its rather rustic, sometimes vegetal character that intrudes too far into the wine, never quite lives up to the reputation it has in Australia. The winery released its first Chardonnay in 1982, and it has not been widely praised; certainly, the 1987 tasted of candy with rather artificial, unvarietal characteristics. Lastly, travelers to Australia may want to search out some of the rare blends that Penfolds releases every several years from some of its best lots of wine, designated simply by a bin number. While I have never tasted any, some of the top Australian wine authorities claim that these are even greater than the Grange Hermitage, which would be amazing if true. Penfolds is a winery to search out for its red wines, but avoid its white wines, and if you can afford it, don't miss the opportunity to try one of the greatest red wines made in the world, the Grange Hermitage.

PETALUMA (SOUTH AUSTRALIA)

1985 Botrytis Rhine Riesling Red Capsule	C	92
1985 Chardonnay	C	90
1984 Coonawarra Red Table Wine	C	87
1985 Coonawarra Red Table Wine	C	89

This luxury winery in Adelaide is producing extremely high quality wines that connoisseurs from all over the world are taking very seriously. Until recently, their brilliant winemaker, Brian Croser, has been buying grapes from cooler microclimates in Australia and making one of the great sweet Rieslings to come from that country, as well as a stunning red wine that is primarily a blend of Cabernet Sauvignon and Shiraz, and a very age-worthy Chardonnay. As Petaluma's own vineyards come into production (starting with the 1985 Chardonnay from their Mount Lofty Vineyard), it will be interesting to see whether any new direction in either style or texture takes place. Of the current releases, the 1985 Botrytis Riesling is a true Beerenauslese-style wine. The low alcohol and high residual sugar are balanced beautifully by the crisp acidity essential for the wine's longevity. Ripe apricot and peach aromas jump from the glass. Very rich and sweet with outstanding complexity and balance, it is one of the finest late-harvest dessert Rieslings I have tasted from Australia. The new 1985 Chardonnay shows an intensely flavored, full-bodied character and is reminiscent of the rich, very ripe, full-bodied yet well-balanced wines from such California Chardonnay specialists as Mount Eden and Chalone. It has intensely buttery, applelike, floral fruit, a smoky, intense complexity, toasty richness, and quite a long, crisp finish; it should last for another 3–5 years. Petaluma also produces a red proprietary wine called simply Coonawarra, which is a blend of Cabernet Sauvignon and Shiraz. The 1985 shows a very rich, deep bouquet of spicy oak, black currants, and mineral scents, being a full-bodied wine with excellent aging potential. Quite powerful and concentrated, it finishes superbly and should last at least through most of the decade of the nineties. The 1984 is a bit lighter but shares the same style with its rich, oaky, blackcurrant fragrance, and ripe, sweet, grapy smells; it reminded me of a blend of a French Pomerol and a top California Cabernet Sauvignon. These are among the best and most expensive wines from Australia.

PEWSEY VALE (BAROSSA)

I have not seen any recent vintages of Pewsey Vale wines, but I have good notes on both their off-dry Spätlese-style Riesling and their more nectarlike Beerenauslese-style Riesling from previous vintages. Certainly this winery seems to do an outstanding job with the Riesling grape from its own vineyard in the cooler microclimate of the Barossa Mountains. Prices are surprisingly fair for the two Rieslings.

REDBANK (VICTORIA)

1985 Cabernet Sauvignon Avoca	C	?
1985 Cabernet Sauvignon Redbank	C	85
1985 Long Paddock	C	76
1985 Sally's Paddock	C	87

1985 Shiraz   C   74

This small winery with a production of less than 2,500 cases has a reputation for producing very powerful, intense, age-worthy red wines. My experience has been limited to their offerings from the excellent 1985 vintage from the Pyrenees area of Victoria. The wines I tasted were quite variable. The 1985 Shiraz was opaque in color but overly oaky and quite short and lean on the palate. The 1985 Long Paddock also had a very intense color and a good bouquet, but once again it was quite short on the palate. The best Redbank wine I tasted was the Sally's Paddock, which smelled of mint and black currants, with an intense, long, rich, velvety texture, and a soft, delectable finish. It should be drunk over the next 4–5 years. The Avoca Cabernet Sauvignon showed much the same minty, blackcurrant bouquet, and like all of the Redbank wines was impressively deep in color, but it had excessively high acids that gave a tart edge to it. Perhaps the fruit will fatten out and the acidity will be less annoyingly high in 4–5 years. Lastly, the Redbank Cabernet Sauvignon, which is preposterously priced, had tons of jammy, fleshy flavors and good, tart acids, but the wine's size and weight seemed out of proportion; however, it is a very interesting wine.

REDMAN (COONAWARRA)

Redman, one of the most famous and historically respected estates in the Coonawarra district of southern Australia, is known for its red wines. However, the only vintages that I have seen recently, the 1983 Cabernet Sauvignon and the 1983 Claret, are probably no longer commercially available. The Claret was a blend of grapes from several different vineyards, and both it and the Cabernet Sauvignon were mediocre wines at best, but I hesitate to be too critical of this winery, which has an excellent reputation in Australia.

REYNELLA (SOUTHERN VALES)

1985 Cabernet/Merlot/Malbec   B   84

1985 Cabernet Sauvignon Coonawarra   B   85

1985 Chardonnay McLaren Vale   B   85

1986 Chardonnay McLaren Vale   B   87

1987 Chardonnay McLaren Vale	B	87
1982 Vintage Port	B	90
1983 Vintage Port	B	86

I had had a number of disappointing experiences with the wines of Reynella in the late seventies and early eighties, but with the infusion of capital from the huge Hardy company, the quality of recent wines under winemaker Geoff Merrill has soared. This 50,000-case producer is now turning out very good Chardonnay, a good Cabernet Sauvignon, and one of the best vintage ports from Australia. In the last three vintages, the Chardonnays have improved greatly, with the 1987 and 1986 showing a toasty, oaky, hazelnut quality to the vibrant apple and buttery fruit, and a full-bodied, well-balanced feel on the palate. The Cabernet Sauvignon shows good, straightforward, blackcurrant fruit, has good body, and a lush finish with some moderate tannins to resolve. It should drink beautifully for another 5–6 years. The Vintage Port is quite outstanding in 1982 and could easily pass in a blind tasting for one of the better Portuguese vintage ports. At its low price, it is an astonishing bargain. The 1983 Vintage Port is a bit lighter, but nevertheless quite concentrated with a big, rich, tarry, blackberry and plummy bouquet. Both of the Vintage Ports should last for at least 20 years. This winery's prices have not caught up with its new level of quality, so I recommend that readers give the wines of Reynella a serious look.

ROSEMOUNT (COONAWARRA)

1985 Cabernet Sauvignon Show Reserve Coonawarra	C	85
1987 Chardonnay Estate	B	86
1986 Chardonnay Roxburgh	D	92
1987 Chardonnay Roxburgh	D	93
1986 Chardonnay Show Reserve	B	88
1987 Chardonnay Show Reserve	B	90
1986 Diamond Reserve Red Table Wine	A	84

1986 Semillon	A	85

1985 Semillon Botrytis	B	93

1985 Shiraz	B	72

This winery in Coonawarra has an outstanding track record with its white wines, particularly Chardonnay, and it has also had either the good fortune or the aggressive public relations needed to get the world's media to give it a great deal of attention. Prices tend to be moderately high, but the quality has consistently been good in spite of a few hiccups with several of the vintages in the mid-eighties that caused some to say there was a falling off in quality. The best wines are certainly those marked Show Reserve, as well as the Roxburgh Chardonnay. The Roxburgh always exhibits a hefty amount of toasty, smoky oak, yet it seems to have the requisite amount of rich apple and buttery-popcorn fruit needed to sustain that oak. The Chardonnay Estate is usually the most open-knit, filled with tropical-fruit aromas and flavors, and with a supple, delicious finish. It is a medium- to full-bodied wine, and the 1987 is a good example of this Chardonnay. The 1987 Show Reserve Chardonnay shows the influence of more toasty oak, offering up riper, richer, pineapple-scented, buttery fruitiness and slightly more body. While these wines appear to require drinking within several years of the vintage, older examples have aged better than I would have suspected, so the safe period in which to imbibe your Rosemount Chardonnays is usually within 4–5 years of the vintage.

The other good white wine made here is the Semillon, of which both the 1987 and 1986 show a plump, full, flavorful feel on the palate, with enough acidity for balance and freshness. They are among the top dozen Semillon and Sauvignon Blancs made in Australia. Rosemount has also introduced a great sweet dessert wine made from the Semillon grape that has been affected by the botrytis fungus. The 1985 is a spectacular wine; bright gold with an immense bouquet of honey, crème brûlée, fruit, and new oak, it is a long, rich, sweet, well-balanced wine with a staggering finish. This Château Yquem imitation should be drunk over the next 7–8 years. As for the red wines, they have been more spotty, sometimes showing surprising inconsistency from bottle to bottle. I remember a good 1982 Cabernet Sauvignon/ Malbec blend from the Hunter Valley, but the Cabernets from Coonawarra have often been too tart and lean, although the 1985 Show Reserve shows good blackcurrant fruit, spicy oak, and an attractive suppleness even today. It is not a blockbuster, nor will it last more than 7–8 years, but for drinking over the next 4–5 years, it is quite well done. Rosemount wines clearly merit most of the publicity they have received.

ROTHBURY ESTATE (HUNTER VALLEY)

1987 Chardonnay Broken Back Vineyard	B	88
1986 Chardonnay Reserve	B	90
1987 Chardonnay Reserve	B	90
1985 Hermitage/Cabernet Sauvignon Broken Back Vineyard	B	89
1987 Sauvignon Blanc Broken Back Vineyard	A	86
1987 Semillon Broken Back Vineyard	A	85
1985 Semillon/Sauternes	B	85

With a production closing in on 100,000 cases, one would suspect that the wines of Rothbury Estate would taste a bit more commercial than they do. These are unbelievably serious wines that are among the very finest made in Australia. In fact, I would argue that the Chardonnays might well be the most consistently superb Chardonnays made in the land down under. Both 1987s exhibit a judicious use of new oak barrels to impart a toasty, complex, apple-butter fruitiness, have full body, good acidity, and surprisingly rich, long finishes. They are big wines, but never tiring to drink. The Reserve just has a bit more depth and character. The 1986 Reserve with its full-intensity bouquet of rich fruit and subtle oak, and long, flowing flavors is extremely harmonious but should be drunk over the next 2 years, whereas the 1987s will probably last several years longer. The 1987 Sauvignon Blanc and Semillon from the Broken Back Vineyard in Hunter Valley are two fine examples of these varietals, showing a touch of oak, well-delineated fruit and varietal character, and a medium-weight, elegant style. The Sauvignon has crisp acids and lingers on the palate in a very graceful, elegant style. The Semillon exhibits a bit more toasty new oak that has very fine acids and a lemony, waxy fruitiness. As for the sweet Semillon/Sauternes, it is not up to the level of some top producers such as Peter Lehmann or Rosemount, but it has quite a bit of stuffing, yet its low acidity gives it a rather heavy-handed feel on the palate; it is bursting with decadent, rich, sweet fruit. One does not see much of the red wines from Rothbury Estate in the marketplace, but should you see the 1985 Hermitage/Cabernet Sauvignon from the Broken Back Vineyard, it is a very powerful, ripe, rich wine with a touch of oak, plenty of tannin, layers of peppery cassis, tarry fruit, and enough potential to last in a cool cellar for another 7–10 years if not longer. Prices for Rothbury Estate wines are surprisingly modest for the quality.

ST. HUBERTS (YARRA VALLEY)

1982 Cabernet Sauvignon	B	65
1986 Chardonnay	B	72
1984 Shiraz	B	73

I remember the first wines I tasted from the moderate-sized St. Huberts winery in the Yarra Valley: the 1977 and 1978 Cabernet Sauvignons. These were quite complex, rich, rather classically made wines, fully justifying the media attention this winery had received in Australia. The wines listed above all left me quite disappointed, as they not only failed to represent their varietal character properly, but they lacked concentration, were a bit clumsy, and overall were unusual wines that were simply not very pleasant to drink. At present, this winery, which started off with so much promise, cannot be recommended.

SAXONVALE (HUNTER VALLEY)

1986 Chardonnay Bin 1 Hunter Valley	A	83
1987 Chardonnay Bin 1 Hunter Valley	A	82
1985 Hermitage Hunter Valley	A	86
1986 Sauvignon Blanc Hunter Valley	A	80
1987 Sauvignon Blanc Hunter Valley	A	78
1982 Shiraz Hunter Valley	A	85

1983 Shiraz Hunter Valley   A   85

Situated in the lower Hunter Valley, this 50,000-case winery makes reliably good wines that in many ways resemble the typical Australian philosophy for making red and white wines. They all offer gobs of up-front, soft, fat fruit, a touch of oak, and ripe, round finishes. The Chardonnays, particularly the Bin 1, show a good bit of pungent, smoky oak to go along with the lemon, buttery, applelike fruit. The Shiraz has been consistently good, especially in the vintages listed above, although there does seem to be some bottle variation (probably from bad shipping). The wines are loaded with peppery, blackcurrant fruit and have lush, rich textures with 5 more years of life ahead of them. The 1985 Hermitage is the best of the red wines listed. The winery also produces a very dull Gewürztraminer, an overoaked white burgundy, and a consistently refreshing Semillon.

SEPPELT (BAROSSA)

1984 Cabernet Sauvignon Black Label	A	86
1985 Cabernet Sauvignon Black Label	A	87
1987 Chardonnay Reserve Bin	A	87
1984 Great Western Brut Sparkling Wine	B	79
N.V. Seppelt Old Strafford Tawny Port	B	90
N.V. Seppelt Para-Port Bin 110	C	93
N.V. Seppelt Show Muscat	C	93
N.V. Seppelt Show Tokay	C	92
N.V. Seppeltsfield Show Amontillado D.P. 116	C	88
N.V. Seppeltsfield Show Fino D.P. 117	C	88
N.V. Seppeltsfield Show Oloroso Sherry D.P. 38	C	92
1985 Shiraz Black Label	A	85

Seppelt, one of Australia's largest wineries, has a sterling record when I look through my tasting notes. Rarely is a wine less than good, and many of the limited-edition wines of Seppelt are simply extraordinary, especially their fortified wines. For value, one of the finest bargains in Chardonnay in the world must be the 1987 Seppelt Reserve Bin Chardonnay, which is a fairly dramatic wine with a good lashing of oak, ripe fruit, full body, plenty of depth, and mouth-filling flavors. It should be drunk over the next several years. The winery's Black Label Cabernet Sauvignon is also quite excellent, exhibiting a rich, soft, velvety style with a pleasing marriage of oak and intense, jammy fruit. The 1985 probably has a bit more length and aging potential than the 1984. The 1985 Shiraz Black Label offers the same voluptuous, lush qualities as the Cabernet Sauvignon but adds a peppery, blackberry component. As for the sparkling wine, I have had better examples than the recent 1984 Brut, but perhaps it was not the best bottle of this particular sparkling wine, which is usually one of the best made in Australia.

Lastly, Seppelt specializes in limited quantities of sherry- and port-styled wines, which are simply world class and profoundly complex. Given their quality and potential longevity, they qualify as great values when one compares their prices to similar-quality ports from Europe. The Show Fino has a beautiful, fresh, lively, delicate bouquet of nuts and fruit, tastes dry, and has excellent balance. The Show Amontillado is deeper in color, still relatively dry on the palate, but long, rich, fresh, and exuberant with a great deal of aromatic complexity. The Show Oloroso is an unctuous, decadently rich, caramel-colored sherry with sensational richness, a great finish, and medium-dry taste; it must be drunk to be believed. A super value is the Old Strafford Tawny Port, a 6-year-old, orange-and-ruby-colored port that has heaps of velvety, sweet, complex fruit, and a huge bouquet of fruitcake and grilled nuts. It competes favorably with the finest tawny ports from Portugal. The new release of Para-Port Bin 110 is 16 years old and is immensely rich with an enormous bouquet of chocolate, coffee, and Oriental spices interwoven with ripe berries. Quite full-bodied and unctuous, it makes a sensational after-dinner drink. Lastly, the Show Tokay and Show Muscat are dense, unctuous, fortified wines, brown in color, approximately 8–10 years old, sensationally complex with heady fragrances of ripe fruit, caramel, spices, and nuts. Not surprisingly, the Muscat is slightly more aromatic and penetrating than the Tokay. These are all compelling wines that merit significant attention even though their limited quantities will make them difficult to find.

CHÂTEAU TAHBILK (GOULBURN)

1984 Cabernet Sauvignon	B	90
1985 Cabernet Sauvignon	B	90
1985 Marsanne	A	75
1987 Rhine Riesling	A	82
1984 Shiraz	B	90
1985 Shiraz	B	86

Château Tahbilk is the star of Australia's viticultural area called the Goulburn Valley. Wine has been made here since the nineteenth century, and Tahbilk is renowned for its full-bodied, rustic, very rich, and age-worthy red wines, which are among the longest-lived reds of Australia. As for the whites, while the winery is excited by its Marsanne, a vertical tasting I did of seven vintages left me more impressed with the older vintages than the younger ones, but there wasn't one wine in the entire vertical tasting that I would go out and buy. Additionally, the Riesling tends to be made in a rather full, rich style, but one that still has the varietal flowery character with scents and flavors of apples and minerals. The glories of this winery are its Shiraz and Cabernet Sauvignon. Both the 1984s and 1985s are outstanding examples of what these two grapes can do in Australia when made in a traditional, unfiltered style. Both are massive wines with the 1984s showing a bit more body and opulence of fruit than the more tannic, backward 1985s. The Cabernet Sauvignon is an admirably concentrated, powerfully constructed wine that should last for at least 10–15 more years. As for the Shiraz, it has the same power as the Cabernet Sauvignon and adds to it a peppery, tarry character, making quite an enormous impact on the palate. While they can be drunk now, ideally they should be cellared until the early 1990s. Given their prices, they are among the greatest values in the world for age-worthy, serious red wines, and I enthusiastically recommend them.

TALTARNI (VICTORIA)

1984 Cabernet Sauvignon	B	82
1987 Fumé Blanc	B	84
1983 Shiraz	B	78

The Taltarni operation, a sister to the Clos du Val winery in California, raised eyebrows and caused a rush to wine merchants when their 1978 Cabernet Sauvignon and Shiraz were released. Both were massive, unbelievably rich, age-worthy wines packed with power, flavor, and tannin. I was an enthusiastic purchaser of these wines, and the Cabernet Sauvignon at 10 years of age is still not ready to drink; the Shiraz is just coming into its own. Both wines should have 10–15 more years of evolution left in them. In fact, the Cabernet Sauvignon may turn out to resemble a downsized version of the great Penfolds Grange Hermitage. Since the 1978s, I have felt the Taltarni wines have become significantly lighter in style, less interesting, and perhaps too overzealously filtered and cleaned up at the expense of flavor and character. There is nothing at all wrong with the above wines, and only when one compares them with what this winery did in 1977, 1978, and 1979 does one become disappointed. The Fumé Blanc is certainly good with its subtle herbaceous bouquet and crisp, flinty, fresh-fruit flavors. The Cabernet Sauvignon tastes like a high-tech wine with decent fruit, a touch of oak, but no real character, in other words, a shadow of what the winery produced in 1978. The same can be said for the Shiraz. Unfortunately, I do not believe these are isolated examples of mediocre vintages of Taltarni wines; I think they do reflect the direction in which the winery is heading, which is a shame when you consider how much character and personality the 1978s still have.

TOLLANA (BAROSSA)

I have not tasted the most recent releases from Tollana, but having followed the wines from this very large winery over several vintages, I was left with the impression that at best all of Tollana's wines, which come from grapes grown in the Barossa area, are rather one-dimensional, commercial wines with no great flavor depth or dimension.

TYRRELLS (NEW SOUTH WALES)

1983 Cabernet Sauvignon	A	83
1984 Cabernet Sauvignon	A	84
1983 Cabernet Sauvignon/Merlot	A	72
1986 Chardonnay	A	82
1987 Chardonnay	A	84
1987 Chardonnay Vat 47	B	86
1987 Fumé Blanc Wood-Matured	A	77
1984 Long Flat Red	A	85
1985 Long Flat Red	A	84
1987 Long Flat White	A	84
1986 Pinot Noir	B	74
1986 Semillon	A	65

This gigantic winery in the lower Hunter Valley produces an enormous range of wines, of which some of my favorites include their inexpensive Long Flat Red with its plummy, ripe, round generosity, and supple flavors, and Long Flat White with its fresh, clean, aromatic character and decent fruit. The varietal wines are led by the Vat 47 Chardonnay, which is very, very good and can last 5–6 years. The other wines suffer immensely in quality and are often rather dull, overly tired wines without a great deal of distinction or character. Perhaps shipping has something to do with the oxidized character that some of the wines have taken on after arriving in other countries. When I think of Tyrrells, I usually think of the excellent value in the Long Flat Red, which should be drunk within 3–4 years of its release, and the Long Flat White, which should be drunk within a year of its release.

VASSE FELIX (WESTERN AUSTRALIA)

1984 Cabernet Sauvignon	B	88

1985 Cabernet Sauvignon	B	85

Vasse Felix is a small producer in the Margaret River area of Western Australia specializing in making Cabernet Sauvignon in the image of a famous Médoc in Bordeaux. Both the 1984 and 1985 show elegant, cigar-box, herbaceous, blackcurranty aromas, medium to full body, soft tannins, and a graceful, supple finish. While quite drinkable now, they should not be cellared beyond 1992.

VIRGIN HILLS (VICTORIA)

1984 Cabernet Sauvignon	B	75

1985 Cabernet Sauvignon	B	85

Another tiny winery making less than 1,000 cases of very good Cabernet Sauvignon, Virgin Hills is located in a cool-climate, high-altitude area in Victoria. The 1984 Cabernet Sauvignon tasted surprisingly acidic and lean, but it did display a fine cedary, blackcurrant aroma. The 1985 is a much richer, deeper wine with excellent depth of fruit, full body, and none of the annoying excessive acidity of the 1984.

WOLF BLASS (VICTORIA)

1983 Cabernet Sauvignon President's Selection Black Label	C	88

1984 Cabernet Sauvignon President's Selection Black Label	C	90

1982 Cabernet Sauvignon/Shiraz Black Label	C	87

1983 Cabernet Sauvignon/Shiraz Black Label	C	87

1984 Cabernet Sauvignon/Shiraz Black Label	C	90

1987 Chardonnay	B	?

The highly promoted Wolf Blass winery wins plenty of medals in Australian wine competitions and a taste of their red wines explains why. While the 1987 Chardonnay shows a rather simple, one-dimensional, apple fruitiness, the red wines all share a voluptuous texture, are opulently fruity with intense bouquets of cedarwood, toasty oak, and peppery black currants. They are wines that are meant to be drunk upon release but certainly show the ability to age for 5–7 years. As a general rule, the top vintages have been 1982 and 1984, where there is more richness in the wines than in the very good, even excellent 1983s. These are among the most seductive and flamboyant red wines from Australia, and although prices are on the high side, the quality is clearly in the bottle.

WYNDHAM ESTATES (SOUTH AUSTRALIA)

1982 Cabernet Sauvignon Bin 444 Hunter Valley	A	86
1983 Cabernet Sauvignon Bin 444 Hunter Valley	A	84
1984 Cabernet Sauvignon Bin 444 Hunter Valley	A	87
1986 Cabernet/Merlot Bin 888 Hunter Valley	B	89
1985 Cabernet/Shiraz Hunter Valley	A	84
1985 Chardonnay Bin 222 Hunter Valley	A	75
1986 Chardonnay Bin 222 Hunter Valley	A	84
1987 Chardonnay Hunter Valley	B	87
1985 Hermitage Bin 555 Hunter Valley	A	87
1985 Late-Harvest Riesling Botrytis Hunter Valley	B	87
1984 Merlot Hunter Valley	A	85
1985 Oak Cask Chardonnay Hunter Valley	A	72
1985 Pinot Noir Hunter Valley	A	85
1986 Semillon Hunter Valley	A	82

With a production of over 1,000,000 cases, of which 25% is exported to 22 countries all over the world, Wyndham Estates and its boisterous winemaker, Bryan McGuigan, have effectively penetrated many foreign marketplaces by pricing their wines at what skeptics claim is intentionally under the competition. There is no doubting the appeal these wines have for the mass consumer. By and large the lineup of reds is stronger than the overoaked white wines, but the new 1987 Hunter Valley Chardonnay (which inexplicably comes in a Bordeaux-shaped bottle) shows that the winery is sensitive to criticism as it has toned down the oak and produced the best Chardonnay I have yet tasted from Wyndham Estates. As for the other Chardonnays, if you like the taste of splinters in your mouth, you will probably enjoy them more than I did, as they seem to stress oak over fresh, lively fruit.

The bargains among the red wines are rather amazing. First, there is an authentic-tasting 1985 Pinot Noir that sells at an amazingly low price. It has good color, an expansive, velvety palate, and fine depth and length. Merlot has become a hot commodity in certain foreign markets, and the 1984, at a ridiculously low price, is smooth, silky, quite long, and satisfying. As for the single-bin Cabernet Sauvignons and Hermitage wines, they have shown considerable bottle variation, no doubt due to poor storage and shipping conditions, but at their best the Hermitage is concentrated, peppery, and plump, offering quite a hedonistic mouthful of full-bodied wine. The Cabernet Sauvignon offers plentiful amounts of smoky, toasty oak, rich, blackcurrant fruit, and behaves as if it wanted to be the famous BV Private Reserve from California. Certainly, the 1984 seems to have more to it than the 1983 or 1982, and it can be cellared for another 3–4 years. The red wines all share the creamy, opulent, lavishly rich, oaky style that Wyndham Estates undoubtedly knows consumers love. By the way, don't ignore the winery's excellent medium-sweet, crisp, impeccably styled, floral, delicate Riesling, which is also a sensational buy. Finally, the winery's entry into the double-digit-priced Cabernet/Merlot market is its 1986 Bin 888 Cabernet/Merlot from the Hunter Valley. Given two months of skin contact in rotary tanks, this 75% Cabernet Sauvignon, 25% Merlot blend is stuffed with crunchy, succulent, black-cherry and blackcurrant fruit, shows a good touch of vanillin and toasty oak, is quite full-bodied, very rich and long, and should drink beautifully for another 6–7 years. If these wines sound delicious, they are, and furthermore, they are unquestionably some of the best wine bargains in the world.

YALUMBA (BAROSSA)

N.V. Clocktower Port   A   86

This winery makes dry table wines, but far and away its best wine, an extraordinary value, is its Clocktower Port, a nonvintage blend that tastes like a fine Portuguese tawny. A rich berry and buttery nutlike bouquet is followed by an unctuous, well-balanced, heady, alcoholic port that provides immense satisfaction at an extremely low price.

YARRA YERING (YARRA VALLEY)

1984 Chardonnay	B	74
1985 Cabernet Sauvignon	B	85
1986 Chardonnay	B	84?
1987 Chardonnay	B	87
1986 Semillon	B	?
1987 Semillon	B	84
1984 Shiraz	B	65

Yarra Yering, a small boutique winery located in the Yarra Valley, is one of the leading proponents of making Australian wines more balanced and elegant. My tasting notes to date have shown mixed results, with some bad, musty, lean, acidic bottles from either improper blending at the winery or poor shipping afterward. Certainly, the 1985 Cabernet Sauvignon showed a great deal of promise and rich fruit as opposed to the 1984, which despite its dense color was heavy, overripe, and clumsy. The 1984 Shiraz was also disappointing, with a vegetal, odd character. It's hard to know exactly where this winery fits in the scheme of things in Australia given its spotty performance to date.

YERINGSBERG (YARRA VALLEY)

1985 Cabernet Sauvignon	C	86
1986 Chardonnay	C	86

1987 Chardonnay   C 88

Producing less than 600 cases, this is one of Australia's smallest wineries. The quality of the two Chardonnays I have tasted from Yeringsberg showed a skilled winemaker and high-quality fruit. Both the 1987 and 1986 have complex orange-, lemon-, tropical-fruit-scented bouquets, full body, and voluptuous textures; both should be drunk over the next several years. The Cabernet Sauvignon shows intense, deep, ruby/purple color, a full-bodied, rich, curranty grapiness, and some moderate tannins to resolve; it should last for another 5–6 years. The prices are on the high side for Australian wine, but then so is the quality.

10. ARGENTINA, BULGARIA, CHILE, GREECE, HUNGARY, LEBANON, NEW ZEALAND, SWITZERLAND, UNITED KINGDOM, YUGOSLAVIA

ARGENTINA

Mediocre Quality but Good Potential

I suspect few people realize that Argentinians rank among the world leaders in per capita consumption of wine. Not only do these fun-loving people drink plenty of wine, but the country is also the fifth leading producer of wine in the world, making 275 million cases of wine from 750,000 acres of vineyards. While Argentina has lagged behind Chile in promoting its wines to the outside world, it is beginning to become a bit more export conscious. Are the wines of interest? The white wines from well-known grapes such as Sauvignon, Semillon, and Chardonnay have been uninteresting and rather clumsy, but the red wines, while not yet comparable with the best from Chile, are fat, soft, spicy, decent wines at bargain prices. The best red wines are from Cabernet Sauvignon, Syrah, and Merlot grapes. Pinot Noir is made, but it fares no better in Argentina than in most other places outside Burgundy.

In my research for this book I tasted over one hundred white, red, and rosé wines from Argentina, and the average score was 68 points, which in short tells the distressing story of the current quality of Argentine wines in the marketplace. While the potential for better quality is present, the white wines are either oxidized and bizarre, or overly acidic and neutral. The red wines suffer from a number of defects including washed-out, diluted flavors from excessive vineyard yields or a lack of selection in the winery, and old, musty flavors from unclean, old wooden barrels. Sadly, a general lack of grip and focus was noted in even the adequately made wines. None of the insipid current releases from the following wineries can be recommended: **Navarro, Michel Torino, Trapiche, Andean, Clos du Moulin, Comte de Valmont, Bodegas Lavaque, Saint Felicien, Fond de Pave,** and **Bodegas y Vinedos Giol.**

The best wineries in my tastings (with wines that merited scores only in the high seventies) were **Humberto Canale** and **Etchart,** and some bottlings from **Aberdeen-Angus.**

BULGARIA

Inexpensive Plonk

Although they have not yet caught on in America, a visit to virtually any merchant in the United Kingdom will reveal bins of cheap Bulgarian Merlot, Chardonnay, and Cabernet Sauvignon. Most cost between $4 and $5 a bottle, offering straightforward, simple fruit that must be drunk within 3–4 years of the vintage. The wine producers are of little relevance since everything to date is coming from one of the government-run cooperatives. I would stay away from the $6 and $7 a bottle "reserve" wines that the shrewd Bulgarians are marketing, since these cask-aged wines simply don't have the fruit to hold up to the wood. All things considered, a cheap Bulgarian Chardonnay or Merlot is not such a bad gamble.

CHILE

High Quality, Modest Prices

Chile, if you have not already learned by now, is making very serious, complex wines. Prices are ridiculously low in some cases, and this is a country (politics aside) that should be looked at with great interest by consumers desiring a terrific bargain in wine. The best producers and their top wines currently in the marketplace are listed below.

Sauvignon Blanc—For Sauvignon Blanc fermented in stainless steel, bottled early for freshness, and of absolutely first-rate quality, look for the 1988 and 1987 **Canepa** and 1988 **Errazuriz Panquehue.**

Chardonnay—Chardonnay is good, but not yet exciting. Look for the 1987 and 1988 soft, very fruity, tasty wines from **Cousino Macul.**

Cabernet Sauvignon—For the last several years, the finest Cabernets have come from two wineries, **Santa Rita** and **Cousino Macul.** Santa Rita's 1985 and 1986 Cabernets are unbelievable for their prices of less than $8 a bottle. In an escalating order of quality, Santa Rita produces a "120" for $4, a Cabernet Sauvignon "Medalla Real" for $7.50, and a Cabernet Sauvignon "120 Estate" for $9. Cousino Macul's less rich but elegant, herbaceous, cedar-scented Cabernets are available in a regular cuvée and a top of the wine, excellent "Antiguas Reserva." Look for the 1984 and 1985 regular Cabernet and the 1981 and 1982 Antiguas Reserva.

Two other reliably good producers of Cabernet Sauvignon are **St. Morillon** and **Los Vascos.** The 1983 St. Morillon at $5 is a great bargain, and the 1984 and 1985 Los Vascos at $4 are even greater values.

Sparkling wine—**Valdivesco's** nonvintage Brut at $7 is a solid, well-made sparkling wine.

Interestingly, two of the most highly promoted brands of Chilean wine, **Torres** and **Concho y Toro**, are not of the same level of quality as the aforementioned producers. However, the Torres vineyards are young, and given the impeccable quality of this firm's Spanish wines, one can only expect better and better things from their Chilean operation. As for Concho y Toro, they may be realizing the competitive edge enjoyed by Santa Rita and Cousino Macul, because their 1984 Castillero del Diablo appears to be the most serious Cabernet Sauvignon they have yet made and is capable of challenging the best of Chile.

Other wineries of Chile that are producing somewhat bland, commercial wines include **Santa Carolina**, **Tarapaca**, and **Undurraga**.

GREECE

Is There Life Beyond Retsina?

When Greece entered the Common Market in 1981, we started to see some serious attempts, on a limited basis, at promoting the drinking of Greek wines. The results have been predictable. Consumers found the wines oxidized, poorly made, and bizarre. In the case of Retsina, Greece's one legitimate contribution to viticulture, most non-Greeks found it akin to chewing on a pine tree—a notoriously odd wine. I had not bought a Greek wine in almost three years when researching this book, so I decided to see what was in the market in 1989. Retsina, whether you find it obnoxious or not, is still out there, and if you have to try it, look for the **Metaxas** Retsina as it is the best. For a dry rosé try the "Roditys" made by **Cambas**. At $3.50 it is a good bargain but is not vintage dated, so knowing whether it is a fresh bottle will be difficult until you pull the cork. The best dry red wines come from the island of Cephalonia. Look for the **Calliga** "Monte Nero" (pricey at $9) and "Ruby Red" ($6.50); they are two of the best red wines made in Greece. For a sweet red wine, the "Mavrodaphne" of **Achaia Clauss** (Greece's largest wine producer) will taste vaguely like a Recioto from Italy.

HUNGARY

Unrealized Potential

Every once in a while an innovative importer will come back from Hungary with an assortment of samples from that country's wine producers. Some of the wines will taste quite decent, particularly in view of the low prices. Then the importer orders the wines, they arrive months later, and lo and behold, they vary in taste and quality from bottle to bottle. Hungary's biggest problems are consistency and its ignorance of twentieth-century tastes and expectations. Yes, there is the overly promoted **Bull's Blood**, but even this wine is no longer of the quality it once was. Additionally, there are the sweet Tokays that have a certain following in the international marketplace. However, most of these wines are not what they are cracked up to be. Hungary has the potential to provide sound, everyday table wines at bargain-basement prices, but at present, they are losing out to more quality-oriented countries such as Chile, Australia, and their Eastern Bloc neighbor, Bulgaria.

LEBANON

One World-Class Red Wine
Amid the Chaos

The top wine of the Middle East is a story in itself. Thirty kilometers (18 miles) from the savage and senseless civil war that has torn apart Beirut is **Château Musar,** a winemaking estate founded in the thirties and one that makes superlative wines from a blend of Cabernet Sauvignon, Syrah, and Cinsault. Owner/winemaker Serge Hochar has had vintages wiped out because no harvesters would risk their lives to pick the grapes, but still he continues. His wine training came from his father and a stint in Bordeaux, but the wines made here remind me of the best and most complex Châteauneuf-du-Papes. They are quite full-bodied, very fragrant, rich, and supple enough to drink young, but if the very good 1966 and exquisite 1969 or 1970 tasted recently are any indication, they will last 10, even 20 years. The vintages now on the market are the 1975, 1977, 1978, 1979, and 1980. Retailing for less than $12 a bottle, the wines are undeniable bargains given the quality. The 1977 is deeper and has more potential than the 1975. The 1979 is gorgeously fragrant and velvety, as is the 1980. Musar is still relatively unknown; as long as the disastrous civil war continues to rage, the future is uncertain here, but this estate does indeed produce outstanding wine.

NEW ZEALAND
The New Darling of the Wine Media

Mention the words "cool climate" and many a wine writer will be searching for the next junket to discover the undiscovered great wines of country XYZ. New Zealand is a case in point. Has anyone noticed the press this country has been getting of late? I feel I must be among only a few writers left in the world who have not taken a free business trip to New Zealand to taste these remarkable new wines from this hot new "cool climate" viticultural paradise. However, I have done a little homework and at least tasted as many of these wines as I could get my lips on. After wading through all the hype, one does see a potential from this country that may well justify the enthusiasm exhibited by top tasters such as England's Jancis Robinson, who is decidedly a pro–New Zealander.

Initially, it was the Sauvignon Blancs that elicited most of the excitement from the wine press. Certainly I have found excellent Sauvignons from the likes of **Selaks, Kumeu River, Nautilus, Mouton Estate, Montana,** and **Cape Mentelle,** but I have also tasted quite a few unappetizing, excessively vegetal Sauvignons that make me wonder about all the hype.

As for Chardonnay, the New Zealanders are just beginning to learn how to handle all of their cool-climate acids. Full malolactic fermentation, lees contact, and new barrels are making their appearance, and the results look to be some pretty stunning Chardonnays from wineries such as **Kemeu River, Te Mata, Matua Valley, Nobilo,** and **Corbans.**

New Zealand's early attempts with Cabernet Sauvignon and Merlot ranged from annoyingly herbaceous to atrociously vegetal wines. The newer styles have purged some of these veggies, and the Merlots and Cabernets from **Te Mata, Kumeu River, Matua Valley,** and **C. J. Pask** are showing gobs of plummy, blackcurrant fruit, and more and more class, but the nasty vegetal streak remains in evidence.

I do not have any enthusiasm for New Zealand Pinot Noir or Gewürztraminer, but the Germanic varietals Müller-Thurgau and Riesling look to have potential in the hands of wineries such as **Selaks, Wines, Delegats,** and **Collard Brothers.**

Is all the excitement over New Zealand's wines generated by recent press coverage justified? Not completely, but this country has some very fine wines that are becoming increasingly competitive with the finest in the world.

SWITZERLAND

If It Were Not for the Prices

The only bargain I have ever discovered in Switzerland was to fly to Geneva, rent my car there, then drop my car off in Paris at the conclusion of my trip. By originating my rental in Switzerland, I avoided France's 33% tax on car rentals. One does not visit Switzerland on a budget. Like everything else in the country, its wines are frightfully expensive—always have been, always will be. Although one might quibble over the price, the quality of many Swiss wines is very good, especially the fragrant, richly fruity wines made from a grape called Chasselas that does better in Switzerland than anywhere else. The Chasselas white wines appear not only under the grape's own name, but also under the names Fendant, Dezaley, and Neuchâtel. Switzerland has 35,000 acres of vineyards in every one of its cantons, but the top vineyards are centered either on the steep slopes above Lake Geneva in an area called Vaud, or further east around the town of Sion in an area called Valais. The Chasselas grape, or Fendant as it is called in Valais, produces a very aromatic white wine that at its best suggests a Condrieu in bouquet, and a medium-bodied, stainless-steel-fermented, yet fleshy Chardonnay in texture and weight. If it were not so expensive (usually $10–16 a bottle), it would be quite popular. It is Switzerland's best white wine. Red wine, the best of which is called Dole and is a blend of Pinot Noir and Gamay, is an adequate, serviceable red, though never worth its stiff price tag. Following are the top producers of Switzerland and their best wines:

Domaine du Mont d'Or—Look for the rich Fendant and decent Dole.

Gerard Pinget—The white Chasselas called Dezaley Renard is one of the two best white wines of Switzerland.

J & P Testuz—For my money, Switzerland's best winery, making rich, perfumed, delicious Fendant and Dezaley under the Domaine L'Arbalete label. Only the price of $20 or more a bottle is a problem.

UNITED KINGDOM

*Courageously Trying to Overcome the
Impossible Weather*

Several years ago Robin Young, the well-known English wine writer and consumer advocate for *Decanter* magazine, proposed to me a mystery "blind tasting." No information was given and I scored all the wines. Every wine I tasted was below average except for one light, floral, pretty wine that made it to 80, or just barely above average. They were all English wines. English wines have the wretched weather of that country to overcome, as anyone who visited England during the summers of 1985 or 1986 can attest. Furthermore, the grapes that can be grown successfully are unusual German clones developed for cold, wet, northerly climates. Given the bizarre names of the varietals, such as Madeleine Angevine, Gütenborner, Huxelrebe, Ortega, Wrotham, Schonburger, and Reichensteiner, plus the high labor costs of making English wine, the bold truth is that English wine is an expensive mediocrity. Should you want to experience a $10-a-bottle, neutral, insipid wine, then I suggest you look for the products of several of the more successful wineries. **Lamberhurst** (England's biggest vineyard) makes decent quaffing wines that are clean and correct, and **Wootton** turns out pleasant if innocuous Seyval Blanc, Müller-Thurgau, and Schonburger.

YUGOSLAVIA

Caveat Emptor!

Regrettably, most of the Yugoslavian wine available is unacceptable, with no redeeming social value despite prices of less than $3 a bottle. This does not have to be the case because there are good Yugoslavian wines made, but importers seem content to buy the lowest commercial grade of swill and sell it off to the public as a "value"! Stay away from heavily promoted brands such as **Avia** and **Nadia**. Better-quality Yugoslavian wines exist, but apparently no one wants to spend the extra 10% to bring them here.

APPENDIX

ESTIMATED MATURITY CHARTS

Explanation of the Charts

Following is the estimated range of years over which the listed châteaux's wines should be consumed for the specific vintage. Keep in mind the following points.

1. If you like the way a wine tastes when young, don't hesitate to enjoy it in spite of what the chart may say.
2. I have had to make several assumptions, the primary ones being that the wine was purchased in a healthy state, and you are cellaring the wine in a cool, humid, odor and vibration free environment that does not exceed 68° F in the summer.
3. The estimates are an educated guess based on how the wine normally ages, its quality, balance, and depth for the vintage in question.
4. The estimates are conservative in the sense that good storage conditions are essential. I have assumed a maturity based on my own palate, which tends to prefer a wine more fresh and exuberant over one which has begun to fade, but which may still be quite delicious and complex.

Consequently, if you have cool, ideal cellars, the beginning year in the estimated range of maturity may err in favor of drinking the wine on the young side. I presume most readers would prefer, given a choice, to open a bottle too early rather than too late, and this philosophy has governed my projected maturity period for each wine.

How to Read the Charts

N/T = No recent or no tasting experience.

Now = Totally mature, and not likely to improve; this wine should be drunk up.

Now—1993 = The wine has entered its plateau of maturity where it should be expected to remain until 1993, at which time it may begin to slowly decline.

1992—2010 = This is the estimated range of years in which I believe the wine will be in its plateau period—the years over which it will be at its best for drinking. Please keep in mind that Bordeaux wines from top vintages tend to decline slowly (just the opposite of Burgundy) and a top wine from an excellent vintage may take 10–15 years to lose its fruit and freshness after the last year in the stated plateau period.

? = This signifies that the only experience to date has been one unfavorable rating and judgment is reserved.

THE TOP CHÂTEAUX OF BORDEAUX—1975–1986

CHÂTEAU	1986	1985	1983	1982	1981	1979	1978	1976	1975
L'Arrosée	1993–2010	Now–2003	Now–1999	1990–2005	Now–1996	Now–1995	Now–1998	N/T	N/T
Ausone	1993–2005	1993–2005	1993–2010	1996–2020	Now–1997	1992–2005	1990–2005	Now–2000	Now–1995
Batailley	1998–2010	1993–2000	1990–2000	1990–2005	Now–1996	1990–2000	Now–2000	Now–1994	1989–2000
Bel Air	?	1989–1994	1993–2005	1990–2000	Now–1993	Now–1995	Now–1995	Now–1990	Now–1992
Beychevelle	1996–2010	1989–1997	1993–2005	1995–2010	Now–1997	Now–1997	1990–1998	Now–2000	1990–2005
Bon Pasteur	1992–2005	Now–1994	1989–1996	1992–2005	Now–1991	Now	Now–1990	Now	Now
Boyd-Cantenac	1992–2000	Now–1998	1993–2005	1992–2008	Now–1990	Now–1992	Now–2000	Now	1993–2005
Branaire-Ducru	1991–1999	Now–1995	Now–1998	1992–2007	Now–1998	Now–1994	Now–1994	Now–1992	Now–2005
Brane Cantenac	1992–2005	1989–1997	1990–2005	Now–2000	1989–1995	Now–1996	Now–1996	Now–1992	Now–1994
Brillette	1990–2002	Now–1992	Now–1992	Now–1998	Now–1993	Now–1991	Now–1990	N/T	N/T
Cadet-Piola	1993–2005	1990–1998	1992–2007	1992–2005	Now–1995	Now–1992	Now–1993	Now–1992	Now–1994
Calon-Segur	1996–2010	1990–2000	1990–1997	1998–2020	Now–1994	Now–1995	Now–1994	Now–1990	Now–1997
Canon	1993–2010	1993–2007	1995–2015	1992–2020	1990–2000	1990–2005	1992–2005	Now–1994	1992–2010
Canon de Brem	1994–2005	1992–2003	1992–2003	1990–2005	Now–1996	1989–1998	Now–1992	Now	Now–1990
Cantenac-Brown	N/T	N/T	1990–2000	1994–2005	1991–2004	Now–1995	Now–1995	Now–1990	1989–2005
Cantemerle	1990–1998	Now–1997	1990–2000	Now–1996	Now–1995	Now–1993	Now–1995	Now–1989	1992–2003
Certan-Giraud	Now–1995	Now–1993	Now–1992	Now–1996	Now–1992	Now–1993	Now–1990	Now	Now–1993
Certan de May	1995–2015	1991–2003	1990–2005	1992–2010	1992–2005	1989–2000	Now–1996	Now–1992	Now–1998
Chasse-Spleen	1995–2015	1993–2010	1990–2000	1990–2000	Now–1998	Now–1996	1990–2005	Now–1996	1990–2005
Cheval Blanc	1992–2008	Now–1996	1992–2003	1992–2010	1990–2000	1990–1998	1990–2005	Now–1992	Now–2000
Clerc-Milon	1998–2020	1995–2005	1990–2000	Now–2000	Now–1995	Now–1993	Now–1992	Now–1992	Now–1996

THE TOP CHÂTEAUX OF BORDEAUX—1975–1986 (Continued)

CHÂTEAU	1986	1985	1983	1982	1981	1979	1978	1976	1975
Clos des Jacobins	1990–2000	Now–1993	Now–1998	1992–2005	Now–1995	Now–1996	Now–1996	Now–1992	Now–1995
Clos René	1991–1995	Now–1993	Now–1996	Now–1995	Now–1991	Now–1990	Now	Now	Now–1996
La Conseillante	1991–2005	Now–1996	1990–1998	1990–2000	Now–2000	Now–1992	Now–1992	Now	Now–1992
Cos d'Estournel	1995–2010	1991–2010	1990–2005	1992–2008	1989–1996	Now–1997	Now–2000	Now–1993	1990–2000
Domaine de Chevalier	1995–2015	1993–2005	1993–2005	1996–2010	Now–1997	Now–1997	Now–2000	Now–1992	1990–1998
La Dominique	1994–2008	Now–1993	Now–1998	1990–2007	1990–2000	Now–1995	Now–1995	N/T	Now–1996
Ducru-Beaucaillou	1995–2015	1992–2010	1993–2005	1996–2010	1992–2008	Now–1995	Now–2005	Now–1993	1990–2000
Duhart-Milon Rothschild	1995–2005	1991–2000	1995–2005	1995–2010	1992–2003	Now–1992	Now–1993	Now	Now
L'Eglise-Clinet	1990–2003	1990–2005	Now–1996	Now–1998	Now–1992	Now–1992	Now	Now	Now–1993
L'Enclos	1990–1995	Now–1993	Now–1993	1990–2000	Now–1994	Now–1990	Now–1991	Now	Now–1992
L'Evangile	Now–1995	1991–2015	1990–2003	1992–2010	Now	Now–1991	Now–1991	Now	Now–1993
Figeac	1990–2005	Now–1998	Now–1985	1991–2008	Now–1993	Now–1991	Now–1993	Now	Now–1992
Forts de Latour	1996–2010	1991–2000	1991–2001	1992–2008	1990–2003	1989–1996	Now–2000	Now	Now–1995
Fonbadet	1990–1997	Now–1992	1992–2000	1990–1996	Now–1994	Now–1992	Now–1992	Now	N/T
Fourcas-Hosten	N/T	1991–1997	1993–2000	1991–1998	1990–1996	N/T	N/T	N/T	1990–2000
Le Gay	1998–2010	1995–2008	1993–2005	1998–2010	Now	1989–1996	1990–1999	Now	1990–2005
Giscours	?	Now–1995	Now–1993	Now–1993	Now–1995	1990–2003	1992–2006	Now–1990	1992–2010
Gloria	1990–1998	Now–1997	Now–1995	Now–1993	Now	Now	Now–1992	Now	Now–1995
Grand-Puy-Lacoste	1993–2015	1989–2005	1993–2000	1994–2010	Now–1993	Now–1992	Now–1996	Now	Now–1993
Grand-Puy-Ducasse	1990–2000	Now–1997	Now–1994	Now–1995	Now–1992	Now–1990	Now–1990	Now	Now–1992
La Grave Trigant	1990–1997	Now–1993	Now–1995	1989–2000	Now–1988	Now–1992	Now–1990	Now	Now–1992
Gruaud-Larose	2000–2025	1991–2003	1990–2004	1998–2020	1990–2000	Now–2003	1992–2008	Now–1990	1992–2010

Haut-Bages-Libéral	1995–2020	1991–2005	1992–2003	1990–2000	1990–2000	1990–2000	Now–1994	Now–1995	Now–1993	1989–2003
Haut-Bailly	1990–2000	Now–1996	1990–1997	1990–2000	1990–2000	Now–1996	Now–1996	Now–1993	Now	Now
Haut-Batailley	1991–2010	Now–1993	1989–2000	1990–2005	1990–2003	Now–1993	Now–1992	Now–1992	Now	Now–1992
Haut-Brion	1995–2015	1991–2005	1993–2005	1992–2015	1991–2003	1990–2003	1990–2005	Now–2000	Now–1992	Now–1994
Haut-Marbuzet	1991–2003	Now–1997	Now–1998	1990–2005	1990–2005	Now–1994	Now–1992	Now–1993	Now	Now–1995
D'Issan	1993–2003	1989–1997	1990–2003	Now–2000	Now–2000	Now–1996	Now–1993	Now–1996	Now	Now–1993
Kirwan	1992–1996	1990–1997	1991–2003	Now–2000	Now–2000	Now–1991	Now–1990	Now–1991	Now	Now
Lafite-Rothschild	1998–2015	1993–2008	1998–2015	1996–2025	1992–2008	1992–2005	1992–2005	1991–2005	1990–2010	1989–2015
Lafon-Rochet	1996–2008	1992–1999	1993–2010	1990–2005	Now–1996	Now–1996	Now–1992	Now–1991	Now	Now–1996
La Lagune	1996–2010	1990–2000	1992–2003	1992–2010	Now–1992	Now–1993	Now–1993	1990–2003	Now–1992	1991–2003
Lafleur	2000–2025	1995–2015	1995–2010	1995–2020	Now	1990–2010	1990–2010	1990–2003	Now	1992–2025
La Fleur Pétrus	1990–1996	Now–1997	Now–1997	Now–2000	Now–1995	Now–1995	Now–1993	Now–1991	Now	1990–2005
Lanessan	N/T	Now–1996	1990–2000	1992–2003	Now–1991	Now–1991	Now–1990	Now–1992	Now	1989–2003
Lascombes	1992–2000	Now–1997	Now–2003	Now–2001	Now–1992	Now–1992	Now–1992	Now–1992	Now	Now–2003
Langoa-Barton	1998–2010	1992–2002	1992–2000	1993–2008	1990–2000	1990–2000	Now–1991	Now–1992	Now	1990–2005
Latour	1996–2010	1992–2008	1995–2008	1996–2020	1992–2006	1990–2000	1990–2000	1992–2010	Now–1994	1992–2020
La Tour-Haut-Brion	1990–2000	1990–1997	1991–2000	1994–2010	1990–1998	1990–1998	Now–1997	1991–2003	Now	1992–2010
Latour à Pomerol	1995–2010	1992–2005	1990–2000	1992–2005	1989–1996	1989–1996	Now–1995	Now–1993	Now	Now–1996
Léoville-Barton	1997–2020	1992–2007	1995–2005	1995–2010	1990–1996	1990–1996	Now	Now–1994	Now	Now–1998
Léoville-Las Cases	1998–2025	1991–2005	1996–2015	1998–2025	1993–2005	1993–2005	1990–1998	1993–2008	Now–1991	1990–2010
Léoville-Poyferré	1997–2020	1989–1998	1996–2005	1996–2015	1990–1996	1990–1996	Now–1996	Now–1992	Now	Now–1996
La Louvière	Now–1997	Now–1994	Now–1992	Now–1993	Now	Now	Now	Now	N/T	Now–1990
Lynch-Bages	1996–2020	1990–2005	1992–2005	1991–2008	Now–1993	Now–1992	Now–1992	Now–1990	Now	Now–1998
Magdelaine	?	1991–2003	1992–2003	1992–2010	1990–1995	1990–1995	Now–1994	Now–1993	Now	Now–1996

THE TOP CHÂTEAUX OF BORDEAUX—1975–1986 (Continued)

CHÂTEAU	1986	1985	1983	1982	1981	1979	1978	1976	1975
Malescot St.-Exupéry	N/T	1989–1997	1993–2000	1991–2003	1990–1996	Now–1995	Now–1996	Now	1989–1996
Château Margaux	2000–2030	1994–2008	1998–2025	1992–2015	1993–2003	1990–2003	1990–2005	Now	Now–1991
Maucaillou	N/T	Now–1993	Now–1993	Now–1994	Now	Now	Now	Now	Now
Meyney	1995–2010	1991–2005	1990–2003	1990–2005	1989–1997	Now–1996	Now–1996	Now	Now–1996
La Mission-Haut-Brion	1995–2012	1991–2005	1992–2003	1994–2010	1991–2002	1990–2000	1990–2005	Now	1992–2015
Montrose	1995–2015	1992–2000	1990–1997	1992–2004	1990–1997	Now–1999	Now–1996	Now–1996	1990–2005
Mouton-Baronne-Philippe	1995–2010	Now–1997	1992–2000	1990–2000	Now–1996	N/T	N/T	Now	Now–1993
Mouton-Rothschild	1996–2030	1992–2010	1995–2008	1996–2020	1991–2000	Now–1996	Now–1995	Now–1997	1993–2008
Les-Ormes-de-Pez	1991–1996	Now–1992	Now	Now–1993	Now	Now	Now	Now	Now–1993
Palmer	1994–2010	1990–2000	1992–2008	1990–2000	1990–1997	1993–2005	Now–2005	Now–1992	Now–2000
Pape-Clément	1993–2010	1990–2000	Now	Now–1992	Now	Now	Now	Now	Now–1996
Pavie	1995–2010	1993–2005	1992–2000	1990–2000	1990–1995	Now–1994	Now–1990	Now	Now–1996
Pavillon Rouge de Margaux	1996–2008	1990–2000	Now–1993	Now–1994	Now–1992	–	–	–	N/T
Petit-Village	1991–2001	Now–1994	Now–1995	Now–1998	Now–1992	Now–1991	Now	Now	Now
Pétrus	1998–2025	1995–2015	1993–2005	1992–2015	1993–2008	1992–2010	Now–1996	Now	1992–2025
Pichon Longueville Baron	1991–2005	Now–1993	1990–1996	1990–1996	Now–1993	Now–1992	1990–2000	Now	Now–1991
Pichon Lalande	1994–2015	1989–2002	1990–2002	1990–2005	1989–1997	Now–1996	Now–1999	Now–1990	Now–1998
Le Pin	1990–2000	Now–1997	Now–1996	Now–2000	Now–1994	–	–	–	–
Pontet-Canet	1998–2015	1992–2005	1993–2002	1992–2005	Now–1993	Now–1991	1989–1996	Now	Now–1993
Potensac	1991–1998	Now–1996	1989–1993	1990–2000	Now–1992	Now	Now	Now	N/T
Pougeaux	1993–2010	1990–2005	1990–1997	1992–2005	Now–1991	Now–1993	Now–1995	Now	1989–1995

Prieuré-Lichine	1994–2010	Now–1995	1990–2003	1992–2005	Now–1991	Now–1990	Now–1992	Now	Now
Rausan-Ségla	1993–2005	Now–1997	1993–2003	Now–1997	Now	Now	Now	Now	Now
Rauzan-Gassies	?	1991–2000	1993–2000	Now–1998	Now–1991	Now–1991	Now–1995	Now	1990–1996
Rouget	1991–1999	1993–2005	1990–1996	1993–2009	1990–1994	N/T	Now–1993	Now	1990–1995
St.-Pierre-Sevaistre	1992–2007	1989–1998	1990–1998	1990–2002	1990–2000	Now–1996	Now–1996	Now	1989–1994
de Sales	Now–1994	Now–1993	Now–1991	Now–1993	Now	Now	Now	Now	Now
Sociando-Mallet	2000–2025	1995–2015	1996–2010	2000–2025	1990–1996	1990–1995	1992–2005	Now–2000	1992–2010
Soutard	1997–2015	1996–2010	1993–2003	1995–2005	Now–1996	Now–1997	Now–1996	Now	1990–2000
Talbot	1995–2015	1990–2005	1993–2005	1995–2008	Now–1996	Now–1995	Now–2000	Now–1992	Now–1995
du Tertre	1993–2008	?	1993–2001	1990–2005	1989–1996	Now–1996	Now–1998	Now	Now
Trotanoy	1993–2007	1990–2000	1992–2001	1991–2010	1991–2002	Now–1996	Now–1995	Now–1992	Now–1998
Vieux-Château-Certan	1993–2008	Now–1997	1990–2000	1990–2005	Now–1996	Now–1995	Now–1996	Now	Now–2000

RED BURGUNDY—1976–1987

WINE	1987	1986	1985	1984	1983	1982	1980	1979	1978	1976
Comte Armand Pommard Clos des Epeneaux	1991–1996	1990–1994	1990–2000	?	1992–1996	Now	Now	Now	Now–1993	Now–1996
Robert Arnoux Vosne-Romanée Les Suchots	Now–1994	Now–1993	Now–1996	?	1990–1995	Now	Now–1992	Now	Now–1994	?
Bichot-Clos Frantin Vosne-Romanée Les Malconsorts	1990–2000	Now–1996	1991–2003	?	1990–1998	Now	Now	Now	Now–1993	?
P. Bourée Charmes-Chambertin	N/T	1990–1995	1992–2003	N/T	1993–2000	Now–1993	Now–1993	Now–1992	Now–1995	N/T
P. Bourée Clos de la Roche	N/T	1990–1995	1990–2000	N/T	1993–2003	Now–1993	Now–1992	Now–1992	Now–1995	N/T
R. Chevillon Nuits St.-Georges Les Saint Georges	1990–1997	Now–1995	1991–2000	N/T	1993–2000	Now	Now–1993	Now	Now	N/T
R. Chevillon Nuits St.-Georges Les Vaucrains	1990–1997	Now–1995	1992–2003	1989–1993	1992–2002	Now	Now–1993	Now	Now	N/T
Courcel Pommard Rugiens	1990–1996	Now–1995	1990–2000	N/T	1989–1995	Now	Now–1993	Now–1991	Now–1995	1990–1998
J. Drouhin Charmes-Chambertin	1990–1997	1989–1994	1990–2003	N/T	—	—	—	—	—	—
J. Drouhin Griotte-Chambertin	1992–2003	1990–1995	1992–2004	N/T	—	—	—	—	—	—
Drouhin-Larose Chambertin Clos de Bèze	1991–2000	Now–1993	1990–2000	N/T	1992–2000	Now	Now	Now–1993	Now–1995	1989–1996
Drouhin-Larose Bonnes Mares	1991–2000	Now–1993	1990–1998	N/T	1990–1996	Now	Now	Now–1992	Now–1995	Now–1995
Dujac Bonnes Mares	1992–2001	1990–2000	1993–2005	Now–1992	1990–1997	Now	Now–1992	Now	Now–1996	1990–2000
Dujac Charmes-Chambertin	1992–2003	1990–2000	1992–2005	Now–1992	1989–1997	Now	Now–1992	Now	Now–1996	1990–2000
Dujac Clos de la Roche	1992–2005	1991–2002	1993–2005	Now–1992	1991–2000	Now	Now–1993	Now	Now–2000	1990–2003
Dujac Clos St.-Denis	1992–2005	1990–2000	1992–2005	Now–1992	1991–2000	Now	Now–1993	Now	Now–2000	1990–2003
René Engel Grands-Echézeaux	1991–2000	Now–1995	1990–2003	N/T	Now	N/T	N/T	N/T	N/T	N/T
Faiveley Chambertin Clos de Bèze	1994–2008	1990–1997	1993–2008	1990–1996	1993–2008	Now–1995	Now–1994	Now–1997	1990–2005	1989–1996
Faiveley Charmes-Chambertin	1992–2000	1990–1997	1990–2004	N/T	—	Now–1992	Now–1993	Now–1994	Now–1996	N/T
Faiveley Corton Clos des Cortons	1993–2000	1990–1998	1992–2002	1990–1995	—	Now–1992	Now–1996	Now–1992	Now–1996	N/T
Faiveley Mazis-Chambertin	1993–2000	1991–1999	1993–2005	Now–1995	1993–2005	Now–1993	Now–1993	Now–1994	Now–2000	N/T
Machard de Gramont Nuits St.-Georges Les Haut Pruliers	1991–1998	Now–1994	1991–2003	N/T	1990–1996	Now–1992	Now–1994	Now–1993	Now–1996	N/T
Machard de Gramont Pommard Le Clos Blanc	1990–1996	Now–1993	1992–2002	N/T	1990–1996	Now–1993	Now–1994	Now–1992	Now–1996	N/T
Jean Grivot Clos Vougeot	1990–1998	1990–1995	1990–1998	N/T	1990–1994	Now	Now	N/T	N/T	N/T
Jean Gros Clos Vougeot	—	—	—	N/T	1993–2000	Now	1990–1995	Now–1992	Now–2000	N/T
Jean Gros Richebourg	1992–2003	1990–1996	1992–2005	Now–1993	1993–2002	Now–1992	Now–1996	Now	Now–1999	N/T
Hospices de Beaune Beaune Clos des Avaux	1991–2002	Now–1995	1990–2005	Now	1992–2000	Now	Now–1992	Now	Now–1998	Now
Hospices de Beaune Beaune Nicolas Rollin	1992–2003	Now–1997	1990–2005	Now	1992–2000	Now	N/T	N/T	N/T	Now

Hospices de Beaune Corton Charlotte Dumay	1993–2004	1990–1999	1991–2005	Now–1992	Now	Now–1994	Now–1993	Now–1993	Now–2000	Now
Hospices de Beaune Corton Docteur Peste	1993–2004	1990–1999	1991–2005	Now–1993	1993–2005	Now	Now–1994	Now–1996	Now–2005	Now
Hospices de Beaune Mazis-Chambertin	1993–2007	1991–2003	1992–2008	1990–1995	1995–2008	Now	Now–1997	Now–1995	1990–2010	N/T
Hospices de Beaune Pommard Dames de la Charité	1992–2002	Now–1996	1990–2005	Now–1992	N/TNow	N/T	N/T	N/T	Now–1994	1990–2003
Hospices de Beaune Savigny Les Beaune Arthur Girard	1992–2005	1990–2002	1992–2005	1990–1994	1992–2002	Now	Now–1994	N/T	1990–2005	N/T
Hospices de Beaune Volnay Blondeau	1992–2003	Now–1997	1990–2003	Now	N/T	Now	Now–1992	N/T	N/T	N/T
Hospices de Beaune Volnay Santenots Jehan de Massol	1992–2003	Now–1995	1990–2003	Now	N/T	Now–1992	Now–1992	Now	N/T	N/T
Hudelot-Noëllat Clos Vougeot	1990–1996	Now–1992	1991–2001	N/T	1990–1998	Now	Now–1993	N/T	N/T	N/T
Louis Jadot Beaune Clos des Ursules	1990–1998	Now–1998	Now–1998	N/T	1990–2000	N/T	N/T	N/T	N/T	N/T
Louis Jadot Bonnes Mares	1992–2000	Now–1994	1992–2002	N/T	N/T	N/T	N/T	N/T	N/T	N/T
Louis Jadot Chambertin Clos de Bèze	1992–2002	Now–1994	1992–2002	N/T	1993–2003	N/T	N/T	N/T	N/T	N/T
Louis Jadot Chambolle-Musigny Les Amoureuses	1991–2001	Now–1994	1991–2001	N/T	N/T	N/T	N/T	N/T	N/T	N/T
Louis Jadot Chapelle-Chambertin	1992–2002	Now–1994	1990–2000	N/T	N/T	N/T	N/T	N/T	N/T	N/T
Louis Jadot Clos Vougeot	1992–2002	Now–1994	1992–2002	N/T	1993–2005	Now	N/T	N/T	Now–1995	Now–1993
Louis Jadot Gevrey-Chambertin Clos St.-Jacques	1992–2005	Now–1994	1991–1999	N/T	N/T	Now	N/T	N/T	N/T	N/T
Henri Jayer Echézeaux	1992–2000	1992–2000	1993–2003	1990–1994	1990–1997	Now–1993	Now–1995	Now–1991	Now–1998	N/T
Henri Jayer Nuits St.-Georges Meurgers	1992–2000	1990–1996	1992–2000	Now–1993	1990–1998	Now–1993	Now–1995	Now–1992	Now–1996	N/T
Henri Jayer Richebourg	1993–2005	1992–2000	1993–2005	1990–1996	1993–2005	Now–1995	Now–2000	Now–1993	Now–2001	N/T
Henri Jayer Vosne-Romanée Les Brûlées	1993–2002	1990–1997	1992–2002	Now–1994	1990–2000	Now–1995	Now–1995	Now–1991	Now–1995	N/T
Henri Jayer Vosne-Romanée Clos Parantoux	1992–2000	1990–1997	1992–2000	Now–1994	1990–2000	Now–1992	Now–1993	Now–1991	Now–1995	N/T
Jayer-Gilles Echézeaux	1992–2000	Now–1996	1992–2001	N/T	1990–2000	Now–1992	Now–1992	N/T	N/T	N/T
P. Leclerc Gevrey-Chambertin Les Cazetiers	1991–2000	1991–1997	1991–2003	Now–2003	1992–2000	Now–1993	Now–1994	Now–1993	N/T	N/T
P. Leclerc Gevrey-Chambertin Combe Aux Moines	1991–2000	1991–1997	1991–2003	Now–1992	1992–2000	Now–1993	Now–1994	Now–1993	N/T	N/T
R. Leclerc Gevrey-Chambertin Combe Aux Moines	1991–1998	Now–1995	1991–2000	Now–1992	Now–1997	Now–1992	Now–1992	Now	N/T	N/T
Leroy Beaune Grèves	N/T	N/T	1992–2006	N/T	N/T	N/T	N/T	N/T	N/T	Now–1997
Leroy Chambertin	N/T	N/T	1995–2010	N/T	N/T	N/T	N/T	N/T	1990–2000	1990–2010
Leroy Clos Vougeot	N/T	N/T	1995–2007	N/T	N/T	N/T	N/T	N/T	1990–1998	1990–2005
Leroy Mazis-Chambertin	N/T	N/T	1995–2008	N/T	N/T	N/T	N/T	N/T	N/T	N/T
Leroy Nuits St.-Georges Perdrix	N/T	N/T	1993–2007	N/T	N/T	N/T	N/T	N/T	N/T	N/T
Leroy Nuits St.-Georges Richemonde	N/T	N/T	1993–2007	N/T	N/T	N/T	N/T	N/T	N/T	N/T
Leroy Pommard Epenots	N/T	N/T	1993–2007	N/T		N/T	N/T	N/T	N/T	N/T

RED BURGUNDY—1976–1987 (Continued)

WINE	1987	1986	1985	1984	1983	1982	1980	1979	1978	1976
Leroy Ruchottes-Chambertin	N/T	N/T	1995-2010	N/T	N/T	N/T	N/T	N/T	N/T	N/T
Leroy Savigny Les Serpentières	N/T	N/T	1994-2008	N/T	N/T	N/T	N/T	N/T	N/T	N/T
H. Lignier Clos de la Roche	1992-2002	1990-1996	1993-2005	Now-1992	1992-2002	Now	Now-1992	Now	Now-1996	N/T
Maume Mazis-Chambertin	1994-2002	1992-2000	1993-2008	1990-1993	1995-2010	Now	1992-2002	Now-1998	N/T	N/T
Méo-Camuzet Clos Vougeot	1990-1997	Now-1994	Now-1998	N/T	N/T	1991-1998	N/T	N/T	N/T	N/T
Méo-Camuzet Richebourg	1992-2001	1990-1996	1991-2001	N/T	N/T	N/T	N/T	N/T	N/T	N/T
Méo-Camuzet Vosne-Romanée Les Brûlées	1992-2000	Now-1995	Now-1996	N/T	N/T	N/T	N/T	N/T	N/T	N/T
Moine-Hudelot Richebourg	1992-2000	1990-1995	1992-2002	N/T	N/T	N/T	N/T	N/T	N/T	N/T
Mongeard-Mugneret Clos Vougeot	1993-2000	1990-1996	1992-2001	Now	1993-2001	Now	Now	Now	Now	Now
Mongeard-Mugneret Grands-Echézeaux	1994-2002	1990-1996	1993-2003	Now	1993-2005	Now	Now-1994	Now	Now-1994	Now
Mongeard-Mugneret Richebourg	1992-2000	Now-1995	1990-1998	Now	N/T	N/T	N/T	N/T	N/T	N/T
H. de Montille Pommard Rugiens	1993-2003	1990-1997	1993-2005	Now-1991	1995-2005	Now-1997	1991-2005	N/T	1990-2005	N/T
G. Mugneret Clos Vougeot	1992-2000	Now-1995	1993-2005	Now	1993-2001	Now	Now-1993	Now	Now-1998	N/T
G. Mugneret Echézeaux	1992-2000	Now-1995	1993-2005	Now	1993-2001	Now	Now-1992	Now	Now-1996	N/T
G. Mugneret Ruchottes-Chambertin	1993-2005	Now-1996	1995-2008	Now	1993-2003	Now	Now-1995	Now	Now-2000	N/T
A. Mussy Pommard Epenots	1990-2000	Now-1996	1991-2003	Now	1992-1999	Now	1990-1997	Now-1996	Now-1999	N/T
Perrin-Rossin Morey St.-Denis Monts Luisants	1992-2001	1992-2000	Now-1998	N/T	Now	N/T	N/T	N/T	N/T	N/T
Perrin-Rossin Nuits St.-Georges Les Richemondes	1992-2003	1990-1998	1992-2005	N/T	Now	N/T	N/T	N/T	N/T	N/T
Ponsot Chambertin	1990-2003	Now-1997	1992-2005	Now	1993-2005	Now	N/T	N/T	N/T	N/T
Ponsot Clos de la Roche Vieilles Vignes	1992-2005	Now-1998	1993-2005	Now	1993-2007	Now	1993-2010	Now-1999	1990-2003	Now-2001
Ponsot Clos St.-Denis Vieilles Vignes	1992-2005	Now-1998	1993-2005	Now	1993-2007	Now	1992-2005	Now-1999	1990-2000	Now-2000
Pothier-Rieusset Pommard Rugiens	1991-2000	Now-1996	1990-2003	Now	1993-2000	Now	Now-1996	1990-2000	1990-2003	1990-2000
Pousse d'Or Volnay La Bousse d'Or	1990-1996	Now-1994	1990-2001	Now	1990-1995	Now	Now-1992	Now	Now-1998	1990-2000
DRC Grands-Echézeaux	1994-2006	1992-2000	1992-2010	1990-1995	1993-2008	Now-1992	Now-1998	Now-2000	1990-2010	1992-2005
Domaine de la Romanée-Conti Richebourg	1995-2008	1992-2003	1994-2012	1990-1995	1995-2010	Now-1994	Now-2000	1991-2005	1992-2012	Now
Domaine de la Romanée-Conti Romanée-Conti	1997-2010	1993-2005	1995-2010	1990-1995	1992-2007	Now-1994	Now-2000	Now-2003	1990-2010	Now-1992
Domaine de la Romanée-Conti Romanée-St. Vivant	1995-2008	1992-2003	1995-2010	1990-1995	1994-2007	Now-1994	Now-2000	1990-2000	1992-2008	Now
Domaine de la Romanée-Conti La Tache	1996-2010	1992-2005	1995-2012	1990-1995	1995-2010	Now-1993	Now-2004	1992-2010	1992-2012	Now-1992
J. Roty Charmes-Chambertin	1993-2000	1990-1996	1992-2002	Now	Now-1992	Now	Now-1994	Now-1991	Now-1998	N/T

J. Roty Mazy-Chambertin	1993–2003	1990–1997	1994–2004	Now	Now–1994	Now	Now–1993	Now–1991	Now–1998	N/T
G. Roumier Bonnes Mares	1993–2000	1992–2002	1992–2000	Now–1993	1993–2005	Now–1992	Now–1992	Now–1990	Now–1996	1992–2005
G. Roumier Chambolle-Musigny Les Amoureuses	1992–2000	1991–2000	1992–2000	Now–1992	1993–2003	Now	Now–1992	Now	Now–1996	1992–2003
G. Roumier Ruchottes-Chambertin	1994–2003	1993–2004	1993–2003	N/T	1995–2005	Now	Now–1994	N/T	1990–2000	N/T
G. Roumier Clos Vougeot	1993–2001	1993–2004	1992–2000	Now–1993	1993–2003	Now	Now–1993	N/T	1990–2000	1993–2006
A. Rousseau Chambertin	1994–2003	1990–1998	1992–2004	Now–1994	1993–2008	Now	Now–1995	Now–1992	?	1990–2000
A. Rousseau Chambertin Clos de Bèze	1992–2002	1990–1998	1992–2004	Now–1994	1993–2008	Now	Now–1995	Now	?	1990–2000
A. Rousseau Clos des Ruchottes	1992–2000	1990–1995	1990–2000	Now–1992	1990–1997	Now	Now–1992	Now	?	N/T
A. Rousseau Gevrey-Chambertin Clos St. Jacques	1992–2000	Now–1996	1990–2000	Now–1992	1990–1999	Now	Now–1995	Now	Now	1990–2000
B. Serveau Chambolle-Musigny Les Amoureuses	1990–1996	Now–1995	Now–1998	Now	1990–1998	Now	Now	Now	Now	N/T
R. Sirugue Grands-Echézeaux	1990–1997	1989–1994	1990–1998	Now	1992–2000	Now	Now	Now	Now	N/T
J. Tardy Clos Vougeot	1991–1999	1989–1996	1990–1998	Now	1992–2004	Now	Now	Now	Now–1995	N/T
Tollot-Beaut Corton Bressandes	1990–1996	Now–1995	1990–1998	Now	1991–2000	Now	Now	Now	Now–1992	1990–1998
J. Trapet Chambertin Vieilles Vignes	1991–1997	1992–1997	Now–1995	Now–1992	Now	Now	Now	Now	Now	Now

SELECTED CALIFORNIA CABERNET SAUVIGNON—1970-1986

WINE	1986	1985	1984	1983	1982	1981	1980
Beaulieu Private Reserve George de Latour (Napa)	N/T	1993-2005	1990-2000	Now-1995	1990-2005	Now-1997	1990-2005
Beringer Private Reserve (Napa)	1992-2003	1993-2005	1990-2000	1990-1996	1990-2000	Now-1991	Now
Buehler (Napa)	1990-1996	1992-1999	Now-1997	Now-1994	Now-1995	Now-1993	1990-1997
Burgess (Napa)	1991-2000	1992-2003	1990-2000	1990-1995	1990-1995	Now-1990	Now-1991
Carmenet (Sonoma)	1992-2005	1992-2005	1990-2003	1990-2000	Now-1998	—	—
Caymus Estate (Napa)	N/T	1992-2005	Now-1998	1989-1994	Now-1994	Now-1993	1989-1998
Caymus Special Selection (Napa)	N/T	N/T	N/T	Now-1995	1990-2000	Now-1997	1991-2005
Chappellet (Napa)	N/T	1994-2005	1992-2003	1992-1998	1990-1996	1990-1995	1990-2000
Clos du Val (Napa)	N/T	Now-1995	Now-1994	1989-1998	Now-1992	Now-1993	Now-1992
Diamond Creek (Napa) All Three Vyds	1991-2000	1990-1997	1990-2003	1991-1996	Now-1996	Now-1993	Now-1995
Dominus (Napa)	1991-2005	1990-2005	1990-2000	1992-2005	—	—	—
Duckhorn Three Palms Vineyard Merlot (Napa)	N/T	1990-2010	1990-2000	N/T	N/T	Now-1994	N/T
Dunn (Napa)	1992-2003	1992-2005	1990-2000	1991-1997	Now-1996	Now-1993	1992-2002
Dunn	1994-2007	1995-2010	1994-2008	1994-1999	1990-2008	Now-1997	—
Forman (Napa)	1992-2000	1992-2000	1990-2000	1990-2000	—	—	—
Grgich Hills (Napa)	N/T	1992-2003	1990-2000	1991-1997	1990-2000	N/T	N/T
Groth (Napa)	Now-1997	Now-1998	Now-1995	Now-1993	Now-1992	—	—
Gundlach-Bundschu Rhine Farm Merlot and Cabernet	1990-1998	1990-1998	Now-1996	Now-1995	Now-1994	Now	Now
Heitz Martha's Vyd (Napa)	N/T	N/T	1991-2010	1993-2005	1990-2003	Now-1994	1990-2004
Wm Hill Reserve (Napa)	1993-2000	1993-2004	1992-2000	1990-1995	Now-1995	1990-1995	1990-2007
Johnson-Turnbull (Napa)	N/T	1993-2002	1992-1998	1990-1994	Now-1992	Now	Now-1990
Jordan (Sonoma)	N/T	1990-1997	Now-1994	Now-1992	Now-1992	Now-1990	Now-1993
Kistler (Sonoma)	1992-2000	1994-2005	1993-2003	1990-1996	Now-1994	1990-1998	1990-1997
Laurel Glen (Sonoma)	1991-2000	1992-2005	Now-1998	Now-1993	Now	Now-1993	Now-1992
Louis Martini (Napa)	N/T	N/T	Now-1992	Now-1992	Now-1994	Now-Now	
Matanzas Creek Merlot (Sonoma)	1990-1995	Now-1993	Now-1991	Now	Now	—	—
Mayacamas (Napa)	N/T	N/T	1993-2007	1993-2000	1994-2010	1990-2005	1992-2010
Robert Mondavi Reserve (Napa)	1990-2003	1990-1997	Now-1996	Now-1995	Now-1993	Now-1994	Now-1995
Château Montelena (Napa)	1993-2005	1994-2010	1992-2005	1993-2000	1990-2002	1989-1996	1990-2002
Monticello (Napa)	1993-2005	1992-2004	1990-2005	Now-1994	Now	—	—
Mount Eden (Santa Cruz)	N/T	1990-2000	1989-1995	N/T	N/T	Now-1993	Now
Opus One (Napa)	N/T	N/T	1990-1997	Now-1993	Now-1994	Now	Now-1993
Joseph Phelps Insignia (Napa)	1992-2005	1993-2003	1990-2000	1993-2000	Now-1996	Now-1995	1991-2005
Joseph Phelps Eisele (Napa)	1995-2005	1992-2005	1992-2002	1993-1999	Now-1997	1992-2002	—
Pine Ridge (Napa)	1994-2005	1995-2010	1993-2003	—	—	—	1990-2005
Ridge Monte Bello (Santa Cruz)	1992-2000	1995-2015	1993-2015	—	Now	1993-2006	1990-2005
Rubicon (Napa)	N/T	1994-2005	1992-2003	1992-2000	1990-2003	Now-1998	Now-1995
Shafer (Napa)	Now-1997	Now-1994	Now-1993	1990-1994	Now-1993	Now	Now
Silver Oak (All Three Vyds)	1990-2000	1990-2003	Now-2000	1991-1996	Now-1996	Now-1994	Now-1992
Simi Reserve (Sonoma)	1993-2005	1992-2005	N/T	N/T	1990-2000	N/T	N/T
Spottswoode (Napa)	1992-2003	1992-2005	1990-2002	1992-1998	Now-1999	—	—
Stag's Leap Cask 23 (Napa)	1990-2000	1992-2000	Now-2000	1990-2000	—	—	—
Sterling (Napa)	1993-2002	1993-2005	N/T	1992-1997	N/T	N/T	Now-1993
Tudal (Napa)	1991-2002	1992-2003	1990-2000	1990-1995	Now-1996	N/T	N/T
Villa Mt. Eden (Napa)	N/T	N/T	N/T	N/T	Now-1993	Now-1991	1990-2000

1979	1978	1977	1976	1975	1974	1973	1972	1971	1970
1992–2005	Now–1995	Now–1994	1994–2020	Now–1998	Now–1992	Now	Now	Now	Now–2000
Now–1990	Now–1992	Now	N/T	N/T	N/T	N/T	N/T	N/T	N/T
1990–1994	1991–2000	—	—	—	—	—	—	—	—
Now	Now	Now	Now–1990	Now	Now	Now	—	—	—
—	—	—	—	—	—	—	—	—	—
Now–1998	Now–1994	Now–1993	Now–1997	Now–1993	Now–1995	Now–1995	—	—	—
1990–2000	Now–1995	—	Now–2005	Now–2005	—	—	—	—	—
Now–1993	Now–1994	Now–1992	Now–1992	Now	Now	Now–1993	—	—	—
1990–1996	Now–1992	Now–1991	Now–1990	Now	Now	Now–1990	Now	—	—
Now–1992	Now–1993	Now	Now–1993	Now–1990	Now–1991	N/T	N/T	N/T	N/T
—	—	—	—	—	—	—	—	—	—
N/T	Now–1991	—	—	—	—	—	—	—	—
—	—	—	—	—	—	—	—	—	—
Now–1995	—	—	—	—	—	—	—	—	—
—	—	—	—	—	—	—	—	—	—
—	—	—	—	—	—	—	—	—	—
—	—	—	—	—	—	—	—	—	—
—	—	—	—	—	—	—	—	—	—
1990–2003	Now	Now	Now–1993	1989–2001	1990–2008	Now–2000	—	Now–1996	Now–2001
Now–1995	Now–1997	—	—	—	—	—	—	—	—
Now	—	—	—	—	—	—	—	—	—
Now–1990	Now	Now	Now	—	—	—	—	—	—
Now–1994	—	—	—	—	—	—	—	—	—
Now–1994	—	—	—	—	—	—	—	—	—
Now	Now	Now	Now	Now	Now	Now	Now	Now	Now
—	—	—	—	—	—	—	—	—	—
1990–2000	1990–2000	Now–2000	1992–2005	Now–1996	1992–2010	1990–2010	—	Now–1995	1990–2010
Now–1996	Now–1998	Now	Now–1990	Now–1992	Now–2000	Now–1990	—	Now	Now–1998
Now–1995	Now–2003	Now	Now–1994	Now	Now	—	—	—	—
—	—	—	—	—	—	—	—	—	—
Now–1992	Now–1992	N/T	Now	Now	Now–2000	1993–2020	—	N/T	N/T
Now	—	—	—	—	—	—	—	—	—
1991–2001	Now–1993	Now–1990	1993–2010	Now	Now–1993	—	—	—	—
Now–1998	Now–2000	Now–1992	—	Now–2003	—	—	—	—	—
—	—	—	—	—	—	—	—	—	—
—	Now–2003	1993–2015	Now	Now–1997	1990–2010	Now	Now–1994	Now–1993	1990–2010
Now–1993	Now–1992	—	—	—	—	—	—	—	—
Now	Now–1990	—	—	—	—	—	—	—	—
Now	N/T	N/T	N/T	N/T	N/T	N/T	—	—	—
N/T	N/T	N/T	N/T	N/T	Now–1991	—	—	—	—
—	—	—	—	—	—	—	—	—	—
Now	Now–1995	Now–1990	—	—	Now	—	—	—	—
Now–1992	1989–1998	Now–1993	1990–1997	1990–1997	Now–2000	Now–1998	—	—	—
—	—	—	—	—	—	—	—	—	—
Now–1993	Now–2000	N/T	N/T	N/T	Now–1998	—	—	—	—

INDEX

ABOUT THE AUTHOR

ROBERT M. PARKER, JR., is the author and publisher of *The Wine Advocate* and the author of *Bordeaux: The Definitive Guide for the Wines Produced Since 1961* and *The Wines of the Rhône Valley and Provence.* He is a contributing editor for *Food & Wine* magazine, and the wine columnist for *Connoisseur* magazine. He lives with his wife of 20 years, Patricia and daughter, Maia, in Parkton, Maryland.

Much of the material in this book is based upon tastings and research done by Robert Parker in conjunction with the publishing of *The Wine Advocate*, an independent consumer's guide to fine wine that is issued six times a year. A one-year subscription to *The Wine Advocate* costs $30.00 for delivery in the continental United States, $35.00 for Canada, and $55.00 for air-mail delivery anywhere in the world. Subscriptions or a sample copy may be obtained by writing to The Wine Advocate, P.O. Box 311, Monkton, MD. 21111.